THE
ALL ENGLAND
LAW REPORTS
1994

Volume 4

Editor-in-chief
PETER HUTCHESSON LLM
Barrister, New Zealand

Editor
CAROLINE VANDRIDGE-AMES LLM

London
BUTTERWORTHS

UNITED KINGDOM Butterworth & Co (Publishers) Ltd,
Halsbury House, 35 Chancery Lane, **London** WC2A 1EL
and 4 Hill Street, **Edinburgh** EH2 3JZ

AUSTRALIA Butterworths, **Sydney, Melbourne, Brisbane, Adelaide, Perth, Canberra** and **Hobart**

CANADA Butterworths Canada Ltd, **Toronto** and **Vancouver**

IRELAND Butterworth (Ireland) Ltd, **Dublin**

MALAYSIA Malayan Law Journal Sdn Bhd, **Kuala Lumpur**

NEW ZEALAND Butterworths of New Zealand Ltd, **Wellington** and **Auckland**

PUERTO RICO Butterworth of Puerto Rico Inc, **San Juan**

SINGAPORE Butterworths Asia, **Singapore**

SOUTH AFRICA Butterworths Publishers (Pty) Ltd, **Durban**

USA Butterworth Legal Publishers, **Carlsbad**, California and **Salem**, New Hampshire

ISBN for the complete set of volumes: 0 406 85159 X
for this volume: 0 406 031754

© Butterworth & Co (Publishers) Ltd 1994

Printed and bound in Great Britain by William Clowes Ltd, Beccles and London

House of Lords

The Lord High Chancellor of Great Britain: Lord Mackay of Clashfern

Lords of Appeal in Ordinary

Lord Keith of Kinkel
Lord Goff of Chieveley
Lord Jauncey of Tullichettle
Lord Browne-Wilkinson
Lord Mustill

Lord Slynn of Hadley
Lord Woolf
Lord Lloyd of Berwick
Lord Nolan
Lord Nicholls of Birkenhead

Court of Appeal

The Lord High Chancellor of Great Britain

The Lord Chief Justice of England: Lord Taylor of Gosforth
(President of the Criminal Division)

The Master of the Rolls: Sir Thomas Henry Bingham
(President of the Civil Division)

The President of the Family Division: Sir Stephen Brown

The Vice-Chancellor: Sir Richard Rashleigh Folliott Scott

Lords Justices of Appeal

Sir Brian Thomas Neill
Sir Martin Charles Nourse
Sir Iain Derek Laing Glidewell
Sir Alfred John Balcombe
Sir Thomas Patrick Russell
Dame Ann Elizabeth Oldfield Butler-Sloss
Sir Murray Stuart-Smith
Sir Christopher Stephen Thomas Jonathan
  Thayer Staughton
Sir Michael Mann
Sir Donald Henry Farquharson
Sir Anthony James Denys McCowan
  (Senior Presiding Judge for England and
  Wales)
Sir Alexander Roy Asplan Beldam
Sir Andrew Peter Leggatt

Sir Johan Steyn
Sir Paul Joseph Morrow Kennedy
Sir David Cozens-Hardy Hirst
Sir Simon Denis Brown
Sir Anthony Howell Meurig Evans
Sir Christopher Dudley Roger Rose
Sir Leonard Hubert Hoffmann
Sir John Douglas Waite
Sir John Ormond Roch
Sir Peter Leslie Gibson
Sir John Stewart Hobhouse
Sir Denis Robert Maurice Henry
Sir Mark Oliver Saville
Sir Peter Julian Millett
Sir Swinton Barclay Thomas
Sir Robert Andrew Morritt

High Court of Justice

The Lord High Chancellor of Great Britain
The Lord Chief Justice of England
The President of the Family Division
The Vice-Chancellor
The Senior Presiding Judge for England and Wales
The puisne judges of the High Court

Chancery Division

The Lord High Chancellor of Great Britain
The Vice-Chancellor

Sir John Evelyn Vinelott
(retired 30 September 1994)
Sir Jean-Pierre Frank Eugene Warner
(retired 30 September 1994)
Sir Jeremiah LeRoy Harman
Sir John Leonard Knox
Sir William Aldous
Sir Donald Keith Rattee
Sir John Frank Mummery
Sir Francis Mursell Ferris
Sir John Murray Chadwick
Sir Jonathan Frederic Parker
(Vice-Chancellor of the County Palatine
of Lancaster)

Sir John Edmund Fredric Lindsay
Dame Mary Howarth Arden
Sir Edward Christopher Evans-Lombe
Sir Robin Raphael Hayim Jacob
Sir William Anthony Blackburne
Sir Gavin Anthony Lightman
Sir Robert Walker
Sir Robert John Anderson Carnwath
Sir Colin Percy Farquharson Rimer
(appointed 3 October 1994)

Queen's Bench Division

The Lord Chief Justice of England

Sir Haydn Tudor Evans
(retired 30 September 1994)
Sir Ronald Gough Waterhouse
Sir Frederick Maurice Drake
Sir Christopher James Saunders French
Sir Iain Charles Robert McCullough
Sir Oliver Bury Popplewell
Sir William Alan Macpherson of Cluny
Sir Philip Howard Otton
Sir Michael Hutchison
Sir Richard Howard Tucker
Sir Robert Alexander Gatehouse
Sir Patrick Neville Garland
Sir Michael John Turner
Sir John Downes Alliott
Sir Harry Henry Ognall
Sir Konrad Hermann Theodor Schiemann
Sir John Arthur Dalziel Owen
Sir Francis Humphrey Potts
Sir Richard George Rougier
Sir Ian Alexander Kennedy
Sir Nicholas Addison Phillips
Sir Robin Ernest Auld

Sir Malcolm Thomas Pill
Sir Stuart Neill McKinnon
Sir Mark Howard Potter
Sir Henry Brooke
Sir Thomas Scott Gillespie Baker
Sir Igor Judge
Sir Edwin Frank Jowitt
Sir Michael Morland
Sir Mark Waller
Sir Roger John Buckley
Sir Anthony Brian Hidden
Sir John Michael Wright
Sir Charles Barrie Knight Mantell
Sir John Christopher Calthorpe Blofeld
Sir Peter John Cresswell
Sir Anthony Tristram Kenneth May
Sir John Grant McKenzie Laws
Dame Ann Marian Ebsworth
Sir Simon Lane Tuckey
Sir David Nicholas Ramsay Latham
Sir Christopher John Holland
Sir John William Kay
Sir Richard Herbert Curtis

[continued on next page]

Queen's Bench Division *(continued)*

Sir Stephen John Sedley
Dame Janet Hilary Smith
Sir Anthony David Colman
Sir Anthony Peter Clarke
Sir John Anthony Dyson
Sir Thayne Forbes
Sir Michael Alexander Geddes Sachs
Sir Stephen George Mitchell
Sir Rodger Bell
Sir Michael Guy Vicat Harrison
Sir Bernard Anthony Rix

Dame Anne Heather Steel
Sir William Marcus Gage
Sir Jonathan Hugh Mance
Sir Andrew Centlivres Longmore
Sir Thomas Richard Atkin Morison
Sir Richard Joseph Buxton
Sir David Wolfe Keene
 (appointed 3 October 1994)
Sir Andrew David Collins
 (appointed 11 October 1994)

Family Division

The President of the Family Division

Sir Anthony Bruce Ewbank
Sir Anthony Barnard Hollis
Sir Mathew Alexander Thorpe
Sir Edward Stephen Cazalet
Sir Alan Hylton Ward
Sir Robert Lionel Johnson
Sir Douglas Dunlop Brown
Dame Joyanne Winifred Bracewell

Sir Michael Bryan Connell
Sir Jan Peter Singer
Sir Nicholas Allan Roy Wilson
Sir Nicholas Peter Rathbone Wall
Sir Andrew Tristram Hammett Kirkwood
Sir Christopher Stuart-White
Dame Brenda Marjorie Hale

CITATION

These reports are cited thus:

[1994] 4 All ER

REFERENCES

These reports contain references to the following major works of legal reference described in the manner indicated below.

Halsbury's Laws of England

The reference 26 *Halsbury's Laws* (4th edn) para 577 refers to paragraph 577 on page 296 of volume 26 of the fourth edition of *Halsbury's Laws of England*.

The reference 7(1) *Halsbury's Laws* (4th edn reissue) para 267 refers to paragraph 267 on page 177 of reissue volume 7(1) of the fourth edition of *Halsbury's Laws of England*.

Halsbury's Statutes of England and Wales

The reference 40 *Halsbury's Statutes* (4th edn) 734 refers to page 734 of volume 40 of the fourth edition of *Halsbury's Statutes of England and Wales*.

The reference 19 *Halsbury's Statutes* (4th edn) (1994 reissue) 497 refers to page 497 of the 1994 reissue of volume 19 of the fourth edition of *Halsbury's Statutes of England and Wales*.

The Digest

(formerly *The English and Empire Digest*)

The reference 37(2) *Digest* (Reissue) 424, *2594* refers to case number 2594 on page 424 of the reissue of green band volume 37(2) of *The Digest*.

The reference 27(1) *Digest* (2nd reissue) 330, *2849* refers to case number 2849 on page 330 of the second reissue of green band volume 27(1) of *The Digest*.

Halsbury's Statutory Instruments

The reference 17 *Halsbury's Statutory Instruments* 305 refers to page 305 of volume 17 of the grey volumes series of *Halsbury's Statutory Instruments*.

The reference 14 *Halsbury's Statutory Instruments* (1994 reissue) 201 refers to page 201 of the 1994 reissue of volume 14 of the grey volumes series of *Halsbury's Statutory Instruments*.

Cases reported in volume 4

Digest of cases reported in volume 4

House of Lords petitions

This list, which covers the period 4 October to 15 December 1994, sets out all cases which have formed the subject of a report in the All England Law Reports in which an Appeal Committee of the House of Lords has, subsequent to the publication of that report, refused leave to appeal. Where the result of a petition for leave to appeal was known prior to the publication of the relevant report a note of that result appears at the end of the report.

Chancery plc v Ketteringham [1994] 4 All ER 96, CA. Leave to appeal refused 24 November 1994 (Lord Jauncey of Tullichettle, Lord Mustill and Lord Nicholls of Birkenhead)

Fetch v Gurney (Inspector of Taxes) [1994] 3 All ER 731, CA. Leave to appeal refused 31 October 1994 (Lord Keith of Kinkel, Lord Mustill and Lord Nolan)

R v North Humberside and Scunthorpe Coroner, ex p Jamieson [1994] 3 All ER 972, CA. Leave to appeal refused 13 December 1994 (Lord Jauncey of Tullichettle, Lord Mustill and Lord Lloyd of Berwick)

CORRIGENDA

[1994] 3 All ER

p 899. **Graysim Holdings Ltd v P & O Property Holdings Ltd.** Counsel for Graysim were instructed b⁷ *A Banks & Co* as principals.

[1994] 4 All ER

p 305. **Re Leyland DAF Ltd.** Line *h* 2: for '£291,528' read '£2,915·28'. Line *h* 4: for '£667,108' rea⁴ '£6,671·08'.

p 468. **Beoco Ltd v Alfa Laval Co Ltd.** Counsel for the first defendant were instructed by *Davies Arnol* *Cooper* and counsel for the plaintiff were instructed by *Herbert Smith* and not as printed. Page 477, lin *g* 2. Insert the following after '... adjournment of the trial': 'so that the question of the alternative basis ⁶ quantum could be investigated and payment into court made, and secondly, because he said that the firs⁴

p 826. **Crédit Suisse v Beegas Nominees Ltd.** Line *j* 1: for 'regard' read 'disregard'.

p 883. **Barclays Bank plc v Glasgow City Council, Kleinwort Benson Ltd v Glasgow City Council.** Lin⁴ *d* 5: for 'legality' read 'illegality'. Page 889, line *h* 2: after 'that I have' insert 'not'.

Sutherland and others v Gustar (Inspector of Taxes)

COURT OF APPEAL, CIVIL DIVISION

SIR DONALD NICHOLLS V-C, LEGGATT AND HENRY LJJ

7, 8, 22 FEBRUARY 1994

Income tax – Case stated – Determination of appeal by commissioners – Request for case stated – Jurisdiction of commissioners to state case – Appeal – Partnership – Whether one partner entitled to appeal against commissioners' determination without consent of other partners – Whether that partner 'the appellant' for the purposes of appeal to High Court by way of case stated – Taxes Management Act 1970, s 56.

In 1990 a medical practice appealed to the General Commissioners against assessments on the partnership for the years 1976–77 to 1987–88. The main point of contention concerned the deductibility of each of the six partners' personal expenses. Prior to the hearing, five of the partners reached agreement with the inspector of taxes on the level of each partner's expenses. The inspector estimated B's expenses as sixth partner and arrived at a figure of assessable profits, which was accepted by all partners except B. At the hearing before the commissioners, B sought to challenge the other partners' claims for personal expenses, but the commissioners refused to allow him to address them on those expenses and adjourned the hearing to enable the inspector and B to agree on the level of his expenses. The commissioners later determined the assessments on the figures agreed between the inspector and the five doctors as adjusted to reflect the agreed level of B's expenses. B expressed his dissatisfaction with the determination, believing that the agreement reached between the inspector and the five partners was too generous to them, and requested the commissioners to state a case for the opinion of the High Court pursuant to s 56[a] of the Taxes Management Act 1970. By a notice of motion the five partners (including the personal representative of the fifth, who had died) sought a declaration that B was not 'the appellant' for the purposes of s 56 of the 1970 Act so that the commissioners did not have jurisdiction to state a case. They contended that 'the appellant' could only be the whole partnership of six partners and that consequently dissatisfaction with the commissioners' determination could not be declared by B alone on behalf of the partnership. The Crown and B however contended that B could properly be regarded as 'the appellant' and as being dissatisfied with the commissioners' determination. The judge held that 'the appellant' within the meaning of s 56 could only be the whole partnership and that neither the commissioners nor the Crown were entitled to regard the dissatisfaction declared by B or his request for the case to

---

a   Section 56, so far as material, is set out at p 4 *h j*, post

be stated as being on behalf of the partnership and orderd the case to be removed from the file. The Crown and B appealed.

Held – Having regard to the procedural code for tax appeals set out in Pt IV of the 1970 Act, it was clear that Parliament's intention was that one jointly assessed taxpayer should have a right of appeal even if the other person or persons named in the assessment did not wish to appeal. Accordingly, any person assessed to tax, whether alone or jointly with others, was entitled to bring an appeal to the general or special commissioners under s 31 of the Act in respect of the assessment. In the case of a joint assessment on partnership profits, the notice of appeal was given on behalf of all those assessed. It triggered an appeal against the assessment, but did not enable the person giving notice to conduct the appeal as though he was acting for all the partners, since he had authority only to act for himself unless of course his co-partners authorised him to act on their behalf. Notice of the hearing had to be given to the other partners, who were all appellants for the purposes of the 1970 Act, and their concurrence was needed if the appeal was to be settled or abandoned. By parity of reasoning, the same position applied under s 56 of the Act in relation to an appeal from the commissioners to the High Court. Thus, a person who was dissatisfied with the commissioners' determination of an appeal might 'declare his dissatisfaction to the commissioners who heard the appeal' whether the assessment was raised on himself alone or jointly with others and then require the commissioners to state and sign a case for the opinion of the High Court. It followed that B, as one of the partners jointly assessed, was entitled to declare his own dissatisfaction with the commissioners' determination and that sufficed to trigger the appeal mechanism to the High Court. The appeal would therefore be allowed and the case stated would be re-listed (see p 6 g to j, p 7 b c, p 9 f g and p 10 b c, post).

Notes

For case stated to the High Court on questions of fact and law, see 23 *Halsbury's Laws* (4th edn reissue) para 1703.

For the Taxes Management Act 1970, s 56, see 42 *Halsbury's Statutes* (4th edn) (1993 reissue) 209.

Cases referred to in judgment

Harrison (Inspector of Taxes) v Willis Bros [1965] 3 All ER 753, [1966] Ch 619, [1966] 2 WLR 183, CA.

Johnson v Stephens and Carter Ltd [1923] 2 KB 857, [1923] All ER Rep 701, CA.

Lewis v Daily Telegraph Ltd (No 2) [1964] 1 All ER 705, [1964] 2 QB 601, [1964] 2 WLR 736, CA.

MacKinlay (Inspector of Taxes) v Arthur Young McClelland Moores & Co (a firm) [1990] 1 All ER 45, [1990] 2 AC 239, [1989] 3 WLR 1245, HL; *rvsg* [1988] 2 All ER 1, [1989] Ch 454, [1988] 2 WLR 1117, CA; *rvsg* [1986] STC 491, [1986] 1 WLR 1468.

Rodriguez v Speyer Bros [1919] AC 59, [1918–19] All ER Rep 884, HL.

Seal & Edgelow v Kingston [1908] 2 KB 579, CA.

Sharpey-Schafer v Venn (1955) 34 ATC 141.

Tomlinson v Broadsmith [1896] 1 QB 386, CA.

Whitehead v Hughes (1834) 2 Cr & M 318, 149 ER 782, Exch.

Cases also cited or referred to in skeleton arguments

a Collet v Hubbard (1846) 2 Coop temp Cott 94, 47 ER 1069, LC.
Davey & Co v Alby United Carbide Factories Ltd (19 March 1914, unreported), Ch D.
Hood-Barrs v IRC (No 3) (1959) 39 TC 209, CA.
Hutcheon & Partners v Hutcheon 1979 SLT (Sh Ct) 61.
b Nicholson v IRC [1975] STC 245, 50 TC 287, CA.
Petch v Gurney (Inspector of Taxes) [1992] STC 892, Ch D.
Sun Life Assurance Co of Canada v Jervis [1944] 1 All ER 469, [1944] AC 111, HL.
Valleybright Ltd (in liq) v Richardson [1985] STC 70.

c **Appeal**
The Crown and Dr David Barnes appealed against a decision of Lindsay J on 7 May 1993 ([1993] STC 399) whereby, on the motion of Drs Heinz Peter Berg, David Wayman, Bridget Hiscock and Margaret Wise and Mrs Linda Sutherland in her capacity as personal representative of Dr Robert Sutherland (the applicants), it was ordered that the case stated by the General
d Commissioners for the division of Hertford be removed from the file. The grounds of appeal were, inter alia, that the judge had erred in holding that neither the commissioners nor the Crown was entitled to regard the dissatisfaction declared or the requirement of a case to be stated by Dr Barnes as being on behalf of the whole partnership of six doctors which alone
e comprised 'the appellant' for the purposes of s 56 of the Taxes Management Act 1970. The facts are set out in the judgment of the court.

Launcelot Henderson (instructed by the Solicitor of Inland Revenue) for the Crown.
Dr Barnes appeared in person.
c Roger Thomas (instructed by Hempsons) for the applicants.

Cur adv vult

22 February 1994. The following judgment of the court was delivered.

f **SIR DONALD NICHOLLS V-C.** Under s 111 of the Income and Corporation Taxes Act 1988 income tax payable in respect of partnership profits is the subject of a joint assessment made in the partnership name. This does not have the effect of making a partnership an entity for taxing purposes. It means only that the liability of the partners to pay income tax on the partnership profits is a joint liability of all of them, not a several liability of each. The use of the
g partnership name is a piece of machinery (see Harrison (Inspector of Taxes) v Willis Bros [1965] 3 All ER 753 at 757, [1966] Ch 619 at 639). The question raised by these appeals is whether one partner is entitled to appeal from an assessment, either to the General or Special Commissioners or from them to the High Court, contrary to the wishes of the other partners. The statute
h makes no special provision for appeals against joint assessments, and there is no authority on the point.

The statutory provisions
Income tax appeals are regulated by Pt IV of the Taxes Management Act 1970. Section 31(1) provides that 'an appeal may be brought against an assessment to tax' by a notice of appeal given within a 30-day time limit to the

tax inspector or other officer in question. When an assessment is made on one person the position is straightforward. It is clearly implicit in s 31(1) that an appeal may be brought by that person. However, standing by itself s 31(1) gives no guidance on what is to happen if the assessment is joint: do all the persons assessed have to join in a notice of appeal?

Although s 31(1) gives no guidance on this, some of the subsequent sections contain provisions which only work satisfactorily if, in the case of a joint assessment, 'the appellant' means both or all the persons who were the subject of the assessment. Foremost among these is s 54, which is concerned with settling appeals by agreement. Section 54(1) provides:

> '... where a person gives notice of appeal and, before the appeal is determined by the Commissioners, the inspector ... and the appellant come to an agreement ... that the assessment or decision under appeal should be treated as upheld without variation, or as varied in a particular manner or as discharged or cancelled, the like consequences shall ensue for all purposes as would have ensued if, at the time when the agreement was come to, the Commissioners had determined the appeal and had upheld the assessment or decision without variation, had varied it in that manner or had discharged or cancelled it, as the case may be.'

It could not be right that, in the case of an appeal against an assessment on a partnership, one partner could launch an appeal in the teeth of opposition from his fellow partners and then bind his partners to whatever terms he alone might agree with the tax inspector by way of settlement of the appeal. Similarly with s 54(4), which applies when 'a person who has given notice of appeal' notifies the inspector that he does not wish to proceed with the appeal. When that happens s 54(1) applies as though 'the appellant' and the inspector had come to an agreement that the assessment under appeal should be upheld. Subsection (4), like sub-s (1), envisages that the appellant and the tax inspector are the only persons interested in the outcome of the appeal. Further, s 50(1) requires the commissioners to give notice of the day for hearing appeals to every 'appellant' and to the tax inspector or other officer. There is no procedure for notifying a person who is a party to an assessment but who has not himself appealed.

Accordingly, it is said, the right of appeal to the commissioners under s 31 must be capable of being exercised only by all the partners in the case of an assessment on a partnership. Moreover, and this is the next step in the argument, this must equally be so at the further stage in the appeals process, which is by way of case stated to the High Court. Section 56(1) provides:

> 'Immediately after the determination of an appeal by the Commissioners, the appellant or the inspector ... if dissatisfied with the determination as being erroneous in point of law, may declare his dissatisfaction to the Commissioners who heard the appeal.'

Section 56(2) provides that, having declared his dissatisfaction, 'the appellant' or the inspector may within 30 days require the commissioners to state and sign a case for the opinion of the High Court. In these provisions, it is said, the appellant must be all the persons assessed in the case of a joint assessment.

The problem

There is force in this argument. The difficulty we have with it is the exposed position in which it would leave individual partners. A joint assessment can be enforced against any partner in the full amount, leaving him to pursue his partners for their share of the partnership assessment. In the ordinary way there is little difficulty in practice. Faced with an assessment, the partners agree on whether to appeal to the commissioners against the tax inspector's decision. Similarly, if they have appealed to the Special or General Commissioners, they will discuss whether to challenge the commissioners' decision and take the matter even further, to the High Court. They will agree on what they should do.

But partners do not always have the same interest in challenging an assessment. What is important to one partner may not matter to another. Similar divergences of interest, and differences of view about what is the best course for the partnership, can and do arise regarding other aspects of partnership business. Here, as elsewhere in the law, the courts evolved practical solutions. In the context of litigation, the courts devised procedures which protect a would-be plaintiff partner by permitting him to go ahead with court proceedings but also protect the partners who do not wish to become embroiled in the proceedings. The traditional means used to achieve this end was for the minority partner to be permitted to bring the proceedings in the name of the partnership. Every partner is an agent of the firm, a principle now enshrined in s 5 of the Partnership Act 1890. But the other partners had to be protected by an adequate indemnity.

There are many instances of this procedure being followed. For example, in *Whitehead v Hughes* (1834) 2 Cr & M 318, 149 ER 782 Bayley B observed that 'one of several partners has a clear right to use the names of the other partners'. If the others object they may apply for an indemnity against the costs to which they might be subjected by the use of their names. This was approved by Sir Gorrell Barnes P in *Seal & Edgelow v Kingston* [1908] 2 KB 579 at 582 and by Lord Finlay LC in *Rodriguez v Speyer Bros* [1919] AC 59 at 69, [1918–19] All ER Rep 884 at 890. Those were cases of claims brought by a partnership. The same approach was applied to claims brought against a partnership firm (see *Tomlinson v Broadsmith* [1896] 1 QB 386 esp at 392 per Rigby LJ).

An alternative approach is to treat partners, so far as litigation is concerned, in the same way as other joint contractors. If one joint contractor is unwilling to join the other in pursuing a claim on the contract, the one may bring proceedings himself so long as he joins the other as an additional defendant in the proceedings. That procedure is now embodied in RSC Ord 15, r 4(2). Rule 4(2) was introduced in 1962, but the notes to the rule in *The Supreme Court Practice 1993*, vol 1, para 15/4/1 record that this rule embodied the previous law and practice. In *Johnson v Stephens and Carter Ltd* [1923] 2 KB 857 at 861, [1923] All ER Rep 701 at 702–703 Atkin LJ referred to *Whitehead v Hughes* and left open the question whether it was still the law that one partner can use his co-partner's name as plaintiff against his will.

These solutions do not provide an answer in the present case. There is no machinery for the commissioners to require a would-be appellant, proceeding in the name of all the partners, to provide an indemnity for his co-partners. Nor is there machinery whereby an appellant partner, proceeding in his own name, may add his unwilling co-partners as additional respondents to his appeal. Further, Parliament cannot have intended that the commissioners would become involved in sorting out disputes between partners about whether an appeal by one of them should be permitted to go ahead and, if so, on what terms so far as his co-partners are concerned. The would-be appellant might, indeed, always apply to the Chancery Division for an order, for example, requiring his co-partners to concur in pursuing an appeal on being appropriately indemnified. But there are tight time limits for giving notices of appeal, and there must be some solution to this problem which does not require one partner to have recourse to the court before he can appeal against a joint assessment.

How, then, can the pieces be made to fit together? They do not slot neatly into place. On the one hand, the statutory scheme for appeals is not geared to cases where a single assessment is made on more than one person and the taxpayers disagree about what should be done. On the other hand, Parliament cannot be taken to have intended that in such a case one of the persons assessed should have no right of appeal, and that he should be worse off than a joint contractor who seeks to pursue a claim against the wishes of the other joint contractor. Parliament cannot have intended that he should be worse off than defendants against whom judgment is entered on a joint claim; one of them may appeal without the concurrence of the co-defendants. Before us the Revenue joined forces with Dr Barnes in submitting that fairness and justice require that, like any other taxpayer, a taxpayer named in a joint assessment should himself have a right of appeal.

The statutory solution

In these circumstances it would be easy to retreat into adopting a literal approach to the construction of the statutory provisions, while criticising the much-maligned parliamentary draftsman for compelling the court to reach an unsatisfactory result, and adding as a rider an expression of pious hope that Parliament will take an early opportunity to reconsider the matter.

We do not think that is the right approach. Legislation is to be interpreted so as to give effect to Parliament's presumed intention, so long as this is clear, provided always the language of the statute fairly admits of the interpretation in question. Here, having carefully considered the procedural code for tax appeals set out in Pt IV of the Taxes Management Act 1970, we are of the clear view that Parliament must have intended that one jointly assessed taxpayer shall have a right of appeal even if the other person or persons named in the assessment do not wish to appeal. Accordingly, s 31 is to be construed as enabling any person assessed to tax to bring an appeal in respect of the assessment, whether he has been assessed alone or jointly with others.

In the latter case, in contemplation of law the notice of appeal is given on behalf of all those assessed in the sense, but only in the sense, that the notice effectually triggers an appeal against the joint assessment. This does not enable the person giving the notice then to conduct the appeal as though he were acting for all the partners. He has authority only to act and speak for himself, unless his co-partners authorise him to act for them. If they do not, and if they wish to pursue a different line, they may do so. But an appeal against the joint assessment having been set in motion, they, along with the partner who gave the notice of appeal, are appellants for the purposes of the 1970 Act. Accordingly, notice of the hearing must be given to them, and their concurrence is needed if the appeal is to be settled or abandoned pursuant to s 54.

This will not give rise to any difficulty when the appeal is heard. At the hearing of the appeal, the commissioners will hear evidence and submissions from any partner who wishes to attend or be represented, as well as the inspector. The commissioners will then uphold or vary or discharge the assessment appropriately. In rare cases when justice so requires, plaintiffs in court proceedings may be separately represented (see *Lewis v Daily Telegraph Ltd (No 2)* [1964] 1 All ER 705, [1964] 2 QB 601). The procedure in front of the commissioners admits of similar flexibility in the case of appellants.

By parity of reasoning a like position obtains under s 56 concerning an appeal from the commissioners to the High Court. A person who is dissatisfied with the commissioners' determination of an appeal may 'declare his dissatisfaction to the commissioners who heard the appeal'. In our view he may do this whether the determination is in respect of an assessment of himself alone or of himself jointly with others. In the latter case as much as the former, the consequence under the statute is that the person who has declared his dissatisfaction may then require the commissioners to state and sign a case for the opinion of the High Court.

This construction of the legislation will not expose partners who do not wish to appeal to the risk of being ordered to pay costs. It is not the practice for orders as to costs to be made in respect of appeals to the General or Special Commissioners. Regarding appeals to the High Court, the judge will have no difficulty in seeing that costs orders reflect the justice of the case and that, in the ordinary run of things, a partner who dissociates himself from an unsuccessful appeal is not ordered to bear any costs.

Before us there was some debate on whether disagreement over the prosecution of an appeal to the commissioners or to the court was a difference arising as to an 'ordinary matter' connected with the partnership business for the purposes of s 24(8) of the Partnership Act 1890. Section 24 sets out rules governing the rights and duties of partners, which apply subject to any express or implied agreement between the partners. Under s 24(8) differences as to ordinary matters may be decided by a majority of the partners. We do not consider that this provision bears on the point before us. If a partner seeks to assert that the prosecution of an appeal by his co-partner is in breach of a term of their contract of partnership, either express or implied by the statute, he may pursue that claim with the partner, if necessary in court proceedings. Likewise if a majority of partners wish to assert that, by reason of the terms of their partnership, they are entitled to withdraw an appeal. These are not matters for the commissioners or for the Revenue.

The facts

The facts of this case are set out in the decision of Lindsay J ([1993] STC 399). We need refer only to the essentials. Dr Barnes was a partner in a medical practice comprising six general practitioners at Broxbourne, Hertfordshire. In July 1989 the tax inspector raised 15 assessments or further assessments against the partnership for the years 1976–1977 to 1987–88. The partnership's accountants, Messrs Hereward Philips, acting on behalf of all the partners appealed against the assessments. Before the appeal was heard by the General Commissioners discussions took place in May 1990 between Hereward Philips and the inspector. By now Hereward Philips no longer acted for Dr Barnes. They acted only for the other five partners. Unhappily, disagreements within the partnership had reached such a state that the five partners had commenced proceedings against Dr Barnes in the Chancery Division seeking dissolution of the partnership.

The main point of contention with the Revenue concerned the deductibility of certain expenses. Assessment of income tax on a partnership involves the tortuous process summarised by Vinelott J in *MacKinlay (Inspector of Taxes) v Arthur Young McClelland Moores & Co (a firm)* [1986] STC 491 at 504–505, [1986] 1 WLR 1468 at 1474–1475. This summary was approved by Lord Oliver when the case reached the House of Lords (see [1990] 1 All ER 45 at 48–49, [1990] 2 AC 239 at 249). Suffice to say, and we state this very shortly, the expenses deductible in arriving at the profits of a partnership include, as one would expect, the 'general expenses' such as rent of the partnership premises and staff salaries and also 'personal expenses' incurred by individual partners wholly and exclusively for the purposes of the partnership business. Here the expenses in issue were personal expenses claimed by the doctors for items such as cars and telephones at home. Hereward Philips, acting for the five doctors, reached agreement with the inspector regarding their personal expenses. Dr Barnes declined to agree those expenses. So the appeal proceeded in front of the Hertford General Commissioners.

Unfortunately, two irregularities occurred. Dr Barnes accused the five doctors of knowingly making excessive claims for their personal expenses, but the commissioners refused to allow Dr Barnes to address them regarding these expenses. That was clearly wrong. The amount of these expenses was an integral element in the calculation of the taxable profits of the partnership. Second, although this only came to light later, one of the three commissioners who heard the appeal was disqualified. The assessments under appeal included further assessments raised out of time pursuant to leave given by a commissioner under s 41 of the 1970 Act. Section 41(2), as it then stood, provided that a commissioner who gives such leave shall take no part in the hearing of an appeal from that assessment. Here one of the commissioners who heard the appeal was the commissioner who had given leave to raise the further assessments made by the inspector in July 1989. So he ought not have taken any part in the proceedings or to have been present. Plainly this was an oversight, but the statute is clear. No doubt this irregularity was capable of being waived by all concerned, but it has not been waived by Dr Barnes.

The upshot of the hearing on 6 June was that the commissioners accepted the figures agreed between the inspector and the five doctors for their expenses, and the figures agreed between the inspector and Dr Barnes for his expenses, and determined the assessments accordingly. The further assessments for the years 1976–77 to 1982–83 were reduced to nil, the further assessments for the years 1983–84 and 1984–85 were reduced a little, the further assessments for the years 1985–86 and 1986–87 were increased by about £2,500, and the main assessment for the year 1987–88 was increased from £150,000 to almost £155,500. Overall there was a substantial reduction.

Dr Barnes was unhappy at the outcome. He declared his dissatisfaction at once in a letter to the clerk to the commissioners:

'I wish to declare my dissatisfaction with the refusal of the Commissioners to permit me in law to present argument in full that the accounts and explanations submitted by the above partnership to the Inland Revenue were incomplete and untrue. I am a member of that partnership.'

Thereafter, within the 30-day time limit prescribed by s 56(2) of the 1970 Act, he wrote to the clerk on 3 July requiring the commissioners to state and sign a case for the High Court. In that letter Dr Barnes expressed concern at the commissioners' failure, among other matters, to make a finding of negligence, wilful default or fraud. His case, not to mince words, is that the partnership has been dishonestly evading the payment of tax. This serious allegation, we must add, is firmly denied by the five doctors. With allegations of this nature being made, it is not at all surprising that at the trial of the dissolution action the judge made an order for the dissolution of the partnership. That was on 15 March 1991. Millett J held that Dr Barnes' conduct made it unreasonable for the other five doctors to continue in partnership with him.

The case stated

Eventually, at a date in 1992 which does not appear, the commissioners stated a case for the High Court. We need not go into the reasons for the delay. One of the questions raised in the stated case is whether the commissioners were justified in refusing to hear Dr Barnes on the other partners' expenses claims. On 6 April 1993 four of the five doctors, and the personal representative of the fifth doctor who had died, issued an application seeking to strike out the stated case, primarily on the ground that the commissioners had no jurisdiction to state a case at the request of Dr Barnes alone.

Lindsay J acceded to the application on 7 May 1993. He held that, whatever the position might have been had Dr Barnes purported to speak and write on behalf of the partnership, as to which he said nothing, given the way Dr Barnes did express himself the triggering events required for stating a case under s 56 of the 1970 Act had not been complied with. It was the whole partnership of six doctors which alone comprised 'the appellant', and Dr Barnes did not declare the dissatisfaction of the partnership with the commissioners' decision. He declared his own dissatisfaction. Before us are appeals against that decision, brought by the Crown and by Dr Barnes.

It follows from what we have set out earlier that we must part company with the judge on his conclusion. As one of the persons jointly assessed, Dr Barnes was entitled to declare *his* dissatisfaction with the commissioners' decision, and this sufficed to trigger the appeal mechanism to the High Court in respect of that decision.

Grounds for dissatisfaction

A further matter relied on in the application to strike out the case stated was that Dr Barnes has no ground for being dissatisfied with the commissioners' determination. The submission runs as follows. Dr Barnes is seeking to increase the assessments, not reduce them. If he believes tax fiddling has been going on, he may get in touch with the tax inspector. That he has already done. It was then for the inspector to pursue the matter if he saw fit to do so. Dr Barnes has discharged any obligations he might have in this regard. It is not for him to seek to increase the assessments above the amounts set by the inspector. The appeal procedure is not the proper method for Dr Barnes to air grievances about the alleged conduct of his former partners (see *Sharpey-Schafer v Venn* (1955) 34 ATC 141). The case stated should be struck out as frivolous, vexatious and an abuse of the process of the court.

On this we agree with the judge. If (as we have found) the hearing by the commissioners was irregular, and Dr Barnes was wrongly refused an opportunity to address them on the expenses he challenged, then clearly he has grounds for dissatisfaction with their decision. Of course the commissioners may not need to hear a party if, having heard the other side, they are minded to decide in favour of that party and make a determination in the terms he seeks. That was not this case.

Conclusion

We shall therefore allow these appeals, set aside the judge's order, and dismiss the application dated 6 April 1993. Given the procedural irregularities we have mentioned, it is difficult to see how the case stated can have any result other than setting aside the commissioners' determination and remitting the matter for a fresh hearing before different commissioners. Mr Thomas for the applicants was not in a position to consent to such an order, and so the case stated will have to be re-listed. We would couple with this order an indication that the case should be re-listed as soon as possible. The case relates to a hearing before the General Commissioners which took place almost four years ago.

Appeal allowed. Leave to appeal to the House of Lords refused.

Siew Ling Choo   Barrister.

Welsh Development Agency v Redpath Dorman Long Ltd

COURT OF APPEAL, CIVIL DIVISION

GLIDEWELL, SIMON BROWN AND PETER GIBSON LJJ

8, 9 FEBRUARY, 17 MARCH 1994

Pleading – Amendment – Leave to amend after expiry of limitation period – Plaintiffs claiming damages for negligence – Limitation period expiring – Plaintiffs seeking leave to amend statement of claim – Amendment constituting new claim – Whether plaintiffs entitled to leave to amend statement of claim – Limitation Act 1980, s 35(1)(3) – RSC Ord 20, r 5(5).

In July 1992 the plaintiffs issued a summons for leave to amend their statement of claim in their action for damages against the defendant consulting engineers who had advised them on the development of an industrial estate. In particular, the plaintiffs sought leave to add claims for negligent misstatement in respect of structural advice given by the defendants and set out in reports dated December 1985 and August 1987. The summons was heard in May 1993. The judge refused the plaintiffs' application, holding (i) that since under s 35(1)[a] of the Limitation Act 1980 any new claim made on amendment would be deemed to have been commenced on the same date as the original action, if it was reasonably arguable that the relevant limitation period had expired before an amendment in the action was made so that s 35(1) might deprive the

a   Section 35, so far as material, is set out at p 16 *e* to *h*, post defendants of a limitation defence they would otherwise have had, the onus would then be on the plaintiffs to show either that they were within the limitation period or that the amendment came within the provisions of s 35(5) and RSC Ord 20, r 5(5)[b] as a new cause of action arising out of substantially the same facts as were already in issue, but that the court retained a discretion whether or not to allow the amendment, (ii) that the claims in relation to the 1985 report appeared to be outside the six-year limitation period for negligent misstatement (which expired in September 1992, six years after the expiry of the primary limitation period in contract) as at May 1993 and consequently any amendment to allow the addition of those new claims would give the plaintiffs what might be the unfair advantage of relation back under s 35(1) and (iii) that while there was no Limitation Act objection to the amendment in respect of the 1987 report it was so closely bound up with the similar claims under the 1985 report that it would be better not to allow an amendment confined to the 1987 report. The plaintiffs appealed, contending that the judge was wrong to conclude that unless a claim came within one of the exceptions provided by the rules, leave to amend could not be given if the limitation period had expired at the time when the court was considering whether to grant leave, since the relevant date for that period was the date at which the application for leave was made and if, at that date, the limitation period had not expired s 35(3) did not apply and, further, that the judge had erred in refusing to allow the amendment in respect of the 1985 report. The defendants appealed against the judge's further decision granting the plaintiffs leave to add claims in respect of additional factory units on the grounds that the claim for breach of contract was not a new claim for the purposes of s 35 and that the parallel claim in tort fell within Ord 20, r 5(5).

Held – (1) The provision of s 35(3) of the 1980 Act that 'neither the High Court nor any county court shall allow a new claim ... to be made in the course of any action after the expiry of any time limit under this Act ...' admitted of only one interpretation which was that the relevant date for expiry was the date at which the amendment was actually made, which by definition could be no earlier than the date at which leave was granted to make the amendment. Accordingly, a new claim under s 35(5) could not be made by amendment until the pleading was actually amended, so unless a case came within one of the exceptions, leave could not be given after the time limit had expired and that applied even if the limitation period had not expired at the date when the application for leave to amend was made (see p 22 c to e, p 24 b c and p 26 j, post); dictum of Hirst J in *Bank of America National Trust and Savings Association v Chrismas, The Kyriaki* [1994] 1 All ER 401 at 414–415 applied; *Kennett v Brown* [1988] 2 All ER 600 overruled.

    (2) In cases where, if amendment were to be allowed, s 35(1) would operate to give an advantage to the plaintiff by depriving the defendant of a limitation defence, leave to amend by adding a new claim should not be given unless the plaintiff could show that the defendant did not have a reasonably arguable case on limitation which would be prejudiced by the new claim, or could bring himself within RSC Ord 20, r 5. The judge was therefore correct in refusing to allow the amendment to plead misstatement in respect of the claims which appeared to be time-barred and, once he had reached that decision, his decision not to allow a similar amendment confined to the claims in the 1987 report was

---

b   Rule 5, so far as material, is set out at p 16 j to p 17 b, post

a matter for his discretion, with which the court would not interfere. The plaintiffs' appeal would accordingly be dismissed (see p 26 *f* to *j*, post); dictum of Purchas LJ in *Grimsby Cold Stores Ltd v Jenkins & Potter (a firm)* (1985) 1 Const LJ 362 at 370 applied; *Leicester Wholesale Fruit Market Ltd v Grundy* [1990] 1 All ER 442 distinguished.

(3) The question whether a new cause of action arose out of substantially the same facts as those already pleaded was essentially a matter of impression and since the judge had clearly taken all the relevant factors into account when granting the plaintiffs leave to amend by adding claims in contract and tort in respect of the additional factory units his decision was not open to challenge. The defendants' appeal would accordingly be dismissed (see p 18 *b*, p 19 *b e f* and p 26 *j*, post).

Notes

For amendment of a writ after expiry of the limitation period, see 37 *Halsbury's Laws* (4th edn) paras 274, 277, and for cases on the subject, see 37(1) *Digest* (Reissue) 264–265, 1732–1737.

For the Limitation Act 1980, ss 14A, 35, see 24 *Halsbury's Statutes* (4th edn) (1989 reissue) 662, 690.

Cases referred to in judgment

Bank of America National Trust and Savings Association v Chrismas, The Kyriaki [1994] 1 All ER 401.
Chaplin v Boys [1968] 1 All ER 283, [1968] 2 QB 1, [1968] 2 WLR 328, CA; *affd* [1969] 2 All ER 1085, [1969] 3 WLR 322, HL.
Grimsby Cold Stores Ltd v Jenkins & Potter (a firm) (1985) 1 Const LJ 362, CA.
Holland v Yates Building Ltd (1989) Times, 5 December, CA.
Howe v David Brown Tractors (Retail) Ltd (Rusons Engineering Co Ltd, third party) [1991] 4 All ER 30, CA.
Kennett v Brown [1988] 2 All ER 600, [1988] 1 WLR 582, CA.
Leicester Wholesale Fruit Market Ltd v Grundy [1990] 1 All ER 442, [1990] 1 WLR 107, CA.
Letang v Cooper [1964] 2 All ER 929, [1965] 1 QB 232, [1964] 3 WLR 573, CA.
Pirelli General Cable Works Ltd v Oscar Faber & Partners (a firm) [1983] 1 All ER 65, [1983] 2 AC 1, [1983] 2 WLR 6, HL.
Ronex Properties Ltd v John Laing Construction Ltd (Clark Nicholls & Marcel (a firm), third parties) [1982] 3 All ER 961, [1983] QB 398, [1982] 3 WLR 875, CA.
Société Commerciale de Réassurance v ERAS (International) Ltd [1992] 2 All ER 82n, CA.
Steamship Mutual Underwriting Association Ltd v Trollope & Colls (City) Ltd (1986) 6 Con LR 11, CA.

Cases also cited or referred to in skeleton arguments

Birmingham City DC v C Bryant & Son Ltd (1987) 9 Con LR 128.
Caparo Industries plc v Dickman [1990] 1 All ER 568, [1990] 2 AC 605, HL.
Leicester Wholesale Fruit Market Ltd v Grundy (No 2) (1990) 53 BLR 1, CA.
London Congregational Union Inc v Harriss & Harriss (a firm) [1988] 1 All ER 15, CA.

Interlocutory appeal

The plaintiffs, the Welsh Development Agency (the agency), appealed from the order of Judge John Hicks QC, hearing official referees' business made on

a 10 May 1993, refusing them leave to amend their statement of claim to add claims that structural advice given by the defendants, Redpath Dorman Long Ltd (trading as RDL Engineering Services) (RDL), in connection with the agency's development of East Moors Industrial Estate, Cardiff, and set out in two reports dated December 1985 and August 1987 amounted to negligent misstatement on the ground that those claims were barred under s 35 of the
b Limitation Act 1980. RDL appealed against that part of the judge's order granting the agency leave to make amendments to add claims in respect of an additional ten factory units. The facts are set out in the judgment of the court.

Donald Keating QC and Keith Bush (instructed by Eversheds Phillips & Buck, Cardiff) for the agency.
c Brian Knight QC and Martin Bowdery (instructed by Mark Galloway, Croydon) for RDL.

Cur adv vult

d 17 March 1994. The following judgment of the court was delivered.

GLIDEWELL LJ. On 10 May 1993 Judge Hicks QC hearing official referees' business gave judgment on the plaintiffs' application to amend their statement of claim in three different respects and also to amend their reply. The judge granted leave for the amendments to the statement of claim under two heads,
e but refused the application relating to the third head. He also gave leave for the proposed amendment of the reply. The plaintiffs now appeal against his refusal to grant leave for the amendment under the third head. The defendants appeal against the judge's grant of leave to amend the statement of claim under one of the other two heads.

f Basic facts
The Welsh Development Agency (the agency) are a statutory body who in 1980 owned and wished to develop the East Moors Industrial Estate, Cardiff. The estate included the site of the former East Moors Steelworks, with some adjoining land. The agency engaged the defendants, Redpath Dorman Long
g Ltd (trading as RDL Engineering Services) (RDL), who are consulting engineers to design the substructure of a number of factory units on a part of the estate known as the Tharsis site. At the relevant time the level of this site had been raised by tipping; the agency allege that the part of the Tharsis site outside the boundary of the former steelworks had been tipped to a greater
h depth than the area inside the boundary.
On 18 September 1980 RDL submitted a report to the agency which recommended that certain parts of the structure of the factory buildings should be based on piled foundations, but that the floor slabs of the factory units should not be piled. The agency allege that they accepted the
j recommendations in this report and constructed 12 factory units on the Tharsis site numbered 50 to 56 and 68 to 72, with floor slabs unsupported by piling. These units included two, Nos 50 and 51, which were constructed on sites partly within and partly without the boundary of the former steelworks. The agency allege that the 12 units were constructed between October 1980 and November 1981.
Units 50 and 51 were both leased by the agency to the same tenant, Huntleigh Technology Ltd (Huntleigh). The agency allege that in or about

November 1985 Huntleigh reported to them that the floor slab of unit 51 *a* appeared to have settled. The agency requested RDL to investigate the matter and to report, which RDL did by a report received in December 1985. RDL reported that the floor slab had indeed settled by up to 55 mm at the centre of the building. They concluded that this settlement was probably due to a leak in a water main close to unit 51, was not due to any inadequacy in design, and was unlikely to continue. *b*

In March 1987 the agency allege that Huntleigh complained about settlement of the floor slab in unit 50. The agency again requested RDL to report, which they did in August 1987. They found that two sections of the floor slab in unit 50 had settled, but the agency allege that RDL represented that this was not due to any defect in design and would be unlikely to continue sufficiently to disturb Huntleigh's manufacturing processes. RDL also *c* reported that the settlement in unit 51 appeared to have stopped.

The agency allege that despite these reports settlement of the floor slabs of both buildings continued. As a result by 1990 it became impossible for Huntleigh to continue to occupy either building, because they used sensitive high technology equipment which had to be kept level. The agency therefore *d* relocated Huntleigh to two other units on the estate (not on the Tharsis site).

The action

The writ in this action was issued on 3 July 1990. By it the agency claimed for—

'loss and/or damages suffered as a result of the Defendant's breach of *e* contract and/or negligent acts and/or omissions in its capacity as consulting engineer engaged by the Plaintiff ...'

The statement of claim was served on 3 January 1991. Although the indorsement of the writ had framed the cause of action as being both in *f* contract and in tort, the statement of claim pleaded:

'By reason of the said engagement the Defendants owed the Plaintiffs a duty to exercise the degree of skill and care normally to be expected of Consulting Civil Engineers in relation to the design of site works and sub-structure works associated with the said buildings and when advising *g* the Plaintiffs on matters related thereto.'

Paragraph 17 of the pleading specifically alleged:

'The settlements of the floor slabs of the said Units were caused by the negligence ... of the Defendants their servants or agents.' *h*

This pleading was followed in the usual way by particulars of the negligence.

It is common ground that although the writ had alleged breach of contract, the statement of claim was based purely upon the tort of negligence.

The defence was served on 23 March 1991. Negligence, damage and causation were all put in issue. Moreover the defence contained the following *j* specific pleas:

'20. Further or alternatively, it is denied that the sums pleaded in paragraph 18 are recoverable in law in respect of the cause of action pleaded in the Statement of Claim ...

23. Any cause of action (otherwise denied) is statute barred pursuant to the Limitation Act 1980.'

Paragraph 20 is a plea that, even if the damage was suffered, the damages claimed are irrecoverable in tort because they are damages for purely economic loss. In this appeal we are not concerned with this issue. It is the plea of limitation in para 23 of the defence which gives rise to the issues in this appeal.

By their reply dated 9 May 1981, the agency pleaded that RDL were estopped from relying on the provisions of the Limitation Act 1980 by reason of the agency's reliance on RDL's reports of December 1985 and August 1987.

The relevant law and its application

The effect of ss 2 and 5 of the Limitation Act 1980 is that the basic limitation period for actions in tort or in contract is six years from the date when the cause of action accrues. There is, however, this important difference, that a cause of action in contract accrues when the breach of contract occurs, whereas a cause of action in tort accrues when the damage for which the action is brought occurs. This, as this action illustrates, is particularly relevant in relation to claims for breach of a duty of care in the design or construction of a building. It is accepted that in this case the duty of care imposed upon RDL by their contract with the agency was broken, if at all, when they reported on 18 September 1980. The cause of action for RDL's breach of the duty imposed on them in tort, however, only accrued when the damage to the floor slab of any individual building occurred. In other words, there may well be a series of different dates for the accrual of causes of action in relation to the different factory units. It is notoriously difficult to ascertain when damage of this sort first occurred, but it is possible to say that the damage must have occurred not later than a given date, eg November 1985 in the case of factory unit No 51, when it was ascertained that the floor slab of that unit had settled.

It follows that the primary limitation period in contract expired on 18 September 1986, whereas the primary limitation period in tort would probably have expired at a variety of different dates for the different units. If it is correct to say that damage first occurred no later than the date when the settlement of the floor slab was observed, then for unit 51 the primary limitation period expired not later than November 1991, and for unit 50, where the settlement was observed in March 1987, the limitation period expired not later than March 1993.

There are two further sections of the 1980 Act which are relevant in this appeal. Section 35 is particularly relevant to the amendments here in issue. We shall consider it in detail later. Section 14A of the Act was added by s 1 of the Latent Damage Act 1986 in order to deal with the problem that damage to a building may occur but remain latent until after a primary limitation period has expired. Under the law before this amendment of the statute, a plaintiff who did not discover the damage until the six years had passed might therefore have lost his right of action. This was the position in *Pirelli General Cable Works Ltd v Oscar Faber & Partners (a firm)* [1983] 1 All ER 65, [1983] 2 AC 1; as a result of the decision of the House of Lords the plaintiffs in that case were held to be barred by the expiry of the limitation period from pursuing their action.

The effect of s 14A is to add an alternative limitation period in such a case. The section applies to 'any action for damages for negligence'. If in such an action a plaintiff has suffered damage, but can show that he did not for some time either know that such damage had been caused nor that the damage was attributable to the negligence of the defendant, the limitation period extends to whichever is the later of six years from the date on which the cause of action

accrued or three years from the date on which the plaintiff obtained the
necessary knowledge in order to bring his action.

The amendments sought and the judge's decision upon them

By a summons issued on 14 July 1992 the agency sought leave to amend the
statement of claim in the following respects. (1) To frame their claim in breach
of contract as well as in tort. The judge granted leave for the amendments
under this head, and there is no appeal by RDL against this part of his order.
(2) To add claims in respect of an additional ten factory units, since the
unamended statement of claim related only to units 50 and 51. The judge
granted leave to make the amendments sought under this head. It is against
this part of his order that RDL appeal. (3) To add claims that the advice given
by RDL in the reports of December 1985 and August 1987 amounted to
negligent misstatement, which of itself gave the agency a right of action. The
judge refused leave to make the amendments sought under this head. It is
against this part of his order that the agency now appeal. (4) The agency also
sought leave to amend the reply in order to plead reliance on s 14A of the 1980
Act. The judge granted leave to make this amendment, and there is no appeal
against this part of his decision.

The power of the court to allow amendments

Section 35 of the 1980 Act contains the following provisions which are
relevant to this appeal:

'(1) For the purposes of this Act, any new claim made in the course of
any action shall be deemed to be a separate action and to have been
commenced ... (b) ... on the same date as the original action.

(2) In this section a new claim means ... (a) the addition or substitution
of a new cause of action ...

(3) Except as provided by ... rules of court, neither the High Court nor
any county court shall allow a new claim within subsection (1)(b) above ...
to be made in the course of any action after the expiry of any time limit
under this Act which would affect a new action to enforce that claim ...

(4) Rules of court may provide for allowing a new claim to which
subsection (3) above applies to be made as there mentioned, but only if the
conditions specified in subsection (5) below are satisfied, and subject to
any further restrictions the rules may impose.

(5) The conditions referred to in subsection (4) above are the
following—(a) in the case of a claim involving a new cause of action, if the
new cause of action arises out of the same facts or substantially the same
facts as are already in issue on any claim previously made in the original
action ...'

The rules of court referred to in s 35(4) are to be found in RSC Ord 20, r 5.
So far as is material this provides:

'(1) Subject to ... the following provisions of this rule, the Court may at
any stage of the proceedings allow the plaintiff to amend his writ, or any
party to amend his pleading, on such terms as to costs or otherwise as may
be just and in such manner (if any) as it may direct.

(2) Where an application to the Court for leave to make the amendment
mentioned in paragraph ... (5) is made after any relevant period of
limitation current at the date of issue of the writ has expired, the Court

a
may nevertheless grant such leave in the circumstances mentioned in that paragraph if it thinks it just to do so ...

(5) An amendment may be allowed under paragraph (2) notwithstanding that the effect of the amendment will be to add or substitute a new cause of action if the new cause of action arises out of the same facts or substantially the same facts as a cause of action in respect of

b
which relief has already been claimed in the action by the party applying for leave to make the amendment.'

The effect of these provisions taken together, in relation to this appeal, is as follows. (a) A new cause of action is a 'new claim' within s 35. The court may not allow a new claim to be made after the expiry of a limitation period which

c
would affect a new action to enforce such a claim unless the new cause arises out of the same or substantially the same facts as those already in issue in the action. (b) If the court does allow a new claim to be made by amendment, it shall be deemed to have been commenced when the writ in the original action was issued.   (c) If, when the court is considering whether to allow an

d
amendment, the limitation period for a new action has not expired, the claim is not caught by s 35(3). Order 20, r 5(1) then permits the court to allow the amendment without any particular requirement being satisfied.   (d) However, if the court has power to allow an amendment, whether this be because the period of limitation for a new action has not expired or because the claim is based on substantially the same facts as those already in issue in the action,

e
the court retains a discretion whether or not to allow the amendment.

RDL's appeal against the leave to add claims relating to the ten further units

As we have already said, the statement of claim as originally filed related only to the damage alleged in the floor slabs of factory units 50 and 51. The

f
principal amendment allowed under this head was the addition to the pleading of a new para 16A, which reads:

'As a result of receiving a report in October 1990, from consultants instructed to investigate the settlements to the floor slabs of Units 50 and 51, the Plaintiffs instructed the said consultants to investigate the floor

g
slabs of the other 10 units. The said investigation, carried out between November 1990 and May 1992 revealed that the slabs of the said other units had also suffered differential settlements, which were continuing to increase. The magnitude of the differential settlements ranged from 32 mm (Unit 52) to 107 mm (Unit 54).'

h
Consequential amendments were allowed to refer to the added 10, or as appropriate to the 12, units throughout the pleading. In addition an additional sub-paragraph was added to para 18, which pleaded that the businesses carried on by the tenants of the other ten units did not suffer interference by reason of the settlement of the floor slabs in their units, that the agency therefore did not

j
propose at present to carry out any remedial works in those units, and that the loss suffered by the agency at the time of the amendment was therefore the diminution in the value of the freehold reversions to the ten units.

This is in very marked contrast to the claim in respect of units 50 and 51 in which the total of damages claimed for reconstruction of the floor slabs and for relocating the tenants giving credit for the cost of piling which was not incurred in 1980 amounts to £750,000 in round figures.

We can summarise the judge's reasoning for allowing the amendments under this head as follows.

(1) He started by deciding that the correct approach was to assume that the amendments which he had already allowed to add the plea of breach of contract had been made. In this respect we are confident that he was correct, and indeed this is made clear by the fact that there has been no appeal in relation to his allowing the addition of the plea of breach of contract. The judge concluded, and again we agree, that 'The cause of action is the same and accrued at the same time'. It follows that it was his view that a claim in contract with regard to the ten additional buildings was not 'a new claim' for the purposes of s 35.

At this stage of the judge's judgment, he had not reached his decision on negligent misstatement, and he therefore did not take the possibility of allowing those amendments into account, again quite properly. Moreover he was not concerned with a possible limitation period resulting from s 14A of the 1980 Act, because in *Société Commerciale de Réassurance v ERAS (International) Ltd* [1992] 2 All ER 82n this court decided that the phrase in s 14A 'any action for damages for negligence' is limited to actions for damages for negligence where the duty of care arises solely in tort and does not apply to claims for a duty alleged to arise in contract.

(2) The judge then turned to consider a claim in tort in relation to the ten additional units. He considered first whether such a claim would be a 'new claim' within s 45. He adopted the definition of a cause of action given by Diplock LJ in *Letang v Cooper* [1964] 2 All ER 929 at 934, [1965] 1 QB 232 at 242:

'A cause of action is simply a factual situation the existence of which entitles one person to obtain from the court a remedy against another person.'

The judge then concluded that the amendment to the claim in tort by reason of the settlement of the floor slabs in the ten additional units would raise a new claim for the purposes of s 35.

In doing so, the judge based himself largely upon the decision of this court in *Steamship Mutual Underwriting Association Ltd v Trollope & Colls (City) Ltd* (1986) 6 Con LR 11. In that case the plaintiff building owners had commenced an action against the contractors, the architects and the structural engineers for damages for alleged defects in the air-conditioning plant in the building. Two-and-a-half years after the delivery of the statement of claim, the plaintiffs applied to amend it to claim also damages for alleged defects in the structure of the walls. This court concluded that the amendments would relate to a new cause of action. May LJ said (at 36):

'In the present case, if one remembers what a cause of action is (for instance, to refer back to the dictum in *Letang*), if one looks to the size of this particular building, to its complexities, to other matters of degree, to the statement of claim before the proposed reamendment ... I feel bound to agree with the learned judge where he concluded, having referred to the cases on what is a cause of action, the statement of claim in both its original and amended form related only to the air conditioning. I think that its effect was to narrow the causes of action so that they became confined to breaches of contract concerned with air conditioning and negligence resulting in damages to the air conditioning. In the light of the definitions of a cause of action already referred to, I do not think one can

a   look only to the duty on a party, but one must look also to the nature and
extent of the breach relied upon, as well as to the nature and extent of the
damage complained of in deciding whether, as a matter of degree, a new
cause of action is sought to be relied upon.'

Lloyd LJ and Caulfield J agreed.

b   It followed that the judge could only allow this amendment if he concluded
that it came within Ord 20, r 5(5), ie the cause of action in tort in relation to the
ten additional units arose out of the same or substantially the same facts as the
cause of action already pleaded in relation to units 50 and 51. He concluded
that substantially all the relevant facts had already been pleaded in the
unamended statement of claim plus the amendment to add the breach of
c   contract, and thus allowed these amendments also.

Mr Knight QC, for RDL, submits that there is not what he calls 'sufficient
overlap' between the claims in relation to units 50 and 51 and those in relation
to the other ten units to justify the judge's decision. He makes the following
points in support of this general submission. (a) The ground conditions below
units 50 and 51 were significantly different from those between the other units,
d   because part of the land on which the first two units had been constructed was
filled to a greater depth than the old steelworks site. Thus, the differential
settlement in relation to units 50 and 51 was greater. (b) The nature of the
tenants' usage, and thus the loading of the slabs, is or may well be different.
(c) The time when settlement began appears to be different. (d) The nature
of the damages claimed is totally different, as we have already explained.

e   We are not confident that the difference in the nature of the damages claim
is a relevant consideration, but we agree that the other points advanced by Mr
Knight are relevant. Nevertheless, as the judge, said whether or not the new
cause of action arises out of substantially the same facts as that already pleaded
is substantially a matter of impression. It is not suggested that the judge
f   misdirected himself in any way, and since it is clear that he took all the relevant
factors into account, we are of the opinion that he was entitled to come to the
conclusion to which he did come on this issue. We cannot fault this part of his
judgment in any way and we would therefore dismiss RDL's appeal.

g   *The agency's appeal against the refusal to allow amendment to claim for
negligent misstatement*

Under this head the agency are seeking leave to add to their statement of
claim three paragraphs. In the first of these they seek to allege (para 19):

h   'The statements made by the Defendants in their December 1985 and
August 1987 reports were made in circumstances under which they were
likely to be relied upon by the Plaintiffs and which gave rise to a duty of
care owed by the Defendants to the Plaintiffs namely a duty to take
reasonable care to ensure that the Plaintiffs did not suffer loss, including
economic loss, by reason of such reliance.'

j   In para 20 it is sought to plead that the representations made in the reports,
which had already been pleaded in earlier paragraphs of the statement of claim,
were made negligently. Particulars of negligence are given. The intended para
21 reads:

'By reason of the Defendants' said negligence the Plaintiffs have suffered
loss and damage. PARTICULARS Had the December 1985 report revealed
the fact that settlement of the slab of unit 51 was due, or possibly due, to

inadequacy in design or had the Defendants advised the Plaintiffs to commission an independent investigation the Plaintiffs would have commissioned a full and thorough investigation of the cause of the settlement and the inadequacies in the design of the floor slabs of all 12 units, as particularised under paragraph 17 above, would have been revealed. The Plaintiffs would therefore have been made aware of their causes of action against the Defendants in contract and/or negligence within 6 years of such causes of action accruing. If, therefore, which is not admitted, the Plaintiffs are unable to pursue against the Defendants causes of action which they would otherwise have had, by reason of the expiry of the relevant limitation periods, the said inability has been caused by the negligence of the Defendants and has resulted in the Plaintiffs being deprived of their right to recover the selfsame damages as are particularised under paragraph 18 above.'

It is important to note in relation to this part of the appeal that the plaintiffs' summons for leave to amend the statement of claim was issued on 14 July 1992.

We hope we do justice to the judge's admirable judgment if we summarise his conclusion on this part of the case as follows.

(1) The cause of action alleged here arose, not when the allegedly negligent report was made, but when the plaintiffs suffered damage as a result. In the case of the December 1985 report, this was when the primary limitation period for an action in contract expired, ie 18 September 1986. In tort as we have already made clear the date at which the primary limitation periods expired is less certain, though in respect of unit 51 it appears that it expired not later than November 1991 and for unit 50 not later than March 1993.

(2) The earliest date of expiry of a cause of action for negligent misstatement was therefore 18 September 1992, ie six years after 18 September 1986. However, the latest date for the expiry of such a cause of action was probably well after the date of the judge's judgment.

(3) If the plaintiffs' application had been heard before 18 September 1992, the earliest limitation period for a claim in negligent misrepresentation would not have expired. In that circumstance, s 35(3) would not have applied, and the court would have had an unrestricted discretion to allow these amendments under Ord 20, r 5(1).

(4) But the application was not heard until May 1993. Section 35(3) of the 1980 Act provides that the court shall not—

'allow a new claim ... to be made in the course of any action after the expiry of any time limit under this Act which would affect a new action to enforce that claim ...'

A new claim cannot be 'made' by amendment until the pleading is actually amended, so unless a case comes within one of the exceptions leave cannot be given after the time limit has expired. This applies even if the limitation period had not expired at the date when the application for leave to amend was made.

(5) Therefore some at least, but probably by no means all, of the claims for negligent misstatement were outside their primary limitation periods when the court was considering whether to allow amendment.

(6) However, such claims might still have been inside the alternative limitation period provided by s 14A of the 1980 Act.

(7) These were clearly 'new claims', ie the addition of one or more new causes of action under s 35 and Ord 20 r 5. Such causes of action did not arise

a   out of substantially the same facts as the causes of action already pleaded. Therefore the amendments could only be allowed if the defendant could not reasonably argue that the relevant period of limitation (which in practice in relation to some of the causes of action meant the s 14A period) had expired.

(8) The approach of the court should differ according to the nature and effect of the proposed amendments. If the amendment adds a 'new claim' and
b   the relevant limitation period expired between the date of the writ and the date of the amendment, s 35(1) will, after amendment, deprive the defendants of a limitation defence they would otherwise have had. In such a case 'the onus is on the plaintiffs to show that they are within the statutory limits and satisfy the conditions prescribed by the statute and the rules'.

(9) If, however, the amendment, though clearly adding a new claim, alleges
c   that at the date of the amendment either the primary limitation period or the s 14A limitation period has not expired, the amendment should be allowed, unless it is so clear on the facts that the relevant limitation period has expired that if a fresh action were brought it would be struck out under RSC Ord 18, r 19 as being an abuse of process (see *Ronex Properties Ltd v John Laing*
d   *Construction Ltd (Clark Nicholls & Marcel (a firm), third parties)* [1982] 3 All ER 961 at 966, 968, [1983] QB 398 at 405, 407–408 per Donaldson LJ and Sir Sebag Shaw).

(10) Where issues of both kinds arise or may arise, the court's approach should be that set out in para (8) above. Any injustice to the defendants by depriving them of a limitation defence they would otherwise have would thus
e   be avoided, while the plaintiffs can commence a fresh action to which, if they are correct, limitation will not be a defence.

(11) The correct test to apply in this case in relation to the amendment alleging negligent misstatement in the December 1985 report was that set out in para (8) above. This was because, at the date the judge was considering the
f   application for leave to amend, the primary limitation period for this cause of action appeared to have expired, ie on 18 September 1992. Thus amendment to allow the addition of this claim would give the plaintiffs what might be the unfair advantage of relation back under s 35(1).

(12) As to the claim based on the August 1987 report, the judge said that Mr Knight conceded that there was no Limitation Act objection to this part of the
g   amendment. The judge concluded that the amendment would not be struck out as being an abuse under Ord 18, r 19. Nevertheless he said:

> '... since it is closely bound up with the similar claim under the 1985 report, which the plaintiffs will have to pursue by separate action, if at all,
h   I consider that in all the circumstances it would be better not to allow an amendment confined to the 1987 report.'

For these reasons the judge refused leave to allow the amendment under this head.

j   *Argument for the agency*

Mr Keating QC for the agency challenges two major parts of the judge's reasoning. Firstly, he argues that the judge was wrong to conclude, as summarised at para (4) above, that unless a new claim comes within one of the exceptions provided by the rules, leave for the amendment cannot be given if the limitation period has expired at the time when the judge is considering whether to grant leave. Mr Keating argues that the relevant date for this period is the date at which the application for leave is made. If, at that date, the limitation period has not expired, s 35(3) does not apply.

In support of this argument, Mr Keating relies upon the wording of Ord 20, r 5(2):

'Where an application to the Court for leave to make the amendment ... is made after any relevant period of limitation current at the date of issue of the writ has expired, the Court may nevertheless grant such leave ...'

This, submits Mr Keating, interprets s 35(3) so as to make it clear that it is the date of application which is the relevant date. If this were not so, the plaintiffs' right to amend would depend on purely arbitrary factors, such as when the court could hear the application for leave or how long it took the court to deliver judgment after hearing the application.

In our judgment the judge's decision on this issue was entirely correct. The wording of s 35(3) of the 1980 Act, which reads:

'... neither the High Court nor any county court shall allow a new claim ... to be made in the course of any action after the expiry of any time limit under this Act ...'

is so clear as to admit of only one interpretation. That is that the relevant date is the date at which the amendment is actually made, which by definition must be no earlier than the date at which leave is granted to make the amendment. We are glad to see that this decision agrees with that reached by Hirst J in *Bank of America National Trust and Savings Association v Chrismas, The Kyriaki* [1994] 1 All ER 401 at 414–415.

The judge appreciated that, at least in theory, the difference between the wording of s 35(3) and that of Ord 20, r 5(2) could create a lacuna in a case where the application for leave was made before but was not considered until after the limitation period expired. Theoretically it might be argued that in such a case the court would have no power to allow an amendment even if the case clearly came within, for example, Ord 20, r 5(5). The judge said:

'I have come to the conclusion that the resolution of this problem is to be found in the fact that Ord 20, r 5(2) is an enabling, not a restrictive, provision. The key word is "nevertheless" which enables the obstacle otherwise posed by a "late" application to be overcome, but does not imply that an earlier application cannot take advantage of the rule if it otherwise applies and its provisions are needed in order to escape the prohibition of s 35(3).'

It is not necessary for us to reach a decision on this point, but we see the force of the judge's reasoning.

Before we turn to Mr Keating's second major argument, we must consider two earlier decisions of this court on the effect of s 35(1) and (3) of the 1980 Act. The first is *Kennett v Brown* [1988] 2 All ER 600, [1988] 1 WLR 582. This was a decision of a court comprising Lord Donaldson MR and Parker LJ. That case has recently been considered by this court in *Howe v David Brown Tractors (Retail) Ltd (Rusons Engineering Co Ltd, third party)* [1991] 4 All ER 30. We adopt gratefully from the judgment of Stuart-Smith LJ in that case the following summary of *Kennett v Brown* (at 36–37):

'... the plaintiff suffered personal injuries in a road accident and brought an action against the first defendant claiming damages. Subsequently the second defendant was joined as a party. Shortly after the expiry of three years from the accident the first defendant served a contribution notice on the second defendant. He claimed an indemnity in respect of any liability he might incur to the plaintiff and damages for personal injury. The first defendant applied for directions, and the district registrar held that there could be no claim by the first defendant in respect of his own injuries until he had applied under s 33 of the Limitation Act 1980 to disapply the provisions of s 11. He stood the application over. [We add that the district registrar made it clear that if the application under s 33 were not made, the contribution notice should be struck out.] On appeal to the judge in chambers by the first defendant it was held that it was for the second defendant to raise the limitation defence in the contribution proceedings and, if and when he did so, for the first defendant to apply under s 33. The appeal to the Court of Appeal was dismissed. It is important to appreciate that that case turned solely on the construction of s 35 of the 1980 Act. There was no question of the addition of a party to the proceedings, since the second defendant was already properly joined as a party in the contribution proceedings. The claim in respect of the first defendant's personal injury was a new claim within the meaning of s 35(1)(b).'

In *Kennett v Brown* [1988] 2 All ER 600 at 602–603, [1988] 1 WLR 582 at 585 Lord Donaldson MR said that the question which was at the heart of that appeal was, when did the s 35(3) point fall to be considered? He continued:

'So I look at the wording of the subsection. Parliament must be deemed to have been aware of the way in which, subject to special provisions made in rules of court, the Limitation Acts have always been applied, namely as procedural bars which a defendant to a particular claim could raise if he wished, but which he was not obliged to raise if he did not wish. If the view of the statute which is put forward by counsel for [the defendant] is accepted, it would be necessary in every case where a new claim falling within s 35(1)(b) was raised after the expiry of the limitation period for the person raising the claim to make an application under s 33 to have the Limitation Act 1980 disapplied. I can see no reason of policy why that should be the case and why Parliament should ever have intended it, and so I approach the words in s 35(3), "neither the High Court nor any county court shall allow a new claim ... to be made in the course of any action", without feeling that I am in any way bound by the literal meaning of those words. In s 11 and the various other sections the wording of the 1980 Act is "An action ... shall not be brought". We know that Parliament does not mean by that that no action shall be brought; it means that no action shall succeed. I see no reason why the words here, "neither the High Court nor any county court shall allow a new claim ... to be made", should receive any other construction.'

Lord Donaldson MR then said that the new claim contained in the contribution notice was not dependent on a prior application by the first defendant under s 33, but that the second defendant could plead s 35(3) in his defence.

In *Howe's* case Nicholls LJ and Stuart-Smith LJJ felt able to distinguish and thus not be bound by the decision in *Kennett v Brown*. In our view we cannot take that course. We believe that if we are not to follow that decision, we are obliged to say boldly that the reasoning in *Kennett v Brown* was wrong. We are able to do so because that was a decision of a court consisting of two Lords Justices in an interlocutory matter, in extemporary judgments. We, though also sitting on an interlocutory appeal, are a court of three Lords Justices. That we have the power to disagree with, and overrule, a previous decision of a court of two Lords Justices in an interlocutory appeal is clear from the decision of this court in *Chaplin v Boys* [1968] 1 All ER 283 at 288, 293, 296, [1968] 2 QB 1 at 23, 30, 36, per Lord Denning MR, Lord Upjohn and Diplock LJ.

Our difficulty with the decision in *Kennett v Brown* is that it appears to be based on a wrong interpretation of s 35(3) and to disregard the effect of s 35(1). If the claim in the contribution notice were not struck out, or an order made under s 33 disapplying s 11, the effect of s 35(1) would then be that the contribution notice would be deemed to have been served on the date of the plaintiff's writ in the action. Thus the second defendant would be deprived of his limitation defence. Section 35(3) could not then, as it were, reinstate this defence—indeed, in our view s 35(3) is not a provision which creates a defence, but a mandatory direction to a court dealing either with an application to amend a new claim or an application to strike out a new claim added without leave, by amendment or (as in *Kennett v Brown*) by way of a contribution notice. For these reasons we conclude that *Kennett v Brown* was wrongly decided.

This brings us to the second decision to which we have referred, *Holland v Yates Building Ltd* (1989) Times, 5 December. The court consisted of Browne-Wilkinson V-C and Beldam LJ. It was an appeal against a decision of a judge that an order giving leave to join two men as defendants should be set aside. The appeal was not opposed, and we apprehend was therefore not argued to any great extent. In his judgment allowing the appeal Browne-Wilkinson V-C cited *Kennett v Brown* as authority for the proposition:

'In cases under s 35 of the Limitation Act 1980 it was wrong to seek to determine the question whether or not the cause of action against the new party was statute-barred unless and until the party sought to be joined had pleaded a defence under the 1980 Act.'

Since we have concluded that *Kennett v Brown* was wrongly decided, it follows that in our view *Holland v Yates Building Ltd* should not be treated as authoritative.

We now turn to consider the second argument advanced by Mr Keating in support of the agency's appeal. This is that the judge was wrong in the approach which he adopted, as summarised as para (8) above, namely that if it is reasonably arguable that the relevant limitation period has expired before an amendment is made, so that s 35(1) may deprive the defendants of a limitation defence they would otherwise have, the onus is on the plaintiffs to show that the amendment comes within the provisions of s 35(5) and Ord 20, r 5(5).

In making this submission Mr Keating relies upon a passage in a judgment of Glidewell LJ, with which Fox LJ agreed, in *Leicester Wholesale Fruit Market Ltd v Grundy* [1990] 1 All ER 442 at 445–447, [1990] 1 WLR 107 at 111–113. In that case the plaintiffs issued a writ against six defendants. Two-and-a-half months later, before the writ had been served on any defendant, they amended it without leave by adding a further four defendants. One of those defendants sought an order under Ord 15, r 6(2) that he should cease to be a party to the action. The basis of his application was that at the time when the writ was amended the limitation period of six years had already expired. The registrar refused the application but the judge allowed it on appeal. The plaintiffs appealed to this court.

a   In his judgment, after quoting the relevant parts of s 35, Glidewell LJ said
([1990] 1 All ER 442 at 445, [1990] 1 WLR 107 at 111):

'It follows, therefore, that if at the time when a further defendant is
added to an action by amendment he has a limitation defence which he
could raise if the plaintiff then issued a new writ against him, but if that
defence would not have been available to the defendant at the time when
b   the writ was originally issued, he should not be joined as a defendant
because he would thus be deprived of a defence which would then have
been available to him.'

He then went on to say, however, that there was no evidence in that case
that if the writ was statute-barred when it was amended to add the additional
c   defendants, it was not so barred when it was originally issued. In other words
the issue between the parties was whether the cause of action had arisen over
six years before the date when the writ was originally issued, or on a much
more recent date as the statement of claim alleged, that is to say some three
years before the issue of the writ. Glidewell LJ said:

d   'Of course, if the second is correct there is no question of limitation. If
the first is correct there would have been a limitation defence if Hallams
had been a party from the start.'

He did not say this in terms, but it is thus apparent that in that case s 35(1)
gave no advantage to the plaintiffs. He concluded ([1990] 1 All ER 442 at 447,
e   [1990] 1 WLR 107 at 113):

'In my judgment, the proper approach in circumstances such as these is
for the court to ask itself: if at the time when the writ was amended the
plaintiff had instead issued a fresh writ against the same defendant, could
that defendant have successfully applied to strike out the action on the
f   ground that the limitation period had expired and the action was thus an
abuse of the process of the court? If the answer to that question is No, then
I can see no reason why exactly the same result should not be achieved by
amending the writ to add the defendant as a defendant instead of issuing a
new piece of paper. Therefore, in my view, the test should be the same.'

g   The test to be applied in such circumstances Glidewell LJ derived from the
decision of this court in Ronex Properties Ltd v John Laing Construction Ltd (Clark
Nicholls & Marcel (a firm), third parties) [1982] 3 All ER 961 at 966, [1983] QB 398
at 405. He quoted a passage from the judgment of Donaldson LJ in which he
said:

h   'Where it is thought to be clear that there is a defence under the
Limitation Act, the defendant can either plead that defence and seek the
trial of a preliminary issue or, in a very clear case, he can seek to strike out
the claim on the ground that it is frivolous, vexatious and an abuse of the
process of the court ...'

j   Adopting the test Glidewell LJ had enunciated, this court allowed the
appeal.
In the present case the judge appreciated that in Leicester Wholesale Fruit
Market Ltd v Grundy on the facts referred to above s 35(1) gave no advantage to
the plaintiff, and he therefore indicated that he would have adopted the test
applied in that case if the circumstances had been similar: see that part of his
judgment which we have sought to summarise at para (11) above.

Unfortunately, *Leicester Wholesale Fruit Market Ltd v Grundy* [1990] 1 All ER 446 at 447, [1990] 1 WLR 107 at 113 created confusion by saying that a passage in a judgment of Purchas LJ in the earlier decision of this court in *Grimsby Cold Stores Ltd v Jenkins & Potter (a firm)* (1985) 1 Const LJ 362 was both obiter and wrong. In that case Purchas LJ had said (at 370):

'Leave to add a new party should not be given unless it can be shown that the defendant did no[t] have a reasonably arguable case on limitation which would be prejudiced by the additional new claim. I agree with Watkins L.J. that, as a result of the new evidence in the form of the report attached to the affidavit, the appellants have at least a strong arguable case that the damage was suffered more than six years before the date of the application to amend and that, therefore, this application should not be granted. Any prejudice to the applicant plaintiff can to a large extent be mitigated, if it exists, by having recourse to the ordinary process of issuing a fresh writ.'

In the present case the judge correctly said that the *Grimsby Cold Stores* case was on its own facts a case to which s 35(1) did apply so as to give an advantage to the plaintiff. The judge treated Glidewell LJ's remarks about Purchas LJ's judgment as obiter—he was too polite also to say that he was wrong—and thus felt able, in the present case, to adopt the test enunciated by Purchas LJ.

We now wish to make it clear that, though the test applied in the *Leicester Wholesale Fruit Market* case was the correct test in the circumstances of that case, in which s 35(1) gave the plaintiff no advantage, it was unnecessary for the decision in that case to disagree with what Purchas LJ said in the *Grimsby Cold Stores* case. Our view is that the judge was correct in concluding that where s 35(1) does, or may well, give the plaintiff an advantage, a different test, namely that enunciated by Purchas LJ in the *Grimsby Cold Stores* case, should be applied. In such a case, leave to amend by adding a new claim should not be given unless the plaintiff can show that the defendant does not have a reasonably arguable case on limitation which will be prejudiced by the new claim, or can bring himself with Ord 20, r 5.

We should add that the court in *Holland v Yates Building Ltd* also relied on the judgment of Glidewell LJ in the *Leicester Wholesale Fruit Market* case as being of general application and not limited to its own particular facts. For this reason also we regard the decision in *Holland* as one which should not be followed.

We therefore agree with the judge's decision not to allow an amendment to the statement of claim to plead a new claim for negligent misstatement in the December 1985 report. Once he had reached that decision, his decision also not to allow an amendment to plead misstatement in the August 1987 report was a matter for his discretion, with which this court cannot and should not interfere.

For the reasons set out above, we dismiss both the agency's appeal and RDL's appeal.

Appeals dismissed.

Raina Levy   Barrister.

Re Rex Williams Leisure plc

COURT OF APPEAL, CIVIL DIVISION
RUSSELL, STAUGHTON AND HOFFMANN LJJ
28, 29 MARCH, 27 APRIL 1994

Company – Director – Disqualification – Disqualification order – Evidence – Form of evidence – Affidavit – Oral evidence – Submission of no case to answer – Defendants wishing to preserve right to make submission of no case to answer – Defendants seeking direction enabling them to give evidence orally at hearing – Whether defendants required to file evidence in affidavit form before hearing – Company Directors Disqualification Act 1986, s 16(1) – Insolvent Companies (Disqualification of Unfit Directors) Proceedings Rules 1987, rr 4, 6.

Company – Director – Disqualification – Disqualification order – Evidence – Hearsay evidence – Affidavit filed by official appointed by Secretary of State to obtain information from employees and directors of company – Whether information based on notes of interviews with directors and employees inadmissible in evidence as hearsay – Companies Act 1985, s 447.

Company – Director – Disqualification – Disqualification order – Hearing – Postponement – Pending civil proceedings – Whether hearing of application for disqualification order should be postponed pending determination of civil proceedings against director.

In April 1990 an administration order was made in respect of a company which carried on a gaming and amusements business. The statement of affairs showed an estimated deficiency of £4·4m owing to creditors. On 27 April 1992 the Secretary of State applied for disqualification orders under s 8[a] of the Company Directors Disqualification Act 1986 against two former directors of the company and filed affidavit evidence in support of his application to show that it was expedient in the public interest that the orders be made. One of the affidavits filed in support was made by a chartered accountant who had been authorised by the Secretary of State to investigate the company's affairs and was based on notes he made of interviews with the directors and employees of the company when exercising his powers under s 447[b] of the Companies Act 1985 to require a company or person in possession of a company's documents to produce those documents and provide an explanation of them. Instead of filing evidence in answer as contemplated by r 6[c] of the Insolvent Companies (Disqualification of Unfit Directors) Proceedings Rules 1987, the directors applied to the court for (i) an order striking out those parts of the affidavit evidence put forward on behalf of the Secretary of State which recorded or exhibited statements by persons other than the directors themselves on the ground that such evidence was hearsay and inadmissible, (ii) a declaration that the directors were entitled to appear at the hearing and give evidence or call witnesses without first having filed affidavit evidence, thereby preserving their right to submit that there was no case to answer without revealing their own

---

a   Section 8, so far as material, is set out at p 32 *j* to p 33 *a*, post
b   Section 447, so far as material, is set out at p 31 *h* to p 32 *a*, post
c   Rule 6 is set out at p 34 *c d*, post

evidence and (iii) an order staying the disqualification application pending the determination of a civil action concerning the same issues brought by the company against one of the directors. The court refused the application and the directors appealed, contending, first, that s 16(1)^d of the 1986 Act entitled them to 'give evidence or call witnesses' without any prior obligation to file affidavit evidence in answer pursuant to r 6 of the 1987 rules and that if the 1987 rules operated to exclude oral evidence they would be ultra vires as purporting to exclude the right conferred in s 16(1) and, second, that the third party statements contained in the affidavits filed in support were inadmissible in the absence of some statutory exception to the hearsay rule.

Held – The appeal would be dismissed for the following reasons—

(1) Although s 16(1) of the 1986 Act gave a respondent to disqualification proceedings the right to give evidence or adduce the evidence of other witnesses at the hearing of the application for his disqualification, that right was not absolute, since it was qualified by the procedure set out in the 1987 rules, rr 4^e and 6 of which made it plain that a respondent who wished to oppose the making of a disqualification order would have to file any evidence he wished the court to take into consideration in the form of affidavits within the time specified. The court clearly retained a residuary discretionary control over its own procedure, which it might exercise to allow, for example, a witness in proceedings under the 1986 Act to supplement his affidavit with oral evidence in chief before being cross-examined, but the circumstances in which such evidence would be allowed at the hearing were exceptional and neither party was entitled to insist on it. The 1987 rules were not however ultra vires in advancing the point at which the respondent would be required to decide whether he intended to call evidence, since that change was essentially a procedural matter and it was within the power of the 1986 Act to make rules governing the procedure of the court in disqualification proceedings. It followed that the directors were obliged to file affidavit evidence in answer before the hearing and were not entitled as of right to wait until the hearing to give oral evidence or call witnesses (see p 34 *b* to *f*, p 36 *d* to *g*, p 41 *e* to *h* and p 42 *b*, post).

(2) Evidence in the form of third party statements obtained under s 447 of the 1985 Act by the Secretary of State when investigating the affairs of a company to determine whether it was expedient in the public interest to wind up the company, which was admissible on a winding-up petition under s 124A^f of the Insolvency Act 1986 despite the fact that it was hearsay, was also impliedly admissible in disqualification proceedings under s 8 of the 1986 Act. Moreover, the mere fact that there was no provision similar to r 3(2)^g of the 1987 rules, the effect of which was to make any assertion in the official receiver's report (whether or not within his personal knowledge) prima facie evidence of its truth, which applied to assertions in affidavits sworn for the Secretary of State in support of a disqualification application did not entail that they were inadmissible, since subordinate legislation such as the 1987 rules

---

d   Section 16(1), so far as material, provides: '... on the hearing of [an application for   a disqualification order] the [person against whom the order is sought] may appear and himself give evidence or call witnesses.'

e   Rule 4, so far as material, is set out at p 34 *h*, post

f   Section 124A, so far as material, is set out at p 39 *e*, post

g   Rule 3(2) is set out at p 33 *d*, postz

a could not repeal an exception to the hearsay rule which Parliament had impliedly created by primary legislation in s 8 of the 1986 Act. The question whether hearsay evidence which was untested by cross-examination of the informant might be insufficient to satisfy the burden of proving that a director was unfit against opposing evidence would depend on the circumstances of the particular case, and the fact that the Secretary of State might need to reinforce

b his case by affidavits from the appropriate informants was no reason why their hearsay evidence under s 447 should be inadmissible in disqualification proceedings. There were accordingly no grounds for striking out any parts of the affidavits filed in support (see p 39 *f g j* to p 40 *a j* and p 41 *b e f j* to p 42 *b*, post); *Re Armvent Ltd* [1975] 3 All ER 441 and *Re St Piran Ltd* [1981] 3 All ER 270 applied.

c (3) The fact that the Secretary of State had a public duty to apply for the disqualification of unfit company directors meant that he should not be held up indefinitely by other proceedings over which he had no control. The disqualification proceedings would not therefore be stayed pending determination of the administrators' action (see p 41 *d* to *f* and p 42 *b*, post).

d Decision of Sir Donald Nicholls V-C [1993] 2 All ER 741 affirmed.

Notes

For the disqualification of company directors, see 7(1) *Halsbury's Laws* (4th edn reissue) paras 569–585, and for cases on the subject, see 9(2) *Digest* (2nd reissue) 119–123, 4156–4169.

e For the Companies Act 1985, s 447, see 8 *Halsbury's Statutes* (4th edn) (1991 reissue) 516.

For the Company Directors Disqualification Act 1986, ss 8, 16, see ibid 781.

For the Insolvency Act 1986, s 124A, inserted by s 60(3) of the Companies Act 1989, see ibid 849.

f For the Insolvent Companies (Disqualification of Unfit Directors) Proceedings Rules 1987, rr 3, 4, 6, see 4 *Halsbury's Statutory Instruments* (1992 reissue) 539, 540.

Cases referred to in judgments

Armvent Ltd, Re [1975] 3 All ER 441, [1975] 1 WLR 1679.

g *City Investment Centres Ltd, Re* [1992] BCLC 956.

Grosvenor and West-End Railway Terminus Hotel Co Ltd, Re (1897) 76 LT 337, CA.

Keypak Homecare Ltd, Re [1990] BCLC 440.

Koscot Interplanetary (UK) Ltd, Re [1972] 3 All ER 829.

Laurie v Raglan Building Co Ltd [1941] 3 All ER 332, [1942] 1 KB 152, CA.

h *Moonbeam Cards Ltd, Re* [1993] BCLC 1099.

Practice Note [1921] WN 356.

R v Erdheim [1896] 2 QB 260, [1895–9] All ER Rep 610, CCR.

R v Harris (Richard) [1970] 3 All ER 746, [1970] 1 WLR 1252.

R v Scott (1856) Dears & B 47, 169 ER 909, CCR.

SBA Properties Ltd, Re [1967] 2 All ER 615, [1967] 1 WLR 799.

j *St Piran Ltd, Re* [1981] 3 All ER 270, [1981] 1 WLR 1300.

Travel and Holiday Clubs Ltd, Re [1967] 2 All ER 606, [1967] 1 WLR 711.

Cases also cited or referred to in skeleton arguments

Allied Produce Co Ltd, Re [1967] 3 All ER 399, [1967] 1 WLR 1469.

Arab Monetary Fund v Hashim (No 7) [1993] 4 All ER 114, [1993] 1 WLR 1014, CA.

Arrows Ltd (No 4), Re [1993] 3 All ER 861, [1993] Ch 452, CA.

Carecraft Construction Co Ltd, Re [1993] 4 All ER 499, [1994] 1 WLR 172.
Jazzgold Ltd, Re [1994] 1 BCLC 38.
Jones v A-G [1973] 3 All ER 518, [1974] Ch 148, CA.
Lombard Shipping and Forwarding Ltd, Re [1993] BCLC 238.
London and County Securities Ltd v Nicholson [1980] 1 WLR 948.
Noble Trees Ltd, Re [1993] BCLC 1185.
Pergamon Press Ltd, Re [1970] 3 All ER 535, [1971] Ch 388, CA.
Savings and Investment Bank Ltd v Gasco Investments (Netherlands) BV [1984] 1 All ER 296, [1984] 1 WLR 271.
Secretary of State for Trade and Industry v Langridge [1991] 3 All ER 591, [1991] Ch 402, CA.
Tasbian Ltd, Re (No 2) [1991] BCLC 59, CA.

Interlocutory appeal
Frank John Warren and Peter Allan Sealey, former directors of Rex Williams Leisure plc, appealed from the decision of Sir Donald Nicholls V-C ([1993] 2 All ER 741, [1994] Ch 1) made on 3 December 1992 dismissing their applications for (i) an order that the application by originating summons dated 27 April 1992 issued by the Secretary of State for Trade and Industry that the defendants be disqualified under s 8 of the Company Directors Disqualification Act 1986 be struck out on the ground that it was an abuse of the process of the court for that application to be heard while civil proceedings concerning the same issues were pending, (ii) a declaration that the directors were entitled under s 16(1) of the 1986 Act to give oral evidence at the hearing without first having served or filed affidavit evidence and (iii) an order that certain evidence in the affidavits filed in support of the originating summons be struck out on the ground that it was hearsay and inadmissible. The facts are set out in the judgment of Hoffmann LJ.

Clive Hugh Jones (instructed by *Garstangs*, Bolton) for the directors.
Elizabeth Gloster QC and *Guy Newey* (instructed by *Simone Higgins*) for the Secretary of State.

Cur adv vult

27 April 1994. The following judgments were delivered.

HOFFMANN LJ. This is an appeal by leave of the judge from three interlocutory rulings of Sir Donald Nicholls V-C ([1993] 2 All ER 741, [1994] Ch 1). They concern the procedure to be followed in an application by the Secretary of State for Trade and Industry to have company directors disqualified. Two of them raise questions of general importance. One is whether a respondent to such an application must file his evidence in opposition before the hearing or whether he can wait until then and give or call oral evidence. The other is whether the Secretary of State as applicant can rely upon statements taken from third parties in the course of an official investigation into the affairs of a company.

(1) *The facts*
   The directors (respondents to the application to disqualify) are Mr Frank Warren and Mr Peter Sealey. Mr Warren is, among other things, a boxing promoter. Mr Sealey is a solicitor. Both were directors of a company called

a
Rex Williams Leisure plc. Its principal business was the supply of amusement machines. It obtained a quotation on the unlisted securities market. Members of the public subscribed for shares. Early in 1988 it appears to have entered into some kind of transaction to buy from Mr Warren the shares in another company which he controlled for over £2m. In the end the purchase did not proceed. But as part of the transaction the company on 21 March 1988 paid Mr

b
Warren £200,000. Mr Sealey authorised the payment. After the share sale fell through, Mr Warren did not return the money. It remained unpaid on 30 April 1990, when the company was placed in administration. The estimated deficiency for creditors is £4·4m.

(2) Procedural steps so far

c
The joint administrators sued Mr Warren for the return of the £200,000. He gave notice of intention to defend the action. For the last three years the action has been asleep. The last thing that happened was on 9 January 1991, when a summons for summary judgment issued by the administrators was adjourned to the judge.

d
On 2 April 1991 the Secretary of State took an interest. There is no evidence as to why, but the chances are that he had received a report from the administrators under the Insolvent Companies (Reports on Conduct of Directors) (No 2) Rules 1986, SI 1986/2134. This requires administrators within six months of the date of the administration order to furnish the Secretary of State with a report on the persons who have been directors within

e
the preceding three years. At any rate, the Secretary of State authorised Mr Desmond High, a chartered accountant, to investigate the £200,000 payment pursuant to s 447 of the Companies Act 1985.

Section 447 is one of a battery of powers contained in Pt XIV of the Companies Act 1985, which is headed 'Investigation of Companies and their

f
Affairs; Requisition of Documents'. The best known is s 432(2), which empowers the Secretary of State to appoint inspectors to investigate the affairs of a company and report if it appears to him that there are circumstances suggesting various kinds of misconduct, including misfeasance by the persons concerned in its management. Section 431, more rarely used, provides for inspection on the application of some of the members or the company itself.

g
Sections 442 and 446 deal with more limited investigations into share ownership and share dealings. Section 447 has the sidenote 'Secretary of State's power to require production of documents'. For present purposes, these are the relevant provisions of s 447, as amended by s 63 of the Companies Act 1989:

h
'... (3) The Secretary of State may at any time, if he thinks there is good reason to do so, authorise an officer of his or any other competent person, on producing (if so required) evidence of his authority, to require a company to produce to him (the officer or other person) forthwith any documents which he (the officer or other person) may specify.

j
(4) Where by virtue of sub-section ... (3) the Secretary of State or an officer of his or other person has power to require the production of documents from a company, he or the officer or other person has the like power to require production of those documents from any person who appears to him or the officer or other person to be in possession of them ...

(5) The power under this section to require a company or other person to produce documents includes power—(a) if the documents are produced

... (ii) to require that person, or any other person who is a present or past *a* officer of, or is or was at any time employed by, the company in question, to provide an explanation of any of them ...

(8) A statement made by a person in compliance with such a requirement may be used in evidence against him.'

The product of a s 447 investigation will therefore consist primarily of documents which were already in existence but also explanations and *b* commentary by former officers or employees. It is an offence knowingly or recklessly to provide an explanation which is false in a material particular (s 451). But, unlike an inspector under ss 431 or 432, a person authorised to conduct an investigation under s 447 is not required to write a report expressing his opinion in the matters under investigation. His formal duty is *c* simply to gather information.

Informally, however, Mr High told the investigations division at the Department of Trade and Industry that as a result of his investigations, he had come to the conclusion that Mr Warren and Mr Sealey had acted unlawfully and in breach of their fiduciary duties to the company. They had simply extracted its cash. The result was that the Secretary of State decided to apply *d* to the court under s 8 of the Company Directors Disqualification Act 1986 for the disqualification of Mr Warren and Mr Sealey as directors on the ground that their conduct made them 'unfit to be concerned in the management of a company'.

Sections 6 to 10 of the 1986 Act provide for various circumstances in which *e* such an application may be made. The most common is under s 6, which deals with persons who have been directors of insolvent companies and whose conduct shows them to be unfit. If it appears to the Secretary of State 'expedient in the public interest' that a disqualification order should be made under s 6, he may either make the application himself or, in the case of a person who has been a director of a company in compulsory liquidation, he may direct *f* that the application be made by the official receiver. In either case, the information upon which the Secretary of State will act in deciding whether an application for a disqualification order is expedient in the public interest will be primarily derived from the 'office-holder' (ie the liquidator, administrator or administrative receiver). He has a statutory duty under s 7 of the 1986 Act *g* and also under the Insolvent Companies (Reports on Conduct of Directors) (No 2) Rules 1986 to report to the Secretary of State on matters which may indicate that a director is unfit.

An alternative route is s 8 of the 1986 Act, which can be used even if the company has not become insolvent. Leaving out reference to a number of statutory powers which do not for present purposes matter, these are the *h* relevant provisions of that section, as amended by s 198(2) of the Financial Services Act 1986:

'(1) If it appears to the Secretary of State from a report made by inspectors under section 437 of the Companies Act ... or from information *j* or documents obtained under section 447 ... of the Companies Act ... that it is expedient in the public interest that a disqualification order should be made against any person who is or has been a director or shadow director of any company, he may apply to the court for such an order to be made against that person

(2) The court may make a disqualification order against a person where, on an application under this section, it is satisfied that his conduct in

a
relation to the company makes him unfit to be concerned in the management of a company.'

In this case the Secretary of State applied under s 8 of the 1986 Act.

b
The procedure governing applications for disqualification orders is for the most part contained in the Insolvent Companies (Disqualification of Unfit Directors) Proceedings Rules 1987, SI 1987/2023 (the disqualification rules). Rule 2(a) says that an application in the High Court shall be made by originating summons and that the appropriate provisions of the Rules of the Supreme Court shall apply accordingly, except when the disqualification rules make provision to inconsistent effect. The Secretary of State issued the originating summons in these proceedings on 27 April 1992.

c
Rule 3 of the disqualification rules is headed 'The case against the respondent'. It reads as follows:

d
'(1) There shall, at the time when the summons is issued, be filed in court evidence in support of the application for a disqualification order; and copies of the evidence shall be served with the summons on the respondent.

(2) The evidence shall be by one or more affidavits, except where the applicant is the official receiver, in which case it may be in the form of a written report (with or without affidavits by other persons) which shall be treated as if it had been verified by affidavit by him and shall be prima facie
e
evidence of any matter contained in it.

(3) There shall in the affidavit or affidavits or (as the case may be) the official receiver's report be included a statement of the matters by reference to which the respondent is alleged to be unfit to be concerned in the management of a company.'

f
The evidence filed by the Secretary of State under r 3(1) and (2) consisted of three affidavits. One was by Mr Burns, a deputy inspector of companies. It was fairly formal and said pursuant to r 3(3) that the matters upon which the Secretary of State would rely were those concerning the £200,000 payment. The second affidavit was by Mr Copp, one of the administrators. He exhibited
g
his affidavit in the RSC Ord 14 application, setting out the results of his investigations. The third was by Mr High. He explained the progress of his investigations, describing and exhibiting some of the documents which he had obtained and his notes of the explanations which he had been given. He recorded his conclusion that the payment had been unauthorised, unlawful
h
and in breach of fiduciary duty.

Ordinarily, the next step would have been for the directors to file their evidence in answer. This is what is contemplated by r 6 of the disqualification rules, to which I shall return in a moment. But instead, on 10 July 1992, the directors took out a summons seeking the following relief. First, an order striking out the summons on the ground that it was an abuse of process for the
j
application to be heard while the action to recover the £200,000 was still proceeding. Sir Donald Nicholls V-C had little difficulty in refusing this application and I shall deal with it last. Secondly, a declaration that the directors were 'entitled' to appear at the hearing and give evidence or call witnesses without having filed affidavit evidence. Thirdly, an order striking out those parts of the affidavits of Mr Copp and Mr High which recorded or exhibited statements by persons other than the directors themselves. The

summons was adjourned to Sir Donald Nicholls V-C who refused all three applications. The directors appeal. *a*

(3) *Oral evidence or affidavits?*
The directors claim that they need not file affidavit evidence in answer. Instead, they say that they are entitled as of right to wait until the hearing and then give oral evidence or call witnesses. Or if the court has a discretion in the *b* matter, they say that it should be exercised in favour of ordering pleadings followed by a trial with oral evidence.

The disqualification rules are not the most hospitable terrain on which to mount such a submission. Rule 6 provides:

'(1) The respondent shall, within 28 days from the date of service of the *c* summons, file in court any affidavit evidence in opposition to the application he wishes the court to take into consideration and shall forthwith serve upon the applicant a copy of such evidence.
(2) The applicant shall, within 14 days from receiving the copy of the respondent's evidence, file in court any further evidence in reply he wishes the court to take into consideration and shall forthwith serve a copy of that *d* evidence upon the respondent.'

The imperative 'shall' in r 6(1) suggests that if the respondent wants his evidence taken into consideration, he *must* file it within the stipulated time. Perhaps it could have been clearer still: 'shall file in court any *affidavit* evidence' might at first sight leave open the possibility that he could adduce *e* other forms of evidence (eg oral evidence) which does not have to be filed in court.   But then why does it say 'he wishes the court to take into consideration'? Presumably he wishes the court to take all his evidence into consideration. These words only make sense if they mean that the evidence he wishes the court to take into consideration must be filed on affidavit. *f* Furthermore, r 6(3), which deals with the Secretary of State's evidence in reply, makes it clear that it must be on affidavit. How is this to be done unless the respondent has filed affidavits?

The question is put beyond doubt if one takes into account the way the 1987 disqualification rules amended the previous version in the Insolvent Companies (Disqualification of Unfit Directors) Proceedings Rules 1986, SI *g* 1986/612. In the 1986 rules, r 6 said that the respondent 'may' within 28 days file affidavit evidence. It left out the words 'he wishes the court to take into consideration'. Now 'may' has been replaced by 'shall'. And to the various notices which by r 4 have to be indorsed on the originating summons, the 1987 rules have added the following: *h*

'(e) that any evidence which the respondent wishes to be taken into consideration by the court must be filed in court in accordance with the time limits imposed under Rule 6 (the provisions of which shall be set out on the summons).'

This could hardly be clearer. In the face of this language Mr Jones (who *j* appeared for the directors) has deployed some of the familiar weaponry of statutory construction: the argument from a priori incredulity (it is impossible to believe that the legislator intended by such language to take away such a fundamental human right) and the various forms of argument from inconsistency with other parts of current and earlier legislation. Some of these linguistic arguments would carry greater weight if the Companies Act 1985 and a associated legislation were the work of a single faultless author. In fact, the legislation is a vast legislative mosaic, the work of many hands, parts of which date back to the Companies Act 1862 (25 & 26 Vict, c 89) and the Bankrupt Law Consolidation Act 1849 (12 & 13 Vict c 106). Interpretation must take this into account.

b I could simply say that the language of the disqualification rules is now so clear as to be impervious to arguments of this kind. But out of respect to Mr Jones's skilful argument, I shall deal with them in more detail.

(a) History

c Mr Jones pointed out that when a power to disqualify directors was first introduced in s 217 of the Companies Act 1929, the procedure was assimilated to that of the misfeasance summons, a summary procedure which went back to the Companies Act 1862: see r 66 of the Companies (Winding-up) Rules 1929, SR & O 1929/612 (L 16). Misfeasance summonses had originally followed the traditional Chancery procedure of having all the evidence on affidavit, but in 1921 the Companies Court adopted a more common law

d approach. Astbury J issued a *Practice Note* [1921] WN 356:

'In a recent case tried in this Court various defects in the present practice relating to the trial of misfeasance summonses ... were made apparent. The practice of allowing witnesses to give their evidence in chief by affidavits, prepared or settled for them by others, in cases where real
e disputes of fact exist and/or where various charges of misfeasance or breach of trust are involved, is open to grave objection, and when numerous or complicated issues of law or fact exist, the points relied upon are under the practice at present prevailing, as and when occasion demands, amended or raised for the first time and from time to time during the progress of the trial, which causes confusion, recalling of
f witnesses, possible injustice, waste of time and increased costs ... in future the practice in these cases shall be as follows: On the return of the summons the Registrar shall give directions as to whether points of claim and defence are to be delivered or not, as to the taking of evidence wholly or in part by affidavit or orally, as to cross-examination, and generally as to the procedure on the summons. No report or affidavit shall be made or
g filed until the Registrar shall so direct.'

Rule 66 of the 1929 rules reflected this *Practice Note*, providing that no affidavit or report was to be filed in advance of the first appointment before the registrar and giving him a wide discretion 'as to the taking of evidence wholly or in part
h by affidavit or orally'. Mr Jones says that against this background of practice, the legislation on disqualification reflected an expectation that the procedure would be primarily oral. Section 217(2) of the Companies Act 1929 said that the official receiver should give the respondent not less than ten days' notice of his intention to make an application 'and on the hearing of the application that person may appear and himself give evidence or call witnesses'. This was the
j language of trial at common law rather than Chancery affidavits. Section 217(2) has been carried forward into successive statutes dealing with disqualification and still exists as s 16(1) of the 1986 Act. Therefore, said Mr Jones, the disqualification rules should not be construed to exclude the oral procedure envisaged by Astbury J in an appropriate case: where 'real disputes of fact exist and/or various charges of misfeasance or breach of trust are involved'. The present was such a case. Mr Jones went so far as diffidently to

suggest that if the 1987 disqualification rules *did* exclude oral evidence by or on behalf of the respondent, they would be ultra vires as purporting to exclude a right conferred by Parliament in s 16(1) of the 1986 Act.

No doubt there are many cases in which the most effective method of trial is to have a brief statement of the issues and then have the protagonists into the witness box as soon as possible to tell their stories in their own words. It happens daily in county courts all over the land. But in the High Court it has been largely abandoned. The 1987 disqualification rules are only part of a general trend towards greater emphasis on written procedure in advance of the hearing, which is also reflected in the rules for the exchange of witness statements (RSC Ord 38, r 2A) and the use of skeleton arguments. Misfeasance proceedings under s 212 of the Insolvency Act 1986 are once more tried on affidavits: see the Insolvency Rules 1986, SI 1986/1925. So the short answer to Mr Jones's submission based on the history of disqualification procedure is that times have changed. The advantage of allowing both sides to discover each other's cases in detail before trial and cross-examination is perceived to outweigh the loss of spontaneity and the increase in costs at the pre-trial stage.

As for the submission of ultra vires, I do not think that s 16(1) and its predecessors were ever intended to confer an absolute right to give or call oral evidence. Even the *Practice Note* [1921] WN 356 and the subsequent Companies (Winding-up) Rules 1929 gave the court power to direct that evidence should be wholly by affidavit. All that has happened is that this has become the norm. So in my judgment, 'give evidence or call witnesses' confers a right to give evidence or adduce the evidence of other witnesses, but the manner in which that may be done is a matter for the rules.

Of course the court retains a residuary discretionary control over its own procedure (see, for example, RSC Ord 2, r 1). A judge will commonly allow a witness in proceedings under the 1986 Act to supplement his affidavit with a few answers in chief before being cross-examined. And no doubt if a respondent wishes to call a witness over whom he genuinely has no influence and who has refused to swear an affidavit, the court will allow him to do so on subpoena. But the circumstances in which oral evidence in chief will be allowed at the hearing are exceptional and neither applicant nor respondent is entitled to insist on it.

(b) *No case to answer*

Mr Jones said that a requirement that the directors put their evidence on affidavit would deprive them of an effective opportunity to submit that they had no case to answer. A submission of no case to answer, ie that there is no evidence upon which a notional jury *could* find for the plaintiff or applicant, is, in civil proceedings without a jury, an arcane and almost obsolete procedure of which the collective experience of the court could recall only one instance. The reason for its disappearance is that in *Laurie v Raglan Building Co Ltd* [1941] 3 All ER 332 at 337, [1942] 1 KB 152 at 155 Lord Greene MR (with whom the other two members of the Court of Appeal agreed) said that the proper practice is for the judge to refuse to rule on a submission of no case to answer unless counsel for the defendant has said that he proposes to call no evidence. If this is the invariable practice, a submission of no case to answer would appear to offer no advantage over closing one's case without calling evidence and submitting that the plaintiff has not discharged the burden of proof.

Mr Jones accepted that, one way or the other, he would have to elect whether or not to call evidence. But he said that in an ordinary civil trial, he *a* could postpone this decision until after the applicant's evidence had been tested by cross-examination. Even if there had been an order for exchange of witness statements under Ord 38, r 2A, so that his right to call evidence was conditional on having served a witness statement, he could still decide not to call the witness. If so, the witness statement could not be used as evidence against him: see r 2A(4). But once he and his witnesses had committed

b themselves to affidavit, their evidence was available for both sides.

This may represent a difference between trial on affidavits and trial with oral evidence preceded by exchange of witness statements. But I do not regard the difference as sufficient to cast any doubt upon the construction or vires of the disqualification rules. Until Ord 38, r 2A, a litigant had a privilege to withhold until trial the contents of the proofs taken from his witnesses. Now it can be

c made a condition of his calling their evidence that he should have waived that privilege in advance of the trial. Likewise, the disqualification rules advance the moment at which a respondent must elect whether or not he is going to call evidence. Both changes are in my view purely procedural and within the rule-making power to regulate the 'practice and procedure' of the court

d exercising jurisdiction under ss 6 to 10 of the 1986 Act: see s 21(2) of the Act, applying s 411 of and para 2 of Sch 8 to the Insolvency Act 1986.

(c) Expense

Mr Jones next submitted that to require affidavits to be filed often placed an unfair burden upon respondents to disqualification applications. Affidavits

e were expensive. They were usually drafted by lawyers. Respondents whose companies had become insolvent tended to be short of money. It would be much cheaper if they could simply go into the witness box and tell their stories. Mr Jones, who has great experience of the Companies Court, said that disqualification applications not infrequently went undefended because the

f director could not afford to oppose them.

I think, speaking for myself, that this was Mr Jones's best point. The 'cards-on-the-table' philosophy, as exemplified by Ord 38, r 2A and the disqualification rules, may save costs overall by promoting settlements and shortening oral hearings. But it does undoubtedly produce a 'front-loading' of the costs at the pre-trial stage when affidavits or witness statements have to be

g prepared. This is capable of being used oppressively, enabling the state or the richer party to drown his opponent in documents and testimony. I do not suggest that anything of the kind has happened in this case, but it is something which requires careful handling on the part of the department and vigilance on the part of the registrar and judges.

h But although I think that the point has substance, it does not advance Mr Jones's argument in this case. It is a general complaint about the spirit of the times rather than a reason for not giving the disqualification rules the effect they were obviously intended to have.

j *(4) The use of hearsay*

The second point of principle is the use by the Secretary of State, in the affidavits of Mr High and Mr Copp and their exhibits, of statements made to them by third parties. The statements by the respondents themselves are of course admissible at common law as admissions. But the remaining statements are at common law inadmissible under the hearsay rule. They can be admissible in disqualification proceedings only by virtue of some statutory exception to that rule.

Miss Gloster QC, who appeared for the Secretary of State, relied upon an *implied* exception in the case of information obtained under statutory powers which the Secretary of State is required to take into account in deciding whether it is expedient in the public interest that certain proceedings should be brought under the Companies Act 1985 or associated legislation. In such cases she says that there is an implied hearsay exception which allows the court to receive the same information in evidence.

The exception originates in two decisions of Pennycuick J sitting in the Companies Court in 1967: *Re Travel and Holiday Clubs Ltd* [1967] 2 All ER 606, [1967] 1 WLR 711 and *Re SBA Properties Ltd* [1967] 2 All ER 615, [1967] 1 WLR 799. Each concerned a winding-up petition presented by the Board of Trade under s 169(3) of the Companies Act 1948, which said that the Board could present such a petition on the just and equitable ground if it appeared from a report of inspectors appointed under s 169(1) or (2) (now ss 431 and 432 of the 1985 Act) that it was expedient to do so. In *Re Travel and Holiday Clubs* [1967] 2 All ER 606 at 609, [1967] 1 WLR 711 at 715 Pennycuick J said:

'It seems to me that it would not be in accordance with the apparent intention of the section that where inspectors appointed under the Act have made a report, the court should not be entitled to look at that report and accept it not as hearsay evidence, but as material of a different character altogether and should have to be satisfied anew by evidence of the ordinary nature as to the facts found in the report.'

In *Re SBA Properties Ltd* he distinguished a case concerning a report of inspectors under the Companies Act 1862, in which the Court of Appeal had said that the report was not 'evidence in a court of justice of the existence of any fact mentioned in it': per Lord Esher MR in *Re Grosvenor and West-End Railway Terminus Hotel Co Ltd* (1897) 76 LT 337 at 338. Under s 169(3), Pennycuick J said the question was—

'whether the court can treat the inspectors' report, not as evidence in the ordinary sense, but as material on which, if it is not challenged, the court can proceed to make a winding-up order on the ground that it is just and equitable so to do.' (See [1967] 2 All ER 615 at 621, [1967] 1 WLR 799 at 806.)

These decisions left two matters for later clarification: first, the somewhat mysterious distinction between 'evidence' and 'material', and secondly, the suggestion that if the report was 'challenged', it might cease to be evidence or 'material', leaving all the relevant facts to be proved de novo.

Both points were resolved by later decisions. *Re Koscot Interplanetary (UK) Ltd* [1972] 3 All ER 829 shows recognition that the report is hearsay evidence and that s 169(3) of the 1948 Act (by then replaced by s 35 of the Companies Act 1967) created an implied statutory exception to the hearsay rule. In *Re Armvent Ltd* [1975] 3 All ER 441, [1975] 1 WLR 1679 the petition was opposed. Templeman J said:

'It seems to me even if the report of the inspectors is challenged nevertheless it ought to be treated as prima facie evidence and that it ought to be left to a judge in any case having read the report and having seen the witnesses to make up his own mind whether it is just and equitable to wind up the company. The whole machinery of the inspectors' report was evolved in order to enable the Secretary of State to present a winding-up

a petition where the Secretary of State considers the public interest so demands. It would be unfortunate if once the Secretary of State has reached that conclusion on proper grounds based on the inspectors' detailed report, that the court should be right back to square one and start again as though the inspectors had never come on the scene at all.' (See [1975] 3 All ER 441 at 446, [1975] 1 WLR 1679 at 1685–1686.)

b Finally in *Re St Piran Ltd* [1981] 3 All ER 270 at 276, [1981] 1 WLR 1300 at 1306 Dillon J referred to the principle which had evolved as an exception to the hearsay rule and stated its basis as follows:

c '... it would be nonsensical if the court could not take the report into consideration in deciding whether it was just and equitable that the company should be wound up when by the very terms of s 169(3) of the 1948 Act, as of s 35 of the 1967 Act, it is on the basis of his consideration of the report that the Secretary of State has concluded that it is expedient that the winding-up petition should be presented or that the company should be wound up.'

d The provisions which derive from s 169(3) of the 1948 Act have been amended and extended on a number of occasions. The latest version is s 124A of the Insolvency Act 1986, which was inserted by the Companies Act 1989. These are the relevant provisions:

e '(1) Where it appears to the Secretary of State from—(a) any report made or information obtained under Part XIV of the Companies Act 1985 (company investigations, &c) ... that it is expedient in the public interest that a company should be wound up, he may present a petition for it to be wound up if the court thinks it just and equitable for it to be so ...'

f Thus the material which the Secretary of State may take into consideration includes whatever is gathered under the inspection and investigation powers of Pt XIV of the 1985 Act, including s 447.

Miss Gloster says that if the exception applies to public interest petitions under s 124A of the Insolvency Act 1986, it should equally apply to disqualification applications under s 8 of the 1986 Act. The relevant phrase-

g ology of the two sections is almost identical. Sir Donald Nicholls V-C found the analogy a powerful one and so do I.

But Mr Jones submitted that disqualification applications were quite different from public interest petitions for winding up. In the latter, no particular facts had to be proved. In *Re Armvent Ltd* [1975] 3 All ER 441 at 443,

h [1975] 1 WLR 1679 at 1683 Templeman J said:

'I am not here to establish whether every charge made by the inspectors and every conclusion is right. In my judgment there is no way by which the truth about this company can be established save by winding-up.'

j All that the evidence had to establish was that it was in the public interest that the company should be wound up to enable the official receiver to investigate its affairs. But in a disqualification application the Secretary of State must prove facts which show that the director is unfit.

In my judgment these distinctions go to weight rather than admissibility. In a disqualification application, hearsay evidence untested by cross-examination of the informant may be insufficient to satisfy the burden of proof against opposing evidence. It will depend upon the facts and probabilities of each case.

Once the Secretary of State knows from the opposing affidavits which material
facts are seriously in dispute, he may be well advised to reinforce his case by   *a*
affidavits from the appropriate informants. But that is no reason why their
hearsay evidence obtained under s 447 of the 1985 Act should be inadmissible.
Much of what they say may be uncontested, in which case it would have been
a waste of time and money to insist that they swear affidavits.

Mr Jones relies upon two further arguments on construction. First, he draws   *b*
attention to s 447(8) of the 1985 Act, which I have quoted above. He says that
if the statute expressly makes the respondent's own statements admissible
against him, surely it follows that statements by other people are not. In my
judgment, however, s 447(8) has nothing to do with the hearsay rule. At
common law a statement by a party to litigation is always admissible against
him. No statutory exception to the hearsay rule is needed. Section 447(8) is one   *c*
of a number of sections scattered over various statutes which are intended to
deal with a different problem, namely an early nineteenth century opinion that
statements made under statutory compulsion were not 'voluntary' for the
purposes of the confession rule in criminal proceedings. In fact this view was
decisively rejected in R v Scott (1856) Dears & B 47, 169 ER 909, but starting   *d*
with s 17(8) of the Bankruptcy Act 1883 (46 & 47 Vict c 52), Parliament has been
constantly vigilant in case it should again raise its head. The result is that
powers to obtain information in the Companies Act 1985, Insolvency Act 1986
and associated legislation are almost invariably accompanied by a provision
that the answers are to be admissible against the informant. They may have
served little purpose except to stir up arguments of the expressio unius variety   *e*
(see, for example, R v Erdheim [1896] 2 QB 260, [1895–99] All ER Rep 610 and R
v Harris [1970] 3 All ER 746, [1970] 1 WLR 1252), and in Re Keypak Homecare Ltd
[1990] BCLC 440 Harman J (probably unfairly) declared one of them to be
absolutely meaningless. But they were not intended as exceptions to the rule
against hearsay.   *f*

Mr Jones based a similar argument on r 3(2) of the disqualification rules,
which I have already quoted. The 1986 version of the rules had merely equated
the official receiver's report to an affidavit. It said that the report 'shall be
treated as if it had been verified by affidavit by him'. The 1987 version added
the words 'and shall be prima facie evidence of any matter contained in it'. The   *g*
effect of these words is to make any assertion in the report, whether or not
within the personal knowledge of the official receiver, prima facie evidence of
its truth: see Re City Investment Centres Ltd [1992] BCLC 956 and Re Moonbeam
Cards Ltd [1993] BCLC 1099. There is no similar provision for assertions in
affidavits sworn on behalf of the Secretary of State and so Mr Jones says that if
the amendment was necessary to make hearsay admissible in reports by the   *h*
official receiver, it must follow that it is not admissible in affidavits.

The formal answer to this submission is that subordinate legislation such as
the disqualification rules cannot repeal an exception to the hearsay rule which
Parliament has impliedly created by primary legislation in s 8. The more
realistic answer is that it is indeed odd that in reports by the official receiver *any*   *j*
hearsay should be admissible, whereas affidavits should be limited to hearsay
which is admissible under specific exceptions such as s 8 or the Civil Evidence
Act 1968. The new r 3(2) seems another example of legislation which has not
been sufficiently thought through and, in a praiseworthy attempt to improve
or clarify one detail of the law, produces inconsistency or uncertainty in other

parts. But this is not in my judgment sufficient to prevent statements obtained
under s 447 of the 1985 Act from being impliedly admissible in proceedings
under s 8 of the Company Directors Disqualification Act 1986. It is therefore
unnecessary for me to deal with the Secretary of State's alternative
submissions that the hearsay passages in the affidavits should not be struck out
because they might be admissible under the 1968 Act or Ord 38, r 3. Sir Donald
Nicholls V-C dealt separately with hearsay statements, exhibited documents
and conclusory assertions, but I agree that there are no grounds for striking out
any parts of the affidavits and the appeal against his ruling therefore fails.

(5) Stay pendente lite

Finally, I return to the first order sought on the directors' summons, which
was an order striking out the disqualification proceedings as an abuse of
process because they were launched while the action by the administrators to
recover the £200,000 was still proceeding. This action, as I mentioned earlier,
has been dormant for more than three years. In this court, Mr Jones put
forward the more modest proposal that there should be a stay of these
proceedings until the action had been concluded. Even this was not pursued
with great enthusiasm. For my part, I think it would be quite absurd. The
Secretary of State has a public duty to apply for the disqualification of unfit
directors. He cannot be held up indefinitely by other proceedings over which
he has no control.

(6) Conclusion

I think that the judgment of Sir Donald Nicholls V-C was entirely right and
I would dismiss this appeal.

STAUGHTON LJ. I agree that this appeal should be dismissed. Of the two
points which seem to me most significant, the first is whether the Insolvent
Companies (Disqualification of Unfit Directors) Proceedings Rules 1987, SI
1987/2023, are ultra vires.

It is said that they are, if and to the extent that they do not allow a
respondent to call evidence unless he has filed an affidavit of the proposed
witness. That is said to conflict with s 16(1) of the Company Directors
Disqualification Act 1986, which provides that the person against whom an
order is sought 'may appear and himself give evidence or call witnesses'.

The 1986 Act contemplates in s 21, although somewhat indirectly, that rules
may be made. In my judgment it enables rules to deal with how evidence shall
be given and witnesses called; and in particular it permits a requirement that
affidavits shall first be filed. This is essentially a rule as to how the right
conferred by s 16(1) shall be exercised, and not a derogation from that right.

The second point that has troubled me concerns hearsay evidence. RSC Ord
41, r 5 provides that, subject to a number of exceptions which do not apply in
the present case, 'an affidavit may contain only such facts as the deponent is
able of his own knowledge to prove'.

How then can the Secretary of State be entitled to use affidavits of
information and belief in disqualification proceedings? As Hoffmann LJ has
shown, this stems from an implied statutory provision as to the use of hearsay
as evidence, or at any rate as provisional evidence until it is challenged. That
doctrine is now of respectable antiquity, having been established between 1967

and 1975. I would for my part have hesitated to accept it when first propounded. But as it has existed for a substantial period of time, during which relevant statutory provisions have been replaced and re-enacted or amended, I would not now alter it.

RUSSELL LJ. I also agree.

Appeal dismissed. Leave to appeal to the House of Lords refused.

Carolyn Toulmin   Barrister.

Re Barn Crown Ltd

CHANCERY DIVISION (COMPANIES COURT)
JUDGE RICH QC
20, 21, 24 JANUARY 1994

Company – Winding up – Disposition of property – Disposition of property after commencement of winding up – What constitutes a disposition – Insolvency Act 1986, s 127.

Payment into a bank account of a company which is in credit after the commencement of winding-up proceedings against the company does not constitute a disposition of property of the company in favour of the bank and therefore is not caught by s 127[a] of the Insolvency Act 1986 (see p 51 *j* to p 52 *d*, post).

Re Mal Bower's Macquarie Electrical Centre Pty Ltd (in liq) [1974] 1 NSWLR 254 and *Re J Leslie Engineers Co Ltd (in liq)* [1976] 2 All ER 85 considered.

Notes

For the relation back of winding-up orders, see 7(2) *Halsbury's Laws* (4th edn reissue) paras 1698–1700.

For the Insolvency Act 1986, s 127, see 4 *Halsbury's Statutes* (4th edn) (1987 reissue) 809.

Cases referred to in judgment

Gray's Inn Construction Co Ltd, Re [1980] 1 All ER 814, [1980] 1 WLR 711, CA.
Joachimson (N) v Swiss Bank Corp [1921] 3 KB 110, [1921] All ER Rep 92, CA.
Leslie (J) Engineers Co Ltd (in liq), Re [1976] 2 All ER 85, [1976] 1 WLR 292.
Loteka Property Ltd (in liq), Re [1990] 1 Qd R 322, Qld SC.
McGuinness Bros (UK) Ltd, Re (1987) 3 BCC 571.
Mal Bower's Macquarie Electrical Centre Pty Ltd (in liq), Re [1974] 1 NSWLR 254, NSW SC.
Mersey Steel and Iron Co Ltd v Naylor Benzon & Co (1884) 9 App Cas 434, [1881–85] All ER Rep 365, HL.
Midland Bank Ltd v Reckitt [1933] AC 1, [1932] All ER Rep 90, HL.

---

a   Section 127, so far as material, is set out at p 43 *g*, post

a *National Australia Bank Ltd v KDS Construction Services Pty Ltd* (1987) 163 CLR 668, Aust HC.

National Commercial Banking Corp of Australia Ltd v Batty (1986) 160 CLR 251, Aust HC.

Taylor v Plumer (1815) 3 M & S 562, [1814–23] All ER Rep 167, 105 ER 721.

b *Underwood (A L) Ltd v Bank of Liverpool and Martins, A L Underwood Ltd v Barclays Bank* [1924] 1 KB 775, [1924] All ER Rep 230, CA.

Cases also cited

French's (Wine Bar) Ltd, Re [1987] BCLC 499.

London and Mediterranean Bank, Re, Bolognesi's Case (1870) LR 5 Ch App 567.

c *Maran Distributors Pty Ltd (in liq), Re* (1992) 11 ACLC 167, Qld SC.

Norfolk Plumbing Supplies Pty Ltd v Commonwealth Bank of Australia (1992) 10 ACLC 158, NSW SC.

Westpac Banking Corp v Merlo [1991] 1 NZLR 560, NZ CA.

Application

d By notice of application, Malcom John Mears, the liquidator of Barn Crown Ltd (the company), applied for an order declaring that the receipt of £37,134·30 by the respondent, Banco Bilbao Vizcaya (the bank), constituted dispositions of the company's property which were void under s 127 of the Insolvency Act 1986. The facts are set out in the judgment.

e *Andrew Feldman* (instructed by *Clifford Harris & Co*) for the liquidator.

Thomas Lowe (instructed by *Bazley White & Co*) for the bank.

JUDGE RICH QC. The order to wind up this company was made on 19 f February 1992, and the applicant was appointed liquidator. He applies by application dated 30 May 1993 for a declaration that the receipt of amounts totalling £37,134·30 by the bank between 23 October 1991 and 24 February 1992 constituted dispositions of the company's property which were void pursuant to s 127 of the Insolvency Act 1986.

The form of the application is in the winding-up proceedings. The g Insolvency Rules 1986, SI 1986/1925, provide for such applications 'under the Act or Rules'. Section 127 provides:

> 'In a winding up by the court, any disposition of the company's property … made after the commencement of the winding up is, unless the court otherwise orders, void.'

h It follows therefore that such an application and any application by a respondent for the validation of any disposition is an application under the 1986 Act.

The application continues by seeking an order that the bank pay the j liquidator the said sum of £37,000-odd. Although counsel could not point to the provisions of the rules which provide for the making of such order on such an application, I was referred to the decision of Harman J in *Re McGuinness Bros (UK) Ltd* (1987) 3 BCC 571, in which he assumes such jurisdiction and to *Re J Leslie Engineers Co Ltd (in liq)* [1976] 2 All ER 85, [1976] 1 WLR 292, where Oliver J made such an order on an application by summons. I accept that where the declaration is made under s 127 upon an application to which the person who has the benefit of the disposition is a party, it is appropriate to make an order for payment, but as I think only in such cases.

The bank admits that such payments as are referred to in the application were made to it after the commencement of the winding up by the presentation of the petition on 13 September 1991. 23 October 1991 is 14 days after the advertisement of that petition. Payments in the form of third party cheques were accepted by the bank, collected by it on the company's behalf and credited to the company's account. After allowing for £2,854·68, which stood to the company's credit at the date when the liquidator was appointed and has been paid to him, and £800, which was paid to the company in cash, the sum of £37,134·30 claimed represented the total receipts into the company's account over the period.

By affidavit dated 6 May 1993 the bank's solicitor had disputed whether the receipt by the bank of these sums constituted dispositions of the company's property. Upon opening on behalf of the liquidator Mr Feldman therefore sought leave to amend the application to seek alternative relief, namely a declaration that payment out from the company's account did constitute such dispositions and an order for payment of a like sum.

Mr Lowe for the bank claimed that to allow such an amendment nearly two years after the winding-up order had been made raised a possibility of prejudice to the bank because on the application, as originally made, it would not have been necessary to investigate the reasons for the payments, whereas in order to determine whether such dispositions as were involved in the making of payments should be validated, it would be necessary to know whether, for example, they were made in respect of debts incurred before or after the commencement of the winding up, and such investigation, if not made promptly, would be difficult.

I am not certain that there really is such a distinction between the two claims, having regard to the basis upon which the actual order for payment was arrived at by the Court of Appeal in Re Gray's Inn Construction Co Ltd [1980] 1 All ER 814, [1980] 1 WLR 711. The risk of such prejudice was, however, in any event, sufficiently overcome by an agreement on the basis of which the amendment was allowed. It was agreed on behalf of the liquidator to limit any claim for repayment to £16,094·96 or such larger sum not exceeding £20,000 as might be proved in the liquidation within six months of 20 January 1994. On that basis the bank, for itself, agreed not to seek validation of any dispositions in excess of such sums. The amendment was therefore allowed.

In the event, however, the amendment, except in so far as it limited the scope of any order for payment which would result from a declaration on the application as originally made, proved an unnecessary complication in the proceedings. Mr Lowe did not dispute that the payments out of the account did constitute dispositions of the company's property, but, as was accepted by Mr Feldman, they were not dispositions of such property to the bank. Although Mr Feldman reserved the right to claim payment of such sums from the bank on grounds other than mere restitution, he accepted that any such claim ought to be pleaded in some way, and he therefore accepted that it would not be appropriate for me to make an order for payment by the bank on the present application unless I held that the receipts by the bank did constitute dispositions of the company's property.

Mr Lowe accepted that if such receipts did constitute such dispositions, then it would be appropriate to make an order upon the present application for payment in the agreed form. Thus, the sole issue for my determination is whether receipts by the bank did constitute dispositions of the company's property.

It was further agreed for the purposes of determining that issue that the company's account with the bank should be treated as having been in credit at all material times. As a matter of fact this was not strictly accurate because for some three days the account was overdrawn because some cheques which had been paid into it had been dishonoured. The liquidator did not, however, seek to found any claim upon that fact, and I therefore, by agreement, treat the account as having been in credit at all material times.

The application, as originally made, relied upon some observations of Buckley LJ in *Re Gray's Inn Construction Co.* In that case the Court of Appeal reversed a decision of Templeman J where he held that payments of cheques to a bank in circumstances where the company was throughout running an overdraft were not dispositions of property within the predecessor of s 127 of the 1986 Act. Buckley LJ said ([1980] 1 All ER 814 at 818, [1980] 1 WLR 711 at 715):

> 'The judge proceeded on the basis, which he held to be the position in law, that payment of moneys to the credit of a company's account, whether it is in credit or not, do not constitute a disposition of the company's property. That is a view with which, with deference to the judge, I feel unable to agree. When a customer's account with his banker is overdrawn he is a debtor to his banker for the amount of the overdraft. When he pays a sum of money into the account, whether in cash or by payment in of a third party's cheque, he discharges his indebtedness to the bank pro tanto. There is clearly in these circumstances, in my judgment, a disposition by the company to the bank of the amount of the cash or of the cheque. It may well be the case, as counsel for the bank has submitted, that in clearing a third party's cheque and collecting the amount due on it, the bank acts as the customer's agent, but as soon as it credits the amount collected in reduction of the customer's overdraft, as in the ordinary course of banking business it has authority to do in the absence of any contrary instruction from the customer, it makes a disposition on the customer's behalf in its own favour discharging pro tanto the customer's liability on the overdraft. Counsel for the bank was constrained in the course of the argument to accept that this is so. In the present case the company's account with the bank was overdrawn, so I need not consider what the position would have been if any cheque had been paid in when the account was in credit, but I doubt whether even in those circumstances it could be properly said that the payment in did not constitute a disposition of the amount of the cheque in favour of the bank.'

Mr Feldman has shown me that the writers of various textbooks on company and on banking law have not challenged this dictum as to the position which did not arise in that case, namely a payment in when the account was in credit. Naturally such dictum, falling from Buckley LJ, although obiter, commands the greatest of respect.

Harman J also made some observations in *Re McGuinness Bros (UK) Ltd* (1987) 3 BCC 571 which might be taken to support this dictum, although if it was so intended, it was also clearly obiter because *McGuinness* was also a case of an overdrawn account. I cite from his judgment, where he said (at 574):

'However, the matter stands that in law all the dispositions of the
company's property after the winding-up are void. It is clear that   *a*
payments out of or into the bank account are dispositions of property.
That follows from *Gray's Inn Construction* and was indeed well-known long
before that case was decided.'

The only reasoned explanation to which my attention has been drawn for
reaching the same conclusion in respect of an account out of which the bank   *b*
makes a disposition in its own favour, discharging, pro tanto, the customer's
liability on the overdraft, to quote Buckley LJ's explanation of the position of
the overdrawn account, and one which places the receipts of the cheques
which it collects on the customer's behalf to the credit of the customer's
account to be held to the customer's order, is found in a passage in Professor   *c*
Goode's *Principles of Corporate Insolvency Law* (1990) pp 187–188 under the
heading 'Payments into a bank account'. He said:

'Where the company pays cash (as opposed to a cheque) into its account,
the payment constitutes a disposition of its property, whether or not the
account is in credit, for ownership of the cash passes to the bank. If the   *d*
account is in credit the company acquires a corresponding claim against
the bank, which would be recorded by a credit of the payment to its
account, so that the net effect of the transaction is simply to convert an
asset of the company from one form, cash, into another, a claim on the
bank. Hence in terms of its effect the breach will usually be a merely   *e*
technical one, but the position would be otherwise if the bank were to
become insolvent before the company had withdrawn the amount
credited. The position is somewhat different in the case of a cheque.
Deposit of the cheque with the bank for the purpose of collection is not in
itself a disposition within section 127 where the company's account is in
credit, for the bank collects purely as agent and has no interest of its own   *f*
in the cheque. The position is otherwise where the company owes money
to the bank, for it then acquires a lien on the cheque and if the view
expressed above is correct this constitutes a disposition for the purpose of
section 127. When the bank collects the cheque for the company it
receives the payment initially as agent for the company but immediately   *g*
borrows it back as part of the banker-customer relationship and credits the
borrowing to the customer's account. The collection process itself
involves the disposition of an asset of the company, for the bank
surrenders the customer's cheque, which represents both a negotiable
instrument and the embodiment of a claim against the drawer, in
exchange for payment, so that one form of property belonging to the   *h*
company is converted into another. Crediting of the proceeds of the
cheque to an account already in credit is a further, albeit technical,
disposition of the company's property, for its claim against the bank to
money had and received in respect of the proceeds collected is replaced by
a new claim against the bank in its capacity as borrower, as recorded by the   *j*
credit to the account. Similarly, where the account is overdrawn the effect
of the bank's act in crediting the proceeds is to apply the moneys collected
on the company's behalf in discharge of the debt due to the bank and
thereby to extinguish *pro tanto* the company's claim against the bank in
respect of the sum collected. The original asset thus disappears in the
same way as where the proceeds are credited to an account not in

overdraft, but with the very different result that the bank obtains a preference over other creditors, so that the breach of section 127 is no longer technical.'

Mr Feldman adopts this passage as his argument for the declaration originally sought, and I certainly treat the views of Professor Goode with respect and do not differ from them lightly. In his reasoning Professor Goode accepted that the deposit of the cheque by the company with the bank does not involve a disposition because the bank is the company's agent. Nevertheless he treated the conversion of the property in the cheque into a debt from the bank to the company as a disposition of the company's property. To equate such transformation with a disposition does not appear to me to accord with ordinary English usage wherein a disposition connotes the transfer or alienation of an asset not its mere conversion into a different form which is nonetheless as much within the control of the owner.

If Professor Goode's construction does not accord with ordinary usage I certainly see no reason to give other than the natural meaning to a section which seeks to override property rights, particularly when the avoidance of such transactions as Professor Goode would bring within the definition does not appear to me to be necessary in order to avoid the mischief of preference of creditors, at which he, as I think rightly, says that the section is aimed.

Mr Feldman found himself constrained to accept that if this reasoning of Professor Goode is right then the mere payment of a debt to the company by making out a cheque which converts one chose in action into another (an action on the cheque) is also a disposition of the company's property. Indeed it appears that in *Mersey Steel and Iron Co Ltd v Naylor Benzon & Co* (1884) 9 App Cas 434, [1881–85] All ER Rep 365 a debtor was advised that such was the effect of s 153 of the Companies Act 1862, which was to the same effect as s 127 of the 1986 Act. The debtor therefore refused to pay such sums which became due in accordance with a contract with the company after the presentation of a petition to wind it up. The House of Lords held that because of such advice the debtor should not be held to have repudiated the contract, but Lord Selborne LC made this comment on that advice (9 App Cas 434 at 441, [1881–85] All ER Rep 365 at 369):

'On the 10th of February, which was before the winding-up order was made, and while that state of affairs still continued, the company by their secretary wrote to say that they thought (being so far correct and thinking rightly) that the objection was not well founded in law ...'

I accept that parenthetic observation on the advice that led to the withholding of payment, and I think that it is not enough to constitute a disposition, that a transaction involves a conversion of a chose in action, or even the property in a negotiable instrument into a chose more nearly in possession.

In the Supreme Court of New South Wales, Street CJ considered the meaning of the word 'disposition' in *Re Mal Bower's Macquarie Electrical Centre Pty Ltd (in liq)* [1974] 1 NSWLR 254. He held (what Mr Lowe is not minded to support in this case) that a payment out of money by a bank is not a disposition; but in doing so he made some observations which I do find helpful in analysing the process of collection of a third party's cheques on behalf of a company against whom a petition had been presented. He said (at 257–258):

'The phrase, "disposition of the property" in s. 227 has a statutory origin in England well back in the last century. I have been unable to trace the phrase to its source, but it seems likely to have originated from the word "dispone", used in Scottish law as a word meaning "to transfer or alienate". The *Oxford Dictionary* includes, as one of the meanings of "dispone"—"Sc.Law. To make over or convey officially or in legal form (1555)." The same work includes, in the definition of "disposition", "— spec. in Law, the action of disponing." The word "disposition" in one or other of its forms, and in varying contexts, is a commonplace in revenue statutes. There is, however, little guidance to be had from examining such other contexts, apart from noting that the concept associated with the use of such word involves the presence of both a disponor and a disponee. There is, in my view, great force in Mr. McLelland's argument that the paying by a bank of a company's cheque, presented by a stranger, does not involve the bank in a disposition of the property of the company so as to disentitle the bank to debit the amount of the cheque to the company's account. The word "disposition" connotes in my view both a disponor and a disponee. The section operates to render the disposition void so far as concerns the disponee. It does not operate to affect the agencies interposing between the company, as disponor, and the recipient of the property, as disponee. As was put in the course of argument, if a company, after presentation of the petition, delivered goods to a carrier consigned to a purchaser, the purchaser would face the avoidance of the transaction under s. 227, but the carrier would not be placed in the position of a tortious handling of the goods. Again, if a company were to send its wages clerk up to the bank to cash the weekly wages cheque and bring back the proceeds for making out the paypackets, the payment of the cheque would involve no disposition of the company's property: the company's property belonged to it just as much when it was in the bank as when it was in the form of cash in the hands of the wages clerk. The element of disposition only enters into the situation when something passes out from the company to a disponee. It is the passing to the disponee which is the relevant disposition avoided by s. 227. Taking further the example of a wages cheque, the giving by a company to the employee of his wages out of the cash brought back by the wages clerk would be disposition of the property of the company to the employee. Alternatively, if the company gave to the employee directly a cheque for him to present to collect for himself, the handing over of that cheque would be a conditional disposition within s. 227. The intermediary functions fulfilled by the bank in respect of paying cheques drawn by a company in favour of and presented on behalf of a third party do not implicate the bank in the consequences of the statutory avoidance prescribed by s. 227.'

In *Re J Leslie Engineers Co Ltd (in liq)* [1976] 2 All ER 85, [1976] 1 WLR 292 Oliver J likewise identified the act of disposition by reference to the receipt by the disponee. Two sums were in issue in that case. One of £250 was paid to the first respondent, a Mr Greaves, by five money orders bought by a director, Mr Hadrys, with the company's cash, drawn from the company's bank account by a cheque for cash. The other was a sum of £800 paid to the respondent by a cheque drawn on Mr Hadrys' personal account, but, unknown to Mr Greaves, backed, when it had to be represented, by a company cheque in favour of Mr

Hadrys paid into Mr Hadrys's joint account with his wife at the same bank as the company's account to enable the cheque given to Mr Greaves to be met. Oliver J dealt with the application to treat the payment of the £250 as void as follows ([1976] 2 All ER 85 at 89, [1976] 1 WLR 292 at 297):

'It is submitted by counsel for the respondents that the "dispositions" which were avoided by s 227 of the [Companies Act 1948] do not include such dispositions as are constituted by the payments to the respondents in this case; that "the dispositions" at which the section is aimed are the initial dispositions only—that is to say the encashments of the two cheques—and it is against Mr Hadrys alone that any claim will lie. I cannot think that as a general proposition that can be right. It seems to me to be wholly immaterial, so long as one is dealing with the company's property, whether the purported disposition is made by the company or by a third party, or whether it is made directly or indirectly. I feel, therefore, no difficulty—and, I may add, no doubt—about the initial payment of £250. The banknotes received from the bank were as much the company's property, and identifiable as such, as were the moneys in the account, and it seems to me to make not the slightest difference that Mr Hadrys took the banknotes and converted them into money orders payable to Mr Greaves. There was, throughout, a clearly identifiable property of the company which passed directly from the company's hands (in the person of Mr Hadrys, its controlling director) to those of the respondents: see, for instance, *Taylor v Plumer* (1815) 3 M & S 562, [1814–23] All ER Rep 167. That disposition was, in my judgment, quite clearly invalidated by the section unless and until this court otherwise orders.'

By contrast, the disposition of the company's property in the case of the £800 took place when the cheque was paid to Mr Hadrys, not when Mr Hadrys' cheque to Mr Greaves was met. Oliver J continues ([1976] 2 All ER 85 at 89–90, [1976] 1 WLR 292 at 297–298):

'The second payment, however, creates, to my mind, very much greater difficulty. The disposition which counsel for the liquidator attacks is not the drawing of the cheque to Mr Greaves or the sending to him of that cheque, and it is not—or it is not *alone*—the drawing by Mr Hadrys of the cheque on the company's account. It is the application by the bank of the funds in the joint account to meet Mr Greaves's cheque when it was re-presented. That, says counsel, was the disposition of the company's property which is avoided and which gives the liquidator the right to recover the sum claimed from the respondents. It must be remembered that the invalidation of a disposition of the company's property and the recovery of the property disposed of, are two logically distinct matters. Section 227 of the 1948 Act says nothing about recovery: it merely avoids dispositions and is in these terms [which the judge set out]. What is the appropriate remedy in respect of the invalidated disposition is a matter not regulated by the Act and that has to be determined by the general law. In order to succeed against the respondents, the liquidator does not necessarily have to demonstrate a transaction invalidated by s 227 for there may be claims to recover moneys paid on other grounds. He does, however, have to show a right of recovery, and it is counsel for the liquidator's contention that he does that if he demonstrates that the transaction is one which is bitten by s 227 and persuades the court that it ought not to validate it. I think that I should say straightaway that, although, as I have said, I cannot accept that the respondents were not aware that they were contracting with a limited company, I cannot on the evidence before me find any indication that when payment of the £800 was made, or indeed at any material time, the respondents knew or had any reason to suspect that the funds to meet it had been provided by the company. I cannot, therefore, treat the case as one of a collusive payment, and I think that I must accept that, so far as the respondents were concerned, they thought that the moneys were being paid by Mr Hadrys or his wife out of their own resources. Looking at the transaction in stages, there was clearly no disposition of any property of the company when the cheque in favour of the respondents was first sent and presented. When the cheque on the *company's* account was drawn and presented there quite clearly *was* a disposition of the company's property, and one which is, unless validated, avoided by s 227. But that cheque was paid in with a number of other cheques and, after allowing for the overdraft, the moneys represented by the cheque became mixed with Mr Hadrys's own moneys, throwing up a credit balance of some £950.' (Oliver J's emphasis.)

I think I have to read on later in this judgment, where Oliver J made this observation on what constituted the property of the company ([1976] 2 All ER 85 at 91, [1976] 1 WLR 292 at 299):

'"The property of the company" for the purposes of s 227 was, as it seems to me, not the credit balance in the account owed by the bank to Mr and Mrs Hadrys, but the sum total of the rights of the company created by the transactions leading up to the creation of that balance. I do not think that the meeting, out of the credit balance held by the bank to the order of Mr and Mrs Hadrys, of the re-presented cheque in favour of the respondents was a disposition of the property of the company simply because the company could by appropriate proceedings have obtained a declaration of charge on that credit balance.'

This appears to me to be a more practical approach to the definition of the moment at which the company's property is disposed of than what appeared to me to be an over-technical analysis of the banking process in the passage which Mr Feldman adopted from Professor Goode, as his argument.

I derive assistance also in analysing the effect of banking transactions for the purposes of this section from another Australian case, decided by McPherson J in the Queensland Supreme Court, *Re Loteka Property Ltd (in liq)* [1990] 1 Qd R 322. I should incidentally pay tribute to Mr Lowe's industry which has brought these and other Commonwealth authorities, not all of which is it necessary for me to cite, to the court's attention. In that case the liquidator sought, as the applicant before me does by the amended application, to recover from a bank which did not freeze the operation of the account of a company against whom a petition for winding up had been presented (but which account remained in credit) sums paid out of such account. The judge recounts the effect of depositing a cheque in an account which is in credit by citing a passage from another case (see [1990] 1 Qd R 322 at 328). His account is not, I think materially different from Professor Goode's. It reads, quoting from *National Australia Bank Ltd v KDS Construction Services Pty Ltd* (1987) 163 CLR 668 at 676:

'The effect of the receipt by a bank of a cheque deposited by a customer to the credit of his current account turns upon the terms of the contract between the bank and its customer. In the ordinary course of business when a customer deposits a cheque to the credit of his account, the bank becomes his agent for collection of the cheque from the paying bank and, if the customer's account is in credit, the collecting bank borrows the proceeds from the customer when collected: *Joachimson v. Swiss Bank Corporation* ([1921] 3 KB 110 at 127, [1921] All ER Rep 92 at 100), *A. L. Underwood Ltd v. Bank of Liverpool* ([1924] 1 KB 775 at 791, [1924] All ER Rep 230 at 236). If the customer's account is in debit, the proceeds are applied in reduction of the overdraft. In either situation the collecting bank does not become a holder for value of the cheque at any time before it is cleared: *A. L. Underwood Ltd v. Barclays Bank* ([1924] 1 KB 775 at 804–805, [1924] All ER Rep 230 at 240–241); *National Commercial Banking Corporation of Australia Ltd v. Batty* ((1986) 160 CLR 251 at 273). In collecting the proceeds the collecting bank exhausts the operation of the cheque (*A. L. Underwood Ltd v. Bank of Liverpool*), notwithstanding that the paying bank holds it thereafter as a voucher on account of its customer the drawer: *Midland Bank Ltd v. Reckitt* ([1933] AC 1 at 14, [1932] All ER Rep 90 at 94).'

The reference to the status of the paid cheque as a voucher prompts a question which Professor Goode did not address: 'What is the effect of declaring the disposition of the cheque void?' If the drawer's bank is bound to return it as remaining the company's property, is it to be treated on such return as still being a valuable instrument? Is, for example, the fact that it is out of date to be disregarded? And if so, on what basis? Is the fact that it has been paid to be disregarded, although there is no basis on which the disposition to the company which is made by the payment of the cheque is to be avoided by s 127 of the 1986 Act?

McPherson J was concerned with a claim to avoid not payments into the company's account but payments out of it. He went on from his description of the processing of a cheque to conclude that in the case of a payment out of the account there is of course a disposition to the payee but that it takes place upon the delivery of the cheque. He dealt, however, with the effect of the presentation of a cheque as follows ([1990] 1 Qd R 322 at 328–329):

'In paying the customer's cheque, the bank debits the customer's account with the amount of the cheque drawn in favour of the stranger. In doing so, the bank, if the customer's account is overdrawn, lends its own money to the customer. That involves no disposition of the customer's property to the bank. Equally, if the account is sufficiently in credit to meet the cheque, no disposition of property of the customer takes place in favour of the bank. The amount standing to the credit of the customer's account is simply diminished thus reducing pro tanto the indebtedness of the bank to the customer. It is the payee of the cheque that receives the benefit of the proceeds of the cheque. All that happens between customer and banker in an adjustment of entries in the statement recording the accounts between them ...'

I think that the collection of a cheque, which is what I am concerned with, can be similarly analysed. In collecting payment upon a cheque the bank credits the customer's account with the amount of the cheque. If the account is already in credit, no disposition of the property of the customer takes place in favour of the bank. The amount standing to the credit of a customer's account is increased in return for the surrender of the cheque which becomes a voucher for payment. It is the drawer of the cheque whose property is disposed of. All that happens between the customer and the banker is an adjustment of entries in the statement recording the accounts between them.

I would accordingly decide the sole issue left for my determination, after the various agreements and concessions to which I have referred, against the liquidator. I would therefore refuse the declaration sought and the application as originally made. On the amended application, it is conceded by the bank that the payments were dispositions and since Mr Feldman has given the liquidator's undertaking not to seek repayment of any of these sums from the payees, who are of course not before the court, there does not appear to me to be any reason why I should not grant that declaration as against the bank.

For the reasons which I have already given, however, I would refuse an order for payment by the bank, leaving the liquidator to seek payment if he is so advised by proceedings in which his grounds for so claiming can be fully pleaded.

Application dismissed.

Evelyn M C Budd   Barrister.

Practice Direction

Practice – Pre-trial or post-judgment relief – Anton Piller order – Ex parte application – Order representing serious restriction on rights of persons bound by its terms – Consistent approach to be adopted in relation to form and carrying out of order – New standard form of order – Guidelines.

Practice – Pre-trial or post-judgment relief – Mareva injunction – Worldwide Mareva injunction – Pre-trial injunction – Injunction restraining disposal of assets outside jurisdiction – Ex parte application – Order representing serious restriction on rights of persons bound by its terms – Consistent approach to be adopted in relation to form and carrying out of order – New standard form of order – Guidelines.

Practice – Pre-trial or post-judgment relief – Mareva injunction – Injunction restraining removal of assets out of or disposal within jurisdiction – Ex parte application – Order representing serious restriction on rights of persons bound by its terms – Consistent approach to be adopted in relation to form and carrying out of order – New standard form of order – Guidelines.

(1) The granting of a Mareva injunction or Anton Piller order is a matter for the discretion of the judge hearing the application. However, it is desirable that a consistent approach should in general be adopted in relation to the form and carrying out of such orders, since they represent serious restrictions on the rights of those persons subjected to them imposed after hearing only the applicant's case on an ex parte application. This practice direction sets out guidelines for the assistance of judges and those who apply for these orders.

(2) Attached to this practice direction are new standard forms of the following orders: annex 1, Anton Piller order; annex 2, worldwide Mareva injunction; and annex 3, Mareva injunction limited to assets within the jurisdiction. These forms, inevitably, are complicated, but their language and layout are intended to make it easier for persons served with these orders to understand what they mean. These forms of order should be used save to the extent that the judge hearing a particular application considers there is a good reason for adopting a different form.

(3) The following matters should be borne in mind in relation to an ex parte application for any of these orders.

(A) *On an application for either a Mareva or an Anton Piller order*

1. Where practicable the papers to be used on the application should be lodged with the judge at least two hours before the hearing.

2. An applicant should be required, in an appropriate case, to support his cross-undertaking in damages by a payment into court or the provision of a bond by an insurance company. Alternatively, the judge may order a payment by way of such security to the applicant's solicitor to be held by the solicitor as an officer of the court pending further order.

3. So far as practicable, any application for the discharge or variation of the order should be dealt with effectively on the return date.

(B) *On an application for an Anton Piller order*

1. (a) As suggested in *Universal Thermosensors Ltd v Hibben* [1992] 3 All ER 257 at 276, [1992] 1 WLR 840 at 861 the specimen order provides for it to be served by a supervising solicitor and carried out in his presence and under his supervision. The supervising solicitor should be an experienced solicitor, having some familiarity with the operation of Anton Piller orders, who is not a member or employee of the firm acting for the applicant. The evidence in support of the application should include the identity and experience of the proposed supervising solicitor. (b) If in any particular case the judge does not think it appropriate to provide for the order to be served by a supervising solicitor, his reasons should be expressed in the order itself.

2. Where the premises are likely to be occupied by an unaccompanied woman and the supervising solicitor is a man, at least one of the persons attending on the service of the order should be a woman: see para 2(3) of the standard form of order and footnote b.

3. Where the nature of the items removed under the order makes this appropriate, the applicant should be required to insure them: see Sch 3, footnote e of the standard form.

4. The applicant should undertake not to inform any third party of the proceedings until after the return date: see Sch 3, para 6.

5. In future, applications in the Queen's Bench Division will no longer be heard by the judge in chambers. In both Chancery and Queen's Bench Divisions, whenever practicable, applications will be listed before a judge in such a manner as to ensure that he has sufficient time to read and consider the papers in advance.

6. On circuit, applications will be listed before a High Court judge or a Circuit Judge, sitting as a judge of the High Court specially designated by the Presiding Judge to hear such applications.

(4) If an Anton Piller order or Mareva injunction is discharged on the return date, the judge should always consider whether it is appropriate that he should assess damages at once and direct immediate payment by the applicant.

(5) This practice direction applies to all Divisions of the High Court.

By direction of the Lord Chief Justice, Lord Taylor, with the concurrence of the President of the Family Division, Sir Stephen Brown, and the Vice-Chancellor, Sir Donald Nicholls.

28 July 1994

Annex 1

[Heading]

Order to allow entry and search of premises

IMPORTANT:

NOTICE TO THE DEFENDANT

(1) This order orders you to allow the persons mentioned below to enter the premises described in the order and to search for, examine and remove or copy the articles specified in the order. This part of the order is subject to restrictions. The order also requires you to hand over any of the articles which are under your control and to provide information to the plaintiff's solicitors, and prohibits you from doing certain acts. You should read the terms of the order very carefully. You are advised to consult a solicitor as soon as possible.

(2) Before you the defendant or the person appearing to be in control of the premises allow anybody onto the premises to carry out this order you are entitled to have the solicitor who serves you with this order explain to you what it means in every day language.

(3) You are entitled to insist that there is nobody [or nobody except Mr ...] present who could gain commercially from anything he might read or see on your premises.

(4) You are entitled to refuse to permit entry before 9.30 am or after 5.30 pm or at all on Saturday and Sunday.

(5) You are entitled to seek legal advice, and to ask the Court to vary or discharge this order, provided you do so at once, and provided that meanwhile you permit the supervising solicitor (who is a solicitor acting independently of the plaintiff) and the plaintiff's solicitor to enter, but not start to search: see para 3.

(6) If you ... the defendant disobey this order you will be guilty of contempt of Court and may be [sent to prison or] fined or your assets seized.[a]

THE ORDER

An application was made today [date] by counsel [or solicitors] for ... the plaintiff to Mr Justice [...]. Mr Justice [...] heard the application and read the affidavits listed in Sch 6 at the end of this order.

As a result of the application IT IS ORDERED by Mr Justice [...] that:

---

a   Delete the words 'sent to prison' in the case of a corporate defendant. This notice is not a substitute for the indorsement of a penal notice.

Entry and search of premises and vehicles on the premises

1. (1) The defendant must allow Mr/Mrs/Miss ... : ('the supervising solicitor'), together with Mr ... a solicitor of the Supreme Court, and a partner in the firm of the plaintiff's solicitors ... and up to ... other persons being [their capacity] accompanying them, to enter the premises mentioned in Sch 1 to this order and any vehicles on the premises so that they can search for, inspect, photograph or photocopy, and deliver into the safekeeping of the plaintiff's solicitors all the documents and articles which are listed in Sch 2 to this order ('the listed items') or which Mr ... believes to be listed items. The defendant must allow those persons to remain on the premises until the search is complete, and if necessary to re-enter the premises on the same or the following day in order to complete the search.

(2) This order must be complied with either by the defendant himself or by a responsible employee of the defendant or by the person appearing to be in control of the premises.

(3) This order requires the defendant or his employee or the person appearing to be in control of the premises to permit entry to the premises immediately the order is served upon him, except as stated in para 3 below.

Restrictions on the service and carrying out of para 1 of this order

2. Paragraph 1 of this order is subject to the following restrictions.

(1) This order may only be served between 9.30 am and 5.30 pm on a weekday.

(2) This order may not be carried out at the same time as any police search warrant.

(3) This order must be served by the supervising solicitor, and para 1 of the order must be carried out in his presence and under his supervision. [At least one of the persons accompanying him as provided by para 1 of this order shall be a woman.][b]

(4) This order does not require the person served with the order to allow anyone [or anyone except Mr ...] who could gain commercially from anything he might read or see on the premises if the person served with the order objects.

(5) No item may be removed from the premises until a list of the items to be removed has been prepared, and a copy of the list has been supplied to the person served with the order, and he has been given a reasonable opportunity to check the list.

(6) The premises must not be searched, and items must not be removed from them, except in the presence of the defendant or a person appearing to be a responsible employee of the defendant.

(7) If the supervising solicitor is satisfied that full compliance with sub-para (5) or (6) above is impracticable, he may permit the search to proceed and items to be removed without compliance with the impracticable requirements.

Obtaining legal advice and applying to the court

3. Before permitting entry to the premises by any person other than the Supervising Officer and the plaintiff's solicitors, the defendant or other person appearing to be in control of the premises may seek legal advice, and apply to

---

b   The words in brackets in (3) are to be included in a case where the premises are likely to be occupied by an unaccompanied woman and the superivising solicitor is a man.

the Court to vary or discharge this order, provided he does so at once. While
this is being done, he may refuse entry to the premises by any other person, and *a*
may refuse to permit the search to begin, for a short time (not to exceed two
hours, unless the supervising solicitor agrees to a longer period).

Delivery of listed items and computer print-outs
4. (1) The defendant must immediately hand over to the plaintiff's solicitors *b*
any of the listed items which are in his possession or under his control.

(2) If any of the listed items exists only in computer readable form, the
defendant must immediately give the plaintiff's solicitors effective access to
the computers, with all necessary passwords, to enable them to be searched,
and cause the listed items to be printed out. A print-out of the items must be
given to the plaintiff's solicitors or displayed on the computer screen so that *c*
they can be read and copied. All reasonable steps shall be taken by the plaintiff
to ensure that no damage is done to any computer or data. The plaintiff and
his representatives may not themselves search the defendant's computers
unless they have sufficient expertise to do so without damaging the
defendant's system. *d*

Disclosure of information by the defendant
5. (1) The defendant must immediately inform the plaintiff's solicitors: (a)
where all the listed items are; and (b) so far as he is aware: (i) the name and
address of everyone who has supplied him, or offered to supply him, with
listed items; (ii) the name and address of everyone to whom he has supplied, or *e*
offered to supply, listed items; and (iii) full details of the dates and quantities of
every such supply and offer.

(2) Within ... days after being served with this order the defendant must
prepare and swear an affidavit confirming the above information.
f

Prohibited acts
6. (1) Except for the purpose of obtaining legal advice, the defendant must
not directly or indirectly inform anyone of these proceedings or of the contents
of this order, or warn anyone that proceedings have been or may be brought
against him by the plaintiff until [...]^c.
g
(2) [Insert any negative injunctions.]

EFFECT OF THIS ORDER
1) A defendant who is an individual who is ordered not to do something
must not do it himself or in any other way. He must not do it through others
acting on his behalf or on his instructions or with his encouragement. *h*
2) A defendant which is a corporation and which is ordered not to do
something must not do it itself or by its directors officers employees or agents
or in any other way.

UNDERTAKINGS
The plaintiff, the plaintiff's solicitors and the supervising solicitor gave to *j*
the court the undertakings contained in Schs 3, 4 and 5 respectively to this
order.

---

c   The date to be inserted here should be the return date or, if sooner, seven days from the date of
     the order.

DURATION OF THIS ORDER

Paragraph 6(2) of this order will remain in force up to and including [: :19] (which is 'the return date'), unless before then it is varied or discharged by a further order of the court.[d] The application in which this order is made shall come back to the court for further hearing on the return date.

VARIATION OR DISCHARGE OF THIS ORDER

The defendant (or anyone notified of this order) may apply to the court at any time to vary or discharge this order (or so much of it as affects that person), but anyone wishing to do so must first inform the plaintiff's solicitors.

NAME AND ADDRESS OF PLAINTIFF'S SOLICITORS

The plaintiff's solicitors are: [Name, address and telephone numbers both in and out of office hours.]

[INTERPRETATION OF THIS ORDER

1) In this order 'he' 'him' or 'his' include 'she' or 'her' and 'it' or 'its'.

2) Where there are two or more defendants then (unless the context indicates differently) (a) references to 'the defendants' mean both or all of them; (b) an order requiring 'the defendants' to do or not to do anything requires each defendant to do or not to do it; (c) a requirement relating to service of this order, or of any legal proceedings, on 'the defendants' means on each of them; and (d) any other requirement that something shall be done to or in the presence of 'the defendants' means to or in the presence of one of them.]

SCHEDULE 1

The premises

SCHEDULE 2

The listed items

SCHEDULE 3

Undertakings given by the plaintiff

1) If the court later finds that this order or carrying it out has caused loss to the defendant, and decides that the defendant should be compensated for that loss, the plaintiff will comply with any order the court may make.

[2] As soon as practicable to issue a writ of summons [in the form of the draft writ produced to the court] [claiming appropriate relief.]]

3) To [swear and file an affidavit] [cause an affidavit to be sworn and filed] [substantially in the terms of the draft produced to the court] [confirming the substance of what was said to the court by the plaintiff's counsel/solicitors.]

4) To serve on the defendant at the same time as this order is served upon him (i) the writ (ii) a notice of motion/summons for ... 19 and (iii) copies of the affidavits and copiable exhibits containing the evidence relied on by the plaintiff. [Copies of the confidential exhibits need not be served, but they must be made available for inspection by or on behalf of the defendant in the presence of the plaintiff's solicitors while the order is carried out. Afterwards they must be provided to a solicitor representing the defendant who gives a written undertaking not to permit the defendant to see them or copies of them

---

d   The date should be the earliest practicable return date.

except in his presence and not to permit the defendant to make or take away any note or record of the exhibits.]

5) To serve on the defendant a copy of the supervising solicitor's report on the carrying out of this order as soon as it is received and to produce a copy of the report to the Court.

6) Not, without the leave of the court, to use any information or documents obtained as a result of carrying out this order except for the purposes of these proceedings or to inform anyone else of these proceedings until after the return date.

[7)]^e

SCHEDULE 4

Undertakings given by the plaintiff's solicitors.

1) To answer at once to the best of their ability any question whether a particular item is a listed item.

2) To return the originals of all documents obtained as a result of this order (except original documents which belong to the plaintiff) as soon as possible and in any event within two working days of their removal.

3) While ownership of any item obtained as a result of this order is in dispute, to deliver the article into the keeping of solicitors acting for the defendant within two working days from receiving a written undertaking by them to retain the article in safe keeping and to produce it to the court when required.

4) To retain in their own safe keeping all other items obtained as a result of this order until the Court directs otherwise.

SCHEDULE 5

Undertakings given by the supervising solicitor

1) To offer to explain to the person served with the order its meaning and effect fairly and in everyday language, and to inform him of his right to seek legal advice and apply to vary or discharge the order as mentioned in para 3 of the order.

2) To make and provide to the plaintiff's solicitors a written report on the carrying out of the order.

SCHEDULE 6

Affidavits

The judge read the following affidavits before making this order:

1) ...

2) ...

---

e   In appropriate cases an undertaking to insure the items removed from the premises shall be
     included.

Annex 2

[Heading]

Injunction prohibiting disposal of assets worldwide

IMPORTANT

NOTICE TO THE DEFENDANT

(1) This order prohibits you from dealing with your assets up to the amount stated. The order is subject to the exceptions at the end of the order. You should read it all carefully. You are advised to consult a solicitor as soon as possible. You have a right to ask the court to vary or discharge this order.

(2) If you disobey this order you will be guilty of contempt of court and may be [sent to prison or] fined or your assets may be seized.[f]

THE ORDER

An application was made today [date] by counsel for [or solicitors] for ... the plaintiff to Mr Justice [...]. Mr Justice [...] heard the application and read the affidavits listed in Sch 2 at the end of this order.

As a result of the application IT IS ORDERED by Mr Justice [...] that:

1. *Disposal of assets*

1) The defendant must not (i) remove from England and Wales any of his assets which are in England and Wales whether in his own name or not and whether solely or jointly owned up to the value of £ ... or (ii) in any way dispose of or deal with or diminish the value of any of his assets whether they are in or outside England or Wales whether in his own name or not and whether solely or jointly owned up to the same value. This prohibition includes the following assets in particular: (a) the property known as ... or the net sale money after payment of any mortgages if it has been sold; (b) the property and assets of the defendant's business known as ... (or carried on at ...) or the sale money if any of them have been sold; and (c) any money in the accounts numbered ... at ...

2) If the total unincumbered value of the defendant's assets in England and Wales exceeds £ ... the defendant may remove any of those assets from England and Wales or may dispose of or deal with them so long as the total unincumbered value of his assets still in England and Wales remains above £ .... If the total unincumbered value of the defendant's assets in England and Wales does not exceed £ ..., the defendant must not remove any of those assets from England and Wales and must not dispose of or deal with any of them, but if he has other assets outside England and Wales the defendant may dispose of or deal with those assets so long as the total unincumbered value of all his assets whether in or outside England and Wales remains above £ ... .

2. *Disclosure of information*

1) The defendant must inform the plaintiff in writing at once of all his assets whether in or outside England and Wales and whether in his own name or not and whether solely or jointly owned, giving the value, location and details of all such assets.

---

f   Delete the words 'sent to prison' in the case of a corporate defendant. This notice is not a substitute for the indorsement of a penal notice.

2) The information must be confirmed in an affidavit which must be served on the plaintiff's solicitors within days after this order has been served on the defendant.

EXCEPTIONS TO THIS ORDER

1) This order does not prohibit the defendant from spending £ ... a week towards his ordinary living expenses [and £ ... a week towards his ordinary and proper business expenses] and also £ ... a week [or a reasonable sum] on legal advice and representation. But before spending any money the defendant must tell the plaintiff's solicitors where the money is to come from.

[2] This order does not prohibit the defendant from dealing with or disposing of any of his assets in the ordinary and proper course of business.]

3) The defendant may agree with the plaintiff's solicitors that the above spending limits should be increased or that this order should be varied in any other respect but any such agreement must be in writing.

EFFECT OF THIS ORDER

1) A defendant who is an individual who is ordered not to do something must not do it himself or in any other way. He must not do it through others acting on his behalf or on his instructions or with his encouragement.

2) A defendant which is a corporation and which is ordered not to do something must not do it itself or by its directors officers employees or agents or in any other way.

THIRD PARTIES

1) *Effect of this order.* It is a contempt of court for any person notified of this order knowingly to assist in or permit a breach of the order. Any person doing so may be sent to prison, fined, or have his assets seized.

2) *Effect of this order outside England and Wales.* The terms of this order do not affect or concern anyone outside the jurisdiction of this court until it is declared enforceable or is enforced by a court in the relevant country and then they are to affect him only to the extent they have been declared enforceable or have been enforced UNLESS such person is: (a) a person to whom this order is addressed or an officer or an agent appointed by power of attorney of such a person; or (b) a person who is subject to the jurisdiction of this Court and (i) has been given written notice of this order at his residence or place of business within the jurisdiction of this Court and (ii) is able to prevent acts or omissions outside the jurisdiction of this Court which constitute or assist in a breach of the terms of this order.

3) *Set off by banks.* This injunction does not prevent any bank from exercising any right of set off it may have in respect of any facility which it gave to the defendant before it was notified of the order.

4) *Withdrawals by the defendant.* No bank need inquire as to the application or proposed application of any money withdrawn by the defendant if the withdrawal appears to be permitted by this order.

[SERVICE OUT OF THE JURISDICTION AND SUBSTITUTED SERVICE

1) The plaintiff may serve the writ of summons on the defendant at ... by ....

2) If the defendant wishes to defend the action he must acknowledge service within ... days of being served with the writ of summons.]

UNDERTAKINGS
The plaintiff gives to the court the undertakings set out in Sch 1 to this order.

DURATION OF THIS ORDER
This order will remain in force up to and including : :19 ('the return date'), unless before then it is varied or discharged by a further order of the court[g] . The application in which this order is made shall come back to the court for further hearing on the return date.

VARIATION OR DISCHARGE OF THIS ORDER
The defendant (or anyone notified of this order) may apply to the court at any time to vary or discharge this order (or so much of it as affects that person), but anyone wishing to do so must first inform the plaintiff's solicitors.

NAME AND ADDRESS OF PLAINTIFF'S SOLICITORS
The plaintiff's solicitors are:
[Name, address and telephone numbers both in and out of office hours].

[INTERPRETATION OF THIS ORDER
1) In this order 'he' 'him' or 'his' include 'she' or 'her' and 'it' or 'its'.
2) Where there are two or more defendants then (unless the context indicates differently) (a) references to 'the defendants' mean both or all of them; (b) an order requiring 'the defendants' to do or not to do anything requires each defendant to do or not to do it; (c) a requirement relating to the service of the order, or of any legal proceedings, on 'the defendants' means on each of them.]

SCHEDULE 1
Undertakings given to the court by the plaintiff
1) If the court later finds that this order has caused loss to the defendant, and decides that the defendant should be compensated for that loss, the plaintiff will comply with any order the court may make.
2) As soon as practicable the plaintiff will [issue and] serve on the defendant [a] [the] writ of summons [in the form of the draft writ produced to the court] [claiming appropriate relief] together with this order.
3) The plaintiff will cause an affidavit to be sworn and filed [substantially in the terms of the draft affidavit produced to the court] [confirming the substance of what was said to the court by the plaintiff's counsel/solicitors].
4) As soon as practicable the plaintiff will serve on the defendant a [notice of motion] [summons] for the return date together with a copy of the affidavits and exhibits containing the evidence relied on by the plaintiff.
5) Anyone notified of this order will be given a copy of it by the plaintiff's solicitors.
6) The plaintiff will pay the reasonable costs of anyone other than the defendant which have been incurred as a result of this order including the costs of ascertaining whether that person holds any of the defendant's assets and that if the court later finds that this order has caused such a person loss, and decides that the person should be compensated for that loss, the plaintiff will comply with any order the court may make.
[7) The plaintiff will not without the leave of the court begin proceedings against the defendant in any other jurisdiction or use information obtained as

---

g   The date should be the earliest practicable return date

a result of an order of the court in this jurisdiction for the purpose of civil or criminal proceedings in any other jurisdiction.

8) The plaintiff will not without the leave of the court seek to enforce this order in any country outside England and Wales [or seek an order of a similar nature including orders conferring a charge or other security against the defendant or the defendant's assets].]

SCHEDULE 2

Affidavits

The judge read the following affidavits before making this order:

1) ...

2) ...

Annex 3

[Heading]

Injunction prohibiting disposal of assets in England and Wales

IMPORTANT

NOTICE TO THE DEFENDANT

(1) This order prohibits you from dealing with your assets up to the amount stated. The order is subject to the exceptions at the end of the order. You should read it all carefully. You are advised to consult a solicitor as soon as possible. You have a right to ask the court to vary or discharge this order.

(2) If you disobey this order you will be guilty of contempt of court and may be [sent to prison or] fined or your assets may be seized[h].

THE ORDER

An application was made today [date] by counsel [or solicitors] for ... the plaintiff to Mr Justice [...]. Mr Justice [...] heard the application and read the affidavits listed in Sch 2 to this order.

As a result of the application IT IS ORDERED by Mr Justice [...] that:

1. *Disposal of assets*

1) The defendant must not remove from England and Wales or in any way dispose of or deal with or diminish the value of any of his assets which are in England and Wales whether in his own name or not and whether solely or jointly owned up to the value of £ .... This prohibition includes the following assets in particular: (a) the property known as ... or the net sale money after payment of any mortgages if it has been sold; (b) the property and assets of the defendant's business known as ... (or carried on at ...) or the sale money if any of them have been sold; and (c) any money in the accounts numbered ... at ...

2) If the total unincumbered value of the defendant's assets in England and Wales exceeds £ ..., the defendant may remove any of those assets from England and Wales or may dispose of or deal with them so long as the total unincumbered value of his assets still in England and Wales remains above £ ....

---

h   Delete the words 'sent to prison' in the case of a corporate defendant. This notice is not a substitute for the indorsement of a penal notice.

2. *Disclosure of information*

1) The defendant must inform the plaintiff in writing at once of all his assets in England and Wales whether in his own name or not and whether solely or jointly owned, giving the value, location and details of all such assets. The information must be confirmed in an affidavit which must be served on the plaintiff's solicitors within days after this order has been served on the defendant.

EXCEPTIONS TO THIS ORDER

1) This order does not prohibit the defendant from spending £ ... a week towards his ordinary living expenses [and £ ... a week towards his ordinary and proper business expenses] and also £ ... a week [*or* a reasonable sum] on legal advice and representation. But before spending any money the defendant must tell the plaintiff's solicitors where the money is to come from.

[2) This order does not prohibit the defendant from dealing with or disposing of any of his assets in the ordinary and proper course of business.]

3) The defendant may agree with the plaintiff's solicitors that the above spending limits should be increased or that this order should be varied in any other respect but any such agreement must be in writing.

EFFECT OF THIS ORDER

1) A defendant who is an individual who is ordered not to do something must not do it himself or in any other way. He must not do it through others acting on his behalf or on his instructions or with his encouragement.

2) A defendant which is a corporation and which is ordered not to do something must not do it itself or by its directors officers employees or agents or in any other way.

THIRD PARTIES

1) *Effect of this order.* It is a contempt of court for any person notified of this order knowingly to assist in or permit a breach of the order. Any person doing so may be sent to prison, fined, or have his assets seized.

2) *Set off by banks.* This injunction does not prevent any bank from exercising any right of set off it may have in respect of any facility which it gave to the defendant before it was notified of the order.

3) *Withdrawals by the defendant.* No bank need inquire as to the application or proposed application of any money withdrawn by the defendant if the withdrawal appears to be permitted by this order.

[SERVICE OUT OF THE JURISDICTION AND SUBSTITUTED SERVICE

1) The plaintiff may serve the writ of wummons on the defendant at ... by ....

2) If the defendant wishes to defend the action he must acknowledge service within ... days of being served with the writ of summons.]

UNDERTAKINGS

The plaintiff gives to the court the undertakings set out in Sch 1 to this order.

DURATION OF THIS ORDER

This order will remain in force up to and including : :19 ('the return date') unless before then it is varied or discharged by a further order of the court[i] . The

---

i   The date should be the earliest practicable return date.

application in which this order is made shall come back to the court for further hearing on the return date.

VARIATION OR DISCHARGE OF THIS ORDER

The defendant (or anyone notified of this order) may apply to the court at any time to vary or discharge this order (or so much of it as affects that person), but anyone wishing to do so must first inform the plaintiff's solicitors.

NAME AND ADDRESS OF PLAINTIFF'S SOLICITORS

The plaintiff's solicitors are:

[Name, address and telephone numbers both in and out of office hours].

[INTERPRETATION OF THIS ORDER

1) In this order 'he' 'him' or 'his' include 'she' or 'her' and 'it' or 'its'.

2) Where there are two or more defendants then (unless otherwise stated) (a) references to 'the defendants' mean both or all of them; (b) an order requiring 'the defendants' to do or not to do anything requires each defendant to do or not to do it; and (c) a requirement relating to service of this order or of any legal proceedings on 'the defendants' means on each of them.]

SCHEDULE 1

Undertakings given to the court by the plaintiff

1) If the court later finds that this order has caused loss to the defendant, and decides that the defendant should be compensated for that loss, the plaintiff will comply with any order the court may make.

2) As soon as practicable the plaintiff will [issue and] serve on the defendant [a] [the] writ of summons [in the form of the draft writ produced to the court] [claiming appropriate relief] together with this order.

3) The plaintiff will cause an affidavit to be sworn and filed [substantially in the terms of the draft affidavit produced to the court] [confirming the substance of what was said to the court by the plaintiff's counsel/solicitors].

4) As soon as practicable the plaintiff will serve on the defendant a [notice of motion] [summons] for the return date together with a copy of the affidavits and exhibits containing the evidence relied on by the plaintiff.

5) Anyone notified of this order will be given a copy of it by the plaintiff's solicitors.

6) The plaintiff will pay the reasonable costs of anyone other than the defendant which have been incurred as a result of this order including the costs of ascertaining whether that person holds any of the defendant's assets and that if the court later finds that this order has caused such person loss, and decides that such person should be compensated for that loss, the plaintiff will comply with any order the court may make.

SCHEDULE 2

Affidavits

The judge read the following affidavits before making this order:

1) ...

2) ...

Cheltenham and Gloucester Building Society v Building Societies Commission

CHANCERY DIVISION

SIR DONALD NICHOLLS V-C

24, 25 MAY, 8 JUNE 1994

Building society – Transfer of business – Transfer of business to existing company – Transfer agreement – Terms of transfer agreement – Cash payments – Parent of existing company proposing to make payments to voting members of building society of less than two years' standing – Whether such payments lawful – Building Societies Act 1986, s 100(9).

A banking group wished to take over the plaintiff building society's business for £1·8bn. The plaintiff proposed to enter into a conditional transfer agreement with an existing company, C & R, which was wholly owned through an intermediate holding company by the banking group. It was proposed that C & R's parent company would offer cash bonuses totalling £1·8bn to be allocated in the following way: £500 to each shareholding member of the plaintiff; £500 to each borrowing member in respect of each mortgaged property, £500 to each employee and pensioner; and a proportionate cash payment, equal to about 10% of the amount in each account, with a likely maximum payment of £10,000 in any one case to each shareholding member of the plaintiff and each holder of a deposit account with the plaintiff or its Guernsey subsidiary. The plaintiff's directors supported the proposal. The Building Societies Commission however considered that in certain respects the proposed terms were outside the powers of the plaintiff and were unlawful. The plaintiff brought proceedings against the commission seeking a declaration, inter alia, that it was within the plaintiff's powers under s 97(1)[a] of the Building Societies Act 1986 to transfer its business to C & R on terms that the proposed cash payments would be made by the successor's parent company and that such payments were not prohibited by s 100(9)[b] of the 1986 Act, which prevented an existing successor company from offering cash bonuses to voting members who had held their shares for less than two years.

Held – The transfer of the business of a building society on terms that cash payments would be made by an existing company to voting members of the building society of less than two years' standing was unlawful as being contrary to s 100(9) of the 1986 Act and, on a proper construction of the Act, the proposal that such payments would be made by the parent company of the proposed successor was outside what was authorised by the Act, just as much as if the payments were made by the successor company itself. Parliament's intention in relation to the 1986 Act was clearly to limit the short-term financial gains which could be offered as inducements to members to vote in favour of a transfer and, consequently, if the members were prepared to approve terms

---

a   Section 97(1) provides: 'A building society may, in accordance with this section and the other
     applicable provisions of this Act, transfer the whole of its business to a company (its
     "successor").'

b   Section 100(9) is set out at p 70 *e f*, post

whereby part of the cash on offer would be paid to employees, pensioners and depositors (ie non-members) that was a matter for them. It followed, first, that the proposal that cash payments should be made by C & R's parent company was unlawful and, second, that the proposed payments to holders of deposit accounts and other non-members was not prohibited by the Act and might be made if approved by the shareholding and borrowing members of the plaintiff (see p 71 *d* to *f h* to p 72 *e* and p 73 *c* to *e g h*, post).

Notes

For transfer of business of building societies, see 4(2) *Halsbury's Laws* (4th edn reissue) paras 787–796.

For the Building Societies Act 1986, ss 97, 100, see 5 *Halsbury's Statutes* (4th edn) (1993 reissue) 585, 589.

Summons

The plaintiff, Cheltenham and Gloucester Building Society (C & G), applied to the court, inter alia, for a declaration that it was within the powers of the plaintiff under s 97 of the Building Societies Act 1986 to transfer its business to Chambers & Remington Ltd upon terms that certain cash payments would be made by Chambers & Remington's immediate holding company, Lloyds Bank Financial Services (Holdings) Ltd, pursuant to the scheme described in the draft transfer statement and that such cash payments were not prohibited by s 100(1) or (9) of the 1986 Act or by any other provision. The defendant was the Building Societies Commission. The facts are set out in the judgment.

Jonathan Sumption QC, Richard Sykes QC and *Malcolm Waters* (instructed by *Slaughter & May*) for C & G.
Philip Heslop QC, Stephen Richards and *Stephen Moverley Smith* (instructed by the *Treasury Solicitor*) for the commission.

Cur adv vult

8 June 1994. The following judgment was delivered.

SIR DONALD NICHOLLS V-C. Cheltenham and Gloucester Building Society, or C & G for short, is one of the largest building societies in the country. It is also one of the most profitable. The Lloyds Bank group wishes to take over C & G's business and is offering £1·8bn. The directors of C & G support the proposal. They believe that, freed from the borrowing restrictions affecting building societies and with access to the bank's treasury, the business will be able to borrow more cheaply. There are other advantages. Lloyds Bank will make further capital available, and the business can take advantage of the bank's distribution strengths.

Under the Building Societies Act 1986 the transfer of the business of a building society, and the terms of the transfer, must be approved by prescribed resolutions of the members. The society must also obtain the confirmation of the Building Societies Commission. Under the Act the commission is entrusted with supervisory functions in respect of building societies. The commission is concerned to promote the financial stability of building societies generally, and to administer the statutory system of regulation of building societies.

Herein lies the difficulty which has arisen. The commission considers that in some respects the proposed terms are outside the powers of C & G and are unlawful. The disagreement raises questions of fundamental importance about the meaning of the statutory provisions. This is virgin territory, because no building society has yet transferred its business to an already existing institution. To resolve this difference of opinion without delay, C & G has brought these proceedings against the commission, seeking declarations.

Building societies

Building societies, as they exist today, are creatures of statute. They occupy an honoured place in the social and economic history of the last two centuries. In their original form, in the early days of the nineteenth century, building societies were small unincorporated mutual associations or clubs. Sometimes there were as few as 10 or 20 members. The members, of whom there was a set number, joined together to save money with the society, each member subscribing by regular instalments for his share of a given nominal amount. The fund established was available for members to use for building a house. Later this was extended to buying a house. Money advanced to members for this purpose was in the nature of a loan, secured by a mortgage. When all the shares were fully subscribed and each member had a house, the society was dissolved and the accumulated surplus distributed. In contrast to these 'terminating' societies were 'permanent' societies. This was a later development. Permanent societies had a constantly changing membership, and did not terminate when all the shares had been fully subscribed.

Building societies have been subject to statutory control for a long time. The first comprehensive legislation, enabling societies to be incorporated, was the Building Societies Act 1874. Now all societies are incorporated bodies under s 5 of the 1986 Act. They have only such powers as they are given by the Act, either expressly or by way of necessary implication.

By way of background I should mention two further features. As time has passed, the number of building societies has fallen, but the size of the continuing societies has increased by leaps and bounds. Temporary, or terminating, societies have ceased to exist. Many of the permanent societies have become national rather than local, with widespread branch networks as we know them today. They have a membership rivalling or far exceeding that of the largest limited companies. The largest societies have 10 or 20 times as many members as the number of shareholders in ICI, the company with the largest share register. Many societies are household names. In 1900 there were 2,286 societies with 585,000 members and total assets of £60m. Now there are only 84 societies, but they have 37 million members and total assets of £277bn, a colossal sum. There are seven million borrowing members.

The history of C & G is perhaps not untypical of a large and successful society. Cheltenham and Gloucestershire Benefit and Building and Investment Association was formed in August 1850. In 1878 the association was incorporated as Cheltenham and Gloucestershire Permanent Mutual Benefit Building Society. It changed to its present name in 1918. In recent years C & G has grown enormously, partly as a result of mergers. It has 230 branch offices, and assets of over £17bn. Ranked by total assets, it is now the sixth largest society. It has 825,000 shareholding members who are entitled to vote, and 370,000 borrowing members also entitled to vote. In addition, C & G has 61,000 depositors. Depositors are, in law, creditors of the society and not members, and they are not entitled to vote. C & G also has a wholly owned subsidiary in Guernsey, C & G Channel Islands Ltd. This is a bank, with 3,000 depositors.

The second feature to be noted is that, unlike shareholders of an ordinary public limited company, the members of a building society do not have a significant financial stake in the profits of the society. In general, they do not have a right to participate in the profits. Neither borrowing members nor shareholding (or investing) members receive a dividend out of profits comparable to the dividends paid by public limited companies. In 1993 the income and expenditure account of C & G showed a pre-tax profit of £202m, and its balance sheet included very substantial reserves. Its general reserve stood at £864m. C & G may draw upon these reserves for the payment of interest and bonuses (r 36 of C & G's rules) but in practice, in this and other societies, profits are not distributed as such to members.

Building Societies Act 1986

The 1986 Act conferred on building societies the powers they need for carrying on business: power to raise funds by issuing shares to members and by borrowing money and receiving deposits, power to make advances to members secured on land, and so forth. The powers conferred by the Act also enable societies to offer a much wider range of services than those traditionally associated with building societies. Societies were authorised to undertake estate agency services and conveyancing services and act as land management agents. They were authorised to provide money transmission services, foreign exchange services, and services relating to the purchase or sale of investments. They were enabled to act as payments agents, mortgage investment agents, insurance agents, managers of personal equity plans, managers of pension unit trust schemes and administrators of pension schemes.

Inevitably, the existence of these wider powers in the financial services field meant that different societies would evolve in different ways and at different speeds. The government anticipated that some societies might reach a stage when the constraints appropriate to a building society would unreasonably hamper their further development. Accordingly the Act introduced a new power enabling a society to slough off its building society skin and emerge, shining and vigorous, as an authorised institution under what is now the Banking Act 1987.

The transfer provisions

This new power is contained in a small group of sections, ss 97 to 102. Section 97(1) is the basic enabling provision. It empowers a society to transfer the whole of its business to a successor company, in accordance with the provisions of the 1986 Act.

The broad scheme is that a building society enters into an agreement, called a transfer agreement, with its successor. The transfer agreement must contain certain provisions. The agreement is conditional on the transfer and the terms of the transfer agreement being approved by prescribed resolutions, called transfer resolutions, passed by the members of the society. The society must send to the members a transfer statement setting out in full the information needed for the members to reach an informed decision. The statement has to be approved by the commission.

The transfer agreement is also conditional on confirmation of the transfer and its terms by the commission. The commission does not have a general discretion to give or withhold confirmation. The commission has some dispensing powers, but essentially its role is to see that all the prescribed statutory requirements have been fulfilled. If they have, and if the commission is satisfied on certain points, the commission must confirm the transfer (s 98(2)). If the commission gives the necessary confirmation, all the property, rights and liabilities of the society are automatically transferred to and vest in the successor on a date described as the vesting date. The society is dissolved on the same date.

The successor company may be a company specially formed by the society for the purpose of carrying on the society's business. Or it may be an existing company, with a going-concern business of its own, which will assume the future conduct of the society's business. In the latter case the transfer is in the nature of a take over. In either case the commission must be satisfied that the successor company will become, or will remain, an authorised institution for the purposes of the Banking Act 1987 (s 98(3)(c), as amended).

The perceived mischief

Parliament was concerned that these transfer procedures should not be operated for the wrong reasons. The procedures were intended to facilitate natural, organic development. They were not intended to provide a means whereby an outside institution might take over a building society business by tempting members with the offer of a substantial cash bonus. There was an obvious risk that members might snap up such an offer, regardless of the best long-term interest of their society and secure in the knowledge that they could transfer their money to a safe haven with another building society once the transfer had gone through. When the Building Societies Bill was presented to Parliament in December 1985, HM Treasury issued a consultative paper, 'Conversion of building societies to company status', which directed attention at this perceived mischief:

> 'This could precipitate a rush of conversions involving a rapid, disruptive and damaging change to the building society movement, as well as liquidity problems for newly converted companies. As was the initial experience in the USA with conversions of mutually-based savings and loan associations to joint-stock status, there could be large speculative movements of funds between societies on rumours of impending conversions.'

The safeguards

The Act therefore contains safeguards. The first safeguard is in the transfer resolutions. A high level of membership approval has to be forthcoming. Such an important change in the nature of the business of a building society should not be made without the strong support of the membership. Where the successor is a specially formed company the transfer must be approved by two resolutions: a borrowing members' resolution, passed by a majority of the borrowing members, and a shareholders' resolution, passed on a poll by three-quarters of the members voting, being a poll at which at least 20% of the members qualified to vote voted. Where the successor is an existing company, the hurdles are even higher. The shareholders' resolution must still be passed by at least three-quarters of the members voting. In addition, it must be passed either by at least 50% of the members qualified to vote or by qualified shareholders representing not less than 90% of the total value of the shares held by shareholders qualified to vote (Sch 2, para 30). The commission may relax these requirements in 'rescue' cases (para 30(4)).

These requirements represent a formidable obstacle in the case of a transfer to an existing company. It is one thing to obtain the approval of a high percentage of the shareholders who are sufficiently interested to vote. It is an altogether different matter to persuade a high percentage of the electorate to take the trouble to turn out and vote.

Even so, the protection this affords against the perceived mischief is limited. It is limited, because the prospect of an immediate cash or other bonus is precisely the incentive which could be expected to overcome membership apathy and produce positive action from the members when asked to vote on transfer resolutions. So the Act contains a second set of safeguards. To prevent speculative investment in building societies, the Act places limits on the distributions and benefits which may be made available to members. Where rights are conferred to acquire shares in priority to other subscribers, the right must be restricted to members who held shares for a two-year period (s 100(8)). In the case of a transfer to a specially formed company, no distribution of funds is permitted save to members who have no right to vote (s 100(10)). Where the successor is an existing company, subject only to the special exception for members who have no right to vote, any distribution of funds to members of the society is confined to members who have held shares throughout a two-year period (s 100(9)). I shall refer to those members as two-year members, in contrast to newly joined members. Section 100(9) provides:

'Where the successor is an existing company, any distribution of funds to members of the society, except for the distribution required by subsection (2)(b) above, shall only be made to those members who held shares in the society throughout the period of two years which expired with the qualifying day; and it is unlawful for any distribution to be made in contravention of the provisions of this subsection.'

This subsection lies at the heart of the present dispute.

The proposed cash payment to all C & G members

I can now identify the principal matter in dispute. C & G is proposing to enter into a conditional transfer agreement with an existing company, Chambers & Remington Ltd, which I shall call 'the proposed successor'. The proposed successor is wholly owned, through an intermediate holding company, Lloyds Bank Financial Services (Holdings) Ltd, by Lloyds Bank plc. I shall refer to the intermediate holding company as 'the parent of the proposed successor'. In short, the proposal is that the business of C & G will be transferred to the proposed successor. The proposed successor will become a public limited company and an authorised institution under the Banking Act 1987. It will be renamed 'Cheltenham and Gloucester plc'. Lloyds Bank and the parent of the proposed successor will join in the transfer agreement. Stated shortly, the parent of the proposed successor will pay £500 to each shareholding member of C & G, £500 to each borrowing member in respect of each mortgaged property, £500 to each employee and pensioner, and a proportionate cash payment to each shareholding member and also to each holder of a deposit account with C & G or its Channel Islands subsidiary. The proportionate payments will be proportionate to the amount in the recipient's account, with a top limit of about £100,000. The distribution percentage is likely to be in the region of 10%, so the maximum sum a member or depositor will receive is likely to be about £10,000. The total of all these payments will be the sum of £1·8bn.

Special provision is made for the statutory cash bonus required to be paid by s 100(2)(b) to certain members who are not eligible to vote on the transfer resolutions. The sum involved here, up to £5m, is comparatively small, and I need not elaborate further on this. Nothing turns on this provision.

If the proposed transfer agreement had been simply an agreement between C & G and the proposed successor, with the cash payments coming from the proposed successor, the agreement would clearly have been unlawful. That would have been so even if the payments had come from the proposed successor's own existing assets, without any need to borrow. The proposal would have fallen foul of the prohibition in s 100(9), because under the proposal the payments are being made to all the members, not just the two-year members. The number of members involved is considerable. About 27% of C & G's shareholding members are newly joined members.

That is not the proposal in the present case. Here the proposed transfer agreement is different. Here the cash payment is coming, not from the proposed successor itself, but from the parent company of the proposed successor without any right to reimbursement by the successor. Does this make a difference? It would be surprising if it did. That would emasculate s 100(9). All an existing institution need do would be to undertake a simple capital reconstruction and pass assets up to a newly-created parent. Then the parent company could do what the existing institution cannot. The parent company could use its newly acquired assets for the purpose of the take over. The parent company could offer a cash bonus to all the members of the building society which its subsidiary is seeking to take over. The cash bonus could be offered to newly joined members as well as two-year members.

The thrust of C & G's case is that the language of the Act does not permit of an interpretation which would render such a transaction unlawful. If the use of the assets of the parent company rather than of the subsidiary is a loophole, it is a loophole for which Parliament has made no provision. How Parliament would have decided to deal with the loophole is not clear. The government is currently reviewing the working of the 1986 Act. The court cannot, under the guise of interpretation, stop up this loophole.

An exhaustive provision

I am unable to accept these submissions. I have reached this conclusion by the following route. Under the statute the terms of transfer must be set out in the transfer agreement made with the successor: 'a building society must .... agree ... with its successor in a transfer agreement on the terms of the transfer ...' (s 97(4)). This envisages that all the terms will be set out in the agreement. That is the prescribed statutory mechanism. A building society has no power to transfer its business save by operating this mechanism.

Secondly, and following on from this, s 100(1) enables those terms to include provision for part of the funds of the society or its successor to be distributed among members of the society in consideration of the transfer, subject to the limitation in s 100(9). Section 100(1) provides:

'Subject to subsections (2) to (10) below, the terms of a transfer of business by a building society to a company which is to be its successor may include provision for part of the funds of the society or its successor to be distributed among ... members of the society, in consideration of the transfer.'

The next step is to note that, in the case of a transfer to an existing company, the successor company needs no authorisation from the Building Societies Act to make a cash payment, described somewhat awkwardly as a distribution of part of its funds, to members of the society in consideration of the transfer. Members of the society are not members of the successor company, and the successor company is not a building society. Its power to apply part of its assets in this way derives from, and depends upon, its own memorandum and articles of association. But, despite this, s 100(9) is plainly directed at restricting the cash payments a successor company may make to members of the society in consideration of the transfer. The legislation seeks to achieve that result by making the s 100(1) power subject to the s 100(9) restriction. Whatever a successor's own constitution may provide, the terms of a transfer agreement cannot include a term under which the successor will make a cash distribution to newly joined members.

In my view, and this is the final step, this scheme makes no sense unless s 100(1), with its appendant limitations and prohibitions in sub-ss (8) to (10), is treated as a compendious and exhaustive statement of the provision which may be included in the terms of transfer for the payment of cash to members of a society in consideration of the transfer. Otherwise, although the successor is prohibited from applying its funds to newly joined members in contravention of s 100(9), other companies in the group of which the successor company is part may do so. I am unable so to read these provisions. Parliament cannot have intended that to be the position.

I recognise that s 100(1) is expressed in permissive terms, and that it is not one of the 'regulated terms' with which the terms of the transfer agreement are obliged to comply by s 97(4)(b): see s 100(12). But s 100(9) is a regulated term, and the whole of s 100 is an applicable provision of the Act with which the transfer must accord if it is to be authorised by the Act: see s 97(1) and (2).

Mr Sumption QC sought to draw a distinction between the funds of a successor and the funds of other companies in the same group. The funds of the successor, like the funds of the society itself, are available for use in the society's business. It is these funds alone which s 100(9) is seeking to safeguard. This argument is not persuasive. Section 100(9) is not concerned to protect excessive distributions of funds. Section 100(1) sets no ceiling on the amount of funds which may be distributed. Section 100(9) has a different purpose, as I have explained. It restricts the persons to whom a distribution may be made, not the amount of the distribution.

Mr Sumption also submitted that to read s 100(1) as I have done has the result of compelling the successor to pay for the transfer with assets otherwise available for use in the transferred business, and of precluding another company in the successor's group from applying 'new money' for this purpose. This is a hollow argument. I see no reason to doubt that, in the present case, the principal reason why the price will be paid by the parent of the transferee company, and not the transferee company itself, is the perceived need to sidestep s 100(9) and offer cash bonuses to all the members, not just the two-year members. If Lloyds Bank wishes to use 'new money', there are several ways by which an additional £1·8bn could be injected into the proposed successor.

Payments to non-members

a   I turn to the second issue. The members of C & G comprise shareholding (investing) members and borrowing members. As already noted, under the proposed transfer agreement, payments will be made to non-members: £500 to each employee and pensioner, and a proportionate cash payment to each depositor with C & G or its subsidiary. In my view the position here is quite b different from that discussed so far. Section 100(9) is an important feature of the legislative scheme. It evinces an intention by the legislature to prohibit cash distributions to newly joined members of a society. Such cash distributions are declared to be unlawful. Section 100(8) and (10) is likewise concerned with prohibiting certain distributions and benefits. All three of these subsections are concerned with making payments to, or conferring rights c on, members of the society.

By way of contrast, I can detect no prohibitory intention regarding distributions to non-members. This is not surprising. It is the members of the society who will decide whether to pass the transfer resolutions. They, and they alone, have the power to vote. For reasons already mentioned, d Parliament was concerned to limit the short-term financial gains which could be offered as inducements to members to vote in favour of a transfer. None of this has any relevance to non-members. They have no votes. They have no say in whether the transfer agreement will be approved.

In principle, therefore, if the members are prepared to approve terms whereby part of the cash on offer will be paid to employees and pensioners and e depositors, that is a matter for them.

Of course, if a building society is proposing to distribute its own funds to non-members as part of the transfer arrangements, one would need to find a source for the power enabling the society to do so. That power does not lie in s 100(1), because that subsection authorises payments only to members. f However, that is not what is proposed in the present case. Here, the payment is being made by another company, which (I assume) has power under its own constitution to apply its funds in this way.

That, therefore, leaves only the question whether the transfer agreement may properly include a term whereby a third party agrees to make certain payments to non-members of the society. I can see no reason why not. Plainly, g the transfer agreement may include terms other than regulated terms. I can see nothing in the legislation to indicate that a third party may not join in a transfer agreement made between a society and its successor. I do not consider s 97(5) is a clear indication in that regard. What I do see, and have already stated, is that when taken with s 100(9), and when one has the underlying purpose of h that provision in mind, s 100(1) and its appendant limitations are to be read as an exhaustive statement of the provision which may be included in the terms of transfer for the payment of cash to members in consideration of a transfer. For the reason I have given, payments to non-members stand on a different footing.

j

Directors' interests

The remaining issue is wholly separate and discrete. All the directors of C & G are shareholding members. Some of them are also borrowing members, and some of them are employed under service agreements which would become obligations of the proposed successor on the vesting date. Others have the prospect of being offered a share option by Lloyds Bank under its share option scheme. The rules of C & G contain a common form provision

precluding a director from voting on contracts in which he is interested and
from being counted in the quorum present at the meeting. Rule 30.2 provides:

'No director shall vote as a director in regard to any contract, or proposal
therefor, in which he is interested, whether directly or indirectly, or upon
any matter arising thereout, and if he shall so vote his vote shall not be
counted nor shall he be reckoned in estimating a quorum when any such
contract, or proposal therefor, is under consideration.'

'Contract' includes any transaction or arrangement. This prohibition may be
suspended or relaxed, at any time and to any extent, by resolution at a general
meeting of the society (r 30.3).

The question which has arisen is whether the board of C & G as presently
constituted can enter into the proposed conditional transfer agreement, on
behalf of the society, without the directors waiving the benefits they would
receive if the transfer proceeds to completion. The Act envisages that such an
agreement will be made, and that thereafter the members will consider
whether to pass the requisite transfer resolutions approving the transfer and its
terms: see s 97(4)(b) and (c). But how can this be done when, on the face of it,
all the directors of C & G are disqualified from passing a board resolution
approving the transfer agreement on behalf of the society? The interests of the
C & G directors, far from being unusual, must be exactly what one would
expect. One would expect the directors of a building society to be
shareholding members.

The commission submitted that the C & G directors are disqualified, but
that when the transfer resolutions are passed this may operate to ratify what
they have done. This is not attractive. It would mean that, if the C & G board
goes ahead and enters into a proposed conditional agreement, the building
society would not have agreed conditionally with a successor in a transfer
agreement pursuant to s 97(4)(b). The society would not have done so,
because no valid board resolution would have been passed before the transfer
resolutions were put to the members. This would not accord with the
statutory scheme.

In my view the key lies in the fact that the proposed transfer is conditional
on the passing of the requisite transfer resolutions by the members: see
cl 4(A)(ii) and (iii) of the proposed transfer agreement. The interest which the
directors have under the agreement can never materialise unless the
agreement is approved by the requisite shareholders' resolutions. Such an
approval by the members will achieve the object underlying r 30.2. C & G will
not become bound by the votes of interested directors. It will become bound
only if and when the shareholders so resolve.

In this circumstance it would be absurd if the directors had to seek the
members' approval twice over in respect of the same transaction: first, to
suspend r 30.2 so as to enable the board to approve the transfer agreement
conditionally on subsequent approval by the members and then, secondly and
later, after the board has entered into the conditional agreement on behalf of C
& G, to approve the agreement itself. This would be to construe r 30.2 in a way
which makes no practical sense in the context of this statutory scheme. In my
view, given that completion is conditional upon the members passing the
transfer resolutions, the benefits the directors will or may acquire on
completion are not interests precluding them from voting on the conditional
transfer agreement.

a It goes without saying that the transfer statement sent to the members must spell out, prominently and unequivocally, all the interests the directors have in the society and all the benefits they may acquire on completion. The members need to have brought home to them that the board which has considered the terms of the transfer and entered into the conditional transfer agreement is composed of individuals all of whom have a financial interest in the transfer. *b* That is information material to the members' decision, and the commission will be concerned to see this information is provided. If the information is not provided, the commission will not confirm the transfer: see s 98(3)(a). So, once more, the transfer agreement would not proceed to completion.

c *Order accordingly.*

Celia Fox   Barrister.

1 Taittinger and others v Allbev Ltd and others

COURT OF APPEAL, CIVIL DIVISION
SIR THOMAS BINGHAM MR, MANN AND PETER GIBSON LJJ
14, 15, 17, 25 JUNE 1993

Passing off – Geographical name – Geographical name descriptive of particular district of France – Plaintiffs a class of producers within that district – Champagne – Non-alcoholic beverage made from elderflowers produced and offered for sale in England under description 'Elderflower Champagne' – Whether likelihood of substantial damage to plaintiffs' goodwill.

European Economic Community – Proportionality – Penalty – Penalty for non-compliance with Community legislation – Regulation – Injunction to restrain breach of regulation – Whether injunction breaching principle of proportionality – Council Regulation (EEC) 823/87, art 15(5).

In 1991 the defendants, who were the producers and wholesalers of mainly non-alcoholic drinks, produced and marketed in England a non-alcoholic carbonated drink under the name 'Elderflower Champagne'. It was sold in bottles of the size, colour and shape usually associated with champagne and was corked with a reusable mushroom-shaped cork. The front label included the word 'elderflower' in large cursive script, with the word 'champagne' below that in smaller but distinct block letters. The back label included a short history of the drink as a traditional English drink and a list of its ingredients. It was sold in various retail outlets at a price of around £2·45 per 75 cl bottle. The plaintiffs, a representative of the French champagne producers and the bodies which regulated the production of wines using French appellations d'origine, subsequently brought an action in passing off for damages and an injunction to restrain the defendants from using the word 'champagne' in relation to their product and in assertion of a right under art 15(5) of Council Regulation (EEC) 823/87, the effect of which was to prohibit the use of the name 'champagne' for the description and presentation of drinks other than wine unless there was no risk of confusion. The plaintiffs contended, in particular, that if the

defendants continued to market their product there would be a blurring or
erosion of the uniqueness that attended the word 'champagne' so that the
exclusive reputation of the champagne houses would be debased. The judge
held (i) that although there had been a misrepresentation in the defendants'
labelling which was calculated to deceive prospective purchasers (albeit a small
section of the public) into thinking that the defendants' product was
champagne or in some way associated with it, there was no likelihood of
substantial damage to the champagne houses' business, reputation or goodwill
and consequently the passing off action failed and (ii) that since the plaintiffs
had suffered no actionable damage there was no basis on which to grant
injunctive relief under art 15(5) of Regulation 823/87. The plaintiffs appealed.

Held – It was a reasonably foreseeable consequence that a non-alcoholic
carbonated drink marketed as 'Elderflower Champagne' which was neither
champagne nor associated with its producers would erode the goodwill in the
distinctive and exclusive name 'champagne' with serious adverse
consequences for the champagne producers, who would be entitled to an
injunction restraining all use of the word 'champagne' in connection with the
drink. It was also clear that a more than minimal risk of confusion was
produced by use of the name 'Elderflower Champagne', which accordingly
contravened art 15(5) of Regulation 823/87 and since there was nothing
disproportionate in the grant of injunctive relief to restrain further
infringement of art 15(5) the champagne producers were prima facie entitled to
an injunction under Community law. Since all the requirements for a valid
cause of action in passing off were satisfied and in the absence of any
exceptional features which might justify withholding injunctive relief on the
grounds of public policy, the court would grant the injunction sought by the
plaintiffs, which did not prevent the defendants from selling their product but
prohibited them from using the word 'champagne' in doing so. The court
would also grant an injunction restraining the defendants from acting contrary
to art 15(5) of Regulation 823/87. The plaintiffs' appeal would accordingly be
allowed (see p 84 *a* to *c e*, p 86 *b g h*, p 88 *d* to *j*, p 90 *g* to *j*, p 91 *d* to *g j*, p 92 *a*,
p 94 *e f*, p 95 *c* to *g j* and p 96 *c*, post).

Erven Warnink BV v J Townend & Sons (Hull) Ltd [1979] 2 All ER 927 applied.

Wineworths Group Ltd v Comité Interprofessionel du Vin de Champagne [1992] 2
NZLR 327 considered.

Notes
For the ingredients of an action for passing off, see 48 *Halsbury's Laws* (4th edn)
para 144, and for cases on the subject, see 47(2) *Digest* (Reissue) 338–424, *2243–2758*.

Cases referred to in judgments
Bollinger (J) v Costa Brava Wine Co Ltd [1959] 3 All ER 800, [1960] Ch 262, [1959]
    3 WLR 966.
Bollinger (J) v Costa Brava Wine Co Ltd (No 2) [1961] 1 All ER 561, [1961] 1 WLR
    277.
Bulmer (H P) Ltd v J Bollinger SA [1978] RPC 79, CA.
Burberrys v J C Cording & Co Ltd (1909) 26 RPC 693.
Deutsche Milchkontor GmbH v Federal Republic of Germany [1983] ECR 2633.
Erven Warnink BV v J Townend & Sons (Hull) Ltd [1979] 2 All ER 927, [1979] AC
    731, [1979] 3 WLR 68, HL; *affg* [1980] RPC 31, Ch D.

Guccio Gucci SpA v Paolo Gucci [1991] FSR 89.
IRC v Muller & Co's Margarine Ltd [1901] AC 217, [1900–3] All ER Rep 413, HL.
Reckitt & Colman Products Ltd v Borden Inc [1990] 1 All ER 873, [1990] 1 WLR 491, HL.
Singer Manufacturing Co v Loog (1882) 8 App Cas 15, HL; *affg* (1880) 18 Ch D 395, CA.
Sodastream Ltd v Thorn Cascade Co Ltd [1982] RPC 459, CA.
Spalding (A G) & Bros v A W Gamage Ltd (1915) 84 LJ Ch 449, HL.
Stringfellow v McCain Foods (GB) Ltd [1984] RPC 501, Ch D and CA.
Vine Products Ltd v Mackenzie & Co Ltd [1969] RPC 1.
Wineworths Group Ltd v Comité Interprofessionel du Vin de Champagne [1992] 2 NZLR 327, NZ CA; *affg* [1991] 2 NZLR 430, NZ HC.

Cases also cited or referred to in skeleton arguments
Akerhielm v De Mare [1959] 3 All ER 485, [1959] AC 789, PC.
Amministrazione delle Finanze dello Stato v Simmenthal SpA Case 106/77 [1978] ECR 629.
Amsterdam Bulb BV v Produktschap voor Siergewassen Case 50/76 [1977] ECR 137.
Angus (George) & Co Ltd, Re application by (1943) 60 RPC 29.
Anklagemyndigheden v Hansen & Søn I/S Case C-326/88 [1990] ECR I-2911.
Birmingham Vinegar Brewery Co Ltd v Powell [1897] AC 710, HL.
British Broadcasting Corp v Talbot Motor Co Ltd [1981] FSR 228.
Bryant & May Ltd v United Match Industries Ltd (1933) 50 RPC 12.
Burgess v Burgess (1853) 3 De G M & G 896, [1843–60] All ER Rep 90, 43 ER 351, CA.
Chelsea Man Menswear Ltd v Chelsea Girl Ltd [1987] RPC 189, CA.
Comet BV v Produktschap voor Siergewassen Case 45/76 [1976] ECR 2043.
County Sound plc v Ocean Sound Ltd [1991] FSR 367, CA.
Gouriet v Union of Post Office Workers [1977] 3 All ER 70, [1978] AC 435, HL.
Habib Bank Ltd v Habib Bank AG Zurich [1981] 2 All ER 650, [1981] 1 WLR 1265, CA.
Holmes v Pipers Ltd [1914] 1 KB 57, DC.
Institut National des Appellations d'Origine des Vins et Eaux-de-Vie v Andres Wines Ltd (1980) 40 DLR (4th) 239, Ont HC.
Iron-Ox Remedy Co Ltd v Co-op Wholesale Society Ltd (1907) 24 RPC 425.
Jarman & Platt Ltd v I Barget Ltd [1977] FSR 260, CA.
Johnson (R) & Co v Archibald Orr Ewing & Co (1882) 7 App Cas 219, HL.
Lego System A/S v Lego M Lemelstrich Ltd [1983] FSR 155.
McDonald's Hamburgers Ltd v Burgerking (UK) Ltd [1987] FSR 112, CA.
Parker Knoll Ltd v Knoll International Ltd [1962] RPC 265, HL.
Payton & Co Ltd v Titus Ward & Co Ltd (1899) 17 RPC 58, CA.
Procureur de la République v Michelangelo Rivoira (Administration des Douanes Françaises intervening) Case 179/78 [1979] ECR 1147.
Saxlehner v Apollinaris Co [1897] 1 Ch 893.
Schlüter v Hauptzollamt Lörrach Case 9/73 [1973] ECR 1135.
Seixo v Provezende (1865) LR 1 Ch App 192, LC.
Singer Manufacturing Co v Wilson (1876) 2 Ch D 434, CA.
Slazenger & Sons v Feltham & Co (1889) 6 RPC 531, CA.
Société Française Radio-Electrique v West Central Wireless Supplies (1928) 45 RPC 276.
Star Industrial Co Ltd v Yap Kwee Kor (trading as New Star Industrial Co) [1976] FSR 256, PC.

Stoke-on-Trent City Council v B & Q (Retail) Ltd [1984] 2 All ER 332, [1984] AC 754, HL.
Treasure Cot Co Ltd v Hamley Bros Ltd (1950) 67 RPC 89.
Unitex Ltd v Union Texturing Co Ltd [1973] RPC 119, CA.
Von Colson and Kamann v Land Nordrhein-Westfalen Case 14/83 [1984] ECR 1891.

Appeal
The plaintiffs, Taittinger (who sued on behalf of itself and of all other persons who produced wine in the Champagne district of France and shipped such wine to England and Wales), Comité Interprofessionel du Vin de Champagne and Institut National des Appellations d'Origine, appealed from the order of Sir Mervyn Davies sitting as a judge of the High Court in the Chancery Division made on 8 February 1993 whereby he dismissed the plaintiffs' action against the defendants, Allbev Ltd and Guy John Corbett Woodall and Sheila Woodall (trading as Thorncroft Vineyard), in passing off and in assertion of a right under art 15 of Council Regulation (EEC) 823/87, as amended by Council Regulation (EEC) 2043/89, seeking damages and an injunction restraining the defendants from using the word 'champagne' in relation to a beverage that they produced and marketed under the name 'Elderflower Champagne'. The facts are set out in the judgment of Peter Gibson LJ.

Charles Sparrow QC and *Nicolas Bragge* (instructed by *Monier-Williams*) for the plaintiffs.
Stuart Isaacs QC and *Neil Calver* (instructed by *Batten & Co*, Yeovil) for the defendants.

Cur adv vult

25 June 1993. The following judgments were delivered.

PETER GIBSON LJ (giving the first judgment at the invitation of Sir Thomas Bingham MR). 'Elderflower Champagne' is the name given by the defendants to a beverage which they first marketed in October 1991 and is now widely available from health food shops as well as from retail outlets from which both alcoholic and non-alcoholic drinks are sold, for example J Sainsbury plc. The first defendant, Allbev Ltd, a producer and wholesaler of mainly non-alcoholic drinks but also of some wines, produces Elderflower Champagne and the second defendant, a partnership between Dr Guy Woodall and his wife, Mrs Sheila Woodall, trading as Thorncroft Vineyard, advertises, markets, distributes and sells it wholesale. It is sold in two sizes of bottle, of 75 cl and 25 cl. Most of its sales are of the larger size bottle, the attractive get-up of which makes it look like a champagne bottle. But it is not a product of the Champagne district of France, it is not made from the grape and it is non-alcoholic. It is a drink made from elderflowers, sugar, citric acid and lemons to which carbonated water is added.

The use by the defendants of the word 'champagne' came to the attention of the champagne producers of France. In the last three decades no group had been more vigorous than the champenois in asserting their rights. No less than 64 instances were given in evidence of steps taken in England since 1960 to ensure that the name of champagne is only used commercially to refer to wine from the Champagne district of France. In February 1992 proceedings were commenced, initially only by the first plaintiff, Taittinger, against Allbev Ltd.

Taittinger, one of the great champagne houses, sues in a representative capacity for all who produce wine in Champagne and ship such wines to England and Wales. Subsequently the second and third plaintiffs were joined as plaintiffs and the partnership of Dr and Mrs Woodall as a defendant. The second plaintiff is Comité Interprofessionel du Vin de Champagne, a body established with legal personality under French law and having amongst its objects the defence of interests of persons involved in the production of wines sold under the Appellation d'Origine Champagne. The third plaintiff is Institut National des Appellations d'Origine, an organ of the French government and having legal personality under French law. Its objects include the regulation of the production of wines entitled to the French Appellations d'Origine and the protection of users of those wines.

The plaintiffs sued both in passing off and in assertion of a right under Council Regulation (EEC) 823/87 (as amended), laying down special provisions relating to quality wines produced in specified regions of the European Community. They sought permanent injunctions and also applied for an interlocutory injunction restraining the defendants from using the word 'champagne' in relation to Elderflower Champagne. Mr Robert Reid QC, sitting as a deputy judge of the High Court in the Chancery Division, on 15 April 1992 would have granted an injunction against passing off until trial but for an undertaking to the like effect being offered to the court and accepted. The drink continued to be sold but without the word champagne as part of its name on the label.

The trial of the action took place in January 1993 before Sir Mervyn Davies, sitting as a judge of the High Court. In a reserved judgment on 8 February 1993 he accepted the concession of the defendants that a valuable goodwill belonging to Taittinger and the champagne houses it represents had been built up in the name champagne and he held that there had been a misrepresentation by the defendants in their labelling of the bottles of Elderflower Champagne which was calculated to deceive. But he found that the plaintiffs failed to establish a likelihood of substantial damage and so he held that the claim in passing off failed. He also declined to exercise his discretion to afford any relief under Community law. Accordingly he dismissed the action and ordered an inquiry as to damages on the plaintiffs' cross-undertaking in damages which they had been required to give when the defendants gave their undertaking to the court.

The plaintiffs now appeal. They say that they are entitled to permanent injunctions against the defendants both in passing off and in reliance on their right under Regulation 823/87. The defendants cross-appeal, claiming that there was no or no material misrepresentation by them and that in so far as the judge had held that they were in breach of the regulation he was wrong in law; they also claim that an injunction would infringe the principle of proportionality.

The facts

The word 'champagne' is distinctive of a sparkling alcoholic wine produced in, and only in, Champagne. It is usually sold in a green 75 cl bottle with a dimpled bottom and a mushroom-shaped cork held down with wire, the cork and neck being covered in foil. The style of the label will vary from make to make but the label often shows the name of the champagne in a cursive script with the name 'champagne' in block letters underneath. Champagne is a quality drink, associated in the minds of the public with celebratory occasions, and it retails in the United Kingdom from about £7·50 upwards.

Elderflower Champagne retails at about £2·45 a 75 cl bottle. It is marketed, in that form, in a bottle of approximately the size, colour and shape usually associated with champagne, although the glass appears to be thinner and the defendants say that the bottle is purchased from a cider bottle manufacturer. It is corked with a mushroom-shaped cork, but, unlike a champagne cork, which has to be of a shape that requires compression to insert into the neck of the champagne bottle, the Elderflower Champagne cork is reusable. The cork is also wired, though unlike that for a champagne cork, the wire appears unnecessary for a bottle containing not fermented but carbonated liquid. At the time of the trial, save for bottles sold to Sainsbury, there was no foil over the wired cork and neck. For bottles sold to Sainsbury, at Sainsbury's request, foil covered the wired cork and neck, and the foil used by the defendants bore the emblem of a bunch of grapes on two sides of the neck and on the top but at a time when the word 'Champagne' was deleted from the label. Since then, foil without that emblem has been used on bottles sold to Sainsbury. There is a front label headed 'Thorncroft' on a gold background. Below that there are various words printed on a white background. At the top there is the word 'traditional' in small print. Underneath there is the prominent word 'Elderflower' in a large cursive script and beneath that in smaller but distinct block letters is the word 'Champagne'. The word 'Champagne' was deleted after Mr Reid's ruling in April 1992 but after the trial 'Champagne' has reappeared on the label but in a cursive script like 'Elderflower'. Below that, the words 'the natural non alcoholic sparkling refreshment' are printed in yet smaller print. Representations of small white flowers are shown on a green background surrounding the white central area of the label. The back label reads:

> 'Elderflower Champagne is a delightfully refreshing traditional drink with a provenance dating back to the middle ages. The distinctive flavour of fresh elderflowers, reminiscent of lychees and muscat grapes, imparts to it a length and body more commonly found in wine than in a soft drink. Elderflowers also have a reputation for warding off colds and flu, and for cooling and cleansing the system. Serve chilled, and refrigerate after opening.'

The ingredients (which I have already stated) are given and at the bottom of the label is 'Thorncroft Vineyard' with its address. We have been told that the word 'Vineyard' no longer appears on the bottle label. The 25 cl bottle has the same labels but a screw cap.

The suggestion that the defendants' 'Elderflower Champagne' is a traditional drink with a provenance dating back to the middle ages seems to me on the evidence to be a creative interpretation of what was known to Dr Woodall. Whilst there is a seventeenth century literary reference to an infusion of elderflowers in small ale, the earliest publication containing a recipe for homemade 'elderflower champagne' that was produced in evidence was dated 1949; further the fizzy drink to which the published recipes refer depended on fermentation for its fizz, was mildly alcoholic and used white wine vinegar and no carbonated water. However, the judge expressed himself satisfied that the defendants' product might be regarded as a modern type of 'elderflower champagne' produced commercially. Certainly there is no evidence of any commercial sales of 'elderflower champagne' until the defendants' product was marketed.

Dr Woodall is the moving spirit among the defendants. He formed Allbev Ltd to produce the elderflower cordial that he decided to produce first on a commercial scale. When that venture prospered, other 'hedgerow' products were made and in 1989 he decided to expand the range of elderflower drinks to Elderflower Champagne. His evidence was that he knew of a drink called 'elderflower champagne' from his grandmother and from recipe books and he was most keen to retain the traditional name, but he positively did not want people to believe that the product was alcoholic.

Winter months are not the best months for sales of a refreshing drink like Elderflower Champagne but nevertheless over 20,000 75 cl and over 12,000 25 cl bottles were sold from November 1991 to January 1992. In May, June and July 1992, although the word 'Champagne' was deleted from the label in accordance with the undertaking to the court, sales averaged over 12,000 75 cl bottles a month. Sales then fell away, but rose sharply to nearly 24,000 75 cl bottles in February 1993, the month when the judge gave his judgment.

The judge heard evidence from a number of witnesses called on behalf of the plaintiffs who were experienced in the wine trade. They included Mr A W Gunn, the managing director of the English distributor of the champagne house, Pol Roger. In his witness statement he referred to what Danckwerts J said in *J Bollinger v Costa Brava Wine Co Ltd* (*No 2*) [1961] 1 All ER 561 at 563, [1961] 1 WLR 277 at 282:

> '... [Champagne] is and has for a long time been known to the trade and the public in the United Kingdom as "Champagne", and as such has acquired a high reputation ... In particular ... Champagne is a wine specifically associated with occasions of celebration so that (in addition to sales to persons who regularly buy wine) it is purchased on such occasions from time to time by many persons who are not in the habit of buying wine for consumption and are not educated in the nature or qualities of different kinds of wine.'

Mr Gunn agreed with that and said:

> '... I can say that the finding is as true today as it was when it was made, especially the last remarks concerning the public's knowledge of wines. If anything the last remark may be even truer today than then, as in the last 10 or 15 years, sales of wine have increased and the number and range of customers have widened enormously; and while it is true that more people know more about wine now than in 1960, an even greater number who are "not educated in the nature or qualities of different kinds of wines" have started buying wine. I believe this enormous widening to have resulted from the market change in the Wine Trade retail structure, now dominated by the major supermarkets. Wine has become widely available as an everyday commodity on supermarket shelves, to be picked up by the customer.'

He also pointed out that there were many non-alcoholic wines now gaining a presence in the market, including many non-alcoholic or low alcohol sparkling drinks. Mr M D Campbell, the director of buying for Thresher, the largest drinks retailing chain in the country, and Mr J H Brind, the central buyer of wines at Waitrose, the supermarket division of the John Lewis Partnership, gave similar evidence.

These and several other witnesses gave evidence of the likelihood, though
not of the actuality, of confusion between the defendants' Elderflower
Champagne and champagne or of a mistaken belief that the defendants'
product had something to do with champagne.   Mr Isaacs QC for the
defendants objected to that evidence, and the judge referred to certain
authorities to the effect that questions as to confusion or being deceived are for
the court and that opinions on those questions are inadmissible in evidence.
But he also referred to the remarks of Kerr LJ in *Sodastream Ltd v Thorn Cascade
Co Ltd* [1982] RPC 459 at 468 to the effect that trade witnesses can give as
admissible evidence their opinions on the likely reactions of others in relation
to matters which are within the sphere of their work, and to the similar
remarks of Browne-Wilkinson V-C in *Guccio Gucci SpA v Paolo Gucci* [1991] FSR
89 at 91. The judge did not rule on this question because he, independently of
that opinion evidence, reached the same conclusion as the witnesses. We too
have not heard argument on this question as it has not been necessary to take
into account that evidence for the purpose of this appeal, but I cannot forbear
to comment that the good sense of what Kerr LJ and Browne-Wilkinson V-C
said seems to me to be obvious.

Passing off
      The authoritative modern formulation of what constitutes the tort of
passing off is contained in *Erven Warnink BV v J Townend & Sons (Hull) Ltd* [1979]
2 All ER 927, [1979] AC 731 (the *Advocaat* case). In that case Lord Diplock
pointed out that the tort had been extended beyond the classic form of it
whereby the tortfeasor misrepresented his goods as the goods of someone else.
He referred to the seminal speech of Lord Parker in *A G Spalding & Bros v A W
Gamage Ltd* (1915) 84 LJ Ch 449 at 450 where the right the invasion of which is
the subject of passing off actions was identified as the 'property in the business
or goodwill likely to be injured by the misrepresentation'. Lord Diplock also
referred to the classic statement by Lord Macnaghten of the concept of
goodwill: 'It is the benefit and advantage of the good name, reputation and
connection of a business. It is the attractive force which brings in custom.'
(See *IRC v Muller & Co's Margarine Ltd* [1901] AC 217 at 223–224, [1900–3] All
ER Rep 413 at 416.) This recognition that what the law protects by a passing
off action is a trader's property in his business or goodwill enabled the court in
the *Spalding* case to give protection to a plaintiff trader whose goodwill was
injured by another trader selling goods which he correctly represented to be his
own but misrepresented to be goods of a quality superior to that of the
plaintiff's goods. Lord Diplock identified five characteristics which must be
present in order to create a valid cause of action for passing off:

> '(1) a misrepresentation (2) made by a trader in the course of trade, (3) to
> prospective customers of his or ultimate consumers of goods or services
> supplied by him, (4) which is calculated to injure the business or goodwill
> of another trader (in the sense that this is a reasonably foreseeable
> consequence) and (5) which causes actual damage to a business or
> goodwill of the trader by whom the action is brought or (in a quia timet
> action) will probably do so.' (See [1979] 2 All ER 927 at 932–933, [1979] AC
> 731 at 742.)

Lord Diplock pointed out that even if all five characteristics are present, it does
not follow that the court is bound to conclude that there has been an actionable

wrong; but he held that all those characteristics were present in the *Advocaat* case and that as there was no exceptional feature which justified on grounds of public policy withholding a remedy, an injunction would lie.

Lord Fraser similarly described five essential facts which have to be shown in a passing off action (see [1979] 2 All ER 927 at 943–944, [1979] AC 731 at 755–756). I only need mention the fifth as this was referred to by the judge and much relied on by Mr Isaacs:

'... that he has suffered, or is really likely to suffer, substantial damage to his property in the goodwill by reason of the defendants selling goods which are falsely described by the trade name to which the goodwill is attached.'

The adjective 'substantial' was not used by Lord Diplock to qualify his reference to damage, nor, I note, is it used by Lord Oliver in his recent reduction to three elements (essentially goodwill, misrepresentation, damage) of what has to be proved in order to succeed in a passing off action (see *Reckitt & Colman Products Ltd v Borden Inc* [1990] 1 All ER 873 at 880, [1990] 1 WLR 491 at 499). I take Lord Fraser to be saying that there must be more than trivial or minimal damage, and I observe that this appears to have been the view too of Slade LJ in *Stringfellow v McCain Foods (GB) Ltd* [1984] RPC 501 at 546.

Lord Diplock in the *Advocaat* case specifically approved the extension to the law of passing off made by Danckwerts J in *J Bollinger v Costa Brava Wine Co Ltd* [1959] 3 All ER 800, [1960] Ch 262. That case first recognised that there could be goodwill attaching to the name 'champagne' which was shared by a large number of traders using that name as distinctive of their wines and which could be protected in a passing off action against traders who had no goodwill in that way but sought to make use of the reputation and goodwill of champagne. At the trial Danckwerts J in *J Bollinger v Costa Brava Wine Co Ltd (No 2)* [1961] 1 All ER 561 at 567, [1961] 1 WLR 277 at 291 held, on evidence to which the judge in the present case likened the evidence put before him, that champagne was distinctive of the wine produced in Champagne, that a substantial portion of the public, being 'persons whose life or education has not taught them much about the nature and production of wine, but who from time to time want to purchase "Champagne", as the wine with the great reputation', was likely to be misled by the misrepresentation constituted by the description by the defendant in that case of its wine as 'Spanish champagne' and that it was a deliberate case of passing off which should be restrained by an injunction.

The judge's approach, which was entirely correct, was to follow the guidance given in the *Advocaat* case. He went through Lord Diplock's five essential characteristics, considering whether on the facts they had been established.

First, he considered whether the defendants were guilty of any misrepresentation, a question which he rightly characterised as one of the most important in the present case. He was of the clear view that the labelling of the defendants' product constituted a misrepresentation in that the front label of their bottle indicates that it contains a champagne that is being sold under the name 'Elderflower'. He pointed out, in my view correctly, that no great importance is to be attached to the back label. That is not likely to attract the close attention of many purchasers. Mr Isaacs challenged the conclusion of the judge on misrepresentation, pointing to features of the labelling, get-up and retail selling, such as the price of the Elderflower Champagne, which he said

should have led the judge to conclude that there was no misrepresentation. I
cannot agree. It appears to my eye plain that there was a misrepresentation
that the defendants' product was champagne or in some way associated with
it. It was called champagne and the impression the name conveyed is strongly
reinforced by the get-up with so many features of a typical champagne bottle
present. Some who notice that it is non-alcoholic might well think that a
non-alcoholic champagne has been produced by the champagne producers in
the same way that non-alcoholic wine and beer have been produced. But I
would go further on misrepresentation than the judge did. To my mind it is of
cardinal importance in this case that, as the defendants accept, champagne is
distinctive exclusively of a sparkling wine produced in Champagne. It is to be
noted that the present case differs from several other champagne cases cited to
us in which much of the evidence had been directed to whether champagne
had become a generic term as other wines had done, no longer distinctive of
wine produced in a particular area. Mr Isaacs disclaimed any intention to argue
that champagne was a generic term. But once it is accepted that champagne is
so distinctive, I do not see how it is possible to market a product as Elderflower
Champagne, which was made in Surrey, without making a representation that
is a falsehood. Mr Isaacs also challenged the finding of misrepresentation on
the ground that there was no material misrepresentation. But that argument
went to the question of confusion to which I will shortly come.

The judge then moved to the second and third characteristics which, so far
as relevant, are that the misrepresentation was made by a trader in the course
of trade to ultimate consumers of goods supplied by him. He said that they
were present and that is not challenged.

He next turned to the fourth characteristic, whether the misrepresentation
was calculated to injure the business or goodwill of the champagne houses in
the sense that this was a reasonably foreseeable consequence. He considered
first whether the misrepresentation was calculated to injure and second
whether or not any intent bore on the question. He referred to the opinion
evidence of the plaintiffs' witnesses, of which I have already made mention,
and said:

> 'It is evidence which of course goes to show that the defendants'
> misrepresentation is calculated to deceive, that is to say is likely to lead the
> public, or a part of the public, into buying the defendants' merchandise in
> the belief that it is champagne. But if the evidence is put aside, so that I am
> obliged to use my own judgment in the matter, I come to the same
> conclusion as the witnesses.'

He then explained that whereas the average member of the public seeing a
bottle of Elderflower Champagne at a price of £2·45 would examine the bottle
and by inspecting the label have any misrepresentation dispelled, there was
another relevant section of the public. He continued:

> 'There is the simple unworldly man who has in mind a family
> celebration and knows that champagne is a drink for celebrations. He may
> know nothing of elderflower champagne as an old cottage drink. Seeing
> "Elderflower" on a label with below the word "Champagne" he may well
> suppose that he is buying champagne. Since the simple man I have in
> mind will know little of champagne prices, he is likely to suppose that he
> has found champagne at a price of £2·45. I do not mean that I now refer to
> any majority part of the public or even to any very substantial section of

the public, but to my mind there must be many members of the public who would suppose that the defendants' "Elderflower" is champagne. Thus it is that I find it established that the defendants' misrepresentation is a misrepresentation that is calculated to deceive.'

This, therefore, is a plain finding of fact by the judge that many members of the public who are prospective purchasers of champagne would be deceived into thinking that the defendants' product was champagne. In my judgment there was evidence before the judge from which he could properly reach that conclusion, and I refer in particular to the evidence of Mr Gunn, Mr Campbell and Mr Brind on the growth in the wine-buying public not educated in the nature and qualities of different kinds of wine. The judge only referred to those who thought Elderflower Champagne was champagne. It seems to me at least as likely that a not insignificant number of members of the public would think that it had some association with champagne, if it was not actually champagne. In this context it is worth recalling that Danckwerts J in J Bollinger v Costa Brava Wine Co Ltd (No 2) [1961] 1 All ER 561 at 564, [1961] 1 WLR 277 at 282 recognised that a large number of people would not have been deceived by the description Spanish champagne and said:

> 'Moreover, when the case is tried in an atmosphere of educated persons, many of whom are well acquainted with the qualities of various wines, it may seem absurd that persons should be deceived by what may appear to be a transparent impersonation.'

Nevertheless, he held that a substantial portion of the public would be misled. It is right not to base any test on whether a moron in a hurry would be confused, but it is proper to take into account the ignorant and unwary (see Singer Manufacturing Co v Loog (1882) 8 App Cas 15 at 18 per Lord Selborne LC).

Lord Diplock's phrase 'calculated to injure', as he himself made plain, does not import a test of actual intention to injure: it is sufficient that this should be the reasonably foreseeable consequence of the misrepresentation. The judge held that the defendants did not intend to deceive or to ride on the back of the goodwill possessed by the champagne houses and did not find that Dr Woodall adopted the Elderflower Champagne get-up with the intention of causing the public to believe that what he was selling was champagne. There is no appeal by the plaintiffs on this, but as Mr Sparrow QC for the plaintiffs rightly stressed, the absence of subjective intention does not prevent the court from concluding that objectively it was a reasonably foreseeable consequence of the misrepresentation that injury to the plaintiffs would result. The judge himself said that his finding on subjective intention was of no service to the defendants as respects the first four characteristics identified by Lord Diplock because intent was not a necessary ingredient of the tort of passing off.

One might have expected the judge to turn at that point to the fifth characteristic identified by Lord Diplock, having apparently dealt with the first four. But surprisingly he then said: 'Since I find that there has been a material misrepresentation, I move on to items (4) and (5) as mentioned by Lord Diplock', and he went on to consider whether it was a reasonably foreseeable consequence of such misrepresentation that it would cause actual damage to the champagne houses' business or goodwill. I feel bound to say that this is inconsistent with his earlier treatment of the fourth characteristic, as is the way he then treats his earlier finding that many members of the public out to purchase champagne would be deceived into thinking that Elderflower

Champagne was champagne. He thereafter refers to those members of the public as 'a small section of the public' which then becomes 'the very small section of the public that I have referred to above'. In fact what the judge addresses is not the fourth and fifth but only the fifth characteristic.

But before I turn to that, I should express my conclusion on the fourth characteristic. In my opinion there was ample evidence that, objectively assessed, it was a reasonably foreseeable consequence of the misrepresentation that injury to the champagne houses' goodwill would result. It was accepted that they had a valuable goodwill in the exclusively distinctive name champagne, yet Dr Woodall was using the name 'champagne' to describe his drink (as was expressly stated in a press release put out by the defendants and as is manifest). Dr Woodall himself accepted in cross-examination that obviously there was a likelihood of confusion in the use by the defendants of the word 'Champagne', and he clearly wanted to use the name 'champagne' to promote sales of their product.

Part of his cross-examination went as follows:

'Q. So, you want to add the word "Champagne" to this label because you think it will help you sell more bottles? A. (Pause) ...

Sir Mervyn Davies. Well, come along—you do want to use the word "Champagne", do you not? A. Yes, my Lord.

Q. That is why you are fighting the action, presumably. A. Well, I want to use the word "Elderflower Champagne" and it's as simple as that.

Mr Sparrow. But you have got "Elderflower" here. A. Yes.

Q. You want to use the word "Champagne", do you not? A. I would prefer to replace "Sparkling Elderflower", which I've already indicated is an unsatisfactory description and has been questioned by the trading standards officials with the proper name for the product which I consider to be Elderflower Champagne.

Q. Because you think that will help you to sell more bottles. A. Well, I don't try to do things in business in order to diminish my sales.

Q. That is a rather ungracious affirmative response, but an affirmative response nonetheless, is it not? A. Yes.'

To all this can be added the judge's own finding that many members of the public would be deceived, quite apart from my own view that there would be members of the public who would think that the defendants' product is in some way connected with champagne. In my judgment the misrepresentation was plainly calculated to injure the plaintiffs' goodwill.

In relation to the fifth characteristic, that the misrepresentation should have caused or would probably cause actual damage to the champagne houses' goodwill, the judge held that the plaintiffs did not establish a likelihood of substantial damage. He reached this conclusion in this way. He posed the question whether it was really likely that the goodwill in the name champagne would be substantially affected if the defendants continued to sell Elderflower Champagne and answered that in the negative, the effect on the plaintiffs' reputation being in his view nil or minimal. He gave his reason as being that those who bought Elderflower Champagne in the belief that it was champagne made up a very small section of the public and he coupled that conclusion with the fact that the defendants' activities were on a small scale as compared with those represented by the plaintiffs. He further pointed to the absence of indication of any likely large-scale enlargement of the defendants' operation.

I have already adverted to the inconsistency between his finding that many members of the public would be deceived when buying Elderflower Champagne and the description of them as constituting a very small section of the public. The deception of many members of the public cannot be de minimis. To this I would add the confusion of those who would think that the defendants' product had some association with champagne, if it was not actually champagne. Further, it cannot be right that the larger the scale of the activities of a trader suing in passing off, the less protection it will receive from the court because of a comparison with the scale of the activities of a defendant who trades on a smaller scale. The question is whether the relevant activities of the defendants are on such a small scale leading to such a small injury that it can be ignored. On the evidence of the defendants' sales, I find it impossible to say that that is the case here.

But in my judgment the real injury to the champagne houses' goodwill comes under a different head and although the judge refers to Mr Sparrow putting the point in argument, he does not deal with it specifically or give a reason for its undoubted rejection by him. Mr Sparrow had argued that if the defendants continued to market their product, there would take place a blurring or erosion of the uniqueness that now attends the word 'champagne', so that the exclusive reputation of the champagne houses would be debased. He put this even more forcefully before us. He submitted that if the defendants are allowed to continue to call their product 'Elderflower Champagne', the effect would be to demolish the distinctiveness of the word champagne, and that would inevitably damage the goodwill of the champagne houses.

In the *Advocaat* case [1980] RPC 31 at 52 Goulding J held that one type of damage was 'a more gradual damage to the plaintiffs' business through depreciation of the reputation that their goods enjoy'. He continued: 'Damage of [this] type can rarely be susceptible of positive proof. In my judgment, it is likely to occur if the word "Advocaat" is permitted to be used of alcoholic egg drinks generally or of the defendants' product in particular.' In the House of Lords in that case Lord Diplock referred to that type of damage to goodwill as relevant damage, which he described as caused 'indirectly in the debasement of the reputation attaching to the name "advocaat" ...' (See [1979] 2 All ER 927 at 930–931, [1979] AC 731 at 740.)

In *Vine Products Ltd v Mackenzie & Co Ltd* [1969] RPC 1 at 23 Cross J, commenting with approval on the decision of Danckwerts J in *J Bollinger v Costa Brava Wine Co Ltd (No 2)*, said:

'[Danckwerts J] thought, as I read his judgment, that if people were allowed to call sparkling wine not produced in Champagne "Champagne," even though preceded by an adjective denoting the country of origin, the distinction between genuine Champagne and "champagne type" wines produced elsewhere would become blurred; that the word "Champagne" would come gradually to mean no more than "sparkling wine;" and that the part of the plaintiffs' goodwill which consisted in the name would be diluted and gradually destroyed.'

That passage was referred to approvingly by Gault J in *Wineworths Group Ltd v Comité Interprofessionel du Vin de Champagne* [1992] 2 NZLR 327 at 341. In that case the sale of Australian sparkling wine under the name champagne was held to constitute passing off. The New Zealand Court of Appeal upheld the decision of Jeffries J, who had held ([1991] 2 NZLR 432 at 450): 'By using the word champagne on the label the defendant is deceptively encroaching on the

reputation and goodwill of the plaintiffs.' Jeffries J had no doubt that if relief
was not granted the plaintiffs would most certainly suffer damage if the word
was used on all or any sparkling wine sold in New Zealand. He thought the
ordinary purchaser in New Zealand without special knowledge on wines was
likely to be misled. Gault J, after agreeing with Jeffries J on deception, said
([1992] 2 NZLR 327 at 343):

> 'I find the issue of damage or likely damage to the goodwill with which
> the name "Champagne" is associated equally obvious in light of the
> finding that there is in fact an established goodwill in New Zealand. I have
> no doubt that erosion of the distinctiveness of a name or mark is a form of
> damage to the goodwill of the business with which the name is connected.
> There is no clearer example of this than the debasing of the name
> "Champagne" in Australia as a result of its use by local wine makers.'

By parity of reasoning it seems to me no less obvious that erosion of the
distinctiveness of the name champagne in this country is a form of damage to
the goodwill of the business of the champagne houses. There are undoubtedly
factual points of distinction between the New Zealand case and the present
case, as Mr Isaacs has pointed out, and he placed particular reliance on the fact
that in the New Zealand case as well as in *J Bollinger v Costa Brava Wine Co Ltd
(No 2)*, the court held that there was a deliberate attempt to take advantage of
the name champagne, whereas in the present case the judge found no such
specific intention. In general it is no doubt easier to infer damage when a
fraudulent intention is established. But that fact does not appear to have
played any part in the reasoning on this particular point either of Jeffries J or of
Sir Robin Cooke P, who thought the case exemplified the principle that a
tendency to impair distinctiveness might lead to an inference of damage to
goodwill (see [1992] 2 NZLR 327 at 332), or of Gault J; nor in logic can I see why
it should. It seems to me inevitable that if the defendants, with their not
insignificant trade as a supplier of drinks to Sainsbury and other retail outlets,
are permitted to use the name 'Elderflower Champagne', the goodwill in the
distinctive name champagne will be eroded with serious adverse consequences
for the champagne houses.

In my judgment therefore the fifth characteristic identified in the *Advocaat*
case is established. I can see no exceptional feature to this case which would
justify on grounds of public policy withholding from the champagne houses
the ordinary remedy of an injunction to restrain passing off. I would therefore
grant an injunction to restrain the defendants from selling, offering for sale,
distributing and describing, whether in advertisements or on labels or in any
other way, any beverages, not being wine produced in Champagne, under or
by reference to the word champagne. That injunction, I would, emphasise,
does not prevent the sale of the defendants' product, provided it is not called
champagne.

Council Regulation (EEC) 823/87
The plaintiffs rely on Council Regulation (EEC) 823/87, as amended by
Council Regulation (EEC) 2043/89. The former regulation contains lengthy
recitals which make abundantly clear the purpose intended to be achieved
thereby. The following are relevant:

> 'Whereas, in order to protect producers from unfair competition and
> consumers from error and fraud, the terms "quality wine produced in a

specified region" and "quality sparkling wine produced in a specified region" should be reserved for wines which comply with Community provisions, although the use of traditional specific designations in accordance with the provisions of the producer Member States should be permitted; whereas a list of such traditional specific designations should be drawn up so that they are known to all Member States ...

Whereas the marketing of beverages not covered by the wine sector and of certain basic raw materials used to produce these beverages under names normally used to designate wines is liable to mislead the consumer as to the nature and origin of the product thus described and to injure the interests of wine producers;

Whereas, with a view to informing consumers correctly and providing appropriate protection for the legitimate interests of wine producers, it is necessary ... to permit direct or indirect use of such names for other beverages only where any risk of confusion as to the nature, origin, source or composition of the beverage in question is ruled out ...

Whereas, in order to preserve the particular quality characteristics of quality wines psr, Member States should be allowed to apply additional or more stringent rules governing the production and movement of quality wines psr, in accordance with fair and traditional practices.'

Article 1(2) of that regulation, as amended by art 1 of the later regulation, refers to certain quality wines psr (produced in specified regions) including quality sparkling wines psr.

Article 15(1) of that regulation, as amended by art 13 of the later regulation, reads:

'... the specific terms traditionally authorized, as provided for in paragraph 2, by the national legislation of the producer Member State, to designate particular wines may be used, respectively, only for the wines listed in Article 1(2) ...'

Article 15(2) refers to 'champagne' in relation to France. Article 15(5), as amended, reads:

'The following may be used for the description and presentation of a beverage other than a wine or grape only if there is no risk of confusion as to the nature, origin or source and composition of such beverage ... a traditional specific term referred to in paragraph 2.'

Thus, put shortly, only if there is no risk of such confusion can the word champagne be used for the description and presentation of a drink like Elderflower Champagne.

By art 16 of the former regulation, each member state is responsible for the control and protection of the quality wines psr marketed in accordance with the regulation.

The regulation is of course directly applicable and so it confers enforceable rights on persons within member states. That much is common ground.

In accordance with art 16 the United Kingdom has issued regulations which make it an offence in this country not to comply with art 15(5). The current regulations are the Common Agricultural Policy (Wine) Regulations 1992, SI 1992/672, which require the Minister of Agriculture, Fisheries and Food and the Wine Standards Board to enforce art 15(5) against a wholesaler here who

fails to comply with the article. Those regulations do not confer rights on
private persons like the plaintiffs.

The judge, after setting out the rival contentions before him that there was
a risk of confusion caused by the use of the name 'Elderflower Champagne' and
that there was no such risk, cited from the decision of the Court of Justice of
the European Communities in *Deutsche Milchkontor GmbH v Federal Republic of
Germany* [1983] ECR 2633 at 2634. There the court referred to the principle that
it is for member states to ensure that Community regulations are implemented
within their territory and said (in para 2):

> 'In so far as Community law, including its general principles, does not
> include common rules to this effect, the national authorities when
> implementing Community regulations act in accordance with the
> procedural and substantive rules of their own national law.'

The judge said that in the absence of common rules he had to act in
accordance with the substantive rules of English law, and this required him to
consider whether there should be an injunction restraining the defendants
from infringing art 15(5); that afforded him a discretion which he decided to
exercise so as to keep the situation in Community law the same as it is in
English law and, accordingly, having refused the injunction against passing off,
he refused the injunction sought under Community law.

I have serious doubts whether the judge's approach was correct on the facts
found by him; but it is unnecessary to say more about that as in view of the
conclusion that I have reached on passing off, it is clear that a more than
minimal risk of confusion is produced by the use of the name 'Elderflower
Champagne' for the defendants' product. Accordingly, art 15(5) is contravened
and prima facie an injunction to prevent such contravention is the appropriate
remedy for the plaintiffs.

Mr Isaacs nevertheless argued that the injunction sought by the plaintiffs
prohibiting the contravention of Regulation 823/87, as amended, would
offend the Community principle of proportionality as going too far. The
applicability of the principle is well-established but, having regard to the clear
purpose of the regulation, it seems to me plain beyond argument that there is
nothing disproportionate in the grant of an injunction to restrain further
contravention by the defendants.

Accordingly I would grant an injunction restraining the defendants from
acting contrary to Regulation 823/87, as amended, by using the name
champagne for the description and presentation of their Elderflower
Champagne or any other beverage not being wine produced in Champagne,
where there is any risk of confusion as to the nature, origin or source and
composition of such beverage.

For these reasons, with all respect to the very experienced judge, I would
allow the appeal, discharge the inquiry as to damages and grant the injunctions
which I have indicated.

MANN LJ. I have had the advantage of reading in draft the judgment of Peter
Gibson LJ. I am in agreement with it and add a few words of my own because
I differ from the judge.

The plaintiffs established that the word 'champagne' has acquired a public
goodwill as denoting a sparkling wine which is produced in the Champagne
district of France. The judge held that the goodwill was part of the trading

assets of the first appellant and those whom it represents. The appellants are entitled to have their goodwill protected against a deceptive use of the word 'champagne', and a deceptive use can be constituted either by a misrepresentation that a drink is champagne or by a misrepresentation that a drink (or other product) has an association or connection with the business which owns the public goodwill (see *H P Bulmer Ltd v J Bollinger SA* [1978] RPC 79 at 99, 117, 142). The judge concluded that the defendants' product represented itself to be a champagne. There was material to warrant this conclusion in the obverse label and in the bottle's shape, colour and closure. However, having regard to the retail price and the non-alcoholic content, I think the preferable conclusion is that the defendants' product represents itself as having an association or connection with the business which has the goodwill. That is an untrue representation. However, the representation is not actionable unless it is likely to damage the appellants' goodwill.

The judge found that the appellants had not established a 'likelihood of substantial damage'. The reasons for his conclusion were that those who buy 'Elderflower Champagne' in the belief that it is champagne are few in number and that the defendants' activities are (at least as yet) on a relatively small scale. With respect to the judge, these reasons are not decisive against the appellants. Their case was and is, that the word 'champagne' has an exclusiveness which is impaired if it is used in relation to a product (particularly a potable product) which is neither champagne nor associated or connected with the businesses which produce champagne. The impairment is a gradual debasement, dilution or erosion of what is distinctive (see Sir Robin Cooke P in *Wineworths Group Ltd v Comité Interprofessionel du Vin de Champagne* [1992] 2 NZLR 327 at 332). The consequences of debasement, dilution or erosion are not demonstrable in figures of lost sales but that they will be incrementally damaging to goodwill is in my opinion inescapable. On this basis I would grant injunctive relief as claimed.

I am also of the opinion that the appellants are entitled to injunctive relief under European law. Article 15(5) of Council Regulation (EEC) 823/87 inhibits the use of the name 'champagne' in relation to a beverage where there is 'risk of confusion as to the nature, origin or source ... of' the beverage. The purpose of the inhibition is to be found in the recitals to the regulation and in particular the twentieth of them which refers to the provision of 'appropriate protection for the legitimate interests of wine producers'. Article 15(5) is directly applicable and art 16 makes its enforcement the responsibility of member states. Under English law an injunction is an available method of enforcement and its availability at the suit of an individual is unaffected by the availability of criminal processes to public authorities (see, as to that availability, the Common Agricultural Policy (Wine) Regulations 1992, SI 1992/672, reg 3). Had the judge granted an injunction in respect of the national law then he would also have granted an injunction in respect of European law. I respectfully doubt if this was the correct approach: once there is a risk of confusion, then subject to the principle of proportionality an injunction should issue without any further requirement. However, it suffices for me to say that an injunction is appropriate in respect of the national law, that an injunction is appropriate in respect of European law and that it is not disappropriate (de minimis apart) to prohibit that which gives rise to a risk of confusion. I also would allow the appeal.

SIR THOMAS BINGHAM MR. I have had the advantage of reading in draft the judgment of Peter Gibson LJ, with which I am in complete agreement.

Since on two points I differ from the judge, and since the case has aroused some public interest, I very briefly summarise my own reasons for agreeing that the plaintiffs' appeal should be allowed.

In *H P Bulmer Ltd v J Bollinger SA* [1978] RPC 79 at 93–95 Buckley LJ described the action for passing off in this way:

> 'To succeed on this part of the appeal the respondents must establish that the appellants have committed the tort of passing off, a form of civil actionable wrong which does not depend upon any legislation but is recognised as an actionable wrong by the general law of the land. A man who engages in commercial activities may acquire a valuable reputation in respect of the goods in which he deals, or of the services which he performs, or of his business as an entity. The law regards such a reputation as an incorporeal piece of property, the integrity of which the owner is entitled to protect. This does not, of course, mean that he is entitled to protection against legitimate competition in the market. If A's goods have acquired a reputation on the market connected with a particular name, mark or get-up, A cannot complain if the value of that reputation is depreciated by B coming on to the market with similar goods which acquire a reputation which owes nothing to the name, mark or get-up associated with A's goods. A can, however, complain if B in the course of his operations uses in connection with his goods the name, mark or get-up associated with A's goods or one so closely resembling it as to be likely to lead to confusion on the market between the goods of A and those of B. By so doing B wrongfully appropriates to himself part of the reputation belonging to A and so infringes the integrity of A's property in that reputation. This proprietary right recognised by the law is not a right in the name, mark or get-up itself: it is a right in the reputation or goodwill of which the name, mark or get-up is the badge or vehicle: *Singer v Loog* ((1880) 18 Ch D 395 at 412), per Lord Justice James; ((1882) 8 App Cas 15 at 26–27, 38–39), per Lord Chancellor Selborne; Lord Watson; *Burberrys v Cording* ((1909) 26 RPC 693 at 701), per Parker, J.; *A. G. Spalding Bros. v A. W. Gamage Ltd.* ((1915) 84 LJ Ch 449 at 450) per Lord Parker. Upon analysis it seems to me to be clear that in principle this must be so. If B has made use of a name, mark or get-up which has become distinctive of A's goods, B does not damage or interfere with A's right or ability to use that name, mark or get-up but he does, or may be likely to damage A in respect of his trade, that is to say, in respect of his, A's enjoyment of an exclusive right to make use on the market of the reputation of his goods. What is damaged or liable to be damaged is that reputation. It is this which A is entitled to have protected. If B sells goods which are not A's goods in such a way as to give the impression that they are A's goods, A may be injured in respect of his trade in either or both of two ways. He may lose sales of his own goods which he might otherwise have made, and the reputation which his goods enjoy may be depreciated by the confusion of B's goods with his so that A's competitive position in the market may be weakened. Moreover the exclusivity of the association of the name, mark or get-up with A's business might, perhaps, be shown to be itself a valuable asset as a powerful means of bringing A's goods to the notice of the public, thus maintaining and promoting A's competitive position on the market. It has

not, however, been suggested that modern advertising techniques have made it possible for a name to acquire an intrinsic value of its own as an advertising asset. Such a suggestion (if feasible at all in any case) would have to be supported by evidence of a kind which is wholly absent from, and would seem to me most unlikely to be available in, the present case. I accordingly proceed upon the established basis (see the cases just cited) that a claim to relief against passing off cannot be based upon an alleged right of property in a name, nor in a mark or get-up. It is injury, or the likelihood of injury, to the reputation of A's goods or business, that is to say his goodwill, that founds the cause of action. If B's conduct has not the effect of damaging, or being likely to damage A in respect of his trade, B is not guilty of the tort of passing off. [He then referred to authority and continued:] Goodwill is undoubtedly a form of property. It is, in my judgment, against infraction of this incorporeal property that the law will protect a plaintiff in a passing off action. So I think that in the present case one should keep prominently in mind the question whether what the plaintiffs have done (for, having regard to the form of the present action, the roles of the plaintiffs and the defendants are the reverse of what is usual) has injured or is likely to injure the defendants in their trade as makers of Champagne.'

Although there have, since this judgment, been other summaries of the ingredients of the cause of action in passing-off, notably in the speeches of Lord Diplock and Lord Fraser in *Erven Warnink BV v J Townend & Sons (Hull) Ltd* [1979] 2 All ER 927 at 932–933, 943–944, [1979] AC 731 at 742, 755–756, the ruling of Buckley LJ has never to my knowledge been criticised, varied or superseded. But it is now, as I understand, clear that a defendant need not, to be liable, misrepresent his goods to be those of the plaintiff if he misrepresents his goods or his business as being in some way connected or associated with the plaintiff's.

The plaintiff's first task in a passing off action is to prove an established commercial reputation distinctively attached to his goods or his services. That was not in issue in this case. The judge held:

> 'The word champagne is distinctive exclusively of a sparkling wine that is produced in the Champagne district of France as shown on a map that was produced. It is admitted that a valuable reputation and goodwill has been built up in the name 'champagne', such goodwill being part of the trading assets of the first plaintiff and those represented by the first plaintiff.'

In the United Kingdom, and throughout most of the world, that distinctiveness has been tenaciously and vigilantly protected by the champagne houses. The nature, origin or source and composition of a bottle of champagne are accordingly clear. I shall use the noun 'Champagne' with a capital C to refer, and refer only, to the first plaintiffs' distinctive product.

Most, if not all, commercial products convey a statement as to what they are. The first issue in this case is as to the statement conveyed by the defendants' product. The plaintiffs' case is very clear. They say that the product is represented to be Champagne. They rely, first and foremost, on the label which so describes the contents of the bottle. They also rely, but to a lesser extent, on the appearance of the bottle, particularly the use of green glass, the use of a mushroom-shaped cork and a wire retaining device (which of course have a specific function in the case of Champagne but are unnecessary with a product such as this where there is no pressure to withstand) and, in the case of bottles sold through J Sainsbury plc, the use of gold foil to enclose the neck of the bottle, the cork and the wire retaining device.

The defendants' case is equally clear. That product is not, they say, represented to be Champagne but 'Elderflower Champagne', a traditional English country drink unrelated to Champagne. They contend that any suggested association with Champagne is negatived by this description, by the statement that the drink is non-alcoholic, by the label indicating that the cork is resealable, by the use of the English trade-name Thorncroft, by the absence of any reference to France, by the text of the label on the back of the bottle and by the price, a small fraction of the price of the cheapest Champagne, at which the product is sold.

The judge understood the label to be indicating that the bottle contained a Champagne being sold under the name 'Elderflower'. In reaching this conclusion he took account of, because he expressly referred to, the get-up of the product. This is certainly a possible understanding of the representation which the defendants made through their product as marketed. But I would myself be inclined to read the overall representation as being not that the contents were Champagne but that the product was in some way associated with or connected with or derived from Champagne. I am fortified in this conclusion by the reflection that no one in this country would ever, either here or on holidays in Europe, have seen a bottle labelled 'Champagne' which was not Champagne.

If I am right (or the judge was right) as to the representation made, it must follow that this was a misrepresentation.

The second major issue was whether the defendants' misrepresentation, if it was such, was likely to injure the business or goodwill of the first plaintiffs, whether (in other words) there was a risk of confusion. The judge concluded that 'there must be many members of the public who would suppose that the defendants' "Elderflower" is champagne'. The plaintiffs supported this finding, the defendants challenged it. Both parties relied on the features already touched on when considering the representation made.

It is obvious that no discerning, or moderately discerning, buyer of wine would mistake the defendants' product for Champagne. But there is nothing in the evidence to suggest that the great mass of the urban population of this country have ever heard of elderflower champagne, a product never (so far as the evidence shows) exploited commercially at any time up to now. I accept the judge's view that many such buyers would be subject to confusion. Even if 'Elderflower' and the price and the absence of alcohol made it plain that this was not Champagne, neither these nor other features would in my view dispel the belief, in many minds, that the product was in some way connected with or derived from Champagne.

It was on the issue of damage that the judge found against the plaintiffs, somewhat inconsistently, as they submitted. He held:

'The effect on the plaintiffs' reputation will in my view be nil or minimal. I say that because those who buy Elderflower Champagne in the belief that it is champagne make up the very small section of the public that I have referred to above; and that consideration is coupled with the fact that the defendants' activities are on a small scale (as compared with those represented by the plaintiffs). Furthermore, there was no indication of any likely large-scale enlargement of the defendants' operation. Since the plaintiffs do not establish a likelihood of substantial damage, the passing off claim fails.'

Plainly, those with any knowledge of wine will not buy the defendants' product instead of Champagne. It is also hard to imagine anyone buying the defendants' product instead of Champagne for a celebratory occasion for which he would otherwise buy Champagne. Even on those sporting occasions when the consumer's intention is not so much to drink the contents of the bottle as to spray it around, the defendants' product would be unsuitable as the bottle would not, even if shaken, produce the necessary head. Like the judge, I do not think the defendants' product would reduce the first plaintiffs' sales in any significant and direct way. But that is not, as it seems to me, the end of the matter. The first plaintiffs' reputation and goodwill in the description 'Champagne' derive not only from the quality of their wine and its glamorous associations, but also from the very singularity and exclusiveness of the description, the absence of qualifying epithets and imitative descriptions. Any product which is not Champagne but is allowed to describe itself as such must inevitably, in my view, erode the singularity and exclusiveness of the description 'Champagne' and so cause the first plaintiffs damage of an insidious but serious kind. The amount of damage which the defendants' product would cause would of course depend on the size of the defendants' operation. That is not negligible now, and it could become much bigger. But I cannot see, despite the defendants' argument to the contrary, any rational basis upon which, if the defendants' product were allowed to be marketed under its present description, any other fruit cordial diluted with carbonated water could not be similarly marketed so as to incorporate the description 'champagne'. The damage to the first plaintiffs would then be incalculable but severe.

Differing as I do from the judge on the damage issue, but agreeing with him on the other passing off issues, I would allow the plaintiffs' appeal and grant appropriate injunctive relief. This conclusion is not in my view offensive to the common sense or the fairness of the situation. The defendants are plainly very anxious to describe their product as 'Elderflower Champagne' rather than as 'Elderflower' (the description used while the interlocutory injunction was in force) or some variant such as 'Elderflower Sparkling Drink'. Why? Because a reference to champagne imports nuances of quality and celebration, a sense of something privileged and special. But this is the reputation which the Champagne houses have built up over the years, and in which they have a property right. It is not in my view unfair to deny the defendants the opportunity to exploit, share or (in the vernacular) cash in on that reputation, which they have done nothing to establish. It would be very unfair to allow them to do so if the consequence was, as I am satisfied it would be, to debase and cheapen that very reputation.

Even if I agreed with the judge on the damage issue, which for the reasons given I do not, I would not agree with his conclusion on the Community law issue. The effect of art 15(5) of Council Regulation EEC 823/87, in its unamended and its amended form, was to prohibit use of the name 'champagne' for the description and presentation of a beverage other than wine unless there was no risk of confusion as to the nature, origin or source and composition of such beverage. The judge held that there was a risk of such confusion, and I agree. The ordinary means of protecting the legitimate interests of wine producers and ensuring the supply of correct information to consumers, the objective specified in the twentieth recital of the regulation, is by restraining the prohibited act.   Under domestic law the grant of an injunction no doubt remains discretionary, but where the plaintiff's Community law right is infringed and no undertaking is offered by the defendant I would expect the grant of an injunction to follow in any ordinary circumstances.   The absence of substantial damage would not ordinarily justify the refusal of an injunction, in my judgment, since the regulation clearly treats as critical not the likelihood of damage but the risk of confusion.   Nor does the existence of a means of enforcement through the criminal law in my view deprive an aggrieved producer of his right to seek appropriate redress in the civil courts.   I can see nothing disproportionate in restraining a defendant from doing the very act, but no more than the very act, which the regulation prohibits.   On this point also I would allow the plaintiffs' appeal.   I do not find it necessary, in order to give judgment, to seek a ruling from the Court of Justice of the European Communities, a possibility which was raised but not pressed.

Appeal allowed. Leave to appeal to the House of Lords refused.

22 November 1993.   The Appeal Committee of the House of Lords (Lord Templeman, Lord Jauncey of Tullichettle and Lord Mustill) refused leave to appeal.

L I Zysman Esq   Barrister.

Clark and another v Chief Land Registrar and another
Chancery plc v Ketteringham

COURT OF APPEAL, CIVIL DIVISION

NOURSE, KENNEDY AND ROCH LJJ

19–21, 24 JANUARY, 5 MAY 1994

Land registration – Charging order – Protection on register – Caution – Caution registered at Land Registry to protect charge over or interest in property – Land Registry registering subsequent charge over same property, in one case without notice to cautioners – Whether cautioners in first case entitled to indemnity from registrar – Whether cautioners' interest in land having priority over subsequently registered charge – Whether charging order giving cautioners charge over legal estate – Land Registration Act 1925, ss 55, 56(2), 83(2) – Charging Orders Act 1979, s 2(1)(b)(iii).

In the first case, the plaintiffs, who were judgment creditors, obtained a charging order on a property owned by the two debtors under a statutory trust for sale.   The plaintiffs subsequently protected that order by registering cautions at the Land Registry.   Shortly thereafter the second defendant made a loan of £92,000 to the debtors, who executed a legal charge over the property to secure the loan.   The charge was presented to the Land Registry for registration

but, instead of giving notice of the charge to the plaintiffs as required by s 55 of
a the Land Registration Act 1925 and r 218 of the Land Registration Rules 1925 so
that they could object to the registration, the Land Registry registered the
charge without giving such notice, thereby giving the charge on the face of the
register priority over any equitable charge created in favour of the plaintiffs by
their charging order. The property was later sold by the mortgagee but the
b balance of the proceeds after the mortgage was paid off was insufficient to
satisfy both the plaintiffs' and the second defendant's charges. The plaintiffs
sought as against the Chief Land Registrar and the second defendant a
declaration that they were entitled to an indemnity from the registrar under
s 83(2)ᵃ of the 1925 Act in respect of their loss suffered by reason of the denial of
the priority over the second defendant as a result of the Land Registry's failure
c to serve notice pursuant to the cautions. The judge held that the plaintiffs were
entitled to an indemnity from the registrar for failure to give them notice of a
charge over the land subsequently registered by the second defendant. The
registrar appealed, contending (i) that the plaintiffs had not suffered any loss as
the result of the failure to give them notice pursuant to their caution because by
d remaining on the register the caution had the effect that the second defendant
had to satisfy the interests of the plaintiffs as the cautioners before he was
entitled to satisfy his own charge and (ii) that the plaintiffs' charging order only
gave the plaintiffs a charge over the beneficial interest of the judgment debtors
in the property and not a charge over their legal interest and therefore it did not
take priority over the second defendant's charge.
e   In the second case, a property development company agreed to grant the
defendant a long lease of a flat in a block which they planned to construct. A
caution protecting the defendant's estate contract in respect of the flat was
subsequently registered at the Land Registry. The developers later negotiated
a loan facility from the plaintiffs and agreed to secure the loan by granting them
f a charge over the freehold of the building under construction. The defendant
consented to the registration of the legal charge, which was in turn executed
and entered in the charges register. Following completion of the building work,
the defendant went into occupation of the flat without having been granted the
agreed lease. By the time he obtained an order against the developers for
specific performance of the original agreement they were in financial difficulties
g and the plaintiffs were seeking to enforce their charge against them free of the
defendant's estate contract. The deputy judge followed the decision in the first
case and upheld the plaintiffs' claim on the ground that mere registration of the
defendant's caution did not give his estate contract priority over the plaintiff's
subsequently registered charge. The defendant appealed.

h
Held – The appeal in each case would be dismissed for the following reasons—
(1) On their true construction, ss 54 to 56ᵇ of the 1925 Act were clearly
intended to describe the nature and effect of cautions by instituting a procedure
(as amplified by the 1925 rules) under which a person interested in registered
land could ensure that he was warned of any proposed dealing and given an
j opportunity to assert priority for his interest and, accordingly, the mere fact
that a caution had been lodged at the Land Registry to protect an interest in land
did not entitle the cautioner to assert priority for that interest over subsequently
registered charges. In particular, s 56(2) provided that a caution should not

a   Section 83(2) is set out at p 100 g, post
b   Sections 54 to 56, so far as material, are set out at p 104 g to p 105 d, post

prejudice the claim or title of any person and that it should have no effect *a* whatever except as was provided in the Act, namely s 55 and the 1925 rules, r 220(3) of which stipulated that one of the methods of conferring priority was the registration of the dealing subject to a notice protecting the cautioner's interest. Moreover, the fact that a caution was an 'entry' on the register for the purpose of s 20(1)^c of the 1925 Act could not elevate what was essentially a procedure and not an interest in land to a state and effect not given to it by ss 54 *b* to 56. It followed that in each case the subsequently registered charge had priority over the cautioners' interest in the land and that the judge was correct in ruling that the plaintiffs were entitled to an indemnity from the registrar in respect of their loss (see p 105 *e* to *h*, p 106 *g h*, p 107 *d e* and p 108 *g* to *j*, post); *Barclays Bank Ltd v Taylor* [1973] 1 All ER 752 applied; *Parkash v Irani Finance Ltd* *c* [1969] 1 All ER 930 distinguished.

(2) In the first case it was clear, as a matter of construction, that the charging order expressly referred to the debtors' legal and beneficial interest in the property and was effective to create a charge over the legal estate in the land and not merely their interest in the proceeds of sale, and neither s 2(1)^d of the Charging Orders Act 1979 nor RSC Ord 50, rr 1 to 4 (which detailed the *d* procedure for obtaining a charging order) nor any technical breach of the rules of court could alter the clear effect of that order. The judge's decision on the charging order point was accordingly correct (see p 103 *d* to *g*, and p 108 *j*, post).

Decision of Ferris J [1993] 2 All ER 936 affirmed.

Notes   *e*
For the right to indemnity, see 26 *Halsbury's Laws* (4th edn) paras 1061–1074, and for cases on the subject, see 39(1) *Digest* (Reissue) 158, *1645–1647*.

For cautions against dealings, see 26 *Halsbury's Laws* (4th edn) paras 1346–1366, and for cases on the subject, see 39(1) *Digest* (Reissue) 173–176, *1695–1707*.

For priorities on registered conveyancing, see 26 *Halsbury's Laws* (4th edn) *f* para 922, and for a case on the subject, see 39(1) *Digest* (Reissue) 172, *1693*.

For rectification of the register, see 26 *Halsbury's Laws* (4th edn) paras 1054–1060, and for cases on the subject, see 39(1) *Digest* (Reissue) 155–158, *1629–1644*.

For the Land Registration Act 1925, ss 20, 55, 56, 83, see 37 *Halsbury's Statutes* (4th edn) 538, 565, 566, 590.

For the Charging Orders Act 1979, s 2, see 22 *Halsbury's Statutes* (4th edn) *g* (1991 reissue) 374.

For the Land Registration Rules 1925, r 218, see 16 *Halsbury's Statutory Instruments* (1994 reissue) 369.

Cases referred to in judgments   *h*
Barclays Bank Ltd v Taylor [1973] 1 All ER 752, [1974] Ch 137, [1973] 2 WLR 293, CA.

---

c   Section 20(1), so far as material, provides: 'In the case of a freehold estate registered with an
    absolute title, a disposition of the registered land or of a legal estate therein ... for valuable   *j*
    consideration shall, when registered, confer on the transferee ... an estate in fee simple ... or
    other legal estate expressed to be created in the land dealt with ... subject—(a) to the
    incumbrances and other entries, if any, appearing on the register ...'
d   Section 2(1), so far as material, provides: 'a charge may be imposed by a charging order only on
    ... (b) any interest held by a person as trustee of a trust ... if the interest is in [inter alia, land] ...
    and ... (iii) in a case where there are two or more debtors all of whom are liable to the creditor
    for the same debt, they together hold the whole beneficial interest under the trust
    unencumbered and for their own benefit.'

Kitney v MEPC Ltd [1978] 1 All ER 595, [1977] 1 WLR 981, CA.
a *Parkash v Irani Finance Ltd* [1969] 1 All ER 930, [1970] Ch 101, [1969] 2 WLR 1134.
White Rose Cottage, Re [1964] 1 All ER 169, [1964] Ch 483, [1964] 2 WLR 396; *affd in part* [1965] 1 All ER 11, [1965] Ch 940, [1965] 2 WLR 337, CA.

Cases also cited or referred to in skeleton arguments
b *Irani Finance Ltd v Singh* [1970] 3 All ER 199, [1971] Ch 59, CA.
National Westminster Bank Ltd v Allen [1971] 3 All ER 201, [1971] 2 QB 718.
Perry v Phoenix Assurance plc [1983] 3 All ER 60, [1988] 1 WLR 940.
Stevens v Hince (1914) 110 LT 935.

c **Appeals**

Clark and anor v Chief Land Registrar and anor
The first defendant, the Chief Land Registrar, appealed from the decision of
Ferris J ([1993] 2 All ER 936, [1993] Ch 294) hearing an application by originating
summons on behalf of the plaintiffs, Richard Clark and June Erica Clark, given
d on 28 August 1992 whereby he declared (1) that pursuant to s 2(1) of the Land
Registration and Land Charges Act 1971 the plaintiffs were entitled to an
indemnity under s 83 of the Land Registration Act 1925 in respect of loss arising
from the failure by the registrar, on the presentation by the second defendant,
Peter Edward Jones, of a legal charge dated 7 December 1990 over the property
known as Spinners Corner, 10 Blyton Close, Beaconsfield, Buckinghamshire,
e registered under title no BM 52084 at HM Land Registry, to give to the plaintiffs
notice under s 55 of the Land Registration Act 1925 and r 218 of the Land
Registration Rules 1925, SR & O 1925/1093 warning them as cautioners and (2)
that the plaintiffs as chargees under a charging order nisi made on 3 August 1990
and a charging order absolute made on 21 November 1990 over the property did
f not by virtue of cautions against dealings registered on 16 August and 29
November 1990 respectively have priority over the interest of the second
defendant as proprietor of a legal charge dated 7 December 1990 which was
entered on the register on 11 December 1990. The facts are set out in the
judgment of Nourse LJ.

g *Chancery plc v Ketteringham*
The defendant, Ralph Daniel Ketteringham, appealed from the decision of
David Neuberger QC, sitting as a deputy judge of the Chancery Division, given
on 23 September 1993 whereby he declared that a legal charge in respect of
property at 3 Alton Road, Parkstone, Poole, Dorset registered by the plaintiffs,
h Chancery plc, on June 27 1988 had priority over the interest of the defendant
under an estate contract in respect of a flat which was part of that property and
in respect of which a caution had entered on the proprietorship register on 11
March 1988. The facts are set out in the judgment of Nourse LJ.

j *James Munby QC* and *Peter Crampin QC* (instructed by the *Treasury Solicitor*) for
the Chief Land Registrar.
Edward Nugee QC and *Jock Craven* (instructed by *Hunters*) for Mr and Mrs Clark.
Anthony Allston (instructed by *Hobson & Arditti*) for Mr Jones.
Daniel Gerrans (instructed by *Trevanions*, Poole) for Mr Ketteringham.
Ernest Scamell (instructed by *Fladgate Fielder*) for Chancery plc.

Cur adv vult

5 May 1994. The following judgments were delivered.

a

NOURSE LJ.

Introduction

The main question arising on these appeals (the caution point) is whether a caution against dealings lodged in respect of registered land gives the cautioner *b* anything more than a right to be warned of a proposed dealing or entry on the register and a right to assert priority for the interest in respect of which it is lodged. In both courts below that question was answered in the negative. Now the registrar in the first case and the cautioner in the second ask us to hold that the priority sought is achieved by the lodging of the caution and no more. This question, which appears to be fundamental to the system of registered *c* conveyancing in this country, depends on the true construction and effect of the material provisions of the Land Registration Act 1925.

In the first case, *Clark v Chief Land Registrar*, an anterior question (the charging order point) also arises. It is said by the registrar that the charging order in respect of which the caution was lodged in that case created a charge *d* over interests in the proceeds of sale of land, not over the land itself, with the result that it created no interest capable of being protected on the register. The plaintiff cautioners, Mr and Mrs Richard Clark, to whom the charging order was granted, say that it created a charge over the land, although they accept that, if it did not, the result contended for by the registrar would follow. In the court below Ferris J ([1993] 2 All ER 936, [1993] Ch 294) decided this question also in *e* favour of Mr and Mrs Clark. It depends on the true construction and effect of the charging order. Since it was made in standard form, the question again appears to be one of some general importance.

On a superficial view of the matter, it might be thought curious that the Chief Land Registrar, whose function is rather to adjudicate in contests between *f* competing interests in registered land than to take sides in them, should have entered into a dispute on questions such as these. The explanation is that Mr and Mrs Clark claim an indemnity under s 83(2) of the 1925 Act, which provides:

'Where an error or omission has occurred in the register, but the register is not rectified, any person suffering loss by reason of such error or *g* omission, shall, subject to the provisions of this Act, be entitled to be indemnified.'

The admitted omission here was a failure to give to Mr and Mrs Clark a warning to which they were entitled by reason of the lodging of their caution. In arguing the questions, the registrar seeks to protect the public purse against the *h* consequences of the omission by establishing that Mr and Mrs Clark have suffered no damage in respect of which they are entitled to be indemnified. In the court below he also contended that Mr and Mrs Clark's proper remedy was to seek rectification of the register (the rectification point). Again that contention was rejected by Ferris J and it was abandoned during the argument *j* in this court.

The stance adopted by the registrar has had the paradoxical result that on each of the outstanding points he has put forward an argument contrary to that which he might have been expected to put forward. Thus, on the caution point, acknowledged weaknesses in the drafting of the 1925 Act have been exploited in order to promulgate a view of a caution which, if correct, would both a contravene the view consistently taken by his predecessors and blur, if not eliminate, the distinction between a caution and a notice. On the charging order point, he has argued that an order in standard form, almost universally adopted but not previously questioned, did not have the effect which it was clearly intended to have.

The hearing of the appeal in *Clark v Chief Land Registrar* was fixed to start on b 19 January 1994, with an estimated length of three days. Later a direction was made for the hearing of the appeal in *Chancery plc v Ketteringham* at the same time, but for some reason which is not clear the time allocated for the hearing of both appeals remained three days. It was evident from the skeleton arguments lodged in the latter case that counsel intended to advance detailed arguments on the caution point which had not been advanced in the court c below in *Clark* and would now be advanced on the appeal. The parties to both appeals having opted for them to be heard together, we decided to start by hearing argument on the caution point, in order not to detain the parties in *Ketteringham* longer than was necessary.   Moreover, since Mr Gerrans for Mr Ketteringham accepted that if the appeal on the caution point failed in *Clark*, d then, subject to two additional points, Mr Ketteringham's appeal must also fail, we heard argument by the appellants in both appeals and then completed the argument in *Clark*, allowing Mr Gerrans a right of reply as well as Mr Munby QC, for the registrar. At that stage, a majority of the court being of a clear opinion that the appeal on the caution point in *Clark* must fail and that there was nothing in either of Mr Gerrans's additional points, it became unnecessary e for us to call on Mr Scamell, for Chancery plc, to answer Mr Ketteringham's appeal.

Even without Mr Scamell being heard, the argument on the caution point lasted for two and a half days. We then heard a day and a half's argument on the charging order point, the parties in *Ketteringham* having withdrawn. Now f the convenient course is to take the questions in their logical order and, like Ferris J, to deal first with the charging order point. Both points being relatively straightforward, I propose to treat only of their essentials.

Clark v Chief Land Registrar

The material facts are fully set out in the judgment of Ferris J ([1993] 2 All ER g 936, [1993] Ch 294). They need not be repeated at length. I will state the most important of them.

Mr and Mrs Jeffrey Jarvis were the registered proprietors with title absolute of Spinners Corner, Beaconsfield, Bucks. They were joint tenants of it both at law and in equity. They held the legal estate on trust for sale and the proceeds h of sale in trust for themselves as joint tenants. On 5 June 1990 Mr and Mrs Clark obtained judgment against them in proceedings in the Queen's Bench Division for a sum of just under £215,000. By an order nisi made in those proceedings on 3 August 1990 Mr and Mrs Jarvis's 'interest' in Spinners Corner was charged with the payment of that sum together with interest and costs. The order j recited the reading of an affirmation of Mr Merrick, an articled clerk with Mr and Mr Clark's solicitors, from which it was said to appear (inter alia) that Mr and Mrs Jarvis had 'a beneficial interest' in Spinners Corner. In his affirmation, Mr Merrick stated that it was sought 'to impose a charge on the freehold land known as Spinners Corner ... which property is registered at HM Land Registry under Title No. BM52804'. He also said that he was informed and verily believed that Mr and Mrs Jarvis were 'the beneficial freehold owners' of it and

that that fact appeared from the office copy entries on the register which the
court had already ordered to be produced.

On 16 August 1990 Mr and Mrs Clark caused a caution to be lodged at the
Land Registry against dealings with Spinners Corner. The application was
supported by a statutory declaration in standard form made by a partner in their
solicitors, who declared that they were interested in the land as the chargees of
the charging order nisi dated 3 August 1990.

On 21 November 1990 a charging order absolute was granted. Having recited
the reading of Mr Merrick's affirmation and the order nisi, it ordered that the
'interests' of Mr and Mrs Jarvis in Spinners Corner should stand charged with
the amount needed to satisfy the judgment. On 29 November a further caution
was lodged in respect of that order.

On 7 December 1990 Mr and Mrs Jarvis, as part of the compromise of an
action in the Chancery Division brought against them by Mr Jones, the second
defendant in this action, executed a legal charge of Spinners Corner in his
favour. That legal charge was presented for registration at the Land Registry on
11 December 1990. I take up the narrative in the words of Ferris J ([1993] 2 All
ER 936 at 939–940, [1993] Ch 294 at 300–301):

> 'It was then that the mistake on the part of the Land Registry occurred.
> What should have happened was that, on presentation of Mr Jones's charge
> for registration, the Land Registry ought to have given notice to the Clarks
> under s 55 of the Land Registration Act 1925 and r 218 of the Land
> Registration Rules 1925, SR & O 1925/1093. On receipt of that notice the
> Clarks would have had an opportunity to object to the registration of the
> charge in favour of Mr Jones. Nobody doubts that they would have availed
> themselves of that opportunity ... Unfortunately the Land Registry failed
> to serve the requisite notice on the Clarks, with the result that they
> remained in ignorance of the charge in favour of Mr Jones. That charge
> was duly registered, the registration being effective on 11 December 1990,
> the date when it was lodged for registration.'

The subsequent history of the matter and the basis of Mr and Mrs Clark's claim
for an indemnity are dealt with by the judge (see [1993] 2 All ER 936 at 940–941,
[1993] Ch 294 at 301–302).

The charging order point

The operative part of the order nisi was expressed to charge Mr and Mrs
Jarvis's 'interest' in Spinners Corner. Their interest in the property was the
entire legal and beneficial interest. It would therefore seem clear, as a matter of
construction, that the order was effective to charge the land, not merely their
interests in the proceeds of sale, it being immaterial for this purpose that it was
only the beneficial interest that was recited in the order. It would also seem
clear, as a matter of construction, that the order absolute, by charging Mr and
Mrs Jarvis's 'interests' in the property, had the like effect.

Mr Munby and Mr Crampin QC, both of whom argued this point on behalf
of the registrar, would not allow the orders this simple effect. They said that
they must be construed in the light of the provisions of s 2(1) of the Charging
Orders Act 1979, RSC Ord 50, rr 1 to 4 and Forms 75 and 76 in App A and the
notes thereto; and that, when so construed, they were effective only to charge
the interests in the proceeds of sale and not the land itself. Ferris J, although he
rejected it, was evidently impressed by this line of argument.

a   For my part, I wholly reject the registrar's approach. Admittedly the orders were made in the unmodified Forms 75 and 76, when they might more appropriately have been made in a modified form. Even that is not clear because, as Mr Nugee QC, for Mr and Mrs Clark, pointed out, the unmodified forms might still be appropriate to orders made, as these could only have been made, under s 2(1)(b)(iii) of the 1976 Act. But suppose that they were made in *b* the wrong form and that there was in consequence some technical breach of the rules. How can that alter the clear effect of the orders themselves? The registrar's argument did not answer that question. Indeed, much of it was directed towards the desirability of the registry's being able to ascertain the ambit of a charge without having to look beyond the order itself. That no doubt could be achieved by making more stringent provision in the legislation. For *c* present purposes it is an irrelevance. We must construe the orders in the only way we know, remembering that the registrar can be in no better a position as against Mr and Mrs Clark than Mr and Mrs Jarvis would have been.

   If an order of the court refers to a person's interest in a specified property without specifying what that interest is, it is both permissible and necessary to *d* look for enlightenment to the evidence which is read into the order. Here both orders recited the reading of Mr Merrick's affirmation, which stated his information and belief that Mr and Mrs Jarvis were the beneficial freehold owners of the property as appearing from the office copy entries on the register which the court had already ordered to be produced. Those entries did indeed disclose that Mr and Mrs Jarvis were the registered proprietors of the property *e* with title absolute and without any joint proprietorship restriction, thus demonstrating the accuracy of Mr Merrick's information and belief. It is therefore impossible to say that the orders, in referring to Mr and Mrs Jarvis's 'interest' or 'interests' in the property, did not refer to both legal estate and beneficial interest. Moreover, Mr Merrick stated that it was sought to impose a charge on the freehold land. In all the circumstances it is clear beyond *f* argument that the orders were both intended and effective to charge the land and not merely the interests in the proceeds of sale.

   For these reasons, I think that Ferris J's decision of the charging order point was correct.

g *The caution point*

   On the footing that the charging orders created a charge over the land, the registrar contends, in the alternative, that the caution lodged in respect of the order absolute on 29 November 1990 gave and continues to give Mr and Mrs Clark's charge priority over Mr Jones's charge. If this contention were correct, *h* Mr and Mrs Clark would have suffered no damage as a result of the failure to warn the caution and would have no need of an indemnity. However, under advice, they have taken the view that it would be wrong for them to seek to succeed on a ground that was clearly bad, especially when, had it been good, Mr Jones would appear to have had an unanswerable claim for an indemnity in their place.

j   In *Megarry and Wade's The Law of Real Property* (5th edn, 1984) p 196 the following reference is made to the Land Registration Act 1925:

> 'The legislation has received comparatively little judicial interpretation, and much therefore depends upon the practice of the Land Registry. The Registry has to handle great numbers of transactions and at the same time provide a prompt and reliable service to the public. The system is therefore

a branch of public administration as well as of property law. In view of the *a* deficiencies of the Act, it is not surprising that the Registry does not always interpret it correctly. Everyday conveyancing requires clear and rapid guidance, even where the clarity does not exist in the law. The Registry has succeeded in constructing a smooth-running machine out of legislation of exceptionally low quality, which is in need of a thorough overhaul.'

Anyone who has had frequent experience of dealings with the Land Registry *b* would wish to indorse this general statement of its achievement. But it must be said at once that this is one of those cases where the legislation has not been correctly interpreted.

The area in which this case falls is the protection of third parties' interests in registered land. The methods of protection prescribed in Pt IV of the 1925 Act *c* are four in number: notices (ss 48 to 52); cautions (ss 53 to 56); inhibitions (s 57); and restrictions (s 58). Cautions are divided into those against first registration and those against dealings. Here we are concerned with cautions against dealings. Although experience has shown that there is some overlapping between the various methods of protection, it seems reasonable to start from an assumption that their basic functions were intended to be different. Thus in *d* any consideration of the effect of a caution against dealings it is to be borne in mind that the general effect of a notice, as stated in s 52(1), is that a disposition by the proprietor takes effect subject to all estates, rights and claims which are protected thereby; in other words, a notice automatically gives priority to the interest it protects. *e*

I turn to ss 53 to 56, which appear under the subheading 'Cautions'. Section 53, which deals with cautions against first registration, can be disregarded except to observe that its language contains nothing to suggest that the lodging of such a caution achieves priority for the interest in respect of which it is lodged. The sections which deal with cautions against dealings are ss 54 and 55. Section 56 deals with cautions generally. *f*

The marginal note to s 54 is 'Cautions against dealings'. Subsection (1) provides:

'Any person interested under any unregistered instrument, or interested as a judgment creditor, or otherwise howsoever, in any land or charge registered in the name of any other person, may lodge a caution with the *g* registrar to the effect that no dealing with such land or charge on the part of the proprietor is to be registered until notice has been served upon the cautioner: Provided that a person whose estate, right, interest, or claim has been registered or protected by a notice or restriction shall not be entitled (except with the consent of the registrar) to lodge a caution in respect of *h* such estate, right, interest, or claim ...'

The marginal note to s 55 is 'Effect of cautions against dealings'. It provides:

'(1) After any such caution against dealings has been lodged in respect of any registered land or charge, the registrar shall not, without the consent *j* of the cautioner, register any dealing or make any entry on the register for protecting the rights acquired under a deposit of a land or charge certificate or other dealing by the proprietor with such land or charge until he has served notice on the cautioner, warning him that his caution will cease to have any effect after the expiration of the prescribed number of days next following the date at which such notice is served; and after the expiration a of such time as aforesaid the caution shall cease unless an order to the contrary is made by the registrar, and upon the caution so ceasing the registered land or charge may be dealt with in the same manner as if no caution had been lodged.

(2) If before the expiration of the said period the cautioner, or some person on his behalf, appears before the registrar, and where so required by b the registrar gives sufficient security to indemnify every party against any damage that may be sustained by reason of any dealing with the registered land or charge, or the making of any such entry as aforesaid, being delayed, the registrar may thereupon, if he thinks fit to do so, delay registering any dealing with the land or charge or making any such entry for such period as he thinks just.'

c

The marginal note to s 56 is 'General provisions as to cautions'. Subsection (2) provides:

'A caution lodged in pursuance of this Act shall not prejudice the claim or d title of any person and shall have no effect whatever except as in this Act mentioned.'

Those are the material provisions of the 1925 Act appearing under the subheading 'Cautions'. It is those provisions which were clearly intended to describe their nature and declare their effect. If viewed in isolation, they give e no support at all to the notion that the lodging of a caution against dealings automatically achieves priority for the interest in respect of which it is lodged. What they do is to institute a procedure whereby a person interested in the land may ensure that he is warned of any proposed dealing and given an opportunity to assert priority for his interest. The procedure is amplified by rr 218 to 221 of the Land Registration Rules 1925, one of the methods of conferring priority f specified by r 220(3) being the registration of the dealing subject to a notice protecting the cautioner's interest. If that is not enough to refute the suggestion that priority is achieved by the lodging of the caution and no more, the provisions of s 56(2) are conclusive. The first part of that subsection, in contrast to the language of s 52(1), provides that a caution shall not prejudice the claim or g title of any person; the second that it shall have no effect whatever except as is mentioned in the Act. That effect is to be found in s 55 as amplified by rr 218 to 221; not in the peripheral provisions of which mention must be made hereafter.

As Sir Robert Megarry and Sir William Wade have observed, the legislation h having received comparatively little judicial interpretation, much depends on the practice of the Land Registry. Since 1958 the repository of that practice has been *The Law and Practice of Registered Conveyancing*, the first edition of which was produced in that year by two former chief land registrars, Sir George Curtis and Mr Theodore Ruoff. Under the subheading 'Cautions against dealings', j they said (p 727):

'There is nothing in the Land Registration Act which expressly suggests that the caution gives constructive notice of the cautioner's claim, right or interest, and it certainly does not confer any kind of priority. Nor does it prejudice the claim or title of any person and has no effect whatever except as stated in the Act.'

In the current edition (dating from 1991) edited by three other former chief land registrars, that passage reads (at para 7-03):

'There is nothing in the Land Registration Act which states that the caution gives constructive notice of the cautioner's claim, right or interest. It does not prejudice the claim or title of any person and has no effect whatever except as stated in the Act.'

The substantive amendment to the first of these two passages, ie the deletion of the words 'and it certainly does not confer any kind of priority', was made in the second edition (1965), edited by Mr Ruoff alone, where a footnote referred to the decision at first instance in *Re White Rose Cottage* [1964] 1 All ER 169, [1964] Ch 483 (see below).

In *Barclays Bank Ltd v Taylor* [1973] 1 All ER 752 at 757, [1974] Ch 137 at 147 Russell LJ, in delivering the judgment of this court, said of a caution against dealings lodged in order to protect the interest of the purchasers under a contract for the purchase of land:

'The caution lodged on behalf of the [purchasers] had no effect whatever by itself on priorities: it simply conferred on the [purchasers] the right to be given notice of any dealing proposed to be registered ... so that they might have the opportunity of contending that it would be a dealing which would infringe their rights and to which the applicants for the registration were not as against them entitled. The limited function of such a caution is stressed by s 56(2) ...'

Having observed that the purchasers' caution did not and could not confer on their equitable entitlement or interest any priority over the bank's equitable charge, Russell LJ continued:

'We should add that counsel for the [purchasers] was quite unable to point to any provision in the statute which stated that their caution as such gave them priority in respect of their equitable interest over the earlier equitable interest of the bank under its mortgage. If such had been the intention of the legislature, it would not have been difficult for the statute to have so provided ...'

The views expressed by the authors and successive editors of *The Law and Practice of Registered Conveyancing* and by this court in *Barclays Bank Ltd v Taylor* are decisive of the caution point. They have the very great merit of having been based essentially on those provisions—ss 54 to 56 of the 1925 Act—which were clearly intended to describe and declare the nature and effect of cautions against dealings. They show that it is for that purpose unnecessary to look beyond those provisions. The deletion of Sir George Curtis' and Mr Ruoff's original firm opinion that cautions do not confer any kind of priority, an opinion which is as correct now as it was then, is of no significance. The lack of priority remains implicit in the revised version. Moreover, the attempts made in argument to depreciate the manifest value of the views expressed in *Barclays Bank Ltd v Taylor* were unsuccessful.

The principal consequence of the arguments advanced on behalf of the registrar and Mr Ketteringham was to demonstrate the unwisdom of straying from ss 54 to 56 to other provisions of the 1925 Act. It is hardly surprising that counsel were able to extract from legislation 'of exceptionally low quality' provisions which, on a myopic view, give some semblance of support for those *a* arguments. None of those provisions can prevail over the clear effect of ss 54 to 56.

In this court, as in the courts below, the appellants relied principally on s 59(1) and (6) of the 1925 Act and *Parkash v Irani Finance Ltd* [1969] 1 All ER 930, [1970] Ch 101. For the reasons given by Ferris J, I agree with him that those provisions and that decision do not assist them (see [1993] 2 All ER 936 at 949–950, [1993] Ch 311–313). For myself, I am certain that Plowman J, a judge of *b* great experience in conveyancing matters, did not intend to suggest that a caution had much the same effect as a notice.

The other provision of the 1925 Act on which the appellants mainly relied was s 20(1)(a). While I would certainly accept that cautions, once recorded in the registry, are 'entries ... appearing on the register' within that provision and *c* that what it means is 'subject to rights and interests created by any document or transaction recorded as an entry' (see *Kitney v MEPC Ltd* [1978] 1 All ER 595 at 602, [1977] 1 WLR 981 at 989) like Ferris J, I am unable to see how it can elevate cautions to a status and effect not given to them by ss 54 to 56. The same answer can be given to an argument based on that part of r 220(3) which *d* empowers the registrar to order that the caution shall continue to have effect.

In my view Ferris J's decision of the caution point was, like his decision of the charging order point, correct. As I have said, the registrar's contention as to the rectification point was abandoned during the argument in this court. There can be no doubt that the judge's decision of that point was also correct.

e *Chancery plc v Ketteringham*

The facts of this case can be briefly stated. On 23 December 1987 three individuals trading as B & C Developments (B & C) agreed to grant Mr Ketteringham a long lease at a low rent of one of the flats in a block they were intending to construct on freehold premises owned by them at Parkstone in *f* Dorset and of which they were registered as the proprietors with title absolute on 3 February 1988. On 11 March 1988 a caution protecting Mr Ketteringham's estate contract in respect of the flat was registered in the proprietorship register. B & C then negotiated a loan facility from Chancery plc on terms that the latter would be granted security by way of a charge over the freehold of the premises. An approach having been made to Mr Ketteringham in May, on 3 June 1988 his *g* solicitors wrote to the Land Registry, with a copy to B & C's solicitors, referring to his caution and stating:

'Please accept this letter as a consent to the registration of a legal charge in favour of [Chancery plc].'

h On 8 June 1988 B & C executed a legal charge over the freehold of the premises in favour of Chancery plc and on 27 June the charge was entered in the charges register. In August 1989 Mr Ketteringham went into occupation of the flat, no lease having been granted to him by B & C. In 1991 he obtained orders for specific performance of the agreement to grant him a lease, but by that time *j* B & C were in financial difficulties and Chancery plc was seeking to enforce its charge against them. Mr Ketteringham maintained that the registration of his caution gave his estate contract priority over Chancery plc's charge. On 27 August 1992 Chancery plc issued an originating summons against him in the Chancery Division claiming declarations to the contrary effect.

The proceedings came on for trial before Mr David Neuberger QC, sitting as a deputy judge of the Chancery Division. By that time the decision of Ferris J

in *Clark v Chief Land Registrar* had been decided and reported. So far as the
caution point was concerned, it seemed to the deputy judge that the only
significant difference between the two cases was that in the former the charge
was registered without the necessary warning having been given to Mr and Mrs
Clark, whereas in the latter Mr Ketteringham had been requested to give his
consent to the registration of Chancery plc's charge and had done so. However,
it was conceded by Mr Ketteringham that that was not a ground for
distinguishing the two cases and that, if he was to succeed, the deputy judge
would have to refuse to follow the decision of Ferris J. In a reserved judgment
delivered on 23 September 1993 the deputy judge followed the decision of
Ferris J and granted the declarations sought by Chancery plc.

Two additional points arise in this case. Before the deputy judge Mr Gerrans
submitted that the decision of Ferris J was inconsistent with the decision of this
court in *Re White Rose Cottage* [1965] 1 All ER 11, [1965] Ch 940, which had not
been cited in the earlier case. That submission was rejected by the deputy
judge, mainly on the ground that the decision and reasoning in *Re White Rose
Cottage* were fully compatible with the conclusion reached by Ferris J. Mr
Gerrans repeated his submission in this court, but I respectfully agree with and
adopt the view of the deputy judge.

Mr Gerrans also based an argument on s 107(1) of the 1925 Act, an argument
which was not available to the Chief Land Registrar in *Clark*. That subsection
starts by providing that a registered proprietor may in general enter into any
contract in reference to the land or charge in like manner as if it had not been
registered. It continues:

'subject to any disposition for valuable consideration which may be
registered or protected on the register before the contract is completed or
protected on the register, the contract may be enforced as a minor interest
against any succeeding proprietor in like manner and to the same extent as
if the land or charge had not been registered.'

Mr Gerrans submitted that Chancery plc's charge was not registered before Mr
Ketteringham's estate contract was 'protected on the register' by the caution;
that Chancery plc was a 'succeeding proprietor'; and that the estate contract
therefore had priority over the charge. The short answer to this submission is
that although the estate contract was indeed 'protected' by the procedure
instituted by ss 54 to 56, it is again impossible for a provision such as s 107(1) to
give it a priority not given to it by those sections.

Accordingly, there being nothing in either of Mr Gerrans's additional points,
I think that the deputy judge's decision of the caution point was also correct.

I would dismiss both appeals.

KENNEDY LJ. I agree.

ROCH LJ. I also agree.

Appeals dismissed. Leave to appeal to the House of Lords refused.

Carolyn Toulmin   Barrister.

Vitol SA v Norelf Ltd, The Santa Clara

QUEEN'S BENCH DIVISION (COMMERCIAL COURT)

PHILLIPS J

23, 30 APRIL 1993

Contract – Repudiation – Anticipatory breach – Communication of acceptance of repudiation by conduct – Buyers of cargo repudiating contract for breach of term limiting time for delivery – Neither party taking further steps to perform contract – Sellers incurring loss on resale of cargo – Sellers subsequently claiming damages from buyers for anticipatory breach of contract – Whether failure by sellers to perform further contractual obligations constituting acceptance of repudiation.

The plaintiff buyers entered into a contract with the defendant sellers for the purchase of a cargo of propane at a price of $US400 per tonne. The contract provided that the cargo was to be shipped from Houston and set out dates in March 1991 when the vessel was expected to arrive, berth and leave Houston. The contract also required both parties to perform a number of actions after the loading of the cargo, including the tender of a bill of lading by the sellers. On 8 March the buyers sent a telex to the sellers, asserting that they had been advised that the vessel would not complete loading until 9 March which was outside the agreed contractual period for delivery of between 1 and 7 March and that in view of the breach of that condition they would have to reject the cargo and repudiate the contract. The vessel completed loading and thereafter neither party took any further steps to perform the contract. The sellers subsequently resold the cargo on 15 March at a price of $US170 per tonne. The first communication between the parties following the buyers' rejection telex was a letter from the sellers claiming approximately $US1m in damages on the basis of the difference between the contract price of the propane and the price obtained by the sellers on resale. The claim was referred to arbitration. The arbitrator held that the buyers' rejection telex constituted an anticipatory breach of contract and that the sellers' failure to take any further steps to perform the contract constituted sufficient communication of acceptance of the buyers' repudiation of the contract. The buyers appealed against the second part of the arbitrators' award, contending that termination of a contract on an anticipatory breach was governed by the same principles of offer and acceptance which applied to the formation of a contract and that as a result failure to perfom contractual obligations, being mere inactivity, could not in law constitute acceptance of the repudiation of a contract.

Held – There was no reason why acceptance of an anticipatory repudiation of a contract by one party should not be undertaken by either words or conduct which made it plain that the innocent party was responding to the repudiation by treating the contract as at an end and, while it might be more difficult to indicate acceptance of the repudiation by conduct alone, it was possible for a party to do so either by taking action that was incompatible with his own continued performance of the contract or by simply failing further to perform his own contractual obligations. Failure to progress an arbitration was a good example of inactivity that was likely to be equivocal, but in other types of contractual relationship where the parties were bound to perform specific acts in relation to one another, a failure to perform an act which a party was obliged to perform if

the contract was to remain alive might be very significant and, where such
conduct followed a renunciation, the obvious inference would be that the
innocent party was responding to the repudiation by treating the contract as at an
end. Accordingly, simple failure to perform contractual obligations was capable
of constituting the acceptance of an anticipatory repudiation of a contract by the
other party. It followed that the buyers' appeal would therefore be dismissed (see
p 114 *g* to p 115 *b d*, post).

Dictum of Viscount Simon LC in *Heyman v Darwins Ltd* [1942] 1 All ER 337 at
341 applied.

Dictum of Winn LJ in *Denmark Productions Ltd v Boscobel Productions Ltd*
[1968] 3 All ER 513 at 527 considered.

Notes

For rights of innocent party to a contract, see 9 *Halsbury's Laws* (4th edn) paras
551–558, and for cases on the subject, see 12(2) *Digest* (2nd reissue) 286–297, 6400–
6431.

Cases referred to in judgment

Allied Marine Transport Ltd v Vale do Rio Doce Navegacao SA, The Leonidas D [1985] 2
All ER 796, [1985] 1 WLR 925, CA.
Braithwaite v Foreign Hardwood Co [1905] 2 KB 543, CA.
Denmark Productions Ltd v Boscobel Productions Ltd [1968] 3 All ER 513, [1969] 1 QB
699, [1968] 3 WLR 841, CA.
Fercometal SARL v Mediterranean Shipping Co SA, The Simona [1988] 2 All ER 742,
[1989] AC 788, [1988] 3 WLR 200, HL.
Heyman v Darwins Ltd [1942] 1 All ER 337, [1942] AC 356, HL.
Holland v Wiltshire (1954) 90 CLR 409, Aust HC.
MSC Mediterranean Shipping Co SA v BRE Metro Ltd, The Leonidas [1985] 2 Lloyd's
Rep 239.
Sinason-Teicher Inter-American Grain Corp v Oilcakes and Oilseeds Trading Co Ltd
[1954] 3 All ER 468, [1954] 1 WLR 1394, CA; *affg* [1954] 2 All ER 497, [1954] 1
WLR 935.

Appeal

The plaintiffs, Vitol SA (Vitol), appealed with leave of the court against the final
arbitration award made by Mr Iain Milligan QC on 23 November 1992 whereby
he held that the anticipatory breach by the plaintiffs of a contract for the purchase
of a cargo of propane from the defendants, Norelf Ltd (Norelf), was accepted by
Norelf as repudiation of the contract by reason that Norelf's conduct thereafter in
failing to take any further steps to perform the contract after the receipt of the
telex constituted sufficient communication of acceptance. The facts are set out in
the judgment.

Andrew Popplewell (instructed by *Holman Fenwick & Willan*) for Vitol.
Jeremy Cooke QC (instructed by *Clyde & Co*) for Norelf.

Cur adv vult

30 April 1993. The following judgment was delivered.

PHILLIPS J. This is an appeal brought with leave of the court against a final
arbitration award made by Mr Iain Milligan QC. It raises the question of the

a nature of the conduct which is capable in law of constituting acceptance of an anticipatory repudiation of a contract.

The facts

On 11 February 1991 the plaintiffs, Vitol SA (Vitol), entered into a contract with the defendants, Norelf Ltd (Norelf), under which Norelf sold to Vitol a cargo of *b* propane. The propane was sold on cif terms and the contract was expressly subject to Incoterms 1990 with subsequent amendments for cif sales. It was not, however, a typical cif contract. It was for a specific cargo to be loaded aboard the vessel, Santa Clara, at Houston and the contract provided dates in March 1991 when the vessel was expected to arrive, berth and leave from Houston. The contract dealt with the passing of title as follows:

c
> 'Title, beneficial ownership and risk of loss shall pass from seller to buyer when the product reaches the flange connecting the shore line with the vessel line at the loading port. Thereafter the product shall be carried by seller as carrier and the carriage shall be governed by the terms and conditions of the Asbatankvoy charter party. The price quoted includes the cost of carriage.'

d The contract required both parties to perform a number of actions after loading of the cargo. Most significantly, Norelf were, on the arbitrator's finding, obliged to tender a bill of lading and Vitol were obliged to pay for the propane. The latter obligation would not arise until 30 days after the bill of lading date. The arbitrator has referred to other performance obligations on Norelf after completion of *e* loading, without specifying what these were, and I assume that this was on the basis that the term that I have just cited and other terms to which I need not refer left Norelf under personal contractual obligation in relation to carriage and delivery after tender of the customary cif documents.

On 8 March 1991 Vitol sent Norelf a telex in the following terms:

f
> 'It was a condition of the contract that delivery would be effected 1–7 March 1991 ... We are advised that the vessel is not likely to complete loading now until some time on 9 March—well outside the agreed contractual period. In view of the breach of this condition we must reject the cargo and repudiate the contract. We do however reserve our position to claim damages in these circumstances.'

g At the time that this telex was sent the vessel was still loading. She completed loading and sailed on the following day. Thereafter neither party took any further steps to perform the contract.

The price that Vitol had agreed to pay for the propane was $US400 per tonne. *h* When Vitol rejected the cargo the price was falling and it continued to fall throughout March. On 12 March at the latest, Norelf began attempting to resell the cargo and succeeded in so doing on 15 March at a price of $US170 per tonne.

On the arbitrator's findings the first communication between the parties after Vitol's rejection telex of 8 March was a letter to Vitol from Norelf's solicitors on *j* 9 August 1991 claiming approximately $US1m on the basis of the difference *i* between the contract price of the propane and the price achieved by Norelf on resale. This claim was referred to arbitration. In the arbitration Vitol maintained their stance that they were entitled to reject the cargo because, in breach of contractual condition, it was loaded out of time. Other points were also relied upon to justify the rejection. None succeeded. The arbitrator held that Vitol's rejection telex constituted an anticipatory breach of contract, and that finding is not challenged.

By this appeal Vitol challenges the following paragraph in the arbitrator's award:

'31. It also follows from those conclusions that the rejection telexes constituted an anticipatory breach of the contract by Vitol. Unless that breach was accepted by Norelf, it was of no effect (see *MSC Mediterranean Shipping Co SA v BRE Metro Ltd, The Leonidas* [1985] 2 Lloyd's Rep 239 at 240): thus, subject to any question of estoppel, which does not arise in this instance, the breach could have been remedied by withdrawal of the rejection contained in the telexes at any time before it was accepted. However, the breach was never remedied and, in my opinion, the tenor of the rejection telexes was such that the failure of Norelf to take any further step to perform the contract which was apparent to Vitol constituted sufficient communication of acceptance (see *Sinason-Teicher Inter-American Grain Corp v Oilcakes and Oilseeds Trading Co Ltd* [1954] 2 All ER 497 at 502–504, [1954] 1 WLR 935 at 942–944, affirmed [1954] 3 All ER 468, [1954] 1 WLR 1394 and *Fercometal SARL v Mediterranean Shipping Co SA, The Simona* [1988] 2 All ER 742 at 748, [1989] AC 788 at 800–801).'

The arbitrator did not make any finding as to the precise moment in time when Norelf's failure further to perform the contract communicated to Vitol an acceptance of their repudiation resulting in the termination of the contract. The reason why he had no need to do so is apparent from the following paragraphs of his award, addressing the issue of damages:

'33. The first obligation which Norelf failed to perform under the contract which would have been apparent to Vitol was the tender of the Santa Clara bill of lading pursuant to clause A8 of Incoterms 1990. That would not have become apparent, however, until several days after Monday 11 March 1991, on which date Norelf informed Vitol by telex that the Santa Clara had completed loading on 9 March 1991. (I note that the bill of lading named Norelf as the consignees, not as the shippers, and also that it was dated 18 March 1991.) 34. The Propane market cif North West Europe was falling throughout March 1991. Despite attempts to resell the Santa Clara cargo which had begun at latest on 12 March 1991, it was not resold until Friday 15 March 1991. The resale price was $US170 per mt and I have reached the conclusion that that was greater than, or equal to, the available market price for this particular cargo whenever the breach was accepted after 11 March 1991. Norelf do not claim damages calculated by reference to any price lower than $US170 per mt. Consequently, damages are to be assessed by reference to that price in accordance with s 50(3) of the Sale of Goods Act 1979.'

Vitol's contentions

Mr Popplewell for Vitol based his submissions upon the proposition that termination of a contract upon an anticipatory repudiation is governed by the same principles of offer and acceptance as formation of a contract. In support of this proposition he relied upon the following passage in the judgment of Winn LJ in *Denmark Productions Ltd v Boscobel Productions Ltd* [1968] 3 All ER 513 at 527, [1969] 1 QB 699 at 731:

'It seems to me that the process of ending or indeed of varying a contract by repudiation is the converse of that of making the same contract; each process operates by offer and acceptance, or their equivalents; each is essentially bilateral. Where A and B are parties to an executory contract, if A intimates by word or conduct that he no longer intends, or is unable, to perform it, or to perform it in a particular manner, he is, in effect, making an offer to B to treat the contract as dissolved or varied so far as it relates to the future. If B elects to treat the contract as thereby repudiated, he is deemed, according to the language of many decided cases, to 'accept the repudiation' and is thereupon entitled: (a) to sue for damages in respect of any earlier breach committed by A *and* for damages in respect of the repudiation; (b) to refrain from himself performing the contract any further. On the other hand, if B elects in such a situation, or is taken by reason of silence to have elected, *not* to treat the contract as at an end, he may require A to perform any contractual obligations as they fall due in the future (provided that he himself performs any simultaneous or precedent obligation) including, as a particular example, the making of payments for which the contract provides. In such a case the contract remains in force for the advantage or disadvantage, as events fall out, of either party.' (Winn LJ's emphasis.)

Mr Popplewell submitted that where party A commits an anticipatory breach of contract, a subsequent breach by party B of one of his contractual obligations cannot, of itself, amount to acceptance of party A's repudiation. His primary submission was, however, that a failure to perform contractual obligations, being mere inactivity, cannot in law constitute acceptance under the principles governing offer and acceptance in the law of contract. In support of this proposition he relied upon the series of decisions where parties have unsuccessfully sought to rely upon inactivity to demonstrate consensual determination of an agreement to arbitrate and, in particular the comments of Goff LJ in *Allied Marine Transport Ltd v Vale do Rio Doce Navegacao SA, The Leonidas D* [1985] 2 All ER 796 at 805, [1985] 1 WLR 925 at 937.

Norelf's contentions

Mr Cooke QC for Norelf challenged both of Mr Popplewell's propositions. He submitted that the doubts expressed by Winn LJ before he advanced the analysis in the passage that I have cited were well-founded. He submitted that where party A repudiates a contract, party B will accept that repudiation and bring the contract to an end if, by words or conduct, he demonstrates that he is treating the contract as at an end, and that the conduct need not be conduct of which party A is aware. Thus, if in a contract for the sale of specific or ascertained goods the buyer indicates his intention to reject the goods and the seller then sells the goods to a third party, that act constitutes acceptance of the buyer's repudiation without the need for any communication to the buyer and notwithstanding that it would otherwise constitute a breach of contract on the part of the seller.

In support of his submissions Mr Cooke relied upon the analysis of that difficult case, *Braithwaite v Foreign Hardwood Co* [1905] 2 KB 543, which formed part of the speech of Lord Ackner in *Fercometal SARL v Mediterranean Shipping Co SA, The Simona* [1988] 2 All ER 742 at 748–751, [1989] AC 788 at 801–805. He also relied upon a finding by Dixon CJ in *Holland v Wiltshire* (1954) 90 CLR 409 at 416, where a purchaser of land had repudiated a contract by failing to tender payment, that the seller's 'election to treat the contract as discharged by the purchasers' breach was sufficiently manifested by his proceeding to advertise the property for sale, and by his selling it'.

Whether, where a buyer renounces his future obligation to pay for goods, the seller can accept the repudiation by selling to a third party without communicating to the buyer the fact that he is doing so, is a question of importance. It is a question that might well have arisen in the present case, for Norelf might have contended that their sale of the propane to a third party constituted acceptance of Vitol's repudiation. This argument was not, however, advanced and it is not necessary for me to decide whether an innocent party can accept an anticipatory repudiation by conduct which is not communicated to the party in anticipatory breach. I have, however, to consider whether the decision in *Braithwaite v Foreign Hardwood Co*, as explained by Lord Ackner, is incompatible with the analysis of Winn LJ in *Denmark Productions Ltd v Boscobel Productions Ltd*. I do not think that it is. Many contractual offers are capable of acceptance by conduct which is not communicated to the offeror. If it be right to treat a refusal by a buyer to accept the goods as an offer to the seller to treat the contract as at an end, I see no reason in principle why that offer should not, if the language used or the surrounding circumstances are appropriate, be deemed to invite acceptance by selling the goods in question to a third party without prior communication to the defaulting buyer.

In the present case, communication is not in issue. The arbitrator has found that Vitol were well aware of the conduct on the part of Norelf that amounted, on the arbitrator's finding, to acceptance of repudiation. The issue is a narrow one. The conduct in question was a failure to take further steps to perform the contract. Can such conduct amount in law to acceptance of a repudiation?

The analogy with contractual offer and acceptance made by Winn LJ cannot be applied precisely. Anticipatory repudiation comes in many forms and some have little similarity with a contractual offer. Acceptance of a repudiation comes closer to acceptance of a contractual offer, for what is required is words or conduct which makes it plain that the innocent party is responding to the repudiation by treating the contract as at an end. The position was clearly stated by Viscount Simon LC in a much-cited statement in *Heyman v Darwins Ltd* [1942] 1 All ER 337 at 341, [1942] AC 356 at 361:

'... the other party may rescind the contract, or (as it is sometimes expressed) "accept the repudiation", by so acting as to make plain that, in view of the wrongful action of the party who has repudiated, he claims to treat the contract as at an end, in which case he can sue at once for damages.'

I see no reason why acceptance of repudiation should not be effected by acts as opposed to by words. It may be more difficult by actions to indicate that one is responding to a repudiation by treating the contract as at an end, but in many circumstances there will be actions that the innocent party can take which will achieve this result. Nor can I see any reason why the act in question should not be one which, but for the fact that it is a response to a repudiation, would itself be a breach of contract. Mr Popplewell argued that in such circumstances the response of the innocent party will always be equivocal—it will not be apparent that the act is a response to the repudiation. He relied on the *Fercometal* case as an example of this. That was a case where the innocent party initially responded to the repudiation by affirming the contract. In such circumstances a subsequent breach by the innocent party of one of his own contractual obligations is unlikely to be or to be seen as a response to the repudiation. Where, however, the innocent party does not respond to a repudiation by affirmation, but proceeds to take action that is incompatible with his own continued performance of the contract, it may be quite clear that he is responding to the repudiation by treating the contract as at an end.

Can the innocent party demonstrate acceptance of a repudiation simply by failing further to perform his own contractual obligations? Again, Mr Popplewell submitted that he could not, and for the same reason inactivity is bound to be equivocal. Again, I cannot agree. It depends upon the circumstances. Failure to progress an arbitration is a good example of inertia that is likely to be equivocal. But in other types of contractual relationship where the parties are bound to perform specific acts in relation to one another, a failure to perform an act which a party is obliged to perform if the contract remains alive may be very significant. It is not difficult to envisage circumstances in which, if such conduct follows a renunciation, the obvious inference will be that the innocent party is responding to the repudiation by treating the contract as at an end.

I do not have to decide whether the failure on the part of Norelf to tender to Vitol a bill of lading, or any of the subsequent unspecified failures to perform the contract which were apparent to Vitol, gave clear indication to Vitol that, in view of Vitol's wrongful action, Norelf were treating the contract as at an end. That is a question of fact for the arbitrator. What I have to decide is whether, as a matter of law, mere failure to perform contractual obligations can ever constitute acceptance of an anticipatory repudiation by the other party. In my judgment, for the reasons that I have given, it can. It follows that this appeal must be dismissed.

Appeal dismissed.

K Mydeen Esq   Barrister.

Webb v EMO Air Cargo (UK) Ltd
(Case C-32/93)

COURT OF JUSTICE OF THE EUROPEAN COMMUNITIES (FIFTH CHAMBER)
JUDGES MOITINHO DE ALMEIDA (PRESIDENT OF CHAMBER), JOLIET, RODRÍGUEZ IGLESIAS, GRÉVISSE (RAPPORTEUR) AND ZULEEG
ADVOCATE GENERAL TESAURO
21 APRIL, 1 JUNE, 14 JULY 1994

European Economic Community – Equality of treatment of men and women – Equal working conditions – Dismissal – Dismissal because of pregnancy – Woman employed for indeterminate period, but initially to provide maternity leave cover – Maternity leave replacement finding herself pregnant shortly after appointment – Replacement dismissed because of pregnancy – Whether inability of woman to fulfil specific task for which she had been recruited a relevant consideration – Whether comparison between woman on maternity leave and man absent for same length of time for medical or other reasons appropriate – Whether dismissal because of pregnancy contrary to European law – Sex Discrimination Act 1975, ss 1(1), 5 (3) – Council Directive (EEC) 76/207, arts 2(1), 5(1).

The appellant was engaged in July 1987 by the employer to cover the job of an employee who would be taking maternity leave at the end of the year. The appellant's contract was for an indeterminate period and it was envisaged that she would continue in her employment following the other employee's return. The employer required the appellant to start work immediately in order to undertake six months' training before the employee she was replacing left to have her baby. Two weeks after starting work, the appellant discovered that she too was pregnant and when she informed the employer of that fact she was dismissed. She made a complaint to an industrial tribunal that the employer had unlawfully discriminated against her on the grounds of her sex, contrary to s 1(1)(a)ᵃ of the Sex Discrimination Act 1975, by dismissing her because of her pregnancy. The tribunal dismissed her claim on the ground that the real reason for her dismissal was her anticipated inability to carry out the primary task for which she had been recruited, namely to cover the job of the pregnant employee during the latter's absence on maternity leave. The Employment Appeal Tribunal and the Court of Appeal subsequently upheld the industrial tribunal's decision. The appellant appealed to the House of Lords, which inclined to the view that there had been no unlawful discrimination because it was the appellant's non-availability during the relevant period that was the critical factor and that (applying the comparison required under s 5(3)ᵇ of the 1975 Act) if a man had been recruited for the same purpose he would have been similarly dismissed if he had told the employer that he would be absent for medical or other reasons during the pregnant employee's absence of maternity leave, but considered that it should construe the applicable domestic legislation so as to accord with the interpretation by the Court of Justice of the European Communities of Council Directive (EEC) 76/207 on the implementation of the principle of equal treatment for men and women in respect of employment matters, and in particular arts 2(1)ᶜ and 5(1)ᵈ, which defined the principle as meaning that there should be 'no discrimination whatsoever on grounds of sex either directly or indirectly by reference in particular to marital or family status' and guaranteed men and women the same working conditions without discrimination on grounds of sex. The House of Lords accordingly stayed the proceedings and referred to the European Court for a preliminary ruling the question whether it would be discriminatory on the grounds of sex, contrary to Directive 76/207, for an employer to dismiss a female employee who because of her pregnancy would be unable to carry out, at the time when her services were required, the particular job for which she was applying or for which she had been engaged.

Held – The Community legislature intended by means of Directive 76/207 to implement in member states the principle of equal treatment for men and women in employment matters and clearly acknowledged (i) the legitimacy, in terms of that principle, of protecting a woman's biological condition during and after pregnancy and the special relationship between a woman and her child over the period following pregnancy and childbirth and (ii) more recently, that special protection should be given to women by prohibiting dismissal during the period from the beginning of pregnancy to the end of their maternity leave. In that context there could be no question of comparing the situation of a woman who found herself incapable, by reason of pregnancy discovered shortly after the conclusion of the employment contract, of performing the task for which she

---

a   Section 1(1), so far as material, provides: 'A person discriminates against a woman ... if—(a) on
     the ground of her sex he treats her less favourably than he treats or would treat a man ...'
b   Section 5(3), so far as material, is set out at p 126 a, post
c   Article 2(1), so far as material, is set out at p 127 b, post
d   Article 5(1), so far as material, is set out at p 127 c, post

had been recruited with that of a man similarly incapable for medical or other reasons, since pregnancy was in no way comparable with a pathological condition (including illness attributable to pregnancy which manifested itself after the period of maternity leave) or unavailability for work on non-medical grounds, both of which were situations that might justify the dismissal of a woman without discriminating on the ground of sex. The availability of an employee was necessarily, for the employer, a precondition for the proper performance of the employment contract, but the protection afforded by Community law to a woman during pregnancy and after childbirth could not be dependent on whether her presence at work during maternity was essential to the proper functioning of the undertaking in which she was employed and any contrary interpretation would render ineffective the provisions of Directive 76/207. Accordingly, in circumstances such as those of the appellant, termination of a contract for an indefinite period on the ground of pregnancy could not be justified by the fact that the woman was prevented, on a purely temporary basis, from performing the work for which she had been engaged. Moreover, the fact that the main proceedings concerned a woman who was initially recruited to replace another employee during the latter's maternity leave but who was herself found to be pregnant after her recruitment could not affect the answer to be given to the national court. It followed that art 2(1) read with art 5(1) of Directive 76/207 precluded dismissal of an employee who had been recruited for an unlimited time with a view, initially, to replacing another employee during her maternity leave and who could not do so because, shortly after her recruitment, she was herself found to be pregnant (see p 127 *e f h* to p 128 *g*, post).

Habermann-Beltermann v Arbeiterwohlfahrt, Bezirksverband Ndb/Opf eV Case C-421/92 [1994] IRLR 364 and *Handels- og Kontorfunktionærernes Forbund i Danmark v Dansk Arbejdsgiverforening* Case C-179/88 [1990] ECR I-3979 considered.

Notes

For dismissal of an employee on the ground of pregnancy, see 16 *Halsbury's Laws* (4th edn reissue) para 343.

For the Community law principle of equal treatment of men and woman as regards working conditions, including conditions governing dismissal, see 52 *Halsbury's Laws* (4th edn) para 21·13.

For the direct effect of Community law, see 51 *Halsbury's Laws* (4th edn) paras 3·41–3·48.

For the Sex Discrimination Act 1975, ss 1, 5, see 6 *Halsbury's Statutes* (4th edn) (1992 reissue) 756, 759.

Cases cited

Dekker v Stichting Vormingscentrum voor Jong Volwassenen (VJV-Centrum) Plus Case C-177/88 [1990] ECR I-3941.

Habermann-Beltermann v Arbeiterwohlfahrt, Bezirksverband Ndb/Opf eV Case C-421/92 [1994] IRLR 364, CJEC.

Handels- og Kontorfunktionærernes Forbund i Danmark v Dansk Arbejdsgiverforening Case C-179/88 [1990] ECR I-3979.

Hofmann v Barmer Ersatzkasse Case 184/83 [1984] ECR 3047.

Marleasing SA v La Comercial Internacional de Alimentación Case C-106/89 [1990] ECR I-4135.

Reference

By order dated 26 November 1992 the House of Lords ([1992] 4 All ER 929, [1993] 1 WLR 49) referred to the Court of Justice of the European Communities for a preliminary ruling under art 177 of the EEC Treaty a question (set out at p 126 h j, post) on the interpretation of Council Directive (EEC) 76/207 of 9 February 1976 on the implementation of the principle of equal treatment for men and women as regards access to employment, vocational training and promotion, and working conditions. The question was raised in the course of an appeal by Carole Louise Webb to the House of Lords from the decision of the Court of Appeal (Glidewell, Balcombe and Beldam LJJ) ([1992] 2 All ER 43) on 20 December 1991 dismissing her appeal from the decision of the Employment Appeal Tribunal (Wood J, Mr T S Batho, Mr A C Blyghton, Mrs M L Boyle and Mrs M E Sutherland) ([1990] ICR 442) given on 14 February 1990 dismissing her appeal from the decision of the industrial tribunal (Mr D S Laughton chairman) sitting at London (North) dated 29 March 1988 and entered on 7 April 1988 dismissing her claim against her employer, EMO Air Cargo (UK) Ltd, on the ground that she had not been unfairly dismissed on 30 July 1987. Written observations were submitted on behalf of Mrs Webb, by Laura Cox and Deborah King, barristers, instructed by Susan James, solicitor, Hillingdon Legal Resource Centre, the United Kingdom, by John Collins, of the Treasury Solicitor's Department, acting as agent, and by Derrick Wyatt QC, of the Bar of England and Wales, the Commission of the European Communities, by Nicholas Khan, of the Legal Service, acting as agent. Oral observations were presented to the court on behalf of Mrs Webb, the United Kingdom and the Commission. The language of the case was English. The facts are set out in the opinion of the Advocate General.

1 June 1994. **The Advocate General** (**G Tesauro**) delivered the following opinion (translated from the Italian).

Mr President, Members of the Court,

1. The question referred to the court by the House of Lords for a preliminary ruling concerns the interpretation of certain provisions of Council Directive (EEC) 76/207 of 9 February 1976 on the implementation of the principle of equal treatment for men and women as regards access to employment, vocational training and promotion, and working conditions.

The national court seeks in particular to establish whether the principle of equal treatment for men and women, as expounded in the directive, precludes the dismissal of a pregnant woman who has been recruited on the basis of a contract for an indeterminate period but for the specific purpose—initially—of replacing another female employee during the latter's maternity leave.

2. A summary of the relevant Community and national legislation is necessary in order to understand the terms of the question.

According to art 2(1) of Directive 76/207, 'the principle of equal treatment shall mean that there shall be no discrimination whatsoever on grounds of sex either directly or indirectly by reference in particular to marital or family status'. Article 5(1) provides that 'application of the principle of equal treatment with regard to working conditions, including the conditions governing dismissal, means that men and women are to be guaranteed the same conditions without discrimination on grounds of sex'. Finally, art 2(3) states that the directive 'shall be without prejudice to provisions concerning the protection of women, particularly as regards pregnancy and maternity'.

Still on the subject of conditions relating to dismissal, mention should be made of art 10 of Council Directive (EEC) 92/85 of 19 October 1992 on the introduction of measures to encourage improvements in the safety and health at work of pregnant workers and workers who have recently given birth or are breastfeeding. That article prohibits the dismissal of female workers 'during the period from the beginning of their pregnancy to the end of the maternity leave ... save in exceptional cases not connected with their condition which are permitted under national legislation and/or practice and, where applicable, provided that the competent authority has given its consent'. However, Directive 92/85 has not yet entered into force; its transposition into national law is to be accomplished by 19 October 1994.

3. With regard to the relevant national legislation, the Employment Protection (Consolidation) Act 1978 prohibits unfair dismissal (s 54), and dismissal on the ground of pregnancy is considered unfair (s 60). However, those provisions do not apply when, as in the case under consideration, dismissal takes place during the initial two years of the employment relationship (s 64).

The Sex Discrimination Act 1975 also defines and prohibits, as constituting direct discrimination on grounds of sex, the situation in which a woman is accorded, on account of her sex, less favourable treatment than that accorded to a man (s 1(1)(a)). The Act also prohibits indirect discrimination, which consists in applying to a woman a requirement or condition which, although applying equally to a man, is to the woman's detriment or is in any event more difficult for her to comply with (s 1(1)(b)). Section 2 of the 1975 Act states that the provisions relating to sex discrimination against women are to be read as applying equally to the treatment of men, except with regard to the special treatment afforded to women in connection with pregnancy or childbirth. Section 5(3) is of particular interest inasmuch as it provides that a comparison of the cases of persons of different sex or marital status 'must be such that the relevant circumstances in the one case are the same, or not materially different, in the other'. Lastly, for the purposes of the present case, s 6(2) of the 1975 Act states that it is unlawful for an employer to discriminate against a woman employed by him by dismissing her or subjecting her to any other detriment.

4. I now turn to the facts of the case. By letter of 26 June 1987, EMO Air Cargo (UK) Ltd (EMO) engaged Mrs Webb as an import operations clerk, subject to a probationary period of three months. At her interview Mrs Webb was told that the job was available because another import operations clerk, Mrs Stewart, was pregnant. In order to be capable of replacing Mrs Stewart, who intended to go on working until the end of the year and to return to her job after maternity leave, Mrs Webb needed to undergo training for a period of six months: she therefore started work on 1 July 1987. Let me make it quite clear at this point that, as the industrial tribunal's reconstruction of the facts plainly reveals, Mrs Stewart's return would by no means have entailed the dismissal of Mrs Webb, a fact which confirms that the latter's contract was for an indeterminate period.

Two weeks after starting work, Mrs Webb realised that she too was pregnant, a state of affairs which led the managing director of EMO to tell her that he had no choice but to dismiss her. On 30 July 1987 Mrs Webb accordingly received a letter which, after reminding her that the position she held had become vacant on account of the pregnancy of another employee, stated: 'Since you have only now told me that you are also pregnant I have no alternative other than to terminate your employment with our company.'

5. The industrial tribunal, before which Mrs Webb brought proceedings contesting her dismissal, dismissed her claim that she had been the victim of direct discrimination on grounds of sex, holding instead that the real reason for her dismissal had been the fact that it would have been impossible for her to carry out the primary task for which she had been recruited, namely to replace Mrs Stewart during the latter's absence on maternity leave. The national court reached that conclusion on the ground that a male employee, engaged for the purpose of replacing a female employee during the latter's pregnancy, would also have been dismissed if he had requested leave of absence during the period in question.

Mrs Webb's subsequent appeals, first to the Employment Appeal Tribunal ([1990] ICR 442) and then to the Court of Appeal ([1992] 2 All ER 43), were both unsuccessful. She finally appealed to the House of Lords ([1992] 4 All ER 929, [1993] 1 WLR 49), which decided that it would be appropriate to seek a preliminary ruling from the court on the following question:

'Is it discrimination on grounds of sex contrary to Council Directive (EEC) 76/207 for an employer to dismiss a female employee ("the appellant") (a) whom he engaged for the specific purpose of replacing (after training) another female employee during the latter's forthcoming maternity leave, (b) when, very shortly after appointment, the employer discovers that the appellant herself will be absent on maternity leave during the maternity leave of the other employee, and the employer dismisses her because he needs the job holder to be at work during that period, (c) had the employer known of the pregnancy of the appellant at the date of appointment, she would not have been appointed, and (d) the employer would similarly have dismissed a male employee engaged for this purpose who required leave of absence at the relevant time for medical or other reasons?'

6. Before we turn to the substance of that question, some attention should be given to the issue, raised on several occasions in the course of the proceedings, of the applicability of Directive 76/207 to the case under consideration, bearing in mind that the dispute is between two persons governed by private law and the court has not so far held that directives have horizontal direct effect.

In that connection, the first point to note is that in applying national law, regardless of whether the provisions in question were adopted before or after the directive, 'the national court called upon to interpret it is required to do so, as far as possible, in the light of the wording and the purpose of the directive in order to achieve the result pursued by the latter and thereby comply with the third paragraph of Article 189 of the Treaty'. (See the judgment in *Marleasing SA v La Comercial Internacional de Alimentación* Case C-106/89 [1990] ECR I-4135 at 4159 (para 8)).

In view of the fact that the national court seeks the interpretation of a directive which has already been transposed into national law, the answer may be of assistance to it for the purposes of interpreting and applying the relevant provisions of the Sex Discrimination Act 1975. Moreover, the House of Lords itself stated in the order for reference that 'it is for a United Kingdom court to construe domestic legislation in any field covered by a Community directive so as to accord with the interpretation of the directive as laid down by the European Court' (see [1992] 4 All ER 929 at 939, [1993] 1 WLR 49 at 59).

7. That said, the first question which arises is whether dismissal in a case such as this constitutes direct discrimination on grounds of sex within the meaning of the directive. For that purpose it must be ascertained whether the material reason for the dismissal applies without distinction to workers of both sexes or whether, on the contrary, it applies only to one of the sexes.

It is quite clear that termination of an employment contract on the ground of pregnancy applies only to women and therefore constitutes direct discrimination on grounds of sex. The court has already had occasion to give a ruling to that effect, both in *Dekker v Stichting Vormingscentrum voor Jong Volwassenen (VJV-Centrum) Plus* Case C-177/88 [1990] ECR I-3941 with respect to the refusal to appoint a pregnant woman, and in *Handels- og Kontorfunktionærernes Forbund i Danmark v Dansk Arbejdsgiverforening* Case C-179/88 [1990] ECR I-3979 (the *Hertz* case) with respect to the dismissal of a pregnant woman. In connection with the latter situation, which corresponds to the present case, the court stated that 'the dismissal of a female worker on account of pregnancy constitutes direct discrimination on grounds of sex, as [does] a refusal to appoint a pregnant woman'. (See the judgment in the *Hertz* case [1990] ECR I-3979 at 3998 (para 13).)

8. The view that a refusal to appoint and/or a decision to dismiss on the ground of pregnancy can relate only to women, thus constituting direct discrimination on grounds of sex, implies—obviously—that substantive equality between men and women as regards employment precludes any consideration, either when taking up employment or during the employment relationship, of a factor which—by definition—only affects women. It follows, therefore, from the reasoning underlying the judgments in the *Dekker* and *Hertz* cases—and how could it be otherwise—that Directive 76/207 must be construed so as to achieve substantive equality, and not mere formal equality which would constitute the very denial of the concept of equality.

Consequently, the dismissal of a female employee for the sole reason that she is pregnant is contrary to art 5(1) of Directive 76/207, inasmuch as it constitutes—at least in principle—direct discrimination on grounds of sex. (From this perspective, art 10 of Directive 92/85, which prohibits the dismissal of female workers during the period from the beginning of their pregnancy to the end of maternity leave, save in exceptional cases not connected with their condition, merely confirms the interpretation of art 5(1) set out here.)

9. However, the national court points out that in the present case, unlike the *Dekker* case, the unequal treatment is not directly based on the female employee's pregnancy but is the result of her inability to carry out, during a particular period, the task for which she had specifically been engaged. In other words, Mrs Webb was not dismissed because of her pregnancy but because her condition would have prevented her from working during the period in which she should have replaced Mrs Stewart.

It is, indeed, difficult to separate and to distinguish pregnancy from inability to work for a specific length of time which coincides moreover with the duration of maternity leave. In such cases, absence from work is in fact determined by the pregnancy, that is to say, by a condition which only affects women. While it may be true that the woman in question was engaged for the purpose of replacing for a short time another employee during the latter's maternity leave, the fact remains that she was engaged on the basis of a contract for an indefinite period and therefore her inability to carry out the task for which she was engaged affects only a limited period in relation to the total length of the contract.

10. The court's recent judgment in *Habermann-Beltermann v Arbeiterwohlfahrt, Bezirksverband Ndb/Opf eV* Case C-421/92 [1994] IRLR 364 is of considerable significance with regard to the point at issue. In that case, the court was asked to rule on the lawfulness of the termination of an employment relationship—whether by annulment or avoidance of the contract—in circumstances in which the unequal treatment was not based directly on the woman's pregnancy but was the result of the prohibition on night-time work during pregnancy, laid down by art 2(3) of Directive 76/207.

The court established that in the circumstances the questions submitted for a ruling related to a contract without a fixed term in relation to which, consequently, the prohibition on night-time work by pregnant women could take effect only for a limited period, and concluded that 'the termination of a contract without a fixed term on account of the woman's pregnancy ... cannot be justified on the ground that a statutory prohibition, imposed because of pregnancy, temporarily prevents the employee from performing night-time work', that is to say the work for which she had been specifically engaged (see [1994] IRLR 364 at 367 (para 25)).

11. In my view, the circumstances of the present case call with even greater justification for a similar conclusion, in view of the fact that the termination of the employment relationship is not connected with a statutory prohibition, as in the case just mentioned, but was occasioned simply by the employer's concern to avoid possible financial or in any event organisational burdens arising from the need to engage an employee to perform—on a temporary basis—the tasks which the female employee who was subsequently dismissed had been recruited to carry out. (In the present case, moreover, it seems that the employer would not have to shoulder special financial burdens since the relevant national legislation makes entitlement to allowances during maternity leave subject to a series of conditions which Mrs Webb did not satisfy. In any event, however, it scarcely needs reiterating that, as expressly stated by the court in *Dekker* [1990] ECR I-3941 at 3973 (para 12), discrimination cannot be justified by the financial loss which an employer who appointed a pregnant woman would suffer for the duration of her pregnancy.) It follows that the dismissal of the employee in question owing to the fact that, because of her pregnancy, she would not have been able to fulfil one of the (express or implied) terms of the relevant contract—an inability which is however temporary in relation to the duration of the contract—must therefore be considered incompatible with the principle of equal treatment as laid down in Directive 76/207.

From that point of view it is of no significance whatever, even though the national court lays emphasis on it in the question submitted, that the employer would not have recruited the person in question if he had been aware of her pregnancy. In that connection, suffice it to say that the dismissal cannot in any case be considered lawful when the appellant herself, as the order for reference reveals clearly enough, was not aware of her condition. (In my view, moreover, whether or not the parties are aware of the pregnancy at the time they enter into an employment relationship is, for the purposes of a valid employment relationship and—a fortiori—of a possible dismissal, actually irrelevant save in exceptional cases to be assessed individually (see my opinion in *Habermann-Beltermann* Case C-421/92 [1994] IRLR 364 at 369 (para 12).) That is the corollary, although only implicitly, of the judgment in *Habermann-Beltermann*, in which the court had been called upon to take that factor into account for the purposes of its ruling.

12. It has been argued, however, that in the present case the question of unequal treatment does not even arise, inasmuch as the employer would also have dismissed a male employee who had asked for leave of absence, whether for medical or other reasons, over the same period in which he was meant to replace the female employee absent on maternity leave. Such 'proof' purports to confirm that the dismissal arose exclusively from the need for the holder of the post in question to be at work during the period in question.

In other words, in a case such as this, dismissal should not be classified as (direct) discrimination on grounds of sex, inasmuch as the underlying cause (inability to perform the contract during a predetermined period of time) would lead to the same consequences with respect to a male employee in the same situation. That line of reasoning presupposes, however, that the circumstances of a pregnant woman are comparable to those of a male employee who is unable, for medical or other reasons, to work during a given period.

13. That possibility is expressly contemplated in the question submitted by the national court. What is more, it is clear from the order for reference that the problem has been raised in precisely those terms by the various national courts who have had occasion to deal with the case, precisely in order to verify in accordance with s 5(3) of the 1975 Act whether there exists treatment which is in effect accorded only to men that can serve as a basis for comparison with that accorded to a woman in the appellant's situation and, more particularly, whether it is permissible to compare a woman's inability to work on account of maternity and a man's inability to work, whether or not on medical grounds.

In that connection it seems to me of no avail to rely on the judgment in *Hertz* Case C-179/88 [1990] ECR I-3979 esp at 3999 (paras 14–17) in which the court considered that the dismissal of a female employee on account of repeated absences through illness, even though the illness may be attributable to pregnancy or confinement, does not constitute direct discrimination on grounds of sex if those absences occur after the period of maternity leave and would also lead in the same circumstances to the dismissal of a male employee. (That judgment may certainly not be construed as meaning that the court has recognised as permissible (or even justifiable) the dismissal of a woman who is absent from work for a reason (illness) connected with pregnancy. Closer examination reveals that the court's decision turned on the fact that Mrs Hertz's illness began after her return to work at the end of her maternity leave. The implication is that an illness connected with pregnancy is covered by the directive, thus rendering dismissal unlawful, to the extent that such illness occurred during maternity leave, that is to say during a period defined by the member states for the purposes of the derogation referred to in art 2(3) of Directive 76/207.)

In that case, the same conditions (a number of absences over a certain period) were applied to workers of both sexes. In the present case, on the other hand, the termination of the employment relationship resulted from a condition (pregnancy) which indisputably affects women alone.

14. The judgment in *Hertz* serves to demonstrate, if anything, that absence through illness may not be equated with absence on maternity leave. To the extent to which that judgment holds that it is not discriminatory to dismiss an employee on account of absences through an illness which, while it may be attributable to pregnancy or confinement, began after the end of the maternity leave, it follows a fortiori that pregnancy may not be equated with illness. An inference which can be drawn, however obvious it may sound, is that a sick woman is to be treated in the same way as a sick man, whatever the cause of her

illness. A pregnant woman, on the other hand, may not simply on account of her pregnancy be placed at a disadvantage to such an extent as to be excluded from the employment sector.

Nor does it seem to me to be possible a fortiori to draw comparisons, although these were referred to in the course of the proceedings, between a woman on maternity leave and a man unable to work because, for example, he has to take part in a sporting event, even if it were the Olympic Games. Other considerations apart, a sportsman, even a champion (whether a man or a woman) is confronted with a normal choice reflecting his needs and priorities in life; the same cannot reasonably be said of a pregnant woman, unless the view is taken—but it would be absurd—that a woman who wishes to keep her job always has the option of not having children.

15. In view of the foregoing observations, I see no need to tackle the question raised by the Commission in the course of the proceedings concerning hypothetical situations in which the contract at issue is not, as in the present case, for an indefinite period but is for a fixed term, in the circumstances limited to the period in which a female employee who has just been engaged would have to be absent on maternity leave.

Nor do I find it necessary to reflect on the various devices suggested by the Commission in order to spare the employer the attendant financial consequences when it transpires that a female employee who has just been engaged will not be able, even if only temporarily, to do the work required of her. Whether or not the contract of employment may be suspended and/or the terms of the contract modified as a result of a female employee being unable to work during a given period are at present matters still governed by national law, provided—of course—that such practices do not lead to a breach of the principle of equal treatment. (Although Directive 92/85, which is due to enter into force on 19 October 1994, imposes on member states a series of unconditional obligations with regard to the treatment of female employees during maternity leave, it still leaves them the option of making pay and the grant of certain allowances subject to the requirement of previous employment for a given period not in excess of 12 months, immediately prior to the anticipated date of the employee's confinement (art 11).)

16. In the light of the foregoing considerations, therefore, I propose that the court give the following answer to the questions submitted by the House of Lords:

> Articles 2(1) and 5(1) of Directive (EEC) 76/207 preclude an interpretation of national law which permits the dismissal of a woman engaged on the basis of an employment contract for an indefinite period on the ground that the employee in question must—on account of pregnancy—be absent from work during the period in which she would have had to replace another female employee, herself absent on maternity leave.

14 July 1994. The **COURT OF JUSTICE** (Fifth Chamber) delivered the following judgment.

1. By order of 26 November 1992, received at the court on 4 February 1993, the House of Lords referred to the court for a preliminary ruling under art 177 of the EEC Treaty a question on the interpretation of Council Directive (EEC) 76/207 of 9 February 1976 on the implementation of the principle of equal

treatment for men and women as regards access to employment, vocational training and promotion, and working conditions.

2. That question was raised in proceedings between Mrs Webb and EMO Air Cargo (UK) Ltd (hereinafter 'EMO').

3. It appears from the order for reference that in 1987 EMO employed 16 persons. In June one of the four employees working in the import operations department, Mrs Stewart, found that she was pregnant. EMO decided not to wait until her departure on maternity leave before engaging a replacement whom Mrs Stewart could train during the six months prior to her going on leave. Mrs Webb was recruited with a view, initially, to replacing Mrs Stewart following a probationary period. However, it was envisaged that Mrs Webb would continue to work for EMO following Mrs Stewart's return. The documents before the court show that Mrs Webb did not know she was pregnant when the employment contract was entered into.

4. Mrs Webb started work at EMO on 1 July 1987. Two weeks later, she thought that she might be pregnant. Her employer was informed of this indirectly. He then called her in to see him and informed her of his intention to dismiss her. Mrs Webb's pregnancy was confirmed a week later. On 30 July she received a letter dismissing her in the following terms: 'You will recall that at your interview some four weeks ago you were told that the job for which you applied and were given had become available because of one of our employees becoming pregnant. Since you have only now told me that you are also pregnant I have no alternative other than to terminate your employment with our company.'

5. Mrs Webb then brought proceedings before the industrial tribunal, pleading direct discrimination on grounds of sex and, in the alternative, indirect discrimination.

6. The relevant national legislation in this case is the Sex Discrimination Act 1975. It is apparent from the documents before the court that Mrs Webb cannot rely either on s 54 of the Employment Protection (Consolidation) Act 1978, which prohibits unfair dismissal, or on s 60 of that statute, which provides that dismissal on the ground of pregnancy constitutes unfair dismissal. Under s 64, workers who have been employed for less than two years are not entitled to claim that protection.

7. Section 1(1) of the Sex Discrimination Act 1975 provides:

'A person discriminates against a woman in any circumstances relevant for the purposes of any provision of this Act if—(a) on the ground of her sex he treats her less favourably than he treats or would treat a man …'

8. Section 2 provides:

'(1) Section 1, and the provisions of Parts II and III relating to sex discrimination against women, are to be read as applying equally to the treatment of men, and for that purpose shall have effect with such modifications as are requisite.

(2) In the application of subsection (1) no account shall be taken of special treatment afforded to women in connection with pregnancy or childbirth.'

9. Under s 5(3):

'A comparison of the cases of persons of different sex or marital status under section 1(1) ... must be such that the relevant circumstances in the one case are the same, or not materially different, in the other.'

10. Lastly, s 6(2) of the 1975 Act provides:

'It is unlawful for a person, in the case of a woman employed by him at an establishment in Great Britain, to discriminate against her ... (b) by dismissing her, or subjecting her to any other detriment.'

11. The industrial tribunal dismissed Mrs Webb's action. It held that she had not been directly discriminated against on grounds of sex. In its view, the real and significant reason for Mrs Webb's dismissal was her anticipated inability to carry out the primary task for which she had been recruited, namely to cover the job of Mrs Stewart during the latter's absence on maternity leave. According to the industrial tribunal, if a man recruited for the same purpose as Mrs Webb had told his employer that he would be absent for a period comparable to the likely absence of Mrs Webb, he would have been dismissed.

12. The industrial tribunal also held that Mrs Webb had not suffered indirect discrimination. More women than men were likely to be unable to do the job for which they had been recruited because of the possibility of pregnancy. However, according to the industrial tribunal, the employers had shown that the reasonable needs of their business required that the person recruited to cover for Mrs Stewart during her maternity leave be available.

13. Appeals by Mrs Webb, first to the Employment Appeal Tribunal ([1990] ICR 442) and then to the Court of Appeal ([1992] 2 All ER 43), were unsuccessful. Mrs Webb was granted leave by the Court of Appeal to appeal to the House of Lords.

14. The House of Lords ([1992] 4 All ER 929, [1993] 1 WLR 49) found that the special feature of this case lay in the fact that the pregnant woman who was dismissed had been recruited precisely in order to replace, at least initially, an employee who was herself due to take maternity leave. The national court is uncertain whether it was unlawful to dismiss Mrs Webb on the ground of her pregnancy, or whether greater weight should be attached to the reasons for which she was recruited.

15. Taking the view that it should construe the applicable domestic legislation so as to accord with the interpretation of Directive 76/207, as laid down by the court, the House of Lords stayed proceedings and submitted the following question for a preliminary ruling:

'Is it discrimination on grounds of sex contrary to Council Directive (EEC) 76/207 for an employer to dismiss a female employee ("the appellant") (a) whom he engaged for the specific purpose of replacing (after training) another female employee during the latter's forthcoming maternity leave, (b) when, very shortly after appointment, the employer discovers that the appellant herself will be absent on maternity leave during the maternity leave of the other employee, and the employer dismisses her because he needs the job holder to be at work during that period, (c) had the employer known of the pregnancy of the appellant at the date of appointment, she would not have been appointed, and (d) the employer would similarly have dismissed a male employee engaged for this purpose who required leave of absence at the relevant time for medical or other reasons?'

16. As is apparent from the documents before the court, the question submitted for a preliminary ruling relates to a contract of employment concluded for an indefinite period.

17. According to art 1(1), the purpose of Directive 76/207 is to put into effect in the member states the principle of equal treatment for men and women as regards access to employment, including promotion, and vocational training and as regards working conditions.

18. Article 2(1) of Directive 76/207 states that 'the principle of equal treatment shall mean that there shall be no discrimination whatsoever on grounds of sex either directly or indirectly by reference in particular to marital or family status'. Under art 5(1), 'application of the principle of equal treatment with regard to working conditions, including the conditions governing dismissal, means that men and women shall be guaranteed the same conditions without discrimination on grounds of sex'.

19. As the court ruled in *Handels- og Kontorfunktionærernes Forbund i Danmark v Dansk Arbejdsgiverforening* Case C-179/88 [1990] ECR I-3979 at 3998 (para 13) (the *Hertz* case) and confirmed in its judgment in *Habermann-Beltermann v Arbeiterwohlfahrt, Bezirksverband Ndb/Opf eV* Case C-421/92 [1994] IRLR 364 at 366 (para 15), the dismissal of a female worker on account of pregnancy constitutes direct discrimination on grounds of sex.

20. Furthermore, by reserving to member states the right to retain or introduce provisions which are intended to protect women in connection with 'pregnancy and maternity', art 2(3) of Directive 76/207 recognises the legitimacy, in terms of the principle of equal treatment, first, of protecting a woman's biological condition during and after pregnancy and, second, of protecting the special relationship between a woman and her child over the period which follows pregnancy and childbirth (see the *Habermann-Beltermann* case [1994] IRLR 364 at 367 (para 21) and *Hofmann v Barmer Ersatzkasse* Case 184/83 [1984] ECR 3047 at 3075 (para 25)).

21. In view of the harmful effects which the risk of dismissal may have on the physical and mental state of women who are pregnant, have recently given birth or are breastfeeding, including the particularly serious risk that pregnant women may be prompted voluntarily to terminate their pregnancy, the Community legislature subsequently provided, pursuant to art 10 of Council Directive (EEC) 92/85 of 19 October 1992 on the introduction of measures to encourage improvements in the safety and health at work of pregnant workers and workers who have recently given birth or are breastfeeding, for special protection to be given to women by prohibiting dismissal during the period from the beginning of their pregnancy to the end of their maternity leave.

22. Furthermore, art 10 of Directive 92/85 provides that there is to be no exception to, or derogation from, the prohibition on the dismissal of pregnant women during that period, save in exceptional cases not connected with their condition.

23. The answer to the question submitted by the House of Lords, which concerns Directive 76/207, must take account of that general context.

24. First, in response to the House of Lords' inquiry, there can be no question of comparing the situation of a woman who finds herself incapable, by reason of pregnancy discovered very shortly after the conclusion of the employment contract, of performing the task for which she was recruited with that of a man similarly incapable for medical or other reasons.

25. As Mrs Webb rightly argues, pregnancy is not in any way comparable with a pathological condition, and even less so with unavailability for work on

non-medical grounds, both of which are situations that may justify the dismissal of a woman without discriminating on grounds of sex. Moreover, in the *Hertz* case the court drew a clear distinction between pregnancy and illness, even where the illness is attributable to pregnancy but manifests itself after the maternity leave. As the court pointed out, there is no reason to distinguish such an illness from any other illness (see [1990] ECR I-3979 at 3999 (para 16)).

26. Furthermore, contrary to the submission of the United Kingdom, dismissal of a pregnant woman recruited for an indefinite period cannot be justified on grounds relating to her inability to fulfil a fundamental condition of her employment contract. The availability of an employee is necessarily, for the employer, a precondition for the proper performance of the employment contract. However, the protection afforded by Community law to a woman during pregnancy and after childbirth cannot be dependent on whether her presence at work during maternity is essential to the proper functioning of the undertaking in which she is employed. Any contrary interpretation would render ineffective the provisions of Directive 76/207.

27. In circumstances such as those of Mrs Webb, termination of a contract for an indefinite period on grounds of the woman's pregnancy cannot be justified by the fact that she is prevented, on a purely temporary basis, from performing the work for which she has been engaged (see the *Habermann-Beltermann* case [1994] IRLR 364 at 367 (para 25) and the Advocate General's opinion in this case (paras 10 and 11 above)).

28. The fact that the main proceedings concern a woman who was initially recruited to replace another employee during the latter's maternity leave but who was herself found to be pregnant shortly after her recruitment cannot affect the answer to be given to the national court.

29. Accordingly, the answer to the question submitted must be that art 2(1) read with art 5(1) of Directive 76/207 precludes dismissal of an employee who is recruited for an unlimited term with a view, initially, to replacing another employee during the latter's maternity leave and who cannot do so because, shortly after recruitment, she is herself found to be pregnant.

Costs

30. The costs incurred by the United Kingdom and the Commission of the European Communities, which have submitted observations to the court, are not recoverable. Since these proceedings are, for the parties to the main proceedings, a step in the action pending before the national court, the decision on costs is a matter for that court.

On those grounds, the court (Fifth Chamber), in answer to the question referred to it by the House of Lords by order of 26 November 1992, hereby rules: art 2(1) read with art 5(1) of Council Directive (EEC) 76/207 of 9 February 1976 on the implementation of the principle of equal treatment for men and women as regards access to employment, vocational training and promotion, and working conditions precludes dismissal of an employee who is recruited for an unlimited term with a view, initially, to replacing another employee during the latter's maternity leave and who cannot do so because, shortly after her recruitment, she is herself found to be pregnant.

Carolyn Toulmin   Barrister.

Hindcastle Ltd v Barbara Attenborough Associates Ltd and others

COURT OF APPEAL, CIVIL DIVISION

SIR STEPHEN BROWN P, ROSE AND MILLETT LJJ

13, 14, 15 JUNE 1994

Landlord and tenant – Assignment of lease – Obligation to pay rent – Assignment by original lessee to company assignee – Express covenant by assignee with lessor to pay rent included in licence to assign – Assignee with licence of lessor reassigning lease – Assignee going into liquidation – Disclaimer of lease by liquidator – Lessor claiming from original lessee rent falling due after disclaimer – Whether obligation to pay rent remaining with original lessee or any surety for original lessee notwithstanding disclaimer as onerous property – Insolvency Act 1986, s 178(4).

In 1983 the plaintiff granted a 20-year lease of property to the first defendant. Four years later the first defendant assigned the lease, with the lessor's consent, to the second defendant pursuant to a licence to assign. The licence contained a covenant under which the second defendant agreed with the lessor to pay the rent and observe and perform the covenants of the lease during the remainder of the 20-year term. The third defendant joined in the licence to assign in order to guarantee the performance of the obligations undertaken by the second defendant, but his obligations as surety were limited to expire in 1993. In 1989 the second defendant assigned the lease to a company, P Ltd, with the lessor's consent. In 1992 P Ltd went into voluntary liquidation and shortly thereafter the liquidator gave notice of disclaimer of the lease pursuant to s 178[a] of the Insolvency Act 1986, which provided in sub-s (4) that a disclaimer (a) determined the rights, interests and liabilities of the company in or in respect of the property disclaimed, but (b) did not, except so far as was necessary for the purpose of releasing the company from any liability, affect the rights or liabilities of any other person. The lessor subsequently issued two writs against the defendants, claiming arrears of rent in respect of different rental periods, and in both actions the judge awarded the lessor summary judgment against all the defendants. The second and third defendants appealed, contending inter alia that their liability to pay the rent ceased on disclaimer of the lease since there was no relevant distinction to be drawn between the position of a surety for the then bankrupt original lessee and the original lessee with an unbroken chain of indemnity from the bankrupt assignee in the sense that each of them was liable to the lessor and was entitled to be indemnified by the bankrupt's estate.

Held – The disclaimer of a lease under s 178 of the 1986 Act by the liquidator of a company which had taken an assignment of the lease from an intermediate assignee did not operate to determine the liability of the original lessee and any surety for the original lessee to pay the rent due under the lease, since the effect of a disclaimer was to extinguish the liability of the bankrupt assignee to pay the rent and to replace it by the different and distinct statutory liability under s 178(6) to compensate any person who had sustained loss and damage in

---

a   Section 178, so far as material, is set out at p 132 *c* to *e*, post

consequence of the disclaimer. Moreover, it was not necessary to extinguish the liability of the original lessee to the lessor in order to release the liability of the bankrupt assignee to indemnify him, having regard to the fact that s 178(4)(a) served to determine all the liabilities of the bankrupt assignee in respect of the disclaimed property (including not only the liability to pay rent to the lessor but also the liability to indemnify the original lessee for his liability to pay the rent to the lessor) and that s 178(4) served in effect to abrogate the right of the original lessee to claim an indemnity from the bankrupt assignee without any necessity to abrogate the obligation of the original lessee to pay the lessor. It followed that s 178(4)(b) did not extinguish the continuing liability of the first defendant after the disclaimer of the lease by the liquidator of P Ltd. The appeal would accordingly be dismissed (see p 135 *c* to *h*, p 136 *c* to *e*, p 137 *c* to *f* and p 138 *f*, post).

W H Smith Ltd v Wyndham Investments Ltd (1994) Times, 26 May approved.

Stacey v Hill [1901] 1 KB 660 and Warnford Investments Ltd v Duckworth [1978] 2 All ER 517 considered.

Notes

For disclaimer of onerous property by a liquidator, see 7(2) Halsbury's Laws (4th edn reissue) paras 1862–1877.

For disclaimer of onerous property on bankruptcy and liquidation, see 3(2) Halsbury's Laws (4th edn reissue) paras 460–477 and 27(1) ibid paras 536–537, and for cases on the subject, see 5(1) Digest (2nd reissue) 43–51, 7632–7708.

For the Insolvency Act 1986, s 178, see 4 Halsbury's Statutes (4th edn) (1987 reissue) 842.

Cases referred to in judgments

Hill v East and West India Dock Co (1884) 9 App Cas 448, HL; affg (1882) 22 Ch D 14, CA.

Smith (W H) Ltd v Wyndham Investments Ltd (1994) Times, 26 May.

Stacey v Hill [1901] 1 KB 660, CA.

Warnford Investments Ltd v Duckworth [1978] 2 All ER 517, [1979] Ch 127, [1978] 2 WLR 741.

Cases also cited or referred to in skeleton arguments

AE Realisations (1985) Ltd, Re [1987] 3 All ER 83, [1988] 1 WLR 200.

Finley, Re, ex p Clothworkers' Co (1888) 21 QBD 475, CA.

Harding v Preece (1882) 9 QBD 281.

Katherine et Cie Ltd, Re [1932] 1 Ch 70, [1931] All ER Rep 125.

Levy, Re, ex p Walton (1881) 17 Ch D 746, [1881–85] All ER Rep 548, CA.

Morris (D) & Sons Ltd v Jeffreys (1932) 148 LT 56, [1932] All ER Rep 881.

Smyth v North (1872) LR 7 Exch 242.

Thompson and Cottrell's Contract, Re [1943] 1 All ER 169, [1943] Ch 97.

Appeal

The second and third defendants, CIT Developments Ltd and Patrick John Whitten (the first defendant's surety), appealed with leave of the judge from the orders of Simon Goldblatt QC sitting as a deputy judge of the High Court on 14 October 1993 whereby he granted the plaintiff, Hindcastle Ltd, summary judgment in respect of arrears of rent after 8 December 1992 reserved by the underlease of premises known as the Second Floor of 297, Oxford Street,

London W1 made between the plaintiff and the first defendant, Barbara
Attenborough Associates Ltd, and dated 20 October 1983, in circumstances
where the underlease had been further assigned by the second defendant (the
first assignee of the underlease) to Prest Ltd (the second assignee of the
underlease) and subsequently disclaimed on 8 December 1992 by the liquidator
of Prest Ltd. The first defendant took no part in the appeal. The facts are set
out in the judgment of Millett LJ.

David Oliver QC and *Carolyn Walton* (instructed by *Stallards*) for the second and
    third defendants.
Jonathan Arkush (instructed by *Chethams*) for the plaintiff.

MILLETT LJ (giving the first judgment at the invitation of Sir Stephen
Brown P). This is an appeal with the leave of the judge by the second and third
defendants from two orders both dated 14 October 1993 of Mr Simon Goldblatt
QC, sitting as a deputy judge of the High Court in the Queen's Bench Division,
whereby he gave summary judgment under RSC Ord 14 for arrears of rent due
under a lease after the lessee had gone into insolvent liquidation and the
liquidator had disclaimed the lease.

The second defendant is an intermediate assignee of the lease which entered
into a direct contractual relationship with the lessor. The third defendant is a
surety which guaranteed the contractual obligations of the second defendant.
The first defendant is the original lessee under the lease. The deputy judge
gave judgment against all three defendants, but the first defendant, which I
understand is now also in liquidation, has not appealed.

The question for decision is whether the disclaimer of a lease under s 178 of
the Insolvency Act 1986 by the liquidator of a company which has taken an
assignment of the lease operates to determine the liability of the original lessee
and any surety for the original lessee, for the position of an intermediate
assignee of the lease which has entered into a direct contractual relationship
with the lessor is indistinguishable from that of the original lessee. Although
in form the appeal is an appeal from the decision of the deputy judge, it is, in
reality, an appeal 15 years out of time from a decision of Megarry V-C in 1979,
and it has been argued by the same counsel who appeared for the unsuccessful
party in that case.

The lease was granted on 20 October 1983 for a term of 20 years from 12
September 1983 at an initial rent of £13,626 p a with periodic upwards only rent
reviews. It was made between the plaintiff as lessor and the first defendant as
original lessee. It was not assignable except with the consent of the lessor. In
1987 it was assigned to the second defendant pursuant to a licence to assign
which contained a covenant on the part of the second defendant with the lessor
to pay the rent and observe and perform the covenants in the lease during the
remainder of the term thereby granted. The third defendant joined in the
licence to assign in order to guarantee the performance of the obligations
thereby undertaken by the second defendant. The obligations of the third
defendant as surety were limited to expire after the end of ten years from the
date of the lease.

In 1989 the second defendant assigned the lease to Prest Ltd (the company).
The assignment was made with the lessor's consent. In 1990 the company and
the lessor agreed that the rent payable under the lease in accordance with the
rent review provisions should thenceforth be £37,500 p a. None of the

defendants took any part in the negotiations which led to the revised rent. On 31 October 1992 the company went into creditors' voluntary liquidation. On 8 December 1992 the liquidator gave notice of disclaimer of the lease pursuant to s 178 of the Insolvency Act 1986. No one has applied for a vesting order under s 181 of the 1986 Act and the time limit for doing so prescribed by the Insolvency Rules 1986, SI 1986/1925, has now expired, though it may of course be extended by the court. Writs were issued by the lessor claiming arrears of rent in respect of different rental periods. The writs were issued on 28 January 1993 and 22 July 1993 respectively, and summary judgment in both actions was entered against all the defendants following the deputy judge's judgment in November 1993.

The effect of a disclaimer by the liquidator of an insolvent company is laid down by s 178 of the 1986 Act, and in particular by sub-ss (4) and (6) thereof. Subsection (4) provides:

'A disclaimer under this section—(a) operates so as to determine, as from the date of the disclaimer, the rights, interests and liabilities of the company in or in respect of the property disclaimed; but (b) does not, except so far as is necessary for the purpose of releasing the company from any liability, affect the rights or liabilities of any other person.'

Subsection (6) provides:

'Any person sustaining loss or damage in consequence of the operation of a disclaimer under this section is deemed a creditor of the company to the extent of the loss or damage and accordingly may prove for the loss or damage in the winding up.'

Provisions in identical terms are contained in s 315 of the 1986 Act in relation to disclaimer by the trustee in bankruptcy of an individual bankrupt.

Provisions to the like effect have been contained in every Companies Act since the right to disclaim onerous property was first extended from personal to corporate insolvency by the Companies Act 1929, and in every Bankruptcy Act since the Bankruptcy Act 1883. The 1986 Act introduced two changes primarily of a procedural character, though having some substantive effect. Before the 1986 Act the liquidator of an insolvent company needed the leave of the court to disclaim in all cases, whereas a trustee in bankruptcy did not need such leave in most cases, and in particular did not need leave to disclaim a lease unless the bankrupt had sublet the premises or mortgaged the lease and the lessor, sublessee or mortgagee had objected to the disclaimer after being given notice thereof. The changes introduced by the 1986 Act brought the law and practice of disclaimer in corporate insolvency into line with that prevailing in personal bankruptcy. They were not without substantive effect, however, for the court had normally refused leave to disclaim where this would prejudice the lessor by discharging a surety from liability. Under the 1986 Act, however, the lessor has no opportunity to object to the disclaimer taking effect.

Mr Oliver QC, who appeared for the second and third defendants, acknowledged that the changes introduced by the 1986 Act did not affect the consequences of a disclaimer, which are laid down by s 178(4) and (6) in substantially the same terms as the corresponding provisions of the Bankruptcy Acts of 1883 and 1914. For ease of exposition I shall, throughout the rest of this judgment, refer to the relevant provisions of the earlier legislation by the numbers of the corresponding provisions in the 1986 Act, that is to say sub-ss (4) or (6).

The consequences of disclaimer of leasehold property have been considered by the courts on a number of occasions. The leading authorities, which consist of one decision of the House of Lords on the effect of the Bankruptcy Act 1869 and one decision of this court on the effect of the Bankruptcy Act 1883, established that there is a clear distinction between the case where the lease was still vested in the original lessee immediately before the disclaimer (which is not the present case) and the case where it was vested in an assignee of the original lessee (which is). The burden of Mr Oliver's submissions was that there is no relevant distinction to be drawn between the position of a surety for the bankrupt original lessee and the original lessee with an unbroken chain of indemnity from the bankrupt assignee. Each of them is liable to the lessor and is entitled to be indemnified by the bankrupt's estate. I shall deal in turn with the two situations as they appear from the relevant authorities.

1. *Lease vested in the original lessee*

Disclaimer by the trustee in bankruptcy of the lessee determines the lease and the lessee's obligations thereunder, with the result that the liability of any surety for the lessee is necessarily discharged. This was decided in *Stacey v Hill* [1901] 1 KB 660, a decision of this court. Two grounds for the decision can be detected.

(i) No other person being interested in the lease, the determination of the lessee's rights and liabilities thereunder, including his right to possession, has the effect of determining the lease altogether and accelerating the reversion. The effect of determining the liability of the lessee is to discharge the surety, for the secondary liability of a surety cannot survive the extinction of the primary guaranteed debt.

(ii) Subsection (4)(b) does not have the effect of preserving the liability of the surety, because the existence of the surety's right of indemnity by the principal debtor makes it necessary to release the surety if the bankrupt's estate is to be released from liability.

Two points may be noticed. (1) The first and main ground for the decision, in which all three Lords Justices concurred, was that the determination of the lessee's rights and obligations had the effect of determining the lease. The lessee's right to possession being determined, and there being no one else with a similar right, there was no obstacle to the lessor's resumption of possession with a view to re-letting the property. Strictly speaking, it was unnecessary to decide that the lease was determined or the reversion accelerated; it was sufficient for the decision that the liabilities of the lessee under the lease had been determined. (2) The second ground for the decision, to which only two of the Lords Justices subscribed, is not fully explained in the judgments and is not as straightforward as it appears at first sight. I shall have to return to this aspect of the case later.

2. *Where the lease is vested in an assignee*

Prior to the Bankruptcy Act 1883 a disclaimer by the trustee in bankruptcy of an assignee of the lease had no effect on the continuing liability of the original lessee or his surety. This was decided by the House of Lords in *Hill v East and West India Dock Co* (1884) 9 App Cas 448. That case was decided under the Bankruptcy Act 1869, the relevant provisions of which were in very different terms from those introduced by the Bankruptcy Act 1883, and which in particular did not include any provision corresponding to sub-s (4)(b). The House of Lords held that the determination of the rights and liabilities of the assignee, which took effect by way of a deemed surrender of the lease, operated only as between the lessor and the bankrupt assignee; so far as the original lessee was concerned, the lease continued to subsist (as did his liability) unless and until the lessor resumed actual possession and brought the lease to an end for all purposes.

Two points may be made about that decision. (1) Mr Oliver submitted that the concept of a lease continuing to exist but having no owner is not a particularly easy one to grasp; nor is it easy to understand what obstacle there is to the lessor's resumption of possession and re-letting the property, seeing that the right to possession of the bankrupt assignee has been determined and that he is the only person entitled to possession as against the lessor. These difficulties are inherent in the decision itself; they do not derive from the potential reactivation of the lease by the making of a vesting order, since there was no power to make such an order prior to the Bankruptcy Act 1883. Both suggested difficulties disappear, however, once it is recognised that the question is not whether the lease actually exists or not, but whether it is to be deemed or treated as continuing to exist. The result of the decision in *Hill v East and West India Dock Co* (1884) 9 App Cas 448 is that, as between the lessor and the bankrupt assignee, the lease is *deemed* to have been surrendered; as between the lessor and the original lessee and his surety, it is not deemed to have been surrendered. In the real world a lease must either exist or not. In the world of statutory hypothesis, however, there is no such requirement.

(2) The basis of the decision in *Hill v East and West India Dock Co* is that the liability of the original lessee is a primary and direct liability and is not dependent on the continued liability of the assignee. There are two separate and distinct obligations, and the statutory determination of the one does not discharge the other. In *Stacey v Hill* [1901] 1 KB 660, by contrast, there was only one obligation, namely that of the lessee, though two different parties were liable in respect of it; and the statutory determination of that obligation necessarily discharged the liability of both of them.

The question, therefore, is what difference, if any, to the liability of the original lessee and any surety for him resulted from the introduction in 1883 of sub-s (4)(b); for we are bound in this court by the decision in *Hill v East and West India Dock Co* to hold that an original lessee is not discharged from his liability to the lessor by reason of the disclaimer of the lease by the liquidator of an assignee 'except so far as is necessary for the purpose of releasing the company [that is to say the insolvent assignee] from any liability'.

This question was considered by Megarry V-C in a characteristically clear and comprehensive judgment in *Warnford Investments Ltd v Duckworth* [1978] 2 All ER 517, [1979] Ch 127. He held that the introduction of sub-s (4)(b) by the Bankruptcy Act 1883 made no difference. Accordingly, he applied *Hill v East and West India Dock Co* and distinguished *Stacey v Hill* [1901] 1 KB 660. He pointed out that the situations dealt with by the two cases were entirely different. In the one case the lease itself was determined and with it the liability of the bankrupt, and the guaranteed liability having been brought to an end the surety was necessarily discharged. In the other the liability of the original lessee was primary and direct, and was not dependent on any continued liability on the part of the bankrupt. Megarry V-C dealt with the argument that the liability of the original lessee was determined (or more accurately not preserved) by sub-s (4)(b) by saying that the bankrupt's estate was not released from liability in any event: any loss sustained by reason of the disclaimer was susceptible of proof under sub-s (6) (a provision which has been in every Bankruptcy Act since 1869). The only question was whether the proof should be lodged by the lessor or by the original lessee. If the original lessee *was* discharged from liability, the proof would be lodged by the lessor; if not, it would be lodged by the original lessee, relying on the chain of indemnity. In either case, the bankrupt's estate would not be released from liability. Since the discharge of the original lessee did not in fact lead to the release of the bankrupt estate, it could not be necessary in order to secure its release.

If that reasoning is correct, then in my judgment the second ground of the decision in *Stacey v Hill* cannot be supported; for there is no relevant distinction to be drawn between the position of the original lessee and that of a surety for the bankrupt assignee, each being liable to the lessor and having a claim for indemnity against the bankrupt estate. Either the determination of the liability to the lessor results in the release of the bankrupt estate or it does not, and if it does not (whether because of sub-s (6) or otherwise) then the discharge of the person entitled to be indemnified is not necessary for the purpose of securing the release of the bankrupt estate from liability.

But in my judgment this part of the reasoning of Megarry V-C is untenable. It is necessary to distinguish between two quite different liabilities of the bankrupt estate. There is, first, the liability which is put an end to by the disclaimer; in the present case, for example, the liability to pay the rent due under the lease. There is, secondly, the statutory liability under sub-s (6) which replaces it, that is to say the liability to compensate any person who has sustained loss or damage in consequence of the disclaimer. These liabilities may or may not be identical in amount, but they are different and distinct liabilities, the effect of a disclaimer being to extinguish the one and to replace it by the other. In my judgment, when sub-s (4)(b) speaks of something being 'necessary for the purpose of releasing the company from any liability', the words 'any liability' refer to a liability of the first kind and not the second. There are two reasons for this. In the first place, the effect of the disclaimer under sub-s (4) must be determined as an anterior question before the identification of the party sustaining loss as a result and the quantification of his loss can be undertaken for the purposes of proof under sub-s (6). In the second place, the bankrupt's estate can never be released from its potential liability under sub-s (6). In my judgment, therefore, sub-s (4)(b) means: 'necessary for the purpose of releasing the company from any such liability as aforesaid', that is to say a liability in or in respect of the property disclaimed and capable of being determined by sub-s (4)(a).

The rejection of this part of the reasoning of Megarry V-C, however, also disposes of Mr Oliver's main argument, which is that sub-s (4) should be given a purposive construction; that its purpose is to release the bankrupt estate from liability to the greatest extent possible; that this means giving sub-s (4) that effect which would lead to the smallest possible claim under sub-s (6); and that this in turn means extinguishing the liability of the original lessee and substituting a claim by the lessor, who would inevitably have a smaller claim than the original lessee, since the lessor, being able to re-let the premises, would have to give credit for the current rental value of the premises, whereas the original lessee would have nothing for which he could be required to give credit. The whole elaborate argument breaks down, however, once it is recognised that the amount of the loss sustained by reason of the disclaimer and provable under sub-s (6) cannot be considered until the effect of the disclaimer under sub-s (4) has first been determined.

It follows in my judgment (and to this extent I disagree with the judgment of Megarry V-C) that the case of the original lessee with an unbroken chain of indemnity cannot be distinguished from that of the surety of the bankrupt lessee by praying in aid the existence of sub-s (6). The question, however, remains: is it necessary to extinguish the liability of the original lessee to the lessor in order to release the liability of the bankrupt assignee to indemnify him? The question only has to be asked to be answered in the negative. It cannot be necessary to extinguish the liability of the original lessee in order to release the estate of the bankrupt: it is sufficient to extinguish the liability of the bankrupt assignee to indemnify the original lessee. Moreover, the extinction of the liability of the bankrupt estate to indemnify the original lessee is in my judgment the plain effect of the subsection. Subsection (4)(a) determines all the liabilities of the bankrupt assignee in respect of the disclaimed property. These are not restricted to liabilities owed to the lessor. They include not only the liability to pay the rent to the lessor, but also the liability to indemnify the original lessee in respect of rent payable to the lessor: both in my judgment are equally 'liabilities in respect of the disclaimed property'. In order to release the estate of the bankrupt assignee from its liability to indemnify the original lessee, however, it is necessary to extinguish the right of the original lessee to be indemnified; what sub-s (4)(b) does is to make it clear that the liability of a bankrupt assignee is determined notwithstanding its effect on the right of the original lessee to an indemnity against his liability.

This was the solution adopted by Judge Paul Baker QC in *W H Smith Ltd v Wyndham Investments Ltd* (1994) Times, 26 May. He said:

> '... I see no difficulty in abrogating the right of the original lessee to claim an indemnity from the assignee without any necessity to abrogate the obligation of the original lessee to pay the lessor. To compensate for the loss of the right to be indemnified against future rent, the original lessee can prove for any loss or injury under s 178(6). I may add, with all respect, that I do not see the necessity for any equation between the lessee's claim for injury and that of the lessor as expounded by Megarry V-C in the passage set out above. The position as I see it is that the liability of the assignee to indemnify the original lessee against *future* payments of rent is removed and a right to assess the loss and prove for it once and for all is substituted without regard to claims for loss or injury from any other party.' (Judge Paul Baker QC's emphasis.)

Mr Oliver's response to this solution was to submit that we are precluded from adopting it by the decision of this court in *Stacey v Hill* [1901] 1 KB 660. We are, of course, bound by that decision and by both grounds for it, and we cannot take refuge in the fact that the second ground for the decision has not won universal acceptance, or that the first ground was sufficient for the decision, or that the second ground is not fully explained. Mr Oliver submitted that the solution which I have suggested (and which was adopted by Judge Paul Baker) was equally open to the court in *Stacey v Hill*; and that since that court undoubtedly decided that it was necessary to discharge the surety in order to release the bankrupt lessee, it must be taken to have decided that it was not sufficient (or appropriate or possible) to leave the surety's obligation unaffected and extinguish his right to indemnity; and that the same must necessarily apply to the case of an original lessee.

As a strict matter of stare decisis, that submission is not acceptable. We are bound by what the court in *Stacey v Hill* actually decided, but not by any conclusion which can be logically deduced from what was decided but which was neither argued nor considered. But in any case I do not accept the submission. The right of the surety to be indemnified by the principal debtor, although arising from contract express or implied, is inherent in the relationship between them. It is co-extensive with and arises eo instanti as his liability. The two may be regarded as inseparable; or, as is sometimes said, as two sides of the same coin. It would, in my judgment, require very clear statutory language to deprive a surety of his right to indemnity while leaving his liability unimpaired. No such language is to be found in sub-s (4)(b), and it is not surprising that the possibility of extinguishing the surety's right to indemnity while leaving him exposed to liability did not occur to any member of the court, except possibly Romer LJ who rejected it. No such inhibitions need constrain the court when considering the position of the original lessee. His obligation arises when he takes the lease; it continues after assignment. If he is prudent, therefore, he takes a covenant of indemnity from his assignee when he assigns the lease. But his right to indemnity is quite separate from his obligation. The two arise at different times and by virtue of different instruments; and the existence of the obligation in no sense imports the right. Like Judge Paul Baker, I see no objection to abrogating the right of the original lessee to an indemnity from the assignee (and replacing it with a statutory right to prove in the assignee's bankruptcy under sub-s (6)) without any necessity to abrogate the obligation of the original lessee to the lessor; and in my judgment we are not precluded by the decision in *Stacey v Hill* from deciding that that is the effect of sub-s (4).

In an alternative and subordinate submission, Mr Oliver submitted that the liability of the second and third defendant extended only to the initial rent reserved by the lease and not to the increased rent agreed between the company and the lessor in accordance with the provisions of the rent review clause. That agreement was reached without reference to the second or third defendants. The question depends on the true construction of the covenants entered into by the second and third defendants in the licence to assign.

The second defendant covenanted with the lessor:

'that as from the date when the Lessee's estate and interest in the Lease shall be assigned to the assignee pursuant to the Licence hereinbefore contained and thenceforth during the residue of the term created by the Lease the Assignee will pay the rents thereby reserved ...'

That takes one back to the lease in order to ascertain what was the amount of the rent reserved thereby during the relevant rental period. That takes one to cl 5 of the lease, which (so far as material) provided:

'*IT IS HEREBY FURTHER AGREED AND DECLARED* as follows:—

The yearly rents reserved by this Lease are those stated in or ascertained in accordance with this Clause ...

(2) The yearly rent shall be:—(a) until the first review date the yearly rent of thirteen thousand six hundred and twenty six pounds (13,626) and (b) during each successive review period a yearly rent equal to the yearly rent previously payable hereunder or such revised yearly rent as may be ascertained as herein provided whichever be the greater and

(3) Such revised yearly rent for any review period may be agreed at any time between the Lessor and the Lessee or (in the absence of agreement) determined ...'

(I should add that the word 'lessee' was defined as including the original lessee and its successors to title.)

Accordingly, on the plain construction of the language of the lease, the rent reserved by the lease after the first review date was the rent agreed between the lessor and the then lessee in accordance with cl 5(2)(b) and (3) of the lease. Indeed, the argument that the only rent which the second defendant has covenanted to pay and which the third defendant has covenanted to guarantee is £13,626 is completely untenable since that rent was reserved by the lease until the first review date and not afterwards.

In a powerful argument, Mr Oliver submitted that the time has come to re-examine the position of the original lessee. The continuing liability of the original lessee after assignment of the lease and the possible operation of a rent review clause has been the subject of a report by the Law Commission, and may well merit consideration by Parliament. We are not concerned with that, but only with a narrower question: the continuing liability of the original lessee after the disclaimer of the lease by the liquidator of his assignee. In my judgment his liability was established by *Hill v East and West India Dock Co* (1884) 9 App Cas 448, a decision of the House of Lords which is binding on us, and the introduction of sub-s (4)(b) by the Bankruptcy Act 1883 has not affected it. Accordingly, for my part, I would dismiss this appeal.

ROSE LJ. I agree.

SIR STEPHEN BROWN P. I agree that the appeal shall be dismissed for the reasons given by Millett LJ.

Appeal dismissed. Leave to appeal to the House of Lords refused.

Carolyn Toulmin   Barrister.

R v Inner West London Coroner, ex parte Dallaglio and another

COURT OF APPEAL, CIVIL DIVISION

SIR THOMAS BINGHAM MR, FARQUHARSON AND SIMON BROWN LJJ

23, 24 MAY, 10 JUNE 1994

Coroner – Inquest – Bias – Judicial review – Adjournment of inquests into deaths of victims of river disaster pending outcome of criminal proceedings – Coroner refusing to resume inquests on conclusion of criminal proceedings – Coroner using words 'unhinged' and 'mentally unwell' to describe relatives of victims – Mothers of two victims seeking judicial review of coroner's decision – Whether coroner's decision indicating appearance of bias – Whether inquests should be resumed – Coroners Act 1988, ss 8(3), 11(5)(b), 16(3) – Coroners Rules 1984, r 36.

The deceased were two of the 51 who died following a collision between a dredger and a passenger launch in August 1989. The inquests were later adjourned on the intervention of the DPP pending the outcome of criminal proceedings against the master of the dredger. As a result of a misunderstanding, a bereaved mother, L, was denied sight of her son's body. On her subsequent unsuccessful application for an exhumation order, the coroner expressed his belief to the relevant authorities that L had been deeply affected psychologically in her grief and was by no means acting rationally. He also referred to some of the relatives and survivors as being 'mentally unwell'. L, together with another bereaved mother, D, later contacted journalists to discuss her conviction that she had been denied access to her son's body to prevent discovery of the fact that his hands had been amputated for identification purposes. Following that meeting, the journalists published an article in a popular Sunday newspaper in which they implied that there had been a cover-up. The coroner thereafter met the journalists in an attempt to persuade them to retract the implication and to set the record straight and in the course of that meeting, according to one of the journalists, the coroner described L as 'unhinged' and displayed an attitude of hostility towards her. In July 1992, after the conclusion of the criminal proceedings, the coroner wrote to the families of the 51 victims to canvass their views on any resumption of the inquests. On 22 July the coroner refused (i) to remove himself on the ground of apparent bias, as requested by a number of the bereaved families, or (ii) to resume the inquests, suggesting that only a minority of the families consulted had favoured a resumption and clearly implying that the majority wished the whole episode ended. L and D applied for judicial review of the coroner's decisions. The court refused their application and L and D appealed, contending that the use of the word 'unhinged' and the reference to the number of 'mentally unwell' relatives betrayed an attitude of some hostility, however unconscious, towards L and members of the action group so that when it came to evaluating the responses to his letter canvassing views on the resumption of the inquests, the coroner belittled the case for those seeking resumption and, doubtless unconsciously, exaggerated the numbers of those opposed. The coroner accepted that the expression 'unhinged' was unfortunate, but contended that while it was one thing to believe that the applicants had been behaving irrationally it was quite another to feel hostility

towards them. He contended, further, that the court in its discretion should
not grant relief since it would be futile to remit to a new coroner the decision
whether to resume the inquests, the scope of which would be confined, in
accordance with ss 8(3)[a] and 11(5)(b)[b] of the Coroners Act 1988 and r 36[c] of the
Coroners Rules 1984, to evidence directed solely to ascertaining the identity of
the deceased, the time and place of death and by what means the deceased
came by his death. The applicants however contended that that approach was
difficult to reconcile with the legislative policy underlying s 8(3)(d), which
made provision for wider scrutiny of the relevant facts by a jury in cases where
death occurred in circumstances, the continuance or possible recurrence of
which was 'prejudicial to the health or safety of the public'.

Held – (1) Where a decision was impugned on the ground of apparent bias the
court seised of the challenge had to consider all the evidence for itself so as to
reach its own conclusion as to whether there was a real danger, meaning a real
risk or real possibility, of injustice having occurred as a result of bias in the
sense that the decision-maker, either consciously or not, was pre-disposed or
prejudiced against one party's case for reasons unconnected with the merits of
the issue. In cases where the applicant expressly disavowed any suggestion of
actual bias, the court had necessarily to consider whether there was a real
danger that the decision-maker was unconsciously biased and, by the time the
legal challenge came to be resolved, the court was no longer concerned strictly
with the appearance of bias but rather with establishing the possibility that
there was actual although unconscious bias. The applicant accordingly had to
demonstrate not a real possibility that the coroner's decision would have been
different but for the bias, but that the real danger of bias had affected the
decision in the sense of having caused the decision-maker, albeit unconsciously, to weigh the competing contentions and so decide the merits
unfairly. On the facts, expressions used by the coroner that one of the relatives
of the disaster victims was 'unhinged' and some others were 'mentally unwell'
indicated a real possibility that he had unconsciously allowed himself to be
influenced against the applicants and other members of the action group by a
feeling of hostility towards them and that he had undervalued their case that
the inquests should be resumed (see p 151 *f* to p 152 *d*, p 153 *h j*, p 160 *b* to *e*,
p 161 *b c f*, p 162 *h* and p 163 *e f h*, post); *R v Gough* [1993] 2 All ER 724 applied.

(2) It was for the individual coroner to recognise and resolve the tension
between ss 8(3) and 11(5)(b) of the 1988 Act and r 36 of the 1984 rules. The
inquiry was bound to stretch wider than strictly required for the purposes of a
verdict and the question of how much wider was pre-eminently a matter for
the coroner whose rulings on the matter would only exceptionally be
susceptible to judicial review. In the circumstances, any fresh coroner to
whom the cases were now remitted would need, for the proper exercise of his

a   Section 8, so far as material, is set out at p 154 *f*, post
b   Section 11(5)(b), so far as material, provides: 'An inquisition ... shall set out, so far as such
    particulars have been proved—(i) who the deceased was; and (ii) how, when and where the
    deceased came by his death ...'
c   Rule 36 provides: '(1) The proceedings and evidence at an inquest shall be directed solely to
    ascertaining the following matters, namely—(a) who the deceased was ; (b) how, when and
    where the deceased came by his death; (c) the particulars for the time being required by the
    Registration Acts to be registered concerning the death.
    (2) Neither the coroner nor the jury shall express any opinion on any other matters.'

s 16(3)^d discretion, to consider what would be the proper scope of any resumed inquest and, in particular, whether a full inquest now would be a practicable proposition and whether it would satisfy any worthwhile purposes. Moreover, although there would be formidable difficulties in resuming the inquests nearly five years after the disaster and although no one could pretend that such a proceeding would be a satisfactory alternative to the public inquiry so long denied the applicants, it was not necessarily the case that a fresh coroner would be bound to refuse a resumption. Indeed, the decision to be made under s 16(3) was of a highly discretionary character and in no way circumscribed by a need to find exceptional circumstances, only 'sufficient cause'. The coroner's decisions would therefore be quashed and the matter remitted to a coroner for a different district for a fresh decision to be taken under s 16(3) on whether to resume the adjourned inquests. The appeal would accordingly be allowed (see p 154 *j* to p 155 *f*, p 156 *b*, p 161 *d* to *f* and p 163 *j* to p 164 *a e* to *j*, post); *R v North Humberside and Scunthorpe Coroner, ex p Jamieson* [1994] 3 All ER 972 considered.

Notes

For adjournment of inquest when criminal charges are made before the verdict, see 9 *Halsbury's Laws* (4th edn) para 1114.

For the Coroners Act 1988, ss 8, 11, 16, see 11 *Halsbury's Statutes* (4th edn) (1991 reissue) 559, 564, 569.

For the Coroners Rules 1984, r 36, see 5 *Halsbury's Statutory Instruments* (1994 reissue) 367.

Cases referred to in judgments

Associated Provincial Picture Houses Ltd v Wednesbury Corp [1947] 2 All ER 680, [1948] 1 KB 223, CA.

R v Chief Constable of the Thames Valley Police, ex p Cotton [1990] IRLR 344, CA.

R v Crown Court at Bristol, ex p Cooper [1990] 2 All ER 193, CA.

R v Gough [1993] 2 All ER 724, [1993] AC 646, [1993] 2 WLR 883, HL.

R v HM Coroner for Western District of East Sussex, ex p Homberg (1994) 158 JP 357, DC.

R v North Humberside and Scunthorpe Coroner, ex p Jamieson [1994] 3 All ER 972, [1994] 3 WLR 82, CA.

R v Sussex Justices, ex p McCarthy [1924] 1 KB 256, [1923] All ER Rep 233, CA.

Appeal

The applicants, Eileen Dallaglio and Margaret Lockwood-Croft, the mothers of Francesca Dallaglio and Shaun Lockwood-Croft (who had both drowned on 20 August 1989 following the collision of the dredger MV Bowbelle with the passenger launch MV Marchioness), appealed from the decision of the Divisional Court (Neill LJ and Mantell J) made on 17 July 1993 dismissing their application for judicial review of the decisions of HM Coroner for Inner West London made on 22 July 1992 refusing (i) to remove himself as coroner on the ground of apparent bias and (ii) to resume the inquests into the deaths of Francesca Dallaglio and Shaun Lockwood-Croft. The facts are set out in the judgment of Simon Brown LJ.

---

d   Section 16, so far as material, is set out at p 142 *j*, post

Jeremy Sullivan QC and *Paul Stinchcombe* (instructed by *Colin Wilson*) for the coroner.
Daniel Brennan QC (instructed by *Pannone Napier*, Sheffield) for Mrs Dallaglio.
Daniel Brennan QC and Terry Munyard (instructed by *Christian Fisher & Co*) for Mrs Lockwood-Croft.

Cur adv vult

10 June 1994. The following judgments were delivered.

SIMON BROWN LJ (giving the first judgment at the invitation of Sir Thomas Bingham MR). Shortly before 2 am on Sunday, 20 August 1989, tragedy struck on the River Thames. Although it was a fine moonlit night, two vessels collided near Southwark Bridge. One was a dredger, the MV Bowbelle; the other a passenger launch, the MV Marchioness. The Marchioness had been chartered for a night-time pleasure cruise with a disco and bar on board. It was a birthday celebration with 127 passengers and a crew of 4. Following the collision the Marchioness sank very quickly. 51 were drowned, 80 survived. The majority of those who died were young, aged between 18 and 30. Twenty-four bodies were found in the wreck, a further 27 were recovered from the river during the course of the following week. Two of those recovered from the river were Francesca Dallaglio, aged 19, and Shaun Lockwood-Croft, aged 26, respectively the first applicant's daughter and the second applicant's son.

All 51 bodies were taken to Westminster mortuary, within the jurisdiction of HM Coroner for Inner West London. Accordingly, it fell to that coroner, Dr Paul Knapman, to hold inquests into their deaths: see s 8 of the Coroners Act 1988. These inquests he formally opened and adjourned in the weeks immediately following the disaster. In February 1990 he indicated that he would commence the inquest hearings on 23 April 1990, taking them in two parts: in part one he would hear the forensic and identification evidence relating to the issues of who died, when and from what cause; in part two, the eye witnesses and technical evidence in relation to the remaining issue of how the deceased came by their deaths.

When the hearing began on 23 April, the relatives of seven of the deceased, including Mrs Dallaglio, objected to a two-stage inquest so that in the event the coroner heard only 44 part-one inquests. Then, on 26 April, as had been fore-warned, the Director of Public Prosecutions intervened: Captain Henderson, the master of the Bowbelle, had been charged under s 27(4)(b) of the Merchant Shipping Act 1970. The inquests had to be adjourned pursuant to s 16(1)(b) of the 1988 Act and r 27 of the Coroners Rules 1984, SI 1984/522.

As will appear, there followed over the next two and a quarter years two sets of criminal proceedings and two investigations, although not—this was a decision apparently taken by the then Prime Minister—a public inquiry. By late June 1992, however, all criminal proceedings had been concluded and the coroner had to decide whether to resume the inquest under the provisions of s 16(3) of the 1988 Act:

'After the conclusion of the relevant criminal proceedings ... the coroner may ... resume the adjourned inquest if in his opinion there is sufficient cause to do so.'

On 22 July 1992, in circumstances and for reasons to which I shall have to return, the coroner announced his decision not to do so. That, crucially, is the decision sought to be impugned in the present judicial review proceedings.

Its consequence, say the applicants, is that, uniquely amongst modern tragedies involving extensive loss of life, the Marchioness disaster will have been the subject of neither a public inquiry nor a full inquest. Most of the other disasters, it appears, have been the subject of both. Although, however, the applicants (and indeed other applicants too until their funds ran out) sought to include *Wednesbury* unreasonableness amongst their proposed grounds of challenge to the coroner's decision, leave was granted on one ground only, that of apparent bias, and it is solely upon that issue that the case has been contested (see *Associated Provincial Picture Houses Ltd v Wednesbury Corp* [1947] 2 All ER 680, [1948] 1 KB 223).

On 17 July 1993 the Divisional Court (Neill LJ and Mantell J) dismissed the motion. The applicants now appeal to this court.

With that short introduction let me return to the facts, first to indicate in broad outline what, apart from the inquest, has been happening over recent years, and then to set out in necessarily greater detail the circumstances in which the apparent bias challenge arises.

Broad outline

The first trial of Captain Henderson took place in April 1991 (a year after the inquest had been halted on the DPP's intervention). The jury was unable to agree. Captain Henderson was retried in July 1991 but again the jury disagreed. In the usual way the prosecution then decided to proceed no further and a not guilty verdict was entered. In neither trial did Captain Henderson give evidence.

Meanwhile an investigation into the collision had been carried out by inspectors from the Marine Accident Investigation Branch (MAIB) of the Department of Transport. That had begun almost immediately after the collision and a full report had been sent to the Secretary of State for Transport in June 1990. On 15 August 1991, following the conclusion of proceedings against Captain Henderson, it was published. That report, although specifically addressed to the collision, by no means satisfied the Marchioness Action Group. They, from the outset, had been pressing for a full public inquiry. The group commissioned a critique of the MAIB report and, at a meeting with the Secretary of State for Transport on 22 October 1991, explained their misgivings. As a result, on 20 December 1991, he asked Mr John Hayes, the Secretary General of the Law Society, to conduct a further inquiry with the following terms of reference:

'In the light of the Marchioness/Bowbelle disaster to examine the handling since 1980 by the Department of Transport of its responsibility for the safety of vessels on rivers and inland waters and to report on the effectiveness of the present approach. The inquiry should take account of developments in the field of marine safety at the international level.'

The Hayes Report, entitled *Report of the Inquiry into River Safety* (Cm 1991), was published on 7 July 1992. Amongst its important recommendations was this:

'2.5.8 There should be an early review of the rescue arrangements and equipment on the Thames which should take account of the Marchioness/ Bowbelle disaster and the views of those who witnessed it. The results should be published and it should be undertaken by an independent person. The recommendations from such a review should be disseminated widely and considered as a basis for action by Riparian and Canal Authorities. It will need to be wider in scope than the present POLACAP emergency plan.'

A press release issued by the Department of Transport on the date of publication of the Hayes Report included this passage:

'Mr Hayes recommended that there should be an early review of the rescue arrangements and equipment on the Thames. The Government has given careful consideration to the recommendation but has concluded that a further review of this kind would not be justified. Action is, however, being taken to ensure that the lessons from the Marchioness/ Bowbelle disaster have been fully assimilated. In addition, Thames rescue arrangements and equipment will also be examined by the relevant District Marine Safety Committee as part of its wider review.'

Meanwhile, a private prosecution had been instituted by a bereaved relative, Mr Ivor Glogg, against the company owning the Bowbelle and four of its directors. A preliminary hearing of these proceedings took place at Bow Street Magistrates' Court on 19 August 1991. A charge of corporate manslaughter was included. The proceedings were finally concluded on 24 June 1992 when the charges against the company and the directors were dismissed by the chief stipendiary magistrate. It was these proceedings which had necessitated the continuing adjournment of the inquests after Captain Henderson's discharge. Upon their conclusion the coroner was at last able to take his decision under s 16(3) of the 1988 Act.

Apparent bias: the facts

As I shall come to explain, two central facts lie at the heart of the applicants' complaint of apparent bias. One is that at a meeting with two journalists on 24 March 1992 the coroner described Mrs Lockwood-Croft as 'unhinged'. The second is that, when on 22 July 1992 he came to give his reasons for refusing to resume the inquests, he gave the clear impression that a substantial majority of the relatives of the deceased were opposed to such a resumption, whereas that was not in fact the case. Marrying these two together, the applicants, as members of the group passionately wanting a full inquest into the deaths of their loved ones, contend that when it came to weighing their wishes against the wishes of those who wanted the matter closed, the coroner regarded them as troublesome and unreasonable and unfairly gave their views short measure.

Given that this court must now form its own view upon the possibility of bias on the coroner's part and must to that end consider the context in which his comments came to be made, it is necessary to examine the facts in some detail, particularly with regard to the coroner's dealing with Mrs Lockwood-Croft. Let me take matters chronologically.

The coroner's first meeting with Mrs Lockwood-Croft was on 25 April 1990 during the part-one inquest hearing. She had been desperately anxious to see her son's body once it was recovered from the river but was prevented from doing so, first by a police officer acting as coroner's officer whilst the body lay in the mortuary, then by an undertaker upon the body's release. Each had claimed to be acting on the coroner's instructions. The coroner invited Mrs Lockwood-Croft and her solicitor into his private room, explained that he had given no such instructions, and apologised for what had happened. What almost certainly happened is that the coroner's officer and undertaker, anxious to spare Mrs Lockwood-Croft the distress of viewing her son's body in its putrefied state, had lied about their instructions. Their efforts were misguided although well-intentioned.

Shaun's body having been buried without Mrs Lockwood-Croft seeing it, she began to have nightmares and developed a fixation that the body in the grave was not his. She accordingly applied for an exhumation order, first to the Home Office, then to the coroner of the district where the body lay, then to the chancellor of the diocese of Guildford. In writing to the latter's registrar on 22 May 1991, the coroner spoke of his belief 'that Mrs [Lockwood-Croft] has been deeply psychologically affected in her grief and is by no means acting rationally', explained how she had been wrongly prevented from seeing the body and continued:

> 'In deciding whether to allow exhumation it might be tempting to allow this to proceed. My misgivings are that Mrs [Lockwood-Croft] is totally obsessed by this aspect of the death. There are a number of mentally unwell relatives and survivors who mutually support each other ... that said, I may say "the legal system" has resulted in them being treated rather uncaringly, in as much as that now, nearly two years after the event, the report (a reference to the MAIB Report) on how it occurred has still not been published!'

Exhumation was finally refused in late 1992.

On 21 August 1991 the coroner wrote to the families of each of the deceased, inviting their views upon a future resumption of the inquest. He suggested that after a trial it was 'very unusual to resume an inquest' but that 'one of the factors which I may legitimately bear in mind is the views of the relatives'. He then continued:

> 'There is the risk of the whole matter deteriorating into an unseemly squabble. There are those who vociferously clamour for "a public inquiry"; there are those who have come to terms with their grief, yet to whom each new headline is a painful reminder ...'

The letter ended thus:

> 'I think it best if you made up your mind in the tranquillity of your own home. There is the danger of one faction or another applying pressure and seeking to persuade you to their point of view. Perhaps you could write to me indicating your views. I rather think that those in favour of resuming the inquest will certainly make their views known, but it would be nice for those with no strong feelings to write also.'

During early 1992, in the course of her extensive efforts to secure an exhumation order, Mrs Lockwood-Croft wrote a number of letters seeking information from various sources. It appears to have been during this period that she first learned of one distressing feature of this case: her son's hands, in common with those of 25 of the 27 bodies recovered from the river, had been surgically removed so that fingerprints could be obtained before they deteriorated further. In answering her many questions, the coroner explained that this had been done to assist the identification process and because of the impossibility of taking fingerprints in the normal manner. His letter of 17 February 1992 concluded:

> 'Whereas many relatives have been most appreciative of our efforts and have kindly said so, it is a matter of disappointment to myself and my Coroners' Officers that others have directed their energies to continued criticism without regard to the difficult and stressful circumstances.'

I come next to a most regrettable incident: the publication on 22 March 1992 in the *Mail on Sunday* of an article under the bold headline 'COVER-UP!' Understandably distressed about the removal of her son's hands, and still deeply upset at not having seen his body before burial, Mrs Lockwood-Croft became convinced that the one explained the other: that the coroner had denied her access to her son's body to prevent her discovering that his hands had been amputated. She got in touch with Mrs Dallaglio and together they decided to contact the press. A meeting was arranged with the *Mail on Sunday* at a Kensington hotel where they spoke to two representatives of that newspaper, Ms Reid, the associate editor, and Ms Allen, a journalist. Two days before publication the coroner was contacted and gave his detailed explanations as to what had occurred. These, however, were substantially ignored. The article referred to Mrs Lockwood-Croft's distress at not being able to see her son's body and of her discovery that his hands had been removed and continued:

> 'So what went wrong? Why was Margaret, through police obstinacy or ignorance, never allowed to pay her last respects to Shaun? She has fought a long lone battle to discover the truth. After a series of letters and telephone calls to Coroner Dr Paul Knapman it was only a month ago that he first confessed that both of Shaun's hands had been removed during the postmortem ... What is so alarming about the Marchioness affair is that so many bodies were mutilated and so many families kept in the dark. Today the Marchioness families will only discover the truth thanks to Margaret Lockwood-Croft.'

The article concluded:

> 'Today Margaret still cannot mourn properly. "I have been told half truths for nearly three years now", she said. "There should be a proper inquiry. Only then will I, and all the mothers like me, ever lay our children truly to rest."'

The coroner read the article and was much concerned by its contents. Through the editor he arranged to see Ms Reid and Ms Allen and on 24 March 1992 they came to his office. 'The purpose of the meeting', the coroner has deposed, 'was to seek to persuade them voluntarily to retract the implication of a cover-up, and to attempt to get them to set the record straight in order to placate the understandable concerns of the other relatives who were already ringing up, wishing to know if the hands had been severed from their children and, if so, why'.

The meeting lasted about an hour. Ms Reid's sworn account of it includes this:

> 'He said that he did not consider that it was responsible journalism for us to run a story based on what Margaret Lockwood-Croft has said, "Because surely you realise that she is unhinged". I particularly recall his use of the word "unhinged" as it is offensive and not an everyday word or a word that I would normally use. It was clear to me that Dr Knapman did not regard Mrs Lockwood-Croft as a serious and bona fide complainant. He appeared to dismiss everything that she had said because of her state of mind.'

Whilst he does not recall using the word 'unhinged' to describe Mrs Lockwood-Croft, the coroner says that it would be 'an accurate lay description' of the view he had formed of her psychological state of mind. It was, he says, 'an objective judgment of the medical condition of a person who has suffered a tragic and traumatic loss', someone suffering from what he, a registered medical practitioner who over the years has dealt as coroner with the deaths of some 50,000 people, feels qualified to diagnose as abnormal grief reaction or post-traumatic stress disorder. He has, he says, the greatest sympathy for Mrs Lockwood-Croft and in no way was his description of her meant to be disparaging. But that was not, it is right to say, Ms Reid's impression. She says that the coroner 'showed no sympathy for Mrs Lockwood-Croft or what she had been through and his whole attitude towards her was one of hostility'.

Although there is much that could be said about the rights and wrongs of the *Mail on Sunday* article and what seems to me the ill-judged if not positively mischievous role played in this affair by the journalists, it is, I think, sufficient for present purposes to note just the following. First, that the newspaper refused to publish any sort of retraction or correction. Secondly, that the coroner's complaint to the Press Complaints Commission was, on 7 August 1992, upheld to the extent that the newspaper was criticised for suggesting a cover-up and for not having published the coroner's explanation of how police officers and undertakers had misinterpreted or falsified his instructions in their attempts to save the families the distress of seeing decomposed bodies. Thirdly, that there seems no good reason to doubt that the photographs of Shaun Lockwood-Croft's naked body lying on the table before the two journalists at the meeting on 24 March, were placed there, not, as they thought, simply to shock them, but rather, as the coroner has deposed, so that they could form their own view as to whether it was not in truth a kindness to have spared the families the sight of the bodies recovered from the river. Not long after the disaster, Mrs Lockwood-Croft had at her own request been shown these photographs; the coroner disputed her description, with which the newspaper article opened, that they showed 'his body was almost perfect physically'. Fourthly, the vice of the article lay not merely in its false assertion of a cover-up but in its needless revelation to other families that many of the deceased's hands had been removed, coupled with the suggestion that this may well have been unnecessary. Inevitably this must have occasioned distress to many relatives and to what purpose? No doubt identification procedures involving the use of amputated hands, as to the need for which there appear to be two schools of thought, should be reviewed. But such an article was hardly the best way to achieve that.

On 25 March 1992, the day after his meeting with the *Mail on Sunday* journalists, the coroner wrote to Mr Storr at the Home Office to explain what had arisen with regard to Mrs Lockwood-Croft. The letter concluded:

'In summary I believe Mrs [Lockwood-Croft] is not acting in a rational manner by reason of her unresolved grief. She is one of the prime movers in the Marchioness Action Group who regularly hold press conferences for the media who are always ready to listen. They are very angry people. However it will be noticed that it is the same few people, many of whom are survivors, who purport to represent all relatives. I am concerned about the relatives of all the 51 people who died, most of whom have put the memory of the disaster behind them and have rebuilt their lives, and to whom each upsurge of media interest is distressing. I may say the main thrust of criticism from the action group is that there has been no Public Enquiry, and that now, two and a half years after the disaster, I have still been prevented from holding a full inquest by operation of the law. They feel "Authority" has let them down, and quite frankly I agree with them.'

I pass on some three months to 3 July 1992. By then, it will be recalled, the various criminal proceedings had finally been brought to a close by the dismissal of the corporate manslaughter prosecution. The coroner accordingly had to reach a decision under s 16(3) of the 1988 Act. On 3 July 1992 he again wrote to all the bereaved families to canvass their views upon the question whether or not to resume the inquests. Having briefly summarised the history, the letter continued:

'Before I decide whether, after all this time, it is advisable to resume the inquests (and this cannot be done before the autumn) I would like to know the feelings of relatives. I would be less than honest if I did not convey some misgivings. An inquest cannot result in the apportionment of blame, still less censure or prosecution. It must only consider "How" the deceased came by their death and this merely means "by what means", not "in what broad circumstances". Many may take the view this has been answered already. Some relatives have come to terms with their grief and each item of media interest merely serves to heighten their distress. Some relatives channel a great deal of their energies into Action Groups. The criticism has been voiced to me that certain people are giving the appearance of speaking for everybody when this is not so. The decision is one for me, and I must remind you that an inquest is conducted by the Coroner on behalf of the Crown. Nevertheless I shall bear in mind the views of all interested parties and I would be grateful if you or your solicitor would write to me before 18th July indicating your views. In any event I will hear legal submissions on Wednesday 22nd July 1992, at 10.00 am in open Court.'

On 9 July 1992, while still awaiting replies to that letter, the coroner provisionally booked a large hall in Westminster for a full inquest hearing to take place in November.

I come finally to 22 July 1992, the date of the decisions under challenge. I say 'decisions' because there are in fact three. There is first the coroner's refusal to recuse himself on grounds of apparent bias as he was asked to do at the start of the hearing by counsel for a number of the bereaved families; secondly, his decision not to resume the inquest into the death of Francesca Dallaglio (one of those for whom no part-one inquest had been heard); thirdly, his decision not to resume the inquest into Shaun Lockwood-Croft's death for the purpose of a part-two hearing. Such an approach, however, seems to me unnecessarily to complicate the case. The coroner could not have resumed the inquest merely to complete the part-one hearings: any resumption would have required him by law to complete the inquest hearings in full. And that, indeed, had been explained to counsel for the seven families in April 1990 when they had elected not to embark on part-one hearings and been repeatedly alerted to the potential consequences of that decision. Nothing, moreover, would be gained by separate consideration of the coroner's refusal to recuse himself. The ground of apparent bias is either made out or not. If it is, then clearly the coroner should have recused himself; if not, then he had no need to. Nor need I do more than note that upon the application that he recuse himself the coroner sat and deliberated together with his deputy.

Having refused to recuse himself the coroner then considered whether or not to resume the inquests. After hearing submissions he decided not do so. He stated his reasons in these terms:

> 'The Marchioness sank on 20th August 1989. Inquests into all persons who died were opened within a few days and a joint inquest for all except those who requested adjournment was held from 23rd to 26th April 1990 when evidence of 104 witnesses was heard. This was adjourned at the request of the Director of Public Prosecutions because criminal proceedings were to take place, and has had to remain adjourned since, by operation of law.
>
> Subsequently the Captain of the Bowbelle has had a trial by jury on two occasions ending with a verdict of not guilty being entered. Attempts to commit certain directors to trial for manslaughter have recently failed. The MAIB report upon the reasons for the Marchioness Disaster was published in August 1991. Publication of a report into River Safety (the Hayes Enquiry) has recently been published.
>
> I have invited views of relatives and other parties in writing and have heard submissions in open Court. It appears considerably less than half advocate a resumption with nothing approaching a consensus view upon the scope desired. Indeed it would require at least three separate types of inquest to attempt to satisfy the disparate views of this minority. In any event some of the questions raised fall outside the province of a Coroner's jury. The wishes of this minority are only one factor, for I must consider the views of those relatives who wish the whole episode ended, and other factors, such as certain witnesses [who] have given evidence in four different courts thus far. Moreover I must consider whether public interest would be served by a resumption.
>
> Statute dictates that I should only resume the inquest after a criminal trial "if there is sufficient cause to do so". If the inquest was resumed it would be necessary to start all over again, at the earliest more than three years after the incident, and after a previous inquest, two trials, one unsuccessful committal and two reports.
>
> Although I realise the decision will not be universally popular I do not consider there are sufficient reasons to embark upon the wholly exceptional course of resuming the inquest.'

It is to the third paragraph of those reasons that particular criticism has been directed, in particular the suggestion that only a minority of the bereaved families consulted favoured a resumption, the clear inference being that the majority 'wish[ed] the whole episode ended'. That that was indeed the implication, or at least well capable of being so understood, is perhaps best illustrated by reference to the coroner's own counsel's skeleton argument submitted to the Divisional Court before the underlying facts had come to light. Basing his written submissions on the coroner's stated reasons, Mr Sullivan QC referred to 'the overwhelming majority of relatives who do not wish to have those inquests resumed'.

When this was challenged by the applicants and the responses to the coroner's letter of 3 July 1992 were produced, it emerged that 16 families (including the family of two of the deceased) were opposed to a resumption; 19 favoured it; and the remaining 15 expressed no views, indeed, for the most part, were abroad and had not replied.

So much for the facts, although I should perhaps note that even that quite lengthy summary is but the tip of an iceberg of material put before the court.

Apparent bias: the law

The test to be applied when a decision is impugned on grounds of apparent bias is now authoritatively established by the House of Lords decision in *R v Gough* [1993] 2 All ER 724, [1993] AC 646. The House was there concerned to resolve a pre-existing conflict on the authorities, some of which favoured a test of whether there was a real danger of bias by the decision-maker, others a test of whether a reasonable person might reasonably suspect bias on the decision-maker's part. *R v Gough* has resolved this conflict in favour of the more stringent test, that of a real danger of bias.

The central passages in Lord Goff's speech are these:

'... bias is such an insidious thing that, even though a person may in good faith believe that he was acting impartially, his mind may unconsciously be affected by bias ... the approach of the law has been ... to look at the relevant circumstances and to consider whether there is such a degree of possibility of bias that the decision in question should not be allowed to stand ... it is not necessary that actual bias should be proved; and in practice the inquiry is directed to the question whether there was such a degree of possibility of bias on the part of the tribunal that the court will not allow the decision to stand ... Since ... the court investigates the actual circumstances, knowledge of such circumstances as are found by the court must be imputed to the reasonable man ... if, in the circumstances of the case (as ascertained by the court), it appears that there was a real likelihood, in the sense of a real possibility, of bias ... justice requires that the decision should not be allowed to stand.' (See [1993] 2 All ER 724 at 728, 730, 735, [1993] AC 646 at 659–660, 661, 667–668.)

In conclusion Lord Goff said:

'... I think it unnecessary, in formulating the appropriate test, to require that the court should look at the matter through the eyes of a reasonable man, because the court in cases such as these personifies the reasonable man; and in any event the court has first to ascertain the relevant circumstances from the available evidence, knowledge of which would not necessarily be available to an observer in court at the relevant time. Finally,.for the avoidance of doubt, I prefer to state the test in terms of real danger rather than real likelihood, to ensure that the court is thinking in terms of possibility rather than probability of bias. Accordingly, having ascertained the relevant circumstances, the court should ask itself whether, having regard to those circumstances, there was a real danger of bias on the part of the relevant member of the tribunal in question, in the sense that he might unfairly regard (or have unfairly regarded) with favour, or disfavour, the case of a party to the issue under consideration by him ...' (See [1993] 2 All ER 724 at 737–738, [1993] AC 646 at 670.)

Lord Woolf said:

'... I agree that the correct test to adopt in deciding whether a decision should be set aside on the grounds of alleged bias is that given by Lord Goff, namely whether there is a real danger of injustice having occurred as a result of the alleged bias ... the courts have long recognised that bias operates in such an insidious manner that the person alleged to be biased may be quite unconscious of its effect ... When considering whether there is a real danger of injustice, the court gives effect to the maxim [that justice must not only be done but be seen to be done], but does so by examining all the material available and giving its conclusion on that material. If the court having done so is satisfied there is no danger of the alleged bias having created injustice, then the application to quash the decision should be dismissed.' (See [1993] 2 All ER 724 at 738, 740, [1993] AC 646 at 671, 672, 673.)

From *R v Gough* I derive the following propositions:

(1) Any court seised of a challenge on the ground of apparent bias must ascertain the relevant circumstances and consider all the evidence for itself so as to reach its own conclusion on the facts.

(2) It necessarily follows that the factual position may appear quite differently as between the time when the challenge is launched and the time when it comes to be decided by the court. What may appear at the leave stage to be a strong case of 'justice [not] manifestly and undoubtedly be[ing] seen to be done', may, following the court's investigation, nevertheless fail. Or, of course, although perhaps less probably, the case may have become stronger.

(3) In reaching its conclusion the court 'personifies the reasonable man'.

(4) The question upon which the court must reach its own factual conclusion is this: is there a real danger of injustice having occurred as a result of bias? By 'real' is meant not without substance. A real danger clearly involves more than a minimal risk, less than a probability. One could, I think, as well speak of a real risk or a real possibility.

(5) Injustice will have occurred as a result of bias if 'the decision-maker unfairly regarded with disfavour the case of a party to the issue under consideration by him'. I take 'unfairly regarded with disfavour' to mean 'was pre-disposed or prejudiced against one party's case for reasons unconnected with the merits of the issue'.

(6) A decision-maker may have unfairly regarded with disfavour one party's case either consciously or unconsciously. Where, as here, the applicants expressly disavow any suggestion of actual bias, it seems to me that the court

must necessarily be asking itself whether there is a real danger that the decision-maker was unconsciously biased.

(7) It will be seen, therefore, that by the time the legal challenge comes to be resolved, the court is no longer concerned strictly with the appearance of bias but rather with establishing the possibility that there was actual although unconscious bias.

(8) In the circumstances of the present case the court must therefore ask itself: is there a real danger that the coroner unfairly (though unconsciously) regarded with disfavour the case of those seeking a resumption of the inquest? Or: is there a real danger that the coroner was unconsciously prejudiced against this group? Or, as Neill LJ put it in the Divisional Court:

'... is there a real danger that in deciding ... not to resume the inquests Dr Knapman was influenced, consciously or unconsciously, to a material degree by his views ... about the Marchioness action group?'

(9) It is not necessary for the applicants to demonstrate a real possibility that the coroner's decision would have been different but for bias; what must be established is the real danger of bias having affected the decision in the sense of having caused the decision-maker, albeit unconsciously, to weigh the competing contentions, and so decide the merits, unfairly.

Apparent bias: arguments

I have already touched on the applicants' argument in these proceedings. The use of the word 'unhinged' was, they submit, clearly offensive and insulting. Although directed specifically towards Mrs Lockwood-Croft, Mrs Dallaglio shares precisely the same distress at what has happened and so feels similarly insulted. Amongst the synonyms for 'unhinged' suggested by *Roget's Thesaurus* are 'barmy' and 'deranged'. Such language, counsel submits, betrays an attitude of mind towards Mrs Lockwood-Croft of some hostility, however unconscious. And this appears to have extended equally to the other members of the action group: note the reference in the coroner's May 1991 letter to 'a number of mentally unwell relatives', the implicit aversion towards those 'who vociferously clamour for a public enquiry', the 'faction' who may seek to pressurise others to their point of view (letter of August 1991), the 'very angry people ... who purport to represent all relatives' (letter of March 1992) and who 'are giving the appearance of speaking for everybody when this is not so' (letter of July 1992).

Small wonder, therefore, submit the applicants' counsel, that when it came to evaluating the responses to his circular letter of 3 July 1992, the coroner belittled the case for those seeking a resumption of the inquest and, although no doubt unconsciously, exaggerated the numbers of those opposed.

Mr Sullivan for the coroner argues the contrary. He accepts, rightly in my judgment, that the expression 'unhinged' was most unfortunate. He points out, however, that the fact that grief causes some people to become mentally unbalanced does not mean that those who recognise and mention this are on that account to be regarded as prejudiced against them. It is one thing to believe the applicants to have been behaving irrationally; quite another to feel hostility towards them. On the contrary, Mr Sullivan submits, the letters primarily relied upon by the applicants may be seen to contain expressions of sympathy: the coroner regards them as having been 'treated rather uncaringly' (letter of May 1991) and the very day after describing Mrs Lockwood-Croft as 'unhinged', he wrote: 'They [the action group] feel "Authority" has let them down and quite frankly I agree with them'.

As to the coroner's reference to the numbers of those respectively seeking and opposing resumption of the inquest, Mr Sullivan submits that read literally there is nothing inaccurate in the stated reasons for the decision and that in any event it was for those wanting a resumption—which the coroner stated would be 'very unusual' after criminal proceedings—to make good their case for it; the coroner was entitled, counsel appears to suggest, to treat those expressing no view as being against a resumption.   That seems to me a difficult submission.

There is one other of Mr Sullivan's arguments on the issue of apparent bias which I should deal with.   Bereaved parents at an inquest, he submits, are hardly to be equated with 'a party to the issue under consideration' within Lord Goff's formulation: an inquest is rather an inquisitorial process charged with establishing certain specified facts.   The state of mind of relatives or, indeed, the coroner's attitude towards them, is simply irrelevant to that process.   That, of course, in one sense is true.   But it seems to me that the question of apparent bias here arises not in connection with the conduct of an inquest, but rather with the anterior question whether the inquest should be resumed or not, whether, in short, there should be an inquest at all.   The relatives are clearly interested parties with regard to that issue and, indeed, as Mr Sullivan accepts, by seeking their views upon it, the coroner implicitly recognised these to be a relevant consideration for the purposes of reaching his decision.   He may well not have been obliged to consult the families, but having done so he was clearly bound to deal fairly and judicially with their views.

Apparent bias: conclusions

I have found this a difficult case and, indeed, my views have wavered during the course of the hearing.

Mr Sullivan's arguments are undoubtedly powerful ones and if it were necessary for the applicants to establish as a probability that the coroner was biased against them in reaching his decision whether or not to resume the inquests, in my judgment they would clearly fail in the attempt.   As it is, however, all that the applicants need show is in the first instance an appearance of bias and then on an examination of all the facts a real possibility that the coroner may unconsciously have felt resentful towards them in such a way as to have influenced his approach to their case for a resumption.

For a judicial officer to say publicly of someone that they are unreliable because 'unhinged' shows, I have no doubt, an appearance of bias: such a description is not merely injudicious and insensitive but bound to be interpreted as a gratuitous insult.   I say 'publicly' because, given the manner in which the two journalists had handled the original story, there was little doubt that they would broadcast anything else they felt might discredit the coroner.   As to the crucial second limb, I find myself in the last analysis unable to discount the real possibility that the coroner unconsciously allowed himself to be influenced against the applicants and the other members of the action group by a feeling of hostility towards them.   There remains to my mind not a probability but a not insubstantial possibility that he thought them trouble-makers and in the result unfairly undervalued their case for a resumption.

Discretion

That conclusion, however, is not necessarily decisive of this challenge. Mr
Sullivan submits that it would be futile now to remit to a fresh coroner the
decision whether or not to resume this inquest and accordingly that the court
in its discretion should refuse to do so. The reasons why he submits it would
be futile are essentially these. First, that the various difficulties of resumption
referred to by the coroner when making his decision in July 1992 have now
inevitably become more acute still by the passage of a further two years: some
witnesses are abroad, some dead, the recollection of all must have faded.
Secondly, that those most actively concerned to secure a full inquest clearly
hope to achieve by it far more than it could possibly deliver. Even discounting
entirely their original hope that an inquest would 'examine the identification
procedures used on the deceased and get to the bottom of the decision to
remove the hands from many of the bodies'—a wish expressed in Mrs
Lockwood-Croft's affidavit but one which everybody now concedes could not
possibly be satisfied by an inquest—there will nevertheless remain efforts to
expand the scope of the inquest well beyond its proper limits. The action
group has, after all, campaigned throughout for a public inquiry. That refused,
the group would seek to turn any fresh inquest into one.

To some extent, as the arguments before us acknowledge, the strength of
this submission depends in part upon the view taken as to the true scope of an
inquest inquiry. Is this to be confined, as Mr Sullivan submits, to evidence
directed solely to ascertaining 'by what means' the deceased came by his death,
solely, that is, once the identity of the deceased and the date and locality of
death are established? That, certainly, appears at first blush to be the approach
now dictated by *R v North Humberside and Scunthorpe Coroner, ex p Jamieson*
[1994] 3 All ER 972, [1994] 3 WLR 82. And yet, as Mr Brennan QC contends,
such an approach is difficult to reconcile with the legislative policy apparently
underlying s 8(3)(d) of the 1988 Act, namely the requirement:

> 'If it appears to a coroner ... that there is reason to suspect ... (d) that the
> death occurred in circumstances the continuance or possible recurrence of
> which is prejudicial to the health or safety of the public or any section of
> the public, he shall proceed to summon a jury ...'

As Morland J suggested in *R v HM Coroner for Western District of East Sussex,
ex p Homberg* (1994) 158 JP 357 at 381:

> '... r 36 should not be so interpreted as to defeat the purpose of section
> 8(3)(d) ... If "the proceedings and evidence" are narrowly confined, the
> answers to the "how" question will not serve the purpose of the section,
> the prevention or reduction of the risk of future injuries in similar
> circumstances.'

It is early days to be revisiting the ground so fully covered in *Jamieson* and I
for my part think it unnecessary for present purposes to say more than this:
that in any s 8(3) case the coroner should have particularly in mind what the
court said in para 14 of its conclusions in *R v North Humberside and Scunthorpe
Coroner, ex p Jamieson* [1994] 3 All ER 972 at 991, [1994] 3 WLR 82 at 101:

> 'It is the duty of the coroner as the public official responsible for the
> conduct of inquests, whether he is sitting with a jury or without, to ensure
> that the relevant facts are fully, fairly and fearlessly investigated. He is

bound to recognise the acute public concern rightly aroused where deaths occur in custody. He must ensure that the relevant facts are exposed to public scrutiny, particularly if there is evidence of foul play, abuse or inhumanity. He fails in his duty if his investigation is superficial, slipshod or perfunctory. But the responsibility is his. He must set the bounds of the inquiry.'

That, of course, was a s 8(3)(a) case, but its adaptability to a s 8(3)(d) context is obvious. It is, in short, for the individual coroner to recognise and resolve the tension existing between ss 8(3) and 11(5)(b) of the 1988 Act and r 36. The inquiry is almost bound to stretch wider than strictly required for the purposes of a verdict. How much wider is pre-eminently a matter for the coroner whose rulings upon the question will only exceptionally be susceptible to judicial review.

Applying that approach to the present circumstances, it seems to me that any fresh coroner to whom this case were now remitted would need, for the proper exercise of his s 16(3) discretion, to consider first what would be the proper scope of any resumed inquest. Whether or not his views about that would satisfy the action group may be doubted. But the better questions are surely these: would a full inquest now be a practicable proposition and would it satisfy any worthwhile purposes?

Although there must inevitably be formidable difficulties in resuming these inquests now, nearly five years after the disaster, and although no one could pretend that such a proceeding would be a satisfactory alternative to the public inquiry so long denied these applicants, I for my part am not prepared to say that a fresh coroner would be bound to refuse a resumption. The decision to be made under s 16(3) is of a highly discretionary character and in no way circumscribed by a need to find exceptional circumstances, only 'sufficient cause'. The coroner states that 'only rarely' are inquests resumed after criminal proceedings but, of course, the section itself expressly envisages, rather than discourages, such a course.

Given that many of the survivors and eye witnesses have still to give their full evidence, and none of the rescue services and those who engaged them; indeed that despite the plethora of other proceedings, some only of the potential witnesses have yet given full evidence and that for the most part directed to issues other than would properly arise at an inquest hearing, it might perhaps still be worth holding one. Many, indeed, were the reasons suggested by the applicants' counsel for allowing a resumption. I confess to finding few as persuasive or eloquent as a letter from two grieving parents, Mr and Mrs Garnham, in response to the coroner's circular of 3 July 1992:

'Personally [we] want this inquest to continue, hoping at least some of the questions not yet answered can be. The main question being HOW was it possible for 51 young and healthy people to die in the middle of London on a Saturday on a very busy river even at that time of night, what happened to rescue and emergency services, that so many had to lose their lives, much of this rescue remains a mystery. Perhaps you can find the answer for us.'

I, therefore, would reject Mr Sullivan's futility argument. And I would do so with some relief. As Bingham LJ pointed out in a natural justice context in R v

Chief Constable of the Thames Valley Police, ex p Cotton [1990] IRLR 344 at 352: 'This is a field in which appearances are generally thought to matter.'

The truth of that, indeed, could hardly be better illustrated than by what Mr Brennan tells us of the applicants' feelings in this very case: they have found it intolerable that so crucial a decision should be taken against what they perceive to be a background of insult and animosity; they would find refusal hard to accept from another coroner; if, however, the decision were fairly taken, they would reluctantly accept it.

I, therefore, would quash this decision and remit the matter to a coroner for a different district for a fresh decision to be taken under s 16(3) whether to resume these adjourned inquests.

I add just this footnote. No one should interpret this judgment as a condemnation of Dr Knapman. Almost without exception he handled the many difficulties he faced not merely with sensitivity but with an evident sympathy for the bereaved families. Understandably, and indeed justifiably, riled by an unfair article in the *Mail on Sunday*, he was guilty of but a single intemperate comment. The case should serve as a reminder to all judicial officers of the almost invariable unwisdom of ever talking to the press about any aspect of current legal proceedings.

FARQUHARSON LJ. In the early hours of 20 August 1989 occurred one of the worst tragedies to take place on the River Thames since the 1939–45 war. The Marchioness, a motor vessel with 141 passengers on board, was in collision with a dredger, the Bowbelle, near Southwark Bridge. As a result no less than 51 young people lost their lives; 24 were found aboard the Marchioness whilst the bodies of the remainder were recovered from the river during the course of the following week.

The bodies were taken to Westminster mortuary which is within the jurisdiction of the respondent who is the coroner for Inner West London. An inquest was formally opened and immediately adjourned. There were further adjournments from time to time until a preliminary hearing took place on 27 February 1990. The coroner proposed that the inquiry should be held in two parts, the first relating to identification and the medical cause of death and the second being devoted to the important issue of how the victims came by their death. The part one hearing took place in the cases of 44 out of the 51, including that of the second applicant's son, between 23 and 26 April 1990.

At that point the Director of Public Prosecutions intervened by informing the coroner that criminal proceedings under s 32 of the Merchant Shipping Act 1988 were being instituted against Captain Henderson, the skipper of the Bowbelle. This inevitably caused delay and in the event considerably more delay than was anticipated. The trial of Captain Henderson did not begin at the Central Criminal Court until 3 April 1991. The jury was unable to agree on its verdict and a re-trial took place in the following July, this time at St Albans. The result was the same, with the jury once more being unable to agree. In accordance with practice, the prosecution at this point offered no further evidence against Captain Henderson and he was acquitted. The coroner was then confronted with another difficulty. On the day that the second trial of Captain Henderson began, the husband of one of the victims of the disaster successfully applied for process against the company which owned the Bowbelle and four of its employees. Summonses for manslaughter were granted, but the committal proceedings were not heard until 25 June 1992, when all the accused were discharged.

Meanwhile two reports had been commissioned. The first by the Marine Accident Investigation Branch (the MAIB) was an inquiry into the disaster and the report was published on 15 August 1991. The second, the Hayes Report (Cm 1991), which made recommendations on river safety, was completed on 7 July 1992.

The criminal proceedings, as is apparent from this chronology, caused prolonged delays in the proceedings before the coroner, as they were only completed some three years after the sinking of the Marchioness. The coroner was then faced with the need to decide whether the inquests should proceed, bearing in mind the criminal proceedings which had taken place, the reports which had been published and the consequent delay. Anticipating this problem would arise, he had written letters to the bereaved relatives from time to time, seeking their views. In this correspondence he identified two groups of relatives, one being more active than the other. This is illustrated in a letter dated 21 August 1991, which said:

'It is now over two years since the tragedy and the inquest stands adjourned. After a trial it is very unusual to resume an inquest, but a Coroner may do so "if he considers there is sufficient reason to do so". Whilst not putting matters to a vote, one of the factors which I may legitimately bear in mind is the views of the relatives. There is the risk of the whole matter deteriorating into an unseemly squabble. There are those who vociferously clamour for "a public inquiry"; there are those who have come to terms with their grief, yet to whom each new headline is a painful reminder; there are those who support the private prosecution for manslaughter, which is ongoing; there are those who wish the inquest resumed in order to explore further criticism in the MAIB report, or believe it will answer "why my relative died". I would also say this to you. I think it best if you made up your mind in the tranquillity of your own home. There is the danger of one faction or another applying pressure and seeking to persuade you to their point of view. Perhaps you could write to me indicating your views. I rather think that those in favour of resuming the inquest will certainly make their views known, but it would be nice for those with no strong feelings to write also.'

The group of which both the present applicants were members had set up a Marchioness Action Group to protect and further the interests of the relatives. It is plainly arguable that the coroner had this group in mind when referring to 'a faction'. This is borne out by a further letter he wrote to the relatives a year later when again inviting opinions as to whether the inquest should be resumed. It is dated 3 July 1992 and in the relevant passage states:

'Some members have come to terms with their grief and each item of media interest merely serves to heighten their distress. Some relatives channel a great deal of their energies into Action Groups. The criticism has been voiced to me that certain people are given the appearance of speaking for everybody when this is not so.'

When the inquest was resumed on 22 July 1992 a submission was made to the coroner that he should recuse himself on the grounds of apparent bias. After retiring to consider the submission the coroner rejected it. He then heard further submissions as to whether he should resume the part one hearings, and what aspects of part two. In the result he decided not to resume the inquest at all. It is this decision which is the subject of the present appeal.

The charge of bias against the coroner was principally based on an incident which occurred in March 1992. The second applicant had wished to see her son's body before he was buried. She was not permitted to do so either by the police at the mortuary or by the undertaker she instructed. The explanation given in each case was that they were following the coroner's instructions. In fact the coroner had given no such instructions and the refusal to allow the inspection was due to a misunderstanding.

When the bodies of 25 of the victims were recovered it was necessary for them to be identified. This was potentially difficult because of their exposure to the elements before being recovered. The police who were responsible for establishing the identities had the authority of the coroner to remove the hands from the bodies for the purpose of fingerprinting. It was said that such mutilation was necessary because the condition of the bodies affected the fingers to some degree and it was only practicable to take prints at the laboratory. The relatives of the deceased were not aware that this step had been taken. When the second applicant learned of it she arranged to meet and be interviewed by representatives of the *Mail on Sunday*. As a result, on 22 March 1992 there was published in that newspaper an article with the heading in heavy print 'Cover-Up'.

It was an emotionally charged article clearly imputing that the coroner had refused inspection of the bodies to conceal the fact that the hands had been removed. It said that it was only a month before that the coroner first 'confessed' that both of Shaun's hands—the second applicant's son—were removed during the post mortem.

It is clear that this allegation was totally untrue and no doubt the coroner was incensed when he read the article. He therefore asked the associate editor and a colleague to come to his office to discuss the matter. He wished 'to seek to persuade them voluntarily to retract the implication of a cover-up; and to attempt to get them to set the record straight in order to placate the understandable concerns of the other relatives who were already ringing up, wishing to know if the hands had been severed from their childrens' bodies and if so why'.

There is no dispute that the coroner showed the journalists photographs of Shaun's body. It was his purpose to demonstrate that they could not be used as a basis for identification. The journalists state that they thought the coroner's purpose was to shock them. They claim that the coroner then told them that he did not consider it was responsible journalism to run the story based on what the second applicant had said 'because surely you realise she was unhinged'. The journalists are firm that this expression was used. The coroner does not recall using it but it is clear that it represented his thinking. On the totality of the affidavits the Divisional Court was satisfied that those words were used by the coroner.

The facts were reported back to the second applicant who has expressed her indignation at being so described.

To support the charge of bias the applicants also point to a letter written by the coroner on 22 May 1991 to the registrar of the diocese of Guildford. The second applicant had applied to the bishop for a faculty to exhume her son's body, as she had an illogical feeling that it might have been the body of another victim. It was in this context that the coroner's letter was written. He expressed his views of the second applicant in the following extracts:

'Let me say at the outset that I believe that Mrs [Lockwood-Croft] has been deeply psychologically affected in her grief and is by no means acting rationally ... My misgivings [about the exhumation] are that Mrs [Lockwood-Croft] is totally obsessed by this aspect of the death. There are a number of mentally unwell relatives and survivors who mutually support each other'.

Not only has the second applicant objected to this assessment. Other members of the bereaved families felt affronted at being described as 'mentally unwell'.

Finally in this context, in a letter to a Home Office official dated 25 March 1992 he wrote:

'... I believe Mrs [Lockwood-Croft] is not acting in a rational manner by reason of her unresolved grief. She is one of the prime movers in the Marchioness Action Group who regularly hold press conferences for the media who are always ready to listen. They are very angry people'.

Whilst looking at this letter it is worth remarking that in conclusion the coroner made this point:

'I may say the main thrust of criticism from the action group is that there has been no Public Enquiry, and that now, two and a half years after the disaster, I have still been prevented from holding a full inquest by operation of the law. They feel "Authority" has let them down and quite frankly I agree with them.'

When the coroner announced that he was not going to proceed with the inquest, which under the Coroners Act 1988 was a decision for him to make, he said that he had invited views of relatives and other parties in writing and had heard submissions in open court. He went on to say that considerably less than half advocated a resumption. In fact 19 families were in favour of proceeding and that of course was substantially less than half of the relatives of the 51 victims. The applicants claim that this statement was misleading inasmuch as the coroner had received letters from only 16 families who did not want the inquest to proceed. Such a misleading statement, it is argued, further supports the charge of bias, because the coroner had assumed that those who failed to respond to his inquiry would have been in favour of halting the inquest.

For my part, I do not find this submission convincing. The coroner was not misleading anybody. As Mr Sullivan QC points out, the inquests had been adjourned and the coroner was simply indicating the number of those who wanted to reactivate the inquests as distinct from those who had not so expressed themselves. It was not the same as a head count with votes for and against. I would discount the 'numbers' criticism as having any relevance to the issue of bias.

There have been no submissions that the coroner was guilty of actual bias in the sense that reflected his state of mind. The complaint is that because of the matters discussed above he was showing apparent bias. There was indeed no basis for suggesting that the coroner was actually biased. The various affidavits and other documents in these proceedings clearly demonstrate that he was most concerned about the welfare of the bereaved families and he repeatedly consulted them. Indeed, the lengths he went to showed that his actions went far beyond those normally expected of a coroner. His letter to the Home Office showed his sympathy with their anxieties. The question remains, was he apparently biased against the applicants and those relatives of the victims who took an active part in the Marchioness action group and campaigned for an inquiry or for the inquests to be resumed?

A recent decision of the House of Lords has clarified the law relating to bias. Lord Goff said in *R v Gough* [1993] 2 All ER 724 at 737–738, [1993] AC 646 at 670:

> 'Accordingly, having ascertained the relevant circumstances, the court should ask itself whether, having regard to those circumstances, there was a real danger of bias on the part of the relevant member of the tribunal in question, in the sense that he might unfairly regard (or have unfairly regarded) with favour, or disfavour, the case of a party to the issue under consideration by him ...'

Applying that test to the present case, the court must ask itself whether in all the circumstances described above there was a real danger of bias on the part of the coroner. As already pointed out, there is no question of actual bias here. Neither is it necessary for the applicants to show that the coroner was aware that he was displaying bias. The question that has to be posed is 'Does it appear that there was a real danger of bias on the part of the coroner affecting his decision not to proceed with the inquests?'

While the tone of the coroner's letters suggest that he was antipathetic to the group comprising the most active relatives, this factor on its own would not produce an affirmative answer. Neither would the reference to 'a number of mentally unwell relatives and survivors', in the letter of 22 May 1991, though both these features are relevant. The vital matter is the reference to the second applicant being 'unhinged'.

While not accepting that he used that expression, the coroner has never disguised his belief that the second applicant was, and is, suffering from abnormal grief reaction or post-traumatic stress disorder. He points out quite correctly that the fact he had made such a diagnosis does not mean that he is in any way biased against her or hostile to her interests.

The coroner says that he has always acted courteously to the applicants and to all the other bereaved relatives. This is apparent from his letter of 17 February 1992 to the second applicant in reply to her peremptory demand for assistance in her own letter of 22 January 1992.

Neither of the applicants were parties to the proceedings in the sense that they were witnesses at the inquests, save perhaps on matters of identity, but the coroner recognised that they were of course highly interested parties in general terms. They were interested in the sense that they were pressing for the inquests to continue. It is in that capacity that they were sensitive to any manifestation of bias.

I recognise, as the coroner points out in his affidavit, that the function of a coroner differs from that of a judge. The coroner plays an investigative role and is in consequence in a much closer relationship to the parties than a judge would ever be. The coroner explains that it is sometimes necessary to invoke the assistance of the press when seeking evidence and gives an example of how that had been successfully done in the past. None the less in the present case the interview with the press was not to seek information for the better a discharge of the coroner's functions but to persuade them to withdraw and apologise for an article which had understandably given him offence. For my part, I would say that it is wrong or at least undesirable for anybody sitting in a judicial capacity to discuss the case he is trying or preparing to try with anybody else, or to make any public comment about it (see *R v Crown Court at Bristol, ex p Cooper* [1990] 2 All ER 193). The trouble which such activities cause

b is illustrated both by that case and the present.

Bearing all those matters in mind one returns to the question whether in all the circumstances of the present case it appears that there was a real danger of bias on the part of the coroner.

With considerable reluctance I am driven to the conclusion that there was such a danger. The relevant circumstances include the fact that this inquest

c arose out of a national tragedy, that the relatives of the deceased were deeply affected by the disaster, that the relatives were much incensed that there had been no public inquiry, that the absence of such an inquiry made them all the more anxious that the inquest should proceed, and that the reference to the second applicant in this context led to an apprehension of bias which was real.

d Even if there was an apparent danger of bias, it remains a matter for the decision of the court whether it should grant judicial review of the coroner's decision not to proceed with the inquest. Through no fault of his the delays have been considerable. It is now nearly five years since the tragedy and the resumption of the inquests will lay a heavy burden on the coroner who has to conduct it. On the other hand, the absence of an appropriate inquiry in the past

e coupled with the apprehension on the part of the relatives of bias by the coroner persuades me that the motion should be granted and that a new coroner should be appointed to consider whether or not to resume the inquests.

f **SIR THOMAS BINGHAM MR.** I have had the benefit of reading in draft the judgments of Simon Brown and Farquharson LJJ. I agree with them that this appeal should be allowed for the reasons which they give.

The importance of these appeals to all concerned leads me to give reasons of my own. I give these gratefully adopting the summary of the facts given by Simon Brown and Farquharson LJJ.

g It has long been regarded as essential that judicial decision-makers should, so far as reasonably possible, resolve disputes coming before them on their legal and factual merits, uninfluenced by extraneous prejudice or predilection or personal interest. The qualification 'so far as reasonably possible' is necessary because judicial decision-makers are human beings upon whom

h multifarious experiences and influences inevitably leave a mark. The decision-maker should consciously shut out of his decision-making process any extraneous prejudice or predilection of which he is aware; but he cannot shut out an extraneous prejudice or predilection of which he is unaware. The name given by the law to extraneous prejudice or predilection or personal interest in

j this context is bias.

It not infrequently happens that judges find themselves called upon to criticise, sometimes in strong terms, parties or witnesses appearing before them. The subjects of such criticisms are apt to complain that the judge was prejudiced or biased against them. But such complaints will carry no weight with an appellate court provided the criticisms were based on material properly before the judge in that case and were not, in the light of that material, inappropriate. In such a case there is no element of extraneous prejudice or predilection and hence, in the eyes of the law, no question of bias.

From the House of Lords recent decision in *R v Gough* [1993] 2 All ER 724, [1993] AC 646 it is clear that bias may fall for consideration in three classes of case. The first class comprises cases of actual bias. These are cases in which a decision-maker is shown, in fact and for whatever reason, to have been influenced in his decision-making by prejudice, predilection or personal interest. Such cases are very rare. *R v Gough* was not such a case. Nor is the present case. But the law is very clear and very emphatic: where a decision is shown to have been tainted by actual bias it cannot stand.

The second class comprises cases in which the decision-maker has a direct pecuniary interest, however small, unless negligible, in the subject matter of the decision. In such cases it is irrelevant that the interest has had no effect on the decision in question. 'The nature of the interest is such that public confidence in the administration of justice requires that the decision should not stand' (see *R v Gough* [1993] 2 All ER 724 at 730, [1993] AC 646 at 661). It is rather as if, in such cases, the law presumes bias.

The third class comprises cases in which there is no actual bias and no direct pecuniary interest giving rise to a presumption of bias. It was the bounds of this third class which were in issue in *Gough*. The House of Lords was there called upon to choose between two tests for inclusion in this class, both of the rival tests finding support in authority. One test was whether a reasonable and fair-minded person sitting in the court and knowing all the relevant facts would have had a reasonable suspicion that a fair trial was not possible because of bias on the part of the decision-maker. The second was whether there was a real likelihood, or danger, of bias. The House of Lords unanimously upheld the second of these tests, expressed in terms of real danger, to make clear that it is possibilities, not probabilities, which matter. This decision shows, as it seems to me, that the description 'apparent bias' traditionally given to this head of bias is not entirely apt, for if despite the appearance of bias the court is able to examine all the relevant material and satisfy itself that there was no danger of the alleged bias having in fact caused injustice, the impugned decision will be allowed to stand. The famous aphorism of Lord Hewart CJ in *R v Sussex Justices, ex p McCarthy* [1924] 1 KB 256 at 259, [1923] All ER Rep 233 at 234 that 'justice ... should manifestly and undoubtedly be seen to be done' is no longer, it seems, good law, save of course in the case where the appearance of bias is such as to show a real danger of bias. In the present case the court's task is to ascertain the relevant circumstances and ask itself whether, having regard to these circumstances, there was a real danger of bias on the part of HM Coroner for Inner West London in the sense that he might have unfairly regarded with disfavour the cases of the applicants as parties to an issue under consideration by him.

In approaching the answer to this question, the special position of a coroner in England and Wales must be borne in mind. His role is quite unlike that of any other judicial officer. He, through his officer, gathers the relevant evidence, and I can readily accept that it would on occasion be appropriate to approach the press for information. He decides which witnesses should be called and which statements should be read. He examines the witnesses. In all these respects his role is quite unlike that of a judge as we know it. His function is indeed closer to that of a juge d'instruction than to that of a judge presiding over contested proceedings between adversaries. Thus his role is different. It is also very difficult and sensitive, because issues concerning the death of those *a* they love are naturally of great moment to those they leave behind, and sometimes to the public at large. That is why, after so many centuries, inquests continue to be held. There is, however, as I think, nothing in the coroner's role which indicates that he is, or should be, subject to any lower standard of impartiality than other judicial decision-makers: if anything, his central and dominant role in the conduct of an inquest might be said to call for a higher *b* standard since those interested in the proceedings are, to an unusual extent, dependent on his sense of fairness.

Like the Divisional Court, and like Simon Brown and Farquharson LJJ, I do not myself draw an inference of bias from the coroner's statement that fewer than half the relatives and other parties advocated a resumption of the *c* inquests. It was true that fewer than half of the relatives and other parties represented before him had written to ask that the inquests be resumed. Almost as many had written to ask that the inquests should not be resumed. It was reasonable for him to suppose that those who did not answer were indifferent whether the inquests were resumed or not, and he had no reason to *d* believe that his letters had not reached the addressees. Whether viewed on its own or as part of a composite picture, his statement on this matter in my view suggests no real danger of bias.

We must on the evidence accept, as the Divisional Court did, that the coroner described Mrs Lockwood-Croft as 'unhinged'. This causes me concern for three main reasons:

e (1) The first is the choice of expression. Had the coroner described Mrs Lockwood-Croft as distracted by grief, or as suffering from post-traumatic stress disorder, no valid objection could have been taken. Anyone might in her position suffer in the same way, and to make such a suggestion in such terms would not disparage her. But 'unhinged' is in common parlance a pejorative *f* expression, clearly suggesting that the views of a person so described are not deserving of full credence.

(2) The expression was used by the coroner as part of his argument put to the journalists who called on him that it was not responsible journalism to publish an article based on such an unreliable source. The coroner was in effect saying that the newspaper should not have published the article in reliance on *g* what Mrs Lockwood-Croft had said because she was 'unhinged' and so not a reliable source.

(3) In other letters the coroner used language which suggested that he regarded the applicants and others involved in the action group as an unrepresentative, mentally unwell, faction. The representations made by such *h* a body could not reasonably be expected to be judged on their objective merits.

These considerations lead me to conclude that there was here a real danger that the coroner might have unfairly regarded with disfavour the cases of the applicants as parties to an issue under consideration by him. The judgment of the Divisional Court does not persuade me to a contrary view. The coroner *j* was not of course obliged to put out of his mind the fact that the applicants were distracted by grief, if that was his judgment, but he was obliged to evaluate their representations on their objective merits and to recognise, if this was his view, that the absence of a full public inquiry might have prolonged or exacerbated their grief.

It follows that in my opinion the coroner should have recused himself when asked to do so. Justice accordingly requires that his decision not to resume the inquests must be quashed and this question must now be the subject of decision by a different coroner.

I reach this decision with regret. The coroner reacted to this horrific tragedy with energy and public spirit. He went to great lengths to treat the bereaved with sympathy and understanding. He had, it need hardly be said, no intention to be unfair and no consciousness of being so. He might have decided against resumption of the inquests anyway. He was, it would seem, and understandably, concerned that the death of over 50 young adults in the heart of London on a fine August night had not been thought to merit a full public inquiry contrary to the almost invariable practice when such catastrophes occur. The present proceedings may fairly be seen as a by-product of that decision. The issue for this court is, however, the single limited question raised above. Conscious though I am of the great difficulty in which the coroner was placed, I nevertheless feel bound to reach the conclusion I have expressed.

I make two further points, each of them important. First, I would warn the applicants against undue optimism that another coroner will take a different view on the resumption of the inquests. There are very powerful grounds— among them the lapse of time, the existence of other reports and the interest of those bereaved who have succeeded in putting this terrible tragedy behind them—against resumption. I should not for my part be taken as viewing the resumption with favour or, for that matter, disfavour. I am only holding that the decision whether the inquests should be resumed or not should be taken by a coroner about whose ability to resolve the question on the objective merits as he sees them there can be no room for doubt.

Secondly, I wish to reject the argument advanced for the coroner that the applicants should not be granted relief since resumption of the inquests, if ordered, could lead to no useful result. The basis of this argument, founded on the recent decision of this court in *R v North Humberside and Scunthorpe Coroner, ex p Jamieson* [1994] 3 All ER 972, [1994] 3 WLR 82 was that the inquests could only investigate how the deceased came by their deaths, to which the only proper answer would be, as is already known, that they died by drowning following the collision between the Marchioness and the Bowbelle. *Jamieson's* case was specifically directed to the verdict of lack of care in the context of deaths in custody, but the court's ruling was of wider application and it is true that if these inquests were to be resumed the verdicts which the coroner could properly leave open to the jury at the end would be both limited and predictable. The court did not, however, rule that the investigation into the means by which the deceased came by his death should be limited to the last link in the chain of causation. That would not be consistent with the court's conclusion in *R v North Humberside and Scunthorpe Coroner, ex p Jamieson* [1994] 3 All ER 972 at 991, [1994] 3 WLR 82 at 101 (para 14) which emphasised the need for full, fair and fearless investigation and the exposure of relevant facts to public scrutiny, and it would defeat the purpose of holding inquests at all if the inquiry were to be circumscribed in the manner suggested. It is for the coroner conducting an inquest to decide, on the facts of a given case, at what point the chain of causation becomes too remote to form a proper part of his investigation. That question, potentially a very difficult question, is for him. If these inquests were to be resumed, and I emphasise if, the question would have to be answered by the new coroner, exercising his judgment as best he can on all the information available in the knowledge that, wherever he drew the line, his ruling would be unwelcome to some. It is, however, clear, as was

accepted by counsel for the applicants in argument, that the treatment of the
bodies of the deceased after death could not form part of a properly conducted
inquest.

Appeal allowed. Leave to appeal to the House of Lords refused.

L I Zysman Esq   Barrister.

R v Secretary of State for the Environment, ex parte Lancashire County Council

R v Secretary of State for the Environment, ex parte Derbyshire County Council

QUEEN'S BENCH DIVISION (CROWN OFFICE LIST)

JOWITT J

24, 25, 26, 27, 28 JANUARY 1994

*Local authority – Local Government Commission – Restructuring of local
government – Policy guidance – Guidance urging substantial increase in unitary
authorities at expense of existing two-tier structure of local government – Secretary
of State issuing policy guidance on restructuring of local government and directing
commission to review local authorities having regard to policy guidance – Local
authorities seeking judicial review of Secretary of State's guidance and directions –
Whether policy guidance being outside Secretary of State's powers and unlawful –
Local Government Act 1992, s 13.*

*Local authority – Local Government Commission – Restructuring of local
government – Policy guidance – Guidance urging substantial increase in unitary
authorities at expense of existing two-tier structure of local government – Secretary
of State issuing policy guidance on restructuring of local government – Secretary of
State rejecting commission's recommendations and directing further review –
Commission directed to conduct review having regard to policy guidance – Whether
Secretary of State bound to implement commission's recommendations – Whether
Secretary of State having power to direct further review of wide-ranging scope –
Local Government Act 1992, s 15(6).*

In November 1993 the Secretary of State, pursuant to his powers under s 13ᵃ of
the Local Government Act 1992, issued policy guidance to the Local
Government Commission on the replacement of the existing two-tier
structure of local government with unitary authorities. Paragraph 3 of the new
policy guidance acknowledged that in some areas the commission might wish
to recommend a continuation of the existing two-tier structure, but stated that
the government expected that to be the exception and that the result would be
a substantial increase in the number of unitary authorities in both urban and
rural areas.   At about the same time the Secretary of State received the

---

a   Section 13, so far as material, is set out at p 171 *fg*, post

commission's report on county council D, which recommended the creation of two unitary authorities and the continuation of the existing two-tier structure of local government in respect of the rest of the county. The Secretary of State decided not to accept the commission's recommendations and directed it to conduct a further review of D pursuant to his powers under s 15(6)[b] of the 1992 Act. That direction expressly required the commission to have regard to the 1993 policy guidance when conducting its review and to consider inter alia whether there should be a new set of recommendations replacing the existing ones in their entirety. D applied for judicial review of the Secretary of State's 1993 policy guidance, his decision not to give effect to the commission's recommendations and his direction to the commission to conduct a further review. D contended (i) that any statement of the Secretary of State's policy of what he expected by way of an outcome to a review should not add a further criterion to the statutory criteria in s 13(5), which required the commission, in conducting its review, to consider whether the need to reflect the identities and interests of the local communities and to secure effective and convenient local government made it desirable to recommend a particular change in order to satisfy those needs or some or any of them, and should not, under the guise of guidance, amount in fact to a direction, (ii) that once the Secretary of State had directed an inquiry he would be bound to give effect to the commission's recommendations (with or without modifications) unless he could show good cause for his decision not to do so and (iii) that the reference to 'revised recommendations' in s 15(6) did not permit a further review of such wide-ranging breadth as had been proposed.

In the second case, the Secretary of State instructed the commission to suspend its review of county council L following publication of the draft version of the 1993 policy guidance. Shortly thereafter he directed the commission to conduct a fresh review of L taking account of the new policy guidance. L also applied for judicial review of the Secretary of State's 1993 policy guidance and his subsequent direction to the commission on the ground that the document went beyond guidance, as a means of steering a conclusion in one direction rather than another, and was unlawful.

Held – (1) The Secretary of State was entitled, in his guidance to the commission, to reflect his policy and to say what it was, provided he considered it was relevant to a consideration of the statutory criteria laid down by s 13(5) of the 1992 Act, which were all-embracing. It was also legitimate for the Secretary of State to state his belief that unitary authorities were in general more likely to fulfil the statutory criteria than a two-tier system of local government. However, when the Secretary of State expressed his hope as to the end result of a review, the language he used had to be examined critically to see whether, on a fair reading, it conveyed the message to the commission that the government's hoped-for result was to be seen as an end in itself. Language which conveyed that message would be unlawfully either adding a fresh criterion or undermining the existing statutory criteria or both. On a fair reading by members of the commission the sentence complained of in the 1993 guidance conveyed a message that the government's hoped-for result was to be seen as an end in itself and its effect was clearly to undermine the statutory criteria laid down by s 13 of the Act. It followed that the Secretary of State had

---

b   Section 15(6), so far as material, is set out at p 179 j, post

acted unlawfully in giving policy guidance to the commission which urged a
substantial increase in the number of unitary authorities at the expense of
existing two-tier structures and consequently that those parts of the Secretary
of State's directions which required the commission to conduct reviews of D
and L having regard to the 1993 policy guidance were also unlawful (see p 173 *j*
to p 174 *a d e* and p 177 *a* to *c e f*, post).

(2) The Secretary of State had an unfettered discretion under s 17(1)ᶜ of the
1992 Act to decide whether to exercise his powers and give effect to the
commission's recommendations.   If, having considered those recommendations, the Secretary of State decided to direct the commission to conduct a
further review pursuant to s 15(6) of the Act, there was nothing in s 15(6) to
suggest either that he had to find fresh evidence before he could invoke that
power, or that, when considering whether to direct a further review, he could
not take account of his own policy and decide that, on a reconsideration, with
better enlightenment about the potential benefits of a move to unitary
authorities, the respondents to the review might see matters differently and
the commission might make a different set of recommendations. Moreover, it
was also clear that the ambit of s 15(6), which was intended to provide an
effective revising procedure, was sufficiently broad to allow the Secretary of
State to direct a further review of any matter set out in the commission's report
without imposing any limits on the type or nature of the review to be
undertaken. On the facts, D's separate challenges to the decision letter and the
direction to the commission to conduct a further review failed, since the
Secretary of State was able to show that he had proper grounds for deciding not
to put the commission's recommendations into effect and since the language
of s 15(6) was apt to include the use which he had made of the revising
procedure. The applications for judicial review would accordingly be allowed
in part (see p 177 *h* to p 178 *b*, p 179 *e* to *g* and p 180 *e f j* to p 181 *b*, post).

Notes

For local government changes under the Local Government Act 1992, see 28
Halsbury's Laws (4th edn) para 1070B.

Cases referred to in judgment

Associated Provincial Picture Houses Ltd v Wednesbury Corp [1947] 2 All ER 680,
[1948] 1 KB 223, CA.
Laker Airways Ltd v Dept of Trade [1977] 2 All ER 182, [1977] QB 643, [1977] 2
WLR 234, CA.

Applications for judicial review

R v Secretary of State, ex p Lancashire CC
Lancashire County Council (Lancashire) with the leave of Laws J given on 9
December 1993 applied for judicial review of the November 1993 policy
guidance on the restructuring of local government given by the Secretary of
State for the Environment to the Local Government Commission under
powers conferred on him by s 13 of the Local Government Act 1992 and his
direction of 22 November 1993 to the commission to conduct a review of
Lancashire having regard to the 1993 policy guidance on the ground that that
guidance, which urged a substantial increase in unitary authorities over the

---

c   Section 17(1), so far as material, is set out at p 177 *j*, post

existing two-tier structure of local government, was unlawful. The relief
sought was orders of certiorari quashing the 1993 policy guidance and
direction. The facts are set out in the judgment.

R v Secretary of State, ex p Derbyshire CC

Derbyshire County Council (Derbyshire) with the leave of Laws J given on 9
December 1993 applied for judicial review of (i) the November 1993 policy
guidance on the restructuring of local government given by the Secretary of
State for the Environment to the Local Government Commission under
powers conferred on him by s 13 of the Local Government Act 1992, (ii) the
Secretary of State's decision refusing to implement recommendations made by
the commission following its review of Derbyshire and (iii) his direction of 29
November 1993 to the commission to conduct a further review of Derbyshire
having regard to the 1993 policy guidance on the grounds that the 1993 policy
guidance, which urged a substantial increase in unitary authorities over the
existing two-tier structure of local government, was unlawful, that the
Secretary of State was bound to implement the commission's
recommendations and that s 15(6) of the 1992 Act did not permit a further
wide-ranging review. The relief sought was orders of certiorari quashing the
1993 policy guidance, the Secretary of State's decision and his direction. The
facts are set out in the judgment.

Duncan Ouseley QC and *Clive Lewis* (instructed by *G A Johnson* , Preston) for
Lancashire.

Elizabeth Appleby QC and *Clive Lewis* (instructed by *John McElvaney*, Matlock) for
Derbyshire.

Andrew Collins QC and *Robert Jay* (instructed by the *Treasury Solicitor*) for the
Secretary of State.

JOWITT J. There are two motions before the court, following leave to move
given by Laws J. The first to be argued is an application by Lancashire County
Council to quash the November 1993 policy guidance given by the Secretary of
State for the Environment to the Local Government Commission under
powers given him by s 13 of the Local Government Act 1992 and to quash his
direction to the commission given on 22 November 1993 to conduct a review
of Lancashire under that section and to have regard in so doing to his
November 1993 policy guidance.

The second application to be argued is made by Derbyshire County Council
to quash the same policy guidance and to quash a decision by the Secretary of
State not to give effect to the recommendations of the commission following
a review of Derbyshire and the direction he gave to the commission purporting
to be given under ss 13 and 15 to conduct a further review of Derbyshire and
to have regard to that policy guidance.

The attack upon the policy guidance is common to both applications but
whereas Lancashire's attack on the review direction is consequential upon the
first attack and stands or falls with it, Derbyshire's attack on the review
direction in its case, as well as being consequential upon the first attack, is
based also on a free-standing ground as is its attack on the decision not to give
effect to the commission's recommendations.

I shall deal first with the common attack on the policy guidance and the
consequential attack on the review directions, and then with Derbyshire's

a free-standing attack on the decision not to implement and on the review direction in its case.

The facts in relation to the two cases, which it is necessary to relate in order to understand the issues, can be stated quite briefly. I begin, though, with an outline of the relevant statutory provisions in order to place the facts in context. It will be necessary later in this judgment to return in greater detail to *b* a consideration of some of the statutory provisions.

The Local Government Act 1992 is, by its preamble, 'An Act [among other things] to make new provision ... in relation to local government in England for effecting structural, boundary and electoral changes'.

Section 12 sets up the Local Government Commission.

c Section 13(1) requires it, when so directed by the Secretary of State, to review the areas he designates and recommend to him whether he should make such structural, boundary or electoral changes as are specified in its recommendations or whether he should make no changes.

Section 13(5) sets out criteria to which the commission is to have regard in *d* deciding what it should recommend.

Section 13(6) empowers the Secretary of State to give directions to the commission as to the exercise of its functions under s 13, including a power to direct that it shall, in the exercise of those functions, have regard to guidance given by him as to matters to be taken into account.

e Section 14(1) defines a structural change in relation to a non-metropolitan area as a replacement of two-tier with single-tier local government; that is the replacement of the present system whereby the administration of local government and the provision of services are shared by county councils and district councils with what are referred to as unitary authorities, which are to be the local government administrators and providers within their respective *f* areas.

Section 15(1) to (4) deals with the commission's procedures.

Section 15(7) empowers the Secretary of State to give directions in relation to the commission's procedures to which it must have regard.

Section 15(6) empowers the Secretary of State, after he has already received *g* the commission's report on a review, to direct it to conduct a further review of an area to which the report relates and make revised recommendations as respects that area.

In addition to empowering him to give procedural guidance, s 15(7) also gives the Secretary of State powers in relation to a direction under s 15(6) *h* which mirror his powers under s 13(6) in relation to a direction under sub-s (1) of that section.

Under s 17 the Secretary of State may decide to give effect by the making of an order to all or any of the recommendations arising from a review under ss 13 or 15 with or without modifications. Section 28(1) defines modifications as *i* including additions, alterations and omissions.

An order effecting a structural change takes effect when a draft order, having been laid before both Houses of Parliament, has been approved by resolution of each House: s 26(2).

The Secretary of State may, under s 17, decide not to accept any of the recommendations. In that event, no changes are made and there is no need for any draft order to be laid before Parliament.

FACTS

Derbyshire	a

The original direction to review Derbyshire (and other counties) was given on 23 July 1992. The direction required the commissioners to have regard to the policy guidance and the procedural guidance dated July 1992. (In fact the procedural guidance is dated June 1992 but nothing turns on this.)

I shall return to the policy guidance and concern myself at the moment with	b
the procedural guidance. It envisages four stages.

At stage one of a review the commission publicises the fact that there is to be a review and draws attention to the framework within which the commission is required to operate. This is a reference to the commission's statutory duty under s 15(2) to inform interested parties of the procedural and	c
policy guidance issued to it by the Secretary of State. It is a matter for the commission whether or not at this stage to put forward options for consideration.

At stage two, the commission prepares draft recommendations, which take account of the policy guidance and, at stage three, it publicises and seeks response to them.	d

Stage four of the review deals with the report to the Secretary of State of the commission's recommendations and the publicity to be given to them.

The procedural guidance also refers to procedures should there be a direction for a further review.

The commission's draft recommendations were published in May 1993 and	e
various options for change to unitary authorities were discussed in it. Two draft recommendations were made. The first was that the existing two-tier structure of local government should be replaced by several unitary authorities. The second was that the county should be divided into two unitary authorities, the City of Derby and the rest of the county.

In this document the commission laments that it has heard directly from just	f
a very small fraction of the people of Derbyshire, most of whom say they know little or nothing about the review. It recognises that many of those who have taken the trouble to respond to the commission's invitations for views have a special interest of one kind or another.

The commission's report to the Secretary of State is dated November 1993.	g
It is a detailed report covering the investigations undertaken and the responses received and canvassing the pros and cons for the various options which have been considered. The recommendation was that there should be two unitary authorities, Derby City and in the area taking in Chesterfield, Bolsover and North East Derbyshire. The recommendation was that the rest of the county	h
of Derbyshire should continue with two tiers of local government.

While the commission was conducting its review new policy guidance was under consideration by the Secretary of State. Views had been sought on a new draft, and in the same month that the commission's report on Derbyshire was received the new policy guidance was issued, the November 1993 policy	j
guidance.

On 27 November 1993 the Secretary of State wrote to Sir John Banham, the chairman of the commission. I shall return to this letter. It suffices for the moment to say that the Secretary of State was not prepared to accept the recommendations on Derbyshire, and he informed Sir John in the letter that he was directing the commission to conduct a further review of Derbyshire pursuant to s 15(6). The formal direction is dated 29 November 1993 and para 3 a of this direction requires the commission to have regard to the new policy guidance and to the new November 1993 procedure guidance.

Lancashire
No review has so far been conducted by the commission under the 1992 Act in relation to Lancashire. On 2 September 1993 a direction was given by the Secretary of State to the commission to conduct a review of Lancashire. He
b directed the commission to have regard to the 1992 policy and procedure guidance.

I have referred already to the fact that the draft which culminated in the November 1993 policy guidance had been published while the commission was still at work on the Derbyshire review. The draft was in fact issued on 30
c September 1993. On 18 October 1993 the Secretary of State gave the direction ordering the suspension of the review for Lancashire and other counties.

On 22 November 1993 the Secretary of State gave a further direction to the commission to review Lancashire (and other counties). The commission was directed for the purpose of this review to have regard to the November 1993
d policy and procedural guidance.

THE ISSUES

The construction of s 13(1), (5) and (6)
Section 12 assigns to the commission the role of carrying out the functions assigned to it by s 13.
e Those functions, so far as they are relevant for present purposes, are to be found in sub-ss (1) and (5):

'(1) If the Secretary of State so directs, the Local Government Commission shall, in accordance with this Part and any directions given under it—(a) conduct a review of such areas in England as are specified in
f the direction or are of a description so specified; and (b) recommend to the Secretary of State as respects each of those areas either—(i) that he should make such structural, boundary or electoral changes as are specified in the recommendations; or (ii) that he should make no such changes ...
(5) Any structural, boundary or electoral changes recommended to the Secretary of State under this section shall be such as appear to the Local
g Government Commission desirable having regard to the need—(a) to reflect the identities and interests of local communities; and (b) to secure effective and convenient local government.'

It will be seen that sub-s (1) requires the commission, when so directed by the
h Secretary of State, to conduct a review and to recommend either that there should be structural changes or that there should be no changes for the area under review.

By virtue of sub-s (5) if change is recommended it must be such as appears to the commission to be desirable having regard to paras (a) and (b). In other
j words, taking into account the needs set out in those paragraphs and how and to what extent the change under consideration would help to satisfy any of those needs, the commission considers it desirable to recommend the change and so recommends. It is, therefore, the effect of the change in helping to satisfy any or all of the needs set out in either or both of the two paragraphs which enables the commission to recommend it. Absent that effect, the commission has no power to recommend change and the recommendation should then be for no change.

A consideration of paras (a) and (b) suggests that the question whether and to what extent a proposed change will satisfy any of these needs may produce a number of different answers. It might be such as to satisfy all the needs set out. It might satisfy only some, one or none. One need might be satisfied at the expense of making satisfaction of another need harder to attain. One proposed change may do more to satisfy the needs than another. The overall indication may be in favour of retaining the status quo, either because proposed changes will do nothing to satisfy any of the needs, or because a step forward in satisfying one of them will be more than offset by the step backwards in satisfying another.

At one stage Mr Collins QC tentatively espoused a different construction of sub-s (5) in response to questions by me. This was to the effect that, provided the Secretary of State's policy guidance did not conflict with the statutory criteria, it might add further criteria so that the commission had to consider what recommendations were desirable and, in so doing, have regard both to the statutory and policy guidance criteria. In other words, what is desirable was not to be governed solely by the need to reflect identities and interests and to secure effective and convenient local government.

I was at one time attracted by this construction; hence my questions to Mr Collins on the point. I have, though, rejected it, and Mr Collins has withdrawn his tentative support for it. The statutory criteria seem to me to be all-embracing, and I read s 13(5) as requiring the commission to consider and answer the question: does the need to reflect the identities and interests of local communities and to secure effective and convenient local government make it appear to the commission desirable to recommend a particular change in order to satisfy those needs or some or any of them?

What, then, is the permissible ambit of the Secretary of State's policy guidance? His power under s 13(6) is to give directions to the commission as to the exercise of its functions under s 13. That takes one to sub-s (5). The direction may require the commission to have regard to the guidance he gives. That must mean 'have regard to his guidance when exercising those functions'.

It follows, in my judgment, that the guidance which the Secretary of State can give must relate and be restricted to the consideration by the commission of the desirability of recommendations for change or for retaining the status quo in so far as they relate to the satisfaction of the needs set out in sub-s (3)(a) and (b).

Mr Collins accepts this. He accepts that the criteria which the commission has to consider are those and only those set out in paras (a) and (b) of sub-s (5); it is not open to the Secretary of State to add any further criterion. Mr Collins rightly cautions me, though, that one must not read guidance, or steering towards a goal, as amounting in itself to laying down a criterion. I accept this.

I have to ask myself whether the guidance given by the Secretary of State in the November 1993 document includes matters which are outwith the scope permitted by s 13(6). If the answer to this question is Yes, then to the extent that guidance falls outside the permitted scope, the Secretary of State exceeded his powers and his guidance was unlawful.

If the answer to the question is No, then a further question has to be asked: was the guidance complained of given in a form which, on a proper reading, amounts not to guidance but direction? If it does not go beyond guidance, there is no illegality. If it takes the form of direction, then it is to that extent unlawful as also being outwith the Secretary of State's powers.

Policy

a   It is clear that although the Secretary of State has wide powers to modify the commission's recommendations, he cannot transform them so that they become a different animal. It is a question of degree. Although, therefore, he might modify a recommendation of no change by, for example, altering a boundary, it is difficult to see how he could lawfully modify a recommendation

b   for no change so that it became a recommendation for change from a two-tier to a unitary structure for local government. It follows from this that although it must be obvious that Parliament would not have enacted this legislation had it not thought that the restructuring of local government held out the prospect of improvement and that change is capable of promoting the objectives set out in paras (a) and (b) of s 13(5), the Secretary of State has no power to lay a draft

c   order for change in structure before Parliament unless and until he receives the enabling recommendation for change from the commission.

This does not mean that the Secretary of State is not entitled to have a policy in relation to the restructuring of local government. The commission's role is to recommend. The concept of a recommendation envisages that another will

d   make a decision and that in making it he will exercise a judgment. This is confirmed by the Secretary of State's powers to require a further review and to decide not to implement recommendations or to implement all or some of them with or without modifications. The role of the commission vis-à-vis the Secretary of State in relation to restructuring local government is to provide him with a basis upon which he can decide whether to lay a draft order before

e   Parliament. In making such a decision, he is clearly entitled to have reference to his own policy.

Is the Secretary of State entitled to reflect his policy in the guidance he gives? Is he entitled to say how he thinks a proper consideration of the statutory criteria will affect the answer to the question: should there be maintenance of

f   the status quo or should there be change?

Mr Collins submits that the answers to these questions should all be in the affirmative. Mr Ouseley QC for Lancashire and Miss Appleby QC for Derbyshire do not speak quite with one voice. Miss Appleby provides affirmative answers with two caveats, which Mr Collins accepts: any statement of the Secretary of State's policy or what he expects by way of an outcome to a

g   review must not add a further criterion to the statutory criteria and must not, under the guise of guidance, amount in fact to a direction.

Mr Ouseley submits that although the Secretary of State may say in his guidance what his policy is, he may not do so in terms which indicate the outcome which he desires. To do so goes beyond giving guidance and is

h   unlawful. His desire as to a particular result is irrelevant and to require the commission to have regard to what is irrelevant is unlawful.

It is accepted, though, on behalf of both applicants that guidance may lawfully suggest how different factors might be weighted in relation to one another and that this may have the effect of steering a conclusion in one

j   direction rather than another. In my judgment this concession is rightly made. The concept of guidance goes beyond simply providing a checklist of factors which the commission should take into account. To guide someone is to lead, steer or point someone in a particular direction.

In my judgment the Secretary of State is entitled, in the guidance he gives to the commission, to reflect his policy and to say what it is provided he considers (and is not *Wednesbury* unreasonable in so considering) that it is relevant to a consideration of the statutory criteria (see *Associated Provincial Picture Houses*

Ltd v Wednesbury Corp [1947] 2 All ER 680, [1948] 1 KB 223). I do not find any
Wednesbury unreasonableness in the Secretary of State's view as to the
relevance of his policy. It is, therefore, legitimate for him to say that his belief
is that unitary authorities are in general more likely to fulfil the statutory
criteria than a two-tier system of local government. To say this serves a
threefold purpose. (1) It focuses the commission's attention on the need to
consider whether this is so. (2) Since the policy guidance has to be circulated
by the commission (s 15(2)(b)) and the commission may reflect the ministerial
view of its draft recommendations, it is more likely that the pros and cons of
the case for change will be ventilated. (3) If this has been done, the
commission is better able to make its own decision and, if it recommends no
change, to justify that recommendation so that the Secretary of State is better
able to evaluate the recommendations he receives. Nor do I see that those who
wish to see no change will be inhibited in putting forward their case by what
they learn of ministerial views from the policy guidance.

When, though, the Secretary of State expresses his hope as to the end result
of a review, the language he uses has to be examined critically to see whether
on a fair reading it conveys the message to the commission that the
government's hoped-for result is to be seen as an end in itself and that the
recommendation, therefore, of such a result by the commission will be within
its proper remit under s 13 even though it is made as a result of attaching less
importance to the statutory criteria than would have been attached to them
without such a message. Language which conveyed this message would be
unlawful either by adding a fresh criterion or undermining the statutory
criteria or both.

In saying this I am influenced by two factors. First is the fact that a body of
people, though experienced in their own fields (and I bear in mind that four
members of the commission are lawyers and one was a member of the
commission's forerunner, the English commission under the Local Government Act 1992), are unlikely to approach ministerial guidance on the basis that
its legality must first be questioned before regard is had to it.

The second is that it would be quite understandable for a commission
member (conscious of the duty to have regard to such guidance in reaching a
decision) to take the view that guidance couched in terms which do not
obviously convey the message that all that is being stated is the government's
view that regard to the statutory criteria is likely in most cases to point to the
desirability of change and only exceptionally to the maintenance of the status
quo, is intended to set down a further criterion to be taken into account in
reaching a decision.

The November 1993 policy guidance

I can turn now to the passages in the 1993 policy guidance of which
complaint is made. Mr Ouseley, but not Miss Appleby, makes complaint about
the final sentence of para 11.

Paragraph 11 reproduces para 10 of the July 1992 policy guidance but with
the addition of the final sentence, which is new to the 1993 document.

> 'There need be no maximum or minimum size for the area or population
> covered by a unitary authority. There should be no presumption that each
> authority should deliver all its services in-house; where it is efficient and
> cost-effective to do so, the Government encourages authorities to buy in
> services from the private and voluntary sectors. Authorities may also

a make arrangements jointly with neighbouring authorities under Section 101 of the Local Government Act 1972, Section 1 of the Local Authorities (Goods and Services) Act 1970 or under function-specific legislation. The Commission should have regard to the need to establish authority areas such that authorities can carry out their functions effectively, and do so in ways which meet community interests. Unitary authorities covering

b either a very large area or a very small population will need a specially strong justification, because of concerns in the former case about remoteness and in the latter about the effectiveness of service delivery.'

The sentence complained of undoubtedly expresses a view as to the circumstances in which a unitary authority is seen to be undesirable. A very

c large area, such as most counties, is unlikely to provide a suitable basis for a unitary authority because of the problem of remoteness. An area with a very small population, such as some district councils which might aspire to unitary status, is likely to have problems about providing effective services.
This sentence seems to me to be no more than obvious common sense, and I see no ground for criticising the addition of this sentence to the 1992

d guidance, either taken on its own or coupled with the other matter of complaint to which I shall come in a moment. Guidance must not take the form of direction, but this sentence does not in my view come within a mile of amounting to direction. I have well in mind the decision of the Court of Appeal in *Laker Airways Ltd v Dept of Trade* [1977] 2 All ER 182 at 199, [1977] QB 643 at 714, where Roskill LJ, speaking of the difference between guidance and

e direction, said:

'The difference was well put by counsel for the plaintiffs when he submitted that guidance is assistance in reaching a decision proffered to him who has to make that decision, but that guidance does not *compel* any

f particular decision. Direction on the other hand, especially in the context of s 4, is compulsive in character. It requires the person to whom the direction is given to decide as directed. It deprives him of any freedom of decision, of any power to make his own decision as opposed to that which he is directed to make.' (My emphasis.)

g Lawton LJ observed ([1977] 2 All ER 182 at 208, [1977] QB 643 at 724–725):

'The statutory word is "guidance", not "direction". The Secretary of State can point out the way to be followed. He can tell the [Civil Aviation Authority] what policy is to be applied in the performance of its functions … The word "guidance" has the implication of leading, pointing the way,

h whereas "direction" even today echoes its Latin root of regere, to rule.'

The only complaint directed by Miss Appleby, for Derbyshire, against the 1993 document and the principal complaint made by Mr Ouseley, for Lancashire, is directed against the final sentence of para 3:

j 'Unitary authorities can reduce bureaucracy and costs and improve the coordination and quality of services. The Commission should examine each area which the Secretary of State directs it to review to see whether a unitary structure would better reflect the identities and interests of local communities, and secure convenient and effective local government. In considering its recommendations, the Commission should weigh the costs of change, including transitional costs, against the benefits of its proposals (see paragraphs 8 to 10). The Government does not wish to impose a

national blueprint for reform, or to require the wholesale abolition of
either district or county councils. In some areas the Commission may
wish to recommend a continuation of the existing two-tier structure. But
the Government expects that to be the exception, and that the result will
be a substantial increase in the number of unitary authorities in both urban
and rural areas.'

That final sentence is new to the 1993 document. In its place, para 3 of the 1992
policy guidance had as its final sentence the following:

'But the Government expects to see a substantial increase of the number
of unitary authorities as a result of the Commission's reviews.'

There was added to the 1993 document a new para 4, which did not appear at
all in the 1992 document.

'The Government attaches great importance to local consensus;
proposals which are put forward by groups of authorities will be an
important starting point for the Commission. Where those proposals
demonstrate that a range of options including amalgamations of districts
or disaggregations of counties has been fully considered, along with the
implications for individual services (as indicated in Annex B), the
Government expects the Commission to give them particular weight.
Proposals to make existing authorities unitary authorities will therefore
demand special scrutiny by the Commission unless it is clear that the
proposers have also considered other options. The Commission will wish
to measure proposals from local authorities against expressed views from
those outside local government.'

It is submitted by Mr Ouseley that the new para 4 gives an added sting to the
sentence complained of in para 3. I do not see this.

What, then, of the sentence at the end of para 3? It is important that this
sentence is read in its context in order to ascertain its meaning and effect so far
as the commission is concerned. Mr Collins has stressed various phrases in
para 3. It begins by saying only that unitary authorities can reduce bureaucracy
and so forth. The commission is told only to see *whether* a unitary structure
will better satisfy the statutory criteria. The government does not wish to
impose a national blueprint for reform or to require the wholesale abolition of
district or county councils, and in some areas the commission may wish to
recommend a continuation of the existing two-tier structure. Mr Collins drew
my attention as well to passages in paras 4 to 9 and 11 to 13 of the document,
all of which I have in mind.

I have to ask myself what, on a fair reading and seen in context, the final
sentence of para 3 would mean to the members of the commission, bearing in
mind, and I regard this as important, the change in wording between the 1992
and the 1993 versions. As Mr Collins accepts, it is a matter of impression. It is
not susceptible to a lengthy exegesis. I am mindful of what I said earlier in this
judgment of the need to examine critically language which states a desired
outcome. The word 'expects' can have a variety of meanings from 'thinks' or
'hopes' at one end of the spectrum to 'requires' at the other. As used in this
sentence, it places a good deal of emphasis on a looked-for objective. Bearing
in mind the sentence in the earlier guidance which it has supplanted, I do not
think a commissioner would simply say the Secretary of State has not
expressed his meaning very happily (a criticism Mr Collins might be prepared

a to accept). In my judgment on a fair reading by members of the commission, this sentence conveys the message that the government's hoped-for result is to be seen as an end in itself, so that the recommendation of such a result by the commission will be within its proper remit under s 13, even if it is made as a result of attaching less importance to the statutory criteria than would have been attached to them without such a message. In my judgment, the effect of

b the sentence is to undermine the statutory criteria and add a further criterion.

As I have made clear already, none of this is to say that the Secretary of State is not entitled to say what his policy is and how he thinks a proper consideration of the statutory criteria is likely to point in the large majority of cases to a unitary form of local government rather than a two-tier form. Prudence suggests the desirability, additionally, of suitably underlining the fact

c that this is his guidance as to how the commission might find the statutory criteria are best achieved.

The effect of my conclusion, however, about this sentence, expressed as it is, is that its inclusion in the policy guidance was outwith the Secretary of State's powers to give guidance and was unlawful.

d The applicants attack the sentence on the basis also that it amounts to a direction and not simply to guidance. As to this, I think one must have regard to the make-up of the commission. Brief biographical details concerning its members are to be found in exhibit 1 to Mr Easteal's affidavit filed in the Derbyshire case on behalf of the commissioners. Reminding myself of what was said in the *Laker Airways* case about the difference between guidance and

e direction, I do not think the membership of the commission would feel directed by the sentence complained of. In my view the mischief of this sentence is the one I have already identified. The effect of my ruling is that that part of the two directions to conduct reviews which require the commission to have regard to the November 1993 policy guidance is unlawful because of the

f unlawful sentence in that guidance. I shall seek the assistance of counsel as to how my ruling should be translated into relief.

DERBYSHIRE'S SEPARATE CHALLENGES

I come now to Derbyshire's challenges to the decision letter and to the direction to the commission to conduct a further review.

g One ground is common to both challenges. It is said that the Secretary of State had no ground upon which he could properly decide not to give effect to the commission's recommendations contained in its report on Derbyshire and no ground upon which he could properly decide to direct a further review. It is submitted that he required evidence upon which he could fault the report

h before he could decide upon either of these courses and that he had none.

To say that absent any ground for criticism based on evidence the Secretary of State is not entitled to decide against giving effect to the commission's recommendation is to say that once he directs an inquiry he will be bound to give effect to its recommendations, either with or without modifications, unless he can show good cause for his failure. I find myself quite unable to read

j such a fetter into the Secretary of State's statutory powers. Section 17(1) provides that 'he may, if he thinks fit, by order give effect to all or any of the recommendations, with or without modifications'. This is not a requirement that the Secretary of State shall do something 'unless'. The statutory provision imposes no duty at all to act. It is permissive, and the Secretary of State need only exercise the power conferred on him if he thinks fit. To my mind, the words used could not more clearly confer an unfettered discretion on the

Secretary of State to decide not to exercise his powers. Such a decision, I would
hold, is not reviewable. (I am not called upon in this case to consider whether a
a decision by the Secretary of State to exercise his powers would be reviewable
and I express no view about that.)

If, though, I should be wrong in this, I am satisfied that the Secretary of State
did have material upon which he could decline to implement the
recommendations and that the same material justified him in directing a b
further review if in law (and I do not need to decide this) he needed such
material.

Miss Appleby draws my attention to the decision letter of 27 November 1993
and to para 8 in the affidavit of Mr Young, an under-secretary in the
Department of the Environment. In the decision letter written to Sir John
Banham the Secretary of State wrote: c

'... after considering the Commission's recommendations for
Derbyshire ... I am not at present satisfied that the proposals in respect of
these two areas meet the criteria in section 13(5) of the Local Government
Act 1992.'
d

He goes on to speak of his direction for a further review under s 15(6) and
writes in his concluding paragraph:

'This decision is not a reflection on the work which the Commission has
done in connection with these two reviews. As you yourself recognised in
your letter to me of 8 November, there have been representations from e
many of the councils in these areas requesting that the areas be reviewed
again in the light of the new policy guidance. That revised guidance lays
greater emphasis on the importance of local consensus and the desirability
of unitary authorities. I believe that the local authorities and people of
Derbyshire ... should be given the chance of being reviewed under the f
new guidance.'

In his affidavit Mr Young said that in deciding to give a direction for a further
review, the Secretary of State had not been influenced by the representations
he had received. This is not disputed, and it is unnecessary, therefore, to
consider them. In para 8 Mr Young said, in reference to what the Secretary of g
State had said in his letter about the criteria contained in s 13(5):

'I should take this opportunity to clarify the final sentence of this
passage. It was not intended to imply that the Secretary of State was of the
view that the Commission's recommendations were outwith the
parameters set by section 13(5) of the Act. Rather, that the Secretary of h
State had formed the judgment that, even in the context of the original
policy guidance, the Commission's recommendations did not, in his view,
best reflect the identities and interests of local communities or best secure
effective and convenient local government.'

Miss Appleby submits that once the Secretary of State conceded that the j
commission's recommendations were not outwith the statutory parameters,
there could be no ground for faulting its recommendations and therefore no
ground either for declining to implement them or for directing a further
review. She took me through the commission's report to demonstrate the
thoroughness of its work, the extent to which it had considered various
options and rejected them because they failed to satisfy one or other of the

a statutory criteria, and how the commission considered it had made the only set of recommendations open to it.

The fallacy in this submission is the assumption that only one set of recommendations can satisfy the statutory criteria. The report shows that there were options which offered a better chance than other options of satisfying para (b) but which had to be rejected because they failed to satisfy, b or fell short in the extent to which they satisfied, para (a). A judgment of this nature involves striking a balance, but it may not necessarily be the only balance which can be struck and still be said to have had proper regard to the statutory criteria. Where the case in support of para (b) is very strong, it may be a proper decision, which has had regard to both criteria, to recommend that option notwithstanding that local support for it may be lukewarm.

c Mr Collins pointed out some interesting parts of the report in relation to public support for change. A poll survey recorded a 54% support for the general principle of unitary authorities and that in every district authority more people supported the general principle than opposed it. None the less, as appears from para 60 of the report:

d 'The Commission found no groundswell of opinion outside the City of Derby and North East Derbyshire that local government in Derbyshire needed drastic reform indeed, there was strong support for the present structure. This was confirmed by MORI. This, the Commission judges, partly reflects the nature of the area but also a general feeling that in the e past the two tiers have worked reasonably well together.'

Mr Collins makes two points which I judge to be sound. There is nothing in s 15(6) to suggest that the Secretary of State must find fresh evidence before he can invoke his power to direct a further review. Secondly and allied to this, when the Secretary of State considers the exercise of this power, he is making f a judgment and is entitled to take into account his policy; it is legitimate for him to consider in weighing the satisfaction of the needs in para (a) against those in para (b) that a wrong balance may have been struck and that on a reconsideration, with better enlightenment about the potential benefits of a move to unitary authorities, respondents to the review may see things differently and the commission may make a different set of recommendations.

g In my judgment, if it is necessary for the Secretary of State to show he had grounds for the decision he made not to put into effect the recommendations and to direct a further review, he is able to show that he had proper grounds. The attack on this basis fails.

Miss Appleby makes a final attack on the direction to the commission to h conduct a further review. The direction is expressed to be made in pursuance of the Secretary of State's powers under both ss 13(1) and 15(6), but the operative part of the direction follows the wording of the latter provision. Miss Appleby submits that this is in fact a direction under s 15(6). Mr Collins invites me to consider its lawfulness on that basis and I do.

Section 15(6) provides:
j
'Where the report on a review is submitted to the Secretary of State under subsection (4) above, he may, if he thinks fit, direct the Local Government Commission to conduct a further review of any area to which the report relates and to make revised recommendations as respects that area ...'

I have referred already to the power to give guidance provided by s 15(7).

Miss Appleby's attack turns upon a consideration of the ambit of the
direction and the proper construction of s 15(6). It is common ground that the *a*
direction requires the commission to conduct a further review of Derbyshire
and that in conducting such a review it will have to consider whether all or any
of its present recommendations should stand, whether any of them should be
altered, whether any new ones should be made, and whether there should be
a new set of recommendations replacing the present ones in their entirety.   *b*

Miss Appleby submits that s 15(6) does not permit a further review of such a
wide-ranging breadth. The subsection speaks of revised recommendations,
and what the Secretary of State has directed is a review of a kind which he has
no power to direct.

To consider this point it is necessary to look at the words used in the statute
first in the context of the Secretary of State's power under s 17(1) to make his *c*
own modifications, and second against the factual background of making
adjustments when recommendations have already been made.

If it is borne in mind that a further review is likely to take time and be costly
(this is clear from the material before me) it might be expected that if all he had
in mind were revisions of a modest order, a Secretary of State, for practical *d*
reasons as well as in the public interest, would avoid the delay and expense of
a further review and exercise his own powers to modify. It is true there might
be cases in which he might consider that although he had no substantial
modifications in mind, he would be helped by the conclusions produced by a
further review. To my mind, though, this does not undermine the fact that the *e*
powers given under s 17(1) point to the intention of Parliament to provide in
s 15(6) for a wider-ranging revision than the Secretary of State might be
minded to undertake under his own statutory powers. This is consistent with
the wording of s 15(6) which allows the Secretary of State to direct a further
review of any area to which the report relates, without imposing any limit as
to size. The words used are apt to include the whole of the area to which a *f*
report relates.

Miss Appleby appeared to me to be suggesting that revised
recommendations, in order to fall within the subsection, would need to be
substantially in the form of the original recommendations, though with
amendments to some or all of them individually and that a new *g*
recommendation, not recognisable as an amended version of an original one,
would not fall within it.

If this were right, what would that mean in practical terms?
Recommendations which recommend change for some parts of a county and
none for other parts (as in the Derbyshire case) divide the county into different *h*
areas. If a new recommendation (new in the sense I have just considered)
cannot be made, the commission would really be restricted to recommending
changes to the boundaries delineated in its original recommendations. It
would not be possible, for example, to recommend creation of a further
unitary authority because this would be a new recommendation. The fact is
that areas within a county are like the pieces of a jigsaw puzzle. If one piece is *j*
restyled by moving it into or out of unitary status or by adding to or decreasing
its size, this inevitably has a knock-on effect on the other pieces, which cannot
all remain as originally recommended.

If Miss Appleby's submission were correct, then the more flawed a set of
recommendations, and consequently the more they might be in need of drastic
revision, the less apt s 15(6) would be to provide an effective revising

a procedure. In my judgment her submission as to the restrictive ambit of the subsection would greatly reduce its utility. The word 'revised', as it is used, should be construed purposively and not narrowly.

Revised recommendations are the product of the act of revising, and to revise is to look again at something, to re-examine something in order to improve or amend it (see the *Shorter Oxford English Dictionary*). These words

b are apt to include the use which the Secretary of State has made of the revising procedure provided by s 15(6).

I reject also Miss Appleby's submissions concerning the construction of s 15(6). Accordingly, Derbyshire's separate challenges fail.

There were other challenges relating only to Derbyshire set out in its

c grounds, but these have not been pursued and I need say nothing about them.

Applications allowed in part by striking out the final sentence of para 3 of the November 1993 policy guidance.

Dilys Tausz   Barrister.

d

Deutsche Ruckversicherung AG v Walbrook Insurance Co Ltd and others

e # Group Josi Re (formerly known as Group Josi Reassurance SA) v Walbrook Insurance Co Ltd and others

f QUEEN'S BENCH DIVISION (COMMERCIAL COURT)

PHILLIPS J

15–17, 21, 22 MARCH, 21 APRIL 1994

Affidavit – Admissibility in evidence – Affidavit in support of interlocutory
g *injunction – Affidavits containing material from report prepared by Department of Trade and Industry – Report setting out opinions of DTI inspectors – Whether rules of procedure precluding deponent from relying on intermediate source of information as ground for seeking interlocutory relief – Whether deponent only entitled to rely on original sources of information admissible as evidence at trial – RSC Ord 41, r 5(2).*

h
Bank – Documentary credit – Irrevocable credit – Circumstances in which court may restrain beneficiary from drawing on credit – Interlocutory injunction – Reinsurers opening letters of credit in favour of reinsured – Reinsurers purporting to avoid underlying contracts of reinsurance for fraudulent misrepresentation and/or non-disclosure – Reinsurers seeking to restrain beneficiaries from drawing on letters
j *of credit on ground that such conduct fraudulent once underlying contracts avoided – Whether court should restrain reinsured from drawing on letters of credit – Factors to be considered.*

Between 1973 and 1980 the plaintiff reinsurers, a German company in the first action and a Belgian company in the second, concluded a number of reinsurance contracts with the defendant insurance companies. In 1983 the

reinsurers granted letters of credit to the reinsured in consideration of the
reinsured making over substantial loss reserves to them. The reinsurers *a*
subsequently brought separate actions against the reinsured, claiming inter alia
declarations that the reinsurance contracts and letters of credit were illegal,
unenforceable and void on the ground that the reinsurers had violated English
law by carrying on insurance business in the United Kingdom without the
necessary statutory authorisation and an order restraining the reinsured from *b*
assigning, charging or presenting documents or drawing on the letters of
credit. The reinsurers obtained ex parte injunctions which were later set aside
on the basis that the illegality of the underlying reinsurance contracts did not
taint the letters of credit. Shortly before that hearing, however, the reinsurers
had made substantial amendments to their points of claim (without making
any application for relief at that point) to the effect that the reinsurance *c*
contracts had been avoided for fraudulent misrepresentation and/or
non-disclosure. In particular, the reinsurers alleged that the directors of the
underwriting agency to which they had delegated the placing, administration
and handling of reinsurance had fraudulently appropriated overriding
commission payable under the reinsurance contracts which should have been *d*
paid to the reinsured, that the directors' dishonest conduct (which constituted
a moral hazard) was a material matter, the non-disclosure of which by the
reinsured entitled the reinsurers to avoid the contracts and that since the
reinsured no longer enjoyed any right to payments under those contracts they
could not properly draw on the letters of credit. The reinsurers issued
summonses in each action, claiming interlocutory injunctions restraining the *e*
reinsured from drawing on (or alternatively disposing of the proceeds of) the
letters of credit. The affidavits filed in support of those claims relied largely on
the contents of a Department of Trade and Industry report of investigations
into the activities of certain of the defendant companies. The reinsured by
cross-summonses sought to strike out of the affidavits those sections which *f*
referred to the DTI report together with the report exhibited to the affidavits.
They contended that although RSC Ord 41, r 5(2)[a] provided that an affidavit
sworn for the purpose of being used in interlocutory proceedings could contain
'statements of information or belief with the sources and grounds thereof',
under that rule a deponent could only properly rely on original sources of
information which would be admissible as evidence at the trial and that the *g*
DTI report, which set out the inspectors' opinions based on the evidence they
had considered, did not satisfy that requirement.

Held – (1) The power of the court to grant an interlocutory injunction was one
that should be flexible and not fettered by the technical rules of admissibility of *h*
evidence that applied at trial. Accordingly, for the purposes of obtaining
interlocutory relief, RSC Ord 41, r 5(2) enabled a deponent to put before the
court facts which he was not able of his own knowledge to prove without
requiring him, at that stage, to identify as the source of his information or belief
an original source of evidence which would be admissible at trial. Indeed, the *j*
object of Ord 41, r 5(2) militated against placing that restriction on the natural
meaning of the words and, in a situation of urgency, a plaintiff might well not
have time to identify or trace evidence which would be admissible at the trial.
Clearly an original source would normally carry much more weight than an

---

a Rule 5, so far as material, is set out at p 188 *g* post.

a intermediate source, and where original sources were known they had to be identified, but it did not follow that intermediate sources could not be referred to or relied on since, ultimately, it was for the court to weigh all the material to decide whether the plaintiff had made out his case. On the facts, the reinsurers were entitled to rely on the DTI report in their affidavits in support of their claims to interlocutory relief. The reinsured's applications to strike out

b those sections in the affidavits which referred to the report would therefore be dismissed (see p 191 a to g, post); Re SBA Properties Ltd [1967] 2 All ER 615 not followed.

(2) It was clearly established that the court would not grant an injunction restraining a bank from making a payment under a letter of credit unless it was

c satisfied that there was a clear prima facie case that the beneficiary was acting fraudulently in drawing on the credit. There was however no basis for the suggestion that the court should apply a different test when considering an application to restrain a beneficiary (rather than a bank) from effecting payment under a letter of credit. A beneficiary could not be held to be fraudulent if he drew on a letter of credit in circumstances where he was

d uncertain as to the validity of his right to payment under the underlying contract, since the plaintiff seeking to enjoin would have to do no more than persuade the court that there was a seriously arguable case that the claim under the underlying contract was invalid, which would effectively deprive the beneficiary of much of the benefit which a letter of credit was intended to

e bestow. On the contrary, the correct contractual inference was that the beneficiary should be entitled to draw on the letter of credit provided he had a bona fide claim to payment under the underlying contract. To succeed on their application for injunctions against the reinsured, therefore, the reinsurers had to establish that, in drawing on the letters of credit, the reinsured would be acting fraudulently in that they would be claiming payment to which they

f knew they had no entitlement (see p 196 a to f and p 197 d e, post); Edward Owen Engineering Ltd v Barclays Bank International Ltd [1978] 1 All ER 976 applied; Bolivinter Oil SA v Chase Manhattan Bank [1984] 1 All ER 351n considered.

(3) Although there was a clear prima facie case that the directors of the underwriting agency had acted fraudulently as alleged, it was not clear that

g that was a material matter which should have been disclosed, since the fact that overriding commission was being diverted did not, on the face of it, have any impact on the risks being reinsured. Moreover, where the materiality of the fraud was said to be no more than a moral hazard, it would be an affront to common sense that the cover of the insured or reinsured should be at risk

h because of failure to disclose a fraud committed on itself of which only the fraudster was aware. It was therefore doubtful whether the reinsurers had validly avoided the contracts of reinsurance and in those circumstances the reinsurers had not made out a clear case that the reinsured would be acting fraudulently if they drew on the letters of credit. The applications for

j injunctions restraining the reinsured from so doing would accordingly be dismissed. The alternative claim for injunctions restraining disposal of the proceeds of the letters of credit would also be dismissed, largely due to the difficulty of establishing any proprietary claim on the part of the reinsurers to moneys paid by the banks under the letters of credit (see p 198 d, p 199 b, p 200 g to j, p 201 b and p 202 j, post); Re Hampshire Land Co [1896] 2 Ch 743 applied; Fitzherbert v Mather (1785) 1 Term Rep 12 considered.

Notes

For letters of credit in general, see 3(1) *Halsbury's Laws* (4th edn reissue) paras   *a*
252–256.

For restraint of payment under letters of credit on the ground of fraud, see
3(1) *Halsbury's Laws* (4th edn reissue) paras 289–290.

For the contents of affidavits in interlocutory proceedings, see 17 *Halsbury's
Laws* (4th edn) para 314.
                                                                                  b

Cases referred to in judgment

Agip (Africa) Ltd v Jackson [1992] 4 All ER 451, [1991] Ch 547, [1991] 3 WLR 116,
    CA.
American Cyanamid Co v Ethicon Ltd [1975] 1 All ER 504, [1975] AC 396, [1975] 2
    WLR 322, HL.   *c*
Belmont Finance Corp Ltd v Williams Furniture Ltd [1979] 1 All ER 118, [1979] Ch
    250, [1978] 3 WLR 712, CA.
Blackburn Lowe & Co v Vigors (1887) 12 App Cas 531, HL.
Bolivinter Oil SA v Chase Manhattan Bank [1984] 1 All ER 351n, [1984] 1 WLR
    392n, [1984] 1 Lloyd's Rep 251, CA.   *d*
*Chao (trading as Zung Fu Co) v British Traders and Shippers Ltd (NV
    Handel-maatschappij J Smits Import-Export, third party)* [1954] 1 All ER 779,
    [1954] 2 QB 459, [1954] 3 WLR 496, CA.
*Container Transport International Inc v Oceanus Mutual Underwriting Association
    (Bermuda) Ltd* [1984] 1 Lloyd's Rep 476, CA.
Dong Jin Metal Co Ltd v Raymet Ltd [1993] CA Transcript 945.   *e*
El Ajou v Dollar Land Holdings plc [1994] 2 All ER 685, CA.
Fitzherbert v Mather (1785) 1 Term Rep 12, 99 ER 944.
Grosvenor and West-end Rly Terminus Hotel Co Ltd, Re (1897) 76 LT 337, CA.
Hampshire Land Co, Re [1896] 2 Ch 743.
Harbottle (R D) (Mercantile) Ltd v National Westminster Bank Ltd [1977] 2 All ER   *f*
    862, [1978] QB 146, [1977] 3 WLR 752.
Houghton (J C) & Co v Northard Lowe & Wills Ltd [1928] AC 1, [1927] All ER Rep
    97, HL.
Howe Richardson Scale Co Ltd v Polimex-Cekop (21 June 1977, unreported), QBD;
    affd [1978] 1 Lloyd's Rep 161, CA.
Malas (trading as Hamzeh Malas & Sons) v British Imex Industries Ltd [1958] 1 All   *g*
    ER 262, [1958] 2 QB 127, [1958] 2 WLR 100, CA.
Metall und Rohstoff AG v Donaldson Lufkin & Jenrette Inc [1989] 3 All ER 14, [1990]
    1 QB 391, [1989] 3 WLR 563, CA.
Newsholme Bros v Road Transport and General Insurance Co Ltd [1929] 2 KB 356,
    [1929] All ER Rep 442, CA.   *h*
Owen (Edward) Engineering Ltd v Barclays Bank International Ltd [1978] 1 All ER
    976, [1978] QB 159, [1977] 3 WLR 764, CA.
Pan Atlantic Insurance Co Ltd v Pine Top Insurance Co Ltd [1993] 1 Lloyd's Rep 496,
    CA; *affd* [1994] 3 All ER 581, [1994] 3 WLR 677, HL.
Savings and Investment Bank Ltd v Gasco Investments (Netherlands) BV [1984] 1 All   *j*
    ER 296, [1984] 1 WLR 271.
SBA Properties Ltd, Re [1967] 2 All ER 615, [1967] 1 WLR 799.
Siskina (cargo owners) v Distos Cia Naviera SA, The Siskina [1977] 3 All ER 803,
    [1979] AC 210, [1977] 3 WLR 818, CA and HL.
United City Merchants (Investments) Ltd v Royal Bank of Canada [1982] 2 All ER
    720, [1983] 1 AC 168, [1982] 2 WLR 1039, HL.

a *United Trading Corp SA v Allied Arab Bank Ltd* [1985] 2 Lloyd's Rep 554n, CA.

Summonses

The plaintiffs, Deutsche Ruckversicherung AG, a German reinsurance company, and Group Josi Re (formerly known as Group Josi Reassurance SA), a Belgian reinsurance company (the reinsurers), issued separate writs on 30 b July 1993 and 17 August 1993 respectively against the defendant insurance companies, including Walbrook Insurance Co Ltd (the reinsured), claiming declarations that certain reinsurance contracts made between them, together with letters of credit opened in favour of the reinsured, were illegal, unenforceable and void.   In July 1993 the reinsurers obtained ex parte injunctions restraining the reinsured from drawing on the letters of credit.   On c 21 December 1993 Clarke J set aside those injunctions on the ground that illegality of the underlying contracts would not taint the letters of credit. Shortly before that hearing the reinsurers made substantial amendments to their pleadings, alleging that they had avoided the contracts of insurance for fraudulent misrepresentation and/or non-disclosure, but reserved those points d for a subsequent hearing.   The reinsurers issued summonses in each action on 21 January 1994 claiming an interlocutory injunction to restrain the reinsured from drawing on the letters of credit.   The reinsured issued cross-summonses on 9 March 1994 seeking to strike out under RSC Ord 41, r 6 those parts of the reinsurers' affidavit in support which referred to a Department of Trade and Industry report on certain of the defendant companies as their source of e information and belief.   The applications were heard in chambers, but the judgment was delivered in open court.   The facts are set out in the judgment.

Andrew Bartlett QC and *Marion Egan* (instructed by *Cameron Markby Hewitt*) for the reinsurers.

f *Stewart Boyd QC* and *David Joseph* (instructed by *Freshfields*) for the reinsured.

Cur adv vult

21 April 1994. The following judgment was delivered.

g **PHILLIPS J.** I am concerned with two actions which are now consolidated. The second is almost, but not quite, a carbon copy of the first.   The defendants in each action are the same.   They are insurance companies which belonged to a pool for some or all of the period 1974 to 1980.   The plaintiffs in the first action are a German reinsurance company.   The plaintiffs in the second action h are a Belgian reinsurance company.   Pleadings and proceedings in the second action have so closely mirrored those in the first that I can in this judgment deal with both at the same time.   I shall refer to the plaintiffs in each action as 'the reinsurers' and the defendants in each action as 'the reinsured'.   As this nomenclature indicates, the reinsured and the reinsurers were party to a j number of reinsurance contracts concluded between 1973 and 1980.   The reinsured claim that there is due to them under these contracts sums which greatly exceed the premiums paid.

In the course of 1983 the reinsurers procured the opening of a number of letters of credit in favour of the reinsured.   In the first action these were issued by Vereins-und Westbank, Hamburg and confirmed by Citibank in London.   In the second action the letters of credit were issued by Chase Manhattan Bank in

London. The letters of credit were in the same terms and provided for the
payment against sight of drafts accompanied by debit notes covering the   *a*
liability of the reinsurers for outstanding loss reserves up to specified
maximum amounts. It seems that before these letters of credit were issued, the
reinsured had been permitted to retain substantial reserves in respect of
potential liabilities of the reinsurers. The letters of credit were provided in
consideration of the reinsured making over these loss reserves to the   *b*
reinsurers.

In each action, as originally pleaded, the reinsurers claimed declarations that
the reinsurance contracts were illegal, unenforceable and void. The basis of
this claim was that the reinsurers had violated English law by carrying on
insurance business in the United Kingdom without the authorisation required
by statute. The reinsurers thus sought to rely upon their own illegality in order   *c*
to escape from onerous contractual obligations. The reinsurers further
claimed that the letters of credit were also illegal, void and unenforceable and
sought, inter alia, an order restraining the reinsured from assigning, charging,
presenting documents or drawing upon the letters of credit.

In July 1993 the reinsurers obtained ex parte injunctions restraining the   *d*
reinsured from drawing on the letters of credit. On 21 December 1993 Clarke
J set aside these injunctions. He held that illegality of the underlying contracts
of reinsurance would not taint the letters of credit.

Shortly before the hearing before Clarke J the reinsurers made substantial
amendments to their points of claim in each action. These amendments
averred that the contracts of insurance had been duly avoided for fraudulent   *e*
misrepresentation and/or non-disclosure. Clarke J was not invited to consider
any application for relief based upon these amendments. That matter was
reserved for a subsequent hearing.

THE NATURE OF THE FRAUD ALLEGED   *f*

The reinsurers allege that the members of the pool delegated to HS Weavers
(Underwriting) Agencies Ltd (Weavers) the placing, administration and
handling of reinsurance. It is alleged that at all material times Messrs Driver
and/or Wilson and/or Henry Weavers were directors and directing minds of
Weavers. It is further alleged that five of the defendant members of the pool   *g*
were in common ownership and/or control with Weavers and that Messrs
Driver and/or Wilson and/or Henry Weavers were directors and/or directing
minds of those defendants. The reinsurance contracts provided for the
payment, or perhaps more accurately the retention, of 5% 'overriding
commission'. The reinsurers contend that this overriding commission should
have been credited to the reinsured but that Driver, Wilson and Henry   *h*
Weavers improperly diverted the overriding commission into their own
pockets. This state of affairs, so the reinsurers contend, created a moral hazard
and, in consequence, was a material fact which should have been disclosed
both at the times that the contracts of reinsurance were placed and at the times
that the letters of credit were issued. On 19 November 1993 the reinsurers   *j*
purported to avoid the contracts of reinsurance on the ground of this
non-disclosure. The reinsurers contend that, in consequence of their
avoidance of the contracts of reinsurance, the reinsured no longer enjoy any
right to payments under those contracts, so that they cannot properly draw on
the letters of credit. The reinsurers have issued summonses in each action
claiming an interlocutory injunction restraining the reinsured from drawing

a on the letters of credit. As an alternative they have issued summonses claiming interlocutory injunctions restraining the reinsured from disposing of the proceeds of the letters of credit.

THE CROSS-SUMMONSES

b The affidavits in support of the reinsurers' claims to interlocutory relief rely very largely upon the contents of a Department of Trade and Industry report of investigations under s 432(2) of the Companies Act 1985 into London United Investments plc and C R Driver & Co Ltd (in liq). I shall refer to this report as 'the DTI report'. By their cross-summonses the reinsured seek to strike out those parts of the reinsurers' affidavits that refer to the DTI report, together with the DTI report exhibited to the affidavits. If these applications by the c reinsured are successful, the reinsurers' applications must fail in limine. I propose, accordingly, to consider the cross-summonses first.

THE AFFIDAVITS

The reinsurers were members of a pool on whose behalf business was d conducted by Inter Community Reinsurance Agency BV (ICRA). The affidavits upon which the reinsurers primarily rely were sworn by Mr Howard Kaye, a solicitor of Messrs Cameron Markby Hewitt. I propose to quote from the third affidavit of Mr Kaye in the first action passages which are, essentially, duplicated in the second action.

e '2. The facts and matters herein are true to the best of my knowledge, information and belief and, save where otherwise appears, are derived from: (a) my own knowledge; (b) information supplied by Mr Pieper, a director of the plaintiffs; (c) the Department of Trade & Industry's report into London United Investments plc ("LUI") and C R Driver & Co Ltd f ("Driver Ltd") published on 23 September 1993, which is exhibited to Sarah Isaacs' first affidavit in this action sworn on 23 November 1993, marked "SEI 1". 3. The DTI report reveals fraudulent conduct relevant to and in relation to reinsurance contracts between the plaintiffs and the Defendants ... *The DTI report*   7. The authors of the DTI report are Angus Gilroy FCA and William Gage QC. Their original remit, which g widened somewhat in the course of their investigations, was to investigate payments of commission on reinsurance contracts involving Weavers. The investigation included payment of overriding commission on contracts between the Weavers' pool and the ICRA pool. 8. Overriding commission is defined by the DTI inspectors as: "A commission paid by h the reinsurer to the reinsured, as a contribution to the expenses of the reinsured and as a reward for introducing business, commonly calculated as a percentage of premium." Mr Pieper and Mr Threadgold have confirmed that it is their understanding that overriding commission is paid to the reinsured. 9. The authors of the DTI report interviewed 88 j witnesses and were provided with written statements or agreed notes of telephone conversations with others. The witnesses included Weavers' personnel, brokers and reinsurers. The authors had wide powers under the Companies Act 1985 to require production of documents and they obtained documents from Weavers, brokers and reinsurers. 10. Although it has not been possible to do more than begin independent investigation of the facts and matters reported by the authors in view of the short time

which has elapsed since the publication of the report and the absence of
discovery in these proceedings. I believe them to be true.'   *a*

Mr Kaye then goes on, over 43 paragraphs, to set out the facts and matters
that he believes to be true on the basis of the DTI report, indicating by
reference to paragraph numbers the relevant sections of the report relied upon
in relation to the individual matters. These can be summarised as follows.
(1) Driver, Henry Weavers and Wilson were directors and directing minds of   *b*
London United Investments plc (LUI), which company wholly owned and
controlled five of the reinsured, namely Kingscroft, Walbrook, El Paso, Lime
Street and Mutual (KWELM) and also Weavers. (2) Driver, Henry Weavers
and Wilson were directors and directing minds of Weavers. (3) Weavers
acted as agents for the reinsured in placing the reinsurance contracts and   *c*
Driver, Henry Weavers and Wilson acted on behalf of Weavers and the
reinsured in this respect. (4) Driver, Henry Weavers and Wilson set up a
number of Liechtenstein Anstalten associated with a Mr Graham A P Smith
(the Smith companies). (5) Driver, Henry Weavers and Wilson agreed with
the agents of the reinsurers that overriding commission, usually 5%, would be
charged on the reinsurance premiums. (6) This overriding commission   *d*
should properly have been paid to the reinsured. (7) Driver, Henry Weavers
and Wilson ensured that the documentation seen by the reinsured made no
mention of this overriding commission. (8) Driver, Henry Weavers and
Wilson diverted the overriding commission to the Smith companies. Between
1970 and 1989 approximately $US 50m was diverted in this way.   *e*

Grounds for striking out
The reinsured seek to strike out those parts of Mr Kaye's affidavits which
rely upon the DTI report as the source of his information and belief. The
application is made pursuant to RSC Ord 41, r 6, which provides: 'The Court   *f*
may order to be struck out of any affidavit any matter which is scandalous,
irrelevant or otherwise oppressive.'

Mr Boyd QC for the reinsured argues that the parts of the affidavits to which
he objects are irrelevant and oppressive because the relevant rule, on its true
construction, does not permit Mr Kaye to rely upon the DTI report as the
source of his information and belief. That rule is Ord 41, r 5(2), which   *g*
provides:

'An affidavit sworn for the purpose of being used in interlocutory
proceedings may contain statements of information or belief with the
sources and grounds thereof.'
                                                                      h
It is Mr Boyd's submission that, under this rule, a deponent can only
properly rely upon original sources of information that would be admissible as
evidence at the trial. The DTI report, so he submits, does not satisfy that
requirement.

In support of this submission Mr Boyd referred me first to *Re Grosvenor and*   *j*
West-end Rly Terminus Hotel Co Ltd (1897) 76 LT 337 and to *Re SBA Properties Ltd*
[1967] 2 All ER 615, [1967] 1 WLR 799. These cases support the general
proposition that a DTI report under s 432 of the Companies Act 1985, or the
predecessor of that section, is not evidence in a court of law of the existence of
any fact mentioned in it. Neither decision bears on the question of whether a
DTI report can properly be relied upon as providing the sources and grounds

a of information or belief of a deponent to an affidavit sworn for the purpose of being used in interlocutory proceedings. Only one decision bears on that question, *Savings and Investment Bank Ltd v Gasco Investments (Netherlands) BV* [1984] 1 All ER 296, [1984] 1 WLR 271, and Mr Boyd's submissions were founded largely upon that decision. In that case the plaintiffs were seeking an interlocutory injunction to preserve their security in shares in respect of which

b they claimed to have an interest. They filed an affidavit in which they referred to a report made by inspectors who had been appointed to investigate one of the defendant companies under the Companies Act 1948. They relied, in particular, on criticisms made by the inspectors of the conduct of the controlling shareholder of another of the defendants. The plaintiffs applied, successfully, under Ord 41, r 6 to strike out the references to the inspectors'

c report in the affidavit. The reasons given by Peter Gibson J for acceding to this application appear from a passage in his judgment ([1984] 1 All ER 296 at 305–306, [1984] 1 WLR 271 at 282–283):

d 'Neither counsel has been able to cite any authority which elucidates the scope of what is or is not permitted by Ord 41, r 5(2). It is obvious from r 5(2) itself that it operates as an exception from the primary rule of evidence stated expressly in Ord 41, r 5(1) that a person may only give evidence as to "facts", which he "is able of his own knowledge to prove". Rule 5(2), by including statements of information or belief, plainly allows the adduction of hearsay. It also allows a statement of belief, that is to say

e an opinion; but in its context that belief must be that of the deponent, and such statements will have no probative value unless the sources and grounds of the information and belief are revealed. To my mind the purpose of r 5(2) is to enable a deponent to put before the court in interlocutory proceedings, frequently in circumstances of great urgency,

f facts which he is not able of his own knowledge to prove but which, the deponent is informed and believes, can be proved by means which the deponent identifies by specifying the sources and grounds of his information and belief. What r 5(2) allows the deponent to state that he has obtained from another must, in my judgment, be limited to what is admissible as evidence. Take, for example, a case where there are

g unsuccessful without prejudice discussions to settle an action, in the course of which a statement is made by a party which is highly relevant to an issue in interlocutory proceedings. I apprehend that the court would strike out from an affidavit made by another party who heard the statement any reference to such statement having been made, as it would

h not be admissible as evidence and so would be irrelevant. So too, in my judgment, a statement in an affidavit referring to other forms of inadmissible evidence should be treated as irrelevant. That would include statements of opinion not being within any recognised exception to the general principle to which I have referred. Further I find it impossible to accept counsel for SIB's submission that it is sufficient in order to comply

j with r 5(2) that the deponent should identify only the source to him of his information even though it is clear that that source was not the original source. Thus, if the deponent was informed of a fact by A, whom the deponent knows not to have firsthand knowledge of the fact but who had obtained the information from B, I cannot believe that it is sufficient for the deponent to identify A as the source of the information. That, to my

mind, would largely defeat the requirement that the sources and grounds
should be stated and would make it only too easy to introduce prejudicial *a*
material without revealing the original source of hearsay information by
the expedient of procuring as the deponent a person who receives
information second hand. By having to reveal such original source and not
merely the immediate source, the deponent affords a proper opportunity
to another party to challenge and counter such evidence, as well as *b*
enabling the court to assess the weight to be attributed to such evidence.
Even in a period in which the court's practice on interlocutory motions is
governed by the rules laid down in *American Cyanamid Co v Ethicon Ltd*
[1975] 1 All ER 504, [1975] AC 396 and accordingly the court avoids
determination of the facts at that stage, it is still common experience that
many cases do not progress beyond and are decided by the outcome of an *c*
interlocutory motion. In my judgment the court ought not to allow in
affidavits to be used in interlocutory proceedings material which cannot
be proved because it is mere opinion or is otherwise inadmissible. This is
the more important in cases like the present when the material sought to
be adduced will never be adjudicated on at the trial, because, as is common *d*
ground, it is not relevant to the issues at the trial. In the present case it is
not, of course, the opinion of any Tom, Dick or Harry that is in question
but the opinion of a statutory fact-finding body which has given its
opinion after a lengthy inquiry and after obtaining evidence from those
whose duty it was to give that evidence. The inspectors in the present case
are an eminent Queen's Counsel and a chartered accountant and they have *e*
manifestly been painstaking in the preparation of their reports. I have no
reason to think that the inspectors have not done their work carefully and
well. I would willingly give the report a special evidential status if I could,
but the consistent approach of the courts in the winding-up cases has been
to accept that the contents of an inspectors' report are only opinions and *f*
inadmissible save for the statutory justification for treating the reports in
winding-up proceedings as material on which the court could act if that
material was not challenged in a proper way. That is so even though r 30
of the Companies (Winding-up) Rules 1949, SI 1949/330, allows a
verifying affidavit for a petition to be sufficient prima facie evidence of the
statements in the petition and the statutory form of affidavit allows the *g*
deponent to state his belief without stating the source of his information.
That approach is inconsistent with affording any wider recognition to the
reports as evidence.'

Mr Boyd submitted that, in the present case, the DTI report merely set out the *h*
opinions of the inspectors based upon the evidence that they had considered
and that those opinions could not properly be relied upon by Mr Kaye as
sources of information and belief.

Mr Bartlett QC for the reinsurers submitted that, in *Savings and Investment
Bank Ltd v Gasco Investments (Netherlands) BV*, the plaintiffs were seeking to rely *j*
upon opinion evidence in its narrow sense, that is opinion of the probity of
conduct, rather than opinion as to the existence of facts. He submitted that
Peter Gibson J's decision should be restricted to excluding from affidavit
evidence reference to inadmissible opinion in the former sense. I do not find it
possible to read Peter Gibson J's judgment subject to this limitation. The
report with which he was dealing, just as the report in the present case, plainly

consisted largely of conclusions of fact based upon evidence considered by the inspectors. I consider that the *Gasco Investments* case fully supports Mr Boyd's submissions. Having carefully considered the decision in that case, however, I have concluded that it is not one which I am able to follow. I agree with Peter Gibson J that the purpose of r 5(2) is to enable a deponent to put before the court, frequently in circumstances of great urgency, facts which he is not able of his own knowledge to prove. Having regard to that purpose I cannot, with great respect, follow the judge in concluding that, at the interlocutory stage, a deponent must identify as the source of his information or belief an original source of evidence which will be admissible at the trial. The object of the rule militates against placing this restriction upon the natural meaning of its words. In a situation of urgency a plaintiff may well not have time to identify or trace evidence which will be admissible at the trial. If he has learned of facts via an intermediate source which there is good reason to believe will, itself, have had access to primary sources of information, I can see no good reason for precluding the plaintiff from relying upon that intermediate source as a ground for seeking interlocutory relief. Perhaps the most important form of interlocutory relief is the injunction. It seems to me that the power of the court to grant an interlocutory injunction is one that should be flexible and not fettered by the technical rules of admissibility of evidence that apply at a trial.

The weight to be attached to a statement of belief in an affidavit that depends upon sources and grounds other than the knowledge of the deponent will, of course, depend upon the nature of those sources and grounds. An original source will normally carry much more weight than an intermediate source, and where original sources are known, they must be identified. But it does not follow that intermediate sources cannot be referred to or relied upon. Ultimately it must be for the court to weigh all the material in order to decide whether the applicant has made out his case for the interlocutory relief sought.

In their report the DTI inspectors specifically identify some of the original sources for their conclusions of fact. In other parts of their report they do not do so. The plaintiffs prepared a schedule seeking to identify original source material for the inspectors' relevant findings of fact. They were not wholly successful, but they identified sufficient original source material to justify Mr Kaye advancing in his affidavit his belief as to the material facts, even if, contrary to my view, it was necessary for him to identify original sources of information.

For these reasons the applications to strike out parts of the reinsurers' affidavits must be dismissed.

THE FACTS

The reinsured have not sought to adduce any evidence to controvert most of the allegations of fact made by the reinsurers. On the material that they have placed before me, I find that the reinsurers have established a clear prima facie case in relation to seven of the eight matters that I summarised earlier in this judgment. I need to deal in a little more detail with the first matter: the question of the directing minds of the reinsured companies.

Directing minds

The pleadings and the reinsurers' affidavits suggested that it was their case that Driver, Henry Weavers and Wilson were directing minds of KWELM but not of the other reinsured companies. In the course of his submissions Mr

Bartlett expanded the reinsurers' case to allege that Driver, Henry Weavers and Wilson were the directing minds of all the reinsured companies. Mr *a* Bartlett undertook to seek leave to amend his pleadings to reflect this case.

The concept of the directing minds of a company becomes relevant when it is necessary to consider the knowledge or intention of the company. This necessity can arise in a number of different situations in the field of both criminal and civil law. Where a company is no more than a corporate vehicle *b* for the activities of an individual who owns almost all its shares, there will usually be no difficulty in identifying that individual as the directing mind of the company. Where the company is directed by a number of individuals, each performing different functions, the identification of the relevant directing mind can be more difficult. Affidavit evidence has been filed on behalf of the reinsured that gives information in relation to the shareholdings and *c* directorships of some of the reinsured companies. Wilson, Weavers and Driver are not shown to have been the majority shareholders of any of those companies, although the ultimate beneficial ownership of a number of them at the relevant times is not clear. LUI did not become the owner of Kingscroft, El Paso and Mutual until 1987 or 1988. So far as LUI itself is concerned, Wilson, *d* Weavers and Driver were minority shareholders, holding between them during most of the material period approximately 10% of the total issued share capital. During that period Driver, Weavers and Wilson were on the boards of KWELM and for much of that period on the board of LUI, together with other directors who were always in the majority. Taken as a whole, the evidence does not clearly establish that Wilson, Weavers and Driver were, in their *e* capacity as directors, the directing minds of any of the relevant companies other than Weavers.

All of the reinsured companies had delegated to Weavers as their agent the function of obtaining reinsurance cover and, in these circumstances, the exercise of trying to identify a directing mind or minds within the individual *f* companies in relation to this activity does not seem to me to be a realistic one. Mr Bartlett's broader submission was that Driver, Weavers and Wilson, as those to whom the placing of reinsurance had been delegated by each of the reinsured companies, were the directing minds of those companies in relation to reinsurance and that the knowledge of those three gentlemen was to be *g* attributed to the reinsured companies both because they were the relevant directing minds of those companies and because they were the agents of those companies. In my judgment this over-complicates the analysis. In considering the knowledge of the reinsured companies one should simply apply the principles that govern the circumstances in which the knowledge of an agent *h* who is instructed to place reinsurance falls to be attributed to his principal.

The principles governing restraint of payment under letters of credit

There is an abundance of authority that the contract that exists between a bank that issues a letter of credit or a performance guarantee and the *j* beneficiary in whose favour it is issued has to be considered independently from the underlying transaction to which it relates. Allegations of breach of the underlying transaction will not justify an attempt to restrain the beneficiary from claiming or the bank from making payment under a letter of credit. To this principle there is an exception where fraud is alleged. The nature of that exception has been put in issue in the present case.

The reinsurers' case

a   Mr Bartlett contends that an application for an injunction restraining payment under a letter of credit is subject to the guidelines laid down by the House of Lords in *American Cyanamid Co v Ethicon Ltd* [1975] 1 All ER 504, [1975] AC 396. The court first has to consider whether the plaintiff has made out a seriously arguable case for substantive relief (the threshold test). If he has, the

b   court has to consider whether damages will be an adequate remedy. If they will, an injunction will not normally be granted. If they will not, the court then has to consider other factors which affect the balance of convenience. One of these factors is the special role that a letter of credit plays in international trade.

    Mr Bartlett contends that where an injunction is sought to restrain a bank from paying under a letter of credit, fraud is relevant at two stages. No cause

c   of action will lie against a bank for making payment under a letter of credit unless the bank knows that the letter of credit is being drawn upon fraudulently. Thus the plaintiff has to pass the threshold of showing that there is a seriously arguable case, not merely that the drawer is fraudulent, but that the bank knows this. Then when the balance of convenience is considered, a

d   special factor weighs in the scale. It is the policy of the law, save in cases of fraud or illegality, not to interfere by injunction with the operations of banks under letters of credit and similar instruments, but to leave the plaintiff to his remedy against the beneficiary for breach of the underlying contract. Where an injunction is sought against a bank, the plaintiff must make out a clear case of fraud to the knowledge of the bank.

e   It is Mr Bartlett's submission that the *Cyanamid* guidelines apply equally where an injunction is sought to prevent the beneficiary from drawing on a letter of credit but that they are likely to have different results. The beneficiary and the plaintiff will both be parties to the underlying transaction. The letter of credit will be conditional payment in respect of the plaintiff's obligations

f   under that transaction. If for any reason the plaintiff's obligations have not arisen, it will be a breach of contract for the beneficiary to draw on the letter of credit. Thus, the threshold question is whether the plaintiff has a seriously arguable case that, having regard to the underlying transaction, the beneficiary has no right to draw on the letter of credit. Mr Bartlett accepts, however, that there remains a special factor to be considered when the balance of

g   convenience is weighed. The court will not grant an injunction unless the plaintiff makes out a case of fraud. But, so Mr Bartlett submits, a beneficiary will be acting fraudulently if he draws on the letter of credit in circumstances where he is in doubt as to whether or not the plaintiff is under obligation to him under the underlying transaction. Only if the beneficiary believes in his

h   entitlement to payment can he honestly draw on the letter of credit. If the plaintiff satisfies the court that there is a seriously arguable case that the beneficiary has no such belief, an injunction should be granted.

The reinsured's case

j   Mr Boyd did not attempt an analysis of the legal basis of the special rule in relation to letters of credit and the fraud exception to it. He simply submitted that the nature of that rule and of its exception is clear on authorities which bind me. An interlocutory injunction will not be granted to restrain payment under or drawing upon a letter of credit unless the plaintiff makes out a clear case that the beneficiary is acting fraudulently in drawing upon the letter of credit. Where an injunction is sought against a bank, the plaintiff must show

that the bank knows that the beneficiary is acting fraudulently. Where an
injunction is sought against a beneficiary, a sufficient case of fraud will not be   a
made out unless the plaintiff demonstrates that the beneficiary knows that he
has no right to draw on the letter of credit.

The correct approach

I admired Mr Bartlett's skilful attempt to rationalise this area of the law   b
within the familiar *Cyanamid* guidelines. I have not, however, found it possible
to reconcile his approach with binding authority. The majority of the cases
involve injunctions sought against banks. Here the comparatively recent
foundations of our law are to be found in *Edward Owen Engineering Ltd v
Barclays Bank International Ltd* [1978] 1 All ER 976, [1978] QB 159 and the cases
cited in it. That case involved a performance guarantee, but the Court of   c
Appeal held that the same principles applied as applied to a letter of credit.
Lord Denning MR adopted this statement of principle from the judgment of
Kerr J in *R D Harbottle (Mercantile) Ltd v National Westminster Bank Ltd* [1977] 2
All ER 862 at 870, [1978] QB 146 at 155:

> 'It is only in exceptional cases that the courts will interfere with the   d
> machinery of irrevocable obligations assumed by banks. They are the
> life-blood of international commerce. Such obligations are regarded as
> collateral to the underlying rights and obligations between the merchants
> at either end of the banking chain. Except possibly in clear cases of fraud
> of which the banks have notice, the courts will leave the merchants to   e
> settle their disputes under the contracts by litigation or arbitration ... The
> courts are not concerned with their difficulties to enforce such claims;
> these are risks which the merchants take. In this case the plaintiffs took
> the risk of the unconditional wording of the guarantees. The machinery
> and commitments of banks are on a different level. They must be allowed
> to be honoured, free from interference by the courts. Otherwise, trust in   f
> international commerce could be irreparably damaged.' (See [1978] 1 All
> ER 976 at 983, [1978] QB 159 at 171.)

Browne LJ approved this passage from the judgment of Kerr J ([1978] 1 All ER
976 at 985, [1978] QB 159 at 174):
                                                                                         g
> '"I am not saying that in such cases [that is, cases where parties have
> entered into confirmed letters of credit] the courts would not again
> assume jurisdiction. Indeed, as was said in some of the authorities, in
> cases of obvious fraud to the knowledge of banks, the courts may preclude
> banks from fulfilling their obligations to third parties. But in the present   h
> case there is simply a contractual dispute between the plaintiffs and their
> customers in Libya, in which the rights and wrongs are not clear, though
> as mentioned above I assume that the rights are on the side of the
> plaintiffs. They will unfortunately have to pursue those rights against the
> buyers as best they can."'
                                                                                         j
These principles have been followed repeatedly in subsequent cases.

In a number of instances the courts have purported to apply the *Cyanamid*
test in a case such as this: *Howe Richardson Scale Co Ltd v Polimex-Cekop* [1978] 1
Lloyd's Rep 161 at 165 per Roskill LJ, *Dong Jin Metal Co Ltd v Raymet Ltd* [1993]
CA Transcript 945 per Lloyd LJ and *United Trading Corp SA v Allied Arab Bank
Ltd* [1985] 2 Lloyd's Rep 554n. Only in this last case did the court consider the

nature of the threshold test. This raised the question of the cause of action
where an injunction is sought to prevent a bank paying under a performance
bond. Both parties agreed, having regard to *Siskina (cargo owners) v Distos Cia
Naviera SA, The Siskina* [1977] 3 All ER 803, [1979] AC 210, that a cause of action
had to be demonstrated. Negligence was selected as the most plausible cause
of action. Ackner LJ held that 'the evidence of fraud must be clear, both as to
the fact of fraud and as to the bank's knowledge' and went on to define the
Cyanamid threshold test as follows:

> 'Have the plaintiffs established that it is seriously arguable that, on the
> material available, the only realistic inference is that [the beneficiaries]
> could not honestly have believed in the validity of its demands on the
> performance bonds?' (See [1985] 2 Lloyd's Rep 554 at 561.)

The nature of the cause of action in a case such as this has not often been
considered by the courts. Ackner LJ remarked that in America, which is the
source of the fraud exception, it is not necessary for a plaintiff to demonstrate
a cause of action against a bank (see [1985] 2 Lloyd's Rep 554 at 561). In *United
City Merchants (Investments) Ltd v Royal Bank of Canada* [1982] 2 All ER 720 at
725, [1983] 1 AC 168 at 184 Lord Diplock stated:

> 'The exception for fraud on the part of the beneficiary seeking to avail
> himself of the credit is a clear application of the maxim ex turpi causa non
> oritur actio or, if plain English is to be preferred, "fraud unravels all". The
> courts will not allow their process to be used by a dishonest person to
> carry out a fraud.'

This raises the question of whether, as an exception to the *Siskina* principle,
the court will intervene by injunction to prevent the perpetration of a fraud. In
Bolivinter Oil SA v Chase Manhattan Bank [1984] 1 Lloyd's Rep 251 at 254
Donaldson MR accepted the following proposition:

> 'The Court should grant an injunction restraining payment under a
> letter of credit or performance guarantee where the result of payment is
> likely to be to permit the ultimate beneficiary to profit from his own fraud
> at the expense of the Plaintiff ... The basis of the jurisdiction is not the
> power of the Court to grant an injunction restraining a breach of contract.
> The Plaintiff does not have to establish that the payment enjoined would
> constitute a breach of contractual duty owed to the Plaintiff by the Bank.
> The basis of the jurisdiction is wider—the power of the Court to intervene
> where necessary to prevent fraud. The Plaintiff has to show that his legal
> rights are threatened by the fraud of the beneficiary.'

The threshold test suggested by Ackner LJ of asking whether it is seriously
arguable that fraud is the only realistic inference is a puzzling one, combining
as it does two very different standards of proof. Furthermore, the requirement
that there must be clear evidence of the bank's knowledge of fraud is academic
once the proceedings have reached the inter partes stage. At this point the
evidence of fraud will be placed simultaneously before the court and before the
bank, which is party to the proceedings (see the discussion in the *United Trading
Corp* case [1985] 2 Lloyd's Rep 554 at 560). If the court concludes that there is
clear evidence of fraud, it will necessarily conclude that the bank has acquired
knowledge of the fraud.

The difficulty of analysing in terms of legal principle this area of the law is compounded by the fact that, so far as I am aware, there is no reported case where the court, in inter partes proceedings, has approved the grant of an injunction on the basis of the fraud exception. What is, in my view, clearly established by the authorities is that the court will not grant an injunction restraining a bank from paying under a letter of credit unless the court is satisfied that there is a clear prima facie case that the beneficiary is acting fraudulently in drawing on the credit.

I turn to consider Mr Bartlett's submission that a different test falls to be applied where an injunction is sought against the beneficiary. It seems to me that the effect of Mr Bartlett's submissions is to deprive the letter of credit of any special status so far as the beneficiary is concerned. If a beneficiary is to be held to be fraudulent if he draws on a letter of credit in circumstances where he is uncertain as to the validity of his right to payment under the underlying contract, the plaintiff seeking to enjoin him will have to do no more than persuade the court that there is a seriously arguable case that the claim under the underlying contract is invalid. This will rob the beneficiary of much of the benefit which a letter of credit is intended to bestow. Where a letter of credit is issued by way of conditional payment under an underlying contract, I do not consider that it is correct to imply a term into the underlying contract that the beneficiary will not draw on the letter of credit unless payment under the underlying contract is due. On the contrary, I consider that the correct contractual inference that should normally be drawn is that the beneficiary will be entitled to draw on the letter of credit provided that he has a bona fide claim to payment under the underlying contract. If this is correct, there is no basis for the suggestion that the court should apply a different test when considering an application to restrain a beneficiary, rather than a bank, from effecting payment under a letter of credit.

When one turns to the authorities, they lend no support to the distinction that Mr Bartlett seeks to establish. In *Malas (trading as Hamzeh Malas & Sons) v British Imex Industries Ltd* [1958] 1 All ER 262, [1958] 2 QB 127 buyers sought to restrain sellers from drawing on a letter of credit on the ground that payment was not due under the underlying sale transaction. In denying the plaintiffs their injunction, Jenkins LJ said that the system of financing transactions by letter of credit—

> 'would break down completely if a dispute between the vendor and the purchaser were to have the effect of "freezing", if I may use the expression, the sum in respect of which the letter of credit was opened.' (See [1958] 1 All ER 262 at 263, [1958] 2 QB 127 at 129.)

In *R D Harbottle (Mercantile) Ltd v National Westminster Bank Ltd* [1977] 2 All ER 862, [1978] QB 146 the plaintiffs sought to restrain, among others, the beneficiaries from drawing on performance guarantees. Kerr J held that it might well be right that the beneficiaries had no right to payment under the guarantees, but that the case fell well short of established fraud. In these circumstances, of his own motion, he discharged the ex parte injunction that had been granted against the beneficiaries. In *Howe Richardson Scale Co Ltd v Polimex-Cekop* [1978] 1 Lloyd's Rep 161 Donaldson J had held at first instance that there was a strong prima facie case that the beneficiaries of a bank guarantee were not entitled, under the underlying transaction, to draw on the guarantee, but refused to grant an injunction restraining them from doing so.

The Court of Appeal upheld this decision. In the *Bolivinter Oil* case [1984] 1 Lloyd's Rep 251 an ex parte injunction was obtained restraining the beneficiaries from drawing upon and the banks from paying under a performance guarantee. The banks applied successfully to discharge the injunction, and this decision was upheld by the Court of Appeal. No appeal was made by the beneficiaries. The evidence indicated that they had no right to claim under the underlying contract, but did not clearly establish that their claim was made fraudulently. Because there was no appeal against the injunction granted against the beneficiaries, the Court of Appeal allowed it to stand. The court indicated however (at 256–257):

> '... it has the effect of breaching the great and fundamentally important separation maintained by the Courts between the rights of the parties under the underlying contract ... and the rights of one of them under the independent banking contract.'

Finally, in *Dong Jin Metal Co Ltd v Raymet Ltd* [1993] CA Transcript 945 the Court of Appeal rejected the submission that a different test applied where an injunction was sought against a beneficiary from that which applied when an injunction was sought against a bank.

In the light of these authorities, and for the reasons given earlier in this judgment, I have concluded that there is no difference in what the reinsurers have to establish to obtain their injunctions in this case from that which they would have to establish if they were seeking injunctions against the banks which have issued or confirmed the letters of credit. They must establish that, in drawing on the letters of credit, the reinsured will be acting fraudulently in that they will be claiming payment to which they know they have no entitlement.

I should add, that in advancing the arguments that he did in relation to this area of the case, it seems to me that Mr Bartlett was seeking to reopen issues decided against him in the earlier proceedings before Clarke J. Mr Boyd was content to rest his case on the merits, rather than on any plea of issue estoppel, and I have dealt with the law in some detail out of deference to the detailed arguments advanced by Mr Bartlett.

What must the reinsurers prove?

In order to justify the grant of an injunction, the reinsurers must prove that if the reinsured draw on the letters of credit, they will do so fraudulently in the knowledge that they have no right to payment under them. The reinsurers contend that the reinsured have no right to payment under the letters of credit because the underlying contracts which gave rise to those rights have been validly avoided. In so far as there is an issue as to that, the reinsurers have sought to persuade me that that issue will clearly fall to be resolved in the reinsurers' favour at trial—so clearly indeed that my judgment to that effect will suffice to preclude the reinsured from drawing bona fide on the letters of credit and, in consequence, justify the grant of an injunction restraining them from doing so.

The issue of the validity of the reinsurers' purported avoidance of the contracts of reinsurance raises difficult questions of fact and law. I have concluded that the issues of law are not ones which it would be appropriate for me to determine on an interlocutory hearing pursuant to the powers conferred on me by Ord 14A. These issues have been argued at some length, but having regard to the provisional views that I have formed in relation to them, I can deal with them quite briefly.

The reinsurers' case on the avoidance of the contracts of insurance can be summarised as follows. (1) Wilson, Weavers and Driver were acting fraudulently in misappropriating the overriding commission that should have been credited to the reinsured. (2) This fraudulent conduct was a material factor which would influence the conduct of a prudent insurer when considering whether to take the risk. Had they known of it, the reinsurers would not have been prepared to take the risk. (3) Knowledge of this conduct was imputed to each of the reinsured companies by virtue of the fact that Wilson, Weavers and Driver were the directing minds of those companies in relation to reinsurance. Accordingly, they were obliged to disclose this to the reinsurers. (4) Wilson, Weavers and Driver, as the agents placing the reinsurance on behalf of the reinsured, were obliged to disclose all material facts within their knowledge, including the fact of their fraudulent conduct. (5) The reinsurers did not learn of the fraudulent conduct until they received the DTI report, whereupon they validly avoided the contracts of reinsurance for non-disclosure. The reinsured join issue in relation to each of these contentions.

I have found that there is a clear prima facie case that Wilson, Weavers and Driver acted fraudulently as alleged. On the affidavit evidence as it stands, the reinsurers' agents who negotiated the reinsurance were unaware of the diversion of the overriding commission. There is, however, a relevant question in relation to this matter which has not been addressed in the affidavits sworn on behalf of the reinsurers. How did it come about that no mention of the overriding commission appeared in the reinsurance treaties themselves?

Materiality

Mr Bartlett submitted that the dishonest conduct of Wilson, Weavers and Driver constituted a moral hazard and that therefore it was axiomatic that it was a material matter that should have been disclosed. I see the force of the argument that reinsurers are likely to be disinclined to accept risks from brokers or agents who have behaved dishonestly, but where the dishonest conduct has no impact on the risks being reinsured, I question whether it can entitle the reinsurers to avoid contracts placed by such brokers or agents on the ground of non-disclosure. The doctrine of non-disclosure is founded in equity. Avoidance in circumstances such as those of this case is liable to have results that are inequitable. Reinsurance is a vital aspect of the security provided by an insurer. If dishonesty of a broker entitles all who have dealt with that broker to avoid their contracts on the ground of non-disclosure of moral hazard, the result can impact harshly not only on the reinsured but on the primary insured. I would not expect the trial judge in this case to make a more generous finding of the ambit of materiality than that which a strict application of the law requires. The Court of Appeal has recently in *Pan Atlantic Insurance Co Ltd v Pine Top Insurance Co Ltd* [1993] 1 Lloyd's Rep 496[b] clarified the test of

---

b Subsequent to the proceedings herein the decision of the Court of Appeal in *Pan Atlantic Insurance Co Ltd v Pine Top Insurance Co Ltd* [1993] 1 Lloyd's Rep 496 has been affirmed by the House of Lords (see [1994] 3 All ER 581, [1994] 3 WLR 677).

materiality laid down in *Container Transport International Inc v Oceanus Mutual Underwriting Association (Bermuda) Ltd* [1984] 1 Lloyd's Rep 476. Steyn LJ held:

> '... as the law now stands, the question is whether the prudent insurer would view the undisclosed material as probably tending to increase the risk.' (See [1993] 1 Lloyd's Rep 496 at 506.)

Whether the fact that Driver, Weavers and Wilson were diverting overriding commission was a matter which the prudent reinsurer would view as probably tending to increase the risk is a question of fact which will have to be resolved at the trial. I would simply observe that the fact that overriding commission was being diverted does not, on the face of it, have an impact on the risks being reinsured.

Imputation of knowledge

There is an issue between Mr Bartlett and Mr Boyd as to why it is that an insured or reinsured is affected by non-disclosure of facts which are known to the agent who effects the insurance or reinsurance, but not to the insured or reinsured. Mr Bartlett submits that this is because the agent owes an obligation to disclose all material facts within his own knowledge. Mr Boyd submits that it is because the knowledge of the agent is imputed to his principal. This issue may seem of no significance, but it has relevance in relation to a more fundamental issue in relation to imputed knowledge.

Mr Bartlett relied upon this statement by Hoffmann LJ in *El Ajou v Dollar Land Holdings plc* [1994] 2 All ER 685 at 702:

> 'The circumstances in which the knowledge of an agent is imputed to the principal can vary a great deal and care is needed in analysing the cases. They fall into a number of categories which are not always sufficiently clearly distinguished ... First, there are cases in which an agent is authorised to enter into a transaction in which his own knowledge is material. So, for example, an insurance policy may be avoided on account of the broker's failure to disclose material facts within his knowledge, even though he did not obtain that knowledge in his capacity as agent for the insured. As Lord Macnaghten said in *Blackburn Lowe & Co v Vigors* (1887) 12 App Cas 531 at 542–543: "But that is not because the knowledge of the agent is to be imputed to the principal but because the agent of the assured is bound as the principal is bound to communicate to the underwriters all material facts within his knowledge."'

Mr Boyd submitted that the passage cited from the speech of Lord Macnaghten represented a minority view in *Blackburn Lowe & Co v Vigors*. The majority view expressed in that case was that the knowledge of the broker was imputed to his principal. Having considered that case, I agree with Mr Boyd. Lord Halsbury LC approved this statement (12 App Cas 531 at 535–536, 537):

> '... the principal is to be as responsible for any knowledge of a material fact acquired by his agent employed to obtain the insurance as if he acquired it himself ... When a person is the agent to know, his knowledge does bind the principal.'

A careful reading of the speech of Lord Watson has persuaded me that he also considered that the knowledge of a broker effecting insurance fell to be imputed to his principal (see 12 App Cas 531 at 537–538). Lord FitzGerald adopted the reasoning of Lord Halsbury LC and Lord Watson.

The reason for the debate that I have just addressed was a dispute between Mr Bartlett and Mr Boyd as to the applicability to a case such as the present of an exception to the rule whereby the knowledge of an agent is imputed to the principal. This exception was stated by Buckley LJ in *Belmont Finance Corp Ltd v Williams Furniture Ltd* [1979] 1 All ER 118 at 126, [1979] Ch 250 at 261 as follows:

'... it is a well-recognised exception from the general rule that a principal is affected by notice received by his agent that, if the agent is acting in fraud of his principal and the matter of which he has notice is relevant to the fraud, that knowledge is not to be imputed to the principal.'

That rule dates back to *Re Hampshire Land Co* [1896] 2 Ch 743 and has been applied in a number of different circumstances (see *J C Houghton & Co v Northard Lowe & Wills Ltd* [1928] AC 1, [1927] All ER Rep 97, *Newsholme Bros v Road Transport and General Insurance Co Ltd* [1929] 2 KB 356, [1929] All ER Rep 442 and *Chao (trading as Zung Fu Co) v British Traders and Shippers Ltd (NV Handel-maatschappij J Smits Import-Export, third party)* [1954] 1 All ER 779, [1954] 2 QB 459).

Mr Bartlett submitted that the essence of the rule was that the court will not infer that a company has knowledge of a fact known to an agent or director of the company in circumstances where, because of the agent's or director's fraud or other breach of duty to the company, it would be contrary to common sense to draw such an inference. Mr Bartlett submitted, however, that the rule had no application in a case such as the present. The rule that here applied was that where an agent's fraud, default or wrongdoing caused loss or prejudice to two parties, the loss or prejudice should fall on the party by whom the agent was trusted or employed or who took the risk of the agent's wrongdoing. This principle dated back to the decision of Lord Mansfield in *Fitzherbert v Mather* (1785) 1 Term Rep 12, 99 ER 944.

I have found this area of the law one of great difficulty. Where a director or a broker commits a fraud on a company which has a direct impact on a risk which is placed on behalf of that company with insurers or reinsurers, I can see the force of the argument that the rule in *Re Hampshire Land Co* should give way to the rule in *Fitzherbert v Mather*. Where, however, the materiality of the fraud is said to be no more than moral hazard I find it an affront to common sense that the cover of the insured or reinsured should be at risk because of failure to disclose a fraud committed on itself of which only the fraudster was aware. In such circumstances my inclination would be to apply the rule in *Re Hampshire Land Co*.

For these reasons it is not clear to me that the reinsurers have validly avoided the contracts of reinsurance. On the contrary, my provisional view is that they probably have not done so. In these circumstances the reinsurers have not made out a clear case that the reinsured will be acting fraudulently if they draw on the letters of credit and the applications for injunctions restraining them from so doing will be dismissed.

The claims for injunctions restraining disposal of the proceeds of the letters of credit

I turn to the alternative claim that the reinsurers make for an interlocutory injunction restraining the reinsured from disposing of any sums that they may draw under the letters of credit. This is not a claim for Mareva relief. The reinsurers accept that those who presently have the conduct of the reinsured's affairs will not seek to put their assets beyond the reach of the reinsurers in order to deny them the fruits of these proceedings. The relief is sought pursuant to Ord 29, r 2 on the basis that the reinsurers have a seriously arguable claim to a proprietary interest in the proceeds of the letters of credit.

There are, in my judgment, a number of problems confronting the reinsurers in seeking this relief. Foremost among these is the difficulty of establishing any proprietary claim on the part of the reinsurers to moneys paid by the banks under the letters of credit.

In the first action the reinsurers seek to rely upon the terms of a 'trust agreement' concluded with the reinsured on 5 July 1983. The problem in respect of this is that the reinsurers have purported to rescind it on the same grounds of non-disclosure as they have invoked when purporting to avoid the contracts of reinsurance. As Mr Boyd pointed out, if the avoidance is valid, no trust can arise under the trust agreement. If the avoidance is invalid, no challenge can be made of the reinsured's entitlement to moneys drawn under the letters of credit.

In relation to both actions Mr Bartlett advanced an alternative argument. He contended that if the reinsurers draw under the letters of credit moneys to which they have no entitlement because the underlying contracts of re-insurance have been duly avoided, the reinsurers will acquire 'a proprietary claim in equity to trace the proceeds of the letters of credit, based on an equitable right in the nature of a constructive trust'.

This seemed a surprising proposition, having regard to the fact that the reinsurers would have no proprietary interest in the moneys in question prior to their payment to the reinsured by the banks. As the argument developed it became apparent that Mr Bartlett was seeking to advance the frontiers of our law by inviting me to recognise the existence in this case of what has been described in the United States as a remedial trust. The American Law Institute's *Restatement of the Law, Restitution* (1937) § 160, describes this as follows:

> 'Where a person holding title to property is subject to an equitable duty to convey it to another on the ground that he would be unjustly enriched if he was permitted to retain it, a constructive trust arises.'

Such a trust has been recognised in a number of Commonwealth jurisdictions. In *Metall und Rohstoff AG v Donaldson Lufkin & Jenrette Inc* [1989] 3 All ER 14 at 57, [1990] 1 QB 391 at 479 Slade LJ considered whether such a trust could arise under English law:

> 'The extent to which a constructive trust can properly be treated as a remedy is far from clearly defined in the authorities. The position is stated thus in *Snell's Principles of Equity* (28th edn, 1982) p 193: "In some jurisdictions the constructive trust has come to be treated as a remedy for many cases of unjust enrichment; whenever the court considers that the property in question ought to be restored, it simply imposes a constructive trust on the recipient. In England, however, the constructive trust has in general remained essentially a substantive institution; ownership must not be confused with obligation, nor must the relationship of debtor and creditor be converted into one of trustee and *cestui que* trust. Yet the attitude of the courts may be changing; and although the constructive trust is probably not confined to cases arising out of a fiduciary

relationship, it is far from clear what other circumstances suffice to raise it or how far it can be employed as a species of equitable remedy to enforce legal rights." However, the authors of Goff and Jones *The Law of Restitution* (3rd edn, 1986), p 78, after a comprehensive review of the authorities, state their views as follows: "Equity's rules were formulated in litigation arising out of the administration of a trust. In contrast restitutionary claims are infinitely varied. In our view the question whether a restitutionary proprietary claim should be granted should depend on whether it is just, in the particular circumstances of the case, to impose a constructive trust on, or an equitable lien over, particular assets, or to allow subrogation to a lien over such assets." While we have had the benefit of very full argument on almost all other aspects of the law involved in this case, we have neither heard nor invited comprehensive argument as to the circumstances in which the court will be prepared to impose a constructive trust de novo as a foundation for the grant of equitable remedy by way of account or otherwise. Nevertheless, we are satisfied that there is a good arguable case that such circumstances may arise and, for want of a better description, will refer to a constructive trust of this nature as a "remedial constructive trust".'

I fear that the circumstances of this case provide barren ground in which to attempt to nurture a remedial constructive trust. Mr Bartlett has failed to persuade me that there is any basis upon which his clients can assert a proprietary interest in moneys that may be paid to the reinsured by banks, out of the banks' own funds, pursuant to obligations undertaken under letters of credit. True it is that the reinsurers will have to reimburse those banks, directly or indirectly, but I cannot see how that can give rise to a proprietary claim to the moneys advanced by the banks. Mr Bartlett referred me to *Agip (Africa) Ltd v Jackson* [1992] 4 All ER 451, [1991] Ch 547. That case involved a payment made by way of international banking transfers, where the British paying bank took a delivery risk by paying with its own funds some hours before it received the transfer that originated from the plaintiffs' bank in Tunisia. The Court of Appeal held that on those facts it was possible to trace in equity the payment made by the British bank as originating from the plaintiffs' funds in Tunisia. I do not consider the special facts of that case can be applied so as to enable a payment made by a bank under a letter of credit to be treated as a payment of funds beneficially owned by the opener of the credit.

More generally, the claim to relief which Mr Bartlett advances would, if well-founded, be available in every case where a plaintiff challenged the right of a beneficiary under a letter of credit to payment under the underlying transaction. Such relief would clot what has been described as the lifeblood of international commerce as surely as an injunction restraining drawing on the credit.

For these reasons I am not prepared to grant the injunctions sought under Ord 29, r 2.

Applications dismissed.

K Mydeen Esq   Barrister.

Littrell v United States of America (No 2)

COURT OF APPEAL, CIVIL DIVISION

NOURSE, ROSE AND HOFFMANN LJJ

19, 20, 21 OCTOBER, 12 NOVEMBER 1993

Constitutional law – Foreign sovereign state – Immunity from suit – Treaty regulating stationing of member states' forces in each other's territory – Member of US Air Force sustaining injury through treatment by US medical personnel at US military base hospital – Serviceman claiming damages against United States government – Whether treaty relevant to plaintiff's claim – Whether conduct of US government being exercise of sovereign immune authority – Agreement regarding the Status of Forces of Parties to the North Atlantic Treaty 1951, art VIII, para 5.

The plaintiff brought proceedings in England against the United States government and the United Kingdom Ministry of Defence, claiming damages for personal injuries arising out of medical treatment administered in 1987 by US Air Force personnel at a US military hospital in England. The plaintiff was a member of the US Air Force at the time, but he contended that his claim ought to be decided according to English law, since it fell within art VIII, para 5ᵃ of the Agreement regarding the Status of Forces of Parties to the North Atlantic Treaty 1951, to which both the United Kingdom and United States governments were parties and which was incorporated into English municipal law by virtue of the Visiting Forces Act 1952 and arrangements made thereunder. Article VIII, para 5 provided inter alia that where claims arose out of the acts of members of a visiting force done in performance of an official duty for which the sending state was responsible and which caused damage to third parties in the territory of the receiving state where the visiting force was located, the cost incurred in satisfying those claims would be payable by the receiving state and the sending state in the proportion 25:75. The Ministry of Defence applied for an order that it cease to be a party to the action, which the deputy judge granted on the ground that art VIII, para 5 of the treaty agreement did not confer on the plaintiff any right of action against the United Kingdom government, since the term 'third parties' did not include 'members of a visiting force' such as the plaintiff. The United States government subsequently applied for and obtained an order that the English court had no jurisdiction to entertain the plaintiff's claim on the ground that the United States government was immune from suit. The plaintiff appealed against that judge's order and the case proceeded on the revised basis that the treaty agreement was not in fact incorporated into English law. The plaintiff contended that since the treaty agreement was not part of English law, sovereign immunity was instead governed by the principles of customary international law to the extent that they were part of English municipal law and that, on current principles, the conduct of the United States government that gave rise to the plaintiff's claim should be characterised as acta jure gestionis (of a private or commercial law character in relation to which the defendant government would not be immune from suit) and not as acta jure imperii (the exercise of sovereign immune authority), with the result that the

---

ᵃ   Paragraph 5, so far as material, is set out at p 208 *c d*, post

government now had no immunity in relation to personal injury claims in tort. The United States government accepted that the treaty agreement was not part *a* of English law, but contended that it was none the less appropriate to take it into consideration since in 1951 the parties to the agreement, which defined the consensual basis on which the US troops entered the United Kingdom, could not have contemplated that claims against sovereign states would be outflanked by a later change in customary international law and therefore any *b* such change subsequent to the treaty agreement which imposed greater liability on a state by reducing sovereign immunity had to give way to the agreement prevailing between the NATO powers.

Held – (1) The terms of a treaty conferring immunity on a foreign state were *c* ineffective in English law unless confirmed by the enactment of Parliament and, in the absence of statutory enactment, it was the common law including the incorporated rules of customary international law which identified and defined the extent of sovereign immunity and it was the common law in operation at the time when the claim was made which was determinative. If the contracting parties wished their relationship to be unaffected by changes in *d* international law it would be open to them so to provide in the treaty agreement itself, or by further agreement, but in the absence of incorporation of such a treaty into municipal law, the rights of individuals would remain unaffected. It followed that the treaty agreement under consideration was clearly irrelevant to the plaintiff's claim and that the deputy judge should have *e* so ruled and dismissed the action against the Ministry of Defence on that ground and consequently any matters relating to the construction of terms of the treaty did not arise for determination. The question whether the United States government was immune from suit accordingly depended on whether the plaintiff's claim could be characterised as acta jure gestionis or acta jure imperii (see p 210 *h* to p 211 *c*, p 216 *a* to *e* and p 217 *h j*, post); *The Parlement* *f* *Belge* (1879) 4 PD 129 applied.

(2) When deciding whether the conduct of a foreign state should be characterised as acta jure gestionis or acta jure imperii the court would look at all the circumstances in relation to the nature of the activity giving rise to the plaintiff's claim and its context and decide whether those factors together *g* characterised the activity as sovereign or non-sovereign. The activity under consideration was the medical treatment by the United States government in one of its base hospitals of a member of its armed forces in the context of its maintenance of those forces in the United Kingdom. The nature of the treatment, the identity of those involved and the place where it was given were *h* factors which together pointed irresistibly to the conclusion that the judge was right in characterising the activity as jure imperii. It followed that the plaintiff could not bring an action in the English courts for damages for personal injuries arising out of allegedly negligent medical treatment carried out at a US military hospital on a US military base in England on the ground that the *j* treatment, which was in the context of the United States government's maintenance of its forces in the United Kingdom, was an act in the exercise of United States sovereign authority and was therefore immune from suit. The appeal would accordingly be dismissed (see p 213 *b* to *e*, p 216 *f j* and p 217 *c d f* to *j*, post); dicta of Lord Wilberforce in *I Congreso del Partido* [1981] 2 All ER 1064 at 1072, 1074 applied.

Notes

For sovereign immunity from suit, see 8 *Halsbury's Laws* (4th edn) para 410, and for cases on the subject, see 1(1) *Digest* (2nd reissue) *69–72, 546–555.*

For visiting forces, see 41 *Halsbury's Laws* (4th edn) paras 127–142, and for cases on the subject, see 39(2) *Digest* (Reissue) *37–38, 224–227.*

For the Visiting Forces Act 1952, see 3 *Halsbury's Statutes* (4th edn) 935.

Cases referred to in judgments

British Airways Board v Laker Airways Ltd [1984] 3 All ER 39, [1985] AC 58, [1984] 3 WLR 413, HL.

Chow Hung Ching v R (1948) 77 CLR 449, Aust HC.

Chung Chi Cheung v R [1938] 4 All ER 786, [1939] AC 160, PC.

Cia Naviera Vascongada v Cristina, The Cristina [1938] 1 All ER 719, [1938] AC 485, HL.

Claim against Empire of Iran (1963) 45 ILR 57, FDR Fed Const Ct.

Coleman v Tennessee (1878) 97 US 509, US SC.

Exemption of US Forces, Re (1943) 4 DLR 11, Can SC.

Feres (executrix) v US (1950) 340 US 135, US SC.

I Congreso del Partido [1981] 2 All ER 1064, [1983] 1 AC 244, [1981] 3 WLR 328, HL.

Littrell v USA [1992] 3 All ER 218.

Maclaine Watson & Co Ltd v Dept of Trade and Industry [1989] 3 All ER 523, sub nom *J H Rayner (Mincing Lane) Ltd v Dept of Trade and Industry* [1990] 2 AC 418, [1989] 3 WLR 969, HL.

Parlement Belge, The (1879) 4 PD 129; *rvsd* (1880) 5 PD 197, [1874–80] All ER Rep 104, CA.

Philippine Admiral (owners) v Wallem Shipping (Hong Kong) Ltd [1976] 1 All ER 78, [1977] AC 373, [1976] 2 WLR 214, PC.

Schooner Exchange, The v McFaddon (1812) 7 Cranch 116, US SC.

Secretary of State in Council of India v Kamachee Boye Sahaba (1859) 13 Moo PCC 22, 15 ER 9, PC.

Trendtex Trading Corp v Central Bank of Nigeria [1977] 1 All ER 881, [1977] QB 529, [1977] 2 WLR 356, CA.

Victory Transport Inc v Comisaria General de Abastecimientos y Transportes (1964) 336 F 2d 354, US Ct of Apps (2nd Cir).

Walker v Baird [1892] AC 491, PC.

Wright v Cantrell (1943) 44 SR (NSW) 45, NSW SC.

Cases also cited or referred to in skeleton arguments

A-G for Canada v A-G for Ontario [1937] AC 326, PC.

A-G v De Keyser's Royal Hotel Ltd [1920] AC 508, [1920] All ER Rep 80, HL.

Baronci v Ospedale del Bambino Gesu (1956) 24 ILR 215.

Buchanan (James) & Co Ltd v Babco Forwarding and Shipping (UK) Ltd [1977] 3 All ER 1048, [1978] AC 141, HL.

Buttes Gas and Oil Co v Hammer (Nos 2 and 3), Occidental Petroleum Corp v Buttes Gas and Oil Co (Nos 1 and 2) [1981] 3 All ER 616, [1982] AC 888, HL.

Ciniglio v Indonesian Embassy (1966) 65 ILR 268.

Collision with Foreign Government Owned Motor Car (Austria) Case (1961) 40 ILR 73.

Empresa Exportadora de Azucar v Industria Azucarera Nacional SA, The Playa Larga [1983] 2 Lloyd's Rep 171, CA.

Fothergill v Monarch Airlines Ltd [1980] 2 All ER 696, [1981] AC 251, HL.
IRC v Exxon Corp [1982] STC 356, [1982] 1 WLR 999.
Sengupta v Republic of India [1983] ICR 221.
US Government v IRSA (1966) 65 ILR 262.

Interlocutory appeal
The plaintiff, Ricardo Louis Littrell, appealed from the decision of Sir Gervase
Sheldon (sitting as a judge of the High Court) made on 8 June 1992 that the
court had no jurisdiction to entertain his claim for damages for personal
injuries and loss against the United States government arising out of medical
treatment between December 1987 and 23 October 1989, which was
negligently administered to the plaintiff by US Air Force medical personnel at
the military hospital, RAF Lakenheath, Suffolk, on the ground that the United
States government was immune from suit. The plaintiff had originally brought
proceedings against the Ministry of Defence as second defendant, but on 14
November 1991 Robert Carnwath QC (sitting as a deputy judge of the High
Court) ([1992] 3 All ER 218) had acceded to an application by the defendant that
it cease to be a party to the action on the ground that the provisions of the
Agreement regarding the Status of Forces of Parties to the North Atlantic
Treaty 1951 (London, 19 June 1951; TS 3 (1955); Cmd 9363) did not confer on
the plaintiff any right of action against the United Kingdom government. The
facts are set out in the judgment of Rose LJ.

Maurice Mendelson QC, Andrew Buchan and *Malcolm Shaw* (instructed by
    Cunningham John & Co, Thetford) for the plaintiff.
Charles Falconer QC and *Timothy Saloman QC* (instructed by *Nabarro Nathanson*)
    for the United States government.

Cur adv vult

12 November 1993. The following judgments were delivered.

ROSE LJ (giving the first judgment at the invitation of Nourse LJ). The
plaintiff, Ricardo Louis Littrell, with the leave of the judge, appeals against a
decision of Sir Gervase Sheldon sitting as a judge of the High Court on 8 June
1992. He ordered, on the defendant's application under RSC Ord 12, r 8(1)(h),
that the court decline jurisdiction on the ground that the defendant is immune
from suit. As will appear, the argument before this court has not proceeded on
the same basis as before the judge.
　　The plaintiff was a staff sergeant in the United States Air Force stationed for
five years prior to December 1987 in the United Kingdom. He developed
asthma. On 1 December 1987 he suffered an asthma attack at home and was
taken for treatment to the United States military hospital at the United States
base at Lakenheath. The treatment involved the administration of an
intravenous drip, by reason of which the plaintiff claims he lost the use of his
right arm. He was discharged from the United States Airforce in August 1989
as being medically unfit. He now lives in the United States and receives a
disability pension from the United States government.
　　In the United States he claimed compensation. This was rejected by letter in
December 1989 on two grounds: first, his treatment met acceptable standards
of medical care; secondly, his claim was barred by the doctrine established by

'the Supreme Court in *Feres (executrix) v US* (1950) 340 US 135, namely that the United States government was not liable under the Federal Tort Claims Act for injuries to servicemen sustained on active duty as a result of the negligence of others in the armed forces.

The plaintiff did not take matters further in the United States. But on 21 November 1990 he issued a writ in England naming the United States of America as first defendant and the United Kingdom's Ministry of Defence as second defendant. On 14 November 1991 Mr Robert Carnwath QC ([1992] 3 All ER 218), sitting as a deputy judge of the High Court, struck out the action against the second defendant on the ground that the Agreement regarding the Status of Forces of Parties to the North Atlantic Treaty 1951 (London, 19 June 1951; TS 3 (1955); Cmd 9363) (SOFA) (to which I will come later) did not, on its proper construction, confer on the plaintiff any right of action against the United Kingdom government. Sir Gervase Sheldon followed the deputy judge's construction of SOFA. The plaintiff's appeal against the deputy judge's decision has been abandoned. For it is now common ground between the parties that, contrary to the basis on which the matter proceeded before the deputy judge, SOFA, as such, has never been incorporated into English municipal law: the statement upon which the parties relied below in 18 *Halsbury's Laws* (4th edn) para 1611 is inaccurate.

The submissions before this court have been directed to two questions. First, what if any relevance to the plaintiff's claim has SOFA? Secondly, should the defendant's conduct giving rise to the plaintiff's claim be characterised as acta jure gestionis (ie of a private or commercial law character in relation to which the defendant government is not immune from suit) or acta jure imperii (ie the exercise of sovereign immune authority).

Before setting out the rival contentions it is convenient to identify the potentially material terms of SOFA and the legislation.

SOFA was made in June 1951 between the parties to the North Atlantic Treaty. It has been ratified by the governments of the United Kingdom and the United States of America. It regulates the stationing of the forces of member states in each other's territory. I adopt Sir Gervase Sheldon's summary.

'It deals with a variety of problems likely to arise in such circumstances—from the obligation of the members of the visiting force "to respect the law of the receiving State" (art II) (ie "the Contracting Party in the territory of which the force ... is located") (art I); to exemptions from passport, visa and immigration regulations (art III); to the need for driving permits (art IV); to the wearing of uniform (art V); to the possession and carriage of arms (art VI); and to the respective jurisdictions of the receiving state and the "sending State" (ie "the Contracting Party to which the force belongs") in criminal and disciplinary matters (art VII). Article IX deals with such diverse subjects as the purchase by members of the visiting forces of goods and services, as to the provision for the Force of buildings, facilities and services and as to the employment of local labour. Article IX, para 5, also provides that "When a force ... has at the place where it is stationed inadequate medical or dental facilities, its members or their dependants may receive medical and dental care, including hospitalisation, under the same conditions as comparable personnel of the receiving State". Taxation is the subject of art X, and customs that of art XI.'

Article VIII deals with claims for personal injury and damage to property resulting from the activities of a visiting force or its members. By para 4:

'Each Contracting Party waives all its claims against any other Contracting Party for injury or death suffered by any member of its armed services while such member was engaged in the performance of his official duties.'

Paragraph 6 deals with tort claims against members of visiting forces arising from acts not committed in the performance of official duties and para 7 with claims arising from the unauthorised use of official vehicles. Paragraph 9 precludes an immunity claim by a sending state for the member of its force against local civil jurisdiction except in relation to enforcement of judgments arising from the performance of official duties. Paragraph 5 provides:

'Claims (other than contractual claims and those to which paragraph 6 or 7 of this Article apply) arising out of acts or omissions of members of a force or civilian component done in the performance of official duty, or out of any other act, omission or occurrence for which a force or civilian component is legally responsible, and causing damage in the territory of the receiving State to third parties, other than any of the Contracting Parties, shall be dealt with by the receiving State in accordance with the following provisions ...'

Provisions follow which set out the procedure for dealing with claims and they include an agreement in sub-para 5(e)(i) for the distribution between the contracting parties of the cost incurred in satisfying claims of 25% to the receiving state and 75% to the sending state where one sending state is responsible.

The Visiting Forces Act 1952 enacted a variety of provisions, notably in relation to criminal jurisdiction, to enable the government to ratify SOFA although the Act itself makes no reference to SOFA (see 177 HL Official Report (5th series) cols 451–452 per Lord Simonds LC). Section 9 establishes machinery for satisfying civil claims but the jurisdictional basis for such claims is not referred to in the Act. The Visiting Forces (Designation) Order 1954, SI 1954/634, made under s 1(2) of the Act, designated the United States as one of the countries to which the Act applied. Section 8(2) of the Act enabled an Order in Council to exempt a visiting force or its members from the operation of specified enactments and to confer on such a force or its members any privilege or immunity to the extent, in each case, appropriate to home forces. Such an order was made by the Visiting Forces and International Headquarters (Application of Law) Order 1965, SI 1965/1536.

The State Immunity Act 1978 removed, by s 5, state immunity 'as respects proceedings in respect of (a) death or personal injury; or (b) damage to or loss of tangible property, caused by an act or omission in the United Kingdom'. But s 16(2) excluded from the ambit of that Act proceedings in relation to armed forces of a state while present in the United Kingdom and expressly made the 1978 Act subject to the Visiting Forces Act 1952. Accordingly, save for a submission on behalf of the defendant as to the inference to be drawn from s 16(2) as to the legislature's then state of mind, it is common ground that the 1978 Act is for present purposes immaterial.

The Crown Proceedings (Armed Forces) Act 1987 repealed s 10 of the Crown Proceedings Act 1947 so as to permit proceedings for death or personal injury caused by a member of the armed forces while on duty to be brought against the Crown by a member of those forces.

Against that background I turn to the submissions made to this court.

As to the first question, Mr Mendelson QC, who did not appear below, submitted on behalf of the plaintiff that, contrary to the submission made below, SOFA is irrelevant to the present claim. Immunities of the sovereign state itself are not referred to in SOFA and form no part of it. Further or alternatively SOFA is not part of English law by legislation or otherwise. Although parts of it were anticipated by the provisions of the 1952 Act, art VIII of SOFA, in so far as it provides a jurisdictional basis for claims, as distinct from the machinery for dealing with them, was not so enacted. The only exceptions, immunities and privileges conferred by the 1965 order pursuant to the power contained in s 8(2)(a) of the 1952 Act relate not to immunity from tortious liability but to a miscellany of such comparatively minor matters as fire regulations and weed control. SOFA not being part of English municipal law, sovereign immunity is governed by customary international law to the extent that that is part of English municipal law. Mr Mendelson accepted that, in 1951 at the time of SOFA, at common law the United States had immunity from the jurisdiction of the English courts in relation to tortious claims.

For the United States, Mr Falconer QC submitted that SOFA set out the basis on which NATO states consented to forces of other states being stationed on their territory. That consent involved the immunity, in relation to tortious and analogous claims, of the sovereign himself and individual members of the visiting force. SOFA only permitted claims by outsiders; alternatively, claims by insiders could be made only against individual members of the visiting force and not against the sovereign. Customary international law must give way to agreement between the parties. At the date of SOFA customary international law had four relevant principles. (i) A sovereign's power was absolute within his own territory and the extent of the immunity of a friendly visiting sovereign and a member of his forces depended on the host sovereign's consent (see *The Schooner Exchange v McFaddon* (1812) 7 Cranch 116 and *Chung Chi Cheung v R* [1938] 4 All ER 786 at 794, [1939] AC 160 at 170). (ii) In the absence of express agreement, the extent of such immunity depended on what consent to immunity was to be implied from the host state's invitation (see the *Schooner Exchange* case 7 Cranch 116 at 139 and *Coleman v Tennessee* (1878) 97 US 509 at 515). (iii) The visiting sovereign himself enjoyed absolute immunity in relation to everything (see *I Congreso del Partido* [1981] 2 All ER 1064 at 1070, [1983] 1 AC 244 at 261, per Lord Wilberforce). (iv) Individual members of visiting forces enjoyed some, not clearly defined, immunity at least in relation to activities within their own lines not affecting the property or persons of the host state and in exercising jurisdiction relevant to the maintenance of an efficient and disciplined force available to the sovereign (see *Wright v Cantrell* (1943) 44 SR (NSW) 45, *Re Exemption of US Forces* (1943) 4 DLR 11 and *Chow Hung Ching v R* (1948) 77 CLR 449 esp at 475 per Dixon J).

Against that background of customary international law, Mr Falconer accepted that SOFA was not, as such, enacted into English law although the parts of it which were reflected in the Visiting Forces Act 1952 were, he said, either a confirmation or a cutting down of existing immunities and in the latter case amounted to waiver by a consenting state for which no legislation was required. The 1952 Act and the House of Lords debate which preceded it showed that the legislature thought they were enacting art VIII of SOFA and, although the 1952 Act conferred no immunity, the legislature regarded the position between states as being governed by it (see 177 HL Official Report (5th series) cols 463–464 referred to without objection). Accordingly, he submitted, it is appropriate to look at SOFA as defining the consensual basis on which United States troops entered the United Kingdom. No legislation was required because, save in relation to criminal cases, SOFA created no additional immunities which did not already exist. He also tentatively submitted in reliance on dicta in *The Parlement Belge* (1879) 4 PD 129 at 149 and *Chow Hung Ching v R* (1948) 77 CLR 449 at 482 per Dixon J that, as SOFA was part of the basis on which the United Kingdom sovereign invited troops into the United Kingdom to help maintain peace, no legislative approval was required. Accordingly, submitted Mr Falconer, any change in customary international law subsequent to SOFA and imposing greater liability on a state by reducing sovereign immunity has to give way to the agreement prevailing between the NATO powers. They could not have contemplated that claims against sovereign states, for which, in particular, a proportionate distribution of the cost had been agreed, would be outflanked by a subsequent change in customary international law. Accordingly, the adoption by the House of Lords in *I Congreso del Partido* of a restrictive doctrine of sovereign immunity (to the nature of which I will come later) does not avail the plaintiff in the light of SOFA; and s 16(2) of the 1978 Act shows that the legislature intended the existing code of SOFA should continue to apply to the regime for visiting forces.

I have set out the substance of Mr Falconer's arguments in relation to the first question in some detail in deference to the enthusiasm and skill with which they were advanced. For my part, however, the answer to the first question is clear and simple. SOFA has no relevance to this plaintiff's claim.

In *The Parlement Belge* Sir Robert Phillimore held that the terms of a treaty conferring immunity are ineffective in English law unless confirmed by the enactment of Parliament. Any other conclusion would permit the Crown by entering into a treaty to legislate without Parliament's consent. In the ensuing hundred years there has been no authority cited to this court which questions that principle. On the contrary, in *Walker v Baird* [1892] AC 491 the Privy Council held that reliance on a treaty as justifying interference with private rights affords no defence in municipal law and the passage which Mr Falconer relied on in the judgment of Dixon J in *Chow Hung Ching v R* (1948) 77 CLR 449 at 475 specifically emphasises the primacy of the common law. At the heart of Mr Falconer's submission, unsupported by authority, was the distinction he sought to draw between a treaty which increases immunity (which he accepts requires statutory enactment) and a treaty which merely reflects or reduces existing immunity (which he says does not require legislation).

For my part, I am unable to accept that there is any such distinction in principle or on authority. Article VIII, para 5 of SOFA was never enacted. It provides a jurisdictional basis for claims against members of a force of a sovereign state which, on Mr Falconer's analysis of customary international law at the time, could not otherwise have been made. In any event, I know of no authority which suggests that construing a treaty is a proper way of ascertaining rights in municipal law. In the present case the treaty admitted the troops, determined the interstate relationship of the contracting parties and conferred status on the visiting forces. But, in the absence of statutory enactment, it is the common law including the incorporated rules of customary international law, which identifies and defines the extent of sovereign immunity. And in my judgment it is the common law at the time when the claim is made which is determinative. I am unable to accept that the viability of the plaintiff's claim should be determined by the state of customary international law as reflected in the common law 40 years ago. If, as Mr Falconer suggested, the high contracting parties wished *their* relationship to be unaffected by changes in international law it would have been open to them so to provide in SOFA and it is still open to them so to provide by further treaty. But in the absence of incorporation of such a treaty into municipal law, the rights of *individuals* will remain unaffected.

Accordingly, SOFA is, in my judgment, irrelevant to this plaintiff's claim and the deputy judge should have so ruled and dismissed the action against the Ministry of Defence on this ground. It follows that whether, having regard to the terms of art XVI of SOFA, the English courts have any jurisdiction to construe it, or if they have, what the true construction should be, are both matters which, in my judgment, do not arise for determination.

I turn to the second question, which is capable of briefer response. It is common ground that the speech of Lord Wilberforce in *I Congreso del Partido* [1981] 2 All ER 1064 at 1070, [1983] 1 AC 244 at 262 sets out the relevant approach to characterisation of the activity on which the plaintiff relies as jure gestionis or jure imperii. He said, in relation to the limitation engrafted onto the principle of immunity of states, which became part of English law by virtue of *Philippine Admiral (owners) v Wallem Shipping (Hong Kong) Ltd* [1976] 1 All ER 78, [1977] AC 373 and *Trendtex Trading Corp v Central Bank of Nigeria* [1977] 1 All ER 881, [1977] QB 529:

> '... the so-called restrictive theory, arises from the willingness of states to enter into commercial, or other private law, transactions with in-dividuals. It appears to have two main foundations. (a) It is necessary in the interest of justice to individuals having such transactions with states to allow them to bring such transactions before the courts. (b) To require a state to answer a claim based on such transactions does not involve a challenge to or inquiry into any act of sovereignty or governmental act of that state. It is, in accepted phrases, neither a threat to the dignity of that state nor any interference with its sovereign functions.'

Lord Wilberforce adopted with approval a passage in the judgment of the Federal Constitutional Court of the German Federal Republic in *Claim against Empire of Iran* (1963) 45 ILR 57 at 80:

> 'As a means for determining the distinction between acts *jure imperii* and *jure gestionis* one should rather refer to the nature of the State transaction or the resulting legal relationships, and not to the motive or purpose of the State activity. It thus depends upon whether the foreign State has acted in exercise of its sovereign authority, that is in public law, or like a private person, that is in private law.' (See [1981] 2 All ER 1064 at 1071, [1983] 1 AC 244 at 263–264.)

Lord Wilberforce said ([1981] 2 All ER 1064 at 1072, [1983] 1 AC 244 at 265):

> 'Under the restrictive theory the court has first to characterise the activity into which the defendant state has entered. Having done this, and (assumedly) found it to be of a commercial, or private law, character, it

may take the view that contractual breaches, or torts, prima facie fall within the same sphere of activity. It should then be for the defendant state to make a case ... that the act complained of is outside that sphere, and within that of sovereign action.'

He cited with approval a passage from a judgment of the Second Circuit Court of Appeals in *Victory Transport Inc v Comisaria General de Abastecimientos y Transportes* (1964) 336 F 2d 354 at 360:

'The purpose of the restrictive theory of sovereign immunity is to try to accommodate the interest of individuals doing business with foreign governments in having their legal rights determined by the courts, with the interest of foreign governments in being free to perform certain political acts without undergoing the embarrassment or hindrance of defending the propriety of such acts before foreign courts.' (See [1981] 2 All ER 1064 at 1073, [1983] 1 AC 244 at 265–266.)

Lord Wilberforce concluded ([1981] 2 All ER 1064 at 1074, [1983] 1 AC 244 at 267):

'... in considering, under the restrictive theory, whether state immunity should be granted or not, the court must consider the whole context in which the claim against the state is made, with a view to deciding whether the relevant act(s) on which the claim is based should, in that context, be considered as fairly within an area of activity, trading or commercial or otherwise of a private law character, in which the state has chosen to engage or whether the relevant act(s) should be considered as having been done outside that area and within the sphere of governmental or sovereign activity.'

For the plaintiff, Mr Mendelson submitted that there is no immunity in tort in relation to personal injury claims. There is, he said, a rebuttable presumption of liability either because it is presumed that causing personal injury is an act jure gestionis because anyone can do it or because states have decided as a matter of policy that they will remove immunity. The context of the activity should not, he submitted, be too widely drawn and it is the nature of the transaction and not its motive or purpose which is determinative. Such questions should be asked as: are these acts which only a government can do? Is specialist military equipment or are specialist military premises involved? Does the activity involve acts which the soldier was committing under orders, such as being required to undergo innoculation prior to foreign service? Would entertaining a claim involve interference with the smooth performance of government functions? Would the claim involve investigating sensitive or confidential matters? By these sort of yardsticks Mr Mendelson submitted that the activity here was jure gestionis.

Mr Falconer elicited four relevant propositions from the speech of Lord Wilberforce. (1) The court must consider the whole context of the claim to determine whether the relevant act was fairly within the activity of a private law character. (2) The activity must first be characterised as sovereign or non-sovereign: if sovereign there is immunity; if non-sovereign there is no immunity unless the state can make a case that the particular act complained of is outside the non-sovereign sphere. (3) Focus must be on the nature of the activity, not its purpose. (4) The purpose of the restrictive theory is to accommodate the interests of individuals doing business or otherwise having private relations with foreign governments in having their rights determined by the courts with the interests of foreign governments in being free from interference in performing sovereign acts without the need to defend or justify those acts in a foreign court.

As a matter of first impression, it would, to my mind, be astonishing if the present plaintiff were able, in a foreign court, to recover from the state in whose forces he served, in respect of treatment provided by that state as an adjunct to that service, compensation on a basis not sustainable in the courts of the state which he served. Such a conclusion would constitute a clear and undesirable interference with the relationship between a state and its armed forces.

As a matter of analysis, I am not in the present case assisted by concepts of the burden of proof or presumptions. In the light of Lord Wilberforce's speech, the court has to look at all the circumstances in relation to the nature of the activity and its context and decide whether those factors together (no one factor being in itself determinative) characterise the activity as sovereign or non-sovereign. The activity here for consideration was the medical treatment by the United States government in one of its base hospitals, of a member of its forces, in the context of its maintenance of those forces in the United Kingdom. I have no hesitation in concluding that, in particular, the nature of the treatment, the identity of those involved and the place where it was given are factors which, together, point irresistibly to the conclusion that the judge was right in characterising this as jure imperii.

Accordingly, although, for the reasons given, I differ from the judge on the first question, I would dismiss this appeal.

HOFFMANN LJ. Mr Ricardo Littrell is an American citizen resident in Kentucky who in 1987 was serving as a staff sergeant in the United States Air Force stationed at RAF Mildenhall in Suffolk. He suffered from asthma and attended the United States military hospital at the nearby United States Air Force base at RAF Lakenheath for treatment. He says that on 1 December 1987 attempts were made to inject him through a catheter inserted into his arm which, by reason of the negligence of the medical staff, caused him to lose the use of the arm. As a result of this misfortune, he was in 1989 invalided out of the US Air Force with a disability pension. But he wishes also to bring a claim against the United States government in tort.

Mr Littrell cannot bring such an action in the United States because by federal law the United States government, like the United Kingdom government before the passing of the Crown Proceedings (Armed Forces) Act 1987, is immune from suit for injuries to servicemen 'where the injuries arise out of or are in the course of activity incident to service' (see *Feres (executrix) v US* (1950) 340 US 135). He therefore sues in England where the alleged tort took place. But the United States claims that in an English court it is also entitled to immunity from suit on the ground that it is a foreign sovereign. It asks the court to decline jurisdiction. Sir Gervase Sheldon, sitting as a judge of the High Court, upheld the immunity and dismissed the action.

A claim to state immunity in respect of an action for personal injury would ordinarily fail because s 5 of the State Immunity Act 1978 says in terms: 'A State is not immune as respects proceedings in respect of ... personal injury ... caused by an act or omission in the United Kingdom.' But s 16(2) says that s 5 does not apply to 'proceedings relating to anything done by or in relation to the armed forces of a State while present in the United Kingdom ...' The question must therefore be determined according to the common law.

The first ground upon which the judge held immunity to exist was that the extent of the United States government's liability for the acts of its servicemen stationed in this country was governed by a treaty made in 1951 between the United States, the United Kingdom and other NATO countries entitled Agreement regarding the Status of Forces of Parties to the North Atlantic Treaty 1951 (London, 19 June 1951; TS 3 (1955); Cmd 9363). In art VIII, para 5 of that treaty the United States accepted a limited responsibility to contribute to compensation to 'third parties' for the tortious acts of its servicemen in the United Kingdom but no more. The judge, following the judgment of Mr Robert Carnwath QC ([1992] 3 All ER 218) sitting as a deputy judge of the High Court in parallel proceedings brought by Mr Littrell against the United Kingdom Ministry of Defence, held that the term 'third parties' did not include other American servicemen. The treaty did not expressly say that the United States was to be immune in respect of any other claims but, as the judge rightly observed, the treaty was concluded against the background of an apparently settled rule of customary international law according absolute immunity to a foreign sovereign in a municipal court (see *Cia Naviera Vascongada v Cristina, The Cristina* [1938] 1 All ER 719 at 721, 723, [1938] AC 485 at 490–491, 493–494). Accordingly, said the judge, the effect of the treaty was that the United States was to be liable as provided in art VIII, para 5 but not otherwise.

Since 1951 customary international law has changed and that change has been reflected in the common law of England. It now distinguishes between acts jure imperii in respect of which the foreign sovereign is still entitled to immunity and acts jure gestionis in respect of which he is not. Mr Littrell claims that his medical treatment was an act jure gestionis. But the judge held that this change could not affect the construction of the treaty, which was the governing instrument:

'... subject to subsequent legislation the situation created by treaty can be changed only by treaty or by some other form of agreement between the states concerned.'

In my view the judge was wrong to regard the treaty as relevant. Mr Littrell was asserting a claim in private law in an English municipal court. Whether or not he is entitled to pursue such a claim cannot depend upon the terms of a treaty between sovereign states because:

'The transactions of independent States between each other are governed by other laws than those which Municipal Courts administer: such Courts have neither the means of deciding what is right, nor the power of enforcing any decision which they may make.' (See *Secretary of State in Council of India v Kamachee Boye Sahaba* (1859) 13 Moo PCC 22 at 75, 15 ER 9 at 28–29 per Lord Kingdown.)

The terms of a treaty cannot confer immunity upon anyone in an English municipal court unless they have been incorporated in an Act of Parliament. Thus in *The Parlement Belge* (1879) 4 PD 129 Sir Robert Phillimore decided that if a mail vessel belonging to the King of the Belgians was not immune from arrest as sovereign property at common law, such immunity could not be conferred by a treaty on mail carriage concluded between Belgium and the

United Kingdom. The Court of Appeal found it unnecessary to decide this question because it considered that immunity existed at common law (see (1880) 5 PD 197, [1874–80] All ER Rep 104). But no doubt has ever been cast on Sir Robert Phillimore's decision. The Visiting Forces Act 1952 did give effect to certain aspects of the treaty and, as appears from the debate on the Second Reading in the House of Lords, was introduced to enable this country to ratify it (see 177 HL Official Report (5th series) cols 451–452). But it confers no statutory immunities upon the United States. No doubt this was because the absolute immunity which then existed at common law was thought to be sufficient.

Mr Falconer QC, who appeared for the United States government, accepted the general principle that treaties were not justiciable but said that there was an exception in the case of treaties to regulate the conduct of foreign forces in the United Kingdom. In his celebrated judgment in *The Schooner Exchange v McFaddon* (1812) 7 Cranch 116, Marshall CJ considered a case in which a sovereign 'allows the troops of a foreign prince to pass through his dominions ...' In such a case, he said, it would be a derogation from the grant of permission if the domestic sovereign attempted to exercise jurisdiction over the troops during their passage. Mr Falconer relied upon this case for the proposition that the immunities of visiting forces are governed by the terms upon which they have been invited. In this case, such terms were embodied in the NATO Status of Forces treaty.

I do not think that it is possible to derive from the *Schooner Exchange* case the broad proposition that the immunities of a foreign sovereign in a municipal court for the acts of his forces in this country are governed by the terms upon which they have been invited. All it says is that consent to the passage of troops implies that they and their sovereign will have those immunities which, as Marshall CJ says, are 'consonant to the usages and received obligations of the civilised world', that is, in accordance with customary international law. This point was made with customary clarity by Dixon J in *Chow Hung Ching v R* (1948) 77 CLR 449 at 482:

> '... by admitting a very special description of men, viz. an organized body of the armed forces of a foreign nation and by imposing no condition subjecting the force to local law either altogether or in any particular respect, the Crown impliedly undertakes that the force shall be governed by its own discipline and military tribunals to the exclusion of the local jurisdiction *and the common law gives effect to the implication.*' (My emphasis.)

No doubt the courts may look at a treaty to see whether the foreign forces are here by invitation. This would not offend against the rule that treaties are not justiciable: as Lord Oliver of Aylmerton said in *Maclaine Watson & Co Ltd v Dept of Trade and Industry* [1989] 3 All ER 523 at 545, [1990] 2 AC 418 at 500, the conclusion of a treaty is as much a fact as any other. This, I think, is the element of truth in Mr Falconer's assertion that the courts may take account of treaties of peace. The termination of a state of war has consequences in private law and the court may therefore examine the treaty to see whether peace has been concluded. But this does not mean that it can enforce the terms of the treaty. Mr Falconer attempted to take the supposed principle still further and, relying on a submission by Sir Richard Webster A-G in *Walker v Baird* [1892] AC 491 at 497, said that the courts could also give effect in municipal law to a 'treaty having for its object the preservation of peace ...' The NATO treaty fell within that description, as was apparent from its resounding preamble, and so by association did the treaty concerning the status of NATO forces.

In my view there is no authority to support such a broad proposition. I should have thought that the NATO treaty was the very paradigm of a treaty which could not possibly be justiciable in a municipal court. As for the treaty on the status of forces, I think that a court could look at it as part of the material for deciding whether a particular unit of foreign troops qualified for the immunities accorded by customary international law to visiting forces. But whether, as against his own subjects, the sovereign can agree to greater immunities, depends upon his domestic constitution. Perhaps there are countries in which the government may accord to foreign troops the right to pillage its citizens without redress in their own courts. But in England this would require an Act of Parliament.

In my judgment, therefore, the judge should not have allowed himself to be, as Lord Diplock put it in *British Airways Board v Laker Airways Ltd* [1984] 3 All ER 39 at 49, [1985] AC 58 at 85, 'beguiled into construing' the NATO Status of Forces treaty. He had no jurisdiction to do so and it has nothing to do with the case. Likewise, I think that the deputy judge was wrong to attempt to construe the treaty in the proceedings against the Ministry of Defence. He should have dismissed the action on the short ground that the treaty upon which the plaintiff based his claim was not justiciable. I should say that I sympathise with the judge for having taken the course he did, because counsel for the Ministry of Defence conceded that the treaty had somehow been incorporated into English municipal law. But this concession was in my judgment wrong and since the point went to jurisdiction, it should have been taken by the court.

The question in this case is therefore whether in accordance with the common law as laid down in *I Congreso del Partido* [1981] 2 All ER 1064, [1983] 1 AC 244, the act which forms the basis of the claim was jure imperii or jure gestionis. The judge, as an alternative ground for his decision, held that it was the former. I agree and I think that it would be difficult to improve upon the reasoning by which the judge came to that conclusion. In *I Congreso del Partido* [1981] 2 All ER 1064 at 1074, [1983] 1 AC 244 at 267 Lord Wilberforce said that the court—

> 'must consider the whole context in which the claim against the state is made, with a view to deciding whether the relevant act(s) on which the claim is based should, in that context, be considered as fairly within an area of activity, trading or commercial or otherwise of a private law character, in which the state has chosen to engage or whether the relevant act(s) should be considered as having been done outside that area and within the sphere of governmental or sovereign activity.'

The context in which the act took place was the maintenance by the United States of a unit of the US Strategic Air Force in the United Kingdom. This looks about as imperial an activity as could be imagined. But it would be facile to regard this context as determinative of the question. Acts done within that context could range from arrangements concerning the flights of the bombers (plainly jure imperii) to ordering milk for the base from a local dairy or careless driving by off-duty airmen on the roads of Suffolk. Both of the latter would seem to me to be jure gestionis, fairly within an area of private law activity. I do not think that there is a single test or 'bright line' by which cases on either side can be distinguished. Rather, there are a number of factors which may characterise the act as nearer to or further from the central military activity.

In the present case I think that the most important factors are the answers to the following questions. First, where did it happen? In cases in which foreign troops are occupying a defined and self-contained area, the authorities on customary international law attach importance to whether or not the act was done within the 'lines' or 'the rayon [ie radius] of the fortress' (see Oppenheim *International Law* (1905) p 483). Secondly, whom did it involve? Acts involving only members of the visiting forces are less likely to be within the jurisdiction of local municipal courts than acts involving its own citizens as well. Thirdly, what kind of act was it? Some acts are wholly military in character, some almost entirely private or commercial and some in between.

In this case, RAF Lakenheath was, in spite of its name and the presence of an RAF officer for liaison duties, wholly within the control of the US Air Force. The act took place at the military hospital within the base. It involved only US personnel. And the operation of a military hospital, although no doubt requiring much the same skills as the operation of a civilian hospital, is a recognised military activity. If the case had concerned an assault within the base by one American serviceman on another, I think that under customary international law the English courts would have declined both civil and criminal jurisdiction. Why should it exercise civil jurisdiction because the injury was inflicted by negligence? Mr Mendelson QC says that the reason is that an assault would have been a disciplinary offence and an assertion of jurisdiction would have interfered with the foreign sovereign's right to discipline his own troops. An action for medical negligence, on the other hand, involves no interference with military matters.

I do not agree. First, the United States engages its troops on the basis of *Feres (executrix) v US* (1950) 340 US 135, the doctrine by which it is immune from suit by servicemen for injuries incident to service. For an English court to allow visiting US servicemen to sue their government would clearly be an interference with this aspect of the relationship between the troops and their sovereign. Secondly, the plaintiff's action involves the claim that the treatment which he received in the military hospital fell below the standard which an English court would consider reasonable. In my judgment, however, the standard of medical care which the United States affords its own servicemen is matter within its own sovereign authority.

In my judgment, therefore, the act of which Mr Littrell complains was clearly on the jure imperii side of the line and the judge was right to dismiss the action.

NOURSE LJ. I agree with both judgments and, on the decisive question whether the acts complained of by the plaintiff were jure imperii or jure gestionis, with the judgment of Sir Gervase Sheldon at first instance. The plaintiff was being treated by the United States of America in the performance of its sovereign function of maintaining its armed forces in this country. The appeal is dismissed.

Appeal dismissed. Leave to appeal to the House of Lords refused.

Carolyn Toulmin   Barrister.

Jordan v Norfolk County Council

CHANCERY DIVISION

SIR DONALD NICHOLLS V-C

10, 11 MAY 1994

Valuer – Valuation – Valuation of expert – Mandatory Order – Review – Council trespassing on plaintiff's land – Council cutting down trees in process of laying sewage pipe on plaintiff's land – Order requiring council to carry out tree, hedge and shrub replacement 'so far as reasonably practicable' – Plaintiff's expert drawing up plans without regard to cost of reinstatement work – Estimated cost vastly exceeding cost contemplated when order made – Whether court having jurisdiction to review order – Whether phrase 'reasonably practicable' including cost.

The plaintiff owned a strip of disused railway line embankment adjoining his garden which was about 200 yards in length and 20 to 30 yards wide. In 1989 the county council went onto the embankment and caused a sewage pipe to be laid through the plaintiff's land, without his agreement, cutting down many trees in the process. At the hearing of the plaintiff's claim against inter alia the council, the judge held that the council had committed a trespass and, declining to award the plaintiff damages in lieu of a mandatory injunction, ordered the council to remove the sewage pipe and reinstate the site to its former condition by carrying out certain works to the reasonable satisfaction of the plaintiff's consulting engineer. Paragraph 8 of the mandatory order required the council to replace 'all trees hedges and shrubs on the site destroyed or damaged as a result of the Defendants' operations on the site so far as reasonably practicable with trees hedges and shrubs of equal maturity ... the extent of such work to be determined by a landscape architect to be nominated by the consulting engineer ...' The judge also ordered the council to pay the plaintiff £25,000 in damages, which was the value of the site as building land. The plaintiff's landscape architect, in his draft report, estimated the cost of reinstatement work (including a scheme to transport and replant semi-mature trees) at between £230,000 and £300,000. In contrast, the council's expert put forward a tree planting scheme costing between £20,000 and £25,000. The council subsequently applied to the court for a determination that the plaintiff's expert had adopted an erroneous approach in his draft report which took no account of the cost of the proposed reinstatement work and was therefore at variance with the 'reasonably practicable' requirement in para 8 of the order. The plaintiff contended that the court had no jurisdiction to intervene and give directions to an expert appointed by the court even if that expert had made a mistake.

Held – Where an order of the court compelled a party to comply with its terms so far as was 'reasonably practicable', that phrase was sufficiently general to embrace considerations beyond what was physically feasible and was apt to include financial considerations. Accordingly, where the cost of complying with a mandatory order vastly exceeded what could have been in the contemplation of the court, the court had power to review its decision so as to achieve the original object of the order to the extent that that could be done without imposing an unjust burden on the party required to comply with its terms. On the facts, however reprehensible the council's conduct had been, the judge in his order could not have intended to make it pay over £200,000 to restore to its original condition a site that was then worth £25,000 and para 8 of the order, properly construed, could not have that effect. The court would therefore order that a new landscape architect should start afresh with producing a new scheme to restore the strip of land and, in determining the extent of the tree, hedge and shrub replacement under para 8, the landscape architect should prescribe items only in so far as their cost would be reasonable having regard to the nature and value of the site. The council's application would accordingly be allowed (see p 222 *f g j* to p 223 *a d e j* to p 224 *a c e* to *g*, post).

Jones v Sherwood Computer Services plc [1992] 2 All ER 170 distinguished.

Notes

For third party valuations and the principles on which the court will interfere, see 32 *Halsbury's Laws* (4th edn) para 23, and for cases on the subject, see 34 *Digest* (Reissue) 447–449, 3648–3652.

For contractual valuation in general, see 49 *Halsbury's Laws* (4th edn) paras 4–7, and for cases on the subject, see 49 *Digest* (Reissue) 47–49, *174–186*.

Cases referred to in judgment

Cristel v Cristel [1951] 2 All ER 574, [1951] 2 KB 725, CA.
Jones v Sherwood Computer Services plc [1992] 2 All ER 170, [1992] 1 WLR 277, CA.

Cases also cited

Ainsworth v Wilding [1896] 1 Ch 673.
Arenson v Arenson [1975] 3 All ER 901, [1977] AC 405, HL.
Campbell v Edwards [1976] 1 All ER 785, [1976] 1 WLR 403, CA.
Dean v Prince [1954] 1 All ER 749, [1954] Ch 409, CA.
Dodd Properties (Kent) Ltd v Canterbury City Council [1979] 2 All ER 118, [1980] 1
     WLR 433; *rvsd* [1980] 1 All ER 928, [1980] 1 WLR 433, CA.
Ford-Hunt v Raghbir Singh [1973] 2 All ER 700, [1973] 1 WLR 738.
Gale (decd), Re [1966] 1 All ER 945, [1966] Ch 326, CA.
Lodge Holes Colliery Co Ltd v Wednesbury Corp [1908] AC 323, HL.
R v Cripps, ex p Muldoon [1984] 2 All ER 705, [1984] QB 686, CA.
Tito v Waddell (No 2) [1977] 3 All ER 129, [1977] Ch 106.

Application

Norfolk County Council applied to the court to vary part of an order made by Andrew Park QC sitting as a deputy judge of the High Court in the Chancery Division on 1 October 1993 whereby he ordered the council to reinstate the land belonging to the plaintiff, Clifton Jordan, to its former condition. The facts are set out in the judgment.

Francis Barlow (instructed by *Mills & Reeve*, Norwich) for the plaintiff.
Jeremy Sullivan QC and *Paul Stinchcombe* (instructed by *Hughmans*, agents for
     Nicholas Hancox, Norwich) for the council.

SIR DONALD NICHOLLS V-C. This application is a sequel to the trial of an action which took place last July over a period of 11 days before Mr Andrew Park QC, sitting as a deputy judge of the High Court in the Chancery Division.

The plaintiff, Mr Clifton Jordan, lives at 4 Crane Close, Dereham, Norfolk. His garden runs alongside a disused railway line embankment. Mr Jordan owns a strip of the embankment about 200 yards in length. The strip is 20 to 30 yards wide. At its highest point the embankment is about 12 or 13 feet above the level of the surrounding land. On the far side of the embankment are open fields. On the near side Mr Jordan's house is part of a residential building estate.

In 1989 Norfolk County Council went onto the embankment, that is Mr Jordan's land, and proceeded to construct there a sewer along the side of the embankment furthest from Mr Jordan's house. This was in connection with a major supermarket development. They cut down many trees. All this was done without leave from Mr Jordan. This was, as the judge held, a trespass. Indeed the judge was very critical of the council's conduct. He said the council came out of it very badly. The judge considered the council had been high-handed and discourteous in its attitude towards Mr Jordan, that it had treated him unreasonably and arrogantly, that it had chanced its arm and had made untrue and misleading statements.

The judge declined to award damages in lieu of a mandatory order for the removal of the pipe. He made an order that within seven months, that is by 1 May 1994, the council and its co-defendant Key Markets Ltd should remove the sewer and reinstate the site to its former condition by carrying out certain works. The works were to be carried out to the reasonable satisfaction of Mr Jordan's consulting engineer, Mr Wright. The works were set out in nine paragraphs in the judge's order. The sewer and the manhole chambers were to be removed, the trench was to be back-filled, the affected areas of the embankment were to be covered with topsoil and reseeded, and all fencing which had been damaged or removed was to be replaced or repaired.

Paragraph 8, which is the crucial paragraph for the purposes of this application, sets out the following as one of the items of work to be done:

'... replacing all trees hedges and shrubs on the site destroyed or damaged as a result of the Defendants' operations on the site so far as reasonably practicable with trees hedges and shrubs of equal maturity (subject as to the trees to a limit of 60 semi-mature trees) the extent of such work to be determined by a landscape architect to be nominated by the consulting engineer hereinafter referred to by reference to photographic evidence and local knowledge ...'

The judge ordered payment of damages of £25,000 plus interest. That sum was arrived at in this way. In 1989, before the trespass, Mr Jordan's strip of the embankment was worth some £50,000. That was because this land was the subject of planning permission for residential development. After removal of the sewer, at 1993 values, the land would be worth about £25,000. The judge awarded Mr Jordan the difference between these two amounts because, before the drain pipe was installed, Mr Jordan was planning to sell the land to a developer. Because of the trespass he lost that opportunity and he should be recompensed accordingly.

The judge's order was made on 1 October. What happened afterwards was that Mr Wright nominated Mr Paul Mathews to determine the extent of the work required by para 8. Mr Mathews was instructed, so it seems, early in February. He produced a draft report to the council on 11 March. The draft sets out details of the work required, with estimated costs at between £230,000 and £300,000.

The council was aghast at this amount. These figures were way beyond anything either party or the judge contemplated or could have contemplated when he made his order. At the trial, although there was much contention over whether damages should be awarded in place of an injunction, there was no discussion about the likely cost of reinstatement works. What there was before the judge, by way of background, was evidence about the value of the site. I have mentioned the judge's conclusion in that regard. In addition, under his claim for damages, Mr Jordan had particularised the cost of replacing trees removed by the council when laying the drain as £2,350. The trees were largely if not entirely self-sown trees, ash and oak and so forth, that one commonly sees on railway embankments, especially those no longer used and pruned by British Rail. Over the years the trees had matured. Mr Jordan's pleaded case was that £2,350 was an estimate of the cost of replacing about 60 trees. Mr Jordan's expert recommended tree planting at a cost of £12,000 out of a total landscaping expenditure of £27,000.

It was against that background that the judge decided that the council should remove the drain and reinstate the site. In his judgment, the judge, addressing the question of what remedy should be granted to Mr Jordan, said:

'... the injunction should require the land to be reinstated as far as is reasonably practicable to what was its condition before the trespass occurred.'

The judge rejected the claim for damages in respect of the removal of the trees. He said:

'... if my suggestion that the injunction should require the defendants to take reasonable steps to reinstate the land is adopted, I think that it would be inappropriate to award damages on this account.'

The item to which the judge was referring in that passage was a claim for the cost of the replacement of the trees and fencing.

The judge summarised his conclusion in similar terms:

'Both defendants should be ordered within a specified period from judgment (which I suggest should be three months) to dig up and remove the drain from Mr Jordan's land and to reinstate the land as far as is reasonably practicable in the circumstances to its state before November 1989. The precise wording of the order may need discussion.'

I now have before me an application by the council relating to the unexpected state of affairs which has arisen. Since the application relates to carrying out the trial judge's order, it would have been much better if the application had been made to him. However, neither party made arrangements in that regard, nor did either party submit to me that I should adjourn the application for hearing by Mr Park. Accordingly, since both parties were before me, I decided to hear the application and not put them to the extra expense an adjournment would involve.

The council seeks an extension of time within which to carry out its obligations. The parties are agreed that I should extend the period until 31 December 1994. Secondly, the council seeks in effect a determination that Mr Mathews has adopted an erroneous approach in his draft report. The council's expert has put forward a tree planting scheme which would cost between £20,000 and £25,000. There would be a mix of 200 feathered trees, whips and shrubs, together with 46 ash trees with a size range of 20 to 30 cm. In five years the ash would have reached a height of 25 feet or so, and the whips and shrubs a height of 10 to 15 feet.

In contrast to this, Mr Mathews has produced a scheme which takes no account at all of cost. He has looked to see what is physically feasible, and then set out a scheme which would reproduce the state of the site in 1989 as nearly as may be. Some of the trees removed had a girth exceeding one metre. Mr Mathews could not locate replacement trees of this size, so he has taken the largest trees available with a girth of 60 to 70 cm. Such trees are, of course, hugely expensive, and the operation of planting them with the necessary root ball is a major one. A three-year guarantee and maintenance period has been provided for, including a water supply by trickle-fed irrigation system. In the result, his draft report estimates ground preparation and preparatory works at £27,500. The supply and planting of semi-mature trees, shrubs and plants is estimated to cost nearly £110,000. Of this, the biggest item is £80 each for 41 ash trees with a girth of 60 to 70 cm. Shading for the trees is estimated at £2,500, and mulch at over £2,000. The supply and installation of the irrigational system and a sprinkler are estimated to cost £15,000. Maintenance of planting and of the irrigation system and of the fencing is estimated to cost another £4,000. There will be 12 site visits over three years at a cost of £150 per visit, making a total of £1,800. The guarantee costs for replacement stock are estimated at over £46,000. Finally, the removal of the irrigation system in due course, and making good access and fencing, no doubt after the three-year period of maintenance is completed, is estimated to cost another £7,000, making a grand total of some £231,000. (I add that with autumn planting the cost would be somewhat less.)

The council submitted that, contrary to this scheme, the phrase 'reasonably practicable' in para 8 of the judge's order requires some regard to be had to expense. In my view the phrase 'so far as reasonably practicable' in para 8 is sufficiently general for it to embrace matters additional to the physical feasibility of planting replacement trees of the same maturity. In this area there is very little nowadays which is not physically feasible if enough money is spent. Hence in this context the phrase is apt to include financial considerations.

Take a simple example. Ash trees of the necessary girth (of equal maturity) may be obtainable but only from some distant part of the country. This would involve mammoth transport costs and horrendous planting expenses on this narrow site. Ash trees obtainable in this way could not fall within the obligation to replant 'so far as reasonably practicable' with trees of equal maturity. No doubt the limit of 60 semi-mature trees was inserted as a form of long stop limit, and that limit must have been aimed at giving the council a degree of financial protection. The tree-planting obligation was not to be open-ended. Nevertheless, I do not think the presence of this express limit is sufficient to restrict the generality of the earlier phrase to physical feasibility alone.

This, however, is not the end of the matter. To conclude that cost is an element the landscape architect should take into account does not afford guidance on the weight he should attach to this element. How is he to balance the type of trees required for reinstatement against their cost? At what point is he to reject an item as too expensive? I think the answer to these questions is that in determining what should be the extent of the tree, hedge and shrub replacement, the landscape architect should prescribe items insofar, but only insofar, as their cost would be reasonable, having regard to the nature and value of the site.

Mr Jordan has been severely wronged by his local county council, a powerful body. It rode roughshod over his rights. But for his tenacity it would have got away with this. The remedy afforded to Mr Jordan ought fairly to reflect this and his justified sense of outrage. The local authority can have no complaint on this score. But the remedy must be reasonably proportionate to the wrong. This is a stretch of disused railway embankment adjoining Mr Jordan's house. On the far side are open fields. The trees formerly on the site were not of high amenity value to him as a screen. The site itself is ripe for development. If and when developed, the surface will be lowered and levelled and most of the trees on it will be grubbed out. As building land it is worth £25,000 or so. But for the council's wrongful act, Mr Jordan would have sold the site in 1989 for that purpose. The land in those building boom days was worth about £50,000. In the action Mr Jordan sought and has been awarded damages on that footing.

I cannot believe that, however reprehensible was the council's conduct, the judge intended to make an order which would impose on the council in respect of this land in those circumstances an obligation to plant trees and shrubs at a cost of over £200,000. That, frankly, would be absurd. The cost of the exercise would be altogether disproportionate to the benefit it would confer on Mr Jordan. That would make no sense at all. I do not believe that, properly construed, para 8 had that effect. The pipe was to be removed and the embankment made good, but some sense of proportion was to be observed over the replanting operation.

Mr Barlow submitted that the court has no jurisdiction to intervene and, in effect, give directions to the expert appointed by the court. The parties to an agreement appointing an expert to determine an issue between them are bound by his decision, even if he makes a mistake, provided he acts honestly: see *Jones v Sherwood Computer Services plc* [1992] 2 All ER 170, [1992] 1 WLR 277. I am unable to accept this. Even in the field in which *Jones v Sherwood* is concerned, the expert's decision will not be binding on the parties if the expert departed his instructions in a material respect: see [1992] 2 All ER 170 at 179, [1992] 1 WLR 277 at 287 per Dillon LJ. But quite apart from this, I cannot accept the analogy. I am concerned with the carrying out of a court order. If there is disagreement between the parties on the proper interpretation of the order, the court has jurisdiction to decide that dispute. The court's power to do so is not ousted by the fact that, having marked out the extent of the defendant's obligation by the words in dispute, the order goes on to provide that a nominated expert shall determine what in fact needs to be done to satisfy the obligation.

If I should be wrong so far, I would still reach the same conclusion by another route. The order gave the parties liberty to apply. That would have been implicit even if it had not been expressed. The parties have liberty to apply to the court in connection with the carrying out of the order. Where the order is a mandatory order requiring a party to carry out certain works, and after the order has been made it comes to light that the cost of carrying out of the works vastly exceeds anything contemplated by anyone when the order was made, in my view the court must have power to review the position.

Otherwise the order will operate in a way that the judge did not intend. That cannot be right. Accordingly, in this case, para 8 should now be reviewed so as to achieve the object the judge had in mind so far as this can be done without imposing an altogether unjust burden on the council.

Mr Barlow submitted that the court has no jurisdiction in that regard either. A final order has been made. The arguments addressed to me by the council should have been addressed to the trial judge. The application is an assault on the terms of the order itself. It is an appeal by other means and I should not entertain it. This being a final order, the court has no power to vary or amend it. The case does not fall within any of the limited exceptions to the general principle.

I am unable to accept the conclusion for which Mr Barlow contended. The discovery that the cost involved is so vast is an unforeseen change of circumstance. The court may then review the position: see *Cristel v Cristel* [1951] 2 All ER 574 at 577, [1951] 2 KB 725 at 731 per Denning LJ.

The council seeks a further item of relief. It seeks a variation of the judge's order by replacing Mr Mathews with a new independent landscape architect to be nominated in default of agreement between the parties by the president of the Landscape Institute. On this the council case is, in effect, that the scheme produced by Mr Mathews is, in its elaboration and extravagance, so far removed from anything one might have reasonably expected that the council can no longer be expected to have confidence in Mr Mathews' suitability for this particular assignment.

I have not found this an easy point. In the end, I think the council is entitled to be concerned at Mr Mathews' continuing to act as the independent landscape architect in this case. For the reason advanced by the council, it would be better, if a new scheme has to be produced, that the new scheme should be produced by a different hand. This is not to cast any cloud over Mr Mathews' professional skill and expertise. Rather it will be easier and preferable for a different expert to start afresh than for Mr Mathews to be asked to prune his present draft or to start anew. Since it is now apparent there is such a vast area of dispute between the parties on how the replanting should be carried out, it is better for there to be a new expert, who will come in without any preconceptions and not having had any prior involvement.

I shall make an order accordingly. In determining the extent of the tree, hedge and shrub replacement under para 8, the new landscape architect will have regard to the views expressed in this judgment on the proper interpretation of that paragraph.

Application allowed.

Celia Fox   Barrister.

Smith New Court Securities Ltd v Scrimgeour Vickers (Asset Management) Ltd and another (Roberts, third party)

COURT OF APPEAL, CIVIL DIVISION

NOURSE, ROSE AND HOFFMANN LJJ

25, 26, 28 OCTOBER, 1–4, 8 NOVEMBER 1993, 17 FEBRUARY 1994

Damages – Measure of damages – Fraudulent misrepresentation – Party induced to purchase shares by fraudulent misrepresentation – Assessment of value of shares for fraud damage – Whether value being difference between price paid and price of shares on open market – Whether value being difference between price paid and price if market had known of fraud.

On 21 July 1989 the plaintiff company, SNC, purchased a parcel of ordinary shares in company F at a price of 82·25p per share, totalling over £23m. The first defendant company, SVAM, sold the shares to SNC as broker on behalf of the second defendant company, C, to which they had been charged by way of security. In September 1989 there was a serious decline in the market price of F shares as a result of a fraud (which was unrelated to the transaction involving the sale of shares to SNC) perpetrated on F which dramatically reduced the company's net worth. SNC eventually sold its holding of F shares at a significant loss and subsequently issued proceedings against SVAM, claiming that it had been induced to purchase the shares by one or more fraudulent misrepresentations made on behalf of C. The judge found that two of the representations had been made in circumstances which entitled SNC to recover damages equivalent to the difference between the price paid and the true value of the shares on 21 July, that, by reason of the unconnected and then undiscovered fraud, the value of each share on the date of sale was only 44p and, further, that it was on the basis of that value and not the price at which the shares would have changed hands in the market that SNC was entitled to recover. The judge awarded SNC damages of £10,764,005, being the difference between the purchase price (£23,146,321) and the value of the shares at 44p each (£12,382,226). C appealed, contending inter alia that SNC was only entitled to recover on the basis of the price at which the shares would have changed hands, being 82·25p or at all events not less than 78p each, rather than the price which would have been paid if the market had known about the fraud which had been revealed. SNC challenged that part of the judge's ruling that not all the alleged incidents of fraud had been proven.

Held – Where a party had been induced to purchase shares by fraudulent misrepresentation on the part of the vendor, the court would assess the damages recoverable by the innocent purchaser as the difference between the price paid and the price which, absent the misrepresentation, the shares would have fetched on the open market and not on the price which would have been paid if the market had known about the fraud. The assumption that the market knew everything it actually knew on the date of sale, without being influenced by the misrepresentation itself, was clearly a rational principle on which to calculate the loss which directly flowed from the representation on the relevant date, in contrast to the assumption that the market was omniscient (in the sense that it knew everything material to the price of the shares which was in fact the case), which was entirely arbitrary and allowed the damages to be increased or diminished by any fact or event which, unknown to anyone, actually existed or occurred before the relevant date, provided that it had emerged before the trial. It followed that the correct measure of damages was the difference between what SNC paid for the shares (82·25p per share) and the price which, absent the fraudulent misrepresentation, the parcel of shares would have fetched on the open market on the date of sale. Since 78p was the market price on the date in question, the loss was 4·25p per share and therefore the damages which SNC was entitled to recover, on the broader basis that all the incidents of fraud had been made out, would have to be reduced from £10,764,005 to £1,196,010. C's appeal would accordingly be allowed to that extent (see p 235 *b* to *f*, p 237 *e* to *j* and p 239 *b*, post).

Waddell v Blockey (1879) 4 QBD 678 and dictum of Lord Atkin in Clark v Urquhart, Stracey v Urquhart [1930] AC 28 at 68 applied.

Notes

For fraudulent misrepresentation in general, see 31 *Halsbury's Laws* (4th edn) paras 1057–1062, and for cases on the subject, see 34 *Digest* (Reissue) 330–344, 2566–2726.

For measure of damages for misrepresentation, see 31 *Halsbury's Laws* (4th edn) paras 1107–1109, and for cases on the subject, see 34 *Digest* (Reissue) 383–387, 3126–3166.

Cases referred to in judgment

Clark v Urquhart, Stracey v Urquhart [1930] AC 28, HL.

Doyle v Olby (Ironmongers) Ltd [1969] 2 All ER 119, [1969] 2 QB 158, [1969] 2 WLR 673, CA.

Lynall v IRC [1971] 3 All ER 914, [1972] AC 680, [1971] 3 WLR 759, HL.

Naughton v O'Callaghan (Rogers and ors, third parties) [1990] 3 All ER 191.

Twycross v Grant (1877) 2 CPD 469, CPD and CA.

Waddell v Blockey (1879) 4 QBD 678, CA.

Appeals

The second defendant, Citibank NA (Citibank), appealed from that part of the judgment of Chadwick J ([1992] BCLC 1104) given on 25 March 1992 whereby he (1) gave judgment for the plaintiff, Smith New Court Securities Ltd (SNC), against Citibank for £10·764m together with interest, being damages for fraudulent misrepresentation claimed by SNC in its action against the first defendant, Scrimgeour Vickers (Asset Managment) Ltd (SVAM), and Citibank arising out of an oral agreement made on 21 July 1989 whereby SNC had agreed to buy from SVAM 28,141,424 ordinary shares of 10p each in the company known as Ferranti International Signal plc at a price of 82·25p per share and (2) dismissed SNC's action against SVAM and (3) in third party proceedings, ordered the third party, Christopher Nigel Roberts, to indemnify Citibank against its liability under the order. Citibank appealed and SNC appealed from the dismissal of its claim against SVAM. The facts are set out in the judgment of the court.

Jonathan Sumption QC and *Anthony Mann QC* (instructed by *Wilde Sapte*) for Citibank.

Anthony Grabiner QC, Ian Glick QC and *John McCaughran* (instructed by *Ashurst Morris Crisp*) for SNC.

Cur adv vult

17 February 1994. The following judgment of the court was delivered.

NOURSE LJ. On 25 March 1992 Chadwick J ([1992] BCLC 1104), in a judgment reserved after a trial extending over some 25 days, gave judgment for the plaintiff, Smith New Court Securities Ltd (SNC), against the second defendant, Citibank NA (Citibank) for £10·764m, together with interest and a part of SNC's costs. The judge dismissed the action as against the first defendant, Scrimgeour Vickers (Asset Management) Ltd (SVAM). In third party proceedings he ordered the third party, Christopher Nigel Roberts, to indemnify Citibank against its liability under the order and to pay its costs of defending the action.

SNC is a member of the International Stock Exchange and a leading market maker in the City of London. SVAM, also a member of the Stock Exchange, is a company within the Citicorp group. Citibank is another company within that group, having offices in London from which it carries on its business as a bank. At the material time Mr Roberts was employed by Citibank as the head of its private banking department. He was also an executive director of SVAM and a member of the Stock Exchange.

SNC's claim arises out of its purchase, on 21 July 1989, of 28,141,424 ordinary shares of 10p in Ferranti International Signal plc (Ferranti) at a price of 82·25p each, about £23m in all. SVAM sold the shares to SNC as broker on behalf of Citibank, to which they had been charged by a United States company, Parent Industries Inc, as security. SNC's case is that it was induced to purchase the shares by one or more fraudulent misrepresentations made by Mr Roberts on behalf of Citibank.

SNC's purchase was concluded in the course of a telephone conversation which took place in the late afternoon of 21 July, the three representations on which it relies having allegedly been made earlier in the day. Chadwick J found that the first representation was not made, but that the second and third were made in circumstances entitling SNC to recover damages equivalent to the difference between the price paid and the true value of the shares on 21 July. He also found that, by reason of another unconnected and then undiscovered fraud, the value of each share at that date was only 44p. He held, as a matter of law, that it was on the basis of that value, not the price at which the shares would have changed hands in the market, that SNC was entitled to recover. The difference between the purchase price (£23,146,321) and the value of the shares at 44p each (£12,382,226) was £10,764,005, the amount of the judgment entered in the action.

Citibank, but not Mr Roberts, has now appealed to this court, contending, first, that the judge's findings as to the second and third representations were against the weight of the evidence; secondly, and in any event, that SNC is only entitled to recover on the basis of the price at which the shares would have changed hands in the market on 21 July 1989, being 82·25p or at all events not less than 78p each. SNC has put in a respondent's notice, the main burden of which is that the judge ought to have found that the first representation was made as well as the second and third.

Thus each side attacks a part of the judge's findings. The documents adduced below were few in number. The evidence consisted largely of the statements and oral testimony of numerous witnesses. We have had to go minutely into that evidence; the hearing in this court, relatively little of which was taken up with arguments on the law, having lasted for eight full days. After careful reflection, we have come to a clear view that there is a conflict in the judge's findings which goes to the very root of his decision on the facts. The question is how it ought to be resolved. It has been a difficult and anxious question, to which we have devoted much thought. In the end we have had to stand back from the minutiae of the evidence and assess its broad effect. That is how we propose to deal with it now.

After an introductory section and others dealing with SNC's claim and the third party proceedings, the judge gave a full account of the background to the events of 21 July 1989, none of which is controversial and none of which need be repeated (see [1992] BCLC 1104 at 1110–1114). He then turned to the standard of proof and the weight to be given to the evidence of Mr G A Lewis and Mr A S Abrahams, the two directors of SNC who were the principal participants and witnesses on its behalf.

Under this heading, the judge made two preliminary observations. The first was that in examining the evidence in support of the allegations that Mr Roberts made representations on 21 July 1989 which he knew to be false, he kept in mind that convincing proof was required to displace the presumption that a person in Mr Roberts's position could be expected to act honestly. He continued (at 1115):

'Secondly, the circumstances in which Mr Lewis and Mr Abrahams prepared their evidence in advance of the criminal proceedings against Mr Roberts, and the manner in which they gave that evidence, make it necessary to approach the evidence which they have given in this trial with extreme caution.'

Having summarised, in seven numbered paragraphs, the circumstances in which that evidence was prepared and having stated that the Criminal Justice Act statements of Mr Lewis and Mr Abrahams were, as a result, in substantially identical terms, the judge said (at 1115–1116):

'The effect of this process was that any independent recollection which either Mr Lewis or Mr Abrahams might have had as to the events of 21 July 1989 was likely to have become coloured by the recollection of the other. No doubt Mr Holt, and SNC's solicitors, thought they were acting in the best interests of SNC; but a process better calculated to devalue the evidence of the two principal witnesses for the prosecution in the criminal proceedings—and, subsequently, in the civil proceedings in this court— would be difficult to imagine.'

The judge then quoted from the explanations given by Mr Abrahams and Mr Lewis in the criminal proceedings for the virtual identity between their statements. He described their evidence as disingenuous and continued (at 1116):

'In my judgment, Mr Lewis and Mr Abrahams each sought, deliberately, to mislead the jury in the criminal proceedings as to the true process by which their Criminal Justice Act statements were prepared. The true position did not emerge until full discovery was made, belatedly, in the course of the trial of the civil action in this court. I do not accept their explanations, given in this court, that they had forgotten, at the time when they gave evidence in January 1991, the circumstances in which their Criminal Justice Act statements had been prepared one year earlier. In these circumstances it would, in my view, be unsafe to make a finding of dishonesty against Mr Roberts on the unsupported evidence of Mr Lewis and Mr Abrahams. I approach the examination of the events of 21 July 1989 on the basis that little, if any, weight can be given to their evidence where it is in conflict with that given by Mr Roberts.'

That is an important section of the judge's judgment, to which we will return in due course. At this point it is convenient to turn away from it and to say something more about the three representations on which SNC relies.

SNC's case, as pleaded, and supported mainly by the evidence of Mr Lewis and Mr Abrahams, was to the following effect.

(1) The first representation was made over the telephone by Mr Roberts to Mr Lewis and Mr Abrahams in a conversation which began at 9.43 am. It was that SNC would be in competition with two other bidders interested in purchasing the Ferranti shares, namely Citicorp and another, unnamed, bidder not within the securities industry. SNC's case was that on the basis of that representation it decided to bid 82p per share.

(2) The second representation was made at the outset of a midday meeting at SNC's offices which Mr Roberts had been invited to attend in a further telephone conversation held at 10.42 am. The purpose of the meeting was for him to hear SNC's bid and to bring with him, in sealed envelopes, the two competing bids. On arrival, Mr Roberts said that, although he had not brought any sealed envelopes with him, he would disclose the bids made by the two competing bidders once SNC had made its bid. It was implicit in what Mr Roberts said that the competing bids existed. SNC's case was that, in the light of Mr Roberts's promise to disclose the other bids, it would not have made its bid of 82p per share but for that representation.

(3) The third representation was made by Mr Roberts at the same meeting immediately after SNC had bid 82p per share. It was that Citicorp had bid in the region of 75 to 77p per share and that Aeritalia, an Italian state-owned defence contractor, had bid 81p per share. SNC's case was that it had been induced by that representation to agree to keep its bid open until 4.30 pm, when Citibank accepted it.

The judge dealt with the events of 21 July 1989 (see [1992] BCLC 1104 at 1116–1126). As to the 9.43 am conversation, he said there was no doubt that Mr Roberts told SNC that there were at least two other parties interested in purchasing the Ferranti shares and that one of them was a market maker, Citicorp Scrimgeour Vickers (CSV), another company within the Citicorp group; the implication being that the other interested party was not a market maker (see [1992] BCLC 1104 at 1117–1118). The only witnesses to what Mr Roberts said in the 9.43 am conversation were Mr Lewis and Mr Abrahams.

Following that conversation a meeting, which has come to be known as the pricing meeting, was held in Mr Abrahams's office to discuss whether SNC should bid for the Ferranti shares. In addition to Mr Abrahams and Mr Lewis, four others were present, including Mr David Marks, a director of SNC on the market making side. Having found that those present were told that SNC would be bidding in competition with a bidder from outside the securities industry, the judge said (at 1119):

> 'I am satisfied, therefore, that whatever Mr Roberts may have actually said in the course of the 9.43 am telephone conversation, the effect of what he said was that Mr Lewis and Mr Abrahams came to believe that SNC would be in competition with a bidder from outside the securities industry; and that they expressed that belief to the meeting at which the decision to bid 82p per share was taken.'

The judge added that he was also satisfied that that belief was an important factor in the deliberations which led to the decision to bid. He reaffirmed that view (see [1992] BCLC 1104 at 1121).

At 10.42 am, after the pricing meeting, Mr Lewis, in the presence of Mr Abrahams, telephoned Mr Roberts in order to inform him that SNC had decided to bid for the Ferranti shares and to ask him to attend at its offices, so that the bid could be made in person. It was arranged that Mr Roberts would come over to SNC's offices at about midday. Mr Lewis's evidence was that during that conversation he asked Mr Roberts to bring the other two bids with him in sealed envelopes. The judge found that Mr Roberts understood, by the end of that conversation, that Mr Lewis was expecting him to bring the other two bids with him, but he did not accept Mr Lewis's evidence as to the sealed envelopes. He accepted Mr Roberts's evidence that Mr Lewis suggested that SNC's bid could be treated as if it were a 'sealed bid' or were a bid in a sealed envelope; meaning that only he should see it, and that he would be expected to accept it or not at a meeting face to face. These matters were dealt with by the judge (see [1992] BCLC 1104 at 1121–1122).

Although the judge accepted Mr Roberts's account of the 10.42 am conversation as substantially correct, he rejected his initial claim that the only purpose of having a sealed bid by SNC was to ensure confidentiality (see [1992] BCLC 1104 at 1122–1123).

Mr Roberts arrived at SNC's offices shortly after midday, when a meeting took place between him, Mr Lewis, Mr Abrahams and Mr David Marks. Mr Roberts did not have any sealed envelopes containing bids from other parties with him. The judge found that he told the meeting that he would disclose the competing bids after SNC had made its bid and further that, if he had not given that assurance, SNC would not have made the bid which it did make.

SNC's bid of 82p per share was made orally at the midday meeting. Mr Roberts's response was that the bid was very close to the figure his client was seeking. He said that his client wanted 83p per share; and asked if SNC would raise its bid. Mr Lewis, or Mr Abrahams, said that they would not do so. Relying principally on the evidence of Mr David Marks, and recording that Mr Lewis and Mr Abrahams gave evidence to the same effect, the judge found that Mr Roberts told them that Aeritalia had bid 81p per share for the Ferranti shares, whereas the true position was that it had not made a bid for them, either at that price or at all. The judge dealt with these matters (see [1992] BCLC 1104 at 1123–1124).

The judge stated his conclusions as to the three representations (at 1129):

'For the reasons which I have set out in this judgment, I am satisfied that Mr Roberts made the second and third representations at the midday meeting and in the circumstances alleged. Having regard to the need for convincing proof, and to the fact that the only evidence available is that of Mr Lewis and Mr Abrahams, I am not satisfied that the first representation was made in the earlier telephone conversations in the morning of 21 July 1989 in sufficiently unequivocal terms for it to form the basis for an action in deceit; although, as I have said, it is clear that whatever was said by Mr Roberts in those telephone conversations led SNC to think that it was in competition with other bidders. I am satisfied—and, indeed, the contrary was not argued—that the second and third representations were false; and that Mr Roberts knew that those representations were false.'

The essence of Citibank's case on the facts, as advanced by Mr Sumption QC on its behalf, is that the judge's adverse findings in regard to the second and third representations were based on speculative inferences about what was inherently likely to have happened, each of which depended on other speculative inferences about what was inherently likely to have happened at some earlier stage. It was said that that was a wholly inappropriate basis on which to make findings of fraud against Mr Roberts, especially when they depended substantially on the discredited evidence of Mr Lewis and Mr Abrahams. The essence of SNC's case on the facts, as advanced by Mr Grabiner QC on its behalf, was that the judge's finding as to the first representation was inconsistent with his findings as to the second and third, his finding as to the first being heavily influenced by his wrongful rejection of the evidence of Mr Lewis and Mr Abrahams.

The crucial issue in the case is whether Mr Roberts, on any one or more of the three occasions alleged by SNC, deliberately and so as to influence its bid, led SNC to believe that there was another bidder for the Ferranti shares outside the securities industry. If he did, it is either common ground or unchallengeable that the representation was, as Mr Roberts knew, false and, further, that SNC's bid of 82p per share was, in part, influenced by it.

In our view the judge's analysis of the evidence before him gives rise to a number of difficulties.

First, although he made no general comment on the demeanour, consistency, or content of the evidence of Mr Lewis and Mr Abrahams, he concluded that little if any weight could be given to their evidence where it was in conflict with that given by Mr Roberts. His reason for coming to that conclusion was that they had sought deliberately to mislead the jury in the criminal proceedings as to the process by which their Criminal Justice Act statements had been prepared. But that was not an adequate reason for rejecting their evidence on the critical issues in the civil proceedings. That is particularly so if, as it must be, regard is had to the consistency of their accounts throughout and the confirmation they received at important points from Mr David Marks, a witness whose evidence was accepted substantially in its entirety.

Secondly, the judge made no general comment on the demeanour, consistency or content of the evidence of Mr Roberts. He accepted Mr Roberts's account of what was said about a 'sealed bid' in the 10.42 am conversation, but, in apparent contradiction, he rejected Mr Roberts's initial explanation as to the purpose of the sealed bid. Further, he rejected Mr

Roberts's evidence that at the midday meeting he had not referred to other bids but had merely identified the level of interest from CSV and Aeritalia.

Thirdly, the judge found that the second and third representations were made at the midday meeting and that they were, as Mr Roberts knew, false. He so found principally in reliance on the evidence of Mr Marks, but also, it would appear, in partial reliance on that of Mr Lewis and Mr Abrahams. Yet, as next appears, he was not prepared to find that the first representation, which was closely similar, had also been made.

Fourthly, the judge found that during the 9.43 am conversation Mr Roberts told SNC that there were two other interested parties, one a market maker, CSV, and the other, impliedly, from outside the market. The effect of what Mr Roberts said was such that Mr Lewis and Mr Abrahams 'came to believe that SNC would be in competition with a bidder from outside'; what he said 'led SNC to think that it was in competition with other bidders'; and the pricing meeting was informed accordingly. But the judge was not satisfied that 'the first representation was made ... in sufficiently unequivocal terms for it to form the basis for an action in deceit'. This appears to be a surprising conclusion in view of the findings that the second and third representations were made. It is explained by the judge on the ground of 'the need for continuing proof' (the meaning of which is not clear) and the fact that SNC's only evidence as to the 9.43 am conversation came from Mr Lewis and Mr Abrahams.

Fifthly, the judge found that the believed presence of a bidder from outside the securities industry was an important factor to those at the pricing meeting, though not the only factor; it was 'very material' in deciding what to bid. Yet this meeting preceded the making of the representation which he found proved. He found that, without a promise at the midday meeting to disclose the other bids, SNC would not have bid; yet he also found that the decision to bid 82p had already been made at the pricing meeting and such a bid was in fact made before disclosure of the other bids.

The judge's third, fourth, and fifth findings taken together make it very difficult, if not impossible, to separate reliance by SNC on the second and third representations from reliance on what Mr Roberts said in the 9.43 am conversation, which the judge found did not amount to a representation. Yet he did not address this difficulty. Furthermore, Mr Roberts's evidence was that, both at 9.43 am and at midday, he had indicated interest, but not bids, from others. The judge rejected this account in relation to the midday meeting and also found that what Mr Roberts said at 9.43 am led SNC to believe that there were other bidders. But he did not reject Mr Roberts's account of the 9.43 am conversation. Nor did he specifically address the consequential dichotomy in his findings. The only apparent reason for not finding that the first representation was made was the judge's reluctance to accept the evidence of Mr Lewis and Mr Abrahams because of what they had said in the Crown Court. For the reasons already given, this was an inadequate basis for disregarding their evidence.

This court is always reluctant to interfere with a judge's findings of primary fact. But in the present case we are driven to conclude that Chadwick J's finding that the first representation was not proved cannot stand. We so conclude for the following reasons, shortly stated.

(1) The judge's reason for not accepting the evidence of Mr Lewis and Mr Abrahams was inadequate.

(2) His finding that SNC were at 9.43 am led to think that there were other bidders is virtually tantamount to a finding that a representation was then made.

(3) His acceptance of Mr Roberts's evidence as to what was said about a sealed bid in the 10.42 am conversation appears to be irreconcilable with his rejection of Mr Roberts's initial evidence as to the purpose of a sealed bid and his evidence that, at the midday meeting, he had not referred to other bids.

(4) Events at the pricing meeting and the making of the second and third representations as found by the judge are all inexplicable unless the first representation had also been made.

(5) The judge failed to stand back and consider his finding as to the first representation in the light of his findings as to the second and third. Had he done so, we have little doubt that he would have been driven to conclude, as we do, that the first representation was also made.

We emphasise that, like the judge, we have sought to keep it well in mind that convincing proof is required to displace the presumption that a person in Mr Roberts's position can be expected to act honestly. But that presumption was displaced by the judge's findings as to the second and third representations. Despite the remarkable absence from the judgment of any general comment on the demeanour, consistency or content of the evidence of Mr Roberts, we cannot accept Mr Sumption's submission that the judge made no assessment of his reliability and proceeded only by way of intellectual inference. Having found Mr Roberts's evidence in relation to the second and third representations to be unreliable, the judge could only reasonably have found it to be so in relation to the first representation as well. We would only add that Mr Roberts's evidence, accepting, as it did, part of what Mr Lewis and Mr Abrahams said about the 9.43 am and 10.42 am telephone conversations, but then putting an improbable twist on it on each occasion, appears on its face to have been highly questionable.

It follows that the first ground in SNC's respondent's notice is made out. We find that the first representation was made. The judge's findings in relation to the second and third representations, namely that they were false, made fraudulently and induced SNC to make its bid (ultimately of 82·25p per share) apply equally to the first representation. Accordingly, like the judge, although on a broader basis, we proceed to consider the damages to which SNC is entitled.

Ascertaining the true measure of damages recoverable by SNC is complicated by the unusual and dramatic events which affected the Ferranti share price after the sale to SNC on 21 July 1989 but before the fraudulent nature of the representations had been discovered in December of the same year. On the date of sale the screen price, ie the price at which market makers were willing to deal in relatively small parcels, stood at 89p. It declined steadily over the summer. On 11 August the company published its accounts for the year ended 31 March 1989. These contained nothing which had not already been made known to the market before 21 July. But on 11 September 1989 the directors announced that information had come to their attention which required a restatement of the 1989 accounts. Dealings in the shares were suspended. On 29 September 1989 the chairman sent a letter to shareholders telling them that Ferranti had been the victim of a gigantic fraud perpetrated by a Mr Guerin, an American arms dealer. It had paid him a very substantial price for the shares in his company on the basis of fictitious contracts and accounts. The discovery reduced the company's net worth from £371m to £200m and its profits in the previous year from £29m to £11m. There is no suggestion that Citibank knew anything about Mr Guerin's fraud when it sold the shares on 21 July 1989.

When trading in Ferranti shares resumed on 3 October, the screen price was 55p. On 17 November the company published its revised audited accounts. These showed that the effects of Mr Guerin's fraud were even worse than the chairman had predicted. The screen price fell further. Until then, SNC had retained all the shares which it bought in July. But on 20 November 1989 it gradually began to trickle them onto the market. Over the following months it obtained prices ranging from 49p down to 30p. By 30 April 1990 it had sold them all.

The remedies available to a party who has been induced to enter into a contract by a fraudulent misrepresentation are rescission and damages. Rescission is a restitutionary remedy which allows the defrauded party to recover the property with which he has parted under the contract and return the benefit which he received. It is however a necessary condition of this remedy in English law that the plaintiff should be able to make substantial restitution in specie of the property which he has received. If SNC had retained the shares, it would have been able to return them and claim repayment of the full price, even though the value of the shares had fallen. But, no doubt after weighing the commercial risks of winning the action against the possibility of a further decline in the Ferranti share price, it decided to sell. Thereby it lost the right to rescission. In the case of a fungible asset like quoted shares, the rule which requires restitution in specie is a hard one. Not every legal system would insist upon it, particularly in a case of fraud. But SNC accepted that it could not pursue the claim to restitution and abandoned it at the trial.

The damages claimed in the statement of claim were the difference between the price paid (82·25p) and the 'true value' of the shares on the date of acquisition. There was no claim for any form of consequential loss such as additional money spent in reliance on the truth of the representation (see *Doyle v Olby (Ironmongers) Ltd* [1969] 2 All ER 119, [1969] 2 QB 158). Furthermore, SNC accept and aver that the date upon which the loss must be ascertained is the date of acquisition. The measure of damages is, in Lord Atkin's words, 'the actual damage directly flowing from the fraudulent inducement' (see *Clark v Urquhart, Stracey v Urquhart* [1930] AC 28 at 68). Depreciation of the value of the shares by market forces operating after the date of acquisition does not flow directly from the fraudulent inducement, but from the purchaser's decision to retain the shares and accept the hazards of the market rather than sell at once (see *Waddell v Blockey* (1879) 4 QBD 678).

The argument has therefore turned upon what is meant by the true value of the shares on 21 July 1989. Citibank says that it is the price for which, absent the misrepresentations, the shares could have been sold in the market. This could not on any view have been less than 78p, which was the price SNC was willing to pay for a bought deal. The judge decided that it was the price which would have been paid if the market had known about the fraud which was revealed in September. This, after hearing expert evidence, he determined at 44p.

Before looking at the authorities, we examine the matter in principle. Although judges sometimes speak of 'real' or 'true' or sometimes even 'intrinsic' value, it must be borne in mind that value in money is not a property internal to a thing like its weight or size. It is the price which on certain given assumptions would have been paid for that thing in the market. Varying the assumptions will vary the value. So, for example, if one assumes that only a restricted class of people are allowed to buy, its value may be very different from what it would have been on a sale in the open market, ie on the assumption that anyone could buy.

One of the most important elements in valuation is what assumption should be made about the information which was available to the market. This is well illustrated by the decision of the House of Lords in *Lynall v IRC* [1971] 3 All ER 914, [1972] AC 680, in which shares were worth £4 10s on the assumption that the market knew about the board's plans for a public flotation and £3 10s on the assumption that it did not.

What assumptions as to information should be made for the purposes of determining the loss caused by the fraudulent misrepresentation? It seems to us that there are only two possibilities. The first is to assume that the market knew everything it actually did know but was not influenced by the misrepresentation itself. The second is to assume that the market was omniscient, ie it knew everything relevant to the price of the shares which was in fact the case. The first solution is a rational principle upon which to calculate the loss which directly flowed from the representation on the relevant date. The second is in our view entirely arbitrary and allows the damages to be increased or diminished by any fact or event which, unknown to anyone, actually existed or occurred before the relevant date, provided that it has emerged from the womb of time before the trial. Assume, for example, a purchaser fraudulently induced to buy shares for 80p on a date when the price which they would have fetched in the market was 60p. He cuts his losses and sells for that price a week later. A month later it emerges that on the date when he bought, the board were negotiating a favourable contract which, if known about, would have resulted in the shares trading at 85p. On the assumption of omniscience, the damages are zero. This cannot be right.

In our view Chadwick J could only have assumed the market to know about the September revelations by applying a general assumption of omniscience. He formulated the principle as follows ([1992] BCLC 1104 at 1143):

> 'In ascertaining the plaintiff's loss under the basic rule events subsequent to the acquisition can be taken into account only if, and insofar as, they are relevant for the purpose of ascertaining the true value of the shares at the time of the acquisition. A subsequent depreciation in the value of the shares caused by events which have no natural or proximate connection with the circumstances existing at the time of the acquisition must be disregarded.'

In other words, all 'circumstances existing at the time of the acquisition'—everything in the world that was the case—and any subsequent events having a natural and proximate connection with those circumstances, can be taken into account to ascertain the 'true value' of the shares.

We can see no difference in principle between assuming market knowledge of the unconnected fraud revealed in September and assuming knowledge of the board negotiations in the example we have given. The judge thought that such an assumption was justified by the cases. But omniscience seems to us such an arbitrary and irrational assumption that we are reluctant to declare it English law unless clearly bound by authority to do so.

The main authority upon which the judge relied was *Twycross v Grant* (1877) 2 CPD 469, which was concerned with a false prospectus deemed fraudulent by s 38 of the Companies Act 1867. Trading in the market had been on the basis of the prospectus. It is important to bear in mind that the statutory fraud was a failure to disclose the existence of certain contracts, so that absent the fraud, the market would by definition have known the relevant facts. The defendant claimed that the value of the shares at the date of purchase was the price at which they were trading on the Stock Exchange. Giving the judgment of the Common Pleas Division, Lord Coleridge CJ rejected this submission (at 489–490):

'... if the jury thought (as they well might, and probably did,) that the quotation on the Stock Exchange did not shew a real, but only a delusive value caused by the fraudulent nature of the prospectus and the mode in which the shares were manipulated by the defendants and others in concert with them, the jury were not only justified in disregarding, but were bound to disregard, such delusive and factitious value ... There is no evidence whatever that the shares ever had any value except that which resulted from the wrongful acts of the defendants; and it would be contrary to all principle to allow them to take advantage of their own wrong, and claim credit for the market-price of the shares, when but for their own concealment of the contracts in question there is no reason to suppose that the shares would have had any market value at all.'

This passage shows, if we may say so, a very simple and understandable rule, namely that in determining the value of the property, one assumes the misrepresentation not to have been made. It does not require any assumption that the market knew facts which it would not have known whether the misrepresentation had been made or not. The judgment of the Common Pleas Division was affirmed by the Court of Appeal and it is upon certain passages and an illustration in the judgments of Cockburn CJ and Bramwell LJ that Chadwick J relied in holding that the case required him to value the shares upon an assumption of omniscience.

There is in our view nothing in the judgments of the Court of Appeal to suggest that it intended to go further than the principle laid down by Lord Coleridge CJ. There is perhaps some slightly loose language in dealing with arguments which do not touch upon the present issue. Thus Bramwell LJ, addressing the argument that the business might have been destroyed by some subsequent disaster, said (at 504): 'But in that case the thing would not have been worthless through its intrinsic and inherent defect.' The words 'intrinsic and inherent defect' were taken by Chadwick J as indicating that anything which could be described as an inherent defect in the property must be taken into account, whether the market would have known of it or not. But in our view Bramwell LJ's whole judgment is predicated on the assumption that if the promoters had disclosed to the market the information which had been fraudulently concealed, the shares would have been worthless: '... if it had been said there was a contract to pay a company-maker 48,500*l.*, to launch, or float, or finance the company—about one seventh of its capital—no one knowing that would have taken shares in it.' (See at 2 CPD 469 at 504.) The phrase 'intrinsic and inherent defect' is used only by way of contrast with a subsequent event and against a background which assumes that, absent the fraudulent non-disclosure, it would have been known to the market.

The only real support for the judge's principle is in a casual illustration given by Cockburn CJ in repelling the same analogy with loss caused by subsequent events. He said that if a man buys a horse 'on the false representation that it has won some great race' and it later catches some disease and dies, he cannot recover the whole price (see 2 CPD 469 at 544). He must give credit for what the animal was actually worth at the time of the purchase. But, said Cockburn CJ, it would be different if, after he got the animal home, it died 'of some latent disease inherent in its system at the time he bought it'. In that case, the horse was 'by reason of the latent mischief worthless when he bought'. If the use of the term 'latent' was intended to mean that the purchaser could recover the full price even though buyers in the ordinary market would neither have discovered the defect nor required a warranty against latent diseases, then this example is difficult to reconcile with principle. But because Cockburn CJ was addressing an altogether different point, namely the distinction between matters which affected the value at the time of the sale and loss caused by subsequent events, it is difficult to know exactly what he had in mind. We certainly do not believe that he intended to embrace the omniscience theory with all its consequences.

The essence of Mr Grabiner's powerful argument for SNC was that in a case in which the purchase had been induced by a fraudulent misrepresentation and the purchaser had acted entirely reasonably in retaining the shares, it was unjust that the risk of catastrophic events, like the discovery of Mr Guerin's fraud, should fall upon the innocent purchaser rather than the fraudulent vendor. We see the force of this argument, but in our view the injustice, if any, stems from the rigidity of two rules which Mr Grabiner does not challenge. These are, first, the denial of a restitutionary remedy (which would leave the risk of subsequent devaluation of the shares on the fraudulent vendor) unless there can be restitution of the very same shares in specie and, secondly, the rule in *Waddell v Blockey* (1879) 4 QBD 678, which requires the damages to be calculated as at the date of the sale (compare *Naughton v O'Callaghan (Rogers and ors, third parties)* [1990] 3 All ER 191). The effect of these rules cannot in our judgment be overturned by introducing the startling concept of omniscience into the mundane process of valuation.

In our judgment, therefore, the correct measure of damages was the difference between 82·25p and the price which, absent the misrepresentation, the parcel of shares would have fetched on the open market on 21 July 1989. Mr Sumption submitted that on the evidence accepted by the judge, that price was 82·25p a share. That was the price which SNC decided to bid before any representation had been made. But that submission is undermined by our finding that the 9.43 am representation was made and that the pricing meeting acted upon it. The judge found that in the absence of a representation, SNC would have offered 78p for a bought deal. He thought that Citibank would not have accepted this price: it would have preferred to deal in-house with CSV. But there was no evidence that CSV would have offered a higher price. It too was wanting a bought deal. It follows that, in our view, 78p was the market price on the date in question. The loss flowing from the misrepresentation was therefore 4·25p a share and the damages must be reduced from £10,764,005 to £1,196,010, being the difference between the price paid (£23,146,321) and the value of the shares at 78p each (£21,950,311).

It remains for us to deal with three questions of costs raised by SNC. Chadwick J's leave for SNC to enter a cross-appeal on these questions not having been sought or obtained, Mr Sumption submitted that we were precluded from dealing with them by s 18(1)(f) of the Supreme Court Act 1981. We are satisfied that that provision has no application in this case. The judge ordered Citibank to pay to SNC its costs of the action, but only from and after 20 December 1990 and limited in relation to the costs of the trial to 75% of those costs. He also refused to give SNC a certificate for three counsel.

The judge's reason for relieving Citibank from bearing 25% of the costs of the trial was expressed thus:

'My concern is that this trial ran for some time more than was necessary, due not only to the way in which Mr Lewis and Mr Abrahams had been prepared in their earlier witness statements, but also by the nature of the discovery made by the plaintiffs. It was necessary, I think, to call Mr Abrahams back at least twice and Mr Lewis more than once, too, I think.'

The 25% discount was based on the judge's view that a total of approximately six days of the trial had been thrown away. Although we have disagreed with the judge's evaluation of the evidence of Mr Abrahams and Mr Lewis in these proceedings, we think that his decision on this point, and also his refusal to grant a certificate for three counsel, were within his discretion and cannot be interfered with by this court.

The judge's decision to disallow SNC's costs incurred before 20 December 1990 came about in this way. The writ was issued on 6 January 1990 against SVAM as the sole defendant. Citibank was not joined until 19 December 1990. It was an issue in the action whether the representations made by Mr Roberts were made by him as agent for Citibank or as agent for SVAM. The judge decided that, at the time of the midday meeting at any rate, Mr Roberts was acting on behalf of Citibank. He found that Citibank alone was responsible, vicariously, for the representations made by Mr Roberts at that meeting (see [1992] BCLC 1104 at 1129).

In dealing with this question, the judge pointed out that SNC had originally alleged that Mr Roberts was acting in the transactions on behalf of SVAM, and that that allegation had been traversed in SVAM's defence served on 20 February 1990. He continued:

'As from the outset of the action therefore—or, more accurately, within a month of the outset of the action—the plaintiffs knew that Mr Roberts's agency was in issue. I am told that they resisted an application in or about April 1990 to join Citibank as a defendant. In those circumstances, I can see no reason why Citibank should be required to pay costs incurred during a period in which it was plain that they were a candidate to be a defendant; but equally plain that the plaintiffs were resisting their joinder.'

Mr Grabiner submitted that the judge was wrong to conclude that SVAM was not also liable to SNC. That is a question on which we do not propose to enter. His alternative submission was that the judge in any event erred in principle or gave a decision which was plainly wrong. He took us through the material events and evidence in order to show that SNC had no reason to suppose that Mr Roberts had been acting on behalf of Citibank, whereas SVAM and Citibank, who knew that he had been, did not say so.

We respectfully think that Mr Grabiner's alternative submission is correct. It can, we believe, be put more broadly still. SVAM and Citibank having been closely connected both in the group of which they were members and in this transaction, and Mr Roberts having been an executive director of the one and the head of the private banking department of the other, SNC did nothing unreasonable in acting as it did. Moreover, both companies have throughout been represented by the same solicitors and counsel and it is not suggested that the costs as a whole during the period in question were increased.

We propose that Chadwick J's order should be varied by substituting the sum of £1,196,010 for that of £10,764,005 in paras (2)(i) and (3)(i) thereof and by deleting the words 'such costs to commence on 20th December 1990' from para (2)(iii) thereof. To that extent the appeal will be allowed.

Appeal allowed in part. Leave to appeal refused.

Carolyn Toulmin   Barrister.

Balkanbank v Taher and others

QUEEN'S BENCH DIVISION (COMMERCIAL COURT)

CLARKE J

18, 19, 20, 29 APRIL 1994

Practice – Pre-trial or post-judgment relief – Mareva injunction – Worldwide Mareva injunction – Pre-trial injunction – Counterclaim – Jurisdiction – Plaintiff obtaining interim relief in aid of substantive action proceeding in Irish court – Court discharging injunction by consent on failure of Irish action and directing an inquiry into damages – Defendants seeking to advance counterclaims in respect of losses sustained by reason of the injunction – Whether court having jurisdiction to entertain counterclaims in respect of claim for interim relief – Whether originating summons seeking Mareva relief an 'action' for purposes of procedural rules – Whether court retaining discretion whether to order plaintiff to pay damages to defendants – Civil Jurisdiction and Judgments Act 1982, s 25, Sch 1, art 24 – RSC Ord 28, r 7(1).

In 1990 the plaintiff bank issued proceedings in Ireland against the defendants alleging fraud in respect of a joint venture agreement and, at the same time, applied for and obtained a Mareva injunction restraining the defendants from dealing with their assets within the jurisdiction of the Irish court. The bank subsequently issued an originating summons in the English court seeking worldwide Mareva relief as against the defendants, which was granted pursuant to s 25[a] of the Civil Jurisdiction and Judgments Act 1982, which enabled the English courts to give effect to art 24[b] of the Convention on Jurisdiction and the Enforcement of Judgments in Civil and Commercial Matters 1968 (which was set out in Sch 1 to the 1982 Act) by providing interim relief in aid of substantive proceedings already commenced or about to be commenced in another convention country, subject to the standard form of undertaking as to damages. At the trial of the substantive Irish action, the

a   Section 25, so far as material, is set out at p 244 j to p 245 a, post
b   Article 24 is set out at p 246 e, post

court rejected the bank's principal allegation of fraud and discharged the Irish injunction. Shortly thereafter, the English court made a consent order discharging the worldwide Mareva injunction and directed that there be an inquiry into the damages sustained by the defendants by reason of the English injunction which the bank ought to pay. The defendants claimed that they had suffered catastrophic losses as a result of the English injunction and sought to advance various counterclaims against the bank under RSC Ord 28, r 7(1)^c, which provided that a defendant to an 'action begun by originating summons', who alleged that he had any claim or was entitled to any relief or remedy against the plaintiff in respect of any matter, might make a counterclaim in the action in respect of that matter instead of bringing a separate action. The bank however contended that the court had no jurisdiction to entertain the counterclaims on the ground that a s 25 application made by originating summons was not an 'action' within the meaning of Ord 28, r 7(1), which was confined to actions in which the plaintiff asserted a substantive right. The defendants also claimed that the court no longer had a discretion whether to award damages to them because it had already exercised its discretion in making the earlier consent order.

Held – (1) An application for interim relief under s 25 of the 1982 Act was not an 'action' begun by originating summons within the meaning of RSC Ord 28, r 7, which, on its true construction, limited the availability of a counterclaim to those actions where the plaintiff claimed substantive relief and thereby submitted to the jurisdiction of the court in respect of any claim which the defendant might wish to advance on the merits. In particular, Ord 28, r 7 was not intended to confer on a defendant to a s 25 application for interim relief the right to make a counterclaim on the merits, since that construction would in effect confer jurisdiction on the English court over substantive claims commenced or about to be commenced in the courts of another convention country and was inconsistent not only with the 1968 convention, which made no provision for a defendant to counterclaim on the merits in the convention country in which interim relief under art 24 had been obtained, but also with s 25 of the 1982 Act itself, which was intended to ensure that substantive proceedings in another convention country were carried forward to best advantage, not to confer jurisdiction on the English court which it would not otherwise have had. It followed that the court did not have jurisdiction under Ord 28, r 7 to entertain a counterclaim in proceedings commenced by originating summons for the purpose of obtaining interim relief under s 25 of the 1982 Act in support of an action on the merits brought in the court of another convention country. The defendants' counterclaims would accordingly be struck out (see p 250 *d* to *f g h* and p 251 *j* to p 252 *b j* to p 253 *d*, post); *Channel Tunnel Group Ltd v Balfour Beatty Construction Ltd* [1993] 1 All ER 664 considered.

(2) An undertaking in damages was given to the court, not the defendant, and, although it was for the defendant to make a claim under it, it was for the court to decide whether it was appropriate to order the plaintiff to pay damages in any particular case. Moreover, the question whether the court had exercised its discretion to order a plaintiff to pay damages to the defendant in respect of losses sustained as a result of a Mareva injunction would clearly

---

c   Rule 7(1) is set out at p 244 *h*, post

depend on the facts of the particular case. On the facts, the court had not yet exercised its discretion and accordingly it retained a discretion to be exercised thereafter (see p 256 *h*, p 258 *b c g h* and p 259 *j*, post); *Norwest Holst Civil Engineering Ltd v Polysius Ltd* (1987) Times, 23 July and *Financiera Avenida v Shiblaq* (1991) Times, 14 January considered.

Per curiam. The order made on an application for an inquiry into damages should spell out clearly what, if any, residual discretion is left to be exercised later and it should, for example, be possible to tell on the face of the order whether the plaintiff is to pay the amount ascertained on the inquiry (see p 260 *c*, post).

Notes
For counterclaim to originating summons, see 37 *Halsbury's Laws* (4th edn) para 558.

For undertakings and inquiries as to damages, see 24 *Halsbury's Laws* (4th edn reissue) paras 982–986, 987, and for cases on the subject, see 28(4) *Digest* (2nd reissue) 396–406, 6856–6970.

For the Civil Jurisdiction and Judgments Act 1982, s 25, Sch 1, art 24, see 11 *Halsbury's Statutes* (4th edn) (1991 reissue) 1116, 1149.

As from 1 December 1991 Sch 1 to the 1982 Act was substituted by the Civil Jurisdiction and Judgments Act 1982 (Amendment) Order 1990, SI 1990/2591.

Cases referred to in judgment
Babanaft International Co SA v Bassatne [1989] 1 All ER 433, [1990] Ch 13, [1989] 2 WLR 232, CA.
Barclays Bank Ltd v Rosenberg Ltd (1985) 135 NLJ 633.
Channel Tunnel Group Ltd v Balfour Beatty Construction Ltd [1993] 1 All ER 664, [1993] AC 334, [1993] 2 WLR 262, HL.
Cheltenham and Gloucester Building Society v Ricketts [1993] 4 All ER 276, [1993] 1 WLR 1545, HL.
CSI International Co Ltd v Archway Personnel (Middle East) Ltd [1980] 3 All ER 215, [1980] 1 WLR 1069, CA.
Derby & Co Ltd v Larsson [1976] 1 All ER 401, [1976] 1 WLR 202, HL.
Fawsitt, Re, Galland v Burton (1885) 30 Ch D 231, CA.
Financiera Avenida v Shiblaq (1991) Times, 14 January, [1990] CA Transcript 973.
Haiti (Republic) v Duvalier [1989] 1 All ER 456, [1990] 1 QB 202, [1989] 2 WLR 261, CA.
Liberia (Republic) v Gulf Oceanic Inc [1985] 1 Lloyd's Rep 539, CA; *affg* (29 March 1994, unreported), QBD.
Metal Scrap Trade Corp Ltd v Kate Shipping Co Ltd, The Gladys [1990] 1 All ER 397, [1990] 1 WLR 115, HL.
Norwest Holst Civil Engineering Ltd v Polysius Ltd (1987) Times, 23 July, [1987] CA Transcript 644.
Siskina (cargo owners) v Distos Cia Naviera SA, The Siskina [1977] 3 All ER 803, [1979] AC 210, [1977] 3 WLR 818, HL.
Vardon's Trusts, Re (1885) 31 Ch D 275, CA.
X v Y [1989] 3 All ER 689, [1990] 1 QB 220, [1989] 3 WLR 910.
Zygal Dynamics plc v McNulty [1989] CA Transcript 571.

Applications
On 8 October 1990 the plaintiff, Balkanbank, issued an originating summons against the defendants, Naser Taher, Kevin McGrath, Via Holdings Ltd, Taher

Meats (Ireland) Ltd, Balkan International Ltd and Bank of Credit and Commerce International SA, seeking, in aid of substantive Irish proceedings, a Mareva injunction restraining the defendants from dealing with their assets worldwide. The injunction was granted by Waller J pursuant to s 25 of the Civil Jurisdiction and Judgments Act 1982 and was made subject to the standard form of undertaking as to damages. On 13 May 1992, following the collapse of the Irish action, Evans J made a consent order discharging the Mareva order and ordered that there be an inquiry as to damages. On 25 February 1994 Clarke J directed that there be a hearing on the effect of the consent order in terms of the court's discretion to award damages. On 11 March 1994 the first, third and fourth defendants sought to advance a counterclaim under RSC Ord 28, r 7(1), claiming general damages to be assessed by the court for loss caused to each of them by reason of the injunction. On 25 March 1994 Balkanbank applied to the court pursuant to Ord 12, r 8 for an order declaring, inter alia, that the court had no jurisdiction to entertain the counterclaim. At the hearing the judge considered the issues regarding both the counterclaim and the consent order. The hearing and judgment took place in chambers, but Clarke J ruled that the judgment was to be treated as having been delivered in open court. The facts are set out in the judgment.

Timothy Saloman QC and *Robert Bright* (instructed by *Allen & Overy*) for the plaintiff.
Steven Gee QC (instructed by *Bermans*) for the defendants.

Cur adv vult

29 April 1994. The following judgment was delivered.

CLARKE J. There are before the court applications relating to two discrete matters. The first relates to a counterclaim which the first, third and fourth defendants have sought to advance and the second relates to the question whether the court retains a discretion whether to order the plaintiff to pay damages to the defendants. I shall consider the issues relating to the counterclaim first.

Counterclaim

The history of this matter, so far as it is relevant for present purposes, is briefly as follows. In 1990 the plaintiff (Balkanbank) wished to make certain allegations of fraud against some of the defendants. On 3 October 1990 Balkanbank issued proceedings in Ireland claiming certain moneys which it said belonged to it and claiming damages, inter alia, for fraud against the first defendant (NT), Taher Investments Ltd, which is now the third defendant (VHL), the fourth defendant (TMIL) and the fifth defendant (BIL). The dispute arose out of a joint venture agreement between Balkanbank and VHL. VHL was controlled by the Taher family including NT. BIL was a joint venture company. It is not necessary at present to set out either the true nature of the joint venture or the detail of the allegations.

On the same day, 3 October 1990, Balkanbank obtained a Mareva injunction against each of the defendants in the Irish action limited to assets within the jurisdiction of the Irish court. On the morning of 8 October the Irish injunction was varied by consent. On the same day Balkanbank obtained a worldwide

Mareva injunction from this court which was granted by Waller J. The defendants have alleged non-disclosure of material facts before Waller J, although it is not at present necessary for me to consider the validity or otherwise of that allegation. The order was made under s 25 of the Civil Jurisdiction and Judgments Act 1982 in aid of Balkanbank's substantive proceedings in Ireland. It was granted because of the reliance placed by Balkanbank upon the alleged fraud of the defendants.

The proceedings were commenced by originating summons which gave the addresses of NT, TMIL and BIL as in Ireland while that of VHL was given as in Liechtenstein. I am not concerned with Kevin McGrath or the Bank of Credit and Commerce International SA (the second and sixth defendants). I shall therefore disregard them in what follows. There has never been a hearing of the originating summons, although on 10 October 1990 there was a variation of the order made by Waller J after discussion between the parties. There very rarely is a hearing of the originating summons in the case of applications of this kind. The defendants did not at that stage enter an acknowledgment of service.

The trial of the action in Ireland began before Blayney J in April 1991. It was long and expensive. Blayney J gave judgment on 12 February 1992. Balkanbank's principal allegations of fraud failed, although NT and TMIL were ordered to account for certain sums to Balkanbank. BIL made a counterclaim against Balkanbank claiming that it was in breach of contract in failing to transfer certain shares in Air Via, but the counterclaim failed. The Irish Mareva injunction was discharged and the court in Ireland subsequently directed that there be an inquiry as to damages suffered by the defendants by reason of the injunction. That inquiry has not yet taken place.

Waller J's order was made on the basis of certain undertakings which were given to the court by Balkanbank. The undertaking as to damages was in the usual form as follows:

'To abide by any Order which this Court may make as to damages, in case this court may hereafter be of the opinion that the Defendants or any of them have suffered any by reason of this order which the Plaintiff ought to pay.'

On 24 April 1992 NT, VHL and TMIL obtained a Mareva injunction against Balkanbank in aid of their claim for damages under that undertaking. On 13 May 1992 Evans J made a consent order discharging the worldwide Mareva injunction as against NT, VHL and TMIL and ordered—

'that there be an inquiry as to what damages the First, Third and Fourth Defendants herein or any of them have or has suffered as a result of the making of the said Order of 8 October which the Plaintiff ought to pay.'

The hearing of that inquiry has now been fixed to begin in October 1994. Since May 1992 there have been many interlocutory skirmishes between the parties to which it is not necessary for me to refer at present, although I should mention that BIL says that it has suffered loss as a result of the injunction and its claim too is to be heard in October.

The defendants' primary case is that they have suffered catastrophic losses as a result of the English injunction. It is common ground that the Taher group has collapsed. The defendants say that as a result of the English injunction they lost the support of the banks with the result that they were unable to continue in business. The defendants' claims are now pleaded in detail. They are denied by Balkanbank, which says that the group would have collapsed in any event. In the alternative it says, inter alia, that the losses were caused by the Irish injunction and/or by the allegations themselves. These points were first raised in a letter from Messrs Allen & Overy dated 14 January 1994, in which they said this:

'In our clients' submission, quite apart from the question whether your clients' evidence will be accepted, your clients have failed (i) to distinguish between the effect, if any, of the Irish and English orders and (ii) to distinguish between the effect, if any, of those orders, or either of them, and the effect, if any, of the allegations made in either the Irish or the English proceedings.'

Those points have now been pleaded in para 13 of Balkanbank's points of defence.

Some of the defendants now wish to advance counterclaims which they have pleaded in points of counterclaim attached to their points of claim. The counterclaims fall into two parts. The first is a counterclaim by VHL. In the inquiry VHL claims that it has suffered very substantial losses as a result of the English injunction. Mr Gee QC for the defendants says that that is VHL's primary case, but that it wishes to argue in the alternative that the same losses were caused by the breach by Balkanbank of certain alleged implied terms of the joint venture agreement and/or of certain alleged breaches of fiduciary duties which it is said to have owed VHL. VHL has also alleged that Balkanbank is bound to account for any profits made from an investment in a company in Gabon.

The second counterclaim is brought by NT, TMIL and VHL. It is for a declaration that the losses were caused by reason of the Irish injunction within the meaning of the undertaking which Balkanbank gave to the court in Ireland.

Mr Saloman QC for the plaintiff submits that the court has no jurisdiction to entertain the counterclaims or, if it has, that it should not exercise it. It is convenient to consider the question of jurisdiction first.

Jurisdiction to counterclaim

Mr Gee submits that the defendants are entitled to counterclaim under RSC Ord 28, r 7(1). Indeed, as I understand it, that is the only rule upon which he relies so that if the court does not have jurisdiction under it he accepts that there is no other basis upon which the defendants can counterclaim. Order 28, r 7(1) provides as follows:

'A defendant to an action begun by originating summons who has acknowledged service of the summons and who alleges that he has any claim or is entitled to any relief or remedy against the plaintiff in respect of any matter (whenever and however arising) may make a counterclaim in the action in respect of that matter instead of bringing a separate action.'

Mr Gee submits that a defendant to such an action has a right to counterclaim and that since these defendants are defendants to the action begun by this originating summons they have a right to counterclaim.

The plaintiff's claim for interim relief was made under s 25 of the 1982 Act, which provides as follows:

'The High Court ... shall have power to grant interim relief where—(a) proceedings have been or are to be commenced in a Brussels or Lugano

Contracting State other than the United Kingdom ... and (b) they are or will be proceedings whose subject-matter is within the scope of the 1968 Convention as determined by Article 1 (whether or not that or any other Convention has effect in relation to the proceedings).'

An application under s 25 has to be made by originating summons under RSC Ord 5, r 3. Mr Gee submits that such a proceeding is an 'action begun by originating summons' within the meaning of Ord 28, r 7(1). His argument may be summarised as follows.

(1) By s 100 of the Judicature Act 1873 an 'action' was defined as a 'civil proceeding begun by writ or in such other manner as may be prescribed by rules of court'. In *Re Fawsitt, Galland v Burton* (1885) 30 Ch D 231 it was held by the Court of Appeal that the rules must not be taken as being or as intended to be inconsistent with the 1873 Act and that since RSC 1883, Ord 55, r 3 provided that certain civil proceedings must be commenced by originating summons and not by writ it followed that a proceeding so commenced was an 'action' for the purposes of a rule relating to appeal to the Court of Appeal. *Re Fawsitt, Galland v Burton* was followed by the Court of Appeal in *Re Vardon's Trusts* (1885) 31 Ch D 275.

(2) Section 225 of the Supreme Court of Judicature (Consolidation) Act 1925, which was in the same terms as s 100 of the 1873 Act, provided:

'In this Act, unless the context otherwise requires the following expressions have the meanings hereby assigned to them respectively, that is to say:—"Action" means a civil proceeding commenced by writ or in such other manner as may be prescribed by rules of court ...'

By s 31 of the Interpretation Act 1889, in the absence of a contrary intention, expressions in the rules have the same meaning as in the 1925 Act. The relevance of those provisions is that they were the statutes in force when Ord 28, r 7 was first introduced, which was in the Rules of the Supreme Court (Revision) 1962, SI 1962/2145, although some other parts of Ord 28 were amended by the Rules of the Supreme Court 1965.

(3) The equivalent provisions which are in force at present are s 151 of the Supreme Court Act 1981 and s 11 of the Interpretation Act 1978. They are to the same effect.

(4) The jurisdiction to grant relief by counterclaim was contained in s 39 of the 1925 Act. Sections 36 to 44 of that Act (including s 39) were in effect re-enacted in s 49 of the 1981 Act, which provides, inter alia:

'(2) Every ... court shall give the same effect as hitherto—(a) to all ... counterclaims ... and, subject to the provisions of this or any other Act, shall so exercise its jurisdiction in every cause or matter before it as to secure that, as far as possible, all matters in dispute between the parties are completely and finally determined, and all multiplicity of legal proceedings with respect to any of those matters is avoided.'

The court has jurisdiction under Ord 28, r 7 in a case such as this in order to effectuate the purpose enshrined in that section.

(5) It follows that the originating summons in the instant case claiming interim relief under s 25 of the 1982 Act is or begins an 'action begun by originating summons' within the meaning of Ord 28, r 7(1) so that the defendants are in principle entitled to counterclaim against the plaintiffs.

(6) There is no restriction on the type of claim which can be advanced by counterclaim. It does not have to be connected with the plaintiff's claim, although if it is appropriate the court will direct that the counterclaim proceed by separate action in England under Ord 28, r 7(3).

Mr Saloman does not quarrel with the above analysis save to submit that, in its context, Ord 28, r 7 should be construed as being confined to actions begun by originating summons in which the plaintiff asserts a substantive right. He submits that the rule cannot have been intended to confer upon a defendant to an originating summons, which claims only interim or interlocutory relief, the right to make a claim on the merits.

In this regard he points, in particular, to a claim such as that advanced by the plaintiff in this case. The plaintiff wished to proceed on the merits in Ireland. Jurisdiction was conferred on the Irish court by arts 1, 2 and 6(1) of the European Convention on Jurisdiction and the Enforcement of Judgments in Civil and Commercial Matters 1968 (set out in Sch 1 to the 1982 Act and subsequently amended). The English courts would not have had jurisdiction on the merits under the 1968 convention. The plaintiffs would not have been able to serve the writ out of the jurisdiction under Ord 11. The only relief which the plaintiff could seek under the 1968 convention in England was provisional relief under art 24, which provides as follows:

'Application may be made to the courts of a Contracting State for such provisional, including protective, measures as may be available under the law of that State, even if, under this Convention, the courts of another Contracting State have jurisdiction as to the substance of the matter.'

Mr Saloman further points to the fact that under the convention the obtaining of interim relief under art 24 does not have the effect of conferring upon the courts of the state where such relief is obtained jurisdiction on the merits which it would not otherwise have under the convention. By art 6.3 a person domiciled in a contracting state may be sued by way of counterclaim in the court where the original claim is pending. In the instant case that would be the court in Ireland. There is no provision in the 1968 convention to the effect that a person against whom interim relief is obtained under art 24 may counterclaim on the merits in the state in which the interim relief is obtained.

Mr Gee accepts that the convention does not contemplate a counterclaim of this kind being advanced in the court where the interim relief is obtained, but submits that that is nevertheless the effect of Ord 28, r 7.

In my judgment there is considerable force in Mr Saloman's submissions. The effect of Mr Gee's submissions if they are right is that where, for example, a plaintiff seeks interim relief in England in support of a substantive claim which has not yet been commenced in the state which has jurisdiction over it, the defendant obtains the right to counterclaim on the merits and thus to make the English court the court first seised of the substantive dispute, which may in turn have the effect of depriving the court which would have had jurisdiction of the jurisdiction which it would have had by reason of art 21, or at least of persuading it to stay the proceedings under art 22. It would I think be surprising if the English rules of procedure had that effect.

Mr Gee submits however that they do. In addition to the statutory provisions referred to above he draws attention to a number of cases in which the court has refused to hold that the purpose of the plaintiff's claim is relevant to the rights conferred upon a defendant by Ord 28, r 7. It is convenient to consider the various cases to which I was referred in chronological order.

In *Derby & Co Ltd v Larsson* [1976] 1 All ER 401, [1976] 1 WLR 202 the plaintiffs brought an action on the merits in England. It was held by the House of Lords that by doing so they had submitted themselves to the risk of a counterclaim under Ord 15, r 2 (which is the equivalent rule to Ord 28, r 7 but which applies to actions begun by writ) so that the counterclaim was 'properly brought against a person duly served within the jurisdiction' for the purposes of Ord 11, r 1, which applied by reason of Ord 15, r 3(5). Lord Russell said ([1976] 1 All ER 401 at 415, [1976] 1 WLR 202 at 205):

> 'If a person chooses to commence proceedings in this jurisdiction he lays himself open to the possibility of a counterclaim by the defendant as well as to a defence. The rules of court permit it subject to compliance with time requirements.'

The underlying basis of that decision and indeed of the rules is that where a plaintiff makes a claim in England he submits to the jurisdiction of the English court and thus exposes himself to a counterclaim brought by the defendant. That case was concerned only with a claim by the plaintiffs on the merits. The question for decision here is whether the same principle applies where the relief sought is not of a substantive nature.

In *Republic of Liberia v Gulf Oceanic Inc* [1985] 1 Lloyd's Rep 539 the second plaintiffs (LPRC) entered into a contract with a third party for the purchase of a large quantity of crude oil to be shipped from the Gulf. LPRC was owned and controlled by the Republic of Liberia (ROL). LPRC entered into a contract of affreightment with the defendants (GOI) which contained an arbitration clause. GOI nominated an arbitrator on the basis it was entitled to claim in the arbitration against ROL on the ground that ROL was a party to the contract as the undisclosed principal of LPRC. ROL and LPRC issued a writ claiming against GOI a declaration that LPRC and GOI were the only parties to the contract, a declaration that the appointment of the arbitrator by GOI in relation to a claim against ROL was null and void and an injunction restraining all the defendants from taking any further step in the arbitration. GOI counterclaimed a declaration that ROL were parties to the contract of affreightment and damages against ROL for breach of contract or in tort for inducing a breach of the contract by LPRC. They also claimed damages in the alternative against LPRC.

The plaintiffs applied for an order striking out the counterclaim except in so far as it claimed a declaration that LPRC were the only parties to the contract on the ground, inter alia, that the counterclaim ought to have been brought by separate action under Ord 15, r 5 or that it was otherwise an abuse of the process of the court. Order 15, r 5 is the equivalent of Ord 28, r 7(3).

The plaintiffs' application was rejected by both Lloyd J (29 March 1984, unreported) and the Court of Appeal. The Court of Appeal applied the principles set out in *Derby & Co Ltd v Larsson*. Oliver LJ said ([1985] 1 Lloyd's Rep 539 at 544):

> 'I am bound to say that I know of no ground upon which the question raised by the plaintiffs in this case, namely whether they are or are not parties to a particular contract, can be elevated to the status of some special form of proceeding, with special rules which cannot be "subverted", merely because the object of the exercise is to determine

whether the plaintiff is bound by a contractual term of a particular type, viz. an arbitration clause. It seems to me to be a perfectly ordinary action for a declaration commenced in reliance on the Court's general jurisdiction to make declarations, and the mere fact that its purpose is to ascertain whether or not an arbitration clause is binding does not, in my judgment, put it into some special sacrosanct category of proceeding in which a counterclaim is not to be permitted to be made within the ordinary principles applicable under O. 15.'

That passage seems to me to set out the decision of the court. Mr Gee submits that what the plaintiff is seeking to do here is to rely upon the purpose of the application under s 25 of the 1982 Act and to put it in a special sacrosanct category of proceeding in which a counterclaim is not to be permitted to be made under Ord 28, r 7(1).

The distinction between that case and the instant case is, however, that whereas there the relief sought by the plaintiff was substantive relief, the relief sought here is interim relief in support of an action on the merits elsewhere. There is thus nothing in the decision in that case which leads to the conclusion that Mr Saloman's submissions should be rejected.

In *Metal Scrap Trade Corp Ltd v Kate Shipping Co Ltd, The Gladys* [1990] 1 All ER 397, [1990] 1 WLR 115, in an action begun by originating summons, the plaintiffs claimed a declaration that arbitrators had no jurisdiction in respect of a dispute between the parties on the ground that there was no arbitration agreement between them. The defendants counterclaimed the damages which they had been seeking in the arbitration. The plaintiffs applied for an order striking out the counterclaim under Ord 28, r 7(3), without prejudice to their case that they were entitled to a stay of the counterclaim under s 1 of the Arbitration Act 1975. The House of Lords refused the application, but stayed the counterclaim pursuant to the inherent jurisdiction of the court pending the determination of the question whether there was a valid arbitration agreement between the parties.

Order 28, r 7(3) provides:

'If it appears on the application of a plaintiff against whom a counterclaim is made under this rule that the subject-matter of the counterclaim ought for any reason to be disposed of by a separate action, the Court may order the counterclaim to be struck out or may order it to be tried separately or make such other order as may be expedient.'

The opinion of the majority was given by Lord Brandon. It was held that the defendants were entitled to counterclaim and that it was irrelevant that the defendant might not be able to obtain leave to serve his counterclaim out of the jurisdiction. It was further held that the separate action referred to in Ord 28, r 7(3) meant an action which could be proceeded with in the High Court in England (see [1990] 1 All ER 397 at 409, [1990] 1 WLR 115 at 130 per Lord Brandon). It was thus held that the plaintiffs were not entitled to an order that the counterclaim be struck out or stayed under Ord 28, r 7(3). A stay was however ordered under the inherent jurisdiction of the court so that the matter could be further considered when it had been determined whether there was a valid arbitration agreement. In the course of his speech Lord Brandon approved the passage from the judgment of Oliver LJ in the *Republic of Liberia* case quoted above (see [1990] 1 All ER 397 at 407–408, [1990] 1 WLR 115 at 127–128).

Both those cases were thus cases in which the plaintiffs' claim was for substantive relief and are not, in my judgment, decisions contrary to the plaintiff's argument in the instant case. They do not focus at all upon a possible distinction between claims brought by a plaintiff for substantive relief of some kind and claims brought for interim or interlocutory relief of the kind which Balkanbank sought here.

In *Republic of Haiti v Duvalier* [1989] 1 All ER 456, [1990] 1 QB 202 the plaintiff issued a writ in England claiming interim relief under s 25 of the 1982 Act in aid of substantive proceedings in France. It was held by the Court of Appeal that the writ could be served out of the jurisdiction in France under Ord 11, r 1(2) without the leave of the court. It was argued on behalf of the defendant that the claim made by the writ was not a claim which by virtue of the 1982 Act the court had power to hear and determine because it was an application for interim relief only and was not a cause of action so that the court had no jurisdiction to hear and determine it because of the decision of the House of Lords in *Siskina (cargo owners) v Distos Cia Naviera SA, The Siskina* [1977] 3 All ER 803, [1979] AC 210.

Staughton LJ rejected that argument. He said ([1989] 1 All ER 456 at 462–463, [1990] 1 QB 202 at 211–212):

> 'Since the enactment of s 25, *either* a claim for interim relief is itself a cause of action *or* there can be proceedings and a claim without a cause of action. Which solution one chooses is merely a matter of semantics; there is no need to make such a sterile choice and I do not do so … It is agreed that the action, begun by writ, ought properly to have been begun by originating summons: see Ord 5, r 3. However, it is also agreed that nothing turns on that point in the present case.' (Staughton LJ's emphasis.)

It may thus be said that Staughton LJ took the view that a proceeding begun by originating summons for interim relief under s 25 is an action begun by originating summons. That is true, so far as it goes. But he was not considering whether such a proceeding fell within Ord 28, r 7(1), so that that expression of view does not, in my judgment, carry the defendants' argument very far.

In *X v Y* [1989] 3 All ER 689, [1990] 1 QB 220 the plaintiffs obtained leave ex parte to serve a writ out of the jurisdiction upon a defendant in Saudi Arabia in support of a claim for injunctive relief under s 25 of the 1982 Act in aid of proceedings in France. Mr Anthony Diamond QC held that the court had jurisdiction to grant leave under Ord 11, r 1(1)(b) notwithstanding the fact that that sub-paragraph was in identical terms to sub-para (i) which was considered by the House of Lords in *The Siskina*. The defendant had relied upon the following passage from the speech of Lord Diplock which sets out the ratio of the decision ([1977] 3 All ER 803 at 825, [1979] AC 210 at 256):

> 'To come within the sub-paragraph the injunction sought in the action must be part of the substantive relief to which the plaintiff's cause of action entitles him; and the thing that it is sought to restrain the foreign defendant from doing in England must amount to an invasion of some legal or equitable right belonging to the plaintiff in this country and enforceable here by the final judgment for an injunction.'

It was submitted that since the rule remained the same the application for injunctive relief under s 25 could not be served out of the jurisdiction because the plaintiff was not entitled to substantive relief in England. Mr Diamond QC rejected that argument on the basis that, as Kerr LJ pointed out in *Babanaft International Co SA v Bassatne* [1989] 1 All ER 433 at 442, [1990] Ch 13 at 30, the whole purpose of s 25 was to reverse the decision in *The Siskina* and to enact art 24 of the 1968 convention (see [1989] 3 All ER 689 at 696–697, [1990] 1 QB 220 at 228). He thus gave a new construction to the words of the rule in the light of the enactment and purpose of s 25.

A similar approach should in my judgment be adopted to the construction of Ord 28, r 7. But Mr Gee submits that the reasoning in that case leads to the conclusion that there was here an 'action begun by originating summons' within the meaning of Ord 28, r 7. As I understand it, the argument proceeds as follows. Order 11, r 1(1) applies where 'in the action begun by writ' the case falls within one of the sub-paragraphs of the rule. Order 11, r 9(1) makes Ord 11, r 1 apply to originating summonses. Thus, in the case of an originating summons, Ord 11, r 1 applies to an 'action begun by originating summons'. If an originating summons begins an 'action' for the purposes of Ord 11 it must equally do so for the purposes of Ord 28, r 7.

I see the force of that submission, but, in my judgment, it is to construe the rules too narrowly and not to have proper regard to the purpose of each. The effect of the cases is to give full effect to art 24 of the 1968 convention and to s 25 of the 1982 Act. If the defendants' argument is correct the combined effect of s 25 and the rules is to confer jurisdiction on the English court over substantive claims which the parties to the convention cannot have intended. In my judgment Ord 28, r 7(1) should not be construed to have that effect unless there is binding authority requiring me so to construe it or there is no other sensible construction of the rule.

As to binding authority, neither the cases to which I have referred nor any of the other cases which were cited are authority for the proposition that the rule should be so construed. As to the rule itself, Mr Gee submits that in the light of the statutory provisions to which I referred earlier there is no sensible construction other than to apply the definition of 'action' in s 151 of the 1981 Act and to hold that this was an action begun by originating summons. I do not accept that submission. In all the Judicature Acts to which I have referred, namely those in 1873, 1925 and 1981, the definition section begins 'unless the context otherwise requires'.

In my judgment the context does otherwise require. It requires that in Ord 28, r 7(1) the expression 'action begun by originating summons' should be limited to those actions begun by originating summons in which the plaintiff seeks some substantive relief. Although I am not directly concerned with Ord 15, r 2 I think it likely that that rule should be similarly restricted so far as writs are concerned. As indicated above, the rationale of the rule is that discussed in *Derby & Co Ltd v Larsson* [1976] 1 All ER 401, [1976] 1 WLR 202, namely that where a plaintiff makes a claim in England he submits to the jurisdiction of the court. That appears to me to make perfect sense where the claim is a claim for substantive relief such as a claim for damages or a claim for a declaration. It does not seem to me to make sense where the relief sought is interim relief in aid of proceedings elsewhere.

If the effect of Ord 28, r 7(1) is as suggested by Mr Gee, it is, I think, rather remarkable that no such suggestion has apparently been made in the past. Although I have concentrated upon an application under s 25 of the 1982 Act, it appears to me that there may be other types of application to which similar

a considerations would apply. Examples are applications under s 12(6) of the
Arbitration Act 1950, such as applications for security for costs, or other
applications under that Act such as applications for leave to enforce an award
as a judgment or order of the court under s 26. Such applications must be made
by originating summons. It would, as it seems to me, be very remarkable if the
effect of making an interlocutory application of that kind was to expose the
b applicant to a counterclaim of any type whatever on the part of the defendant
to the summons.

There is no case which suggests that Ord 28, r 7 (or indeed Ord 15, r 2)
should be construed as suggested by Mr Gee. On the other hand, the recent
decision of the House of Lords in *Channel Tunnel Group Ltd v Balfour Beatty
Construction Ltd* [1993] 1 All ER 664, [1993] AC 334, although it was not
c concerned with the construction of the rules of court and thus is not directly
relevant to the question which arises for decision here, gives some support for
the approach which I have adopted. Both Lord Mustill (who made the
principal speech with which all members of the committee agreed) and Lord
Browne-Wilkinson (with whom Lord Keith and Lord Goff agreed) drew
d attention to the fact that there are other cases not covered by s 25 of the 1982
Act where the court has power to grant interim relief in aid of substantive
proceedings elsewhere.

Lord Browne-Wilkinson said that the English court has power to grant an
injunction under s 37 of the Supreme Court Act 1981 subject to only two limits,
namely (i) that the court must have personal jurisdiction over the defendant in
e the sense that he can be duly served either personally or under Ord 11 (other
than under Ord 11, r 1(1)(b)) and (ii) that the plaintiffs have a cause of action
under English law (see [1993] 1 All ER 664 at 668, [1993] AC 334 at 342). He
rejected the suggestion that the court has to be satisfied, at the time it grants
interlocutory relief, that the final order, if any, will be made by an English
f court.

Lord Mustill said that there is power to grant an interlocutory injunction
under s 37 of the 1981 Act in aid of any of the following classes of claim (see
[1993] 1 All ER 664 at 686–687, [1993] AC 334 at 362–363). (1) A claim in an
English domestic arbitration (where the court would have a discretion whether
or not to stay an action on the merits under s 4(1) of the 1950 Act); (2) a claim
g in an English non-domestic arbitration (where the court would be bound to
grant a stay); (3) a claim in a foreign arbitration where the claim would in
principle be justiciable in England (subject to the arbitration agreement), either
because the defendant could be served in England or because leave to serve out
of the jurisdiction could in principle be obtained under Ord 11.

h Lord Mustill said that it makes no difference whether or not the English
proceedings were commenced in breach of the arbitration clause.

It follows from the speeches of both Lord Mustill and Lord
Browne-Wilkinson that the court has a much wider power to grant a Mareva
injunction over assets within the jurisdiction in aid of proceedings elsewhere
j than is included in s 25. It appears to me that, at least in cases where the writ
or originating summons claims only interim relief, the same considerations
apply to such applications as I have set out above in connection with Ord 28,
r 7. Moreover, if (as hinted by Lord Browne-Wilkinson) the House of Lords
should in some future case depart from the decision in *The Siskina* (as
subsequently modified) the same considerations would apply in such a case
(see [1993] 1 All ER 664 at 669, [1993] AC 334 at 343). It would I think be very
surprising if a claim for interim relief, whether made under s 25 of the 1982 Act

in aid of proceedings in a convention country or under s 37 of the 1981 Act in
aid of proceedings in a foreign jurisdiction or in a foreign arbitration, gave the
defendant a right to counterclaim subject only (as is conceded by Mr Gee) to
arts 21 and 22 of the convention, the principles of forum conveniens and other
similar considerations such as those stemming from an exclusive jurisdiction
clause.

The speech of Lord Mustill seems to me to support the proposition that
where interim relief is sought in England in aid of proceedings elsewhere
(whether the relief is sought under s 25 of the 1982 Act or under s 37 of the 1981
Act) the role of the English court should be regarded as subordinate to the role
of the foreign court. As to arbitration, see the *Channel Tunnel Group* case [1993]
1 All ER 664 at 688, [1993] AC 334 at 364.

As to s 25, Lord Mustill said this ([1993] 1 All ER 664 at 689, [1993] AC 334 at
365–366):

'Let us take first the case where the English court, before which no
proceedings have been brought except for interim relief, makes an order
under s 25 of the 1982 Act in support of an action brought in the courts of
a foreign state. Here, it is obvious that the court is not making an order in
an English action. By granting the order, the court does not engage itself
at all in the resolution of the dispute, but merely seeks to make the
resolution of the dispute by the foreign court more effective. It is a
free-standing item of ancillary relief. Next, let it be assumed that the
foreign proceedings take the shape of an arbitration, rather than litigation.
Once again, if the English court grants an interlocutory injunction by way
of interim protection under s 37 of the 1981 Act it is not playing any part
in the decision of the dispute, but is simply doing its best to ensure that the
resolution by the arbitrators is fruitful. Common sense and logic suggest
that the analysis must be the same where the application for the
interlocutory injunction is associated with the commencement of an
action which the court is obliged to stay. Common sense, because it
cannot be right that by starting the action the plaintiff automatically
forfeits any right to ancillary relief to which he would otherwise be
entitled. Logic, because the purpose of the stay is to remove from the
court the task of deciding the substantive dispute, so that it can be
entrusted to the chosen tribunal. This is what the court is bound to do, by
virtue of the [Convention on the Recognition and Enforcement of Foreign
Arbitral Awards (New York, 10 July 1958; TS 20 (1976); Cmnd 6419]. But
neither the arbitration agreement nor the convention contemplate that by
transferring to the arbitrators the substance of the dispute, the court also
divests itself of the right to use the sanctions of municipal law, which are
not available to the arbitrators, in order to ensure that the arbitration is
carried forward to the best advantage. I thus see no difficulty in principle
in an order which combines a mandatory stay with an interlocutory
injunction by way of interim relief.'

If Mr Gee's argument were to be accepted the effect of an application by a
plaintiff under s 25 would be to entitle a defendant to advance a substantive
counterclaim relating to subject matter of any kind whatsoever regardless of its
connection with the subject matter of the plaintiff's claim. To allow him to do
so would not be consistent with the approach to s 25 which seems to me to
underlie Lord Mustill's speech because it would or might permit or require the

English court to play a part in the decision of the dispute. It would not then be,
as Lord Mustill put it, 'a free-standing item of ancillary relief'.

The only purpose of s 25 is to ensure that the proceedings in say Ireland (or
other convention states) are carried forward to best advantage, not to confer
jurisdiction on the English court which it would not otherwise have had.

The House of Lords refused to grant an interlocutory injunction in the
Channel Tunnel Group case, but its approach in my judgment supports the
conclusion which I have reached. That is that an application for interim relief
under s 25 of the 1982 Act is not an 'action' begun by originating summons
within the meaning of Ord 28, r 7. The reason is that the context so requires.
The rationale for the rule was that where a plaintiff brings a claim on the merits
he submits to the jurisdiction of the court in respect of any claim which the
defendant may wish to advance on the merits. The same rationale does not
apply to an application for a free-standing item of ancillary relief in aid of
proceedings elsewhere.

For these reasons I have reached the conclusion that the court does not have
jurisdiction to entertain the defendants' counterclaim, which must therefore
be struck out.

If that conclusion is correct, none of the other points which relate to the
counterclaim arises. However, since they were argued before me I shall
shortly state my conclusions upon them.

Is counterclaim still possible?

Mr Saloman submits that a counterclaim can only be advanced by a
defendant while he is still a defendant to the action brought by the plaintiff and
that the plaintiff's action came to an end at the latest when the injunction was
discharged by Evans J on 13 May 1992. In this connection he refers to the
scheme for the conduct of proceedings begun by originating summons which
is laid down by Ord 28, r 4. Mr Gee submits on the other hand that the
proceedings brought by the originating summons are still extant because the
inquiry as to damages remains to be determined.

I was referred to the decision of the Court of Appeal in *CSI International Co
Ltd v Archway Personnel (Middle East) Ltd* [1980] 3 All ER 215, [1980] 1 WLR 1069,
where it was held that a counterclaim which had been raised under Ord 15, r 2
could no longer be brought when the plaintiff had obtained judgment on his
claim and that judgment had been satisfied. As Roskill LJ put it, after that there
was no longer still extant any action by the plaintiffs in which the defendants
could properly counterclaim against them (see [1980] 3 All ER 215 at 220, [1980]
1 WLR 1069 at 1075). The Court of Appeal thus regarded the relevant question
to be whether at the time that the defendant wishes to proceed with his
counterclaim the action brought by the plaintiffs is still extant. I accept Mr
Gee's submission that another way of putting the same question is to ask
whether the action is still pending.

Applying that approach I have reached the conclusion that the action is still
extant or pending. Since May 1992 the parties have been preparing for the
inquiry as to damages. A number of orders of the court have been made in that
connection. In addition there have been contempt proceedings. In these
circumstances it appears to me that the action remains on foot for various
purposes and that if the court had jurisdiction it would not be too late to
entertain a counterclaim.

Acknowledgment of service and discretion

By Ord 28, r 7(1) the acknowledgment of service is a condition precedent to the making of a counterclaim. There was much debate at the hearing as to the steps if any which the defendants had taken to this end. It is not necessary for me to engage in that debate here save to say this. No attempt to acknowledge service was made until this year. An acknowledgment of service has however now been entered. It was entered as recently as 14 April. I accept Mr Saloman's argument that the defendants had deliberately decided not to enter an acknowledgment earlier. On the other hand it is I think clear that it did not occur to the defendants or their advisers to advance a counterclaim until very recently.

Mr Saloman submits that the defendants need leave to acknowledge service out of time. Mr Gee submits that that is not so because by RSC Ord 12, r 6(2) leave is not required to enter acknowledgment of service out of time; it is only required to do any act later than the act should have been done if the defendant had acknowledged service in time. He submits that there is no such act in this case. Mr Gee is I think strictly correct as a matter of construction of the rule.

The question then arises whether the defendants would now need leave to take any of the steps set out in Ord 28, r 7(2), which provides as follows:

'A defendant who wishes to make a counterclaim under this rule must at the first or any resumed hearing of the originating summons by the Court but, in any case, at as early a stage in the proceedings as is practicable, inform the Court of the nature of his claim and, without prejudice to the powers of the Court under paragraph (3) the claim shall be made in such manner as the Court may direct under rule 4 or rule 8.'

Mr Gee submits that the defendants did inform the court of the counterclaim at as early a stage as was practicable because they did so as soon as reasonably practicable after they received the letter from Allen & Overy dated 14 January 1994 which is quoted above.

I reject that submission. In my judgment, the rule contemplates that any counterclaim will be notified as early in the proceedings as is reasonably practicable so that if no counterclaim is notified at a reasonably early stage it is too late to counterclaim later as of right. The rule does not mean that the defendant has a right to counterclaim whenever he might subsequently think up a counterclaim, provided only that he has a reasonable excuse for not thinking of it before. It follows that, in my judgment, the defendants would need the leave of the court to advance a counterclaim now.

Mr Saloman submits that it is now too late for such leave to be granted. Mr Gee submits, on the other hand, that the points which the defendants seek to raise are closely related to the matters which will, in any event, be before the court at the inquiry and that the proper course would be to allow the counterclaims to proceed. The principal points made by Mr Saloman may be summarised as follows.

(1) The present position is the result of choices made by the defendants who chose not to acknowledge service when they should have done and chose not to make a claim against Balkanbank at that time. (2) The defendants chose not to counterclaim in the Irish proceedings except in the case of the counterclaim advanced by BIL, which failed. (3) The defendants had the relevant knowledge of the relevant facts at an early stage but nevertheless chose not to counterclaim in Ireland. Any counterclaim could and should have been

advanced at the same time as that advanced by BIL. (4) The delay in advancing the counterclaims has been, as Mr Saloman described it, mammoth, since it is now April 1994 whereas the defence in Ireland was served in January 1991. (5) There has been no satisfactory explanation for the delay. (6) The extent of the alleged losses has been known all along so that this is not a case in which the defendants can say that they have only just learned the true facts. (7) If leave were granted now the scheme of the convention would be flouted because Balkanbank cannot now rely upon arts 21 and 22 as they could have done earlier. (8) The lawyers in Ireland are familiar with the underlying facts. (9) The addition of the counterclaims would require the calling of more witnesses and the adducing of more evidence than will at present be required at the inquiry.

There is, in my judgment, some force in these points, but I have reached the conclusion that they are outweighed by the considerations advanced by Mr Gee. The counterclaim which VHL now seeks to advance could, in principle, have been included in the proceedings before Blayney J, except that, as I have already stated, the defendants did not think to do so at that time. Even now they say that the cause of their losses was the English worldwide injunction. As I understood Mr Gee, they only advance the case that the losses were caused by breach of contract or by breach of fiduciary duty in the alternative, that is if the losses were not caused by the English or Irish injunctions but, as Balkanbank now asserts in para 13 of the points of defence, by the making of the allegations. They only made the allegation for the first time after they had received the letter dated 14 January to which I have already referred.

There is evidence that it is now too late to counterclaim in Ireland. But there seems no good reason why the defendant should not be able to proceed with a claim in Ireland for damages for breach of the joint venture agreement or for breach of fiduciary duties against Balkanbank by seeking appropriate leave under their equivalent of our Ord 11. There is no suggestion that the counterclaims would now be out of time if pursued in Ireland or indeed elsewhere. Nor is it suggested that the defendants could not proceed in Ireland because of arts 21 or 22 of the 1968 convention. In these circumstances it seems to me that the question should be whether it is more appropriate in the interests of the parties and the ends of justice that the defendants should be permitted to counterclaim here or whether they should be compelled to do so in Ireland, or perhaps elsewhere.

I have reached the conclusion that, despite the considerations advanced by Mr Saloman, the answer to that question is that if the court had a discretion it should exercise it by allowing the counterclaim to proceed here. The questions: what losses have been suffered by the defendants and whether such losses were caused by the English injunction or by the Irish injunction or by the allegations made by Balkanbank, are already to be decided in the inquiry in these proceedings. The only further questions raised by VHL's counterclaim are: what terms are to be implied into the joint venture agreement, what if any fiduciary duties were owed to VHL and whether there were any breaches of such implied terms or of such duties. I see no reason why those questions should not also be conveniently decided by the English court. Mr Saloman submits that they would involve much further evidence. That may be, but that evidence will have to be deployed somewhere. I can see no reason why it should not be deployed here; I feel sure that the parties' English lawyers would be well able to advance their clients' respective cases. If there is any issue which it would be convenient to try discretely from the others the court can make an appropriate order to that effect, but given the way that Balkanbank seeks to defend the defendants' claims in the inquiry, if I had a discretion, I would exercise it in favour of the defendants.

I would permit them to advance both classes of counterclaim, although I am far from saying that it would be appropriate to grant a declaration of the kind sought. That would be a matter for the trial judge.

I would just add two points. The first is that although I would exercise my discretion in that way if there were jurisdiction to counterclaim, that fact does not persuade me to take any different view on jurisdiction. The reasons which I gave earlier remain sound. The second is that thought might be given in the future to whether it would be desirable in cases of this kind to extend the undertaking in damages or to take some other step in order to give the court jurisdiction to award damages which the plaintiff alleges were caused not by the injunction wrongfully obtained by him, but by some cause for which the plaintiff was also responsible as a matter of law, but in respect of which the court would otherwise have no jurisdiction.

Discretion to award damages

There is an issue between the parties as to whether the court retains a discretion whether to award damages to the defendants other than BIL. Mr Gee submits that the court no longer has such a discretion by reason of the order of Evans J dated 13 May 1992. It is common ground that the court retains its discretion in the case of BIL because its claim for damages has only recently been added to the inquiry and the order relevant to BIL expressly leaves the question open. It is also common ground that if the court retains its discretion in relation to the claims of the other defendants the question how the discretion should be exercised should be left to the hearing of the inquiry, although it does seem to me that further thought should be given to whether that is indeed the most sensible course.

Mr Gee submits that the effect of the order of Evans J is to deprive the court of the discretion, which it previously had, to decide whether or not to order Balkanbank to pay damages to the defendant. Mr Saloman submits, on the other hand, that the court retains its discretion unless and until it exercises it and that it is reasonable to infer that Evans J was not exercising a discretion because the order he made was made by consent.

I have been referred to a number of authorities which are relevant to this question, although some of them are unreported, and they do not all seem to me to be entirely satisfactory. In considering them it is I think important to have in mind that the undertaking in damages is given to the court and, although it is for the defendant to make a claim under it, it is for the court to decide whether it is appropriate to order the plaintiff to pay damages in any particular case. It does not therefore seem to me to be a matter which can be dealt with solely by the agreement of the parties, although there is of course nothing to prevent a particular plaintiff from paying damages to a particular defendant without the intervention of the court.

It is convenient to repeat the undertaking and the order. The undertaking was:

'To abide by any Order which this Court may make as to damages, in case this court may hereafter be of the opinion that the Defendants or any of them have suffered any which the Plaintiff ought to pay.'

a   It is common ground that the court has a discretion whether to order the plaintiff to pay damages where the defendants have sustained loss caused by the injunction. The court is not in my judgment bound to order damages to be paid even where the injunction is discharged. Whether it does so or not will depend on the circumstances of the case.

By the consent order of Evans J dated 13 May 1992 the injunction was
b   discharged and it was ordered—

'that there be an inquiry as to what damages the First, Third and Fourth Defendants herein or any of them have or has suffered as a result of the making of the said Order of 8 October which the Plaintiff ought to pay.'

If I were construing that order unassisted by authority I would hold that it does
c   not amount to an order that Balkanbank must pay whatever losses were suffered by the defendants as a result of the injunction. I would hold that the court retains a discretion whether or not so to order and that the expression 'which the Plaintiff ought to pay' gives support for that view. Mr Gee however submits that that expression is not concerned with the exercise of a discretion by the court but merely reflects the fact that the court will not award all loss
d   caused by the injunction but only that loss properly recoverable having regard for example to the ordinary rules as to remoteness of damage. I am bound to say that unassisted by authority I would not hold that it was so limited.

Mr Gee submits however that the order must be construed in its historical context. He referred me to the following form in *Seton's Forms of Judgments and*
e   *Orders* (7th edn, 1912) vol 1, p 507–508:

'An inquiry whether the Deft has sustained any and what damages by reason of the injunction granted by the order dated &c., and which the Plt ought to pay according to his undertaking contained in the said order; And in case it shall appear that any such damage has been sustained, It is
f   ordered that the Plt do pay to the Deft, within one month from the date of the Master's certificate to be made pursuant to this order, the amount which shall be thereby certified for such damages, and also pay to the said Deft his costs of the said inquiry ...'

I observe that that order is in a different form from the order of Evans J because
g   it contains an order to pay whereas the latter does not.

In *Barclays Bank Ltd v Rosenberg Ltd* (1985) 135 NLJ 633 Evans J, on the basis of a concession made by counsel, referred the question whether the injunction should have been granted to the person who was undertaking the inquiry as to damages. It is not clear what the terms of the order in that case were.

h   In *Norwest Holst Civil Engineering Ltd v Polysius Ltd* (1987) Times, 23 July the Court of Appeal said that the approach adopted by Evans J was wrong and that it was for the judge to decide whether the injunction should have been granted and if (and only if) he decided that it should not would any question of an inquiry arise. The court was I think struck by the fact that it was for the judge to decide the question of principle, whereas the inquiry might be conducted by
j   a master.

In *Zygal Dynamics plc v McNulty* [1989] CA Transcript 571, the relevant facts were briefly as follows. An application was made for the discharge of an injunction, for an inquiry as to damages and for an order that the plaintiff pay the amount of any damages found due. The judge made an order in substantially the same terms as the order of Evans J in the instant case, although he made it clear that he intended that all points should be open at the hearing of the inquiry including whether the injunction had been rightly granted. It was argued in the Court of Appeal (at least initially) that the judge should have considered whether the injunction was properly granted before ordering an inquiry. That argument was not accepted.

The Court of Appeal held that the intention of the order was plain from the judge's remarks, namely that all points were to be open and it further held that, while greater care might be required as to the form of the order in future cases, there was no need to change the form of the order made in order to achieve that intention. The effect of that decision is that, depending upon the circumstances, the form of order made by Evans J in this case is or may be wide enough to give the court hearing the inquiry power to exercise its discretion whether or not to order the plaintiff to pay damages. It seems to me to follow that this form of order does not by itself and without more preclude the exercise of the discretion.

I was however also referred to another decision of the Court of Appeal, namely *Financiera Avenida SA v Shiblaq* (1991) Times, 14 January, on appeal from a decision of Saville J, which had been made on 21 October 1988. On the hearing of an inquiry the question arose whether the court retained a discretion whether to order the plaintiff to pay damages. The order was in the same form as here. Saville J held that no suggestion had been made when the inquiry was ordered that the court should reserve the exercise of its discretion. He then said:

> 'In those circumstances the words in the order upon which Mr Crystal relies mean, in my view, no more than that the defendant should recover those damages (if any) to which he is entitled as a matter of law.'

Mr Gee relies upon that passage. By the time that the case came before the Court of Appeal a transcript of the first hearing before Saville J had been obtained which showed that the question of discretion had been reserved. The Court of Appeal accordingly remitted the case to the judge in order to enable him to exercise the discretion whether or not to order damages to be paid. It did so because Saville J had not exercised his discretion at the first hearing. It did not comment upon the meaning of the words in the order but held in effect that notwithstanding the wording of the order Saville J had not exercised the discretion of the court.

Mr Saloman relies upon that decision in this way. He says that the question whether the discretion has been exercised depends upon the facts of the particular case and that that decision shows that it does not automatically follow from the form of words in the standard order that the discretion has been exercised. I accept that submission, which is in my judgment consistent with the decision of the Court of Appeal in the *Zygal* case.

In the course of his judgment in the *Financiera* case Lloyd LJ made some general observations which are reflected in the more recent decision of the Court of Appeal in *Cheltenham and Gloucester Building Society v Ricketts* [1993] 4 All ER 276, [1993] 1 WLR 1545. Neill LJ set out a number of general principles applicable to the enforcement of a cross-undertaking in damages. They include the following ([1993] 4 All ER 276 at 281–282, [1993] 1 WLR 1545 at 1551):

> '(2) The undertaking, though described as an undertaking as to damages, does not found any cause of action. It does, however, enable the party enjoined to apply to the court for compensation if it is subsequently

established that the interlocutory injunction should not have been
granted. (3) The undertaking is not given to the party enjoined but to the
court. (4) In a case where it is determined that the injunction should not
have been granted the undertaking is likely to be enforced, though the
court retains a discretion not to do so. (5) The time at which the court
should determine whether or not the interlocutory injunction should have
been granted will vary from case to case. It is important to underline the
fact that the question whether the undertaking should be enforced is a
separate question from the question whether the injunction should be
discharged or continued. (6) In many cases injunctions will remain in
being until the trial and in such cases the propriety of its original grant and
the question of the enforcement of the undertaking will not be considered
before the conclusion of the trial. Even then, as Lloyd LJ pointed out in
Financiera Avenida v Shiblaq (1991) Times, 14 January, [1990] CA Transcript
973, the court may occasionally wish to postpone the question of
enforcement to a later date. (7) Where an interlocutory injunction is
discharged before the trial the court at the time of discharge is faced with
a number of possibilities. (a) The court can determine forthwith that the
undertaking as to damages should be enforced and can proceed at once to
make an assessment of the damages ... (b) The court may determine that
the undertaking should be enforced but then direct an inquiry as to
damages in which issues of causation and quantum will have to be
considered. It is likely that the order will include directions as to pleadings
and discovery in the inquiry. In the light of the decision of the Court of
Appeal in *Norwest Holst Civil Engineering Ltd v Polysius Ltd* (1987) Times, 23
July, [1987] CA Transcript 644, the court should not order an inquiry as to
damages and at the same time leave open for the tribunal at the inquiry to
determine whether or not the undertaking should be enforced. A decision
that the undertaking should be enforced is a precondition for the making
of an order of an inquiry as to damages. (c) The court can adjourn the
application for the enforcement of the undertaking to the trial or further
order. (d) The court can determine forthwith that the undertaking is not
to be enforced. (8) It seems that damages are awarded on a similar basis
to that on which damages are awarded for breach of contract. This matter
has not been fully explored in the English cases ...'

Paragraph 7(c) must I think be read in the light of the decision in the *Zygal*
case because it is implicit in that decision that, as is conceded by Mr Gee (and
as has been done in the case of BIL), it is permissible in an appropriate case to
leave the question whether the discretion should be exercised to the person
hearing the inquiry, at least if the inquiry is to be heard by a judge. Peter
Gibson LJ appears to have taken that view although he draws attention to the
fact that the court in *Zygal* was not told of the decision in *Norwest Holst* (see
[1993] 4 All ER 276 at 287–288, [1993] 1 WLR 1545 at 1557).

It is not necessary for me to resolve this question in the instant case, because
the authorities in my judgment show that there must be an exercise of the
court's discretion at some stage. If the court has not exercised its discretion it
must I think retain it, as occurred in both *Zygal* and *Financiera*, notwithstanding
the terms of the order. I accept the submission of Mr Saloman that it is most
unlikely that Evans J intended to exercise any discretion when he made the
consent order. In these circumstances I have reached the conclusion that the
court retains its discretion whether to order Balkanbank to pay damages to the

defendants, although as indicated above it does seem to me that if Balkanbank wish to argue that it should not, it should state the grounds upon which it relies *a* and consideration should be given to that question being resolved before the inquiry, in accordance with the approach stated by the Court of Appeal in *Norwest Holst*.

I would add two points. The first is that, having considered the authorities, I remain of the view that, on the true construction of the order of Evans J, the *b* court retains a discretion and would if necessary so hold. There does not seem to me to be any binding decision to the contrary and I would respectfully disagree with the passage quoted above from the judgment of Saville J in *Financiera*.

The second point is that it does seem to me that care should be taken in the *c* future to consider whether and how the discretion should be exercised at the time that the application for an inquiry is made. The order made at that time should spell out clearly what if any residual discretion is to be left to be exercised thereafter. It should for example be possible to tell on the face of the order whether the plaintiff is to pay the amount ascertained on the inquiry.

d

Order accordingly.

K Mydeen Esq   Barrister.

e

R v R

COURT OF APPEAL, CRIMINAL DIVISION

EVANS LJ, ROUGIER AND DOUGLAS BROWN JJ

20 DECEMBER 1993, 26 JANUARY 1994

f

Criminal evidence – Expert Evidence – Legal professional privilege – Items subject to legal privilege – Meaning of 'made' – Appellant providing blood sample for DNA testing at his solicitors' request – Scientist giving expert opinion evidence based on sample – Whether expert's evidence admissible against appellant – Whether sample *g* *'made' for purpose of legal proceedings – Whether sample protected by legal privilege – Police and Criminal Evidence Act 1984, s 10(1)(c).*

The appellant was charged with six counts of indecent assault, rape and incest. During the prosecution case, the trial judge granted leave permitting *h* representatives of the Crown Prosecution Service to interview a scientist who had carried out DNA tests at the request of the defendant's solicitors on a blood sample provided by the appellant to his general practitioner for that purpose at the request of his solicitors. The judge subsequently ruled that the evidence of the scientist, who had been subpoenaed as an expert witness for the prosecution, was admissible against the appellant. The scientist duly gave *j* evidence in relation to one of the counts, a charge of incest. The appellant was convicted on that count and four other counts and sentenced to three years' imprisonment. He appealed against conviction on the ground that the judge had erred in admitting the scientist's evidence in respect of the blood sample, which had been given to his solicitors in confidence and was thus inadmissible as an item 'subject to legal privilege' within s 10(1)(c) of the Police and Criminal

Evidence Act 1984. The Crown however contended that s 10 of the Act was limited to items which were 'made' in connection with legal proceedings and that a blood sample could not be said to have been so 'made'.

Held – A sample of blood provided by a defendant to his general practitioner at the request of his solicitors and for the purposes of his defence in criminal proceedings was clearly given in circumstances of confidence. The statutory definition of 'subject to legal privilege' in s 10 of the 1984 Act accordingly applied to enable the defendant to object to the blood sample being produced in evidence or to oral evidence of opinion based on it, since the sample constituted an item 'made' in the general sense of 'brought into existence' for the purposes of legal proceedings. It followed that the appellant's sample of blood was an item 'subject to legal privilege' within s 10(1)(c) of the Act and that the appellant was entitled to object to its production or to opinion evidence based on it. The court was however satisfied that no miscarriage of justice had occurred, despite the fact that the trial judge had erred in admitting privileged evidence without the appellant's consent, since there was ample evidence of the appellant's guilt, quite apart from the weight which the jury might have placed on the scientist's expert evidence. The proviso to s 2[a] of the Criminal Appeal Act 1968 would therefore be applied and the appeal would be dismissed (see p 265 e to p 266 b d e j, post).

Dictum of Lord Denning MR in *Harmony Shipping Co SA v Davis* [1979] 3 All ER 177 at 181 and *W v Edgell* [1990] 1 All ER 835 considered.

Notes

For legal professional privilege, see 13 *Halsbury's Laws* (4th edn) paras 71–85, and for cases on the subject, see 18 *Digest* (2nd reissue) 154–169, *1379–1482.*

For the Police and Criminal Evidence Act 1984, s 10, see 12 *Halsbury's Statutes* (4th edn) (1994 reissue) 860.

For the Criminal Appeal Act 1968, s 2, see ibid, 391.

Cases referred to in judgment

Harmony Shipping Co SA v Davis [1979] 3 All ER 177, sub nom *Harmony Shipping Co SA v Saudi Europe Line Ltd* [1979] 1 WLR 1380, CA.

R v King [1983] 1 All ER 929, [1983] 1 WLR 411, CA.

Ventouris v Mountain, The Italia Express [1991] 3 All ER 472, [1991] 1 WLR 607, CA.

W v Edgell [1990] 1 All ER 835, [1990] Ch 359, [1990] 2 WLR 471, CA.

Case also cited

R v Quinn [1990] Crim LR 581, CA.

Appeal against conviction

The appellant, R, appealed against his conviction on 9 October 1992 in the Crown Court at Wolverhampton before Judge Evans QC and a jury on three counts of incest and two counts of indecent assault for which he was sentenced to three years' imprisonment on the ground, inter alia, that the judge had erred in admitting for the prosecution the evidence of an expert instructed on behalf

---

a   Section 2, so far as material, provides: ' ... the Court may, notwithstanding that they are of the opinion that the point raised in the appeal might be decided in favour of the appellant, dismiss the appeal if they consider that no miscarriage of justice has actually occurred.'

of the appellant based on a blood sample obtained in circumstances of legal
privilege. The facts are set out in the judgment of the court.

Anthony Barker QC (assigned by the *Registrar of Criminal Appeals*) for the
appellant.
Christopher Hotten (instructed by the *Crown Prosecution Service,*
Newcastle-under-Lyme) for the Crown.

At the conclusion of the argument the court announced that the appeal would
be dismissed for reasons to be given later.

26 January 1994. The following judgment of the court was delivered.

EVANS LJ. The appellant was charged on six counts of indecent assault, rape
and incest at the Crown Court at Wolverhampton in October 1992. During the
prosecution case, the judge was asked to permit representatives of the Crown
Prosecution Service to interview a scientist who had carried out DNA tests at
the request of the defence solicitors on a blood sample provided by the appellant
to his general practitioner for that purpose. Leave was granted, and
subsequently the judge ruled that the evidence of the scientist, who had been
subpoenaed as a witness for the prosecution, was admissible against the
appellant. The scientist, Dr Rysiecki, duly gave evidence in relation to one
count, count 5, a charge of incest. The appellant was convicted on this and on
four other counts, and he was sentenced to three years' imprisonment. He now
appeals against his conviction on all counts.

At the conclusion of the appeal hearing on 20 December 1993, we stated that
in our view the submission of Mr Barker QC for the appellant that the evidence
was not properly admitted was correct, but that we were satisfied that no
miscarriage of justice had occurred and that the proviso under s 2(1) of the
Criminal Appeal Act 1968 should be applied. We therefore dismissed the appeal
and we now give our reasons for doing so.

The question whether the prosecution was entitled to call as an expert
witness a duly qualified person who had previously been consulted by the
appellant's solicitors, and who had advised them accordingly, is one of general
interest and importance, and we shall consider it first as a matter of principle. It
was common ground that the two-stage approach adopted by the prosecution
in the present case—asking first for permission to interview the expert, and then
for leave to call her as a witness—was strictly unnecessary, though fully
understandable as a matter of caution. The sole question is whether her
evidence was properly admitted on behalf of the prosecution.

There is no property in a witness: see *Harmony Shipping Co SA v Davis* [1979] 3
All ER 177, [1979] 1 WLR 1380, applied in a criminal case in *R v King* [1983] 1 All
ER 929, [1983] 1 WLR 411. The prosecution therefore cannot be prevented
from approaching or calling a witness, merely because he (or she) has previously
been consulted by the defence.

The evidence which any such witness may give is limited, however, by the
normal rules of legal professional privilege. These may protect
communications between the witness and the defence solicitors, assuming that
they were made in contemplation of legal proceedings etc, but they do not
prevent the expert from giving his or her opinion on the matters in issue. In

Harmony Shipping Co SA v Davis, Lord Denning MR explained the position as follows ([1979] 3 All ER 177 at 181, [1979] 1 WLR 1380 at 1385):

> 'Many of the communications between the solicitor and the expert witness will be privileged. They are protected by legal professional privilege. They cannot be communicated to the court except with the consent of the party concerned. That means that a great deal of the communications between the expert witness and the lawyer cannot be given in evidence to the court. If questions were asked about it, then it would be the duty of the judge to protect the witness (and he would) by disallowing any questions which infringed the rule about legal professional privilege or the rule protecting information given in confidence, unless, of course, it was one of those rare cases which come before the courts from time to time where in spite of privilege or confidence the court does order a witness to give further evidence. Subject to that qualification, it seems to me that an expert witness falls into the same position as a witness of fact. The court is entitled, in order to ascertain the truth, to have the actual facts which he has observed adduced before it and to have his independent opinion on those facts.'

Archbold's Criminal Pleading Evidence and Practice (45th edn, 1993), para 12-18 is to the same effect:

> 'The rule in civil proceedings that legal privilege attaches to confidential communications between solicitors and expert witnesses but not to the expert's opinion or the chattels or documents upon which the expert has based his opinion applies also in criminal proceedings. Accordingly, no such privilege attaches to a document in the possession of a handwriting expert which emanated from a defendant and was sent by him to his solicitors for examination by the expert: *R. v. King* ([1983] 1 All ER 929, [1983] 1 WLR 411, CA). See also *Harmony Shipping Co. S.A. v Saudi Europe Line Ltd.* (sub nom *Harmony Shipping Co SA v Davies* [1979] 3 All ER 177 at 181, [1979] 1 WLR 1380 at 1385, CA).'

It is not suggested that in the present case Dr Rysiecki gave any evidence regarding communications between her and the defence solicitors. The fact that such communications had taken place, as distinct from the communications themselves, was not privileged in any event. The dispute centres on the fact that her evidence was based on a blood sample which the appellant had provided so that her advice could be obtained. The sample was taken by his general practitioner and was given to his solicitors in conditions of confidence which may be said generally to have been privileged.

Mr Barker's submission to the judge was founded on the proposition that the appellant cannot be required to incriminate himself. This is reflected in the rule that a witness cannot be required to answer questions which might incriminate him of any offence (modified when the appellant himself gives evidence and can be cross-examined by virtue of the Criminal Evidence Act 1898), and in the appellant's present right of silence at all stages after his arrest.

In our judgment, the issue has to be decided by the application of the rules of legal professional privilege. These may reflect some wider or more general principle, as Mr Barker submits, but the question, it seems to us, is whether, and if so to what extent, Dr Rysiecki's evidence should have been excluded on grounds of legal privilege.

Mr Hotten for the prosecution, to whom we are greatly indebted for his *a* submissions, told us that the blood sample which had been provided by the defence solicitors to the expert was not produced in court and was not exhibited in her witness statement. It is possible, even likely, that the sample had ceased to exist as such, by reason of the tests carried out upon it. Therefore, he submitted, the sample formed no part of her evidence, and she was entitled to give her opinion in accordance with the rule stated in *Harmony Shipping Co SA v* *b* *Davis* [1979] 3 All ER 177, [1979] 1 WLR 1380. He relied in particular upon the passing reference to legal privilege in *W v Edgell* [1990] 1 All ER 835 at 846, [1990] Ch 359 at 416. There, the expert witness instructed by the plaintiff's solicitors had examined the plaintiff himself, and no question of an 'item' or sample arose. The plaintiff claimed public interest immunity for her report, but he was unsuccessful. *c*

This submission was initially persuasive, but in our judgment it must be rejected. It is not a case where the witness's opinion was based on examination and testing of a sample obtained in non-privileged circumstances, or of the appellant himself. If she had been asked to test a sample lawfully obtained previously by the police when the appellant was in custody—as to which, we *c* shall comment further below—then her evidence could have been given with no question of legal privilege arising. But as it was, the opinion evidence she gave was based on the sample she had received from the defence solicitors. Her opinion was as to the DNA properties of the appellant's blood, but it was based on that sample and she could not have given her evidence without it. The fact *e* that it was not exhibited, and may no longer exist, does not alter this fact.

We turn, therefore, to consider the status of the sample provided by the appellant to his solicitors and then made available to Dr Rysiecki for the purpose of obtaining her advice in connection with the pending charges against him. The sample could not have been obtained from the appellant without his consent, and the consent was given for that limited purpose. Could the *f* prosecution take advantage of the fact that they were able to have access to the sample, or at least to Dr Rysiecki's opinion based on the sample, notwithstanding that the appellant had not consented to them doing so? Just as there is no property in a witness, so also, as a general proposition, evidence is not excluded by reason of the circumstances in which it has become available to *g* the party wishing to call it. The question, therefore, remains one of privilege, and legal professional privilege in particular.

The obtaining of intimate samples from a person in police detention is governed by s 62 of the Police and Criminal Evidence Act 1984. The suspect must consent in writing and the statutory procedure must be followed. The *h* statute has no application when the defendant is not in custody, and so no question arises of the prosecution being entitled under the statute to produce in evidence the blood sample which was obtained from the defendant for his solicitors, as in the present case. If the sample, or evidence derived from it, was tendered by the prosecution as a non-PACE Code sample then its admission would be governed by the fairness provisions of s 78 of the 1984 Act or by the *j* court's general discretion to exclude evidence which, although admissible in law, is unduly prejudicial to the defendant. But none of these questions arise if the sample, or evidence derived from it, is privileged. There is no discretion to admit privileged material without the defendant's consent, except possibly in exceptional circumstances which do not arise here.

a   Section 9 of the 1984 Act protects 'items subject to legal privilege' from police powers of search and seizure, and these are defined in s 10:

'(1) Subject to subsection (2) below, in this Act "items subject to legal privilege" means—(a) [communications between a professional legal adviser and his client]; (b) [communications made in contemplation of legal proceedings]; and (c) items enclosed with or referred to in such
b   communications and made—(i) in connection with the giving of legal advice; or (ii) in connection with or in contemplation of legal proceedings and for the purposes of such proceedings, when they are in the possession of a person who is entitled to possession of them.
(2) Items held with the intention of furthering a criminal purpose are not
c   items subject to legal privilege.'

It is usually documents and oral communications which are the subject of legal privilege, and in the context of civil cases the privilege is that of the party, who may object to questions asked of himself or of his witnesses: see *Phipson on Evidence* (14th edn, 1990) paras 20-02, 20-03. Section 10 of the 1984 Act,
d   however, recognises that 'items' may be the subject of legal privilege in certain circumstances. Whilst it is true that s 10 is concerned to provide a definition of 'subject to legal privilege' for the purposes, inter alia, of limiting the right to search and have access to material under s 9 of the 1984 Act, which could explain why the definition includes 'items' as well as communications, nevertheless in our judgment the statutory definition applies when the issue is whether the
e   defendant can object to the object in question being produced in evidence, or to oral evidence of opinion based upon it.
The object in question in the present case was a sample of the appellant's blood provided by him to his general practitioner at the request of his solicitors and for the purposes of his defence in these criminal proceedings. It was given
f   in circumstances of confidence. That factor is a pre-condition of privilege, although it is not enough to create privilege on its own. We hold that the sample so obtained was an 'item' which was subject to legal privilege in these proceedings, provided that it falls within the express wording of s 10 of the 1984 Act.
Mr Hotten submitted that s 10 is limited to items which are 'made' and that
g   a blood sample cannot be said to have been 'made'. It is even more difficult, he submits, to say that other kinds of samples, such as nail clippings or individual hairs taken as samples, in common parlance are 'made'. In our judgment, however, the word was used in a general sense, certainly wide enough to include 'brought into existence', and a sample of blood obtained and held in a
h   particular container does constitute an 'item ... made' for the purposes of legal proceedings etc. If his submission was correct, it is difficult to identify any kind of object which would be subject to legal privilege under s 10(1)(c), except perhaps a model, made for the purpose of obtaining expert advice. (Documents are communications within s 10(1)(a) and (b).) The significance of 'made',
j   meaning 'brought into existence', in our judgment, is that the privilege does not extend to objects which did not come into existence for the purpose of obtaining legal advice etc (see *Ventouris v Mountain, The Italia Express* [1991] 3 All ER 472, [1991] 1 WLR 607).
Mr Hotten also submitted that legal privilege was excluded by s 10(2) of the 1984 Act on the ground that the sample was 'held with the intention of furthering a criminal purpose', the criminal purpose in question being the

(assumed) guilt of the appellant. Rightly and understandably, he did not press this submission and we need say no more about it.

For these reasons, therefore, we hold that the blood sample was an item 'subject to legal privilege' under s 10(1)(c) of the 1984 Act; that the appellant was entitled to object to its production or to opinion evidence based upon it, and that this ground of appeal is made out. We come therefore, to the operation of the proviso under s 2 of the Criminal Appeal Act 1968.

The proviso

The evidence of Dr Rysiecki which in our opinion was wrongly admitted was relevant only to count 5 of the six-count indictment. That was a charge of incest with the appellant's daughter, then aged 17, as a result of which a child was born. Counts 1 and 2 were charges of indecent assault involving the same daughter when she was under the age of 13 years, and counts 4 and 6 were further charges of incest at dates when the daughter was aged 16 and 18 or 19, respectively. There were guilty verdicts on each of these five counts.

We can assume, in favour of the appellant, that if there was a miscarriage of justice in regard to count 5, by reason of the wrongful admission of privileged evidence, then not only the verdict on that count but also the other guilty verdicts should be set aside.

On count 5, however, there was overwhelming evidence of the appellant's guilt, quite apart from whatever weight the jury may have placed on Dr Rysiecki's expert evidence. Witnesses included the daughter herself and other members of the family who lived in the same household as the appellant and the daughter at the relevant times. They were concerned, not only with the question whether the appellant had intercourse with his daughter at the time when she became pregnant, but also with the defence suggestion, which the jury clearly rejected, that a named individual, who was the daughter's boyfriend for a short time, was the person responsible. One of the family witnesses gave evidence of an admission or possible admission by the appellant that he was responsible. Moreover, the prosecution called an expert witness, Mr Webster, who gave opinion evidence based on DNA samples and whose evidence, understandably, having regard to the advice which, it must be assumed, the defence had received from Dr Rysiecki, was challenged but not contradicted.

The judge's summing up was a model of its kind, and apart from the wrongful admission of privileged evidence, as we have held, the proceedings cannot be criticised in any way.

Mr Barker submits that Dr Rysiecki's evidence must have been accepted by the jury, at the very least, as having strengthened Mr Webster's evidence, and that in consequence it would be wrong to apply the proviso on the ground that no miscarriage of justice actually occurred. Mr Hotten submits that her evidence was no more than the 'icing on the cake' and that there was a powerful case against the appellant, even without it.

This is in many ways a tragic case, and we do not feel that it would be useful or desirable to consider the evidence in greater detail. We are entirely satisfied that no miscarriage of justice has occurred, either in reference to count 5 or to the five counts on which the appellant was convicted, generally, and therefore we dismiss the appeal.

Appeal dismissed.

Kate O'Hanlon　Barrister.

Khanna v Lovell White Durrant (a firm)

CHANCERY DIVISION
SIR DONALD NICHOLLS V-C
4, 5 JULY 1994

b *Practice – Subpoena duces tecum – Setting aside – Application to set aside subpoena – Non-party required to produce documents on a date prior to main trial date – Absence of authority for new practice compelling early production of documents – Whether subpoena defective – Whether interlocutory practice flawed.*

c The plaintiff brought an action against a firm of solicitors claiming damages for professional negligence. The trial, which was expected to last five weeks, was due to commence in November 1994. On 8 June the plaintiff issued a subpoena duces tecum against an assistant solicitor, J, who was employed by another firm of solicitors and who was not a party to the action. The subpoena commanded J to attend court on the day fixed for trial or on the return date *d* specified and to produce certain documents which were retained at his firm's offices. The subpoena was served on J on 14 June and he was informed that it would be heard by the court on 4 July. J applied to set aside the subpoena on the ground, inter alia, that it was defective in that it called for the production of documents on a date other than the day fixed for the main trial and that there was no warrant in the Rules of the Supreme Court for that practice.

e

Held – The court had a wide measure of control over the manner in which a trial would be conducted, including the manner in which it would receive evidence, and consequently the interlocutory practice which had developed of calling for the production of documents specified in a subpoena duces tecum on a date prior to the date of the intended trial was not flawed if it could be *f* done conveniently and without injustice, despite the absence of express authority for the practice in the Rules of the Supreme Court. The practice had much to commend it since, as between the parties to the action, the production of documents pre-trial was likely to save costs and to further the interests of justice rather than impede them and, as to the person to whom the subpoena *g* was addressed, in the ordinary course the date on which he was required to produce documents was a matter of indifference to him. As far as the Chancery Division was concerned, there was no reason why, if the parties to the action so agreed, the clerk of the lists should not fix a date in advance of the main trial for the production of documents in response to a subpoena and if the parties *h* were unhappy with the date fixed the matter could be mentioned to a judge by notice of motion. If the earlier date should prove to be highly inconvenient to a non-party, failing agreement between all concerned, the court would entertain an application by the non-party aimed at resolving the impasse. If however the non-party objected to producing the documents at all in advance of the main trial, the judge who conducted the hearing arranged for production *j* of the documents would decide whether to uphold that objection. On the facts, there was no procedural irregularity since there was a date fixed for the production of documents specified in the subpoena. J's objection to the procedure adopted failed and his application on that ground would accordingly be dismissed (see p 271 *f* to *j*, p 272 *b* to *e h* and p 273 *d*, post).

Dictum of Donaldson MR in *Williams v Williams* [1987] 3 All ER 257 at 261 applied.

Notes

For the form and issue of a writ of subpoena, see 37 *Halsbury's Laws* (4th edn)   a
para 455.

For enforcing or objecting to the production of documents at trial, see 17 *Halsbury's Laws* (4th edn) paras 250, 251.

Cases referred to in judgment   b

Norwich Pharmacal Co v Customs and Excise Comrs [1973] 2 All ER 943, [1974] AC 133, [1973] 3 WLR 164, HL.

Williams v Williams [1987] 3 All ER 257, [1988] QB 161, [1987] 3 WLR 790, CA.

Cases also cited

Burchard v Macfarlane, ex p Tindall and Dryhurst [1891] 2 QB 241, [1891–94] All   c
ER Rep 137, CA.

Elder v Carter, ex p Slide & Spur Gold Mining Co (1890) 25 QBD 194, CA.

Lee v Angas (1866) LR 2 Eq 59, V-C.

Panayiotou v Sony Music Entertainment (UK) Ltd [1994] 1 All ER 755, [1994] 2 WLR 241.

South Carolina Insurance Co v Assurantie Maatschappij 'de Zeven Provincien' NV   d
[1986] 3 All ER 487, [1987] AC 24, HL.

Sunderland Steamship P&I Association v Gatoil International Inc, The Lorenzo Halcoussi [1988] 1 Lloyd's Rep 180.

Summons   e

By a summons dated 29 June 1994 Christopher Jay applied for an order that the writ of subpoena dated 8 June 1994, directed to him and issued out of Chancery Chambers in an action for damages brought by Virender Khanna against Messrs Lovell White Durrant, be set aside on the ground, inter alia, that it was defective in calling for documents to be produced before the court on a date   f
other than that fixed for the trial. The facts are set out in the judgment.

C A Brodie QC and Daniel Gerrans (instructed by Sheridans) for Mr Khanna.
Andrew Edward Mitchell (instructed by Reynolds Porter Chamberlain) for Lovell White Durrant.
Rory Phillips (instructed by Herbert Smith) for Mr Jay.   g

SIR DONALD NICHOLLS V-C. I have before me an application to set aside a subpoena to produce documents, otherwise known as a subpoena duces tecum. The application puts in issue for the first time a practice now being followed in some cases regarding such subpoenas.   h

In this case the subpoena was issued by Mr Virender Khanna in an action brought by him against Lovell White Durrant, the well-known firm of solicitors. The claim in the action is for damages for professional negligence. Lovell White Durrant altogether deny all questions of any negligence on their part. The trial is expected to last five weeks, and is due to commence in   j
November.

The subpoena was issued on 8 June 1994. It is addressed to Mr Christopher Jay, who is employed as an assistant solicitor by Herbert Smith, another well-known firm of solicitors. I need not go into the detail of the documents referred to in the subpoena. They are voluminous. The background lies in the terms of compromise of a previous action, which I shall call 'the first action', in which Mr Khanna was a defendant and in which for a period Lovell White

a Durrant acted as his solicitors. Under the terms of compromise embodied in an order made by Potter J in November 1992, the documents were delivered into the joint custody of Herbert Smith and Sheridans, Mr Khanna's solicitors, for the purpose of identifying the ownership of the documents and their distribution to the owners. No agreement has yet been reached. The documents remain at the offices of Herbert Smith. In the main, the boxes of
b documents specified in the subpoena are the documents held by Herbert Smith pursuant to Potter J's order, and also other documents relating to the first action.

The subpoena was served on Mr Jay on 14 June. He was told that the subpoena would be heard by the court on 4 July. Mr Jay responded with a summons to set aside the subpoena on several grounds, one of which is that the
c subpoena is irregular in that it calls for production of documents at a date other than the day fixed for the trial.

RSC Ord 38, r 14(1) provides that a writ of subpoena must be in one of three prescribed forms, whichever is appropriate. The subpoena before me was issued in the appropriate prescribed form, with one variation. As issued, the
d operative part of the subpoena reads:

> '... we command you to attend at the Royal Courts of Justice, Strand, London ... at the sittings of the Chancery Division, of our High Court of Justice on the day fixed for the trial of the above-named cause/*return date*
> e   *hereof*, notice of which will be given to you and from day to day thereafter until the end of the trial/*hearing* and to bring with you and produce at the place aforesaid on the date notified to you those documents enumerated below as remain at the offices of Herbert Smith ... as are in the joint possession of Messrs Herbert Smith and Messrs Sheridans under an Order of the Honourable Mr. Justice Potter dated 5 November 1992 in the [first
> f   action] ...'

The words I have emphasised, 'the return date hereof', do not appear in the prescribed form, namely form 28 in Appendix A to the Rules of the Supreme Court. The prescribed form requires the person to whom the subpoena is
g addressed to attend at the date fixed for the trial and give evidence on behalf of the party issuing the subpoena, or to bring with him and produce on that date the documents in question. There is no provision for an earlier return date. Under the prescribed form there is no obligation to attend in advance of the trial.

h The plaintiff issued the writ of subpoena in this form so as to avoid the inconveniences and disadvantages which arise from the production of documents at, and not before, the trial. For instance, the person to whom the subpoena is addressed is notified of the date of the trial and he duly attends at court on the appointed day. The trial starts, and in due course he is called to give oral evidence or to produce documents or both. Frequently the
j documents mentioned in the subpoena have not previously been seen by one or other, or either, of the parties. So if the documents are lengthy or numerous or of crucial importance, an adjournment is likely to become necessary to enable the parties' advisers to read the documents and obtain copies. The adjournment may be for a short while but when the documents are voluminous, the trial may have to be adjourned for a day or longer, sometimes a considerable period. Obviously this is very inconvenient.

There may be other reasons why production at the trial is not satisfactory. In some cases, and the present case appears to be one, a party may wish to see the documents before witness statements are prepared. Or a party may wish to see the documents before deciding whether or not to accept a payment into court, or to settle the action on particular terms. Then the absence of the documents is unsatisfactory and out of step with the modern approach. Increasingly, court procedures are designed to require production of evidential material at an earlier rather than a later stage of the proceedings. The emphasis is on the parties knowing the strengths and weaknesses of each other's case as soon as possible, and not being kept in the dark until the trial, by which time increased costs will have been incurred on both sides.

Donaldson MR had these considerations in mind when the case of *Williams v Williams* [1987] 3 All ER 257, [1988] QB 161 was before the Court of Appeal. There the court was concerned with an application for the inspection of documents under the Bankers' Books Evidence Act 1879. The question was whether the Act applied to paying-in slips and paid cheques retained by banks after the conclusion of the transactions to which they relate. Donaldson MR observed ([1987] 3 All ER 257 at 258, [1988] QB 161 at 164):

'Clearly if justice is to be done, Mrs Williams must be able to find out what payments have been made into and out of these charitable accounts and her husband's accounts and by and to whom such payments were made. The question is how this is to be achieved. As the bank concedes, she could obtain a subpoena duces tecum addressed to the appropriate officer of the bank requiring him to attend at the hearing with all documentation in the hands of the bank relating to the accounts of the "charity" and of her husband. However, this would probably, if not inevitably, lead to adjournments in both proceedings in order that the documents could be studied and further inquiries made. If, on the other hand, Mrs Williams and her advisers could have this information in advance of the hearings, the financial and other costs of an adjournment would be avoided and indeed the chances of getting at the truth would be improved.'

Donaldson MR held that the cheques and paying-in slips did not fall within the scope of the 1879 Act, but that an order might be made that the respondent husband obtain these documents from the bank and disclose them to Mrs Williams. Donaldson MR concluded his judgment by saying ([1987] 3 All ER 257 at 261–262, [1988] QB 161 at 169):

'If, however, [the documents] are only discoverable by means of a subpoena duces tecum calling on the appropriate officer of the bank to attend the hearing, I see no reason why the court should not order that the hearing should begin on a specified day and, so far as that day is concerned, be confined to receiving the documents, the remainder of the hearing standing adjourned to a date to be fixed.'

That was seven years ago, in July 1987. Donaldson MR's suggestion indicated a way round the inconveniences and disadvantages I have mentioned. Since then, a practice along the lines suggested by Donaldson MR has grown up, certainly in the Chancery Division and in the Commercial Court, and perhaps elsewhere. The practice has much to commend it. As between the parties to the action, the production of the documents pre-trial is a likely to save costs and to further the interests of justice rather than impede them. As to the person to whom the subpoena is addressed, in the ordinary course the date on which he produces the documents is a matter of indifference to him. Having to produce the documents at all may be inconvenient, for the same reason as being compelled to attend court and give oral evidence may be inconvenient. But usually it makes no difference to him whether he produces b the documents sooner rather than later.

In the present case Mr Jay, through his counsel, has mounted a sustained attack on the regularity of this new practice. The essence of his submissions can be encapsulated as follows. Production of documents as evidence by non-parties is to be contrasted with discovery by parties. In general, and leaving aside special cases such as *Norwich Pharmacal Co v Customs and Excise* c *Comrs* [1973] 2 All ER 943, [1974] AC 133, non-parties cannot be required to give discovery. As to evidence, the appropriate time for this to be produced is the trial. That is the stage at which evidence is adduced. It is produced to the judge conducting the trial, not the parties. Hence the prescribed form for subpoenas, whether to attend and give oral evidence, or to attend and produce specified d documents. The new practice departs from the long-established procedure. The date fixed as the trial date, but with the proceedings on that day confined to production of documents in answer to the subpoena, is not a genuine trial date at all. It is a fiction. The date fixed for that hearing may be many months before the case is ready to be tried, and the judge conducting that hearing may not be the trial judge. There is no warrant in the Rules of the Supreme Court e for such a 'notional' trial date. Any shortcomings flowing from an application of the long-established subpoena procedures must be left to the rules committee and cured by an amendment to the rules.

I accept that, as the new practice has developed, the date fixed as the commencement of the trial, but for the purposes only of receiving documents f from the non-party served with the subpoena, is usually not the date of commencement of the trial in the ordinary sense of that expression. However, that does not mean that the new practice is flawed. The court has a wide measure of control over the manner in which a trial will be conducted, including the manner in which it will receive evidence. If this course is just and g convenient, discrete issues or aspects of the trial can be dealt with separately and on different occasions. An issue such as the assessment of damages can be dealt with separately and later, maybe by a different judge. By parity of reasoning, another matter which pertains to a trial, the receipt of documents produced in response to a subpoena, can be dealt with in advance of everything else falling to be dealt with at the trial and, in that sense, in advance of the main h trial. When this can be done conveniently and without injustice, a different judge from the judge conducting the main trial can be responsible for this part of the trial.

The question which then arises is how the fixing of a trial date for the purpose only of receiving documents in response to a subpoena is to be j achieved. Mr Phillips submitted that this should be a judicial decision. The party who has issued the subpoena must apply to a judge for an appropriate direction, even if the other parties to the action have no objection. A judge should consider the matter, albeit without the advantage at that stage of argument from the person served with the subpoena. Only if the judge, in the exercise of his discretion, so decides should a special date in advance of the main trial be fixed for production of the documents.

I must say that this seems to me to be unnecessarily elaborate and rigid. *a* Interlocutory procedures still differ from court to court, partly for historical reasons but partly also because of differences in the nature of the work. A rule of universal application in all courts and in all circumstances is not needed or appropriate. All I will say is that, as far as the Chancery Division is concerned, I can see no reason why, if the parties to the action so agree, the clerk of the lists should not fix, in advance of the main trial date, an earlier date for the *b* production of documentary evidence in response to a subpoena. He is the officer of the court charged with the fixing of dates for hearings of all kinds before the judges. If the parties are unhappy with a date he has fixed, they can always apply to the judge in charge of the relevant list. So if the parties to the action are unable to agree on this point, the matter must be mentioned to a judge. They should apply by notice of motion to the Chancery motions judge. *c* If they can agree, I can see no reason why they should have to incur the cost of making an application to the judge.

But what of the position of the non-party served with a subpoena? How are his interests to be protected? It must be borne in mind that, in the ordinary way, the date fixed for the trial is fixed by the court in conjunction with the *d* parties' advisers. A non-party served with a subpoena of either sort is not normally brought in at this stage and consulted about whether the date is convenient for him. Of course, if the date fixed for the trial should prove to be highly inconvenient to him for some pressing reason, failing agreement between all concerned the court would entertain an application by the *e* non-party aimed at resolving the impasse.

Against this background there is nothing inherently prejudicial to a non-party if, without reference to him, the party who has issued the subpoena seeks a date for production of the documents earlier than the date fixed for the main part of the trial. As already mentioned, normally the person served with the subpoena will be concerned only with the convenience or inconvenience *f* to him of the particular day. Normally he will be supremely indifferent whether he produces the documents in the course of the main trial or some days or months earlier. His concern about the convenience of the particular day can readily be accommodated by the clerk of the lists or other court officer being in touch with him or his representatives in the same way as would *g* normally be done if he were a party to a proceeding and the hearing date was being fixed by the court. If, unusually, as in the present case, his objection is not to the inconvenience of some particular date but is to producing the documents at all in advance of the main trial, the judge who conducts the hearing arranged for production of the documents will decide whether to *h* uphold that objection. So, in this way, his interests can be fully protected.

Mr Phillips contended that approval of the new procedure will blur the distinction between discovery and evidence. I do not see why it should. The purpose underlying a subpoena to produce documents to the court at trial is the compulsory production of evidence for the trial by a non-party. The new *j* procedure does no more than give effect to that purpose by the means which is just and convenient in today's conditions. The subpoena will remain in the prescribed form. The subpoena will still have to specify the documents in question. The documents will still be produced to the court. It will still be for the judge to rule on which documents should be made available to the parties for inspection or copying, and on what arrangements should be made for the custody of the documents. The rights of the non-party will not be prejudiced a in any way. He will enjoy the same rights in all respects as he enjoys if the documents are required to be produced at the main trial. In the unlikely event, as I have said, that earlier production would of itself be prejudicial to the non-party, the judge will resolve this in the manner in which fairness and justice require.

b Mr Phillips further submitted that it would be unsatisfactory for the documents to be produced to a judge other than the trial judge. The case will not have been opened to him as it would have been to the trial judge. He will not be so well placed to give directions about the use which can be made of the documents or to decide disputes on these issues. I am not impressed by this point. Applications to set aside subpoenas are often heard in advance of the trial by judges other than the trial judge. If a judge considers he is not

c sufficiently well-informed to deal with issues of this nature without delving more deeply than would be sensible for him in advance of the trial, it is always open to him to adjourn the matters in dispute to the main trial.

Accordingly, Mr Jay's objection to the procedure adopted in this case fails. The words in this subpoena which represent a departure from the prescribed

d form are inappropriate and need not and should not be used, but nothing turns on that in this case. Here a date was fixed for the production of the documents specified in the subpoena, so there was no procedural irregularity.

Mr Jay has other grounds on which he seeks to have the subpoena set aside. On these the evidence is not yet complete. I have dealt with the point of general application first, at the request of all parties. It follows that Mr Jay's

e summons to set aside the subpoena on the other grounds will have to be adjourned to be determined at a later date. On that occasion it will be open to Mr Jay to advance any arguments he wishes on why, having regard to the facts of this case, he should not be ordered to produce the documents in advance of the main trial.

f I add three footnotes. First, this is a topic which, despite my conclusions, would merit further consideration by the Supreme Court procedure committee and by the rules committee. Secondly, my observations are addressed only at subpoenas to produce documents. Different considerations apply to subpoenas to attend and give oral evidence because of the difference in the nature of the evidence given in response to such subpoenas. I have heard

g no argument on this issue. Thirdly, Mr Brodie QC advanced an alternative argument prompted initially, it is proper I should acknowledge, by a suggestion from me. He submitted that, in any event, Ord 38, r 13 would lead to the same result. That rule reads:

h '(1) At any stage in a cause or matter the Court may order any person to attend any proceedings in the cause or matter and produce any document, to be specified or described in the order, the production of which appears to the Court to be necessary for the purpose of that proceeding.

(2) No person shall be compelled by an order under paragraph (1) to produce any document at a proceeding in a cause or matter which he could

j not be compelled to produce at the trial of that cause or matter.'

I cannot agree with this submission. I need not go into the history of the rule, and the cases in which an earlier, slightly different, version of the rule was considered. Suffice to say, this rule empowers the court to order any person, including a non-party, to 'attend any proceedings in the cause or matter', and produce documents which appear to the court to be necessary 'for the purpose of that proceeding'. 'That proceeding' harks back to 'the proceedings' which the person may be ordered to attend. A distinction is being drawn between a *a* particular interlocutory or other proceeding in a cause or matter and the entire cause or matter. That this distinction is being drawn is supported by para (2), which limits the documents whose production can be compelled under the order. A person is not compelled to produce at 'a *proceeding* in a cause or matter' a document he could not be compelled to produce 'at the *trial* of that cause or matter'. In my view the phrase 'necessary for the purpose of that *b* proceeding' in para (1) confines the scope of the rule to documents necessary for the purpose of the particular interlocutory or other proceeding at which the person is required to attend.

Application to set aside subpoena on the ground of procedural irregularity dismissed.

c

Celia Fox   Barrister.

National Rivers Authority v Yorkshire Water   *d* Services Ltd

QUEEN'S BENCH DIVISION

SIMON BROWN LJ AND BUCKLEY J

20, 21 OCTOBER, 15 NOVEMBER 1993

e

Water and watercourses – Pollution of river – Causing poisonous, noxious or polluting matter to enter river – Sewage works operating by gravity – Act of unknown third party – Discharge of chemical dangerous to river life into sewer – Chemical flowing through outlet pipe into river – Whether water authority having *f* *'caused' polluting matter to enter river – Whether water authority entitled to rely on statutory defence – Water Act 1989, ss 107(1)(a), 108(7).*

A regional water authority owned and operated a sewage treatment works, which operated largely by gravity. Sewage entered the works where it was treated by a *g* series of processes. The resultant liquid continued to flow by gravity and was discharged through an outlet pipe into a beck which flowed into a river. Both the beck and the river were controlled waters within the meaning of the Water Act 1989. The discharged liquid, although treated, was still sewage and 'poisonous, noxious or polluting matter' for the purposes of s 107(1)(a)[a] of the 1989 Act. The water authority was not however guilty of 'causing' polluting matter to enter *h* controlled waters, contrary to s 107(1)(a), because it discharged sewage effluent into the beck in accordance with a consent granted by the Secetary of State, which contained conditions as to the nature, volume and composition of the effluent discharged. The water authority, in turn, had granted consent to its industrial customers to discharge effluent into the sewers, subject to conditions which, inter *j* alia, excluded the discharge of iso-octonal, which was dangerous to river life. During the night of 13 May 1990 someone made a single discharge of iso-octonal into the sewer which naturally made its way into the works. The National Rivers

---

a   Section 107(1)(a) is set out at p 278 *c d*, post

a Authority subsequently discovered the presence of iso-octonal in the river and brought an information against the water authority, charging it with an offence under s 107(1)(a) of the 1989 Act. The justices upheld the charge and the water authority appealed against the resulting conviction, contending that it had not actively caused the iso-octonal to be present in the effluent and that, in any event, it had a due diligence defence under s 108(7)[b] of the Act since it could not

b reasonably have prevented the discharge. The court quashed the conviction, ruling as a matter of law that the water authority did not cause the iso-octonal to enter controlled waters. The National Rivers Authority appealed, contending (i) that the question of causation was one of fact not law and in view of the water authority's responsibilty for the maintenance and operation of the sewage treatment works and the fact that the ultimate goal of the treatment process was

c the discharge through the outlet pipe of the final effluent, it clearly caused the iso-octonal to enter the river and (ii) that the s 108(7) defence was not available to the water authority, which had been charged with contravening s 107(1)(a), since s 108(7) itself operated to provide a sewage undertaker with a defence to a charge under s 107 'by reason only' of the fact that a discharge of polluting matter

d contravened the conditions of a consent relating to the discharge.

Held – The appeal would be allowed for the following reasons—

(1) The question whether a person had caused poisonous, noxious or polluting

e matter to enter controlled waters contrary to s 107(1)(a) of the 1989 Act was a matter of fact and not of law. Since the reference to causation in s 107(1) did not import either knowlege or negligence with regard to the flow of polluting matter into controlled waters, the fact that sewage treatment works operated by gravity did not exonerate the responsible water authority from having caused polluting matter to enter controlled waters contrary to s 107(1)(a) of the Act, even though

f it could not have prevented the discharge of the pollutant which had been released into the works by an unknown third party. On the facts, the only reasonable conclusion was that the water authority had caused the polluting matter, namely the iso-octonal, to enter controlled waters contrary to s 107(1)(a) of the 1989 Act (see p 279 j to p 280 a and p 281 d, post); dictum of Lord Wilberforce

g in Alphacell Ltd v Woodward [1972] 2 All ER 475 at 479 applied.

(2) The wording of s 108(7) of the 1989 Act was clear and provided a defence only to a charge of contravening the conditions of a consent relating to the discharge of polluting matter from a sewage treatment works and, consequently, s 108(7) did not as matter of law provide a defence to a charge under s 107(1)(a) of

h causing polluting matter to enter controlled waters. Indeed, if s 108(7) had been intended to apply to both ways of committing an offence under s 107 the words of limitation 'by reason only' included in the subsection would be otiose. The water authority was not therefore entitled to rely on the s 108(7) defence. Moreover, findings that the water authority could not reasonably have been

j expected to prevent the iso-octonal from entering the sewers or the works and could not have known of its presence were considerations material to the question of penalities to be imposed, but were not relevant to the issue of liability (see p 280 h to p 281 d, post).

---

b   Section 108(7) is set out at p 280 e f, post

Notes

For the control of pollution in controlled waters, see 49 *Halsbury's Laws* (4th edn) *a*
para 860A, and for cases on 'causing' such pollution, see 49 *Digest* (Reissue) 332,
2540–2542.

As from 25 July 1991 ss 107 and 108 of the Water Act 1989 were replaced by ss 85
and 88 of the Water Resources Act 1991. For ss 85 and 88 of the 1991 Act, see 49
Halsbury's Statutes (4th edn) (1992 Reissue) 802, 806.   *b*

Cases referred to in judgment

Alphacell Ltd v Woodward [1972] 2 All ER 475, [1972] AC 824, [1972] 2 WLR 1320,
     HL; *affg* [1971] 2 All ER 910, [1972] QB 127, [1971] 2 WLR 445, DC.
Brutus v Cozens [1972] 2 All ER 1297, [1973] AC 854, [1972] 3 WLR 521, HL.
Impress (Worcester) Ltd v Rees [1971] 2 All ER 357, DC.   *c*
National Rivers Authority v Welsh Development Agency (1992) 158 JP 506, DC.
North West Water Authority v McTay Construction Ltd (14 April 1986, unreported),
     DC.
Welsh Water Authority v Williams Motors (Cymdu) Ltd (1988) Times, 5 December,
     DC.   *d*
Wrothwell (F J H) Ltd v Yorkshire Water Authority [1984] Crim LR 43, DC.
Wychavon DC v National Rivers Authority [1993] 2 All ER 440, [1993] 1 WLR 125,
     DC.

Case stated

National Rivers Authority (the authority) appealed by way of case stated from the *e*
decision of the Crown Court (Mr Recorder SW Williamson QC and justices) at
Wakefield on 18 March 1992 allowing the appeal of Yorkshire Water Services Ltd
(Yorkshire Water) against its conviction by the Batley and Dewsbury Magistrates'
Court of causing poisonous, noxious or polluting matter to enter controlled
waters, contrary to s 107(1)(a) of the Water Act 1989. The facts are set out in the *f*
judgment of the court.

Shaun Spencer QC and *Gerard Heap* (instructed by Julie Gledhill) for the National
     Rivers Authority.
Stuart Brown QC and *Alaric Dalziel* (instructed by Stuart McFarlane) for Yorkshire
     Water.   *g*

Cur adv vult

15 November 1993. The following judgment of the court was delivered.

                                                                                        h
BUCKLEY J. This is an appeal by National Rivers Authority (the authority) by
way of case stated from the decision of the Crown Court at Wakefield on 18
March 1992. By its decision the Crown Court had allowed the appeal of Yorkshire
Water Services Ltd (Yorkshire Water) against its conviction by the Batley and
Dewsbury Magistrates' Court of causing poisonous, noxious or polluting matter
to enter controlled waters, namely the River Spen, contrary to s 107(1)(a) of the *j*
Water Act 1989.

The following facts emerge from the case stated: from September 1989
Yorkshire Water was the owner and operator of the North Bierley Sewage
Treatment Works. The works operate, as do many others, largely by gravity.
Sewage enters the works via a sewer which leads into an inlet chamber. It flows
into one of two primary tanks where some settlement will take place. From there,

a fluid sewage flows to filter beds where it is treated by bacteria in grazing fauna; the resultant liquid then flows into humus tanks where further settlement takes place. The liquid continues to flow by gravity and is discharged through an outlet pipe into Hunsworth Beck which in turn flows into the River Spen. Hunsworth Beck and River Spen are controlled waters within the meaning of the 1989 Act. That which is discharged into Hunsworth Beck from the works, although treated b as above, is still sewage and 'poisonous, noxious or polluting matter'. Yorkshire Water is not guilty of an offence under the Act because it discharges the sewage effluent into Hunsworth Beck in accordance with a consent granted by the Secretary of State. That consent contains conditions as to the nature, volume and composition of the effluent discharged. Yorkshire Water, in turn, had granted consent to its industrial customers to discharge effluent into the sewers, also c subject to conditions. In particular, these conditions excluded the discharge into the sewer of iso-octonal. In sufficient quantities iso-octonal would impair the efficacy of the works and would itself pass through the works and be discharged into the controlled waters virtually undiluted. It is very dangerous to river life. During the night of 13 May 1990 someone made a single discharge of iso-octonal d into the sewer which inevitably made its way into the works. This had been done with the intention of avoiding detection and Yorkshire Water could not reasonably be expected to prevent the discharge of iso-octonal into the sewer or indeed into the works. Once in the works it was inevitable that a significant proportion of the iso-octonal would be discharged into controlled waters. Because of the presence of the iso-octonal in the effluent it contravened the e conditions of Yorkshire Water's consent from the Secretary of State.

The court concluded:

f 'On the facts and in law, Yorkshire Water Services Limited did not cause iso-octonal to enter controlled waters. Without iso-octonal, the effluent discharged would have been within the limits set by the consent conditions and Yorkshire Water Services Limited is not criminally liable for causing poisonous, noxious or polluting matter to enter controlled waters ... It also appears on the facts that Yorkshire Water Services Limited have a defence under s 108(7) ... The appeal was allowed with costs.'

g In reaching those conclusions it appears that the court had proceeded on the basis of its decision as follows:

'The facts having been found as above, the question of whether Yorkshire Water Services Limited had "caused" polluting matter to enter controlled waters involved a question of law for the Recorder.' (See para 6a of the case h stated.)

I understand that to mean that once the court (Mr Recorder S W Williamson QC and justices) had found the facts which I have recited, the question whether Yorkshire Water caused polluting matter to enter controlled waters was regarded by them as a question of law for the recorder. Although this court is bound by the j contents of the case stated and should not stray into the judgment of the Crown Court which is not annexed to the case but happens to be before us, I am confirmed in this view by a sentence which appears in the penultimate paragraph of the recorder's judgment: 'given that what is alleged here is that Yorkshire Water Services Ltd caused iso-octonal to enter controlled waters, I hold in law and therefore we find that the appellant did not cause iso-octonal to enter controlled waters.' I consider it legitimate to look at the judgment to that limited

extent and in order to resolve any doubt there may be as to finding 6a in the case
stated.   *a*

The questions posed for the opinion of this court are:

'(1) On the facts found by the court, were Sections 107 and 108 of the
Water Act 1989 correctly applied?

(2) On the facts found by the court, was it correct in law to find that
Yorkshire Water Services Ltd had not caused poisonous, noxious or polluting   *b*
matter to enter controlled waters?

(3) On the facts found by the court, was a defence available in any event
under Section 108(7) of the Water Act 1989?'

The first issue concerns the word 'causes' as it appears in s 107(1) of the Act:
                                                                                                           c

'Subject to section 108 below, a person contravenes this section if he causes
or knowingly permits—(a) any poisonous, noxious or polluting matter or any
solid waste matter to enter any controlled waters ...'

Two questions arise: is causation a question of fact or law, and if fact, was the
Crown Court's decision unreasonable?   *d*

Mr Spencer QC for the authority submitted that the question was one of fact
and in view of Yorkshire Water's responsibility for maintenance of the sewage
disposal system and the design and operation of the works, and as the ultimate
and intended aim was the discharge through the outlet pipe of the final effluent,
it clearly caused the substance complained of to enter the river.   *e*

Mr Brown QC for Yorkshire Water submitted that there was no more than a
standing by, no positive act had been done by Yorkshire Water and even if it
caused the discharge generally it did not cause the iso-octonal to be present.

In *Brutus v Cozens* [1972] 2 All ER 1297, [1973] AC 854 the House of Lords
considered the meaning of the word 'insulting' in the Public Order Act 1936 and
concluded that the meaning of an ordinary word of the English language was not   *f*
a question of law. A short citation from Lord Reid will suffice ([1972] 2 All ER 1297
at 1299, [1973] AC 854 at 861):

'The meaning of an ordinary word of the English language is not a question
of law. The proper construction of a statute is a question of law. If the
context shows that a word is used in an unusual sense the court will   *g*
determine in other words what that unusual sense is ... It is for the tribunal
which decides the case to consider, not as law but as fact, whether in the
whole circumstances the words of the statute do or do not as a matter of
ordinary usage of the English language cover or apply to the facts which have
been proved. If it is alleged that the tribunal has reached a wrong decision   *h*
then there can be a question of law but only of a limited character. The
question would normally be whether their decision was unreasonable in the
sense that no tribunal acquainted with the ordinary use of language could
reasonably reach that decision.'

In *Alphacell Ltd v Woodward* [1972] 2 All ER 475, [1972] AC 824 the House   *j*
considered s 21 of the Rivers (Prevention of Pollution) Act 1951. That section was
in the same terms as s 107(1) of the 1989 Act. The case arose out of a case stated
by magistrates which, in effect, posed the question whether 'caused' imported
knowledge or negligence. The House held that it did not and Lord Wilberforce
said: 'In my opinion, "causing" here must be given a common sense meaning and
I deprecate the introduction of refinements ...' (see [1972] 2 All ER 475 at 479,

a [1972] AC 824 at 834). This approach was followed in *F J H Wrothwell Ltd v Yorkshire Water Authority* [1984] Crim LR 43.

I am satisfied that once the facts have been established, whether any party may be said to have 'caused' a certain result is itself a factual conclusion for the tribunal. In the present case, it is clear that it was treated as a matter of law for the recorder. That was wrong. In *Alphacell Ltd v Woodward* [1972] 2 All ER 475 at 479,

b [1972] AC 824 at 834, Lord Wilberforce, before stating that 'causing' should be given a common sense meaning, said:

'The subsection evidently contemplates two things—*causing*, which must involve some active operation or chain of operations involving as the result the pollution of the stream; *knowingly permitting*, which involves a failure to

c   prevent the pollution, which failure, however, must be accompanied by knowledge.' (Lord Wilberforce's emphasis.)

Lord Wilberforce was there giving his understanding of 'causing' as a matter of language. This view, together with others which may be gleaned from the cases, may be used as a guide by courts or tribunals in reaching their own decision on a

d set of facts. It may even be that by reference to such guides, a particular decision of magistrates or a Crown Court could be held unreasonable. But none of this means that the decision of the magistrates or Crown Court on causation is other than a decision of fact.

The facts of *Alphacell Ltd v Woodward* could be likened to the present case save that the works were not sewage works and were not operated by the force of

e gravity. The pollution occurred because the pumps in a settling tank became blocked and the tank overflowed into a stream. Lord Wilberforce said ([1972] 2 All ER 475 at 479, [1972] AC 824 at 834):

'In my opinion, this is a clear case of causing the polluted water to enter the stream. The whole complex operation which might lead to this result was an

f   operation deliberately conducted by the appellants and I fail to see how a defect in one stage of it, even if we must assume that this happened without their negligence, can enable them to say they did not cause the pollution.'

After referring to *Impress (Worcester) Ltd v Rees* [1971] 2 All ER 357, in which a valve on the appellant's fuel tank had been deliberately opened by some third party, an

g unauthorised act wholly unconnected with the appellant's business and in which the court had held that there was so powerful an act by the third party that the appellant did not cause the flow of oil, Lord Wilberforce said ([1972] 2 All ER 475 at 479, [1972] AC 824 at 835):

'I do not desire to question this conclusion, but it should not be regarded as

h   a decision that in every case the act of a third person necessarily interrupts the chain of causation initiated by the person who owns or operates the installation or plant from which the flow took place. The answer to such questions is one of degree and depends on a proper attribution of responsibility for the flow of the polluting matter.'

j   In the present case Yorkshire Water operates the works in a manner which is, according to its design, calculated to direct effluent, after some treatment, into Hunsworth Beck. I regard it as unarguable that because the design of the works utilises the force of gravity Yorkshire Water merely stands by and thus does not cause the outflow. As 'causes' does not import either knowledge or negligence I regard it as equally clear that Yorkshire Water 'caused' the contents of the effluent including the iso-octonal to be discharged into Hunsworth Beck. The fact that the

party responsible for putting the slug of iso-octonal into the sewers might also be
regarded as 'causing' the pollution is neither here nor there. Nor is the finding to   *a*
the effect that Yorkshire Water was not negligent. We were, in the course of
argument, referred to various other authorities including *Wychavon DC v National
Rivers Authority* [1993] 2 All ER 440, [1993] 1 WLR 125 and the transcripts of *Welsh
Water Authority v Williams Motors (Cymdu) Ltd* (1988) Times, 5 December, *North
West Water Authority v McTay Construction Ltd* (14 April 1986, unreported) and   *b*
National Rivers Authority v Welsh Development Agency (1992) 158 JP 506. It seems to
me that all these authorities proceeded on the basis that causation was a question
of fact for the original tribunal and each turned on its own particular facts. In
Wychavon DC v National Rivers Authority the court was, in effect, holding that there
was no evidence to support the conviction. It was not suggesting that whether
the defendant had caused pollution was a question of law.   *c*

It is unnecessary for the court to express any view upon the correctness or
otherwise of any of these decisions which turned on their own facts.

Mr Brown referred us to s 107(5) of the 1989 Act in further support of his
submissions on 'causes'. This section or its predecessor was also considered in
Alphacell v Woodward [1972] 2 All ER 475 at 484, 491, [1972] AC 824 at 840, 849 per   *d*
Viscount Dilhorne and Lord Salmon. It was held not to throw any light on the
meaning given to s 2(1)(a) of the 1951 Act but rather to deal with a special case.

The second issue is the proper construction of s 108(7):

> 'A sewage undertaker shall not be guilty of an offence under section 107
> above by reason only of the fact that a discharge from a sewer or works   *e*
> vested in the undertaker contravenes conditions of a consent relating to the
> discharge if—(a) the contravention is attributable to a discharge which
> another person caused or permitted to be made into the sewer or works; (b)
> the undertaker either was not bound to receive the discharge into the sewer
> or works or was bound to receive it there subject to conditions which were
> not observed; and (c) the undertaker could not reasonably have been   *f*
> expected to prevent the discharge into the sewer or works.'

It is also necessary to recite s 107(6):

> 'A person who contravenes this section or the conditions of any consent
> given under this Chapter for the purposes of this section shall be guilty of an   *g*
> offence and liable ...'

Thus it is clear that there are two ways of committing an offence created by
s 107(6); contravening s 107(1) *or* the conditions of any consent. In this case
Yorkshire Water was charged with contravening s 107(1). Mr Spencer submitted   *h*
that, in those circumstances, s 108(7) did not provide it with a defence because the
words—

> 'by reason only of the fact that a discharge from a sewer or works vested
> in the undertaker contravenes conditions of a consent relating to the
> discharge ...'   *j*

limited the defence to a person who is guilty of an offence under s 107 only
because they have contravened the conditions of a consent. Mr Brown submitted
that the subsection amounts to a 'due diligence' clause which applies to any
contravention of s 107. It seems to me that the difficulty with Mr Brown's
argument is that if the subsection was intended to apply to both ways of
committing an offence created by s 107(6), the words 'by reason only' would be

a otiose. It is true that in this case Yorkshire Water would constantly be committing an offence by contravening s 107(1) but for the provisions of s 108. The reason for that is the finding in the case that the final discharge from the works is, despite treatment, 'poisonous, noxious or polluting matter'. It is difficult to see how Yorkshire Water might contravene their terms of consent without also contravening the terms of s 107(1). However, the findings are

b insufficient to explore that matter fully and in any event the same situation may not pertain with other sewage undertakers within the ambit of the 1989 Act. I conclude that the wording of s 108(7) is clear and provides a defence only to a charge of contravening the conditions of a consent. It does not provide Yorkshire Water with a defence in this case. Right or wrong, that is based on the construction of the subsection and is a question of law. The findings that

c Yorkshire Water could not reasonably be expected to prevent the iso-octonal entering the sewers or the works and could not have known of its presence are considerations material to the question of penalties to be imposed but do not go to liability.

It follows from the above that I would answer questions 1 and 3 in the case, No.

d As to question 2, that I would also answer, No. Not because causation is a question of law, it is not, but because on the facts as stated in the case I consider it unreasonable to reach any conclusion other than Yorkshire Water did cause the polluting matter to enter controlled waters.

e *Appeal allowed. Leave to appeal to the House of Lords refused.*

23 March 1994. The Appeal Committee of the House of Lords gave leave to appeal.

Dilys Tausz   Barrister.

f

National Rivers Authority v Wright Engineering Co Ltd

g QUEEN'S BENCH DIVISION
SIMON BROWN LJ AND BUCKLEY J
20, 21 OCTOBER, 15 NOVEMBER 1993

h *Water and watercourses – Pollution of brook – Causing poisonous, noxious or polluting matter to enter controlled waters – Absolute offence – Engineering Company having oil tank on site – Vandals damaging sight gauge on oil tank – Oil leaking into nearby brook – Whether company having 'caused' polluting matter to enter brook – Whether act of vandals reasonably foreseeable in view of earlier minor incidents of vandalism – Whether justices entitled to dismiss information against company – Water Act 1989, s 107(1)(a).*

j The respondent company, W, operated a light engineering works. W stored heating oil on the works site in a tank which was situated adjacent to a surface water drain, which led to a water course. The brook was controlled water within the meaning of the Water Act 1989. A sight gauge was fitted to the tank and secured by wire. The flow of oil into the sight gauge was controlled by a tap in the form of a stopcock near the base of the tank, but no safety lock had

been fitted to prevent the tap being turned. During the Christmas shutdown
in 1990, the sight gauge was vandalised and the nearby brook was polluted   *a*
with oil which had leaked from the damaged sight gauge. The National Rivers
Authority discovered the presence of the oil in the brook and subsequently
brought an information against W, charging the company with having caused
polluting matter to enter controlled waters contrary to s 107(1)(a)[a] of the Act.
W contended that it had not contravened s 107(1)(a) because the vandalism   *b*
experienced on the night in question was different in nature and extent to the
isolated minor incidents which had occurred in the past and was not
reasonably foreseeable, with the result that the company could not be said to
have 'caused' the oil to enter the brook. The authority, however, contended
that the s 107(1)(a) offence was an absolute one and that since W was aware
that the site was a potential target for vandalism, the damage which occurred   *c*
was reasonably foreseeable as a possible extension to the earlier (albeit
different) forms of vandalism. The justices dismissed the information against
W on the grounds that although the s 107(1)(a) offence was prima facie an
absolute one, the company had not 'caused' the oil to enter controlled waters,
since the discharge of oil was the result of an intervention by a third party and   *d*
the vandalism involved was not reasonably foreseeable because it was out of
all proportion to the earlier and more minor incidents. The authority
appealed.

Held – Although foreseeability would be relevant to any inquiry into whether   *e*
a party 'knowingly permitted' polluting matter to enter into controlled waters
for the purposes of s 107(1)(a) of the 1989 Act, it was of less significance in a
consideration of who or what 'caused' the resulting pollution. Foreseeability
was, however, one factor which a tribunal might consider in seeking to apply
common sense to the question of who or what caused the act of pollution and,
in circumstances involving the acts of vandals, foreseeability was certainly a   *f*
factor to be taken into account. On the facts found, it was open to the justices
to find that the vandals 'caused' the escape of the oil and not W. The fact that
vandalism on a smaller scale and of a different type had occurred in the past
was something which the justices had clearly considered, but understandably
decided was insufficient to alter their view that W had not 'caused' the
discharge of oil. The justices were therefore entitled to acquit W. The   *g*
authority's appeal would accordingly be dismissed (see p 284 *j*, p 285 *e* to *h* and
p 286 *b c*, post).

Dictum of Lord Wilberforce and of Lord Salmon in *Alphacell Ltd v Woodward*
[1972] 2 All ER 475 at 479, 490 applied.

National Rivers Authority v Yorkshire Water Services Ltd [1994] 4 All ER 274   *h*
considered.

Notes

For control of pollution in controlled waters, see 49 *Halsbury's Laws* (4th edn)   *j*
para 860A, and for cases on 'causing' pollution of streams, see 49 *Digest*
(Reissue) 332, 2540–2542.

---

a   Section 107(1)(a), so far as material, provides: '... a person contravenes this section if he causes
    or knowingly permits ... any poisonous, noxious or polluting matter ... to enter any controlled
    waters'

a   As from 25 July 1991 s 107 of the Water Act 1989 was replaced by s 85 of the
Water Resources Act 1991. For s 85 of the 1991 Act, see 49 *Halsbury's Statutes*
(4th edn) (1992 reissue) 802.

Cases referred to in judgments
Alphacell Ltd v Woodward [1972] 2 All ER 475, [1972] AC 824, [1972] 2 WLR 1320,
b   HL.
National Rivers Authority v Yorkshire Water Services Ltd [1994] 4 All ER 274, DC.
Impress (Worcester) Ltd v Rees [1971] 2 All ER 357, DC.
Welsh Water Authority v Williams Motors (Cymdu) Ltd (1988) Times, 5 December,
DC.

c **Case stated**
National Rivers Authority (the authority) appealed by way of case stated by the
justices for the County of Warwickshire in respect of their adjudication as a
magistrates' court sitting at Stratford-upon-Avon on 23 August 1991 whereby
they dismissed an information against Wright Engineering Co Ltd (Wright
d Engineering) that they, on a day between 24 December 1990 and 1 January
1991, at The Willows, Stratford-upon-Avon, did cause to enter controlled
waters, namely the Racecourse Brook, polluting matter, contrary to s 107(1)(a)
of the Water Act 1989. The facts are set out in the judgment of Buckley J.

Roger D H Smith QC (instructed by Mark Knowles) for the authority.
e *James Tillyard* (instructed by *G F Lodder & Sons*, Stratford-upon-Avon) for
Wright Engineering.

Cur adv vult

f 15 November 1993. The following judgments were delivered.

BUCKLEY J (giving the first judgment at the invitation of Simon Brown LJ).
This is an appeal by National Rivers Authority (the authority) by way of case
stated from the decision of the Warwickshire Justices sitting at
Stratford-upon-Avon on 23 August 1991. By their decision the justices
g dismissed an information against Wright Engineering Co Ltd (Wright
Engineering) which alleged that they:

'On a day between the 24th December 1990 and 1st January 1991 at The
Willows, Stratford-upon-Avon, did cause to enter controlled waters,
namely The Racecourse Brook, polluting matter contrary to s 107(1)(a) of
h the Water Act 1989.'

The following facts emerged from the case stated.
Wright Engineering operates a light engineering company from a site in
Masons Road, Stratford-upon-Avon, where they stored heating oil in a 5,000
litre tank which was adjacent to a surface water drain which led to the water
j course. Fitted to the tank was a sight gauge, fixed in an upright position and
secured by wire. The flow of oil into the sight gauge was controlled by a tap
in the form of a stopcock near the base of the tank. No lock was fitted to
prevent the tap being turned. Before the premises were closed for the
Christmas holidays on 21 December 1990 equipment had been cleaned, stored
or secured. Pliers had been used to wind wire tightly round the sight gauge.
During the Christmas shutdown Mr Kelly, on behalf of the authority, visited

Racecourse Brook and found the water was polluted with oil. He discovered
that the oil emanated from Wright Engineering's yard which was awash with
it. It had come from the sight gauge which had been vandalised. But for such
vandalism, the oil would not have leaked.

There had been past incidents of vandalism at Wright Engineering's works,
but these were relatively minor compared with the present incident. Wright
Engineering was aware that the site was a potential target for vandalism but
had not envisaged vandalism of the extent and nature experienced on the night
in question.

Racecourse Brook at The Willows is controlled water and oil is a polluting
matter.

The justices then set out in the case the evidence given by each witness. It
is unnecessary for me to set it out in full. I refer to certain passages later. It
appears that the submissions of the parties to the justices focused mainly on the
question, was the vandalism foreseeable?

The justices were of opinion that although the offence was prima facie an
absolute one, the discharge of oil was the result of an intervention by a third
party and that the vandalism involved was not reasonably foreseeable because
it was out of all proportion to the earlier and more minor incidents.

The questions for the opinion of the High Court were stated in the case as
follows:

'(1) Was there evidence upon which Magistrates could come to the
decision that the type and extent of vandalism was not reasonably
foreseeable?

(2) Whether, despite Section 107(1)(a) of the Water Act 1989 being a
prima facie absolute offence, a person, in circumstances where some form
of vandalism is foreseeable, may properly be acquitted if the act of
vandalism which caused the polluting matter to enter the controlled water
was that of a third party and of a type and extent which was not reasonably
foreseeable but against which precaution could have, but had not in fact,
been taken.'

With the consent of all parties, this appeal was argued immediately following
National Rivers Authority v Yorkshire Water Services Ltd [1994] 4 All ER 274
Counsel in this appeal, Mr Smith QC for the authority and Mr Tillyard for
Wright Engineering, were in court during argument in the earlier appeal and
argument in this appeal was shorter than it might otherwise have been. The
main issue concerned the relevance of foreseeability to 'causes', as that word
appears in s 107(1) of the 1989 Act.

I referred to the speech of Lord Wilberforce in *Alphacell Ltd v Woodward*
[1972] 2 All ER 475 at 479, [1972] AC 824 at 834-835 in the *Yorkshire Water* case.
I would only add a short sentence from the speech of Lord Salmon ([1972] 2 All
ER 475 at 490, [1972] AC 824 at 847):

'I consider, however, that what or who has caused a certain event to
occur is essentially a practical question of fact which can best be answered
by ordinary common sense rather than abstract metaphysical theory.'

In some of the cases to which I referred in the *Yorkshire Water* case,
foreseeability was mentioned. Clearly it will be relevant to any inquiry into
whether a party 'knowingly permitted' (contrary to s 107(1)) but, in my
judgment, that is of less significance in a consideration of 'causes'. I stop short

of Mr Tillyard's assertion that it has no place because where, as here, acts of third parties are involved, a tribunal's task is to look at all the circumstances and arrive at a 'proper attribution of responsibility', to quote Lord Wilberforce. Some of the cases have drawn a distinction between doing a positive act in a chain of causation and passively standing by. Lord Salmon illustrated an aspect of that in *Alphacell Ltd v Woodward* [1972] 2 All ER 475 at 490, [1972] AC 824 at 847 where, after stating that it was plain that the appellants caused the pollution by the active operation of their plant, he continued:

'They certainly did not intend to cause pollution but they intended to do the acts which caused it. What they did was something different in kind from the passive storing of effluent which could not discharge into the river save by an act of God or, as in *Impress (Worcester) Ltd v Rees* [1971] 2 All ER 357, by the active intervention of a stranger, the risk of which could not reasonably have been foreseen.'

That approach was adopted by Lloyd LJ in *Welsh Water Authority v Williams Motors (Cymdu) Ltd* (1988) Times, 5 December. Similarly, there is an obvious factual difference between this case and the *Yorkshire Water* case. Here, the object of the tank was to retain the oil, that object was defeated by vandals who tampered with the sight gauge. In the *Yorkshire Water* case the object of Yorkshire Water's works was to process that which came in through the sewers and then to discharge it through the outlet pipe into Hunsworth Beck. This case is factually in the same class as *Impress (Worcester) Ltd v Rees* [1971] 2 All ER 357.

The cases give guidance, but it must be remembered that each will have its own factual peculiarities. I agree with Lloyd LJ, who stated in *Welsh Water Authority v Williams Motors*:

'...the question is not what was foreseeable by the respondents or anybody else: the question is whether any act on the part of the respondents caused the pollution.'

However, that does not mean that foreseeability is wholly irrelevant. It is one factor which a tribunal may properly consider in seeking to apply common sense to the question: who or what caused the result under consideration.

On the facts found by the justices in this case, namely that vandals had tampered with the sight gauge and opened the tap on the tank, it was certainly open to the justices to find that they 'caused' the escape and not Wright Engineering. The fact of past vandalism on a smaller scale and of a different type was something which the justices clearly considered but, in my view, understandably decided was insufficient to alter their view.

In view of the way the justices framed their questions, I turn briefly to the evidence set out in the case. The evidence clearly showed that the sight gauge had been vandalised and although vandalism had occurred in the past, possibly about once a year, it had not been of this type. Mrs Blaney, the company secretary, referred to previous vandalism but said it had never been a serious problem. She had no reason to suspect that anyone would tamper with the oil. Mr Wright, the director of the company, gave similar but more detailed evidence. In cross-examination he was frank enough to admit that, with hindsight, he should have been aware of the dangers of oil spillage. With hindsight, he realised the tank was clearly a target and that there was a real danger. He also said he was worried that it was easy to remove the old sight glass (gauge) but said that it had been secured by wire tightly wound around it with pliers. Neither this nor any of the other evidence set out in the case alters the views I have expressed.

I turn to the questions posed in the case.

(1) I would answer this, Yes, but stress that, for the reasons given, this question is only of limited relevance.

(2) I do not consider it appropriate to give a simple Yes or No answer to this question because of its emphasis on foreseeability, rather than causation.

On the facts found by the justices and set out in their case, they were entitled to acquit Wright Engineering. I would dismiss the appeal. It only remains for me to thank counsel in both these appeals for their great assistance.

SIMON BROWN LJ. I agree.

Appeal dismissed.

Dilys Tausz   Barrister.

National Rivers Authority v Alfred McAlpine Homes East Ltd

QUEEN'S BENCH DIVISION

SIMON BROWN LJ AND MORLAND J

14, 15 DECEMBER 1993, 26 JANUARY 1994

Water and watercourses – Pollution of river – Causing polluting matter to enter river – Cement washed into river during building operations carried out by company – Employees admitting liability – Employees not exercising controlling mind of company – Whether company liable for acts of junior employees – Water Resources Act 1991, s 85.

The respondent company was engaged in building houses on a residential development. A stream, which was a controlled water within the meaning of s 104 of the Water Resources Act 1991, ran through the site in a man-made culvert and emerged to the north of the development, from where it flowed into a river. In May 1992 the National Rivers Authority inspected the stream and found the water to be cloudy downstream of the building site with a number of dead and distressed fish. The company's site agent and manager both accepted responsibility for the pollution, explaining that it had been caused by cement being washed into the stream during the construction of a water feature on the site. The authority brought an information against the company, alleging that it had caused polluting matter, wet cement, to enter controlled waters contrary to s 85[a] of the 1991 Act. The justices held that there was no case to answer and dismissed the information, holding that while s 85 appeared to create an offence of strict liability, the authority had failed to show that the company itself was liable because neither the site agent nor the site manager were of a sufficiently senior standing within the company to enable

---

a   Section 85, so far as material, is set out at p 289 *g h*, post

them to be categorised as persons whose acts were the acts of the company.
a The authority appealed. The company contended that it was not criminally
liable since neither the site agent not the site manager could be regarded as
exercising the controlling mind and will of the company and since s 85 itself
could not be construed as imposing vicarious liability on companies.

b **Held** – The question in all cases where a company was prosecuted under s 85 of
the 1991 Act was whether as a matter of common sense the company, by some
active operation or chain of operations carried out under its essential control,
caused the pollution of controlled water. Accordingly, a company would be
criminally liable for causing pollution which resulted from the acts or omissions
of its employees acting within the course and scope of their employment when
c the pollution occurred, regardless of whether they could be said to be exercising
the controlling mind and will of the company, save only where some third party
acted in such a way as to interrupt the chain of causation. On the facts, it was
immaterial that those in the company's head office had no direct part in
determining the precise construction which allowed the cement to wash into
d the stream, since it was sufficient that those immediately responsible on site
were employees of the company and acting apparently within the course and
scope of that employment. It followed that unless and until the company called
evidence displacing the inference from the facts, that the pollution resulted
directly from the company's own operation in constructing the water feature,
the justices could not properly find no case to answer. The appeal would
e therefore be allowed (see p 294 *f* to *j*, p 295 *e f j*, p 297 *b c g* to *j*, p 298 *h j* and p 299 *j*
to p 300 *c*, post).

Dictum of Lord Wilberforce, of Viscount Dilhorne and of Lord Salmon in
Alphacell Ltd v Woodward [1972] 2 All ER 475 at 479, 482, 489–491 applied.

Tesco Supermarkets Ltd v Nattrass [1971] 2 All ER 127 distinguished.

f **Notes**
For the control of pollution of controlled waters, see 49 *Halsbury's Laws* (4th
edn) para 860A, and for cases on 'causing' such pollution, see 49 *Digest* (Reissue)
332, 2540–2542.

For Water Resources Act 1991, s 85, see 49 *Halsbury's Statutes* (4th edn) (1992
g reissue) 802.

Cases referred to in judgments
Allen v Whitehead [1930] 1 KB 211, [1929] All ER Rep 13, DC.
Alphacell Ltd v Woodward [1972] 2 All ER 475, [1972] AC 824, [1972] 2 WLR 1320,
h   HL; *affg* [1971] 2 All ER 910, [1972] 1 QB 127, [1971] 3 WLR 445, DC.
Impress (Worcester) Ltd v Rees [1971] 2 All ER 357, DC.
Moses v Midland Railway Co (1915) 84 LJKB 2181, DC.
Mousell Bros Ltd v London & North-Western Rly Co [1917] 2 KB 836, [1916–17] All
   ER Rep 1101, DC.
j *Pepper (Inspector of Taxes) v Hart* [1993] 1 All ER 42, [1993] AC 593, [1992] 3 WLR
   1032, HL.
Seaboard Offshore Ltd v Secretary of State for Transport, The Safe Carrier [1993] 3 All
   ER 25, [1993] 1 WLR 1025, DC; *affd* [1994] 2 All ER 99, [1994] 1 WLR 541, HL.
Sherras v De Rutzen [1895] 1 QB 918, [1895–99] All ER Rep 1167, DC.
Sweet v Parsley [1969] 1 All ER 347, [1970] AC 132, [1969] 2 WLR 470, HL.
Tesco Stores Ltd v Brent London BC [1993] 2 All ER 718, [1993] 1 WLR 1037, DC.

Tesco Supermarkets Ltd v Nattrass [1971] 2 All ER 127, [1972] AC 153, [1971] 2 WLR 1166, HL.

Welsh Water Authority v Williams Motors (Cymdu) Ltd (1988) Times, 5 December, DC.

Wychavon DC v National Rivers Authority [1993] 2 All ER 440, [1993] 1 WLR 125, DC.

Cases also cited or referred to in skeleton arguments
Coppen v Moore (No 2) [1898] 2 QB 306, [1895–99] All ER Rep 926, DC.
Grade v DPP [1942] 2 All ER 118, DC.
James & Son Ltd v Smee, Green v Burnett [1954] 3 All ER 273, [1955] 1 QB 78, DC.
Melias Ltd v Preston [1957] 2 All ER 449, [1957] 2 QB 380, DC.
National Rivers Authority v Wright Engineering Co Ltd [1994] 4 All ER 281, DC.
National Rivers Authority v Yorkshire Water Services Ltd [1994] 4 All ER 274, DC.
Price v Cromack [1975] 2 All ER 113, [1975] 1 WLR 988, DC.
Southern Water Authority v Pegrum [1989] Crim LR 442.
Strutt v Clift [1911] 1 KB 1, DC.
R v Winson [1968] 1 All ER 197, [1969] 1 QB 371, CA.
Wrothwell (F J H) Ltd v Yorkshire Water Authority [1984] Crim LR 43, DC.
Wychavon DC v National Rivers Authority [1993] 2 All ER 440, [1993] 1 WLR 125, DC.

Case stated
National Rivers Authority (the authority) appealed by way of case stated by the justices for the County of Kent, acting in and for the petty sessional division of Tonbridge and Malling, in respect of their adjudication on 11 January 1993 whereby they dismissed the information that the respondent, Alfred McAlpine Homes East Ltd (the company) had, on or about 20 May 1992, at Goldwell Springs, East Malling, Kent, caused polluting matter, namely wet cement, to enter controlled waters within the meaning of s 104 of the Water Resources Act 1991, namely the Ditton Stream, contrary to s 85 of the 1991 Act. The facts are set out in the judgment of Simon Brown LJ.

Camden Pratt QC and *Philip J Marshall* (instructed by *Martin Davies*, Worthing) for the authority.

Marilyn Kennedy-McGregor (instructed by *Laytons*, East Molesey) for the company.

Cur adv vult

26 January 1994. The following judgments were delivered.

SIMON BROWN LJ. The National Rivers Authority Southern Region (the authority) appeal by case stated against the decision of the Tonbridge and Malling Justices sitting at West Malling on 11 January 1993 upholding a submission of no case to answer and dismissing an information laid by the authority against Alfred McAlpine Homes East Ltd (the company). The information alleged that on 20 May 1992 the company caused polluting matter, wet cement, to enter controlled waters, the Ditton Stream, contrary to s 85 of the Water Resources Act 1991.

The facts found by the justices can be shortly stated. The company were engaged at the time in building houses on a new residential development at Goldwell Springs, East Malling. The Ditton Stream (which the company acknowledge was a controlled water within the meaning of s 104 of the 1991 Act) ran through the development in a man-made culvert, emerging to the north of the site where it entered first a lake and then the River Medway. On 21 May 1992 Mr Barker, a water quality engineer employed by the authority, went to inspect the Ditton Stream and found it to be clear upstream of the Goldwell site but, downstream of the site, cloudy and containing a number of dead and distressed fish. During his inspection Mr Barker was approached first by the company's site agent, Mr David Brown, and second by their site manager, Mr Tom Riley. Both were interviewed separately under caution and both accepted responsibility for the pollution, explaining that it had been caused by cement being washed into the stream on 20 May 1992, during construction of a water feature on the Goldwell Springs site.

At the close of the authority's evidence, the company submitted that upon those facts there was no case to answer. The submission was accepted. The justices concluded that although both Mr Riley and Mr Brown took responsibility for the pollution and 'although s 85 did seem to create an offence of strict liability', the authority had failed to show that the company itself was liable. They said this:

> 'We applied the guidelines in *Tesco Supermarkeιs Ltd v Nattrass* [1971] 2 All ER 127, [1972] AC 153 and found that neither Mr Riley nor Mr Brown were of a sufficiently senior standing within the company to enable us to say with confidence that they fell into the category of those whose acts were the acts of the company.'

The question posed for the opinion of this court is:

> 'Whether [the justices] were correct to conclude that an offence under s 85 of the Water Resources Act 1991 could only be committed by a company if the offence was committed by a person exercising the "controlling mind and will" of the company, such as a director, manager, secretary or some similar officer of the company, and therefore correct to find that there was no case to answer and to dismiss the information.'

Section 85(1) provides, so far as relevant:

> 'A person contravenes this section if he causes or knowingly permits any poisonous, noxious or polluting matter ... to enter any controlled waters.'

So far as material it is in identical terms to s 2(1) of the Rivers (Prevention of Pollution) Act 1951. The starting point for consideration of this appeal must accordingly be the decision of the House of Lords in *Alphacell Ltd v Woodward* [1972] 2 All ER 475, [1972] AC 824. There are helpful passages to be found in all five speeches. Let me, however, cite from just two. First, from Lord Wilberforce ([1972] 2 All ER 475 at 479, [1972] AC 824 at 834–835):

> 'The subsection evidently contemplates two things—*causing*, which must involve some active operation or chain of operations involving as the result the pollution of the stream; *knowingly permitting*, which involves a failure to prevent the pollution, which failure, however, must be accompanied by knowledge. I see no reason either for reading back the

word "knowingly" into the first limb, or for reading the first limb as, by deliberate contrast, hitting something which is unaccompanied by knowledge. The first limb involves causing and this is what has to be interpreted. In my opinion, "causing" here must be given a common sense meaning and I deprecate the introduction of refinements, such as causa causans, effective cause or novus actus. There may be difficulties where acts of third persons or natural forces are concerned but I find the present case comparatively simple. The appellants abstract water, pass it through their works where it becomes polluted, conduct it to a settling tank communicating directly with the stream, into which the polluted water will inevitably overflow if the level rises over the overflow point. They plan, however, to recycle the water by pumping it back from the settling tank into their works; if the pumps work properly this will happen and the level in the tank will remain below the overflow point. It did not happen on the relevant occasion due to some failure in the pumps. In my opinion, this is a clear case of causing the polluted water to enter the stream. The whole complex operation which might lead to this result was an operation deliberately conducted by the appellants and I fail to see how a defect in one stage of it, even if we must assume that this happened without their negligence, can enable them to say they did not cause the pollution. In my opinion, complication of this case by infusion of the concept of mens rea, and its exceptions, is unnecessary and undesirable. The section is clear, its application plain ... There are two previous decisions which call for brief comment. The first is *Moses v Midland Railway Co* (1915) 84 LJKB 2181 which was decided upon similar terminology in s 5 of the Salmon Fishery Act 1861. The cause of the escape of the polluting creosote was a defective tap in the tank wagon which did not belong to the railway company but to a private owner. The conclusion that the railway company had not caused it to flow was, I should have thought, inevitable. The second is *Impress (Worcester) Ltd v Rees* [1971] 2 All ER 357. The appellants had placed a fuel oil tank near, although not adjacent to, the River Severn. The oil escaped through a valve which was not kept locked. The Divisional Court found that it was an inevitable conclusion of fact that some unauthorised person had opened the valve for purposes unconnected with the appellants' business. They held that the opening of the valve was of so powerful a nature that the conduct of the appellants was not a cause of the flow of oil. I do not desire to question this conclusion, but it should not be regarded as a decision that in every case the act of a third person necessarily interrupts the chain of causation initiated by the person who owns or operates the installation or plant from which the flow took place. The answer to such questions is one of degree and depends on a proper attribution of responsibility for the flow of the polluting matter.' (Lord Wilberforce's emphasis.)

Second, this passage from Lord Salmon's speech ([1972] 2 All ER 475 at 489–491, [1972] AC 824 at 847–849):

'The nature of causation has been discussed by many eminent philosophers and also by a number of learned judges in the past. I consider, however, that what or who has caused a certain event to occur is essentially a practical question of fact which can best be answered by ordinary common sense rather than abstract metaphysical theory. It seems to me that, giving the word "cause" its ordinary and natural meaning, anyone may cause something to happen, intentionally or negligently or inadvertently without negligence and without intention … The appellants clearly did not cause the pollution intentionally and we must assume that they did not do so negligently. Nevertheless, the facts … to my mind make it obvious that the appellants in fact caused the pollution. If they did not cause it, what did? There was no intervening act of a third party nor was there any act of God to which it could be attributed. The appellants had been responsible for the design of the plant; everything within their works was under their control; they had chosen all the equipment. The process which they operated required contaminated effluent being pumped round their works until it came to rest in an open tank which they sited on the river bank. If the pumps which they had installed in this tank failed to operate efficiently the effluent would necessarily overflow into the river. And that is what occurred. It seems plain to me that the appellants caused the pollution by the active operation of their plant. They certainly did not intend to cause pollution but they intended to do the acts which caused it. What they did was something different in kind from the passive storing of effluent which could not discharge into the river save by an act of God or, as in *Impress (Worcester) Ltd v Rees* [1971] 2 All ER 357, by the active intervention of a stranger, the risk of which could not reasonably have been foreseen. The appellants relied strongly on *Moses v Midland Railway Co* (1915) 84 LJKB 2181. In that case a private owner's tank wagon filled with creosote formed part of a train being driven by the defendants. At the beginning of the journey the wagon was subjected to careful examination by the defendants which revealed no defect. There was, however, a latent defect in one of its taps. Whilst the train was travelling along the banks of a river this defect caused creosote to leak into the river and polluted it so that many fish were killed. On a charge under s 5 of the Salmon Fishery Act 1861 the justices held that the defendants had not caused the pollution, and that decision was upheld by the Divisional Court. The facts were strikingly different from those of the present case. The wagon was not owned by the defendants, they were in no way responsible for its design or maintenance; they exercised no control over the defective tap; and they had no knowledge or means of knowledge of the latent defect which caused the leak. The decision, which to my mind is not relevant to this appeal, may well have been correct on its facts although the judgments as reported are not very satisfactory. The appellants contend that even if they caused the pollution still they should succeed since they did not cause it intentionally or knowingly or negligently. Section 2(1)(*a*) of the Rivers (Prevention of Pollution) Act 1951 is undoubtedly a penal section. It follows that if it is capable of two or more meanings then the meaning most favourable to the subject should be adopted. Accordingly, so the argument runs, the words "intentionally" or "knowingly" or "negligently" should be read into the section immediately before the word "causes". I do not agree. It is of the utmost public importance that our rivers should not be polluted. The risk of pollution, particularly from the vast and increasing number of riparian industries, is very great. The offences created by the 1951 Act seem to me to be prototypes of offences which "are not criminal in any real sense, but are acts which in the public interest are prohibited under a penalty": *Sherras v De Rutzen* [1895] 1 QB 918 at 922, [1895–99] All ER Rep 1167 at 1169 per

Wright J referred to with approval by my noble and learned friends, Lord
Reid and Lord Diplock, in *Sweet v Parsley* [1969] 1 All ER 347 at 350, 360,
[1970] AC 132 at 149, 162. I can see no valid reason for reading the word
"intentionally", "knowingly" or "negligently" into s 2(1)(a) and a number
of cogent reasons for not doing so. In the case of a minor pollution such as
the present, when the justices find that there is no wrongful intention or
negligence on the part of the defendant, a comparatively nominal fine will
no doubt be imposed. This may be regarded as a not unfair hazard of
carrying on a business which may cause pollution on the banks of a river.
The present appellants were fined £20 and ordered to pay in all £24 costs. I
should be surprised if the costs of pursuing this appeal to this House were
incurred to the purpose of saving these appellants [£44]. If this appeal
succeeded and it were held to be the law that no conviction could be
obtained under the 1951 Act unless the prosecution could discharge the
often impossible onus of proving that the pollution was caused
intentionally or negligently, a great deal of pollution would go unpunished
and undeterred to the relief of many riparian factory owners. As a result,
many rivers which are now filthy would become filthier still and many
rivers which are now clean would lose their cleanliness. The legislature no
doubt recognised that as a matter of public policy this would be most
unfortunate. Hence s 2(1)(a) which encourages riparian factory owners not
only to take reasonable steps to prevent pollution but to do everything
possible to ensure that they do not cause it.'

Perhaps rather oddly, that decision appears not to have been placed before
the justices in the present case. Their approach seems rather to have been
dictated by the earlier decision of the House of Lords in *Tesco Supermarkets Ltd
v Nattrass* [1971] 2 All ER 127, [1972] AC 153 (not cited in *Alphacell* although two
members of the Appellate Committee were party to both). To *Tesco v Nattrass*
I shall return. First, however, it is important to see how the company seek to
explain and distinguish *Alphacell*.

Mrs Kennedy-McGregor treated us to a most able and sustained argument
ranging over the whole field of corporate criminal liability. We were referred
to many authorities. Let me try to summarise her case. It comes, I believe,
essentially to this:

(1) A company can only be criminally liable in one of two ways, either (a) by
being held vicariously liable for the acts of its servants or agents, or (b) by being
identified with individuals held to represent its controlling mind and will—the
acts and state of mind of these individuals being deemed to be those also of the
company itself.

(2) *Alphacell* is properly to be regarded as a category (b) case.

(3) This case is distinguishable from *Alphacell*, there being nothing
equivalent here to the storage system designed and operated by the controlling
officers of the defendant company there.

(4) Given, as all accept, that neither the site agent nor the site manager can
possibly be regarded as exercising the respondent company's controlling mind
and will, it can accordingly only be found criminally liable were this court (for
the first time, it is suggested) to determine that s 85 of the 1991 Act should be
construed so as to impose vicarious liability upon companies—liability, that is,
for their servants or agents.

(5) Vicarious liability is only imposed by the law in three circumstances: (i) By the clear words of the statute itself as, for example, under s 163 of the Licensing Act 1964: 'a person shall not ... either himself or by his servant or agent ...' (ii) In delegation cases, namely where the offence is of such a character that it can only be committed by the person who delegates, the relevant duty therefore being held non-delegable. *Mousell Bros Ltd v London & North-Western Railway Co* [1917] 2 KB 836, [1916–19] All ER Rep 1101 and *Allen v Whitehead* [1930] 1 KB 211, [1929] All ER Rep 13 are said to be examples of this class of case. (iii) By application of what Professor Glanville Williams calls the 'extended construction principle'. This principle has been applied to offences which are described in terms applicable equally to both employer and servant, offences where the actus reus is, for example, to 'sell', to be 'in possession', to 'keep', to 'use', to 'present'. Illustrations were cited to us.

(6) The court should not impose vicarious liability in respect of s 85 of the 1991 Act. It is, counsel submits, unnecessary to do so to achieve the object of the legislation. Nor is there anything in the statutory language to suggest such an approach. Indeed, Mrs Kennedy-McGregor submits, the court should shrink from such an approach, producing as it does (to use the words of Professor Glanville Williams) 'a tyrannous combination' of strict and vicarious responsibility whereby the company can be rendered criminally liable for something it did not do and knew nothing about and may indeed actually have forbidden.

To my mind the difficulty with this whole elaborate argument is that it breaks down at least as early as stage (2). Assuming, without deciding, that the dichotomy suggested at stage (1) is both sound and absolute, I for my part see *Alphacell* as an illustration of vicarious liability rather than a case where the House of Lords concluded that those representing the directing mind and will of the company had themselves personally caused the polluting matter to escape. The failure in the pumps which was the immediate cause of the pollution was unexplained; but there was certainly nothing to link it to any senior officer in the company. True, none of their Lordships' speeches specifically referred to the company's servants or agents as such; nor did they expressly use the language of vicarious liability. But to my mind the whole tenor of the judgments is consistent only with that approach. How else distinguish *Moses v Midland Railway Co* (1915) 84 LJKB 2181 in the way they did? Why else, in discussing *Impress (Worcester) Ltd v Rees* [1971] 2 All ER 357, does Lord Wilberforce speak of 'some unauthorised person' having opened the valve 'for purposes unconnected with the appellant's business', and 'the act of a third person' having interrupted 'the chain of causation initiated by the person who owns or operates the installation or plant from which the flow took place'; and Lord Salmon refer to 'the active intervention of a stranger, the risk of which could not reasonably have been foreseen'? Why do the speeches stress the clear analogy between this statutory offence of causing pollution and the common law public nuisance cases which plainly recognise a master's liability for his servant's acts? Why, similarly, does Lord Salmon speak of the section as one 'which encourages riparian factory owners not only to take reasonable steps to prevent pollution but to do everything possible to ensure that they do not cause it'?

And only such an approach seems to me consistent too with later decisions of the Divisional Court directed to subsequent enactments of this same provision. Take Lloyd LJ's judgment in the Divisional Court in *Welsh Water Authority v Williams Motors (Cymdu) Ltd* (1988) Times, 5 December, with regard to s 32(1)(a) of the Control of Pollution Act 1974. There, a delivery company, whilst filling the defendants' storage tank with diesel oil, spilled some oil, which eventually found its way into controlled waters. In upholding the defendants' acquittal, Lloyd LJ said this:

> '[The delivery company] were independent contractors ... They were not in any sense under the control of the respondents in the way they carried out and fulfilled their functions under the contract ... It was no different from that of an ordinary domestic householder who finds that his tank has been overfilled by the oil company ... Giving the word "cause" its ordinary common sense meaning, as Lord Wilberforce says we must, I can find no positive act in any chain of operations by the respondents here which could be said to have caused the pollution.'

The implication from these various dicta is surely unmistakeable: an employer is liable for pollution resulting from its own operations carried out under its essential control, save only where some third party acts in such a way as to interrupt the chain of causation.

Is the present case then properly distinguishable from *Alphacell Ltd v Woodward* [1972] 2 All ER 475, [1972] AC 824 in point of fact? I believe not, at least not on the evidence as it stood before the justices at the close of the authority's case. I see no difference in principle between the design and maintenance of a storage tank for pollutants (*Alphacell*), and the carrying on of building operations involving the use of pollutants (here, cement to construct a water feature), each occurring on land adjacent to controlled waters. Either system, if ineffectively devised or operated, can result equally in the escape of polluting material into the adjacent stream.

It accordingly seems to me nothing to the point that those in the company's head office here may well have had no direct part in determining the precise system of construction which allowed this cement to wash into the Ditton Stream. It is sufficient that those immediately responsible on site (those who in the event acknowledged what had occurred) were employees of the company and acting apparently within the course and scope of that employment. Certainly it could not be said of them (in contradistinction to the independent contractors responsible for the pollution in the *Welsh Water Authority* case) that 'they were not in any sense under the control of the [company] in the way they carried out and fulfilled their functions under the contract'. In my judgment, therefore, unless and until the company were themselves to call evidence displacing the clear inference otherwise arising from the facts found—that the pollution resulted directly from the company's own operation in constructing the water feature—it seems to me that the justices could not properly find here no case to answer. On the contrary, there appears to me to have been the clearest possible case.

It accordingly becomes unnecessary to examine in detail the later stages of Mrs Kennedy-McGregor's argument. Concluding as I do that the case falls four-square within the *Alphacell* principle, this is no occasion to attempt any general exegesis of vicarious liability in criminal law.

There are, however, a number of further matters I should briefly touch upon in deference to the width of counsel's submissions and researches. First, the draft criminal code produced (largely by Professor Sir John Smith QC) in 1989 as Law Commission Report No 177. Clause 29 of this code deals with vicarious liability; cl 30 with corporate liability. In essence, cl 29 would provide for liability for an act done by another only if that other is '(a) specified in the definition of the offence as a person whose act may be so attributed; or (b) acting within the scope of his employment or authority and the definition of the offence specifies the element in terms which apply to both persons'. Clause 30(1) would provide that: 'A corporation may be guilty as a principal of an offence not involving a fault element by reason of—(a) an act done by its employee or agent, as provided by section 29; or (b) an omission, state of affairs or occurrence that is an element of the offence.'

Paragraph 10.4 of the notes upon the draft code comments in respect of clause 30:

> '*Offences of strict liability.* Vicarious liability for offences of strict liability may attach to corporations as to other persons. Or a corporation may, for example, be the occupier of a building from a chimney of which dark smoke is emitted; or its activities may cause polluting matter to enter a stream. Then, like any other person, it can be liable for the emission or for causing the pollution, without fault on its part.'

Footnoted to that paragraph is reference inter alia to s 31(1)(a) of the Control of Pollution Act 1974. Quite how cl 30(1)(b) relates to Mrs Kennedy-McGregor's various categories of corporate criminal liability I remain unclear; I am, however, comforted in my conclusion on the present appeal by what I understand to be Professor Smith's view that one way or another a company is criminally liable if its 'activities' cause pollution—if, that is, its activities have involved 'an omission, state of affairs or occurrence'. Surely they have here.

Second, I should say a word about *Tesco Supermarkets Ltd v Nattrass* [1971] 2 All ER 127, [1972] AC 153, the decision which persuaded the justices that a company can only be liable under s 85 of the 1991 Act if the act which most immediately causes pollution is that of someone representing the controlling mind and will of the company. That, at least, is how I understand the justices' decision here. *Tesco v Nattrass* however was concerned with a very different situation. What was there in question was not whether the company was liable under an offence section, but rather whether it was entitled to invoke a defence section. That an offence (under s 11(2) of the Trade Descriptions Act 1968) was prima facie committed by the company through one of its employees acting on its behalf was not only clear but, indeed, the necessary assumption upon which the entire argument proceeded. What was in issue was whether the manager who was most directly at fault was 'another person' (ie a person other than the company itself) within the meaning of the defence section (s 24(1)(a) of the 1968 Act). The answer was Yes, because he was not of sufficient standing to be identified with the company itself as being or having its directing mind and will. Given, as I think established by *Alphacell*, that a company under s 85 *can* be guilty of causing pollution by the acts of its servants or agents—just as a company can be guilty of offering to supply goods under the provisions of s 11(2) of the 1968 Act—*Tesco v Nattrass* provides no assistance whatever in the present circumstances; the 1991 Act simply affords no relevant defence akin to that arising under s 24(1)(a) of the 1968 Act.

Nor, in my judgment, is any light shed on the present appeal by the recent
decisions in *Seaboard Offshore Ltd v Secretary of State for Transport, The Safe Carrier*   *a*
[1993] 3 All ER 25, [1993] 1 WLR 1025[b] and *Tesco Stores Ltd v Brent London BC*
[1993] 2 All ER 718, 1993] 1 WLR 1037. In *Seaboard* the Divisional Court allowed
a shipowner's appeal. Professor Smith, whilst trenchantly criticising much of
the court's reasoning, nevertheless approved its conclusion:

> 'The statute in the present case, in terms, imposes a personal duty on the   *b*
> owner "to take all reasonable steps to secure that the ship is operated in a
> safe manner". If the owner has taken all reasonable steps, it would seem to
> contradict the statute to convict him because someone else has behaved
> negligently.' (See his commentary at [1993] Crim LR 612 at 613.)

Here the corresponding duty upon the company was not 'to take all   *c*
reasonable steps' to avoid pollution; rather it was not to cause pollution.

In *Tesco Stores Ltd v Brent London BC* [1993] 2 All ER 718, [1993] 1 WLR 1037,
just as in *Tesco v Nattrass*, both the company and its employee were prima facie
liable under the offence section; unlike in *Tesco v Nattrass*, however, the
Divisional Court held in *Tesco v Brent* that the company could not invoke the   *d*
relevant defence section, there s 11(2) of the Video Recording Act 1984. Section
11(2), so the Divisional Court held, fell to be construed so as to attribute to the
company the employee's own state of mind. Right or wrong (and Professor
Smith suggests the latter (see [1993] Crim LR 612 at 625)), the decision has no
bearing on the present appeal.

I come finally to Mrs Kennedy-McGregor's reliance—pursuant to *Pepper*   *e*
(Inspector of Taxes) v Hart [1993] 1 All ER 42, [1993] AC 593—upon a statement
made by Lord Jowitt LC, during the House of Lords debate in 1951 upon the
Rivers (Prevention of Pollution) Bill:

> 'On the last occasion I said that I was inclined to think that if some
> worker, either by mistake or by malice aforethought, opened the wrong   *f*
> stopcock and allowed effluent to enter the river, the company would be
> responsible. I do not think that is right. It would not be right to say that
> the company "causes or knowingly permits"—and I stress "knowingly"—
> effluent to enter a stream unless the act has been done by some person for
> whom the company was responsible.' (See 172 HL Official Reports (5th   *g*
> series) col 508.)

Assuming for present purposes that the preconditions laid down in *Pepper v
Hart* for consulting Hansard in this fashion are here satisfied, there nevertheless
appear to me two insuperable obstacles in the company's path. First, that this
court is now in any event bound by the authoritative approach to s 85 of the   *h*
1991 Act determined by the House of Lords in *Alphacell Ltd v Woodward* [1972]
2 All ER 475, [1972] AC 824. Second, and more fundamentally still, that Lord
Jowitt LC's reference to 'some person for whom the company [is] responsible'
surely cannot refer, as Mrs Kennedy-McGregor has to submit it does, to 'a
senior officer' representing the controlling mind and will of the company.
Rather, the expression seems to me altogether more apt to describe a servant   *j*
acting within the course of his employment or an agent discharging his duties
under his principal's control. In short, subject only to the somewhat puzzling

---

b   Subsequent to the proceedings herein the decision of the Divisional Court in *Seaboard Offshore
      Ltd v Secretary of State for Transport, The Safe Carrier* [1993] 3 All ER 25, [1993] 1 WLR 1025 has
      been affirmed by the House of Lords (see [1994] 2 All ER 99, [1994] 1 WLR 541).

reference to a worker's 'mistake', Lord Jowitt LC's statement to my mind
a supports rather than contradicts the view which I have formed regarding the
scope of this offence—the view implicit, as I believe, in *Alphacell*.

It follows that I, for my part, would answer the question posed here by the
justices in the negative, adding only that the question to be asked in all cases
where a company is prosecuted under s 85 of the 1991 Act is whether as a matter
b of common sense the company by 'some active operation or chain of
operations' caused the pollution of the stream. As Lord Wilberforce observed,
difficulties may arise 'where acts of third persons or natural forces are
concerned'. In my judgment, however, no such difficulty arises from the mere
fact that most such operations are necessarily undertaken by the company's
servants or agents.

c Having answered in that way the question raised by the case stated, it further
follows that in my judgment the authority's appeal succeeds and the matter
must be remitted to the justices for rehearing.

MORLAND J. In May 1992 the respondents were constructing a new
d residential development at Goldwell Springs, East Malling. Through the site in
a culvert ran the Ditton Stream which beyond the site emerged into a lake
which flowed into the River Medway. On the site a water feature was being
constructed. Somehow, cement from this work entered the stream, polluting
it and killing fish.

On 21 May a water quality engineer of the appellants inspected the site, when
e the site agent and the site manager employed by the respondents admitted that
on the previous day cement had been washed into the stream during the
construction of the water feature. No point was taken before the magistrates
or before us that the admissions of the site agent and the site manager were not
admissible against the respondents.

On 28 September 1992 the respondents appeared before the magistrates at
f West Malling, charged with the offence of causing polluting matter, namely
wet cement, to enter controlled waters within the meaning of s 104 of the
Water Resources Act 1991, namely the Ditton Stream, contrary to s 85(1) of that
Act. At the conclusion of the prosecution case, Mrs Kennedy-McGregor
submitted, no doubt with the same excellence and skill that she has argued the
g case before us, that the respondents had no case to answer. The submission was
successful and the appellants have appealed by way of case stated.

The question for the opinion of the court is: whether the magistrates were
correct to conclude that an offence under s 85 of the 1991 Act could only be
committed by a company if the offence was committed by a person exercising
h the 'controlling mind and will' of the company, such as a director, manager,
secretary or some similar officer of the company, and therefore correct to find
that there was no case to answer and to dismiss the information.

My answer to the question is unhesitantly No. Indeed, any other answer
would render important environmental legislation almost entirely nugatory.

The question that the magistrates had to ask themselves when deciding on
j the respondent's submission was: 'Is there sufficient evidence upon which a
bench of magistrates, directing itself correctly in law and acting reasonably,
could find the case proved, assuming no more evidence is called?'

There was no issue as to the basic factual situation. Cement being used in the
construction of the water feature by the respondents polluted the stream.

Mrs Kennedy-McGregor submitted that although s 85(1) of the 1991 Act
created an offence of strict liability, guilt could only arise if the pollution was

caused by the respondent company through its directorate, or at least senior management, exercising the company's controlling mind and will. There was no evidence of that in this case.

Otherwise, she submitted, the respondent company could only be criminally liable if s 85(1) created an offence whereby a company became vicariously liable for offences in reality committed by their servants or agents. It would be exceptional if this were the case because invariably a statute creating vicarious liability also gives a 'due diligence' defence so that an employer or principal who had done everything that could be reasonably expected of him was not penalised as, for example, in *Tesco Supermarkets Ltd v Nattras* [1971] 2 All ER 127, [1972] AC 153. Other cases of strict liability imposed upon companies can be explained because a positive duty is imposed which could not be avoided by delegation, as, for example, in *Mousell Bros Ltd v London & North-Western Railway Co* [1917] 2 KB 836, [1916–17] All ER Rep 1101.

Mrs Kennedy-McGregor also submitted that s 85(1) of the 1991 Act created an offence of strict liability encompassing the world at large and not classes or sections of people such as users of vehicles, sellers of goods or licensees of public houses. It should be interpreted strictly, especially in the absence of any due diligence defence. If Parliament had intended not only the actual polluter to be criminally liable but also his principal or the company by whom he was employed, Parliament would have specifically said so by imposing vicarious liability by the insertion in the section of the words 'whether by himself, his servant or agent'.

Despite the skill and cogency of Mrs Kennedy-McGregor's arguments and her attempt to distinguish *Alphacell Ltd v Woodward* [1972] 2 All ER 475, [1972] AC 824 on the basis of the inherent design fault in the pumping system (see Viscount Dilhorne's speech [1972] 2 All ER 475 at 479, [1972] AC 824 at 836) and that thus the causative act of pollution was by the controlling mind and will of the company, in my judgment, her arguments are fallacious if the relevant words of s 85(1) of the 1991 Act are given a purposive interpretation.

The object of the relevant words of s 85(1) and the crime created thereby is the keeping of streams free from pollution for the benefit of mankind generally and the world's flora and fauna. Most significantly deleterious acts of pollution will arise out of industrial, agricultural or commercial activities. The damage occasioned may take years to repair and often at a cost running into thousands or millions of pounds. The act or omission by which the polluting matter enters a stream may result from negligence or may not. It does not matter. In almost all cases the act or omission will be that of a person such as a workman, fitter or plant operative in a fairly low position in the hierarchy of the industrial, agricultural or commercial concern.

In my judgment, to make the offence an effective weapon in the defence of environmental protection, a company must by necessary implication be criminally liable for the acts or omissions of its servants or agents during activities being done for the company. I do not find that this offends our concept of a just and fair criminal legal system, having regard to the magnitude of environmental pollution, even though no due diligence defence was provided for.

In my judgment, the dicta in *Alphacell Ltd v Woodward* entirely support this interpretation, although the question for the House was whether 'knowingly' qualified 'causes' in the earlier 1951 Act.

Lord Wilberforce said ([1972] 2 All ER 475 at 479, [1972] AC 824 at 834–835):

a   'In my opinion, this is a clear case of causing the polluted water to enter the stream. The whole complex operation which might lead to this result was an operation deliberately conducted by the appellants and I fail to see how a defect in one stage of it, even if we must assume that this happened without their negligence, can enable them to say they did not cause the pollution. In my opinion, complication of this case by infusion of the

b   concept of mens rea, and its exceptions, is unnecessary and undesirable. The section is clear, its application plain. I agree with the majority of the Divisional Court ([1971] 2 All ER 910, [1972] 1 QB 127) who upheld the conviction, except that rather than say that the actions of the appellants were *a cause* of the pollution I think it more accurate to say that the appellants caused the polluting matter to enter the stream ... it should not

c   be regarded as a decision that in every case the act of a third person necessarily interrupts the chain of causation initiated by the person who owns or operates the installation or plant from which the flow took place. The answer to such questions is one of degree and depends upon a proper attribution of responsibility for the flow of the polluting matter.' (Lord

d   Wilberforce's emphasis.)

It can be strongly argued that the respondents by their activities directly caused the flow of polluting matter into the stream. It is difficult to see in principle why it should matter whether those activities are essentially mechanical by their plant or essentially manual by their servants or agents. The

e   forbidden result is the same.

Viscount Dilhorne said ([1972] 2 All ER 475 at 482, [1972] AC 824 at 838–839):

'It was the operation of the works which led to the flow of liquid to the tanks. It was that operation which, with the system they had installed, led to the liquid getting into the river ... In these circumstances I see no escape

f   from the conclusion that it was the acts of the appellants that caused the pollution. Without their acts there would not have been this pollution. It was their operation of their works that led to the liquid getting into the tanks and their failure to ensure that the pumps were working properly that led to the liquid getting into the river.'

g   Lord Salmon said ([1972] 2 All ER 475 at 491, [1972] AC 824 at 848–849):

'If this appeal succeeded and it were held to be the law that no conviction could be obtained under the [Rivers (Prevention of Pollution) Act 1951] unless the prosecution could discharge the often impossible onus of proving that the pollution was caused intentionally or negligently, a great

h   deal of pollution would go unpunished and undeterred to the relief of many riparian factory owners. As a result, many rivers which are now filthy would become filthier still and many rivers which are now clean would lose their cleanliness. The legislature no doubt recognised that as a matter of public policy this would be most unfortunate. Hence s 2(1)(*a*) which

j   encourages riparian factory owners not only to take reasonable steps to prevent pollution but to do everything possible to ensure that they do not cause it.'

Although Lord Salmon was dealing with an entirely different point, 'mens rea', in my judgment, if, to succeed in such prosecutions, the authorities had to prove that the company by its 'controlling mind and will' caused the pollution rather than criminal liability vicariously by some human intervention by their

servants or agents in the company's activities, the effectiveness of the relevant
part of s 85(1) of the 1991 Act would be lost and the filthiness of rivers increased. *a*

I see no reason why Parliament as a matter of policy should not have placed
on principals, whether companies or others, the responsibility of
environmental protection. They are best placed to ensure that streams are not
polluted during their activities by their servants or agents. They can do this by
training, discipline, supervision and the highest standard of maintenance of *b*
plant.

As my interpretation of the words of the section is made without hesitation
or doubt, I do not consider it appropriate to consider the views recorded in
Hansard of Lord Jowitt LC during debate on the bill that became the 1951 Act.

In my judgment if the magistrates had directed themselves correctly in law
they must have found a case to answer. *c*

I would allow the appeal and order that the case be reheard by a fresh bench
of magistrates.

*Appeal allowed. Leave to appeal to the House of Lords refused but the court certified in
accordance with s 1(2) of the Administration of Justice Act 1960 that the following point *d*
of law of general public importance was involved: Whether a company may be liable for
the acts of its servants acting in the course of their employment in causing polluting
matter to enter controlled waters in contravention of s 85 of the Water Resources Act
1991, regardless of whether or not those servants were of such position within the
company that they could be said to be exercising the controlling mind or will of the
company.* *e*

Dilys Tausz   Barrister.

Re Leyland DAF Ltd
Re Ferranti International plc

CHANCERY DIVISION   *g*

LIGHTMAN J

12, 13, 14, 26 JULY 1994

*Company – Receiver – Appointment by debenture holder – Liability of receiver – Joint
administrative receivers appointed by debenture holders of two companies – *h*
Receivers informing company employees that their contracts of employment would
continue – Receivers asserting that they had not thereby adopted contracts or
assumed personal liability in respect of them – Employees claiming contractual
payments following redundancy – Whether receivers having adopted contracts of
employment – Whether receivers personally liable for contractual payments – If so, *j*
whether receivers' liability co-extensive with that of respective companies –
Insolvency Act 1986, s 44(1)(b).*

The applicants were the administrative receivers of two companies, L and F.
The receivers of L were appointed on 3 February 1993 and on the same day,
following accepted practice, they wrote to all employees saying that they

contemplated causing the company to continue to pay remuneration to them
in accordance with their contracts of employment but that they did not and
would not adopt those contracts or assume any personal liability in relation to
their present or future employment. The receivers of F were appointed on 1
December 1993 and on the following day they wrote to all employees
informing them that the company would remain their employer, that the
receivers themselves were not and would not become their employer and that
they had not assumed and would not assume any personal liability in relation
to their employment or adopt their contracts of employment. The receivers of
both companies continued to pay the employees' wages, but many employees
were made redundant over the succeeding months and those employees were
contractually entitled to various payments including pay in lieu of notice,
pension and redundancy payments, holiday pay and other benefits. The
receivers applied to the court seeking the following directions: (i) whether they
had 'adopted' the employees' contracts of employment for the purposes of
s 44(1)(b)[a] of the Insolvency Act 1986, which provided that an administrative
receiver was personally liable on any contract of employment adopted by him
in the carrying out of his functions, (ii) if so, whether their personal liability in
respect of those contracts could be legally excluded and (iii) if there was no legal
exclusion, whether their liability was co-extensive with that of the respective
companies. The respondents to the applications were individual employees
who had been made redundant and who represented different categories of
employee in the two companies, each with different types of contractual
entitlement against their employer. They contended that the receivers had
adopted their contracts of employment and could not exclude their personal
liability because although s 44 of the Act specifically permitted a receiver to
contract out of personal liability in the case of contracts entered into by him as
receiver, no such proviso applied to adopted contracts.

Held – (1) In cases of receivership the word 'adopted' in s 44(1)(b) of the 1986
Act was to be given the special meaning of 'treated as continuing in force'. On
that definition, it was clear from the letters written by the receivers of L and F
indicating that they contemplated causing the company to continue to pay
remuneration in accordance with the employees' contracts of employment that
they had adopted those contracts and the receivers' accompanying
protestations that, by so treating the contracts as continuing, they did not and
would not adopt the contracts of employment could not negate or qualify the
legal effect of their actions (see p 313 *j* to p 314 *b d* and p 319 *f*, post); *Powdrill v
Watson* [1994] 2 All ER 513 followed.

(2) On its true construction, s 44 of the 1986 Act did not prohibit limitation
by agreement of an administrative receiver's personal liability for adopted
contracts of employment. Indeed, the statutory policy was not to confer a right
on employees out of which they could not contract, but to prevent receivers
encouraging expectations of payment and then disappointing them. In order to
exclude personal liability however nothing less than a contract to that effect
would do and the court would be slow to infer that the employees had entered
into such a contract, surrendering their statutory protection, unless it was
evident that they had given a full and informed consent. On the facts, it was
clear beyond question that no such contract had been concluded because, in

---

a   Section 44, so far as material, is set out at p 312 *h j*, post

each case, the receivers' letter was no more than a unilateral declaration of non-liability and could not reasonably have been understood by the recipient employees as an offer requiring acceptance or rejection. Even if the letters did constitute offers, it would be totally unrealistic and unfair to treat the continued performance by the employees of their contracts of employment as an acceptance of a new contract excluding the statutory incident of personal liability, since any such exclusion would have had no immediate practical effect on the employees. The receivers in each case were accordingly personally liable on the adopted contracts of employment (see p 315 c d e f, p 316 c to e h and p 319 f, post); Jones v Associated Tunnelling Co Ltd [1981] IRLR 477 applied; Re Specialised Mouldings Ltd (13 February 1987, unreported) disapproved.

(3) While there might be some doubt whether Parliament really intended such a windfall for employees, the only tenable construction of s 44 of the 1986 which reflected the special protection afforded to employees under the legislation was that the liability of an adopting receiver was co-extensive with that of the company and covered all liabilities (whenever incurred and of whatever kind) arising under the adopted contract of employment. It was also plain, on the language of s 44, that such liability attached at and from the date of adoption and was not retrospective to the date of appointment. It followed that, in the absence of any limitation by agreement, the receivers' liability was co-extensive with that of the respective company (see p 317 d to f and p 319 d f g, post).

Notes

For effect of appointment of administrative receiver, see 7(2) Halsbury's Laws (4th edn reissue) paras 1159, 1196, 1399.

For the Insolvency Act 1986, s 44, see 4 Halsbury's Statutes (4th edn) (1987 reissue) 762.

As from 24 March 1994, s 44 of the 1986 Act was amended by s 2 of the Insolvency Act 1986 in relation to contracts of employment adopted on or after 15 March 1994.

Cases referred to in judgment

Anchor Line (Henderson Bros) Ltd, Re [1936] 2 All ER 941, [1937] Ch 1, CA.
Atlantic Computer Systems plc, Re [1992] 1 All ER 476, [1992] Ch 505, [1992] 2 WLR 367, CA.
Botibol (decd), Re, Botibol v Botibol [1947] 1 All ER 26.
Davis (S) & Co Ltd, Re [1945] Ch 402.
Diesels and Components Pty Ltd, Re [1985] 2 Qd R 456, (1985) 9 ACLR 825, Qld Full Ct.
Greenwood v Martins Bank Ltd [1933] AC 51, [1932] All ER Rep 318, HL.
Jones v Associated Tunnelling Co Ltd [1981] IRLR 477.
Lawson (Inspector of Taxes) v Hosemaster Machine Co Ltd [1966] 2 All ER 944, [1966] 1 WLR 1300, CA.
Leyland Daf Ltd v Automotive Products plc [1994] 1 BCLC 245, Ch D and CA.
Mack Trucks (Britain) Ltd, Re [1967] 1 All ER 977, [1967] 1 WLR 780.
Nicoll v Cutts [1985] BCLC 322, CA.
Phoenix Bessemer Steel Co, Re, ex p Carnforth Haematite Iron Co (1876) 4 Ch D 108, CA.
Powdrill v Watson [1994] 2 All ER 513, CA; affg [1994] 2 BCLC 118.
R v Grantham [1984] 3 All ER 166, [1984] QB 675, [1984] 2 WLR 815, CA.

R v Lockwood [1986] Crim LR 244, CA.
Specialised Mouldings Ltd, Re (13 February 1987, unreported), Ch D.

Application

John Andrew Talbot and Murdoch Lang McKillop, joint administrative receivers of Leyland DAF Ltd and Ferranti International plc, applied pursuant to s 35(1) of the Insolvency Act 1986 for, inter alia, directions as to whether they had adopted the employment contracts of the representative respondents, being, in the case of Leyland DAF, Ronald Douglas Cadge and Robert Sumner, and in the case of Ferranti, Maureen Grundy and John Ernest Parry, and whether the applicants were personally liable under s 44(1)(b) of the 1986 Act to make certain contractual payments to the respondents. The facts are set out in the judgment.

Patrick Elias QC and *Mark Phillips* (instructed by *Wilde Sapte* and *Allen & Overy*) for the receivers.
Charles Purle QC and *David Bean* (instructed by *Rowley Ashworth*) for the respondents.

Cur adv vult

26 July 1994. The following judgment was delivered.

LIGHTMAN J.

1. INTRODUCTION

I have before me originating applications by the administrative receivers of Leyland DAF Ltd (Leyland Daf) and Ferranti International plc (Ferranti) seeking directions whether they have adopted certain contracts of employment between their respective companies and these companies' employees and if so as to the extent (if any) of the personal liability assumed.

The applications raise important and far-reaching questions as to the meaning and effect of s 44(1)(b) of the Insolvency Act 1986. This section imposes on administrative receivers personal liability in respect of contracts of employment adopted by them. Section 19(5) of the 1986 Act provides that sums payable in respect of debts and liabilities incurred during an administration under contracts of employment adopted by an administrator shall be charged on the property of the company in administration in his custody or under his control. The legislature was impelled to make these specific provisions (initially in ss 50(1)(b) and 37(3)(b) of the Insolvency Act 1985, replaced by and consolidated in the sections in the 1986 Act) providing special protection for employees in case of both administrative receivership and administration by the lack of protection under the pre-existing law made apparent by the decision of the Court of Appeal in *Nicoll v Cutts* [1985] BCLC 322. Section 37(1) of the 1986 Act provides like protection in case of non-administrative receiverships. The meaning and effect of s 19(5) was considered by Evans-Lombe J and the Court of Appeal in *Powdrill v Watson* [1994] 2 BCLC 118; *affd* [1994] 2 All ER 513. The decision of the Court of Appeal occasioned the legislature to give second thoughts to this special protection and whether it went too far, and to pass the Insolvency Act 1994 which strictly limits that protection in case of contracts adopted on or after 15 March 1994 by administrators and administrative receivers, but not non-administrative receivers. The applications before me

concern contracts adopted (if adopted at all) by administrative receivers prior
to that date, and accordingly must be decided without regard to the provisions
of the 1994 Act. The problems raised on these applications and in *Powdrill* are
not isolated incidents. I am told that between 1987 and 1994 there have been
27,210 administrative receiverships and 1,172 administrations. Accordingly,
whilst the 1994 Act lays down the code for the future in respect of adoptions by
administrative receivers and administrators, since it is not retrospective and
does not extend to adoptions by non-administrative receivers, for many
contracts *Powdrill* and the applications before me will be test cases. An appeal
from the decision of the Court of Appeal in *Powdrill* is due to be heard by the
House of Lords on 5 December 1994. It is proposed that, whatever I decide, the
losing party will seek to 'leapfrog' the Court of Appeal and obtain a hearing of
an appeal by the House of Lords at the same time as the pending appeal in
Powdrill so as to obtain definitive guidance on both sections.

Sections 19(5) and 44(1)(b) plainly have an affinity, but their language and
operation are not identical. Accordingly, the decision of the Court of Appeal is
not necessarily determinative of the issues before me. In these circumstances,
it seems to me appropriate that I should in my judgment give a full and detailed
judgment reviewing the statutory legal context in which the sections fall to be
considered, and first reach a view of my own as to the construction and ambit
of s 44; and then, and then only, consider whether this view is confirmed or
precluded by the decision in *Powdrill*.

2. FACTS AND QUESTIONS RAISED

The parties have helpfully agreed the facts and questions to be answered in
respect of both companies and I can set these out briefly.

Leyland Daf

(1) History of receivership

(a) The Leyland Daf receivers were appointed on 3 February 1993, following
the collapse of Leyland Daf's Dutch parent company. At the date of the
appointment Leyland Daf owed approximately £570m to secured and
unsecured creditors.

(b) Leyland Daf owned six plants over the country and employed 5,371
individuals. The monthly wage bill was £7m and the Leyland Daf receivers had
no access to cash to fund it. On the day of their appointment the Leyland Daf
receivers wrote to all employees a letter (the Leyland Daf letter) intended to
state their attitude to future trading and the status of employment contracts
during the period of receivership trading. The key terms of the letter are as
follows:

> '... the receivers currently contemplate causing the Company, for such
> period as the receivers think fit, to continue to pay remuneration to you in
> accordance with your contract of employment ... Section 44(1)(b) of the
> Insolvency Act 1986 provides that an administrative receiver of a company
> is "personally liable on any contract of employment adopted by him in the
> carrying out of his functions". The receivers have not adopted, do not
> adopt, and will not at any future date adopt your contract of employment
> with the Company ... Section 44(1)(b) also provides that "an
> administrative receiver of a company is personally liable on any contract
> entered into by him in the carrying out of his functions (except in so far as

the contract otherwise provides)". The receivers themselves have not intended to enter nor do they intend to enter into any contract of employment with you. Nevertheless, to avoid any doubt, it is stressed that in any event the receivers have not assumed and will not at any future date assume any personal liability in relation to your present or future employment.'

The Leyland Daf receivers intended to pay, and in fact paid, employees' wages post-receivership as and when the liability to pay arose. Sending this letter followed the accepted practice in receivership cases.

   (c) On 12 February 1993, 1,552 employees were made redundant. On 16 February 1993 a further 74 employees were made redundant. These redundancies were made within the 14-day period provided in s 44 of the 1986 Act. Between 26 March 1993 and 10 September 1993, 957 employees were made redundant. As a consequence of the circumstances at the time, contractual notice was not given to these employees.

   (d) As a result of Leyland Daf's continued trading and a series of sales between 24 April 1993 and March 1994, 2,700 jobs were saved. This was achieved on the assumption that the claims of any employees not transferred to the purchasers would fall to be dealt with in a subsequent liquidation.

(2) The contractual position of the employees
   (a) There are two classes of employee: (i) 'Workshop employees', represented by the second respondent, Mr Sumner. There are 582 former employees who fall into this category. Mr Sumner was a fitter and latterly a workshop inspector for various Leyland Daf companies from 1958 until he was dismissed on 31 March 1993. His contract is in essence set down in the collective agreement covering pay, working practices and conditions of employment. (ii) 'Staff employees', represented by the first respondent, Mr Cadge. There are 375 former employees who fall into this category. Mr Cadge was a principal engineer who had been employed since September 1946 and was made redundant on 26 March 1993. His contract is primarily set out in the letter dated 2 February 1981.

   (b) The contracts of employment of these employees are contained in a series of collective agreements, letters sent to individual employees and Leyland Daf employee manuals. Under these contracts the employees are or may be entitled to benefits under six heads:

   (i) Notice
   (a) Workshop employees are generally entitled to one week's notice for each year of service up to a maximum of 12 weeks. Mr Sumner was entitled to 12 weeks' notice, making a claim (subject to mitigation) of £291,528. (b) Staff employees have different periods of notice. Mr Cadge is entitled to three months' notice, making a claim (subject to mitigation) of £667,108.

   (ii) Pensions
   The letters sent to employees encouraged them to join the pension scheme and advised them that unless they contracted out it would be assumed that they wished to be a member. (a) Mr Sumner's claim for pension payments falling due during his notice period is £116·61. (b) Mr Cadge's claim for pension payments falling due during his notice period is £266·84. The total value of the potential claims under this head together with claims in respect of medical insurance is £148,463·45.

(iii) Redundancy policy

Leyland Daf had a negotiated redundancy policy. The minimum sum payable was six weeks' pay. The provision for payment of compensation for loss of office, which constitutes an element of severance pay, is not contractually binding. The relevant policy document on employee redundancy compensation is stated in terms that the payment for compensation for loss of office 'is neither a right nor a contractual entitlement'. (a) Mr Sumner would have a claim under this policy of £4,372·92. (b) Mr Cadge would have a claim under this policy of £12,315·84.

(iv) Company car policy

Certain employees claim to be entitled to purchase their cars on termination at a discounted price. There are 142 employees who qualified for this benefit. Mr Cadge's loss for being unable to participate in the car purchase scheme is £692·51. The opportunity to purchase cars on termination was not part of the contracts of employment. The relevant policy document setting out the principles applicable states in terms that 'this policy does not establish any contractual entitlement or "right" to the privilege of discounted cars'.

(v) Medical and accident insurance

Some employees (and in particular Mr Cadge, but not Mr Sumner) were entitled to participate in Leyland Daf's BUPA scheme.

(vi) Holiday pay

(a) Mr Sumner was entitled to 25 days' holiday in accordance with cll 3 to 12 of the collective agreement. His claim to holiday pay is £291·53. (b) Mr Cadge's claim to holiday pay arises under cll 1 to 5 and 1 to 6 of the staff employment terms and conditions. He claims £307·90 under this head. The total potential claims to holiday pay are £143,573·41. (c) Part VII of the Employment Protection (Consolidation) Act 1978 (as amended) provides for the national insurance fund to guarantee employees the payment of certain debts owing from insolvent employers. The employees of Leyland Daf either have been paid, or are entitled to be paid the guaranteed sums out of this fund. Their claims against the Leyland Daf receivers fall to be reduced accordingly, although the Secretary of State is subrogated to those claims. Payment out of the fund accordingly does not affect any liability of the receivers.

(3) Questions raised

The questions raised by the Leyland Daf receivers are as follows. (1) Whether the contracts of employment of Mr Cadge and Mr Sumner were adopted by the receivers as such in carrying out their functions as administrative receivers within the meaning of s 44 of the 1986 Act. (2) Assuming that the contracts were adopted, whether the receivers in principle are personally liable on such contracts to make payment (together with interest or not) in respect of the following: (a) sums payable by way of damages for wrongful dismissal effected by them during the receivership: (i) in lieu of contractual notice under the respondents' contracts of employment; (ii) in respect of pension benefits to the extent that such benefits would have accrued to the respondents during their contractual notice periods; (iii) sums payable under the Leyland Daf's policies in relation to private medical insurance and accident insurance that the first respondent was entitled to; (b) holiday pay falling due by reason of the respondents' contract of employment; (c) sums payable under Leyland Daf's redundancy policy; (d) sums payable to the first respondent under Leyland Daf's car policy. (3) Whether such of the sums referred to above as the court directs should be paid to the respondents: (a) forthwith; or (b) on the vacation of office by the receivers; or (c) on the winding up of Leyland Daf.

Ferranti

(1) History of the receivership

On 1 December 1993 the Ferranti receivers were appointed. They were appointed receivers of Ferranti International plc, Ferranti Control Group plc, Ferranti International Holdings Ltd, Dundridge College Ltd, ISC Technologies Ltd and Ferranti Dynamics Ltd. I shall call the companies collectively 'Ferranti'. At the date of the appointments Ferranti owed approximately £111m to secured creditors, £5m to preferential creditors and £44·7m to unsecured creditors.

Ferranti's business was organised into four business units within which there were a number of different operations located throughout the UK. There were approximately 3,200 employees and the monthly wage bill was about £4·7m. The businesses of the Ferranti group were sophisticated and highly complex. Whether the businesses survived depended upon the continued performance of hundreds of contracts and on Ferranti's ability to secure future contracts. This gave rise to a number of difficulties and approximately 70 members of the Ferranti receivers' staff were used to conduct urgent investigations.

To ensure that Ferranti had the funds to continue trading whilst the Ferranti receivers carried out their investigations, the Ferranti receivers borrowed £5m on the basis of personal liability.

On 2 December 1993 (the day after their appointment) the Ferranti receivers wrote to all employees a letter (the Ferranti letter) intended to inform them in unambiguous terms that there was no question of the Ferranti receivers adopting their contracts of employment if they were kept on after the 14-day period stipulated in s 44(2) of the 1986 Act and that there was no intention on the part of the Ferranti receivers to incur any personal liability on those contracts of employment. The key terms of the letter are:

'(1) The Receivers themselves are not and will not become your employer. (2) On the contrary, the Companies have remained and, for so long as your employment continues, will remain your employer. (3) The Receivers have not assumed, and will not at any future date assume, any personal liability in relation to your employment. (4) Section 44(1)(b) of the Insolvency Act 1986 provides that an administrative receiver of a company is "personally liable on any contract of employment adopted by him in the carrying out of his functions". The Receivers have not adopted, do not adopt and will not at any future date adopt, your contract of employment with the Companies. (5) Section 44(1)(b) also provides that "an administrative receiver of a company is personally liable on any contract entered into by him in the carrying out of his functions (except in so far as the contract otherwise provides)". The Receivers themselves have not intended to enter nor do they intend to enter into any contract of employment with you. Nevertheless, to avoid any doubt, it is stressed that in any event the Receivers have not assumed and will not at any future date assume any personal liability in relation to your present or any future employment.'

The Ferranti receivers caused Ferranti to pay the employees' wages for the periods in which they continued to work.

On 10 December 1993, 611 employees were made redundant. The redundancies were discussed with the management and unions of Ferranti but it was impracticable to give the employees contractual notice. These redundancies were made within the 14-day period provided by s 44 of the 1986 Act.

Since 16 December 1993, 106 employees have been made redundant, 7 of whom were employed on the executive contract and the remaining 99 on the non-executive contract. As at 26 April 1994, 2,243 employees were still employed by the Ferranti group.

As a result of Ferranti's continued trading, two of the business units have been sold to GEC and 1,017 jobs saved. There is, at present, interest in the remaining business units.

(2) The contractual position of the employees

There are two classes of employee employed under one of two standard forms of contract: (a) Executive staff', represented by Mr Parry. This contract applies only to senior managers and 85 members of staff who were employed under this contract at the commencement of the receivership. Mr Parry was a materials manager at Ferranti's Oldham site. His employment with Ferranti began on 11 August 1986 and he was made redundant on 14 January 1994. Subject to mitigation, Mr Parry's claim is for £27,062·17. (b) Non-executive staff', represented by Mrs Grundy. This contract applies to all other grades of staff and 3,108 members of staff who were employed under this contract at the commencement of the receiverships. Mrs Grundy was a process worker at Ferranti's Oldham site. Her employment began on 28 March 1977 and she was made redundant on 4 February 1994. Subject to mitigation, Mrs Grundy's claim is for £4,564·33. Under their contracts the respondent employees are or may be entitled to benefits under five heads:

(i) Notice

(a) Under cl 12 of the executive contract, Mr Parry was entitled to six months' notice of termination and claims £17,336·52. The total potential claims under this head are £1,397,012. (b) Non-executive staff are entitled to four weeks' notice plus an additional week for every year after five years' service up to a maximum of 12 weeks. Mrs Grundy was entitled to 12 weeks' notice and claims £1,845·72. The total potential claims under this head are £356,054. There is a potential claim of £570,000 by Mr Davies, the former finance director who is one of a number of 'super-employees'.

(ii) Severance payment

(a) Under a severance payment and redeployment agreement dated 14 April 1991 Mr Parry was entitled to a severance payment of one month's pay plus five weeks' pay, totalling £6,376·63. The total potential claims under this head are £108,037. (b) Under the severance payment and redeployment agreement Mrs Grundy was entitled to a severance payment of one month's salary plus the maximum additional severance payment of 12 weeks' pay under cl 5. Her claim is for £2,514·80. The total potential claims under this head are £385,029.

(iii) Holiday pay

(a) Under the executive contract Mr Parry was entitled to 33 days of paid holiday. Under cl 6(d) of his contract, holiday pay on termination was calculated based on the number of completed weeks of service from 1 January

until the date of termination, less holiday taken. Mr Parry claims £132·85.
(b) Under the non-executive contract Mrs Grundy was entitled to 37 days of
paid holiday. Holiday pay on termination was calculated based on the number
of completed weeks of service from 1 January until the date of termination less
holiday taken. Mrs Grundy claims to be entitled to 2½ weeks of holiday pay
totalling £132·85. The Ferranti receivers believe that her claim is for £76·91.
The total potential claims for holiday pay are £50,218, of which £12,375 is the
potential liability to Mr Davies.
    (iv) Pensions
    (a) Mr Parry was a member of Ferranti's pension scheme. Clause 9 of the
executive contract refers to the Ferranti pension schemes. Mr Parry entered the
Ferranti pension scheme. (b) Mrs Grundy was a member of Ferranti's pension
scheme.   The booklet given to employees is referred to in cl 5 of the
non-executive contract. The booklet provides that 'the Company meets the
balance of the cost of providing the Scheme benefits' and '[t]he Company ... has
undertaken to meet the balance of the cost, as advised by the Scheme's actuary,
of providing all the Scheme benefits.' The claims for payment to the pension
scheme are considerable. The personal liability of the receivers in respect of
these claims is not in issue before me. Under the non-executive contract there
are claims for damages for non-payment of pension contributions of £39,086.
Under the executive contract the claims total £361,296. Mr Davies has a claim
for £60,000.   If the Ferranti receivers are personally liable to meet the
contributions required to top up the pension scheme for the year commencing
1 April 1993, the liability is approximately £4,485,000 notwithstanding the fact
that part of that liability is due in respect of the period prior to the appointment
of the receivers.
    (v) Mr Parry's company car
    Under cl 2.4 of his contract Mr Parry was provided with a car. The total claim
for motor cars is £8,157 under the non-executive contract and £22,986 under the
executive contract. Mr Davies has a claim for £15,387.
    The employees of Ferranti either have been paid, or are entitled to be paid,
the guaranteed sums out of the National Insurance Fund. Their claims against
the Ferranti receivers fall to be reduced accordingly, although the Secretary of
State is subrogated to those claims. Any personal liability of the receivers is
accordingly unaffected by payments out of the fund.
    The total liability of the Ferranti receivers to employees who have been
made redundant since 15 December 1993 is about £1,735,000. In addition there
is a claim by the pension fund trustees (which again is not in issue before me)
of £4,485,000 and potential liabilities to those staff still employed of
£10,114,000. The Ferranti receivers' potential personal liability is accordingly
over £17m.

(3) Questions raised
    The questions raised by the Ferranti receivers are as follows. (1) Whether
the contracts of employment of Mrs Grundy and Mr Parry were adopted by the
receivers as such in carrying out their functions as administrative receivers
within the meaning of s 44 of the 1986 Act. (2) Assuming that the contracts
were adopted, whether the receivers in principle are personally liable on such
contracts to make payment (together with interest or not) in respect of the
following: (a) sums payable by way of damages for wrongful dismissal effected
by them during their receivership: (i) in lieu of contractual notice under the

respondents' contracts of employment; (ii) in respect of pension benefits to the extent that such benefits would have accrued to the respondents during their contractual notice periods; (iii) in respect of health care scheme benefits to which the second respondent was entitled by reason of cl 5 of his contract of employment to the extent that such benefits would have accrued to the second respondent during his contractual period; (iv) in respect of the benefits of the provision of a motor car to the second respondent in accordance with cl 2.4 of his contract of employment to the extent that such benefits would have accrued to him during his contractual period; (b) sums due to the first respondent in respect of holiday pay falling due by reason of cl 3 of the first respondent's contract of employment; (c) sums due to the second respondent in respect of holiday pay falling due by reason of cl 6(d) of the second respondent's contract of employment; (d) sums due to the respondents under the terms of a severance payment and redeployment agreement dated 14 February 1991. (3) Whether such of the sums referred to in (2) above as the court directs should be paid, should be paid to the respondents: (a) forthwith; or (b) on vacation of office by the receivers; or (c) on the winding up of Ferranti.

3. RELEVANT LEGAL CONTEXT

Before examining the relevant legislation, it is, I think, appropriate to consider the rights and duties of employees and receivers under the pre-existing law which, subject to the changes thereby effected, remain in force.

(a) Liquidation and receivership expenses

In the case of a liquidation, a liquidator is ordinarily required to pay out of the assets of the company as liquidation expenses in priority to other creditors, not merely new debts incurred by the liquidator on behalf of the company, but also sums due under continuing obligations, e g under contracts of employment and supply agreements, which the liquidator chooses to continue (or 'adopt', as it is expressed in the cases: see Re Anchor Line (Henderson Bros) Ltd [1936] 2 All ER 941, [1937] Ch 11 and Re S Davis & Co Ltd [1945] Ch 402) for the benefit of the winding up, in respect of and limited to the period of liquidation. But there is no requirement of a receiver in a receivership to make any such payment. The reason for the distinction is that in the case of a liquidation the creditor is precluded during the liquidation from taking proceedings against the company to enforce his right to payment, but there is no such constraint on the creditor in case of a receivership (see Re Atlantic Computer Systems plc [1992] 1 All ER 476 at 482–486, [1992] Ch 505 at 520–525).

(b) Receivers' liability under contracts

(1) New contracts

It has always been a regular feature of a floating charge that it authorises the receiver to enter into contracts in the name and on behalf of the company, an authority which terminates on liquidation. Under the law of contract, a receiver should incur no personal liability under the contract any more than any other agent. But since the enactment of s 87(2) of the Companies Act 1947, which was immediately superseded by s 369(2) of the Companies Act 1948, statute has imposed personal liability on the receiver, 'except in so far as the contract otherwise provides'. Such liability is not a term of the contract but a statutory incident (see Lawson (Inspector of Taxes) v Hosemaster Machine Co Ltd

[1966] 2 All ER 944 at 950, [1966] 1 WLR 1300 at 1313). The current legislation in respect of the imposition of this incident is contained in the first part of s 44(1)(b).

(2) Continuing contracts

The appointment of a receiver out of court does not automatically determine continuing contracts (eg of employment or for the supply of goods) in effect at the date of his appointment unless the contract expressly or implicitly provides to the contrary or could no longer be performed consistently with the appointment and role of the receiver (see *Re Mack Trucks (Britain) Ltd* [1967] 1 All ER 977 at 982, [1967] 1 WLR 780 at 786, approved by Dillon LJ in *Nicoll v Cutts* [1985] BCLC 322 at 325). In the case of continuing contracts (subject to one qualification) the receiver is entitled on behalf of the company to require the employee or supplier to continue to honour the contracts. The qualification is that the insolvency of the company may amount to a declaration of inability to meet engagements when they become due and on this ground may entitle the employee or supplier to treat the contract as discharged (see *Re Phoenix Bessemer Steel Co, ex p Carnforth Haematite Iron Co* (1876) 4 Ch D 108).

(c) Pre-receivership liability

Pre-receivership unsecured debts and liabilities of the company continue after receivership as debts of the company, but they are debts which (save and to the extent that they are statutorily preferred under the provisions of the 1986 Act) the receiver is under no obligation to pay, whether personally or out of the charged assets. Save with the statutory exception of certain public utilities (s 233 of the 1986 Act) the creditor may (if his contract terms so permit) refuse to continue to supply or refuse to enter into a new contract with the company unless arrears are paid or the receiver accepts personal liability or both (see *Leyland Daf Ltd v Automotive Products plc* [1994] 1 BCLC 245 and the earlier cases which led to the statutory limitation on the exercise of monopoly power by utilities to achieve this advantage, cited in Lightman and Moss *Law of Receivers of Companies* (1986) p 60, n 2a). If the receiver accedes to such a demand, the creditor will obtain priority over other creditors including those on whom the status of preferential creditor is specifically conferred by the 1986 Act.

(d) Fraudulent trading

Under s 213 of the 1986 Act, if in the course of the winding up of a company it appears that the business of the company has been carried on with intent to defraud the creditors of the company, the court may on the application of the liquidator declare that any persons who were knowingly parties to the carrying on of the business in such manner are liable to make such contribution (if any) to the company's assets as the court thinks proper. The required intent to defraud is subjective, and not objective, and accordingly it is necessary to show that there was either an intent to defraud or a reckless indifference whether or not the creditors were defrauded (see *R v Lockwood* [1986] Crim LR 244). But there is a sufficient intent to defraud if credit is obtained at a time when the person knows that there is no good reason for thinking that funds will become available to pay the debt when it becomes due or shortly afterwards. It is unnecessary to establish knowledge that funds will never become available (see *R v Grantham* [1984] 3 All ER 166, [1984] QB 675).

A receiver carrying on the business of a company is exposed to a claim for fraudulent trading if he allows debts or liabilities to be incurred by the company (of particular relevance in this case) under continuing contracts during the receivership for which he has no personal liability and in respect of which he knows there is no good reason for thinking that they can or will be paid. Honesty requires no less. The responsibility of receivers in respect of such creditors has perhaps been insufficiently regarded in the past. Section 213 of the 1986 Act has scope for application in situations such as that which arose in *Nicoll v Cutts* [1985] BCLC 322 (see below).

4. THE DECISION IN NICOLL v CUTTS

Nicoll v Cutts [1985] BCLC 322 was decided whilst the Insolvency Bill 1985 was progressing through Parliament. In that case Mr Nicoll, the company's managing director, was the company's only working director. He was in charge of the day-to-day running of the company. He had a five-year contract and an annual salary of £7,500. Mr Nicoll was injured and spent five or six months in hospital. After the appointment of receivers no step was taken to determine Mr Nicoll's contract. Instead, Mr Nicoll discussed the company's business with the receiver from his hospital bed. At no stage did the receiver make it clear (or even suggest) to Mr Nicoll that it was not his intention to pay him for the services which he was providing. Subsequently Mr Nicoll was given notice terminating his employment which was effective about two months after the appointment of the receiver. Mr Nicoll claimed his salary for the period during which his employment had not been terminated. The receiver replied that he had no personal liability to pay and that Mr Nicoll could only prove for this remuneration in the company's liquidation which had supervened. In view of the company's insolvency, such a proof would not have resulted in any dividend. Mr Nicoll contended that it made no sense that an employee whose service contract is continued by the bank's receiver in order to assist in realising the company's assets to the best advantage should, as remuneration for the period of that continuation of his service contract, be relegated to a claim against the company and get nothing. The Court of Appeal held that, whilst they had considerable sympathy for Mr Nicoll, they could do nothing because the court had no power to order the receiver to pay him. This holding, that the receiver was not liable to pay for services provided by an employee, was the trigger for legislative reform.

5. SECTIONS 44 AND 19(5) OF THE 1986 ACT

The 1986 Act included two provisions for the protection of employees in the case of an administrative receivership in s 44 and in the case of an administration in s 19. These sections read as follows:

'44.—(1) The administrative receiver of a company—(a) is deemed to be the company's agent, unless and until the company goes into liquidation; (b) is personally liable on any contract entered into by him in the carrying out of his functions (except in so far as the contract otherwise provides) and on any contract of employment adopted by him in the carrying out of those functions; and (c) is entitled in respect of that liability to an indemnity out of the assets of the company.

(2) For the purposes of subsection 1(b) the administrative receiver is not to be taken to have adopted a contract of employment by reason of anything done or omitted to be done within 14 days after his appointment ...'

'19 ... (4) [The administrator's] remuneration and any expenses properly incurred by him shall be charged on and paid out of any property of the company which is in his custody or under his control at that time in priority to any security to which section 15(1) then applies.

(5) Any sums payable in respect of debts or liabilities incurred, while he was administrator, under contracts entered into or contracts of employment adopted by him or a predecessor of his in the carrying out of his or the predecessor's functions shall be charged on and paid out of any such property as is mentioned in subsection (4) in priority to any charge arising under that subsection. For this purpose, the administrator is not to be taken to have adopted a contract of employment by reason of anything done or omitted to be done within 14 days after his appointment.'

Both sections have one thing in common, namely the concern to make specific provision in the case of contracts of employment 'adopted' by the receiver and administrator. The subject of both sections is the same, namely adopted contracts. But there are in particular two immediately apparent and significant distinctions between the two sections: (a) s 44(1)(b) imposes personal liability on the receiver, who is entitled to an indemnity out of and a charge on the assets in the hands of the receiver, whilst s 19(5) merely creates a charge on the assets the subject of the administration; and (b) under s 44(1)(b) the receiver's liability is 'on' the adopted contracts, whilst under s 19(5) the charge is limited to sums payable in respect of debts and liabilities incurred whilst he is an administrator under the adopted contract. In short, the intended legal consequences are different.

The statutory purpose of these sections was to overrule the effect of *Nicoll v Cutts* [1985] BCLC 322 (see *Re Atlantic Computer Systems plc* [1992] 1 All ER 476 at 486, [1992] Ch 505 at 524 per Nicholls LJ). But whilst Parliament clearly wished to be seen to act, it was less anxious to make plain what it had done, and this has given rise to the issues in this action.

6. THE ISSUES

The issues raised on the application are threefold: (1) the meaning of 'adoption' and whether in this case Leyland Daf and Ferranti adopted the contracts of employment of their employees; (2) if the answer to (1) is in the affirmative, whether the personal liability of the receivers in respect of such adopted contracts (a) can legally be excluded and if so (b) whether it was in this case; and (3) if the answer to (2) is to the effect that there was no exclusion, the extent of the obligations under the adopted contracts to which personal liability extends.

(1) Meaning of adoption

The word 'adoption' in respect of a contract has a variety of different meanings in different contexts. It may mean 'novation' (see eg *Greenwood v Martins Bank Ltd, Botibol v Botibol* [1933] AC 51 at 57, [1932] All ER Rep 318 at 321 per Lord Tomlin and *Re Botibol (decd)* [1947] 1 All ER 26 at 28 per Evershed J). It may (in case of a contract entered into by an agent without authority) mean 'ratify'. Adoption, however, in cases of receivership has a special meaning. 'What is meant by saying that a receiver has power to "adopt" a pre-receivership contract is that he may refrain from repudiating it' (see *Re Diesels and Components Pty Ltd* [1985] 2 Qd R 456 at 459 per McPherson J). Adoption has the same meaning in the context of a liquidation when the question arises whether the liquidator has so acted as to render the liability to the other party part of the costs of the liquidation, as opposed to a mere provable debt (see *Re Anchor Line (Henderson Bros) Ltd* [1936] 2 All ER 941, [1937] Ch 1 and *Re S Davis & Co Ltd* [1945] Ch 402). Accordingly, as it seems to me, in the context of s 44, the word 'adopted' must be given the meaning 'treated as continuing in force'. It is fair to say that this is the view expressed in *Lightman and Moss* pp 203–206 and I can see no reason to resile from it (or indeed the views expressed on some of the other issues raised on these applications).

No distinction can be drawn, as it seems to me, from the meaning of the word 'adopted' in ss 44 and 19. The construction of the word in the context of s 19 adopted by the Court of Appeal (Dillon and Leggatt LJJ) in *Powdrill* [1994] 2 All ER 513 at 520, 521 is to this very effect, namely the express or implied acceptance of the contract's continuance, a restatement of the language of Professor Goode in *Principles of Corporate Insolvency Law* (1990), cited with approval by Evans-Lombe J and by Dillon LJ, namely acts or acquiescence after expiry of the 14-day period indicative of the intention to treat the contract as on foot.

In these circumstances there can be no dispute that the contracts of employment of the employees of Leyland Daf and Ferranti were adopted by the respective receivers. The protestations by the receivers in their letters that they were not, by so treating the contracts as continuing, adopting them cannot negate or qualify the legal effect of their actions.

(2) Exclusion of liability

Before considering questions of exclusion it is appropriate to consider the character of the liability imposed on the receiver by s 44. It seems to me quite clear that the character is the same as that imposed on receivers who contract without excluding personal liability. The liability is not a term of the contract, but a statutory incident of it.

(a) Power to exclude

Mr Purle QC for the employees submits that the language and policy of the 1986 Act precludes any arrangement or agreement between the receiver and employee excluding this personal liability. He draws attention to the way that s 44 of the 1986 Act specifically permits a receiver to contract out of personal liability in the case of contracts entered into by him as receiver, and the absence of any like provision in respect of adopted contracts, and he stresses the statutory policy underlying the section to protect employees, which (he says) would be undermined if the receiver could as a matter of course contract out of his liability.

There are, as it seems to me, a number of answers to this submission. First, as a matter of language, the proviso requiring a provision in the contract excluding personal liability if personal liability is to be avoided in case of contracts entered into by the receiver is quite inapposite in case of the adoption of a contract by the receiver. The act of adoption does not require and in any ordinary case will not take the form of a contract between the receiver and employee, and accordingly a statutory proviso that liability may be excluded by a term in the contract would not be appropriate. Accordingly I do not think that the absence of an express provision for an agreement excluding personal liability in the case of adopted contracts is of particular significance.

Of far greater significance are the facts that: (i) in many cases it may only be sensible for a receiver to adopt a contract of employment if he can agree some limitation on his personal liabilities, his only alternative being to dismiss. I can see no reason why Parliament should forbid him to enter into such an agreement, which may be for the benefit of the employees as well as himself; (ii) the receiver can in any event dismiss and re-engage employees on terms excluding personal liability. Again, I can see no reason why this should be necessary instead of an agreement to allow the existing employment to continue, but excluding personal liability. There is plainly nothing to prevent receivers in new contracts of employment contracting out of personal liability.

As it seems to me, the statutory policy is not to confer upon employees a basic right which they cannot contract out of, but to prevent receivers encouraging expectations of payment and then disappointing them; and in particular the unfair exploitation of employees by receivers, in the absence of the unequivocal and informed agreement of the employees, taking the benefit of their services without at the same time accepting legal responsibility for payment.

I can see no hint of, or reason for, any statutory prohibition on employees contracting out of the protection afforded by s 44. I am comforted by the fact that in *Powdrill* [1994] 2 BCLC 118 at 127 Evans-Lombe J at first instance took the same view in respect of administrators contracting out of s 19(5). The Court of Appeal expressed no view on the question as it did not arise.

(b) Actual exclusion

For exclusion of the statutory incident of personal liability, it is plain that what is required is a contract to this effect between the receiver and the affected employees and nothing less will do. The statutory incident of personal liability should be capable of removal whatever the capacity in which the receiver contracts for its removal, whether personally or as agent for the company. But as it seems to me, the court should be slow to infer that the employees have entered into such contract surrendering their statutory rights unless it is plain that they have given a full and informed consent.

Mr Elias QC has very properly in this context brought to my attention the case of *Jones v Associated Tunnelling Co Ltd* [1981] IRLR 477. The Employment Appeal Tribunal (albeit obiter) gave consideration in that case to the question how far the assent to a variation in the contractual terms of employment should be implied from the mere failure of an employee to object to the unilateral alteration by the employer of the terms of his employment contained in a statutory statement. Browne-Wilkinson J, giving the decision of the tribunal in a passage which I gratefully adopt, said (at 481):

'In our view, to imply an agreement to vary or to raise an estoppel against the employee on the grounds that he has not objected to a false record by the employers of the terms actually agreed is a course which should be adopted with great caution. If the variation relates to a matter which has immediate practical application (eg, the rate of pay) and the employee continues to work without objection after effect has been given to the variation (eg, his pay packet has been reduced) then obviously he may well be taken to have impliedly agreed. But where, as in the present case, the variation has no immediate practical effect the position is not the same. It is the view of both members of this Tribunal with experience in industrial

relations (with which the Chairman, without such experience, agrees) that
it is asking too much of the ordinary employee to require him either to
object to an erroneous statement of his terms of employment having no
immediate practical impact on him or be taken to have assented to the
variation. So to hold would involve an unrealistic view of the inclination
and ability of the ordinary employee to read and fully understand such
statements. Even if he does read the statement and can understand it, it
would be unrealistic of the law to require him to risk a confrontation with
his employer on a matter which has no immediate practical impact on the
employee. For those reasons, as at present advised, we would not be
inclined to imply any assent to a variation from mere failure by the
employee to object to the unilateral alteration by the employer of the terms
of employment contained in a statutory statement.'

It seems to me clear beyond question that neither the Leyland Daf nor the
Ferranti letter was or should reasonably have been understood by the recipient
employees as an offer requiring acceptance or rejection. They constituted
merely unilateral declarations of 'non-liability'. But even if they did constitute
offers, since the exclusion of personal liability of the receiver had no immediate
practical effect on the employees, it would be totally unrealistic and unfair to
treat the continued performance by the employees of their contracts of
employment as an acceptance of a new contract by way of variation of their
contract of employment excluding the statutory incident of personal liability.
The statutory personal liability accordingly continues to attach to the receivers.

Mr Elias did at one point submit that a more relaxed attitude should be
adopted in inferring an arrangement or agreement to displace personal liability.
He explained with conviction the heavy burden on receivers on taking office,
the impracticality of obtaining written acceptances by employees of offers
within the statutory 14-day period, and the damaging consequences for all
concerned if the receiver is obliged in order to protect himself from personal
liability to dismiss all employees and then re-engage them. He also made a plea
that the finding of the requirement for an agreement excluding liability
operated harshly on receivers who had acted and developed an established
practice based upon the decision in *Re Specialised Mouldings Ltd* (13 February
1987, unreported, but referred to by Dillon LJ in *Powdrill* [1994] 2 All ER 513 at
520–521) to the effect that sending letters in terms of the Leyland Daf and
Ferranti letters was effective to exclude personal liability.

I can only respond that Parliament in the 1986 Act plainly did not intend that
liability in respect of adopted contracts should be avoided by anything less than
liability under new contracts entered into by the receiver. The receiver was
given the free choice between adoption and repudiation: he was not given the
third free choice of adoption in the absence of agreement of the employees
without assuming personal liability. This may be unfortunate for the receiver
and the receivership, but would negate the protection intended for employees
and restore the position to that prevailing in *Nicoll v Cutts* [1985] BCLC 322.

As regards reliance on the decision in *Re Specialised Mouldings* and the
established practice of insolvency practitioners based upon it, it is difficult to
believe that there was not involved on the part of such practitioners some
degree of wishful thinking. This decision in *Re Specialised Mouldings* cannot (as
Dillon LJ pointed out in *Powdrill*) have been intended by the judge as a
precedent in other cases. Certainly even before *Powdrill* the decision, given

without reasons, was regarded by lawyers at best as one 'to be treated with caution' (see eg Marshall and Broomhead *Employment Insolvency Handbook* (1992) pp 22–25), and was indeed authoritatively stated to be wrong (see Professor Goode in *Principles of Corporate Insolvency Law* p 101).

By the end of his argument I think that Mr Elias fairly and correctly accepted that nothing less than a contract with the employees was required, in effect conceding that the decision in *Re Specialised Mouldings Ltd* was not even arguably sustainable.

(c) *Extent of liabilities*

Mr Elias has submitted that as a matter of construction of s 44 there are three possible alternatives regarding the extent of the liabilities assumed by the 'adopting' receiver: (1) all liabilities whenever incurred of whatever kind under the adopted contract; (2) liabilities incurred under the contract whilst receiver; (3) liabilities for services rendered to the company during the receivership.

The second alternative equates the liability of the receiver to that of the administrator in respect of adopted contracts under s 19(5) as held in *Powdrill*. The third alternative equates the liability to that imposed in respect of contracts adopted on or after 15 March 1994 under the 1994 Act.

Whilst there may be doubt whether Parliament really intended such a windfall for employees and indeed anything more than the third alternative as the antidote to *Nicoll v Cutts* [1985] BCLC 322, as a matter of language, it seems to me the only tenable construction is the first alternative. As Leggatt LJ said in respect of a related question in *Powdrill* [1994] 2 All ER 513 at 525: 'Whatever the consequences for insolvency law ... the point is in my judgment too plain for argument.' Section 44(1)(b) equates the statutory incident of personal liability of the receiver in the case of liability on employment contracts adopted by the receiver in carrying out his functions to the statutory incident of personal liability on new contracts which do not exclude personal liability entered into by him in the carrying out of his functions. In both cases the liability is co-extensive with that of the company. I can find no handle within the language used on which to fasten any limitation, nor could Mr Elias suggest any.

Mr Elias has helpfully and forcibly addressed me as to the damaging consequences that will ensue from such a construction on receiverships and the achievement of corporate rescues which the 1986 Act is designed to achieve. He submits that the first construction should be rejected because it (a) goes beyond the mischief in *Nicoll v Cutts* which s 44(1)(b) was designed to remedy; (b) involves receivers being required to assume blind open-ended commitments; (c) creates difficulties for receivers and in particular in respect of distributions and the discharge of the receivership; and (d) subverts the rescue culture in respect of companies in difficulties which the 1986 Act was designed to promote.

(i) As regards remedying the mischief revealed by the decision in *Nicoll v Cutts*, the mischief could be remedied in a multitude of ways and it seems to me that all three alternative constructions remedy the mischief: the mischief rule affords no light as to which construction should be adopted.

(ii) I am concerned that the decision by receivers whether or not to adopt employment contracts (a course which may be critical to saving a business and the jobs of employees) if the decision is to be made within the statutory 14 days must frequently be made without any adequate opportunity to investigate, let alone evaluate, the possible claims in respect of which an open-ended personal liability is to be assumed. The potential liability makes adoption a risky course which receivers must think twice about (and on occasions consult their appointors) before undertaking. The answer to this dilemma for receivers, as I read the 1986 Act, is that if they are not prepared to take this risk, they must decline to adopt. Any other answer, limiting their exposure, must be found in legislation (as in the 1994 Act) and not a forced construction of the 1986 Act.

(iii) As regards distribution and discharge, I recognise that the personal liability on adopted contracts will continue to subsist until the liability is discharged and that this may create problems in the way of distribution of realisations and the discharge of the receivership. But the problem is no different in kind from that posed in respect of new contracts entered into by the receiver which do not exclude personal liability. The receivers may be compelled to proceed on a 'worst case' estimate, but this course is not an unfamiliar one, eg when there is outstanding litigation, and to insist on protection by way of indemnity, security or otherwise before they pay their appointor or agree to be discharged. Whilst I appreciate the practical advantages for the receiver and receivership in this respect of adopting the other constructions and the disincentive which my preferred construction may create on the adoption of employment contracts, I do not think that this construction is so obviously unreasonable that another should be adopted which finds no like basis in the statutory language.

(iv) As regards the rescue culture which prevails today, no doubt one of the most important resources of a business over which a receiver is appointed is likely to be the employees, and it will facilitate a rescue if the receiver can keep the workforce together without incurring any or any substantial personal liability. But the legislation recognises that the employees in respect of their labour are not to be treated in the same way as other suppliers of goods and services under continuing contracts. They merit special protection. They are specially vulnerable and unlikely to have the muscle to be able to insist (as may some other suppliers under continuing contracts) on payment or special treatment in respect of sums already accrued due or to accrue in the future. I do not think it is inconceivable or absurd to infer from s 44 of the 1986 Act that Parliament intended the receiver, if he intended to exploit this resource, to honour the employees' contracts in full; nor do I think it inconceivable or absurd to infer that Parliament may have considered that the real issue in many cases such as the present is not really one of personal liability of the receivers, but of priorities in payment between the debenture holder (generally a bank) and the employees. This is the case here where the assets of both companies subject to the crystallised floating charge are more than ample to pay the employees in full. The receiver has a charge on these assets to secure his liability. When the assets are not sufficient or there is any risk of the personal liability exceeding the value of the assets to which the receiver can look for payment, no doubt the receiver can and will before incurring personal liability require an indemnity from his appointor. It may be that this 'priority' of the employees may deter some rescues; some appointors will not wish to take the risk that the costs of discharging all liabilities to employees under adopted contracts will fall upon them if the rescue fails to achieve a sufficient return. But I cannot think that this consequence must be seen to be so inconsistent with the legislation or its purpose as to deny the employees under adopted contracts the protection which prima facie the language affords them.

I should add that nothing decided in *Powdrill* on the different wording of s 19(5) impinges on my decision as to the extent of the liability imposed on receivers by s 44(1)(b).

7. DATE OF COMMENCEMENT OF PERSONAL LIABILITY

I have been asked to decide the date on which the personal liability of the receiver attaches, namely retrospectively to the date of appointment or the date of adoption. This question does not have the significance it would have if I had reached a different view on the extent of liabilities arising on adoption. Mr Elias argues that retrospectivity to the date of appointment has the advantages (a) of consistency with the practice in liquidation where payment as a liquidation expense for continuing services and supplies runs from the date of liquidation; (b) of certainty, avoiding possible difficult inquiries as to the date of adoption; and (c) of harmonising with the existing preference given to employees which relates to the period immediately prior to the appointment. But it seems to me plain on the language of the section that liability attaches at and from the date of adoption and is not retrospective to the date of appointment. By virtue of s 44(2), this will be on the fifteenth day after the appointment or the earliest date thereafter on which adoption takes place. It would appear that it is not legally possible for a receiver deliberately to adopt a contract earlier than the fifteenth day though this may be thought the only or best method of holding on to essential employees. Earlier than this date he can, however, contract to adopt after the statutory period for taking stock has expired or contract immediately to assume an equivalent obligation.

8. ANSWERS TO QUESTIONS

In view of my decision on the construction of the 1986 Act, the answer to all questions raised is simple, namely the receivers (i) have adopted the contracts of employment, (ii) have not contracted out of their personal liability, and (iii) are personally liable co-extensively with the companies in respect of all contractual (but no other) liabilities under the contracts of employment of the employees irrespective of the dates on which they accrued or the periods in respect of which the liability arose.

The receivers are bound to pay forthwith, as they are bound to discharge forthwith all immediate obligations under new contracts they enter into without an exclusion of personal liability. It is common ground that the receivers have no obligation to pay interest: any such obligation can only arise when and if the employees sue for payment. This is clearly correct.

It is, I think, agreed that there is no dispute as to which of the items detailed in the originating application are contractual. The detailed answers are as follows:

Leyland Daf

1. The contracts of employment of the first respondent Mr Cadge and the second respondent Mr Sumner have been adopted by the administrative receivers of Leyland Daf in the carrying out of their functions as such receivers within the meaning of s 44 of the 1986 Act.

2(1) The administrative receivers in principle are personally liable on such contracts to make payments in respect of the following: (a) sums payable by way of damages for wrongful dismissal effected by them during the receivership: (i) in lieu of contractual notice under the respondents' contracts of employment; (ii) in respect of pension benefits, to the extent that such benefits would have accrued to the respondents during their contractual notice periods; (iii) in respect of Mr Cadge's entitlement under Leyland Daf's policies in relation to private medical insurance and accident insurance; (b) all holiday pay falling due under the respondents' contract of employment. But the administrative receivers are not liable to pay: (c) under Leyland Daf's redundancy policy compensation for loss of office, or (d) under Leyland Daf's company's car policy for loss of opportunity to purchase cars at a discounted price on termination of employment.

(2) The administrative receivers are not presently liable to pay interest on any sum so due.

(3) The sums referred to in 2 above should be paid to the respondents forthwith.

Ferranti International plc

1. The contracts of employment of the first respondent Mrs Grundy and the second respondent John Parry have been adopted by the administrative receivers of Ferranti in the carrying out of their functions as such receivers within the meaning of s 44 of the 1986 Act.

2(1) The administrative receivers in principle are personally liable on such contracts to make payments in respect of the following: (a) sums payable by way of damages for wrongful dismissal effected by them during the receivership: (i) in lieu of contractual notice under the respondents' contracts of employment; (ii) in respect of pension benefits, to the extent that such benefits would have accrued to the respondents during their contractual notice periods; (iii) in respect of health care schemes benefits, to which the second respondent was entitled by reason of cl 5 of his contract of employment to the extent that such benefits would have accrued to him during his contractual notice period; (iv) in respect of the benefit of the provision of a motor car to Mr Parry in accordance with cl 2.4 of his contract of employment, to the extent that such benefits would have accrued to him during his contractual notice period; (b) all sums due to Mrs Grundy in respect of holiday pay falling due by reason of cl 3 of her contract of employment; (c) all sums due to John Parry in respect of holiday pay falling due by reason of cl 6(d) of his contract of employment; (d) all sums due to the respondents under the terms of the severance payment and redeployment agreement dated 14 February 1991.

(2) The administrative receivers are not presently liable to pay interest on any sum so due.

3. The sums referred to in 2 above should be paid to the respondents forthwith.

Declarations accordingly.

Celia Fox   Barrister.

R v Inspectorate of Pollution and another, ex parte Greenpeace Ltd

COURT OF APPEAL, CIVIL DIVISION

GLIDEWELL, SCOTT AND EVANS LJJ

1, 3 SEPTEMBER 1993

Judicial review – Application for judicial review – Application for leave to apply for judicial review – Grant of leave – Applicant seeking to challenge executive decision authorising action by third party – Court granting leave to apply for judicial review, but refusing to grant stay of decision pending hearing of substantive application – Grant of stay would adversely affect third party's operations – Principles to be applied by court in deciding whether to grant stay.

The respondent government departments granted an authorisation under the Radioactive Substances Act 1960 to a company, BNFL, to operate a thermal oxide reprocessing plant. BNFL subsequently applied for and obtained a variation of the existing authorisation to enable it to complete a ten-week testing programme involving the discharge of radioactive waste before the plant went into operation. The applicant, an environmental protection organisation which was concerned about the levels of radioactive discharge from the plant, sought to challenge the variation of the authorisation and applied to the High Court for leave to apply for judicial review by way of an order of certiorari to quash the respondents' decision to grant the variation. The judge granted leave to apply for judicial review, but refused to grant a 14-day stay on the implementation of the varied authorisation pending a full hearing of the application on the grounds that the governmental body charged with the task of deciding whether the plant could be operated safely had issued the variation of the authorisation, that the additional radioactive discharge from the plant would be contained within the permitted volumes, that BNFL would suffer substantial financial loss as a result of delay in the testing process and that the applicant had given no cross-undertaking in damages to compensate the third party for any financial loss it might suffer and was unlikely to be able to do so. The applicant appealed, contending (i) that where interlocutory relief in the form of a stay was sought in judicial review proceedings, a requirement that an undertaking in damages be given as a condition of the grant of relief was inappropriate and (ii) that there was fresh material relating to the testing procedure (which was to be in three phases with increasing quantities of liquid effluent and aerial activity) which might have enabled the judge to adopt a half-way position and grant a five or six-day stay to take effect at the beginning of the second and more detrimental phase. BNFL contended that there was nothing in the fresh evidence to invalidate the balance of convenience reasons given by the judge in justification of his decision.

Held – Where the real purpose of interlocutory relief in a judicial review case was to prevent executive action by a third party in pursuance of rights which had been granted by the decision under attack and that purpose was pursued by an application for a stay of the decision, the court, in considering whether to grant the stay, should look to the substance rather than the form of the application and apply the same principles as would have been applicable if the application had been for an interlocutory injunction. It followed that the judge had applied the correct principles on the balance of convenience in refusing the stay, since the variation allowed for the discharge of radioactive material within permitted limits and the applicant had given no cross-undertaking in damages. Moreover (Evans LJ dissenting), the additional evidence available since the hearing of the application was not sufficient to invalidate the judge's refusal to grant the stay as the balance of convenience rationale applied as much to the 14-day delay to the testing period as to the proposed shorter delay. The appeal would accordingly be dismissed (see p 324 d e, p 326 e to j, p 327 a f to j and p 328 a to d, post).

American Cyanamid Co v Ethicon Ltd [1975] 1 All ER 504 and dictum of Lord Diplock in Hadmor Productions Ltd v Hamilton [1982] 1 All ER 1042 at 1046 applied.

Notes

For judicial review generally, see 37 Halsbury's Laws (4th edn) paras 567–583, and for cases on the subject, see 16 Digest (Reissue) 321–435, 3362–4797.

For the Radioactive Substances Act 1960, see 47 Halsbury's Statutes (4th edn) 755.

As from 27 August 1993, the 1960 Act was repealed by the Radioactive Substances Act 1993, s 50, Sch 6. For the 1993 Ac which replaces the 1960 Act, see 47(S) ibid 133.

Cases referred to in judgments

American Cyanamid Co v Ethicon Ltd [1975] 1 All ER 504, [1975] AC 396, [1975] 2 WLR 316, HL.

Hadmor Productions Ltd v Hamilton [1982] 1 All ER 1042, [1983] 1 AC 191, [1982] 2 WLR 322, HL.

R v Secretary of State for Education and Science, ex p Avon CC [1991] 1 All ER 282, [1991] 1 QB 558, [1991] 2 WLR 702, CA.

Cases also cited or referred to in skeleton arguments

M v Home Office [1993] 3 All ER 537, [1994] 1 AC 377, HL.

Minister of Foreign Affairs, Trade and Industry v Vehicles and Supplies Ltd [1991] 4 All ER 65, [1991] 1 WLR 550, PC.

R v Secretary of State for the Home Dept, ex p Muboyayi [1991] 4 All ER 72, [1992] 1 QB 244, CA.

Interlocutory appeal

The applicant, Greenpeace Ltd, appealed with leave from that part of the judgment of Brooke J given on 1 September 1993 whereby, having granted the applicant leave to apply for judicial review by way of an order of certiorari to quash the decision of the respondents, HM Inspectorate of Pollution and the Minister of Agriculture, Fisheries and Food (the departments), dated 25 August 1993, to issue a variation of authorisations granted to British Nuclear Fuels plc (BNFL), an interested party, under the Radioactive Substances Act 1960 for the discharge of radioactive waste from their plant at Sellafield, Cumbria, he refused to grant the applicant a stay of the departments' decision to issue the variation pending the hearing of the substantive application. The facts are set out in the judgment of Glidewell LJ.

Owen Davies (instructed by *Sarah Jane Burton*) for Greenpeace.
Kenneth Parker QC and *Mark Shaw* (instructed by the *Treasury Solicitor*) for the
    departments.
George Newman QC and *Alan Griffiths* (instructed by *Freshfields*) for BNFL.

GLIDEWELL LJ. This is an appeal by Greenpeace Ltd against a decision of
Brooke J given two days ago on the afternoon of 1 September 1993, when,
having granted Greenpeace leave to apply for judicial review of the decision of
the respondents, HM Inspectorate of Pollution and the Minister of Agriculture,
Fisheries and Food (the departments), to issue a variation of an authorisation
under the Radioactive Substances Act 1960 in relation to the premises of British
Nuclear Fuels plc (BNFL) at Sellafield, he then refused an application for a stay
of the departments' decision to issue the variation. It is against the refusal to
grant a stay that this appeal lies.

Put shortly, the position is that the application concerns the thermal oxide
reprocessing plant which has been constructed by BNFL at Sellafield, formerly
Windscale, in Cumbria.

The proposed construction of that plant was the subject of a lengthy inquiry
in 1977, after which an unusual statutory process was followed by which
planning permission was given by Parliament for the construction of the plant.
Construction then started and was completed in February 1992. So far, the
plant, which is designed for the reprocessing of nuclear fuel from certain
nuclear power stations, has not operated.

There is already in existence an authorisation from the departments to
operate the plant. It is, however, apparently common ground that, in the
event, a new authorisation will be needed before the plant is operated as BNFL
intend to operate it. Before that stage is reached, however, BNFL wish to go
through a testing programme which will occupy approximately ten weeks.
The evidence before us says that it is the fourth phase of a five-stage testing
programme, the fifth stage of which will come after the final authorisation has
been given. Rather than applying for a specific authorisation for the testing
programme, BNFL applied to the departments for a modification of the
existing authorisation. It was that which was granted to them and which is the
subject of the challenge by Greenpeace.

Before Brooke J neither BNFL (who were not, of course, parties to the
proceedings as such, but who had been notified and were present at the
hearing) nor the departments objected to leave being granted by the judge. At
present, a date has been fixed for the hearing of that application in substance
by Otton J on 14 September. We are told by Mr Newman QC for BNFL that
they are still pressing for a slightly earlier date, but we must work on the basis
that the hearing will be on 14 September, with the judgment, presumably,
shortly thereafter.

While they have not objected to the grant of leave, both the departments
and BNFL are, I apprehend, going to argue strenuously that the substantive
application should be refused. Indeed, Mr Newman has now made it clear that
they are going to argue that Greenpeace have no locus standi to make this
application at all.

Those, however, are not matters that need concern us because leave has
been granted. On the application for a stay, Brooke J was in this initial
difficulty: first of all, until recently, as a general principle, stays against
departments of the Crown were very rare creatures. The judge, basing himself

upon the decision of this court in *R v Secretary of State for Education and Science, ex p Avon CC* [1991] 1 All ER 282, [1991] 1 QB 558, concluded that he did indeed have jurisdiction to grant a stay. The matter has not been canvassed before us and the hearing has proceeded on the basis that the judge did indeed have jurisdiction, had he been minded to grant a stay.

That then, however, raised for the judge this difficult question (on which, so far as I know, there is no authority): where it is sought to stay a decision of a government department, and the effect of granting the stay will be to affect detrimentally the operations of a third party who is not party to the proceedings, what is the proper approach for the court, from which the stay is sought, to adopt?

If the third parties are made third parties to the proceedings, as they could be, and if an interlocutory injunction were sought against them, then the answer to the question would be clear: the court would then apply the normal principles it applies when an interlocutory injunction is sought, those laid down in *American Cyanamid Co v Ethicon Ltd* [1975] 1 All ER 504, [1975] AC 396.

In this case, that did not happen because BNFL were not made parties and no interlocutory injunction has been sought against them. It is quite clear, in my view, that Brooke J treated this application for a stay, in a sense, as if it were an application for an interlocutory injunction against BNFL, and he applied the principles he would have applied had he been considering such an application. In my judgment, he was entirely right to do so. If a third party would be affected by a decision on an application for a stay but is not made a party to the proceedings as a respondent to an application for an injunction, then, in my view, nevertheless, the same principles should be followed.

The matters which the judge took into account in exercising his jurisdiction on those principles were these: firstly, a major reason for not granting a stay is that it was the governmental body charged with the task of deciding upon whether this plant could properly and safely be operated which had issued the amendment to the authorisation, that is to say HM Inspectorate of Pollution and the Minister of Agriculture, Fisheries and Food.

There was evidence before the judge, as there is before us, that the additional radioactive discharge from the plant which will result from this testing process taking place will not be uncountable, but will be very small indeed. Moreover, the evidence is that it will not require any alteration of BNFL's existing authorisation to discharge radioactive material either into the air or in liquid form into the sea. Those discharges will be contained within the volumes permitted by that authorisation.

Added to that, the judge had evidence which clearly impressed him that if, as a result of a stay, the commissioning testing process is held up and, in the end, BNFL are permitted to go ahead with the operation of the reprocessing plant, there is at least a risk (they put it higher than that; they say it is probable) that they will suffer a loss as a result of the delay. They quantify that at approximately £250,000 a day. Presumably they are already suffering loss as a result of not having got the plant into operation since it was completed in February 1992. That is the sort of figure that they are claiming.

It is not, of course, entirely clear that they will necessarily suffer a loss if they are subjected to two weeks' delay, because the process of making a decision as to whether they can go ahead with the operation of the reprocessing plant after the testing procedure is still subject to decisions of ministers which, even if they come down in favour of BNFL, will not necessarily be made in a timescale which would result in a delay for two weeks or so having any effect at all. Nevertheless, there was the evidence and it impressed Brooke J.

On the other hand, he had to balance that against the very real concern of members of Greenpeace. There was evidence, which Greenpeace are presumably going to adduce at the hearing before Otton J and at any other hearings which are open to them, challenging the scientific evidence which was accepted by the departments. Put very shortly, if I understand it correctly, it is Greenpeace's stance that any additional emission of irradiated material into the atmosphere is harmful and should not be permitted unless there is some clear benefit. They argue that the reprocessing plant has no beneficial effect. It exists purely to enable BNFL to make money.

Those are the battle lines and those are the points which the judge had to weigh. As I have said, he weighed them upon normal principles. In the end he made his decision on the basis of the balance of convenience. At the end of his judgment he said:

> 'Balancing, as I must, all the arguments that have been brought before me when I decide how to exercise my discretion to grant a stay, I am bound to say that I am very considerably influenced by the evidence which BNFL have put before the court as to the likely financial loss they will suffer, and as to Greenpeace's likely inability to pay for that financial loss, if BNFL can indeed show (about which I express no view at all) that a delay in operating the plant for a fortnight will incur losses of this kind, coupled with the expert view of the [departments] as to the minimal effect of the level 4 commissioning of [the reprocessing plant].'

At the hearing before Brooke J, no offer was made by Greenpeace to give an undertaking as to damages suffered by BNFL should they suffer any; the sort of undertaking that would normally be required if an interlocutory injunction were to be granted.

I bear in mind that the judge said that he was influenced by the evidence about Greenpeace's likely inability to pay for that financial loss, but he had earlier remarked that he had not been offered an undertaking. If we were dealing with this matter purely on the material which was before the judge, I would find no difficulty at all. This was essentially a matter for the discretion of the judge. On that basis there would be nothing which would entitle us to say that the judge was clearly wrong or failed to take into account any relevant consideration and thus we could not possibly differ from the exercise of that discretion.

It is, however, said that there are two related new matters which do entitle us to take a completely different approach. The first is that there was produced before us when we had a first initial hearing of this matter on the evening of the same day as the judge gave his decision, 1 September, a document produced at the request of Mr Shuttleworth, representing BNFL, by a Mr Hallington, who is the commissioning support manager, which made it clear that the present testing process is going to be in three phases.

The first phase, what is called 'initial activities', putting it shortly (and, I hope, not too inaccurately), involves charging vessels in the plant with uranium nitrate; that will occupy seven days. That process started yesterday morning and so, presumably, on that timescale, will be completed by Thursday morning of next week.

The second phase, which is expected to last some five weeks thereafter, up to the end of the sixth week, involves starting up the evaporator, which involves a more intensive use and testing of the plant.

The initial phase, it is said, will create no liquid effluent and an infinitesimal level of aerial activity; the second phase will create some liquid effluent and an estimate of aerial discharge which is given in the letter.

I remind myself that they are still within the very small amount to which the evidence relates, but obviously the second phase is going to create relatively a greater quantity of discharge than the first.

It has been suggested to us by Mr Davies for Greenpeace that, even if we feel unable to disagree with the judge as to the totality of the stay, it would, nevertheless, be possible and proper to adopt a half-way position by granting a stay which would take effect at the beginning of the second phase of this testing on Thursday of next week, to operate until Otton J gave his decision, which would, presumably, be over a period of five or six days in total.

The basis of Mr Davies's argument is that, in that way, the somewhat more detrimental discharges would be avoided and, at the same time, the total loss to BNFL, if any, would obviously be substantially less because of the delay: instead of being 14 days, it would be, as I have said, five or six.

He urges upon us that that presents us with a new situation and creates new factors which we could properly take into account to enable us to exercise our discretion afresh without in any way trespassing upon the normal principles on which this court acts when it is considering the exercise of a judge's discretion.

To that, Mr Newman for BNFL replies that the argument of Mr Davies is simply, with respect to him, illogical. He submits that since the judge, taking into account whatever risk there was from a discharge over the period until Otton J's hearing, balancing the points made against granting the stay, decided that the balance of convenience did not favour granting a stay, we could not possibly conclude that for a lesser period of discharge and for a lesser amount of discharge, the balance of convenience did justify granting a stay; if we did we should simply be tinkering improperly with the exercise of the judge's discretion.

Mr Newman reminds us of a passage from the speech of Lord Diplock in *Hadmor Productions Ltd v Hamilton* [1982] 1 All ER 1042 at 1046, [1983] 1 AC 191 at 220–221, in which his Lordship said:

'... I cannot agree that the production of additional evidence before the Court of Appeal ... is of itself sufficient to entitle the Court of Appeal to ignore the judge's exercise of his discretion and to exercise an original discretion of its own. The right approach by an appellate court is to examine the fresh evidence in order to see to what extent, if any, the facts disclosed by it invalidate the reasons given by the judge for his decision. Only if they do is the appellate court entitled to treat the fresh evidence as constituting in itself a ground for exercising an original discretion of its own to grant or withhold the interlocutory relief.'

Mr Newman submits that there was nothing in the fresh evidence which invalidates the reasons given by the judge for his decision. Having been swayed initially, I must confess, by Mr Davies's persuasive argument to the contrary, I find myself in agreement with Mr Newman's argument.

For those reasons, I conclude that we are not in a position, even if we wished to, to disagree with the exercise by Brooke J of his discretion not to grant a stay and I would dismiss the appeal.

SCOTT LJ. I agree. At the end of Brooke J's judgment there appears this note:

'Leave to appeal was granted on the basis that the judge said he considered that the principles on which judges exercised their discretion in public law cases on interlocutory applications warranted the consideration of the Court of Appeal.'

The application, now on appeal before us, that prompted that note was an application for interlocutory relief. The interlocutory relief in question is a stay of the decision of HM Inspectorate of Pollution and the Minister of Agriculture, Fisheries and Food, made on 25 August 1993, to authorise British Nuclear Fuels plc (BNFL) to commence the commissioning of the Sellafield plant.

The evident purpose of the application for interlocutory relief is to prevent BNFL from commencing the commissioning that, pursuant to the authorisation granted on 25 August, they are entitled to commence. The purpose is to prevent them commencing that commissioning pending the determination of the question whether the decision is or is not tainted with some degree of illegality and ought to be set aside.

This interlocutory purpose could as well, and in my opinion more straightforwardly, have been pursued by means of an application against BNFL, who would first have had to be made a party to the proceedings, for an interlocutory injunction.

In my opinion, if the real purpose of interlocutory relief in a judicial review case is to prevent executive action by a third party being carried out pursuant to the decision under attack, the more suitable procedure would be to have the third party in question joined and then to seek an interlocutory injunction against that party, rather than to seek a stay of the decision. If, however, the purpose is pursued, as it has been in the present case, by an application for a stay of the decision rather than by an application for an interlocutory injunction against the third party, the courts should, in my opinion, look to the substance rather than to the form, and apply the same principles to the application as would have been applicable had the application been for an interlocutory injunction.

Brooke J dealt with the application for a stay which was before him in a manner that seems to me to have been indistinguishable from the manner in which he would have dealt with an application for an interlocutory injunction. In dealing with the application in that way, the judge took into account the possible effect of the stay upon BNFL; he took account of the fact that no cross-undertaking in damages had been offered; he took account of the evidence as to the degree of contamination that commissioning might cause, and he took account of the opinion of the Inspectorate of Pollution. In applying himself in that manner to the matter before him, in my judgment, the judge acted correctly and applied the correct principles.

Mr Davies has argued that, where interlocutory relief in the form of a stay is sought in judicial review proceedings, a requirement that an undertaking in damages be given as a condition of the grant of the interlocutory relief is not in accordance with practice and is inappropriate.

I make no comment on previous practice in this regard. Mr Davies may well be right. But if the purpose of the interlocutory stay is, as here, to prevent executive action by a third party in pursuance of rights which have been granted by the decision under attack, then, in my judgment, to require a cross-undertaking in damages to be given is, as a matter of discretion, an entirely permissible condition of the grant of interlocutory relief and in general, I would think, unless some special feature be present, a condition that should be expected to be imposed. Therefore, I think that Brooke J directed himself correctly in taking into account the matters regarding BNFL's financial position and regarding the absence of a cross-undertaking to which I have referred.

As to the additional material placed before this court and the question whether that material entitles this court to grant, either in whole or in part, the stay that the judge has refused to grant, I agree with and would not wish to add anything to what Glidewell LJ has already said.

I agree that the appeal should be dismissed.

EVANS LJ. I have the misfortune to differ from Glidewell and Scott LJJ on one point, but I should emphasise that otherwise I would adopt and gratefully acknowledge their analysis of the issues.

The circumstances now are different from what they were when the matter came before Brooke J only two days ago. The first difference is that details of the testing process are now known from a document which was produced to us on Wednesday evening by Mr Newman QC for British Nuclear Fuels plc (BNFL) and subsequently exhibited by Mr Shuttleworth in his second affidavit. What the document shows, which is relevant for present purposes, is that phase 1 of level 4 of the commissioning process involves a straightforward process of transferring the uranium nitrate by road tanker to (what I will call, I hope, accurately) the 'site tankage'. The second change is that phase 1 has now started. BNFL started it following their successful resistance to the application for a stay pending the hearing of this appeal on Wednesday evening. Phase 1 is estimated to occupy seven days and will, therefore, on the face of it, be completed on Thursday, September 8. The issue before us now, for practical purposes, is whether BNFL should then proceed to stage 2, which involves commencing the process of priming the evaporator. It seems to me that that involves the beginning of the process of introducing uranium into the machinery if, as I hope, that is an accurate way of describing it.

Before Brooke J, the question was whether the start should be delayed for 14 days. There is no indication that he knew anything of the different stages which were involved. I respectfully agree that we cannot fault his decision and should not interfere with it. Now the question is whether on Friday, September 10 BNFL should proceed to stage 2 or whether they should wait until the conclusion of the hearing before Otton J on September 13. The transition from phase 1 to phase 2 represents, as I understand the evidence, a considerable threshold. At stage 1 there is said to be an infinitesimal level of emission, no contamination of the machinery and no effluent which will require subsequent disposal. It is at stage 2 that the risks which the applicant apprehends will begin. Moreover, the loss suffered by BNFL, if any, as a result of a stay, will consist of four or five days' delay in about mid-November upon a number of major assumptions which I need not rehearse here.

Mr Newman says that this issue is encompassed by Brooke J's decision. I respectfully disagree. I do not know what the judge would have said if he had been told that stage 1 could proceed without risk, or without any substantial risk, but had been asked to delay stage 2 by a mere four or five days. That is the present situation and, in my judgment, the court's discretion should be exercised in these circumstances in favour of the applicant to that extent. I would also feel that we were entitled to substitute our own answer to that different question in the circumstances which I have outlined.

Appeal dismissed.

Bebe Chua   Barrister.

R v Inspectorate of Pollution and another, ex parte Greenpeace Ltd (No 2)

QUEEN'S BENCH DIVISION (CROWN OFFICE LIST)

OTTON J

14, 15, 16, 29 SEPTEMBER 1993

Judicial review – Application for judicial review – Locus standi of applicant – Sufficient interest – Company authorised to discharge radioactive waste from premises – Company granted variation of authorisations to test new plant – Environmental protection organisation concerned at extent of radioactive discharge – Organisation having international profile and 2,500 supporters in area of new plant – Whether organisation having sufficient interest to apply for judicial review of executive decision to vary authorisations – Supreme Court Act 1981, s 31(3) – RSC Ord 53, r 3(7).

Judicial review – Availability of remedy – Discretion of court to grant relief – Statutory authorisation – Company authorised to discharge radioactive waste from premises – Government departments granting variation of authorisations to enable testing of new plant – Environmental protection organisation concerned at increasing levels of radioactive discharge applying for judicial review of executive decision – Whether judicial review should be granted – Whether variation of authorisations valid or justified – Whether new authorisations required for testing process – Radioactive Substances Act 1960, ss 6(1), 8(1)(4)(7) – Council Directive (Euratom) 80/836, art 6.

Public health – Waste disposal – Radioactive waste – Statutory authorisation – Company authorised to discharge radioactive waste from premises – Company obtaining variation of authorisations to enable testing of operation of new plant – Whether variation of authorisations valid or justified – Radioactive Substances Act 1960, ss 6(1), 8(1)(4)(7) – Council Directive (Euratom) 80/836, art 6.

A company, BNFL, which reprocessed spent nuclear fuel, was authorised by the respondent govenment departments to discharge liquid and gaseous radioactive waste from its premises under authorisations granted pursuant to s 6(1)[a] of the Radioactive Substances Act 1960. In 1992 BNFL applied for new

---
a   Section 6(1) is set out at p 337 *d e*, post

authorisations to include the proposed operation of its new thermal oxide reprocessing plant. Pending the grant of the new authorisations, BNFL also applied for and obtained a variation of the existing authorisations to enable it to test the new plant before it became fully operational. An environmental protection organisation with an international standing was concerned about the levels of radioactive discharge from the site and applied for judicial review by way of an order of certiorari to quash the respondents' decision to vary the existing authorisations and an injunction to stay the implementation of the varied authorisations, which would halt the proposed testing of the new plant pending a decision on BNFL's main application. The applicant, which had 2,500 supporters in the area where the plant was situated, contended (i) that the variations were unlawful since they concerned an operation which was different in description and kind from that for which the original authorisations had been granted and, as such, they constituted an anticipation of new authorisations not yet granted under s 8(1)^b of the 1960 Act, rather than a variation of existing authorisations capable of being made under s 8(7) and (ii) that the respondents' decision not to consider the justification for the tests in the light of the emissions of radioactivity entailed in the running and decontaminating of the plant was impeachable, given their obligation under the 1960 Act and art 6^c of Council Directive (Euratom) 80/836 to ensure that the process for which the variation was sought was justified in terms of its overall benefits and the point that, if the main authorisations were ultimately refused, the testing would have been carried out without any justification. The respondents contended that s 6(1) of the 1960 Act, as amplified by s 8(4), permitted BNFL to dispose of any radioactive waste from its premises and permitted variation of the original authorisations to allow the testing process to take place. BNFL contended that the applicant had failed to establish a 'sufficient interest in the matter' to which the application related, as required by s 31(3)^d of the Supreme Court Act 1981 and RSC Ord 53, r 3(7)^e, and accordingly had no locus standi to make the application.

Held – (1) When deciding whether an applicant for judicial review had a sufficient interest in the matter to which the application related, the court hearing the substantive application should take into account, in the exercise of its discretion, the nature of the applicant, the extent of his interest in the issues raised, the remedy which he sought to achieve and the nature of the relief sought. Having regard to the fact that the applicant was an entirely responsible and respected body with a genuine interest in the issues raised, that it had 2,500 supporters in the area where the plant was situated, who might not otherwise have an effective means of bringing their concerns before the court if the applicant were denied locus standi, that the primary relief sought was an order of certiorari and not mandamus, which, even if granted, would still leave the question of an injunction to stop the testing process pending determination of the main issues in the discretion of the court and that the applicant had been actively involved in the consultation process relating to BNFL's application to operate the new plant, it was clear that the applicant had a 'sufficient interest

---

b   Section 8, so far as material, is set out at p 338 *a* to p 339 *b*, post
c   Article 6, so far as material, is set out at p 344 *j* to p 345 *a*, post
d   Section 31(3) is set out at p 349 *b c*, post
e   Rule 3(7) is set out at p 349 *c*, post

in the matter' to be granted locus standi (see p 349 *h*, p 350 *c e f* and p 351 *c d j*, post); dictum of Lord Donaldson MR in *R v Monopolies and Mergers Commission, ex p Argyll Group plc* [1986] 2 All ER 257 at 265 applied; dictum of Lord Roskill in *IRC v National Federation of Self-Employed and Small Businesses Ltd* [1981] 2 All ER 93 at 117 considered; *R v Secretary of State for the Environment, ex p Rose Theatre Trust Co* [1990] 1 All ER 754 not followed.

(2) On its true construction, s 6(1) of the 1960 Act permitted BNFL to dispose of any relevant radioactive waste (as defined in the authorisations) on or from its premises including the plant on site which was used for the purpose of any undertaking carried on by the company and thereby conferred on BNFL a wide power to extend or contract its activities on site under its licences, in pursuance of its objectives but subject to strict independent regulatory control. Moreover, it was open to the respondents to permit the disposal of radioactive waste resulting from the testing process under the existing authorisations, since the relevant radioactive waste was a constant definition of waste or solids resulting from all gases arising from operations at the company's premises, as distinct from the identity of the new plant or the substance (oxide) producing the waste. The respondents were accordingly entitled to exercise their power to vary the existing authorisations because the variations did not extend the description of radioactive waste set out in the original authorisations and did not authorise disposals of new types of radioactive waste. It followed that the respondents had not exercised their powers unlawfully by permitting BNFL to implement the testing process for the new plant by the variation route in order to avoid the consultation process, which was only mandatory in respect of new authorisations (see p 341 *g* to p 342 *a g*, p 334 *j* to p 344 *b e* to *g* and p 352 *a*, post).

(3) Although there was a general obligation on the authorising bodies to consider the health and safety aspect when deciding whether to permit the discharge of radioactive waste which would result from the testing process and, in particular, whether the levels involved would pose a significant risk to the health and safety of the public, there was no obligation on them to address the wider issues which were already under consideration through the consultation process triggered by the main applications. It was clear that the respondents had taken account of the wider issues of justification before reaching their decision to grant the variations, because they were aware that the issues of justification for the operation of the new plant, which had been raised in the consultation process, had in fact been considered by ministers who favoured granting the new authorisations sought by BNFL. It was also clear that the need for testing was established in terms of its overall benefit and that the requirement of art 6 of Directive 80/836 was satisfied, since the matters considered by the regulating bodies included the advantages which the testing would produce and therefore there was a justification in advance. The justification ground of the application would accordingly be dismissed. It followed that the substantive application would also be dismissed (see p 345 *b c*, p 346 *b* to *f* and p 352 *a*, post).

Notes

For the nature and scope of judicial review, locus standi and certiorari, see 1(1) Halsbury's Laws (4th edn reissue) paras 60, 64, 116–117, and for cases on the subject, see 16 *Digest* (Reissue) 388–433, 4237–4773.

For the Radioactive Substances Act 1960, ss 6, 8, see 47 *Halsbury' Statutes* (4th edn) 761, 764.

As from 27 August 1993, the 1960 Act was repealed by the Radioactive Substances Act 1993, s 50, Sch 6. Sections 6, 8, 18 and 19 of the 1960 Act have now been replaced by ss 1, 2, 13, 16, 17 and 47 of the 1993 Act. For those replacement sections, see 47(S) *Halsbury's Statutes* (4th edn) 135, 136, 147, 150, 152, 183.

For the Supreme Court Act 1981, s 31, see 11 *Halsbury's Statutes* (4th edn) (1991 reissue) 991.

Cases referred to in judgment

Associated Provincial Picture Houses Ltd v Wednesbury Corp [1947] 2 All ER 680, [1948] 1 KB 223, CA.

Borowski v Minister of Justice of Canada [1981] 2 SCR 575, Can SC.

Covent Garden Community Association Ltd v Greater London Council [1981] JPL 183.

Finlay v Minister of Finance of Canada [1986] 2 SCR 60, Can SC.

IRC v National Federation of Self-Employed and Small Businesses Ltd [1981] 2 All ER 93, [1982] AC 617, [1981] 2 WLR 722, HL.

McNeil v Nova Scotia Board of Censors [1976] 2 SCR 265, Can SC.

R v Chief Adjudication Officer, ex p Bland (1985) Times, 6 February, DC.

R v Dept of Transport, ex p Presvac Engineering Ltd (1989) Times, 4 April, DC.

R v Hammersmith and Fulham London BC, ex p People before Profit Ltd (1981) 80 LGR 322.

R v Monopolies and Mergers Commission, ex p Argyll Group plc [1986] 2 All ER 257, [1986] 1 WLR 763, CA.

R v Secretary of State for Social Services, ex p Child Poverty Action Group (1984) Times, 16 August; rvsd (1985) Times, 8 August, [1985] CA Transcript 405.

R v Secretary of State for Social Services, ex p Child Poverty Action Group [1989] 1 All ER 1047, [1990] 2 QB 540, [1989] 3 WLR 1116, CA.

R v Secretary of State for the Environment, ex p Rose Theatre Trust Co [1990] 1 All ER 754, [1990] 1 QB 504, [1990] 2 WLR 186.

R v Stroud DC, ex p Goodenough (1980) 43 P & CR 59, DC.

Thorson v A-G of Canada [1975] 1 SCR 138, Can SC.

Application for judicial review

Greenpeace plc applied with leave of Brooke J given on 1 September 1993 for judicial review by way of an order of certiorari to quash the decision of the respondents, HM Inspectorate of Pollution and the Minister of Agriculture, Fisheries and Food, dated 25 August 1993, granting applications by British Nuclear Fuels plc (BNFL) for variations of authorisations under the Radioactive Substances Act 1960 to discharge radioactive waste from its premises at Sellafield, Cumbria, in order to test its new thermal oxide processing plant. BNFL took part in the proceedings as an interested party. The facts are set out in the judgment.

Michael Beloff QC and *Owen Davies* (instructed by *Sarah Jane Burton*) for Greenpeace.

Kenneth Parker QC and *Mark Shaw* (instructed by the *Treasury Solicitor*) for the respondents.

George Newman QC and *Alan Griffiths* (instructed by *Freshfields*) for BNFL.

Cur adv vul

29 September 1993. The following judgment was delivered.

OTTON J. This is an application by Greenpeace Ltd for judicial review of a decision by HM Inspectorate of Pollution (HMIP) and the Minister of Agriculture, Fisheries and Food (MAFF) dated 25 August 1993 to grant applications by British Nuclear Fuels plc (BNFL) for variations of authorisations under the Radioactive Substances Act 1960 (as amended) to discharge radioactive waste from BNFL's premises at Sellafield, Cumbria, in order to test BNFL's (new) thermal oxide processing plant (THORP).

The testing has already commenced, but is in its early stages, in advance of a final decision whether or not to approve BNFL's applications to discharge such waste into the sea and atmosphere as and when THORP were to commence regular operations. It is Greenpeace's case that the decision to allow testing was not lawfully made.

BNFL, pursuant to the objects clause in its memorandum of association, has been carrying out the reprocessing of irradiated nuclear fuel on a commercial basis for electricity generating companies since 1971. In particular para 4(1) provides:

'To design, manufacture, supply or deal in nuclear fuel; to carry out any processing and re-processing of fissile material and nuclear fuel; to manufacture, supply or deal in radio-active substances; to operate nuclear reactors and other irradiation facilities; to produce, use and dispose of heat and electricity generated by nuclear power stations; to design, manufacture, supply or deal in plant, equipment and apparatus of a kind used in or in connection with any of the foregoing activities.'

It has appeared as a party interested.

HMIP was established in 1987 when the existing Industrial Pollution Inspectorate, Radiochemical Inspectorate and the Hazardous Waste Inspectorate were merged into a unified inspectorate. HMIP is part of the Department of the Environment but acts as an independent inspectorate and is responsible, inter alia, for the authorisation and regulation of non-nuclear industrial pollution, regulation for the disposal of radioactive waste, research on pollution control and radioactive waste disposal and for giving expert advice to government and industry. So far as the disposal of radioactive waste is concerned, some 8,000 premises are controlled by HMIP under the 1960 Act, including nuclear power plants, defence establishments, research establishments, radioactive waste disposal sites and industrial plants where radioactive sources are used.

Under the 1960 Act HMIP and MAFF each regulate the disposal of radioactive waste from premises subject to a nuclear site licence. HMIP pays particular attention to the effects of any disposal on the environment. MAFF pays particular attention to the consequences of such a disposal for the food chain, fisheries and the marine environment in general.

Greenpeace Ltd is the corporate identity of Greenpeace UK, the United Kingdom national office of Greenpeace International (incorporated in the Netherlands as Stichting Greenpeace Council). It is a well-known campaigning organisation which has as its prime object the protection of the natural environment.

BACKGROUND

One of the principal operations at BNFL's site at Sellafield is the reprocessing of spent nuclear fuel to recover reusable uranium and plutonium and separate out the radioactive waste products. The reprocessing of spent nuclear fuel from Magnox nuclear reactors has been carried on at Sellafield since the early 1950s. Magnox nuclear reactors are gas-cooled graphite moderated reactors using Magnox-clad fuel, built in the 1960s, on which the United Kingdom's first nuclear power programme was based. They are likely to cease operating by the early years of the next century. Some Magnox reactors are already being decommissioned. BNFL is also undertaking a significant programme of post-operational decontamination and decommissioning of redundant plant. By way of replacement, they wish in addition to THORP to commission the enhanced actinide removal plant to reduce discharges from the existing plant.

These operations produce radioactive waste. Gaseous wastes are discharged from the Sellafield site by a number of chimney stacks and other outlets on the site. Liquid wastes, treated where necessary by the site effluent treatment systems, are collected together and monitored prior to discharge from the site via sea pipelines. In 1978 Parker J recommended in his Report on the Windscale Inquiry, and Parliament authorised, the construction of a high technology thermal oxide reprocessing plant (THORP) for the reprocessing of spent nuclear fuels at Sellafield. THORP is designed to perform the same function as the Magnox reactors but in relation to the next generation of reactors. The existing facilities at Sellafield for reprocessing spent Magnox fuels are not suitable for the reprocessing of spent oxide fuels. Thus BNFL have constructed a new plant to reprocess spent oxide fuels from the later generation of thermal reactors. This plant is in the process of completion.

BNFL are in possession of 'authorisations' which permit them to discharge liquid and gaseous radioactive waste from the Sellafield site. The existing authorisations were issued between 1986 and 1990. Their conditions and limitations are reviewed every four years by HMIP and MAFF to ensure that discharges continue to be as low as reasonably achievable.

In April 1992 BNFL submitted applications for new authorisations in respect of the Sellafield site as a whole to take account of the review of their existing operations and to include the proposed operation of THORP and the enhanced actinide removal plant. Draft certificates of authorisation were prepared to assist the public consultation process. The applications by BNFL, the draft authorisations and supporting explanatory memoranda, were put out to consultation in November 1992. That consultation period closed on 25 January 1993. For convenience I refer to these applications as 'the main' or 'the operational' applications.

In the meantime, BNFL sought approval from HMIP to commence the uranium commissioning or testing phase for THORP.

On 25 November 1992 BNFL wrote to HMIP:

'BNFL has welcomed the start of the public consultation period for the new Sellafield discharge authorisations (ie the main or operational authorisations). However, we are still concerned that we have not received approval to commence the uranium commissioning phase for THORP, a step that would minimise the delay to the operation of THORP whilst remaining within the current site discharge authorisation levels. This is despite a statement by your own staff ... that there are no waste management safety or technical reasons for not commencing uranium commissioning on the timescale that had previously been agreed with HMIP.'

On 29 January 1993 HMIP replied:

'We are advised that it would not be appropriate to agree to an amendment to the Implementation Documents for the existing authorisation in order to permit emissions of radioactive waste from parts of the THORP plant as part of commissioning trials. If however, you wish to proceed with this aspect of commissioning trials the inspectorate and MAFF would be prepared to consider the variation of the *existing* gaseous and liquid authorisations to permit the discharge of radioactive wastes from the THORP plant arising only from commissioning trials. The variation would only permit testing, would be for a limited period and would be strictly without prejudice to their consideration of the current applications for discharges arising from the reprocessing of spent fuels. *The variation would involve public consultation.*'

On 5 February the chief executive of BNFL wrote:

'My letters intended to convey the message that we wish to expedite uranium commissioning in THORP in order to mitigate the considerable cost being incurred by the company due to the delay in receiving the new Sellafield Site Discharge Authorisation. As I understand it, the course of action you propose in your letter would have just the opposite effect. The public consultation period on the new Sellafield Site Discharge Authorisation has already ended and it is not unreasonable for us, therefore, to expect a decision on the new authorisation within a few weeks. If we proceed along the line suggested in your letter and seek a variation of the existing authorisation, then that itself could take far longer than the remaining procedures on the new authorisation. Clearly an absolute nonsense ... What we cannot understand is why additional points of discharge cannot be added to the schedule under the *present* authorisation provided our total discharges are within the limits of that present authorisation.'

To which Dr Marshall, head of the North West Region HMIP, replied on 5 February:

'Authorising departments are advised that it would not be appropriate to agree to an amendment to the Implementation Documents for the existing authorisation in order to permit emissions of radioactive waste from parts of the THORP plant as part of testing the plant. The new points of discharge would be in respect of plant which was not included in the existing authorisation and for which there would be no opportunity for representations by statutory consultees and the public. I confirm that to proceed by way of a variation would, realistically, involve a period of at least 12 weeks from receiving your application depending upon the number of responses resulting from the public consultation, before any variation could be granted.'

This letter represents the high point of Greenpeace's application. BNFL were seeking to obtain approval for testing by variation of the conditions of the existing authorisation. HMIP were taking the line that to do even this required a consultation process which would trigger representations by the statutory consultees and the public. Greenpeace argue that HMIP and MAFF were entirely correct and that BNFL were wrong. The fact remained, however, that the main authorisation was likely to be given (or withheld) before the consultation process had taken place and authorisation given (or withheld) for the testing of the plant. To cut a long story short, BNFL again applied for testing permission and HMIP and MAFF then indicated that they would consider an application for variations to the existing authorisations, thus avoiding the need for consultation.

In May 1993 HMIP and MAFF sent a report to the Secretary of State for the Environment and the Minister of Agriculture, Fisheries and Food. This stated:

'The inspectorates are satisfied that the systems of controls provided by the conditions in the draft (main) authorisations would be adequate and conform to the latest standard of conditions and requirement which are being brought to bear on all licensed sites in the UK.'

The inspectorates also concluded that 'the provisions of the draft authorisations would effectively protect human health, the safety of the food chain, and the environment generally'. After consideration of the report the Secretary of State and the minister announced that there would be a further round of public consultation to enable comments to be received on the 'wider issues' which had arisen during the original consultation period and on the 'justification for the operation of THORP'.

On 30 June 1993 BNFL made formal application for a variation to the existing authorisations to permit level 4 testing of THORP and issued draft authorisations.

Greenpeace's antennae had picked up this activity. On 16 July Lord Melchett, the executive director, wrote to BNFL, the Secretary of State and the minister expressing Greenpeace's deep concern. On 22 July HMIP and MAFF announced that they were minded to grant a variation of BNFL's existing authorisations to discharge liquid and gaseous radioactive waste so that such uranium could be used to test THORP. They had concluded that:

'The radiological impact of the emissions from testing THORP (ie with uranium in its natural and depleted state) would be very small, less than 0.001% of the average dosed to the United Kingdom population from natural background radiation [and] there would be no increase to the existing limits of emissions from Sellafield.'

Greenpeace were informed by both of the authorising authorities and invited to comment by 12 August.

On 29 July 1993 Greenpeace applied for leave to apply for judicial review before Hutchison J. The application was refused on the grounds that there was as yet no decision to review and the application was premature.

On 4 August the further consultation period on the wider issues in connection with the applications for the main authorisations opened and is due to continue until 4 October 1993. A decision as to whether to grant, refuse or to order a public inquiry is not anticipated before the mid to end of October. On 19 August the authorising agencies indicated that they were minded to grant testing authorisations and asked whether BNFL required a hearing on such variations. This offer was not taken up.

On 25 August the authorising departments decided to grant 'variations' to its existing liquid and gaseous discharge authorisations to take effect from 2 September.   Greenpeace were informed.   On 1 September Brooke J gave Greenpeace leave to apply for judicial review but refused a stay of the implementation of the varied authorisations (ie to stop the testing).   He granted leave to appeal to the Court of Appeal.   On the following day the revised 'variations' became effective and phase 1 of the level 4 testing began at midnight.   On 3 September the Court of Appeal dismissed the appeal of Greenpeace against the judge's refusal to grant a stay (see [1994] 4 All ER 321). The hearing of the substantive matter came before me on 14 September.   I wish to express my appreciation and gratitude to counsel and solicitors for all parties on the efficient and expeditious manner in which the matter was prepared for trial.

STATUTORY FRAMEWORK

This is contained in the Radioactive Substances Act 1960 (as amended).

'6.   *Disposal of radioactive waste.*—(1) Subject to the provisions of this section, as from the appointed day no person shall, except in accordance with an authorisation granted in that behalf under this subsection, dispose of any radioactive waste on or from any premises which are used for the purposes of an undertaking carried on by him, or cause or permit any radioactive waste to be so disposed of, if (in any such case) he knows or has reasonable grounds for believing it to be radioactive waste ...

18.   *Meaning of "radioactive material", "radioactive waste"* ... (1) In this Act "radioactive material" means anything which, not being waste, is either a substance to which this subsection applies or an article made wholly or partly from, or incorporating, such a substance ...

(4) In this Act "radioactive waste" means waste which consists wholly or partly of—(a) a substance or article which, if it were not waste, would be radioactive material, or (b) a substance or article which has been contaminated in the course of the production, keeping or use of radioactive material, or by contact with or proximity to other waste falling within the preceding paragraph or this paragraph ...

19.   *General interpretation provisions.*—(1) In this Act, except in so far as the context otherwise requires, the following expressions have the meanings hereby assigned to them respectively, that is to say ... "the chief inspector" means the chief inspector appointed under subsection (2) of section 11A of this Act; "disposal", in relation to waste, includes the removal, deposit or destruction thereof, the discharge thereof, whether into water or into the air or into a sewer or drain or otherwise, or the burial thereof, whether underground or otherwise, and "dispose of" shall be construed accordingly ... "premises" includes any land, whether covered by buildings or not, including any place underground and any land covered by water ... "substance" means any natural or artificial substance, whether in solid or liquid form or in the form of a gas or vapour; "undertaking" includes any trade, business or profession, and, in relation to a public or local authority, includes any of the powers or duties of that authority, and, in relation to any other body of persons, whether corporate or unincorporate, includes any of the activities of that body ...'

('Waste' is also defined to distinguish it from radioactive waste which I do not read.)

'**8. Supplementary provisions as to authorisation of disposal and accumulation of radioactive waste.**—(1) The power to grant authorisations under subsection (1) of section six of this Act in respect of the disposal of radioactive waste on or from ... (b) any premises situated on a site in respect of which a nuclear site licence is for the time being in force, or (c) any premises situated on a site in respect of which, after the revocation or surrender of a nuclear site licence, the period of responsibility of the licensee has not come to an end, shall be exercisable by the chief inspector and the Minister of Agriculture, Fisheries and Food; and the disposal of radioactive waste on or from any such premises shall not be treated as authorised thereunder unless it is so authorised by both the chief inspector and the Minister.

(2) Before granting an authorisation to which the preceding subsection applies, the chief inspector and the Minister of Agriculture, Fisheries and Food shall each consult with such local authorities, local fisheries committees, statutory water undertakers or other public or local authorities as appear to him to be proper to be consulted by him ...

(4) Any authorisation under section six or section seven of this Act may be granted either in respect of radioactive waste generally or in respect of such one or more descriptions of radioactive waste as may be specified in the authorisation; and any such authorisation may be granted subject to such limitations or conditions as the chief inspector or, as the case may be, the chief inspector and the Minister think fit.

(4A) On any application being made the chief inspector shall, subject to any directions under this section, send a copy of the application to each local authority in whose area, in accordance with the authorisation applied for, radioactive waste is to be disposed of or accumulated.

(5) On granting any such authorisation, the chief inspector or, as the case may be, the chief inspector and the Minister—(a) shall furnish the person to whom the authorisation is granted with a certificate containing all material particulars of the authorisation; and (b) shall, subject to any directions under this section, send a copy of the certificate to each local authority ...

(6) Any such authorisation shall have effect as from such date as may be specified therein: and in fixing that date, in the case of an authorisation where copies of the certificate are required to be sent as mentioned in paragraph (b) of subsection (5) of this section, the chief inspector or, as the case may be, the chief inspector and the Minister—(a) shall have regard to the time at which those copies may be expected to be sent, and (b) shall fix a date appearing to him or them to be such as will allow an interval of not less than twenty-eight days after that time before the authorisation has effect, unless in his or their opinion it is necessary that the coming into operation of the authorisation should be immediate or should otherwise be expedited.

(7) The chief inspector or, as the case may be, the chief inspector and the Minister by whom an authorisation has been granted under section six or section seven of this Act may at any time revoke the authorisation, or may vary it—(a) where the authorisation has effect without limitations or

conditions, by attaching limitations or conditions thereto; (b) where the authorisation has effect subject to limitations or conditions, by revoking or varying any of those limitations or conditions or by attaching further limitations or conditions thereto.

(8) On revoking or varying an authorisation granted under section six or section seven of this Act, the chief inspector or, as the case may be, the chief inspector and the Minister shall give notice thereof to the person to whom the authorisation was granted ...

11. *Procedure in connection with registrations and authorisations.*— (1) Before the chief inspector and the Minister of Agriculture, Fisheries and Food—(a) refuse an application for an authorisation under section six of this Act, or (b) attache any limitations or conditions to such an authorisation, or (c) vary such an authorisation, otherwise than by revoking a limitation or condition subject to which it has effect, or (d) revoke such an authorisation, the person directly concerned [ie BNFL] shall, and such local authorities or other persons whom the Secretary of State and the Minister consider appropriate may, be afforded the opportunity of appearing before, and being heard by, a person appointed for the purpose by the Secretary of State and the Minister ...

(4) In this section "the person directly concerned", ... in relation to an authorisation under section six of this Act, means the person applying for the authorisation or the person to whom the authorisation was granted, as the case may be [ie BNFL]; and any reference to attaching limitations or conditions to such an authorisation is a reference to attaching limitations or conditions thereto either in granting the authorisation or in the exercise of any power to vary it.'

Section 11A(1) deals with the appointment of inspectors and chief inspectors which I do not read. Section 12 concerns the power of the Secretary of State to give directions to the chief inspector.

In addition to these elaborate statutory provisions, it is also government policy that all controllable radiation exposure should be kept as low as reasonably achievable, in accordance with relevant principles of the International Commission on Radiological Protection, in compliance with the Euratom Treaty and the European Council Directives (to which I shall refer later). These lay down the basic standards for the health protection of the general public and workers against the dangers of ionising radiation, that discharges of radioactivity shall be controlled in such a way that any environmental effects from such radiation would be acceptable and that the radiological impact on members of the public will be within national and international dose limits. Dose limits are derived from Council Directive (Euratom) 80/836. Account is also taken of advice from the National Radiological Protection Board.

THE ISSUES

By these proceedings Greenpeace seeks to challenge (i) the inspectorate's decision to grant the applications to vary the existing authorisations in order to test the THORP plant and (ii) their decision to determine the application while the main applications for authorisation for the permanent operation of the plant were pending. They also seek to impeach the inspector's decision not to consider the justification for the tests in the light of the emissions of radioactivity entailed in the running and decontaminating of the plant (the 'lawfulness' issue).

Greenpeace seeks an order of certiorari to bring up and quash the decision, and an injunction to stay the implementation of the applications for a variation of the existing authorisations, i e to stop testing pending a decision in favour of the main operation of the THORP plant.

Originally the revised form 86A contained six grounds in support of the application. However, as matters progressed the applicant's skeleton argument contained only two grounds. I need not deal with those that were not pursued.

BNFL contests whether Greenpeace has a sufficient interest in the matter to which the application relates. They contend that the matter is the decision of the chief inspector and MAFF to make the testing variations to BNFL's authorisations for the Sellafield site. Thus unless the court is satisfied at the substantive hearing that the applicant does have sufficient interest in the matter to which the application relates the applicant is not entitled to the relief sought (the locus standi issue).

The lawfulness issue

The first ground concerns the lawfulness of the procedure adopted. Greenpeace submits that the variations to the authorisations are unlawful because they are not a variation of the present authorisations capable of being made under s 8(7). They are an anticipation of the new authorisations not yet granted under s 8(1). Mr Michael Beloff QC for Greenpeace submits that when one examines the language of the 1960 Act and the authorisations and the variations thereto, it was the clear purpose of the legislation that any purported variation must relate to plant that existed at the time of the grant of the original authorisation. The purported variations involve or encompass an operation which is different in description and kind from that for which the original authorisations were granted. He submits that it is not a proper or lawful variation of a condition or limitation to include an entire new plant and the source of that new plant's emissions by way of a variation. He relies heavily upon the precise language of HMIP's letter of Dr Marshall dated 5 February to which I have referred.

The respondents have always accepted that the full operation of the THORP plant must be the subject of fresh or main authorisations which will require the statutory consultation process. Thus, Mr Beloff submits, that there is no difference in principle between the main or full operation and the testing or commissioning stage. It is illogical not to require a consultation stage before considering whether or not to permit testing. Further, it would be wrong in principle to construe s 8 in such a way that such an authorisation of any kind had been granted to permit *any* subsequent increase in its operation and the carrying on of a fresh operation would only involve variation of the authorisation and hence remove from the public consultation process such proposed fresh operations.

He further submits that, on a proper construction of s 6(1), any authorisation granted in relation to 'any premises which are used for the purpose of any undertaking' only covers plant on the premises when the original authorisation was granted. It cannot include THORP which was not in existence at that time. Likewise the expression 'the premises occupied by the company at Sellafield' etc in the certificate of authorisation must again be construed as an authorisation to dispose of 'relevant' waste from the premises which was to be discharged when the authorisation was given (ie 1986). Not to so construe would result in any new process being authorised by variation. This cannot have been the intention of the legislature in framing a strict regulatory statute concerning such a sensitive issue as nuclear safety. In short, the power of the inspectors to vary an authorisation under s 8(7)(b) may be exercised to strengthen or relax a limitation or condition. This power extends only to matters peripheral to the core activity; it does not permit variation of the core activity itself. Similarly, the authorising bodies have unlawfully varied the authorisation so as to permit the disposal of radioactive waste of a different description from the description of radioactive waste, the disposal of which was authorised by the original authorisation.

Mr Kenneth Parker QC, leading counsel for the respondents, submits that s 6(1), as amplified by s 8(4), and the words 'undertaking', 'premises' and 'radioactive waste' as defined create a very wide concept and, when properly construed, the Act, the language of the authorisations and their variations and in particular the definitions of the individual words and phrases do not bear the construction contended for by Greenpeace. He submits that the authorised person is free to alter and/or expand the *operations* carried on by him on the relevant premises at the date of authorisation provided he complies with the conditions of the authorisation. In practice the conditions imposed as to the amount and manner of waste disposal have the effect of materially restricting the nature and extent of such activities. The scope and structure of the authorisation and restrictions are not confined to the operations or disposal of radioactive waste only at the time of enactment of the authorisation. Such a narrow construction would severely restrict the operations which BNFL were licensed to perform. There is thus no obligation to go by way of the authorisation with consultation route if the variation without consultation route is permissible. It may be that as a matter of policy the respondents and/ or BNFL have elected to go by way of the consultation process for the main variations; this has no bearing upon whether or not a variation is permissible to permit commissioning or testing.

Conclusion

In reaching my conclusions I start with s 6(1).

(1) On my construction s 6(1) permits BNFL to dispose of any radioactive waste (as defined in s 18(4)) on or from 'premises' as defined in s 19(1), ie 'any land whether covered by buildings or not', ie Sellafield. Although I have been referred to the use of 'plant' elsewhere in the documentation, there is no reference to 'plant' or any qualification of the definition of 'premises'. Premises as defined is much wider and as a matter of construction includes the plant on site. Plant must be situated on land whether covered by buildings or not.

(2) The premises must be used for the purpose of any 'undertaking' carried on by BNFL as defined (which is not seriously in dispute) that testing of THORP falls within the definition.

(3) Such 'disposal' (s 19(1)) includes the discharge of radioactive waste into water or into the air.

(4) (Perhaps most important.) Such disposal must be in accordance with authorisations granted by the authorising bodies.

Thus there is a wide power vested in BNFL to extend or contract their activities on site under their licence, in pursuance of their objectives but subject to strict independent regulatory control.

I then turn to consider authorisation under s 8(4). Any authorisation under s 6 may be granted in respect of radioactive waste specified in the authorisation and subject to such conditions or limitations as the authorising bodies think fit. It is thus necessary to consider the language of the main body of each authorisation before or above the conditions and limitations. In each authorisation there is a general paragraph which is of particular importance. It provides, so far as material:

> 'The Secretary of State ... and the Minister ... in accordance with section 6(1) ... and section 8(4) of the ... Act ... hereby authorise ... [BNFL] to dispose of relevant waste from the premises ... at Sellafield by discharging it into: 1. "The atmosphere" (gaseous waste), and 2. "The sea" ... (liquid waste) ... Subject to the conditions and limitations specified below.'

By ss 11 and 21 of the Interpretation Act 1978 any expression used in the authorisation must bear the same meaning as in the statute. Thus BNFL can dispose of any relevant waste from their 'premises'. Plant does not enter into the ambit of the authorisation, thus 'premises' must again include the THORP plant.

'Relevant waste' is defined in each authorisation. By condition 14(1) of the liquid waste authorisation it means:

> 'Radioactive waste in the form of a continuous aqueous phase together with (a) Solids resulting from the neutralisation of radioactive waste prior to discharge, and (b) Other solids so far as it is not reasonably practicable to exclude them.'

In the gaseous authorisation, relevant waste is defined at condition 13(1) and means: 'Radioactive waste in the form of gases, mists and dusts arising from the operations of the company at Sellafield.'

In other words, the relevant waste is a constant definition of waste as solids resulting from all gases etc arising from operations of BNFL at Sellafield as distinct from the identity of the plant (THORP) or the substance (oxide) producing it.

Under s 8(7) the inspectors may at any time revoke the authorisation or may vary it:

> '(b) where the authorisation has effect subject to limitations or conditions, by revoking or varying any of those limitations or conditions, or by attaching further limitations or conditions thereto.'

This power is very wide but not unlimited as the respondents contend. Any variation to the conditions or limitations cannot have the effect of widening the general terms of the authorisation. They can however be used both to relax or make more stringent the conditions governing the disposal of relevant waste.

Are the variations themselves outside the scope of the authorisations?

Gaseous waste

Condition 2 provides that BNFL 'Shall not dispose of relevant waste except by means of (a) Stacks designed, constructed or maintained for that purpose' and is varied thus: 'In condition 2(a), after "maintained for that purpose" insert: "and in the case of relevant waste arising only from the testing of the THORP Stack".' Thus relevant waste is a constant both in the authorisation and in the variation. The effect of the variation still only permits the disposal of relevant waste. There is no extension or increase in the disposal of relevant waste even though there is an added stack (THORP stack) contributing to the relevant waste.

The rest of the variations ensure that, inter alia: (1) BNFL use only unirradiated uranium and uranium compounds derived from natural and depleted uranium as opposed to spent nuclear fuel; (2) disposals of relevant waste shall not exceed stringent and defined limits; and (3) should permission for reprocessing (ie the main authorisation of THORP) not be given BNFL will be required to undertake decontamination of the plant.

Liquid waste

Similarly the variations to the liquid waste authorisation still only permit the disposal of relevant waste as defined. This is even more clear than in the gaseous context; here the authorisation itself (as opposed to the conditions and limitations in the gaseous certificate) authorises disposal of radioactive waste by discharging it into the sea from the seaward end of the pipelines constructed and maintained for that purpose. Thus there is no increase in the discharge points.

This may not have been immediately obvious to Dr Marshall when he wrote in the terms that he did on 5 February and upon which the applicants place such reliance: 'The new points of discharge would be in respect of plant which was not included in the existing authorisation ...' He could not have been referring to the liquid waste authorisation and if he had the gaseous waste authorisation in mind then I am satisfied that the addition of the THORP stack in the schedule attached to the conditions was permissible. It did not alter the character of or increase the discharge of relevant waste. In argument, the applicant did not seek to draw any distinction between the two authorisations. Both either fell or survived. I am further satisfied that the rest of these variations have the same effect as those I have summarised in the gaseous variations.

As a result of this analysis of the statute as amended, the two certificates of authorisation, their conditions and limitations, and the variations under challenge, I conclude that I must reject the construction for which the applicant contends. It was open to the respondents to permit the disposals of relevant waste resulting from testing with unirradiated uranium under the existing authorisations. The authorisations which were in force before the 1993 variations permitted BNFL to discharge relevant waste (gaseous and liquid) from both magnox and oxide fuels. The relevant waste includes radioactive waste from uranium (whether natural, depleted or fissile). However I wish to emphasise that I am not expressing a view whether the main applications could have been effected by the variation route, ie without consultation. The real question for me to determine was whether the power to vary was properly exercised.

In my judgment it was. The variations do not extend the description of radioactive waste not already included within the original authorisations. The variations do not authorise disposals of new descriptions of radioactive waste. It is irrelevant that the relevant waste will emanate from new plant. The authorisation entitles BNFL to carry out its operations at its premises at Sellafield and this generic authorisation is sufficiently wide to cover the testing of the new THORP plant with natural and depleted uranium. The authorisation permits disposal by discharging relevant waste into the atmosphere from stacks (legitimately extended to include the THORP stack) and into the sea via the existing pipelines.

I must also reject the assertion that it was illogical for the respondents to require the main applications to proceed by the consultation process and the testing authorisation without. There is no mandatory obligation upon the authorising bodies to undertake consultation for proposed authorisations or variations. For *authorisations*, they have a wide discretion as to consultation. By s 8(2) Parliament empowers the authorising bodies to consult only with such local authorities, local fisheries etc 'as appears proper to "them" to be consulted by "them".' As to *variations*, the Secretary of State and minister may in their discretion afford an opportunity to be heard by 'such local authorities or other persons whom the Secretary of State and Minister consider appropriate'.

Greenpeace has been consulted in respect of the main application. Greenpeace does not seek to impugn the exercise of the Secretary of State's discretion as to variations. Finally, the fact that a policy decision was taken to invoke or extend the consultation process cannot impugn the decision either to adopt the variation procedure or the decision itself to allow testing.

It must follow, in my judgment, that I cannot accept Greenpeace's suggestion that the respondents (I emphasise the respondents as opposed to BNFL) unlawfully exercised their powers by permitting BNFL to test by the variation route (rather than the authorisation route) in order to avoid consultation or to cut corners or to shut out the consultation process. If the respondents (or BNFL) decided or elected to go by the variation procedure it was open for them to do so in law. Furthermore, the respondents' decision to proceed by variation was not inconsistent with the decision to proceed by fresh authorisation for the main or operational application. Similarly, it was not irrational in the *Wednesbury* sense (see *Associated Provincial Picture Houses Ltd v Wednesbury Corp* [1947] 2 All ER 680, [1948] 1 KB 223); this course of action was open to them.

I therefore reject the application on that ground.

The justification point

Greenpeace's second ground is that, when considering the application for a variation, the authorising bodies were obliged to ensure that the process for which the variation was sought was justified. This, he said, was an implied requirement of the scheme under the principal Act. Counsel referred to para 46(a) of the *Radioactive Substances Act 1960: a guide to the administration of the Act* (1982) issued by the Department of the Environment, which provides that 'All practices giving rise to radioactive waste must be justified, ie the need for the practice must be established in terms of its overall benefits'. This phrase (it is submitted) covers THORP in both its testing and operational modes. I was also referred to art 6 of Council Directive (Euratom) 80/836 as amended by Council Directive (Euratom) 84/467, which provides:

'a. Various types of activity resulting in an exposure to ionising radiation shall have been justified in advance by the advantages which they produce ... b.   All exposure shall be kept as low as reasonably achievable ...'

It is submitted that no discharge of radioactivity of any kind can be justified unless there is a consideration of the factors relating to environmental impact, economics, health and safety, and all other relevant facts and matters.   If at the end of the day the main authorisations are refused there would have been no justification for the testing at all.

In my judgment, there was a general obligation on the authorising bodies when considering whether to permit the discharges necessary for *testing* to consider the health and safety aspect and in particular whether the amount of radioactive waste to be discharged would pose a significant risk to the health or safety of the public.   However, this consideration in my judgment was confined to the testing process; there was no obligation upon the authorising bodies to consider the wider issues which were already under consideration through the consultation process as extended relating to the main operation.

In his affirmation Dr Bryce, head of the pollution policy division of HMIP, declares:

'HMIP and MAFF considered that the radiological impact to the public and to the environment from the discharge of radioactive waste which would result from the discharges arising from testing THORP would be extremely small.   The variations permit a total discharge during testing of 600 kilogrammes of uranium.   HMIP and MAFF Inspectors concluded that the doses to the critical group (that is, the most exposed members of the public) resulting from the 10 week testing period would correspond to less than 0·02 microsieverts per year.   That is significantly less than the [National Radiological Protection Board] recommendation of 300 microsieverts per year for new plant and only 0·001 per cent of the average dose to an individual of 2,200 microsieverts per year resulting from natural background radiation to a member of the UK population.   To put this in perspective, a passenger taking a single flight to Spain would receive, as a result of exposure to cosmic radiation, a dose approximately 500 times greater than the annual dose received by a member of the critical group from the testing of THORP.   It was concluded that exposures resulting from the THORP testing would be as low as reasonably achievable.'

These conclusions are not accepted in their entirety by Greenpeace.   I give full weight to the comments of Mr David Sumner on the question of the justification for the variations.   However, it is not for me to accept or to reject what Dr Bryce says, it is whether that evidence was such which enabled the decision to be taken.   Thus I proceed to consider Dr Bryce's further observations:

'On any view, the size of the doses in issue here are significantly lower than any recommended standard.   Indeed, because of the extremely low levels of radioactivity which would be released from testing THORP using natural or depleted uranium, it was not necessary to increase the existing limits for the discharge of gaseous or liquid radioactive waste from the Sellafield site.   In practice, because the discharges from Sellafield are below the existing authorisation limits there would be a very small increase in the actual amount of radioactive discharges from the site.'

Clearly these were highly material considerations for the regulating bodies to consider before coming to their conclusions. This consideration alone, in my judgment, meets the justification argument, it was not necessary to go into social and economic issues arising out of the main authorisation.

However, I am equally satisfied that the regulating bodies did take account of wider issues of justification before reaching their decision. They were aware from the terms of the minister's letter that the wider issues of justification for the operation of THORP which had been raised in the process of consultation had in fact been considered by ministers and that ministers were minded to conclude that authorisations should be granted. In other words, there was a distinct possibility that the main operation would in fact be authorised.

I am satisfied that in proceeding in the way that they did the requirement of para 46 of the Guidelines was satisfied. So far as testing was concerned, this was a practice giving rise to radioactive wastes, the need for the testing was established 'in terms of its overall benefit'. Likewise the requirement under art 6 of the directive was satisfied. The 'type of activity resulting in an exposure to ionising radiation' covers the testing process during which there occurs a disposal of natural and artificial radioactive substances (art 2). The matters taken into account by the regulating bodies included the advantages which the testing would produce and thus there was a 'justification in advance'. Furthermore, when considering art 6 it is also relevant to bear in mind that the need for THORP was considered at the planning stage (the Parker Report on the Windscale Inquiry) and during the parliamentary process before approval was given. This inevitably took into account many more relevant issues, including the benefit and disbenefit analysis to assess the economic value of the THORP installation. Thus in a broad sense THORP had already been 'justified in advance'. In my view art 6 does not require that such matters be re-evaluated either under art 6 or under s 6 of the 1960 Act.

I must therefore reject the second ground upon which this application is based.

LOCUS STANDI

Mr George Newman QC, leading counsel for BNFL, the party directly affected by the decision under review, submits that in principle and on authority Greenpeace has failed to establish a sufficient interest in the matter to which the application relates and that accordingly the grant of leave should be set aside and in the exercise of my discretion I should disallow the application on that ground, however I may have found on the merits of the case.

In advancing this argument Mr Newman was careful to preface his submissions by emphasising that this issue does not question the sincerity of Greenpeace and its supporters for the causes it supports. BNFL do not seek to question the legitimacy of Greenpeace's objectives and views. The question at issue is not the extent of its reputation and the extent to which it is known nationally and internationally or the integrity of its aims.

Mr Newman took me through an extensive and helpful review of the authorities on the point, which included: *Covent Garden Community Association Ltd v Greater London Council* [1981] JPL 183, *R v Stroud DC, ex p Goodenough* (1982) 43 P & CR 59, *IRC v National Federation of Self-Employed and Small Businesses Ltd* [1981] 2 All ER 93, [1982] AC 617, *R v Hammersmith and Fulham London BC, ex p People before Profit Ltd* (1981) 80 LGR 322, *R v Secretary of State for Social Services, ex p Child Poverty Action Group* (1984) Times, 16 August; *rvsd* (1985) Times, 8 August, *R v Chief Adjudication Officer, ex p Bland* (1985) Times, 6 February, *R v Secretary of State for Social Services, ex p Child Poverty Action Group* [1989] 1 All ER 1047, [1990] 2 QB 540 and *R v Secretary of State for the Environment, ex p Rose Theatre Trust Co* [1990] 1 All ER 754, [1990] 1 QB 504, a decision of Schiemann J. I do not need to explore that decision in any great detail.

In particular he relied upon the speeches in the House of Lords in *IRC v National Federation of Self-Employed and Small Businesses Ltd*. This concerned a decision by the Inland Revenue Commissioners in respect of the tax affairs of the 'Fleet Street casuals' not to investigate tax lost in earlier periods. The applicants were a federation representing the self-employed and small businesses. It was held that the applicants did not have a sufficient interest in the matter to which the application related. The federation was merely a body of taxpayers which had shown no sufficient interest in that matter to justify their application for relief and the federation had completely failed to show any conduct of the revenue which was ultra vires or unlawful. In particular he relied upon extracts from three of the speeches. Lord Wilberforce said ([1981] 2 All ER 93 at 96, [1982] AC 617 at 630):

> '... it will be necessary to consider the powers or the duties in law of those against whom the relief is asked, the position of the applicant in relation to those powers or duties, and the breach of those said to have been committed.'

From Lord Diplock ([1981] 2 All ER 93 at 101, [1982] AC 617 at 636):

> '... the questions (1) what was the public duty of the Board of Inland Revenue of which it was alleged to be in breach, and (2) what was the nature of the breaches that were relied on by the federation ... need to be answered in the instant case before it is possible to say whether the federation has "a sufficient interest in the matter to which the application relates"',

and per Lord Fraser ([1981] 2 All ER 93 at 108, [1982] AC 617 at 646):

> 'The correct approach ... is ... to look at the statute under which the duty arises, and to see whether it gives any express or implied right to persons in the position of the applicant to complain of the alleged unlawful act or omission.'

He also submitted that the analysis of Schiemann J in *ex p Rose Theatre Trust Co* was a correct statement in principle, notably where he set out the following propositions ([1990] 1 All ER 754 at 766, [1990] 1 QB 504 at 520):

> '1. Once leave has been given to move for judicial review, the court which hears the application ought still to examine whether the applicant has a sufficient interest. 2. Whether an applicant has a sufficient interest is not purely a matter of discretion in the court. 3. Not every member of the public can complain of every breach of statutory duty by a person empowered to come to a decision by that statute. To rule otherwise would be to deprive the phrase "a sufficient interest" of all meaning. 4. However, a direct financial or legal interest is not required. 5. Where one is examining an alleged failure to perform a duty imposed by statute it

is useful to look at the statute to see whether it gives an applicant a right enabling him to have that duty performed. 6. Merely to assert that one has an interest does not give one an interest. 7. The fact that some thousands of people join together and assert that they have an interest does not create an interest if the individuals did not have an interest. 8. The fact that those without an interest incorporate themselves and give the company in its memorandum power to pursue a particular object does not give the company an interest.'

Mr Newman takes as his starting point the context of the 1960 Act. He submits that Parliament's purpose in passing the statute is to permit such activities subject to regulation by the designated statutory authorities, not to forbid them altogether. There are built into the statutory framework provisions for consultation in respect of new authorisations and even variations. Thus, there is no express or implied right to persons in the position of Greenpeace to complain of the alleged unlawful act or omission. He analysed the position of Greenpeace in relation to the statutory duties and powers. He emphasised that Greenpeace's primary object is:

'In the United Kingdom and internationally to promote, encourage, further, establish, procure and achieve the protection of wildlife and the elimination of threats and damage to the environment or the global environment of the earth.'

Thus Greenpeace asserts that it represents a wider public interest. This demonstrates that the complaint is in furtherance of Greenpeace's general campaign against the use of radioactive material and the disposal of radioactive waste. Greenpeace merely subscribes to a different view as to the risks associated with such activities from that formed by the authorities charged by statute to regulate and control these activities. Thus Greenpeace's complete opposition to authorising the disposal of radioactive waste is fundamentally incompatible with the statutory scheme adopted by Parliament in the 1960 Act. The fact that an individual or a pressure group has commented on a proposed decision and those comments have been considered by the statutory authorities does not confer on the individual or pressure group a sufficient interest in the decision to challenge the decision by proceedings for judicial review. To hold otherwise, he submits, would be to discourage the statutory authorities from inviting or considering comments from the public beyond their statutory obligations to do so.

He further analyses the challenge to the lawfulness of the procedure and comments:

'This is the classic case of the busybody. The nub of Greenpeace's complaint is that, although it has itself the opportunity to make comments the decision is flawed because some person or body should have been consulted. Allegations that procedural rights have not been respected are properly vindicated by those entitled to those rights and not by a pressure group which itself has no practical complaint.'

In any event, he submits the case does not fall within the exceptional category envisaged by the House of Lords of 'flagrant and serious breaches of the law' or 'exceptionally grave or widespread illegality' or 'a most extreme case' which would justify an exceptional approach to the question of 'sufficient interest' (see *IRC v National Federation of Self-Employed and Small Businesses Ltd* [1981] 2 All ER 93 at 104, 108, 120, 99, [1982] AC 617 at 641, 647, 662, 633 per Lord Diplock, Lord Fraser of Tullybelton, Lord Roskill and Lord Wilberforce).

Conclusions

The requirement of a sufficient interest emerges from s 31(3) of the Supreme Court Act 1981:

'No application for judicial review shall be made unless the leave of the High Court has been obtained in accordance with rules of court; and the court shall not grant leave to make such an application unless it considers that the applicant has a sufficient interest in the matter to which the application relates.'

RSC Ord 53, r 3 (7) provides:

'The Court shall not grant leave unless it considers that the applicant has a sufficient interest in the matter to which the application relates.'

In reaching my conclusions I adopt the approach indicated by Lord Donaldson MR in *R v Monopolies and Mergers Commission, ex p Argyll Group plc* [1986] 2 All ER 257 at 265, [1986] 1 WLR 763 at 773:

'The first stage test, which is applied on the application for leave, will lead to a refusal if the applicant has no interest whatsoever and is, in truth, no more than a meddlesome busybody. If, however, the application appears to be otherwise arguable and there is no other discretionary bar, such as dilatoriness on the part of the applicant, the applicant may expect to get leave to apply, leaving the test of interest or standing to be re-applied as a matter of discretion on the hearing of the substantive application. At this second stage, the strength of the applicant's interest is one of the factors to be weighed in the balance.'

This approach was followed and developed by Purchas LJ in *R v Dept of Transport, ex p Presvac Engineering Ltd* (1989) Times, 4 April when, after considering the decision of the House of Lords in *IRC v National Federation of Self-Employed and Small Businesses Ltd* , he said:

'Personally I would prefer to restrict the use of the expression locus standi to the threshold exercise and to describe the decision at the ultimate stage as an exercise of discretion not to grant relief as the applicant has not established that he had been or would be sufficiently affected.'

Thus I approach this matter primarily as one of discretion. I consider it appropriate to take into account the nature of Greenpeace and the extent of its interest in the issues raised, the remedy Greenpeace seeks to achieve and the nature of the relief sought.

In doing so I take into account the very nature of Greenpeace. Lord Melchett has affirmed thus:

'Greenpeace International has nearly 5 million supporters worldwide; Greenpeace UK has over 400,000 supporters in the United Kingdom and about 2,500 of them are in the Cumbria region, where the BNFL plant is situated. Greenpeace is a campaigning organisation which has as its prime object the protection of the natural environment.'

Greenpeace International has also been accredited with consultative status with the United Nations Economic and Social Council (including United Nations General Assembly). It has accreditation status with the United Nations Conference on Environment and Development. They have observer status or the right to attend meetings of 17 named bodies including Parcom (Paris Convention for the Prevention of Marine Pollution from Land Based Sources).

BNFL rightly acknowledges the national and international standing of Greenpeace and its integrity. So must I. I have not the slightest reservation that Greenpeace is an entirely responsible and respected body with a genuine concern for the environment. That concern naturally leads to a bona fide interest in the activities carried on by BNFL at Sellafield and in particular the discharge and disposal of radioactive waste from its premises and to which the respondents' decision to vary relates. The fact that there are 400,000 supporters in the United Kingdom carries less weight than the fact that 2,500 of them come from the Cumbria region. I would be ignoring the blindingly obvious if I were to disregard the fact that those persons are inevitably concerned about (and have a genuine perception that there is) a danger to their health and safety from any additional discharge of radioactive waste even from testing. I have no doubt that the issues raised by this application are serious and worthy of determination by this court.

It seems to me that if I were to deny standing to Greenpeace, those it represents might not have an effective way to bring the issues before the court. There would have to be an application either by an individual employee of BNFL or a near neighbour. In this case it is unlikely that either would be able to command the expertise which is at the disposal of Greenpeace. Consequently, a less well-informed challenge might be mounted which would stretch unnecessarily the court's resources and which would not afford the court the assistance it requires in order to do justice between the parties. Further, if the unsuccessful applicant had the benefit of legal aid it might leave the respondents and BNFL without an effective remedy in costs. Alternatively, the individual (or Greenpeace) might seek to persuade Her Majesty's Attorney General to commence a relator action which (as a matter of policy or practice) he may be reluctant to undertake against a government department (see the learned commentary by Schiemann J on 'Locus Standi' [1990] Pub L 342). Neither of these courses of action would have the advantage of an application by Greenpeace, who, with its particular experience in environmental matters, its access to experts in the relevant realms of science and technology (not to mention the law), is able to mount a carefully selected, focused, relevant and well-argued challenge. It is not without significance that in this case the form 86 contains six grounds of challenge but by the time it came to the substantive hearing before me, the Greenpeace 'team' (if I may call them that) had been able to evaluate the respondents' and BNFL's evidence and were able to jettison four grounds and concentrate on two. This responsible approach undoubtedly had the advantage of sparing scarce court resources, ensuring an expedited substantive hearing and an early result (which it transpires is helpful to the respondents and to BNFL). This line of reasoning has some support from the approach to be found in a line of cases in the Supreme Court of

Canada (see *Thorson v A-G of Canada* [1975] 1 SCR 138, *McNeil v Nova Scotia Board of Censors* [1976] 2 SCR 265, *Borowski v Minister of Justice of Canada* [1981] 2 SCR 575 and *Finlay v Minister of Finance of Canada* [1986] 2 SCR 607 esp the judgment of Le Dain J; see also the helpful and imaginative commentary of the authors Supperstone and Goudie *Judicial Review* (1992) pp 335–356 and 338–340).

I also take into account the nature of the relief sought. In *IRC v National Federation of Self-Employed and Small Businesses Ltd* the House of Lords expressed the view that if mandamus were sought that would be a reason to decline jurisdiction. Here, the primary relief sought is certiorari (less stringent) and, if granted, the question of an injunction to stop the testing pending determination of the main applications would still be in the discretion of the court. I also take into account the fact that Greenpeace has been treated as one of the consultees during the consultation process and that they were invited (albeit with other non-consultees) to comment on the 'minded to vary' letter.

It follows that I reject the argument that Greenpeace is a 'mere' or 'meddlesome busybody'. I regard the applicant as eminently respectable and responsible and its genuine interest in the issues raised is sufficient for it to be granted locus standi.

I should add that Lord Roskill in *IRC v National Federation of Self-Employed and Small Businesses Ltd* [1981] 2 All ER 93 at 117, [1982] AC 617 at 659 approved the commentary to Ord 53 in *The Supreme Court Practice 1989* (see now *The Supreme Court Practice 1993* vol 1, para 53/1–14/11) that the question of whether the applicant has a sufficient interest appears to be—

'a mixed question of fact and law; a question of fact and degree and the relationship between the applicant and the matter to which the application relates, having regard to all the circumstances of the case.'

Thus it must not be assumed that Greenpeace (or any other interest group) will automatically be afforded standing in any subsequent application for judicial review in whatever field it (and its members) may have an interest. This will have to be a matter to be considered on a case by case basis at the leave stage and if the threshold is crossed again at the substantive hearing as a matter of discretion.

I also bear this consideration in mind when I respectfully decline to follow the decision of Schiemann J in *R v Secretary of State for the Environment, ex p Rose Theatre Trust Co* [1990] 1 All ER 754, [1990] 1 QB 504. Suffice it to say that the circumstances were different, the interest group had been formed for the exclusive purpose of saving the Rose Theatre site and no individual member could show any personal interest in the outcome. In any event his decision on the locus standi point (as indeed is mine) was not central to his decision.

In exercising my discretion I would grant Greenpeace standing in this case. If I had found in their favour on the grounds advanced, the question of what relief would have been appropriate would still have been within my discretion. Although I would probably have granted an order of certiorari to strike down the decision, it would have been a matter of considerable argument and further representation before I would have taken the further step of granting an injunction to end the testing. In case this case goes any further, I say no more on that particular point.

In the event, having granted in my discretion Greenpeace leave to make this application on behalf of its members on these matters of considerable interest to the public, I cannot find for Greenpeace on the merits of the application. It must therefore be refused.

Application dismissed.

Mary Rose Plummer   Barrister.

R v Secretary of State for the Environment and others, ex parte Greenpeace Ltd and another

QUEEN'S BENCH DIVISION (CROWN OFFICE LIST)

POTTS J

7–11, 14–17 FEBRUARY, 4 MARCH 1994

Judicial review – Availability of remedy – Discretion of court to grant relief – Statutory authorisation – Company obtaining authorisations to operate thermal oxide reprocessing plant – Environmental protection organisation and local authority seeking judicial review of decision to grant authorisations and Secretary of State's further decision not to call in applications or hold public inquiry – Whether judicial review should be granted – Whether justification for authorisations in terms of overall benefit a legal requirement – Whether legislation to be construed to accord with relevant Community directive – Whether decision not to hold inquiry flawed – Whether environmental impact assessment a legal requirement – Radioactive Substances Act 1993, ss 13, 16, 24(2) – Council Directive (Euratom) 80/836, arts 6, 13 – Council Directive (EEC) 85/337.

In 1983, following a public inquiry and parliamentary debate, a company, BNFL, which carried on the business of reprocessing spent nuclear fuel obtained full planning permission to construct a thermal oxide reprocessing plant on its site. On completion of the new plant in 1992 BNFL applied for new authorisations for the discharge of radioactive waste to sea and air in order to commence operations. The Inspectorate of Pollution and the ministry responsible for regulating the disposal of radioactive waste on nuclear sites prepared draft authorisations which they made available for public consultation over a ten-week period. After considering 84,000 responses, including responses from an environmental protection organisation and the local authority for the area where the plant was situated, the ministers concluded that no new matters had been raised by the consultation and responses which would cause them to reconsider the terms of the draft authorisations, which in their view would effectively promote human health, the safety of the food chain and the environment generally. A further consultation took place in 1993 to consider wider policy issues which had not been addressed earlier, such as the justification for the new plant and proposed emissions of radioactivity in terms of overall benefit and the non-proliferation implications of an increasing stockpile of plutonium. In December 1993 the Secretary of State and the ministers granted the new authorisations pursuant a to ss 13[a] and 16[b] of the Radioactive Substances Act 1993. The environmental protection organisation and the local authority subsequently applied for judicial review of the decision granting the authorisations and of the Secretary of State's earlier decision not to exercise his discretion under s 24(2)[c] of the 1993 Act to call in BNFL's applications for new authorisations and to hold a local inquiry. The applicants contended inter alia (i) that the authorisations

b had not been lawfully granted, since the ministers' decision that there was no legal obligation to justify the grant of the authorisations, and thereby a particular practice resulting in the discharge of radioactive waste, was inconsistent with the exercise of powers under ss 13 and 16 of the 1993 Act, which should be construed in accordance with arts 6[d] and 13[e] of Council Directive (Euratom) 80/836 (and international standards recognised by the

c government) which required the issue of prior justification to be addressed, (ii) that the decision not to hold an inquiry was flawed, since the Secretary of State had to decide not only whether he and the ministers had sufficient information to enable them to reach a decision on the contentious issues, but also (a) whether they could be further assisted by the testing of material which would

d take place in such an inquiry and (b) whether it was in the public interest that an inquiry should be held and (iii) that the ministers were under a legal duty to provide and make available an environmental impact assessment in accordance with the provisions of Council Directive (EEC) 85/337 governing the assessment of the environmental effects of projects likely to have significant effects on the environment, which applied to the proposed

e operation of the new plant, but not its construction as it predated the directive.

Held – The application would be dismissed for the following reasons—

(1) There was no reason why ss 13 and 16 of the 1993 Act should not be construed to accord with Directive 80/836 and, in particular, arts 6 and 13, which required the issue of justification in terms of net benefit to be considered prior to the grant of any authorisation for the discharge of radioactive waste, notwithstanding that the Act itself was silent on the matter of prior justification. Directive 80/836 was concerned with the justification of particular practices affecting particular individuals in particular circumstances and it was clear that there had been no justification of the activity of thermal oxide reprocessing at BNFL's new plant involving the decision-maker being satisfied that the benefits flowing from the activity outweighed the detriments. It followed that there was a legal obligation to justify the grant of the authorisations in terms of net benefit and that the ministers had erred in concluding that justification was not relevant in the context of the exercise by them of their functions under the Act (see p 365 h, p 368 f to h and p 384 h, post).

(2) Although the ministers had erred in law in failing to consider at the outset whether the proposed emissions of radioactivity were justified, their general approach to justification could not be faulted. The minister had in fact carried out a careful process of weighing the benefits against the detriments in reaching the conclusion that the balance came down on the side of

a   Section 13, so far as material, is set out at p 357 g h, post
b   Section 16, so far as material, is set out at p 357 j to p 358 b, post
c   Section 24(2) is set out at p 358 f g, post
d   Article 6, so far as material, is set out at p 359 d, post
e   Article 13, so far as material, is set out at p 359 g, post

justification. In particular, they were entitled to conclude that there was a good economic case for proceeding with the new thermal oxide reprocessing plant, that dry storage was not a true alternative to reprocessing and that compliance with international and national standards on radiation dose limits, targets and constraints would protect the public from unacceptable health risks. The ministers were accordingly entitled to conclude that the proposed emissions were justified (see p 375 *j* to to 376 *d* and p 384 *h*, post).

(3) On a true construction of Directive 85/337, the construction of the thermal oxide reprocessing plant, the bringing into operation of the plant and the consequent discharges were one project which predated the directive. It followed that the directive did not apply to the project and, as a result, that the ministers were not under a legal duty to provide an environmental impact assessment complying with the provisions and standards laid down in the directive before the grant of the authorisations. In any event, although no formal assessment had taken place, it was clear that the information provided and made available for consultation by the inspectorates and ministers met the subsequent requirements of the directive (see p 377 *e* to *g* and p 384 *h*, post).

(4) In exercising his discretion under s 24(2) of the 1993 Act whether to direct a local inquiry, the Secretary of State had adequately and properly addressed the matters relevant to his decision, since the consultation procedures adopted met the necessary requirements and he was satisfied that he was in a position to take account of the representations and to weigh the economic, health and environmental factors in deciding whether to grant the authorisations. Moreover, although it was arguable that a minister sensible to the scale of representations and the desirability of allaying public anxiety would have directed a public inquiry, that was not the issue. The Secretary of State, in refusing to direct a local inquiry, acted lawfully within the wide powers conferred on him by Parliament, since had he applied his mind genuinely and rationally to the issue of whether to hold an inquiry and his decision not to do so could not therefore be impugned (see p 379 *e*, p 382 *b* to *d*, p 383 *a b* and p 384 *e* to *h*, post); dictum of Lord Lowry in *Brind v Secretary of State for the Home Dept* [1991] 1 All ER 720 at 737–738 applied.

Notes

For atomic energy and radioactive substances in general, see 16 *Halsbury's Laws* (4th edn) paras 224–500.

For control of radioactive waste, see 16 *Halsbury's Laws* (4th edn) paras 361, 362 and for cases on the subject, see 20 *Digest* (Reissue) 228, *2300–2301*.

For public inquiries concerning radioactive substance rules, see 16 *Halsbury's Laws* (4th edn) para 268.

For the Radioactive Substances Act 1993, ss 13, 16, 24, see 47(S) *Halsbury's Statutes* (4th edn) 147, 150, 159.

Cases referred to in judgment

Associated Provincial Picture Houses Ltd v Wednesbury Corp [1947] 2 All ER 680, [1948] 1 KB 223, CA.

Binney v Secretary of State for the Environment (1983) Times, 8 October.

Brind v Secretary of State for the Home Dept [1991] 1 All ER 720, [1991] 1 AC 696, [1991] 2 WLR 588, HL.

Bushell v Secretary of State for the Environment [1980] 2 All ER 608, [1981] AC 75, [1980] 3 WLR 22, HL.

a   *Council of Civil Service Unions v Minister for the Civil Service* [1984] 3 All ER 935, [1985] AC 374, [1984] 3 WLR 1174, HL.
Duke v GEC Reliance Ltd [1988] 1 All ER 626, [1988] AC 618, [1988] 2 WLR 359, HL.
Ionising Radiation Protection, Re, EC Commission v Belgium Case C-376/90 [1993] 2 CMLR 513, CJEC.
b   *Marleasing SA v La Comercial Internacional de Alimentación SA* Case C-106/89 [1990] ECR 1–4135.
Nottinghamshire CC v Secretary of State for the Environment [1986] 1 All ER 199, [1986] AC 240, [1986] 2 WLR 1, HL.
Padfield v Minister of Agriculture, Fisheries and Food [1968] 1 All ER 694, [1968] AC 997, [1968] 2 WLR 924, HL.
c   *R v Nat Bell Liquors Ltd* [1922] 2 AC 128, [1922] All ER Rep 335, PC.
R v Rochdale Health Authority, ex p Rochdale Metropolitan BC (1992) 8 BMLR 137, DC.
Secretary of State for Education and Science v Tameside Metropolitan Borough [1976] 3 All ER 665, [1977] AC 1014, [1976] 3 WLR 641, HL.
d   *Twyford Parish Council v Secretary of State for the Environment* [1992] 1 CMLR 276.
von Colson and Kamann v Land Nordrhein-Westfalen Case 14/83 [1984] ECR 1891.
Webb v EMO Air Cargo (UK) Ltd [1992] 4 All ER 929, [1993] 1 WLR 49, HL.

Application for judicial review
e   Greenpeace Ltd and Lancashire County Council (Lancashire) applied with leave of Laws J granted on 13 January 1994 for judicial review by way of: (i) an order of certiorari to quash the decision of the first respondent, the Secretary of State for the Environment, not to call in applications by British Nuclear Fuels plc (BNFL) for authorisations under the Radioactive Substances Act 1960 (replaced by the Radioactive Substances Act 1993) to discharge radioactive
f   waste from their plant at Sellafield, Cumbria, and hold a public inquiry; (ii) an order of certiorari to quash the decision of the second and third respondents, the Chief Inspector of HM Inspectorate of Pollution and the Minister of Agriculture, Fisheries and Food, dated 17 December 1993, to grant authorisations to BNFL under the Act to discharge radioactive waste from their premises at Sellafield. BNFL took part in the proceedings as an interested
g   party. The facts are set out in the judgment.

Andrew Collins QC, Owen Davies and *James Cameron* (instructed by *Sarah Jane Burton*) for Greenpeace.
Nicholas Blake (instructed by *Sarah Jane Burton*, agent for *Max Winterbottom*,
h   Preston) for Lancashire.
Stephen Richards and *J Turner* (instructed by the *Treasury Solicitor*) for the respondents.
George Newman QC and *Alan Griffiths* (instructed by *Freshfields*) for BNFL.

i   *Cur adv vult*

4 March 1994. The following judgment was delivered.

POTTS J. The applicants apply for judicial review of: (1) a decision by the Secretary of State for the Environment dated 15 December 1993 refusing to exercise his powers under s 12(B) of the Radioactive Substances Act 1960 and/

or s 24 of the Radioactive Substances Act 1993, (a) to call in the applications by British Nuclear Fuels plc (BNFL) for authorisations under the Act to discharge radioactive waste from their plant at Sellafield, Cumbria, and (b) to cause a local inquiry to be held; (2) a decision made by the Secretary of State for the Environment, the Chief Inspector of HM Inspectorate of Pollution (the chief inspector) and the Minister of Agriculture Fisheries and Food (the minister) dated 17 December 1993 to grant authorisations under the Act to BNFL.

Leave to apply was granted by Laws J on 13 January 1994. Laws J directed expedition and the hearing commenced on 7 February 1994.

The applicants seek the following relief. (1) An order of certiorari to bring up and quash the Secretary of State's decision of 15 December 1993 not to call in the applications for authorisations and hold a public inquiry. (2) (Not applicable.) (3) An order of certiorari to bring up and quash the decision of the chief inspector and the minister dated 17 December 1993 to grant authorisations to BNFL pursuant to s 13 of the 1993 Act to discharge radioactive waste from their premises at Sellafield. (4) A declaration that no authorisation can be lawfully granted unless the authorising body shall have first been satisfied that the proposed emissions of radioactivity are justified in that the activity giving rise to these emissions produces a net benefit to the public taking into account detriment inherent in increased radiation emissions. (5) A declaration that no authorising authority can be so satisfied as in (4) above without a public inquiry at which the purported economic advantages of operating a thermal oxide reprocessing plant (THORP) can be examined and weighed against the perceived detriments. (6) A declaration that no authorisation or discharges can be lawfully granted without there first being provided and made available an environmental impact assessment that meets the substantive requirements of Council Directive (EEC) 85/337 and provides a sufficient basis for assessment of the environmental impact of the operation of THORP.

THE PARTIES AND OTHER RELEVANT BODIES

Greenpeace Ltd is the corporate identity of Greenpeace UK, the United Kingdom National Office of Greenpeace International (incorporated in the Netherlands as Stichting Greenpeace Council). Its prime object is the protection of the natural environment.

Lancashire County Council is a statutory consultee by virtue of Lancashire's proximity to Sellafield and its long coastline.

Her Majesty's Inspectorate of Pollution (HMIP) was established in 1987 when existing inspectorates were merged. HMIP is part of the Department of Environment and the Secretary of State for the Environment has ministerial responsibility for it but it acts as an independent inspectorate. It is responsible for the authorisation and regulation of non-nuclear industrial pollution, regulations for the disposal of radioactive waste, research on pollution control and radioactive waste disposal and for giving advice to government and industry. HMIP has statutory responsibilities in respect of the disposal of radioactive waste. HMIP and the Ministry of Agriculture, Fisheries and Food (MAFF) each regulate the disposal of radioactive waste from premises subject to a nuclear site licence. HMIP is concerned with the effects of any such disposal on the environment. MAFF is concerned with the consequences of such disposal on the food chain, fisheries and the marine environment in general. The inspectorates have extensive experience of regulation at a Sellafield and have granted various authorisations permitting the disposal of liquid, solid and gaseous radioactive wastes from the site since 1960.

BNFL (an interested party) carries on the business of reprocessing spent nuclear fuel at its site at Sellafield, Cumbria. BNFL is a public limited company whose shares are owned by or on behalf of the Secretary of State for Trade and Industry. BNFL was set up to fulfil the purposes of the Atomic Energy Act 1971
b to facilitate the commercial development of nuclear fuel. BNFL is the holder of a site licence in respect of Sellafield under the Nuclear Installations Act 1965.

The International Commission on Radiological Protection (ICRP) makes recommendations on radiological protection. The commission is a long established non-governmental, independent body of scientific experts drawn from countries throughout the world. It sets its own agenda. It considers
c developments in knowledge on all factors concerning radiological protection. These include the biological effects of radiation exposure and risks to health from radiation exposure. The commission also advises on the need for standards, the form of such standards and the criteria appropriate for maximising radiation protection. Recommendations and statements from ICRP are
d openly published.

The National Radiological Protection Board (the NRPB) advises the government of the United Kingdom on all aspects of the radiological protection. The NRPB was established by the Radiological Protection Act 1970. The function of the NRPB is to carry out research about protection from radiation hazards and to provide advice to those, including government
e departments, with responsibilities in the United Kingdom in relation to the protection from radiation hazards either of the community as a whole or of particular sections of the community. The Act also gives the NRPB the power to provide technical services. The NRPB has a staff of about 340, about 270 of whom are scientific or technical.

THE STATUTORY BACKGROUND

The Radioactive Substances Act 1993 came into effect on 27 August 1993. It is a consolidating measure, replacing the Radioactive Substances Act 1960. The material provisions are as follows:

f Section 13(1) of the 1993 Act (which replaced s 6(1) of the 1960 Act) provides:

'Subject to section 15, no person shall, except in accordance with an authorisation granted in that behalf under this subsection, dispose of any radioactive waste on or from any premises which are used for the purposes of an undertaking carried on by him, or cause or permit any radioactive
g waste to be so disposed of, if (in any such case) he knows or has reasonable grounds for believing it to be radioactive waste.'

Section 16(3) (formerly s 8(1) of the 1960 Act) provides:

'In England, Wales and Northern Ireland, the power to grant authorisations under section 13(1) in respect of the disposal of radioactive
h waste on or from any premises situated on a nuclear site shall be exercisable by the chief inspector and the appropriate Minister; and the disposal of radioactive waste on or from any such premises in England, Wales or Northern Ireland shall not be treated as authorised under section 13(1) unless it is so authorised by both the chief inspector and that Minister.'

Section 16(5) (formerly s 8(2) of the 1960 Act) provides:

'Before granting an authorisation under section 13(1) in respect of the disposal of radioactive waste on or from premises situated on a nuclear site, the chief inspector and, where the premises are in England, Wales or Northern Ireland, the appropriate Minister shall each consult with such local authorities, relevant water bodies or other public or local authorities as appear to him to be proper to be consulted by him.'

The 'appropriate Minister' is, for England and Wales, the Minister of Agriculture, Fisheries and Food (s 47(1)).

Section 23 of the 1993 Act confers powers on the Secretary of State for the Environment to give directions in relation to applications:

'(1) The Secretary of State may, if he thinks fit in relation to ... (b) an application for an authorisation under section 13 or 14 ... give directions to the chief inspector requiring him to take any of the steps mentioned in the following subsections in accordance with the directions.

(2) A direction under subsection (1) may require the chief inspector so to exercise his powers under this Act as—(a) to refuse an application ... or (b) to effect or grant an authorisation, attaching such limitations or conditions (if any) as may be specified ... or (c) to vary [an] ... authorisation ... (d) to cancel or revoke (or not to cancel or revoke) [an] ... authorisation.'

Section 24 of the Act provides:

'(1) The Secretary of State may—(a) give general directions to the chief inspector requiring him to refer applications under this Act for registrations or authorisations ... to the Secretary of State for his determination, and (b) give directions to the chief inspector in respect of any particular application requiring him to refer the application to the Secretary of State for his determination.

(2) Where an application is referred to the Secretary of State in pursuance of directions given under this section, the Secretary of State may cause a local inquiry to be held in relation to the application ...

(4) After determining any application so referred, the Secretary of State may give the chief inspector directions under section 23 as to the steps to be taken by him in respect of the application.'

Section 28 of the Act provides that before the chief inspector and the appropriate minister refuse an application for an authorisation under s 13 or attach limitations or conditions to such an authorisation or vary it or revoke it:

'the person directly concerned shall, and such local authorities ... whom [the ministers] consider appropriate, may be afforded the opportunity of appearing before, and being heard by, a person appointed for the purpose ...'

Articles 30 and 31 of the Euratom Treaty (TS 1 (1973); Cmnd 5179) are relevant. They provide:

'30. Basic standards shall be laid down within the Community for the protection of the health of workers and the general public against the dangers arising from ionizing radiations. The expression "basic

standards" means: (a) maximum permissible doses compatible with
adequate safety; (b) maximum permissible levels of exposure and
contamination; (c) the fundamental principles governing the health
surveillance of workers.

31. The basic standards shall be worked out by the Commission after it
has obtained the opinion of a group of persons appointed by the Scientific
and Technical Committee from among scientific experts and in particular
public health experts, in the Member States. The Commission shall obtain
the opinion of the Economic and Social Committee on these basic
standards. After consulting the European Parliament the Council shall ...
establish the basic standards ...'

The Council of the European Communities established the basic standards
for the health protection of the general public and workers against the dangers
of ionising radiation by Council Directive (Euratom) 80/836 of 15 July 1980 (as
amended). Title III provides for the 'Limitation of Doses for Controllable
Exposures', art 6 of which is as follows:

'The limitation of individual and collective doses resulting from
controllable exposures shall be based on the following general principles:
(a) the various types of activity resulting in an exposure to ionizing
radiation shall have been justified in advance by the advantages which
they produce ...'

This replaced (in September 1984) a provision:

'(a) every activity resulting in an exposure to ionizing radiation shall be
justified by the advantages which it produces; (b) all exposures shall be
kept as low as reasonably achievable; (c) without prejudice to Article 11,
the sum of the doses and committed doses received shall not exceed the
dose limits laid down in this Title for exposed workers ... and members of
the public ...'

Article 13 provides:

'*Exposure of the population as a whole*
1. Each Member State shall ensure that the contribution to the exposure
of the population as a whole from each activity is kept to the minimum
amount necessitated by that activity, taking account of the principles set
out in Article 6(a) and (b).
2. The total of all such contributions shall be kept under review ...'

Council Directive (EEC) 85/337 of 27 June 1985 is also relevant. So far as it
is material it provides:

'*Article 1*
1. This Directive shall apply to the assessment of the environmental
effects of those public and private projects which are likely to have
significant effects on the environment.
2. For the purposes of this Directive: "project" means:—the execution
of construction works or of other installations or schemes,—other
interventions in the natural surroundings and landscape including those
involving the extraction of mineral resources; "developer" means: the
applicant for authorization for a private project or the public authority
which initiates a project; "development consent" means: the decision of

the competent authority ... which entitles the developer to proceed with
the project ...

Article 2

1. Member States shall adopt all measures necessary to ensure that,
before consent is given, projects likely to have significant effects on the
environment by virtue, *inter alia*, of their nature, size or location are made
subject to an assessment with regard to their effects ...

Article 3

The environmental impact assessment will identify, describe and assess
in an appropriate manner, in the light of each individual case and in
accordance with Articles 4 to 11, the direct and indirect effects of a project
on the following factors:—human beings, fauna and flora,—soil, water,
air, climate and the landscape,—the inter-action between the factors
mentioned in the first and second indents,—material assets and the
cultural heritage.

Article 4

1. Subject to Article 2(3), projects of the classes listed in Annex I shall be
made subject to an assessment in accordance with Articles 5 to 10.

2. Projects of the classes listed in Annex II shall be made subject to an
assessment, in accordance with Articles 5 to 10, where Member States
consider that their characteristics so require.'

Article 5 and Annex III specify the information to be supplied by the developer
of a project which is subject to an environmental impact assessment. Annex II
sets out the projects subject to art 4(2). Paragraphs 1 and 2, 'Agriculture' and
'Extractive Industry', are to be noted. Paragraph 3 indicates 'Energy Industry'.
Paragraph 3(h) identifies: 'Installations for the reprocessing of irradiated
nuclear fuels' as a project subject to art 4(2).

Background

The history of nuclear operations on the Sellafield site dates back to 1947.
Nuclear fuel from Magnox reactors has been reprocessed at Sellafield for more
than 30 years.

Reprocessing has been carried out on a commercial basis for both United
Kingdom and overseas customers since 1971. Since 1971 the site has been
owned and operated by BNFL, apart from a small area belonging to the United
Kingdom Atomic Energy Authority. The site consists of a plant to handle and
store spent fuel, for reprocessing spent fuel and for the generation of
electricity. BNFL is in possession of authorisations issued under the
Radioactive Substances Act 1960 to enable them to lawfully discharge
radioactive waste into the atmosphere, 'gaseous discharges' and into the Irish
Sea 'liquid discharges'.

Between 1971 and 1977 BNFL sought planning permission for a thermal
oxide reprocessing plant (THORP) designed to reprocess spent oxide fuel from
nuclear reactors. A public inquiry presided over by Sir Roger Parker was held
to consider this application and various related matters. The inquiry heard
evidence over some 100 days in 1977. The Parker Report on The Windscale
Inquiry arising from the inquiry was presented to Parliament on 26 January
1978. The report recommended that outline planning permission be given in
respect of BNFL's application. The report was debated in Parliament on 22

March 1978 (see 946 HC Official Report (5th series) cols 1537–1676).
a On 15 May 1978 there was a further debate on the Town and Country Planning (Windscale and Calder Works) Special Development Order 1978, SI 1978/523, and outline permission was granted (see 950 HC Official Report (5th Series) cols 111 –182). Full planning permission was applied for and obtained by BNFL in 1983. Construction of THORP was subsequently begun and was completed
b in February 1992. BNFL has also built an enhanced actinide removal plant (EARP) to treat liquid waste streams on the site, both for Magnox reprocessing and from THORP before being discharged to the sea. Since 1980 BNFL has been required to stop the discharge of certain types of liquid waste from Magnox reprocessing and store them on the site until EARP becomes operational. It is intended that EARP will treat this backlog of stored wastes.

c   In April 1992 in order to operate THORP, BNFL applied for new authorisations for discharges of radioactive waste to sea and air from the Sellafield site. After considering the applications the inspectorates prepared draft new authorisations. They made these available for public consultation. Consultation began on 16 November 1992 and lasted for ten weeks. Some
d 84,000 responses to the consultation were received by the inspectorates in total.

    The inspectorates considered the responses, including those of the first applicant, Greenpeace Ltd (Greenpeace) and the second applicant, Lancashire County Council (Lancashire). Lancashire contributed to the consultation by commissioning a report from their scientific advisory body, Radiation
e Monitoring in Lancashire (RADMIL). Lancashire urged that the issues raised by the applications for authorisation could only be resolved by public inquiry. The inspectorates reported to the ministers (ie the Secretary of State for the Environment and the Minister of Agriculture Fisheries and Food) in May 1993. In their report they concluded that no points had been raised by the
f consultation and the responses thereto to cause them to reconsider the terms of their draft authorisations. The inspectorates stated that they had reached the view that—'the provisions of the draft authorizations would effectively protect human health, the safety of the food chain and the environment generally'. But the inspectorates further pointed out that a number of wider policy issues had been raised during the consultation. These related to the
g justification for nuclear fuel reprocessing generally, and for THORP in particular, to the non-proliferation implications of an increasing stockpile of plutonium and security risks. The inspectorates reported that they had not addressed these issues.

    From the beginning of the consultation period Greenpeace had sought to
h persuade the inspectorates that they were required as a matter of law to consider whether the emissions of radioactivity from THORP were justified in terms of there being a net benefit. Further, by letters of 9 February, 28 June and 5 July 1993, the executive director of Greenpeace urged the Secretary of State to call in the applications and cause a public inquiry to be held. On 13 July 1993 a minister at the Department of the Environment informed Greenpeace that a
i decision whether or not to hold a public inquiry would be taken after the second round of consultations.

    On 28 June 1993 the ministers had announced that a further round of consultation would be undertaken to provide an opportunity for the wider issues referred to by the inspectorate in their report to be considered. The ministers' position at that time is summarised in 'Radioactive Substances Act

1993, Decision by the Secretary of State for the Environment and the Minister
of Agriculture, Fisheries and Food in respect of an application from British
Nuclear Fuels for authorisations to discharge radioactive wastes from the
Sellafield site' (the decision document):

'13. When the ministers had considered the report from the
Inspectorates and these other papers, they made a further announcement
on 4 August. In this announcement they concluded that: (i) The draft
authorisations fully satisfied the requirements of the Act; (ii) all
substantive and relevant issues raised in the first consultation had been
adequately considered by the Inspectorates; (iii) in framing their draft
authorisations the Inspectorates had applied the relevant principles
underlying the Government's objectives for radioactive waste
management.
14. In the light of this the Ministers stated they were minded to
conclude that the authorisations should be granted on the terms proposed
by the Inspectorates.
15. The Ministers also considered the wider issues raised during the first
consultation and which the Inspectorates had not addressed. They
concluded that these issues were not relevant in the context of the exercise
by them of their functions under the legislation, though they noted that a
number of respondents had argued that they were.
16. The Ministers considered the additional documents which had been
prepared on these wider issues and came to the view that even if the wider
issues had been relevant, they would still have been minded to conclude
that the authorisations should be granted on the terms proposed by the
Inspectorates. The Ministers recognised however that the further
information provided by these papers had not been made available for
wider comment and said that their final decisions would not be taken until
after further consultation.'

The second round of consultations started on 4 August 1993 with the
publication of the following documents to the consultees. (a) 'Statement of
Government Policy on Reprocessing and Operation of Thermal Oxide Reprocessing Plant at Sellafield'. (b) 'Further material on the Environment
Aspects of the Operation of THORP' (BNFL). (c) 'The Economic and
Commercial Justification for THORP' (BNFL). (d) 'Report on the Public
Consultation conducted by HMIP and MAFF'. The second consultation was
to come to an end on 4 October 1993, but responses received after that date
were considered. There were 42,500 responses to the second consultation. Of
these, 12,300 people called for a public inquiry on an individual basis. Of the
statutory local authorities who responded, four were in favour of the operation
of the plant, including Cumbria County Council and Copeland Borough
Council (the local authority areas in which Sellafield is located) while 23 were
opposed. A further 22 did not express an opinion either way. Of these 49
responses, 39 called for a public inquiry. A further 53 responses were also
received from local authorities who were not formally consulted, of which one
was in favour, 30 were against and 22 did not express an opinion either way.
Of these 53 further responses, 46 called for a public inquiry, giving a total of 85
local authorities who requested a public inquiry into the operation of the plant.
Greenpeace responded to the consultation by submitting several volumes of
material. Greenpeace renewed its call for a public inquiry and explained the

a shortcomings of the information available to it for the purposes of consultation. Lancashire renewed its call for a public inquiry (first made in December 1992) and submitted an updated report from RADMIL.

On 15 December 1993 the ministers refused to call in BNFL's applications or to cause a local inquiry into the authorisations to be held, stating that, 'We are satisfied that no issues have been raised which would cause us to conclude that b further consultation or debate is necessary' (see the Secretary of State's statement to the House of Commons on 15 December 1993, 234 HC Official Report (6th series) col 677). On 16 December 1993 the chief inspector and the minister granted BNFL authorisations to discharge gaseous and liquid radioactive waste under the provisions of the Radioactive Substances Act 1993.

c THE ISSUES

The decisions under review raise issues of great importance. It is clear from the responses to the consultation exercises that they have caused anxiety and concern to a substantial number of public bodies and private individuals. In this application Greenpeace has expressed that anxiety and concern on behalf d of its members. Lancashire has done likewise. Both applicants contend that the issues raised can only properly be tested and ventilated at a local inquiry, ie a public inquiry.

I must emphasise that it is not the function of this court to act as a court of appeal from the minister's decision. This court cannot determine the scientific and environmental arguments advanced to ministers or resolve disputes of e fact. It is important to note that s 24(2) of the 1993 Act confers a discretion on the Secretary of State as to whether to cause a local inquiry to be held or not. The essential question for the court is whether the respondents acted unlawfully in reaching any or all of the decisions complained of.

The original grounds upon which relief was sought raised a number of f overlapping issues. As the hearing progressed, it became clear that there were four essential issues. (1) Justification: (a) whether there was a legal requirement to consider justification and (b) whether the finding that the activities giving rise to the discharges permitted by the authorisations were justified was irrational. (2) Environmental impact assessment: (a) whether Council Directive (EEC) 85/337 applied and (b) whether the essential g requirements of the directive were complied with in any event. (3) Consultation. (4) Local inquiry: whether the decision not to hold an inquiry was flawed or irrational.

(1) JUSTIFICATION

h (a) *Was justification required in law?*

The applicants argue that a decision-making process was flawed because of the minister's conclusion that there was no legal obligation to justify the grant of the authorisations. The principle of justification derives from the system of radiological protection recommended by the International Commission on i Radiological Protection. Publication 60 issued by the ICRP (ICRP 60) states (para 112):

'(a) No practice involving exposures to radiation should be adopted unless it produces sufficient benefit to the exposed individuals or to society to offset the radiation detriment it causes. (*The justification of a practice.*) (My emphasis.)

(b) In relation to any particular source within a practice, the magnitude of individual doses, the number of people exposed, and the likelihood of incurring exposures where these are not certain to be received should be kept as low as reasonably achievable, economic and social factors being taken into account. This procedure should be constrained by restrictions on the doses to individuals (dose constraints), or the risks to individuals in the case of potential exposures (risk constraints), so as to limit the inequity likely to result from the inherent economic and social judgements. (The optimisation of protection.)

(c) The exposure of individuals resulting from the combination of all the relevant practices should be subject to dose limits, or to some control of risk in the case of potential exposures. These are aimed at ensuring that no individual is exposed to radiation risks that are judged to be unacceptable from these practices in any normal circumstances. Not all sources are susceptible of control by action at the source and it is necessary to specify the sources to be included as relevant before selecting a dose limit. (Individual dose and risk limits.)'

In *Re Ionising Radiation Protection, EC Commission v Belgium* Case C-376/90 [1993] 2 CMLR 513 at 524 Mr Advocate General Jacobs stated in his opinion that the general principles upon which the system of radiological protection recommended by the ICRP are based are those set out in IRCP 60, para 112 and that: 'Those principles are reflected in Article 6 of [Council Directive (Euratom) 80/836]. The question for the court is whether justification must be considered in the exercise of powers under ss 13 and 16 of the 1993 Act. The Act is silent on how these powers are to be exercised. As stated, the 1993 Act is a consolidating measure replacing the Radioactive Substances Act 1960. The guide to that Act issued by the Department of the Environment in 1982 is relevant as explaining the policy behind the Act and the recommendations of the ICRP and the advice of the NRPB. The relevant paragraphs are:

'*Standards of Control*

41. An expert panel was set up in 1956 to advise on the control of Radioactive Wastes and its report was appended to the White Paper of that name published in November 1959, (Cmnd 884). The government accepted the report and the Radioactive Substances Act 1960 was based on its recommendations. In its acceptance of the report the Government stated that: An important section of the panel's report is concerned with the standards by which the discharge of radioactive waste should be controlled. These standards are not immutable; they will be subject to review from time to time in the light of advice received from international and national advisory bodies. Neither will they provide a charter for the discharge of radioactive waste at will, provided that the discharges remain within specified upper limits; it is the essence of the prudent system of control that discharges should be kept not only within the upper limits of safety, but as far below them as can reasonably be achieved.

42. The International Commission of Radiological Protection (ICRP) is generally regarded as the appropriate body to provide guidance on radiological protection standards. The National Radiological Protection Board (NRPB), established as a national point of authoritative reference on radiological protection standards, has been directed by the Health

a Ministers to give advice on the acceptability of ICRP's recommendations for application in the United Kingdom.

43. The ICRP recommendations provide the basis for the European Community Directive made under the Euratom Treaty, which lays down basic safety standards for the health protection of the general public and workers against the dangers of ionizing radiation. The latest version of b this Directive (80/836 Euratom) was adopted by the European Community on 15 July 1980 ...

46. For the purposes of radiological protection, the basic objectives of radioactive waste management United Kingdom are: (a) that all practices giving rise to radioactive waste must be justified, ie the need for the practice must be established in terms of its overall benefit. (b) radiation c exposure of individuals and the collective dose to the population arising from radioactive wastes shall be reduced to levels which are as low as reasonably achievable, economic and social factors being taken into account. (c) the average effective dose equivalent from all sources including natural background radiation and medical procedures to d representative members of a critical group of the general public shall not exceed 5 mSv (0·5 rem) in any one year.'

Thus, submits Mr Collins QC, counsel for Greenpeace, relying on the guide, it is government policy to apply ICRP standards to radioactive waste management and the control of waste. Since there is nothing in the 1993 Act e to say how the standards should be set for the purposes of authorisation, it is not only lawful but desirable that the announced policy in the guide should be applied in any exercise of the powers conferred by ss 13 and 16 of the Act. To fail to comply with the policy would be to fail to have regard to a material consideration. The ministers' conclusion that there was no legal obligation to f justify the grant of authorisations was such a failure in terms of domestic law. Mr Blake, for Lancashire, likewise relies on the ICRP standards and the guide to the 1960 Act and submits that even without Directive 80/836 the ministers in exercising their powers under the 1993 Act would have been entitled, as a matter of domestic policy, to consider whether the practice giving rise to the emissions created a sufficient social benefit to merit authorisation. To have g applied para 46 of the guide as a relevant consideration would not have been unlawful.

I am unable to accept these submissions. Primary legislation is not to be construed by reference to general policy statements or departmental guidance. There is nothing in the express language of the Act to suggest that justification h is a necessary consideration. If the Act and the guide stood alone the ministers would be entitled to conclude that a true construction of ss 13 and 16 did not require prior justification of the proposed discharges.

The applicants, however, submit that the Act is to be construed consistently with the requirements of the 1980 directive. Mr Richards, for the respondents, j accepts that it is a principle of Community law that national legislation is interpreted, so far as possible, consistently with the requirements of any relevant community directive (see *Marleasing SA v La Comercial Internacional de Alimentación SA* Case C-106/89 [1990] ECR I-4135). The principle does not require the plain meaning of a statute to be distorted but allows words to be read in when a statute is silent. The approach and the principles which govern this court are summarised in the speech of Lord Keith of Kinkel in *Webb v EMO*

Air Cargo (UK) Ltd [1992] 4 All ER 929 at 939–940, [1993] 1 WLR 49 at 59–60, which I respectfully adopt and apply.

'Directive 76/207 does not have direct effect upon the relationship between a worker and an employer who is not the state or an emanation of the state, but nevertheless it is for a United Kingdom court to construe domestic legislation in any field covered by a Community directive so as to accord with the interpretation of the directive as laid down by the European Court, if that can be done without distorting the meaning of the domestic legislation: see *Duke v GEC Reliance Ltd* [1988] 1 All ER 626 at 636, [1988] AC 618 at 639–640 per Lord Templeman. This is so whether the domestic legislation came after or, as in this case, preceded the directive: see *Marleasing SA v La Comercial Internacional de Alimentación SA* Case C-106/89) [1990] ECR I-4135 ... the European Court said in its judgment (at I-4159): "8. In order to reply to that question, it should be observed that, as the Court pointed out in its judgment in Case 14/83 *von Colson and Kamann v Land Nordrhein-Westfalen* [1984] ECR 1891, paragraph 26, the Member States' obligation arising from a directive to achieve the result envisaged by the directive and their duty under Article 5 of the Treaty to take all appropriate measures, whether general or particular, to ensure the fulfilment of that obligation, is binding on all the authorities of Member States including, for matters within their jurisdiction, the courts. It follows that, in applying national law, whether the provisions in question were adopted before or after the directive, the national court called upon to interpret it is required to do so, so far as possible, in the light of the wording and the purpose of the directive in order to achieve the result pursued by the latter and thereby comply with the third paragraph of Article 189 of the Treaty ..." It is to be observed that the provision of Spanish law in issue in that case was of a general character capable of being construed either widely or narrowly. It did not refer specifically to the grounds upon which the nullity of a public limited company might be ordered. If it had done so, and had included among such grounds the case where the company had been formed with the purpose of defrauding creditors of one of the corporators, the Spanish court would have been entitled and bound to give effect to it notwithstanding the terms of the directive. As the European Court said, a national court must construe a domestic law to accord with the terms of a directive in the same field only if it is possible to do so. That means that the domestic law must be open to an interpretation consistent with the directive whether or not it is also open to an interpretation inconsistent with it.'

At one stage in the hearing I expressed the view that if Parliament had wished to introduce an express requirement for justification into the domestic law it had the opportunity to do so when amendments to the 1960 Act were made by the Environmental Protection Act 1990, if not also when the consolidating 1993 Act was passed.

The applicants, however, submit that once the 1980 directive came into force (ie in 1980) legislation was unnecessary. Thereafter domestic legislation would have to be interpreted consistently with it. Their submission is that there is nothing in ss 13 and 16 of the 1993 Act which is inconsistent with the directive. Moreover, there can be no question of rewriting or distorting the

policy of the statute since the directive clearly accords with the policy laid
a down in the guide.

Mr Richards, however, submits that there is nothing in the directive which
requires justification to be considered for the purposes of the present
authorisations. Articles 30 and 33 of the Euratom Treaty (pursuant to which
the directive was adopted) are concerned with laying down 'basic standards'.
b There is nothing in them to suggest that activities complying with the basic
standards may none the less be prevented by reference to the principle of
justification. Article 6 of the directive it is submitted, lays down general
principles but does not impose separate obligations on member states.
Article 13 provides by way of primary obligation that the contribution to the
exposure of the population as a whole from each activity is to be kept to the
c minimum 'necessitated by that activity'. This presupposes the carrying on of
the activity. Reference to the principles in art 6(a) and (b) is a secondary
matter. It would be a distortion of art 13, as well as being inconsistent with the
treaty itself, to construe it as requiring member states to apply the justification
principle so as to prevent the carrying on of the activity in circumstances where
d the primary obligation was complied with.

The respondents further submit that the amended wording of the directive
makes it clear that it is the type of activity, not the carrying on of the activity
at a particular site, that must be justified in advance. The type of activity in the
present case is reprocessing of spent fuel; this type of activity has been justified
by the Parker Report, two parliamentary debates and continued examination
e of the issue in Parliament.

Mr Newman QC for BNFL supports these submissions and goes further. He
argues: (1) that the ICRP principle of justification applies to practices (ie
human activities which increase the overall exposure to radiation) and not to
sources (ie the source of an exposure). The Sellafield site is a source or a group
f of sources. It is not a practice within the ICRP definition. Section 13 of the
1993 Act is concerned with the authorisation of discharges from the Sellafield
site, that is from a source or group of sources. It is not concerned with proving
or reviewing the justification of practices; (2) that art 6 of the 1980 directive is
concerned with the use of the ICRP principles as 'general principles' in the
setting of dose limits, not in the process of authorising site discharges; (3) that
g in so far as Title III of the 1980 directive requires legislative implementation, it
has been implemented by the Ionising Radiations Regulations 1985, SI 1985/
1333, and that there is no need to introduce art 6(a) into the construction of
s 13.

Whether, on their true construction, arts 6 and 13 of the directive require
h justification to be considered for the purposes of authorisations such as the
present might be thought to be a matter for the Court of Justice of the
European Communities. None of the parties to the present proceedings have
suggested that the matter should be referred. I have been left to do the best I
can.

j Article 30 of the treaty and arts 6 and 13 of the directive sit uneasily together
and present problems of construction. Nevertheless, I have reached the
following conclusions. (1) Article 13 makes reference to art 6(a) and thus
justification. It plainly includes art 6(a) as a principle to which regard must be
had by member states. I accept Mr Collins' submission that if Mr Richards'
argument was correct, art 6(a) could have no meaning since justification could
never be applied. In my judgment art 13 makes no sense unless a purposive

construction is given to it so as to 'to take account of' art 6(a) and ensure that
each 'activity' shall have been justified. (2) Mr Richards' argument that it is a
the 'type of activity' not the carrying on of the activity at a particular site that
must be justified in advance, fails. I accept Mr Collins' submission that the
principle of justification would be rendered meaningless if Mr Richards'
construction was upheld. In my view ICRP 60 and the directive are concerned
with justification of particular practices which affect particular individuals in b
particular circumstances. In this case the type of activity is thermal oxide
reprocessing at Sellafield. There has been no justification of this activity
involving the decision maker being satisfied that the benefits flowing from the
activity outweigh the detriment. In my opinion Sir Roger Parker neither
performed this exercise nor purported to do so and I reject Mr Richards'
submission that he did. Likewise, with regard to the parliamentary debates c
and other matters relied on. (3) I reject Mr Newman's first submission
concerning the meaning of 'practice' and 'source' within the context of ICRP
60. ICRP 60 is clearly directed towards a system for the protection of
individuals from particular exposures. I accept Mr Collins' submission that
THORP is the human activity (the practice) which increases overall exposure d
to radiation. The source which comprehends that practice and 'so is within
that practice' is Sellafield. (4) I also reject Mr Newman's other submissions; in
particular that relating to the effect of the 1985 regulations. This submission
was not made or adopted by the respondents despite my inquiry. The
regulations do not implement the whole of the directive. I accept Mr Blake's
submission that the purpose of the regulations is to enforce the standards set e
by national and international authorities and to impose criminal liability for
breach thereof. The directive still applies as a means of interpreting ss 13 and
16.

Thus I conclude that arts 6(a) and 13 of the directive (consistent with ICRP
60, para 112) require justification to be considered for the purpose of f
authorisations such as the present.

This being so, can ss 13 and 16 of the 1993 Act be construed so as to accord,
so far as possible, with the requirements of the directive? Would the plain
meaning of ss 13 and 16 be distorted if justification had to be considered in
advance of the authorisations? My answer to the first question is Yes and to the
second question No. As indicated above, the 1993 Act is entirely silent as to g
justification. There is no reason why, in practice, the justification exercise
cannot be carried out before the grant of authorisations. The ministers have
purported to do this in the present case. Moreover, interpretation of ss 13 and
16 so as to accord with the directive is entirely consistent with the purpose of
the Act as spelt out in the guide. In my judgment, therefore the ministers erred h
in law in concluding that justification was not relevant in the context of the
exercise by them of their functions under the legislation. There was a legal
obligation to justify the grant of the authorisations.

(b) *Was justification properly considered in any event?* j

Mr Blake submits that if the ministers erred as to the legal duty to justify,
this, in itself, would be sufficient foundation for the grant of a declaration in
the terms of para (4) of the relief sought. I cannot accept this submission. If
the ministers in fact considered justification and after careful, rational analysis
of the issues concluded that the emissions were justified, the court, in the
exercise of its discretion, would be entitled to refuse relief despite the error in

law. I take the same view in respect of Mr Collins' submission that the
ministers should have considered justification at the outset as a starting point
and that their failure to consider it then flawed their subsequent decisions.

In order to discharge their functions with regard to justification the
ministers had to balance detriment and benefit arising from the grant of the
authorisations. It is important to note that Mr Collins expressly abandoned
any suggestion that the ministers acted in bad faith. Mr Collins' essential point
is that the only substantial benefit to set against the risk of damage to the health
of persons resulting from the discharges was economic. Thus, it is argued, in
order to properly consider this issue the ministers should have obtained for
themselves all material information. They failed to do this. In particular: (a)
they did not seek to check BNFL's assertions as to future contracts and
viability, (b) they did not insist on seeing a report made for BNFL by Messrs
Touche Ross on the future viability of THORP and disclose it and (c) they did
not properly consider possible alternatives to THORP, namely dry storage.

In order to appreciate the argument it is necessary to refer to the decision
document. The economic aspects are dealt with in paras 124 to 133.
Paragraphs 126, 127 and 128 are particularly relevant:

'Economic Aspects

126. The Ministers are not persuaded that so much weight should be
placed on calculations relating to BNFL's profitability. While it is
important that BNFL should have the resources to be able to fulfil its
financial and environmental obligations, this does not depend on any
particular level of profitability. They have also noted that BNFL's
shareholder is the State.

127. They consider moreover that the wider economic value of THORP
can best be assessed by the market evidence that is available from the
willingness of BNFL and its customers to enter into and maintain
sufficient contracts to fill BNFL's order book for at least the first ten years
of THORP's operation. In their assessment of paragraphs 109–123 above,
the Ministers have found no evidence that the market choices of BNFL or
their customers were being artificially distorted. If they had singly or
collectively found greater economic benefit in another option, such as dry
storage, the Ministers see no reason why they would not be able to
re-negotiate the contracts accordingly.

128. While the Ministers do not wish to place undue weight on the
precise figures put forward by BNFL, they nevertheless have felt it prudent
to consider the criticisms made of them. Accordingly, DTI were asked if
there was anything in the comments put forward which would cause them
concern. Their response was that there was nothing in the representations
which would cause them to challenge the conclusion set out in the
Government Statement, that there was no reason to dissent from the
essential conclusion in BNFL's document, namely that operation of
THORP will bring very substantial benefits to the company. The
Ministers accept that conclusion. Their reasoning on the most significant
points is explained in the following paragraphs.'

In paras 129 and 130 the ministers addressed the cost of decommissioning
THORP and concluded that even doubling the figures used by BNFL for
decommissioning costs this 'would not significantly affect the conclusion that
the operation of the plant would be likely to bring BNFL significant

commercial benefit.' In para 131 the ministers addressed arguments
concerning the use of an 8% discount rate, the cost of krypton-85 abatement
technology and delay in the opening of the Nirex repository.

The paper prepared by BNFL and referred to in the above passages sets out
the commercial economic justification for opening THORP as follows:

'1.4 ... THORP has orders worth in excess of £9000m (nine thousand
million pounds), over half from overseas. Customers have recently
reconfirmed that they wish THORP to be brought into operation as soon
as possible to reprocess their fuel and for their contracts to be fulfilled.
Based on the January 1993 start-up, THORP would have made at least
£500m (Jan 1992 money values) profit for BNFL in its first ten years, after
making full provision for decommissioning costs. Overall BNFL profits
are being eroded at a rate of some £2m (two million pounds) per week as
a result of current delays. On the basis of figures provided by BNFL,
independent accountants and management consultants Touche Ross have
calculated that the operation of THORP over its first ten years will provide
an economic benefit to BNFL, the NPV of which is estimated at some £1.8
Bn (1.8 thousand million pounds) in 1993 money values, using an 8%
discount rate. On the same basis the economic benefit to the UK arising
from the first ten years of THORP operation is some £900m. The plant has
a design life of at least 25 years and has been built to very high technical
and safety standards. The operation of THORP will support some 5,450
jobs, including well over 3,000 in West Cumbria ... The recycling of
plutonium and uranium recovered by THORP enables a very significant
energy resource to be utilised. Recycling of uranium from reprocessing is
already commonplace and use of plutonium as MOX (mixed uranium and
plutonium) fuel in existing reactors is well established technically and is
being progressively commercialised. BNFL anticipates returning
significant quantities of MOX to overseas THORP customers. Since 1976,
all THORP contracts signed with overseas customers contain options for
BNFL to return to those customers the radioactive wastes arising from
reprocessing. It is the government's intention that these options will be
implemented.'

The ministers dealt with the respective contentions as to jobs in para 132 of the
decision document and set out their conclusions in para 133:

'132. The number of jobs produced by the operation of THORP was
disputed by a number of respondents. It was claimed that BNFL had
exaggerated the number of jobs that THORP would support, and also that
the alternative of dry storing the spent fuel would create just as many. The
Ministers have considered these arguments but note that, even on the
conservative estimates of opponents of the plant, THORP would still be a
significant source of employment for the West Cumbria region.

133. In conclusion, the Ministers consider that THORP should provide
benefit for BNFL, its customers seem content, and that this provides a
good economic case for it proceeding. It would also provide a significant
source of employment for the people of West Cumbria.'

Against this background I conclude that the ministers were entitled to rely
on BNFL's figures as to contracts and conclude that there was a good economic

a case for proceeding. In this connection it is important to note para 114 of the decision document:

'The Ministers have considered whether customers have changed their intentions during the consultation period. They have received no letters or representations indicating such a change, and on the contrary there have been letters supporting THORP from the domestic utilities Scottish
b Nuclear and Nuclear Electric, on behalf of the ten Japanese utilities and from the Japanese Ministry for International Trade and Industry. The Ministers have been advised by DTI moreover that no offers have been made by customers to buy out their contracts.'

c As to the Touche Ross report, this was and is a BNFL document. The ministers were entitled to reach a conclusion on the future viability of THORP without seeing it. This was especially the case given their view as to the effect of the BNFL contracts.

The applicants contend that dry storage represents an alternative to reprocessing which the ministers failed properly to investigate. In the report
d of a public local inquiry into objections to the proposed spent fuel store at Torness Power Station, Dunbar, under the Electricity Act 1989 (application for s 36 consent) the inspector noted, inter alia:

'*Proposed fuel route*
e 1.5. SNL already send irradiated fuel elements to Sellafield and has contractual arrangements for further batches of elements. However the company would like to cease to do this for subsequent batches of fuel elements. Instead, after a longer period of storage in the ponds at Torness, they would be taken in the same transport flasks an even shorter distance by private road to a new storage facility within the power station site. The
f application for consent under the Electricity Act 1989 which is the subject of this public inquiry is to provide this storage facility.

Findings of fact
9.16. Long term storage of irradiated AGR fuel at Torness would therefore be a departure from the published Government policy and
g established practice, which involves early transfer to Sellafield, reprocessing, and vitrification.

Recent changes
9.17. The Scottish Office policy witness was not aware of any subsequent Government document that altered these policies. However
h the IPI witness noted that circumstances had changed since 1986, in that there was less economic advantage in obtaining uranium from reprocessing; dry storage had emerged as a practical possibility; and direct disposal of spent fuel, without reprocessing, appeared to be feasible. The reprocessing route no longer appears to offer any immediate and significant advantages, from a waste disposal point of view. The policy
i witness was not aware of any government policy favouring dry storage or direct disposal, but the Government was not committed one way or the other. Long term storage was supported by the Government because it had the advantages that the material would cool down and become less radioactive, and would allow decisions on ultimate disposal to be made in about 30 years time.'

The applicants rely on these passages and submit that when taken with the
other material they show that the ministers did not adequately consider dry
storage as an alternative to reprocessing.   It is further submitted that the
passages raise doubt as to the future of reprocessing as opposed to dry storage;
these considerations were not adequately addressed by the ministers.   They
could only be properly addressed at a public inquiry.

The ministers took the view that dry storage and reprocessing are not true
alternatives (decision document, paras 101 and 108).   They took the view: (a)
that dry storage was merely a postponement of the decision as to what to do
with spent fuel and (b) that dry storage does not have the same function as
reprocessing.   The ministers had regard to the report of the Radioactive Waste
Management Advisory Committee (RWMAC).   Paragraph 104 of the decision
document describes the ministers' approach:

'The Ministers have noted the comments from RWMAC's 11th annual
report quoted by respondents.   However, the Ministers would also draw
attention to the analysis which RWMAC carried out into the radiological
impact of reprocessing on the public and which was published in the same
report.   Here the Committee stated that in terms of radiological impacts
the options of reprocessing and direct disposal of spent fuel were "within
the uncertainties in the estimates ... broadly comparable".   Furthermore
RWMAC's conclusion on the issue of reprocessing oxide fuel was that: "an
illustrative comparison of the waste management impacts of early
reprocessing, delayed reprocessing and not reprocessing at all has
indicated that all three options have impacts which are small and
comparable within the bounds of the uncertainties in the estimates.   There
are therefore no significant waste management reasons for or against early
reprocessing of spent fuel.   However, it may be prudent to reprocess on an
early timescale the spent AGR fuel which has been in store underwater at
Sellafield for some years.   This would require the operation of THORP."'

In my view, the ministers' approach to the rival contentions was not irrational.
There was no failure to investigate and consider dry storage as an alternative
to reprocessing.   It was one that the ministers were entitled to take.   The
inspector's findings and summary of evidence given at the Torness Inquiry
must be seen in context.   The inspector was not considering the provision of
reprocessing facilities.   He was considering whether waste from a nuclear
power station should be stored given that reprocessing facilities were available
elsewhere.   The assertions and findings made at that inquiry are therefore not
directly relevant to issues raised by the present application.   In any event I am
satisfied that the issues which are raised in the passages from the report cited
above were addressed by the ministers in the decision document.

Thus I am unable to accept the submission that the ministers failed to have
regard to or overlooked material considerations in their assessment of the
economic and dry storage aspects.   They were entitled to approach the matter
in the way they did; they were entitled to rely on the material identified by
them and to conclude that there was a good economic case for proceeding not
only for BNFL, but for the people of West Cumbria.   In my judgment the
ministers' approach was neither irrational nor their conclusions perverse.

Whilst adopting the argument advanced by Mr Collins, Mr Blake, on behalf
of Lancashire, has concentrated his submissions on health risk and detriment.
When he opened Lancashire's case he said:

'A public inquiry is needed on these authorisations because the issues relevant to whether these emissions are justified are of such complexity that they cannot be appropriately dealt with in the consultation process. It is not Lancashire's submission that the court should resolve these issues or be familiar with the technical and scientific literature relevant to a full investigation of these issues ...'

As to health risk, he put Lancashire's case thus:

'Any increase of exposure to emissions increases the risk of fatal cancer and other illnesses. The authorisations will result in increases of certain radio-nuclides into the air and sea. The increases that will result are increases over the emissions made in the past. The authorisations will increase actual emissions over previous years and require justification.'

In his final submissions, Mr Blake said:

'The question is not whether the emissions can be accommodated within overall dose limits of 1 mSv, but whether they are acceptable as a risk to health and whether they are justifiable having regard to the balance of advantage over detriment.'

The ministers dealt with these issues in paras 22 to 84 of the decision document and in Annex A thereto. It is no part of my function to resolve scientific issues. The question for me is whether in law the ministers were entitled to reach the conclusions which they did. I see no advantage, therefore, in increasing the length of an already long judgment by quoting at length from the decision document. Nor do I think it necessary to rehearse the detailed arguments advanced by Mr Blake. At times these required a familiarity on my part with the technical and scientific issues which he had at first suggested was unnecessary. In any consideration of the ministers' decision it is to be emphasised that they acted throughout on the advice of the inspectorate and the NRPB, and that that advice followed and applied the standards set out by the ICRP. In a second affidavit dated 31 January 1994, Frances Anne Fry, assistant director of the NRPB, explained the approach of that body to risk:

'2. In setting limits or constraints, ICRP in its Publication 60 has advocated the use of risk data based on continuous exposure over a lifetime. Data to support this recommendation were given in Annex C of Publication 60. In the NRPB response to the ICRP recommendations (Doc NRPB 4, 1, 1993), NRPB concurred with this approach and endorsed the use of ICRP risk factors in setting limits and constraints. In calculating the risks of fatal cancer from a continuous exposure, it is necessary to take account of the probability of an individual dying from other causes. In fact, the annual average risk of fatal cancer from a lifetime exposure at 0.3 mSv per year is 1.1 105, which rounds to 1 in 100,000.

3. Taking account of the "benchmark" risk of 1 in 100,000 per year for new reactors (HSE. The tolerability of risk from nuclear power stations, 1992), taking into account the above risk-dose relationship for continuous exposure and bearing in mind the perspective provided by doses from natural radiation and their variation, the Board recommended a value of 0.3 mSv as an upper limit on the dose constraint for a new source.'

The ministers set out their approach to the recommendations of the advisory
bodies in paras 30, 31 and 32 of the decision document. These are important
paragraphs:

'30. It is possible to use studies of acceptable levels of risk (see paragraph
27 above) and of dose/risk relationship (see paragraph 29 above), to set
dose limits and targets for members of the public. In accordance with
ICRP recommendations and on the advice to the NRPB, the principal dose
limit in the UK for members of the public from all *manmade* sources of
radioactivity (other than medical applications) is one millisievert per year.
This dose limit is incorporated in European Community legislation, and is
applied throughout the European Community and in most other
countries. This compares with an average radiation dose to members of
the UK population of 2·2 millisieverts per year from *natural* background
radiation and an average of 0·3 millisieverts per year from *medical*
applications.
31. Since members of the public may be exposed to radiation from more
than one source of radiation, the UK has also adopted a radiation dose
target of 0.5 millisieverts per year from the operation of any single nuclear
site. Going one step further the National Radiological Protection Board
has recently recommended that no more than 0·3 millisieverts per year
should result from the operation of a single *new plant*.
32. The Ministers consider that compliance with these dose limits and
targets would protect individual members of the public from unacceptable
levels of risk resulting from radioactive waste discharges.' (The ministers'
emphasis.)

In my judgment, the ministers were fully entitled to conclude that compliance
with the dose limits, targets and constraints set out in these paragraphs would
protect the public from unacceptable risks. In so concluding, they were
applying international and national standards. The ministers were entitled to
reject the criticisms made. The stance taken by the ministers could not be said
to be irrational. There is no illogicality in excluding historical dischargers from
consideration in the 0·3 mSv dose constraint; the constraint is aimed at new
sources in order that the overall limit of 1 mSv (from past, present and future
discharges) is complied with.

Mr David William Lord, the Lancashire county analyst, was instrumental in
the establishment of RADMIL (Radioactivity Monitoring in Lancashire).
RADMIL laid a report before the inspectorates during the first round of
consultations and submitted a second report during the second round. The
reports are addressed in the decision document and in the annex.

After analysing the available material, the ministers concluded (decision
document, para 49):

'The Ministers have examined carefully the issues raised on the
radiological assessments undertaken by the Inspectorates to see whether
any required further investigation. They have concluded that this is
unnecessary and that there is no reason to question the basic validity of the
approach adopted by the Inspectorates.'

This conclusion is one the ministers were entitled to come to after
consideration of the issues.

In the decision document the ministers specifically considered 'risks to individuals'. Their conclusions in this regard are crucial and deserve to be set out in full:

'50. Many respondents expressed general concerns about the radiological impact resulting from the proposed radioactive discharges from Sellafield and from THORP. Doses have been calculated by the Inspectorates on the basis of recommendations of ICRP in their publication 26 (ICRP 26) and also where appropriate on the basis of revised data in publication 60 (ICRP 60). For consistency with the earlier documents, the doses quoted in this document are those estimated on the basis of ICRP 26.

51. If discharges took place continuously at the proposed discharge limits, the resulting maximum dose to the critical group, from radioactive discharges from the whole Sellafield site, would be 0·214 millisieverts per year. This represents a risk of fatal cancer of about 1 in a hundred thousand (to be compared with the table in paragraph 24 above). This is within the principal dose limit of one millisievert per year, and is within the UK target for maximum doses resulting from the operation of any single nuclear site of 0·5 millisievert per year.

52. From THORP alone the maximum annual dose would be 0·033 millisieverts per year representing an annual risk of fatal cancer of about 1 in six hundred thousand. This is well within NRPB's recommended target of 0·3 millisieverts for a new plant.

53. The Ministers concluded that the discharge limits contained in the draft authorisations would result in doses which are within the prevailing dose limits and targets, and hence represent risks to members of the critical group which are considered acceptable.'

On the material before them, it was open to the ministers to make the findings expressed in paras 51 and 52. They were entitled to reject RADMIL's contentions, as had the inspectorates, and conclude that the discharge limits set out in the draft authorisations represented acceptable risks to the critical group. They were entitled to go on (and I am satisfied they did) to balance benefit against detriment in the light of these findings. Neither the findings, the conclusions nor the approach to justification could be said to be irrational or perverse. I therefore reject Mr Blake's submissions in this regard.

For completeness, I should say that I considered other subsidiary matters relating to justification. These include the ministers' approach and conclusions in paras 46 and 47 of the decision document regarding, risk, the effect on wildlife, the letter on behalf of the Committee on Medical Aspects of Radiation in the Environment, non-proliferation concerns, spent fuel management and collective dose to world population. In my view, these matters were all properly considered.

In my judgment, the ministers' approach to justification cannot be faulted. The ministers first considered the narrow issues, and concluded at paras 52, 62–63 of the decision document that the discharges were acceptable in terms of risks to the individuals most exposed and in terms of risks to the worldwide population. They then went on to examine the wider issues as if those issues were legally relevant: 'Although the matters are not believed to be relevant to their decisions, the Ministers have considered them as if they were' (para 85). They considered the wider issues under the headings used for the purpose of

grouping together the main points raised in the consultation procedure (see
summary of responses, paras 81ff) and reached specific conclusions on them.
The ministers then reached their conclusions both on the basis of the narrow
issues and on the basis that the wider issues were relevant:

'161. The Ministers are satisfied that they would have reached the same
decision if, contrary to their view, the wider issues fell to be taken into
account. As stated above, they have considered those issues as if they were
legally relevant and have weighed the various risks and benefits, in
particular those arising out of the operation of THORP. In their judgment
there is a sufficient balance of advantage in favour of the operation of
THORP. They are satisfied that the activities giving rise to the discharges
permitted by the authorisations are justified.'

I accept the submission that is made on behalf of the respondents that there is
nothing in that general approach which is open to reasonable criticism. The
ministers carried out a careful process of weighing the benefits against the
detriments in reaching the conclusion that the balance came down on the side
of justification. They were entitled to reach that conclusion. I therefore reject
the submissions made on behalf of the applicants. Although the ministers
erred in law in respects I identified earlier in this judgment, I am satisfied that
the issue of justification was properly addressed by them.

2. *Environmental impact assessment*
Paragraph 64 of the applicant's grounds states:

'no lawful authorisations could have been granted without there first
having been provided and made available an environmental impact
assessment complying with the provisions and standards laid down by
directive 85/337.'

This directive is, so far as material, set out above. The applicants' contention
raises two issues: (i) whether Council Directive (EEC) 85/337 applies in the
present case, and (ii) whether, if so, the requirements of the directive were
complied with in any event. The nub of the applicants' submission is that the
construction of THORP was one project and that the bringing into operation
of the processes within THORP thereby causing emissions was a second. Mr
Collins submits that each project is within the wide expression in para 3(h) of
Annex II of the directive: 'Installations for the reprocessing of irradiated
nuclear fuels'. Unless the applicants can identify two separate projects in this
way, their case under the directive must fail. If there was only one project,
then its commencement predated the 1985 directive and the directive does not
apply to it. The directive does not apply to projects in the pipeline when the
directive came into force: see *Twyford Parish Council v Secretary of State for the
Environment* [1992] 1 CMLR 276.
    The directive applies to the assessment of the environmental effects of
'public and private projects which are likely to have significant effects on the
environment'. 'Project' is defined as 'the execution of construction works or
of other installations or schemes' and 'other interventions in the natural
surroundings and landscape including those involving the extraction of
mineral resources' (art 1.2).
    Mr Collins argues that the discharges into the environment of ionising
radiations constitute an intervention in the natural surroundings. Thus the

a operation of THORP is a second and separate project to which the directive applies.

The definitions in art 1.2 of the directive must be read with arts 2.1 and 4, which identify projects to which the directive applies. THORP falls within Annex II, para 3(h); it is an installation 'for the reprocessing of irradiated nuclear fuels'. It is a distortion of art 1.2 to treat the bringing into operation of b THORP as an intervention 'in the natural surroundings and landscape' (art 1.2). Projects of this nature are identified in Annex II, paras 1 and 2, under 'Agriculture' and 'Extracted industry'. I accept the respondents' submission that the whole thrust of the directive is to require an environmental impact assessment at the outset, that is to say 'at the earliest possible stage in all the technical planning and decision-making processes' (see the preamble to the c directive). Article 2.1 moreover requires member states to make an environmental impact assessment 'before consent is given'. This is in accordance with the preamble which refers to 'development consent'. Development consent means 'the decision of the competent authority ... which entitles the developer to proceed with the project' (art 1.2). In my d judgment such consent in this case means the decision of the competent authority which entitles the developer to proceed with the execution of the installation 'for the reprocessing of irradiated nuclear fuels' (Annex II, para 3(h)). It is a distortion of language to regard the authorisation of emissions as such a decision. That decision was the Town and Country Planning (Windscale and Calder Works) Special Development Order 1978, SI e 1978/523, following upon the Parker Report.

Thus I conclude that on a true construction of the directive, the construction of THORP and the bringing into operation of THORP and consequent discharges were and are one project. That project predated the directive. The directive does not apply to the project. The ministers were therefore not under f a legal duty to provide and make available an environmental impact assessment complying with the provisions and standards laid down in the directive before the grant of the authorisations. The applicants' submissions in this regard therefore fail.

In any event, although no formal environmental impact assessment took g place, I am satisfied that the information provided and made available for consultation by the inspectorates and the ministers met the substantive requirements of the directive. The approach adopted is described by Dr Brown, head of the Radioactive Substances Division of the Department of the Environment in his first affidavit dated 28 January 1994, paras 250/255. Relevant information was included in the BNFL document 'Further Material h on the Environmental Aspect of the Operation of THORP' which was part of the documentation sent to consultees in the second round of consultations. Detailed information about the environmental effects of radioactive discharges under the new authorisations was provided by the inspectorates in the first round of consultation. It has been argued that the applicants did not have information on alternatives to reprocessing and that an environmental impact assessment would have provided such information. The directive sets out in Annex III items of information that the developer should supply:

'2. Where appropriate, an outline of the main alternatives studied by the developer and an indication of the main reasons for his choice, taking into account the environmental effects.'

The crucial words here are 'where appropriate'. I accept the respondents' submission that it is appropriate for a developer to give an outline of the main alternatives before the development takes place, not after the plant has been built when consideration is being given to the acceptable level of discharges from that plant.

3. *Consultation*

By para 67 of their grounds the applicants assert that the second consultation announced in June 1993 was an inadequate forum for resolution of the issues that require determination because:

'(i) the Secretary of State wrongly refused to disclose the Touche Ross study and details of the relevant terms of the commercial contracts to those he was consulting. The presumptions, raw data, rival cost calculations, contained in the study would be necessary material for informed criticism and evaluation of the case for economic justification; (ii) alternatively, failed to obtain the Touche Ross study and/or details of the contract terms from BNFL; (iii) adopted a procedure that deprived himself of the opportunity of informed comments with respect to commercially sensitive documents; such documents, including the actual contracts with suppliers, can be disclosed on a limited basis in a public local inquiry, but not in a written consultation; (iv) adopted a procedure that deprived himself of the benefit of oral examination of disputed evidence; (v) adopted a procedure that deprived himself of the benefit of a reasoned Inspector's report that, amongst other things, could form the basis of public assurance as to the safety of and need for the emissions.'

But when he came to make his final submissions Mr Collins put the matter thus:

'What information should be given will depend upon the nature and purposes of the consultation exercise. Since the economic issue was crucial as it represented the only effective benefits, fuller information ought to have been given. Although lack of proper consultation is potentially a free standing ground, it is better considered as a further reason for an inquiry since the failure to give full information renders the need for an inquiry more pressing.'

Thus the contention that the Secretary of State wrongly refused to disclose the Touche Ross report was not pursued. That report was not the Secretary of State's to disclose in any event. Likewise the contracts. The thrust of the applicants' submissions under this head was that fuller information concerning economic issues could and should have been given. If this was impracticable or impossible, then all the more reason for holding a public inquiry.

The material before me has compelled me to the conclusion that the consultation process satisfied all relevant requirements. I have set out above my reasons for concluding that the ministers were entitled to approach the economic issues in the manner in which they did. That being so nothing turned on the precise detail of contracts, profitability figures and the like. The ministers were entitled to conclude that what mattered was BNFL's assertions concerning contracts in hand, their profitability and their effect on employment in Cumbria. In any event, exhaustive information does not have to be provided in order to have an effective consultation (see *R v Rochdale*

Health Authority, ex p Rochdale Metropolitan BC (1992) 8 BMLR 137 and I accept the respondents' submission in this regard. I therefore reject the applicants' submission that the consultation procedure adopted by the ministers was inadequate.

In para 68 of the grounds it is alleged that—'the consultation embarked on by the Secretary of State was not a genuine consultation on the issues raised therein and/or a sham ... '

As indicated earlier in this judgment, Mr Collins expressly abandoned any suggestion of bad faith on the part of the ministers. I am satisfied on the whole of the available material and in particular from what appears in the decision document itself that the consultation procedure adopted by the ministers was at all times proper. The decision was fairly reached. The ministers applied their minds personally to the issues raised in accordance with the requirements of the 1993 Act. There is in my judgment no good ground for saying that the circumstances of the consultations were such as to create reasonable concern about the fairness of the decision.

4. *Local inquiry*

Section 24(2) of the 1993 Act replaces s 105 and Sch 5, para 12B of the Environmental Protection Act 1990. It provides that 'the Secretary of State may cause a local inquiry to be held ...' The section therefore confers a wide discretion on the Secretary of State to be exercised in accordance with ordinary principles of public law. The discretion must be exercised for the purposes of the Act (see *Padfield v Minister of Agriculture, Fisheries and Food* [1968] 1 All ER 694, [1968] AC 997) and within *Wednesbury* limits (see *Associated Provincial Picture Houses Ltd v Wednesbury Corp* [1947] 2 All ER 680, [1948] 1 KB 223).

I was referred to *Binney v Secretary of State for the Environment* (1983) Times, 8 October, a decision of Webster J. That case concerned s 10 of and Sch 1 to the Highways Act 1980. Paragraph 7 of Sch 1 required the minister to hold a local inquiry in the event of an objection unless (para 7(2)) the minister was satisfied that in the circumstances of the case the holding of an inquiry was unnecessary. The statutory provisions governing the ministers' exercise of discretion therefore differed from those in the present case. Nevertheless certain passages in the judgment of Webster J are of general application. He referred to the dictum of Lord Diplock in *Bushell v Secretary of State for the Environment* [1980] 2 All ER 608 at 611, [1981] AC 75 at 102 and then said:

'In my judgment the object of the Act and the object of the holding of public inquiries under the Act include at least the following two objects. First (and I am adopting and slightly rephrasing part of the dictum of Lord Diplock which I have already cited), to ensure that the minister is able to weigh any conflicting public interests. Secondly ... to ensure that those with the right to make representations have had those representations properly taken into account. It is not sufficient ... that the information which the minister needs is available to him, nor that the issues raised are sufficiently clear to him, because those two considerations wholly omit the much more difficult judgmental function of assessing the information and weighing conflicting views. In my judgment, a minister properly directing himself and acting reasonably, cannot be satisfied ... that public inquiry is unnecessary unless he is satisfied of at least two things, namely that without a public inquiry he can properly weigh any two or more

conflicting issues, and, secondly, that those with the right to make
representations can have their representations properly taken into
account. I do not go so far as to add a third factor, for which [counsel]
contends, that he ought to decide to hold a public inquiry simply to enable
objectors to be able to take the view that they have had a fair hearing. I do
not purport or intend to decide that matter one way or the other.'

Mr Collins submits that the matters relied on to establish that justification was
not properly considered are relevant to the local inquiry issue. But he argues
further that it does not follow that if there was no irrationality as to
justification there was ipso facto no irrationality in failing to set up an inquiry.
In this regard, the Secretary of State had to decide not only whether he and the
ministers had sufficient information to enable them to reach a decision on the
contentious matters but whether (a) they could be further assisted by the
testing of the material which would take place in such an inquiry and (b)
whether reasons relating to the allaying of public concern made it desirable in
the public interest that an inquiry should be held.

Mr Collins submitted that the following matters were relevant in
considering whether there should be an inquiry. (1) The importance of the
decision: there was a substantial increase in emissions of ionising radiation.
(2) The great public concern demonstrated by the responses to the
consultations and the desire of large numbers of people and local authorities
that there should be an inquiry. (3) The quality of the responses. There are
serious scientific and economic matters to be considered which can only be
tested and properly resolved by the experts on each side giving evidence before
an independent inspector. (4) The failure of the ministers to obtain
information about BNFL contracts and the Touche Ross report could be
remedied by examination of appropriate witnesses at an inquiry. (5) The
likelihood that there would be public concern that ministers were deciding
issues when their government had made it clear that its policy and wish was
that THORP should proceed. (6) The need to inform people about radiation
and allay their fears; an inquiry held in public is the best way of informing and
reassuring and of dealing with scaremongering. (7) The need to provide the
Secretary of State with the information resulting from the testing of scientific,
economic and other issues so as to enable him to reach the correct decision in
the public interest. Mr Collins also submits that the Secretary of State took into
account an irrelevant consideration, namely that the ordering of an inquiry
would cause considerable delay with implications of financial loss to BNFL.

In order to assess these points (many of which overlap) it is necessary to
examine the manner in which the Secretary of State considered whether or not
to exercise his discretion to hold an inquiry. Paragraphs 153 to 158 of the
decision document are relevant. It is necessary to quote paras 154 to 158 in full.

'154. In response to the further consultation exercise just under 12,300
requests were received asking for either a hearing or a local inquiry. Many
of those requesting a hearing or inquiry argued that the further
consultation exercise was an inappropriate method of examining the wide
range of important issues which needed to be addressed. It was further
argued that these issues could not be fully explored, with all conflicting
arguments and opinions properly weighed and taken into account, by
correspondence alone; only in a public inquiry or hearing could evidence
be given and tested through cross-examination and an independent

conclusion reached. It was also argued that a public inquiry would provide the most appropriate means of ensuring that any environmental impact of the operation of THORP was properly assessed. None of the respondents who expressed support for the operation of THORP requested a hearing or inquiry, although several did argue that there was no need for one and the authorisations should be granted without further delay.

155. In considering whether to exercise their discretion to hold a hearing or inquiry, the Ministers had regard to a number of matters. They acknowledge first of all that here is genuine public interest in the outcome of their deliberations. This is clear from the number of responses received to the consultation exercise, and the amount of media coverage of the issues (although the media interest has been focused mainly on THORP rather than Sellafield as a whole). Against this they consider that the extensive consultation already carried out, by the Inspectorates and then by the Ministers themselves, has provided an adequate opportunity for people to make full and informed representations, as is evidenced by the quality, quantity and detail of the responses received.

156. They have also have taken account of the large number of respondents who have requested a hearing or an inquiry, including 85 local authorities, but they note also that these do not include the two local authorities—Cumbria County Council and Copeland Borough Council—in whose area Sellafield is situated. The Ministers acknowledge that many might feel they lack reassurance that their representations have been fully taken into account unless all the issues were subjected to the detailed examination that a hearing or inquiry would be able to provide. They wish to emphasise, however, that they have taken great care to give their full consideration to all of the concerns and arguments raised.

157. The Ministers have also considered the extent to which a hearing or inquiry would assist their consideration of the issues raised by this case. They do not accept, as many have argued, that a hearing or inquiry is necessary to enable an independent assessment of the issues, whether it be a hearing or inquiry to look at the narrow issues relevant to the Act or one which explored the wider issues discussed above. They also believe that the nature of the considerations which have been at the forefront of their minds in reaching their decisions on the authorisations is such that further debate on or enquiry into the issues would not bring any fresh considerations to bear or remove any remaining uncertainty.

158. Moreover, and in any event, the Ministers consider that it would not be appropriate to hold a hearing or an inquiry in this case. They are confident that the very large amount of information and argument which has been presented to them provides an adequate basis for them to inform themselves of the weight and substance of the concerns of all interested parties, and to assess and weigh that information and argument. The Ministers have taken great care to ensure that they are conversant with, and understand, the issues which have a bearing on their decisions. They are satisfied that no new issues have been raised in the course of the consultation exercise which would lead them to conclude that further consultation or debate is necessary or desirable. They are also conscious of the considerable delay which a hearing or inquiry could be expected to entail, and the likely financial implications for BNFL of such a delay. The Ministers have therefore decided, in the light of all these matters and after

weighing the arguments of those who sought a hearing or inquiry, that they should exercise their discretion by reaching a decision without further debate or inquiry.'

I have reached the conclusion that in the above passages the Secretary of State adequately and properly addressed all those matters relevant to his decision not to hold a local inquiry. He was satisfied that he was in a position to take account of the representations made (para 156) and to weigh the information received (para 158). Thus the criteria identified by Webster J in *Binney v Secretary of State for the Environment* (1983) Times, 8 October were addressed. I accept that the argument that scientific and economic issues ought to be considered and tested in public is a strong one; but the Secretary of State applied himself to these matters and decided not to order an inquiry. In my judgment he was entitled to take this course given the consultations that had taken place and the information that was available to him. The ministers' assertion (para 158) that that information and argument 'provides an adequate basis for them to inform themselves of the weight and substance of the concerns of all interested parties, and to assess and weigh that information and argument' cannot be faulted.

The applicants have contended that the Secretary of State wrongly took into account the delay that would result from the ordering of an inquiry. It is said that any such delay would be the consequence of the Secretary of State's failure to order an inquiry at an early stage after receipt of the applications. The passage complained of is in para 158 of the decision document quoted above. I am satisfied that when looked at in context, that passage does not bear the interpretation that the applicants seek to place upon it. The passage appears after it is stated that it would not be appropriate to hold a hearing or inquiry in this case. Moreover the passage begins: '... They are also *conscious* of the considerable delay which a hearing or inquiry could be expected to entail ...' (my emphasis). Delay and any consequent financial implications were collateral considerations. In my judgment neither were advanced by the ministers as a reason for concluding as they did. Irrelevant considerations are not taken into account.

The applicants have contended that because of the government's stated support for THORP and the state ownership of THORP, the ministers would appear as judges in their own cause unless an inquiry was held. In his concluding submissions, Mr Collins argued that the ministers did not refer to the need to inform the public to allay fears or concerns about the impossibility of divorcing government from the ministers' decision. These were matters it is said that should have been taken into account in the decision-making process and were not.

No one could dispute the need to properly inform the public of matters such as those under review. Sir Roger Parker referred to this in his report (para 2.1):

'Moreover it was repeatedly stressed by one or other party in the course of the Inquiry that the public are badly informed and should be better informed. I have no doubt whatever that this is so, in the sense that the public should be provided with more in the way of digestible and reliable information. It is the lack of such information which renders the public or some members of it suspicious of those who operate the nuclear industry and exposes them to anxieties which are needless.'

Thus I see the force of Mr Collins' argument. But Parliament entrusted the
ministers with responsibility for making the relevant decisions and gave the
Secretary of State a discretion as to whether or not to direct a local inquiry.
Provided the Secretary of State applied his mind genuinely and rationally to the
issue of whether or not to hold a public inquiry, his decision cannot be
impugned. In this case, there is no evidence that the Secretary of State failed
so to apply his mind.

In *Brind v Secretary of State for the Home Dept* [1991] 1 All ER 720 at 737–738,
[1991] 1 AC 696 at 764–766 Lord Lowry said:

> 'The kind of unreasonableness for which a court can set aside an
> administrative act or decision is popularly called "*Wednesbury*
> unreasonableness*" from the name of the famous case, *Associated Provincial
> Picture Houses Ltd v Wednesbury Corp* [1947] 2 All ER 680, [1948] 1 KB 223,
> in which Lord Greene MR spoke of a decision "so absurd that no sensible
> person could ever dream that it lay within the powers of the authority"
> (see [1947] 2 All ER 680 at 683, [1948] 1 KB 223 at 229). In *Secretary of State
> for Education and Science v Tameside Metropolitan Borough* [1976] 3 All ER 665
> at 671, [1977] AC 1014 at 1026 Lord Denning MR referred to decisions "so
> wrong that no reasonable person could sensibly take that view". In
> *Council of Civil Service Unions v Minister for the Civil Service* [1984] 3 All ER
> 935 at 951, [1985] AC 374 at 410 Lord Diplock, having used irrationality as
> a synonym of *Wednesbury* unreasonableness, said that "It applies to a
> decision which is so outrageous in its defiance of logic or of accepted moral
> standards that no sensible person who had applied his mind to the
> question to be decided could have arrived at it", while in *Nottinghamshire
> CC v Secretary of State for the Environment* [1986] 1 All ER 199 at 202, [1986]
> AC 240 at 247 Lord Scarman, when invited to examine the detail and
> consequences of guidance given by the Secretary of State, said: "Such an
> examination by a court would be justified only if a prima facie case were
> to be shown for holding that the Secretary of State had acted in bad faith,
> or for an improper motive, or that the consequences of his guidance were
> so absurd that he must have taken leave of his senses." These colourful
> statements emphasise the legal principle that judicial review of
> administrative action is a supervisory and not an appellate jurisdiction. I
> recall that in *R v Nat Bell Liquors Ltd* [1922] 2 AC 128 at 156, [1922] All ER
> Rep 335 at 351 Lord Sumner, admittedly speaking of an attempted
> challenge to the validity of court proceedings, said that the superior
> court's jurisdiction was one "of supervision, not of review". I believe that
> the subject is nowhere better discussed than by Sir William Wade in his
> authoritative textbook *Administrative Law* (6th edn, 1988) ch 12 'Abuse of
> Discretion' pp 388–462. The learned author, with the aid of examples
> covering more than a century, clearly demonstrates that what we are
> accustomed to call *Wednesbury* unreasonableness is a branch of the abuse,
> or misuse, of power: the court's duty is not to interfere with a discretion
> which Parliament has entrusted to a statutory body or an individual but to
> maintain a check on excesses in the exercise of discretion. That is why it
> is not enough if a judge feels able to say, like a juror or like a dissenting
> member of the Cabinet or fellow-councillor: "I think that is unreasonable;
> that is not what I would have done." It also explains the emphatic
> language which judges have used in order to drive home the message and

the necessity, as judges have seen it, for the act to be "so unreasonable that no reasonable minister etc would have done it". In that strong, and necessary, emphasis lies the danger. The seductive voice of counsel will suggest ... that, for example, ministers, who are far from irrational and indeed are reasonable people, may occasionally be guilty of an abuse of power by going too far. And then the court is in danger of turning its back not only on the vigorous language but on the principles which it was intended to support. A less emotive, but, subject to one qualification, reliable test is to ask: "*Could* a decision-maker acting reasonably have reached this decision?" The qualification is that the supervising court must bear in mind that it is not sitting on appeal, but satisfying itself whether the decision-maker has acted within the bounds of his discretion. For that reason it is fallacious for those seeking to quash administrative acts and decisions to call in aid decisions of a Court of Appeal reversing a judge's finding, it may be on a question of what is reasonable. To say what is reasonable was the judge's task in the first place and the duty of the Court of Appeal, after giving due weight to the judge's opinion, is to say whether they agree with him. In judicial review, on the other hand, the task of the High Court is as described above, and the task of the Court of Appeal and, when necessary, this House is to decide whether the High Court has correctly exercised its *supervisory* jurisdiction.' (Lord Lowry's emphasis.)

In this passage, Lord Lowry precisely defines the role of the court in the present case. Whether or not I would have directed a public inquiry is neither here nor there. It may be thought that a minister sensible to the scale of representations set out above, and the desirability in allaying public anxiety, would have directed an inquiry. But this is not an issue for me. The essential question is whether the Secretary of State in refusing to direct an inquiry was acting lawfully within the powers conferred upon him by Parliament. Applying the principles of law set out above to the whole of the material adduced before me, I come to the conclusion that he was. He did not err in law; he did not take into account irrelevant considerations. He had regard to all relevant considerations. This decision was not irrational. The applicants therefore fail on this ground also.

5. Conclusion

In the result I refuse to grant the relief sought under paras (1), (5) and (6) of the grounds. In the exercise of my discretion the ministers, having erred in law in the respects I identified earlier in this judgment, for the reasons already given, I refuse the relief sought in paras (3) and (4) of the grounds.

Application dismissed.

Mary Rose Plummer   Barrister.

Brown v KMR Services Ltd
Sword-Daniels v Pitel and others

QUEEN'S BENCH DIVISION (COMMERCIAL COURT)

GATEHOUSE J

23, 24, 28 FEBRUARY, 1–4 MARCH, 13 APRIL 1994

Negligence – Contract – Concurrent remedies – Duty of care – Insurance – Lloyd's underwriting agent – Duty owed to names – Names informing members' agents of wish to follow cautious underwriting strategy – Agents recommending high risk excess of loss syndicates – Agents failing to warn names of dangers of excess of loss reinsurance – Whether agents in breach of contract – Whether agents in breach of duty of care, irrespective of whether name a sophisticated investor or whether agent recommended stop-loss insurance – Whether agents liable for names' losses.

The plaintiff in the first case, SD, became a Lloyd's name in 1986. SD informed his members' agent, on joining Lloyd's, that he wished to follow a low risk conservative underwriting policy and that he could not contemplate the possibility of suffering serious loss, since he was largely dependent on his professional income as a dentist and had only slender assets. The agent gave SD the impression that, while insurance was a risk business, the inevitable occasional loss would be small and that in the unlikely event of substantial underwriting losses he would be protected by personal stop-loss insurance, which he was advised to obtain. From 1987 to 1990 SD's agent placed between 34% and 42% of his allocated premium income limit with 7 (out of a total of 14) syndicates which specialised in catastrophe excess of loss and London market excess reinsurance. The agent however failed to warn SD that in years when one or more catastrophes (e g a hurricane, oil spill and/or earthquake) occurred those high reward/high risk syndicates suffered heavy losses because of the funnelling effect of reinsuring 'excess of loss on excess of loss' and the spiral effect of a small number of syndicates reinsuring each other in successive layers. Several disasters occurred between 1987 and 1990, which, to a considerable extent, came to rest with the names on the excess of loss syndicates, which included SD.

The plaintiff in the second case, B, was a successful business man who began underwriting as a Lloyd's name in 1977. B's early underwriting policy, which he made clear to the members' agent acting on his behalf, was cautious and conservative. The success of his underwriting activities however led B to expand his portfolio, which he did independently, selecting his own syndicates and allocations primarily by reference to profitability. By 1985 B had increased his premium income limit five-fold to £1m and by 1989 he was on 35 syndicates, of which 15 were excess of loss syndicates, amounting to 49% of his premium income limit. At no time did B's agent alert him to the dangers of excess of loss reinsurance. B was aware of those dangers by 1990, yet his allocations to excess of loss syndicates for the year (despite a reduced exposure) were still substantial, totalling 33·6% of his premium income limit. B continued to participate in excess of loss syndicates in 1991 and 1992, but by then he had curtailed his exposure due to the massive losses overtaking the names on the 'disaster' syndicates, including himself.

The plaintiffs brought separate proceedings against their former members' agents, alleging that they had acted negligently and in breach of contract in advising them to join high reward/high risk syndicates, instead of following a conservative underwriting policy, and sought damages suffered in the years 1987 to 1990 and likely to be suffered in open years and declarations for an indemnity. The agents contended, inter alia, (i) that the alleged breach of contract merely provided the occasion for some other independent event to cause the damage and was not the effective cause of the plaintiffs' losses, (ii) in relation to SD, that the recommendation to obtain stop-loss insurance was an integral part of the agent's advice and underwriting strategy and therefore (contrary to the general rule) the proceeds of insurance received should be taken into account in assessing both liability and the quantum of damages and (iii) that in view of the global market losses suffered by Lloyd's syndicates from 1988 to 1990 (4·9%, 19·5% and 27·2% respectively) the plaintiffs should not be entitled to recover damages so that they were better off than the market average performance had their portfolios been composed differently.

Held – (1) Where a Lloyd's name obtained an assurance from his members' agent that only syndicates constituting a low risk conservative underwriting policy would be recommended, the agent would be in breach of contract and in breach of his duty of care if he subsequently recommended high risk excess of loss syndicates contrary to that assurance without first obtaining the name's informed consent. A Lloyd's name was also entitled to expect a warning of the dangers inherent in excess of loss reinsurance syndicates from his members' agent, irrespective of whether he happened to be a sophisticated investor (see p 396 g to j, p 397 j and p 409 e h, post); Sykes v Midland Bank Executor and Trustee Co Ltd [1970] 2 All ER 471 and dictum of Lord Diplock in Saif Ali v Sidney Mitchell & Co (a firm) (P, third party) [1978] 3 All ER 1033 at 1041, 1043 applied.

(2) Where a members' agent placed a Lloyd's name on a high risk excess of loss syndicate in breach of contract, that breach was the effective cause of the name's loss, since the whole purpose of the syndicate's 'excess of loss on excess of loss' contracts was to pay the reinsured party's excess of loss in the event of a relevant catastrophe, subject to the syndicate's own reinsurance protection, and if that protection was not sufficient to cover the loss, the remainder of the excess would be paid by the syndicate itself. The type of loss incurred by the name was also foreseeable (even if its scale was not) and was the natural and obvious consequence of membership of a disaster syndicate. It followed that the agent would be liable for any loss incurred as a result of his breach of contract (see p 398 b to e j to p 399 a, post); H Parsons (Livestock) Ltd v Uttley Ingham & Co Ltd [1978] 1 All ER 525 applied.

(3) On the facts, SD, given his financial circumstances, should have received advice from his member' agent on the dangers of the excess of loss syndicates which he had been recommended to join and on the policy of allocating a substantial part of his premium income limit to such syndicates. Without that advice, SD's agreement to the allocations complained of was an uninformed agreement. If SD had been alerted, it was probable that he would have retained his Lloyd's membership, but insisted on a safer low risk portfolio and since it was impossible to decide what a safer portfolio would have comprised, the only fair conclusion was that he would have suffered the loses claimed. SD's claim for breach of contract was therefore made out. Moreover, the agent's failure to give SD comprehensive advice was a breach of duty which was

unaffected by the advice to procure stop-loss insurance, which merely
a operated to mitigate loss by providing a band of protection within set limits
which could easily be exceeded in the event of serious underwriting loss, and
consequently stop-loss cover was not relevant to the issue of liability or the
assessment of damages. On the question of damages, market average
performance figures were not a useful guide in the assessment of the quantum
b of SD's losses, since it was likely that the alternative low risk portfolio would
not have incurred market average losses, which clearly would incorporate the
heavy losses suffered by the disaster syndicates. SD was accordingly entitled
to recover his actual losses and to an indemnity against future losses on the
open years of the syndicates in question (see p 396 *g* to p 397 *a c j*, p 399 *f* and
p 400 *a*, post); *Bradburn v Great Western Rly Co* [1874–80] All ER Rep 195 applied;
c *Eley v King & Chasemore* (1989) 22 EG 109 considered.

(4) On the facts, B was an independent-minded name who made his own
investment decisions and from 1985 followed a strategy of aggressive
underwriting based on profitability. B was not however given any warning of
the dangers of the high risk excess of loss syndicates which he joined and he
d was entitled to expect such advice from his members' agent, irrespective of
whether he happened to be a sophisticated investor. B's claim for breach of
contract was therefore made out. On the question of damages, it was clear
that, even if the agent had given the necessary warning, B would nevertheless
have continued on a number of the syndicates of which he later complained
and probably would have allocated about 30% of his premium income limit to
e excess of loss syndicates. B's damages and his indemnity for future losses on
open years would accordingly be reduced pro rata (see p 408 *g h*, p 409 *b e h* and
p 410 *j* to p 411 *a*, post).

Notes

f For standard of duty of an agent for reward, see 1(2) *Halsbury's Laws* (4th edn)
para 94, and for cases on the subject, see 1(2) *Digest* (2nd reissue) 279–284, *2219–
2254*.

For insurance at Lloyd's, see 25 *Halsbury's Laws* (4th edn reissue) para 21.

Cases referred to in judgment

Alexander v Cambridge Credit Corp Ltd (1987) 9 NSWLR 310, NSW CA.
*Arbuthnott v Feltrim Underwriting Agencies Ltd, Deeny v Gooda Walker Ltd,
Henderson v Merrett Syndicates Ltd* (1993) Times, 30 December, [1993] CA
Transcript 1472; *affd* sub nom *Henderson v Merrett Syndicates Ltd* [1994] 3 All
ER 506, [1994] 3 WLR 761, HL.
Banque Bruxelles Lambert SA v Eagle Star Insurance Co (1994) 31 EG 68.
Banque Financère de la Cité SA v Westgate Insurance Co Ltd [1990] 2 All ER 947,
[1991] 2 AC 249, [1990] 3 WLR 364, HL.
Bradburn v Great Western Rly Co (1874) LR 10 Exch 1, [1874–80] All ER Rep 195.
Eley v King & Chasemore (a firm) (1989) 22 EG 109, CA.
Galoo Ltd (in liq) v Bright Grahame Murray (a firm) [1994] 1 WLR 1360, CA.
Parry v Cleaver [1969] 1 All ER 555, [1970] AC 1, [1969] 2 WLR 821, HL.
Parsons (H) (Livestock) Ltd v Uttley Ingham & Co Ltd [1978] 1 All ER 525, [1978]
QB 791, [1978] 3 WLR 990, CA.
Quinn v Burch Bros (Builders) Ltd [1966] 2 All ER 283, [1966] 2 QB 370, [1966] 2
WLR 1017, CA.

Saif Ali v Sydney Mitchell & Co (a firm) (P, third party) [1978] 3 All ER 1033, [1980] a
AC 198, [1978] 3 WLR 849, HL.
Sykes v Midland Bank Executor and Trustee Co Ltd [1970] 2 All ER 471, [1971] 1 QB
113, [1970] 3 WLR 273, CA.

Actions

Brown v KMR Services Ltd   b
The plaintiff, Richard Kevin Brown, a Lloyd's name, by a writ issued on 6 May
1992, brought an action against the defendant, KMR Services Ltd (formerly HG
Poland (Agencies) Ltd), claiming (i) damages for underwriting losses incurred
during the period 1987 to 1990 and resulting from membership of a number of
high risk excess of loss syndicates recommended by the defendant in its c
capacity as members' agent in breach of its duty of care and in breach of
contract and (ii) a declaration as to the defendant's liability to indemnify Mr
Brown against further underwriting losses on open years. The facts are set out
in the judgment.

Sword-Daniels v Pitel and ors   d
The plaintiff, Michael Sword-Daniels, a Lloyd's name, by a writ issued on 22
June 1992, brought an action against the defendants, Michael David Walter
Pitel, Poland, Pitel Underwriting Agencies Ltd, Poland & Co Ltd and KMR
Services Ltd, claiming (i) damages for underwriting losses incurred during the
period 1987 to 1990 and resulting from membership of a number of high risk e
excess of loss syndicates recommended by the defendants in their capacity as
members' agents in breach of their duty of care and in breach of contract and
(ii) a declaration as to the defendants' liability to indemnify Mr Sword-Daniels
against further underwriting losses on open years. The facts are set out in the
judgment.
                                                                        f
Adrian Hamilton QC and *Stephen Hofmeyr* (instructed by *D J Freeman*) for Mr
   Brown.
Michael Crane and *Hannah Brown* (instructed by *Hextall Erskine & Co*) for Mr
   Sword-Daniels.
Peregrine Simon QC and *Simon Bryan* (instructed by *Elborne Mitchell*) for the g
   defendants.

Cur adv vult

13 April 1994. The following judgment was delivered.   h

GATEHOUSE J. The plaintiffs in these two actions, heard together, suffered
very serious financial losses as names at Lloyd's in the years of account 1987 to
1990. In addition to accrued losses, they are both likely to suffer further losses
in respect of open years.
    In these actions they claim against their former members' agents damages, j
and declarations for an indemnity, on the ground that the agents acted
negligently and in breach of contract in advising them which syndicates to join
and/or to continue with, and with what premium allocations.
    Both plaintiffs allege that they made known to the agents their desire to
follow a conservative underwriting policy but, in breach of the agent's duty of
care, they were recommended to join, and were not warned about the nature

of, syndicates which were unsuitable as being high reward/high risk, namely
those which wrote a substantial book of Catastrophe Excess of Loss (CAT
XOL) and London Market Excess (LMX) reinsurance. In good years, ie those
which were wholly or largely catastrophe-free, such syndicates generally made
substantial profits for their names. But the insurance market is traditionally
cyclical and there will inevitably come a time when one or more major
catastrophes will occur: when this happens, such syndicates are likely to suffer
disastrous results because of the funnelling effect of reinsuring 'excess of loss
on excess of loss', and the spiral effect of a small number of syndicates
reinsuring each other in successive layers. Put shortly, whereas the basic
principle of direct insurance is to spread the risk among the many, this kind of
reinsurance has the opposite effect: excess of loss reinsurance tends to
concentrate the risk among ever fewer syndicates, with the result that by far
the greater proportion of the loss involved in the original catastrophe,
hurricane, earthquake, oil-rig etc has to be borne by a comparatively few
syndicates.

Before turning to the details of these claims some preliminary points can be
made.

(1) Every individual who wishes to become an underwriting member of
Lloyd's is made unequivocally aware of certain fundamental matters, the most
important of which for present purposes are these. (a) All insurance is a high
risk business and a name can make losses as well as profits. (b) The name has
unlimited liability. If his/her reserves and deposits are insufficient to meet the
name's share of insurance claims written on his or her behalf, the individual
will be liable to the full extent of his/her assets. (c) Except for professional
underwriters, the name is prohibited from engaging in the actual process of
underwriting; this must be left entirely to the judgment and discretion of the
managing agent of each syndicate which the name joins acting through its
active underwriter. (d) This is secured by the name entering into a contract
with a members' agent. If the latter is a combined agent, ie both a members'
agent and a managing (underwriting) agent, total control of the name's
underwriting is vested in that agent. Otherwise, the members' agent is entitled
to, and in fact always does, delegate the actual underwriting to a separate
managing agent. In either case, the name has no say in what risks are to be
underwritten on his/her behalf. The precise contractual provisions between a
name, his members' agent' and, since 1990, the managing agent have varied
over the years. They are fully set out in a recent decision of the Court of
Appeal, referred to later, but the variations do not effect the scope of the
members' agent's duties towards its names.

(2) It follows from the above that a name's choice of members' agent is very
important and the Lloyd's brochure, which is supplied to every prospective
name, emphasises the need to ensure that the name's underwriting philosophy
is compatible with that of the prospective members' agent.

(3) Despite para (1)(a) above, the Lloyd's market has enjoyed a singular
record of success over many years. For instance, in the 40-year period from
1945 to 1985, the market as a whole made a loss in only three. Of course,
individual syndicates vary greatly: some may make a loss even in the good
years for the market as a whole and, similarly, even in disaster years some
syndicates may still make profits. But the overall record up to at least 1985 was
impressive and it is not surprising that membership of Lloyd's increased
greatly, particularly between 1981 and 1988.

(4) Despite the emergence in the mid-80s of serious losses on certain
long-tail business, particularly asbestosis and environmental pollution risks,
membership did not start to decline until 1989, presumably when the effects of
the catastrophes of 1987 and 1988 became widely known.

(5) To those who had the necessary means, membership of Lloyd's offered
considerable advantages. First, the name's capital could be used twice over: to
entitle the name to earn premium income and, at the same time, to earn an
investment income and the chance of capital appreciation. Secondly, if losses
were unfortunately suffered, they could be set against tax on other income.
This was of special benefit in the era of very high personal taxation before 1979,
but it plainly remained a considerable attraction thereafter. Thirdly, there was
perceived to be a certain cachet, particularly in business, in describing oneself
as a 'name at Lloyd's'.

(6) Serious catastrophes had occurred in the past, particularly Hurricane
Betsy in 1965 and Hurricane Alicia in 1983, the first event ever to cause an
insured loss of $US 1bn, but their effects had been reasonably well contained
within the Lloyd's market. What no one anticipated was the size and
frequency of the various disasters that occurred between 1987 and 1990
beginning with the North Europe and United Kingdom windstorm of October
1987, followed by the Piper Alpha rig disaster in July 1988, the Exon Valdez oil
spill, Hurricane Hugo and the San Francisco earthquake in 1989, to name but
some. Losses soared to $US 3·4bn, $US 4·5bn and ultimately to $US 10bn.
These are the losses which, to a considerable extent, have come to rest with the
names on the syndicates in question.

(7) The importance to the name of his members' agent has been mentioned.
It is to the agent that the name turns for his introduction to Lloyd's and then
for advice on all his subsequent underwriting matters, and he pays for the
agent's services by a fee and a percentage of his underwriting profits. There
was no issue between the parties as to the agent's duties. Those relevant to
these actions are, in summary: (a) to advise the name which syndicates to join
and in what amounts, (b) to keep him informed at all times of material factors
which may affect his underwriting, (c) to provide him with a balanced portfolio
and appropriate spread of risk; a balanced spread of business on syndicates
throughout the main markets at Lloyd's, (d) to monitor the syndicates on
which it places the name, and to make recommendations as to whether the
name should increase his share on a syndicate, join a new syndicate, reduce his
share, or withdraw, (e) to keep regularly in touch with the syndicates to which
the name belongs, and (f) to advise and discuss with the name the prospects
and past results of syndicates on which he could be placed.

With those introductory remarks, I turn to consider the facts of the two
actions.

I propose to consider, first, Mr Sword-Daniels's claim because it is
comparatively straightforward, with very little dispute as to the facts.

Mr Sword-Daniels is a dental surgeon practising in partnership with his wife
in Burgess Hill. He also teaches dentistry part-time at Guy's Hospital, where
a fellow part-time teacher, Mr Frank van den Berg, interested him in becoming
a member of Lloyd's. The latter had been a name for many years and had
derived from it a steady though unspectacular income. His members' agent
was John Poland & Co and their representative, who handled his Lloyd's
affairs, was Mr Michael Pitel. Mr van den Berg suggested that he should
introduce Mr Sword-Daniels to Mr Pitel and did so in 1986.

Mr Sword-Daniels's purpose in seeking membership was to establish a reserve of funds which, added to certain endowment policies, he hoped would pay for the private education of his daughters. Mr Pitel explained the general working of Lloyd's, as he would have done to any prospective name, and Mr Sword-Daniels explained his purpose in seeking membership and, in some detail, his means and income. In particular, he made it clear that he had always been a cautious investor who could not contemplate the possibility of suffering serious losses. I have no doubt that Mr Pitel told him, as was also plainly apparent from, among other documents, the Lloyd's brochure and verification form, that membership involved unlimited liability and that insurance was a risk business which could result in losses as well as profits. But the impression left with Mr Sword-Daniels was that when the inevitable occasional losses occurred, they would be small and easily containable. It was a crucial part of Mr Pitel's underwriting philosophy that in the unlikely event of substantial losses, the name would be protected by a personal stop-loss insurance which he recommended to all his names.

It is clear on the evidence that Mr Sword-Daniels was a nervous investor, almost entirely dependant upon professional income and with very slender assets. While accepting the possibility of losses on his underwriting, he wanted a 'safety-first' approach, and was assured of this by Mr Pitel.

There was a conflict between the parties as to whether, as the plaintiff maintained, he was assured by Mr Pitel that he would only be placed on low risk *syndicates* or, as the defendants maintained, the assurance related to low risk *insurance*, ie that his portfolio of syndicates looked at as a whole and protected by personal stop-loss would conform to a conservative low risk approach. The resolution of this issue depends mainly on recollection of what was said in various conversations which took place nearly seven years ago. The plaintiff's version was supported by similar recollections of two witnesses, Professor Mortimer and Mr Howard, both dental surgeons and colleagues of Mr Sword-Daniels who were contemplating Lloyd's membership in 1987. A meeting with Mr Pitel at Guy's Hospital was arranged by Mr Sword-Daniels, who was present himself for part of the time, and Mr Pitel gave a presentation. Both Professor Mortimer and Mr Howard said that they, too, could not contemplate the possibility of serious losses and they were both assured, so they said, that if they joined the Poland agency they would be placed on safe syndicates, the same syndicates as Mr Sword-Daniels was on. There must be doubt as to precisely what was said to Mr Sword-Daniels in 1986: there is room for confusion and there are arguments in favour of both recollections. If I had to choose, I would on balance find that the effect of what Mr Pitel said in 1986 was that he would adopt a safety-first conservative approach to his recommended portfolio; not that he would ensure that every syndicate would be low risk. In the end, I do not think I need to resolve the dispute because, whatever words were used on various occasions, I am satisfied that Mr Sword-Daniels was left with the clear impression that the underwriting strategy to be pursued on his behalf would be a safety-first policy of low risk insurance. Without an assurance to that effect, he would have shied away from becoming a name.

More than one expert witness expressed the view, with which I agree, that in the light of Mr Sword-Daniels's disclosed circumstances, he should have been discouraged from joining Lloyd's. His only substantial asset was a half-share in the equity of his house, which had to be charged to the bank in order to obtain the guarantees totalling £100,000 which were necessary to establish the required minimum of readily realisable assets. Beyond this, his assets were minimal. Although he was a higher-rate taxpayer his professional income at the time was modest, some £32,800 p a and his other income no more than about £2,000 p a, so there was an insubstantial tax cushion to absorb any serious loss.

No complaint is made, of course, that Mr Sword-Daniels should not have been put forward as a suitable member, but I think he was at least close to the bottom end of any suitability scale, and it was clearly the duty of John Poland & Co, acting through Mr Pitel, to make sure that they followed the safety-first approach which had been promised and on which he relied.

How, then, did it come about that in 1987, Mr Sword-Daniels's first year of underwriting, no less than £80,000 out of his allocated premium income of £190,000 was placed with 7 syndicates (out of a total of 14) which, on any view, were 'high risk'? There was debate as to whether the proper description of the syndicates concerned was 'high reward/high risk', or 'higher reward/higher risk'. Again, I do not think it matters: at all material times the professionals in Lloyd's, underwriters, brokers and members' agents, have been well aware of the differing reward/risk categories that can be applied to different syndicates. Obviously, this involves a certain amount of individual judgment. Mr Wilshaw, the principal expert called on behalf of both plaintiffs, divided syndicates into three categories which he described as:

'(1) Standard Risk: Typically those writing a simple direct account where I believe the syndicate loss potential was not significant—of the order of 10% of the stamp. (2) Medium Risk: This category is likely to involve most syndicates. Typically those writing a mixture of direct and reinsurance, with some catastrophe X/L and perhaps even a very small amount of LMX. The loss potential would typically be in the range 10% to 30% of the stamp. (3) High Risk: This would be those syndicates where the loss potential was greater than 30% of the stamp, which to a large extent would be due to their exposure on LMX business.'

He based his categorisation of Mr Sword-Daniels's syndicates on the reports and accounts at each year-end. Those for the year ended 31 December 1985 would have been published in mid-1986 and would have been available to Mr Pitel at the time when he was considering which syndicates to recommend to Mr Sword-Daniels for his first underwriting year.

Even if one uses this simple categorisation, there is obviously room for differing judgments as to which category many syndicates will fall into. The definitions are not hard and fast and other experts, as well as the professional factual witnesses, were entitled to differing opinions. But there was general agreement that syndicates which held themselves out as specialist CAT XOL/ LMX or whose book of business contained a substantial amount of such reinsurance were to be regarded as at the upper end of the reward/risk scale, however defined. In particular, the Gooda Walker syndicates (290 and 298); the Feltrim syndicates (540, 542 and 847), and the two Poland in-house LMX syndicates (104 and 733) and the Aragorn syndicate (384) all fell into this range. On all these except 542, Mr Sword-Daniels participated in 1987, to the extent of 42% of his total allocated premium income limit (pil).

In 1988, when premium income limits were changed from a net to a gross basis, ie adding 25%, the position was much the same. The same seven syndicates had a total allocation of £99,000, which represented just under 40% of Mr Sword-Daniels's total pil of £250,000. There were some adjustments of individual syndicates' allocations consequent on grossing up, but whereas the allocation to 298 remained the same, that to 847 was doubled. There were further variations in 1989, but the allocation to high risk syndicates was at least £92,000 (as I think, although the figures are not wholly clear) or nearly 37% of the total. For the last year in respect of which Mr Sword-Daniels claims in this action, the allocation appears to be £85,000 or 34% of his total pil. So the percentage on high risk syndicates has declined slightly, although there is a curious feature of the 1990 year. Since at least July 1985 there had been an in-house rule in Polands that, as between their main or flag-ship syndicates and the associated LMX syndicates, direct names allocations should be in the proportion of $2\frac{1}{2}$:1. This may have been, in part, because of the difference in capacity, but a more important reason, in my view, was because of the perceived greater volatility of the LMX syndicates. This rule was at least broadly observed in the case of Mr Sword-Daniels for 1987 and 1988, although the proportion was 2:1 rather than $2\frac{1}{2}$:1, but in 1989 it began to be seriously departed from. In that year £20,000 was allocated to the main marine syndicate 108, but £17,000 to the LMX syndicate 733. For 1990 the proportion became simply 1:1, £20,000 in each case.

These figures show a startling portfolio for a name of Mr Sword-Daniels's known means, circumstances and cautious underwriting strategy. I must therefore consider Mr Pitel's approach to find an explanation.

The guidelines he employed can be summarised in this way: (1) allocations on all four of the main Lloyd's sectors, marine, non-marine, aviation and motor. Each traditionally had a cycle of profitable years followed by the occasional loss-making year. Generally the cycles did not coincide so it was a basic tenet to spread premium income over all four.

(2) As a further measure to spread risk, small lines on a number of syndicates within each sector, to even out the effect of individual syndicates suffering a bad year. For a name writing a small total pil, say £100,000, there would not be much scope for this aspect of spread: I think the minimum allocation to any one syndicate was in practice £5,000 because, below this, syndicate fees and costs would considerably erode likely profits. The larger a name's total pil, the more opportunity for spread within each sector.

(3) By 1986 the dire effects of asbestosis and environmental pollution, principally from the USA, had inculcated an extreme wariness of long-tail business in general.

(4) Caution with regard to new syndicates without a well-established track record; thus, a strong preference for those active underwriters who enjoyed a high reputation based on consistently successful results and the general respect of the Lloyd's professional community.

(5) As mentioned already, direct names on Poland-managed syndicates were to have premium allocated to their LMX and main syndicates in the proportion of 1:$2\frac{1}{2}$. Mr Pitel appears to have modified this to 1:2 but that is not of great importance. In 1987 Mr Sword-Daniels was indeed given this allocation. But I agree with Mr Crane that, so far as this principle was based on comparative volatility, as I think it predominantly was, the same logic should have applied to syndicates managed by other agencies. Yet in this area, while £70,000 was allocated to lower risk syndicates, no less than £60,000 was distributed between five in the high or higher risk bracket.

(6) Stop-loss protection. Mr Pitel said he would not have suggested the 1987 allocation to Mr Sword-Daniels without the benefit of stop-loss cover. I have no doubt that this is right. It would have been a very serious misjudgment to have done otherwise.

Stop-loss protection was a central plank of Mr Pitel's policy. It needs comment. First, and obviously, a stop-loss policy only mitigates losses. The name has to bear his own underwriting losses up to the excess point at which his stop-loss policy comes into play. Furthermore, it is only a band of protection thereafter; in the event of a really serious underwriting loss, however remote the possibility may have seemed in 1987, the policy limit may be exceeded. Mr Sword-Daniels's stop-loss policy for that year was £150,000 excess of £30,000. It was put to him that this showed his contemplation and acceptance, however unpalatable, of the possibility of irrecoverable loss of up to £30,000. This is true, but he was clearly led to believe that in practice his losses, if they occurred, would only be a small fraction of this figure: the policy was there as a sure comfort in the event of the unthinkable happening. And it must be remembered that the normal excess point was not less than 10% of the name's pil. If stop-loss underwriters agree to come on risk at a figure lower than that, the premium will become progressively more expensive, thus eroding the name's anticipated profits to an unacceptable extent. In practice, if Mr Sword-Daniels was to take out the stop-loss protection which Mr Pitel strongly advised, he had to accept the excess point offered.

Secondly, stop-loss does not assist cash flow, because it does not respond as and when losses occur. A call may be made upon the name and has to be met, but it will not be until the relevant year is closed, up to two years after the year of the call, and then a further period before the Inland Revenue agrees the tax position, that the stop-loss policy will respond. A new name will not receive a cheque from his underwriting agent during the first three years of his membership, but he may have to pay one or more calls during that period. Mr Pitel said it was almost unheard of for a name to receive a call in his first year of underwriting, but the possibility was there and it was progressively more likely to happen in the second and third years. Mr Sword-Daniels was in the unhappy position of never receiving a cheque, but he had to pay substantial calls. Although stop-loss recoveries came later, they were not there to meet these calls. Mr Sword-Daniels's limited assets were foreseeably at risk. Thirdly, there was the disadvantage that stop-loss insurance could only be placed in the New Year, so the name, who generally had to complete his allocations by 1 December and certainly by the end of the year, did not know for certain by then that he would obtain stop-loss protection or on what terms. The stop-loss insurers' capacity might run out or their terms might harden, as Mr Sword-Daniels found in succeeding years when his excess point went up, the cover narrowed and his premium also increased.

Fourthly, there is a limited capacity for this type of reinsurance within Lloyd's and if it has to be sought elsewhere, there is always the possible danger that the security may prove illusory.

For these reasons, stop-loss cover was only a limited protection for any name, but particularly for Mr Sword-Daniels. It did not convert his portfolio with its large proportion of high or higher risk syndicates into one which reflected a safety-first policy of low risk insurance.

Mr Pitel's other justification for recommending these syndicates was that Walker (290 and 298) and Fagan (540 and 847) were underwriters of the highest reputation who had consistently produced a good record of profits. Fagan had produced a consistent level of 7% or 8%, which although perhaps more modest than most syndicates, Mr Pitel interpreted as showing substantial reserves and reinsurance cover. As to syndicates 104 and 733, these were Poland's own in-house LMX syndicates, controlled by their own active underwriters, who were directors of the combined agency and under the supervision of the chief executive and the board with a 'hands-on' approach. He also said that he was assured by both Walker and Fagan that they had adequate reinsurance in place.

There is a good deal to be said for his appreciation of the position. He himself was on all seven of the syndicates in question, in some cases for double Mr Sword-Daniels's line (though it has to be noted that his high risk exposure was £120,000 out of his total pil of £440,000 in 1987, ie 27% compared to Mr Sword-Daniels's 42%). He himself had stop-loss protection which he evidently thought sufficient at the time, although in the event he has also suffered grievous losses. And he drew particular comfort from the fact that Mr Sword-Daniels's stop-loss premium which was in his view a very low one, was the result of independent stop-loss underwriters' assessment and therefore a confirmation of the low risk profile of the portfolio as a whole. I am not sure that this was justified, at least in 1987, but I have no doubt that Mr Pitel was convinced.

But there were warning signs. In May 1987 Mr Walker, the active underwriter of syndicate 290, ended his report:

'... as we have advised all our Names in the past, this Syndicate is a High Risk by the nature of the business it writes and we have very nearly reached the limit of Reinsurance that it is worth buying. We must always live with the problem which must apply to all Syndicates that in the event of a major loss we could run out of reinsurance protection ...'

Both Fagan and Walker had given Pitel worst case loss estimates of 100%, placing those syndicates at the very top of the risk spectrum. So, reassuring remarks that the underwriters knew their aggregate exposure and were well covered by reinsurance needed to be regarded with a critical eye.

In any case, Mr Pitel's approach is only part of the picture. The name's contract is with his members' agent and it is the agent that is responsible for the name's affairs and for acting as a reasonably competent agent in fulfilling its duties of care. This must necessarily include putting its authorised representative, Mr Pitel in this case, Mr Maclean and Mr Marks in Brown's case, in a position to fulfil those duties.

The Poland board was, on the face of it, one of the strongest boards in Lloyd's. Among others, it had two directors responsible for the names servicing section as well as the active underwriters of both the Poland LMX syndicates. So far as underwriters were alive to the dangers of such syndicates, LMX underwriters were, or should have been. It seems obvious in retrospect that not all specialist underwriters were aware in 1987 of the 'spiral', as it came to be generally referred to later, in 1988–89, but the evidence of Mr Round, the defendants' principal expert witness, as to the inherent risks of LMX syndicates is important. He was asked by Mr Crane:

'Q. ... Are you saying that it appears [LMX underwriters] did not know any more than the average members' agent? A. I think they knew considerably more than the average members' agent but even the underwriters engaged in LMX did not fully understand the effect of the spiral.

Q. Subject to the qualification that the effect of the spiral came as somewhat of a surprise, would you accept the proposition that an LMX underwriter would understand the inherent risks of writing the business? A. Yes.

Q. Would you accept that in so far as writing an excess of loss protection of an excess of loss account, he would understand the potential for accumulation or funnelling? A. Yes.'

That knowledge was therefore available to the Poland board and, if not communicated to the 'names handler', it should have been. It probably was: this was what I understood Pitel to mean when he spoke of 'gearing'. The board was also aware of difficulties faced by its own LMX syndicates which were having to retain greater uninsured exposures because of increase in reinsurance premiums, and one of which (733) reported that the high cost of reinsurance might kill it in three to four years.

In a report by the managing agency division to the Poland board in July 1988 it was said (with reference to the Piper Alpha rig disaster of 6 July):

'Most underwriters have specific Rig X/L programmes protecting this direct loss, but these protections are written by the London Market, and these reinsurers are likewise protected by policies written in the London Market, which will produce the "dreaded" spiral. Some underwriters will/may run out of protection but it will take some years before the final outcome can be established.'

Whether or not Mr Pitel and other agents' representatives were alert to the added spiral effects of LMX reinsurance, it seems a fair inference from this report that the potential dreaded spiral was something already well known to underwriters, and not only LMX underwriters. The author of this report was a Mr NJ Brown, the active underwriter of syndicate 455, which does not appear to have engaged in this type of reinsurance.

I hope Mr Crane and his team will forgive me if I do not deal in further detail with their very full and well-collated submissions. I do not think it necessary because I am satisfied that, on the facts, Mr Sword-Daniels's claim is unanswerable. The evidence was clear that he should have received advice from his members' agent about the syndicates which it was recommended he join, in particular the nature of the higher reward/risk syndicates, in view of his personal circumstances. His slender assets, comparatively modest income, limited underwriting ambitions and, above all, his known unwillingness to face the possibility of serious losses all required a cautious, even pedestrian, underwriting strategy. He was not alerted to the high risk nature of CAT XOL syndicates, nor to the fact that it was proposed to allocate a substantial part of his premium income to such syndicates. Without such advice, his agreement to the allocations in each year of which he complains was an uninformed agreement. The warning that Mr Pitel should have given him need not have been elaborate. All that was required was a brief explanation that, while the syndicates in question usually produced excellent profits in catastrophe-free years, sooner or later a major catastrophe was certain to occur and when it did the loss could be very serious: that if more than one occurred in any one year, however unlikely that might seem on past history, such syndicates might go through their own reinsurance protection: that the danger to the names would be that much greater, and that personal stop-loss insurance was by no means a complete answer.

If Mr Sword-Daniels had been alerted, the question then arises as to what he would probably have done. He might have resigned his membership of Lloyd's, but having gone to the trouble and expense of joining I think this is unlikely. More probably, he would have been frightened off all higher risk syndicates and asked Mr Pitel to think again and suggest a 'safer' portfolio. It is quite impossible to decide what this would have comprised; the permutations are infinite and the overall result can only be entirely speculative. Even syndicates customarily regarded as 'safe' or lower risk can suffer quite substantial losses. Some striking examples were put to Mr Wilshaw. On balance, I think the only fair conclusion is not to guess at what might have been, but simply conclude that Mr Sword-Daniels would not have suffered the losses particularised in his points of claim and, subject to the defences I deal with below, he is entitled to damages in respect of his ascertained losses to date. In my judgment he is also entitled to an indemnity against future losses on those syndicates with open years.

I reach this conclusion on the particular facts of the case. I have not, of course, overlooked Mr Simon QC's submissions concerning the standard of care to be expected of a defendant acting in a professional capacity. The wisdom of hindsight is a constant intruder which one has to try to guard against. I have to do my best to consider the allegations of breach of contract in the context of the latter part of 1986 and thereafter; not in the light of the disasters that have subsequently become apparent. The defendants put in evidence tables showing the support given in the 1989 and 1990 years to four of Mr Sword-Daniels's syndicates which, in the event, have produced his worst losses, by the 15 largest members' agents. There is no doubt that that contemporaneous support was quite considerable. In answer, the plaintiff relied on a short table which on its face revealed some startling statistics. Out of a total Lloyd's membership in 1987 of 30,936 names, only 134 were placed on all four of the same syndicates, of which 31 were Poland names. But this eclectic choice of syndicates, and the table limited to medium/small sized agencies is, I suspect, a good example of unreliable statistics based on hindsight.

The test of liability for professional negligence was restated by Lord Diplock in *Saif Ali v Sidney Mitchell & Co (firm)* (P, third party) [1978] 3 All ER 1033 at 1041 and 1043, [1980] AC 198 at 218 and 220, the latter passage being:

> 'No matter what profession it may be, the common law does not impose on those who practise it any liability for damage resulting from what in the result turns out to have been errors of judgment, unless the error was such as no reasonably well informed and competent member of that profession could have made.'

On the expert evidence of both parties, Mr Sword-Daniels should have been warned of the dangers inherent in his portfolio, but was not. On the evidence I have heard, I conclude that no competent members' agent would have failed to do so at the relevant time.

Proof of breach of contract does not carry the plaintiff home: he also has to establish that the breach was the effective cause of the loss and that the loss was not too remote in law.

As to causation, the defendants submit that it is not enough to establish that the breach caused the plaintiff to be on a particular loss-making syndicate, in other words, that the breach merely set the scene for some other independent event to cause the damage. They referred to *Quinn v Burch Bros (Builders) Ltd* [1966] 2 All ER 283, [1966] 2 QB 370, *Banque Financière de la Cité SA v Westgate Insurance Co Ltd* [1990] 2 All ER 947, [1991] 2 AC 249, *Banque Bruxelles Lambert SA v Eagle Star Insurance Co* (1994) 31 EG 68 per Phillips J, *Galoo Ltd (in liq) v Bright Grahame Murray (a firm)* [1994] 1 WLR 1360 and *Alexander v Cambridge Credit Corp Ltd* (1987) 9 NSWLR 310.

Essentially, the court has to decide whether a breach of contract was an effective cause of the loss or whether it merely provided the occasion for the loss. For example, in the last two cited cases the courts held that while the auditors' negligence had resulted in the respective companies continuing to trade and thus provided the occasion for the loss, it had not caused it. The other cited decisions were each examples of the same principle which, in the end, may require a commonsense approach. In this case it seems to me that the breach was at least an effective cause of the loss. If a name is placed on a CAT XOL syndicate, the whole purpose of the syndicate's 'excess of loss on excess of loss' contracts is to pay the reinsured's excess of loss in the event of a relevant catastrophe, subject to the syndicate's own reinsurance protection. If that protection is not enough, the syndicate pays the remainder of the excess. I find no difficulty in holding that the defendants' breach of contract is causative of loss.

The defendants are, I think, in this further difficulty. If they wished to raise this defence they were in my judgment obliged by RSC Ord 18, rr 8 and 12 to plead and prove what was the effective cause of the loss. I cannot think that the burden lay upon the plaintiff to plead and prove more than he has, e g that the loss was not caused by some novus actus interveniens. Naturally the defendants were anxious to exclude from this trial any consideration of negligent underwriting as the effective cause: that is an issue which will arise in other Lloyd's litigation. Even if established, it would not assist the defendants in this action for they would be answerable for any such negligence (i) in respect of their own managed syndicates, 104 and 733 and (ii) in respect of the other syndicates, to which they had delegated their duty of underwriting on their names' behalf (see *Arbuthnott v Feltrim Underwriting Agencies Ltd, Deeny v Gooda Walker Ltd, Henderson v Merrett Syndicates Ltd* (1993) Times, 30 December. These cases are, I understand, under further appeal but that is the present law[a].

The only possible alternative novus actus must be that the plaintiff's losses were caused simply by bad luck or underwriting misjudgment falling short of actionable negligence. Again, this possibility played no part in the present action, so there is nothing to be said about it except that I do not think it was for the plaintiff to prove the negative.

Remoteness and foreseeability

It is most unlikely that any professional member of Lloyd's foresaw the magnitude of the financial disasters that struck in the middle-to-late 1980s. Certainly those who gave evidence before me were all agreed on this. But

---

a   The House of Lords has affirmed the decision of the Court of Appeal (see *Henderson v Merrett Syndicates Ltd* [1994] 3 All ER 506, [1994] 3 WLR 761).

losses of the type that occurred were undoubtedly foreseeable and in fact foreseen, even though their scale was not. That is enough for the plaintiff (see e g *H Parsons (Livestock) Ltd v Uttley Ingham & Co Ltd* [1978] 1 All ER 525, [1978] QB 791). The plaintiff's losses were the natural and obvious result of his being a member of the 'disaster' syndicates.

I need next to consider whether Mr Sword-Daniels's stop-loss recoveries are to be taken into account. Authority is clear that a plaintiff's damages are not in general reduced by the proceeds of insurance that he has procured (see *Bradburn v Great Western Rly Co* (1874) LR 10 Exch 1, [1874–80] All ER Rep 195 approved and indorsed by all their Lordships in *Parry v Cleaver* [1969] 1 All ER 555, [1970] AC 1).

However, Mr Simon contends that this general rule does not and cannot apply where the advice of which complaint is made includes advice that the plaintiff should procure insurance: in such a case, the insurance is not collateral but an integral part of both the advice and the underwriting strategy. It is, he says, specifically designed to reduce the risk and therefore should be taken into account 'at all stages'. (Which I assume means on both liability and quantum.)

The only decided case relied on is *Eley v King & Chasemore (a firm)* (1989) 22 EG 109, which Mr Simon accepts is not a direct authority but, he says, illustrates the principle. It is certainly not an authority for reducing the quantum of damages by the amount of the insurance proceeds, because quantum was not in issue in that case. The trial judge and the Court of Appeal held that the defendant surveyors had not been negligent, so the question of damages did not arise. What they said was that the advice to the purchaser to take out insurance was very good advice and part of the reason why the surveyor was not negligent. In this case, Mr Pitel's advice (whether the idea originated with him, as I think probable, or with the plaintiff) was not enough to remove the dangers to which he failed to draw Mr Sword-Daniels's attention. His omission was a breach of duty, unaffected by the advice to insure. So stop-loss cover cannot be relevant to liability.

As to quantum, while Mr Simon's reasoning is attractive, it is contrary to settled authority and I must therefore decline to accept it.

Mr Simon's final submissions, which applied to both plaintiffs, involved consideration of the global market losses suffered by Lloyd's syndicates in 1988, 1989 and 1990, which were respectively 4·9%, 19·5% and 27·2%. He contended that the plaintiffs cannot be entitled to recover damages so that they are better off than the market average performance had their portfolios been composed differently.

This is one way of avoiding the impossible task of guessing at the notional make-up of their respective portfolios, had proper warnings been given. Again, the argument has its attraction but it is too rough and ready. I will consider Mr Brown's position separately, but as to Mr Sword-Daniels I do not think his damages should be assessed on the basis that if other, low risk, syndicates had been advised by Mr Pitel these would probably have suffered, overall, the average market loss. Mr Crane points out this defence was not pleaded, so none of the experts had to consider a notional portfolio without CAT XOL/LMX content. But it would have been an impossible task. My guess (that is all it can be, and for what it is worth) is that an alternative low risk portfolio might have made modest losses but equally might have made modest profits. It was not likely to have suffered 'market average' losses: the average figures set out above for each year include the heavy losses suffered by high risk syndicates, so they are not a useful guide. My conclusion is that Mr Sword-Daniels is entitled to recover his actual losses, as pleaded, and is entitled to an indemnity against future losses on the open years of the syndicates in question.

For completeness, I should add that Mr Crane put his case in three alternative ways. First, he submits that where a principal obtains from his agent for reward an assurance that the agency will be performed in a certain manner, the agent will be in breach of contract if he subsequently performs in a different way involving breach of the assurance, without obtaining his principal's informed consent (see *Bowstead on Agency* (15th edn, 1985) art 38). Liability will be established in such a case irrespective of negligence by the agent.

Alternatively, Mr Crane submits that if the agent gives an assurance as to the manner of performing the services, ie in this case an assurance that the plaintiff would be placed on, or recommended to join, syndicates which are low risk (the plaintiff's case) or which overall constitute a low risk conservative portfolio (as the defendants admit), the recommendations actually made and agreed to by the plaintiff involved a breach of the agent's duty of care. This submission does not depend upon evidence of the general professional practice of contemporary Lloyd's members' agents: it depends upon its particular facts.

A further alternative is that, disregarding any specific assurance as to the mode of performance, the portfolios for each of the relevant years of account were grossly inappropriate for a name of the plaintiff's known means and circumstances: no reasonably competent agent would have recommended them.

Since the assurance was given, I do not need to consider the third alternative. In my view the plaintiff is entitled to succeed on both the first and second bases.

The remedies seem to require apportionment between the defendants as follows. In respect of the 1987, 1988 and 1989 years of account, the advice, via Mr Pitel, was that of John Poland & Co Ltd, the third defendants. By a novation agreement of 1 January 1989, HG Poland (Agencies) Ltd, now the fourth defendant, became jointly liable to the plaintiff in respect of the 1989 year losses and solely liable for those in 1990. The action against the first defendant personally has been discontinued. If Mr Crane wishes to have a formal judgment entered against the second defendant, he would be entitled to it, on the basis of breach of common law duty. There was no contractual nexus between the plaintiff and the second defendant but the second defendant would be similarly liable for Mr Pitel's negligence. This is a matter that can no doubt be dealt with when figures are finally agreed and formal judgment comes to be entered.

Mr Brown's case is far more complex. He began underwriting in the 1977 year in a small way, gradually increasing his pil over the years in line with consistently successful results. His portfolio correspondingly expanded until in 1989 he was on 35 syndicates. The details of this expansion and changes are complicated. I have to say that there were a number of areas of his evidence which were unsatisfactory and which I am not able to accept. I have no doubt that when he began underwriting he was as unfamiliar with the workings of Lloyd's as any new name and that his initial approach was one of caution, in line with what he rightly saw as Poland's own general philosophy with regard to names. But in time, I think that approach changed. Mr Brown underplayed his own part in reviewing his Lloyd's 'investment' and the attention he gave to the annual reports and accounts of those syndicates on which he was placed, those that he wished to join, and his respective premium allocations. On certain topics his evidence was rightly characterised by Mr Simon as evasive and his answers to questions contradictory.

Mr Brown is a successful business man, the managing director and sole shareholder of Kevard Textile Machinery Ltd of Huddersfield. After graduating in 1975 from Imperial College, London, with a BSc in mechanical engineering, he spent two years at the London Business School, where he obtained a MSc in business administration and then entered the family business. In 1976, when he was 22 and still at the London Business School, Mr Brown became interested in joining Lloyd's and was introduced by the family insurance brokers to HG Poland (Agencies) Ltd. He first met Mr Denis Sullivan of Polands and his assistant at that time, Mr Ian Maclean, at Lloyd's on 2 March 1976. Polands were held out, and held themselves out, as a long-established and well-respected members' agency with a conservative approach to underwriting. Mr Brown became a mini-name later that year and began underwriting as from 1 January 1977 with a pil of £50,000.

At that time Polands were a relatively small agency and new names were given what was called the 'Poland package', ie allocations of their premium income among syndicates managed by the Poland group and spread over the four main sectors, marine, non-marine, motor and aviation. Mr Brown's initial allocation, which remained unaltered for 1978, 1979 and 1980, was as follows:

	£
Syndicate 108 (Marine)	15,000
Syndicate 105 (Non-Marine)	15,000
Syndicate 560 (Motor)	10,000
Syndicate 103 (Aviation)	5,000
Syndicate 767 (Ajax Engineering)	5,000

In August 1980 Mr Brown told Mr Maclean that he wished to increase his pil to £100,000 and inquired whether Poland had any additional capacity for 1981. Mr Maclean's suggestion, accepted by Mr Brown, was to increase the allocation on 108, 105 and 560 (by £5,000, £15,000 and £20,000 respectively) and to add two further Poland syndicates, namely 733 Marine LMX £5,000, and 104 LMX Non-Marine, also £5,000. This was the occasion when LMX syndicates first appeared in the portfolio and it appears that Mr Maclean also obtained quotations for stop-loss cover, although whether at his own suggestion or at Mr Brown's request is not clear.

In 1982 (and for 1983 and 1984) Mr Brown further increased his pil to £150,000 although in each year £10,000 remained unallocated. No new syndicates were added, but included in the £40,000 total increase were increases in the two LMX syndicates to £10,000 in each case.

For 1985, Mr Brown again increased his pil, this time to £200,000, all allocated. On 14 August 1984 he had written to Mr Maclean:

'Following the visit of myself and father to your offices on 14th August and subsequent consideration of the information supplied regarding the additional syndicates that are seeking new Names I now have pleasure in enclosing schedules of Premium Limits we would seek to secure and changes to existing Limits.'

(Mr Brown's father had also become a member of Lloyd's in 1980.)

The attached schedule is of some interest. Mr Brown had received from Poland and separately, from Ajax (767) statements showing his results for the 1981 account closed on 31 December 1983. On the Poland statement it was clear that the LMX Marine syndicate 733 had produced a handsome gross profit of £1,951 on its underwriting, ie 39% on Mr Brown's 1981 line of £5,000, and LMX Non-Marine syndicate 104 had likewise produced £2,040, nearly 41%. The Motor syndicate 560 had produced only a very small underwriting profit, but the addition of investment appreciation and investment income resulted in a total of £3,234 or about 11% on his line of £30,000. On the other hand Non-Marine syndicate 105 had suffered an overall loss of £2,889 and Ajax 767 a very small gross profit which turned into a loss after deduction of expenses. Marine 108 and Aviation 103 both had poor underwriting results but appreciation of capital and investment income resulted in small gross profits.

These results are mirrored in Mr Brown's requirements for the coming year. He doubled his allocation on the two profitable LMX syndicates and increased 560 by £5,000. He reduced his allocation on 105 by £10,000 and came off the Ajax syndicate altogether. His line was maintained at the same level on 108 and 103. He asked for £50,000 on a syndicate (Higgins and Doble) which was new to his portfolio and not controlled by Poland. In the event, Mr Maclean told him that only £30,000 could be obtained, which left £20,000 still to be allocated. Mr Maclean suggested two further possibilities and sent the accounts of three other syndicates for consideration. Mr Brown rejected these suggestions and decided to deal with the spare £20,000 by increasing still further, to £65,000, his allocation on Motor syndicate 560.

I have set out these figures in detail, showing Mr Brown's requirements for the 1985 year, because they tend to support the following. First, they confirm that Mr Brown was an independent-minded name who, after eight years' experience, made his own decisions. Secondly, those decisions were plainly guided by the profitability or otherwise of syndicates as shown by their most recent results. Even if the pure underwriting result was negligible, nevertheless if the other factors resulted in a good profit, that warranted a large increase in allocation for the following year, as in the case of 560. Thirdly, there was a curious reluctance by Mr Brown to accept that this showed his underwriting strategy at the time and I agree with the criticism of his evidence.

The 1986 underwriting year was a watershed. By mid-1985 Mr Brown had received his underwriting results for the last of the six closed years 1977 to 1982, all of which had been profitable although some syndicates had shown losses. As in the previous closed year, 1981, the 1982 result was almost entirely due to very substantial profits on the two Poland LMX syndicates which amounted to £4,906 and £5,434, each on a £10,000 line. In June 1985 Mr Brown raised the question of increasing his overall pil five-fold to £1m, the limit then permitted by Lloyd's, and he also asked for quotations for stop-loss cover of £400,000 excess of £100,000. This suggested increase required consideration of a large number of extra syndicates managed by agents other than Poland, in order to achieve spread and avoid too great an allocation on any one syndicate. Maclean had the task of obtaining capacity and balancing Mr Brown's potential new allocations with the requirements of all the other names for whom he was responsible. On 21 June he sent Mr Brown the latest accounts of some 21 non-Poland syndicates for consideration. He added some comments and specific recommendations on certain syndicates, but there was of course an implicit recommendation of all these syndicates, subject to capacity being available. As it turned out, no capacity was available on four of the Murray Lawrence syndicates, and of the remainder Mr Brown eventually accepted seven of Mr Maclean's suggestions and rejected ten. Of those accepted only one, the Berry Cotesworth Marine syndicate 536, features in the plaintiff's claim in respect of later years.

Over the following five months there were continuing discussions between Mr Brown and Mr Maclean by letter, telephone, and in meetings either in London or Huddersfield, to iron out the final allocation for 1986. Only some of the matters need mention. In an undated letter, probably written soon after 15 July, five further possibilities were mentioned by Mr Maclean and he enclosed their latest accounts. Mr Brown accepted four of these and all four, namely 271, 298, 290 and 164 feature in the plaintiff's claim in respect of later years.

[I have twice added the qualification 'in respect of later years' because of changes made in Mr Brown's pleaded claim by an amendment in December 1993. Until then his claim covered the underwriting years 1986 and 1987 as well as later years. By the amendment, the claims in respect of 1986 and 1987 were dropped.

This is not surprising. The 1986 year was a very successful one for Lloyd's as a whole, and also for Mr Brown. His gross underwriting result produced £138,886, which, after tax provisions, still left £97,337. This was on a premium income of £1m spread over 30 syndicates. It was pleaded in his particulars of claim:

'Further, the Plaintiff's underwriting profits for the 1986 underwriting year of account of approximately £56,700 [which was a false figure] were considerably lower than the profits which the Plaintiff would have made had his gross premium income of £1,000,000 not been allocated to such a large proportion of excess of loss risks.'

This was a wholly unsupportable plea. In fact, 45% of his net underwriting profits were contributed by the ten XOL syndicates of which complaint is now made. Similarly, the 1987 results produced a net after-tax underwriting profit for that year of £63,282 of which £20,279 came from the ten XOL syndicates.]

The proposed increase in pil to £1m required an increase in Mr Brown's Lloyd's deposit to £500,000. This he provided by means of a bank guarantee; a subject which gave rise to a sharp conflict of evidence. Mr Maclean referred in his evidence-in-chief to a telephone conversation, as follows:

'Although I regarded a Name's willingness to increase his capacity as his own affair, when I learned that Richard Brown was using guarantees from a Bank, which may have been secured against his home, I was a little concerned. Had he deposited cash or shares I would not have been concerned. I asked when we were speaking over the phone if he thought capacity of £1 million was a good idea and he replied "Don't stop me now, Ian".'

This was flatly denied by Mr Brown. The issue is an important one, not only on credibility. If the remark was made, it is consistent with Mr Simon's submission that, in the light of Mr Brown's successful underwriting over the past years and his decision to increase his pil five-fold, it demonstrates a strategy of aggressive underwriting essentially based on profitability, whatever may have been his original strategy in 1976. But it is not inconsistent with Mr Brown's expressed intention merely to increase his investment, and therefore profit potential, with a consequential further spread of risk. I have reconsidered the relevant parts of the transcript with particular care. They confirm the clear impression I formed in the course of the evidence that Mr Maclean's recollection on this issue is to be preferred.

In May 1988 the underwriting results for the 1985 year were published, and all the Poland syndicates except for the two LMX syndicates showed losses, to the great disappointment of the names concerned and, of course, to Mr Maclean and Poland itself. Mr Maclean said that since he joined Poland in 1968 this was the first year he could recall in which their names had lost money. Mr Brown's overall loss was a little over £6,000. A three-page explanation by the managing director was circularised to names.

On 8 June 1988 Mr Brown paid promptly the required balance of his 1985 loss with a covering letter, which said, somewhat opaquely:

'... I would be grateful, bearing in mind the size of my present underwriting income, if you could advise me as to any change in my underwriting portfolio which existed in the 1985 underwriting Year of Account. A comment on how you perceive the future of each of the seven syndicates would also be beneficial. I would like to receive this information before the 22nd of this month.'

Mr Maclean interpreted the first request as a reference to what was known as an 'as if' test, ie what Mr Brown's results would have been for 1985 had he then been on his 1988 syndicates. He sent an appropriate schedule. He did not comment on the future of the seven Poland syndicates, but this had been addressed in the managing director's circular of 17 May, and it may be that there was little to add.

The reason why Mr Brown wanted a reply before 22 June was because he had an appointment on 24 June with another members' agent, Edward Lumley & Sons (Mr Glover), to discuss the possibility of his wife becoming a name. He wanted to take the opportunity of getting a second opinion on his own portfolio. He sent the 'as if' schedule to Mr Glover in advance of the meeting.

Mr Brown's account of this meeting raised a number of questions which were not satisfactorily answered. He said that Mr Glover was reluctant to pass comment on what another members' agent had done, but on being pressed had said: 'If I have any comment to make it is that you may have too many syndicates in the excess of loss category.' Mr Brown said that this was a new expression to him. In fact it was not, for in his evidence-in-chief he said that he had seen the phrase in earlier letters and reports provided by Poland. He said that he did not understand what it meant and it worried him, but he did not ask Glover even for a brief explanation. It was an obvious question, if the information caused him concern, but he gave no satisfactory answer as to why he did not ask Glover there and then. This, despite the fact that at the meeting (or possibly in advance) Glover had annotated all Mr Brown's syndicates on the 'as if' schedule, marking 'XL' where appropriate and grading them all from A to E apparently according to profitability.

Immediately following this meeting Mr Brown wrote to Mr Maclean:

'My first analysis of the 1985 results shows them to be pretty disastrous. I think it is time I began to take a much closer and active interest. Bearing in mind that you have no capacity available, (or have you?), I think I should resign from the following—unless you think to the contrary:

MARINE	108, 725
NON-MARINE	105/9
AVIATION	103, 256
MOTOR	560, 234

If you have no alternative satisfactory capacity then this will reduce my gross capacity by £330,000 and also unbalance the spread by sector, but we can work on increasing the capacity again, balancing the spread by sector and improving the quality of my portfolio for underwriting year 1990 (sic). Another aspect which concerns me is the large percentage of syndicates in my portfolio which write excess of loss to some degree. These are:

MARINE	733, 255, 298, 536
NON-MARINE	104, 257, 290, 760, 216
AVIATION	271.

I would like to know what percentage of each of the above syndicates' business is excess of loss, as one hundred percent would represent £437,000 or 47·5% of my re-jigged portfolio—would you consider this worrying? Can you also furnish me with a list of all syndicates that you have access to. Do you know if any of my Marine syndicates are writing substantial (more than 15%) of their business outside of the Marine area. If so should this affect my strategy? I also think that the percentage of long tail and short tail business should be discussed. I think it important that an early reply or meeting be arranged to discuss and set out the above would be advisable. When is the deadline for change?'

It is clear that more had been discussed than Mr Brown was prepared to accept in his evidence. But he maintained that it was not until a further meeting with a Mr Bowles of Lumleys (by now taken over by Gardner Mountain) over a year later that it was for the first time explained to him that XOL syndicates could potentially lose very large sums, whereupon, he said, he was very worried.

A meeting to discuss his syndicate arrangements for 1989 was arranged by Mr Maclean who made a contemporary note of the alterations then agreed. Of the seven syndicates Mr Brown had suggested he should resign from, he did so from two (103 and 234) and he very substantially reduced his line in four more (105/9, 108,256 and 560). What is more significant is that Mr Brown again increased his pil to £1·3m, now spread over 35 syndicates of which 15 were XOL, amounting to £641,000 or 49% of his total pil. For completeness I list these. The first twelve were common to Mr Wilshaw's 'Category 3' and Sir David Walker's list. (Sir David Walker had produced a report of 'An Enquiry into Lloyd's Syndicate participations and the LMX spiral'.) These 12 were:

Marine:	255, 298, 536 and 733.
Non-Marine:	104, 164 (for the 1989 and 1990 years) 216, 257, 290 and 939.
Aviation:	256 (for the 1989 and 1990 years) and 577.

The other three were in Mr Wilshaw's 'Category 3' but not on Sir David
Walker's list:

Marine: 1021.
Non-Marine: 760.
Aviation: 271.

I am satisfied that Mr Wilshaw's categorisation of these three was justified.

The increase in allocation to 'High/Higher Risk' syndicates over 1988 was
£204,000. This came about by (i) the introduction of three new syndicates, 577,
939 and 1021, (ii) an increase on the 1988 allocation for 216 and (iii) the fact that
two of the syndicates on which Mr Brown had been for the previous three
years (164 and 256) now fell into this category because of a change in
underwriting policy.

On 8 August 1989 Mr Brown and his wife, who had not become a member
of Lloyd's in the previous year but was still considering membership, attended
the second meeting with Lumleys that I referred to previously. This time it
was with Mr Bowles. Mr Porter, who was Kevard Manufacturing's in-house
accountant, also attended. Mr Brown said he took the opportunity to ask Mr
Bowles to look at his portfolio:

'After briefly considering the details of my portfolio I was aghast when
Mr. Bowles said words to the effect of "do you actively pursue a high risk
policy?" Mr. Bowles asked me whether I knew what risks were entailed in
"XOL" and I said that I did not. Mr. Bowles explained to me that these
were what he called "disaster" syndicates and said that if there was a large
catastrophe, these syndicates could potentially lose very large sums.'

After the meeting, Mr Brown, his wife and Mr Porter then lunched with Mr
Maclean. Mr Brown said he was considering increasing his pil to £2m. He also
mentioned his concern at his level of exposure to XOL business 'in its various
guises'. A week later he followed this with a letter which asked for a detailed
review of his premium allocation with [XOL exposure] in mind, by individual
syndicates, and for Mr Maclean's suggestions as to any changes that should be
made for 1990 'to correct any imbalance'. The XOL syndicate details were
sent.

On 6 October Mr Brown attended a buffet luncheon given by Poland for all
its underwriting names and in a follow-up letter Mr Bradley, the managing
director, summarised the points he had made in a speech at the luncheon. This
ended with the following:

'I concluded my talk by saying that it had become quite clear to me that
the vast majority of our names joined Polands to pursue a conservative
underwriting policy, where perhaps the profits were modest, but the
downside for major losses was extremely limited. I believe that this is
what the majority of our Names want, and I intend to see that we achieve
these standards. We intend to pursue a conservative underwriting policy,
with the best possible level of protections, with a view to giving you
modest but certainly consistently profitable results. This is going to be our
policy as an Underwriting Agency in the future. Thank you for staying
with us in 1990, I will see that your loyalty is rewarded.'

This was the policy which Mr Brown said had been the Poland policy when
he joined, and no doubt that is correct. On 12 October, referring to Mr

Brown's contemplated increase of his pil to £2m, Mr Maclean sent him a provisional list of capacity available to Polands for 1990 and asked Mr Brown to let him know the syndicates he was interested in joining. But on 26 October Mr Brown wrote:

'In reply to your letter of 12th October 1989 I can confirm that from the list provided I cannot see how I could increase my premium income to £2,000,000 for 1990, without putting an even greater percentage of my portfolio into the excess of loss area. I think we should consider increasing my premium income to £1,500,000 for 1990 and then review my whole portfolio as to whether some of my existing syndicates should be reduced or dropped, as well as joining new ones. I still require from yourselves an analysis as to whether, in your opinion, my spread is "lop-sided" and, if so, in what areas and how should I redress the balance.'

In the event, no increase in pil for 1990 was made. Mr Brown had become impatient with Mr Maclean and his failure, as Mr Brown saw it, to give advice and answer his questions and it was arranged, late in 1989, that his underwriting affairs should henceforth be looked after by Mr Trevor Marks. Some late rearrangements of the allocation were agreed between Mr Brown and Mr Marks and not only was the total pil kept at £1·3m; only £1·13m was allocated.

This agreed allocation is of interest because Mr Brown was by this date fully aware of the dangers of CAT XOL syndicates. But he only resigned from two, viz 255 and 298. He remained on 13 of the syndicates of which he complains in this action. Of these he reduced his allocation on six, in one case only slightly, but in the other five substantially, his line for 1990 being:

	£000
536	30
1021	25
164	30
216	25
257	30
290	20

On four other syndicates, he kept the same allocation for 1990, viz:

	£000
939	20
256	28
271	37
577	40

On the remaining three syndicates, including the two Poland-managed LMX syndicates, he increased his allocation, viz:

	£000
733 35	(increase, £4,000)
104 40	(increase, £9,000)
760 20	(increase, £7,000)

In total, therefore, Mr Brown allocated £380,000 out of his total pil of £1·13m (33·6%) to high/higher risk syndicates.

This did not appear to be out of line with the Lloyd's market as a whole. On 15 November 1989, just before he handed over to Mr Marks, Mr Maclean had sent Mr Brown a syndicate analysis of his existing allocations, which showed allocations to XOL syndicates totalling 50·2% of his pil, as against an overall market average of 31·4%. A footnote to the analysis pointed out that there was no common method used by underwriters in reporting business written by Lloyd's syndicates, and that the table represented a subjective interpretation of the categories described in syndicate reports and accounts at 31 December 1988. Allowing for the difficulties of consistent definition which were inevitable in such an exercise, the results are significant. The figure of 50·2% compares closely with the figure of 49% mentioned above as Mr Brown's 1989 allocation to high risk syndicates. The figure of 31·4% as the 1989 market average is quite close to the figure of 33·6% for the 1990 allocations agreed between Mr Brown and Mr Marks at a time when the former had become well aware of the dangers of CAT XOL reinsurance.

Mr Marks had agreed that Mr Brown was overexposed to CAT XOL but he assumed that Mr Maclean had given him appropriate advice in the past. There was very little time for any wholesale reallocation of the portfolio, but there was evidently enough time to reduce the exposure quite considerably, as set out above.

As Mr Brown is not claiming in respect of the 1991 year I need not go into the subsequent history except to note the following: (i) in June 1991 he notified Poland of his intention to take legal action with regard to his underwriting affairs; (ii) he departed from the Poland stable at the end of 1991 when he transferred his affairs to Crowe Underwriting Agency Ltd; (iii) he continued with Crowe to write on four syndicates that Mr Wilshaw accepted were still 'high risk'. Although the added spiral effect may have been substantially reduced, they remained CAT XOL syndicates, and finally (iv) that although there was ample time in 1990 to reallocate for 1991 Mr Brown remained for that year on eight of the high risk syndicates of which he makes complaint in his pleadings, with a total allocation to them of £180,000.

I come to the following conclusions in Mr Brown's case.

(1) When he joined Lloyd's in 1976 as a mini-name with a small pil his knowledge of underwriting was minimal and his underwriting policy, made known to Messrs Sullivan and Maclean, was cautious and conservative. This accorded with Poland's own general philosophy which, when explained to him, he said 'suited me fine'.

(2) By 1984, and certainly by 1985, he had become a more sophisticated name, choosing his own syndicates and allocations primarily by reference to profitability as disclosed in the annual reports and accounts of each syndicate.

(3) Mr Maclean sent him, or provided at meetings, the annual reports and accounts of all new syndicates which he suggested/recommended Mr Brown should join, often with brief comments.

(4) Mr Brown did not look at many, if any, of the detailed accounts which were voluminous, but that is not of much importance. He concentrated on historic results as shown in the standard form table of the seven-year results of closed years. He had the opportunity to complete his appreciation of each syndicate's progress since the last closed-year result by reading the underwriters' report on the open years and his future underwriting philosophy, usually a short report, sometimes even laconic.

(5) Whether Mr Brown took advantage of this information is in doubt. In my view, both he and his in-house accountant, Mr Porter, underplayed the extent of Mr Brown's understanding of his existing and potential syndicates and their reports. Mr Brown was devious in some of his evidence, one small example being the part played by Mr Porter on the visit to Lumleys and Poland in August 1989. Mr Brown was an intelligent man, and a man of business, trained in all aspects of business administration including investment philosophy. Although he wrote in June 1988 'I think it is time I began to take a much closer and active interest ...' I am satisfied that he took both a close and active interest in his Lloyd's investment from an earlier stage. He was an independent-minded name who took his own decisions on syndicates and allocations, rejecting Mr Maclean's recommendations when he thought fit.

(6) It seems to me somewhat remarkable that it was not until August 1989 that Mr Brown first learned of the essential nature and danger of catastrophe XOL syndicates. I would have thought that any intelligent person with even a smattering of investment knowledge would have realised that high profits are usually accompanied by high risks. The Poland LMX syndicates had produced such profits. Mr Glover's comment in August 1988, the more significant because it was an implied criticism, reluctantly extracted, should further have alerted Mr Brown and, if his own agent did not give him a satisfactory explanation, it is at least surprising that he made no other inquiries. However, that was his evidence.

(7) Nevertheless, Mr Maclean did not give him any, or any sufficient, warning of the dangers of these syndicates and the expert witnesses, as well as Mr Marks, were agreed that he should have done. Mr Brown was entitled to expect this advice, however sophisticated an investor he may have been (see *Sykes v Midland Bank Executor and Trustee Co Ltd* [1970] 2 All ER 471, [1971] 1 QB 113).

(8) Mr Brown did not tell Mr Maclean at any stage that he was changing his original underwriting philosophy to one whereby he was prepared to gamble for profits or accept high risk syndicates. On the other hand I do not accept his evidence that he expressly affirmed to Mr Maclean the continuing cautious strategy of his early years as a name. His evidence was that he did this 'certainly in 1985'. In fact, I think his strategy did change, particularly in 1985 when he decided on his very large increase in pil for the following year. But whether his strategy altered, and whether Poland assumed this, does not, I think, affect the agent's obligation to give advice on which the name can base an informed consent.

(9) This was not given, and Mr Brown's claim for breach of contract is made out.

(10) I have considered previously the questions of causation, remoteness and foreseeability, and the same conclusions apply in Mr Brown's case.

(11) The question of stop-loss insurance does not arise. Mr Brown did not take out stop-loss insurance in any of the years for which he now claims.

(12) But the question then arises: What damage flows from the defendants' breach of contract? The answer is very different in the two cases. I have no doubt that had his agent given the necessary warning, Mr Brown would nevertheless have continued on a number of the syndicates of which he now complains. This follows from (i) his 1990 allocations after he became aware of the dangers—a reduced exposure but still substantial, including an increase on the two Poland LMX syndicates that had served him so well in the past; (ii) his

1991 allocations—further reduced but still quite significant and (iii) his participation on four such syndicates in 1992 on the advice of his new members' agent, now a much reduced proportion of his total, but, of course, arrived at in the context of a very different appreciation by this stage, in the Lloyd's market, of the massive losses overtaking a number of 'disaster' syndicates. The concluding passages of Mr Brown's cross-examination by Mr Simon are significant:

'Q. Mr Brown, your real complaint, if you have a complaint, is that you should have been warned of the fact that just as catastrophe excess of loss syndicates might produce high profits, so they might produce large losses?
A. Yes.
Q. If you have a complaint, that is the nature of your complaint, is it not?
A. Yes.
Q. Did you need to have that explained? A. Yes.
Q. If it had been explained, it is clear that you would have continued to participate in catastrophe excess of loss syndicates?   A. Only if my members' agent thought strongly about it, and that it was ... it would have to be a good case.'
Q. If your case is that you should have been warned, I suggest to you that you would have had some catastrophe excess of loss business in your portfolio to boost your profits and your approach would have been: which are the best? That is right, is it not? A. I would have wanted to know he wanted me to be in that area and why he wanted me to be on those particular syndicates.
Q. You would know why you might be on excess of loss syndicates— because they produced very good profits. You did not need that explaining to you, did you? A. No.
Q. I suggest to you that you would have wanted to know which were the best regarded, if it is your case that you should have been warned. A. Yes.
Q. If the answer had been that Gooda Walker are the market leaders and Rose Thompson Young have been around since 1818 and Mr Maclean was on it, and if you had been told that Devonshire and Mr Bohling are also market leaders, but you need not bother with the rest—if you had been told that you would have gone on those syndicates and you would have no cause for complaint, would you, Mr. Brown? A. Probably, Yes.
Q. Probably you would have had cause for complaint? A. No, sorry, if that is what he had recommended and I had gone on and it was—he explained to me it was prudent at the time and if it was, I would not have a cause for complaint.'

The syndicates referred to in the penultimate question are 290 and 298 (Gooda Walker) 255 (Rose Thompson Young) and 216 (Devonshire/Bohling). In 1986 these were indeed regarded as market leaders. But I do not think it would be right to assume that Mr Brown would necessarily have agreed to join all these. I am faced with a similar task, as with Mr Sword-Daniels, of guessing what Mr Brown's portfolio would probably have consisted of. The fairest result in this case is, I think, to take a percentage. It is certainly a rough and ready solution but I see no sensible alternative. Had he been given an adequate warning, I think Mr Brown would have allocated about 30% of his total pil to high risk syndicates. Which ones, and in what proportions, it is impossible to decide. Doing the best I can, I think Mr Brown's quantified damages should be reduced pro rata and the indemnity which he is entitled to in respect of future losses on open years should be similarly modified.

One last point needs to be considered. The claim in respect of 1986 and 1987 was abandoned. Mr Hamilton contends that Mr Brown has a separate cause of action for each year in respect of which there was a breach, and is therefore entitled to ignore the profitable years and claim only for the loss making years of 1988, 1989 and 1990. This may strictly be right but it produces what I regard as an unjust result. The failure to advise which is complained of resulted in the plaintiff joining high risk syndicates for 1986 and 1987 which are almost identical with the syndicates in subsequent years (although the allocations vary). It seems to me that the profits made in the profitable years ought to be set off against the subsequent losses on the same syndicates.

Judgment for the plaintiffs.

K Mydeen Esq   Barrister.

Director of Public Prosecutions v Bull

QUEEN'S BENCH DIVISION

MANN LJ AND LAWS J

28 MARCH, 5 MAY 1994

Criminal law – Prostitution – Common prostitute – Male prostitute – Male prostitute charged with loitering in street for purposes of prostitution – Whether male prostitute capable of being common prostitute – Whether offence capable of being committed only by female prostitute – Street Offences Act 1959, s 1(1).

The respondent, a male prostitute, was charged with an offence under s 1(1)[a] of the Street Offences Act 1959 of being a 'common prostitute' and loitering or soliciting in a street or public place for the purpose of prostitution. The magistrates' court subsequently dismissed the information against him on the ground that there was no case to answer since s 1(1) of the 1959 Act only applied to female prostitutes. The Director of Public Prosecutions appealed by way of case stated, contending that s 1(1) was not gender specific in line with the use of 'a person' and 'anyone' in sub-ss (2) and (3) and therefore applied to both male and female prostitutes, that the contrasting reference in s 2(1)[b] to the cautioning of 'a woman' was explained by the fact that, until the Sexual Offences Act 1967, homosexual acts between men were criminal offences and thus cautioning was inappropriate and that it was open to the court to interpret s 1(1) as being applicable to prostitutes who were male, even if that was not the original intention of the provision.

Section 1, so far as material, is set out at p 413 *h j*, post
Section 2(1) is set out at p 414 *a b*, post

Held – On its true construction, the term 'common prostitute' in s 1(1) of the 1959 Act, which made it an offence for a common prostitute to loiter or solicit in a street or public place for the purposes of prostitution, was limited to female prostitutes and did not extend to encompass male prostitutes notwithstanding the use of non-gender specific language in s 1(2) and (3). Confirmation for that interpretation was provided by the Report of the Committee on Homosexual Offences and Prostitution 1957, which resulted in the 1959 Act and which clearly showed that the mischief that the Act was intended to remedy was a mischief created by women. Moreover, the term 'common prostitute' was ordinarily regarded as applying to a woman and it was improbable that Parliament had intended to create a new male offence which was but subtly different from the extant s 32[c] of the Sexual Offences Act 1956, which made it an offence for a man persistently to solicit or importune in a public place for immoral purposes. The appeal would accordingly be dismissed (see p 415 *j* and p 416 *d e h*, post).

Dictum of Darling J in *R v De Munck* [1918–19] All ER Rep 499 at 500 considered.

Notes

For common prostitute, see 11(1) *Halsbury's Laws* (4th edn) paras 386, 393, and for cases on the subject, see 14(2) *Digest* (2nd reissue) 215, 7340–7341.

For the Sexual Offences Act 1956, s 32, see 12 *Halsbury's Statutes* (4th edn) (1994 reissue) 259.

For the Street Offences Act 1959, ss 1, 2, see ibid 285, 286.

For the Sexual Offences Act 1967, see ibid 351.

Cases referred to in judgments

Fothergill v Monarch Airlines Ltd [1980] 2 All ER 696, [1981] AC 251, [1980] 3 WLR 209, HL; *rvsg* [1979] 3 All ER 445, [1980] QB 23, [1979] 3 WLR 491, CA.

Pepper (Inspector of Taxes) v Hart [1993] 1 All ER 42, [1993] AC 593, [1992] 3 WLR 1032, HL.

R v De Munck [1918] 1 KB 635, [1918–19] All ER Rep 499, CCA.

R v McFarlane [1994] 2 All ER 283, [1994] QB 419, [1994] 2 WLR 494, CA.

Wicks v Firth (Inspector of Taxes), Johnson v Firth (Inspector of Taxes) [1983] 1 All ER 151, [1983] 2 AC 214, [1983] 2 WLR 34, HL; *rvsg* [1982] 2 All ER 9, [1982] Ch 355, [1982] 2 WLR 208, CA.

Case stated

The Director of Public Prosecutions appealed by way of case stated by the Metropolitan Stipendiary Magistrate for the Inner London Commission Area in respect of his adjudication as a magistrates' court sitting at Wells Street Magistrates' Court, London W1, on 27 April 1993, whereby he acceded to a submission made on behalf of the respondent, Andrew John Bull, that there was no case to answer to the charge that on 4 December 1992 he, being a common prostitute, did loiter in a street or public place for the purpose of prostitution contrary to s 1(1) of the Street Offences Act 1959. The question for the opinion of the High Court was whether the magistrate was correct in construing s 1(1) of the 1959 Act so as to limit it to the activities of female

---

c   Section 32 is set out at p 414 *c*, post

prostitutes and to exclude from its scope the activities of male prostitutes. The facts are set out in the judgment of Mann LJ.

Jeremy Carter-Manning QC and *John McGuinness* (instructed by the *Crown Prosecution Service*) for appellant.
Adrian Fulford (instructed by *Offenbach & Co*) for the respondent.

Cur adv vult

5 May 1994. The following judgments were delivered.

MANN LJ. There is before the court an appeal by way of case stated. The appellant is the Director of Public Prosecutions and the respondent is Andrew John Bull. The case has been stated by Mr Ian Michael Baker, Metropolitan Stipendiary Magistrate for the Inner London Commission Area, in respect of his adjudication as a magistrates' court sitting at Wells Street Magistrates' Court, London W1, on 27 April 1993. On that day Mr Baker had before him a charge against the respondent to the effect that on 4 December 1992 he, being a common prostitute, did loiter in a street or public place for the purpose of prostitution contrary to s 1(1) of the Street Offences Act 1959. At the conclusion of the prosecution case, counsel for the respondent submitted that there was no case to answer on the basis that s 1(1) applies only to female prostitutes. This submission was upheld by the magistrate, who has now posed this question for the opinion of the court:

'Whether I was correct in construing s 1(1) of the Street Offences Act 1959, so as to limit it to the activities of female prostitutes and to exclude from its scope the activities of male prostitutes.'

The magistrate made certain findings of fact to which I think it unnecessary to refer. Suffice it to say he remarks that had the submission not been accepted he would have held that there was a case to answer.

So far as is material, the long title to the 1959 Act is:

'An Act to make, as respects England and Wales, further provision against loitering or soliciting in public places for the purpose of prostitution ...'

The further provision is to be found in ss 1 and 2. The material subsections of s 1 are sub-ss (1), (2) (as substituted by s 71 of the Criminal Justice Act 1982) and (3):

'(1) It shall be an offence for a common prostitute to loiter or solicit in a street or public place for the purpose of prostitution.
(2) A person guilty of an offence under this section shall be liable on summary conviction to a fine of an amount not exceeding level 2 on the standard scale ... or, for an offence committed after a previous conviction, to a fine of an amount not exceeding level 3 on that scale.
(3) A constable may arrest without warrant anyone he finds in a street or public place and suspects, with reasonable cause, to be committing an offence under this section.'

The material subsection of s 2 is sub-s (1), which provides:

'Where a woman is cautioned by a constable, in respect of her conduct in a street or public place, that if she persists in such conduct it may result in her being charged with an offence under section one of this Act, she may not later than fourteen clear days afterwards apply to a magistrates' court for an order directing that there is to be no entry made in respect of that caution in any record maintained by the police of those so cautioned and that any such entry already made is to be expunged; and the court shall make the order unless satisfied that on the occasion when she was cautioned she was loitering or soliciting in a street or public place for the purpose of prostitution.'

The other legislative provision which is material is the earlier s 32 of the Sexual Offences Act 1956, which provides:

'It is an offence for a man persistently to solicit or importune in a public place for immoral purposes.'

As Mr Jeremy Carter-Manning QC for the appellant pointed out, there are differences between the components of an offence under s 32 and those of an offence under s 1(1) of the 1959 Act. Thus: (i) s 32 requires actual soliciting or importuning, s 1(1) requires either actual soliciting or loitering; (ii) s 32 requires persistence, s 1(1) does not; and (iii) s 32 requires an immoral purpose, s 1(1) requires a prostitutional purpose.

The submission for the appellant was that s 1(1) of the 1959 Act is unambiguous and is not gender specific. Our attention was drawn to the following six factors which were relied upon. (i) The phrase in s 1(1) 'a common prostitute' was linguistically capable of including a male person. The Oxford English Dictionary (2nd edn, 1989), vol XII, p 637 includes within the possibilities for 'prostitute', 'a man who undertakes male homosexual acts fo: payment'. (ii) Lord Taylor CJ has recently said in R v McFarlane [1994] 2 All EF 283 at 288, [1994] QB 419 at 424:

'... both the dictionary definitions and the cases show that the crucia feature in defining prostitution is the making of an offer of sexual service for reward.'

I do not regard this factor as of significance. Lord Taylor CJ was speaking i a case which concerned a woman who had been clipping. (iii) Section 1(2) an (3) of the 1959 Act refer respectively to 'a person' and 'anyone'. (iv) In contras s 2(1) refers specifically to 'a woman'. The reason for this is conjectured by M Carter-Manning to be that until the Sexual Offences Act 1967 homosexual act between men were criminal offences and thus cautioning was inappropriate (v) Since 1967 male prostitution has been in certain circumstances no unlawful and accordingly in the new environment it is open to the court t interpret s 1(1) of the 1959 Act as being applicable to prostitutes who are male 'even if this was not the original intent of the provision'. This in my opinio: is a bold submission. It was based upon observations by Lord Bridge c Harwich in Wicks v Firth (Inspector of Taxes) [1983] 1 All ER 151 at 154, [1983] AC 214 at 230, but Lord Bridge was dealing with a situation where a enactment has been re-enacted in a new context. (vi) Where Parliamen intends to deal with gender specific prostitution it uses specifically the wor 'woman', 'girl' or 'her' as in ss 22, 28, 29, 30 and 31 of the Sexual Offences Ac

1956. See also s 5 of the Sexual Offences Act 1967 as regards a 'woman' living on male prostitution.

It is to be observed, for completeness, that Mr Carter-Manning recognised he could obtain no assistance from the gender provisions of s 6 of the Interpretation Act 1978, because the provision that words importing the feminine gender (as does ordinarily the phrase 'common prostitute') include the masculine is inapplicable to enactments such as the 1959 Act (see Sch 2, Pt I).

Mr Adrian Fulford who appeared for the respondent submitted that the phrase 'common prostitute' was for many years before 1959 (and is now) regarded as a term of art which had the meaning formulated by Darling J when delivering the judgment of the Court of Criminal Appeal in R v De Munck [1918] 1 KB 635 at 637–638, [1918–19] All ER Rep 499 at 500. He said:

'The Court is of opinion that the term "common prostitute" in the statute is not limited so as to mean only one who permits acts of lewdness with all and sundry, or with such as hire her, when such acts are in the nature of ordinary sexual connection. We are of opinion that prostitution is proved if it be shown that a woman offers her body commonly for lewdness for payment in return.'

The statute referred to was s 2(2) of the Criminal Law Amendment Act 1885 which however was gender specific for it spoke of 'women or girls'. Although the decision was in that context, I believe there to be great force in Mr Fulford's submission that 'common prostitute' is ordinarily regarded as signifying a woman. The statute was referring to a common law concept. Mr Fulford drew our attention to the only text which appears to deal with the problem. It is Rook and Ward Sexual Offences para 8.12, where the authors state:

'The better view is that the offence under section 1(1) may be committed as principal only by a woman.'

However, Mr Fulford's main submission was that the court should avail itself of the report which led to the 1959 Act and of the Parliamentary debate upon the Bill for the Act (see Pepper (Inspector of Taxes) v Hart [1993] 1 All ER 42, [1993] AC 593). The availability of a report which led to an Act as an aid to interpretation is discussed in Bennion Statutory Interpretation (2nd edn, 1992) p 450. He cites Fothergill v Monarch Airlines Ltd [1980] 2 All ER 696 at 706, [1981] AC 251 at 281, where Lord Diplock said:

'Where the Act has been preceded by a report of some official commission or committee that has been laid before Parliament and the legislation is introduced in consequence of that report, the report itself may be looked at by the court for the limited purpose of identifying the "mischief" that the Act was intended to remedy, and for such assistance as is derivable from this knowledge in giving the right purposive construction to the Act.'

Section 1(1) of the Act was a result of a recommendation in the Report of the Committee on Homosexual Offences and Prostitution (Cmnd 247) (the Wolfenden Committee) para 256. The relevant chapters of the report are chs VIII and IX and a perusal of them leaves me in no doubt that the committee was concerned only with the female prostitute. Thus, and for example:

'223. It would have taken us beyond our terms of reference to investigate in detail the prevalence of prostitution or the reasons which lead women to adopt this manner of life ...

261 ... The problem of the prostitute is, in terms of numbers, far greater than that of the male importuner and, for that matter, far more of a public nuisance. In any event, we think it would be too easy to evade the formula by a game of "general post" in which an individual prostitute would not loiter in a particular place though the number of prostitutes in that place at a given time might be constant.

262. Our second difficulty related to the criteria which would enable the police to infer that a person was loitering "for the purposes of prostitution." We have in mind the possibility that any woman might, from ignorance or indiscretion, put herself in a position in which she might said to be loitering, and by conduct which was quite innocent give rise to a suspicion in the mind of an observant policeman that she was loitering for the purposes of prostitution.'

It is plain that the 'mischief' that the Act was intended to remedy was a mischief created by women.

The assistance which I derive from the report confirms my strong impression that notwithstanding the use of 'a person' and 'anyone' in sub-ss (2) and (3), s 1(1) of the 1959 Act is confined to women. The term 'common prostitute' is ordinarily regarded as applying to a woman and, importantly, it seems improbable that Parliament intended to create a new male offence which was but subtly different from the extant s 32 of the Sexual Offences Act 1956. Accordingly, I would dismiss this appeal and answer the magistrate's question in the affirmative.

I add this. I have not sought to avail myself of the doctrine in *Pepper v Hart* because in my judgment and with the confirmation afforded by the Wolfenden Committee Report, the legislation is neither ambiguous, obscure nor productive of absurdity. However, I must remark that a curious feature of this appeal was Mr Carter-Manning's voluntary and frank concession, both in opening and in reply, that if the court was to look at the Parliamentary debates it would become plain that s 1(1) of the 1959 Act was intended to be applicable only to women. Had I concluded, as a matter of interpretation, that s 1(1) applied to male prostitutes, then a curious situation would have arisen. The judicially ascertained expressed intention of Parliament would have been at variance with what the court had been told was the actual intention of the promoters. The ensuant problems may have to be addressed if concessions of the type made here are repeated on another occasion.

LAWS J. I agree.

Appeal dismissed.

Dilys Tausz   Barrister.

Grovewood Holdings plc v James Capel & Co Ltd

CHANCERY DIVISION

LIGHTMAN J

7, 8, 19 JULY 1994

Maintenance of action – Champerty – Statutory exemption – Liquidator of insolvent company selling beneficial interest in proceeds of litigation in consideration for contributions towards costs – Whether arrangement within liquidators' statutory exemption from prohibition of maintenance – Whether stay of action should be granted on ground of champertous arrangement – Insolvency Act 1986, ss 165, 166, Sch 4, para 6.

The defendant company acted as stockbroker and adviser to the plaintiff in a transaction which proved disastrous and occasioned its client's collapse. As a result the plaintiff brought an action against the defendant alleging negligence and misrepresentation and claiming damages of £38m. The plaintiff subsequently went into liquidation and, in an attempt to continue the action, the liquidator sought the financial support of the creditors and shareholders, but without success. In order to keep the action going, the liquidator entered into one of two agreements with the backers under which, in return for supplying the necessary funding, they would receive half of the recoveries in the action. The backers were thus able to maintain their anonymity, which they would not have been able to achieve if they themselves had become plaintiffs by acquiring the plaintiff's cause of action. The defendant issued a summons seeking a stay of proceedings on the ground that the action was funded by an arrangement which was agreed to be champertous in that it involved the maintenance of an action in consideration of a promise to give the maintainer a share in the proceeds or subject matter of the action. The plaintiff accepted that the agreement was prima facie champertous, but contended that a liquidator was in effect given exemption under the Insolvency Act 1986 from the law of maintenance and champerty in so far as necessary to conclude such an agreement to achieve some realisation for creditors from the cause of action sued on in the proceedings. The liquidator claimed that the transaction was not a sale of a cause of action which was so exempt, but a sale of one-half of the beneficial interest in the net recoveries and that such a sale was authorised by para 6[a] of Sch 4 to and s 436[b] of the 1986 Act as a liquidator's 'power to sell any of the company's property by public auction or private contract' and was likewise exempt from the application of the law of maintenance and champerty.

Held – A trustee in bankruptcy and a liquidator both had statutory power under ss 165[c] and 166[d] of and para 6 of Sch 4 to the 1986 Act to sell a cause of action on

---

Paragraph 6, so far as material, is set out at p 422 *g*, post

Section 436, so far as material, is set out at p 422 *g h*, post

Section 165, so far as material, provides: '(1) ... where a company is being wound up voluntarily, but subject to section 166 below in the case of a creditors' voluntary winding up. (2) The liquidator may ... exercise any of the powers specified in Part I of Schedule 4 to this Act (payment of debts, compromise of claims, etc).'

Section 166, so far as material, provides: '... (3) Subsection (2) [which provides that the s 165 powers shall not be exercised without leave prior to the creditors' meeting] does not apply in relation to the power of the liquidator [to protect the assets of the company] ...'

terms that the assignees by way of consideration would pay over a share of the recoveries and that power necessarily precluded any challenge to such a transaction on the grounds of maintenance or champerty. There was however no basis in principle or authority for extending the statutory exemption applicable in the case of sales of bare causes of action to sales of the fruits of litigation, which remained subject to the full force and effect of the law of maintenance. In particular, there was a critical distinction to be drawn between a statutory sale of a bare cause of action, which would be ineffective if it did not at the same time confer on such a sale immunity from the otherwise applicable law of maintenance, and a sale of the recoveries (or an interest in the recoveries) in an action, which required no special statutory exemption to enable a trustee in bankruptcy or liquidator to dispose of such property. It followed that the sponsorship agreement was champertous, since the consideration for the assignment of the share of the fruits of litigation was the purchaser's obligation to finance the action, and that the action maintained thereunder was equally champertous and an abuse of the process of the court. The action would accordingly be stayed to prevent a continuing abuse of process, however well intentioned the agreement might be (see p 421 *c*, p 423 *e* to *j*, p 424 *a b f* and p 425 *f g*, post).

Ramsey v Hartley [1977] 2 All ER 673 and *Bang & Olufsen UK Ltd v Ton Systeme Ltd* [1993] CA Transcript 0834 considered.

Notes

For principles of maintenance and champerty, see 9 *Halsbury's Laws* (4th edn) paras 400–404, and for cases on the subject, see 8(2) *Digest* (2nd reissue) 30, 127, *218–219, 1022* and 12(1) ibid 486, *3743–3745*.

For the Insolvency Act 1986, ss 165, 166, Sch 4, para 6, see 4 *Halsbury's Statutes* (4th edn) (1987 reissue) 831, 832, 1056.

Cases referred to in judgment

Bang & Olufsen UK Ltd v Ton Systeme Ltd [1993] CA Transcript 0834.
Giles v Thompson [1993] 3 All ER 321, [1994] 1 AC 142, [1993] 2 WLR 908, HL.
Glegg v Bromley [1912] 3 KB 474, [1911–13] All ER Rep 1138, CA.
Goldsmith v Sperrings Ltd [1977] 2 All ER 566, [1977] 1 WLR 478, CA.
Guy v Churchill (1888) 40 Ch D 481.
Martell v Consett Iron Co Ltd [1955] 1 All ER 481, [1955] Ch 363, [1955] 2 WLR 463, CA; *affg* [1954] 3 All ER 339, [1955] Ch 363, [1954] 3 WLR 648.
Papaloizou, Re (4 December 1980, unreported), Ch D.
Park Gate Waggon Works Co, Re (1881) 17 Ch D 234, CA.
Ramsey v Hartley [1977] 2 All ER 673, [1977] 1 WLR 686, CA.
Seear v Lawson (1880) 15 Ch D 426, CA.
Weddell v J A Pearce & Major (a firm) [1987] 3 All ER 624, [1988] Ch 26, [1987] 3 WLR 592.
Westminster Property Group plc, Re [1985] 2 All ER 426, [1985] 1 WLR 676, CA.
Wild v Simpson [1919] 2 KB 544, [1918–19] All ER Rep 682, CA.

Application

The defendant, James Capel & Co Ltd (Capel), applied by summons for an order that proceedings begun by the plaintiffs, Grovewood Holdings Ltd (Grovewood), be stayed on the ground that the action was being funded pursuant to a champertous arrangement. The application was heard in chambers but judgment was given in open court. The facts are set out in the judgment.

Jonathan Sumption QC and *Paul Wright* (instructed by *Cameron Markby Hewitt*) for Capel.
Rupert Jackson QC and *Simon Monty* (instructed by *Reynolds Porter Chamberlain*) for Grovewood.

Cur adv vult

26 July 1994. The following judgment was delivered.

LIGHTMAN J.

1. INTRODUCTION
I have before me a summons issued on the application of the defendant, James Capel & Co Ltd (Capel), seeking an order that the proceedings be stayed on the ground that the action is being funded pursuant to a champertous arrangement.

2. FACTS
The facts can be shortly stated. In 1989 Capel acted as stockbroker and adviser to the plaintiffs, Grovewood Holdings Ltd (Grovewood), on a successful bid for, and acquisition of, a listed property company known as Local London Group plc. The acquisition proved disastrous and occasioned the collapse of Grovewood, which in December 1991 went into insolvent voluntary liquidation. In May 1992 (prior to liquidation) Grovewood commenced this action against Capel alleging negligence and misrepresentation whilst acting as Grovewood's financial adviser. The claim is now for £38m. The allegation is firmly denied. Since liquidation the liquidator has manfully fought to continue the action. He has sought support from the creditors and shareholders, but in vain. In order to keep the action going, he has been driven to enter into two successive agreements entitled 'sponsorship agreements', with backers under which, in return for the necessary funding, he has agreed that the backers should receive one-half of the recoveries of the action. Authority to enter into agreements with third parties to fund the action was conferred on the liquidator by the duly constituted liquidation committee on 10 December 1991.

The two sponsorship agreements are respectively dated 16 December 1992 and 13 May 1994. They are in substantially the same terms. I am only concerned with the second, which I shall call 'the 1994 agreement'. This is constituted by two documents. I shall give a brief summary of their contents. The first is entitled 'sponsorship agreement' and one only of the two sponsors is party to it. (That sponsor is referred to in the 1994 agreement as 'the sponsor' and the other as 'the provider', and I shall refer to them in the same way.) There are three parties, namely (1) the liquidator, (2) the sponsor and (3) the liquidator's solicitors (the solicitors). After reciting the issue of the writ, the insufficiency of assets in Grovewood to fund the litigation, and the agreement of the sponsor to fund the litigation, it is agreed that: (1) the sponsor shall at his own cost in the name of Grovewood diligently pursue the litigation 'without being subject to the control or interference of the liquidator'; (2) the liquidator shall give the sponsor, so far as the rules and practice of the court permit, all assistance and information requested by the sponsor; (3) the solicitors agree to defer charging the sponsor their reasonable profit costs until determination of the litigation; (4) all recoveries in the action shall be paid into the solicitors' client account and be held on trust to pay (a) all costs, (b) the costs due to the solicitors in respect of the action for the period prior to liquidation, namely £225,000 and (c) as to the balance, 50% to the liquidator and 50% to the sponsor; (5) any insufficiency in the recoveries to meet costs incurred or liability for costs ordered to be paid to Capel is to be made good by the sponsor.

The second document is an agreement to which the sponsor and provider alone are parties. In short, it provides for the sponsor and provider to share the liabilities (and in particular any sum ordered to be paid into court as security for costs) and the 50% share of recoveries. Beyond this, the second agreement enables the sponsor to 'unitise' or sell off to other providers the share of the recoveries to which he is entitled in return for payments of or contributions towards the half share of any security for costs which the sponsor is liable to provide.

Capel have for some time been concerned as to the method adopted by the liquidator to finance the action. The liquidator has not been forthcoming in this regard, and only recently has the general character of the arrangements emerged, and indeed the sponsorship agreements were first disclosed at the hearing. The reason for the liquidator's reticence has been the concern of the sponsors for anonymity, and this has been preserved on production of the sponsorship agreements by masking out their names. This concern may explain why the sponsors have been willing to acquire a share in the recoveries as opposed to acquiring the cause of action, in which case they would have to be plaintiffs and to disclose their identities. This summons was issued on 7 June 1994. In the circumstances I can see no substance in any complaint as to delay by Capel in making the application for a stay.

3. LAW

The general principles of the law of maintenance and champerty are stated in 9 *Halsbury's Laws* (4th edn) para 400:

> 'Maintenance may be defined as the giving of assistance or encouragement to one of the parties to litigation by a person who has neither an interest in the litigation nor any other motive recognised by the law as justifying his interference. Champerty is a particular kind of maintenance, namely maintenance of an action in consideration of a promise to give the maintainer a share in the proceeds or subject matter of the action. Since 1967 both criminal and tortious liability for maintenance and champerty have been abolished; but the abolition of these forms of liability does not affect any rule of law as to the cases in which a contract involving maintenance or champerty is to be treated as contrary to public policy or otherwise illegal.'

There may be maintenance of a plaintiff or a defendant, but champerty is confined to assistance to a plaintiff (or counterclaiming defendant) who is making a claim and agrees to share recoveries in return for the assistance or encouragement. Champerty is often referred to in the cases as an aggravated form of maintenance (see e g *Guy v Churchill* (1888) 40 Ch D 481 at 489).

In *Giles v Thompson* [1993] 3 All ER 321, [1994] 1 AC 142 the House of Lords (i) reaffirmed that the policy underlying the prohibition on champertous agreements was to prevent wanton and officious intermeddling with the disputes of others in which the intermeddler has no interest and where his assistance was without justification or excuse and with a view to division of the spoils; (ii) made plain that the objection to trafficking in litigation gave rise to the continuing denial of recognition to the assignment of a bare right of action; and (iii) gave guidance that, in applying the law of champerty, regard should be had to its origins as a principle of public policy designed to protect the administration and purity of justice and the interests of vulnerable litigants.

It is common ground in this case that the 1994 agreement is prima facie champertous. It is not alleged that the sponsors have the requisite interest or motive to justify or excuse their intermeddling. The issues raised on this application are twofold: (1) whether a liquidator is in effect given exemption from the law of maintenance and champerty in so far as necessary to conclude such an agreement as the 1994 agreement and achieve some realisation for creditors from the cause of action sued on in these proceedings; and (2) whether, if the liquidator has no such exemption, a stay can and should be granted on the ground that the agreement is champertous.

(a) *Liquidators and champerty*

The Bankruptcy Act 1869 (which is the ancestor of modern bankruptcy legislation) provided that all the property (defined to include choses in action) of a bankrupt vested in his trustee in bankruptcy and empowered the trustee in bankruptcy to sell to anyone all the property (likewise defined) of the bankrupt. The Court of Appeal in *Seear v Lawson* (1880) 15 Ch D 426 held that a bare right to sue was included within the term 'property' for the purpose of both provisions and accordingly (by way of statutory exception to the rules against maintenance) the trustee could sell a bare right of action. Jessel MR remarked (at 433):

'The proper office of the trustee is to realize the property for the sake of distributing the proceeds amongst the creditors. Why should we hold as a matter of policy that it is necessary for him to sue in his own name? He may have no funds, or he may be disinclined to run the risk of having to pay costs, or he may consider it undesirable to delay the winding-up of the bankruptcy till the end of the litigation.'

The following year in *Re Park Gate Waggon Works Co* (1881) 17 Ch D 234 the Court of Appeal held that s 95 of the Companies Act 1862 (the ancestor of modern company legislation), which authorised a liquidator to sell the property (similarly defined) of the company, likewise permitted the liquidator to sell causes of action, notwithstanding the rule against maintenance.

In *Guy v Churchill* (1888) 40 Ch D 481 Chitty J held that the statutory authorisation of a sale by a trustee in bankruptcy of a cause of action free from the rules against maintenance extended so far as to permit a sale on terms that the assignees should fight the action at his own expense and share any recoveries with the trustee. He reasoned (at 488–489):

'The policy of the statute appears to be to give power to the trustee, with the sanction of the committee, to make arrangements in reference to *choses in action* which are considered beneficial to the creditors. It would be a strange and inconsistent result to say that although the right of action may be sold out and out it cannot be disposed of on the terms that some part of the fruit of the action if successful shall come back to the bankrupt's estate for division among his creditors ... It would be too fine a distinction to hold that the arrangement ... is void merely because the bankrupt's estate gets back part of any money that may be recovered in the action.'

In *Ramsey v Hartley* [1977] 2 All ER 673, [1977] 1 WLR 686 the Court of Appeal, applying *Guy v Churchill*, held that under the parallel section (s 55) of the Bankruptcy Act 1914, a trustee could validly sell a cause of action in return for an indemnity for costs and 35% of any recovery. Megaw LJ held that the presence of the statutory power of sale distinguished the case (as that of *Guy v Churchill*) from the ordinary run of cases where the assignment of a bare cause of action was held invalid. In this context, he said ([1977] 2 All ER 673 at 680, [1977] 1 WLR 686 at 694): 'You may not automatically bring doctrines from other branches of the law into the statutory code of bankruptcy.'

In *Bang & Olufsen UK Ltd v Ton Systeme Ltd* [1993] CA Transcript 0834 the Court of Appeal affirmed that the law is likewise in respect of a sale by a liquidator of a cause of action in return for a share of recoveries. The statutory power of sale of the cause of action precludes any taint of champerty or maintenance in respect of the transaction. Balcombe LJ, after referring to *Ramsey v Hartley*, said:

'it was held [in that case] that an assignment made by a trustee in bankruptcy is valid if it is within the powers conferred by statute upon the trustee, notwithstanding that it might otherwise be held void for maintenance or champerty, because one may not automatically bring doctrines from other branches of the law into the statutory code of bankruptcy. There would appear to be no valid distinction on this point between the law of bankruptcy and the law of insolvent liquidation. They are both now governed by the Insolvency Act 1986, and there is no relevant difference between the two schedules; Sch 4, which deals with powers of a liquidator, and Sch 5, which deals with powers of a trustee in bankruptcy.'

The powers of a voluntary liquidator are conferred by ss 165 and 166 of and Sch 4 to the Insolvency Act 1986. Paragraph 6 of Sch 4 reads as follows: 'Power to sell any of the company's property by public auction or private contract ...' 'Property' is defined in s 436 as including 'things in action ... and every description of property ... and every description of interest arising out of or incidental to property'.

In short, the statutory language describing the power of sale, the property which may be the subject matter of a sale and the absence of any qualification of the prospective purchaser (implicit in the provision for sale by auction) remains (at least for present purposes) the same as in the earlier legislation.

Accordingly, the authorities established beyond question that both a trustee in bankruptcy and a liquidator are given statutory power to sell a cause of action on terms that the assignees by way of consideration will pay over a share of the recoveries. This statutory power necessarily precludes any challenge on grounds of maintenance or champerty to such an agreement.

Mr Jackson QC for Grovewood does not, and cannot, contend that there was any sale of a cause of action in this case. The sale (if any) was of a one-half beneficial interest in the net recoveries. Such a sale, he says, is likewise authorised by the 1986 Act and likewise is exempt from application of the law of maintenance and champerty and, accordingly, a sale of half the recoveries subject to the purchaser agreeing to pay the costs of the action is free from taint. That the 1986 Act authorises a sale of such an interest (being property of the company) cannot be disputed: what is in issue is (1) whether the 1994 agreement constitutes a sale; and (2) if so, whether such a sale enjoys exemption from the law of maintenance and champerty.

(b) *Sale*

Mr Sumption QC for Capel has submitted that the transaction between the liquidator and the sponsor is not a sale and accordingly is beyond the powers of the liquidator conferred by para 6 of Sch 4: it is merely a funding agreement. He cited *Re Westminster Property Group plc* [1985] 2 All ER 426, [1985] 1 WLR 676, where the general rule is laid down that in the absence of a special context the word 'sale' in a statute denotes an exchange of property for cash. It seems to me however that a special context exists in the 1986 Act and its statutory predecessors. For it is quite clear from all the cases I have referred to and the decision of Browne-Wilkinson V-C in *Re Papaloizou* (4 December 1980, unreported) that a transaction involving a transfer of a cause of action in return for financing an action and a share of recoveries has been treated uniformly by the courts since 1880 as a sale. After reaching this conclusion, I found the decision of Scott J in *Weddell v J A Pearce & Major (a firm)* [1987] 3 All ER 624 at 631, [1988] Ch 26 at 34–35 to this very effect. Since this decision is merely confirmation of the conclusion I had already reached, I have not thought it necessary to cause the parties to incur further costs in making submissions relating to this authority. If a transfer of a cause of action in return for financing an action and a share of recoveries is a 'sale' for the purpose of para 6, so I think must be a transfer of a half beneficial interest in recoveries in return for financing the action.

(c) *Exemption*

The insuperable difficulty, as I see it, in the way of Mr Jackson's submission of the existence of such an exemption is that, in the absence of any agreement by the purchaser to finance the action, a sale of the recoveries in an action (as distinct from the cause of action) has long been regarded as valid and unobjectionable on grounds of maintenance (see *Glegg v Bromley* [1912] 3 KB 474, [1911–13] All ER Rep 1138). No special statutory exemption from the law of maintenance is required to enable a trustee in bankruptcy or liquidator to dispose of such property. In this respect there is a critical distinction between a sale of the recoveries (or an interest in the recoveries) and a sale of a bare cause of action. The statutory power of sale of a bare cause of action would be empty of effect if it did not at the same time confer on such a sale immunity from the (otherwise) applicable law of maintenance and this immunity has by judicial decision been recognised as extending to sales on terms providing for a division of recoveries.

I can see no basis in principle or authority for extending the statutory exemption applicable in the case of sales of bare causes of action to sales of the fruits of litigation, which include provision for the purchasers to finance the litigation. The references in the judgments of Megaw and Balcombe LJJ to not bringing into the law of bankruptcy doctrines applicable in other fields can only be intended to apply to doctrines expressly or by implication inconsistent with the provisions or scheme of the bankruptcy code. So far as the 1986 Act confers powers on liquidators and trustees other than the power to sell bare causes of action, the law of maintenance has full force and effect.

I therefore reach the firm conclusion that the 1994 agreement is champertous since the consideration for the assignment of the share of the fruits is the purchaser's obligation to finance the action, the 1986 Act confers no relevant exemption from the law of champerty and accordingly the proceedings are being maintained champertously.

4. STAY

Mr Sumption submits that, when proceedings are maintained champertously, the proceedings constitute an abuse of process and should be stayed. This appears to me to be both logical and right in any ordinary case. The law of champerty is based on public policy considerations designed to protect both the administration of justice and the defendant from the prosecution of such proceedings. If the court does not intervene, it may be taken to be countenancing this abuse of its process.

Mr Jackson first submits that, even if the proceedings are champertous, the court should not intervene to grant a stay because the liquidator is acting meritoriously in the interests of creditors, because it is the merest technicality that the right assigned is to the fruits rather than the cause of action, and because there is evidence of a wind of change in attitudes to champerty manifested in the imminent changes in the law allowing for the charging of contingent fees subject to certain stringent conditions. I must reject this submission. The law draws distinctions (perhaps fine) between what is and what is not champertous, and where the arrangement falls into the category of champerty and there is no statutory exemption, the court must set its face against such an arrangement however well intentioned it may be.

Mr Jackson secondly submits that I am precluded from taking the action of imposing a stay by the views expressed by Danckwerts J and the Court of Appeal in Martell v Consett Iron Co Ltd [1955] 1 All ER 481, [1955] Ch 363. In that action the defendants had applied for a stay on the ground that the action was being maintained by a third party who did not have a sufficient common interest recognised by the law in the subject matter of the action. Danckwerts J and the Court of Appeal held that the third party did have a sufficient interest but expressed the view obiter that a stay is inappropriate in case of illegal maintenance.

A number of different grounds were given for this view. (1) First and foremost is a ground reflecting the fact that at that time, but no longer maintenance was a criminal offence. The ground was that the course of applying for a stay on this ground involved trying the question whether or not the alleged maintainer was committing a crime in the absence of the accused maintainer (see [1955] 1 All ER 481 at 502, 507, [1955] Ch 363 at 422, 429 per Jenkins and Hodson LJJ). This ground (with the abolition of the criminal offence of maintenance) can no longer have any weight. (2) A second related ground was that, if a stay was to be granted on the ground of maintenance, the criminal taint of illegality could only be purged by discontinuing and starting a fresh action. This would elevate maintenance to a defence to the action which it is not (see [1955] 1 All ER 481 at 502, [1955] Ch 363 at 421–422 per Jenkins LJ)

a
This ground ceases to have any force with the abolition of the crime of maintenance, and the recognition of so many grounds for a stay which do not constitute defences, e g absence of authority of the plaintiff's solicitors, forum non conveniens or the fact that the action is brought for a collateral (improper) purpose. (3) A third related ground was that it would be inappropriate to stop an action before the damage to the applicant necessary to constitute a cause of

b
action for maintenance has occurred (see [1954] 3 All ER 339 at 350–351, [1955] Ch 363 at 388–389 per Danckwerts J). Again with the abolition of the tort of maintenance, the foundation for this ground is removed. (4) Danckwerts J also expressed anxiety at the absence of any precedent where a stay had been granted on this ground. No doubt the criminal and tortious sanctions for maintenance were in the ordinary course sufficient sanctions and deterrents to

c
maintenance with no need for recourse to an application for a stay. The criminal and tortious sanctions have gone. (5) A fifth ground was special to the case of maintenance, and inapplicable to a case of champerty, and may be termed 'mutuality'. It was that if a plaintiff's claim could be stayed for maintenance, so, by parity of reasoning, should a defendant's defence if he is

d
illegally maintained. But in the latter case a stay would be inappropriate, and if an abuse of process were to demand retribution, the defence would have to be struck out and judgment entered for the plaintiff. This would be objectionable as tantamount to holding illegal maintenance of the defendant a ground for holding that the plaintiff is entitled to judgment (see [1955] 1 All ER 481 at 502, 507, [1955] Ch 363 at 422, 429 per Jenkins and Hodson LJJ).

e
Atkin LJ in Wild v Simpson [1919] 2 KB 544 at 564 made 'a not unfavourable comment' on the availability of a stay in the case of champertous proceedings (see Martell v Consett Iron Co Ltd [1954] 3 All ER 339 at 350–351, [1955] Ch 363 at 388 per Danckwerts J). Whether or not the expressions of opinion in Martell remain good law in the case of maintenance where there is no 'aggravation', I have no doubt that I am free in case of a champertous agreement such as the present to grant a stay to prevent a continuing abuse of process which the court as well as Capel have an interest in bringing to an end. If the court can stay proceedings because they were brought for a collateral (improper) purpose, as they can (see Goldsmith v Sperrings Ltd [1977] 2 All ER 566, [1977] 1 WLR 478), the court can likewise stay proceedings if champertous. I have no doubt that in this case a stay should be granted.

I should add that I asked Mr Jackson when he opposed the grant of the stay whether there could be any reality in his opposition, since it appeared inconceivable that a reputable liquidator, such as the liquidator in this case, would or could proceed with an action pursuant to an agreement which was held champertous. He agreed that it was inconceivable, but nonetheless he opposed the stay. In my view, if additional grounds for a stay were required (and I do not think that this is so) I would take the view that the acknowledged impropriety of any liquidator proceeding on the basis of such an agreement was a further reason for granting the stay.

I would wish to make it clear, since the question was discussed before me, that the 1994 agreement (even if otherwise valid) appears to be flawed in two particular respects. First, I cannot see how a liquidator can properly or at all surrender his fiduciary power to control proceedings commenced in the name of the company. Second, I consider the provision for unitisation and further trafficking in the litigation objectionable. Mr Sumption has also objected to the provision for payment of the £225,000 pre-liquidation costs to the solicitors as a *a* preference only to be justified if sanctioned by the court or liquidation committee (see s 165 (1) of and Sch 4, para 1 to the 1986 Act). There is no evidence as to the existence of this sanction, but this sum was due to the solicitors in respect of work done prior to the liquidation and secured by a lien over the solicitors' files. The existence of the lien removes any reality for the 'preference' apparently given. In any event, I do not think that this objection *b* (which is an internal question in the liquidation) is a matter to be explored in these proceedings.

I should however make it clear that in respect of all or any of the deficiencies in the arrangements made between the liquidator and the sponsors no personal criticism can be made of the liquidator, sponsors or the solicitors, for they at all times acted on the advice of specialist insolvency and Chancery counsel—not (I *c* should add) the counsel appearing for Grovewood on this application.

Application allowed.

Paul Magrath Esq   Barrister. *c*

R v Khan (Sultan)

COURT OF APPEAL, CRIMINAL DIVISION

LORD TAYLOR OF GOSFORTH CJ, HUTCHISON AND PILL JJ

10, 27 MAY 1994

Criminal evidence – Exclusion of evidence – Discretion – Tape recorded conversation – Electronic listening device installed on private house without knowledge of owner or occupier – Installation involving civil trespass, damage and invasion of privacy – Recorded conversation showing appellant to be involved in importation of heroin – Whether evidence of tape recorded conversation admissible – Whether evidence should be excluded – Police and Criminal Evidence Act 1984, s 78.

The appellant visited the home of a man whom the police suspected of being involved in the supply of heroin on a large scale. As a result of those suspicions, the police, acting in accordance with the Home Office Guidelines on the use of equipment in police surveillance operations 1984, had installed an aural surveillance device on the exterior of the property without the knowledge or consent of the owner or occupier. By means of that device, the police were able to obtain a tape recording of the conversation that subsequently took place between the appellant and others in the house, in the course of which things were said by the appellant which showed clearly that he was involved in the importation of heroin. The appellant was charged with being knowingly concerned in the fraudulent evasion of the prohibition on the importation of a Class A controlled drug. The judge accepted the Crown's evidence that authority for use of the electronic listening device was given under the 1984 Home Office guidelines for a serious criminal investigation involving the supply of heroin on a large scale, where normal methods of surveillance were impracticable and the use of the device would lead to arrest and conviction, and exercised his discretion to admit evidence of the tape recorded conversation. The appellant pleaded guilty and was sentenced to three years' imprisonment. The appellant appealed, contending that evidence of private conversations on private property was inadmissible and that the judge should have exercised his discretion under s 78 of the Police and Criminal Evidence Act 1984 to exclude the tape recording on the ground that its admission as evidence would have an 'adverse effect on the fairness of the proceedings'. The Crown accepted that the installation of the electronic listening device had involved civil trespass to the outside of the building and some degree of damage and amounted to an intrusion on the privacy of those who believed themselves to be secure from being overheard when they had the crucial conversation, but contended that those factors were of insufficient gravity to outweigh the other factors of the case, all of which militated in favour of concluding that fairness to both sides required admission of the evidence.

Held – (1) It was an established rule of English law that the test of admissibility was relevance and that relevant evidence, even if illegally obtained, was admissible. The importance of upholding rights of privacy was clear, but to establish the inviolability of the home by rendering inadmissible statements made within it would be to introduce a new principle into English law, which was not justified either in terms of the proper protection of private rights or public policy. It followed that evidence of tape recorded conversations obtained by a covert electronic listening device attached by the police to a private house was prima facie admissible against a defendant in a criminal trial (see p 434 *b* to *f j* to p 435 *b*, post); dictum of Lord Diplock in *R v Sang* [1979] 2 All ER 1222 at 1231 applied.

(2) On the facts, the invasion of privacy with the attendant trespass and damage was outweighed by other considerations (such as the fact that the police had acted in accordance with the relevant Home Office guidelines and that the criminal conduct under investigation was of a serious nature) and plainly could not be regarded as having such an adverse effect on the fairness of the proceedings that the court ought to exercise its discretion under s 78 of the 1984 Act to exclude the evidence of the tape recorded conversation. The judge had had ample grounds on which to refuse to exclude the prosecution evidence under s 78 of the Act and, accordingly, the appeal would be dismissed (see p 436 *d* to *f* and p 437 *f* to p 438 *a e f*, post); *Malone v UK* (1984) 7 EHRR 14 considered.

Notes

For admissibility of criminal evidence and discretion to exclude relevant prosecution evidence, see 11(2) *Halsbury's Laws* (4th edn reissue) paras 1059, 1060, and for cases on the subject, see 15(1) *Digest* (2nd reissue) 516–518, 520, 17086–17088, 17097.

For the Police and Criminal Evidence Act 1984, s 78, see 17 *Halsbury's Statutes* (4th edn) (1993 reissue) 228.

Cases referred to in judgment

Chundawadra v Immigration Appeal Tribunal [1988] Imm AR 161, CA.
Malone v UK (1984) 7 EHRR 14, ECt HR.
Pan American World Airways Inc v Dept of Trade [1976] 1 Lloyd's Rep 257, CA.
R v Christou [1992] 4 All ER 559, [1992] QB 979, [1993] 3 WLR 228, HL.

R v Preston [1993] 4 All ER 638, [1994] 2 AC 130, [1993] 3 WLR 891, HL.
R v Sang [1979] 2 All ER 1222, [1980] AC 402, [1979] 3 WLR 263, HL.
R v Smurthwaite [1994] 1 All ER 898, CA.

Cases also cited or referred to in skeleton arguments
R v Ali (Shaukat) (1991) Times, 19 February, CA.
R v Bailey [1993] 3 All ER 513, CA.
R v Jelen (1989) 90 Cr App R 456, CA.
R v Maclean [1993] Crim LR 687, CA.
R v Maqsud Ali, R v Ashiq Hussain [1965] 2 All ER 464, [1966] 1 QB 688, CA.
R v Mills [1962] 3 All ER 298, [1962] 1 WLR 1152, CCA.
R v Quinn (1975) 60 Cr App R 314, CA.
R v Stewart [1970] 1 All ER 689, [1970] 1 WLR 907, CA.

Appeal against conviction
Sultan Khan appealed with leave against his conviction on 10 December 1993 in the Crown Court at Sheffield before Judge Barber and a jury of being knowingly concerned in the fraudulent evasion of the prohibition on the importation of class A controlled drugs, for which he was sentenced on 14 March 1994 to three years' imprisonment, on the ground that the judge should have ruled as inadmissible evidence of a covert tape recording of private conversations on private property, or exercised his discretion to exclude it under s 78 of the Police and Criminal Evidence Act 1984. The facts are set out in the judgment of the court.

Franz Muller QC and *Mark George* (assigned by the *Registrar of Criminal Appeals*) for the appellant.
Stephen Gullick and *Simon Haring* (instructed by the *Crown Prosecution Service*, Sheffield) for the Crown.

Cur adv vult

27 May 1994. The following judgment of the court was delivered.

LORD TAYLOR OF GOSFORTH CJ. The issues to which this appeal gives rise are: (i) whether in a criminal trial evidence as to the terms of tape recorded conversations obtained by means of an electronic listening device attached by the police to a private house without the knowledge of the owners or occupiers was admissible against the defendant; and (ii) if it was admissible, whether the judge should in his discretion have excluded it, having regard to the terms of s 78 of the Police and Criminal Evidence Act 1984.

On 10 December 1993 in the Crown Court at Sheffield before Judge Barber, the appellant pleaded guilty on re-arraignment to being knowingly concerned in the fraudulent evasion of the prohibition on the importation of a Class A drug, heroin. He is now serving a sentence of three years' imprisonment which was imposed on 14 March 1994. His plea of guilty followed the judge's ruling, the correctness of which is challenged in this appeal, brought with the leave of the single judge.

The facts
On 21 July 1992 the appellant and a man called Farooq Nawab, both travelling on the same flight, arrived at Manchester airport from Pakistan.

They had been seated in separate parts of the aeroplane and both went, separately, through the green channel. Both were stopped, searched and interviewed. Nawab was found to be in possession of heroin with a street value of almost £100,000 and a small amount of cannabis resin. He said that he was travelling alone, but admitted knowing the appellant, a distant relative, and said that he had spent a night with the appellant in Pakistan. He did not implicate him in the offence. Nawab was, naturally, arrested and charged.

No drugs were found in the possession of the appellant, who made no admissions and was released without charge. On interview at the police station the following day, he denied any offence and declined to answer most of the questions that were put to him.

On 26 January 1993 the appellant went to an address in Sheffield, the home of a man named Bashforth, on the exterior of which an aural surveillance device had been installed by or at the instance of the South Yorkshire Police. Neither the appellant nor Bashforth nor any occupant of the premises was aware of its presence. It was not expected or foreseen that the appellant would visit the premises. By means of that device, the police obtained a tape recording of the conversation that took place between Bashforth, Nawab's brother, a woman and the appellant. In the course of that conversation, things were said by the appellant which plainly (as his subsequent change of plea confirms) showed that he was involved in the importation of the heroin.

As a result, the appellant was arrested on 11 February 1993. He was interviewed, but made no admissions and was subsequently charged. At the trial it was admitted on his behalf that he had been present at the Sheffield address and that his voice was one of those recorded on the tape. On behalf of the prosecution, who for obvious reasons did not wish to disclose details of the circumstances pertaining to the attachment of the listening device, it was admitted that its attachment had involved a civil trespass and occasioned some degree of damage to the property.

In the absence of the jury, the judge heard evidence to enable him to decide whether to admit the tape recording of the conversations. The Crown accepted that without it there was no case against the appellant and, had it been ruled out, would have offered no evidence. The judge admitted it and, following an amendment to the indictment to add a further count, the appellant pleaded guilty. It was made clear that he did so only on the basis of the judge's ruling, and reserved the right to challenge that ruling.

The evidence at the voire dire

The evidence established that on 9 December 1992 Det Chief Supt Burdiss submitted to Chief Con Wells of South Yorkshire, a request on Form CID/62, dated 2 December 1992, for authority to install the listening device. The reason for the request was said to be that Bashforth was dealing heavily in heroin. It was said that the police had concluded that conventional surveillance methods would be totally inadequate to combat his activities and that the position of the premises was such that policemen, whether on foot or in vehicles, who attempted to watch the premises would easily be seen.

The evidence of the chief constable was that the matter was discussed over some 15 to 20 minutes—though he did not keep a note of the conversation—and that as a result he was satisfied that authority should be granted, as it was. This involved that Mr Wells was satisfied (a) that the investigation concerned serious crime; (b) that normal methods of investigation had been tried and failed, or must from the nature of things be unlikely to succeed if tried; (c) that there was good reason to think that the use of the equipment would lead to arrest and conviction; and (d) that the use of the equipment was operationally feasible.

Det Chief Supt Burdiss, who was head of the drug squad, also gave evidence. He spoke of the discussions he had had with other officers in relation to Bashforth, and said that he was satisfied that the supply of heroin on a large scale was involved, and accepted his officers' assessment that normal surveillance was impracticable. Bashforth, he said, was someone in respect of whom the police desired to gather evidence for a prosecution.

Both these witnesses were cross-examined, with a view to testing their assessment of the situation, and challenging the propriety of the authorisation that was given. Since, in the event, the judge accepted the material parts of their evidence, and it is not on this appeal suggested that his decision in that regard is open to challenge, it is unnecessary to rehearse details of the cross-examination. There were also some other witnesses who gave largely formal evidence, to whom again it is unnecessary specifically to refer.

Material documents

There are, in the United Kingdom, no statutory provisions which govern the use by police of secret listening devices on private property. This is to be contrasted with the position in relation to the interception of public telephone calls or postal communications, now governed by the Interception of Communications Act 1985 (following the decision of the European Court of Human Rights in *Malone v UK* (1984) 7 EHRR 14). It is also to be contrasted with controls in the use of surveillance devices by the Security Service laid down in the Security Service Act 1989.

There are, however, Home Office guidelines on the subject, and in addition the South Yorkshire Police have issued standing orders which plainly are intended to be complementary to the Home Office guidelines.

We must refer to some of the provisions to be found in each of these documents. The Home Office guidelines of 1984 are entitled 'Guidelines on the use of equipment in police surveillance operations'. They make it clear that only chief constables (in cases such as the present) or assistant chief constables (in cases exhibiting features not present in the instant case) are entitled to give authority for the use of such devices. Under the heading 'General' appears the following:

> 'Surveillance equipment has a valuable role to play in many police operations, and the police have a duty to employ appropriate surveillance measures where necessary for the prevention and detection of crime. But it must also be recognised that certain uses of equipment in police surveillance operations may involve encroachment on privacy. The circumstances in which the equipment is used are generally the key factor in determining public attitudes. Most concern is directed towards the use of equipment in circumstances where targets of surveillance might reasonably assume a high degree of privacy, for example in their homes or in a hotel bedroom ... Careful consideration at a senior level in the police service therefore needs to be given in each case to all the circumstances of the particular investigation or operation before the use of equipment for surveillance operations is authorised.'

In relation to the use of covert listening devices the guidelines embody the following statements of principle, among others:

'4. In each case in which the covert use of a listening device is requested the authorising officer should satisfy himself that the following criteria are met: a) the investigation concerns serious crime; b) normal methods of investigation must have been tried and failed, or must, from the nature of things, be unlikely to succeed if tried; c) there must be good reason to think that use of the equipment would be likely to lead to an arrest and a conviction, or where appropriate, to the prevention of acts of terrorism; d) use of equipment must be operationally feasible.

5. In judging how far the seriousness of the crime under investigation justifies the use of particular surveillance techniques, authorising officers should satisfy themselves that the degree of intrusion into the privacy of those affected by the surveillance is commensurate with the seriousness of the offence. Where the targets of surveillance might reasonably assume a high degree of privacy, for instance in their homes, listening devices should be used only for the investigation of major organised conspiracies and of other particularly serious offences, especially crimes of violence ...

8 ... Authorisation of the use of equipment should be for a maximum period of one month, after which a fresh application must be made to the authorising officer if it is desired to continue the operation.

9 The product (ie recordings made by or directly from the surveillance equipment) of the surveillance should be retained only for as long as it is required by the circumstances of the enquiry or by any subsequent court proceedings [and should be destroyed as soon as it is apparent that it is no longer so required] ...

10. It is accepted that there may be circumstances in which material obtained through the use of equipment by the police for surveillance as a necessary part of a criminal investigation could appropriately be used in evidence at subsequent court proceedings. The use outside the police service or the courts of [such] material ... should be authorised only in the most exceptional circumstances ...

11. A central record should be kept at force headquarters ... of each application for the use of listening devices. This should include: a) the nature of the case; b) whether authority was given or refused and by whom; c) broadly how the criteria set out in paragraph 4 were met; and d) the final outcome of the investigation. These records should be retained for a period of at least two years.'

It is unnecessary to cite from the South Yorkshire Police standing orders, which, as one would expect, closely follow the Home Office guidelines and are, in all relevant respects, in identical terms.

Before we pass on to summarise the arguments on behalf of the appellant, it is necessary to cite from one further document to which we were referred. This is a letter, referred to in the index with our papers as 'Home Office Guidelines 1/7/77', and addressed to chief constables. The subject matter of the letter is described thus: 'Use of equipment in police surveillance operations.' The material parts of the letter are the following:

'1. The use of certain equipment in police surveillance operations may involve encroachment on privacy. The principles and procedures relating

to such use have been reviewed in consultation with the Association of
Chief Police Officers and the Commissioner of Police of the Metropolis, *a*
and the following arrangements have been agreed for a trial period of
twelve months from the date of this letter ...

Principles ... 3. Public attitudes to encroachments on privacy depend
less on the particular equipment used than on the circumstances of its use.
On each occasion, therefore, these circumstances need to be considered at *b*
a senior level in the police service before use of equipment is authorised.

4. As a general principle, the primary purpose of using equipment for
aural or visual surveillance should be to help confirm or dispel a suspicion
of serious crime, and not to collect evidence (except where, as in
blackmail, the spoken word is the kernel of the offence).

5. In each case the authorising officer should satisfy himself that use of *c*
the particular equipment is:—a. operationally necessary; b. operationally
feasible; and c. justified in all the circumstances.'

It was, as we believe, to this document that the Home Secretary referred in
a parliamentary written answer on 19 December 1984 when, introducing the *d*
1984 guidelines from which we have already quoted extensively, he said:

'The new guidelines contain more detailed and rigorous procedures than
those in the previous guidance which was issued in 1977 and placed in the
Library of the House in February 1982.' (See 70 HC Official Report (6th
series) written answers cols 157–159.)

It is material, in the context of the argument in the present case, to note the
contrast between para 4 of the 1977 guidelines and para 4(c) and, particularly,
para 10 of the 1984 guidelines.

The appellant's argument

The argument advanced by Mr Muller QC and Mr George in support of their
first contention—that the evidence is inadmissible—can be summarised as
follows.

(a) The installation of the listening device involved trespass upon and
damage to private property. The circumstances in which the damage occurred *f*
arguably constitute the offence of criminal damage within the meaning of
s 1(1) of the Criminal Damage Act 1971. (This latter proposition is disputed by
the Crown, but for present purposes, and without rehearsing the arguments,
we accept its validity.)

(b) There is no statute or established law which governs the installation and
use of such devices by the police in private houses, nor are there any statutory *g*
regulations applicable to their use in circumstances involving trespass and
damage. In the absence of such regulation the ordinary citizen has no means
of knowing what the legal position is when such an invasion of privacy occurs.
Citizens should be entitled to know in what circumstances and subject to what
conditions the police may attach a listening device to private premises. In this
regard reliance is placed on *Malone v UK* (1984) 7 EHRR 14 at 39–41 (paras 66–
68). We need cite only the concluding words of para 67 (at 40):

'... the law must be sufficiently clear in its terms to give citizens an
adequate indication as to the circumstances in which and the conditions
on which public authorities are empowered to resort to this secret and

potentially dangerous interference with the right to respect for private life and correspondence.'

(c) Counsel argued that, since the 1984 guidelines and the South Yorkshire Police standing orders were not generally accessible to the public, their existence did not meet the criticism in (b) above. He accepted that, were there in existence a clear statement of the relevant law by the court, that would be a sufficient substitute for the statutory provision which, he contends, ideally there should be.

(d) In so far as it is permissible to have regard to the 1984 guidelines, counsel suggests that the provisions of para 10 constitute an anomalous departure from what had always previously been accepted to be the position—namely that the product of covert surveillance, whether by means of telephone tapping or a listening device, was used only for the prevention and detection of crime, and not in order to secure a conviction by means of its introduction in evidence.

In this connection counsel referred us to *R v Preston* [1993] 4 All ER 638, [1994] 2 AC 130, and to certain passages in the speech of Lord Mustill. That case is not directly in point here, for their Lordships were there primarily concerned with the interpretation of the Interception of Communications Act 1985, the Act passed as the result of the decision in *Malone v UK*. However, when considering the history and rationale of the power assumed by the executive to intercept private communications in the mail, and later by telegraph and telephone, Lord Mustill pointed out:

> '... although there has been some disagreement about whether the intercept material is in principle capable of being used in court (contrast the majority and minority opinions in the report of the Privy Councillors) [*Interception of Communications* (Cmnd 283 (1957)) (the Birkett Report)] all were agreed that in practice such material is never so employed.' (See [1993] 4 All ER 638 at 650, [1994] 2 AC 130 at 147.)

Lord Mustill noted and described as surprising the emergence of para 10 in the 1984 guidelines, describing it as a departure from previous practice which was itself contradicted a few weeks later by a Home Office White Paper *The Interception of Communications in the United Kingdom* (Cmnd 9438 (1985)), designed to lay the ground for the forthcoming Bill. He cited from paras 7 and 12 of the White Paper passages which made it clear that, in relation to 'the interception of communications on public systems' the Bill would make 'such material generally inadmissible in legal proceedings [and] ensure that interception can be used only as an aspect of investigation, not of prosecution'.

(e) Counsel also relied on *Malone v UK* and the decision in that case to the effect that the United Kingdom was in breach of art 8 of the European Convention on Human Rights (Convention for the Protection of Human Rights and Fundamental Freedoms (Rome, 4 November 1950; TS 71 (1953); Cmd 8989). Putting his argument compendiously, and we hope not unfairly compressing it, what in effect Mr Muller contended was that in the 1985 Act passed as a result of the decision in that case Parliament confirmed that the practice that had obtained prior to the 1984 guidelines should continue, ie that the product of telephone and postal interceptions should not be admissible in evidence; by analogy, evidence obtained from bugging private premises, which is in many respects comparable and the obtaining of which involves similar invasions of privacy, ought not to be admitted; and this is all the more so since the practice of bugging private premises arguably constitutes, absent some clear statutory parameters or decided cases on the propriety and limits of such conduct, a breach of art 8. Moreover, Mr Muller argued, the fact that the evidence involved an invasion of privacy and a degree of illegality was a material factor which should have led to the decision that the evidence was inadmissible.

In our judgment this first submission—that the evidence is *inadmissible*— must be rejected. It is an established rule of English law that the test of admissibility is relevance: relevant evidence, even if illegally obtained, is admissible. After a review of the rather sparse authorities bearing on the subject, the author of *Cross on Evidence* (7th edn, 1990) p 482 summarises the position in these words:

> 'It may therefore be concluded that, under English law, illegally obtained evidence is admissible as a matter of law, provided that it involves neither a reference to an inadmissible confession of guilt, nor the commission of an act of contempt of court.'

In *R v Sang* [1979] 2 All ER 1222, [1980] AC 402 the House of Lords plainly accepted that relevance is the test of admissibility when answering the certified question (which was directed to whether a trial judge had a discretion to exclude evidence—other than evidence of an admission—which was relevant and probative) in the following terms:

> '(1) A trial judge in a criminal trial has always a discretion to refuse to admit evidence if in his opinion its prejudicial effect outweighs its probative value. (2) Save with regard to admissions and confessions and generally with regard to evidence obtained from the accused after commission of the offence, he has no discretion to refuse to admit relevant admissible evidence on the ground that it was obtained by improper or unfair means. The court is not concerned with how it was obtained. It is no ground for the exercise of discretion to exclude that the evidence was obtained as a result of the activities of an agent provocateur.' (See [1979] 2 All ER 1222 at 1231, [1980] AC 402 at 437 per Lord Diplock.)

Counsel for the appellant contend that evidence of the content of conversations in a private house is inadmissible. They conceded the qualification that if (for example by talking at an open window so that their words could be heard by passers-by in the street) the occupants fail to take reasonable precautions to ensure that they are not overheard, the evidence would be admissible; likewise, if one of the participants in the conversation chose to give evidence of it. But the essential thrust of the submission was that private conversations on private property were inviolate, unless and until there exists a clear statement of law informing the public that their privacy may be intruded upon covertly by one means or another.

The importance of upholding rights of privacy, so far as possible, having regard to the need to enforce the criminal law and to the public interest, are fully recognised by the existing guidelines, as well as by art 8 of the 1950 convention. However, to establish the inviolability of the home by rendering inadmissible statements made within it would be to introduce a new principle into English law. Quite apart from the difficulties of defining what the principle was, neither the proper protection of private rights nor public policy require it. On the contrary, there is a strong public interest in the detection of crime and in the use by the police of up-to-date technical devices in appropriate circumstances. It will be remembered that it is only in relation to serious crime and where other means of obtaining evidence and detection are unlikely to prove effective that sanction will be given to the use of such devices.

There are in our judgment only two bases on which evidence of this sort could be excluded. The first is if it were possible (which in our view it is not in the present case) to argue that the prejudicial effect of the evidence exceeded its probative value. The second, and this is the second ground on which the appellant sought to persuade the judge to exclude it, is by reliance on the discretion (preserved by s 82 of the Police and Criminal Evidence Act 1984) which he has at common law (see *R v Sang* [1979] 2 All ER 1222, [1980] AC 402) or on the provisions of s 78 of the 1984 Act. Section 78(1) provides as follows:

> 'In any proceedings the court may refuse to allow evidence on which the prosecution proposes to rely to be given if it appears to the court that, having regard to all the circumstances, including the circumstances in which the evidence was obtained, the admission of the evidence would have such an adverse effect on the fairness of the proceedings that the court ought not to admit it.'

Section 82(3) of the Act provides:

> 'Nothing in this Part of this Act shall prejudice any power of a court to exclude evidence (whether by preventing questions being put or otherwise) at its discretion.'

Since, on any view, the discretion conferred on the judge by s 78 is at least as wide as that identified in *R v Sang* it is only necessary to consider the question of the exercise of discretion under s 78—which is what the judge did. In the course of its judgment in *R v Christou* [1992] 4 All ER 559 at 564, [1992] QB 979 at 988 this court said:

> 'The learned judge held that the discretion under s 78 may be wider than the common law discretion identified in *R v Sang*, the latter relating solely to evidence obtained from the defendant after the offence is complete, the statutory discretion not being so restricted. However, he held that the criteria of unfairness are the same whether the trial judge is exercising his discretion at common law or under the statute. We agree. What is unfair cannot sensibly be subject to different standards depending on the source of the discretion to exclude it.'

The nature of the arguments advanced by counsel for the appellant under this head are, predictably, consistent with those on which they relied on the issue of admissibility. They are, in brief, to the following effect. (1) The conduct of the police in fitting the device which enabled them to obtain the evidence was unlawful in the respects already discussed. (2) There are no statutory provisions and no readily accessible published criteria to inform the public as to the circumstances in which such intrusions on privacy may occur. Unless the terms on which such conduct is to be permitted are, by some such means, known to all, it is unfair to permit the product of it to be used in evidence. (3) Previous practice has been against such material being used in evidence to secure a conviction; its legitimate use has been confined to detection and prevention of crime. (4) Parliament has decided that the product of telephone tapping should not be used in evidence and, since this material was obtained in closely analogous circumstances, the use of it would be unfair. (5) There are grounds for thinking, on the strength of the decision in *Malone v UK*, that the European Court of Human Rights would conclude that there had in the present case been a breach of art 8 of the 1950 convention. (6) There was a breach of para 11 of the guidelines and standing orders in that no proper records were kept. (Before the judge it was also argued that there had been a breach of para 4(b) because it could not properly have been concluded by the officers concerned that normal methods of investigation would, if tried, be unlikely to succeed; but counsel for the appellant have not sought to challenge the judge's conclusion that that contention was not made out.)

Mr Muller developed these arguments before the judge, as he did before us. The judge accepted that, in the absence of statutory authority, the situation was, as Mr Muller contended, riddled with ambiguities and that it was closely analogous to the situation which gave rise to *Malone v UK*. He accepted that there was a breach of para 11. However, having rejected the contention that para 4(b) had been breached, the judge held that there had been no significant breach of the guidelines, and continued:

> '[The prosecution have, properly, admitted] that there has been a civil trespass and some damage to the flat of Mr Bashforth and therefore an arguable breach of art 8 in the absence of statutory authority or clear guidelines available to the public. Allowing for those matters I do not think that they, in my judgment at least, come anywhere near allowing me to exclude this evidence under s 78 of the Police and Criminal Evidence Act.'

In our view this was a conclusion which the learned judge was entitled to reach.

In *R v Smurthwaite* [1994] 1 All ER 898 at 902–903 this court gave guidance as to the correct approach to s 78, stating that the right approach was—

> 'simply to examine the language of the relevant provision in its natural meaning and not to strain for an interpretation which either reasserts or alters the pre-existing law. Viewed in that way the phrase ["including the circumstances in which the evidence was obtained"] ... clearly permits the court to have regard to "the circumstances in which the evidence was obtained" and to exclude it, but only if it "would have such an adverse effect on the fairness of the proceedings the court ought not to admit it". Thus, the fact that the evidence had been obtained by entrapment, or by agent provocateur, or by a trick, does not of itself require the judge to exclude it. If, however, he considers that in all the circumstances the obtaining of the evidence in that way would have the adverse effect described in the statute, then he will exclude it ... "Fairness of the proceedings" involves a consideration not only of fairness to the accused but also, as has been said before, of fairness to the public ...'

The court went on to mention some of the factors which, in a case involving (as that did) the obtaining of evidence by an undercover officer, the judge might take into account. They included the following:

'Was the officer acting as an agent provocateur in the sense that he was enticing the defendant to commit an offence he would not otherwise have committed? What was the nature of any entrapment? Does the evidence consist of admissions to a completed offence, or does it consist of the actual commission of an offence? How active or passive was the officer's role in obtaining the evidence? Is there an unassailable record of what occurred or is it strongly corroborated?' (See [1994] 1 All ER 898 at 903.)

Counsel for the Crown point out that in the present case no crime was incited; no deliberate deceit was practised on the appellant; no misleading information was advanced or pressure placed upon him to induce him to speak; the police did not act oppressively towards him; at the time the conversation was taped the appellant had neither been arrested, interviewed, nor charged; the tape provided a clear record of what was admittedly said by the appellant; and no question arose of the breach of any Codes of Practice under the 1984 Act.

There were, they concede, the elements of civil trespass to the outside of the building and the infliction upon it of some degree of damage; and the fact that as a result there was an intrusion upon the privacy of those who believed themselves to be secure from being overheard when they had the crucial conversation.

As to the argument based on art 8 of the 1950 convention, counsel for the Crown rightly pointed out that it is not (as yet) part of the law of the United Kingdom since it has not been enacted into our statutory law. He referred us to *Chundawadra v Immigration Appeal Tribunal* [1988] Imm AR 161 and *Pan American World Airways Inc v Dept of Trade* [1976] 1 Lloyd's Rep 257. From these authorities it is clear that it is permissible to have regard to the convention, which is of persuasive assistance, in cases of ambiguity or doubt. In the circumstances of the present case the position is neither ambiguous nor doubtful: nor is it incumbent on us to consider whether there was a breach of art 8, and we do not propose to do so.

Counsel argued that, in the circumstances, the factors of trespass, damage and the matters relating to art 8 and the intrusion on privacy were of insufficient gravity to outweigh the other factors to which they had referred, all of which militated in favour of concluding that fairness to both sides required the admission of the evidence. We agree with this submission. We would emphasise, in particular, the fact that in proceeding as they did the police were, so far from acting in an arbitrary or uncontrolled manner, proceeding in accordance with the relevant Home Office guidelines. True it is that these do not have statutory authority; but they had been publicised at least to the extent of being placed in the library of the House of Commons, as the Parliamentary answer that we have cited shows, and plainly regulated and defined the conduct of the police officers. Moreover, what was under investigation was a type of criminal conduct of great gravity. The issues of trespass and damage—we think we can legitimately infer that the damage was slight—are in the circumstances of this case of limited importance, save for their impact upon the issues of privacy and the inviolability of the home which have rightly been emphasised. We would expect there to be devices available, now or in the future, which can pick up even the most private conversations without the need for a trespass. There are, as art 8 recognises, circumstances in which such intrusion is necessary and therefore justifiable in a democratic society. In the circumstances we cannot but think that the judge was right in concluding, as plainly he did, that the invasion of privacy with the attendant trespass and damage was outweighed by other considerations and should plainly not be regarded as having such an adverse effect on the fairness of the proceedings that the court ought to exclude the evidence.

We should also say a word about the third of the arguments relied upon by counsel for the appellant—namely that previous practice appears always to have been not to use material obtained by such means in evidence. While we accept that some support is lent to this contention by the terms of the Home Office guidelines 1977, there can be no doubt that the revised guidelines in 1984 and the terms of the Parliamentary written answer of 19 December 1984 embodied a new approach so far as information obtained otherwise than by means of the interception of the public telephone system was concerned. With due deference to the views expressed by Lord Mustill in the passage we have quoted from *R v Preston* [1993] 4 All ER 638 at 650, [1994] 2 AC 130 at 147, we question whether there was in truth any inconsistency between the terms of para 10 of the 1984 guidelines and the White Paper issued shortly thereafter, because the guidelines were directed to surveillance other than by means of telephone interception (see in particular para 12) whereas the White Paper, as its title and content shows, was directed specifically to telephone interceptions. It must be remembered that in *R v Preston* the House of Lords was (in this context) considering only the question of interception of public telephone lines and construing the 1985 Act.

In all the circumstances, we have concluded without any hesitation that the learned judge had before him ample material on which he could properly exercise his discretion in the way in which he did, and refuse to exclude the evidence under s 78 of the 1984 Act. It follows that this appeal must be dismissed.

Before parting with the case, we wish to comment on the argument addressed to us that the use of bugging devices should be more strictly regulated and the criteria more generally promulgated. The Home Office guidelines, and other documents to which we have referred, certainly prescribe criteria and procedures limiting such use. However, although not a legal rule, 'An Englishman's home is his castle' is a tenet jealously held and widely respected. It is, in our view, at least worthy of consideration as to whether the circumstances in which bugging a private home by the police can be justified should be the subject of statutory control. It may be thought that such control is, by analogy with the 1985 Act, just as desirable for bugging devices as for telephone tapping. Without expressing any concluded view, we simply draw attention to the matter as one deserving of consideration.

Appeal dismissed. The court refused leave to appeal to the House of Lords but certified, under s 33(2) of the Criminal Appeal Act 1968, that the following point of law of general public importance was involved in the decision: whether, in a criminal trial evidence as to the terms of tape recorded conversations obtained by means of an electronic listening device attached by the police to a private house without the knowledge of the owners or occupiers was admissible against the defendant.

4 October 1994. The Appeal Committee of the House of Lords gave leave to appeal.

N P Metcalfe Esq   Barrister.

Broadley v Guy Clapham & Co

COURT OF APPEAL, CIVIL DIVISON

BALCOMBE, LEGGATT AND HOFFMANN LJJ

10, 11 JUNE, 2 JULY 1993

Limitation of action – Personal injury claim – Plaintiff's knowledge – Date of plaintiff's knowledge that injury was significant – Date on which plaintiff first had knowledge that injury attributable to defendant's act or omission – Point when knowledge fixing cause of action – Limitation Act 1980, ss 11, 14.

In 1980 the plaintiff underwent an operation for the removal of a foreign body from her knee. Her condition did not however improve and subsequent examinations revealed nerve palsy of the left popliteal nerve and that the plaintiff had left foot drop. In June 1983 the plaintiff instructed the defendant solicitors, who arranged for her to see an orthopaedic surgeon. He advised the plaintiff that the operation might have been negligent. The defendants took no steps thereafter to obtain a report from the consultant or commence proceedings for medical negligence on the plaintiff's behalf. As a result the plaintiff instructed other solicitors. On 17 August 1990 the plaintiff issued a writ against the defendants, alleging that they had failed to take any or any adequate action and, as a result, the plaintiff's claim for medical negligence had become time-barred under the Limitation Act 1980. The defendants pleaded the 1980 Act, contending (i) that a limitation defence would succeed if the plaintiff's cause of action against them accrued before 18 August 1984, (ii) that the plaintiff's cause of action against them was based on their failure to prosecute her cause of action against the surgeon who performed the operation and the relevant health authority and that cause of action was barred under s 11[a] of the 1980 Act (as defined by s 14[b]) three years from (a) the date of the operation or (b) the date of the plaintiff's knowledge of her cause of action for medical negligence, if later and (iii) that since the three-year period from the date of the operation had expired in August 1983, the plaintiff's cause of action against him would be barred if her knowledge of her cause of action for medical negligence existed before 19 August 1981. The question which arose for determination as a preliminary issue was whether the plaintiff's date of knowledge for the purposes of ss 11 and 14 was before or after 19 August 1981. The judge held that the plaintiff knew before the relevant date that her injury was significant (albeit that she did not have direct knowledge of its cause or pathology) and that while such knowledge did not satisfy s 14(1) it was sufficient to fix the plaintiff with constructive knowledge under s 14(3)(b), namely knowledge that the operation had in some way caused her injury which she might reasonably have been expected to acquire from facts ascertainable with the help of medical or other expert advice. The plaintiff appealed.

---

a   Section 11, so far as material, provides: (4) [Any action for damages for negligence where the damages claimed by the plaintiff include damages in respect of personal injuries of the plaintiff or any other person shall not be brought after the expiration of the three-year] period applicable ... from—(a) the date on which the cause of action accrued; or (b) the date of knowledge (if later) of the person injured ...'

b   Section 14, so far as material, is set out at p 444 c to f, post

Held – A person who alleged that medical negligence had occurred in the course of a surgical operation was fixed with a cause of action for the purposes of s 14(3) of the 1980 Act when he knew, or could have known with the help of medical advice reasonably obtainable, that his injury had been caused by damage resulting from something done or not done by the surgeon during the operation. Knowledge detailed enough to enable the plaintiff's advisers to draft a statement of claim was not required before time began to run and not only went beyond the standard necessary for the purposes of s 14 but also conflicted with the final words of s 14(1), which stipulated that 'knowledge that any acts or omissions did or did not, as a matter of law, involve negligence, nuisance or breach of duty' was 'irrelevant'. On the facts it was clear that by 19 August 1981 the plaintiff had both broad knowledge that the operation had caused an injury to her foot and specific knowledge that the operation had been carried out in such a way as to damage a nerve in her leg thereby causing foot drop. It followed that the judge's decision as to constructive knowledge was correct and effectively meant that the plaintiff's cause of action against the defendant was time-barred under the 1980 Act. The appeal would accordingly be dismissed (see p 446 *a* to *c j* to p 447 *c f* to *h*, p 448 *h* to p 449 *b e g h* and p 450 *b c*, post).

Bentley v Bristol and Weston Health Authority [1991] 2 Med LR 359 overruled.

Notes

For limitation period in personal injury actions and the plaintiff's knowledge in relation to limitation of actions, see 28 *Halsbury's Laws* (4th edn) paras 691–692.

For the Limitation Act 1980, ss 11 and 14, see 24 *Halsbury's Statutes* (4th edn) (1989 reissue) 657, 661.

Cases referred to in judgments

Bentley v Bristol and Weston Health Authority [1991] 2 Med LR 359, DC.

Cartledge v E Jopling & Sons Ltd [1963] 1 All ER 341, [1963] AC 758, [1963] 2 WLR 210, HL.

Central Asbestos Co Ltd v Dodd [1971] 3 All ER 204, [1972] 1 QB 244, [1971] 3 WLR 206, CA; *affd* [1972] 2 All ER 1135, [1973] AC 518, [1972] 3 WLR 333, HL.

Driscoll-Varley v Parkside Health Authority [1991] 2 Med LR 346.

Halford v Brookes [1991] 3 All ER 559, [1991] 1 WLR 428, CA.

Hendy v Milton Keynes Health Authority [1992] 3 Med LR 114.

Nash v Eli Lilly & Co [1993] 4 All ER 383, [1993] 1 WLR 782, CA.

Stephen v Riverside Health Authority [1990] 1 Med LR 261.

Wilkinson v Ancliff (BLT) Ltd [1986] 3 All ER 427, [1986] 1 WLR 1352, CA.

Appeal

The plaintiff, Mrs Maureen Broadley, appealed from the decision of Turner J given on 24 March 1992 whereby it was adjudged, on the hearing of a preliminary issue, that the plaintiff's claim commenced by writ dated 17 August 1990 against the defendant firm of solicitors, Guy Clapham & Co, seeking damages for negligence for failing to take any or any adequate or sufficient action whereby the plaintiff's claim for damages for left foot drop due to negligence of inter alia the surgeon who performed an operation on her knee on 13 August 1980 became statute-barred, was time-barred on the grounds that the plaintiff's date of knowledge for the purposes of s 11 of the a Limitation Act 1980, as defined by s 14(3)(b) of the 1980 Act, was before 19 August 1981. The facts are set out in the judgment of Balcombe LJ.

Rodger Bell QC (instructed by *Leigh Day & Co*) for the plaintiff.
Justin Fenwick QC and *Sue Carr* (instructed by *Pinsent & Co*) for the defendant.

b   *Cur adv vult*

2 July 1993. The following judgments were delivered.

BALCOMBE LJ. This appeal is by the plaintiff, Mrs Maureen Broadley, from
c the judgment of Turner J given on 24 March 1992, whereby on the trial of a
preliminary issue he made a finding which effectively meant that her cause of
action was barred under the Limitation Act 1980.

On 13 August 1980 the plaintiff, then aged 39, underwent an operation at the
Royal Northern Hospital, London N7, for the removal of a 'foreign' or 'loose'
d body from her knee. The surgeon who performed the operation was Mr
Martin Lowy. In his operation notes Mr Lowy noted 'Lateral popliteal nerve
identified and protected', but the next day an examination on the ward
recorded that there was nerve palsy of the left lateral popliteal nerve. On 18
August, in the hospital's department of physical medicine, it was noted that the
plaintiff had left foot drop. She was discharged home from hospital on 28
e August, and attended the department of physical medicine on 4 September
when it was recorded: 'Foot drop complete and not improved.' On 5
September the plaintiff attended her general practitioner who recorded in her
notes of that date: 'Loose body removal from knee. Left foot drop. On
physiotherapy. To see Mr. Lowy 15 September.' On 8 September a discharge
f letter form the hospital to the plaintiff's general practitioner described her
operation, but made no reference to foot drop or to its cause, nerve palsy. On
15 September the plaintiff was again seen by Mr Lowy, who noted: 'No active
dorsiflexion of toes ... She walks with typical dropped foot gait. For lateral
popliteal nerve conduction tests. See one month.' She was seen again by Mr
Lowy on 13 October 1980, who then noted: 'Still no power in dorsiflexion ...
g Nerve conduction tests due 30.10. See one month.'

Nerve conduction tests were not carried out and the plaintiff was not seen
again by Mr Lowy for some years.

It was not until 9 June 1982 that the plaintiff next attended her general
practitioner, and when she did she made no mention of the fact that she
h suffered from left foot drop. On 24 April 1983, as a result of a conversation
with nurses from a hostel next door to where she was then working, the
plaintiff wrote to Mr Lowy referring to her operation and the consequent foot
drop, but says she received no reply. She then decided to consult a solicitor,
and in June 1983 instructed the defendant. He arranged for her to be seen by
an orthopaedic surgeon, Mr Farrington, on 6 July 1983. Mr Farrington told the
plaintiff that in his opinion the operation on her knee might have been
negligent. No report was received from Mr Farrington and no writ was ever
issued by the defendant on behalf of the plaintiff. The plaintiff was
subsequently referred to her present solicitors.

On 17 August 1990 the writ in the present action was issued and was served
soon afterwards. A statement of claim was served on 21 December 1990

alleging negligence on the part of the defendant. Paragraph 7 of the statement of claim is in the following terms:

> '7. The Plaintiff was examined by Mr Farrington on July 6th 1983. Negligently and in breach of the implied terms of the said agreement the Defendants failed to obtain a report from Mr Farrington and failed to take any or any adequate or sufficient action whereby the Plaintiff's claim for medical negligence became statute barred by virtue of the Limitation Act 1980.'

The plaintiff was asked for particulars of her claim for medical negligence and the answers given included the following:

> '... (ii) In the course of an operation on the 13th of August 1980 to remove a loose body from the Plaintiff's left knee surgeons in the employment of the said Health Authority negligently divided and/or damaged the left lateral popliteal nerve. Thereafter no or no adequate measures were taken to repair the nerve such that, by early 1981, the said damage became irreparable. (iii) The Plaintiff was left with a left foot drop caused by the said negligence.'

By his defence the defendant pleaded, inter alia, the Limitation Act 1980.

The plaintiff's writ was issued on 17 August 1990. The defence of limitation will succeed if her cause of action against the defendant accrued earlier than six years previously, ie before 18 August 1984 (see s 5 of the 1980 Act). The plaintiff's cause of action against the defendant is based on his failure to prosecute her cause of action against Mr Lowy and the hospital. That cause of action was barred under s 11 of the 1980 Act, three years from either the date of the operation or the date of the plaintiff's knowledge, if later. The period of three years from the date of the operation expired in August 1983, ie well before 18 August 1984. So the plaintiff's cause of action against the defendant is barred if her knowledge of her cause of action against Mr Lowy and the hospital existed before 19 August 1981. Accordingly, on 2 September 1991 a direction was made that there be tried as a preliminary issue in the action:

> 'Was the Plaintiff's date of knowledge for the purposes of Section 11 of the Limitation Act 1980 and as defined by Section 14 of the Limitation Act 1980 before or after 19th August 1981?'

It was this issue which came before Turner J on 24 March 1992. He had the affidavit and oral evidence of the plaintiff herself, the affidavit evidence of Mr Lowy, and the affidavit evidence of Mr Brian Hanbury Day, a consultant orthopaedic surgeon called on behalf of the defendant. One of the issues raised by Mr Lowy in his evidence, on which he was supported by Mr Day, was whether he told the plaintiff that a complication (ie the injury to the lateral popliteal nerve) had occurred as a result of the operation. On this issue the judge said:

> 'I make no finding on the basis that he did so. I do not find that he did not. It is not necessary for the decision to which I have ultimately come to make any specific finding on that matter.'

However the judge did make the following finding of fact relating to the plaintiff's state of knowledge:

'If it be the fact, as I find, that for at least seven months following the date of this operation the plaintiff, when she walked abroad, by which I mean outside her place of residence, required two sticks, or even one stick, it is plain that she must herself have considered that there was something significantly wrong. I am confident, however, that her attitude of mind was: "This is something that has happened to me. I must just get on with it". That does not mean, in my judgment, that a person having that commendable attitude of mind would not have thought and did not think that the injury was not sufficiently serious to justify the institution of proceedings. I am satisfied that the plaintiff knew that once the significant swelling in the knee had subsided, which it largely had by a month after the date of the operation (see out-patient note for September, made by Mr Lowy) she must have known and indeed did know, that what she was suffering from was something other than a direct and inevitable consequence of the operation that had been performed. By seven months after the operation the ankle and control of the foot was substantially as it had been ever since 15 September 1980 by which I mean not that the leg was still as swollen as it was on that date, but that the condition of nerve palsy which existed then continued, as indeed it has from such date right up to the present time. Even a person as uncomplaining as Mrs Broadley would, I am satisfied, have thought there was something significantly wrong with an ankle that was still ineffective so long after the operation and when, on her own account, and disregarding the probabilities that might be inferred from Mr Lowy's affidavit the ankle had shown no signs of improvement. It follows from this finding that I am satisfied that the plaintiff knew before the relevant date in August 1981 that the injury from which she was suffering—albeit she may not have had direct knowledge of its cause or pathology—was a significant injury.'

This finding of fact is, as Mr Bell QC for the plaintiff accepts, a finding to which the judge was entitled to come on the evidence before him and by which the plaintiff is bound in this court.

The judge then held that this was not, taken alone, sufficient to satisfy s 14(1) of the 1980 Act. However, he went on to find that the provisions of s 14(3)(b) of the 1980 Act fixed the plaintiff with constructive knowledge. This finding is contained in the following passage from his judgment:

'It is common ground that Mrs Broadley did not seek medical assistance in connection with foot drop until long after August 1981. Given that she [said she] had been told by Mr Lowy that the foot drop would recover, the fact that it had shown no signs of recovery by February 1981, let alone by August of that year, would have suggested to a reasonable person in Mrs Broadley's position that it would be sensible at the very least for her to have sought assistance from her GP at the least, if not to have gone back to Mr Lowy and said, and I paraphrase: "Look , Mr Lowy, you said my ankle and foot would get better, but they are as bad as ever they were when you last saw me in September 1980—what is wrong?" That, as it seems to me, is the very least that a person in Mrs Broadley's position would have done, even making allowance for her phlegmatic and non-complaining attitude.'

Accordingly, he answered the question raised in the preliminary issue by
holding that the plaintiff's date of knowledge for the purposes of s 11 of the
1980 Act, as defined by s 14 of that Act, was before 19 August 1981. From that
decision the plaintiff has appealed, asserting that the judge's finding as to her
constructive knowledge was wrong as a matter of law. The defendant has
served a respondent's notice asserting that the judge's findings of fact were
sufficient to establish that the plaintiff had actual knowledge within s 14(1),
and that there was no need to rely on constructive knowledge under s 14(3).

Section 14 of the 1980 Act provides, so far as relevant:

'(1) ... in sections 11 ... of this Act references to a person's date of
knowledge are references to the date on which he first had knowledge of
the following facts—(a) that the injury in question was significant; and (b)
that the injury was attributable in whole or in part to the act or omission
which is alleged to constitute negligence, nuisance or breach of duty ...
and knowledge that any acts or omissions did or did not, as a matter of
law, involve negligence, nuisance or breach of duty is irrelevant.

(2) For the purposes of this section an injury is significant if the person
whose date of knowledge is in question would reasonably have considered
it sufficiently serious to justify his instituting proceedings for damages
against a defendant who did not dispute liability and was able to satisfy a
judgment.

(3) For the purposes of this section a person's knowledge includes
knowledge which he might reasonably have been expected to acquire—(a)
from facts observable or ascertainable by him; or (b) from facts
ascertainable by him with the help of medical or other appropriate expert
advice which it is reasonable for him to seek; but a person shall not be fixed
under this subsection with knowledge of a fact ascertainable only with the
help of expert advice so long as he has taken all reasonable steps to obtain
(and, where appropriate, to act on) that advice.'

We were referred to a number of cases, both in this court and at first
instance, where these provisions have been considered. To some of these I
now turn.

Wilkinson v Ancliff (BLT) Ltd [1986] 3 All ER 427, [1986] 1 WLR 1352 was a
case in this court where the plaintiff had been employed as a driver on road
tankers carrying a particular chemical, exposure to which had caused him to
suffer from bronchial asthma. Slade LJ said ([1986] 3 All ER 427 at 438, [1986]
1 WLR 1352 at 1365):

'In a case such as the present, where the acts and omissions on the part
of the defendants which are complained of are, in broad terms, the
exposure of their employee to dangerous working conditions and their
failure to take reasonable and proper steps to protect him from such
conditions, I think that the employee who has this broad knowledge may
well have knowledge of the nature referred to in s 14(1)(b) sufficient to set
time running against him, even though he may not yet have the
knowledge sufficient to enable him or his legal advisers to draft a fully and
comprehensively particularised statement of claim.'

In *Nash v Eli Lilly & Co* [1993] 4 All ER 383 at 398, [1993] 1 WLR 782 at 799, where the plaintiffs alleged that they had suffered side-effects from the use of the drug Opren, Purchas LJ giving the judgment of the court said:

'It was not, in our judgment, the intention of Parliament to require for the purposes of s 11 and s 14 of the Act proof of knowledge of the terms in which it will be alleged that the act or omission of the defendants constituted negligence or breach of duty. What is required is knowledge of the essence of the act or omission to which the injury is attributable.'

None of the cases in this court is concerned with medical negligence occurring in the course of an operation. However, there are two cases at first instance which are so concerned. The first is *Bentley v Bristol and Weston Health Authority* [1991] 2 Med LR 359, a decision of Hirst J. In that case the plaintiff's sciatic nerve was damaged during the course of an operation on 15 June 1981 for a total left hip replacement, a fact which was known to the plaintiff in August 1981. Hirst J accepted the submission of Mr Bell on behalf of the plaintiff (at 363)—

'that the crucial consideration is knowledge of the act or omission actually alleged to constitute negligence (i.e. in the present case knowledge of some act or omission which constituted a failure to carry out the operation safely), and that such knowledge was only acquired by the plaintiff for the first time when she learnt from Mr. Winkworth [in November 1985] that the cause of her injury might be excessive traction of the nerve.'

He rejected the contrary submission on behalf of the defendant (at 363)—

'that the crucial consideration is broad knowledge of the act which caused the damage (i.e. in the present case the operation per se together with the hospital notes containing the data concerning the operation), and for this purpose knowledge of detailed acts and omissions and the opinion of any individual expert, such as Mr. Winkworth, is not relevant.'

The judge said (at 364):

'... the performance of a surgical operation (ie an act invasive to the plaintiff's body to which the plaintiff has consented) is not the act or omission which is itself alleged to constitute negligence. The act or omission which **is** alleged to constitute negligence in operation cases is some conduct or failure which can affect the safety of the operation. Knowledge of such act or omission will frequently depend on information derived by the plaintiff from the expert opinion, and I reject Mr Bennett's submission that such opinion is irrelevant in this context.'

The second of the operation cases is *Hendy v Milton Keynes Health Authority* [1992] 3 Med LR 114, where Blofeld J distinguished *Bentley's* case on its facts and adopted a much less stringent test of 'knowledge' for the purposes of s 14 of the 1980 Act. He said (at 118):

'The plaintiff may be held within the meaning of section 14 to know if she appreciates in general terms that her problem was capable of being attributed to the operation, even where particular facts of what specifically went wrong or how or where precise error was made is not known to her.'

In my judgment, the test adopted by Hirst J in *Bentley's* case is inconsistent with the general principles as laid down by this court in the cases I have cited and is, indeed, inconsistent with the express provisions of the 1980 Act. His test requires knowledge on the part of the plaintiff of all matters necessary to establish negligence or breach of duty. Such a test conflicts with the final words of s 14(1), 'knowledge that any acts or omissions did or did not, as a matter of law, involve negligence ... or breach of duty is irrelevant.' Hirst J's test requires the plaintiff to know all matters necessary to establish negligence or breach of duty even though he or she may not know the legal label attaching to those facts. That is much too high a test, contrary to both the letter and the clear intent of s 14 and, as Slade LJ said in *Wilkinson v Ancliff (BLT) Ltd* [1986] 3 All ER 427 at 438, [1986] 1 WLR 1352 at 1365, if it were right, certainty would never be achieved in cases such as the present.

In the present case Mr Bell for the plaintiff sought to rely on his successful submission in *Bentley's* case and submitted:

'In a case where the plaintiff's (lost) claim arises from injury suffered as the result of surgery, the act or omission alleged to constitute negligence or breach of duty of which the plaintiff must have (constructive) knowledge must be (can be compendiously described as) some act or omission which could adversely affect the safety of the operation or proper recovery from the operation, such as unreasonable interference with the nerve or failure reasonably to safeguard it from damage, or failure properly to investigate and/or repair the nerve lesion in time.'

It follows from what I have said about *Bentley's* case that I reject this submission.

He also submitted that, even if the plaintiff had consulted a solicitor by the end of February 1981, which was when the period of seven months after the date of her operation, to which the judge had referred, expired, there was no evidence upon which the judge would have been able to find that she would have been fixed by the necessary constructive notice before 19 August 1981. He set out in some detail the steps which would have to be taken, and suggested that the judge could not infer that they would be completed before 19 August 1981. The defendant's skeleton argument provides a conclusive answer to this submission:

'In any event it is absurd for the Plaintiff now to contend that the process of acquiring knowledge would have taken an interminable time—having regard to her pleaded case that she first instructed a solicitor, the defendant, on 14 June 1983 and was first advised by Mr Farringdon of the negligence on the 6th July 1983—a mere three weeks later. Against this factual background it is absurd to say that the defendant had an evidential burden which it failed to discharge or that the Judge reached conclusions which were not supported by the evidence.'

In the course of his argument Mr Fenwick QC for the defendant submitted that the knowledge of the plaintiff necessary for the purposes of s 14 could be considered under four heads.

(1) Broad knowledge. Carrying out the operation to her knee in such a way that something went wrong, namely that it caused foot drop (an injury to her foot). The judge's findings of fact set out above establishes that the plaintiff herself had this broad knowledge by February.

(2) Specific knowledge. Carrying out the operation in such a way as to
a damage a nerve thereby causing foot drop (an injury to her foot). The judge's
findings, which in my judgment are correct, establish that the plaintiff
constructively had specific knowledge by 19 August 1981.

(3) Qualitative knowledge. Carrying out the operation in such a way as
unreasonably to cause injury to a nerve (unreasonably to expose a nerve to a
b risk of injury).

(4) Detailed knowledge (which I take to be knowledge sufficiently detailed
to enable the plaintiff's advisers to draft a statement of claim). In my judgment
qualitative or detailed knowledge goes beyond the standard necessary for the
purposes of s 14 of the 1980 Act. The judge came to the right answer for the
right reasons. I would dismiss this appeal.

c

LEGGATT LJ. The plaintiff knew soon after the operation that something was
wrong with her foot which was not an inevitable consequence of the
operation. So she might reasonably have been expected to ask a doctor what
was wrong. If she had done so, she would have been told that the nerve must
d have been damaged in the operation in a way that was not inevitable. Mr Bell
QC concedes that if that is sufficient to satisfy the statute, the plaintiff's claim
must fail. He argues that the plaintiff's date of knowledge was not reached
until she knew of—

> *e* 'some act or omission which could adversely affect the safety of the
> operation or proper recovery from the operation, such as unreasonable
> interference with the nerve or failure reasonably to safeguard it from
> damage, or failure properly to investigate and/or repair the nerve lesion in
> time.'

The use of the words 'unreasonable', 'reasonably' and 'properly' would only
f be justified if s 14(1)(b) required knowledge that the injury was attributable to
negligence. It is plain from the concluding words of s 14(1) that 'knowledge
that any acts or omissions did or did not, as a matter of law, involve negligence'
is irrelevant. In my judgment the only function of the words 'which is alleged
to constitute negligence' is to point to the relevant act or omission to which the
injury was attributable. It follows that the judge was wrong in *Bentley v Bristol*
g *and Weston Health Authority* [1991] 2 Med LR 359 to hold that knowledge must
be proved of the mechanics of damage to a nerve, and Mr Bell's submission
about the need to establish fault similarly fails. The plaintiff constructively
had, by 19 August 1981, such specific knowledge of an act or omission which
might amount to negligence as would have enabled her to investigate it
h timeously.

For the reasons given by my brethren, whose judgments I have read in draft,
I indorse the judge's conclusion and agree that the appeal should be dismissed.

HOFFMANN LJ. This appeal is an attempt to reopen a question of policy
j which in my judgment was settled by Parliament in 1975. The Limitation Act
1980 was a consolidation Act and s 14 is derived from the Limitation Act 1975.
The latter was Parliament's second attempt to deal with the problem revealed
by *Cartledge v E Jopling & Sons Ltd* [1963] 1 All ER 341, [1963] AC 758, namely
that a cause of action for personal injury may accrue to someone who does not
realise that he has suffered an injury, let alone that he has a legal remedy. The
first attempt was the Limitation Act 1963. This provided that time should not

start to run until the plaintiff had knowledge of various specified matters. But
the drafting of that Act was confusing. In *Central Asbestos Co Ltd v Dodd* [1971]   *a*
3 All ER 204, [1972] 1 QB 244 some judges thought it meant that he should
know that he had a cause of action.   Others thought it was enough that he
knew that his injury had been caused by an act or omission of the defendant.
In the House of Lords, Lord Pearson adopted a middle course, which was to
require knowledge that the defendant had been 'at fault', though not   *b*
necessarily in breach of a legal duty (see [1972] 2 All ER 1135 at 1148, [1973] AC
518 at 541). The case left the law in confusion and the Law Reform Committee
was asked to look at the matter again. Its Twentieth Report (see *Interim Report
on Limitation of Actions: in Personal Injury Claims* (Cmnd 5630)) led to the
Limitation Act 1975.

Section 14(1) clearly rejects any need for the plaintiff to have known that he   *c*
had a cause of action. This is put beyond doubt by the concluding words
'knowledge that any acts or omission did or did not, as a matter of law, involve
negligence, nuisance or breach of duty is irrelevant'. But Mr Bell QC says that
the plaintiff must have known that the defendant's act or omission was capable
of being attributed to some *fault* on his part. This, he says, is the only way in   *d*
which one can give effect to the requirement that the actions or omissions
known to the plaintiff must be 'alleged to constitute negligence, nuisance or
breach of duty' without at the same time offending against the proviso that
knowledge of a cause of action is irrelevant. But, in my judgment, this is no
more than an attempt to revive the principle uniquely espoused by Lord
Pearson in the *Central Asbestos* case [1972] 2 All ER 1135, [1973] AC 518. There   *e*
is nothing in s 14(1) to suggest that Parliament intended to adopt such a
principle. Doing so would have been contrary to the recommendation of the
Law Reform Committee. It had declared itself initially attracted by Lord
Pearson's principle, but—

> 'when we came to contemplate its embodiment in an Act of Parliament,   *f*
> we were driven to reject it because of the difficulties, which we consider
> insuperable, of satisfactorily defining "fault" for this purpose. The
> concept of "fault", short of actionability, is, in our view, necessarily
> imprecise because it contains a considerable subjective element. If a
> concept is imprecise, any definition of it must (assuming that it is   *g*
> practicable at all) itself be imprecise. Yet, if one is aiming at a date of
> knowledge which leads to an extension of time **as of right**, that date must
> be precisely defined.' (See *Interim Report on Limitation of Actions*, para 54.)

I think Mr Fenwick QC was right when he said that the words 'which is
alleged to constitute negligence, nuisance or breach of duty' serve to *identify*   *h*
the facts of which the plaintiff must have knowledge without implying that he
should know that they constitute a breach of a rule, whether of law or some
other code of behaviour. Section 14(1)(b) requires that one should look at the
way the plaintiff puts his case, distil what he is complaining about and ask
whether he had, in broad terms, knowledge of the facts on which that
complaint is based.   *j*

It follows that in my judgment *Bentley v Bristol and Weston Health Authority*
[1991] 2 Med LR 359 was wrongly decided. Mrs Bentley knew in August 1981
that her injuries were attributable to damage caused to the sciatic nerve in the
course of a hip replacement operation. She knew soon afterwards that one
way in which nerves can be damaged in the course of an operation is when they

are retracted to keep them out of the way while the surgeon is working on the hip joint. What she did not know until within the limitation period was that the retraction in her case might have been *excessive*. In holding that until then Mrs Bentley did not have sufficient knowledge for the purposes of s 14(1), Hirst J was in my judgment requiring knowledge that the surgeon had fallen short of some standard of care, whether imposed by law or professional practice. This is not required by the 1980 Act.

The other cases upon which Mr Bell relied do not support the principle for which he contended. In *Stephen v Riverside Health Authority* [1990] 1 Med LR 261 the plaintiff did not know until eight years after her treatment that it could have caused her symptoms. The case would have been different if she had known from the start that the symptoms were attributable to the treatment but thought that they were normal side-effects rather than indicative of negligence or fault. In *Driscoll-Varley v Parkside Health Authority* [1991] 2 Med LR 346 the plaintiff thought that the complications from which she suffered had been caused by the way an operation on her leg had been done. Only later did she discover that the real cause was not the operation but the subsequent removal of her leg from traction. This case is concerned with identification of the act which caused the injury and not with appreciation of whether that act was capable of being attributable to negligence or fault.

In this case the plaintiff knew, or could have known with the help of the medical advice reasonably obtainable, that her injury had been caused by damage to the nerve resulting from something which Mr Lowy had done or not done in the course of the operation. In my judgment this was all the knowledge or imputed knowledge which she needed to have. In *Nash v Eli Lilly & Co* [1993] 4 All ER 383 at 398, [1993] 1 WLR 782 at 799 this court said:

> 'It was not, in our judgment, the intention of Parliament to require for the purposes of s 11 and s 14 of the Act proof of knowledge of the terms in which it will be alleged that the act or omission of the defendants constituted negligence or breach of duty. What is required is knowledge of the essence of the act or omission to which the injury is attributable.'

How does one determine the 'essence' of the act or omission? The purpose of s 14(1), as Lord Donaldson MR pointed out in *Halford v Brookes* [1991] 3 All ER 559 at 573, [1991] 1 WLR 428 at 443, is to determine the moment at which the plaintiff knows enough to make it reasonable for him to *begin* to investigate whether or not he has a case against the defendant. He then has three years in which to conduct his inquiries and, if advised that he has a cause of action, prepare and issue his writ. Ordinarily it will suffice that he knows that the injury was caused by an act or omission of the defendant. But there may be cases in which his knowledge of what the defendant did or did not do is so vague and general that he cannot fairly be expected to know what he should investigate. He will also not have reached the starting point if, in an unusual case like *Driscoll-Varley v Parkside Health Authority*, he thinks he knows the acts and omissions he should investigate but in fact he is barking up the wrong tree. In this case, however, it seems to me clear that the essence of Mrs Broadley's complaint is that her nerve was damaged in the course of the operation. She was asked by way of further and better particulars: 'Please fully particularise the Plaintiff's alleged claim for medical negligence.' This was her answer:

'In the course of an operation on the 13th of August 1980 to remove a loose body from the plaintiff's left knee surgeons in the employment of the said Health Authority negligently divided and/or damaged the left lateral popliteal nerve. Thereafter no, or no adequate measures were taken to repair the nerve such that, by early 1981, the said damage became irreparable.'

No doubt in proceedings against the health authority, the pleading would have been more elaborate. But this is the plaintiff's own distillation of her complaint and it seems to me that stripped of the word 'negligently', it contains nothing which, within a few months of the operation, was not known to her or could have been ascertained from any doctor whom she chose to consult. This was quite enough to make it reasonable for her to commence an investigation into whether or not the acts in question gave rise to a cause of action. I therefore think that the judge came to the right conclusion and that the appeal should be dismissed.

Appeal dismissed. Leave to appeal to the House of Lords refused.

Carolyn Toulmin   Barrister.

Dobbie v Medway Health Authority

COURT OF APPEAL, CIVIL DIVISION

SIR THOMAS BINGHAM MR, BELDAM AND STEYN LJJ

26, 27 APRIL, 11 MAY 1994

Limitation of action – Personal injury claim – Plaintiff's knowledge – Date of plaintiff's knowledge that injury was significant – Discretion to disapply limitation period – Plaintiff failing to issue writ within three-year limitation period – Time running from when plaintiff had knowledge that injury was attributable to act or omission of defendant – Whether plaintiff should know that act or omission tortious – Whether court should exercise discretion to allow action to proceed – Limitation Act 1980, ss 11(4)(b), 14(1), 33.

In April 1973 the plaintiff was admitted to hospital for the removal of a lump in her breast. During the operation, the surgeon considered the lump to be cancerous and performed a mastectomy. Subsequent microscopic analysis showed that the growth was benign. The plaintiff was devastated by the effect of the mastectomy and suffered consequent psychological illness, but she accepted the view of the surgeon that she was fortunate that the growth had not proved to be malignant. In May 1988 the plaintiff heard of a similar case in which a surgeon had been held to have been negligent in removing a breast and appreciated, for the first time, that her breast need not have been removed until the lump had been microscopically examined and found to be malignant. On 5 May 1989 the plaintiff issued proceedings against the defendant health authority, claiming damages in respect of the negligent performance of the operation in 1973. In its defence, the health authority contended that the plaintiff's claim had arisen more than three years before the issue of proceedings and that her cause of action was accordingly time-barred under ss 11(4)(b)[a] and 14(1)[b] of the Limitation Act 1980, which provided that the time limit for actions for personal injuries was three years from the date of knowledge of the person injured, which was defined as the date on which the plaintiff first had knowledge (a) that the injury was significant and (b) that it was attributable in whole or in part to the act or omission which was alleged to constitute negligence. The judge held that the plaintiff's cause of action was statute-barred and declined to exercise his discretion to disapply the three-year limitation period under s 33[c] of the 1980 Act. The plaintiff appealed, contending (i) that until 1988, when she had first known that excision of the lump for microscopic analysis could and should have preceded removal of her breast, she had lacked the requisite knowledge of the crucial act or omission of the surgeon on which her claim was founded and (ii) that knowledge of injury meant knowledge that something had happened which was not an ordinary, normal result of surgery and that something had gone wrong.

Held – (1) Time started to run against a claimant for the purposes of s 14(1) of the 1980 Act when he knew that the injury on which he founded his claim was capable of being attributed to the act or omission of the defendant he wished to sue, irrespective of whether, at that point, he knew that the act or omission was actionable or tortious. It followed that the plaintiff's cause of action was statute-barred under the 1980 Act, since it was clear that she knew within the primary limitation period that she had suffered a significant injury which was attributable to the defendant health authority's act or omission, even though she had not appreciated until after that three-year period that such conduct might be actionable (see p 455 j to p 456 f, p 457 g h, p 458 b c, p 459 b to d, p 461 d e, p 462 a b d, p 463 f g and p 464 b, post); *Nash v Eli Lilly & Co* [1993] 4 All ER 383 and *Broadley v Guy Clapham & Co* [1994] 4 All ER 439 considered.

(2) The court would not however exercise its discretion under s 33 of the 1980 Act to disapply the limitation period, having regard to the lengthy delay after the date of actual knowledge and the fact that the plaintiff could have taken advice and issued proceedings years before she did and that it would now be inequitable to require the health authority to face a claim arising out of events which took place so long ago. The plaintiff's appeal would accordingly be dismissed (see p 460 c d, p 462 b to d and p 464 c, post).

Notes

For limitation period in personal injury actions and the plaintiff's knowledge in relation to limitation of actions, see 28 *Halsbury's Laws* (4th edn) paras 691–692.

For the court's power to override the limitation period in personal injury actions, see ibid para 694, and for cases on the subject, see 32(2) *Digest* (2nd reissue) 461–469, 3443–3458.

For the Limitation Act 1980, ss 11, 14, 33, see 24 *Halsbury's Statutes* (4th edn) (1989 reissue) 657, 661, 686.

Cases referred to in judgments

Bentley v Bristol and Weston Health Authority [1991] 2 Med LR 359, DC.

---

a   Section 11(4)(b) is set out at p 455 b c, post
b   Section 14(1), so far as material, is set out at p 455 c d, post
c   Section 33, so far as material, is set out at p 459 f to j, post

Biss v Lambeth, Southwark and Lewisham Health Authority [1978] 2 All ER 125, [1978] 1 WLR 382, CA.

Broadley v Guy Clapham & Co [1994] 4 All ER 439, CA.

Cartledge v E Jopling & Sons Ltd [1963] 1 All ER 341, [1963] AC 758, [1963] 2 WLR 210, HL; *affg* [1961] 3 All ER 482, [1962] 1 QB 189, [1961] 3 WLR 838, CA.

Central Asbestos Co Ltd v Dodd [1972] 2 All ER 1135, [1973] AC 518, [1972] 3 WLR 333, HL.

Davis v Ministry of Defence (1985) Times, 7 August, [1985] CA Transcript 413.

Halford v Brookes [1991] 3 All ER 559, [1991] 1 WLR 428, CA.

Nash v Eli Lilly & Co [1993] 4 All ER 383, [1993] 1 WLR 782, CA; *rvsg in part* [1991] 2 Med LR 169.

Stephen v Riverside Health Authority [1990] 1 Med LR 261.

Stubbings v Webb [1993] 1 All ER 322, [1993] AC 498, [1993] 2 WLR 120, HL.

Wilkinson v Ancliff (BLT) Ltd [1986] 3 All ER 427, [1986] 1 WLR 1352, CA.

Cases also cited or referred to in skeleton arguments

Davis v City and Hackney Health Authority [1991] 2 Med LR 366.

Driscoll-Varley v Parkside Health Authority [1991] 2 Med LR 346.

Hendy v Milton Keynes Health Authority [1992] 3 Med LR 114.

Ramsden v Lee [1992] 2 All ER 204, CA.

Appeal

The plaintiff, Margaret Neil Dobbie, appealed from the order of Otton J made on 14 February 1992 whereby he ordered that her claim against the defendant, Medway Health Authority, be dismissed on the grounds that the plaintiff's cause of action was time-barred by virtue of ss 11 and 14 of the Limitation Act 1980 and that it would not be equitable to allow the action to proceed under s 33 of that Act. The facts are set out in the judgment of Sir Thomas Bingham MR.

James Badenoch QC and *Neil Sanders* (instructed by *Thomson Snell & Passmore*, Tunbridge Wells) for the plaintiff.
Michael Douglas (instructed by *Brachers*, Maidstone) for the health authority.

Cur adv vult

11 May 1994. The following judgments were delivered.

SIR THOMAS BINGHAM MR. The plaintiff, Margaret Neil Dobbie, issued her writ in this action on 5 May 1989 and amended it on 10 May. In the amended writ and in her statement of claim served in October 1990 she claimed damages for personal injury arising from the negligent performance of an operation on 27 April 1973. The defendant health authority, the Medway Health Authority, was sued as the employer of the consultant surgeon who performed the operation.

In its defence, the health authority pleaded that the plaintiff's claim arose more than three years before issue of proceedings and that her cause of action was accordingly statute-barred. Reliance was placed on ss 11 and 14 of the Limitation Act 1980.

The plaintiff in her reply denied that her action was statute-barred, but if it was she asked the court to exercise its discretion in her favour under s 33 of the Act.

In August 1991 these limitation issues were ordered to be tried as preliminary issues. They were so heard, and on 14 February 1992 Otton J determined both issues against the plaintiff, holding that her cause of action was statute-barred and declining to exercise his discretion in her favour under s 33.

The plaintiff appeals against both these rulings.

The facts

The facts were fully and carefully summarised by Otton J in his judgment. It is unnecessary for present purposes to give more than a brief outline.

In 1972 the plaintiff felt a lump in her left breast. She consulted her general practitioner and was eventually referred to a consultant surgeon who examined her and found a lump in the breast. He advised that she should have the lump excised. She was admitted to Sheppey General Hospital on 26 April 1973 to have the lump removed, with a view to its being the subject of diagnostic examination. There was an issue whether the plaintiff consented to anything more than the removal of the lump, namely whether she also consented to mastectomy if the surgeon considered it necessary, but the judge assumed that her consent was limited to removal of the lump.

At the operation on 27 April 1973 the consultant excised the lump, which appeared to him to be cancerous, and he proceeded to perform a simple left mastectomy. After the operation, the lump was sent for microscopic examination and found to be benign. The hospital authority admits that the lump was not examined microscopically before the breast was removed. Facilities for making such examination were not at the time available at the Sheppey General Hospital, but they were available at another hospital in Chatham.

The plaintiff had not expected her operation to involve more than removal of the lump, or such tissue as was needed for microscopic examination. When she came round from the anaesthetic she was horrified to find that the whole of her left breast had been removed. But she had no reason then to question the surgeon's judgment. When she learned the result of the microscopic examination she accepted the view of the surgeon and a nurse that she was very fortunate that the growth had not proved to be malignant.

The judge found, on very clear evidence, that the effect on the plaintiff of losing her breast had been 'devastating'. She had as a result suffered severe psychological illness, which had in turn affected her physical health and blighted her enjoyment of life.

In May 1988 the plaintiff's daughter told her of a radio programme describing a case similar to hers in which a court had held that the surgeon had been negligent in removing the breast. An article on the front page of the *Sunday Times* for 15 May 1988 reported the case. The plaintiff made contact with the radio station and, through it, with an organisation representing the victims of medical accidents. In due course she consulted solicitors, who issued a writ (as already recorded) on 5 May 1989. In February 1990 a consultant surgeon of high standing advised the plaintiff that the breast should not have been removed until the lump had been excised and examined and found to be malignant. Based on this report, counsel drafted the plaintiff's statement of claim. Although the particulars of negligence were pleaded in a number of subparagraphs, the essential thrust of the case was that the breast should not have been removed until the lump had been microscopically examined and found to be malignant.

Limitation

The ordinary rule is that time begins to run against a claimant when a common law cause of action arises, and the cause of action becomes unenforceable if proceedings have not been started before expiry of a period of years prescribed by statute. This rule may have the harsh effect of defeating what would otherwise be unanswerable claims. But such rules have existed for centuries. They are no doubt designed in part to encourage potential claimants to prosecute their claims with reasonable expedition on pain of being unable to prosecute them at all. But they are also based on the belief that a time comes when, for better or worse, defendants should be effectively relieved from the risk of having to resist stale claims.

To this ordinary rule there are of course exceptions. The exception relevant for present purposes affects personal injury claimants. The need for an exception became clear when it was found that employees disabled by industrial disease did not know (and could not have known) that they suffered from the disease, still less that it was caused by their employers' process, until well after the three-year limitation period for personal injuries had expired.

Statutory attempts to mitigate this problem did not prove satisfactory and in 1971 the Law Reform Committee were invited to reconsider the question. In its Twentieth Report (see *Interim Report on Limitation of Actions: in Personal Injury Claims* (Cmnd 5630)) the committee reviewed the previous history and certain suggested solutions. The committee accepted that time should not begin to run before a claimant had knowledge (actual or constructive) both of his injured condition and of its having been caused by an act or omission of the defendant, but was concerned to decide whether the date of knowledge should arrive (1) on the plaintiff acquiring knowledge of those facts; or (2) on his acquiring knowledge of those facts and also that he has a worthwhile cause of action against the defendant; or (3) at some intermediate point between these states of knowledge, as for example on his becoming aware, in the words of Lord Pearson—

'(as a matter of fact in the same manner as a jury would decide) that the defendants were at fault and that his injuries were attributable to their fault.' (See *Central Asbestos Co Ltd v Dodd* [1972] 2 All ER 1135 at 1151, [1993] AC 518 at 545.)

For reasons given in the report, the committee rejected (2). The committee also rejected (3), taking the view that if there was to be an extension of time from the date of knowledge as of right such date must be capable of precise definition and that the concept of fault lacked the necessary precision. The committee accordingly favoured (1). But it recognised that this test could cause hardship to prospective plaintiffs in a small number of cases, and advised that there should be a residual discretion in the court to extend time even when action had not been brought within three years of the date of knowledge as defined in (1). These recommendations were accepted: they found substantial expression in the Limitation Act 1975, and were in due course consolidated in the Limitation Act 1980.

The 1980 Act, ss 11 and 14

These sections provide (so far as relevant to the present appeal) as follows:

'**11.** *Special time limit for actions in respect of personal injuries.*—(1) This section applies to any action for damages for negligence, nuisance or breach of duty (whether the duty exists by virtue of a contract or of provision made by or under a statute or independently of any contract or any such provision) where the damages claimed by the plaintiff for the negligence, nuisance or breach of duty consist of or include damages in respect of personal injuries to the plaintiff or any other person ...

(3) An action to which this section applies shall not be brought after the expiration of the period applicable in accordance with subsection (4) or (5) below.

(4) Except where subsection (5) below applies, the period applicable is three years from—(a) the date on which the cause of action accrued; or (b) the date of knowledge (if later) of the person injured ...

14. *Definition of date of knowledge for purposes of sections 11 and 12.*—(1) ... in sections 11 and 12 of this Act references to a person's date of knowledge are references to the date on which he first had knowledge of the following facts—(a) that the injury in question was significant; and (b) that the injury was attributable in whole or in part to the act or omission which is alleged to constitute negligence, nuisance or breach of duty; and ... knowledge that any acts or omissions did or did not, as a matter of law, involve negligence, nuisance or breach of duty is irrelevant.

(2) For the purposes of this section an injury is significant if the person whose date of knowledge is in question would reasonably have considered it sufficiently serious to justify his instituting proceedings for damages against a defendant who did not dispute liability and was able to satisfy a judgment.

(3) For the purposes of this section a person's knowledge includes knowledge which he might reasonably have been expected to acquire—(a) from facts observable or ascertainable by him; or (b) from facts ascertainable by him with the help of medical or other appropriate expert advice which it is reasonable for him to seek; but a person shall not be fixed under this subsection with knowledge of a fact ascertainable only with the help of expert advice so long as he has taken all reasonable steps to obtain (and, where appropriate, to act on) that advice.'

This special limitation regime applies to claims (such as the present) based in negligence for damages for personal injuries. It plainly modifies the ordinary rule (expressed in s 11(4)(a)) that time runs from the accrual of the cause of action.

The effect of ss 11(4)(b) and 14(1)(a) is to postpone the running of time until the claimant has knowledge of the personal injury on which he seeks to found his claim. That is 'the injury in question'. The word 'knowledge' should be given its natural meaning (see *Davis v Ministry of Defence* (1985) Times, 7 August). As Lord Donaldson of Lymington MR said in *Halford v Brookes* [1991] 3 All ER 559 at 573, [1991] 1 WLR 428 at 443:

'In this context "knowledge" clearly does not mean "know for certain and beyond possibility of contradiction". It does, however, mean "know with sufficient confidence to justify embarking on the preliminaries to the issue of a writ, such as submitting a claim to the proposed defendant, taking legal and other advice and collecting evidence".'

This test is not in my judgment hard to apply. It involves ascertaining the personal injury on which the claim is founded and asking when the claimant knew of it. In the case of an insidious disease or a delayed result of a surgical mishap, this knowledge may come well after the suffering of the disease or the performance of the surgery. But, more usually, the claimant knows that he has suffered personal injury as soon or almost as soon as he does so.

Time does not begin to run against a claimant until he knows that the personal injury on which he founds his claim is significant within the definition in s 14(2). That gives rise to no issue in this appeal.

The effect of ss 11(4)(b) and 14(1)(b) is to postpone the running of time until the claimant has knowledge that the personal injury on which he founds his claim was wholly or partly attributable to the act or omission of the defendant on which his claim in negligence is founded. 'Attributable to' was construed by May LJ in *Davis v Ministry of Defence* to mean 'capable of being attributed to' and not 'caused by', and I see no reason to question that conclusion. It cannot plausibly be suggested that the words 'act or omission' import any requirement that such act or omission should be actionable or tortious, since that would stultify the closing words of s 14(1) and would moreover flout the recommendation on which the legislation was admittedly founded. In *Wilkinson v Ancliff (BLT) Ltd* [1986] 3 All ER 427 at 436, [1986] 1 WLR 1352 at 1362 reference was made to a submission of counsel based on the use of the words 'act or omission' rather than 'conduct' in s 14(1)(b). I do not understand the court to have accepted that submission. But it is customary in discussing tortious liability to refer to acts and omissions, and I do not think the meaning of s 14(1)(b) would be any different had the reference been to conduct. Time starts to run against the claimant when he knows that the personal injury on which he founds his claim is capable of being attributed to something done or not done by the defendant whom he wishes to sue. This condition is not satisfied where a man knows that he has a disabling cough or shortness of breath but does not know that his injured condition has anything to do with his working conditions. It is satisfied when he knows that his injured condition is capable of being attributed to his working conditions, even though he has no inkling that his employer may have been at fault.

Authority on ss 11 and 14

Reference should be made to two recent decisions of this court in which these sections have been considered.

The first case was *Nash v Eli Lilly & Co* [1993] 4 All ER 383, [1993] 1 WLR 782. In that case a number of plaintiffs claimed damages based on side-effects suffered as a result of taking the drug Opren. Under the heading 'Significant injury' the court accepted as valid a distinction between an expected, or accepted, side-effect and an injurious and unacceptable consequence of taking a drug (see [1993] 4 All ER 383 at 391, [1993] 1 WLR 782 at 791). In considering attributability, the court held ([1993] 4 All ER 383 at 398, [1993] 1 WLR 782 at 799):

> 'It was not, in our judgment, the intention of Parliament to require for the purposes of s 11 and s 14 of the Act proof of knowledge of the terms in which it will be alleged that the act or omission of the defendants constituted negligence or breach of duty. What is required is knowledge of the essence of the act or omission to which the injury is attributable.'

In *Broadley v Guy Clapham & Co* [1994] 4 All ER 439 the plaintiff suffered nerve palsy in her left leg, resulting in foot drop, following an operation on her knee. Balcombe LJ held that the plaintiff's claim was statute-barred because she had, more than the prescribed period before the issue of proceedings, known that the operation had been carried out in such a way that something had gone wrong, causing injury to her foot, or alternatively that the operation had been carried out in such a way as to damage a nerve, thereby causing foot drop. Leggatt LJ, agreeing with Balcombe and Hoffmann LJJ, held that the plaintiff had, on the facts, had constructive knowledge since she had had such specific knowledge, soon after the operation, of an act or omission which might amount to negligence as would have enabled her to investigate it timeously. He said (at 447):

> 'It is plain from the concluding words of s 14(1) that "knowledge that any acts or omissions did or did not, as a matter of law, involve negligence" is irrelevant. In my judgment the only function of the words "which is alleged to constitute negligence" is to point to the relevant act or omission to which the injury was attributable.'

Hoffmann LJ rejected a submission that the plaintiff must know that the defendant's act or omission was capable of being attributed to some fault on his part, and said (at 448):

> 'I think [counsel] was right when he said that the words "which is alleged to constitute negligence, nuisance or breach of duty" serve to *identify* the facts of which the plaintiff must have knowledge without implying that he should know that they constitute a breach of a rule, whether of law or some other code of behaviour. Section 14(1)(b) requires that one should look at the way the plaintiff puts his case, distil what he is complaining about and ask whether he had, in broad terms, knowledge of the facts on which that complaint is based.' (Hoffmann LJ's emphasis.)

These decisions are, I think, consistent with and supportive of the construction of the statutory language set out above, subject to one possible qualification. The requirement that the injury of which a plaintiff has knowledge should be 'significant' is, in my view, directed solely to the quantum of the injury and not to the plaintiff's evaluation of its cause, nature or usualness. Time does not run against a plaintiff, even if he is aware of the injury, if he would reasonably have considered it insufficiently serious to justify proceedings against an acquiescent and creditworthy defendant, if (in other words) he would reasonably have accepted it as a fact of life or not worth bothering about. It is otherwise if the injury is reasonably to be considered as sufficiently serious within the statutory definition: time then runs (subject to the requirement of attributability) even if the plaintiff believes the injury to be normal or properly caused.

In some of the cases judges have used language suggesting that knowledge of fault is needed to start time running. For instance, in *Stephen v Riverside Health Authority* [1990] 1 Med LR 261 at 267, Auld J said:

> '... the question that I have to answer is, "When did she first know that the erythema moist spots etcetera, were capable of being attributed to *excessive* exposure to radiation caused by an *improperly conducted* mammography?"' (My emphasis.)

In *Bentley v Bristol and Weston Health Authority* [1991] 2 Med LR 359 at 364, which was disapproved in *Broadley v Guy Clapham & Co*, Hirst J held that there had to be knowledge of some conduct or failure which could affect the safety of the operation. In *Nash v Eli Lilly & Co* [1991] 2 Med LR 169 at 183 Hidden J described the act or omission complained of as—

> 'providing the plaintiff with a drug which was unsafe in that it caused persistent photosensitivity and *failing to take reasonable and proper steps to protect the plaintiff* from such a condition or consequence.' (My emphasis.)

The situation is complicated when, as often happens, the plaintiff learns of the defendant's act or omission and of the criticism that it was negligent at the same time. But it is necessary to emphasise that knowledge of fault or negligence is not needed to start time running.

The present case: ss 11 and 14

The plaintiff knew when she came round from the anaesthetic that her breast had been removed and she learned very shortly afterwards that the lump which the surgeon had operated to excise had been found to be benign. But she was led to believe (distressed though she was) that the practice followed had been usual and proper, and indeed that she had in the circumstances every reason to count herself fortunate. Not until 1988 (at the earliest) did she know that excision of the lump for microscopic examination could and should have preceded removal of the breast. It was accordingly urged on her behalf that until then she lacked the requisite knowledge, since she lacked knowledge of the crucial act or omission of the surgeon on which her claim against the health authority in negligence is founded. Knowledge of injury in this context means knowledge that something has happened which is not an ordinary, normal result of surgery. There must be knowledge that something has gone wrong. The plaintiff did not gain that knowledge, it was said, until 1988 or even 1990.

Otton J rejected this argument. On her evidence he was entitled to conclude that the plaintiff knew within three years of the operation: (1) that she had been admitted for excision of a lump only; (2) that her left breast had been removed; (3) that the lump when examined had not been malignant but benign; (4) that the decision to remove the breast had been taken before any microscopic test had been carried out; (5) that there had been no facilities for microscopic examination at Sheppey Hospital; (6) that she had not given her consent to the removal of her breast; and (7) that the removal of her breast had caused her acute and prolonged anger, distress and psychological damage as well as physical damage.

Echoing the language of some of the cases, the judge held:

> 'In my judgment, she had broad knowledge of sufficient facts to describe compendiously that her breast had been unnecessarily removed, that something had gone wrong and that this was due to the defendants' negligence and further (or in the alternative) that it had been removed without her consent. Even though she might not have had the knowledge to enable her counsel to draft a fully and comprehensively particularised statement of claim, in my view she had knowledge of the nature referred to in s 14(1)(b) sufficient to set time running against her both in negligence and trespass.'

The judge's reasoning is in my view open to criticism in two respects. (1) He was wrong to refer to the breast being 'unnecessarily' removed, to something going wrong and to the health authority's negligence. These matters were on a correct construction of s 14 irrelevant. (2) Section 11 does not apply to actions in trespass, for which no extension of time is in law permissible (see *Stubbings v Webb* [1993] 1 All ER 322, [1993] AC 498). The judge directed himself in accordance with authority as it stood when he gave judgment, and it was not until later that the House of Lords' decision altered the law.

But I am in complete agreement with the judge's conclusion. The personal injury on which the plaintiff seeks to found her claim is the removal of her breast and the psychological and physical harm which followed. She knew of this injury within hours, days or months of the operation and she, at all times, reasonably considered it to be significant. She knew from the beginning that this personal injury was capable of being attributed to, or more bluntly was the clear and direct result of, an act or omission of the health authority. What she did not appreciate until later was that the health authority's act or omission was (arguably) negligent or blameworthy. But her want of that knowledge did not stop time beginning to run.

The judge was right to hold that the plaintiff's claim was statute-barred and I would dismiss the appeal against that finding.

Constructive knowledge: s 14(3)

Since the judge held the plaintiff to have had actual knowledge he held it strictly unnecessary to consider whether she had constructive knowledge. But in case his primary conclusion was displaced, he considered this question and gave reasons for concluding that she had. I do not in any way dissent from these reasons, but since I share his primary conclusion I need not explore this aspect.

The exercise of discretion: s 33

Section 33 provides, so far as material, as follows:

'(1) If it appears to the court that it would be equitable to allow an action to proceed having regard to the degree to which—(a) the provisions of section 11 or 12 of this Act prejudice the plaintiff or any person whom he represents; and (b) any decision of the court under this subsection would prejudice the defendant or any person whom he represents; the court may direct that those provisions shall not apply to the action, or shall not apply to any specified cause of action to which the action relates ...

(3) In acting under this section the court shall have regard to all the circumstances of the case and in particular to—(a) the length of, and the reasons for, the delay on the part of the plaintiff; (b) the extent to which, having regard to the delay, the evidence adduced or likely to be adduced by the plaintiff or the defendant is or is likely to be less cogent than if the action had been brought within the time allowed by section 11 ... or (as the case may be) by section 12; (c) the conduct of the defendant after the cause of action arose, including the extent (if any) to which he responded to requests reasonably made by the plaintiff for information or inspection for the purpose of ascertaining facts which were or might be relevant to the plaintiff's cause of action against the defendant; (d) the duration of any disability of the plaintiff arising after the date of the accrual of the cause of action; (e) the extent to which the plaintiff acted promptly and reasonably once he knew whether or not the act or omission of the defendant, to which the injury was attributable, might be capable at that time of giving rise to an action for damages; (f) the steps, if any, taken by the plaintiff to obtain medical, legal or other expert advice and the nature of any such advice he may have received.'

In reliance on these provisions it was argued that the court's discretion should be exercised in the plaintiff's favour. The delay in bringing proceedings was caused by her belief, fostered by the health authority, that she had been properly treated. Most of the salient facts were not in dispute and most of the evidence was documentary. The case could be tried without prejudice to the health authority despite the lapse of time.

The judge did not consider it equitable to allow the action to proceed. He held that the evidence would be less cogent than if the action had been brought timeously, that the health authority would be prejudiced on the issue of consent, that the plaintiff should reasonably have taken advice sooner and that the time had come when the surgeon should not have to meet this complaint.

I approach this aspect on the basis that the plaintiff is a grievously injured woman who has suffered much and whose claim, if allowed to proceed, might prove to be very strong. But the delay in this case, after the date of actual knowledge, is very lengthy indeed. The plaintiff could have taken advice and issued proceedings years before she did. Sympathetic though anyone reading these papers must be to the plaintiff, it would in my judgment (as in that of the judge) be unfair to require the health authority to face this claim arising out of events which took place so long ago.

I would dismiss the appeal on this ground also.

BELDAM LJ. For many years, as Sir Thomas Bingham MR has pointed out, a plaintiff has been required by statute to commence proceedings before the expiry of a specified period from the date his cause of action accrued. In some circumstances courts of equity provided relief from the strict application of the rule by providing that time did not begin to run until the cause of action was or should have been discovered. So, for example, where his right of action was concealed by equitable fraud or where his action was for relief from the consequences of a mistake, the period of limitation did not begin to run until the plaintiff had discovered the fraud, concealment or mistake or could with reasonable diligence have discovered it (see the Limitation Act 1939, as amended by the Limitation Amendment Act 1980).

By 1963 it had become apparent that in actions for personal injury circumstances could occur which made it equally unfair to hold a plaintiff to the normal period of limitation. The injustice of an inflexible period was demonstrated by *Cartledge v E Jopling & Sons Ltd* [1963] 1 All ER 341, [1963] AC 758. Due to the acts or omissions of the defendant, the plaintiffs contracted an insidious disease which was symptomless until after the period of limitation had expired. Then catastrophic symptoms developed for which they had no remedy. Other circumstances causing injustice appeared. The plaintiff suffered symptoms within the period of limitation but did not know that they were attributable to any act or omission on the part of the defendant. Only after the expiry of the period did he become aware that acts or omissions of the defendant were responsible. This might be because until then medical science had not known that the symptoms could be caused by such acts or omissions; or the plaintiff might have sought medical advice but it was only later when the symptoms had become more serious that the necessary investigations were carried out which indicated that they were attributable to an act or omission of the defendant. In yet a further type of case the plaintiff may have suffered a trivial injury without any consequences of note as a result of an act or omission of the defendant. Some years later when the period of limitation had expired the injury gave rise to far more serious consequences. These problems led to the passing of the Limitation Act 1963 and to the provisions of the Limitation Act 1980 which apply in this case.

Mr James Badenoch QC for the plaintiff has sought to bring himself within the provisions of ss 11 and 14 of the 1980 Act. Section 11 introduces a special time limit for actions in which the damages claimed for negligence, nuisance or breach of duty consist of or include damages 'in respect of personal injuries to the plaintiff ...' Personal injuries are defined in s 38 so that unless the context otherwise requires:

"'personal injuries" includes any disease and any impairment of a person's physical or mental condition, and "injury" and cognate expressions shall be construed accordingly.'

The date of knowledge referred to in s 11(4)(b) refers to the date on which he first had knowledge of the following facts: (a) that the injury in question was significant; and (b) that the injury was attributable in whole or in part to the act or omission which is alleged to constitute negligence, nuisance or breach of duty. In the present case I agree with Sir Thomas Bingham MR that the injury in respect of which the plaintiff claims damages is the loss of her left breast and the severe psychological symptoms which followed. The act or omission of the defendant on which she relies is the act of the surgeon in removing the breast and the omission to carry out a test before doing so which would have indicated that the removal of her breast was unnecessary.

Thus the plaintiff had actual knowledge as required by s 14 within a few days of the operation being performed. In an attempt to escape from the conclusion that the plaintiff's claim is thus statute-barred, Mr Badenoch has advanced arguments based upon an interpretation of the word 'injury' and of the words 'act or omission' which he contends the court should apply by analogy with the interpretation put upon the words in other cases and in particular *Nash v Eli Lilly & Co* [1993] 4 All ER 383, [1993] 1 WLR 782 and *Broadley v Guy Clapham & Co* [1994] 4 All ER 439. His first argument is that the word 'injury' in a case such as the plaintiff's must be given an interpretation which enables the court to distinguish between the normal or expected consequences of successful medical treatment and the consequences of faulty treatment. The man in the street, he argued, would not regard himself as 'injured' by a successful operation. He would only regard himself as injured if he suffered consequences other than those normally to be attributed to the treatment.

I do not believe that the definition in s 38(1) is capable of the expansion which Mr Badenoch seeks to give it.

The interpretation of 'personal injuries' in s 38(1), though plainly not exhaustive, does indicate that 'injury' cannot be qualified by the addition of words implying its source or aetiology. Nor is there any need to import the perception of the reasonable patient.

The patient instanced by Mr Badenoch whose surgeon operates to remove the cause of the patient's symptoms but fails to do so will suffer 'injury' because he will continue to suffer from the symptoms, his health will be impaired and he will need further operative treatment. Whilst he may not know that he has suffered this injury as quickly as a patient whose breast is removed when it need not have been, nevertheless it will not be long before the patient is aware that he has derived no benefit from the operation.

Nor is there any need in such a case to place a strained interpretation on the word 'injury'. Time does not begin to run against such a patient until he knows that it is attributable to an act or omission of the defendant.

Mr Badenoch's arguments do not convince me that the words of ss 11 and 14 create any difficulty. I agree with Sir Thomas Bingham MR that in so far as it has been suggested that the judgments in some cases imply that the plaintiff must have some indication of fault or error in his treatment before he is aware that he has suffered injury, such a requirement is inconsistent with the clear words of s 14.

I also agree that, in the circumstances of this case, the judge was right in the exercise of his discretion not to disapply the provisions of s 11 having regard to the length of time which had elapsed. However I cannot agree with the judge that it is appropriate to take into account the factor which he took from the judgment of Lord Denning MR in *Biss v Lambeth, Southwark and Lewisham Health Authority* [1978] 2 All ER 125, [1978] 1 WLR 382 that there had been prejudice because the action had been hanging over the head of the attendant doctor for so many years. I do not see how such a consideration can apply to a doctor who does not know that any action is contemplated against him.

For these reasons, I agree that the appeal should be dismissed.

STEYN LJ. I agree with everything that Sir Thomas Bingham MR and Beldam LJ have said. I add only a few words of my own.

In the writ, which was issued on 5 May 1989, Mrs Dobbie claimed damages against the Medway Health Authority on the basis of the removal of her left breast on 27 April 1973. Her cause of action accrued on the very day of the operation. Subject to Mrs Dobbie's date of knowledge as defined in the Limitation Act 1980, her claim became statute-barred three years later.

That brings me to s 14(1) of the 1980 Act. That provision defines 'the date of knowledge'. It is the date on which the injured person first had knowledge of four 'facts'. The provision is in conjunctive terms: it requires knowledge of all four facts. On the other hand, it is also exhaustive: no knowledge of any further facts is required. The four facts identified in s 1 are mirrored by the 'facts' referred to in s 14(3), which deals with constructive knowledge. In this case it is unnecessary to consider s 14(3) further.

The first fact mentioned in s 14(1) is that the injury in question was 'significant' in the sense given to that word in s 14(2). The injury in question must mean in this case the removal of Mrs Dobbie's left breast. It was undoubtedly a significant injury. That fact was known to Mrs Dobbie in April 1973. The second indispensable fact under s 14(1) is defined as follows:

'(b) that the injury *was* attributable in whole or in part to the act or omission which *is* alleged to constitute negligence, nuisance or breach of duty ...' (My emphasis.)

Again, the application of these words cause no difficulty in this case. Attributability does not mean legal responsibility. It can only refer to causation. It *is* alleged in the action that the surgeon was negligent in removing Mrs Dobbie's breast. She knew in April 1973 that her injury (the removal of her breast) *was* caused by the act of the surgeon, or in the words of the statute was attributable to him. She therefore had the necessary knowledge of fact (b) at the end of April 1973. Facts (c) and (d) involve knowledge of the identity of the defendant. It is conceded that Mrs Dobbie had knowledge of the identity of the defendant (the health authority) by the end of April 1973. Applying the plain meaning of the words of s 14(1) to straightforward and indisputable facts, the consequence seems to follow that the claim became statute-barred at the end of April 1976.

Mr Badenoch, who appeared before us, argued that there was a missing link in Mrs Dobbie's knowledge. He said that Mrs Dobbie only acquired all the necessary knowledge many years later when she received independent medical advice to the effect that the removal of her breast was not necessary. With due respect to counsel I have to say that his construction of s 14(1) is an artificial and tortured one.

Mr Badenoch conceded that s 14(1) does not require knowledge on the part of the injured person that his injury was caused by the negligence of the defendant. Counsel said that he felt compelled to make this concession because the Law Reform Committee in its Twentieth Report (see *Interim Report on Limitation of Actions: in Personal Injury Claims* (Cmnd 5630)) categorically rejected the need for such knowledge, and the recommendations of the Law Reform Committee were enshrined in the legislation of 1975 and 1980. That is right. But more fundamentally, the concession was inevitable because the plain language of s 14(1) eliminates negligence as one of the facts of which the injured party must have knowledge.

That led counsel to tackle the matter in a different way. He said that the injured party must also know that 'something had gone wrong'. Pertinent to the present case he said that the injured party must know that the mastectomy was 'unnecessary'. He said that the injured party must appreciate the possibility that the operation was negligently performed. He said that the idea was inherent in the concept of an 'injury' in s 14(1). And he also said that the word 'omission' in s 14(1)(b) is capable of indicating what he described as 'a qualitative element', i e something which possibly ought to have been done.

The simple answer to this construction is to be found in the ordinary meaning of the words of s 14(1). The contextual meaning of 'injury' in s 14(1) is a personal injury without any further gloss other than the express definition of 'significant' in s 14(2). The word 'act' does not by itself describe something which ought not to have been done. And it would be impossible to attach a qualitative element to 'omission' but not to 'act'.

Stripped to its essentials counsel's argument is simply an attempt to argue that the injured party must know that he has a possible cause of action. That is not a requirement of s 14(1). Moreover in 1974 the Law Reform Committee rejected a proposal that the injured party must have knowledge 'that he has a worthwhile cause of action' (para 53). The present argument is simply a thinly veiled variant of a possible solution which was rejected by the Law Reform Committee in 1974 and by Parliament in 1975 and 1980.

Counsel submitted that the missing link is to be found in something short of knowledge of negligence. The missing link put forward is remarkably imprecise. In 1974 the Law Reform Committee considered an alternative solution, namely that the plaintiffs' knows 'that the defendants were at fault'. In rejecting this solution the Law Reform Committee commented (para 54):

> 'We were initially attracted by this solution; but, when we came to contemplate its embodiment in an Act of Parliament, we were driven to reject it because of the difficulties, which we consider insuperable, of satisfactory defining "fault" for this purpose. The concept of *"fault", short of actionability*, is, in our view, necessarily imprecise because it contains a considerable subjective element. If a concept is imprecise, any definition of it must (assuming that it is practicable at all) itself be imprecise. Yet, if one

is aiming at a date of knowledge which leads to an extension of time *as of right*, that date must be precisely defined.' (My emphasis.)

The solution so rejected bears a marked similarity to the interpretation now put forward by counsel. But the Law Reform Committee's emphasis on precision in a provision which leads to an extension of time as of right is equally important. There is no room in such a provision for reading words into it which are incapable of precise definition.

For all these reasons I reject Mr Badenoch's interpretation of s 14(1). The claim is statute-barred.

The judge's decision to reject the application to extend time under s 33(1) was plainly right. The length of the delay was too great.

I would also dismiss the appeal.

Appeal dismissed. Leave to appeal to the House of Lords refused.

31 October 1994. TheAppeal Committee of the House of Lords (Lord Keith of Kinkel, Lord Mustill and Lord Nolan) refused leave to appeal.

L I Zysman Esq   Barrister.

Beoco Ltd v Alfa Laval Co Ltd and another

COURT OF APPEAL, CIVIL DIVISION

BALCOMBE, STUART-SMITH AND PETER GIBSON LJJ

1, 2, 3, 21 DECEMBER 1993

Pleading – Amendment – Amendment at trial or hearing – Late amendment substantially altering case against defendant – Whether amendment necessary to enable all issues between parties to be determined – Whether amendment would result in prejudice or injustice to defendant which could not properly be compensated in costs – Whether amendment should be allowed.

Measure of damages – Contract – Breach of warranty – Loss of profit – Supervening event causing greater damage – First defendant supplying defective heat exchanger – Repair to exchanger defective – Plaintiff failing to ensure exchanger properly repaired and tested – Exchanger exploding causing damage to equipment loss of production and loss of profit – Plaintiff claming damages against first defendant for breach of warranty and loss of profit arising from loss in production – Hypothetical damages – Whether damages to be assessed on same basis in contract as in tort – Whether explosion caused by plaintiff's negligence a supervening event – Whether first defendant liable for hypothetical damages for loss of profit during time which would have been taken to make good defective repair had exchanger not been put back in service and exploded.

Costs – Order for costs – Amendment of claim – Late amendment – Whether defendant entitled to costs up to date of late amendment.

The first defendant installed a heat exchanger at the premises of the plaintiff, a company producing refined edible oils. On 24 August 1988, 20 months after its installation, a leak was discovered in the heat exchanger caused by a crack in the outer surface of the casing. The second defendant was employed by the plaintiff to repair the crack. The repair was in fact only partially successful and the heat exchanger failed a pressure test. Nevertheless, without first carrying out any inspection of the repair, which would have revealed that it was defective, the plaintiff put the heat exchanger back into use. Two months later the heat exchanger exploded causing damage to the plaintiff's plant and loss of production. The plaintiff brought an action against the first defendant claiming damages for breach of warranty arising out of defects in the design and workmanship of the heat exchanger, and against the second defendant for breach of contract arising out of the failure to repair the crack as instructed. At the trial of the action the judge gave the plaintiff leave to amend its statement of claim to add a claim that, in the event that the repair was held to be a novus actus, the first defendant was nevertheless liable for damages representing the loss which the plaintiff would inevitably have incurred in replacing or repairing the heat exchanger together with all consequential loss of production and loss of profits. The judge found (i) that the first defendant was liable for breach of warranty because the heat exchanger had defects which were latent until the second defendant repaired part of the crack which had by then appeared, (ii) that the second defendant was liable for breach of contract for its failure to repair the crack as instructed, but (iii) that the cause of the explosion was the plaintiff's recklessness in failing to carry out proper tests to ascertain that the repair to the crack had been successfully carried out. The judge accordingly dismissed the plaintiff's claim against the second defendant entirely and its claim as originally pleaded against the first defendant for the consequences of the explosion, but held that the first defendant was liable for damages to be assessed on the amended claim. The judge ordered the plaintiff to pay the second defendant's costs and the first defendant's costs attributable solely to damages and ordered the first defendant to pay the plaintiff's costs other than those which the plaintiff had to pay to the second defendant. The first defendant appealed against the judge's grant of leave to the plaintiff to amend its statement of claim, the award of damages to the plaintiff on a hypothetical basis of lost profit and the order for costs, while the plaintiff cross-appealed, claiming that the judge should have ordered the first defendant to pay the costs of the second defendant either directly or indirectly.

Held – (1) The guiding principle in giving leave to amend was that all amendments should be allowed at any stage in the proceedings to enable all issues between the parties to be determined, provided that the amendment did not result in prejudice or injustice to the other party which could not properly be compensated in costs. Since an appropriate order for costs would substantially protect the first defendant from any injustice in allowing the late amendment, and since, if the amendment had not been allowed the plaintiff would have been unable to bring a separate action to pursue that claim, which would have amounted to an irreversible injustice to the plaintiff, the appeal against the grant of leave to allow the late amendment would be dismissed (see p 471 *g* to p 472 *a c j* to p 473 *a* and p 480 *h j*, post); *Henderson v Henderson* [1843–60] All ER Rep 378 applied.

(2) The principles for assessing the measure of damages for hypothetical loss in tort were equally applicable where the claim arose out of a breach of contract. In particular, a plaintiff was not entitled to recover damages from the defendant by way of loss of profit which he would have incurred as a result of

the defendant's breach of contract had not some supervening event caused greater damage. The negligence of the plaintiff's engineers, who when they discovered the hitherto latent defect in the heat exchanger, put it back into service without making proper tests to see that the repair had been correctly carried out, in circumstances where they knew of the risk of explosion if it was not, was a supervening event which prevented the plaintiff from recovering damages representing the loss which the plaintiff would have incurred by way of loss of profit on lost production during the period necessary to repair the defect in the heat exchanger. The first defendant was liable, as was accepted, for the costs of replacement of the defective casing of the heat exchanger and such losses, if any, which were incurred on and after 24 August 1988 due to loss of production while the repair was being effected. It was not however liable for hypothetical damages for loss of profit on lost production during the time which would have been taken to make good the defective repair had the exchanger not been put back in service and exploded, since any further repair required had been subsumed in the more extensive repairs required as the result of the explosion which had been the result of the plaintiff's own negligence. The first defendant's appeal would therefore be allowed on the issue of damages (see p 473 *f g*, p 475 *a* to *f h j*, p 477 *c* and p 480 *h j*, post); dictum of Viscount Jowitt in *The Carslogie, Carslogie Steamship Co Ltd v Royal Norwegian Government* [1952] 1 All ER 20 at 24 applied.

(3) In the absence of any special reasons, where a plaintiff made a late amendment which substantially altered the case the defendant had to meet and without which the action would fail, the defendant was entitled to the costs of the action down to the date of amendment. The first defendant had been placed in great difficulty because there had been no proper pleading of the alternative case, no discovery and its experts had had no opportunity to investigate or make any estimate of the proper value of the claim. In those circumstances it was unrealistic to expect the first defendant to make a payment into court or to admit liability for damages to be assessed on the alternative basis. It followed that the first defendant was entitled to its costs down to the date of the amendment, and since in the context of the claim and the expense of the action the amount which would be recovered by the plaintiff was modest, the first defendant should be awarded 85% of its costs after the date of the amendment. The first defendant's appeal would therefore be allowed on the issue of costs and the cross-appeal would be dismissed (see p 478 *e f*, p 479 *g* to p 480 *a g* to *j*, post); *Anglo-Cyprian Trade Agencies Ltd v Paphos Wine Industries Ltd* [1951] 1 All ER 873, *Alltrans Express Ltd v CVA Holdings Ltd* [1984] 1 All ER 685 and *Lipkin Gorman (a firm) v Karpnale Ltd* [1992] 4 All ER 409 applied.

Notes

For measure of damages, see 43 *Halsbury's Laws* (4th edn) paras 986–988 and 12 ibid paras 1164–1165.

For pleading of damage, see 12 *Halsbury's Laws* (4th edn) para 1197.

For exercise of the court's discretion where costs not awarded to successful party, see 37 *Halsbury's Laws* (4th edn) para 717, and for cases on the subject, see 37(3) *Digest* (Reissue) 271–275, 4448–4565.

Cases referred to in judgments

Alltrans Express Ltd v CVA Holdings Ltd [1984] 1 All ER 685, [1984] 1 WLR 394, CA.

Anglo-Cyprian Trade Agencies Ltd v Paphos Wine Industries Ltd [1951] 1 All ER 873.
Bullock v London General Omnibus Co [1907] 1 KB 264, [1904] All ER Rep 44, CA.
Calderbank v Calderbank [1975] 3 All ER 333, [1976] Fam 93, [1975] 3 WLR 586, CA.
Carslogie, The, Carslogie Steamship Co Ltd v Royal Norwegian Government [1952] 1 All ER 20, [1952] AC 292, HL.
Glenfinlas, The [1918] P 363n, [1918–19] All ER Rep 365n.
Haversham Grange, The [1905] P 307.
Henderson v Henderson (1843) 3 Hare 100, [1843–60] All ER Rep 378, 67 ER 313, V-C.
Jobling v Associated Dairies Ltd [1981] 2 All ER 752, [1982] AC 794, [1981] 3 WLR 155, HL.
Kaines (UK) Ltd v Osterreichische Warrenhandelsgesellschaft mbH [1993] 2 Lloyd's Rep 1.
Kingsway, The [1918] P 344, [1918–19] All ER Rep 360, CA.
Lipkin Gorman (a firm) v Karpnale Ltd (1986) [1992] 4 All ER 331, [1987] 1 WLR 987; rvsd in part [1992] 4 All ER 409, [1989] 1 WLR 1340, CA; rvsd in part [1992] 4 All ER 512 , [1991] AC 548, [1991] 3 WLR 10, HL.
Sanderson v Blythe Theatre [1903] 2 KB 533, CA.
Schering Agrochemicals Ltd v Resibel NV SA (4 June 1991, unreported) QBD; affd in part [1991] CA Transcript 1298.
Smith Hogg & Co Ltd v Black Sea and Baltic General Insurance Co Ltd [1940] 3 All ER 405, [1940] AC 997, HL; affg [1939] 2 All ER 855.
Talbot v Berkshire CC [1993] 4 All ER 9, [1993] 3 WLR 708, CA.
Vitruvia Steamship Co Ltd v Ropner Shipping Co Ltd, The Vitruvia 1925 SC (HL) 1.
York, The [1929] P 178, CA.

Cases also cited or referred to in skeleton arguments
Admiralty Comrs v Steamship Susquehanna (owners), The Susquehanna [1926] AC 655, [1926] All ER Rep 124, HL.
Antcliffe v Gloucester Health Authority [1992] 1 WLR 1044, CA.
Besterman v British Motor Cab Co Ltd [1914] 3 KB 181, [1914–15] All ER Rep 1111, CA.
Cutts v Head [1984] 1 All ER 597, [1984] Ch 290, CA.
Elgindata, Re (No 2) [1993] 1 All ER 232, [1992] 1 WLR 1207, CA.
Glenlion Construction Ltd v Beaverfoam (Moreton) Ltd (1983) 134 Fam Law 861, CA.
Jacobs v Schmaltz (1890) 62 LT 121.
Jamal (AKAS) v Moolla Dawood Sons & Co [1916] 1 AC 175, PC.
King v Corke (1875) 1 Ch D 57.
Koch Marine Inc v d'Amica Societa di Navigazione ARL [1980] 1 Lloyd's Rep 75.
Lambert v Lewis [1981] 1 All ER 1185, [1982] AC 225, [1981] 2 WLR 713, HL.
Perestrelloe Cia Ltda v United Paint Co Ltd [1969] 3 All ER 479, [1969] 1 WLR 570, CA.
Porter (J P) Co Ltd v Irving Oil Co Ltd [1954] 3 DLR 295, NS SC.
Scherer v Counting Instruments Ltd (1977) [1986] 2 All ER 529, [1986] 1 WLR 615, CA.
Ströms v Bruks AB v Hutchison [1905] AC 515, HL.
Wasley v Vass [1991] CA Transcript 0714.
Wheeler v Somerfield [1966] 2 All ER 305, [1966] 2 QB 94, CA.

Appeals

The first defendant, Alfa Laval Co Ltd, appealed from the order made by Judge Bowsher QC on 24 February 1992 hearing official referee's business in the action brought by the plaintiff, Beoco Ltd, against the first defendant and the second defendant, Studley Engineering Ltd, for damages for the consequences of the explosion of a heat exchanger in the plaintiff's works on 8 October 1992 whereby the judge granted the plaintiff leave to amend its statement of claim, and further appealed against the judgment of Judge Bowsher QC delivered on 6 April 1992, dismissing the plaintiff's claim against the second defendant and against the first defendant for damages for the consequences of the explosion, but awarding the plaintiff damages to be assessed for hypothetical lost profits on the basis set out in para 5(2) of the statement of claim and further ordering that the plaintiff pay the second defendant's costs and that the first defendant pay the plaintiff's costs of the action (not including the plaintiffs' payment of the second defendant's costs) save that the plaintiff should pay the first defendant's costs hitherto incurred attributable solely to damages. The plaintiff appealed against the order that it should pay the second defendant's costs, claiming that they should be paid by the first defendant. The second defendant took no part in the appeal. The facts are set out in the judgment of Stuart-Smith LJ.

Timothy Stow QC and Freya Newbery (instructed by *Herbert Smith*) for the first defendant.
Brian Knight QC and Tom Weitzman (instructed by *Davies Arnold Cooper*) for the plaintiff.

Cur adv vult

21 December 1993. The following judgments were delivered.

STUART-SMITH LJ (giving the first judgment at the invitation of Balcombe LJ). On Saturday, 8 October 1988 at about 1.30 pm there was an explosion of a heat exchanger at the plaintiff's works at Bootle, Liverpool. Fortunately, no one was injured; but much damage was caused to equipment, including the heat exchanger and even greater economic loss in terms of lost production.

The heat exchanger was installed in February 1987, some 20 months before it blew up. It was supposed to have a life of 20 years.

The plaintiff, formerly known as J Bibby Edible Oils Ltd, extracts from seed, refines and packs various edible oils and processes and sells the residue.

The heat exchanger consisted of a cylindrical steel casing, having an external diameter of about 12 inches and a height of about 15 feet and was installed in one of three similar production lines. Inside the shell were a number of stainless steel tubes looping up and down the length of the casing. The oil to be heated was pumped through the tubes and steam was passed over the tubes so that heat was transferred to the tubes and so to the oil within them. The steam partially condensed in the process and was passed back to the boiler through a closed system for reheating into steam again. The steam was at temperatures of about 250° C or more; the oil required to be heated to from 180° C to 240° C as part of the deodorising process. The steam was under pressure of about 65 bar in the heat exchanger. The casing was not made of a seamless tube, but consisted of three sections of flat steel, each of which was welded to form a cylinder and then the cylinders were welded together along their circumference and closed at each end. The heat exchanger was part of plant provided for the plaintiff by Wimpey Engineering Ltd (Wimpeys). But any claim against them was barred by a contractual time limitation. The plaintiff therefore claimed against the first defendant, which was a sub-contractor to Wimpeys, under a contractual warranty made directly between the plaintiff and the first defendant. The plaintiff contended that there were breaches of warranty in respect of the design, selection of materials and workmanship. The first defendant had in fact sub-contracted the manufacture of the heat exchanger to other sub-contractors, but nothing turns on that.

By amendment the plaintiff also sued the second defendant, who from time to time performed engineering repairs and maintenance on the instructions of the plaintiff. The second defendant's employees came into the matter because on 24 August 1988 a leak was discovered in the heat exchanger. The lagging which surrounds it was removed and there appeared to be a pinhole from which steam was issuing under pressure. Further examination revealed a substantial crack in the outer surface of the casing along the vertical weld. The plaintiff, by its engineers, gave instructions to the second defendant's men to repair the weld. This they purported to do; but they did not do it properly, in the sense that, unknown to them, the crack extended considerably further than the repair which was effected.

Having effected the repair, as it was thought, Mr Jackson, one of the plaintiff's engineers, instructed the second defendant's men to carry out a hydraulic pressure test. This involved pumping water into the heat exchanger to a test pressure of 90 bar. But it failed that test, because it lost pressure. Nevertheless, the next day the plaintiff's engineers decided to put the whole system back into operation again. Before any pressure test was done, still more before the line was put back into operation, there should have been an inspection by radiograph or ultrasound to see if the repair was effective. Had such an inspection taken place it would have revealed that the crack was more extensive than the part that had been rewelded. It was the plaintiff's responsibility to arrange for such an inspection. The failure that caused the explosion was due to this crack.

The trial began before Judge Bowsher QC, sitting as an official referee, on 18 February 1992. Up to that time the only claim made against the first defendants related to the explosion. Paragraph 5(1)(A) of the re-re-re-amended statement of claim, which substantially followed the claim in the writ, was in these terms:

'By reason of the First Defendant's breaches of the above warranties at about 1.30 p.m. on Saturday 8th October 1988 the heat exchanger blew up whilst in use and the Plaintiff has thereby suffered loss and damage and been put to costs and expenses.
Particulars
(1) The cost of repair   £43,525·49
(2) Loss of use of the heat exchanger and
consequent shut down of the Plaintiff
production causing expense and loss of
profit over some 10 weeks   £676,542·00
                                                          £720,067·49'

It was a claim which, together with interest, came to about £1m.

In the course of his opening, the plaintiff's counsel submitted that even if the plaintiff could not establish liability against the first defendant for the explosion, it was, in the alternative, entitled on the pleading, as it then stood, to recover the costs of making good the repairs to the heat exchanger and any consequential loss of profit on the hypothetical basis that, but for the explosion, these would have been incurred. The judge ruled that it was not open to the plaintiff to advance this point on the claim as pleaded.

However, on 24 February 1992, the judge gave the plaintiff leave to make yet a further amendment to its statement of claim in these terms:

> '5(2) As appears above the Plaintiff's primary case is that the First Defendant's breaches of warranty caused the heat exchanger to explode on 8th October 1988. For the avoidance of doubt however it is the Plaintiff's case that, in the event that it is held that the carrying out of the repair weld on 24th August 1988 constituted a novus actus and caused or contributed to the explosion as alleged [by the first defendant] the First Defendant is nonetheless liable to it in damages for breach of such warranties in like sums to those set about above, such sums representing the loss and/or damage which the Plaintiff would inevitably have incurred in replacing, alternatively carrying out some other scheme of repair, to the heat exchanger and including the cost of replacing, alternatively repairing, the heat exchanger together with all consequence [sic] loss of production, loss of profits and/or increased costs of working and/or all other expenses.'

He ordered the plaintiff to pay the costs of and occasioned by the amendment. In his judgment given on 6 April 1992 at the end of the trial, the judge made the following findings.

(1) The first defendant was in breach of warranty in that there were defects in the design and workmanship of the heat exchanger. So far from having a life expectancy of 20 years, it was likely to be nearer 20 months. Until 24 August these defects were latent.

(2) The second defendant was in breach of contract in that it failed to repair the crack as instructed, it repaired only part of it. If it had carried out a second dye penetration test, it would have discovered this. But it was not responsible in any way for the plaintiff's failure to have a radiograph or ultrasound test.

(3) The cause of the explosion was, to use the judge's words, 'the recklessness of the plaintiff in failing to apply to the heat exchanger any proper non-destructive test after causing a repair to be effected to a known defect and before bringing the heat exchanger back into service'. The plaintiff's engineers were well aware of the risk of explosion if the crack was not properly repaired.

Accordingly, he made the following orders. He dismissed the plaintiff's claim against the second defendant. He dismissed the plaintiff's claim against the first defendant, in the respect originally pleaded, for the consequences of the explosion. But he gave judgment against it for damages to be assessed on the basis of the amendment contained in para 5(2) of the re-re-re-re-reamended statement of claim.

As to costs, he ordered (a) that the plaintiff should pay the second defendant's costs, and (b) that the first defendant should pay the plaintiff's costs of the action (not including the costs which the plaintiff had to pay the second defendant); save that the plaintiff should pay the first defendant's costs hitherto incurred attributable solely to damages.

In this appeal the first defendant seeks the following relief.

(1) Leave to appeal from the judge's order of 24 February permitting the amendment. If leave is given and the appeal allowed, judgment will be entered for the first defendant.

(2) Alternatively, the first defendant contends that, as a matter of law, the plaintiff is not entitled to damages on a hypothetical basis of lost profit and that the judge's order directing judgment for damages to be assessed should be set aside to this extent.

(3) In the further alternative, it seeks leave to appeal the judge's order for costs, contending that it should have been awarded the costs of the action down to the date of the amendment in question and thereafter a substantial part of the costs.

The plaintiff cross-appeals on the ground that the judge should have ordered the first defendant to pay the costs of the second defendant either directly or indirectly.

Before opening the appeal, Mr Stow QC, on behalf of the first defendant, sought leave to adduce further evidence. This related to the quantum of costs which, in the opinion of the first defendant's solicitor, would fall upon the first defendant as a result of the judge's order, and also the first defendant's position vis-à-vis its insurers. We decided to look at the evidence de bene esse and to rule on its relevance and admissibility thereafter. I will deal with these matters when I consider the issues to which it is said the evidence relates. I turn to consider the grounds of appeal.

1. Should the judge have given leave to amend to add the alternative claim? This being an exercise of the judge's discretion, this court can only interfere if it can be shown that the judge has either erred in principle in his approach, or has left out of account, or taken into account, some feature that he should, or should not, have considered, or that his decision is wholly wrong, because this court is forced to the conclusion that he has not balanced the various factors fairly in the scale.

The guiding principle in giving leave to amend is that all amendments should be allowed at any stage of the proceedings to enable all issues between the parties to be determined, provided that the amendment will not result in prejudice or injustice to the other party which cannot properly be compensated for in costs.

The main ground upon which Mr Stow opposed the application for leave to amend before the judge was that it was far too late, the first defendant had come to trial prepared to deal with all issues, including quantum. It was impossible to meet the new case without an adjournment of about four months, and it would be a hardship to the first defendant to have a split trial, standing over the assessment of damages on the alternative basis.

The judge rejected Mr Stow's submission. In my judgment, not only is it impossible for this court to say the judge was wrong, but I am quite satisfied that he was correct. If the plaintiff won on its primary case, then the action would go ahead as planned. It was only if the plaintiff's primary case failed that there would have to be an adjournment, further pleadings and discovery, followed by the assessment. Although I recognise that there is undoubtedly some hardship to a defendant who has to face a prolongation of litigation, the disruption and inconvenience caused to people involved in running a business being something that cannot be wholly compensated in costs, an appropriate order for costs in my judgment substantially protects the first defendant from any injustice.

There is a factor which has to be considered on the other side of the scale Unless the plaintiff was permitted to amend to add this alternative claim, it would be unable to bring a separate action to pursue the claim. This is because of the doctrine in *Henderson v Henderson* (1843) 3 Hare 100, [1843–60] All ER Rep 378 that, save in special circumstances, the court will not permit the same parties to reopen the same subject of litigation in respect of matters that might have been brought forward, only because they have from negligence inadvertence or accident, omitted this part of their case (see also *Talbot v Berkshire CC* [1993] 4 All ER 9, [1993] 3 WLR 708). In my judgment, it would be a considerable injustice to the plaintiff, if in truth it has a valid claim on the alternative basis, if it were not permitted to advance it.

Mr Stow's second submission in relation to the amendment arises out of the first defendant's insurance position. The first defendant was insured under a public liability policy. The explosion and consequential damage was clearly an event which was covered by the policy and up till 24 February 1992 insurers had taken over the conduct of the defence: if held liable, they would have to meet the damages and costs. But the claim advanced in the amendment very probably did not fall within the cover afforded by the policy. This obviously put the first defendant in a difficulty, since it had to face for the first time a claim in respect of which it was not insured. There would be likely to be difficult negotiations with insurers as to who should bear any costs if the plaintiff succeeded only on the alternative claim.

After the judge had made his ruling on this amendment, Mr Stow raised this difficulty with the judge. But he did not invite the judge to reconsider his decision on the basis that the problem now faced by the first defendant involved such prejudice that the amendment should not be allowed. He did not do so expressly; nor did he do so by implication.

Mr Stow now submits to this court that the judge erred in principle because he did not take into consideration the prejudice caused to the first defendant by reason of the insurance position. It was in this connection that he sought to introduce the further evidence as to what had occurred as between the first defendant and its insurers. In my judgment, there are two answers to Mr Stow's submissions.

First, since Mr Stow did not invite the judge to reconsider his decision on the amendment, I do not see how he can now say that the judge erred in failing to take it into account. If that is right, any further evidence on the point is quite irrelevant.

Secondly, it is a common feature of litigation of this nature that a defendant faces some claims which are covered by insurance and some which are not. The matter of who bears the costs of defending the action and in what proportions has to be agreed, or if not agreed, settled by litigation. Where the claims are properly pleaded before trial, this will, or should be, settled in good time. Where the problem arises as a result of a late amendment, a similar solution has to be arrived at, if need be by means of a provisional arrangement which may have to be reconsidered after trial. But, although the lateness of the amendment clearly caused extra difficulty to the first defendant, it is no different in kind from that which it would have faced if the case had been timeously pleaded. In my judgment, this ground of appeal affords no basis for disturbing the exercise of the judge's discretion. And the details of the arrangements between the first defendant and insurance is of no relevance.

Finally, in relation to this ground of appeal, I must deal with the submission made by Mr Knight QC, for the plaintiff, that the plaintiff did not need leave to amend at all, because the alternative claim was in some way embraced by the original claim. I cannot accept this. Although the amended pleading purported to claim the same sum as that resulting from the explosion, this was manifestly incorrect. The fact is that the alternative claim was put on an entirely different basis and the calculation was quite different. This is now made clear by the Scott Schedule served since judgment in which the plaintiff claims £21,574 for the cost of repair and £270,000 loss of production in a detailed calculation that differs markedly from the original claim. The judge was quite right to insist on an amendment.

2. The second ground of appeal raises an interesting point of law upon which there does not appear to be any authority directly in point. Can the plaintiff recover damages which he would have incurred by way of loss of profit on lost production during the period necessary to repair the defect in goods or materials supplied by the defendant and caused by his breach of contract, where because of some supervening event those repairs are not carried out or are subsumed in other more extensive repairs?

The supervening event in this case was the negligence of the plaintiff's engineers, who when they discovered the hitherto latent defect in the heat exchanger, put it back into service without making proper tests to see that the repair had been correctly carried out, in circumstances where they knew of the risk of explosion if it was not. But the supervening event might equally have been caused by the breach of contract or negligence of the second defendant, if it had been responsible for making all proper tests before the heat exchanger was put back into service; or it may have been some extraneous event, like a fire in the factory for which no one could be held to blame.

It is common ground in this case that the first defendant is liable for the cost of making good the defective casing of the heat exchanger. This is because what was damaged in the explosion was not a sound heat exchanger with 18 years' life in it, but a defective one with much less. The plaintiff's loss *caused by the explosion* was therefore much less than it would otherwise have been. And it could have recovered from its insurers, or the second defendant as the case may be, only the value of the defective heat exchanger.

Mr Knight submits that the same principle should apply to the loss of profit which could have resulted during the time taken to make good the defect. The cause of action for damages for breach of contract arises at the time of the breach, even though this may not be quantifiable until later. On 24 August 1988, therefore, the plaintiff had a claim against the defendant for breach of contract, the measure of which was the cost of repair and the as yet unquantified claim for lost profit. It is immaterial, he submits, that that loss was never in fact incurred or quantified because of the explosion.

Although there do not appear to be any cases in contract, there are a number of authorities in tort which bear upon the point.

In *The Glenfinlas* [1918] P 363n, [1918–19] All ER Rep 365n the plaintiff's vessel was damaged in a collision with the defendants' vessel, for which the defendants were solely to blame. Temporary repairs were done; permanent repairs were to be done after the war. However, before they were done the vessel struck a mine and sank. Mr Registrar Roscoe awarded the plaintiff the cost of repairs, but not the £160 a day for 12 days that the permanent repairs would have taken.

This decision was approved by the Court of Appeal in *The Kingsway* [1918] P 344, [1918–19] All ER Rep 360, where the decision in *The Glenfinlas* is reported as a note. In that case the repairs had not been done at the time of the assessment of damages, but the plaintiff proved that they would be done. The future loss of profit that was likely to be incurred while they were carried out was recoverable. Pickford LJ distinguished the case from *The Glenfinlas*. He said ([1918] P 344 at 358–359, [1918–19] All ER Rep 360 at 364):

> 'I think the judge was quite right in the view he took. He took the view, and I should agree if it were necessary to decide it, that if at the time of a reference the ship had in fact been lost, as in the case of *The Glenfinlas*, and therefore the repairs never could be done, and there never could be a detention causing loss of profitable employment to the shipowner at all, then these damages could not be recovered. When I say lost, I mean lost by some circumstances outside the collision. Suppose that after the collision damage she had been torpedoed or sunk by perils of the sea, then clearly the shipowner would not have suffered a loss by reason of detention during the effecting of permanent repairs, because he never would or could do them; and the vessel never could be, by reason of the accident, detained from profitable employment, because she had gone and never could get any profitable employment. But that is not this case.'

Scrutton LJ said ([1918] P 344 at 362):

> 'In the Courts of common law two things are perfectly clear. The first thing clear is that when damages which would be otherwise prospective come to be assessed, facts which have actually happened may be taken into account, and when damages are being assessed for a tort which would include some disability of the person or thing injured it may be taken into account that before the damages come to be assessed the person or thing injured has ceased to exist, owing to circumstances not connected with the tort.'

The plaintiff must show that the chattel or equipment in question would have been profitable during the period in question. In *The York* [1929] P 178 at 185 Scrutton LJ gave other examples where it would be impossible to substantiate a claim for damages for loss of profitable time, such as a ship that was detained in ice or subject to an embargo such that she could not trade at all during the period when the repairs were being carried out.

The authority, which in my judgment is of most assistance, is *The Carslogie, Carslogie Steamship Co Ltd v Royal Norwegian Government* [1952] 1 All ER 20, [1952] AC 292. The plaintiff's vessel, the Heimgar, was damaged in a collision with the Carslogie, for which the defendants, owners of the latter vessel, were to blame. Temporary repairs were carried out to the Heimgar to make her seaworthy, but on the way to port where the permanent repairs were to be carried out, she encountered heavy weather and thereby suffered damage which rendered her unseaworthy and requiring immediate repairs. At her destination both sets of repairs were effected concurrently, the work occupying 30 days. Ten days would have been required to effect the repairs to the damage caused by the Carslogie if executed separately. The plaintiffs were held not entitled to loss of profit during the ten days it would have taken to effect them. The House of Lords, in so holding, followed an earlier decision of the House in *Vitruvia Steamship Co Ltd v Ropner Shipping Co Ltd* 1925 SC (HL) 1. Viscount Jowitt said ([1952] 1 All ER 20 at 24, [1952] AC 292 at 301):

> 'I am willing to assume without deciding the question that the collision was *a* cause of her detention. Still, the fact remains that when she entered the dock at New York she was not a profit-earning machine by reason of the heavyweather damage which had rendered her unseaworthy. If there had been no collision she would have been detained in dock for thirty days to repair this damage. I cannot see that her owners sustained any damage in the nature of demurrage by reason of the fact that for ten days out of the thirty she was also undergoing repairs in respect of the collision.' (Viscount Jowitt's emphasis.)

It is important to note that in that case the collision with the Carslogie did not render the Heimgar unseaworthy. The House of Lords distinguished the case from that of *The Haversham Grange* [1905] P 307. In that case the plaintiff's vessel, the Maureen, was damaged in two successive collisions; the first was due partly to the fault of the other ship and partly the plaintiff's; in the second, the other vessel was wholly to blame. But each collision rendered the Maureen unseaworthy. The second tortfeasor was not liable for the loss of profit incurred while the ship was laid up during the repairs, since this was necessarily incurred in making good the damage caused by the first collision, which itself prevented the vessel earning profit. Those were the liability of the first tortfeasor and the plaintiff. Lord Normand said in *The Carslogie* [1952] 1 All ER 20 at 30, [1952] AC 292 at 311:

> '... if the fact is that one of two casualties made the vessel unseaworthy and the other did not, the problem of liability is solved and the time sequence is irrelevant. In *The Haversham Grange* the time sequence was important because the damage suffered by the Maureen in each of the two collisions was enough to make her unseaworthy.'

Similar principles were applied in *Jobling v Associated Dairies Ltd* [1981] 2 All ER 752, [1982] AC 794. The plaintiff was injured through the defendant's breach of statutory duty; in the accident he suffered injuries which disabled him from full employment. However, before trial the plaintiff was found to be suffering from a serious condition, unconnected with the accident, which rendered him incapable of all employment. He could not recover damages for loss of earnings after the illness superseded and prevented him working.

In my judgment, the same principles should apply in contract as in tort in the assessment of damages under this head. This is generally the rule (see *MacGregor on Damages* (15th edn, 1988) paras 234, 239). It can make no difference that the damage to the Heimgar was caused in a collision as opposed to defective repair work carried out under contract by shipbuilders.

Mr Knight advanced two arguments in support of his contention. First, he sought to distinguish *The Carslogie* case on the basis that the first defendant's breach of contract was a cause of the explosion, even if it was only a causa sine qua non in as much as it was the original defect that gave occasion for the inadequate repair. The distinction between causa causans and causa sine qua non has not been much adopted in recent authority, partly no doubt because in *Smith Hogg & Co v Black Sea and Baltic General Insurance Co Ltd* [1940] 3 All ER

405 at 409, [1940] AC 997 at 1003 Lord Wright in effect said that expression causa sine qua non was not material in English law. He said:

'I cannot help deprecating the use of so-called Latin phrases in this way. They only distract the mind from the true problem, which is to apply the principles of English law to the realities of the case. *Causa causans* is supposed to mean a cause which causes, while *causa sine qua non* means, I suppose, a cause which does not, in the sense material to the particular case, cause, but is merely an incident which precedes in the history or narrative of events, but as a cause is not in at the death, and hence is irrelevant.'

But in any event the point is expressly dealt with in the speech of Viscount Jowitt in *The Carslogie* which I have cited.

Secondly, he relies upon an unreported decision in the case of *Schering Agrochemicals Ltd v Resibel NVSA* (4 June 1991, unreported); *affd in part* [1991] CA Transcript 1298. The defendants supplied the plaintiffs with sophisticated equipment for filling plastic bottles with inflammable chemicals. Because of a defect caused by the defendants' breach of contract, the bottles were liable to stay under the capping machine too long; this caused overheating and the consequent risk of fire. Because of an incident which occurred on 8 September 1987, this should have been appreciated by the plaintiffs and the fault corrected. However, it was not and the production line continued in operation till a fire occurred on 30 September. Hobhouse J held that the defendants' breach of contract was a cause of the fire on 30 September, but that the plaintiffs failed to mitigate their loss by taking the line out of action when they should have appreciated the fault and they could not recover for the damage caused by the fire. However, he held that the plaintiffs could recover damages to be assessed on the basis that they would have sustained losses due to loss of production while correcting the defects, even though such loss was not in fact incurred because of the fire. One of the curious features of this case is that this point never seems to have been argued, or indeed pleaded, until the judge permitted an amendment after judgment. The plaintiffs appealed on the ground that the defendants should have been held liable for the consequences of the fire. The majority of the Court of Appeal (Purchas and Scott LJJ) upheld the judge, but on a different basis, namely that the breach of contract of the defendants was not a cause of the fire, the plaintiffs' own negligence breaking the chain of causation. Nolan LJ adopted the judge's reasoning and held there was a failure to mitigate. The majority of the Court of Appeal, therefore, treated the case in precisely the same way as Judge Bowsher did in this case. There was a third party in the *Schering* case from whom the defendants had bought the offending equipment. By a cross-notice of appeal, the third party sought to appeal the judge's decision on damages for the hypothetical loss of profit. It is not at all clear what happened to this cross-appeal, since there is no mention of it in the judgment of the Court of Appeal.

For my part, I do not derive any assistance from the *Schering* case. Hobhouse J's decision was per incuriam, since there was no argument on the point and he, like Judge Bowsher QC, was not referred to the authorities which I have cited. Without knowing what happened to the third party's cross-appeal, it is impossible to conclude that the Court of Appeal gave even tacit support to the proposition contended for by Mr Knight.

Finally, Mr Knight submitted that the judge's decision can be upheld on the alternative basis adopted by Hobhouse J and Nolan LJ in the *Schering* case, namely that the defendant's breach of contract was a cause of the explosion, but the plaintiffs failed to mitigate their loss. With all respect to Mr Knight, I am quite unable to follow this submission. In the first place, he has not appealed the judge's decision on causation; secondly, the majority of the Court of Appeal in the *Schering* case held that the case should have been decided against the plaintiffs on causation, not failure to mitigate; and thirdly, I have not been able to follow why in any event it should make any difference.

For these reasons, I would allow the first defendant's appeal on this ground, the assessment of damages should be limited to the cost of replacement of the defective casing of the heat exchanger and such losses, if any, which were incurred on and after 24 August 1988 due to loss of production while the repair was being effected.

In these circumstances, it is unnecessary to consider the alternative and more limited grounds of appeal raised in the amended notice which related to the terms of the judge's order for the assessment of damages.

3. I turn next to the question of costs. Apart from the costs of and occasioned by the various amendments, including that of the statement of claim on 24 February, which he awarded against the amending party, and the costs attributable to the issue of quantum as it had hitherto been dealt with, which he awarded to the first defendant, the judge gave the plaintiff the whole of the costs of the action against the first defendant.

Mr Stow made the following submissions to the judge: (a) that the first defendant should have the costs down to and including 24 February 1992, because the amendment was fundamental and without it the plaintiff's claim would have failed entirely; (b) that the first defendant should have the bulk of the costs thereafter because the late amendment put the first defendant in a very difficult position from which it could not adequately protect itself by making a payment into court or in any other way. Furthermore, the first defendant was substantially the successful party because the plaintiff was aiming at recovering a sum in the order of £1m, whereas all that it succeeded in getting was judgment for damages to be assessed, which on any basis were likely to be more modest.

The judge rejected these submissions for two main reasons; first, that the first defendant could and should have asked for an adjournment of the trial defendant could have sent a Calderbank letter by which I think he must be understood to mean that the first defendant could have admitted the breach of contract and liability to compensate the plaintiff for any damages found due (see *Calderbank v Calderbank* [1975] 3 All ER 333, [1976] Fam 93).

In my judgment, the judge erred in principle and his order for costs is so manifestly unfair to the first defendant that he cannot have exercised his discretion judicially. As a general rule, where a plaintiff makes a late amendment as here, which substantially alters the case the defendant has to meet and without which the action will fail, the defendant is entitled to the costs of the action down to the date of the amendment. There may, of course, be special reasons why this general rule should not be applied. An example of this is to be found in *Kaines (UK) Ltd v Osterreichische Warrenhandelsgessellschaft mbH* [1993] 2 Lloyd's Rep 1 at 9, where the judge was satisfied that, even if the amendment had been made earlier, the action would have been vigorously resisted. The judge disbelieved the defendant's witnesses and the plaintiff received substantial damages.

Mr Knight argued that the lateness of the amendment was in some way brought about by a late amendment to the defence made on the first day of the trial to raise specifically the causation point that the acts of the plaintiff and/or the second defendant broke the chain of causation between any breach of contract and the explosion. And, he submitted, in any event the first defendant should have anticipated the alternative way in which the claim for damages was put.

I find this argument untenable. First, it is not factually correct; it was the amendment to the defence on 22 August 1991 that quite clearly set up this defence. But, in any event, it ignores the fact that it is for the plaintiff to establish causation in respect of the damage claimed. While the defendant must plead a novus actus interveniens on which he is going to rely, if the plaintiff's claim failed because he fails to establish causation, in the ordinary case the defendant will recover all the costs of the action and not merely those after the service of the defence raising the specific matters.

The judge's reasoning in rejecting Mr Stow's submission was, in my judgment, flawed. First, he appears to have forgotten that Mr Stow did ask for an adjournment. In resisting the application to amend, Mr Stow said it should have been refused or, if it was granted, he requested four months' adjournment to investigate the alternative claim. He never resiled from this at any time before the judge ruled on the amendment.

Secondly, the judge's view that the first defendant could have protected its position by sending a Calderbank letter or admitting liability for damages to be assessed on the alternative basis, in my judgment, wholly ignores the reality of the situation or the difficulty in which the first defendant was placed. It is quite plain that the first defendant could not have made a payment into court. There was no proper pleading of the alternative case, there had been no discovery, and the defendant's experts had no opportunity to investigate or make any estimate of the proper value of the claim. The great advantage to a defendant in making a payment into court is that he can run all defences open to him in the knowledge that, even if some or all of them fail, he may still recover his costs after the date of payment in, if the plaintiff fails to get more.

In those cases where it is for technical reasons not possible to make a payment into court, a Calderbank letter can be written. The effect of such a letter is now enshrined in RSC Ord 22, r 14, which provides:

> 'A party to proceedings may at any time make a written offer to any other party to those proceedings which is expressed to be "without prejudice save as to costs" and which relates to any issue in the proceedings.'

For the same reason that the first defendant could not make a payment into court, it could not make a money offer under Ord 22, r 14. I do not consider that it was reasonable to say that the first defendant should have admitted liability for breach of contract for damages to be assessed. This would have precluded it from arguing other defences, which, although the arguments were not successful, could have been run in a situation where a payment into court or Calderbank offer has been made. Moreover, it seems to me that the first defendant might well have been precluded from arguing that the plaintiff was not entitled to any damages for the hypothetical loss of production.

In my judgment, Mr Stow's submissions are in line with the authorities. In *Anglo-Cyprian Trade Agencies v Paphos Wine Industries* [1951] 1 All ER 873 the plaintiff claimed £2,028, being the full value of certain wine bought by it from the defendant which the plaintiff said was valueless by reason of the defendant's breach of contract. The defendant, while disputing the breach of contract, contended that any defect could be cured by a modest and inexpensive remedy. At trial the plaintiff amended the statement of claim to claim damages on this alternative basis. Devlin J rejected the plaintiff's claim for £2,028, but awarded £52 on the alternative claim. He awarded the defendant the entire costs of the action.

This decision was approved by this court in *Alltrans Express Ltd v CVA Holdings Ltd* [1984] 1 All ER 685, [1984] 1 WLR 394. The plaintiffs claimed £82,500 damages for breach of warranty on the sale of shares. Judgment under RSC Ord 14 was entered for damages to be assessed. The judge assessed them at £2 nominal damages and gave the plaintiffs the costs of the action on the grounds that the defendants could have made a payment into court. This court reversed the order for costs and awarded them to the defendant. The court posed the question 'Who was the successful party?' and said that it was obviously the defendant (see [1984] 1 All ER 685 at 692, [1984] 1 WLR 403); the trial judge had paid far too much attention to the absence of a payment into court of a nominal sum which obviously the plaintiff would not have accepted. The case was very similar to the *Anglo-Cyprian* case, but there had been no late amendment.

In *Lipkin Gorman (a firm) v Karpnale Ltd* (1986) [1992] 4 All ER 331, [1987] 1 WLR 987 the plaintiffs claimed £250,000, including by a late amendment a claim for conversion of a bankers draft in the sum of £3,375. The plaintiffs failed on all but the claim for £3,375. The Court of Appeal ([1992] 4 All ER 409, [1989] 1 WLR 1340) reversing the judge's order, awarded the defendants the costs of the action down to the date of amendment and 80% of the costs thereafter. This was on the basis that the defendants were the winners, subject to there being a discount in respect of the modest extent to which the plaintiffs had succeeded.

What then should be the result in this case? I can see no reason to deprive the first defendant of the costs down to the date of the amendment. Thereafter, they were essentially the winners, since the primary contest related to the damage caused by the explosion. Even on the basis of the judge's conclusion that the defendant would be liable for the hypothetical loss of production, it was a case in which the first defendant should have been awarded a proportion of their costs thereafter, for the reasons I have already given. As it is, in the light of our decision that the only damages that the plaintiff is entitled to recover is the cost of replacing the casing of the heat exchanger and such loss of production that occurred on 24 August as a result of the defect discovered on that day, this is likely to be no more than £21,574·28 now claimed in the Scott Schedule and it may well be less. Although this sum cannot by itself be described as trivial, in the context of a claim for £1m and the enormous expense of this action, it is trivial. It makes no commercial sense to incur costs of this sum to recover such a small sum. And it seems to me very probable that if the first defendant had had a proper opportunity to make a payment into court on the basis that its liability on the alternative claim was limited in the way we have held it to be, it would have done so. A payment in of £21,574 plus interest would obviously not have been accepted and it would have made sound commercial sense to have made it. But, for the reasons I have indicated, the first defendant had no chance to do so. Accordingly, in my judgment, although some discount should be made to reflect the very modest degree of success that the plaintiff achieved, it should not be a large one. I would award the first defendant 85% of its costs after 24 February 1992.

Two further points arise on the question of costs. The first is the application by the first defendant to adduce further evidence consisting of its solicitors' estimate in money terms of the effect of the judge's order for costs. It is said by Mr Stow that this puts flesh on the bones of the judge's order and makes plain the unfairness of it. In my judgment, the evidence should not be admitted because it is quite unnecessary. This court is well aware of the enormous expense involved in a 17-day hearing before the official referee, involving three parties, two of whom are represented by leading and junior counsel and all of whom called expert witnesses. It adds nothing to see the figures, which are in any event only an estimate and not taxed costs.

Secondly, I must deal with the plaintiff's cross-appeal on costs. The judge ordered the plaintiff to pay the second defendant's costs; that was obviously right and Mr Knight does not challenge it. But the judge rejected Mr Knight's submission that the first defendant should be ordered to reimburse the plaintiff in respect of the second defendant's costs. The basis of Mr Knight's argument before the judge, and before this court, was that the plaintiff only joined the second defendant as a defendant because the first defendant blamed the second defendant in its amended defence; therefore it was reasonable for the plaintiff to add it as a defendant. There should, he submitted, be a Sanderson or Bullock order (see *Bullock v London General Omnibus Co* [1907] 1 KB 264, [1904–7] All ER Rep 44 and *Sanderson v Blyth Theatre Co* [1903] 2 KB 533). The judge refused to make such an order: he said the onus was upon the plaintiff to assess the whole of the merits of the case before joining the second defendant.

The fallacy of Mr Knight's argument is this: while an unsuccessful defendant, A, will normally be held liable to pay the costs of a successful defendant, B, whether directly or indirectly, whom he had blamed, that does not apply where the plaintiff fails against both. In such circumstances, A is not ordered to pay the costs of B, even though he may have blamed him. It is, as the judge said, for the plaintiff to decide whether he is going to succeed against either.

Here the plaintiff failed against both defendants on the only claim pleaded against both, namely for the costs consequent upon the explosion. The second defendant is in no way concerned with the alternative claim raised in the amendment. The cross-appeal is misconceived and I would dismiss it.

PETER GIBSON LJ. I agree.

BALCOMBE LJ. For the reasons given by Stuart-Smith LJ, I agree that this appeal should be allowed and the cross-appeal dismissed. I also agree with the orders which he proposes should be made.

Appeal allowed. Cross-appeal dismissed. Leave to appeal to the House of Lords refused.

Carolyn Toulmin   Barrister

Sheldon and others v R H M Outhwaite (Underwriting Agencies) Ltd and others

QUEEN'S BENCH DIVISION (COMMERCIAL COURT)

SAVILLE J

18, 20 OCTOBER 1993

COURT OF APPEAL, CIVIL DIVISION

SIR THOMAS BINGHAM MR, STAUGHTON AND KENNEDY LJJ

13, 14, 30 JUNE 1994

Limitation of action – Postponement of limitation period – Action for breach of contract and duty – Deliberate concealment of relevant facts – Plaintiffs issuing proceedings outside statutory six-year limitation period – Plaintiffs alleging that defendants had deliberately concealed facts relevant to their right of action – Concealment occurring after plaintiffs' cause of action had arisen – Whether running of limitation period postponed – Whether later concealment capable of defeating time bar – Limitation Act 1980, s 32(1)(b).

In April 1992 the plaintiffs, who were Lloyd's names on syndicates managed by the defendant underwriting agency, issued proceedings against the agency and other members' agents, complaining of breaches of contract and duty by the defendants in or before 1982. The defendants by way of defence asserted that the plaintiffs' claim was time-barred as it was not brought within the six-year limitation period prescribed by ss 2 and 5 of the Limitation Act 1980. The plaintiffs however asserted that the running of the limitation period had been postponed under s 32(1)(b)[a] of the 1980 Act because, after their cause of action had arisen, the defendants had deliberately concealed from them facts relevant to their right of action. The judge held, on a preliminary issue of law, that the plaintiffs were entitled to rely on s 32(1)(b) of the Act to overcome the statutory time bar. The defendants appealed, contending that the deliberate concealment (which was alleged to have occurred over a year after the acts complained of) could not operate to postpone the running of the limitation period where it had already begun to run, since the wording of s 32(1)(b) imported no notion of interruption or recommencement of the limitation period and indicated that the deliberate concealment had to occur at the outset when the cause of action would otherwise accrue, in which event it would postpone the running of the limitation period until discovery of the concealment. The plaintiffs contended (i) that in cases of negligent breach, concealment would almost always occur some time after the breach when the defendant came to appreciate his error and took steps to cover it up, and that if such later concealment had no effect on the running of time, s 32(1)(b) would be deprived of much practical substance and (ii) in reliance on the equitable exception to the old statutory limitation rule, that a defendant whose unconscionable conduct had denied the plaintiff the opportunity to sue in time should not in conscience be permitted to plead the statute to defeat a claim brought timeously after the plaintiff had learned or should have learned of it.

---

a   Section 32(1) is set out at p 484 *g h*, post

Held – The appeal would be allowed for the following reasons—

(1) (Staughton LJ dissenting) On its true construction, s 32(1)(b) of the 1980 Act did not suspend or postpone the running of the limitation period in cases where the defendant had deliberately concealed facts relevant to the plaintiff's claim after his action had arisen until the discovery of the concealment, since the language of s 32(1)(b) itself did not operate to interrupt a limitation period which had already begun to run. If the draftsman had intended to provide that time elapsed between accrual of the cause of action and the defendant's concealment should be treated as if it had not elapsed, or that the running of the limitation period should, notwithstanding any earlier running of time, begin again following discovery or reasonable discovery of any concealment, he could easily have do so and, therefore, the inference had to be that that was not an end which he had wished to achieve. The basic rule was that, after a period prescribed by statute, a plaintiff's claim was barred and since the plaintiffs were unable to bring themselves within the s 32(1)(b) exception to that rule they were unable to overcome the statutory time bar (see p 494 *d* to *f*, p 495 *d*, p 504 *c* and p 507 *a* to *c*, post); *Thorne v Heard* [1894] 1 Ch 599, *Beaman v A R T S Ltd* [1949] 1 All ER 465, *Kitchen v Royal Air Forces Association* [1958] 2 All ER 241 and dictum of Megarry V-C in *Tito v Waddell (No 2)* [1977] 3 All ER 129 at 245 considered.

(2) (Per Sir Thomas Bingham MR and Kennedy LJ) Up to 1986 there had been an unjust lacuna in the law which had allowed non-personal injury plaintiffs who could not rely on s 26[b] of the Limitation Act 1939 or s 32 of the 1980 Act to lose their cause of action before they knew they had it. The s 14A and 14B amendments to the 1980 Act (inserted by the Latent Damage Act 1986) had been plainly intended to fill that lacuna by giving unwitting recipients of negligent and unsound advice an extended period in which to sue from the time of discovery, or reasonable discovery, that the advice was unsound. Those later developments showed that it would be unsafe to prefer the plaintiffs' construction of s 32(1)(b) on the basis that the alternative would have involved a risk of unfairness (see p 494 *a* to *d*, p 506 *e* to *g* and p 507 *c*, post).

Notes

For postponement of limitation period where the defendant deliberately concealed facts relevant to plaintiff's right of action, see 28 *Halsbury's Laws* (4th edn) para 917.

For the Limitation Act 1980, ss 2, 5, 14A, 14B, 32, see 24 *Halsbury's Statutes* (4th edn) (1989 reissue) 650, 653, 662, 664, 683.

Cases referred to in judgments

Archer v Moss, Applegate v Moss [1971] 1 All ER 747, [1971] 1 QB 406, [1971] 2 WLR 541, CA.

Armstrong v Milburn (1886) 54 LT 723, [1886–90] All ER Rep 596, CA; *affg* (1885) 54 LT 247, DC.

Beaman v A R T S Ltd [1949] 1 All ER 465, [1949] 1 KB 550, CA.

Betjemann v Betjemann [1895] 2 Ch 474, CA.

Blair v Bromley (1847) 2 Ph 354, 41 ER 979, LC.

Booth v Earl of Warrington (1714) 4 Bro Parl Cas 163, 2 ER 111.

Bulli Coal Mining Co v Osborne [1899] AC 351, [1895–9] All ER Rep 506, PC.

b	Section 26, so far as material, is set out at p 491 *g*, post

Cartledge v E Jopling & Sons Ltd [1963] 1 All ER 341, [1963] AC 758, [1963] 2 WLR 210, HL.

Fothergill v Monarch Airlines Ltd [1980] 2 All ER 696, [1981] AC 251, [1980] 3 WLR 209, HL.

Garner v Wingrove [1905] 2 Ch 233.

Gibbs v Guild (1882) 9 QBD 59, CA; *affg* (1881) 8 QBD 296.

Homfray v Scroope (1849) 13 QB 509, 116 ER 1357.

Hovenden v Lord Annesley (1806) 2 Sch & Lef 607.

King v Victor Parsons & Co (a firm) [1973] 1 All ER 206, [1973] 1 WLR 29, CA.

Kitchen v Royal Air Forces Association [1958] 2 All ER 241, [1958] 1 WLR 563, CA.

Lawrance v Lord Norreys (1890) 15 App Cas 210, [1886–90] All ER Rep 858, HL.

Lynn v Bamber [1930] 2 KB 72.

McCallum, Re, McCallum v McCallum [1901] 1 Ch 143, CA.

Prideaux v Webber (1661) 1 Lev 31, 83 ER 282.

Rhodes v Smethurst (1838) 4 M & W 42, 150 ER 1335.

Thorne v Heard [1894] 1 Ch 599, CA.

Tito v Waddell (No 2) [1977] 3 All ER 129, [1977] Ch 106, [1977] 2 WLR 496, DC.

UBAF Ltd v European American Banking Corp [1984] 2 All ER 226, [1984] QB 713, [1984] 2 WLR 508, CA.

Westlake v Bracknell DC (1987) 19 HLR 375.

Willis v Earl Howe [1893] 2 Ch 545, CA.

Cases also cited or referred to in skeleton arguments

Bartlett v Barclays Bank Trust Co Ltd [1980] 1 All ER 139, [1980] Ch 515.

Bartlett v Barclays Bank Trust Co Ltd (No 2) [1980] 2 All ER 92, [1980] Ch 515.

Eddis v Chichester Constable [1969] 2 All ER 912, [1969] 2 Ch 345, CA.

Iron Trade Mutual Insurance Co Ltd v J K Buckenham Ltd [1990] 1 All ER 808.

Legh v Legh (1930) 143 LT 151, [1930] All ER Rep 565.

Osgood v Sunderland (1914) 111 LT 529.

Summonses

The plaintiffs, John Brooke Sheldon and other names of Lloyd's Syndicates 317 and 661, issued a writ on 29 April 1992 against the defendants, R H M Outhwaite (Underwriting Agencies) Ltd and other members' agents, claiming damages and/or equitable compensation and, by a reamended points of claim, they alleged against the defendants breach of (i) the terms of underwriting agency agreements made by them with the plaintiffs, (ii) fiduciary duty, (iii) general duty of care to the plaintiffs and (iv) that the defendants had deliberately concealed the facts relevant to the plaintiffs' rights against the defendants. In their points of defence served in February 1993, the defendants denied deliberate concealment and asserted that the plaintiffs' claim was time-barred under the Limitation Act 1980. In their points of reply served in July 1993, the plaintiffs alleged that the primary cause of their delay was the deliberate concealment, which in effect postponed the running of the limitation period under s 32(1)(b) of the 1980 Act. The defendants, however, issued a summons pursuant to RSC Ord 18, r 19 to strike out paras 7 to 11 of the plaintiffs' points of reply which referred to the deliberate concealment. The summons was heard in chambers but judgment was given by Saville J in open court. The facts are set out in the judgment of Saville J.

Barbara Dohmann QC and *Tom Beazley* (instructed by *Norton Rose*) for the plaintiffs.

Ian Hunter QC and *Colin Edelman* (instructed by *Denton Hall*) for the first defendant.

Ian Hunter QC and *Jeffrey Gruder* (instructed by *Oswald Hickson Collier & Co*) for the other defendants.

Cur adv vult

20 October 1993. The following judgment was delivered.

SAVILLE J.   The plaintiff Lloyd's names in these proceedings were underwriting members of Syndicates 317 and 661, whose central allegation is that the managers of those syndicates failed properly to perform their responsibilities in regard to the writing and reinsuring of a number of 'run off' contracts in 1981 and 1982. The writ was issued in April 1992 and the points of claim served later that year. In addition to joining issue on the substantive allegations in this pleading, the defendants have raised a plea of limitation. In points of reply the plaintiffs seek to rely upon the 'deliberate concealment' provisions of s 32 of the Limitation Act 1980 as an answer to the plea of limitation. The defendants now seek to strike out the relevant paragraphs of the points of reply on the grounds that the facts and matters pleaded do not bring the matter within s 32 of the 1980 Act.

The submission made by the defendants is that s 32 of the 1980 Act only applies to a deliberate concealment that occurs at the time when the claimant's cause of action arises and not to any later concealment. In the present case it is common ground that some at least of the plaintiffs' pleaded rights of action arose before the end of 1982, whereas the facts and matters alleged by the plaintiffs to amount to deliberate concealment all occurred after the beginning of 1984.

Section 32 of the 1980 Act, as later amended, provides as follows:

'*Postponement of limitation period in case of fraud, concealment or mistake.*— (1) Subject to subsections (3) and (4A) below, where in the case of any action for which a period of limitation is prescribed by this Act, either—(a) the action is based upon the fraud of the defendant; or (b) any fact relevant to the plaintiff's right of action has been deliberately concealed from him by the defendant; or (c) the action is for relief from the consequences of a mistake; the period of limitation shall not begin to run until the plaintiff has discovered the fraud, concealment or mistake (as the case may be) or could with reasonable diligence have discovered it. Reference in this subsection to the defendant include reference to the defendant's agent and to any person through whom the defendant claims and his agent.

(2) For the purposes of subsection (1) above, deliberate commission of a breach of duty in circumstances in which it is unlikely to be discovered for some time amounts to deliberate concealment of the facts involved in that breach of duty.

(3) Nothing in this section shall enable any action—(a) to recover, or recover the value of, any property; or (b) to enforce any charge against, or set aside any transaction affecting, any property; to be brought against the purchaser of the property or any person claiming through him in any case where the property has been purchased for valuable consideration by an

innocent third party since the fraud or concealment or (as the case may be) the transaction in which the mistake was made took place.

(4) A purchaser is an innocent third party for the purposes of this section—(a) in the case of fraud or concealment of any fact relevant to the plaintiff's right of action, if he was not a party to the fraud or (as the case may be) to the concealment of that fact and did not at the time of the purchase know or have reason to believe that the fraud or concealment had taken place; and (b) in the case of mistake, if he did not at the time of the purchase know or have reason to believe that the mistake had been made.

(4A) Subsection (1) above shall not apply in relation to the time limit prescribed by section 11A(3) of this Act or in relation to that time limit as applied by virtue of section 12(1) of this Act.

(5) Sections 14A and 14B of this Act shall not apply to any action to which subsection (1)(b) above applies (and accordingly the period of limitation referred to in that subsection, in any case to which either of those sections would otherwise apply, is the period applicable under section 2 of this Act).'

In support of the defendants' submission, Mr Hunter QC relied upon the fact that the section is expressed to deal with 'postponement' of the limitation period, the fact that the section provides that the limitation period 'shall not begin to run' until the concealment is discovered or should have been discovered, and the fact that, as a matter of general principle, once a limitation period has begun to run, then it continues without interruption. In these circumstances Mr Hunter submitted that the words of the section were wholly inapt to cover a case where a right of action had arisen with a later deliberate concealment. In such a case the limitation period would start to run under the provisions of Pt I of the 1980 Act. If it had been intended to cover such a case, the legislature would not only have used words such as 'suspension' or 'interruption' instead of or in addition to 'postponement' but would also have hardly confined itself to stipulating that the limitation period would not begin to run, since ex hypothesi the case to be covered would be one where on any view the period had begun to run. Furthermore, Mr Hunter submitted that his construction fitted much better with the other two cases dealt with in the section, namely fraud and mistake, where it is clear that the matters preventing time from beginning to run had to be contemporaneous with (as well as part of) the right of action.

I am not persuaded by this argument for the following reasons. In the first place it is, as I understand it, common ground that the expression 'deliberately concealed' in s 32 was used in place of the expression 'concealed by the fraud' found in s 26 of the Limitation Act 1939, because the case law had made clear that 'fraud' in fact encompassed any conduct which could be categorised as unconscionable and which had the effect of concealing the right of action of the plaintiff. In those cases, for example *Beaman v ARTS Ltd* [1949] 1 All ER 465, [1949] 1 KB 550, *Kitchen v Royal Air Forces Association* [1958] 2 All ER 241, [1958] 1 WLR 563 and *King v Victor Parsons & Co (a firm)* [1973] 1 All ER 206, [1973] 1 WLR 29, it is clear that the Court of Appeal were proceeding at least upon the assumption that unconscionable conduct after the wrongdoing giving rise to the right of action could fall within the 'concealed by the fraud' provisions of the 1939 Act. Indeed, the debate was rather the other way round, namely whether in addition the nature of the wrongdoing giving rise to the cause of action itself or the circumstances in which the wrongdoing took place could also amount (without proof of actual deceit or the like) to concealment within the meaning of the then statutory provision. Furthermore, it seems to me that the *Kitchen* decision is an example of a case where subsequent concealment was actually held to preclude reliance on limitation. Mr Hunter submitted that this was because (apparently) the point was not argued, but even if this is so, it seems to me that these cases contain authoritative guidance on the point. The 'concealed by the fraud' provisions were designed (albeit perhaps not very well) to reflect the pre-existing principles of equity which in turn, as it seems to me, did apply to cases where subsequent conduct concealed the plaintiff's rights: see eg *Bulli Coal Mining Co v Osborne* [1899] AC 351 at 363–364, [1895–9] All ER Rep 506 at 509–510. Thus it is perhaps hardly surprising that in these cases no one put forward the present argument.

In the second place, there is nothing to suggest that the 1980 Act was designed to cut down, as opposed to clarifying, the previous width of what is now described as deliberate concealment, nor indeed did Mr Hunter suggest that this was the case, though of course his submission was that the previous law was that which he contended s 32 carried into effect.

In the third place, I do not accept Mr Hunter's analysis of the words used in s 32. Part I of the 1980 Act sets out what it describes as the 'ordinary' time limits but makes them subject to extension or exclusion in accordance with Pt II, where s 32 is to be found. If there is a wrongdoing followed by deliberate concealment, then the ordinary time limit is extended or excluded so that the period runs from the date when the concealment is or ought to have been discovered. Mr Hunter submitted that this would involve the proposition that at any time (or at least up to the expiry of the ordinary period running from the date of the wrongdoing) a deliberate concealment would mean that the time would start again and run for the full period from when the concealment was or ought to have been discovered. This is so, but I do not find it surprising or unacceptable. It seems to me that deliberate concealment can only operate in cases where the plaintiff is unaware of the fact or facts in question relevant to the right of action, for otherwise, ex hypothesi, there could be no concealment. In such cases, at any time up to the expiry of the ordinary period, unconscionable behaviour concealing those facts will have the effect of precluding or at least discouraging the plaintiff from pursuing an existing right of action. In other words, as time goes by the mischief which equity and now the statute seeks to remedy does not reduce. As to a case where the concealment occurs after the ordinary period has expired, my view is that deliberate concealment could not be called in aid, at least so as to enable the plaintiff to mount an effective action, since by that stage the plaintiff has already lost the remedy of the right to sue, so that ex hypothesi the conduct relied upon could not have the effect of concealing a right of action.

Finally, I am not persuaded that the so-called general principle that once time starts to run it runs without interruption is of any assistance. To my mind reliance upon such a principle comes close to begging the question, which is simply whether s 32 does exclude or extend the ordinary time limits when there has been deliberate concealment after the right of action has arisen. In addition I should record that I did not find any assistance in comparing s 32 with other sections of the 1980 Act.

For these reasons I must refuse the defendants' application. It remains to say that, for these same reasons, I must respectfully disagree with the contrary view on subsequent unconscionable behaviour expressed obiter by Megarry V-C in *Tito v Waddell (No 2)* [1977] 3 All ER 129 at 244, [1977] Ch 106 at 245.

In conclusion, I should make clear that nothing in this judgment goes to the question whether or not any of the facts and matters relied upon by the plaintiffs would, if established, amount to deliberate concealment within the meaning of s 32 of the 1980 Act.

Application dismissed.

Interlocutory appeal

The defendants appealed with the leave of the judge.

Ian Hunter QC and *Colin Edelman* (instructed by *Denton Hall*) for the first defendant.

Ian Hunter QC and *Jeffrey Gruder* (instructed by *Oswald Hickson Collier & Co*) for the other defendants.

Barbara Dohmann QC and *Tom Beazley* (instructed by *Norton Rose*) for the plaintiffs.

Cur adv vult

30 June 1994. The following judgments were delivered.

SIR THOMAS BINGHAM MR. This appeal is against a preliminary ruling on an issue of law made by Saville J in the Commercial Court on 20 October 1993. The issue he had to decide was whether the plaintiffs could rely on s 32(1)(b) of the Limitation Act 1980 to overcome a statutory bar otherwise applicable to their claim where the deliberate concealment which they allege occurred after their causes of action had arisen. The judge held that they could. The defendants challenge that ruling.

The plaintiffs were all Lloyd's names on Syndicates 317 and 661 for the year 1982. Those syndicates were managed by the named defendant, R H M Outhwaite (Underwriting Agencies) Ltd. The other defendants in the action were the plaintiffs' members' agents. The plaintiffs complain of acts done or not done in or before 1982. Their writ was not issued until April 1992. Thus their claim is defeated by the six-year limitation period prescribed by the Limitation Act 1980 on which the defendants rely, unless the plaintiffs can show that the running of the limitation period has been postponed under s 32(1)(b) of that Act.

There has been no investigation of the facts. The judge made clear that his judgment did not bear on the question whether any of the facts and matters pleaded by the plaintiffs would, if established, amount to deliberate concealment within the meaning of s 32. Like the judge, this court must approach the legal issue without regard to that question. What matters is that the earliest acts and omissions said to constitute deliberate concealment for purposes of s 32(1)(b) occurred over a year after the breach of contract or duty on which the plaintiffs' claims are founded, and unless such deliberate concealment has the effect of preventing the limitation period beginning to run or suspending or postponing its running the plaintiffs' actions are barred by ss 2 and 5 of the 1980 Act.

Section 32 of the 1980 Act

As amended in 1986 and 1987, s 32 of the Act now provides:

'(1) Subject to subsections (3) and (4A) below, where in the case of any action for which a period of limitation is prescribed by this Act, either—(a) the action is based upon the fraud of the defendant; or (b) any fact relevant to the plaintiff's right of action has been deliberately concealed from him by the defendant; or (c) the action is for relief from the consequences of a mistake; the period of limitation shall not begin to run until the plaintiff has discovered the fraud, concealment or mistake (as the case may be) or could with reasonable diligence have discovered it. References in this subsection to the defendant include references to the defendant's agent and to any person through whom the defendant claims and his agent.

(2) For the purposes of subsection (1) above, deliberate commission of a breach of duty in circumstances in which it is unlikely to be discovered for some time amounts to deliberate concealment of the facts involved in that breach of duty.

(3) Nothing in this section shall enable any action—(a) to recover, or recover the value of, any property; or (b) to enforce any charge against, or set aside any transaction affecting, any property; to be brought against the purchaser of the property or any person claiming through him in any case where the property has been purchased for valuable consideration by an innocent third party since the fraud or concealment or (as the case may be) the transaction in which the mistake was made took place.

(4) A purchaser is an innocent third party for the purposes of this section—(a) in the case of fraud or concealment of any fact relevant to the plaintiff's right of action, if he was not a party to the fraud or (as the case may be) to the concealment of that fact and did not at the time of the purchase know or have reason to believe that the fraud or concealment had taken place; and (b) in the case of mistake, if he did not at the time of the purchase know or have reason to believe that the mistake had been made.

(4A) Subsection (1) above shall not apply in relation to the time limit prescribed by section 11A(3) of this Act or in relation to that time limit as applied by virtue of section 12(1) of this Act.

(5) Sections 14A and 14B of this Act shall not apply to any action to which subsection (1)(b) above applies (and accordingly the period of limitation referred to in that subsection, in any case to which either of those sections would otherwise apply, is the period applicable under section 2 of this Act).'

It is sub-s (1)(b) on which the plaintiffs rely. But the defendants argue that the language of sub-s (1), in providing that the period of limitation shall not in the prescribed circumstances 'begin to run', contradicts the plaintiffs' argument. In the case of an action based on fraud (sub-s (1)(a)) or for relief from the consequences of a mistake (sub-s (1)(c)) the limitation period will not begin to run at all until the fraud or mistake is or should be discovered. But in the case of a breach of contract or a damage-causing breach of duty, not accompanied by contemporaneous deliberate concealment of the cause of action from the plaintiff by the defendant, the limitation period will in the ordinary way begin to run. The defendants accordingly argue that deliberate concealment cannot, on the wording of the statute, operate to postpone the running of the limitation period in a case where it has already begun to run. Deliberate concealment will, they say, either occur at the outset, when the cause of action would otherwise accrue, in which event it will postpone the running of the limitation period until discovery (or imputed discovery) of the concealment, or it will have no effect at all, because the limitation period will already have begun to run and the subsection imports no notion of interruption or recommencement of the limitation period which has already begun to run. The defendants point to ss 29(5) and 34(5) of the 1980 Act and to the Limitation (Enemies and War Prisoners) Act 1945 as examples of drafting techniques used where it was intended to suspend or interrupt the limitation period or cause time to start running again. No such technique, the defendants rightly contend, is to be found in s 32.

These are persuasive and compelling arguments. But the 1980 Act followed 350 years during which questions of limitation have been intermittently addressed, and I do not think one can safely construe s 32(1)(b) in isolation from the developments which preceded it.

Previous history

The Limitation Act 1623 laid down limitation periods for a wide range of civil claims. It admitted no exceptions, save in the case of minors, married women, persons of unsound mind, prisoners and those beyond the seas. The common law courts applied the statute, as they were bound to do, even though it led to what might seem hard decisions: *Prideaux v Webber* (1661) 1 Lev 31, 83 ER 282, *Rhodes v Smethurst* (1838) 4 M & W 42, 150 ER 1335 and *Homfray v Scroope* (1849) 13 QB 509, 116 ER 1357. In the second of these cases Alderson B expressly rejected the view that the limitation period, once it had begun to run, could be interrupted—

'and unless that were so, great inconvenience would follow; for it would be very difficult, in almost every case, to ascertain whether the statute had or had not run, and we should be obliged to take a great many documents and statements, a great many beginnings and endings, and should have to add up those precise periods of time, out of which the six years would have to be made out; so that great inconvenience would result: and therefore it is better to apply the law as it at present stands; it being far better that a particular injury should be inflicted on one individual, than that great inconvenience should be applied to all the community.' (See 4 M & W 42 at 63, 150 ER 1335 at 1344.)

The severity and inflexibility of this statutory rule were mitigated by courts of equity to permit actions to proceed after expiry of the statutory limitation period where the plaintiff's cause of action was founded on or concealed by the fraud of the defendant. *Booth v Earl of Warrington* (1714) 4 Bro Parl Cas 163, 2 ER 111 is a case in which this rule was applied and it was held that the statute should not avail the dishonest defendant. It was felt to be against conscience that a defendant who had deceived the plaintiff should be able to rely on the statute to defeat the plaintiff's claim : see *Hovenden v Lord Annesley* (1806) 2 Sch & Lef 607 at 634 per Lord Redesdale LC. The rule was also applied in cases such as *Blair v Bromley* (1847) 2 Ph 354, 41 ER 979 and *Gibbs v Guild* (1882) 9 QBD 59; *affg* (1881) 8 QBD 296, but in the absence of fraudulent concealment the statutory bar applied, as in *Armstrong v Milburn* (1886) 54 LT 723, [1886–90] All ER Rep 596; *affg* (1885) 54 LT 247.

This equitable rule received some partial recognition in s 26 of the Real Property Limitation Act 1833, which enacted:

'... in every Case of a concealed Fraud the Right of any Person to bring a Suit in Equity for the Recovery of any Land or Rent of which he, or any Person through whom he claims, may have been deprived by such Fraud, shall be deemed to have first accrued at and not before the Time at which such Fraud shall or with reasonable Diligence might have been first known or discovered ...'

The plaintiff relied on this provision in *Willis v Earl Howe* [1893] 2 Ch 545, but unsuccessfully. The defendant's predecessor in title had entered into possession of the land in 1798. The court held that that entry, whether or not it was wrongful, was not fraudulent and had not been concealed. Time therefore started to run against the plaintiff and those through whom he claimed in 1798. Certain later acts of alleged deception were treated as irrelevant, since they did not deprive the plaintiff and those through whom he claimed of their interest. The decision turned on the construction of the section. In *Thorne v Heard* [1894] 1 Ch 599 at 605 Lindley LJ described s 26 as 'legislative recognition and expression of previously well-settled principles in equity', adding that 'those principles were and are applicable to all kinds of property, and not to real property only', but it may be doubted whether this is entirely correct (as Lindley LJ himself appears to have acknowledged in *Betjemann v Betjemann* [1895] 2 Ch 474 at 479).

In *Thorne v Heard* a trustee committed an innocent breach of trust in paying money to a solicitor who converted it and concealed his act from the plaintiff. It was plain that the solicitor could not enjoy the benefit of the statute in any claim against him, but the action was against the trustee and the question was whether the trustee could rely on the limitation defence given to him by s 8 of the Trustee Act 1888. It was argued on the trustee's behalf that he was not party or privy to the solicitor's fraud, and so was entitled to the benefit of the statute, and this argument prevailed. It is, however, apparent from observations of Lindley and A L Smith LJJ that they attached significance to the fact that the solicitor's fraud and concealment took place after the cause of action against the trustee had already accrued (see [1894] 1 Ch 599 at 603, 605, 614–615). But this point does not seem to have been addressed in argument, and the authority of the case must, in my view, be limited.

In *Bulli Coal Mining Co v Osborne* [1899] AC 351, [1895–9] All ER Rep 506 the appellants had fraudulently and furtively mined the respondents' coal, to which (as they knew) they were not entitled. It was argued on their behalf that the equitable rule gave the respondents no protection, since the appellants had taken no steps to conceal their deliberate wrongdoing. The Judicial Committee of the Privy Council rejected this argument, declining to draw any distinction between furtiveness and deliberate concealment. The present question did not arise. In *Lynn v Bamber* [1930] 2 KB 72 the plaintiff alleged both fraudulent misrepresentation and fraudulent concealment, both of which pleas were held to be in principle good to defeat the statutory bar, and the acts relied on to defeat the statute may well have postdated the accrual of the original cause of action. The report of the case does not, however, throw much light on the alleged acts of concealment and in the event there was held to have been no fraud and no concealment, so the authority of this case also for present purposes is limited.

In 1934 the Law Revision Committee under the chairmanship of Lord Wright (and with a notably strong membership) was invited to consider various aspects of the law of limitation, including the scope of the rules on concealed fraud. The committee reported in 1936 (see *The Statutes of Limitation: Fifth Interim Report* (Cmd 5334)) and found that considerable doubt existed, in particular on the interrelationship of the equitable and common law rules. The committee concluded (on this aspect) (para 22):

> 'We think that it is undesirable that this state of obscurity and uncertainty should continue particularly because the actions which are chiefly affected fall within the important category of actions to recover unliquidated damages for a breach of contract or a tort. We are of opinion that a defendant should not be permitted to set up lapse of time which is due to his fraudulent conduct. We desire, accordingly, to make the following recommendation:—(a) that in all cases to which the Statutes of Limitation apply or are applied by analogy, where a cause of action is founded on fraud, committed by the defendant or his agent, or some person through whom he claims, or where a cause of action unconnected with fraud is fraudulently concealed from the plaintiff by the defendant or his agent, or someone through whom he claims, the right of the plaintiff to sue shall be deemed to have first accrued at the time when he discovered such fraud or could with reasonable diligence have discovered it: (b) that the above recommendation shall not apply to any bona fide purchaser for valuable consideration who has not assisted in the commission or concealment of such fraud and who, at the time that he made the purchase, did not know and had no reason to believe that any such fraud had been committed or any such fraudulent concealment had taken place.'

The committee did not address in any more specific way the present problem of fraudulent concealment postdating the breach of contract or duty relied on.

The committee's recommendation was reflected in s 26 of the Limitation Act 1939, which began:

> 'Where, in the case of any action for which a period of limitation is prescribed by this Act, either—(a) the action is based upon the fraud of the defendant or his agent or of any person through whom he claims or his agent, or (b) the right of action is concealed by the fraud of any such person as aforesaid, or (c) the action is for relief from the consequences of a mistake, the period of limitation shall not begin to run until the plaintiff has discovered the fraud or the mistake, as the case may be, or could with reasonable diligence have discovered it ...'

There followed a proviso broadly to the same effect as s 32(3) of the 1980 Act. The Court of Appeal had occasion to consider this section in *Beaman v ARTS Ltd* [1949] 1 All ER 465, [1949] 1 KB 550. On the facts, the plaintiff's cause of action in conversion arose and the defendant's fraudulent concealment of that cause of action took place at the same time. The present issue did not therefore call for decision. It is, however, evident from the judgment of Lord Greene MR that he regarded 'subsequent active concealment of a fraudulent nature' as enough to give the plaintiff the benefit of the statutory postponement (see [1949] 1 All ER 465 esp at 467, [1949] 1 KB 550 esp at 559). He seems to have regarded that as the paradigm case and to have asked himself whether contemporaneous fraudulent concealment had the same effect, concluding that it did.

The question arose more squarely in *Kitchen v Royal Air Forces Association* [1958] 2 All ER 241, [1958] 1 WLR 563. The plaintiff's solicitors failed to issue a writ within the limitation period applicable to fatal accidents claims. Her cause of action against them accrued in May 1946. In October 1946 the alleged tortfeasor told the plaintiff's solicitors it was willing to make (and in fact made) a payment for the benefit of the plaintiff, but the making of the payment was effectively concealed from her by the solicitors. The real issue in the case was whether what happened in October amounted to fraudulent concealment within the meaning of the section, and it was held that it did. But it seems that the court treated the concealment in October as grounds for denying the solicitors' claim to rely on the statute to bar the plaintiff's claim based on her cause of action which had accrued in May. This is perhaps most explicit in the judgment of Parker LJ, who, agreeing with Lord Evershed MR, said ([1958] 2 All ER 241 at 251–252, [1958] 1 WLR 563 at 576):

'That the [solicitors] were negligent towards the plaintiff in May, 1946, I have no doubt and for the reasons given by my Lord. Whether, however, by fraud they concealed the cause of action from the plaintiff is a matter on which I have had considerable doubt. If there was such a concealment, it is to be found and to be found only, in my view, in the events of October, 1946. On the whole, though with considerable hesitation, I have come to the same conclusion as my Lord and I would accept his judgment on this point.'

This plainly supports the plaintiffs' argument. But the support is limited, since it does not appear that argument was directed to the point. This may have been because the non-disclosure in October, if properly regarded as concealment, was a further actionable breach of duty, and the damages recoverable for both breaches of duty were in principle the same. Counsel may well have thought it best to direct his argument to showing that there was no wrongful concealment in October, since if he lost on that it could not help him to succeed on the present point.

Archer v Moss, Applegate v Moss [1971] 1 All ER 747, [1971] 1 QB 406 and *King v Victor Parsons & Co (a firm)* [1973] 1 All ER 206, [1973] 1 WLR 29 both concerned defective building work knowingly carried out and covered up to prevent the defects being discovered for a long time. In each case there was held to have been concealment by fraud within the meaning of s 26.

In 1971 the Law Reform Committee were invited to reconsider the law relating to limitation. Their *Final Report on the Limitation of Actions* (Cmnd 6923) was published in 1977. The committee were agreed that the postponement conferred by s 26 of the 1939 Act should be retained, but advised that the section should be redrafted so as to eliminate the reference to fraud and so give effect to the thrust of the more recent cases. The majority of the committee were content to accept that there would be hard cases, not involving personal injuries, in which a plaintiff would be unable, through no fault of his own, to ascertain before the expiry of the limitation period that he had suffered damage (see para 2.35). A defendant who had not acted unconscionably was thought to be entitled to rely on the statutory defence of limitation, in the interest of certainty. The committee did not consider whether later concealment would prevent time beginning or continuing to run against an earlier cause of action, and made no mention of the observation of Megarry V-C in *Tito v Waddell (No 2)* [1977] 3 All ER 129 at 245, [1977] Ch 106 at 245–246 that if time had already begun to run, he did not think that a supervening fraudulent concealment would start time running again. This expression of opinion, obiter though it was, must of course command very considerable respect.

Section 32 of the 1980 Act, quoted above, gave effect to the spirit, although not the letter, of the Law Reform Committee's recommendation (see para 2.24 of the report). There, for the purposes of construing s 32, the relevant materials end. But it is perhaps relevant to record (irrelevantly for the purpose of construing s 32) how the law now stands.

In its twenty-fourth report (see the *Report on Latent Damage* (Cmnd 9390)) published in November 1984, the Law Reform Committee considered the law of limitation as it affected negligence cases involving latent defects outside the personal injury field. The committee were concerned about cases involving defective building or unsound professional advice in cases where there was no deliberate concealment but where the injured party might be unaware of the defective work or the unsound advice or the resulting damage for many years. The committee recommended (among other things) that in such cases the existing six-year limitation period should be subject to an extension which would allow a plaintiff three years from the date of discovery, or reasonable discoverability, of significant damage (para 4.9). There was to be a longstop of 15 years (para 4.13), but this was not to apply in cases of fraud, deliberate concealment or mistake (para 4.20). Effect was given to these recommendations by the Latent Damage Act 1986, which inserted ss 14A and 14B into the 1980 Act. It is common ground between the parties to these appeals that s 14A, even if applicable to the plaintiffs' claims, will not enable them to defeat the statutory bar pleaded by the defendants. To defeat the statutory bar they must show, as a matter of law, that they are entitled to rely on s 32(1)(b) of the 1980 Act.

The present appeal

I do not think the materials reviewed above yield a very clear answer to the problem raised by this case. Nor do I think that the issue can safely be decided on considerations of practical justice. If, in the seventy-first month following breach of a simple contract, the contract breaker conceals the breach from the potential claimant who is unaware of it, it can fairly be said to be absurd if the claimant then has another six years to sue from the date when he discovers or reasonably should discover the concealment. But if, in the second month after a breach of a simple contract, the contract breaker conceals the breach from the potential claimant who is unaware of it, it would seem unjust that the claimant should in effect be deprived, by the contract breaker, of his opportunity to seek redress. Arguments of this kind, as it seems to me, cancel each other out.

The strongest arguments advanced on behalf of the plaintiffs are in my judgment these.

(1) The equitable exception to the old and unqualified statutory limitation rule rested on the principle that a defendant whose unconscionable conduct had denied the plaintiff the opportunity to sue in time should not in conscience be permitted to plead the statute to defeat the plaintiff's claim provided the claim were brought timeously once the plaintiff learned or should have learned of it. Given that a defendant cannot be said to conceal that of which the plaintiff is already aware, the plaintiffs' construction better reflects this old and salutary equitable principle. The defendants' construction, by contrast, would

allow a defendant, to a greater or lesser extent, to reap the fruits of his own unconscionable conduct.

(2) It seems clear that deliberate breaches of the *Archer v Moss* and *King v Victor Parsons & Co* variety are now squarely covered by s 32(2) of the 1980 Act. That means that many, perhaps most, claims covered by s 32(1)(b) will be claims in negligence. But negligent breaches, not being deliberate, will almost always be breaches of which the defendant is, at the time, unaware. If, therefore, he takes steps to conceal the breach from the plaintiff, such concealment will almost always occur, in such a case, some time after the breach, when the defendant comes to appreciate his error and takes steps to cover it up. To hold that such later concealment has no effect on the running of time may be said to deprive the subsection of much practical substance.

With considerable hesitation, and after more than one change of opinion, I conclude (differing from the judge) that these arguments should not prevail. My reasons are these.

(1) The basic rule is, and has since 1623 been, that after a period prescribed by statute (or applied by courts of equity following the statute) a plaintiff's claim is barred. If these plaintiffs are to defeat the bar pleaded by the defendants they must bring themselves within an exception to the basic rule.

(2) Nothing in the language of s 32 of the 1980 Act suggests that the draftsman intended to create the exception for which the plaintiffs contend. Had he intended to provide that time elapsed between accrual of the cause of action and the defendant's concealment should be treated as if it had not elapsed, or that the running of the limitation period should (notwithstanding any earlier running of time) begin again following discovery or reasonable discovery of any concealment, he could easily have done so, and legislative models were to hand. The inference must be that this was not an end he wished to achieve.

(3) The plaintiffs' construction of s 32 gains no support from consideration of its lineal statutory ancestors, s 26 of the 1939 Act and s 26 of the Real Property Limitation Act 1833.

(4) A purposive construction is of course appropriate where the draftsman's purpose can be discerned, but the pretext of purposive construction is not a warrant for the judge to give the statute an effect which, with the benefit of hindsight, he feels the draftsman would have been well advised to give it. Neither the Law Revision Committee in 1936 nor the Law Reform Committee in 1977 alluded to this problem in their reports or made any recommendation concerning it. The 1939 and 1980 Acts followed and were in part based on these reports. There is nothing to suggest the respective draftsmen had this target in their sights at all, and every reason to suppose that they did not.

(5) In no reported case has it been held, following argument on the point, that supervening concealment entitles a plaintiff to rely on the statutory exception. In *Thorne v Heard* the Court of Appeal appears to have thought, and perhaps held, that supervening concealment did not avail him. In *Beaman's* case the Court of Appeal seems to have assumed, and in *Kitchen's* case its decision may have rested on the view, that supervening concealment did avail him. That was not, however, the obiter opinion of Megarry V-C in *Tito v Waddell (No 2)* and his was the most recent expression of opinion when the 1980 Act was enacted. It cannot in my view be said that authority establishes the exception for which the plaintiffs contend, or even that the 1980 Act was

enacted against a settled background of law of which the draftsman must be taken to have been cognisant.

(6) There was, in my opinion, an unjust lacuna in the law up to 1986, which allowed non-personal injury plaintiffs who could not rely on s 26 of the 1939 Act or s 32 of the 1980 Act to lose their cause of action before they knew they had it. That was a source of concern to some members of the Law Reform Committee in 1977 (see para 2.36 of their report) and may well explain why, just before the 1980 Act was passed, the committee was invited to consider further the limitation aspects of negligence claims arising from latent damage. The amendments made following the committee's further report were plainly intended to fill this unjust lacuna by giving unwitting recipients of negligent and unsound advice an extended period in which to sue from the time of discovery (or reasonable discovery) that the advice was unsound. These later developments do in my view show that it would be unsafe to prefer the plaintiffs' construction on the basis that the alternative would have involved a risk of unfairness. It did; and to some extent at least that was remedied. It would seem at least arguable that these plaintiffs could have relied on that statutory extension.

I would allow this appeal.

STAUGHTON LJ. Either solution to the problem in this appeal can give rise to absurdity. Deliberate concealment might start in one case on the day after the cause of action and last for six years; in another, it might start only on the day before the action would have become time-barred, and then last for one day. If the argument for the underwriting agencies is right, the plaintiffs in the first case would get no extension; if the argument for the names is right, the plaintiffs in the second would enjoy a total limitation period of 12 years. So it is not possible to assert with conviction that Parliament must have intended one solution rather than the other.

Against that background I turn first to the language of the section and other legislative material. Section 32(1) of the Limitation Act 1980 provides that 'the period of limitation shall not begin to run until the plaintiff has discovered the fraud, concealment or mistake ...' That is not at first sight designed to cover the case where there has been no concealment until some time after the cause of action has arisen, so that the period of limitation has begun to run. It would have been more appropriate to use the language of s 29(5): '... the right shall be treated as having accrued on and not before the date of the acknowledgment or payment.'

Nevertheless I do not regard the language of the section as an insuperable obstacle. It can, for example, be treated as providing that the period of limitation which the law regards as appropriate will be one beginning to run after discovery etc. In the Fifth Interim Report of the Law Revision Committee (Cmd 5334) published in 1936 it is said (at para 13):

'... in applying equitable remedies to cases of fraud or mistake, the period of limitation *is not reckoned* until the fraud or mistake is or could, with reasonable diligence, have been discovered.' (My emphasis.)

Is that, in point of language, so different from the wording of s 32(1)?

In fact the Law Revision Committee recommended a solution which accords entirely with the argument for the names in this case. They said (at para 22):

'... in all cases to which the Statutes of Limitation apply or are applied by analogy, where a cause of action is founded on fraud, committed by the defendant or his agent, or some person through whom he claims, or where a cause of action unconnected with fraud is fraudulently concealed from the plaintiff by the defendant or his agent, or someone through whom he claims, the right of the plaintiff to sue shall be deemed to have first accrued at the time when he discovered such fraud or could with reasonable diligence have discovered it.'

Did Parliament intend to depart from that recommendation and produce a different result? Or was the wording of s 26 of the Limitation Act 1939, repeated (in this respect) in the 1980 Act, intended to give effect to that recommendation?

Turning to the numerous cases that were cited, I find only three of direct assistance. The first is *Thorne v Heard* [1894] 1 Ch 599. That case was concerned with a claim to recover the proceeds of sale of property subject to a second mortgage; the money had been misappropriated by the solicitor for the defendants, who were the first mortgagees. In answer to a plea that the claim was barred by lapse of time, the plaintiff relied on the equitable effect of fraud. This was held not to avail him for two reasons: first, the fraud and its concealment occurred after the plaintiff's cause of action had accrued; secondly, it was the fraud and concealment of the solicitor and not of the defendants. That the first ground formed part of the reasoning for the decision is to my mind plain from the judgment of Lindley LJ, and also to some extent from that of A L Smith LJ (see [1894] 1 Ch 599 at 605, 614 respectively).

It follows in my opinion that Saville J was wrong to conclude that 'pre-existing principles of equity ... did apply to cases where subsequent conduct concealed the plaintiff's rights', at all events if some interval of time occurred between the accrual of the cause of action and the subsequent conduct.

The second case which favours the underwriting agencies is the decision of Megarry V-C in *Tito v Waddell (No 2)* [1977] 3 All ER 129, [1977] Ch 106.

To a different effect is *Kitchen v Royal Air Forces Association* [1958] 2 All ER 241, [1958] 1 WLR 563. There the plaintiff claimed damages from her solicitors for negligence in the formulation and prosecution of a claim against an electricity company. The solicitors said that the action was time-barred, and the plaintiff in turn relied on fraudulent concealment.

It was held that the solicitors had been in breach of their duty to their client during the period from November or December 1945 to June or July 1946. Lord Evershed MR held that there was no fraudulent concealment at that stage (see [1958] 2 All ER 241 at 246, [1958] 1 WLR 563 at 569). But there was fraudulent concealment in October and November 1946, after the cause of action against the solicitors had arisen. According to Lord Evershed MR it was a concealment—

'of their having thrown away—and I use that word deliberately—any case which she might have possessed under the Fatal Accidents Act in May, 1946.' (See [1958] 2 All ER 241 at 249, [1958] 1 WLR 563 at 572.)

Parker LJ said:

'That the [solicitors] were negligent towards the plaintiff in May, 1946, I have no doubt and for the reasons given by my Lord. Whether, however, by fraud they concealed the cause of action from the plaintiff is a matter on which I have had considerable doubt. If there was such a concealment, it is to be found and to found only, in my view, in the events of October, 1946. On the whole, though with considerable hesitation, I have come to the same conclusion as my Lord, and I would accept his judgment on this point.' (See [1958] 2 All ER 241 at 251–252, [11958] 1 WLR 563 at 576.)

That decision is plainly inconsistent with the view that concealed fraud, or deliberate concealment, is only relevant if it exists at the moment when the cause of action accrues. But it is said by Megarry V-C in *Tito v Waddell (No 2)* [1977] 3 All ER 129 at 245, [1977] Ch 106 at 245 that the point was not argued, and was decided sub silentio. It is true that it does not feature with any degree of clarity in what Lord Evershed MR described as 'three distinct points for our determination' (see *Kitchen* [1958] 2 All ER 241 at 244, [1958] 1 WLR 563 at 567). And if sub silentio means that the court did not say that it was deciding the point, then the description applies. But at the very least it can be said that the contrary view never occurred to, or at any rate seemed at all plausible to, Lord Evershed MR, Parker and Sellers LJJ, Mr Patrick O'Connor or his junior.

I return to s 32(1) of the 1980 Act. The purpose of the provision in question, as was said for example by Lord Coleridge CJ in *Gibbs v Guild* (1882) 9 QBD 59 at 65, is that a man should not be allowed to take advantage of his own wrong. In my view it is permissible to apply a purposive construction to the section, without doing any great violence to its wording, rather than the 'narrowly semantic approach' criticised by Lord Diplock in *Fothergill v Monarch Airlines Ltd* [1980] 2 All ER 696 at 705, [1981] AC 251 at 280. I would read the section as providing that the period of limitation *shall not be treated as beginning to run* until after discovery of the fraud etc. It is true that this does not exactly equate the plaintiff's remedy with the extent of the wrong; he may well obtain a longer extension than he deserves. But Parliament, which used such a nice adjustment for arbitration proceedings in s 34(5), evidently thought it inappropriate in s 32(1)—perhaps because there might be uncertainty as to the date when deliberate concealment began.

Mr Hunter QC for the underwriting agencies had a point on s 32(3). I am not sure that I fully understood it. But in any event it does not persuade me to adopt his interpretation of s 32(1). I would dismiss this appeal.

KENNEDY LJ. (1) The issue which Saville J had to consider in this case was whether reliance can be placed upon s 32(1)(b) of the Limitation Act 1980 where the alleged deliberate concealment relied upon occurred an appreciable time after the plaintiffs' alleged causes of action arose.

(2) The 1980 Act

Section 2 of the 1980 Act provides: 'An action founded on tort shall not be brought after the expiration of six years from the date on which the cause of action accrued', but by virtue of s 1(2) that ordinary time limit is subject to extension or exclusion in accordance with the provisions of Pt II of the Act, and in Pt II is to be found s 32(1), which, so far as relevant, provides:

'... where in the case of any action for which a period of limitation is prescribed by this Act, either—(a) the action is based upon the fraud of the defendant; or (b) any fact relevant to the plaintiff's right of action has been deliberately concealed from him by the defendant; or (c) the action is for relief from the consequences of a mistake; the period of limitation shall not begin to run until the plaintiff has discovered the fraud, concealment or mistake (as the case may be) or could with reasonable diligence have discovered it ...'

Mr Hunter QC for the appellant defendants invited us to consider with care the words 'the period of limitation shall not begin to run' because, he submits, they show that it is only concealment that takes place before in the normal course of events the period of limitation has begun to run which causes a postponement. Miss Dohmann QC for the respondent plaintiffs submits that the wording of s 32(1) should not be so constrained. If after the cause of action has accrued and the period of limitation has begun to run a fact relevant to the plaintiff's right of action is deliberately concealed from him by the defendant then not only does time cease to run against the plaintiff but the clock returns to zero, and time does not start to run again until the plaintiff has discovered the concealment or could with reasonable diligence have discovered it. And that is the position, she submits, even if at the time of concealment the statutory period of limitation had almost expired, and whether or not the plaintiff was in fact influenced by the act of concealment on the part of the defendant. So although if there is deliberate concealment by a defendant whenever it occurs a plaintiff will usually need the benefit of the statutory provision, the construction for which Miss Dohmann contends can produce a strange result. A more equitable solution, as it seems to me, would be if the act of concealment were to stop the clock running until the plaintiff discovered it or could with reasonable diligence have done so, but as both sides concede that is not an interpretation which can possibly be given to the words of the statute. In my judgment if s 32(1) had to be considered in isolation this court should adopt the interpretation for which Mr Hunter contends, because the words which he emphasises do postulate the period of limitation beginning to run for the first time. Other sections of the 1980 Act do, as it seems to me, lend some support to Mr Hunter's main submission, because they show that where Parliament wished to exclude a period from computation of time it said so in terms (see s 34(5)) and where it wished to postpone the running of time to a date after the accrual of the cause of action it was able to find a suitable formula by means of which to do so (see s 29(5)).

(3) *The early history*

But this statute, like any other, does not have to be considered in isolation. We are entitled to look at the legislative history and the parliamentary purpose, and both sides contend that if we do so we will find support for the positions that they adopt.

In *Prideaux v Webber* (1661) 1 Lev 31, 83 ER 282 the Statute of Limitations was held to be a good bar despite the fact that the King's courts were not available when time was running. In *Hovenden v Lord Annesley* (1806) 2 Sch & Lef 607 at 634 Lord Redesdale LC said of *Booth v Earl of Warrington* (1714) 4 Bro Parl Cas 163, 2 ER 111 that in that case the House of Lords had held—

'the discovery of the fraud, being alleged to be at a subsequent period, and arising out of circumstances collateral, and it being established that such was the fact, a court of equity was well warranted in avoiding the transaction, notwithstanding the statute of limitations: for, pending the concealment of the fraud, the statute of limitations ought not in conscience to run; the conscience of the party being so affected, that he ought not to be allowed to avail himself of the length of time: but after the discovery of the fact, imputed as fraud, the party has a right to avail himself of the statute ...'

That shows the willingness of equity to ameliorate the consequences of the strict application of the Statute of Limitations, but it seems to me to leave in doubt the way in which equity would operate in the circumstances of the present case.

In 1833 Parliament enacted the Real Property Limitation Act, which provided a 20-year limitation period for persons claiming land or rent in equity, but the rigour of that provision was to some extent ameliorated by s 26, which, so far as material, provided:

'... in every Case of a concealed Fraud the Right of any Person to bring a Suit in Equity for the Recovery of any Land or Rent of which he, or any Person through whom he claims, may have been deprived by such Fraud, shall be deemed to have first accrued at and not before the Time at which such Fraud shall or with reasonable Diligence might have been first known or discovered ...'

Chronologically the next case to which our attention has been invited, *Rhodes v Smethurst* (1838) 4 M & W 42, 150 ER 1335, was not a case involving the 1833 Act. It was an action on a promissory note. After the cause of action accrued the debtor died, and no action was commenced for more than six years from the date of the accrual of the cause of action. The Statute of Limitations was invoked. Lord Abinger CB found—

'both authority and reason for concluding that the period of time from which the computation is to begin, is when the action accrued; and that when the statute has once begun to run, any portion of time in which the parties are under disabilities must nevertheless form part of the six years.' (See 4 M & W 42 at 62, 150 ER 1335 at 1343.)

Alderson B, whilst recognising the effect of equity, said that 'if the statute begins to run it must continue to run' (see 4 M & W 42 at 63, 150 ER 1335 at 1344). Although that case did not involve fraud it does, as it seems to me, suggest that the proposition for which Mr Hunter contends, represented the law as it stood in 1838.

In *Homfray v Scroope* (1849) 13 QB 509 at 512, 116 ER 1357 at 1358–1359, an action under the Tithe Act 1836, Lord Denman CJ followed *Rhodes's* case, saying of the statute with which he was concerned that it 'bears the closest analogy to the general Statute of Limitations: and, with regard to them, it is a well known and settled rule, that, where the time has once begun to run, no subsequent disability, however involuntary, will suspend their operation'.

In *Gibbs v Guild* (1882) 9 QBD 59 the plaintiff sought damages for fraudulent misrepresentation, and when the Statute of Limitations was raised asserted that he did not discover and had no reasonable means of discovering the fraud until within the six years before the action was commenced. That being accepted he was in equity entitled to relief. Brett LJ said (at 69):

'It seems to me that there is some little confusion in the expressions used in some cases as to the origin of the cause of action being a fraud. That is not the fraud which raised the equity; but if there was a cause of action, and if its existence was fraudulently concealed from the plaintiff by the defendant who had given that cause of action, it was then that the plaintiff's equity arose notwithstanding that his cause of action had arisen more than six years before.'

Miss Dohmann places reliance upon that passage, which is slightly differently reported in less authoritative reports but I do not find the passage to be of particular assistance in the present case.

In *Armstrong v Milburn* (1886) 54 LT 723, [1886–90] All ER Rep 596 the plaintiff in a solicitor's negligence action, in which the issue of limitation was raised, said that as a result of concealment by the defendant she did not discover and did not have the means of discovering the defendant's negligence until within the six-year period prior to the commencement of the action. In fact no negligence was proved, but Lord Esher MR said (54 LT 723 at 723, [1886–90] All ER Rep 596 at 596):

> '... even if there had been negligence, the plaintiff would still fail, for the Statute of Limitations had run as against her claim, and it is clear that she could have no answer to the defence of the statute unless fraudulent concealment on the part of the defendant were proved ...'

Miss Dohmann relies on the final qualification as suggesting that if fraudulent concealment were proved at whatever date the plaintiff would be able to overcome the limitation defence. In my judgment that is reading too much into a remark which was obiter in a case which did not raise the issue which we have to consider.

In *Willis v Earl Howe* [1893] 2 Ch 545, an action of ejectment, the plaintiff claimed to be the heir to an estate, and the court had to consider s 26 of the 1833 Act. Lindley LJ said, quoting from Lord Herschell in *Lawrance v Lord Norreys* (1890) 15 App Cas 210 at 214, [1886–90] All ER Rep 858 at 860, that to prove a concealed fraud 'the person bringing the suit must shew that he or some person through whom he claims has been by such fraud deprived of the land which he seeks to recover, and that the fraud could not with reasonable diligence have been known or discovered more than the statutory period before the action was brought' (see [1893] 2 Ch 545 at 549–550). In the instant case there was found to be no fraud, and no concealment, so the claim failed.

In 1893 there was published Dr Hewitt's *Treatise on the Statutes of Limitations* in which it is said of s 26 of the 1833 Act that it 'was framed in accordance with the recommendations of the Real Property Commissioners, and was intended to confirm (in the case of suits to recover land or rent) the existing rules of equity as to the effect of fraud upon the operation of the Statutes of Limitations' (see p 206). The author says (p 211):

> 'The rule of Equity as to the effect of fraud upon the Statutes of Limitations is sometimes stated to be that time will not run against a person entitled to a cause of action so long as the existence of the cause of action is fraudulently concealed. But the true rule would seem to be that fraud only affects the operation of the Statutes of Limitations where the original cause of action is based upon fraud, whereby the plaintiff has been deprived of property or has otherwise suffered loss. *If the right of action was wholly unconnected with fraud, the fact that the defendant subsequently concealed the cause of action would not prevent time from running*; and it is submitted that if fraudulent means were adopted in order to effect the concealment, although such fraud might itself give rise to a right of action, it would not keep alive the original cause of action.' (My emphasis.)

Armstrong v Milburn was cited in support of the passage which I have identified.

In *Thorne v Heard* [1894] 1 Ch 599 a solicitor acting for a first mortgagee failed properly to account for moneys received on the sale of the property, to the detriment of the plaintiff, who was the second mortgagee. When the solicitor became bankrupt the facts emerged, and the plaintiff sued the first mortgagee, but was held to be statute-barred because the cause of action accrued when the first mortgagee committed an irrevocable breach of trust by allowing the solicitor to receive the surplus sales' moneys instead of handing them over to the plaintiffs. The fraud of the solicitor was not perpetrated or concealed by the defendant. When acting fraudulently the solicitor was acting in his own interests. Lindley LJ said that *Willis v Earl Howe* decided—

> 'that a fraud committed and concealed, even by the defendant or one of his predecessors in title, would not avail the plaintiff if the fraud and its concealment were subsequent to the wrongful entry which gave the plaintiff or his predecessors a right to bring ejectment.' (See [1894] 1 Ch 599 at 604–605.)

He also said that the 1833 Act 'is a legislative recognition and expression of previously well-settled principles in equity, and those principles were and are applicable to all kinds of property, and not to real property only'. However Lindley LJ qualified that observation in *Betjemann v Betjemann* [1895] 2 Ch 474, where the Statute of Limitations was relied on in a partnership dispute.

The final nineteenth century authority to which our attention was invited is *Bulli Coal Mining Co v Osborne* [1899] AC 351, [1895–9] All ER Rep 506, where the appellants had furtively for years taken the respondents' coal by underground trespass. The Statute of Limitations was held to have no application. Lord James, giving the opinion of the Privy Council, having pointed out that equity follows the law, said ([1899] AC 351 at 363, [1895–9] All ER Rep 506 at 510):

> 'Now it has always been a principle of equity that no length of time is a bar to relief in the case of fraud, in the absence of laches on the part of the person defrauded. There is, therefore, no room for the application of the statute in the case of concealed fraud, so long as the party defrauded remains in ignorance without any fault of his own.'

Of course once again that does not deal with the situation where time has begun to run before any concealment occurs.

In *Re McCallum, McCallum v McCallum* [1901] 1 Ch 143 the plaintiff claimed title to a freehold property and relied on a conveyance of which the plaintiff's father and the defendant, who was the beneficiary of her father's estate, were unaware. The defendant was able to rely on the 1833 Act because although there had been concealment it was by the plaintiff's mother and not by the defendant or the father from whom she derived title. The case is therefore not directly in point, but there are useful observations about the general nature of the equitable jurisdiction, and the extent to which it was reflected in the 1833 Act. Lord Alverstone CJ said (at 150):

> 'As I understand it, the old jurisdiction exercised by the Courts of Equity rested upon the fact that the conscience of the party who was setting up possession as against the title of the true owner was affected, so that he ought not to be allowed to avail himself of the lapse of time.'

And Vaughan Williams LJ said (at 158–159):

'It seems to me that the words of s. 26 sufficiently indicate that the intention of the Legislature, at the time when it enacted a legislative rule respecting the period within which relief might be granted to those seeking to recover any land or rent of which they might have been deprived, was to reserve to Courts of Equity that jurisdiction which those Courts had always exercised to relieve against "concealed fraud" when discovered.'

In the Yorke Prize Essay for the University of Cambridge for 1929, 'Limitation of actions in equity', Mr John Brunyate of Trinity College, Cambridge and the Chancery Bar said, in a chapter on fraud (p 23):

'From the earliest times the Courts of Equity have been chary of applying the Statutes of Limitations in cases of fraud. Sometimes it was thought that length of time would never bar a suit based upon fraud, but the Courts eventually decided that the statutory period, although it would not run while the fraud was undiscovered, would begin to run as soon as the fraud was discovered. This rule was applied both where the cause of action sprang from the fraudulent acts and where the defendant had by later fraudulent acts concealed from the plaintiff an existing cause of action. The rule was developed in applying the Act of 1623, and it is still in force in suits which are still subject to that Act. A similar but not identical rule applicable to suits to recover land or rent was embodied in sect. 26 of the Real Property Limitation Act of 1833 ...'

Miss Dohmann understandably places some reliance on that passage, but it is to be noted that the assertion that the equitable rule applied where the defendant had by later fraudulent acts concealed from the plaintiff an existing cause of action is unsupported by authority, and the researches of counsel have not produced any authority to support it, other than those to which I have referred.

In 1934 the Law Revision Committee was asked to consider, inter alia, 'the circumstances affecting defendants which prevent the periods of limitation from beginning to run, and the scope of the rules as to concealed fraud.' The committee's report was published in 1936 (Cmd 5334), and having looked at various statutory periods of limitation it states (para 7):

'... it has to be remembered that the purpose of the statutes goes further than the prevention of dilatoriness; they aim at putting a certain end to litigation and at preventing the resurrection of old claims, whether there has been delay or not.'

In para 13 of the report it is recognised that 'in applying equitable remedies to cases of fraud or mistake, the period of limitation is not reckoned until the fraud or mistake is or could, with reasonable diligence, have been discovered'. In para 16 the report states:

'At present the only disabilities which operate to suspend the statutory periods of limitation are those which are in existence at the time when the cause of action first comes into being. Any event constituting a disability which arises subsequently is of no effect (*Garner* v. *Wingrove* [1905] 2 Ch. 233). It is, perhaps, conceivable that this rule may cause hardship in certain cases; e.g., where a cause of action accrues to A and he becomes insane before he has had a reasonable time within which to institute proceedings. But such cases must be of very rare occurrence. On the other hand, a rule which would lead to the suspension of a cause of action, if the claimant became subject to a disability at any time whilst the statutory period is running, would in some instances impose grave hardship on defendants. For this reason it seems preferable to leave the present rule as it stands.'

Garner v Wingrove was a case in which a defendant in possession of land was able to take advantage of statutory provisions as to limitation against the owner even though after the time began to run the owner died and title passed to an infant. In dealing with acknowledgment and part payment the 1936 report recognised in para 19 that in some cases time can be made to start afresh, but para 22 does not suggest any such possibility where a cause of action is subsequently concealed by fraud. Indeed, rather the contrary: what it says is—

'As a general rule it is no answer to a plea of the Statutes of Limitation to say that the plaintiff was unaware of the existence of his cause of action until after the expiration of the statutory period. But cases may occur in which such ignorance on the part of the plaintiff is brought about by the fraudulent conduct of the defendant. Either the cause of action may spring from the fraud of the defendant or else the existence of a cause of action untainted in its origin by fraud may have been concealed from the plaintiff by the fraudulent conduct of the defendant. It is obviously unjust that a defendant should be permitted to rely upon a lapse of time created by his own misconduct, but the present state of the law is so obscure and pregnant with difficulties that it must be regarded as uncertain whether a fraudulent defendant can in all cases be prevented from setting up the plea that the action has been brought out of time. Up to a point the law is reasonably clear ...'

The report than refers to s 33 of the 1833 Act and observes:

'... fraudulent statements or fraudulent destruction of evidence after possession has once been obtained have been held not to be sufficient to prevent the Statute from running ...'

Mr Hunter places some reliance upon that observation. The report continues:

'Much of the ground is also covered by the equitable doctrine that a plaintiff is not to be affected by the lapse of time where his ignorance is due to the fraud of the defendant, and he has had no reasonable opportunity of discovering such fraud before bringing his action. The extent, however, of the area within which the equitable doctrine is operative is still a matter of doubt and controversy.'

There is then a discussion of the position before and after the Supreme Court of Judicature Act 1873, with particular reference to the effect of equity upon the common law. The committee concluded that it was 'undesirable that this state of obscurity and uncertainty should continue'. They said: 'We are of opinion that a defendant should not be permitted to set up lapse of time which is due to his fraudulent conduct.' Miss Dohmann invites our attention to that, and to the recommendation in the report which followed it:

'... that in all cases to which the Statutes of Limitation apply or are applied by analogy, where a cause of action is founded on fraud, committed by the defendant or his agent, or some person through whom he claims, or where a cause of action unconnected with fraud is fraudulently concealed from the plaintiff by the defendant or his agent, or someone through whom he claims, the right of the plaintiff to sue shall be deemed to have first accrued at the time when he discovered such fraud or could with reasonable diligence have discovered it.'

For my part, I would accept that if we were considering a statutory provision which enacted that recommendation Miss Dohmann would be in a much stronger position, but the statutory provision with which we are concerned does not say that the right of the plaintiff to sue shall be *deemed to have first accrued* at the time when he discovered the defendant's fraud or could, with reasonable diligence, have discovered it.   Furthermore, the Law Revision Committee's report seems to me to make it abundantly clear that Miss Dohmann cannot really maintain the argument which apparently commended itself to Saville J, namely that prior to the intervention of statute those in the position of her clients enjoyed equitable rights which the statutes should not be interpreted as having taken away.   The fact is that prior to the intervention of statute the position may not have been entirely clear, but generally the rule seems to have been that once time began to run later concealment of the cause of action by the defendant would not interrupt it.

(4) *The Limitation Act 1939*

Instead of following the recommendations of the committee s 26 of the Limitation Act 1939 provided:

'Where, in the case of an action for which a period of limitation is prescribed by this Act, either—(a) the action is based upon the fraud of the defendant or his agent or of any person through whom he claims or his agent, or (b) the right of action is concealed by the fraud of any such person as aforesaid, or (c) the action is for relief from the consequences of a mistake, the period of limitation shall not begin to run until the plaintiff has discovered the fraud or the mistake, as the case may be, or could with reasonable diligence have discovered it ...'

There is then a proviso which for present purposes is not relevant.   In Preston and Newsom *Limitation of Actions* (1st edn, 1940) p 361 the comment is made in relation to s 26 of the 1939 Act—

'where a fraudulent concealment supervenes, a right of action having already accrued, there is nothing in the new provision to stop time running. It deals only with the time when the period of limitation shall "*begin* to run".   If time is running already, the Limitation Act, 1939, s. 26, does not apply ...' (The authors' emphasis.)

Mr Hunter submits that is correct, but Miss Dohmann invites our attention to *Beaman v ARTS Ltd* [1949] 1 All ER 465, [1949] 1 KB 550.   That case concerned a bailee who during the 1939–45 war whilst the plaintiff was abroad disposed of her goods and more than six years later she commenced proceedings for conversion.   It was held in relation to s 26 that the cause of action was not based on fraud, but the Court of Appeal held that the conduct of the defendant did amount to a fraudulent concealment of the cause of action for the purposes of s 26(b).   The court regarded as relevant the bailee's failure to tell the plaintiff what they had done but there was also concealment coterminous with the conversion, so, as I read the judgments, they proceed upon the basis that until the plaintiff learnt what had happened time had not started to run.   For example, Lord Greene MR said ([1949] 1 All ER 465 at 470, [1949] 1 KB 550 at 566):

'This failure to make a proper record was the cause of delay in tracing in what had been done with the goods when the plaintiff came to claim them. I am of opinion that the conduct of the defendants, by the very manner in which they converted the plaintiff's chattels in breach of the confidence reposed in them and in circumstances calculated to keep her in ignorance of the wrong that they had committed, amounted to a fraudulent concealment of the cause of action.'

Similarly Singleton LJ said ([1949] 1 All ER 465 at 472, [1949] 1 KB 550 at 571):

' The disposal of the goods in this way was a fraud on the owner. The reason they did not tell her what they had done with the goods was that they did not wish her to know. There was a chance that she might not come back to this country for many years. By concealing from her what they had done, they concealed from her the right of action which arose on the conversion of the goods.'

In *Kitchen v Royal Air Forces Association* [1958] 2 All ER 241, [1958] 1 WLR 563 the plaintiff succeeded against her former solicitor, who, following the death of her husband, had failed to advise her of her potential claim under the Fatal Accidents Acts and of an offer made in October 1946 by the electricity company involved. The concealment of the offer was held to amount to both a breach of duty and a fraudulent concealment for the purposes of s 26(b) of the 1939 Act, so the claim was not statute-barred. The position taken by the Court of Appeal in relation to the failure to advise in relation to the potential claim is far less clear, and in the circumstances was not critical, so I cannot accept Miss Dohmann's submission that *Kitchen's* case is authority for the proposition that where there is concealment by a defendant sometime after the cause of action has accrued s 26(b) applies. As Sir Thomas Bingham MR has pointed out in his judgment in this case, in *Kitchen's* case that issue did not have to be argued.

In *Cartledge v E Jopling & Sons Ltd* [1963] 1 All ER 341, [1963] AC 758 the House of Lords considered an appeal by plaintiffs who developed pneumoconiosis. The plaintiffs submitted that time should be held only to have run against them from when they knew or could have reasonably be expected to have known of their condition, but Lord Pearce said ([1963] 1 All ER 341 at 351, [1963] AC 758 at 782–783):

'Past cases have been decided on the basis that the time runs from the accrual of the cause of action whether known or unknown and no case has been cited in which the plaintiff's lack of knowledge has prevented the time from running where that lack of knowledge has not been induced by the defendant.'

Turning to s 26 of the 1939 Act, he said that it created 'a special exception' and continued:

'... even in such cases the legislature apparently considered that the right of action accrued in spite of the plaintiff's ignorance, since the Act provides that "the period of limitation shall not begin to run until the plaintiff has discovered the fraud ..." Moreover the Act of 1939 was passed in the light of the earlier cases ... and had the legislature intended to secure a different result it would have said so.'

The clear implication, as it seems to me, is that in the context of the present case time did run from the date of accrual of the cause of action.

Archer v Moss, Applegate v Moss [1971] 1 All ER 747, [1971] 1 QB 406 was a case concerning houses built on unsatisfactory foundations which were then covered. Lord Denning MR said that s 26(b) applied 'whenever the conduct of the defendant or his agent has been such as to hide from the plaintiff the existence of his right of action, in such circumstances that it would be inequitable to allow the defendant to rely on the lapse of time as a bar to the claim' (see [1971] 1 All ER 747 at 750, [1971] 1 QB 406 at 413). As a general proposition that is no doubt correct, but it does not deal directly with the problem we have to resolve. That brings me to what was said obiter by Megarry V-C when giving judgment in *Tito v Waddell (No 2)* [1977] 3 All ER 129 at 245, [1977] Ch 106 at 245:

'Under the Limitation Act 1939, s 26, the effect of fraudulent concealment is that "the period of limitation shall not begin to run until the plaintiff has discovered the fraud ... or could with reasonable diligence have discovered it". If time has already begun to run, I do not think that a supervening fraudulent concealment will start time running again.'

Miss Dohmann submits that Megarry V-C's observations did not and do not represent the law, but if so it is surprising that when Parliament enacted s 26 of the 1939 Act with some modifications as s 32 of the Limitation Act 1980 it did not clarify the position.

(5)   Since the 1980 Act

In August 1980 another Law Reform Committee was asked 'to consider the law relating to—(i) the accrual of the cause of action, and (ii) limitation, in negligence cases involving latent defects (other than latent disease or injury to the person) and to make recommendations'. It reported in 1984 (Cmnd 9390) and Parliament then enacted the Latent Damage Act 1986, which introduced into the 1980 Act ss 14A and 14B. The result is that in an action for damages for negligence other than for personal injuries the starting date for reckoning the period of limitation is the earliest date on which the plaintiff or any person in whom the cause of action vested before him had both the knowledge required for bringing the action and the right to bring it. If, as I believe, the law still is as Megarry V-C found it to be then some deserving plaintiffs who cannot take advantage of s 32(1)(b) will be able to take advantage of s 14A.

The last two authorities on which Miss Dohmann relied were *UBAF Ltd v European American Banking Corp* [1984] 2 All ER 226, [1984] QB 713 and *Westlake v Bracknell DC* (1987) 19 HLR 375. In the *UBAF Ltd* case [1984] 2 All ER 226 at 236, [1984] QB 713 at 728 the Court of Appeal said that if it was within the plaintiff's knowledge whilst they were carrying out their fiduciary duties that the security was inadequate the failure to say so 'would constitute a continuing breach of its fiduciary duty'. If the breach of fiduciary duty continued the problem which we have to consider could not arise. In *Westlake's* case P J Cox QC, sitting as a deputy judge of the High Court, held amongst other things that when a negligent surveyor later sought to reassure house purchasers his conduct amounted to deliberate concealment of facts relevant to the plaintiffs' right of action such as to enable the plaintiffs to invoke s 32 of the 1980 Act. Clearly that part of the decision, if correct, is of considerable assistance to Miss Dohmann, but in my judgment it is not correct, and it is right to point out that there is nothing in the report to suggest that the issue was explored in the way that it has been explored before us.

(6) *Conclusion*

Having now considered in addition to the wording of the 1980 Act the history of the legislation and most of the authorities to which we were referred, I am satisfied that Mr Hunter is right in his submission that reliance cannot be placed on s 32(1)(b) of the 1980 Act where the deliberate concealment relied upon occurred an appreciable time after the cause of action arose. In other words if time has already begun to run the supervening fraudulent concealment will not start it running again.

I would therefore, like Sir Thomas Bingham MR, allow this appeal.

Appeal allowed. Leave to appeal to the House of Lords granted.

L I Zysman Esq   Barrister.

Gidrxslme Shipping Co Ltd v Tantomar-Transportes Maritimos Lda

QUEEN'S BENCH DIVISION (COMMERCIAL COURT)

COLMAN J

28 APRIL, 5, 11 MAY 1994

Practice – Pre-trial or post-judgment relief – Mareva injunction – Discovery in aid of injunction – Arbitration award – Post-award injunction restraining removal of assets out of or disposal within jurisdiction – Worldwide disclosure order – Whether court having unlimited jurisdiction to order disclosure of assets to facilitate enforcement of award – Whether scope of disclosure order limited to extent of Mareva relief – Arbitration Act 1950, s 12(6)(f)(h) – Supreme Court Act 1981, s 37(1).

Arbitration – Award – Enforcement – Mareva relief in aid of enforcement – Disclosure order – Jurisdiction of court to order disclosure to ensure effectiveness of Mareva order – Jurisdiction of court to order disclosure in aid of Mareva order – Scope of disclosure – Arbitration Act 1950, s 12(6)(f)(h) – Supreme Court Act 1981, s 37(1).

The defendant charterers hired a vessel from the plaintiff owners under a time charterparty which included a London arbitration clause. Various disputes subsequently arose in respect of unpaid charter hire which were referred to arbitration. The arbitrator made two interim final awards requiring the charterers to pay the shipowners $US284,392·47 and $US72,957 respectively. By the date of the second award the shipowners had withdrawn the vessel for non-payment of a further instalment of hire and were pursuing another arbitration against the charterers, claiming $US253,396·91 for hire and damages for wrongful repudiation of the time charter by the charterers. The shipowners then made an ex parte application for Mareva relief under s 12(6)(f)^a of the Arbitration Act 1950, which provided that, in relation to a reference to arbitration, the High Court had the same powers to secure the amount in dispute as it had in relation to an action in the High Court. The judge made an order restraining the charterers from dealing with their assets within the jurisdiction and ordered them to disclose on affidavit the nature, value and location of their assets both within and outside the jurisdiction. The charterers applied to restrict the scope of the disclosure order to those assets within the jurisdiction. They contended that a disclosure order could only be made ancillary to, and in aid of, the Mareva injunction itself and therefore a disclosure order could not be more extensive than the Mareva order which the disclosure was designed to make effective. The shipowners contended that the court had unlimited jurisdiction to grant orders for the disclosure of assets outside the jurisdiction in order to facilitate the enforcement of judgments, and therefore the enforcement of arbitration awards which were convertible into judgments by the procedure under s 26 of the 1950 Act and RSC Ord 73, r 10.

Held – (1) The court had jurisdiction under s 12(6)(f) and (h) of the 1950 Act to grant Mareva relief in respect of pending or anticipated arbitrations and there was no reason in principle why such jurisdiction should not be exercised in aid of the enforcement of English arbitration awards, provided that there were grounds for believing that there was a real risk that the party against whom the award had been made might dispose of his assets to avoid execution of the award (see p 513 *f* to *h*, post); *The Rena K* [1979] 1 All ER 397 applied; *Orwell Steel (Erection and Fabrication) Ltd v Asphalt and Tarmac (UK) Ltd* [1985] 3 All ER 747 considered.

(2) Given that the jurisdiction to grant disclosure orders was ancillary to the statutory power under s 37(1)^b of the Supreme Court Act 1981 to grant interlocutory injunctions, it followed that once the court ordered a Mareva injunction in relation to an arbitration claim or award, it had exactly the same jurisdiction to make such a disclosure order against a Mareva respondent. Accordingly, since s 12(6)(f) and (h) of the 1950 Act made the Mareva jurisdiction available in relation to arbitrations, those provisions also made available the court's ancillary power to order disclosure of assets (see p 515 *j* to p 516 *b*, post); *A J Bekhor & Co Ltd v Bilton* [1981] 2 All ER 565 considered.

(3) The court also had jurisdiction under s 37(1) of the 1981 Act, coupled with s 12(6)(f) and (h) of the 1950 Act, to grant a disclosure order and to extend it, in an appropriate case, to assets outside the jurisdiction of the English courts. Moreover, just as the court had jurisdiction to grant a Mareva injunction in aid of execution of an arbitration award, supported by a disclosure order, before it had been converted into a judgment under s 26 of the 1950 Act and RSC Ord 73, r 10, there was no reason why there should not, also in an appropriate case, be a free-standing disclosure order in respect of the losing respondent's assets. The absence of a judgment, as distinct from an award, should make no difference, because it was a matter of policy that arbitration awards should be satisfied and executed. The court accordingly had jurisdiction, by reason of the analogy provided by s 12(6)(f) and (h) of the

---

a   Section 12(6), so far as material, is set out at p 513 *e*, post

b   Section 37(1), so far as material, provides: 'The High Court may by order (whether interlocutory or final) grant an injunction ... in all cases in which it appears to the court to be just and convenient to do so.'

Act, to grant a free-standing disclosure order in support of the enforcement of an arbitration award, notwithstanding that the award had not then been converted into a judgment. It followed that there was a firm jurisdictional basis for an order, made post-judgment or post-award, which included both a Mareva injunction confined to assets within the jurisdiction and a disclosure order in respect of worldwide assets (see p 519 *a* to *e j* to p 520 *a*, post); *Maclaine Watson & Co Ltd v International Tin Council (No 2)* [1987] 3 All ER 886 considered; *Ashtiani v Kashi* [1986] 2 All ER 970 and *Derby & Co Ltd v Weldon (No 2)* [1989] 1 All ER 1002 distinguished.

(4) On the facts, the court had jurisdiction to grant a worldwide disclosure order, because it was ancillary to the two arbitration awards and in support of their enforcement (albeit not in support of Mareva relief) and, as a matter of policy, the judgment or award creditor should have all the information necessary to execute the judgment or award anywhere in the world. The original order would therefore be restored subject to an undertaking that the information disclosed should not be used to attach assets to secure the claim in the third arbitration. The defendants' application would accordingly be dismissed (see p 521 *b e h* to p 522 *b*, post).

Notes

For Mareva injunctions, see 24 *Halsbury's Laws* (4th edn reissue) paras 866–871, and for cases on the subject, see 28(4) *Digest* (2nd reissue) 197–214, *5326–5392*.

For the Arbitration Act 1950, s 12, see 2 *Halsbury's Statutes* (4th edn) (1992 reissue) 585.

For the Supreme Court Act 1981, s 37, see 11 *Halsbury's Statutes* (4th edn) (1991 reissue) 1001.

Cases referred to in judgment

A v C [1980] 2 All ER 347, [1981] QB 956, [1981] 2 WLR 629.

Ashtiani v Kashi [1986] 2 All ER 970, [1987] QB 888, [1986] 3 WLR 647, CA.

Babanaft International Co SA v Bassatne [1989] 1 All ER 433, [1990] Ch 13, [1989] 2 WLR 232, CA.

Bekhor (A J) & Co Ltd v Bilton [1981] 2 All ER 565, [1981] QB 923, [1981] 2 WLR 601, CA.

British Airways Board v Laker Airways Ltd [1984] 3 All ER 39, [1985] AC 58, [1984] 3 WLR 413, HL.

CBS UK Ltd v Lambert [1982] 3 All ER 237, [1983] Ch 37, [1982] 3 WLR 746, CA.

Derby & Co Ltd v Weldon (No 1) [1989] 1 All ER 469, [1990] Ch 48, [1989] 2 WLR 276, CA.

Derby & Co Ltd v Weldon (No 2) [1989] 1 All ER 1002, sub nom *Derby & Co Ltd v Weldon (Nos 3 and 4)* [1990] Ch 65, [1989] 2 WLR 412, CA.

Interpool Ltd v Galani [1987] 2 All ER 981, [1988] QB 738, [1987] 3 WLR 1042, CA.

Lister & Co v Stubbs (1890) 45 Ch D 1, [1886–90] All ER Rep 797, CA.

Maclaine Watson & Co Ltd v International Tin Council (No 2) [1987] 3 All ER 886, [1988] Ch 1, [1987] 1 WLR 1711; *affd* [1988] 3 All ER 257, [1989] Ch 286, [1988] 3 WLR 1190, CA.

Orwell Steel (Erection and Fabrication) Ltd v Asphalt and Tarmac (UK) Ltd [1985] 3 All ER 747, [1984] 1 WLR 1097, DC.

PCW (Underwriting Agencies) Ltd v Dixon [1983] 2 All ER 158, CA.

Rena K, The [1979] 1 All ER 397, [1979] QB 377, [1978] 3 WLR 431.

Siskina (cargo owners) v Distos Cia Naviera SA, The Siskina [1977] 3 All ER 803, [1979] AC 210, [1977] 3 WLR 818, HL.

South Carolina Insurance Co v Assurantie Maatschappij 'de Zeven Provincien' NV, South Carolina Insurance Co v Al Ahlia Insurance Co [1986] 3 All ER 487, [1987] AC 24, [1986] 3 WLR 398, HL.

Third Chandris Shipping Corp v Unimarine SA, The Pythia, The Angelic Wings, The Genie [1979] 2 All ER 972, [1979] QB 645, [1979] 3 WLR 122, DC and CA.

Application

The defendant charterers, Tantomar-Transportes Maritimos Lda, applied to Colman J on 28 April 1994 to restrict the ambit of the second part of his order, made on 19 April on an ex parte application by the plaintiff shipowners, Gidrxslme Shipping Co Ltd, restraining the defendants until further order from removing their assets from the jurisdiction or disposing of, assigning their rights to, charging, mortgaging, encumbering or otherwise dealing with any of their assets within the jurisdiction until the final award in the arbitration between the parties in respect of unpaid charter hire was satisfied, save insofar as the unencumbered value of those assets exceeded $US720,000 and requiring them to make an affidavit disclosing (a) full information concerning the nature and location of all their assets within the jurisdiction, (b) an identification of all vessels owned by the defendants and of all charterparties of all vessels chartered out and/or operated by the defendants, (c) details of all bank accounts where freight, hire and other remuneration in relation to those vessels has been and/or is paid, and   (d) the name of the parties to any arbitrations being pursued in London by the defendants.   The application was heard in chambers but judgment was delivered by Colman J in open court.   The facts are set out in the judgment.

David Bailey (instructed by *Hewett & Co*) for the plaintiffs.
Nigel Jacobs (instructed by *Holmes Hardingham*) for the defendants.

Cur adv vult

11 May 1994.   The following judgment was delivered.

COLMAN J.

Introduction

This is an application on behalf of the defendants, Tantomar-Transportes Maritimos Lda, to restrict the ambit of a disclosure order made alongside a Mareva injunction.   It raises an important point on the appropriate scope of such orders.   That point, shortly, is whether, when the scope of a Mareva injunction is confined to assets *within* the jurisdiction of the English courts, there is jurisdiction to order an affidavit of the defendant's assets *outside* the jurisdiction of the English courts and, if there is, in what circumstances that jurisdiction may appropriately be exercised.

The background to this application can be shortly stated.

The plaintiffs, Gidrxslme Shipping Co Ltd, are the owners of mv Naftilos LS. They let that vessel on time charter to the defendants for 24 months under a time charterparty dated 12 March 1993.   The defendants carry on business in Lisbon.   Various disputes arose.   There was a London arbitration clause and the parties referred their disputes to Mr Bruce Harris, the well-known maritime arbitrator. By an interim final award dated 24 February 1994 (the first award) he awarded that the defendants should forthwith pay to the plaintiff owners $US284,392·47, together with interest and costs. The claim had been in respect of unpaid charter hire. There was then another arbitration as a result of which, on 18 April 1994, Mr Harris issued a further interim final award (the second award) in which he awarded that the defendants should forthwith pay to the plaintiffs $72,957 in respect of more unpaid hire, together with interest and costs. In the meantime, on 2 March 1994 the plaintiffs had withdrawn the vessel for non-payment of another instalment of hire. They immediately started yet another arbitration before Mr Harris in which they claimed $253,396·91 on their hire statement and damages for wrongful repudiation of the time charter by the defendants. They put the damages at $350,000. The total claimed was therefore over $600,000. I refer to this arbitration as 'the third arbitration'.

On 19 April 1994 the plaintiffs' solicitors ascertained that a vessel thought to be owned by the defendants called mv Almar was currently under arrest at Manistry Wharf on the Manchester Ship Canal. They knew of no other tangible assets of the defendants within the jurisdiction. In view of their outstanding claims against the defendants, the plaintiffs' solicitors sought to lodge a caveat against release, but by the time their clerk got to the Admiralty Registry he found that he had missed the boat: it had been released from arrest a few minutes earlier. The next quickest course being to obtain a Mareva injunction against the defendants restraining them from moving from the jurisdiction or otherwise disposing of such assets as they had here, counsel appeared before me later that day and applied ex parte for such an order. There had not been time to prepare an affidavit but Mr Bailey, who appeared on the application, explained the facts very fully and in the usual way undertook that they would be verified by affidavit forthwith.

In the event I made an order, the substance of which was that the defendants were restrained until further order—

'from removing [their] assets from the jurisdiction or disposing of, assigning their rights to, charging, mortgaging, encumbering or otherwise howsoever dealing with any of their assets within the jurisdiction until the Final Award is satisfied, save insofar as the unencumbered value of those assets exceeds U.S.$720,000 ...'

However, it also contained the following paragraph:

'5. The Defendants do, within 7 days of notice of this Order being given under undertaking (2) hereof make and file an affidavit and serve a copy upon the Intended Plaintiffs' Solicitors, Messrs. Hewett & Co. of 8 Crosby Square, London, EC3A 6AQ disclosing: (a) full information concerning the nature and location of all of their assets within the jurisdiction; (b) an identification of all vessels owned by the Defendants and of all charterparties of all vessels chartered out and/or operated by the Defendants; (c) details of all bank accounts where freight, hire and other remuneration in relation to those vessels has been and/or is paid including the following details: (i) the name(s) in which each such account is held; (ii) the number of the account; (iii) the branch of the bank at which the account is held; (iv) the amount of the balance held in the account; (d) The name of the party (i) against whom an Award has recently been published in London in favour of the Defendants which is referred to in paragraph 1(b) and the amount of the Award; (ii) against whom any other arbitration is presently being pursued in London by the Defendants and the date of the hearing if one has been fixed; (e) The name of the Solicitors acting on behalf of the Defendants and the opposite party, in respect of each of the arbitrations referred to at (d) above.'

It will be observed that although the order restraining the movement of assets was confined to assets within the jurisdiction and although para 5(a) is similarly limited, paras 5(b) and 5(c) are not so limited and para 5(d) is not confined to parties domiciled within the jurisdiction.

The order incorporated a provision giving liberty to the defendants to apply on five working hours' written notice to the plaintiffs' solicitors to set aside or vary the order.

The plaintiffs subsequently applied ex parte to extend the injunction so that it applied on a worldwide basis. That application failed since there was no evidence that, if the defendants had any assets abroad, they would dispose of them otherwise than in the ordinary course of their business in order to avoid enforcement of the arbitration awards against them.

The defendants then availed themselves of the liberty to apply to vary the order. Mr Jacobs, on their behalf, appeared on 28 April and submitted that para 5 of the order was too wide in principle and that it ought to have been confined—co-extensively with the restraining order—to vessels, bank accounts and arbitration respondents within the jurisdiction. He said that there was no jurisdiction to go wider than that or, alternatively, it was unduly oppressive to do so. He relied on what was said on such disclosure affidavits in the Court of Appeal in *A J Bekhor & Co Ltd v Bilton* [1981] 2 All ER 565, [1981] QB 923, *Ashtiani v Kashi* [1986] 2 All ER 970, [1987] QB 888 and *Derby & Co Ltd v Weldon (No 2)* [1989] 1 All ER 1002, [1990] Ch 65. In the present case there were no exceptional circumstances to justify a worldwide Mareva injunction even if there were assets abroad and accordingly it could not be said that an affidavit of assets abroad could be justified.

Mr Bailey, for the plaintiffs, submitted that the court had unlimited jurisdiction to grant orders for disclosure of assets outside the jurisdiction for the purpose of facilitating the enforcement of judgments and therefore of arbitration awards which were convertible into judgments by the procedure under s 26 of the Arbitration Act 1950 or s 3(1)(a) of the Arbitration Act 1975 and RSC Ord 73, r 10. He further relied by way of analogy on the power of the courts under Ord 48 to require a judgment debtor to attend for examination as to his assets, including foreign assets (see the judgment of the Court of Appeal in *Interpool Ltd v Galani* [1987] 2 All ER 981, [1988] QB 738). There having been an order of Cresswell J on 8 March 1994 giving leave to enforce the first award as a judgment, he submitted that this was in substance as good as a judgment and therefore there should be an order for disclosure of overseas assets as if Ord 48 applied. Mr Bailey cited the judgment of Kerr LJ in *Babanaft International Co SA v Bassatne* [1989] 1 All ER 433 at 440–441, [1990] Ch 13 at 27–28 in support of his submission that the court did have jurisdiction to order worldwide disclosure of assets and that the decision in *Ashtiani v Kashi* [1986] 2 All ER 970, [1987] QB 888 did not go to jurisdiction.

Having heard these submissions, I indicated at the close of the hearing that my conclusion was that the order should be varied to the effect that the disclosure affidavit should be confined to assets within the jurisdiction and that

a I would give my reasons later. Another related matter, now no longer in issue between the parties, remained to be fully argued and it was thus sensible that I should give judgment on the scope of the affidavit issue at the same time as on the other matter. When the matter came back before the court for such further argument on 5 May it emerged that the parties had compromised the other matter, but in the meantime, on 3 May, judgment had been entered on
b the first award, my order made on 28 April had not been drawn up and Mr Bailey had since encountered the decisions of Millett J and the Court of Appeal in *Maclaine Watson & Co Ltd v International Tin Council (No 2)* [1987] 3 All ER 886, [1987] 1 WLR 1711; *affd* [1988] 3 All ER 257, [1989] Ch 286. He submitted that that authority was highly relevant to my decision and that as it had not previously been cited and as the plaintiffs had in the meantime turned the first
c award into a judgment debt, I ought to review my decision of 28 April to restrict the scope of the disclosure order. There was then further argument on the relevance of that authority which was clearly relevant to the matter in issue, and on the effect of the plaintiffs' having converted the award into a judgment.

d *The jurisdictional basis for Mareva relief*

The application for the Mareva injunction in this case was made by originating summons, being an application for relief under s 12(6)(f) of the 1950 Act. That provides:

e 'The High Court shall have, for the purpose of and in relation to a reference, the same power of making orders in respect of ... (f) securing the amount in dispute in the reference ... as it has for the purpose of and in relation to an action of matter in the High Court.'

f As recognised by Brandon J in *The Rena K* [1979] 1 All ER 397, [1979] QB 377, there is thus created a jurisdiction to grant Mareva injunctions in respect of pending or anticipated arbitrations. The court's jurisdiction in such cases is analogous to the jurisdiction which it has in relation to a pending or anticipated action (see [1979] 1 All ER 397 at 418, [1979] QB 377 at 408). In view of the fact that, as is now firmly established, the court has jurisdiction to grant a Mareva injunction in aid of execution upon application after judgment has been obtained (see *Orwell Steel (Erection and Fabrication) Ltd v Asphalt and Tarmac (UK) Ltd* [1985] 3 All ER 747, [1984] 1 WLR 1097), there is, in my judgment, no reason in principle why the jurisdiction under s 12(6) of the 1950 Act should not be exercised in aid of enforcement of English arbitration awards, provided that there are grounds for believing that there is a real risk
g that the party against whom the award has been made may dispose of his assets to avoid execution of the award.

It is to be observed that in addition to the powers under s 12(6)(f) of the 1950 Act, there is also an express power to make an order for an interim injunction under s 12(6)(h) of the Act. In *The Rena K* [1979] 1 All ER 397 at 418, [1979] QB 377 at 408 Brandon J held that there was power to grant Mareva injunctions under both s 12(6)(f) and s 12(6)(h).

Disclosure orders where there is an arbitration

If there is jurisdiction to grant Mareva injunctions in relation to arbitrations, whether prior to the reference or pre-award in the course of the reference or, as I have held, post-award, is there also jurisdiction to order, in aid of such a

Mareva, the disclosure of the respondent's assets? And is that jurisdiction also exercisable pre-reference, pre-award and post-award?

In order to answer that question it is first necessary to identify the jurisdictional basis of such orders. It is clear from the judgments of the majority in the Court of Appeal in *A J Bekhor & Co Ltd v Bilton* [1981] 2 All ER 565, [1981] QB 923 that the power to order disclosure of assets by the defendant is a derivative of the express statutory power then expressed in s 45(1) of the Supreme Court of Judicature (Consolidation) Act 1925. That simply stated that the High Court 'may grant ... an injunction ... by an interlocutory order in all cases in which it appears to the court to be just or convenient so to do'. At the time when that case was before the Court of Appeal, the Supreme Court Bill, including cl 37, now the Supreme Court Act 1981, s 37(1), was before Parliament. Ackner LJ said ([1981] 2 All ER 565 at 576, [1981] QB 923 at 940):

'Having regard to the authorities referred to above it is now clearly established that the power of the High Court under s 45(1) includes the power to grant an interlocutory injunction to restrain a party to any proceedings from removing from the jurisdiction or otherwise dealing with assets located within the jurisdiction where that party is, as well as where he is not, domiciled, resident or present within that jurisdiction. Clause 37 of the Supreme Court Bill is obviously designed to give statutory effect to those authorities. To my mind there must be *inherent in that power* the power to make all such ancillary orders as appear to the court to be just and convenient to ensure that the exercise of the Mareva jurisdiction is effective to achieve its purpose.' (Ackner LJ's emphasis.)

He continued ([1981] 2 All ER 565 at 577, [1981] QB 923 at 942):

'It is therefore clear that, although the Mareva plaintiff, who has satisfied the guidelines set out by Lord Denning MR in *Third Chandris Shipping Corpn v Unimarine SA* [1979] 2 All ER 972 at 984, [1979] QB 645 at 668, and in particular has provided adequate grounds for believing that there is a risk of the defendant's assets being removed before the judgment or award is satisfied, is in a privileged position, this privilege must not be carried too far. The courts must be vigilant to ensure that the Mareva defendant is not treated like a judgment debtor. It was no doubt with this general principle in mind that Robert Goff J in *A v C* ([1980] 2 All ER 347, [1981] QB 956) was at pains to point out that it would not be right to make general use of the power to enable the plaintiff to discover whether the defendant has any assets here. However, having established the existence of the assets, it may, in a particular case, be necessary for the proper exercise of the jurisdiction that the defendant should provide information about a particular asset in order for the jurisdiction to be properly exercised. Where, as in *A v C*, there are several defendants, the ancillary order might well be designed to obtain information which would enable the court to restrict the injunction to a particular account, and thus enable the judge to decide on what the Mareva injunction should bite.'

Griffiths LJ expressed the need for such orders thus ([1981] 2 All ER 565 at 581, [1981] QB 923 at 947–948):

'The plaintiff must be able to satisfy the court that the defendant has assets within the jurisdiction in order to obtain the injunction and in most cases will probably be able to identify those assets with sufficient particularity to enable the court to make an effective order. In such cases there is no need for discovery, and it would be most oppressive to make an unnecessary order for discovery merely to harass the defendant. However, from time to time cases will arise when, although it seems highly probable that the defendant has assets within the jurisdiction, their precise form and whereabouts are in doubt, or in the case of a number of defendants they may collectively have sufficient assets but there may be doubt about their distribution among themselves. In such cases in order that the Mareva injunction should be effective both the court and the plaintiff require to know the particular assets on which the order should bite. It must be remembered that the underlying reason for making the order is the fear that the defendant may remove his assets and this is most effectively prevented by the plaintiff serving a copy of the injunction on whoever is holding the defendant's assets for the time being. Very often this will be the defendant's bankers, but assets can take many forms and be in the hands of many different persons to whom it is desirable to give notice of the court's order. To my mind the desirability of the power to order discovery is obvious and it is particularly needed in the case of a defendant who has demonstrated himself to be untrustworthy and evasive. But the question remains: does the power exist?'

He, too, identified the jurisdiction as ancillary to the power to grant injunctive relief under s 45(1) of the 1925 Act ([1981] 2 All ER 565 at 582, [1981] QB 923 at 949):

'However, in *A v C* Robert Goff J derived the power to order discovery not only from the rules but also from the power to make the injunction under s 45 of the Supreme Court of Judicature (Consolidation) Act 1925. Counsel for the plaintiffs relies on this power to support the judge's order. If the court has power to make a Mareva injunction it must have power to make an effective Mareva injunction. If the injunction will not be effective it ought not be made. For reasons I have already given it may be necessary to order discovery to make the injunction effective and I would hold that the court has the power to make such ancillary orders as are necessary to secure that the injunctive relief given to the plaintiff is effective. I therefore agree that a judge does have power to order discovery in aid of a Mareva injunction if it is necessary for the effective operation of the injunction.'

Stephenson LJ considered that the power to make a discovery order was based upon the inherent jurisdiction of the court (see [1981] 2 All ER 565 at 585–586, [1981] QB 923 at 953–954).

It is thus reasonably clear that, at least in origin, the jurisdiction to order disclosure of assets had the purpose of facilitating the administration of the injunction by identifying the assets upon which it operated and thereby (i) making it more difficult for the defendant surreptitiously to disobey the order restraining disposal or export abroad of his assets, and (ii) enabling notice to be given to third parties who might have custody of the assets, such as banks or warehouses, so as to bind them to the injunction. The function was not to establish that the Mareva injunction defendant had assets within the jurisdiction, but to ascertain their precise whereabouts and extent.

Consequently, if the jurisdiction to grant disclosure orders arises as a power ancillary to the statutory power under s 37(1) of the Supreme Court Act 1981

to grant interlocutory injunctions, it must follow that once the court orders a *a*
Mareva injunction in relation to an arbitration claim or award, it has exactly
the same jurisdiction to make such a disclosure order against the Mareva
respondent. If s 12(6)(f) and (h) of the 1950 Act make available the Mareva
jurisdiction in relation to arbitrations, they must also make available the
court's ancillary power to order disclosure of assets.

b

The scope of disclosure orders

Following the decision in *A J Bekhor & Co Ltd v Bilton* [1981] 2 All ER 565,
[1981] QB 923 the practice developed of including in orders granting Mareva
injunctions orders for affidavits disclosing the whereabouts of the defendant's
assets not only inside, but also outside the jurisdiction (see eg *CBS UK Ltd v
Lambert* [1982] 3 All ER 237, [1983] Ch 37 and *PCW (Underwriting Agencies) Ltd v*   *c*
Dixon [1983] 2 All ER 158). But in no case was this practice challenged until
Ashtiani v Kashi [1986] 2 All ER 970, [1987] QB 888, in which it was held by the
Court of Appeal (i) that Mareva injunctions should be confined to assets within
the jurisdiction, and (ii) that any ancillary order for disclosure of assets should
be similarly confined. Dillon LJ observed ([1986] 2 All ER 970 at 977–978, [1987]   *d*
QB 888 at 902):

> 'The disclosure of foreign assets cannot be regarded as ancillary to the
> making of a Mareva injunction limited to the English assets. It cannot
> stand on its own feet as a primary exercise of jurisdiction if the Mareva
> exercise is limited to English assets, and it is only valid if so limited as an   *e*
> exception to the principle of *Lister & Co v Stubbs* (1890) 45 Ch D 1, [1886–
> 90] All ER Rep 797 on the practice of the courts.'

Neill LJ dealt with the point more fully ([1986] 2 All ER 970 at 980, [1987] QB
888 at 905):

> 'In the present case we are concerned not only with a Mareva injunction   *f*
> but also with an order for discovery which was made ancillary to the
> injunction. The relevant part of the order for discovery was in these
> terms: "... that the Defendant do disclose the full value of his assets within
> and without the jurisdiction identifying with full particularity the nature
> of all such assets their whereabouts and whether the same be held in his   *g*
> own name or jointly with some other person or persons or by nominees
> or otherwise howsoever on his behalf ..." It is important to remember
> that this is not an action where any proprietary claim is made, nor is it a
> tracing action. It is an action founded on an alleged failure to pay moneys
> due under a contract. What basis is there, therefore, for an order for
> discovery of the defendant's assets? It is not an order for discovery under   *h*
> RSC Ord 24. It seems to me that in the present state of the law the only
> basis for such an order is that it is made in aid of and ancillary to an
> injunction in the Mareva form. The power to order discovery exists, but
> it is a power which exists to make the injunction effective. It seems to me
> to follow that, at any rate prima facie, discovery should be limited, firstly,
> to the ascertainment of assets which will be covered by the Mareva order   *j*
> (in other words, the ascertainment of assets within the jurisdiction), and,
> secondly, at a later stage, to enable the court to consider any application
> by the party enjoined to vary the Mareva injunction. Thus, if a party
> applies to make use of funds which are subject to the Mareva injunction,
> it may become relevant at that stage for the court to inquire whether there

are other assets which are not so subject to which he can have recourse: cf *A J Behkor & Co Ltd v Bilton* [1981] 2 All ER 565 at 572, [1981] QB 923 at 935 per Ackner LJ. There may be other cases where a wider discovery is appropriate, but, as the scope of a Mareva injunction is restricted to assets within the jurisdiction, it seems to me to follow that, certainly in the ordinary way, any discovery in aid of the Mareva should be similarly so restricted. Accordingly, in my judgment the order for discovery that was made in this case was not a proper order to make, and I consider that Sir Neil Lawson was right when he discharged the injunction on the basis of an undertaking and made the order which is the subject of this appeal.'

It was against the background of that body of authority that Millett J had to consider the somewhat unusual point which arose in *Maclaine Watson & Co Ltd v International Tin Council (No 2)* [1987] 3 All ER 886, [1987] 1 WLR 1711. An arbitration award against the ITC had not been satisfied. It had been converted into a judgment, but that, too, remained unsatisfied. Thereupon the plaintiffs had applied for an order under RSC Ord 48, r 1 that a proper officer of ITC should attend court to be orally examined as to the assets of ITC within the United Kingdom. The master refused the order because the ITC was not a body corporate as required by Ord 48. Millett J dismissed the appeal but heard a further motion for a similar order under the inherent jurisdiction of the court. That motion succeeded. Millett J arrived at his conclusion by the following route ([1987] 3 All ER 886 at 891–892, [1987] 1 WLR 1711 at 1716–1717):

'In this case the appellants rightly do not seek a Mareva injunction. There is no reason to believe that the ITC will remove its assets from the jurisdiction in order to defeat execution. The appellants seek only an order for discovery in aid of execution, the procedure of Ord 48 being unavailable. The ITC contend that there is no jurisdiction to make such an order in the absence of a Mareva injunction. It is, however, fallacious to reason from the fact that an order for discovery can be made as ancillary to a Mareva injunction to the conclusion that it cannot be made except as ancillary to such an injunction. The source of the jurisdiction is the same, and so is the ground for exercising it, viz that it appears to the court to be just and convenient to do so ... In the present case the order sought may properly be said to be sought in aid of or for the purpose of implementing of the judgment previously obtained by the appellants. It is, within proper limits, the policy of these courts to prevent a defendant from removing its assets from the jurisdiction or concealing them within it so as to deny a successful plaintiff the fruits of his judgment. This is the policy which underlies the Mareva injunction before and after judgment, pre-trial discovery of assets in aid of the Mareva jurisdiction and Order 48. That policy can only be given effect if a defendant can be ordered when necessary to provide information about the nature and whereabouts of its assets. It can only be given effect in the present case if the court has power to make the order sought. Although Ord 48 is not available, the underlying policy of that order would be forwarded, not frustrated, by the order. There is no doubt that it is just and convenient to make it.'

This conclusion was upheld in the Court of Appeal (see [1988] 3 All ER 257, [1989] Ch 286). The basis of the reasoning in that case was that ITC, having failed to pay the judgment debt, was in breach of an order of the court and, it being the policy of the law that judgments should be enforced and that the

judgment debtor should assist by providing information as to the whereabouts
of his assets, as shown by Ord 48, there was jurisdiction under s 37(1) of the
1981 Act to make an order for disclosure. Such an order would be in support
of the execution of the judgment and it would be just and convenient to make
such an order. In giving the judgment of the court, Kerr LJ said ([1988] 3 All
ER 257 at 380–381, [1989] Ch 286 at 303):

> 'First, we do not accept counsel's contention for the ITC that an attitude
> of total passivity on the part of the ITC in relation to Maclaine Watson's
> attempts to enforce their judgment involves no "invasion of a legal or
> equitable right" of the plaintiffs, to use the phrase of Lord Diplock in
> [Siskina (cargo owners) v Distos Cia Naviera SA] The Siskina [1977] 3 All ER
> 803 at 824, [1979] AC 210 at 256 which he repeated in British Airways Board
> v Laker Airways Ltd [1984] 3 All ER 39 at 46, [1985] AC 58 at 81 and which
> was also used by Lord Brandon in South Carolina Insurance Co v Assurantie
> Maatschappij 'de Zeven Provincien' NV [1986] 3 All ER 487 at 496, [1987] AC
> 24 at 40. Maclaine Watson have an order of the court against the ITC to
> pay to Maclaine Watson the amount of their judgment. The ITC's failure
> to do so is a failure to comply with an order of the court and a breach of an
> obligation owed to Maclaine Watson. As Ralph Gibson LJ pointed out in
> the course of the argument, it matters little whether one speaks of an
> invasion of a plaintiff's right or of a breach of an obligation owed to a
> plaintiff. The court's statutory power to grant an injunction if it appears
> just and convenient to do so, in this case in mandatory form, is not
> excluded by any authority. Second, there is the authority of this court in
> A J Bekhor & Co Ltd v Bilton [1981] 2 All ER 565, [1981] QB 923 and other
> cases that there is an inherent power under what is now s 37(1) to make
> any ancillary order, including an order for discovery, to ensure the
> effectiveness of any other order made by the court. This applies in the
> unusual circumstances of the present case. Since the alternative means of
> appointing a receiver or of making an order under Ord 48 are unavailable,
> the order for disclosure is necessary to render Maclaine Watson's
> judgment against the ITC effective.'

The Court of Appeal thus approved the granting of a mandatory injunction
for the purpose of assisting the enforcement of another order of the court,
namely, the judgment into which the arbitration award had already been
converted. Although, therefore, there was no prior Mareva injunction in
relation to which an order for disclosure of assets could be made as an ancillary
power to the granting of the Mareva, as in Bekhor v Bilton, there was an earlier
judgment against ITC which appeared to have assets overseas and in support
of which the disclosure order could be made as a free-standing mandatory
injunction. The Court of Appeal had already held in Interpool Ltd v Galani
[1987] 2 All ER 981, [1988] QB 738 that Ord 48 could extend to assets outside
the jurisdiction. That being so, and since the enforcement of the judgment was
not confined to assets within the jurisdiction, there was no reason why the
disclosure order should be so confined.

Accordingly, where an English arbitration award has been converted into an
English judgment, there is jurisdiction to order in an appropriate case that the
judgment debtor/arbitration respondent should disclose assets and, if it
appears likely that there are assets abroad, that he should disclose his assets
outside, as well as inside, the jurisdiction. Moreover, such an order can be

made in aid of execution, even if there is no Mareva injunction in aid of execution. If the award has not yet been turned into a judgment—and in this case, that is the position in relation to the second award—there is, in my judgment, no reason in principle why there should not also be jurisdiction under s 37(1) of the 1981 Act, coupled with s 12(6)(f) and (h) of the 1950 Act, to grant a disclosure order and to extend it in an appropriate case to assets outside the jurisdiction of the English courts. The effect of s 12(6) of the 1950 Act is to enable the court to make in relation to a reference those orders which it could have made if the reference had been a High Court action. There is no reason, as a matter of construction of s 12(6), why the analogy of the High Court action should stop upon the making of the arbitration award. Just as there can, in an appropriate case, be a Mareva injunction in aid of execution of the award, supported by a disclosure order, before it has been turned into a judgment, there is no reason why there should not also, in an appropriate case, be a free-standing disclosure order in respect of the losing respondent's assets. The absence of a judgment, as distinct from an award, should make no difference for it is the policy of the law that arbitration awards should be satisfied and executed. Hence the power to convert them into judgments under s 26 of the 1950 Act and Ord 73, r 10. If the award had been a judgment of the court, a free-standing mandatory injunction for disclosure of assets could have been made in support of that order. Accordingly, by reason of the statutory analogy provided by s 12(6)(f) and (h) of the 1950 Act, there must equally be jurisdiction to grant such an order in support of the enforcement of an arbitration award notwithstanding that it has *not* yet been converted into a judgment.

The extension of the use of the Mareva jurisdiction to assets outside the jurisdiction of the English courts was examined in depth by the Court of Appeal in *Babanaft International Co SA v Bassatne* [1989] 1 All ER 433, [1990] Ch 13 and in *Derby & Co Ltd v Weldon (No 2)* [1989] 1 All ER 1002, [1990] Ch 65. While recognising the power of the English courts to grant Mareva injunctions, even in respect of assets outside this jurisdiction in an appropriate case, it was unnecessary in either case to consider the scope of disclosure orders in relation to Mareva injunctions confined to assets within the jurisdiction. However, in *Derby v Weldon (No 2)* [1989] 1 All ER 1002 at 1021, [1990] Ch 65 at 94–95 Neill LJ reaffirmed, albeit obiter, his conviction expressed in *Ashtiani v Kashi* [1986] 2 All ER 970, [1987] QB 888 that disclosure orders should be co-extensive with the scope of the Mareva injunction to which they were ancillary. It is to be observed, however, that both in *Ashtiani v Kashi* and in *Derby v Weldon (No 2)* the courts were concerned with *pre-judgment* orders which included Mareva injunctions. The orders for disclosure were, therefore, orders ancillary to those injunctions. There was no question of there being any other order in support of which a disclosure order could be justified. Where, by contrast, one has the position that a judgment has been already obtained or an award made and where a Mareva injunction in aid of execution is justified, the jurisdiction to make a disclosure order arises both as a power ancillary to and in support of the injunction and independently of the injunction as a power in support of the execution of the judgment or award. It follows that, whereas it may on the facts of the case in question be inappropriate to extend the Mareva injunction to assets outside the jurisdiction—and it is clear from the two authorities cited that such extensions are likely to be rarely justified—very different considerations may apply to disclosure orders in aid of execution. That being so, there is, in my judgment, a very firm jurisdictional basis for an order, made post-judgment or post-award, which includes both a

Mareva injunction confined to assets within the jurisdiction and a disclosure order in respect of worldwide assets.

The appropriate order in the present case

In this case the first award has not been satisfied and has been turned into a judgment. The second award has not been satisfied either but leave to enforce it as a judgment has not yet been given. It may be the subject of proceedings to set it aside for misconduct. The third arbitration is pending. The evidence before me on the ex parte application encompassed all three references. The originating summons applied for and only for an injunction restraining the disposal of assets. It did not refer to an order for disclosure of assets. That would be the normal way of drafting a summons for a Mareva injunction. It is not the practice to refer in the summons in addition to the order for disclosure which is now commonly applied for. It is submitted by Mr Jacobs that inasmuch as the summons applied for a pre-award Mareva injunction in one reference, it is ineffective as a vehicle for an order for disclosure in aid of execution in a totally different reference.

The originating summons was supported by an affidavit which referred to all three arbitrations, indicating how much had been awarded to be paid forthwith under the first award and how much was claimed in the second and third arbitrations. The second award was produced during the hearing. It was thus reasonably clear that the Mareva injunction was applied for both in aid of execution of the first and second awards and as a pre-award injunction in respect of the third arbitration. The same application therefore applied for a Mareva injunction having those two distinct functions. In relation to both such functions it was, as a matter of practice, unnecessary for the originating summons to refer to a disclosure order. Does it make any difference that the disclosure order applied for was for worldwide disclosure and might therefore be available only if the court exercised its jurisdiction to make a free-standing order for disclosure in aid of execution? In my judgment, it does not. Any defendant served with an originating summons for a Mareva injunction can be expected to assume that, coupled with the application, there may be an application for disclosure of assets. In a case where Mareva relief is applied for in aid of execution there is likely to be an ancillary order for disclosure of assets. The fact that the court might base such an order on its jurisdiction to grant a free-standing mandatory order for disclosure of assets worldwide in aid of execution, as distinct from its jurisdiction to grant a disclosure order confined to assets within the jurisdiction and ancillary to the Mareva injunction, cannot require that the originating summons has to be drafted so as to make express reference to that wider jurisdiction. The application is necessarily made ex parte and the first thing the defendant knows of the application is when he is served with the order. It is then open to him to set it aside or vary it by reducing its scope. There can be no conceivable prejudice to him from the form of the originating summons. It was thus open to the court in the present case to accede to the ex parte application for a worldwide disclosure order. The originating summons was in any event issued after the making of the order. There is, for these reasons, nothing in this point.

In the present case the defendants, who have failed to honour the first award and who have subsequently failed to honour the second award, appear to carry on business in Lisbon and are incorporated in Portugal. They claim to have no assets within the jurisdiction except funds held on account of costs by their solicitors and claims in a London arbitration against an English company in a relation to which an award is apparently imminent. There are other pending London arbitrations in which the defendants are claimants, but at least some of the respondents are overseas corporations not within the jurisdiction. The defendants have no bank accounts here. Nothing is known of what assets they have abroad beyond those arbitration claims or the whereabouts of those assets.

b In view of the outstanding and unsatisfied awards against the defendants, amounting in aggregate to $US357,349·47 plus interest and costs, the first award having been converted into a judgment for $US284,392·47, it is, in my judgment, entirely just and convenient in aid of execution of those awards that the defendants should be required to tell the plaintiffs where their assets are, whether inside or outside the jurisdiction of the English courts. It is true that c the defendants have asserted that they have counterclaims in respect of disbursements and bunkers and that they have since the beginning of March 1994 paid a further $US200,000 in respect of further outstanding hire. Although there may be substance in these counterclaims, the fact is that the two awards remain unsatisfied in full and required payment forthwith. They d should therefore be enforced unless the court before which enforcement may be sought considers that enforcement is inappropriate by reason of the counterclaims and the general state of account between the parties. If the plaintiffs now have a disclosure order, they will be able to take such steps as may be available in the countries where the assets are disclosed to exist to enforce the awards or the judgment on the first award. It is right that they e should be able to do so. As I have already indicated, a worldwide Mareva injunction is not justified in this case, although one confined to assets within the jurisdiction is. As I have already explained in this judgment, the disparity of scope between the Mareva injunction and the disclosure order is justifiable where the disclosure order is in aid of execution, as it is in this case.

f Mr Jacobs submitted that if there were to be a worldwide disclosure order, the court should make it on terms that the plaintiffs could not use the information thus acquired to enforce against assets outside the jurisdiction without the leave of this court. He relied on a passage in the judgment of May LJ in *Derby & Co Ltd v Weldon (No 1)* [1989] 1 All ER 469 at 473, [1990] Ch 48 at 55 to the effect that there ought to be as a condition of a worldwide disclosure g order an undertaking by the plaintiff not to take action in any foreign jurisdiction by using the information as to assets thus disclosed without the leave of the English courts. That case was concerned with a pre-trial worldwide Mareva injunction coupled with a worldwide disclosure order. In my judgment, quite different considerations apply in the case of a h post-judgment or post-award disclosure order. In such cases it is just and convenient that the judgment or award creditor should normally have all the information he needs to execute the judgment or award anywhere in the world. It does not need the supervision of these courts to ensure that double execution is not achieved or that the information is not otherwise abused.

j There is, however, an area of protection to which the defendants are certainly entitled. That arises from the purpose for which the worldwide disclosure order is granted. It may only be used for the purposes of execution of the existing judgment or award. It cannot be used to obtain the attachment of assets overseas to secure the claim in the third arbitration.

In the event, the order which I made on 28 April having been reviewed, I have come to the conclusion that my original order of 19 April was within my jurisdiction and entirely appropriate on the facts of this case, subject to the

qualification that the information disclosed cannot be used to attach assets to
secure the claim in the third arbitration and therefore an undertaking must be
given to that effect. The original order will therefore be restored subject to
that undertaking and such minor amendments, if any, as the passage of time
and the events which have occurred since I first made it now require.

Application dismissed. Original order restored subject to undertaking.

K Mydeen Esq   Barrister.

Page v Smith

COURT OF APPEAL, CIVIL DIVISION

RALPH GIBSON, FARQUHARSON AND HOFFMANN LJJ

9, 10, 30 MARCH 1994

*Damages – Personal injury – Psychiatric damage – Nervous shock – Damages claim
for nervous shock – Factors to be considered – Plaintiff directly involved in accident
and not mere bystander – Plaintiff alleging that trauma of accident aggravated
symptoms of myalgic encephalomyelitis – Whether accident caused or materially
contributed to plaintiff's deteriorating condition – Whether plaintiff having to show
that psychiatric injury was foreseeable regardless of direct involvement in accident.*

The plaintiff was involved in a collision with the defendant when the latter
failed to give way when turning out of a side road. The plaintiff was unhurt in
the collision, but the accident caused him to suffer the onset of a bout of
myalgic encephalomyelitis (ME) from which he had suffered for about 20 years
but which was then in remission. Thereafter the plaintiff brought an action
against the defendant claiming damages for chronic and permanent ME which
was likely to prevent him from ever working again. The defendant admitted
that the accident had been caused by his negligence but disputed liability for
damages. The judge however awarded the plaintiff damages of £162,153 on
the ground that once it was established (a) that ME existed and that a relapse
or recrudescence could be triggered by the trauma of an accident of moderate
severity and (b) that nervous shock was suffered by the plaintiff who was
actually involved in the accident, the aggravation of his condition became a
foreseeable consequence for which the defendant was liable. The defendant
appealed, contending (i) that the plaintiff had not proved the causal connection
between the accident and his following condition and (ii) that the judge, in
deciding that the plaintiff's injury was foreseeable, had failed to consider
whether a person of reasonable fortitude would have suffered shock from the
accident as it occurred and had wrongly determined that foreseeability of
injury from nervous shock was not necessary in the case of a plaintiff who had
been directly involved in the accident and was not a mere spectator.

Held – (1) (Per Ralph Gibson LJ) There was no clear evidence from any expert
witness to the effect that other cases had been observed or reported in which
an injury causing no physical injury and no more nervous shock than some
immediate fright had caused either the onset or serious or permanent

a worsening of the symptoms of ME. Accordingly, there was insufficient evidence before the court to warrant the decision that the accident in probability caused or materially contributed to the plaintiff's condition. The defendant's appeal on the ground of causation therefore succeeded (see p 540 e f, post).

b (2) A plaintiff who claimed damages for nervous shock resulting from an accident in which he had escaped physical injury had to show that psychiatric injury was foreseeable and was of a kind that would be suffered by a person of ordinary fortitude and phlegm irrespective of whether he had been directly involved in the accident as opposed to being a mere bystander. If the plaintiff was able to establish liability for nervous shock then the defendant would be liable for all the consequent mental injury sustained by the victim, even though

c it was unforeseen and of a kind that would only be suffered by someone who was particularly vulnerable, and it was at that point that the tortfeasor had to take his victim as he found him and the principle of the eggshell skull was to be applied. On the facts, the plaintiff's injury had not been foreseeable in a person of ordinary fortitude as a result of what happened in the accident. The plaintiff

d had suffered no physical injury at all and had suffered only such fright and shock as any person might be expected to suffer as a result of a collision of moderate severity with some damage to his car but no injury to him. The defendant's appeal would accordingly be allowed (see p 541 h, p 544 f to j, p 547 j to p 548 d, p 552 c to g and p 553 a to d, post); *Hay (or Bourhill) v Young* [1942] 2 All ER 396 applied; *Attia v British Gas plc* [1987] 3 All ER 455 considered.

e

Notes

For liability for nervous shock, see 34 *Halsbury's Laws* (4th edn) para 8, and for cases on the subject, see 17 *Digest* (Reissue) 145–148, *378–393*.

f **Cases referred to in judgments**

Alcock v Chief Constable of the South Yorkshire Police [1991] 4 All ER 907, [1992] 1 AC 310, [1991] 3 WLR 1057, HL.
Attia v British Gas plc [1987] 3 All ER 455, [1988] QB 304, [1987] 3 WLR 1101, CA.
Bonnington Castings Ltd v Wardlaw [1956] 1 All ER 615, [1956] AC 613, [1956] 2 WLR 707, HL.

g *Brice v Brown* [1984] 1 All ER 997.
Chadwick v British Transport Commission [1967] 2 All ER 945, sub nom *Chadwick v British Railways Board* [1967] 1 WLR 912.
Dulieu v White & Sons [1901] 2 KB 669, [1900–3] All ER Rep 353, DC.
Hay (or Bourhill) v Young [1942] 2 All ER 396, [1943] AC 92, HL.

h *Hicks v Chief Constable of the South Yorkshire Police, Wafer v Chief Constable of the South Yorkshire Police* [1992] 1 All ER 690, CA; *affd* [1992] 2 All ER 65, HL.
Hotson v East Berkshire Area Health Authority [1987] 2 All ER 909, [1987] AC 750, [1987] 3 WLR 232, HL.
Hughes v Lord Advocate [1963] 1 All ER 705, [1963] AC 837, [1963] 2 WLR 779, HL.

j *Jaensch v Coffey* (1984) 155 CLR 549, Aust HC.
King v Phillips [1953] 1 All ER 617, [1953] 1 QB 429, [1953] 2 WLR 526, CA.
McGhee v National Coal Board [1972] 3 All ER 1008, [1973] 1 WLR 1, HL.
McLoughlin v O'Brian [1982] 2 All ER 298, [1983] 1 AC 410, [1982] 2 WLR 982, HL.
Malcolm v Broadhurst [1970] 3 All ER 508.
Nicholls v Rushton (1992) Times, 19 June, [1992] CA Transcript 0401.

Overseas Tankship (UK) Ltd v Morts Dock and Engineering Co Ltd, The Wagon Mound (No 1) [1961] 1 All ER 404, [1961] AC 388, [1961] 2 WLR 126, PC.
Smith v Leech Brain & Co Ltd [1961] 3 All ER 1159, [1962] 2 QB 405, [1962] 2 WLR 148.
Wagon Mound, The (No 2), Overseas Tankship (UK) Ltd v Miller [1966] 2 All ER 709, [1967] AC 617, [1966] 3 WLR 498, PC.
Wilsher v Essex Area Health Authority [1988] 1 All ER 871, [1988] AC 1074, [1988] 2 WLR 557, HL.

Appeal

The defendant, Simon Gerald Toby Smith, appealed from the decision of Otton J made on 22 December 1992, whereby the judge ordered that the defendant pay the plaintiff, Ronald Edgar Page, £162,153 in damages for personal injury following a road accident on the ground that the accident, in causing the plaintiff to suffer nervous shock, had materially contributed to his condition of myalgic encephalomyelitis becoming chronic and permanent after the accident. The facts are set out in the judgment of Ralph Gibson LJ.

Colin Mackay QC and *Jennifer Richards* (instructed by *Edward Lewis*) for the plaintiff.
Julian Priest QC and *Andrew Hogarth* (instructed by *Harry R Pearce*, Haywards Heath) for the defendant.

Cur adv vult

30 March 1994. The following judgments were delivered.

RALPH GIBSON LJ. This is an appeal by the defendant, Mr Smith, from the decision of Otton J on 22 December 1992 whereby it was ordered that the plaintiff, Mr Ronald Edgar Page, should have judgment for £162,153 as damages for personal injuries. There is, and was before the judge, no issue as to liability for the traffic accident in which the plaintiff claims to have suffered injury. The contentions of the defendant are that the plaintiff is entitled to no damages for personal injury, or to a much smaller sum.

It is necessary to state the facts in detail in order to examine the submissions of the parties.

The plaintiff is 53 years old. He was driving a Volvo motor car on 24 July 1987 when the defendant drove his car across the plaintiff's path so that the cars collided. The plaintiff, then aged 46, suffered no physical injury whatever. He drove home. Within three hours he felt himself exhausted. A feeling of exhaustion continued. The plaintiff, a school teacher, has not worked since the accident. His case at trial, in November 1992, as stated by the judge, was that for about 20 years he had been afflicted with a condition variously known as myalgic encephalomyelitis (ME), or chronic fatigue syndrome (CFS), or post-viral fatigue syndrome (PVFS), which had manifested itself on sporadic occasions in a mild form. As a result of the accident his condition is, he claimed, now a chronic and permanent state.

Otton J stated eight questions which required to be determined. They were: (1) is there a condition or disease or illness called ME, CFS or PVFS; (2) what are the principal or typical symptoms or characteristics of this condition; (3) what causes it; (4) did the plaintiff suffer from the condition before the accident and, if so, to what extent; (5) did the road traffic accident cause or materially

a contribute to the condition that has prevailed since the accident; (6) if so, if he had it before, to what extent would he have suffered if there had been no accident; (7) the extent, if any, to which the plaintiff has suffered damage as a result of the accident; and (8) if his present condition is attributable to the accident, the level of compensation to which he is entitled after allowance is made for his pre-accident condition and the probable future that he would
b have enjoyed had there been no accident?

Before stating the questions Otton J began his judgment with the following introduction:

'The condition (which I shall refer to as "CFS") is an elusive one. It has not yet been finally determined by medical science. In the meantime, it
c does not always receive the sympathy and understanding it deserves. This scepticism has been manifested by some doctors, and the lack of sympathy is often shown by acquaintances, friends and even the family of the sufferer. This is because there has been a reluctance of the medical profession to recognise CFS as a diagnosable condition and to accept it as a medical condition, and the failure of the public in general to appreciate
d that it is a genuine illness. There is a tendency, even a temptation, to associate the symptoms with sloth, indolence, malingering and hysteria.'

The character and history of the plaintiff was said by Otton J to be 'central to the resolution of the issues'. He set out the story over nine pages. It can be summarised as follows.

e (a) He left school with three A levels. After three years in employment he went in 1965 as a novice to the Sacred Heart Fathers. In January 1966 he suffered dizziness, headaches and sinusitis. The symptoms persisted over many months. His doctor regarded him as neurotic and referred him to Dr Clegg, a psychiatrist. His view was that his condition was 'a mild relative
f depression resulting from his admitted difficulties in adjusting himself to new surroundings'. The plaintiff's account is that the priest in charge, without any explanation, told the plaintiff to leave and not to return. That was the earliest recorded onset of CFS when the plaintiff was aged 23: the judge held that there was an association or 'linkage' between the strain and discipline of the noviciate and the onset of symptoms and their unusually prolonged duration.

g (b) The plaintiff then obtained work as an accounts clerk. His symptoms 'simply went away' without treatment. He continued on that sort of work for three years with different employers. He became disillusioned with the work and the unworthy attitude of his colleagues. In August 1969 he suffered from tension headaches and was prescribed valium at the National Hospital for
h Nervous Diseases. That, as the judge found, may well have been an episode of CFS.

(c) In July 1970 his mother died of cancer. A few days later he was referred to Dr Rollin, a consultant psychiatrist. The judge inferred that it was the knowledge that his mother was suffering from a fatal condition and his distress and concern which precipitated another episode of CFS.

j (d) During 1971 he continued in low-grade clerical work. In February 1972 he was off work for three weeks with bronchitis. In March he was admitted to hospital for a tonsillectomy. The plaintiff asserted that this caused a 'major relapse'. He could hardly walk one month after the operation. He tried to go back to work. He then had five months off until March 1973.

(e) In 1973 there was a record from a psychiatry clinic of the plaintiff attending for 'tension and depression'. In 1975 he visited his doctor on a number of occasions complaining of headache, sinusitis, sickness, diarrhoea, nausea, dizziness, shortness of breath, and pain in his shoulders and back. He was given certificates off work for several weeks.

(f) After a gap in the records, there were recorded eight visits to his doctor between April and November 1978 for sore throats, tiredness, virus infection, and he was off work for periods of time. In 1979 there were records of his complaining to his doctor of breathlessness, tachycardia and pharyngitis and there were similar records in 1980 and 1982.

(g) In 1985 he was off work for two weeks with pleuritis and chest pain. In 1986 he had attended his doctor on three occasions for hay fever and ear infections.

(h) Early in 1987 there began the illness which preceded the accident. He developed a cold and an infection and became 'completely exhausted' again. He was unable to do his work of classroom teaching but did work of marking papers at home. In 1987 he attended his doctor on 15 occasions for sinusitis, debility, exhaustion, poor concentration and muscle aches. He was making some recovery but one of his children became unwell with a viral infection and his recovery was reversed. The plaintiff, after hearing the programme 'Medicine Now' on Radio 4 felt that he had 'some persistent post-viral problem'. The plaintiff wrote to the ME Society and studied the literature relating to that condition. The report of Dr Siklos, dated 26 May 1987, contained the following:

'I am sure he has post-viral fatigue syndrome ... there is little objective evidence that the condition can be improved ... (but) folic acid replacement may be important ... I have (prescribed) folic acid and would be interested to hear how he gets on.'

(i) The course of the plaintiff's work and training was as follows. In 1980 he gave up employment in the commercial world, being disillusioned with the disregard for ethics of his superiors and fellow workers. He wished to 'go into retreat'. He began to draw state benefits in November 1980 and did not return to any form of work until September 1981. He joined a 'charismatic group' within the Roman Catholic Church. He met and married his wife. He decided to fulfil his ambition to read theology. He obtained a degree of Bachelor of Theology at Southampton University, graduating in 1984, and then went to Winchester where he obtained a Certificate of Education in July 1985. He began work as a teacher in a Roman Catholic school in Bury St Edmunds in September 1985. His appointment was confirmed in August 1986.

(j) It was common ground at the trial that the plaintiff's illness in 1987 was a recrudescence of the symptoms of CFS. The plaintiff's case at trial was that gradually the symptoms had decreased and that he was getting better; he saw his doctor on 17 July and discussed when he could return to work; it was his intention to resume work in the autumn term in September 1987.

THE ACCIDENT

(i) The accident occurred on 24 July 1987. The writ was issued in 1990. The plaintiff's pleaded case of March 1990 was that the collision occurred and that, by reason of it, he suffered personal injury. No physical or psychological injury was alleged. In the particulars it was said that he had been suffering—

'acute onset PVFS following an upper respiratory tract infection in early 1987 from which he had largely recovered by July 1987 ... within 24 hours a of the accident the plaintiff experienced severe exacerbation of symptoms and recurrence of PVFS. His symptoms improved minimally up to July 1989 and recovery was very slow. The prognosis was guarded.'

(ii) At trial a number of medical records were agreed including the notes of Dr Dean, the plaintiff's general practitioner. On the main issue no medical b evidence was agreed. The plaintiff called three doctors: Dr Weir, a consultant physician; Dr Wessely, a consultant psychiatrist; and Dr Findley, a consultant neurologist. Their evidence was, in general substance, accepted by the judge. On the issue of whether it was open to the judge to hold that the continuing and worsened condition of the plaintiff had been caused by the accident, parts of their reports should be noted.

c (iii) Dr Weir first saw the plaintiff on 25 March 1992. His note of the accident was as follows:

d 'He has a vivid memory of the accident but did not suffer any severe physical injury requiring hospital treatment. Nonetheless the sudden deceleration of the impact with the other car shook him up considerably and the additional psychological effects of the accident left him feeling very shaky indeed. Two days later he was complaining of moderately severe headache, a stiff neck, stiff knee joints, stiffness of the right hip joint and the muscles of the right hip were painful and bruised. A dominating feature was the presence of severe lethargy ... Symptoms since the e accident: the end of July 1987 marked a ... distinct worsening of the symptoms ... a characteristic feature is an extreme variability of their severity together with a tendency to relapse if he over exerts himself even on days when he feels marginally better. Relapses tend to be precipitated by activity, as previously stated, also virus infections such as colds and flu. f Opinion: there is no doubt that he suffers from CFS and that it is a genuine entity ... it is a disease of the whole person and cannot be defined as either psychological or organic. As to the question whether the road traffic accident caused ... the current condition ... this is definitely the case. There is an undoubted temporal relationship between the occurrence of the accident and the worsening of the symptoms. The combination of g physical and psychological trauma, such as suffered by him in the accident, could easily worsen a whole range of different medical conditions ... the accident contributed very significantly to a worsening of his condition. The prognosis is uncertain; recovery within the next 6 months is a possibility, but ... a longer term illness lasting for up to 10 years or even h longer ... is more likely.'

(iv) Dr Wessely prepared his report on 9 February 1992. He had not seen the plaintiff. He first addressed the question whether there is a condition such as ME, PVFS or CFS. He preferred CFS as a term to describe the condition because 'it makes no unproven aetiological claims'. A patient with the i condition shows no abnormalities on physical examination. It is not due to neuro-muscular disease. It is associated with a high rate of psychiatric disorder. It is not due to hysteria or malingering. The plaintiff at the time of the accident was suffering from CFS, and the viruses that trigger CFS are common and innocuous.

As to whether the plaintiff was recovering at the time of the accident, it was reasonable to assume that he was recovering and would eventually have returned to work. However, the probability of future illnesses was extremely high.   *a*

As to whether the accident contributed to the relapse, that was the most difficult part of the plaintiff's case. The opinion of Dr Wessely was as follows:

'... if CFS/PVFS is solely the result of viral persistence or neuro-muscular disorder, it will be impossible to show that a relapse *b* within 24 hours of the accident would be related to the trauma ... however if ... CFS has both a basis in cerebral dysfunction and links with psychological disorders, then it is far easier to understand what did, after all happen, namely that he did relapse within 24 hours. I suspect that what happened was analogous to the condition of post traumatic stress disorder, a condition in which severe and persistent symptoms may *c* develop after a single traumatic episode ... What is ... more established is that he did suffer "nervous shock"—I note he thought during the accident that he might be about to kill the female passenger involved—and that these nervous shocks would have a significant deleterious effect on the psychological state which ... is already affected in CFS. Thus if one accepts *d* that he was suffering from at least some degree of psychological disorder at the time of the accident ... then it becomes easy to see why the accident could cause a relapse. As to other explanations ... one possibility is that his relapse was actually related to receiving the discouraging material from the ME association ... that only 50% recovery can be expected in one year ... this mis-information may have contributed but I do not think it *e* was causal.'

(v) Dr Findley saw the plaintiff on 1 June 1992. He had the medical records and the reports of Dr Weir and Dr Wessely. His report included the following:

'*The Accident* ... [the plaintiff's] car hit the nearside of the other person's *f* car ... there was no serious personal injury ... However, it is to be emphasised that his car ... was "written off". *Subsequent progress*: ... since [the accident] he has suffered with a fluctuating, at times severe fatigue syndrome which severely interferes with his ability to function ... he is now able to drive, but locally, never more than 12 miles. [Walking 600 yards can cause him to be exhausted for several days.] There is no doubt *g* ... that [he] has suffered throughout most of his adult life with episodes of CFS ... at the time of the ... accident ... [he] was in a recovery phase. There is no doubt from observing patients with this disorder that physical, psychological and infective stresses of all types can result in deterioration in the condition and impair recovery ... the deleterious effects of the *h* accident are likely to have [been] mediated by psychological factors such as "nervous shock" ... although Mr Page tends to underplay his personal injuries in the accident, it is clear that the trauma involved must have been severe to "write off" a large Volvo car, which is renowned for its robust structure ... After being symptomatic for a period now of almost 4 years *j* ... the prognosis in terms of recovery in the short and intermediate term is extremely poor. It is possible ... there will be a slow improvement in his symptoms over time ... many patients, probably 25%, never return to their previous energy levels.'

(vi) It was the opinion of Dr David Kendall, a consultant neurologist who was called for the defendant, that the continuing complaints of the plaintiff after July 1987 had nothing to do with the accident. Dr McKeran, a consultant neurologist who was also called for the defendant, was of the opinion that it was not reasonable to conclude that the plaintiff's condition had been caused by the accident. Their evidence was not accepted by the judge.

(vii) Dr Adrianne Reveley, a consultant psychiatrist, saw the plaintiff in October 1992. She had copies of the medical records and of the reports of Dr Weir, Dr Wessely and Dr Findley. Her record of the plaintiff's account of the accident included the following:

> 'He saw an oncoming car which had swung onto his side of the road. He realised an accident was unavoidable ... The bonnet of the other car was completely squashed ... his car lost a bit of its bumper and its wing was bent ... he drove his car home ... the chassis of his car was bent by the impact. He had no physical injuries at all from the accident. He did not even have bruises from the seat belt.'

(viii) The report contained a long and detailed case history which the judge found to be reliable. The report contained the following passages:

> 'By 7 p.m. [on the day of the accident] he was aware that he was "very tired". The ME literature stressed that sufferers should take plenty of rest, so he went to bed. By the Sunday evening he was as bad as he had felt at the end of March and realised that he was in for a long spell of illness again. He wrote "that he was going to be off work for several months". He realised that he would have to explain in court why he knew at that point that he was going to be ill for months a few days after the accident ... He expected to get back to work, perhaps in 1988, but he did not recover ... it was November 1990 when he understood that he was not going to get better at all. The recovery he had experienced, he realised, was seasonal fluctuation in his ME which gets better in the summer. He keeps his outside interests going and makes sure that he gets outside the house every day. He began prison visiting as a volunteer chaplain in Highpoint Prison, going there twice a week, driving himself the 12 miles there and back. He has no trouble driving ... He is still involved in the local church ... he keeps up his contacts in charismatic renewal ... He had had three traffic accidents in the past. In 1963 he was knocked off his scooter. He was not seriously injured. In 1968 he had a burst tyre on the motorway and in 1970 he hit a parked car. None of these accidents were associated with any physical sequelae. *Current mental state* ... he is happy in himself at present ... he lacks energy and enthusiasm but is at peace with himself and relaxed. He is not pleased with his physical state and would like to be fit and well ... The effect of trauma on ME ... Dr Wessely concludes that the plaintiff suffered "nervous shock" and that the accident would adversely affect a depressive illness of whatever aetiology. I agree ... to some extent ... for this is surely common sense. However, in my view such a "nervous shock", not associated with any physical sequelae at all, nor with any subsequent difficulty driving, is likely to have only a transient slight effect on his mental state ... to judge to what extent the particular "nervous shock" suffered by him ... has affected his subsequent course we must consider the other more powerful reasons why this episode of ME may have been perpetuated.'

Dr Reveley then listed those other reasons. Her report continued as follows:

'Firstly, just before the accident, he had been given a diagnosis which
explained all his symptoms over many years. It would have been a relief
to him to have a diagnosis and confirmation of his years of ill health and
he says that he reads the ME literature with care and follows its advice.
Perhaps ... though the accident was not associated with any direct physical
sequelae, it set up ... an expectation of a relapse ... he did expect to relapse
and expected to be off work for about four months ... perhaps this
expectation was fulfilled. He was not terribly happy teaching which he
found stressful. This is another pressure making it easier for him to stay
off work than to return. The stress of litigation was well known to
perpetuate psychiatric ill health and it is likely that continued attention to
this litigation has prolonged his symptoms. Finally, he is happy and
content with his life as it is. There is no pressure at all to return to work
... it is likely to be a relief to him not to have to work and to have a
diagnosis which allows chronic disability ... he will continue to suffer
episodes for the rest of his life. He is most unlikely to return to teaching.
Conclusion: this accident, which had no physical consequences ... has had
a negligible effect on his lifelong illness and poor prognosis ...'

THE JUDGMENT OF OTTON J

The findings of the judge and the process of his reasoning were, in summary,
as follows.

(i) The judge accepted without hesitation the evidence given by the plaintiff
and his wife.

(ii) He reviewed the medical evidence. It was irreconcilable. In coming to
a conclusion as to which part of the medical evidence he preferred, the
'accident was central'. He reviewed the plaintiff's evidence about the accident
including the fact that he was not physically hurt in any way and that within
three hours of arriving home he felt obviously exhausted as if something
physical had happened.

(iii) The judge considered the evidence as to the damage to the car given by
an insurance motor engineer called for the plaintiff. The damage to the
plaintiff's car was not extensive but it was not economic to repair the car
having regard to its market value and was thus 'a write-off'. Dr Weir had
conceded that he had based his conclusions as to the effect of the accident as a
triggering factor on the fact that the plaintiff was driving a Volvo which was a
write-off. Dr Weir had also formed the view that the plaintiff probably
suffered a whiplash injury to the head.

(iv) The judge noted that Dr Wessely, without going into details of how the
accident happened, attached more importance to nervous shock and the
temporal link between the accident and the deterioration. Dr Findley had
placed emphasis on the fact that the Volvo car was 'written off'.

(v) The judge noted the plaintiff's account to Dr Reveley as recorded by her
and the descriptions recorded by Dr Kendall and Dr McKeran.

(vi) The judge held that the impact was not so severe as the plaintiff's
doctors may have concluded; but, on the other hand, Dr Reveley was
persuaded by the plaintiff's description to her into underestimating the
severity of the impact. On the balance of probabilities there was a collision of
moderate severity. It must have been a frightening experience for the plaintiff
and he did suffer nervous shock in the broad sense of that term.

a   (vii) The judge then addressed question (1): is there a condition or disease or illness called ME? He held that there is a condition known as CFS which may accurately be called a 'syndrome' in that it makes no unproven aetiological claims.

(viii) As to question (2): what are the principal or typical symptoms or characteristics? The judge accepted that it is 'an ill-defined condition with a
b   range of symptoms including malaise, fatigue, headache and exhaustion. There are no abnormal physical signs and investigation is negative'. The judge also said that he accepted Dr Weir's finding from his work in his field that—

> 'a characteristic feature is an extreme variability of their severity together with a tendency to relapse if the patient over exerts himself even
c   > on days when he feels marginally better.'

(ix) As to question (3): what causes it? Otton J held that, on the present stage of medical knowledge, no answer could be given with certainty. He could not accept Dr Wessely's opinion as to 'cerebral disturbance' as a cause but he accepted that Dr Wessely was 'the physician most versed in this
d   particular condition' and the judge accepted 'his analysis and conclusion in broad terms'. Based upon Dr Weir's 'research conclusions' to the effect that relapses tend to be precipitated by activity and virus infections such as colds and flu, the judge found on the balance of probabilities 'that the chronic activation of the immune system is due to an agent provoking this activity
e   probably by as yet an unidentified virus'. Otton J accepted that there is a 'temporal connection'. He also accepted Dr Weir's conclusion that the 'condition can be triggered by a viral infection or emotional stress or the trauma of an accident'; and that Dr Weir had had experience of other patients who have been diagnosed as suffering from CFS as 'a result of the trauma of an accident'. He also accepted Dr Findley's evidence which is based on similar
f   clinical experience.

(x) As to question (4): did the plaintiff suffer from the condition before the accident and, if so, to what extent? Otton J accepted Dr Reveley's opinion that the plaintiff had CFS as far back as 1965 caused by 'the strain of the novitiate'. In 1970, his mother's cancer brought about a further episode. His
g   tonsillectomy in 1972 caused a year's disability from a major 'ME episode'. His history from 1972 to 1986 could be summed up in the words of Dr Findley:

> '... the plaintiff is suffering from a severe fluctuating CFS which has been precipitated on several occasions through his adult life by cerebral illnesses, usually of an upper respiratory tract type and presumed viral
h   > origin.'

Otton J accepted the plaintiff's account of his severe bout of symptoms from February 1987, which were a recrudescence of CFS. This was prolonged by the viral infection 'brought by his child from school'. He was improving during the summer months. He accepted also the evidence of the plaintiff and his wife
j   as to the plaintiff's renewed activity and the evidence of Mrs Flath, the chair of the board of governors, a most responsible and impressive lady. She visited the plaintiff on occasions during the summer of 1987 and noted his improvement during that period of time. On the balance of probabilities the plaintiff was in a recovery stage immediately before the accident and, on the balance of probabilities, he would have returned to school to resume his teaching duties in the autumn of 1987.

(xi) As to question (5): did the road traffic accident cause or materially contribute to the condition which has prevailed since the accident?

(a) The principle of law which Otton J applied in considering this question was stated by him as follows: did the accident, on the balance of probabilities, cause or materially contribute or materially increase the risk of the development or prolongation of the symptoms of CFS which he currently suffers? That test was derived by the judge from the decisions in *Bonnington Castings Ltd v Wardlaw* [1956] 1 All ER 615, [1956] AC 613, *McGhee v National Coal Board* [1972] 3 All ER 1008, [1973] 1 WLR 1 and *Wilsher v Essex Area Health Authority* [1988] 1 All ER 871, [1988] AC 1074. The vital element was, said the judge, that the accident should be a material contribution not merely a minimal or trivial or insignificant contribution.

(b) The finding that the collision was of moderate severity had the effect, said Otton J, of reducing the certainty of Dr Reveley's positive assertion that the trauma had nothing to do with ME or with the plaintiff's continued debility. The finding that the collision was of moderate severity also reduced the reliance that the judge could place upon Dr Weir's conviction that the collision contributed very significantly to a worsening of the plaintiff's condition because the collision had been in fact less severe than Dr Weir had envisaged it as having been. The judge preferred the more cautious approach of Dr Findley that 'the deleterious effects of the accident are likely to have [been] mediated or caused by psychological factors such as "nervous shock"'.

(c) The judge then addressed the question whether any candidates other than the collision can be identified as the *sole* cause of the 'accident'; but that is an obvious error in dictation or transcription and must be taken to mean the 'effects' which followed the accident or the condition of the plaintiff since the accident. Otton J considered the other 'possible causative factors', namely (i) the acquisition by the plaintiff of an expectation of relapse into ME from reading the ME Association literature, (ii) the fact that teaching was stressful for the plaintiff and the accident a relief to him, and (iii) the stress of litigation; and the judge rejected each of them as a sole cause. He also found that a combination of those three factors could not account for the plaintiff's present condition.

(d) The judge emphatically rejected the notion or theory advanced by Dr Reveley that the plaintiff was content with life as it is, even happy, and, having no financial worries, was in a state of equilibrium.

(e) Finally, the juxtaposition of the accident and the recurrence of symptoms could not be described as 'mere coincidence'. He accepted the 'majority view of the experts that physical, psychological and infective stresses of all types can result in deterioration in the condition and impair recovery'. He accepted the answer given by Dr Weir that the accident as an occasion was unique in its combination of factors because it occurred during a period when the plaintiff was unwell. If he had had the accident when he had recovered then he might have had more constitutional strength to recover from it. He also accepted the view of Dr Wessely that had the accident not occurred the plaintiff's recovery was likely to have continued.

(xii) Otton J then considered the contention for the defendant which the judge described as follows. Since the plaintiff had in the accident suffered no physical injury, and if the subsequent relapse was triggered by shock alone, the plaintiff could only recover damages if the defendant could have foreseen the consequences. The plaintiff should fail because it was not reasonably a foreseeable that an accident of such a trivial nature would have had such a devastating effect. Otton J rejected that submission because in fact the accident was not a trivial accident and it was well established that the defendant must in law take the plaintiff as he finds him. He referred to *Malcolm v Broadhurst* [1970] 3 All ER 508 per Lane J, and applied the reasoning there set out. Otton J said:

b   'Once it is established that CFS exists, and that a relapse or recrudescence can be triggered by the trauma of an accident, and that nervous shock was suffered by the plaintiff who was actually involved in the accident, it becomes a foreseeable consequence.'

The nervous shock cases had no relevance because the plaintiff was not a
c spectator of the accident but was directly involved.

(xiii) Otton J then addressed questions (6), (7) and (8) without restating them. They were: to what extent would the plaintiff have suffered if there had been no accident; to what extent has the plaintiff suffered damage as a result of the accident; and what allowance is to be made in assessing damages for his
d pre-accident condition and the probable future that he would have enjoyed had there been no accident.

(a) The judge began by saying that, since the plaintiff was entitled to damages, it was necessary to reflect in the award 'the other factors which I consider also materially contributed to the overall disability'.

(b) Otton J then stated the description given by Mr and Mrs Page of 'what
e happened thereafter', ie after the accident. It is a description of the plaintiff's state and how he lives. He spent all morning in bed on the holiday in Margate in August 1987; he was too tired and exhausted to be with his family. He sleeps until midday in the winter and in the summer gets up a little earlier. The plaintiff's wife always drives, even to camp-sites when they go away on
f holiday, where she does everything, including the erection of a frame tent. The plaintiff sleeps late in the mornings still and only goes out to go to the bank and to visit a prison once a week when he talks to prisoners. He has not mown the lawn since 1987. He never goes for a walk.

(c) As to loss of earnings, it was agreed that the plaintiff would have been earning £14,340 pa if he had remained in his job. In probability he would have
g worked to age 65. The judge applied a multiplier of 10. The full figure was to be reduced because of six factors which the judge listed. They were as follows: (i) to reflect his previous medical history; (ii) his innate vulnerability to episodes before the accident which would have continued had there been no accident; (iii) the limited fields of activity in which he could in any event have
h sought employment; (iv) the stress that teaching would have had upon him had he continued as a teacher; (v) the expectation of symptoms from his previous experience and his reading of the ME literature and the effect it had upon him; (vi) the recurrence of symptoms from the exigencies of life in any event, such as illness, including viral infections, emotional experiences such as
j bereavement in the future, and trauma from possible further accidents.

(d) Therefore, as the judge held, the plaintiff would not have had a full and unbroken period of employment. To reflect those matters the judge reduced the multiplier for future loss of earnings from 10 to 6 and awarded £86,040. Other items of damage were similarly reduced, with adjustments, and in my judgment it is not necessary to consider them separately.

(e) As to general damages, the judge found that 'due to the trauma of the accident, what was previously a mild and sporadic state of CFS had been

promoted to a chronic and permanent state'. That must have caused great
anxiety and grievance and sadness to the plaintiff. Had it not been for the
accident the plaintiff would have recovered, not totally, but to the mild state
that he had enjoyed as evidenced and experienced over the 20 years prior to the
accident. Nevertheless he took into account the plaintiff's condition and the
'vulnerability which would have continued into the future had there been no
accident'. He awarded the sum of £20,000 for general damages.

THE DEFENDANT'S APPEAL

The grounds of appeal are, in summary, as follows.

(1) Upon the evidence it was not open to the judge to hold that the
deterioration or continuation of the plaintiff's symptoms of CFS was caused by
the accident.

(2) If it was open to the judge so to hold, it was not open to him to hold that
the deterioration was more than transitory.

(6) It is convenient to take this ground next. The judge was wrong to direct
himself that the test of causation was whether the defendant's negligence had
materially contributed to the plaintiff's injuries or to their recrudescence. He
should have directed himself that it was necessary for the plaintiff to establish
on the balance of probabilities that the negligence had in fact caused those
injuries.

(3) The judge was wrong to hold that the plaintiff had suffered from
nervous shock as a consequence of the accident because (i) there was no
sufficient evidence that he had so suffered; (ii) the judge failed to direct himself
properly as to what is capable of amounting to nervous shock; and (iii) he
regarded the recrudescence of the plaintiff's symptoms as nervous shock when
there was no evidence that it could be so regarded.

(4) The judge was wrong to hold that the plaintiff's injury was foreseeable;
he failed to apply the principle that it was necessary in law for the plaintiff to
prove that a person of reasonable fortitude might suffer shock from the
accident as it occurred, and wrongly held that foreseeability of injury from
nervous shock was not required in the case of a plaintiff who was involved in
the accident and was not a mere onlooker.

(6) or (7) The judge was wrong to apply the test of whether the accident had
caused or materially contributed or materially increased the risk of the
development or prolongation of symptoms. The proper test was whether the
accident had caused those consequences. In particular the judge was wrong to
hold that the plaintiff was entitled to damages unless some other cause was
shown to have been the sole cause.

(8), (9), (10) and (11) On the facts, a greater allowance or deduction than the
40%, or other deduction allowed by the judge should have been made from the
items of special damages; and the general damages should have been reduced
to allow for the chance that the plaintiff would have suffered a recrudescence
of his condition if the accident had not occurred.

Mr Mackay QC for the plaintiff submitted that the decision of Otton J was
right for the reasons which he gave. The plaintiff's case was, he said, simple
and clear. The defendant, who admitted breach of his duty to other road users,
carelessly drove into the path of the plaintiff. He ought reasonably to have
foreseen that his act might cause some personal injury to the plaintiff and some
damage to his property. In fact it did both. There was ample evidence to
support the finding that the accident caused the plaintiff serious personal
injury. The fact that the type of personal injury and facts sustained was the

a result of the plaintiff's vulnerability or susceptibility, which the defendant could not have foreseen, does not relieve him of liability for it. The damages awarded were right.

CAUSATION OF DAMAGE

Misdirection

b   Apart from the question whether there was sufficient evidence to support the judge's holding that the accident caused the plaintiff's condition after the accident, it was contended for the defendant that the judge misdirected himself in his consideration of the 'other candidates for sole cause'. The submission for the defendant was that where there are several potential operative causes which might have led to the injury of which the plaintiff complains, the *c* plaintiff has to establish on the balance of probabilities that the operative cause which results from the defendant's acts was the cause of his injury. Where a plaintiff has established on the balance of probabilities that a given operative cause or agent led to his injury, but he was exposed to that operative cause or agent both tortiously and non-tortiously by the defendant, he only has to show *d* that the tortious element of the exposure materially contributed to his injury (see *Bonnington Castings Ltd v Wardlaw* [1956] 1 All ER 615, [1956] AC 613). The burden of proof is on the plaintiff at all times. It is never incumbent on a defendant to establish that some other cause, or a combination of other causes, is the sole cause of the plaintiff's injuries. Reference was made to *McGhee v National Coal Board* [1972] 3 All ER 1008, [1973] 1 WLR 1, *Wilsher v Essex Area* *e* *Health Authority* [1988] 1 All ER 871, [1988] AC 1074 and *Hotson v East Berkshire Area Health Authority* [1987] 2 All ER 909, [1987] AC 750.

In my judgment, this submission fails. Otton J did not fail to apply the principles stated in the cases cited; and he did not approach the evidence on the basis that it was for the defendant to prove that some other possible cause was *f* the sole cause of the plaintiff's condition. The steps followed by Otton J, as it seems to me, were as follows. Firstly, for reasons which will require to be examined in detail, he concluded that the view based upon the more cautious approach of Dr Findley was to be preferred, ie that the effects of the accident are likely to have been mediated or caused by psychological facts such as shock. That, as it seems to me, was a provisional conclusion that the accident in *g* probability had materially contributed to the causing of the plaintiff's condition.

Next, the judge proceeded to test that preliminary conclusion by considering and rejecting the other causes as having been, whether singly or in combination, the sole cause of the plaintiff's condition. That process, as I *h* understand the judgment, was part of considering whether it was proved that the accident had materially contributed to the causing of the plaintiff's condition. If the other potential causes were in probability the sole causes of the condition, then the accident could not have contributed materially.

The judge's findings on causation
i   The submissions for the defendant were that the judge's primary findings of fact were unsatisfactory and cannot be supported even if, as I would hold, the judge correctly directed himself in law.

Firstly, it was contended that the judge was wrong to hold that the evidence of Dr Weir and Dr Findley established that in their clinical experience there had been a number of cases in which CFS sufferers who were also the victims of traffic accidents had suffered a relapse in their condition.

Thus, in his judgment, the judge referred to the evidence of Dr Weir as follows:

'... other known causes [of CFS] through his experience include emotional stress, such as from bereavement, and he has treated patients where he is satisfied that their condition has been triggered by the experience of an accident.'

Next, as to Dr Findley, the judge said:

'... he referred to anecdotal instances but he has had a number of road traffic accident patients of his own who have relapsed after a reasonably minor trauma. Bereavement, domestic, financial and work stresses are well-known factors for precipitant of the condition.'

Later the judge concluded:

'I accept without reservation that he has had experience of other patients who have been diagnosed as suffering from CFS as a result of the trauma of an accident. In this regard also I accept Dr Findley's evidence which is based on similar clinical experience.'

There was, it was said, no basis for those findings. Our attention was directed to the passages in the evidence of Dr Weir and of Dr Findley. It was pointed out that no reason was stated as to why the judge regarded the evidence as proving that an accident of the nature and consequences shown to have occurred in this case could cause the recrudescence of symptoms of CFS. No witness said that there had ever been observed such a case before.

Secondly, it was submitted for the defendant that the evidence did not support the judge's finding that the plaintiff, who had been profoundly ill in the early part of 1987, was by early July so much better that in probability he would have returned to work in September 1987; and that the accident resulted in a sudden and grave relapse. The plaintiff referred to two witnesses. He had told his doctor, he said, on 7 July 1987 that he was better and had discussed returning to work in September 1987. He had also discussed returning to work with Mr Peyton who was on the staff of the school where the plaintiff had worked. Further, the judge said in his judgment that Mrs Flath, the chair of the board of governors of the school where the plaintiff worked, had 'visited the plaintiff on occasions during the summer and noted his improvement'. In fact, Mrs Flath had given no such evidence. Mr Peyton's evidence did not support the plaintiff's account: it was that he had seen the plaintiff throughout the summer and 'although the plaintiff indicated ... that he was getting slowly better, my perception of him was that he looked weary. I couldn't see the improvement myself'. He did not recall discussing with the plaintiff his return to work.

As to Dr Dean, he was the plaintiff's general practitioner and the only doctor who had seen the plaintiff at the material time. He was not called on behalf of the plaintiff. He attended on subpoena issued on behalf of the defendant and was called without having provided a statement to the defendant's advisers although his records had been made available. His evidence included reference to his notes to the following effect: on 19 June 1987 'still exhausted all day: some muscle pain in left arm'; and on 17 July 1987 'slightly better' and the giving of a certificate off work for four weeks. The first entry after the accident on 24 July was an entry on 14 August: Dr Dean said that the plaintiff had told

a him that he had been involved in a road accident some little time previously
and had become more exhausted after the accident. If there had been a
significant change in his condition he would have noted it. The note he had
made was 'discussed mind/body interaction' which meant that he had
discussed with the plaintiff the physical symptoms that he might expect in
relation to any emotional state that was likely to prevail, be it caused by the
b accident or not. He had no recollection of discussing with the plaintiff the
possibility of his return to work and believed that he would have noted the fact
if he had had such a discussion. When asked what effect the accident might
have had on the plaintiff and his symptoms, Dr Dean said:

c '... it is my impression that the plaintiff had been quite profoundly
unwell, particularly in March and April and I had had occasion to visit him
at home in early April—and that by 17th July he had made some
improvement from that time when he was profoundly unwell and that
when I saw him after the road traffic accident there had been some relapse
in his symptoms.'

d Dr Dean did not accept the suggestion that the plaintiff in August 1987 had
been 'knocked back to where he had been in March or April 1987': he was,
however, worse than he had been in July.

In answer to these submissions Mr Mackay pointed to the fact that the judge
had accepted the evidence of the plaintiff and his wife. The relationship in time
e between the accident and the worsening of the plaintiff's condition was clear
and impressive. The judge had accepted without reservation the evidence of
Dr Weir and Dr Findley, based upon clinical experience, that 'road traffic
accidents do cause it'. Dr Dean had accepted that the accident had had an effect
on the progress of the plaintiff's condition if only temporary or slight.

f *Conclusion on causation*

In considering whether the plaintiff has established that the condition of
CFS, from which he suffered, was made significantly worse for some period of
time, or permanently, by the accident of July 1987, it is necessary to have in
mind that no doctor claimed to be able to explain how or by what process the
g experience of the accident could have had that effect. The plaintiff's condition
was described as a syndrome, a word which, as I understand it, means a
collection of symptoms which tend to occur together and form a characteristic
pattern but which may not necessarily be always due to the same cause and
which, as Otton J observed, 'makes no unproved aetiological claims'. The
h authority of a doctor to pronounce upon what may or may not, or will or will
not, cause or make worse the symptoms, or render them permanent, comes, as
I understand it, from having observed what has happened in the cases of other
patients with reference to the appearance of the symptoms and what
experience of the patient preceded the appearance, and similarly, with
j reference to worsening and long continuation of symptoms. It is obviously
easier, in such a state of medical knowledge, for a doctor to state what may be
or have been the consequence of certain experiences of the patient with
reference to the appearance, worsening or continuation of symptoms, than to
state with confidence that any particular consequence was in probability the
result of any particular experience. And if he is to assess that a particular
consequence was in probability caused by a particular experience, as
contrasted with that particular consequence possibly having been caused by

that experience, it is to be expected that he can point to some body of a
comparable example observed or reported in clinical experience.

As to the attack upon the judge's finding upon causation, if it were soundly
based upon the evidence of the plaintiff's doctors, and the evidence of the
plaintiff and his wife, then, having regard to the judge's assessment of the
witnesses, I would not think it right to disturb that finding notwithstanding the
fact that the judge was clearly wrong in his recollection of some parts of the b
evidence, such as that given by Mr Peyton and Mrs Flath. That evidence was,
I think, important because the acceptance of the plaintiff as a wholly honest
witness does not mean that he necessarily now recollects the progress of his
condition accurately. Further, although Mr Mackay invited us to accept that
the judge was better placed to assess the progress of the plaintiff's condition
from early 1987 to the accident in July, by way of improvement, and the c
progress of that condition after the accident by way of immediate and
permanent worsening, for my part I find the evidence of Dr Dean, upon
reading it, to be both fair and impressive and to suggest strongly that the
happening of the accident did not have the effect which the plaintiff now
attributes to it. d

The point at which, for my part, the reasoning and conclusion of the judge
on the issue of causation appear to be unsatisfactory is in his application of his
finding about the degree of severity of the collision to the reasoning and
opinions of the doctors: I have referred to it earlier as his provisional
conclusion that the accident in probability had materially contributed to the e
causing of the plaintiff's condition.

The judge's provisional conclusion was based on the following steps.
Firstly, the collision was one of 'moderate severity'. He did not say what that
meant. I take it to mean a summary of what he had found to have happened:
ie a sudden collision with an approaching car which turned across the
plaintiff's path, which had caused him no injury, which 'must have been a f
frightening experience', and which caused the plaintiff 'to suffer nervous shock
in the broad sense of the word'.

Next, that conclusion had, in the view of the judge, the effect of 'reducing
the certainty of Dr Reveley's positive assertion that the trauma had nothing to
do with ME or with the plaintiff's continued debility'. The judge did not g
explain how his finding had, in his view, had that effect. Dr Reveley did not
relate her conclusion to some concept of a collision of 'moderate severity' or
of any lesser severity. She recorded the consequences to the plaintiff of the
collision: the immediate consequences were 'no physical injury at all ... not
even bruises from the seat belt'. Dr Reveley recorded the plaintiff's account of h
the following events including his ability to drive home; his being very tired by
7 pm on the day of the accident; his collecting the hire car on the next day etc.
Her conclusion was that such a 'nervous shock' as had only those
consequences was likely to have only a transient slight effect on the plaintiff's
mental state. Her reasons included the fact that nowhere 'in any of the
descriptions of CFS is trauma referred to as a precipitant'. The fact that Dr j
Reveley accurately described the immediate consequences of the collision does
not mean that her opinion as to the consequences of it to the plaintiff must be
right. On the other hand, the judge's conclusion that the collision was fairly to
be described as one of 'moderate severity' seems to me to have no effect
whatever in suggesting that Dr Reveley's opinion as to the consequences of it
was wrong.

a   The judge next observed that his finding that the collision—

> 'was less severe than that envisaged by Dr Weir reduced the reliance that
> the judge can place upon his conviction that the collision contributed very
> significantly to the worsening of the plaintiff's condition.'

b   The judge did not explain why his finding served only to reduce that reliance.
Dr Weir had not relied upon some particular degree of severity of the collision
as being capable of having the consequences which he attributed to it *although*
it had *not* caused physical injury to the plaintiff. Dr Weir, on the contrary, was
confident that the collision had caused physical injuries and he described them.
It was the 'combination of physical and psychological trauma' which, in his
c   view, 'contributed very significantly to the worsening of his condition'. When
Dr Weir's attention was invited by Mr Mackay to the fact that there had been
no discernible physical injury, Dr Weir did not say that the happening of the
accident alone was sufficient without physical injury but asserted that 'in a
situation like that a very common injury is the whiplash injury' to the neck.
The judge pointed out that there was no evidence of that. Again, Dr Weir did
d   not assert that absence of physical injury mattered not. He said:

> 'Very often the heat of the moment in such a situation masks immediate
> pain and it is a well-recognised characteristic that the bruises sustained in
> such a situation do in fact only manifest themselves up to 24 or even 48
> hours later, and this is particularly the case in whiplash injury and in other
e   > analogous situations on the rugby field or even in the battlefield.'

Next Dr Weir was asked about the psychological side and the effects of an
incident such as this collision. His answer was:

> 'The psychological impact of the sudden realisation immediately prior to
f   > the accident I would consider to be very considerable indeed. There must,
> one presumes, be the instant thought that death is possible and therefore
> the psychological trauma sustained in such a situation would be fairly
> potent.'

g   In cross-examination Dr Weir acknowledged that he had assumed the
accident to have been a 'major' accident. His reference to fear of death was
acknowledged by him to have been an assumption by him. Dealing with what
sort of psychological trauma might cause the symptoms in the plaintiff, he said
that a sudden unexpected loud noise might cause a temporary exacerbation of
his symptoms but not a serious setback or relapse. As to what might cause the
h   plaintiff's symptoms, Dr Weir referred to severe injury, as in a surgical
operation, or, on the psychological side, bereavement, divorce etc. When
asked whether he classed anything suffered by the plaintiff as severe injury, Dr
Weir again did not say that physical injury was not necessary to support his
conclusion but suggested that the plaintiff had in truth suffered physical injury
j   saying:

> 'I think that the plaintiff is possibly underplaying the effects of the injury
> he did in fact suffer in this accident, in that he does actually seem to
> indicate that he suffered some injury; and there is this curious
> phenomenon that people do report the injuries in the heat of the moment
> being masked in their effects.'

Having stated the effect in his view of his finding as to the severity of the
collision upon the opinions of the doctors, the judge expressed his preference   *a*
for the more cautious approach of Dr Findley: 'the deleterious effects are likely
to have [been] mediated or caused by psychological factors such as "nervous
shock"'. It is to be noted that Dr Findley had described the accident as having
caused 'no serious personal injury', and that following the passage cited by the
judge Dr Findley also referred to the plaintiff 'tending to underplay his   *b*
personal injuries' although it was clear that 'the trauma involved must have
been severe to write off a large Volvo motor car'. There was nothing in Dr
Findley's report to suggest that he was taking a different view of what in the
effects of the accident had caused the plaintiff's following condition from that
expressed by Dr Wessely or Dr Weir whose reports had been supplied to him.

Dr Wessely had acknowledged in his report that the most difficult part of the   *c*
plaintiff's case was in showing that the accident had contributed to his relapse.
He suspected that, if CFS is accepted as having a basis in cerebral dysfunction
and links with psychological disorders, then it was easier to understand what
had happened, ie the relapse within 24 hours, as analogous to post-traumatic
stress disorder. He regarded as more established the proposition that the   *d*
plaintiff suffered 'nervous shock' in that he thought that he might be about to
kill the female passenger in the other car and that such a nervous shock would
have a significant deleterious effect on his psychological state.

It seems to me that the submissions for the defendant must be accepted,
namely that there was no clear evidence from any witness to the effect that
other cases had been observed or reported in which an accident causing no   *e*
physical injury, and no more 'nervous shock' than some immediate fright, had
caused either the onset or serious or permanent worsening of symptoms of
CFS. I am unable to accept that the evidence before the court is sufficient to
justify a holding that the accident in probability caused or materially
contributed to the plaintiff's condition.   *f*

THE REQUIREMENT OF FORESEEABILITY

If I am right on the issue of proof of causation, it is not necessary to decide
this point. If I am wrong on the issue of causation, the finding of Otton J will
stand, namely that the accident, which caused to the plaintiff no personal
injury but 'must have been a frightening experience' which caused him to   *g*
suffer 'nervous shock in the broad sense of the word', was the cause of 'the
recrudescence of CFS and of converting that illness from a mild and sporadic
state to one of chronic intensity and permanency'.

The submissions for the defendant advanced by Mr Priest QC were as
follows. If a plaintiff establishes that he has suffered some physical injury, he   *h*
may advance a claim in respect of a recognised psychiatric illness which has
resulted from that physical injury. If a plaintiff has suffered no physical injury,
and his only injuries are a recognised form of psychiatric illness, he may
succeed if the court decides that psychiatric illness was foreseeable in the case
of a person of reasonable fortitude. There is no difference in this respect, it was
submitted, between a bystander and a person directly involved in an event,   *j*
except that the consequences are more likely to be foreseeable in the case of the
latter than in the case of the former. In practical terms, the court closes the
category of plaintiffs by taking the view that a person of reasonable fortitude
can withstand the disasters of life. A shaking up is not treated as a form of
psychiatric illness for these purposes, whether described as nervous shock or
as something else.

a Mr Priest submitted that to introduce the eggshell skull cases, or the eggshell personality cases, into these questions is an error. They are to be considered not when foreseeability is being considered, but at a later stage when damages are considered. When considering foreseeability, the court is always judging matters on the basis of a person of reasonable fortitude.

b Lastly, it was said, once the plaintiff has satisfied the court as to actual physical injury, or as to foreseeable psychiatric illness, then the defendant has to pay the plaintiff damages even if the extent of those damages might not be foreseen; and the plaintiff's unusual sensitivity results in the injuries being more extensive than might have been foreseen.

Reference was made by Mr Priest to *Clerk and Lindsell on Torts* (16th edn, 1989) paras 10–10 to 10–13, 10–153, *Jaensch v Coffey* (1984) 155 CLR 549, *Hay (or*
c *Bourhill) v Young* [1942] 2 All ER 396, [1943] AC 92, *Nicholls v Rushton* (1992) Times, 19 June, *Chadwick v British Transport Commission* [1967] 2 All ER 945, [1967] 1 WLR 912, *Smith v Leech Brain & Co Ltd* [1961] 3 All ER 1159, [1962] 2 QB 405 per Lord Parker CJ, *Brice v Brown* [1984] 1 All ER 997 per Stuart-Smith J, *Alcock v Chief Constable of the South Yorkshire Police* [1991] 4 All ER 907, [1992]
d 1 AC 310, *Hicks v Chief Constable of the South Yorkshire Police, Wafer v Chief Constable of the South Yorkshire Police* [1992] 1 All ER 690 and *Attia v British Gas plc* [1987] 3 All ER 455, [1988] QB 304.

Mr Mackay's submission as first advanced was that, once the plaintiff had proved the causal connection between the accident and his following condition, the plaintiff had sufficiently proved his case because the accident was caused by the defendant's careless driving; before the accident, the
e defendant either foresaw or ought to have foreseen that some form of personal injury, either physical or psychological or both, to the plaintiff, and some damage to his property, was a possible consequence of his careless driving; the fact that the defendant could not reasonably foresee the form of personal injury which the plaintiff in fact sustained was no defence; and the fact that some or
f many or most other people would not have suffered this or even any injury was no defence. He referred to *Overseas Tankship (UK) Ltd v Morts Dock and Engineering Co Ltd, The Wagon Mound (No 1)* [1961] 1 All ER 404, [1961] AC 388, *Hughes v Lord Advocate* [1963] 1 All ER 705, [1963] AC 837, *Dulieu v White & Sons* [1901] 2 KB 669, [1900–3] All ER Rep 353, *The Wagon Mound (No 2), Overseas*
g *Tankship (UK) Ltd v Miller* [1966] 2 All ER 709, [1967] AC 617 and *Malcolm v Broadhurst* [1970] 3 All ER 508. In argument Mr Mackay abandoned any reliance on foresight of damage to property.

Conclusion on foreseeability
h In my judgment, for the reasons which follow, the defendant is entitled to succeed on his appeal on this ground also.

In *King v Phillips* [1953] 1 All ER 617, [1953] 1 QB 429 a taxi cab driver backed his cab into a small boy on a tricycle. The damage to the boy and his tricycle was slight but his mother heard him scream and, looking out of an upstairs window some 70 yards away, saw the tricycle under the taxi cab but could not
j see the boy. He eventually ran home, but his mother had suffered nervous shock, an injury for which she claimed damages. McNair J held that the defendant was under no liability to the mother. On appeal, this court held that the defendant had not, by his servant, the driver, done a legal wrong to the mother for, on the facts as found, and applying the test laid down in *Hay (or Bourhill) v Young* [1942] 2 All ER 396, [1943] AC 92, no 'hypothetical reasonable observer' could reasonably or probably have anticipated that injury either

physical or nervous could have been caused to her by the backing of the taxi without due care and, accordingly, the driver owed no duty to the plaintiff and was not negligent towards her. Denning LJ noted that the claimant in *Hay (or Bourhill) v Young* was not outside the area of contemplation of the defendant motor cyclist so as to be denied recovery if, no matter how remote it was, she had in fact been struck and injured (see [1953] 1 All ER 617 at 622, [1953] 1 QB 429 at 439). He regarded the true principle as being that every driver can and should foresee that, if he drove negligently, he may injure somebody in the vicinity in some way or other; and he must be responsible for all the injuries which he does in fact cause by his negligence to anyone in the vicinity, whether they are wounds or shocks, unless they are too remote in law to be recovered. If he does by his negligence in fact cause injury by shock, then he should be liable for it unless he is exempted on the ground of remoteness. He continued ([1953] 1 All ER 617 at 623, [1953] 1 QB 429 at 441):

> 'Howsoever that may be, whether the exemption for shock be based on want of duty or on remoteness, there can be no doubt since *Hay (or Bourhill) v. Young* that the test of liability for shock is foreseeability of injury by shock. But this test is by no means easy to apply. The test is not what the negligent party himself could reasonably have foreseen, for he rarely has time to foresee anything. The test is what a "reasonable hypothetical observer could reasonably have foreseen": see *Hay (or Bourhill) v. Young* ([1942] 2 All ER 396 at 406, [1943] AC 92 at 111) per LORD WRIGHT. But where must this hypothetical observer be situate? In the driver's seat, or in an observation post on high? It is obvious that much must depend on his powers of observation and the scope of his imagination. One judge may credit him with more foresight than another. One judge may think that he should have foreseen the shock. Another may not.'

The statement that 'the test of liability for shock is foreseeability of injury by shock' was approved by the Privy Council in *The Wagon Mound (No 1)* [1961] 1 All ER 404 at 415, [1961] AC 388 at 426.

In order to test whether injury by shock to the plaintiff was so foreseeable, it is necessary, in my judgment, to consider what at trial is shown to have happened to the plaintiff as a result of the defendant's act or omission. It is not enough to ask what was foreseeable by the defendant at the time of his negligent act. If it were sufficient to show, at that time, that he could reasonably foresee physical injury or injury by shock to any person in the vicinity there would have been no problem to be solved in *Hay (or Bourhill) v Young* because, as Denning LJ said, the defendant there could reasonably foresee that any person in the vicinity might be injured physically and the physical injury might cause injury by shock.

In *Attia v British Gas plc* [1987] 3 All ER 455, [1988] QB 304 the defendants carried out work under contract to the plaintiff's house. As a result of the defendants' negligence, the house was seriously damaged by fire and the plaintiff asserted that she had suffered damage by nervous shock and psychological reaction from seeing her home and possessions burned. The defendants contended, on a preliminary issue, that they could not in law be liable for such damage as a result of the plaintiff watching her property damaged by fire. On that preliminary issue, the plaintiff's claim was dismissed by the judge. This court set aside his order and directed that the claim proceed

a to trial. Dillon LJ, with whose judgment Woolf LJ agreed, noted that there was
in that case no problem of proximity: the defendant knew of the plaintiff, of her
relationship to the house, and had a duty not to start a fire in the house. If she
could prove causation, the question of foreseeability as an aspect of remoteness
remained. Dillon LJ said ([1987] 3 All ER 455 at 458, [1988] QB 304 at 312–313):

b 'Are the defendants right, then, in asserting a priori that it was not
reasonably foreseeable that the plaintiff might suffer any psychiatric illness
as a result of their negligence in starting the fire? It is not necessary that
any particular psychiatric illness should have been foreseen. Whether it
was reasonably foreseeable to the reasonable man, whether a reasonable
onlooker, or, in the context of the present case, a reasonable gas fitter
c employed by the defendants to work in the plaintiff's house, is to be
decided, not on the evidence of psychiatrists as to the degree of probability
that the particular cause would produce the particular effect in a person of
normal disposition ... but by the judge, relying on his own opinion of the
operation of cause and effect in psychiatric medicine, treating himself as
the reasonable man, and forming his own view from the primary facts as
d to whether the chain of cause and effect was reasonably foreseeable (see
McLoughlin v O'Brian [1982] 2 All ER 298 at 312, [1983] 1 AC 410 at 432 per
Lord Bridge). The good sense of the judge is, it would seem, to be
enlightened by progressive awareness of mental illness ([1982] 2 All ER 298
at 320, [1983] 1 AC 410 at 443 per Lord Bridge) ... The question which the
e deputy judge asked himself in the present case was whether it was readily
foreseeable by the defendants that the ordinary householder exposed to
the experience undergone by the plaintiff might break down under the
shock of the event and suffer psychiatric illness as opposed to grief and
sorrow at losing one's home. If "reasonably" is substituted for "readily",
as the judge probably intended, I would for my part indorse that as a
f correct direction. It is not, however, a test of probability as opposed to
possibility.'

Later, in the same case, Bingham LJ said ([1987] 3 All ER 455 at 463, [1988] QB
304 at 319):

g 'Since the defendants were working in the house where the plaintiff
lived, it must have been obvious to them that she would be so closely and
directly affected by their performance of their work that they ought
reasonably to have had her in contemplation as being so affected when
they carried out the work. It is not, I think, contested that the defendants
h owed her a duty to take reasonable care to carry out the work so as to
avoid damaging her home and property. But it is said that the defendants
owed her no duty to take reasonable care to carry out the work so as to
avoid causing her psychiatric damage. This analytical approach cannot, I
think, be said to be wrong, but it seems to me to be preferable, where a
duty of care undeniably exists, to treat the question as one of remoteness
and ask whether the plaintiff's psychiatric damage is too remote to be
recoverable because it was not reasonably foreseeable as a consequence of
the defendants' careless conduct. The test of reasonable foreseeability is,
as I understand it, the same in both contexts, and the result should be the
same on either approach. So the question in any case such as this, applying
the ordinary test of remoteness in tort, is whether the defendant should
reasonably have contemplated psychiatric damage to the plaintiff as a real,

even if unlikely, result of careless conduct on his part.' (Bingham LJ's emphasis.)

That which happened to the plaintiff as a result of the defendant's careless driving was established at the trial by the findings of primary fact of Otton J. There was no physical injury. There was a 'frightening experience'. There was no evidence that it included fear of his own death or fear for the death of the female passenger of the other driver as the plaintiff's doctors had assumed. Such an experience gives rise by itself to no claim to damages. In *Nicholls v Rushton* (1992) Times, 19 June the plaintiff's car collided with that of the defendant's as a result of the defendant's negligence. The plaintiff suffered no physical injury. She claimed damage for severe shock and shaking up. The judge awarded damages on the ground that the plaintiff was involved in the accident, as opposed to being a mere onlooker, so that the onlooker cases did not apply. In this court it was held that there was no evidence of physical injury or psychological injury of any sort and damages could not be awarded for fear or for the shock of the collision.

Otton J did not in this case consider whether, as a result of what happened to the plaintiff in the accident, any psychological injury to the plaintiff as a person of ordinary fortitude was reasonably foreseeable. In rejecting the submissions of Mr Priest, the judge said that this was not a trivial accident and it was well established that the defendant must take the plaintiff as he finds him. I take the reference to 'not a trivial accident' as being a reference to his finding that the collision was one of moderate severity which had the consequences found by him. After reference to *Malcolm v Broadhurst* [1970] 3 All ER 508, in which the claimant had suffered physical injuries in the collision, with the resulting intensification of a pre-existing nervous disturbance, of which the symptoms were continued by the effect of injuries upon her husband, Otton J said that the nervous shock cases relied upon by Mr Priest were irrelevant because the plaintiff in this case had been directly involved.

The fact that this plaintiff was directly involved does not, in my judgment, render irrelevant the question whether injury by nervous shock was reasonably foreseeable as a result of what happened to him in the accident. That fact, of course, makes it much easier for the plaintiff to prove that injury of such a nature was foreseeable. Since the judge did not address the question, it is for this court to decide it upon the basis of the facts found by the judge.

For my part, I have no doubt that such injury was not foreseeable in a person of ordinary fortitude as a result of what happened to the plaintiff in the accident. He suffered no physical injury at all. He suffered such fright and shock as any person may be expected to suffer as a result of a collision of moderate severity with some damage to his car but no injury to him. I have in mind that for this purpose the court should have regard to what may be a reasonably possible result of the collision, even if unlikely. In my judgment it was not foreseeable that the plaintiff should suffer any 'psychiatric damage', or 'psychological injury'. On this ground also I would allow the defendant's appeal and enter judgment for the defendant.

QUANTUM OF DAMAGES

If the defendant had failed on causation and foreseeability, I would not have found it right to interfere with the assessment of damages by Otton J. The task imposed upon the judge was difficult. Before the accident, the plaintiff suffered from CFS. In the view of Dr Wessely, although it was reasonable to assume that before the accident the plaintiff was recovering, the 'probability of future illnesses would be extremely high'. Relapse could be caused by physical injury or psychological factors and by infections such as colds or such as a child may bring home from school. The plaintiff's condition after the accident was described to the judge as fairly constant but he had described his symptoms since the accident to Dr Weir as of—

> 'extreme variability of their severity together with a tendency to relapse if he over exerts himself, even on days when he feels marginally better. Relapses tend to be precipitated by activity … also virus infections such as colds and flu.'

To attribute 60% of future losses of earnings for the rest of his life to age 65, on the basis that he would never work again, to the consequences of the collision was, in my judgment, generous, but it was a conclusion which I think was open to the judge. Similarly, with reference to general damages, I regard the award of £20,000 as on the high side if due allowance is made for what was the likely course of the plaintiff's condition if the accident had not occurred. He suffers the frustration of tiredness but no significant pain. He is able to take part in activities such as prison visiting—not once a week as the judge said but twice—for which purpose, with a round trip of 24 miles, he drives himself. He goes on camping holidays by car. The major difference between his life as it is, and as it would have been, on the judge's findings, is the fact that the greatly variable symptoms are now permanent whereas, without the accident, there was an extremely high probability of such illnesses to which the plaintiff's doctors made no estimate of frequency. As to the point made for the defendant, that the judge should have reduced the general damages to allow for the effect of those concurrent causes in respect of which the judge reduced the future loss of earnings by 40%, the answer, as it seems to me, is that the judge, in fixing £20,000, did allow for those matters.

For the reasons stated, I would allow the defendant's appeal.

FARQUHARSON LJ. For many years the plaintiff has suffered from myalgic encephalomyelitis (ME). The symptoms are not continuous but the plaintiff has from time to time suffered episodes when they were acute. Such episodes usually but not always occur when he has gone through an emotional crisis. The judge examined the plaintiff's medical history with meticulous care at the beginning of his judgment and I do not repeat it here.

By the end of 1986 the plaintiff's symptoms were in remission. He had married, and two children had been born to him and his wife, with a third expected. He was teaching theology at a school in Bury St Edmunds.

In the early part of 1987 the plaintiff's condition deteriorated, due, he thought, to an infection he had contracted from one of his children. His ill health persisted through the first half of the year and he was unable to teach, though some marking was brought from school for him to do at home. However by the beginning of July his doctor was able to detect some improvement, and the plaintiff hoped to resume teaching at the beginning of the new academic year in September.

The accident which is the subject of the present claim occurred on 24 July 1987. The plaintiff's description of what happened as given by him at the trial was to this effect (taken from the judgment):

'He was driving up a steep hill towards his school. As he got to the junction he saw a car coming towards him. It turned straight across the white line to his right and across his path. He tried to steer to the left, he saw the radiator of the other car in front of him, he saw the bonnet of the two cars touching. His car stopped dead from about 30 miles an hour. He was driving a Volvo estate motor car weighing about one and a half tons. He hit the front nearside corner of the other vehicle which was thrown back by the impact. He got out and saw that there were two adult passengers in the car and a loose toddler in the back of the car, which amazed him. He exchanged names and addresses. He was not physically hurt in any way. He telephoned his wife to tell her what had happened. He then drove the car home. It was eventually discovered that the car was damaged beyond economic repair and was treated as a write-off.'

It should be said that the classification of the car as a write-off was attributable to its age and condition rather than to the extent of the damage. Certainly it is clear from the extract from the judgment just cited, that the car could be driven and the plaintiff displayed no clinical signs of injury whether physical or mental.

Within a matter of hours the plaintiff suffered a severe reaction and a reoccurrence of his earlier symptoms. When a few days later he and his family went on holiday to Margate, he was unable to take any part in their recreation and remained in bed. While his health has shown a measure of improvement since then he has not been fit to resume teaching and has never had any kind of job. The damage he has suffered as a result was therefore very considerable and the judge awarded him £147,000 as well as interest and costs.

The judge characterised the accident in this case as one of moderate severity.

There is of course no doubt that an action lies for the careless infliction of nervous shock. It is nowadays regarded as a separate tort. The necessary components are foreseeability, proximity and causation. In the present case no issue arises or could arise on the concept of proximity. The plaintiff as the driver of the car which was struck was closely proximate.

The issue which has divided the parties is the nature of the foreseeability which must be established. The plaintiff's argument is that if an injury is foreseeable, whether that injury be physical or mental, then the tortfeasor is liable for all the damage sustained by the victim, including damage which is not foreseeable. The tortfeasor must take his victim as he finds him and if because of some physical or mental shortcoming his injury is greater than would otherwise be the case he is none the less responsible for that injury. In the present case it would have been obvious to the defendant that by his manner of driving he was creating a real risk that the driver of the other vehicle would suffer some physical injury. In that event, it is argued, he would be liable for any mental injury caused to the plaintiff even though he did not foresee it.

The argument for the defendant is that it is now well established that in nervous shock cases it is necessary to prove that the shock was foreseeable, and was of a kind that would be suffered by a man of ordinary fortitude and phlegm.

In *King v Phillips* [1953] 1 All ER 617 at 623, [1953] 1 QB 429 at 441 Denning LJ said: '... there can be no doubt since *Hay (or Bourhill) v Young* ([1942] 2 All ER 396, [1943] AC 92) that the test of liability for shock is foreseeability of injury by shock.' Denning LJ went on to say that this test is by no means easy to apply. However, the test he propounded was approved by the Privy Council in *Overseas Tankship (UK) Ltd v Morts Dock and Engineering Co Ltd, The Wagon Mound (No 1)* [1961] 1 All ER 404 at 415, [1961] AC 388 at 426 and has been followed in later cases, such as *Malcolm v Broadhurst* [1970] 3 All ER 508 and *Brice v Brown* [1984] 1 All ER 997.

For my part I accept that it is the true test of liability for nervous shock. Furthermore the nature of the mental injury suffered must be such as cannot be withstood by the ordinary man. In *Hay (or Bourhill) v Young* [1942] 2 All ER 396 at 409, [1943] AC 92 at 117 Lord Porter said:

'The driver of a car or vehicle even though careless is entitled to assume that the ordinary frequenter of the streets has sufficient fortitude to endure such incidents as may from time to time be expected to occur in them, including the noise of a collision and the sight of injury to others, and is not to be considered negligent towards one who does not possess the customary phlegm.'

The introduction of this qualification of the right to recover is no doubt for policy reasons. On the other hand, if liability is established for nervous shock the defendant will be liable for all the consequent mental injury sustained by the victim even though it is unforeseen and of a kind that would only be suffered by someone who was particularly vulnerable. This is the point at which the tortfeasor must take his victim as he finds him, and the principle of the eggshell skull is applied (see *Dulieu v White & Sons* [1901] 2 KB 669, [1900–3] All ER Rep 353 per Kennedy J).

In the present case it is evident that the judge adopted the approach suggested by the plaintiff. He says:

'... leading counsel for the defendant submitted ... that the plaintiff suffered no physical injury and therefore if the subsequent relapse was triggered by shock alone he could only recover damages if the defendant could have foreseen the consequences. Here the plaintiff should fail because it was not reasonably foreseeable that the accident of such a trivial nature would have had such a devastating effect. He referred to authorities and passages in *Clerk and Lindsell on Torts* (16th edn, 1989) ... I must respectfully reject that submission. First, on the issue of fact this was not a trivial accident. Second, it is well established that the defendant must take the plaintiff as he finds him. If symptoms are caused or increased by the particular susceptibility of the plaintiff, the defendant is not relieved of responsibility for them ... Once it is established that CFS exists and that a relapse or recrudescence can be triggered by the trauma of an accident and that nervous shock was suffered by the plaintiff who is actually involved in the accident, it becomes a foreseeable consequence. The nervous shock cases relied upon by counsel in my judgment have no relevance. The plaintiff was not a spectator of the accident who suffered shock from what he witnessed happening to another. He was directly involved and suffered the shock directly from witnessing the accident. The remoteness argument therefore must be rejected.'

I would respectfully differ from the judge's approach for the following reasons. (1) He does not apply the test which now represents the law, namely that to establish a case for nervous shock it is necessary to show that nervous shock was foreseeable. (2) He does not apply the limitation of the effect on a man of reasonable fortitude. (3) He finds that the test of foreseeability is satisfied by the fact that the plaintiff suffered the shock directly from experiencing the accident. (4) He finds that the nervous shock cases have no relevance. (5) He presents the eggshell skull principle as a ground for liability rather than establishing the extent of the damage. (6) He accepted the argument on behalf of the plaintiff that foreseeability of physical injury was sufficient to establish liability for nervous shock.

For these reasons, in my judgment, the judge was wrong to hold that the plaintiff had made out his claim. If it was sufficient to establish a case of nervous shock that some physical injury was foreseeable liability would be readily proved. In most cases where two cars collide some physical injury will be foreseen, but that should not make the tortfeasor liable for the victim's nervous shock, as the injury is of a different nature from that actually foreseen.

In my judgment while the nature of the accident was such that at the moment of the defendant's negligent driving some physical injury to the plaintiff was foreseeable, the circumstances taken as a whole do not establish that the defendant could reasonably have foreseen that the plaintiff would suffer any mental injury.

Having arrived at this conclusion on the foreseeability issue it is not necessary for me to examine the question of causation.

I would allow the appeal.

HOFFMANN LJ. The plaintiff, Mr Page, has been diagnosed as suffering from a syndrome of unknown aetiology commonly called ME (myalgic encephalomyelitis) but also known as chronic fatigue syndrome (CFS) and post-viral fatigue syndrome (PVFS). It is characterised by recurrent symptoms of exhaustion unrelieved by sleep, inability to concentrate, persistent headaches and muscular pains after relatively slight exertion. Medical opinion is divided over what causes the syndrome. Some think that it is an unknown virus and others believe that the symptoms are psychosomatic. Mr Page has displayed symptoms on various occasions since 1966, when he was 23. They appear to have been associated with periods of mental stress, such as an unsuccessful attempt to enter a Catholic order, the death of his mother and difficulties at work. One attack in 1972 after the removal of his tonsils kept him away from work for five months. But this was exceptional and he worked as an accounts clerk without serious interruption from March 1973 to February 1980. In July 1981 he married and with the support of his wife studied for a degree in theology and then trained as a teacher. In the autumn of 1985 he obtained employment at a Catholic school near Bury St Edmunds. In February 1987 there was another onset of symptoms following the birth of his third child. They became worse after he caught a cold in March but by July they had improved and he was hoping to be able to return to work when the new term began in September.

On the afternoon of 24 July 1987 the plaintiff was driving his elderly Volvo up West Road in Bury St Edmunds. As he approached an intersection, he saw a Datsun approaching from a side road. He had the right of way and expected it to stop. But it carried on and tried to turn right across his path. There was a collision caused by the negligence of the other driver. This is how Mr Page described the accident in his evidence:

'I see his wheels turn and I begin to think and do this steering to the left. I then see his radiator across in front of me and I realised that there was going to be an accident and before I had time to think of anything else— and it is a most strange impression when something happens so fast that you cannot think—I suddenly saw the bonnets touching so the corners of the bonnets of the two cars were touching and my car just stopped dead from 30 miles an hour. It was just brought to a complete standstill instantly.'

The Volvo was sturdily built and Mr Page was unhurt. He got out and exchanged addresses with the other driver, Mr Smith, who had his wife and small child with him in the car. None of them had been injured. Mr Page telephoned his wife from a public call box to say what had happened and drove home.

A few hours later, however, Mr Page was again feeling exhausted and ill. All the improvement in his condition over the summer was undone. When he went with his wife and three children on holiday to Margate a week later, he could hardly get up in the mornings. But this time he did not improve. The doctors say that he is now very unlikely to get better. He is constantly exhausted and unable to concentrate. It takes him a whole day to absorb the contents of a single letter. Any form of exertion causes headaches and muscular pains. He will probably never work again. The judge found that the accident had caused him 'nervous shock in the broad sense of the word' and that this had caused his symptoms, previously mild and sporadic, to become chronic and permanent. He ordered Mr Smith to pay damages in the sum of about £150,000.

There is no dispute that damages can be recovered for mental or physical illness resulting from the effect of an event upon the mind. That has been the law since *Dulieu v White & Sons* [1901] 2 KB 669, [1900–3] All ER Rep 353. Injury of this kind used to be called 'nervous shock' but the term has gone out of fashion (see *Attia v British Gas plc* [1987] 3 All ER 455 at 462, [1988] QB 304 at 317 per Bingham LJ). It is sometimes called 'psychiatric damage' but its distinguishing feature is its causation rather than its symptoms. It will include, for example, a miscarriage caused by severe fright. I shall for convenience call it damage caused by mental trauma. Such damage is recoverable if it manifests itself in the form of physical or mental illness. It does not include ordinary anxiety, shock, fear or grief, for which the law gives no compensation (see *Hicks v Chief Constable of the South Yorkshire Police*, *Wafer v Chief Constable of the South Yorkshire Police* [1992] 1 All ER 690 and *Nicholls v Rushton* (1992) Times, 19 June).

The conditions of liability for damage by mental trauma are not the same as for ordinary physical injury. After the thorough examination of the subject by the House of Lords in *McLoughlin v O'Brian* [1982] 2 All ER 298, [1983] 1 AC 410 and *Alcock v Chief Constable of the South Yorkshire Police* [1991] 4 All ER 907, [1992] 1 AC 310, I think that the following propositions can be stated. (1) Damage caused by mental trauma is a separate head of damage in the law of negligence with its own conditions of liability. (2) The conditions of liability are foreseeability, proximity and causation. (3) Foreseeability means foreseeability of damage caused by mental trauma. Foreseeability of physical injury is neither necessary nor sufficient. (4) The question of whether damage caused by mental trauma was foreseeable is asked with hindsight, in the light of the accident as it actually happened. (5) For the purposes of foreseeability, the plaintiff must be assumed to be a person of normal fortitude. (6) Normal fortitude is a matter of judicial notice and does not require medical evidence or statistical inquiry. (7) If some damage caused by mental trauma was foreseeable and the other conditions of liability are satisfied, the plaintiff is entitled to be compensated for all damage caused by mental trauma, whether its precise nature and extent were foreseeable or not.

Proposition (1) follows from the later propositions and is expressly stated by Lord Ackner in *Alcock* [1991] 4 All ER 907 at 917, [1992] 1 AC 310 at 400. In proposition (2), the requirement of foreseeability was emphasised in *Hay (or Bourhill) v Young* [1942] 2 All ER 396, [1943] AC 92 and the additional requirement of proximity in *Alcock's* case. The first part of proposition (3) was formulated by Denning LJ in *King v Phillips* [1953] 1 All ER 617 at 623, [1953] 1 QB 429 at 441 and approved by Viscount Simonds in *Overseas Tankship (UK) Ltd v Morts Dock and Engineering Co Ltd, The Wagon Mound (No 1)* [1961] 1 All ER 404 at 415, [1961] AC 388 at 426. Foreseeability of physical injury was held to be unnecessary in *McLoughlin's* case. Proposition (4) is implicit from the way in which the courts have approached the question in all the cases and was expressly stated in *McLoughlin* [1982] 2 All ER 298 at 303, 312, [1983] 1 AC 410 at 420, 432 per Lord Wilberforce and Lord Bridge of Harwich. Proposition (5) was first stated by Lord Porter in *Hay (or Bourhill) v Young* [1942] 2 All ER 396 at 409, [1943] AC 92 at 117 and accepted in *McLoughlin's* case. Proposition (6) is once more implicit in the way all the cases have been decided and was expressly stated by Lord Bridge of Harwich in *McLoughlin* [1982] 2 All ER 298 at 312–313, [1983] 1 AC 410 at 432–433. Proposition (7) is the familiar 'eggshell skull' rule applied to damage by mental trauma and illustrated by *Malcolm v Broadhurst* [1970] 3 All ER 508 at 511, 'there is no difference in principle between an egg-shell skull and an egg-shell personality', *Brice v Brown* [1984] 1 All ER 997 and *Jaensch v Coffey* (1984) 155 CLR 549.

The main debate in this appeal centred on the second part of proposition (3), namely whether the requirement of foreseeability could be satisfied by the fact that the defendant Mr Smith could undoubtedly have foreseen that Mr Page might suffer some form of physical injury.

Mr Mackay QC, who appeared for Mr Page, said that in cases in which the plaintiff was a participant in the accident rather than a bystander, this was enough. The judge accepted this submission. He said:

'The nervous shock cases relied on by Mr Priest QC have in my judgment no relevance. The plaintiff was not a spectator of the accident who suffers shock from what he witnessed happening to another. He was directly involved and suffered the shock directly from experiencing the accident.'

But whether the plaintiff was a participant or a bystander goes to the question of proximity, on which it may well be determinative. So in *Alcock* [1991] 4 All ER 907 at 923, [1992] 1 AC 310 at 407, Lord Oliver of Aylmerton said that cases in which the plaintiff was involved in the accident (like *Dulieu v White & Sons* [1901] 2 KB 669, [1900–3] All ER Rep 353) were not of much assistance in drawing the boundaries of proximity because 'they illustrate only a directness of relationship (and thus a duty) which is almost self-evident from a mere recital of the facts'. There is no doubt that as driver of the vehicle involved in the accident, Mr Page satisfied the requirement of proximity. But proximity is not a substitute for foreseeability. It is an additional requirement. The fact that Mr Page experienced the accident as a participant does not therefore exempt him from proving that damage caused by mental trauma was foreseeable.

The impossibility of using foreseeability of physical injury to satisfy the test of foreseeability of damage caused by mental trauma is shown by the different ways in which the concept is applied. Foreseeability of physical injury means what a reasonable man would have anticipated in the light of the facts known to him before the accident. One considers what Mr Smith should have foreseen as he entered the intersection. But foreseeability of damage caused by mental trauma is judged in the light of the facts of the accident itself.

The cases which state that the test of liability for damage caused by mental trauma is foreseeability of such damage are mainly concerned (like *McLoughlin v O'Brian*) to demonstrate that foreseeability of physical injury is not necessary rather than that it is not sufficient. But the latter must also be true. In *Jaensch v Coffey* (1984) 155 CLR 549 at 595 Deane J, after a thorough examination of the authorities, said:

> '... one finds in the judgments [in *Hay (or Bourhill) v Young*] an implicit (explicit in the case of Lord Porter ([1942] 2 All ER 396 at 410, [1943] AC 92 at 119)) acceptance of a refinement of the ordinary test of reasonable foreseeability of injury which has subsequently received general acceptance: in the case of mere psychiatric injury, the requirement of reasonable foreseeability will not be satisfied unless injury in *that particular form*, as distinct from personal injury generally ... was reasonably foreseeable.' (Deane J's emphasis.)

By 'mere psychiatric injury' I think that the judge meant what I have called damage caused by mental trauma. Later in the same judgment he said (at 604):

> 'The limitations upon the ordinary test of reasonable foreseeability in cases of mere psychiatric injury are conveniently stated in negative form. Two of them have already been mentioned. The first of those is that reasonable foreseeability of risk of personal injury generally will not suffice to give rise to a duty of care to avoid psychiatric injury unassociated with conventional physical injury: a duty of care will not arise unless risk of injury in that particular form was reasonably foreseeable.'

This appears to have been the view of Stuart-Smith J in his illuminating judgment in *Brice v Brown* [1984] 1 All ER 997. Mrs Brice and her eight-year-old daughter Susan were travelling in a taxi which was going too fast and, in attempting to overtake another vehicle, ran head-on into a bus. Mrs Brice suffered minor injuries but Susan suffered a very bad laceration of her forehead which afterwards left a 10 cm scar. Mrs Brice was terrified and distressed. Unfortunately she was afflicted with a hysterical personality disorder which made the consequences much worse than they would have been for a normal person.

Stuart-Smith J said that the plaintiff had to establish, first, that 'the accident caused or materially contributed to the nervous shock' and, secondly, that 'the nervous shock was reasonably foreseeable by the tortfeasor' (see [1984] 1 All ER 997 at 1006–1007). If he did so, he was entitled to compensation for—

> 'nervous shock and such of its direct consequences as were not dissimilar in type or kind, whether or no the same were initially reasonably to be foreseen. Such has been the rule in relation to physical injuries for many years. I can see no reason in principle why mental injury should be in a different category: see *Smith v Leech Brain & Co Ltd* [1961] 3 All ER 1159 at 1162, [1962] 2 QB 405 at 415.'

Later, in deciding that the second requirement of foreseeability had been satisfied, Stuart-Smith J said (at 1007):

'... the tortfeasor could reasonably foresee that nervous shock in the sense to which I have referred would result to a mother of a normally robust constitution in the circumstances which occurred. She was actually present in the vehicle, saw the impeding disaster and was confronted with a child who appeared disastrously injured.'

If all that was necessary was foreseeability of physical injury, the judge would not have needed to go into the question of how a normal mother would have reacted. It would have been enough that Mrs Brice was in the taxi and at risk of being hurt.

I cannot therefore accept Mr Mackay's submission that foreseeability of physical injury is enough. There must be foreseeability of damage caused by mental trauma. The judge expressed no view on this point because, as I understand it, he thought that it was made irrelevant by the fact that Mr Page 'experienced' the accident. But the absence of a finding on this point puts this court at less of a disadvantage than it would have been if we had been concerned with an ordinary question of fact. Instead, the reaction of a man of normal fortitude to such an accident is something of which the court takes judicial notice; as Lord Bridge of Harwich said in *McLoughlin v O'Brian* [1982] 2 All ER 298 at 312, [1983] 1 AC 410 at 432, it is based on a 'consensus of informed judicial opinion'. It is therefore something which this court can decide on the basis of the evidence and the judge's findings about the facts of the accident.

The judge found that the collision was one of 'moderate severity'. Its moderation is shown by the fact that no one sustained injuries of any kind, that Mr Page's vehicle was not so badly damaged that he was unable to drive it home afterwards and that he was able to exchange addresses and then telephone his wife in a normal manner.

It must be emphasised that the question is not whether it could reasonably have been foreseen that the effect of the accident on a person of normal fortitude would have been as extreme as it was for Mr Page. I think it is common ground that it could not reasonably have been foreseen by Mr Smith that the driver of the other car would suffer from ME and have the susceptibility to stress which Mr Page had. The eggshell skull rule (proposition (7) above) means that the question is whether it should have been foreseen that a person of normal fortitude would suffer any damage by mental trauma in the form of actual physical or mental illness.

It was certainly to be expected that a driver in such a collision would be shaken up and suffer some degree of shock. The experience of Pamela Nicholls in the accident which gave rise to *Nicholls v Rushton* (1992) Times, 19 June was something which could certainly have been foreseen. She was not injured but severely shaken up. Her legs felt like jelly and for a few days afterwards she mentally relived the accident and was nervous about driving. The county court judge awarded her £175 but the Court of Appeal said that he was wrong. In the absence of some physical injury or identifiable psychological illness, she could not claim that she had suffered damage by mental trauma.

I accept that it is widely recognised, as Lord Bridge of Harwich said in *McLoughlin v O'Brian* [1982] 2 All ER 298 at 312, [1983] 1 AC 410 at 433—

'an acute emotional trauma, like a physical trauma, can well cause a psychiatric illness in a wide range of circumstances and in a wide range of individuals whom it would be wrong to regard as having any abnormal psychological make-up.'

Nevertheless, if the concept of reasonable foreseeability is to have any content at all, it was not in my judgment reasonably foreseeable that this accident would cause Mr Page compensatable damage by mental trauma. In my view the person of 'customary phlegm' (*Hay (or Bourhill) v Young* [1942] 2 All ER 396 at 409, [1943] AC 92 at 117 per Lord Porter) or 'reasonably strong nerves' (*Alcock v Chief Constable of the South Yorkshire Police* [1991] 4 All ER 907 at 919, [1992] 1 AC 310 at 403 per Lord Ackner) might well have been expected to suffer what the judge called 'nervous shock in the broad sense' but would not have become physically or mentally ill. I therefore think that the foreseeability condition was not satisfied.

The defendant has also challenged the judge's findings on causation and his assessment of the quantum of damages. In view of my conclusion on foreseeability, it is not necessary for me to express an opinion on whether causation was established. I agree with Ralph Gibson LJ that the judge's assessment of the damages is not open to challenge.

I would allow the appeal and enter judgment for the defendant.

Appeal allowed. Leave to appeal to the House of Lords refused.

25 May 1994. The Appeal Committee of the House of Lords gave leave to appeal.

Frances Rustin   Barrister.

McLeod v Commissioner of Police of the Metropolis

COURT OF APPEAL, CIVIL DIVISION

NEILL, HOFFMANN AND WAITE LJJ

3 FEBRUARY 1994

Police – Powers – Entry to private premises without warrant – Entry to prevent apprehended breach of the peace – Whether power of entry restricted to premises where public meeting being held – Police and Criminal Evidence Act 1984, s 17(6).

The plaintiff, who was divorced from her husband, was ordered by the county court to deliver up certain furniture and effects to the husband. Three days before the expiry of the time limit for complying with the order, the husband went to the plaintiff's house with his brother and sister, a solicitor's clerk and two police officers, whose attendance had been arranged by the husband's solicitors. The plaintiff was not at the house at the time and the door was answered by her mother, who had recently had a stroke. The husband and his brother and sister went into the house and proceeded to load furniture into a van. The plaintiff then arrived on the scene and demanded that the furniture be put back in the house, but one of the police officers insisted that the van was not to be unloaded, that the husband should be allowed to drive away and that any disputes should be sorted out later between the parties' solicitors. The plaintiff subsequently brought proceedings in the High Court against the police claiming damages for trespass and breach of duty. The judge dismissed the action on the grounds that the police officers had been carrying out their duty to prevent any breach of the peace which they reasonably apprehended might occur and were entitled to enter and remain on private property without the consent of the owner or occupier in carrying out that duty and that they had not participated in the removal or disturbance of the plaintiff's goods. The plaintiff appealed.

Held – At common law the police had power to enter private premises without a warrant to prevent a breach of the peace occurring there if they reasonably believed a breach was likely to occur on the premises, which power was expressly preserved by s 17(6)[a] of the Police and Criminal Evidence Act 1984. In particular, the police power of entry to prevent a breach of the peace was not restricted to entering premises where public meetings were held. However, before exercising the power of entry onto private premises, the police had to have a genuine belief that there was a real and imminent risk of a breach of the peace occurring and were required to act with great care and discretion, particularly when exercising the power of entry against the wishes of the owner or occupier of the premises. On the facts, the police officers had a lawful excuse for entering the plaintiff's property. The appeal would therefore be dismissed (see p 560 *e* to *j* and p 561 *a*, post).

Thomas v Sawkins [1935] All ER Rep 655 considered.

Notes

For common law power of arrest to prevent breaches of the peace, see 11(1) *Halsbury's Laws* (4th edn reissue) para 709.

For the Police and Criminal Evidence Act 1984, s 17, see 12 *Halsbury's Statutes* (4th edn) (1994 reissue) 866.

Cases referred to in judgments

McGowan v Chief Constable of Kingston upon Hull [1968] Crim LR 34, DC.
Thomas v Sawkins [1935] 2 KB 249, [1935] All ER Rep 655, DC.

Appeal

The plaintiff, Sally McLeod, suing on her own behalf and as the personal representative of the second plaintiff, Margery Mary Mealing deceased, appealed from the judgment of Tuckey J delivered on 12 November 1992 dismissing the plaintiff's claim against the defendant, the Commissioner of Police of the Metropolis, for damages for trespass to land, trespass to goods and breach of duty at the plaintiff's property at 96 Berkley Avenue, Greenford, on 3 October 1989. The facts are set out in the judgment of Neill LJ.

The plaintiff in person.
Simon Walsh (instructed by C S Porteous) for the Commissioner.

NEILL LJ. This is an appeal by Mrs Sally McLeod from the order of Tuckey J dated 12 November 1992 dismissing her claims against the Commissioner of Police of the Metropolis for damages for trespass to land, trespass to goods and

---

a   Section 17, so far as material, is set out at p 559 *b c*, post

breach of duty. The claim arises out of an incident which took place on the afternoon of 3 October 1989.

Mrs McLeod lives at 96 Berkeley Avenue, Greenford. She is a management consultant. She was formerly married to Mr Ian McLeod. They bought 96 Berkeley Avenue as their matrimonial home in 1984 but in April 1986 Mr and Mrs McLeod separated and Mr McLeod went to live elsewhere. In 1987 there were divorce proceedings and in 1988 Mrs McLeod obtained a divorce. At about the time of the institution of the divorce proceedings, Mrs Mealing (Mrs McLeod' s mother), went to live with her daughter at 96 Berkeley Avenue. Mrs Mealing had recently suffered a stroke. It may be noted that Mrs McLeod is also a state registered nurse.

Following the divorce there were proceedings under the Married Women's Property Act 1882 relating to the furniture and other property at 96 Berkeley Avenue. On 30 June 1989 an order was made in the Uxbridge County Court providing for the division of the property in accordance with the list identified in the order. The items belonging to Mr McLeod were to be delivered to his solicitors within 14 days. However, delivery was not effected and on 23 August 1989 Mr McLeod obtained an order from Uxbridge County Court whereby Mrs Registrar Styles ordered Mrs McLeod to make arrangements forthwith for the delivery of the property. That order was backed with a penal notice. Once again, however, something went wrong and on 28 September Mr McLeod went back to Judge Tyrer who made a committal order suspended for seven days in order that the property identified in the list should be delivered on or before 6 October.

On 3 October, three days before the expiry of the judge's deadline, Mr McLeod went to 96 Berkeley Avenue with a van to collect the furniture and other items himself. He went with his brother and sister and was also accompanied by a solicitor's clerk, Mr Logo. In addition, his solicitors had made arrangements for two police officers to be there. Pc White and Pc Strevett, who had been instructed to go to the house over the radio, arrived there at about the same time as Mr McLeod's party in the van. When they arrived at 96 Berkeley Avenue Mrs McLeod was not there; she was at work. The door was opened by Mrs Mealing. Mr McLeod and his brother and sister went in and proceeded to collect the furniture on the list which belonged to Mr McLeod. It amounted to two vanloads. Mr McLeod took the first vanload away and came back for the second load. He was just about to drive away with the second load when Mrs McLeod returned. She was very angry when she saw what had happened and said that the property should be put back in the house. Pc White insisted that the van should not be unloaded and that Mr McLeod should be allowed to drive away. The police officer said any disputes should be sorted out later between the parties' solicitors. Later that evening Mrs Mealing, who had become very distressed about what had happened in the house, was taken to hospital but not detained.

Mrs McLeod's first step after these events was to take criminal proceedings against Mr McLeod and his brother and sister alleging theft but those charges were dismissed. She then instituted civil proceedings. There were three actions. The first action was against the solicitor. It is not necessary to refer to all the claims in that action but it included claims for damages for trespass to land and trespass to goods. The second action was against Mr McLeod, his brother and sister. Here again there were several claims, including damages for trespass to land and trespass to goods. The third action was the action with which we are currently concerned, which is the action against the police. It might have been much simpler if all those three actions could have been heard together. We understand that Mrs McLeod tried to arrange for that to happen but was unable to do so. However that may be, the first two actions came on for hearing before Judge Edwards in the Brentford County Court on various dates between June and October 1992. The hearing concluded on 30 October 1992 when judgment was reserved.

On 10 November 1992 the action against the Commissioner of Police of the Metropolis came on for hearing before Tuckey J in the High Court. The hearing concluded on 12 November when the judge gave judgment dismissing the claim. At that stage Judge Marcus Edwards had not yet given judgment in the county court action and Tuckey J therefore thought it would be better for him not to try to reach a conclusion on any issue with which it was not necessary for him to deal for the purpose of his decision.

On 27 November 1992 Judge Edwards handed down his judgment in the first two actions. The principal issue before Judge Edwards was whether the actions of Mr McLeod, his family and the solicitor had amounted to trespass. It seems clear that immediately after the hearing before Judge Tyrer on 28 September 1989 Mr McLeod had suggested he should go to the house on 3 October and collect his property so that Mrs McLeod would not then have to bother to deliver it. Judge Edwards referred to Mrs McLeod's account of this in his judgment, in which he said:

'The plaintiff says that on 28 September 1989 after Judge Tyrer had made his order giving her until 6 October 1989 to deliver the goods to Mr McLeod, the judge left the courtroom. Mention was then made between her and Mr McLeod & Glenisters [Mr McLeod's solicitors] of Tuesday, 3 October as a possible date for collection. She said that solicitors were to be present, but that she had to speak to her solicitor to make sure he could be there, and that she would write to confirm. A time was proposed, but she never agreed to it, and she never confirmed the day or the hour or indeed had any communication with Mr McLeod or Glenisters between 28 September and 5.30 pm on 3 October 1989 when she returned home to find the McLeods and Glenisters already at the premises.'

The judge then referred in his judgment to the arrangements Mrs McLeod said she had made for the delivery of the furniture early on 6 October. He said:

'I find on the evidence that there was no agreement made between the plaintiff and Mr McLeod for him to collect his goods on 3 October 1989. The contemporary note of counsel, indorsed by Judge Tyrer, makes this clear. If there had been such an agreement, I have no doubt at all that the plaintiff would have made sure that she was present for Mr McLeod's visit, and that she would probably have been accompanied by a solicitor. She would certainly have told her mother in advance. It was quite clear from the events of 3 October 1989 that Mrs Mealing knew nothing of any such proposed visit.'

The judge then considered whether when Mr McLeod's party had arrived on 3 October Mrs Mealing had given permission to them to come in. The judge said that he was satisfied from what he had heard that Mrs Mealing did not give permission. He said:

'Nevertheless the failure of the McLeods and the solicitor to obtain permission from Mrs McLeod meant that their entry was unlawful and a trespass to property.'

He therefore decided the issue of trespass to land in Mrs McLeod's favour. He then turned to the claim for trespass to goods and described what it consisted of, namely the manhandling of property which was involved when Mr McLeod was collecting his own furniture. The judge said:

'Their books and plants had to come off the shelves which the McLeods were collecting, their clothes had to come out of the drawers in a divan bed, and in chests-of-drawers, which Mr McLeod was collecting, and other property was moved around in the rooms of No 96.'

The judge then considered the question of damages. Mrs Mealing had been a party in the action against the McLeods but by the hearing she had died. (She died on 26 January 1992.) In making his assessment of damages the judge decided that Glenisters had not entered the property maliciously or out of spite. He awarded damages against the solicitors in the sum of £750 and interest, and against the McLeods in the sum of £1,200 together with interest and made orders in favour of both Mrs McLeod and her mother's estate in those sums.

I can now return to the third action, the action with which this appeal is concerned. Tuckey J, in his judgment, said he was prepared to accept that Mrs McLeod had not agreed to her husband's proposal about going to the house on 3 October. Tuckey J turned to consider how Mrs McLeod put her case against the police. Having reviewed some of the facts, the judge went on as follows:

'So I turn to the law and an analysis of the way in which the plaintiff puts her case. A police officer has a duty to prevent any breach of the peace which has occurred or which he reasonably apprehends will occur. Pursuant to this duty he is entitled to enter onto and remain on private property without the consent of the occupier or owner (see *Thomas v Sawkins* [1935] 2 KB 249 at 254, 255–256, [1935] All ER Rep 655 at 657–658). This decision is doubted in *Clayton and Tomlinson's Civil Actions against the Police* (2nd edn, 1992) p 242 but the statement of law in *Thomas v Sawkins* is clear and I think that I am bound to follow it. The police contend that they had reasonable grounds for apprehending that a breach of the peace might take place. If they did have such apprehension, they were entitled to enter and remain on the plaintiff's property whether or not Mrs Mealing had given consent for them to do so. It is for this reason that I have not found it necessary to resolve the issue of consent to which I have referred. The plaintiff contends that the police did not have reasonable grounds for apprehending that there might be a breach of the peace and therefore they were trespassers on the property. I reject this contention. They had been told to go to the house on the information of a solicitor that there might be trouble. The history of the matter makes it clear in my judgment that the solicitor's fears were well founded. If Mrs McLeod had been there when her ex-husband's party arrived, I have no doubt that the police constables' role as peacekeepers would have been required. Pc White told me that it was his experience as a police officer that breaches of the peace did occur at events such as these. I have no doubt that he is right about that. The police constables were fully entitled, therefore, in my judgment to fear that a breach of the peace might occur on this occasion. Although Mrs McLeod was not there when they arrived, they were not to know when she might return, and so they were entitled to remain on the premises in my judgment to see the thing through. As it turned out, their intervention was required when Mrs McLeod returned and they then clearly acted with the intention of avoiding a breach of the peace, as I have already explained. It follows from what I have said that I reject the plaintiff's claim based on trespass to land.'

He then turned to consider the allegation against the police in respect of the trespass to goods and he found that the officers did not participate in the removal or disturbance of Mrs McLeod's property. The only possible involvement was that of Pc White who had a list of the property to be taken which he had checked to make certain that only the items on the list were removed. So the judge rejected the claim for trespass to goods as well.

In her appeal to this court Mrs McLeod, who has acted in all of these proceedings in person, and to whose care with which she presented her case I would like to pay tribute, has made it clear that as she has now obtained damages in the other actions, she is not primarily asking for damages. But she says that she is entitled to have the judge's decision overturned and no doubt she is concerned with the order for costs that was made against her.

Her complaints are under three headings. First, she said that the police officers should have made inquiries before entering and that there were two chances to do that; first, when someone from the solicitor's office rang up the police station and said would the police attend; and secondly, when the police officers themselves went there, they ought to have asked to see a copy of the order.

Secondly, she said that there was no breach of the peace and no threat of a breach of the peace. She was not there; the only person who was there was her mother, an elderly lady of 74.

Thirdly, she said they were negligent in failing to give any adequate protection to Mrs Mealing who was greatly distressed by what had happened.

Those were her submissions at the beginning and as indicated in the skeleton argument which she handed to us. As the argument developed, however, it became clear that her main complaint was that the officers had facilitated the trespass by the McLeods and by the solicitor by their presence. They had given Mrs Mealing the impression that she had no option but to open the door. Mrs McLeod says that if those two officers had not been there, and it had not been one of them who had knocked on the door, her mother would have declined to open the door at all and this incident would never have happened. She says the officers should have checked what the order said and if they had done so they would have seen that the order did not give Mr McLeod any right to enter the property.

The real issue in the case, as I see it, is whether the officers had any excuse in law for entering 96 Berkeley Avenue. It is common ground that some excuse is required because it does not appear that there was any consent to the entry by Mrs McLeod or by her mother. The judge found that they took no active part in removing any property and, as I have said, all Pc White did was to check a list of what was being taken. But it is clear they both entered the property and it may be that one of them knocked on the door.

There are two questions which need to be decided. First, in what circumstances, if any, can police officers enter into a private house to prevent a breach of the peace? Secondly, if a right to enter a private house does exist in certain circumstances, did those circumstances exist here?

It is necessary to start by looking at s 17 of the Police and Criminal Evidence Act 1984. That sets out the circumstances in which 'without prejudice to any other enactment, a constable may enter and search any premises ...'

It is to be noted that in s 17(1)(e) it is provided that a constable may enter and search any premises for the purpose of saving life or limb or preventing serious damage to property.

Section 17(5) provides: 'Subject to ... (6) below, all the rules of common law under which a constable has power to enter premises without a warrant are hereby abolished.'

Section 17(6) provides: 'Nothing in ... (5) above affects any power of entry to deal with or prevent a breach of the peace.'

The question can now be reworded: what is the power of entry at common law to deal with or prevent a breach of the peace? We have been referred to two authorities, and Mr Walsh for the Commissioner has said there is no other relevant authority that he has been able to discover.

The principal authority is the decision of the Divisional Court presided over by Lord Hewart CJ in *Thomas v Sawkins* [1935] 2 KB 249, [1935] All ER Rep 655. That was a case where police officers went to a hall where a public meeting which had been extensively advertised was about to take place; the police sergeant in charge of the party was refused admission to the hall but insisted on entering and remaining there during the meeting. The question arose as to whether the police were entitled to take that course.

Lord Hewart CJ, who delivered the first judgment, said ([1935] 2 KB 249 at 254, [1935] All ER Rep 655 at 657):

> 'I think that there is quite sufficient ground for the proposition that it is part of the preventive power, and, therefore, part of the preventive duty, of the police, in cases where there are such reasonable grounds of apprehension as the justices have found here, to enter and remain on private premises.'

Avory J said, in relation to entering premises in connection with an affray ([1935] 2 KB 249 at 255–256, [1935] All ER Rep 655 at 657–658):

> '... I cannot doubt that he has a right to break in to prevent an affray which he has reasonable cause to suspect may take place on private premises.'

He considered, therefore, that the police officers were justified in what they were doing. Lawrence J put the matter as follows ([1935] 2 KB 249 at 257, [1935] All ER Rep 655 at 658):

> 'If a constable in the execution of his duty to preserve the peace is entitled to commit an assault, it appears to me that he is equally entitled to commit a trespass.'

In addition Mr Walsh has provided us with a typed copy of a report of *McGowan v Chief Constable of Kingston upon Hull* [1968] Crim LR 34 before Lord Parker CJ, sitting with Widgery and O'Connor JJ. In that case police officers had gone into a house where a child was being held in a man's arms. The police officers said that they had reason to think that a breach of the peace might occur between the man and his mistress. But a question arose as to whether the mistress had authority to give an invitation to the police officers to come in. Lord Parker CJ when giving his judgment said:

'Regardless of the invitation, there was sufficient to justify the police entering the house on the basis that they genuinely suspected a danger of breach of the peace occurring.'

Those were the two authorities to which we have been referred.

It is right to say that *Thomas v Sawkins* [1935] 2 KB 249 at 254, [1935] All ER Rep 655 at 657 has been subjected to some criticism. The criticism started almost at once with a strong article by Professor Goodhart, 'Thomas v Sawkins: a constitutional innovation' (1936) 6 CLJ 22, in which he expressed misgivings about the decision, which he described as a constitutional innovation. He said in particular that it appeared to infringe the basic principle that the law will not intervene until an offence has actually been committed.

We have been referred to further criticism, to be found in *Clayton and Tomlinson's Civil Actions against the Police* (2nd edn, 1992), and more particularly in a careful analysis of the decision in Feldman *The Law Relating to Entry, Search & Seizure* (1986) pp 324–325, paras 12·12–12·16. It has been suggested that *Thomas v Sawkins* [1935] 2 KB 249 at 254, [1935] All ER Rep 655 at 657 should be limited to public meetings and that there was nothing in that case which justified the right to enter into a private house.

Having had the benefit of argument, I am satisfied that Parliament in s 17(6) has now recognised that there is a power to enter premises to prevent a breach of the peace as a form of preventive justice. I can see no satisfactory basis for restricting that power to particular classes of premises such as those where public meetings are held. If the police reasonably believe that a breach of the peace is likely to take place on private premises, they have power to enter those premises to prevent it. The apprehension must, of course, be genuine and it must relate to the near future.

What then are the facts here? I have set out at some length the judge's reasons. The judge found that the police officers attended to prevent a breach of the peace and that they were reasonable in coming to the conclusion that there was a danger of such a breach. I, for my part, can see no basis for upsetting his decision on these facts. I think it right, however, to add a word of caution.

It seems to me it is important that when exercising his power to prevent a breach of the peace a police officer should act with great care and discretion; this will be particularly important where the exercise of his power involves entering on private premises contrary to the wishes of the owners or occupiers. The officer must satisfy himself that there is a real and imminent risk of a breach of the peace, because, if the matter has to be tested in court thereafter there may be scrutiny not only of his belief at the time but also of the grounds for his belief.

It may be necessary in some future case to consider how far in advance of a possible breach of the peace the right to enter arises. It will depend on the facts of the case, and on the nature and scale of the apprehended breach.

For the purpose of this appeal, however, it is sufficient to say that in my view the officers had a lawful excuse for entering 96 Berkeley Avenue on that afternoon. Accordingly, I would dismiss this appeal.

HOFFMANN LJ. I agree.

WAITE LJ. I also agree.

Appeal dismissed.

18 May 1994. The Appeal Committee of the House of Lords (Lord Keith of Kinkel, Lord Jauncey of Tullichettle and Lord Lloyd of Berwick) refused leave to appeal.

Wendy Shockett   Barrister.

Re Little Olympian Each Ways Ltd

CHANCERY DIVISION

LINDSAY J

7, 8, 11–14, 18 JULY 1994

Costs – Security for costs – Plaintiff 'ordinarily resident' out of the jurisdiction – Test of ordinary residence – Whether plaintiff corporation 'ordinarily resident' where its central control and management abides – RSC Ord 23, r 1(1)(a).

A plaintiff corporation is 'ordinarily resident' out of the jurisdiction for the purposes of RSC Ord 23, r 1(1)(a)[a], which provides that the court may order a plaintiff who is ordinarily resident out of the jurisdiction to give such security for the defendant's costs of the action or other proceedings as it thinks fit, if the central control and management of the company actually abides and is exercised overseas (see p 567 *j* to p 568 *b*, post).

De Beers Consolidated Mines Ltd v Howe [1906] AC 455 and *Unit Construction Co Ltd v Bullock* [1959] 3 All ER 831 applied.

Notes

For court's power to order security for costs where the plaintiff is ordinarily resident out of the jurisdiction, see 37 *Halsbury's Laws* (4th edn) para 299.

Cases referred to in judgment

Adams v Cape Industries plc [1991] 1 All ER 929, [1990] Ch 433, [1990] 2 WLR 657, Ch D and CA.

American Thread Co v Joyce (1913) 6 TC 163, HL.

Arnold v National Westminster Bank plc [1991] 3 All ER 41, [1991] 2 AC 93, [1991] 2 WLR 1177, HL.

Bowring (C T) & Co (Insurance) Ltd v Corsi & Partners Ltd (1994) Times, 28 June, [1994] CA Transcript 0152.

Bradbury v English Sewing Cotton Co [1923] AC 744, [1923] All ER Rep 427, HL.

Brisbane City Council v A-G of Queensland [1978] 3 All ER 30, [1979] AC 411, [1978] 3 WLR 299, PC.

---

a   Rule 1, so far as material, is set out at p 564 *b*, post

Carl-Zeiss-Stiftung v Rayner & Keeler Ltd (No 2) [1966] 2 All ER 536, [1967] 1 AC 853, [1966] 3 WLR 125, HL.

Cesena Sulphur Co Ltd v Nicholson, Calcutta Jute Mills Co v Nicholson (1876) 1 Ex D 428, [1874–80] All ER Rep 1102.

Crozat v Brogden [1894] 2 QB 30, [1891–4] All ER Rep 686, CA.

De Beers Consolidated Mines Ltd v Howe [1906] AC 455, HL.

DSQ Property Co v Lotus Cars Ltd [1987] 1 WLR 127.

Farrer v Lacy Hartland & Co (1885) 28 Ch D 482, CA.

Flender Werft AG v Aegean Maritime Ltd [1990] 2 Lloyd's Rep 27.

Goerz & Co v Bell [1904] 2 KB 136.

Jabbour (Fouad Bishara) v Custodian of Absentee's Property of State of Israel [1954] 1 All ER 145, [1954] 1 WLR 139.

Jones v Scottish Accident Insurance Co Ltd (1886) 17 QBD 421.

Keary Developments Ltd v Tarmac Construction Ltd [1994] CA Transcript 0436.

Kwok Chi Leung Karl v Comr of Estate Duty [1988] 1 WLR 1035, PC.

Mills v Cooper [1967] 2 All ER 100, [1967] 2 QB 459, [1967] 2 WLR 1343, DC.

New Zealand Shipping Co Ltd v Thew (1922) 8 TC 208, HL.

Parkinson (Sir Lindsay) & Co Ltd v Triplan Ltd [1973] 2 All ER 273, [1973] QB 609, [1973] 2 WLR 632, QBD and CA.

Porzelack KG v Porzelack (UK) Ltd [1987] 1 All ER 1074, [1987] 1 WLR 420.

Shah v Barnet London BC [1983] 1 All ER 226, [1983] 2 AC 309, [1983] 2 WLR 16, HL.

Swedish Central Rly Co Ltd v Thompson [1925] AC 495, [1924] All ER Rep 722, HL.

Unit Construction Co Ltd v Bullock [1959] 3 All ER 831, [1960] AC 351, [1959] 3 WLR 1022, HL.

Summons

The respondents, Little Olympian Each Ways Ltd, Mr Michaealious, Mr Pyliotis, Mr Christoferou, Olympic Vocations Ltd and Olympic Holdings Ltd (the defendants) to a petition for relief under s 459 of the Companies Act 1985 by the petitioner, Supreme Travels Ltd (the plaintiff), a company incorporated under the laws of Jersey, applied by way of summons dated 28 March 1994 for an order pursuant to RSC Ord 23 that the plaintiff give security for the defendants costs in the matter on the ground inter alia that the plaintiff was ordinarily resident out of the jurisdiction. The seventh respondent, Star Vacations Ltd took no part in the application. The facts are set out in the judgment.

Robin Potts QC and *David Mabb* (instructed by *Withers*) for the plaintiff.
William Stubbs QC (instructed by *Taylor Joynson Garrett*) for the first, third, fourth and fifth defendants.
Alastair Walton (instructed by *Herbert Smith*) for the second and sixth defendants.

Cur adv vult

18 July 1994. The following judgment was delivered.

LINDSAY J. I have before me a summons dated 28 March 1994, by which some of the respondents to a petition under s 459 of the Companies Act 1985 seek from the petitioner, Supreme Travels Ltd, a company incorporated under the laws of Jersey, security for costs.

The petition, which was presented on 30 August 1991, concerns the affairs of Little Olympian Each Ways Ltd (the company), a company incorporated under the Companies Act 1948. The petitioner claims to hold 1,017,472 preference shares in the capital of the company and to have held them for more than the requisite six months. The respondents to the petition fall into three categories. Star Vacations Ltd, incorporated in Cyprus, is a holding company which was added as seventh respondent in May 1994 and takes no part in the application now before me. The second group is made up of the first, third, fourth and fifth respondents, comprising the company itself and Mr Michaealious, Mr Pyliotis and Mr Christoferou, three individuals who at an earlier stage of the case were referred to as 'the trio'. This category appears by Mr Stubbs QC. The second and sixth respondents, Olympic Vacations Ltd and Olympic Holdings Ltd, are wholly owned subsidiaries of Owners Abroad Group and appear by Mr Walton, who makes common cause with Mr Stubbs. The petitioner appears by Mr Potts QC with Mr Mabb.

As there is a risk of confusion between the respondents to the petition (who are applicants for security for costs) and the petitioner (who is respondent to the application for security for costs) and because so much of the language used in the rules and in the authorities on the subject of security for costs is couched in terms of 'plaintiff' and 'defendant', I hope I shall be forgiven for throughout calling the petitioner 'the plaintiff' and the respondents to the petition 'the defendants'.

This is the second summons for security for costs in this petition. The first was a summons dated 15 October 1991 and it led to an order made on 21 July 1992 by Mr Registrar Buckley that the plaintiff should provide security for the defendants' costs for the period up to but not including the first day of the trial in the sum of £55,000, by way of a bank guarantee from the Royal Bank of Scotland plc. There was provision for a stay on default but there was no default. The order of 21 July 1992, though not expressed as a consent order, was, in the event, as I am told, not opposed by the plaintiff.

The summons now before me, so far as material, reads as follows:

> 'The Petitioner do give security for the Respondents' costs in the above matter to the satisfaction of the Court pursuant to RSC Order 23: (a) on the ground that the Petitioner is and at the date of presentation of the Petition was a company incorporated in Jersey whose registered office is at PO Box 75, Normandy House, Grenville Street, St Helier, Jersey, JE4 9PP, Channel Islands; and (b) further or in the alternative, pursuant to Section 726 of the Companies Act 1985, on the ground that the petitioner will be unable to pay the Respondents' costs if ordered to do so; and (c) further or in the alternative, pursuant to the inherent jurisdiction of the Honourable Court; and that in the meantime all further proceedings be stayed.'

So far as concerns para (b) and as to s 726(1) of the 1985 Act, Mr Stubbs reserves whatever (if any) argument is possible on this point for the Court of Appeal or higher. I am not asked to do anything on that score but to note that reservation. I shall need to return later to consideration of any inherent jurisdiction, but para (a) of the summons invokes Ord 23, r 1(1)(a) and it is to that that I shall first turn. The primary question under Ord 23, r 1(1)(a) has been as to jurisdiction but, as that is a question which does not require a setting out of the issues in the s 459 petition, I shall leave that setting out over until the stage at which it becomes necessary (if it does), namely to the point at which, if I find myself to have jurisdiction, I then move on to consider the discretion I would then have.

RSC Ord 23, r 1, so far as material to this application it reads as follows:

'(1) Where, on the application of a defendant to an action or other proceeding in the High Court, it appears to the Court—(a) that the plaintiff is ordinarily resident out of the jurisdiction ... then if, having regard to all the circumstances of the case, the Court thinks it just to do so, it may order the plaintiff to give such security for the defendant's costs of the action or other proceeding as it thinks just.'

It is convenient to speak of the passage down to the word 'jurisdiction' at the end of (a) as 'jurisdiction' and of the passage after the word 'then' as containing both 'discretion' and 'quantum'. Subject to a point I shall mention shortly, I shall need to divide my judgment principally into corresponding parts but, because the evidence on 'quantum' is very extensive and because, were the plaintiff to succeed on either jurisdiction or discretion, time spent on consideration of that evidence would prove to have been wasted, the issue of quantum has been left as yet unargued and I have not yet even seen the evidence upon it. I shall thus deal with the heading of quantum only if the plaintiff fails and the defendants succeed on both jurisdiction and discretion. The plaintiff argues in point of jurisdiction that, whilst undeniably incorporated out of the jurisdiction, it is not, nor is it shown to be, the onus being on the defendants, 'ordinarily resident out of the jurisdiction' and hence that no order can be made against it under Ord 23, r 1(1)(a).

But before I return to Ord 23 in more detail I should mention two arguments of the defendants which do not rely on the rule. Firstly, it was sought to argue that because the plaintiff had had an earlier award for security of costs made against it, an order which, if not formally a consent order was at least unopposed, and because the plaintiff had not then taken the jurisdiction point it now takes, the plaintiff is, by way of issue estoppel, denied the ability to take the point now. In the course of arguing for issue estoppel, Mr Stubbs came up against this stumbling block: the tense used in Ord 23, r 1(1)(a) is the present tense—'the plaintiff *is* ordinarily resident out of the jurisdiction'. If there were any 'res' which could be said to have been 'judicata' in respect of the earlier award for security, it was that the plaintiff was *then* ordinarily resident out of the jurisdiction. But whether the plaintiff was *then* so resident is now irrelevant; the question is now whether the plaintiff is *now* so resident, an issue not only not yet adjudged but which logically has no necessary relationship with the plaintiff's residence at an earlier date. Estoppel per rem judicatam cannot avail if the only 'res' which can be described as already 'judicata' is strictly irrelevant at the subsequent occasion at which the doctrine is invoked, a subsequent occasion at which not that 'res' but different 'res' fall for decision.

That strict, perhaps surprisingly strict, approach is vividly illustrated in a criminal context in *Mills v Cooper* [1967] 2 All ER 100, [1967] 2 QB 459. At an earlier trial the question of whether the defendant there was a gipsy on 22 December 1965 had been determined against the defendant. At a later trial the issue was whether the defendant was a gipsy on 13 March 1966. In context, being a gipsy meant having a nomadic life with no fixed abode and hence was something that could change from day to day. The Court of Appeal held, even on the assumption that issue estoppel could apply in criminal cases, that it could not apply to estop the defendant from arguing on the second occasion that he was not, on the second occasion, a gipsy because that was a different issue to that decided only shortly before on the first occasion (see [1967] 2 All ER 100 at 103, 105, [1967] 2 QB 459 at 466, 470 per Lord Parker CJ and Diplock LJ). Mr Stubbs, recognising that I am bound by *Mills v Cooper* and finding himself not able to distinguish it, wishes to reserve for the Court of Appeal, should the defendants go there, an argument that *Mills v Cooper* is wrong or inapplicable. Lest the case does go further, I should say that even without *Mills v Cooper* I would not have held the plaintiff to be estopped. A plaintiff might well feel, apropos security for costs, that it would be better to accede to a relatively modest demand for security in a borderline case than to lay out time and money on disputing the jurisdiction. I would have wished not to do anything which would be likely to make a sensible and practical approach of that kind less likely to be adopted by litigants, as I believe would be the case if I were to hold that the unopposed earlier small award lost the plaintiff the jurisdiction argument it now urges, now that a very substantial award is sought. I would thus have been pleased to draw from *Arnold v National Westminster Bank plc* [1991] 3 All ER 41 at 48, 49, [1991] 2 AC 93 at 107 the references to Lord Wilberforce's earlier dictum in *Brisbane City Council v A-G of Queensland* [1978] 3 All ER 30 at 36, [1979] AC 411 at 425 that issue estoppel is to be applied only where the facts are such as to amount to an abuse and to Lord Upjohn's dictum that estoppels are to be applied so as to work justice and not injustice and that the principle of issue estoppel is to be applied to the circumstances of the case with that overriding consideration in mind (see *Carl-Zeiss-Stiftung v Rayner & Keeler Ltd (No 2)* [1966] 2 All ER 536 at 573, [1967] 1 AC 853 at 947). I would, in all the circumstances, have held there to have been nothing abusive here in the plaintiff, now faced with a huge demand for security, taking a point it had not raised when it elected not to oppose the smaller earlier one. I would have held it unjust, on the basis of the earlier order, to bar the plaintiff from a genuine subject of litigation.

A second argument of the defendants outside Ord 23 was an invocation of a suggested inherent jurisdiction to award security for costs, a jurisdiction available, I think it was suggested, in possibly two ways. It could perhaps be used to lead to an award even within areas expressly covered by Ord 23, r 1(1)(a) despite the practice under the rule itself not being to make an award, but, more importantly, it could lead to an award in areas not covered by Ord 23, r 1(1)(a). Under the supposed latter form of inherent jurisdiction, I could, for example, simply say that because the plaintiff is a foreign corporation, is impecunious and, for good measure, is incorporated outside the European Community, I may, without needing to consider where it ordinarily resides, make an order against it. The way Ord 23 is framed puts immense difficulties in the way of an argument for a still-subsisting inherent jurisdiction of such a kind, but I need say nothing by way of decision on the point because Mr Stubbs recognised that the point is better left to the Court of Appeal. Order 23 cannot, says Mr Stubbs, be with total accuracy said in all respects to codify the previous law and practice or to embody it. For example, all awards are now wholly discretionary whereas at an earlier stage awards against plaintiffs resident out of the jurisdiction were as of course or nearly so (see, for example, *Crozat v Brogden* [1894] 2 QB 30, [1891–4] All ER Rep 686) and special provision was earlier made by rule for plaintiffs who founded themselves on judgments, bills of exchange or negotiable instruments (see generally *DSQ Property Co Ltd v Lotus Cars Ltd* [1987] 1 WLR 127 at 132). But, for all that, Mr Stubbs recognises the force of the observations in *C T Bowring & Co (Insurance) Ltd v Corsi & Partners Ltd* (1994) Times, 28 June. There it is said, so far as concerns cases outside s 726 of the 1985 Act in which the courts used to order security in the exercise of their inherent jurisdiction, that the position is now as formulated in the Rules of the Supreme Court and that whilst some theory of an inherent jurisdiction may still remain, the addition of new categories of cases in which awards for security might be made outside the present rules is now a matter not for the exercise of any inherent jurisdiction by judges dealing with matters case by case but for the Rules Committee or Parliament (per Dillon LJ). In the same case, Millett LJ gave his view that there was no inherent jurisdiction whatsoever (cf [1987] 1 WLR 127 at 131). Given the force of the observations in the *Bowring* case in the Court of Appeal, Mr Stubbs reserves to that court argument as to the existence and invocability on the facts of this case of some remaining inherent jurisdiction.

Jurisdiction under Ord 23, r 1

I return, therefore, to Ord 23, r 1(1)(a). It relates, of course, both to individuals and corporations but although, therefore, the language used is the same in both cases, it does not follow from that that matters which may be significant as to residence in the one case are also in the other. In relation to an artificial construct such as a corporation, the notion of 'residence' is applicable only by way of analogy, not even, in some respects, a close one (see *Cesena Sulphur Co Ltd v Nicholson, Calcutta Jute Mills Co v Nicholson* (1876) 1 Ex D 428 at 452, [1874–80] All ER Rep 1102 at 1118, *Goerz & Co v Bell* [1904] 2 KB 136 at 146 and *Unit Construction Co Ltd v Bullock* [1959] 3 All ER 831 at 837–838, [1960] AC 351 at 368). Thus, for example, whilst there is little difficulty in seeing an individual as having two or more residences (if only, say, as between town and country), the position as to companies may be different.

I now turn to a number of arguments put to me on the authorities and my conclusions in relation to them. The addition of the adverb 'ordinarily' does add something of importance to the word 'resident'. It connotes a degree of continuity being required, a reference to the way in which things are usually or habitually ordered (see *Shah v Barnet London BC* [1983] 1 All ER 226 at 233, [1983] 2 AC 309 at 341). Whilst the added word might not have a corresponding effect in the case of an individual, as I see it, it is more difficult for a corporation to be ordinarily resident in more than one place than it would be for it merely to be resident in more than one place. Moreover, the context of Ord 23, r 1(1)(a) is, at lowest, consistent with the propositus having only one ordinary residence. If that is not so one gets to the position, surely uncontemplated, that whereas a man ordinarily resident here could not have an order made against him by reason of his impecuniosity, if he also were to be ordinarily resident out of the jurisdiction then there would be jurisdiction to make an order against him. Both the word 'ordinarily' and the framework of Ord 23 should incline me to a meaning for 'ordinarily resident' such that, other than in exceptional circumstances, I should be able to envisage only one such residence.

The test of residence or ordinary residence (or, correspondingly, being ordinarily resident) is a long established test in tax matters (see e g the *Cesena Sulphur* and *Goerz* cases). Different considerations, though, might well apply to the determination of residence or ordinary residence for the purposes of the United Kingdom taxing statutes and to the determination for other purposes, for example the service of a writ (see *De Beers Consolidated Mines Ltd v Howe* [1906] AC 455 at 459–460 and, more generally, *Goerz* [1904] 2 KB 136 at 144).

Whilst different considerations might well apply to factors determining ordinary residence for tax and for other purposes, so far as concerns individuals, the tests applied in tax cases have without any awkwardness or consciousness of injustice been adopted for other more general purposes (see *Shah* [1983] 1 All ER 226 at 233–234, [1983] 2 AC 309 at 341–342). Ordinary residence is not a term of art (see [1983] 1 All ER 226 at 233, [1983] 2 AC 309 at 340). This conclusion as to individuals suggests one need not be especially shy in this area about adopting the conclusion of tax cases to cases outside tax.

By the time Ord 23 took effect in 1964 there had long been given to the expression 'ordinarily resident' in relation to a trading corporation and tax a meaning that required one to look for where the company's 'central control and management actually abides' (see *De Beers* [1906] AC 455 at 458 per Lord Loreburn LC and *Unit Construction* [1959] 3 All ER 831 at 835, 836, [1960] AC 351 at 363, 365). In the usual way one might be critical of an approach in which, whilst one seeks to find 'ordinary residence' for the purpose of some particular legislation or rule, one asks instead a different question, namely where the central control and management might abide, as such a process involves paraphrasing the enactment and then inquiring not into the enactment but into the paraphrase. However, it is here worth citing Lord Radcliffe in *Unit Construction* [1959] 3 All ER 831 at 836–837, [1960] AC 351 at 366:

'It is true that the law so declared substitutes a judicial formula for the general words of the statute, a form of limitation which one normally seeks to avoid. But, in the circumstances, I believe such a process to have been inevitable, and, in my opinion, the *De Beers* judgment, followed as it is by a number of other judgments of the highest authority which have accepted the same principle, must be treated today as if the test which it laid down was as precise and as unequivocal as a positive statutory injunction. That means that there is no escape from LORD LOREBURN, L.C.'s words: "a company resides for purposes of income tax, where its real business is carried on ... I regard that as the true rule; and the real business is carried on where the central management and control actually abides." I do not know of any other test which has either been substituted for that of central management and control or has been defined with sufficient precision to be regarded as an acceptable alternative to it. To me, at any rate, it seems impossible to read LORD LOREBURN's words without seeing that he regarded the formula he was propounding as constituting *the* test of residence. If the conditions he postulated were present, there was residence; if they were not, other conditions did not suffice to make up residence. And so, I think, his meaning was universally understood, not least in judgments of this House (see *American Thread Co. v. Joyce* ((1913) 6 TC 163 at 165); *New Zealand Shipping Co., Ltd. v. Thew* ((1922) 8 TC 208); *Bradbury v. English Sewing Cotton Co.* ([1923] AC 744, [1923] All ER Rep 427)), for the next twenty years.' (Lord Radcliffe's emphasis.)

Given that there is no insuperable difficulty in adopting the meaning of ordinary residence used in tax cases, given the difficulty in formulating any alternative test and given the emphatic indorsement of Lord Loreburn LC's long established *De Beers* test in *Unit Construction* only a short while before Ord 23 was introduced, it seems to me reasonable to import the 'central management and control' test into Ord 23, r 1(1)(a) as the test intended by the Rules Committee in relation to a corporation, at all events unless I can find some clearly contrary indication appearing from either the context or from authority.

I have not understood there to be any clear indication to the contrary in the context, nor has any authority obliging or even encouraging me to employ some other meaning been shown to me.

Mr Walton mounted an attractive argument for an alternative to Lord Loreburn LC's *De Beers* test based on *Adams v Cape Industries plc* [1991] 1 All ER 929, [1990] Ch 433 and leading to a conclusion based on the passage in *Adams* [1991] 1 All ER 929 at 1015, [1990] Ch 433 at 531, where the Court of Appeal adopted a passage from Pearson J's judgment in *Fouad Bishara Jabbour v Custodian of Absentee's Property of State of Israel* [1954] 1 All ER 145 at 152, [1954] 1 WLR 139 at 146 as follows:

'A corporation resides in a country if it carries on business there at a fixed place of business, and, in the case of an agency, the principal test to be applied in determining whether the corporation is carrying on business at the agency is to ascertain whether the agent has authority to enter into contracts on behalf of the corporation without submitting them to the corporation for approval ...'

Whilst I shall be referring briefly to *Adams*'s case on another point, I see the *Jabbour* and *Adams* approach as being less helpful than the *De Beers* one, chiefly because in *Adams* the Court of Appeal was concerned with the possibly more ephemeral 'presence' or 'residence' of a corporation and not with 'ordinary residence', with its connotation of continuity. Secondly, I prefer *De Beers* because *Adams* was concerned not with the question of whether, to English eyes, a company was in or out of the English jurisdiction but with the question of whether, to English eyes and for the purpose of enforcing in England a foreign court's order, a foreign court could properly have held a corporation to be within that foreign court's jurisdiction for the purpose of making the order against it, a question which would likely to be especially coloured by considerations of comity and reciprocity, issues which have so far played little part in questions of security for costs. So also I prefer *De Beers* to *Kwok Chi Leung Karl v Comr of Estate Duty* [1988] 1 WLR 1035 because what was discussed there was the situs of property and only indirectly that of a person, and the presence or residence of a corporation there spoken of had the quality that it could simultaneously be in several places and hence lacked the connotations which, if I am right above, the word 'ordinarily' under the general context of Ord 23, r 1(1)(a) suggests are to be present (see [1988] 1 WLR 1035 at 1041).

Mr Stubbs, as an alternative approach to the *De Beers* test, ran another argument as follows. The only conceivable candidates for the ordinary residence of the plaintiff are Jersey and England. One can thus prove the ordinary residence to be Jersey by proving it not to be in England. On the test applicable to service here, for example *Jones v Scottish Accident Insurance Co Ltd* (1886) 17 QBD 421—a test looking to a physical presence by an office or an authorised agent here—the plaintiff cannot be said to be resident here and hence must be ordinarily resident in Jersey and thus out of the jurisdiction.

However, service on corporations is now regulated by a separate code not dependent on residence at all (see Ord 65, r 3) and in any event Ord 23, as Mr Potts points out, conspicuously does not require the plaintiff to be not resident here but requires the plaintiff to be ordinarily resident somewhere else. I would thus be uneasy about giving any great weight to an argument that depended on proving an absence of English residence rather than the proving of a foreign one.

Accordingly I propose to adopt the *De Beers* test of central management and control but I am to remember that in applying that test to a non-trading corporation I may need, in the absence of features arising from the carrying on of its business, to look more than otherwise would be the case to the petitioner's corporate activity as, in a different context, was suggested as appropriate in the Court of Appeal in *Adams* [1991] 1 All ER 929 at 1009, [1990] Ch 433 at 524.

The *De Beers* test is such that, in relation to a corporation, it is likely to lead to only one place of ordinary residence (see *Unit Construction* [1959] 3 All ER 831 at 837, [1960] AC 351 at 367–368 per Lord Radcliffe). To that extent it dovetails well with what I have seen to be the context of Ord 23, r 1(1)(a). It is, moreover, very much a question of fact (see *De Beers* [1906] AC 455 at 458 and *Unit Construction* [1959] 3 All ER 831 at 834, [1960] AC 351 at 362–363).

Where the central control and management of a company takes a shape contrary to that required by the company's constitution, the court is not on that account to be deterred from looking to the activity as it is and concluding from it as it would have done had it not been inconsistent with the constitution (see *Unit Construction* [1959] 3 All ER 831 at 834–835, [1960] AC 351 at 363), reversing the Court of Appeal on that point. However, it does not follow from that, as it seems to me, that the company's constitution is irrelevant. Where the company is conducted in a manner consistent with or not inconsistent with its constitution, the consistency between the articles and the factual activity seem to me to buttress one another so as to make less susceptible to challenge a conclusion which is based on both of them than would be a conclusion derived from only one of them.

So far as concerns activities on the part of the companies and the provisions of their respective constitutions, in different cases, hardly surprisingly, different factors have been given different weights. Thus weight has been given to the provision of a company's objects clause, to the place of incorporation, to where the real trade and business of the company is carried on, to where the books of the company are kept, to where the administrative work is done, to where the directors with a full power to disapprove of local steps and to require different ones to be taken themselves met or were resident (*Cesena* (1876) 1 Ex D 428 at 444, 452–456, [1874–80] All ER Rep 1102 at 1109, 1110, 1118–1120); to where directors to whom the management of the company was confided ordinarily met (*Goerz* [1904] 2 KB 136 at 148, *De Beers* [1906] AC 455 at 459 and *Swedish Central Rly Co Ltd v Thompson* [1925] AC 495 at 503); to considerations as to the physical presence of the company, as where it 'keeps house' (*De Beers* [1906] AC 455 at 458); to where the chief office is situate or the company secretary is to be found (*Jones* (1886) 17 QBD 421 at 422–423).

I now turn to the evidence. The plaintiff was incorporated in Jersey on 3 July 1984. Its present paid-up capital is £12 divided into 12 shares of £1 each on which £12 has been paid. Its principal object is that it should be an 'investment trust company', an object which gives no clue as to where it might reside. It has no premises anywhere but it does have a registered office. Its present registered shareholders are B & C Nominees (Jersey) Ltd, B & C Subscribers (Jersey) Ltd, B & C Trustees (Jersey) Ltd and B & C Administrators (Jersey) Ltd, which four companies hold three ordinary shares each and all of which companies have as their address PO Box 75, Normandy House, St Helier, Jersey. That is the address of a Jersey firm of advocates, Messrs Bedell & Christin (B & C). The secretary of the plaintiff is Circle Advisers Ltd, which has the same address as B & C. The memorandum of association of the plaintiff states that its registered office will be situate in Jersey. The present registered office is at the offices of B & C. Amongst the plaintiff's objects is the object of procuring it to be registered or recognised in any part of the world outside the island of Jersey but, so far as can be seen from the evidence, that power has not been exercised. The original, as opposed to present, shareholders in the plaintiff company appear to have been four individuals, each holding three shares, and all having the B & C Jersey address as their address. The plaintiff's articles provide that a general meeting should be held in the island of Jersey once in every calender year; there appears to be no express provision for general meetings to be ordinarily held outside the island. The management of the business of the plaintiff is confided to its directors. Minutes are required to be made by the directors, in books provided for the purpose, of all appointments of officers made by the directors, of the names of the directors present at each meeting of directors and of all resolutions and proceedings of all meetings of the plaintiff, of the directors and of committees of directors. The articles provide that books of account should be kept at what is referred to as the office or at such other place as the directors should think fit and should always be open to inspection of the directors. There is good reason to believe that the original four individual shareholders held not beneficially for themselves but in equal shares for a Captain Lemos and Mr Pipilis, both thought to be residents then of Greece. There is no reason to believe that either of those two thereafter acquired any residence other than Greek. Captain Lemos died intestate domiciled in Greece on 3 December 1989 and on 29 November 1990 letters of administration of all his estate in this country were granted to his son, Christos Lemos of London NW3. The gross value of Captain Lemos's estate in England and Wales and the net estate were both given in the grant as £201,570.

A minute of the first meeting of the plaintiff (held in the Piraeus on 4 July 1984) has been supplied by the plaintiff's solicitors to the defendants. It is, I think, the only minute that has been disclosed, despite requests for more. It indicates that Captain Lemos and Mr John Pipilis were appointed first directors of the plaintiff and that Captain Lemos was chairman. Circle Advisers Ltd were then appointed secretary. At some date in 1986 Captain Lemos had bought the 1,017,472 preference shares in the company of which I earlier spoke. Those preference shares were transferred to the plaintiff. When the share certificate in respect of the preference shares was sent to the plaintiff in May 1986 the plaintiff was given an address in the Piraeus.

On 29 January 1990 the plaintiff was struck off the register in Jersey and dissolved but was restored on 10 June 1991. On the same day that the plaintiff thus sprang back to life in Jersey, there was a grant of letters of administration in the Royal Court of Jersey in respect of the personal estate of Captain Lemos to a Mr John Phillip Kendall.

So much for the past. Coming to the present, Christos Lemos, Captain Lemos's son, has sworn affidavits in which he gives some further details as to the operation of the plaintiff. He says that since reinstatement of the plaintiff to the register on 10 June 1991 he has provided and continues to provide the central management and control of the plaintiff. I attach very little weight to that assertion partly because he fails to indicate to me what he has in mind by the expression 'central management and control' and partly because he gives no concrete examples of his provision of central management and control. Mr Lemos swears that he has been in England since 1965 and has lived and worked here ever since, has a wife and two children here and has since 1981 lived at an address in NW3. I accept that he is resident here and indeed is ordinarily resident here. He deposes that on incorporation of the plaintiff, his father, Captain Lemos, and Mr John Pipilis were directors of the company 'and equal shareholders'. That latter part is incorrect. He says that from his knowledge of his late father's affairs he believes that Mr Pipilis held his shares in the plaintiff as his father's nominee but he gives no greater explanation of why that should be so. He says that after his father's death he set about trying to establish the whereabouts, nature and extent of his father's estate and that he is a beneficiary of his father's estate, including any assets in England or Jersey. I am not told what proportion of Captain Lemos's estate is likely to fall to Mr Lemos, nor that there has been or can be any appropriation to Mr Lemos of some or all of the shares in the plaintiff held for the Jersey estate. Mr Lemos's inquiries led him to ask his present solicitors, Messrs Withers, to investigate the position of the plaintiff. Withers in turn made inquiry of B & C and it was in that way that it was found that the plaintiff had been struck off and it was by way of B & C and Withers at the instigation of Mr Lemos that the plaintiff was restored to the register as I have mentioned.

The s 459 petition was presented, as I have mentioned, on 30 August 1991. It is Mr Lemos's evidence that, by way of new declarations of trust made by the four corporate shareholders, what had been the 50% of the shares in the plaintiff held beneficially for Mr Pipilis, is now held on trust for a body called the Zoodotis Foundation and the other 50% is declared to be held for, in effect, Mr Kendall as Captain Lemos's administrator. Mr Lemos says that the Zoodotis Foundation is a benevolent foundation which was set up by his father to hold the family assets and in particular the family home. He says that the members of the foundation are his mother, his two sisters and his father's private secretary. Whether by that he means to say that the only persons who may benefit by way of the Zoodotis Foundation are those members or whether he means only that the foundation is run by those members is not clear. He goes on to say in evidence that the current position is that the directors of the plaintiff are four partners in B & C (I think I may take it that they are all resident in Jersey). He says that he makes strategic decisions relating to the plaintiff and in particular' in relation to this litigation. The use of the expression 'in particular' suggests that there are strategic decisions as to other aspects of the plaintiff's affairs which he makes but what they might be is not explained. He says that his relationship with B & C and the lines of communication which operate are correctly set out in a letter of 30 June 1994 from a partner in B & C, Advocate Dart, one of the four B & C directors of the plaintiff. Mr Lemos says that the directors of the plaintiff 'take instructions from me', but as he indicates that it is Advocate Dart's letter that correctly sets out his relationship with B & C, it is to that letter that I shall principally look. Indeed, to my mind that letter is the most important explanation of how the affairs of the plaintiff are conducted.

However, before I return to it I shall go next to the affidavit of Mr Adam Taylor of Withers, the plaintiff's solicitors, who also deposes on the subject of the plaintiff's residence. He, too, says that central management and control of the plaintiff is in the hands of Mr Lemos, but again that seems to me more a secondary conclusion or argument rather than the setting out of primary facts. As such I cannot attach any great weight to it, and I see no reason to prefer Mr Taylor's evidence to what can be gleaned from Advocate Dart's letter as Mr Taylor's evidence is likely to be secondhand so far as it concerns how the B & C directors meet and act and react amongst themselves upon their having indicated to them Mr Lemos's wishes or instructions.

Mr Taylor deposes that the shares in the company are the only asset of the petitioner. Large parts of Mr Taylor's affidavit merely recycle passages from Mr Lemos's affidavit but he goes on to state that Mr Lemos takes all material decisions relating to these proceedings and to the plaintiff generally, but, again, I prefer to go to Advocate Dart's letter to find how decisions are taken.

Advocate Dart is a partner in B & C Advocates & Notaries Public of St Helier. He is, as I have mentioned, one of the four partners in B & C who are the only directors of the plaintiff. It is not material that I should examine the position as it might be if they or some of them resigned and if Mr Lemos or others were appointed. Order 23, r 1(1)(a) is directed to the present, not to what will or might be. Advocate Dart's letter of 30 June 1994 shows that the plaintiff gave formal instructions to Withers to act as its solicitors following a board meeting. Mr Potts would emphasise the word 'formal' as if some other instruction had preceded the formal ones and had been given, presumably, by Captain Lemos. There is no detailed evidence of either point and I would expect Withers, naturally wishing to avoid being at personal risk as to costs, to have made clear that they would wish to act only upon the due instructions of the board. Advocate Dart goes on to say, as one would expect, that it was the plaintiff that authorised Withers to issue the petition. It has been Advocate Dart who has inquired into the constitution of Zoodotis and who has explained the position to that body. The plaintiff relies on Mr Lemos to fund the litigation and that (with my emphasis) 'has meant that in practice the directors of Supreme have *allowed* the litigation to be conducted *very much* in accordance with instructions which Mr Lemos gives' to Withers. The word 'allowed' is particularly significant, as is the fact that the instructions given by Mr Lemos are there given to Withers not to the board. Advocate Dart goes on:

> '... if Mr Lemos was ever to give instructions directly to us I would act in accordance with those instructions provided that I was satisfied that they were consistent with Jersey company law and with the interests of Zoodotis and the administrator of the Jersey estate as the person interested in the share capital of Supreme.'

Advocate Dart seems there to distinguish between the four partner-director ('instructions directly to us') and himself ('I would act') but, leaving that aside, it is accepted by Mr Potts that the Jersey company law, as to consistency with which the advocate would need to be satisfied, includes that a board must act with careful regard to the interests of the company and to its shareholders as a whole. Finally, Advocate Dart's letter mentions that following a board meeting the plaintiff opened a bank account on which Mr Lemos is a signatory but his signature requires, if it is to be operative, the countersignature of a director.

Mr Potts argues, rightly in my view, that I must have regard to the shadowy nature of the plaintiff; it has no place of business; it carries on no business; it has only one asset, the shares in the company; it has no branch office or place of business registered in England and its only activity is the conduct of the s 459 petition proceeding in England. Of course, it is implicit in any Ord 23, r 1(1)(a) case that the plaintiff is litigating in England, so that it is difficult to see that fact alone as decisive that the plaintiff is not ordinarily resident out of the jurisdiction. But, in any event, I do not understand that emphasis on the litigation assists the plaintiff. Given that English solicitors are likely to be chary of acting for a company without due instructions from its board, the fact that the plaintiff's sole activity is litigation here underlines that it was the board which resolved to begin that sole activity without which resolution it would have been most unlikely to have been begun, and that the board can by a simple resolution to withdraw instructions from Withers bring the whole of its sole activity to a standstill. Mr Potts accepts that the board has, putting it at its lowest, a power of veto in respect of anything Mr Lemos may propose or wish to be done by the plaintiff, but, relying, he says, upon *Unit Construction*, he argues that a power of veto in the board in Jersey is not the least inconsistent with central management and control being in Mr Lemos in England.

In *Unit Construction* an English parent company had four subsidiaries, one undeniably here and three incorporated and registered in Kenya. The English subsidiary made payments to the African subsidiaries and claimed to be entitled to deduct those payments for the purposes of United Kingdom income tax. It could do so only if the African subsidiaries were resident in the United Kingdom and carrying on a trade wholly or partly in the United Kingdom. The House of Lords held, applying the *De Beers* 'central management and control' test, that the African subsidiaries were resident here. Mr Potts argues that the boards of the African subsidiaries had a power of veto, just as has the board of the plaintiff, but that that did not stop central management and control residing where the parent company, the real manager, was. So also, he says, the plaintiff's board's power of veto should not obscure that real management and control is truly in Mr Lemos in England. I find the parallel unconvincing. In *Unit Construction* the parent company's board had formally resolved that local management in Africa had been so bad that the management of the African subsidiaries 'must be taken over by the directors of the parent company in London (see [1960] AC 351 at 353). The late Mr Frank Heyworth Talbot QC, arguing for the appellant English subsidiary, is recorded as arguing (at 355):

> 'The peculiar feature in the present case is that the boards of the African subsidiaries did not function at all at the material times even as a rubber stamp.'

Lord Radcliffe said that they never purported to function as a board of management. When a board fails to act at all, not even as a rubber stamp, I can see that it may be right to look through its by then wholly theoretical power of veto, but no such case is made out here. The Jersey board may generally accommodate Mr Lemos, but it meets, it gives instructions from time to time to Withers, it opens a bank account, it is kept informed of developments and, if it has acted in the past as Advocate Dart suggests it will for the future, it asks itself whether the implementation of any particular proposals of Mr Lemos are consistent with the best interests of the plaintiff and its shareholders, who do not include Mr Lemos and who hold for beneficiaries who might or might not include Mr Lemos.

Mr Stubbs makes the further important distinction that in *Unit Construction* the English holding company was the sole beneficial shareholder in the African subsidiaries which were wholly owned. Its resolution to take over the management of the African subsidiaries had a constitutional force which Mr Lemos has not achieved and maybe could not achieve. Indeed, the route by which Mr Lemos could impose his will upon the Jersey board should they choose not to implement it is totally unclear and, even it if exists, would take time. There is no real analogy between the African board in *Unit Construction* and the Jersey board of the plaintiff and, in turn, I cannot ignore the power residing in the Jersey board.

I shall now attempt to stand back a little in order to see the whole uncovered picture. I see a company incorporated in Jersey, with a Jersey registered office, with Jersey resident shareholders, with a Jersey board, with a Jersey secretary and with a board that meets as such and which has not surrendered its powers nor had them removed but rather which operates them within what it conceives to be the law of Jersey. It is the Jersey board alone which works the mutation by which, if it so allows or elects, Mr Lemos's personal wishes or proposals or even instructions become an activity of the plaintiff itself. In my judgment, the central management and control of the plaintiff abides in Jersey; it is ordinarily resident out of the jurisdiction.

Discretion

Accordingly, I turn to the discretion I have under Ord 23, r 1(1)(a). I indicated at the outset that I would at this stage, if it arrived, briefly set out the complaints in the petition. The petition has been very substantially amended but, says Mr Potts, its basic complaints remain as they have been from the start, namely that in March 1991 the business and goodwill of the company was transferred to a company referred to as Newco, in return for which Newco assumed the company's liabilities and paid the company £1. The company became a shell and ceased to trade. The plaintiff says the consideration given by Newco was grossly inadequate and that there were breaches of pre-emption provisions which should have operated in the plaintiff's favour as a holder of preference shares in the company, and that the plaintiff complains too, of no notice having been given to it of the EGM of March 1991 at which the arrangements with Newco were apparently approved. The so-called trio, Mr Stubbs's clients, were directors of the company when it sold its business and undertaking to Newco and were not only directors of Newco but also shareholders in Star Vacations Ltd which owned Newco. Star Vacations Ltd sold the shares in Newco (which by then represented the value of the erstwhile business and goodwill of the company and, says the plaintiff, nothing else) to the public company mentioned, Owners Abroad Group, for a price of some £10m. The plaintiff is left, it alleges, with a holding of preference shares in a shell company, whilst the trio and some others have shared in a substantial jackpot, no part of which has come to the plaintiff. The petition will be hotly contested and will be likely to take many weeks to try but Mr Stubbs accepts that this summary, which largely repeats an earlier judgment of mine in May can be taken to be an adequate summary for present purposes.

To revert to my discretion, as to the important consideration of whether an award of security would or would not probably stifle the proceedings, the plaintiff's evidence is startlingly weak. I am told there is a Lemos family shipping business and I am given a figure for Captain Lemos's estate in England. I am told that Mr Lemos has diversified into the financial services business, that he is a member of NASDIM and FIMBRA and that he is the person who has principally funded the petition so far. Beyond that I know nothing of his resources. Nor do I know the means of the Zoodotis Foundation. Mr Taylor of Withers says only this:

'However, whatever the means of Mr Lemos (who is one of the beneficiaries of the Jersey estate of his late father who was a shareholder in Supreme) [I interpose there that that is not correct] or anyone else, I do not believe it is safe to assume that an order for security for costs of the order presently being sought would not have the effect of stifling the petitioner's claim.'

I have been referred to the unreported decision of *Keary Developments Ltd v Tarmac Construction Ltd* [1994] CA Transcript 0436, where Peter Gibson LJ, with whom Butler-Sloss LJ agreed, said:

'Before the court refuses to order security on the ground that it would unfairly stifle a valid claim, the court must be satisfied that, in all the circumstances, it is probable that the claim would be stifled.'

A little later he added:

'However, the court should consider not only whether the plaintiff company can provide security out of its own resources to continue the litigation, but also whether it can raise the amount needed from its directors, shareholders or other backers or interested persons. As this is likely to be peculiarly within the knowledge of the plaintiff company, it is for the plaintiff to satisfy the court that it would be prevented by an order for security from continuing the litigation (see *Flender Werft AG v Aegean Maritime Ltd* [1990] 2 Lloyd's Rep 27).'

The plaintiff's evidence quite fails to satisfy me that an award would stifle its proper claim. That conclusion draws the strength out of another of Mr Potts's submissions, that here the impecuniosity of the plaintiff is the defendant's fault and is a consequence of the very acts complained of in the petition. He says this argument is independent of the stifle argument but, as I see it, if an award is not shown probably to stifle the action, the basic injustice, which is here of a person escaping the consequences of his wounding another by reason only of the severity of the wound, does not arise (see also *Farrer v Lacy Hartland & Co* (1885) 28 Ch D 482 at 485 per Bowen LJ).

Another point that Mr Potts urges is that, just as in the case of an individual resident within the jurisdiction, his impecuniosity is no good ground for an award of security against him, so it should also be no ground against the plaintiff. But why should I treat the plaintiff corporation as if an individual? Of course, if it had been an English corporation within the range of s 726(1) its impecuniosity would have grounded an award against it. I reject this argument as I have no good reason to regard the plaintiff as if resident in England or as if an individual.

Next Mr Potts says that an award is here being sought oppressively. He refers to some errors in computation overstating the costs said to have been spent or to be spent. But if they were errors, as opposed to deliberate, then I see no indication of oppression.

As for the merits of the petition so far as to be borne in mind at this stage, all parties have here had in mind the strictures of Browne-Wilkinson V-C in *Porzelack KG v Porzelack (UK) Ltd* [1987] 1 All ER 1074 at 1077, [1987] 1 WLR 420 at 423, where he says:

'Undoubtedly, if it can clearly be demonstrated that the plaintiff is likely to succeed, in the sense that there is a very high probability of success, then that is a matter that can properly be weighed in the balance. Similarly, if it can be shown that there is a very high probability that the defendant will succeed, that is a matter that can be weighed. But for myself I deplore the attempt to go into the merits of the case unless it can be clearly demonstrated one way or another that there is a high degree of probability of success or failure.'

In the circumstances I have not been taken by either side to the literally thousands of pages of evidence which I am told have already been filed and neither side has sought to convince me of the high degree of probability of their success or of the other's failure. The merits are thus neutral so far as concern my present task. As I have found no argument so far to bar an award of security, I turn to the most general of considerations which, as *Keary* indicates, are as follows:

'The court must carry out a balancing exercise. On the one hand it must weigh the injustice to the plaintiff, if prevented from pressing a proper claim by an order for security. Against that, it must weigh the injustice to the defendant, if no security is ordered and at the trial the plaintiff's claim fails and the defendant finds himself unable to recover from the plaintiff the costs which have been incurred by him in his defence of the claim.'

I have also reminded myself of the broad approach described by Lord Denning MR in *Parkinson & Co Ltd v Triplan Ltd* [1973] 2 All ER 273 at 285–286, [1973] QB 609 at 626. Doing the best I can to conduct the balance as I am required to do, I should, in my judgment, exercise my discretion by making an award of security for costs against the plaintiff. Thus, after an interval, I shall wish to hear argument on the question of quantum of the award.

Application allowed.

Celia Fox   Barrister

T (a minor) v Surrey County Council and others

QUEEN'S BENCH DIVISION
SCOTT BAKER J
26, 27 JULY, 16–19, 22, 23, 25 NOVEMBER 1993, 20 JANUARY 1994

Child – Care – Local authority – Registration of child-minders – Statutory duty of local authority to maintain register – Power to refuse to register child-minder and to cancel registration – Local authority failing to suspend or deregister child-minder under investigation – Infant subsequently injured while in child-minder's care – Whether local authority's failure conferring private law right of action for breach of statutory duty – Nurseries and Child-Minders Regulation Act 1948, s 5.

Negligence – Duty to take care – Existence of duty – Local authority – Child – Care – Negligent misstatement – Statutory duty of local authority to maintain register – Power to refuse to register child-minder and to cancel registration – Local authority deciding not to suspend or deregister child-minder under investigation – Local authority's officer advising infant plaintiff's mother that he could be safely left with child-minder – Infant seriously injured while in child-minder's care – Whether local authority having duty to take reasonable care in exercising its statutory obligations to register and deregister child-minders – Whether local authority liable for negligent misstatement.

The mother of a baby who was less than a year old, the infant plaintiff T, contacted her local social services department to inquire about a full-time child-minder. The department was unable to provide the name of anyone suitable or available at that time. When the mother subsequently saw an advertisement by Mrs W for child-minding she contacted the local authority's nursery and child-minding adviser, B, who confirmed that Mrs W was registered as a child-minder under the Nurseries and Child-Minders Regulation Act 1948 and told her that there was no reason why T could not safely be left in Mrs W's care. In fact, less than three months earlier, another child in the care of Mrs W had been seriously injured, probably through violent shaking. Two case conferences convened by the local authority, at which B was present, were unable to resolve whether Mrs W had caused the injury. As a result, the local authority took no action to deregister Mrs W, although B advised her informally that she should consider minding children between the ages of two and five in future. Soon after T's mother placed him with Mrs W he suffered a non-accidental injury involving serious brain damage similar to the injury suffered by the previous child. T, suing by his mother, brought an action against inter alia the local authority and Mrs W claiming damages for personal injuries. T's claim against the local authority was based on (i) breach of statutory duty for failure to cancel Mrs W's registration pursuant to s 5[a] of the 1948 Act, (ii) breach of a common law duty of care for failure to cancel the registration and (iii) negligent misstatement by the local authority's officer, B. The claim against Mrs W was for breach of contract, negligence and assault.

---

a   Section 5, so far as material, is set out at p 595 c, post

Held – (1) It was clearly the intention of Parliament, in enacting the 1948 Act, that only those persons who were fit to look after children under five should be registered as child-minders and therefore a person could not be so fit, for the purposes of the legislation, when there was an unresolved question about a non-accidental injury suffered by a child who had been in that person's care. Nevertheless, a failure by the local authority to meet its implied obligations under the Act to suspend the child-minder's registration while further investigations were made pending a decision whether or not to cancel the registration did not confer a private law right of action for statutory breach of duty on a child who had been injured while in the care of the minder, since the courts were reluctant to impose on local authorities any liability for breach of statutory duty other than that expressly imposed in the statute. T's claim for breach of statutory duty accordingly failed (see p 595 *g h*, p 596 *e* to *g* and p 597 *g h*, post); dictum of Lord Jauncey in *Hague v Deputy Governor of Parkhurst Prison, Weldon v Home Office* [1991] 3 All ER 733 at 750 applied.

(2) The issues of breach of statutory duty and common law negligence in respect of the exercise of power by a local authority under the 1948 Act ran on parallel lines and, as such, there was no common law duty owed by local authorities to take reasonable care in the exercise of their obligations to register or deregister child-minders. However, if the local authority or its officers informed a parent that there was no reason why a child should not be placed in a particular child-minder's care, when the local authority knew or ought to have appreciated that there was a significant risk in placing the child in that person's care, it might be liable for negligent misstatement. On the facts, it was clear that there was a significant risk to any infant placed in Mrs W's care, another child had recently suffered a serious and unexplained injury while in Mrs W's care and T's mother would not have placed him with her had she known the true position. It followed that, although there was no duty of care based on failure to cancel Mrs W's registration as a child-minder, the local authority was liable for negligent misstatement. There would accordingly be judgment for T against the local authority on that ground and against Mrs W on the grounds of breach of contract, negligence and assault, with damages to be assessed (see p 600 *d e h* to p 601 *c g h*, post); *Hedley Byrne & Co Ltd v Heller & Partners Ltd* [1963] 2 All ER 575 applied; *X and ors (minors) v Bedfordshire CC* (1993) Times, 24 November considered.

Notes

For duty of a local authority to provide for children in need, see 5(2) *Halsbury's Laws* (4th edn reissue) para 1110.

Cases referred to in judgment

A v Liverpool City Council [1981] 2 All ER 385, [1982] AC 363, [1981] 2 WLR 948, HL.

Al-Kandari v J R Brown & Co [1988] 1 All ER 833, [1988] QB 665, [1988] 2 WLR 671, CA.

Anns v Merton London Borough [1977] 2 All ER 492, [1978] AC 728, [1977] 2 WLR 1024, HL.

Caparo Industries plc v Dickman [1990] 1 All ER 568, [1990] 2 AC 605, [1990] 2 WLR 358, HL.

F v Wirral Metropolitan BC [1991] 2 All ER 648, [1991] Fam 69, [1991] 2 WLR 1132, CA.

Hague v Deputy Governor of Parkhurst Prison, Weldon v Home Office [1991] 3 All ER 733, [1992] 1 AC 58, [1991] 3 WLR 340, HL.

Hedley Byrne & Co Ltd v Heller & Partners Ltd [1963] 2 All ER 575, [1964] AC 465, [1963] 3 WLR 101, HL.

Hill v Chief Constable of West Yorkshire [1988] 2 All ER 238, [1989] AC 53, [1988] 2 WLR 1049, HL.

R v Mid-Glamorgan CC, ex p Greig (1988) Independent, 1 June.

Peabody Donation Fund (Governors) v Sir Lindsay Parkinson & Co Ltd [1984] 3 All ER 529, [1985] AC 210, [1984] 3 WLR 953, HL.

R v Inner London Education Authority, ex p Ali (1990) 2 Admin LR 822, DC.

Rowling v Takaro Properties Ltd [1988] 1 All ER 163, [1988] AC 473, [1988] 2 WLR 418, PC.

Smith v Littlewoods Organisation Ltd [1987] 1 All ER 710, [1987] AC 241, [1987] 2 WLR 480, HL.

Sutherland Shire Council v Heyman (1985) 60 ALR 1, Aust HC.

X and ors (minors) v Bedfordshire CC (1993) Times, 24 November; *affd sub nom M (a minor) v Newham London BC, X and ors (minors) v Bedfordshire CC* [1994] 4 All ER 602, [1994] 2 WLR 554, CA.

Yuen Kun-yeu v A-G of Hong Kong [1987] 2 All ER 705, [1988] AC 175, [1987] 3 WLR 776, PC.

Action

The infant plaintiff, T, through his mother and next friend, brought an action by writ issued on 1 March 1991 against the defendants, Surrey County Council, Christine Walton and Martin Walton, claiming damages against the local authority for breach of statutory duty, breach of duty of care and negligence at common law and negligent misstatement and against Mr and Mrs Walton for breach of contract, negligence and assault. The facts are set out in the judgment.

Lionel Swift QC and *Graham Robinson* (instructed by *Blakesley Rice MacDonald*, Chesterfield) for the plaintiff.
Edward Faulkes (instructed by *Barlow Lyde & Gilbert*) for the local authority.
Elizabeth Gumbel (instructed by *Dresdens*) for the Waltons.

Cur adv vult

20 January 1994. The following judgment was delivered.

SCOTT BAKER J.   On 14 June 1989, when Miss H collected her four-month-old son, S, from Mrs Walton, he appeared unwell. He was taken to hospital, where he was admitted to the children's ward. He suffered fits overnight and the following day. He was transferred to Charing Cross Hospital on 16 June. It is now clear that he had suffered an inter-cranial haemorrhage with a localised collection of blood, a subdural haematoma, in the subdural space overlying the brain. The origin was traumatic, either a direct blow to the head or severe shaking. The legacy for S has been epileptic seizures, learning difficulty and behavioural problems.

Just three months later, on 13 September, Miss D received a message to contact Ashford Hospital urgently. Her son T, who is the plaintiff in this action, had been rushed there from the home of the same child-minder, Mrs Walton. He too had suffered a non-accidental injury involving brain damage of a very similar nature to that suffered by S. In his case the medical evidence points overwhelmingly to severe shaking as the cause. As a result, he has suffered seriously impaired vision and mental handicap.

In this action T claims damages for personal injuries against the child-minder, Mrs Walton, and her husband, Mr Walton. He also makes a claim against the local authority based on breach of statutory duty and negligence. The matter is presently before the court on the issue of liability only.

S's case

On 1 June 1989 Mrs Walton was registered as a child-minder by Surrey County Council, the relevant local authority for her area. The Waltons have two children of their own, A, who was born on 11 February 1987 and N, who was born on 8 December 1988. S first went to Mrs Walton on 5 June 1989. When his mother collected him on 13 June she noticed he had a tiny finger-sized bruise on his face. When she mentioned this to Mrs Walton, some reference was made to A possibly having poked him in the face. When she returned him on the morning of 14 June he was fine. That evening about 5.30 pm, when she returned to collect him, it was obvious to Miss H that something was seriously wrong. His head was floppy, his eyes were rolling and his breath was rasping. There were marks on his arms and a reddish purple mark on his head.

I prefer the evidence of Miss H to that of Mrs Walton about the conversation and events at this juncture. I found Mrs Walton very unconvincing in her description of what happened when S's mother came to collect him. Miss H's evidence was that Mrs Walton said there was nothing wrong with S, albeit he had been rather tired and sleeping a lot. It was at Miss H's insistence that S was taken to hospital.

I am satisfied that Mr Walton was at work during the whole of 14 June and therefore could not have been responsible for S's injuries.

At Ashford Hospital S was seen in the accident and emergency department. The doctor there did not think there was anything wrong, but S was kept in overnight to be on the safe side. It was a good thing that he was. One of the nurses asked why S had so many bruises. There were marks on his arm that looked as if he might have been bitten by a child or a small dog. Mrs Walton professed to know nothing about the bruising and did not offer any explanation. The sister thought the marks appeared to be non-accidental injuries. During the night S suffered a number of fits and in due course was transferred to Charing Cross Hospital.

The police became involved. Mrs Walton told them she was unable to say how the mark on the head had been caused. She also told them she had first noticed it at 1.30 pm on the day in question. Had that been so, I would have expected it to be the first thing she told the mother when she came to collect S. The suggestion also emerged, at some stage, although from whom is not clear, that A might have been responsible for the head injury by dropping or throwing a videotape or some other object.

The police kept in touch with Charing Cross Hospital, where it became increasingly clear that S had suffered serious brain damage. In due course the police obtained a statement from Mr Peter Richards, a consultant neurosurgeon at the hospital. He himself did not give evidence, but he made a statement, dated 18 July 1989, in which he said:

'There was some suggestion of an underlying arteriovenous malformation which may have been the source of the haematoma. An angiogram did not clarify the situation too clearly. An abnormal vein was seen but it did not have the typical appearances of an arteriovenous malformation.'

He went on to say that on 23 June an operation was performed to remove the clot. When the surface of the brain was examined, it was noticed that there was an abnormally dilated vein, but this did not have the typical appearance of arteriovenous malformation.

He concluded:

'It is difficult to be certain what has happened here. The combination of a bruise on the head, generalised subarachnoid staining and bilateral retinal haemorrhages is strongly suggestive of a shaking injury although it is possible that because there was an underlying fragile vein, the injury which induced the bleeding was relatively trivial.'

Because the medical evidence was, at that stage, inconclusive it is understandable that no criminal proceedings were brought. I have, however, had the advantage of more detailed and considered evidence. I have heard, in particular, from Dr John Wilson, a senior consultant neurologist at Great Ormond Street, and Dr D P E Kingsley, a consultant neuroradiologist at the National Hospital, Queens Square and at Great Ormond Street. Although neither of these doctors treated S, their evidence leaves me in no doubt about the cause of S's brain damage.

Dr Wilson went carefully through the Charing Cross Hospital notes. His conclusion was that the cause of S's condition was a non-accidental injury. He found it difficult to believe the injury could have been caused by the two-year-old A. He would have had difficulty holding and manipulating a video cassette case or other implement. More than trivial force would have been required. Furthermore, he would have expected S to have cried had he been hurt in this way and Mrs Walton would have heard him cry. But her evidence was that she heard no cry. Dr Wilson's conclusion was that the medical notes were entirely consistent with an injury of traumatic origin. There was no evidence of any arteriovenous malformation and such a cause was essentially inconsistent with the multiple bruises and other visible injuries. He pointed out that an angiogram performed on 16 June did not provide any confirmatory evidence of vascular malformation. Dr Wilson thought the injury was more likely sustained by a direct blow to the head than by shaking and that this direct blow led to contusion of the underlying brain. He reached his conclusions on S entirely independently of what he knew about the case of T.

Dr Kingsley looked at, amongst other things, the four CT scans taken on 16, 18 and 30 June and 7 July as well as the angiogram. He told me he has never seen a haemorrhage of the type suffered by S caused by a cerebral arteriovenous malformation without other stronger CT features. Also, he has never seen a haemorrhage of this type from an arteriovenous malformation at such an early age in the absence of a gross cerebral abnormality. He concluded that the overall appearance of the four scans (and he was considering them progressively in time) indicated a recent traumatic event which appeared likely to have occurred within three to four days of the first examination of 16 June. The progress throughout the next three weeks indicated a severe injury to the head and not one that was likely to have been caused by another child. The presence of extensive surface blood and the subsequent development of low density changes in the cerebral hemispheres indicated a diffuse injury which in his opinion could have been caused either by a direct blow or by shaking. Dr Kingsley was unable to see any evidence of vascular malformation, and was not clear why the possibility of an underlying vascular abnormality was entertained on the original CT scan.

Dr Kingsley went on to comment on the similarity to the changes shown on the CT scans taken after the other child's injury. Both children had suffered subdural haematomas; S's was more localised than that of T. Each was consistent with a shaking injury. The focal nature of S's injury suggested that the injury could have been a direct blow and this was supported by the linear mark on his head.

There is, in my judgment, clear evidence to establish that S's injury was non-accidental and that it was caused whilst in the care of Mrs Walton on 14 June 1989. No evidence was called to refute that of Dr Wilson and Dr Kingsley, and I reach this conclusion without taking into account what happened to T. Having reached this conclusion I note the observation of Dr Kingsley that—

> 'the likelihood of [the damage] being due to non-accidental injury is strengthened by the events which occurred 3 months later to [T] in the care of the same minder.'

That, I think, is a matter of common sense.

T's case

T was born on 14 March 1989. His mother is Miss D and his father Mr H, with whom she had quite a lengthy association. T was born in Ashford Hospital, Middlesex, but it was Miss D's intention to move to Chesterfield, where she and Mr H were together purchasing a house. Although Miss D moved to Chesterfield after her six-week postnatal check, they never in fact lived together in Chesterfield. On 2 May Mr H telephoned to say that he could not go through with the plan to cohabit. The following weeks were an extremely difficult time for Miss D. I have no doubt that it was the arrival of T that precipitated the end of the relationship. Miss D had given up both her home in Colnbrook and a secure well-paid job. She was now living in unfamiliar surroundings as a single mother with a small baby to look after. It was in these circumstances that she found herself with quite strong feelings of rejection of T. These feelings were emotional and she in no way allowed them to affect her practical care of him. I am satisfied that these feelings have no relevance to the disaster that befell T, although Miss Gumbel, on behalf of the Waltons, quite properly probed, in some detail, the possibility that T's injury could have been sustained whilst in his mother's care. I am, however, completely satisfied that it was not.

Through May, June and July Miss D was living in Chesterfield and entertained hopes that her relationship might be saved. When it was clear that it could not, she decided, at about the end of July, to move back to Middlesex. Her plan was to live first with her mother and stepfather and then find somewhere of her own. I shall deal a little later with the circumstances in which she came to use Mrs Walton as her child-minder. On 26 August she moved to Ashford with T.

On Sunday, 27 August Miss D visited Mrs Walton with T and child-minding arrangements were made. On Thursday, 31 August T went to Mrs Walton for the first time and stayed between 10.00 am and 4.00 pm. He went again on the Friday and through the following week, except on the Wednesday. Miss D had by this time obtained a full-time temporary job. On 8 September, when Miss D collected him, Mrs Walton remarked that he looked like a pussy cat, referring to some scratches around his mouth, saying he had scratched himself with his fingernails that were too long. All the scratches faded overnight except one. Miss D was in the habit of making up her diary each day. However, the entry with regard to this was not made until 23 September, when it occurred to Miss D that the incident could be significant. The cut did not disappear overnight, or indeed for some days, and I do not think it could have been caused by T's fingernails. What did cause it, however, remains a mystery.

On Monday, 11 September Miss D spent half an hour in the evening with a social worker, Mrs Pat Wheeler. The reason was to discuss her confused feelings about T. Miss D was considering the possibility of some kind of long-term fostering arrangement. During the course of this meeting Miss D said that she was not particularly happy with Mrs Walton as a child-minder, but could not put her finger on why. In evidence, the only matter Miss D referred to was Mrs Walton's slovenly dress. When she collected him that Monday evening, T seemed perfectly all right.

On the Tuesday, T was with Mrs Walton between 8.30 am and 5.30 pm. When Miss D collected him, his complexion appeared grey and pale. Mrs Walton said he had not had a sleep that afternoon. Both Miss D's mother and a friend who was staying, Sheila O'Brien, noticed that T appeared to be unwell and thought he might be sickening for something. Miss D went to her doctor that evening on her own account, but whatever concerns she had about T were not sufficient for her to mention them to her doctor. That night, however, when she was bathing T she noticed marks in both his ears. They were a mauvey colour and inside the ear at the bottom. They seemed like bruising and appeared to fade when T was in the bath. Miss D's mother, too, saw the marks. T seemed perfectly all right in the morning. I am unable to make any clear findings as to how T came by these marks.

On 13 September Miss D left T with Mrs Walton at about 8.30 am intending to collect him in the evening. At about 1.45 pm she received a message to contact Ashford Hospital urgently. She did and then went straight to the hospital, where T was seriously ill. Both Mr and Mrs Walton were there. Mrs Walton's account of what had happened was that T had been violently sick soon after he arrived at her house. Thereafter she had a doctor's appointment and took T with her. At the appointment the doctor confirmed that she was pregnant. No hint had been given to Miss D of this before, when she agreed to take T on what Miss D was expecting would be a long-term basis.

When she arrived home, she placed T on the sofa with some cushions round him to prevent him rolling off. Mr Walton was at home and the Waltons were expecting friends. She said she planned to change T and then go upstairs and change herself. She put T on the floor to change him and Mr Walton came in from outside. Mr Walton offered to change T and Mrs Walton thought she was upstairs for about 15 minutes. She says that the friends, Mr and Mrs Bush, arrived before she went upstairs to change. Whilst she was upstairs she heard crying but assumed this was T protesting at his nappy being changed. In cross-examination she said she also heard a scream. When she went downstairs she said that T was in Mr Walton's arms and had stopped crying. He was very white and looked seriously ill. His eyes had rolled into his head and looked odd.

Mr Walton's evidence was that T was crying as he changed his nappy. But this was normal crying, just protesting at having his nappy changed. As he was finishing putting clean clothes on, T started to scream really loudly. But this scream was different. Mr and Mrs Bush, he said, were in the living room watching.

Mrs Bush said there was a child crying when they reached the front door and she saw a baby being changed that she assumed was the Walton's own. The baby stopped crying and Mr Walton called her and her husband over to look at him. He looked, in her words, terribly ill. The statement Mrs Bush made to the police was to some extent inconsistent with her evidence. She told the police that when she arrived Mrs Walton was just going upstairs. She then came downstairs with a changing mat and T was whinging on the floor and he started to cry as Mr Walton changed him. He worked up to a scream and then suddenly stopped. When she was called over to look at T, Mrs Walton came downstairs saying, 'not again, please not again'. Mrs Walton denied ever having said any such words.

Mr Bush told the police that T started crying, he thought, when Mr Walton was changing him and that the crying got worse and worse. Mrs Walton then came downstairs and everyone started to panic. His evidence was that Mr Walton was already changing the baby on the floor when they arrived and that he was crying in a normal way; he made no mention of any abnormal crying.

It was clear to all four adults that T's condition was serious and he was immediately taken to Ashford Hospital. What precisely befell T at the Waltons' house that morning cannot be gleaned from the evidence of these four adults. I do not think either Mr or Mrs Bush saw the precipitating event indeed, they probably came on the scene after it had occurred. As to Mr and Mrs Walton I did not, in the light of the whole of the evidence, not least the medical evidence, feel that they were telling me the truth. It is necessary therefore, to turn to the medical evidence next and examine it in some detail.

T was admitted from the accident and emergency unit at Ashford to the paediatric department at West Middlesex. From there he was transferred to Great Ormond Street on the same evening at about 8.30 pm. Robert Crouch was the nurse on duty when T arrived at Ashford. Mr Walton, he said, told him that: 'his colour drained and he became floppy and unresponsive.' He said he had shaken the child in order to make him try and respond. He also said the child had made a couple of good old-fashioned protests during the morning. He also said he had shaken him additionally on the way to hospital. Mr Crouch impressed me as a reliable witness. He said the case stuck in his mind because he was relatively new to nursing and there was a small baby involved who was critically ill. I am therefore confident that he accurately recounted the gist of what Mr Walton had told him. I should add that I am satisfied that any shaking to try and revive him as described to Mr Crouch was not responsible for the injury to T.

When T arrived at Ashford, he was found to be unconscious and floppy and had difficulty in breathing. He was given oxygen and then resumed spontaneous breathing. Blood tests, x-ray examinations and a lumbar puncture were performed and he was transferred to West Middlesex under the care of Dr Husband. There was no sign of any external injury and initially the doctors were looking at the possibility of some infection being the cause of the problem. Dr Husband, the consultant paediatrician at West Middlesex, noted gross bilateral retinal haemorrhages when he looked at his eyes. He could not see any sign of the bruising that Mrs D had seen the previous evening. He arranged for his transfer to Great Ormond Street. However, both Dr Wilson and Dr Robb at Great Ormond Street did notice bruising inside the left ear but only after Miss D had pointed it out to them.

Dr Wilson and Dr Robb were involved with T's treatment at Great Ormond Street. Both gave evidence. Their evidence, although probed in cross-examination, was unchallenged by any evidence called on behalf of the defendants, apart from that of Professor Holt. Dr Wilson has been a consultant neurologist since 1965. He specialises in the investigation and management of child illnesses. He was an impressive witness, who concluded that non-accidental injury was the only satisfactory explanation for what had happened to T. The Ashford Hospital notes were introduced into the case during the course of the trial. Dr Wilson's view was that they disclosed a wide-ranging and appropriate investigation. They disclosed no evidence of infection other than a raised white cell count. This, however, is non-specific and seen quite commonly in cases of children with head injuries. In T's case the white cell count was uniformly high, ie in respect of polymorphs, lymphocytes and monocytes. In the case of bacterial infections, the polymorph count goes up whilst the lymphocyte count stays the same or even falls. Furthermore, the white blood cell count had dropped rather dramatically two days later, which was inconsistent with an overwhelming bacterial infection. Such a rapid fall is consistent with a recovery from a head injury. The whole picture was of the baby's body releasing more white cells in response to trauma. It was also of significance that the evidence of any bacterial infection was so insubstantial that the doctors were able to discontinue treatment with antibiotics at an early stage without disadvantage to T. Another factor was that the blood culture taken at Ashford was subsequently found to be sterile. It should have grown any infecting organisms. In short, there was no sign at Ashford or subsequently of any fulminating infection.

I heard a good deal of evidence about retinal haemorrhages. In my judgment, the retinal haemorrhages suffered by T are compelling evidence in favour of a traumatic injury. An infection, according to Dr Wilson, would only cause retinal haemorrhages if it first caused raised inter-cranial pressure.

The haemorrhages suffered by T were extensive and went to the periphery of the retina. Those caused by infection tend to be local to the optic disc. I shall return to the haemorrhages when I deal with the evidence of Dr Taylor.

T had shown some history of vomiting. Vomiting can be evidence of an infection. But T's vomiting had been intermittent and this is something that is quite common with young children. Dr Wilson's evidence was that whilst he could not be sure of the cause, he was certain in this case that it was not symptomatic of infection.

The picture presented by looking progressively at the brain scans was entirely consistent with physical trauma shortly before the first scan. The facts that T was limp, pale, unresponsive, needed a ventilator and had a stiff neck with arching of the back were all indications of serious injury to the brain. Whilst there was no physical indication of how the trauma could have been inflicted, there was no tenable explanation other than of a non-accidental injury inflicted minutes before he collapsed. The injury suffered by T was a classical response to shaking. This causes a collection of blood, a subdural haematoma. It was Dr Wilson's opinion that T's injuries could not have occurred before he was taken to Mr and Mrs Walton's home on the morning of 13 September.

Dr Stephanie Robb is now a consultant paediatric neurologist at Guys Hospital. In September 1989 she was a senior registrar in neurology at Great Ormond Street. She, like Dr Wilson, never had any serious doubt that T had been subjected to a non-accidental injury. It was her view that the injury must have been suffered within an hour of his being presented to Ashford Hospital. Had it occurred earlier, he would have appeared unwell in the morning, which he had not. She also told me that, in her opinion, the injuries were too severe to have been caused by A.

I found the evidence of Dr Wilson and Dr Robb to be entirely logical and credible and I accept it.

Dr Kingsley, to whom I have already referred with regard to S, referred to CT scans taken on 13 September at 11 pm, on 16 September and on 22 September. His opinion was that the three scans showed a progression of events commencing on 13 September and were strongly in favour of the cause being severe cerebral trauma. This could not have occurred earlier than the morning of 13 September, ie not more than 12 hours before the first scan which puts it at 11 am or 12 noon at the earliest. The radiological changes he saw did not fit with acute infection, whereas they were precisely what you would expect to see where a child has suffered physical trauma. Like S, T had suffered a subdural haematoma which could have been caused by severe shaking. It was his experience that children of that age do not develop subdural haematomas and that they are indicative of non-accidental injury.

Mr David Taylor is a paediatric ophthalmologist. He has been a consultant for 17 years and practises, inter alia, at Great Ormond Street. I found his evidence particularly compelling. He examined T on 11 December 1992 and also saw the Great Ormond Street notes. During the trial he additionally saw the Ashford notes. The Great Ormond Street notes included photographs of the retinal haemorrhages and the CT scan results. He concludes in his report:

> 'The combination of widespread brain swelling, subdural effusions and retinal haemorrhages in a child who has subsequently proved to be physically otherwise normal ie, does not have any metabolic or any other

disease and had not previously suffered from seizures or other illnesses, makes it highly likely that the causation of the problem was a non accidental injury. This could have been by shaking alone or by shaking in combination with asphyxiation. The presence of retinal haemorrhages is not pathognomic of non accidental injury: they occur in a variety of other conditions but they are extremely unusual in ordinary trauma and there is indeed no evidence that there was any form of ordinary trauma in this child ie, there were no bruises or broken bones. I think it highly unlikely that a clumsy resuscitation would have caused these sort of problems without causing external injury and I, therefore, conclude that [T's] current and future problems are caused by a non accidental injury, probably by shaking or shaking combined with asphyxia in the absence of external trauma which occurred on 13th September 1989.'

He expanded somewhat in the course of his evidence, pointing out that these haemorrhages were widespread through the back of the eye and into various levels of the eye. They are caused by sheer forces giving rise to retinal movements. He identified for me in the photographs why the nature of these haemorrhages was so typical of those caused by non-accidental injury of a shaking nature. He sees haemorrhages of this kind approximately five times a year. Sadly, shaking injuries to small babies are far from uncommon. He also mentioned in passing that the bruising in the ear he felt must have been of traumatic origin. This, of course, had been seen by Miss D on the evening of 12 September and whatever caused it therefore occurred too early to have been responsible for T's brain damage. It does, however, suggest that something untoward, of a non-accidental nature, may have happened to T the previous day at Mrs Waltons, but as I have said, I am unable to make any finding on this.

The plaintiff therefore assembled a formidable body of expert evidence that all pointed in one direction. Against this, the Waltons called Professor Holt, emeritus professor of developmental paediatrics at the London Hospital. He retired some four years ago. He concluded:

'The description of the acute episode and collapse suggests to me that he had a convulsion associated with a degree of shock. Such an episode could occur with an acute fulminating infection or with acute head injury. I consider that [T] did suffer an acute infection.'

He relied in support of this conclusion particularly on the high white cell count. Professor Holt had not seen a white cell count as high as in this case following trauma. But then it transpired that Professor Holt had not been concerned in the management of acute head injuries, his particular expertise being brittle bone disease. Indeed it is a long time since he looked after an acutely ill infant. He agreed in cross-examination that there was no positive evidence of infection and I prefer Dr Wilson's explanation for the high white cell count, namely that it was the body's reaction to the trauma.

In the end, Professor Holt agreed that the probable cause of T's problems was non-accidental injury, although he was not prepared to rule out infection. There could, he said, have been both. He also agreed it was unusual to see such extensive retinal haemorrhages with infection. He accepted, too, that it would have to be a fairly forceful shaking to have a sheering effect on the blood vessels.

There is no doubt that, when T was initially treated on 13 September, an acute infection was considered to be a possibility. In time, such a possibility was negatived by the weight of the evidence and all the experts, except Professor Holt, ruled it out. After he had been cross-examined, Professor Holt's position on infection was a good deal more tenuous than it had been in his report. I am satisfied on the whole of the evidence that infection is not a viable explanation as to the cause of T's problems.

One other matter on which Professor Holt differed from the other expert evidence was as to the earliest moment at which the injury could have occurred. He was prepared to go back up to as much as 24 hours, ie the injuries could have occurred when T was in Miss D's care. I reject his evidence in this regard and prefer that of the other experts.

Conclusion on the case against Mr and Mrs Walton

My conclusion on this aspect of the case is that I am satisfied so that I am sure that both S and T suffered non-accidental injuries whilst in the care of Mrs Walton. T's injury was of a shaking nature. That of S could have been either a shaking injury or a direct blow. This conclusion should not be taken as a criticism of those who did not bring criminal proceedings. I have heard a great deal more evidence than was available in 1989. The injury to S can only have been caused by Mrs Walton, as I am satisfied that Mr Walton was at work at the material time. Mr Walton is not eliminated as a candidate for causing the injury to T in the sense of being absent at the material time. On the face of it, therefore, either Mrs Walton or Mr Walton could have been the perpetrator. However, when I come to examine the circumstances I am satisfied that Mrs Walton was responsible. She, on her own account, put T on the floor with a view to changing him. Then she went upstairs. Dr Wilson's evidence was that the injury could have been inflicted minutes before T began to cry, as described by Mr Walton. Mr Walton thought it was the first time he picked up T that he noticed his head was limp. Mr Walton did shake T in an attempt to revive him, but the Bushes were present at the time and I am satisfied that this shaking was not so severe as to cause any damage. I find that Mr Walton was already changing T when the Bushes arrived. I also find that Mrs Walton did utter the words 'not again, please not again', knowing that she had previously caused the injury to S. Further compelling evidence against Mrs Walton is the fact that three months before, she had caused a remarkably similar injury to S. She was unable to tender any explanation how either child could have come by his injuries. In making my finding that Mrs Walton was responsible, I have kept clearly in mind the high standard of proof required in a matter of this gravity. I accept that the burden is on the plaintiff to prove the case against her on the balance of probabilities to a degree commensurate with the seriousness of the allegation.

In the result, I find that the second defendant, Mrs Walton, is liable in breach of contract, negligence and assault. The third defendant, Mr Walton is not liable.

The case against the local authority

It is necessary to examine the circumstances in which the plaintiff came to be placed with Mrs Walton, particularly in the light of events concerning S. On 28 July 1989 Miss D telephoned Ashford social services to inquire about child-minder. I am satisfied she would not have entertained using anyone who was not registered. She spoke to Mr Bodycomb and told him she was then living in Chesterfield, but by September would be back in Ashford and would need a full-time child-minder. He told her there were not many vacancies and took details of T. It was left that he would sort something out and let Miss D have a list. The list did not arrive and Miss D rang again two weeks later, but Mr Bodycomb was on holiday. Eventually she got hold of him on 22 August and he dictated the names of eight child-minders with their addresses and telephone numbers. The reason that he did not give Mrs Walton's name is that he thought her vacancy was already filled with another child, Patel. I accept Mr Bodycomb's evidence on this. She tried all eight names on the list but could get no reply from four. Of the others, two were unsuitable and the other two had no vacancy. That same evening a friend, Carol Walters, telephoned and in the course of conversation mentioned an advertisement she had seen for a child-minder. It turned out to be Mrs Walton. Carol Walters telephoned Mrs Walton and said she had a friend who was looking for a child-minder. Mrs Walton was at this stage thinking of taking on a Mrs Patel, but had made no firm arrangements. Later that night, following the contact made by Carol Walters, Miss D rang Mrs Walton.

During the ensuing conversation, there was some discussion about hours and rates and Mrs Walton said she had looked after two other children. She said one was a boy, whom she was no longer looking after because he had been taken ill. (This was S.) She said he had made a full recovery but she was no longer looking after him. There was some reference to the police having investigated the matter but that this was routine where a child was taken ill when in the care of a child-minder. Miss D told me that her concern was not raised because Mrs Walton seemed so open about it. Miss D arranged to meet Mrs Walton on 27 August.

In the meantime, on 25 August, Miss D telephoned Mr Bodycomb. Her account of the conversation is that she mentioned she had contacted Mrs Walton who was not on his list. She asked for confirmation that she was registered and he said she was. She asked if he was happy for T to be placed in her care and he said 'Yes'. Miss D's diary note reads: 'Spoke to Bodycomb re Christine Walton—he saying OK.'

Mr Bodycomb's recollection of this conversation is unsupported by any note. He said he thought at the time he was speaking to a friend of Miss D. He said he did not think he would have said he was happy for T to be placed with Mrs Walton; it was not his place to say so. In his proof of evidence, dated August 1991, he says Miss D was aware from Mrs Walton that there had been a problem with S. She knew that S had been injured. He went on that he emphasised Mrs Walton had a lively two-and-a-half year old boy and that he felt Miss D was aware of the problem with S, and accordingly he did not go any further because he had no proof that Mrs Walton had caused his injury. In the witness box he said: 'I know I mentioned an accident, an injury, a problem. I can't remember the exact words.'

He said she was dismissive of any discussion about S, giving the impression he had discussed it with the child-minder. He said she came over as very knowledgeable of what had happened and knew there had been a police investigation. In cross-examination, he agreed he was under the impression that Miss D was in possession of the facts, but he did not inquire what facts and that with hindsight perhaps he should have gone further into the matter. In his statement to the police, made on 31 October 1989, Mr Bodycomb said the caller, ie someone stating she was a friend of Miss D, said she was aware of the problems there had been with baby S as, she stated, Mrs Walton had informed her. She asked if there were any other reasons why T should not be placed with Mrs Walton. In response Mr Bodycomb said Mrs Walton had a very lively two-and-a-half year old boy.

There is no evidence that any friend of Miss D ever telephoned Mr Bodycomb. Generally, I found Mr Bodycomb's evidence to be muddled and inconsistent. I do not think he has any reliable recollection of what was said during the telephone conversation of 25 August. It is, however, understandable that having thought subsequently about this tragic case he now thinks he has. I certainly do not think he tried deliberately to mislead me. I prefer the evidence of Miss D as to this important telephone conversation.

I am satisfied that Miss D did telephone, that Mr Bodycomb confirmed Mrs Walton was a registered child-minder and that he left her with the clear impression that in his view there was no reason why T could not be safely left with her. I am satisfied that Miss D was not aware of what had happened to S, or of the unresolved concerns. Mr Bodycomb was not justified in thinking that she was. Had she been told that Mr Bodycomb had not got to the bottom of what had happened to S, she would never have placed him with Mr. Walton. Essentially, the reason she telephoned Mr Bodycomb was to check that Mrs Walton had the stamp of social services' approval.

On Saturday, 26 August Miss D moved back from Chesterfield and on the following day she took T with her to visit Mrs Walton. There was quite a lengthy conversation. If any reference was made to S's 'illness', it was only in passing and his name was not mentioned. Insofar as there is a conflict of evidence as to what was said during this visit, I prefer the account of Miss D to that of Mrs Walton. The visit lasted one-and-a-half to two hours. Miss D was happy with the arrangements and it seemed a happy family home. Miss D's only concern was Mrs Walton's slovenly state of dress which left her with, as she put it, a slight feeling of unease. T began with Mrs Walton the following Thursday.

The state of knowledge of the local authority

Following S's problems on 14 June, a case conference was called on 16 June for 23 June. Some 12 people attended, including Mr Bodycomb and Mr Fayle his superior. Various medical personnel were present, including Dr Husband the paediatrician. At the conference concerns were raised that S had suffered a head injury. Dr Husband explained that the most common way for this sort of injury to be sustained is through shaking. Dr Husband said S had been operated on that day. No congenital malformation was detected in the operation and it could therefore be concluded that the origin of the injury was traumatic. There was some discussion as to whether A might have caused the injury. Dr Husband thought that it was just possible, but he would have expected S to yell if something so violent had happened to him. There was also some discussion about whether it was possible S had suffered an injury before being delivered to the child-minder. This was felt highly unlikely, but worthy of some further inquiries, in particular, from the neurosurgeon a

Charing Cross Hospital. A decision about placing S's name on the child protection register was deferred for this information to be obtained.

Two further observations in the note of this case conference are worthy of comment. First, Sgt Dobbin of the child protection team had 'good feelings' about Mrs Walton and felt she was a very caring and concerned person. Second, Mr Bodycomb thought Mrs Walton had the potential to be a very good minder and had offered her a lot of support since the incident.

A further conference was arranged for 4 July 1989. Many of the same personnel were present, including Mr Bodycomb and Mr Fayle, but not on this occasion, Dr Husband. The conference record records that the notes of this meeting should be read in conjunction with the notes of the earlier meeting. The primary concern of this case conference, and indeed the earlier case conference, was whether any action was needed to protect S, for example whether his name ought to be placed on the child protection register. It was highly relevant whether S was going to be safe with his mother. It was rather less relevant whether he would be safe with Mrs Walton, because he was most unlikely to be minded by her in the future.

The new information at this conference came from Charing Cross Hospital. Sgt Dobbin had spoken to Dr Mendoza three days after the previous conference. Dr Mendoza had said that the operation performed on 23 June was a success. During the operation some small blood vessels had been discovered and removed, which may have contributed to the haemorrhage and the haematoma.

Mr Fayle said he had spoken to Dr Husband, who had been given similar information by Charing Cross about small blood vessels which may have contributed to the problem. Sgt Dobbin also reported information from Charing Cross that S could not have suffered the trauma prior to his delivery to the child-minder. The note of the conference then went on to record:

> 'Moreover, there is a diminished likelihood (although still not an absence of possibility) that [S] suffered a severe trauma in the care of the child-minder Mrs Walton.'

And later:

> 'After some discussion it was felt likely that this bruising (ie on the head, of which there were photographs), had mainly been caused at the child minders, partly by [A] and perhaps partly (in the case of the linear bruise on [S's] scalp) by falling against a sharp object, such as a video.'

I cannot detect, either in the evidence or the case conference note, any foundation for this assertion.

It was concluded that no action was necessary to protect S; that his name would not be placed on the child protection register and that no further conference was necessary.

In my judgment, these two conferences, viewed objectively, left at the very least a question mark about whether S had suffered a non-accidental injury whilst in the care of Mrs Walton. Indeed, Mr Bodycomb accepts as much when he says in his proof that: 'The outcome of both conferences regarding the child-minder was inconclusive.'

What did Mr Bodycomb do about the situation? In his proof of evidence he said he could not pillory Mrs Walton because there was no evidence that she had injured S. If there had been such evidence she would have been deregistered. A little earlier in the same proof he said he had no proof that she had caused his injury. I think he found it hard to contemplate she could have done such a dreadful thing. Indeed, on 21 June, two days before the case conference, there is an entry in the notes made by Mr Bodycomb that he cannot feel Mrs Walton is guilty of any abuse to S or that he was neglected whilst in her care.

Mr Bodycomb planned to meet Mrs Walton on 5 July, the day after the second case conference, and explain that no definite conclusion had been reached about the case of S's injuries. He did not do so because the Waltons were away for a family funeral. In fact he did not go and see her until 28 July. This delay is symptomatic of the general lack of urgency with which the local authority approached the situation.

In 1989, until he left in October, Mr Jonathan Fayle was employed by the local authority as locality team manager for the Ashford locality team. He had overall responsibility for the work of the team, which included social workers and other staff. He was Mr Bodycomb's immediate superior. He chaired the two case conferences with regard to S. In his proof of evidence he says that he thinks Mrs Walton's position as a child-minder was discussed at the second case conference and that it was agreed at the meeting that he and Mr Bodycomb would consider Mrs Walton's position. Mr Bodycomb said in evidence that he did discuss the situation, he thought, on 2 August. Mr Fayle said they had several conversations beginning at the time of S's injuries. Mr Fayle said that during the period of investigation, they agreed she should be advised not to mind. But there was no formal suspension. After the second case conference they decided it would not be right to deregister her, but it would be right to advise her not to take young children. At a very late stage in his evidence Mr Bodycomb said, for the first time, that Mrs Walton's certificate was suspended until they decided she could continue minding. He said he suspended the certificate because of the findings at the case conference. I do not accept that Mrs Walton's certificate was suspended or that she was advised not to mind on an informal basis. Had Mrs Walton's certificate been suspended I think she would have been sent a letter, as she was after T's injury. Furthermore, she said nothing about any suspension and there is no written record of suspension anywhere among the documents I have seen, not even on Mrs Walton's card. Nor is there any evidence of reinstatement.

The first written record after the second case conference is a note made by Mr Bodycomb on Mrs Walton's card in the card index. It reads: 'Vacancy update 26.7.89. One must be over 2 yrs.'

Mr Bodycomb thought the date was wrong and was almost sure it was written after he visited Mrs Walton on 28 July. I think this is probably correct because when he went to see her he wished to ascertain if she wanted to continue minding. On 28 July Mr Bodycomb's notes record:

'Visited Mrs Walton today re the above. She wishes to continue minding. I have recommended that she minds children between 2-5, particularly whilst [A] is still very lively. Maybe registration will need to be changed but will discuss this further with team manager.'

His evidence was that he recommended to her orally that she should only consider taking children between the ages of 2 and 5 while her child was so lively. Mr Bodycomb later told Miss D that he had recommended this strongly to Mrs Walton on 28 July. Mrs Walton's evidence was that Mr Bodycomb came and gave news of S's progress from time to time and that on 28 July she recollects he made a passing remark about minding toddlers rather than babies.

I find that he did make the recommendation he claims, when he went to see Mrs Walton on 28 July. Having seen him for some time in the witness box I am quite satisfied that he did not make the recommendation strongly, albeit that is what he later told Miss D. In any event, the recommendation had no force whatsoever and was the result of an ill thought out compromise in Mr Bodycomb's mind. He had satisfied himself that Mrs Walton was not responsible for S's injury and felt that deregistration would have been unfair to Mrs Walton but, nevertheless, felt he should not do nothing. I am afraid the picture I was left by Mr Bodycomb was one of bumbling inactivity. I do not believe either he or Mr Fayle did anything after the case conference before he went to see Mrs Walton on 28 July. He hoped the problem would go away by Mrs Walton saying that she didn't want to continue child-minding, but he ended up with the uneasy compromise of advising her not to look after children under two because of the perceived possibility that A had been responsible for S's injury. This is a possibility which in my judgment was quite without foundation. He chose to ignore the risk that clearly remained. The truth is that, after two case conferences, it was unresolved how S came by his injury, but one real possibility was that Mrs Walton was responsible. No caring mother who had sat through these two case conferences would have contemplated leaving her small baby with Mrs Walton. Unfortunately, Mr Bodycomb put the interests of the child-minder before those of the child, when the child's interest should, in my judgment, have been his first and paramount consideration.

As regards Mr Fayle's position, although he may have discussed the situation in passing with Mr Bodycomb, I am satisfied he did no more than go along with Mr Bodycomb's decision that Mrs Walton should not be deregistered and be advised to take children over the age of two only. That Mr Fayle in fact exercised a significant supervisory role in this matter over Mr Bodycomb is not supported by any documents. He suggested in evidence that there may have been documents that were destroyed when he left his post in October 1989. I cannot accept that evidence. Mr Fayle gave evidence at the very end of the case and I regret to say that an extremely intelligent man left me with the impression that he was trying to present matters in the light most favourable to the local authority. He did not give the lead that could reasonably have been expected of him after the second case conference.

In my judgment, the crucial feature of this case is not so much the failure of the local authority to deregister Mrs Walton, but the failure to tell Miss D the full facts when she made the inquiry on 25 August. What she needed to know was what the local authority knew, namely that in the light of what had happened, or may have happened, to S there was a serious question mark about the safety of a small child whilst in Mrs Walton's care. Mr Bodycomb did not even say to Miss D that an informal qualification had been put on Mrs Walton's registration in that she had been recommended to take only children over the age of two. Whether or not a child-minder is registered does not stop a mother placing her child with the minder. The legislation only covers placement for reward. What is crucial is that the local authority had information which an inquiring parent could reasonably expect would be passed on.

Subsequent events

Little of the subsequent history is of direct relevance to the issues I have to decide. There is a record in the social services' notes made by Mr Bodycomb on 15 September that records:

'I said I was unaware that Mrs Walton had taken a younger child and had failed to heed the recommendation I had made. He [Mr Walton] said she had been persuaded to take this child.'

I do not accept that Miss D persuaded Mrs Walton to take T. I think the desire that she should take him was mutual.

On 19 September Mr Bodycomb told Mrs Walton her registration was being suspended while further investigations were made. This was indorsed on her card the following day. The registration was ultimately cancelled by letter dated 13 November 1989.

On 20 September 1989 a case conference was held. Neither Mr Bodycomb nor Mr Fayle was present. It is interesting to note, however, that at this early stage there is a written record of Miss D having claimed to have rung Mr Bodycomb and been told in answer to her request whether there was any reason why she should not place T with Mrs Walton that there was not.

On 12 October 1989 Mr Fayle, who was then still the Ashford locality team manager, but was very shortly to leave, wrote a memorandum to Amanda Burge, the assistant area director of social services, enclosing a copy of the earlier case conference minutes. In it he referred to the fact that various statements had been taken in the course of investigation by Det Insp Bloxham and that the final stage was to take statements from the Waltons and Mr Bodycomb. Bearing this letter in mind, I think it is inconceivable that Mr Fayle would, when he left shortly afterwards, have thrown away any material records, eg notes of conversations with Mr Bodycomb, as he suggested in evidence may have been the case. A statement was in fact taken from Mr Bodycomb by the police on 31 October and amongst the documents disclosed by the first defendants is a memorandum by Mr Bodycomb about his involvement with T's placement bearing the same date. I think it is clear from the format of the two documents that the memorandum is related to the making of the statement. The two documents are practically identical.

THE LAW

1. *Breach of statutory duty*

The plaintiff claims that the local authority were in breach of statutory duty and that this sounds in damages. The relevant legislation in force at the material time was the Nurseries and Child-Minders Regulations Act 1948.

Section 1(1) places an obligation on the local authority to keep a register of those who mind children under the age of five for reward. By s 1(4) the local authority may refuse to register a person whom they are not satisfied is a fit person to look after children.

Section 2 gives the local authority power to impose requirements in connection with registration. Those requirements do not include a restriction on the age of the children to be minded. (Local authorities have since been given greater flexibility in the imposition of requirements by s 72 of the Children Act 1989.)

Section 3 deals with the issue of certificates of registration. Section 4 makes it an offence for a child-minder to fail to register or to break a requirement under s 2. Nowhere does the Act provide any sanction on the social services authority for a failure to meet its obligations. Section 5 deals with cancellation of registration. Section 5(b) provides:

'Where ... (b) it appears to the local health authority as respects any premises or person registered under the said section one, that circumstances exist which would justify a refusal under subsection (3) or subsection (4) of that section to register the premises or person, the local health authority may by order cancel the registration ...'

The remainder of the Act is not material.

The plaintiff's claim for breach of statutory duty is pleaded as follows:

'(a) following the injury to a child called S in or about July 1989 whilst in the care of the second defendant in her capacity of child-minder, failed to indorse upon the register of child minders that the second defendant was not registered to look after children under the age of 2 years, alternatively, failed pursuant to s 5 of the 1948 Act, to cancel her registration.

(b) following the said injury to S failed to ascertain that circumstances existed which would justify refusal under s 1(4) of the 1948 Act to register the second defendant as a child-minder and/or failed to act upon the knowledge that such circumstances existed. The plaintiff's case hereunder is that the registration ought to have been cancelled.'

The first allegation is based on the misconception that a registration could be limited to children over the age of two. As a matter of law it could not. In essence therefore the allegation of breach of statutory duty can only be that the first defendants failed to cancel Mrs Walton's registration.

The way the Act works is that s 5 gives the local authority a discretion to cancel a registration where circumstances exist that would justify a refusal to register (s 1(4)). It was clearly the intention of Parliament that only those who are fit to look after children under five should be registered as child-minders. In my judgment, a person cannot be so fit for the purposes of this legislation when there is, as here, an unresolved question about a non-accidental injury.

In principle there is no distinction in the test to be applied when considering on the one hand registration and on the other cancellation of registration. If S's injury had occurred in similar circumstances, but before Mrs Walton was registered, it is inconceivable that the local authority would have proceeded with registration immediately following the second case conference on 4 July.

In evidence Mr Bodycomb agreed there was a real and not fanciful risk to T in placing him with Mrs Walton and that the risk was of non-accidental injury by an adult. I am not confident that Mr Bodycomb, or anybody else at the local authority, ever really addressed his mind properly to the question of cancellation of registration. Several times in his evidence Mr Bodycomb indicated that he was approaching matters from the viewpoint of fairness to Mrs Walton rather than the safety of a child. For example, he said:

'To have proceeded with this [deregistration] would have been acting as both judge and jury on Mrs Walton in circumstances where nothing conclusive had been established against her.'

And on another occasion:

'It is not easy to deregister someone as a child-minder. The county council would need a very good reason for so doing. For example we could be preventing someone from earning her livelihood. It is unusual to deregister anyone.'

That, I think, is getting the emphasis wrong. If, as he clearly did, Mr Bodycomb felt that there was a serious question mark about children under two being minded by Mrs Walton, that should have resulted (1) in suspension whilst the matter was investigated and (2) if the concern was not resolved, in cancellation of the registration.

What I think Mr Bodycomb overlooked is that registration of a child-minder by a local authority will necessarily be seen by parents looking for a minder as a hallmark or stamp of approval, something that can be relied on.

I am in no doubt that the local authority failed to meet their obligations under the Act. They should either have cancelled Mrs Walton's registration or at the very least have suspended it whilst they made vigorous further inquiries. They did neither, but instead made a recommendation to Mrs Walton that she should not in future take young children, a recommendation that had no force whatsoever in law. Indeed it was ignored by Mrs Walton when she took T.

I pause in passing to mention one matter. The Act contains no express power to suspend a registration whilst further investigations are being made pending a decision whether or not to cancel. In my judgment, such a power must be implied and I note it was assumed there was such a power when T's situation came to be considered in September.

It by no means follows that because the local authority failed to meet its obligations under the Act, an action lies against it for breach of statutory duty. It is a question of the true construction of the Act whether an action lies with a private individual for breach of its provisions: see *Clerk and Lindsell on Torts* (16 edn, 1989) p 763 and *Charlesworth on Negligence* (8th edn, 1990) p 852. As far as I am aware, it has not previously been decided whether a breach of duty by a local authority under the Nurseries and Child-Minders Regulations Act 1948 gives rise to a private law claim.

I have read the helpful analysis by Turner J in *X and ors (minors) v Bedfordshire CC* (1993) Times, 24 November. In that case he considered a similar question in relation to the child care legislation. He held that it was not the intention of Parliament to confer a private law right of action on a child injured as the result of a failure by a local authority to comply with the duties imposed on it by virtue of any of the Child Care Acts. I respectfully agree with his reasoning.

The present case, however, falls into a somewhat different category. I agree with Mr Faulkes' analysis on behalf of the local authority that the intention of Parliament was that the local authority should provide information by means of a register and take precautions to ensure appropriate persons and premises were registered and deregistered. The Act was passed for the benefit of the public as a whole and only, in the very broadest sense, for the benefit of children under the age of five (the age to which the legislation then related). The Act is similar to some forms of licensing legislation and it is to be noted that only a limited class of children, namely those under five, minded for reward, fall within the catchment of its benefit.

The fact that the Act itself provides no remedy for any breach by the local authority does not of itself give an individual a right to damages. As Simon Brown J said in *R v Mid-Glamorgan CC, ex p Greig* (1988) Independent, 1 June, (cited with approval by Woolf LJ in *R v Inner London Education Authority, ex p Ali* (1990) 2 Admin LR 822 at 830–831):

> 'In the last analysis, however, I believe that the essential objection to a damages claim ... is not the existence of the default provision but rather the want of any good cause of action. As it seems to me, by no means all breaches of statutory duty by public authorities give rise to any private law claim whatever, irrespective of whether the relevant statute contains default provisions. In my judgment it is only in certain exceptional and well-recognized circumstances that someone, even if particularly damnified by an authority's non-compliance with a statutory duty, can claim damages for such a breach.'

In *Hague v Deputy Governor of Parkhurst Prison, Weldon v Home Office* [1991] 3 All ER 733 at 750, [1992] 1 AC 58 at 170 Lord Jauncey said:

> '... I take from these authorities that it must always be a matter for consideration whether the legislature intended that private law rights of action should be conferred upon individuals in respect of breaches of the relevant statutory provision. The fact that a particular provision was intended to protect certain individuals is not of itself sufficient to confer private law rights of action upon them, something more is required to show that the legislation intended such conferment.'

I can find nothing in the present Act to indicate such an intention. I detect a considerable reluctance on the part of the courts to impose upon local authorities any liability for breach of statutory duty other than that expressly imposed in the statute. In my judgment the claim for breach of statutory duty fails.

2. *Common law negligence*

There are two main strands to the plaintiff's claim. (i) Breach of a duty of care based on failure to cancel the registration, and (ii) a separate breach arising out of negligent misstatement by Mr Bodycomb on the telephone on 25 August.

(i) Failure to cancel the registration

As Turner J pointed out in *X and ors (minors) v Bedfordshire CC*, hitherto, no tort of negligence by a local authority towards children has been recognised. He then cited a passage from Lord Bridge's speech in *Caparo Industries plc v Dickman* [1990] 1 All ER 568 at 573–574, [1990] 2 AC 605 at 617:

'But since [*Anns v Merton London Borough* [1977] 2 All ER 492, [1978] AC 728] a series of decisions of the Privy Council and of your Lordships' House, notably in judgments and speeches delivered by Lord Keith, have emphasised the inability of any single general principle to provide a practical test which can be applied to every situation to determine whether a duty of care is owed and, if so, what is its scope: see *Peabody Donation Fund v Sir Lindsay Parkinson & Co Ltd* [1984] 3 All ER 529 at 533– 534, [1985] AC 210 at 239–241, *Yuen Kun-yeu v A-G of Hong Kong* [1987] 2 All ER 705 at 709–712, [1988] AC 175 at 190–194, *Rowling v Takaro Properties Ltd* [1988] 1 All ER 163 at 172, [1988] A C 473 at 501 and *Hill v Chief Constable of West Yorkshire* [1988] 2 All ER 238 at 241, [1989] AC 53 at 60. What emerges is that, in addition to the foreseeability of damage, necessary ingredients in any situation giving rise to a duty of care are that there should exist between the party owing the duty and the party to whom it is owed a relationship characterised by the law as one of "proximity" or "neighbourhood" and that the situation should be one in which the court considers it fair, just and reasonable that the law should impose a duty of a given scope on the one party for the benefit of the other. But it is implicit in the passages referred to that the concepts of proximity and fairness embodied in these additional ingredients are not susceptible of any such precise definition as would be necessary to give them utility as practical tests, but amount in effect to little more than convenient labels to attach to the features of different specific situations which, on a detailed examination of all the circumstances, the law recognises pragmatically as giving rise to a duty of care of a given scope. Whilst recognising, of course, the importance of the underlying general principles common to the whole field of negligence, I think the law has now moved in the direction of attaching greater significance to the more traditional categorisation of distinct and recognisable situations as guides to the existence, the scope and the limits of the very duties of care which the law imposes. We must now, I think, recognise the wisdom of the words of Brennan J in the High Court of Australia in *Sutherland Shire Council v Heyman* (1985) 60 ALR 1 at 43–44, where he said: "It is preferable, in my view, that the law should develop novel categories of negligence incrementally and by analogy with established categories, rather than by a massive extension of a prima facie duty of care restrained only by indefinable 'considerations which ought to negative or to reduce or limit the scope of the duty or the class of person to whom it is owed'."'

Throughout the second half of the twentieth century, local authorities have been given ever increasing supervisory powers over the care and welfare of children. The core of the current legislation is to be found in the Children Act 1989. It was settled in *A v Liverpool City Council* [1981] 2 All ER 385, [1982] AC 363 that the High Court's wardship jurisdiction could not be used so as to override or circumscribe the exercise by local authorities of their statutory powers. Lord Roskill said ([1981] 2 All ER 385 at 392, [1982] AC 363 at 377):

'I am of the clear opinion that, while the prerogative jurisdiction of the court in wardship cases remains, the exercise of that jurisdiction has been and must continue to be treated as circumscribed by the exercise of the far-ranging statutory code which entrusts the care and control of deprived children to local authorities. It follows that the undoubted wardship jurisdiction must not be exercised so as to interfere with the day-to-day administration by local authorities of that statutory control.'

Parliament has entrusted to local authorities a wide measure of power and responsibility over children and it is desirable that they should be left to exercise those powers and responsibilities as far as possible unhindered by the courts. Of course, as was pointed out by Lord Roskill in the *Liverpool* case, and has been many times since, they are not immune from the remedy of judicial review in an appropriate case.

The problem for the court, in the present case, is very different from that in the *Liverpool* case. Here, the question is whether the local authority owed T a duty to take reasonable care in the exercise of its obligations to register and deregister child-minders. If such a duty does exist, the effect is to bring a particular, but limited, category of child under the umbrella of the duty leaving others outside. The local authority's obligations with regard to child-minding only extended at the time to children under five minded for reward.

Whilst it is true that the courts are more ready to find a duty of care owed where the consequence of a breach is personal injury rather than damage to property and still less mere economic loss, to hold that a duty was owed in the present case would be breaking entirely new ground.

It has been argued that the Nurseries and Child-Minders Regulation Act 1948 falls outside the heart of local authority legislation concerning the care of children and I think it does. Therefore it is said that this case falls outside the category of case with which, for example, Ralph Gibson LJ was concerned in *F v Wirral Metropolitan BC* [1991] 2 All ER 648 at 676, [1991] Fam 69 at 106, where he could see no sufficient reason for the court to create, or declare, the existence of a new right which had not been recognised before.

The question is whether this opens the door to the creation of liability. What we have here is the local authority required by statute to act as a licensing authority. It is going a long way, without more, to hold a licensing authority liable for the misfeasance of a third party when it negligently grants or refuses to cancel a licence. As Lord Goff said in *Smith v Littlewoods Organisation Ltd* [1987] 1 All ER 710 at 728, [1987] AC 241 at 270:

'Now if this proposition is understood as relating to a general duty to take reasonable care *not to cause damage* to premises in the neighbourhood (as I believe that the Lord President intended it to be understood) then it is unexceptionable. But it must not be overlooked that a problem arises when the pursuer is seeking to hold the defender responsible for having failed to *prevent* a third party from causing damage to the pursuer or his property by the third party's own deliberate wrongdoing. In such a case, it is not possible to invoke a general duty of care; for it is well recognised that there is no *general* duty of care to prevent third parties from causing such damage. The point is expressed very clearly in Hart and Honoré *Causation in the Law* (2nd edn, 1985) p 196, where the authors state: "The law might acknowledge a general principle that, whenever the harmful conduct of another is reasonably foreseeable, it is our duty to take precautions against it ... But, up to now, no legal system has gone so far as this ..." The same point is made in Fleming *The Law of Torts* (6th edn,

1983) p 200, where it is said: *"... there is certainly no general duty to protect others against theft or loss."* (Fleming's emphasis.) I wish to add that no such general duty exists even between those who are neighbours in the sense of being occupiers of adjoining premises. There is no general duty on a householder that he should act as a watchdog, or that his house should act as a bastion, to protect his neighbour's house. Why does the law not recognise a general duty of care to prevent others from suffering loss or damage caused by the deliberate wrongdoing of third parties? The fundamental reason is that the common law does not impose liability for what are called pure omissions.'

The point is further illustrated in *Yuen Kun-yeu v AG of Hong Kong* [1987] 2 All ER 705, [1988] AC 175.

Mr Swift QC for the plaintiff argues that the present case is very different from the *Bedfordshire CC* case. There, he says the local authority's powers were discretionary. Here they are specifically defined by statute. I note however that in both s 1(4) and (5) of the 1948 Act the word 'may' rather than 'shall' is used in defining the local authority's obligations.

In my judgment, the issues of breach of statutory duty and common law negligence in respect of the exercise by the local authority of its power under this Act run very much hand in glove. In my judgment, there is no common law duty owed of the nature contended for by the plaintiff and the first strand of the claim fails.

It follows therefore that the plaintiff's claim for negligence fails on all grounds pleaded other than those arising out of the telephone conversation between Mr Bodycomb and Miss D with which I shall now deal.

(ii) Negligent misstatement

Mr Swift contends on this point that there is no question of extending the existing law to create a duty of care where none existed before. He argues that this is a straightforward case of negligent misstatement on the part of Mr Bodycomb on 25 August giving rise to liability in negligence. He points out that in *Yeun Keun-yeu* [1988] AC 175 at 182 counsel for the Attorney General conceded that if the plaintiffs had actually asked the commissioner for his opinion about the company, the situation would have been different and questions of special relationship and negligent misstatement would have arisen.

If Mr Bodycomb had merely told Miss D that Mrs Walton was registered as a child-minder that would not, I think, have given rise to any liability. It would have been an accurate statement; but he went a good deal further. He told her he knew of no reason why T should not go to Mrs Walton, or words to that effect. There was, however, a very good reason why T should not go to Mrs Walton. Another child had recently suffered a serious and unexplained injury whilst in her care. Miss D having made the inquiry, he should have told her whatever he knew that a prudent parent would wish to know before placing a tiny baby with the Waltons. Miss D would not have placed T with Mrs Walton had she known the true position and it avails Mr Bodycomb not at all that he did not know for sure during the phone call that Miss D would in fact decide to place T with her.

In my judgment, the criteria for founding liability for negligent misstatement are met. Mr Bodycomb was at all times acting as the local authority's nursery and child-minding adviser.   He was the only person employed in that capacity for the Ashford area. When he spoke to Miss D on 25 August, he was consulted and speaking as a professional officer with special knowledge and responsibility. He knew, or ought to have known, that what he said would be relied upon. What he said related directly to the safety of the infant plaintiff.   There was, in these circumstances, a special relationship of proximity between Mr Bodycomb and the plaintiff.   I accept Mr Swift's submission that this case falls four square within the principle laid down in *Hedley Byrne & Co Ltd v Heller & Partners Ltd* [1963] 2 All ER 575, [1964] AC 465, but the plaintiff's position is stronger in the present case because he suffered physical injury rather than mere economic loss.

The local authority take one further point. They argue that even if there was a duty of care and a breach of it, such breach was not the cause of the injury to T. Any breach by the local authority, it is contended, was not the effective cause of T's injury. Mr Faulkes went on that it is only in very rare circumstances that a defendant will be held responsible in law for the acts or omissions of a third party. There must, he says, be a very high degree of foreseeability. This type of situation arose in *Al-Kandari v JR Brown & Co* [1988] 1 All ER 833, [1988] 1 QB 665. By a father's solicitor's negligence, the father's passport with his two children on it was left with the Kuwait Embassy. The father was able to get possession of it from the embassy, kidnap the children from the mother's care and remove them from the country. They were never returned. Bingham LJ said ([1988] 1 All ER 833 at 840, [1988] 1 QB 665 at 677):

> 'The judge found against the plaintiff on the ground that it was not reasonably foreseeable that Mr Al-Kandari would be given any opportunity to abduct the children. The correct approach is to consider the breach of duty which has been proved and to ask whether an ordinarily competent solicitor in the defendant's position would have foreseen damage of the kind which actually occurred as a not unlikely result of that breach. Such a solicitor would be mindful that this whole arrangement had been made to ensure that Mr Al-Kandari could not use his passport to spirit the children out of the jurisdiction.'

In the present case Mr Bodycomb knew that Miss D was considering placing T with Mrs Walton. He knew too, or would have done had he stopped to think about it, that had she known the information that was imparted to him at the two case conferences, she would not have placed T with Mrs Walton. He knew that there was a significant risk to any small baby in Mrs Walton's care. In these circumstances I find the local authority liable in negligence to the plaintiff. There will therefore be judgment for the plaintiff against the local authority and Mrs Walton with damages to be assessed.

Judgment for the plaintiff against the local authority and Mrs Walton.

K Mydeen Esq   Barrister.

M (a minor) and another v Newham London Borough Council and others
X and others (minors) v Bedfordshire County Council

COURT OF APPEAL, CIVIL DIVISION

SIR THOMAS BINGHAM MR, STAUGHTON AND PETER GIBSON LJJ

24–28 JANUARY, 23 FEBRUARY 1994

Local authority – Statutory duty – Statutory duty owed in relation to welfare of children – Breach – Whether children and parents affected by breach of statutory duty having right of action – Children and Young Persons Act 1969 – Child Care Act 1980 – Children Act 1989.

Child – Welfare – Local authority – Local authorities' statutory duties in relation to welfare of children – Local authorities failing to take plaintiff children into care – Children suffering ill-treatment and impairment of health – Whether plaintiff children entitled to claim damages for breach of statutory duty – Children and Young Persons Act 1969 – Child Care Act 1980 – Children Act 1989.

Negligence – Duty to take care – Existence of duty – Children – Local authority – Psychiatrist and social worker employed by local authority – Duty owed in relation to welfare of children – Psychiatrist and social worker interviewing child suspected of being subject to sexual abuse – Psychiatrist and social worker wrongly identifying abuser and causing child to be removed from home – Whether local authority, psychiatrist and social worker owing duty of care to child or child's mother in negligence.

Action – Immunity from civil action – Witness – Expert witness – Extent of immunity from civil action – Psychiatrist interviewing child suspected of having been sexually abused at request of local authority – Psychiatrist wrongly identifying abuser and causing child to be removed from home – Whether psychiatrist entitled to immunity from action for negligence – Public interest protected by witness's immunity.

In the first case, the defendant local authority arranged for a child whom social workers suspected had been sexually abused to be interviewed by a psychiatrist and a social worker in the absence of the mother. At the interview the child named the abuser by his first name and the psychiatrist and the social worker wrongly assumed the abuser to be the mother's current boyfriend, who had the same first name and was then living with the mother. The child in fact intended to refer to a cousin who had previously lived at the mother's address. The psychiatrist and the social worker decided that it was necessary to remove the child from the mother's care because she would be unable to protect the child against further abuse by the boyfriend and on the same day the local authority obtained a place of safety order. The mother applied to the judge for an order giving her care and control but, having heard the evidence put forward by the local authority, the judge ordered that the child be made a ward of court, that the local authority be granted care and control, that the child should not return home and that the mother's access be limited. In subsequent proceedings the mother saw, for the first time, a transcript of the child's interview with the psychiatrist and the social worker and realised that the child had not identified her boyfriend as the abuser and that there was no evidence to support that conclusion. The local authority accepted that fact and took steps to rehabilitate the child with the mother and her boyfriend. The child and the mother brought an action against the local authority, the psychiatrist and the health authority which employed her, claiming damages for breach of statutory duty and negligence. They alleged that the defendants had failed to investigate the facts with proper care and thoroughness or to discuss them with the mother and, in doing so, were in breach of their duty under the Child Care Act 1980 to safeguard the welfare of children. The child and the mother claimed that, as a result of their enforced separation and the lack of information given to them, they had suffered anxiety neurosis. On the defendants' application the master struck out the statement of claim as disclosing no reasonable cause of action, holding, inter alia, that the psychiatrist was entitled to the immunity from actions for negligence afforded to a witness. On appeal the judge upheld the master's order. The child and the mother appealed.

In the second case, despite reports from relatives, neighbours, the police, the family's general practitioner, a head teacher, the National Society for the Prevention of Cruelty to Children, a social worker and a health visitor that the plaintiff children were at risk (including risk of sexual abuse) while living with their parents, that their living conditions were appalling and unfit and that the children were dirty and hungry, the defendant local authority rejected recommendations that the children be placed on the Child Protection Register and took little or no action with regard to the children from 1989 until October 1992, when it decided to seek care orders in respect of them. In 1993 the children brought an action against the local authority claiming damages for breach of statutory duty and negligence. They claimed that the authority had failed to have regard to their welfare as required by the Children and Young Persons Act 1969, the 1980 Act and the Children Act 1989 and should have acted more quickly and more effectively when apprised of their condition and that its failure to do so had caused them to suffer ill-treatment and illness and impairment of their health and proper development. On the application of the authority the judge struck out the statement of claim as disclosing no reasonable cause of action. The children appealed.

Held – The appeals would be dismissed for the following reasons—

(1) The duties imposed by the 1969, 1980 and 1989 Acts on local authorities in relation to the welfare of children were so general and unspecific in their terms and conferred on local authorities such wide scope to exercise subjective judgment that it was to be inferred that Parliament did not intend that there should be direct enforcement of the statutes by individuals nor did it intend to confer a private law remedy for breach of local authority duties under the Acts, and (per Staughton and Peter Gibson LJJ) that inference was reinforced by the availability of other remedies, including judicial review, to an aggrieved person. It followed that the statements of claim disclosed no reasonable cause of action for breach of statutory duty and the plaintiffs' claims on that ground had been properly struck out (see p 615 *f* to p 616 *a*, p 628 *d e*, p 631 *j*, p 633 *j*, p 634 *e* to *j* and p 638 *b c*, post).

(2) (Sir Thomas Bingham MR dissenting) Local authorities performing the public law function of caring for children in need, and doctors and health authorities participating in the same process, did not owe a private law duty of care in respect of action or inaction in carrying out that function. A private law duty in negligence would not generally be imposed on a public authority carrying out statutory functions if there was no breach of statutory duty. Furthermore, in the absence of an established category of negligence imposing on local authorities a duty of care in respect of a decision taken in the exercise of their statutory functions whether or not to intervene to protect a child, it would not, applying the incremental approach to the development of the law of negligence, be fair, just and reasonable to impose such a duty on local authorities because of the probability of a large number of claims and the detrimental effect on their resources and the manner in which they would be forced to carry out their functions under the child care legislation if they were held to owe such a duty. It followed that the respective statements of claim of all the children and (Sir Thomas Bingham MR concurring) the mother in the first action disclosed no reasonable cause of action in negligence against the local authorities and those claims had been properly struck out (see p 624 *b*, p 629 *b c*, p 630 *h j*, p 631 *g h*, p 635 *d*, p 637 *b f*, p 639 *g* and p 640 *a*, post); *Hill v Chief Constable of West Yorkshire* [1988] 2 All ER 238 and dictum of Lord Bridge in *Caparo Industries plc v Dickman* [1990] 1 All ER 568 at 574 applied.

(3) (Sir Thomas Bingham MR dissenting) In the first case, although the psychiatrist and social worker owed a duty as professional persons to use reasonable skill and care in their diagnosis, that duty was owed to the local authority or health authority by which they were engaged or employed and not to the child or (Sir Thomas Bingham MR concurring) mother, since neither the child nor her mother had sought the services of the psychiatrist or social worker and they were not, in any meaningful sense, the patient of the psychiatrist or the client of the social worker. It followed that the statements of claim disclosed no cause of action in negligence against the psychiatrist or social worker or their employers and the claims against them had been properly struck out (see p 621 *j* to p 622 *b*, p 629 *e* to p 630 *a*, p 631 *g h* and p 638 *j* to p 639 *e*, post).

Per Sir Thomas Bingham MR and Staughton LJ. The public interest which a witness's immunity from actions for negligence protects is the proper administration of justice. Such immunity is not enjoyed, therefore, by persons who have never become involved in the administration of justice (see p 617 *h* to 618 *c* and p 625 *c d*, post); *Palmer v Durnford Ford (a firm)* [1992] 2 All ER 122 approved.

Notes

For construction of a statute to ascertain whether a civil action lies in respect of a breach of a duty imposed by the statute, see 45 *Halsbury's Laws* (4th edn) para 1282.

For nature of negligence and the duty to take care generally, see 34 *Halsbury's Laws* (4th edn) paras 1–5, and for cases on the subject, see 36(1) *Digest* (2nd reissue) 7–64, *1–325*.

For immunity of a witness in respect of his evidence, see 17 *Halsbury's Laws* (4th edn) para 261, and for cases on the subject, see 22(2) *Digest* (2nd reissue) 137, 143, 215, *7252, 7316, 8247–8248*.

For the Children and Young Persons Act 1969, see 6 *Halsbury's Statutes* (4th edn) (1992 reissue) 136.

For the Children Act 1989 (s 108(7) and Sch 15 of which repealed the Child Care Act 1980), see ibid 387.

Cases referred to in judgments

A v Liverpool City Council [1981] 2 All ER 385, [1982] AC 363, [1981] 2 WLR 948, HL.

Alcock v Chief Constable of the South Yorkshire Police [1991] 4 All ER 907, [1992] 1 AC 310, [1991] 3 WLR 1057, HL.

Caparo Industries plc v Dickman [1990] 1 All ER 568, [1990] 2 AC 605, [1990] 2 WLR 358, HL.

Cocks v Thanet DC [1982] 3 All ER 1135, [1983] 2 AC 286, [1982] 3 WLR 1121, HL.

Cutler v Wandsworth Stadium Ltd (in liq) [1949] 1 All ER 544, [1949] AC 398, HL.

D v National Society for the Prevention of Cruelty to Children [1977] 1 All ER 589, [1978] AC 171, [1977] 2 WLR 201, HL.

Davy v Spelthorne BC [1983] 3 All ER 278, [1984] AC 262, [1983] 3 WLR 742, HL.

Donoghue (or M'Alister) v Stevenson [1932] AC 562, [1932] All ER Rep 1, HL.

E (a minor) v Dorset CC, Christmas v Hampshire CC (7 April 1993, unreported), QBD; *rvsd in part* [1994] 4 All ER 640, CA.

Evans v London Hospital Medical College [1981] 1 All ER 715, [1981] 1 WLR 184.

Everett (pauper) v Griffiths [1921] 1 AC 631, HL; *affg* [1920] 3 KB 163, CA.

F v Wirral Metropolitan BC [1991] 2 All ER 648, [1991] Fam 69, [1991] 2 WLR 1132, CA.

Hague v Deputy Governor of Parkhurst Prison, Weldon v Home Office [1991] 3 All ER 733, [1992] 1 AC 58, [1991] 3 WLR 340, HL.

Hart v John Frame Son & Co (1839) 6 Cl & Fin 193, 7 ER 670, HL.

Hill v Chief Constable of West Yorkshire [1988] 2 All ER 238, [1989] AC 53, [1988] 2 WLR 1049, HL.

Island Records Ltd, Ex p [1978] 3 All ER 824, [1978] Ch 122, [1978] 3 WLR 23, CA.

Lister v Romford Ice and Cold Storage Co Ltd [1957] 1 All ER 125, [1957] AC 555, [1957] 2 WLR 158, HL.

M (a minor) (disclosure of material), Re [1990] 2 FLR 36, CA.

Manda, Re [1993] 1 All ER 733, [1993] Fam 183, [1993] 2 WLR 161, CA.

Marrinan v Vibart [1962] 1 All ER 869, [1963] 1 QB 234, [1962] 2 WLR 1224; *affd* [1962] 3 All ER 380, [1963] 1 QB 528, [1962] 3 WLR 912, CA.

McLoughlin v O'Brian [1982] 2 All ER 298, [1983] 1 AC 410, [1982] 2 WLR 982, HL.

Murphy v Brentwood DC [1990] 2 All ER 908, [1991] 1 AC 398, [1990] 3 WLR 414, HL.

Palmer v Durnford Ford (a firm) [1992] 2 All ER 122, [1992] QB 483, [1992] 2 WLR 407.

R v Brent London BC, ex p Sawyer [1993] CA Transcript 1392.

R v Inner London Education Authority, ex p Ali (1990) 2 Admin LR 822, DC.

R v Mid-Glamorgan CC, ex p Greig (1988) Independent, 1 June.

Ross v Caunters (a firm) [1979] 3 All ER 580, [1980] Ch 297, [1979] 3 WLR 605.

Rowling v Takaro Properties Ltd [1988] 1 All ER 163, [1988] AC 473, [1988] 2 WLR 418, PC.

Roy v Kensington and Chelsea and Westminster Family Practitioner Committee [1992] 1 All ER 705, [1992] 1 AC 624, [1992] 2 WLR 239, HL.

Roy v Prior [1970] 2 All ER 729, [1971] AC 470, [1970] 3 WLR 202, HL.

Saif Ali v Sydney Mitchell & Co (a firm) (P, third party) [1978] 3 All ER 1033, [1980] AC 198, [1978] 3 WLR 849, HL.

Science Research Council v Nassé, BL Cars Ltd (formerly Leyland Cars) v Vyas [1979] 3 All ER 673, [1980] AC 1028, [1979] 3 WLR 762, HL.

Sidaway v Bethlem Royal Hospital Governors [1985] 1 All ER 643, [1985] AC 871, [1985] 2 WLR 480, HL.

T (a minor) v Surrey CC [1994] 4 All ER 577.

Tai Hing Cotton Mill Ltd v Liu Chong Hing Bank Ltd [1985] 2 All ER 947, [1986] AC 80, [1985] 3 WLR 317, PC.

Watson v M'Ewan, Watson v Jones [1905] AC 480, [1904–7] All ER Rep 1, HL.

Yuen Kun-yeu v A-G of Hong Kong [1987] 2 All ER 705, [1988] AC 175, [1987] 3 WLR 776, PC.

Cases also cited or referred to in skeleton arguments

Arenson v Casson Beckman Rutley & Co [1975] 3 All ER 901, [1977] AC 405, HL.

Bolam v Friern Hospital Management Committee [1957] 2 All ER 118, [1957] 1 WLR 582.

Butler (or Black) v Fife Coal Co Ltd [1912] AC 149, HL.

Cabassi v Vila (1940) 64 CLR 130, Aust HC.

Chadwick v British Transport Commission [1967] 2 All ER 945, sub nom *Chadwick v British Railways Board* [1967] 1 WLR 912.

Dawkins v Lord Rokeby (1873) LR 8 QB 255; affd (1875) LR 7 HL 744, [1874–80] All ER Rep 994, HL.

Doe d Murray, Lord Bishop of Rochester v Bridges (1831) 1 B & Ad 847, [1824–34] All ER Rep 167, 109 ER 1001.

Dooley v Cammell Laird & Co Ltd [1951] 1 Lloyd's Rep 271, Assizes.

Driver v William Willett (Contractors) Ltd [1969] 1 All ER 665, Assizes.

Emeh v Kensington and Chelsea and Westminster Area Health Authority [1984] 3 All ER 1044, [1985] QB 1012, CA.

Essex CC v R (note) [1994] Fam 167, [1994] 2 WLR 407.

G v Hounslow London BC (1987) 86 LGR 186.

Gaskin v Liverpool City Council [1980] 1 WLR 1549, CA.

Geddis v Bann Reservoir (Proprietors) (1878) 3 App Cas 430, HL.

Hedley Byrne & Co Ltd v Heller & Partners Ltd [1963] 2 All ER 575, [1964] AC 465, HL.

HIV Haemophiliac Litigation, Re (1990) Independent, 2 October, [1990] CA Transcript 783.

Holtom v Barnet London BC (1993) Times, 30 September.

Home Office v Dorset Yacht Co Ltd [1970] 2 All ER 294, [1970] AC 1004, HL.

Hughes v National Union of Mineworkers [1991] 4 All ER 278.

Lightbody v Gordon (1882) 9 R 934, Ct of Sess.

Lonrho plc v Tebbit [1992] 4 All ER 280, CA.

M (a minor) (child abuse: evidence), Re (note) [1987] 1 FLR 293.

Martine v South East Kent Health Authority (1993) Times, 8 March, [1993] CA Transcript 245.

Mills v Winchester Diocesan Board of Finance [1989] 2 All ER 317, [1989] Ch 428.

Munster v Lamb (1883) 11 QBD 588, [1881–5] All ER Rep 791, CA.

Nottingham CC v P, Re P (minors) (local authority: prohibited steps order) [1993] 3 All ER 815, [1994] Fam 18, CA.

Oxfordshire CC v M [1994] 2 All ER 269, [1994] 2 WLR 393, CA.

Pasmore v Oswaldtwistle UDC [1898] AC 387, [1895–9] All ER Rep 191, HL.

Pickering v Liverpool Daily Post and Echo Newspapers plc [1991] 1 All ER 622, [1991] 2 AC 370, HL.

Puhlhofer v Hillingdon London BC [1986] 1 All ER 467, [1986] AC 484, HL.

R v Local Comr for Administration for the North and East Area of England, ex p Bradford Metropolitan City Council [1979] 2 All ER 881, [1979] QB 287, QBD and CA.

R v Norfolk CC, ex p M [1989] 2 All ER 359, [1989] QB 619.

Rees v Sinclair [1974] 1 NZLR 180, NZ CA.

Rondel v Worsley [1967] 3 All ER 993, [1969] 1 AC 191, HL.

Royal Aquarium and Summer and Winter Garden Society Ltd v Parkinson [1892] 1 QB 431, [1891–4] All ER Rep 429, CA.

Smith v Littlewoods Organisation Ltd (Chief Constable, Fife Constabulary, third party) [1987] 1 All ER 710, [1987] AC 241, HL.

Southwark London Borough v Williams, Southwark London Borough v Anderson [1971] 2 All ER 175, [1971] Ch 734, CA.

Spring v Guardian Assurance plc [1993] 2 All ER 273, CA; *rvsd* [1994] 3 All ER 129, [1994] 3 WLR 354, HL.

Surtees v Kingston-upon-Thames BC, Surtees v Hughes [1991] 2 FLR 559, CA.

Sutcliffe v Thackrah [1974] 1 All ER 859, [1974] AC 727, HL.

Watt v Kesteven CC [1955] 1 All ER 473, [1955] 1 QB 408, CA.

Waugh v British Railways Board [1979] 2 All ER 1169, [1980] AC 521, HL.

West Wiltshire DC v Garland (Cond and ors, third parties) [1993] 4 All ER 246, [1993] Ch 409.

White v Jones [1993] 3 All ER 481, [1993] 3 WLR 730, CA.

Wilson v Colchester Justices [1985] 2 All ER 97, [1985] AC 750, HL.

Wood v Wood 1935 SLT 431, Ct of Sess (OH).

X (a minor) (wardship: restriction on publication), Re [1975] 1 All ER 697, [1975] Fam 47, Fam D and CA.

Interlocutory appeals

M (a minor) and anor v Newham London BC and ors

By notice of appeal dated 7 May 1993 the plaintiffs, a girl now aged 11 and her mother, appealed with leave from the order of Judge Phelan ([1993] 2 FLR 575) sitting as a judge of the Queen's Bench Division of the High Court dated 17 March 1993 whereby he dismissed their appeal against the order of Master Topley dated 19 November 1992 striking out their statement of claim alleging breach of statutory duty and negligence against the defendants, Newham London Borough Council, Newham Health Authority and Dr Eileen Vizard, a psychiatrist employed by the health authority, under RSC Ord 18, r 19 and under the inherent jurisdiction of the court on the grounds that it disclosed no reasonable cause of action and/or was an abuse of the process of the court. The facts are set out in the judgment of Sir Thomas Bingham MR.

X and ors (minors) v Bedfordshire CC

By notice of appeal dated 3 December 1993 the plaintiffs, five brothers and sisters who were now aged between 11 and 3, suing by their next friend, the Official Solicitor, appealed with leave from the order of Turner J ((1993) Times, 24 November) dated 12 November 1993 whereby he ordered that their statement of claim alleging breach of statutory duty and negligence against the defendant, Bedfordshire County Council, be struck out under RSC Ord 18, r 19 and/or under the inherent jurisdiction of the court on the grounds that it disclosed no reasonable cause of action. The facts are set out in the judgment of Sir Thomas Bingham MR.

James Munby QC and *Robert Sherman* (instructed by *Clinton Davis, Cushing & Kelly*) for the plaintiffs in the first appeal.
Edward Faulks (instructed by *Barlow Lyde & Gilbert*) for the local authority.
Allan Levy QC and *Elizabeth-Anne Gumbel* (instructed by *Conway Wood & Co, Harpenden*) for the plaintiffs in the second appeal.
Ian Karsten QC and *Lord Meston* (instructed by *Vizards*) for the county council.
James Holman QC and *Richard Tyson* (instructed by *Field Fisher Waterhouse*) for the health authority and the psychiatrist.

Cur adv vult

23 February 1994. The following judgments were delivered.

SIR THOMAS BINGHAM MR. These two appeals have been heard together. The facts of the two cases, and some of the issues, are quite different. But common to each case is a question of great importance and difficulty: may a child maintain an action for damages (whether for breach of statutory duty or common law negligence) against a local authority for steps taken or not taken in relation to the child by that authority as the responsible social services authority? This question has in each case been answered negatively. The children's claims (as also the mother's claim in the Newham case) have been struck out as disclosing no reasonable cause of action. The plaintiffs in each action appeal. For purposes of these appeals we must assume the plaintiffs' pleaded allegations to be true and capable of proof, although they are strongly contested. Unless the plaintiffs' claims are shown to be plainly unsustainable in law on the basis of their pleaded allegations, the claims should not be struck out.

M (a minor) v Newham London Borough Council

The first plaintiff in this action is a girl born in January 1983 and now aged just 11. She sues by her mother as her next friend. The second plaintiff is the mother, who was 17 when her daughter was born. I shall call these plaintiffs 'the child' and 'the mother'. There was originally a third plaintiff in the action: he lived with the mother and is the father of another of her children, although not of the child. He has withdrawn from the action and is no longer a plaintiff, but it is convenient to continue to refer to him as the third plaintiff.

There are three defendants. The first, the London Borough of Newham, is the local authority with responsibility for child care services in its area. The second is the local health authority. The third is a consultant child psychiatrist employed by the health authority. I shall refer to these defendants as 'the local authority', 'the health authority' and 'the psychiatrist'.

In summary, the factual case pleaded for the child and the mother is as follows. Between 1984 and 1986 the mother and the child had dealings with the local authority's social services department and the health authority. Concern was expressed that the child had been sexually abused. In June 1987, as a result of concern expressed by a health visitor about the mother's care of the child, a social worker employed by the local authority (the social worker) visited the mother's home and obtained details of her situation, including the fact that the third plaintiff was the mother's current boyfriend. The social worker reported his findings to a case conference called by the local authority which decided to place the child on the Child Protection Register on grounds of emotional abuse. During 1987 the mother took the child to see various doctors for advice on problems of urinary infection from which the child was suffering. The doctors could find no physical cause of the infection and were concerned that it might be the result of sexual abuse. An appointment was accordingly made for the child to be examined by the psychiatrist to ascertain whether the child had been sexually abused and, if she had, the identity of the abuser. The mother took the child to see the psychiatrist on 13 November 1987.

On that date the child was interviewed by the psychiatrist in the presence of the social worker but in the absence of the mother. The interview was recorded on videotape. During the session the social worker left the interview room and asked the mother for the names of her father, husband and boyfriend, which she gave.

It is pleaded that the social worker and/or the psychiatrist concluded that the child had been sexually abused and that the third plaintiff was the abuser. In fact the child did not identify the third plaintiff as the abuser but a cousin with the same first name as the third plaintiff who had previously lived at the mother's address. The child said that the abuser had left the mother's home and was not her mother's boyfriend. Had the psychiatrist and the social worker taken a full history of her mother's domestic circumstances or consulted the history the local authority already had or reviewed the child's evidence, they would have ascertained that the third plaintiff was not the abuser and that the abuser was no longer living at the mother's home. At the end of the interview the mother was told by the psychiatrist and the social worker that the child had been sexually abused and that the third plaintiff was the abuser. After the child's interview with the psychiatrist and the social worker the mother asked her privately if the third plaintiff had abused her. The child said he had not. The mother tried to tell the social worker of this denial, but he and the psychiatrist wrongly took this as an attempt to persuade the child to retract the allegation that they understood her to have made.

The psychiatrist and the social worker concluded that the mother would be unable to protect the child against further abuse by the third plaintiff and that she would put pressure on the child to retract her allegation against him and that it was necessary to remove the child from her mother's care. The mother was not asked if she was willing to require the third plaintiff to leave her home. On the same day, on the local authority's application, a place of safety order for 28 days was made by the Newham justices. The local authority's case was that the child had been sexually abused, that she had definitely identified the third plaintiff as the abuser and that there was a risk either of 'direct abuse' or that the mother or others would put pressure on the child to retract her allegation against the third plaintiff.

The mother excluded the third plaintiff and all other men from her home and on 24 November 1987 applied to Anthony Lincoln J for the child to be made a ward of court and for an order giving her care and control. The local authority attended the hearing and adduced evidence to support the same case which had been put to the justices and recommended to the judge that the child be made a ward of court, that it be granted care and control, that the child should not return home and that the mother's access be limited. The judge accepted the local authority's recommendation and made an order expressed to be by consent in the terms which it asked. He adjourned the matter until a date in December, his orders remaining in force until further order. The local authority accordingly placed the child with foster parents. She was approaching her fifth birthday. In December another judge continued the existing arrangements in force, although reducing the mother's access. Up to this time the mother had not seen the video recording or read the transcript of the interview with the child on 13 November 1987.

During these wardship proceedings the mother became pregnant again and another child (D) was born to her. The third plaintiff was the father. Having regard to the previous history involving the child, the local authority obtained an order that D also become a ward of court. In the course of these wardship proceedings the mother obtained sight of the transcript of the interview with the child on 13 November 1987. It was apparent from the transcript that the child had not identified the third plaintiff as the abuser and that there was no evidence to support that conclusion. The local authority was informed and shortly thereafter confirmed that it no longer suspected the third plaintiff of having sexually abused the child. On 21 November 1988 the local authority reported this to Anthony Lincoln J and recommended that the child be rehabilitated with her mother and the third plaintiff. The judge accepted the recommendation and made an order in accordance with it, which was put into effect at once. The child had been separated from the mother for almost a year. In November 1989, on the local authority's application, the wardship of both children was discharged.

The child and the mother plead many allegations of negligence against the defendants. The central allegation is that the defendants failed to investigate the facts with proper care and thoroughness and failed to discuss them with the mother.

The child and the mother complain that as a result of their enforced separation and the lack of information given to them each of them suffered a positive psychiatric disorder diagnosed as anxiety neurosis.

The child and the mother issued proceedings against the three defendants in November 1990. Their statement of claim was heavily amended in October 1992. On 19 November 1992 Master Topley struck out the amended statement of claim as disclosing no reasonable cause of action and as an abuse of the process of the court and dismissed the action. Judge Phelan ([1993] 2 FLR 575), sitting as a judge of the High Court in the Queen's Bench Division, dismissed the appeal of the child and the mother against that order on 17 March 1993. The child and the mother now challenge his decision.

X and ors (minors) v Bedfordshire County Council

The plaintiffs in this action are five children of the same parents who sue by the Official Solicitor as their next friend. The eldest child was born in October 1982 and the youngest in May 1990 so their ages now range between 11 and 3. There is only one defendant in this action, the county council, sued as the local authority responsible for social services in the area where the children and their parents lived. I shall call it 'the county council'.

The facts pleaded on behalf of the children in this action fall into various periods, which it is convenient to separate.

The first period may be said to run from November 1987 to December 1989 and largely concerns the first three children. During this period and before it reports about these children were made to the county council by or through relatives (including the children's grandmother), neighbours, the police, the family's general practitioner, the head teacher of the school which the two older children attended, the National Society for the Prevention of Cruelty to Children (the NSPCC), a social worker and a health visitor. The reports were to the effect that the children were at risk, including the risk of sexual abuse; that the children were locked out of the house for long periods of time with the oldest child (aged five) supervising the next two (aged three and two); that the third child was observed to have an abrasion which could have been caused by a cigarette burn; that the oldest child had been found to be pale, depressed, pathetic and possibly hungry; that the second and third children's bedroom had been observed to be squalid and to have faeces smeared on the wall; that the children's home was in a disgusting state, with the second and third children's beds sodden with urine; that the two older children attended school looking dishevelled and smelly; and that there was concern for the children's emotional well-being. In December 1989 the county council rejected a health visitor's recommendation that the first four children be placed on the Child Protection Register. No case conference was held.

The next period runs from March 1990 to January 1991. During this period it was reported to the county council that the two older children had been seen taking food out of school waste-bins; that the second and third children were still defecating in their bedroom and smearing the walls; that the second and third children were barricaded in their room for up to 14 hours; that they attended school dirty; that the conditions in the children's home had deteriorated further and had been described by the police as appalling and unfit for children; that the second and third children's bedroom was damp and smelly, one bed was broken, the bedding was damp and there was no lighting; and that the appearance of the first and third children was pathetic. A case conference was held in January 1991. It was decided not to place any of the children on the Child Protection Register and not to apply for any court orders.

In July 1991 (and again in May 1992) the children's father asked the county council to take the children into care for adoption. The county council took no action.

For nine days in August 1991 the three older children were placed on their mother's application with foster parents who found them dirty and underfed with poor personal hygiene.

In September 1991 the county council was told that the condition of the second and third children's bedroom had deteriorated; that the children were said to have been locked outside the family home and to have screamed constantly; that the children were left in their bedrooms for long periods and smeared faeces on the windows; and that the second, third and fourth children had been seen stealing food. No action was taken save that respite care was recommended to assist the mother. In November 1991 the mother asked the county council to accommodate the three older children. The county council offered her short-term respite care.

On their mother's application the three older children spent much of the early months of 1992 with foster parents. They gained in weight during this period. In March the county council considered the results of this foster placement. Respite care and monitoring were recommended. In April 1992 the mother asked the county council to remove the second and third children from her care and place them for adoption. In June 1992 the mother told the county council that if it did not remove the children from her care she would batter them. The county council agreed to accommodate the children and they were placed with foster parents.

On 22 June 1992 it was reported to the county council that the children had suffered from neglect and emotional abuse for some time. It was found that their behaviour and physical appearance had improved rapidly after they had been placed with foster parents. The children were placed on the Child Protection Register in the category covering neglect and emotional abuse. The county council took no steps to seek care orders but accepted that the children should not return to live with their parents.

In October 1992 the county council decided to seek care orders in respect of the children and took steps to that end. Interim care orders were made in December 1992 and final orders in April 1993.

The children complain that the county council should have acted more quickly and more effectively. As a result of the county council's failure they say that they suffered ill-treatment and illness, their proper development was neglected and their health was impaired.

The five children issued these proceedings in June 1993. The county council promptly applied to strike out the proceedings. This application was heard by Turner J ((1993) Times, 24 November), who granted it on 12 November 1993. The children appeal against his order.

Statutory duty

As one would expect, Parliament has over many years sought to curb the ill-treatment, neglect and exploitation of children. It was not, however, until 1932 that a duty was laid on local authorities in relation to juveniles in need of care and protection: s 9(4) of the Children and Young Persons Act 1932 obliged a local authority to bring such a juvenile before a juvenile court—

'unless ... they are satisfied that the taking of proceedings is undesirable in the interest of the child or young person ...'

This duty was in substance re-enacted in s 62(2) of the Children and Young Persons Act 1933. The Children Act 1948 elaborated this duty. By s 1 a duty was imposed on a local authority to receive a child into its care if it appeared to the authority (in effect) that the child had no parent or guardian willing or able to look after it and also that the intervention of the authority under the section was necessary in the interests of the welfare of the child. The Children and Young Persons (Amendment) Act 1952 further strengthened this regime of statutory protection. It supplemented s 62 of the 1933 Act by providing in s 2 and para 5 of the Schedule:

'... if a local authority receives information suggesting that any child or young person may be in need of care or protection it shall be the duty of the authority to cause enquiries to be made into the case unless they are satisfied that such enquiries are unnecessary.'

Section 1(1) of the Children and Young Persons Act 1963 was in terms which have since been re-enacted as s 1 of the Child Care Act 1980:

'It shall be the duty of every local authority to make available such advice, guidance and assistance as may promote the welfare of children by diminishing the need to receive children into or keep them in care ...'

The law was further amended by the Children and Young Persons Act 1969, which redefined the grounds on which care proceedings might be brought in a juvenile court. As before, local authorities were obliged to make inquiries if they received information suggesting that there were grounds for bringing care proceedings, unless they were satisfied such inquiries were unnecessary (s 2(1)). Section 2(2) provided :

> 'If it appears to a local authority that there are grounds for bringing care proceedings in respect of a child or young person who resides or is found in their area, it shall be the duty of the authority to exercise their power under the preceding section to bring care proceedings in respect of him unless they are satisfied that it is neither in his interest nor the public interest to do so or that some other person is about to do so or to charge him with an offence.'

The Child Care Act 1980 is the first statute directly in issue in this appeal. It was a consolidating Act. Section 1(1), as already noted, re-enacted s 1(1) of the 1963 Act. Section 2(1) can trace its lineage back to s 1 of the 1948 Act. It provides:

> '2.—(1) Where it appears to a local authority with respect to a child in their area appearing to them to be under the age of seventeen—(a) that he has neither parent nor guardian or has been and remains abandoned by his parents or guardian or is lost; or (b) that his parents or guardian are, for the time being or permanently, prevented by reason of mental or bodily disease or infirmity or other incapacity or any other circumstances from providing for his proper accommodation, maintenance and upbringing; and (c) in either case, that the intervention of the local authority under this section is necessary in the interests of the welfare of the child, it shall be the duty of the local authority to receive the child into their care under this section.'

Section 2(2) required a local authority which had received a child into its care under the section to keep the child in its care, subject to the provisions of the 1980 Act, so long as the welfare of the child appeared to it to require it. But this section did not permit a local authority to keep a child in its care against the wishes of any parent or guardian. Under s 3 a local authority could resolve that the parental rights and duties in relation to a child should vest in the authority, and on objection to the resolution by the party divested of parental rights and duties by the resolution it would be subject to review by a juvenile court. Section 76 of the 1980 Act empowered a Secretary of State to order an inquiry to be held into any matter relating to the functions of a local authority's social services committee, in so far as those functions related to children.

In the Newham case, it has not been suggested that any other or later legislation is relevant to our decision. The events pleaded in that case were complete before the Children Act 1989 came into force on 14 October 1991. But the 1989 Act was in force during the last months of the history of the Bedfordshire case.

It is not necessary or practicable to attempt any comprehensive summary of the Children Act 1989. Germane to the issue in the Bedfordshire appeal is s 17, which provides:

> 'Provision of services for children in need, their families and others.—(1) It shall be the general duty of every local authority (in addition to the other duties imposed on them by this Part)—(a) to safeguard and promote the welfare of children within their area who are in need; and (b) so far as is consistent with that duty, to promote the upbringing of such children by

their families, by providing a range and level of services appropriate to those children's needs.

(2) For the purpose principally of facilitating the discharge of their general duty under this section, every local authority shall have the specific duties and powers set out in Part 1 of Schedule 2 ...

(10) For the purposes of this Part a child shall be taken to be in need if—(a) he is unlikely to achieve or maintain, or to have the opportunity of achieving or maintaining, a reasonable standard of health or development without the provision for him of services by a local authority under this Part; (b) his health or development is likely to be significantly impaired, or further impaired, without the provision for him of such services; or (c) he is disabled ...

(11) ... in this Part—"development" means physical, intellectual, emotional, social or behavioural development; and "health" means physical or mental health.'

In Pt I of Sch 2 to the 1989 Act the Bedfordshire plaintiffs rely on para 4:

'(1) Every local authority shall take reasonable steps, through the provision of services under Part III of this Act, to prevent children within their area suffering ill-treatment or neglect.'

Part III of the 1989 Act deals with local authority support for children and families. The policy of the 1989 Act is, however, made clear by para 7 of Pt I of Sch 2, which requires local authorities to take reasonable steps designed to reduce the need to bring proceedings relating to children.

Section 20 of the 1989 Act provides:

'(1) Every local authority shall provide accommodation for any child in need within their area who appears to them to require accommodation as a result of—(a) there being no person who has parental responsibility for him; (b) his being lost or having been abandoned; or (c) the person who has been caring for him being prevented (whether or not permanently, and for whatever reason) from providing him with suitable accommodation or care ...

(4) A local authority may provide accommodation for any child within their area (even though a person who has parental responsibility for him is able to provide him with accommodation) if they consider that to do so would safeguard or promote the child's welfare.'

Where a child is in the care of a local authority or provided with accommodation by it, duties are imposed on the local authority by ss 22, 23 and 24.

Part V of the 1989 Act is entitled 'Protection of Children'. Most relevant for present purposes is s 47(1) and (8):

'(1) Where a local authority ... (b) have reasonable cause to suspect that a child who lives, or is found, in their area is suffering, or is likely to suffer, significant harm, the authority shall make, or cause to be made, such enquiries as they consider necessary to enable them to decide whether they should take any action to safeguard or promote the child's welfare ...

(8) Where, as a result of complying with this section, a local authority conclude that they should take action to safeguard or promote the child's

welfare they shall take that action (so far as it is both within their power and reasonably practicable for them to do so).'

One of the steps a local authority may take to safeguard or promote a child's welfare is to apply under s 31(1) of the 1989 Act for the child to be placed in its care or under its supervision.

The 1989 Act requires every local authority to establish a procedure for considering representations and complaints by children whom it is looking after or children in need whom it is not looking after or their parents or other interested parties (s 26(3)). It also empowers the Secretary of State to order inquiries (s 81) and to require local authorities to comply with their statutory duty (s 84).

The courts are very regularly called upon to consider whether the imposition of a duty by a particular statute impliedly gives a right of action to a person injured by reason of a breach of that duty. I myself share the regret voiced by Lord du Parcq in *Cutler v Wandsworth Stadium Ltd (in liq)* [1949] 1 All ER 544 at 549, [1949] AC 398 at 410:

> 'Parliament has not by now made it a rule to state explicitly what its intention is in a matter which is often of no little importance, instead of leaving it to the courts to discover, by a careful examination and analysis of what is expressly said, what that intention may be supposed probably to be.'

But the proper approach of the courts to their task of examination and analysis has been clearly and authoritatively laid down, and has not been the subject of debate before us. The governing principles were very helpfully summarised by Lord Jauncey in *Hague v Deputy Governor of Parkhurst Prison, Weldon v Home Office* [1991] 3 All ER 733 at 748–750, [1992] 1 AC 58 at 168–171 and we must apply them.

It is very clear, from the statutes to which brief reference has been made and other statutes not mentioned, that protection of the interests and welfare of children has for many years been a prime object of parliamentary concern. The framework of protection has been developed and refined over the years. Local authorities have increasingly become the primary instrument for giving effect to the intentions of Parliament. To that end, and no doubt in recognition of the very sensitive and difficult questions which are bound to arise, the responsibility for judging what ought or ought not to be done in the case of any given child is in the first instance entrusted to them. There can in this case be no doubt about the class for whose protection the legislation was enacted. Nor can there be doubt about Parliament's intention that the duties imposed upon local authorities should (despite all the inherent difficulties) be competently and conscientiously performed. But I can detect nothing in any of the legislation which persuades me that Parliament intended to confer a right of action on any person who could show, without more, a breach of any of these statutory duties injurious to him. It seems to me fatal to the plaintiffs' contentions (1) that the duties imposed on local authorities were framed in terms too general and unparticular to lend themselves at all readily to direct enforcement by individuals and (2) that the local authorities were accorded so large an area for the exercise of their subjective judgment as to suggest that direct enforcement by individuals was not contemplated. I accordingly agree with both judges that the respective statements of claim disclose no reasonable cause of action for breach of statutory duty and the plaintiffs' claims on that ground were properly struck out.

Common law duty of care

Counsel for the plaintiff children in both actions and the mother in the Newham action invited the court to regard these claims as simple and straightforward applications of principles laid down in authorities such as *Donoghue v Stevenson* [1932] AC 562, [1932] All ER Rep 1, *Saif Ali v Sydney Mitchell & Co (a firm) (P, third party)* [1978] 3 All ER 1033, [1980] AC 198 and *Sidaway v Bethlem Royal Hospital Governors* [1985] 1 All ER 643, [1985] AC 871. The psychiatrist (for whom the health authority were liable) and the social workers in both cases (for whom the local authority and the county council respectively were liable) were persons exercising a professional skill. The child and the mother in the Newham case were patients of the psychiatrist and clients of the social worker. The children in the Bedfordshire case were clients of the county council's social workers. In each case the children and (in the Newham case) the mother were individuals foreseeably likely to be injured by careless acts or omissions on the part of the psychiatrist and the social workers. To find a duty of care in such circumstances involved no incremental extension of existing principles but a conventional application of them.

For the defendants in both actions this attractively simple approach was resisted. It was pointed out that there was no precedent for a successful claim in circumstances such as those before us. It was accordingly necessary for all the plaintiffs to establish not only that injury to them was reasonably foreseeable by the various defendants as a consequence of carelessness on their part and that their relationship with the various defendants had the necessary quality of proximity but also that it was in all the circumstances just and reasonable in the public interest to impose a duty of care. Counsel for the various defendants did not strongly resist the suggestion that carelessness on the defendants' part was foreseeably likely to cause injury to the various plaintiffs. But they did contend that the necessary proximity of relationship was lacking; they did contend that the plaintiffs showed no arguable case on causation; they did contend that the injury suffered was not such as to support a claim for damages; and they advanced a large number of reasons, of law and policy, why a duty of care could not and should not be held to exist in circumstances such as the present. If, contrary to their primary submission, any extension of established principles was here involved, the plaintiffs argued that it was just and reasonable in all the circumstances to impose a duty of care.

I do not think that the facts of these cases are covered by existing authority. The relationship between the child and the mother and the psychiatrist was not on any showing a typical doctor-patient relationship. I am not aware of any previous litigated claim by parent or child against a social worker, and this again cannot be seen as a typical relationship between client and professional person. It is accordingly necessary, in my opinion, to examine the various relationships involved in these cases in a little detail, bearing in mind the principles laid down in recent House of Lords and Privy Council authorities such as *Yuen Kun-yeu v A-G of Hong Kong* [1987] 2 All ER 705, [1988] AC 175, *Rowling v Takaro Properties Ltd* [1988] 1 All ER 163, [1988] AC 473, *Hill v Chief Constable of West Yorkshire* [1988] 2 All ER 238, [1989] AC 53, *Caparo Industries plc v Dickman* [1990] 1 All ER 568, [1990] 2 AC 605 and *Murphy v Brentwood DC* [1990] 2 All ER 908, [1991] 1 AC 398.

The child and the psychiatrist

a   Although the mother took the child to see the psychiatrist, she did not herself seek or instigate the consultation and the psychiatrist was plainly engaged to advise the local authority, not the child or the mother on behalf of the child. It was not therefore a normal doctor-patient relationship.

It is on the other hand clear that the relationship between the psychiatrist b and the child was very direct and personal. The psychiatrist interviewed the child, it would seem at some length. She would have foreseen that if as a result of her questioning she reached erroneous conclusions and if, basing herself on erroneous conclusions, she gave unsound advice, the child was liable to suffer, whether she remained at home to undergo further abuse (if she had suffered abuse) or by separation from her mother (if she had not suffered abuse or was c not likely to continue to do so). She would have recognised the welfare of the child as her paramount concern, not as a matter of legal obligation but of medical duty. Counsel for the health authority and the psychiatrist accepted that the child was the psychiatrist's patient for some purposes, such as confidentiality, but said it was a doctor-patient relationship of a special kind. I d agree; but the child was the psychiatrist's patient in the sense that it was for the child alone that the psychiatrist was (as she knew) being invited to exercise her professional skill and judgment. That would ordinarily lead to the conclusion that the psychiatrist owed the child a duty of care, in the absence of reasons why such a conclusion should not follow, and I am not surprised that in the court below the existence of a duty of care was conceded.

e   It was very strongly urged that this conclusion should not follow because the psychiatrist was entitled to a witness's immunity from actions for negligence. It was accepted that the child's claim did not relate in any way to any evidence the psychiatrist gave in court (because she never gave any), nor to any proof of evidence that the psychiatrist may have provided. But it was said that when f interviewing the child and expressing her conclusions and advising on future action she will have known that, if she concluded that there had been abuse and that the abuser was living with the mother and that separation was desirable, there were likely to be proceedings in which she would be a witness. Accordingly she was entitled to the immunity which the law, on grounds of public policy, affords to those who give or offer or prepare to give evidence in g court. This argument was founded on *Watson v M'Ewan, Watson v Jones* [1905] AC 480, [1904–7] All ER Rep 1, *Marrinan v Vibart* [1962] 1 All ER 869, [1963] 1 QB 234; *affd* [1962] 3 All ER 380, [1963] 1 QB 528, *Saif Ali v Sydney Mitchell & Co (a firm)* (*P, third party*) [1978] 3 All ER 1033, [1980] AC 198 and *Evans v London Hospital Medical College* [1981] 1 All ER 715, [1981] 1 WLR 184.

h   Insofar as this immunity argument rests on a factual inference about the psychiatrist's state of mind, I accept it. The psychiatrist must, I am sure, have appreciated that (depending on her findings and advice) there might very well be court proceedings in which she would be a witness. But there is nothing in *Watson v M'Ewan, Marrinan v Vibart* and *Saif Ali v Sydney Mitchell* to suggest that j a witness is immune from suit in such circumstances. The public interest which these authorities recognise and protect is the proper administration of justice: to that end witnesses must be immune from civil action arising from what they say in court; and that protection must not be circumvented by allowing civil actions based on the earlier stages of preparation of a witness's evidence. But the cases do not indicate that those who have never become involved in the administration of justice at all enjoy immunity. The immunity

of a witness has in the past been treated as analogous to the immunity accorded
to those involved in the conduct of proceedings, and were the immunity as
wide as was claimed, a barrister or a solicitor advising a client whether to
proceed, or an expert advising a client on a factual question with a view to
proceedings, would be immune from actions for negligence: such a result is
however clearly inconsistent with the authority cited. In my opinion Mr
Simon Tuckey QC reached a correct conclusion in *Palmer v Durnford Ford (a
firm)* [1992] 2 All ER 122, [1992] QB 483 and I do not think that case is legally
distinguishable from the present. If that decision cannot be reconciled with the
decision of Drake J in *Evans v London Hospital Medical College* I consider the
former to be more strictly in accord with binding authority. Both Master
Topley and Judge Phelan upheld the defendants' argument on witness
immunity, but I cannot accept that the scope of that immunity is such as to
afford protection in this case.

Imposition of a duty of care on doctors in this context was strongly resisted
on grounds of public policy. Stress was laid on the very difficult, delicate and
judgmental nature of the doctor's task. The imposition of a duty of care would
have adverse practical consequences, causing doctors to act defensively and
indecisively and distracting their attention from the task in hand. It would not
contribute to the maintenance of high standards. It would undermine the
inter-disciplinary co-operation which cases such as the child's demand if some
of those involved were liable in negligence and some were not, and if all were
liable it would make for complex claims, cross-claims and claims for
contribution. It would raise very difficult problems of confidentiality. It
would be very unsatisfactory if claims involving children, perhaps very young
children, could be prosecuted at any time until the children reached the age of
21. Money is not an appropriate remedy.

I see very considerable force in some of these points but they do not in the
end persuade me that it would be just and reasonable on these grounds to deny
a right of action to a child foreseeably injured by an act or omission of a doctor
in circumstances such as the present if it was an act or omission of which no
ordinarily careful and competent member of the medical profession could have
been guilty. I give my reasons briefly.

(1) The extreme difficulty and delicacy of the doctor's task in this context,
and the highly judgmental nature of it, are very relevant. They present any
plaintiff with a formidable task. As always, it will not be enough to show an
error of judgment, or to show that other well-qualified members of the
profession would have taken a different view. It would have to be shown that
the doctor's opinion or conduct fell outside the bounds sanctioned by any
responsible body of professional opinion. It can be assumed that few claims
would succeed.

(2) A doctor's duty in this as in every other professional situation is to
ascertain the facts as best he can, to form the best judgment he can and to give
the soundest advice he can, couching his advice in terms appropriate to the
judgment he has formed. I do not see why a doctor's performance of this duty
in the present context would be inhibited by knowledge that he might be held
liable to a child. He might no doubt be anxious to be as sure as possible before
expressing any opinion, and would be careful to express no opinion stronger
than the facts in his judgment warranted, but both these results are to be
encouraged. I do not think he would be deterred from prompt action where

a the facts appeared to warrant it, since he would be as vulnerable to criticism for failing to advise urgent action when the facts appeared to call for it as for acting precipitately when the facts did not.   The doctor's only certain protection would be sound performance of his professional duty, and that is how it should be.

b (3) I cannot accept, as a general proposition, that the imposition of a duty of care makes no contribution to the maintenance of high standards.   The common belief that the imposition of such a duty may lead to overkill is not easily reconciled with the suggestion that it has no effect.

c (4) I am here concerned with the position of the psychiatrist, who was in a special and direct relationship with the child.   I consider the position of the social workers below.   It by no means follows that if a doctor is subject to a duty the same is true of a policeman, a teacher or a health visitor.   Those relationships must be considered when and if they are in issue.   The potential complexity of litigation is not of itself a ground for denying relief.

d (5) I can well understand that doctors would prefer children and their parents not to see notes and records which they have made of any interview conducted, opinion formed or advice given.   But I see no reason to suppose that difficulties would arise different in kind from those with which the courts are familiar, and which they have developed means to overcome and control (see *D v National Society for the Prevention of Cruelty to Children* [1977] 1 All ER 589, [1978] AC 171, *Science Research Council v Nassé, BL Cars Ltd (formerly Leyland Cars) v Vyas* [1979] 3 All ER 673, [1980] AC 1028 and *Re M (a minor) (disclosure of material)* [1990] 2 FLR 36).

e (6) Limitation periods have been the subject of much consideration and repeated legislation in recent years.   The will of Parliament, reflected in statute, is that minors should be able, on reaching the age of majority, to complain of wrongs done to them before that time.   If the courts were to deny children a right of action which they would otherwise grant on the ground that such delayed litigation would be contrary to public policy, they would in my view be substituting their own view of public policy, quite impermissibly, for that of Parliament.

f (7) It is not suggested that the child could obtain, or ever could have obtained, any redress of any kind against the psychiatrist save by bringing this action.   If she can make good her complaints (a vital condition, which I forbear constantly to repeat), it would require very potent considerations of public policy, which do not in my view exist here, to override the rule of public policy which has first claim on the loyalty of the law: that wrongs should be remedied.

g (8) I agree that money is an inadequate remedy for the injury which the child claims to have suffered.   So it is for the loss of a leg, or an eye, or a life. But it is usually the best the law can do.   If plaintiffs do not want financial recompense they need not claim.   It may be assumed that those representing the child regard it as better than nothing.   It is not for the courts to refuse the only remedy they can give on the ground that plaintiffs are better without it.

j It was argued that even on the basis of the facts pleaded, the psychiatrist's acts and omissions were not the cause of the child's alleged injury, since her separation was the result of orders made by the justices and the judge which necessarily broke the chain of causation.   I cannot accept this as a proposition of law.   Causation is a question of fact.   In some cases a court order may break

the chain of causation, as Balcombe LJ judged to be so in *Re Manda* [1993] 1 All
ER 733 at 743, [1993] Fam 183 at 196. In others it may not, as it did not in *Hart*   a
v John Frame Son & Co (1839) 6 Cl & Fin 193, 7 ER 670 and *Roy v Prior* [1970] 2
All ER 729, [1971] AC 470. I cannot think Balcombe LJ intended to lay down a
rule of law. In this case it might be open to the court to hold that the causative
effect of the psychiatrist's conduct did not end with the making of the court
orders. That possibility is enough to make it improper to strike out.   b

It was argued that the psychiatric disorder suffered by the child was not
damage which the law would recognise as founding a claim for damages in
common law negligence. This submission was based on the speech of Lord
Ackner in *Alcock v Chief Constable of the South Yorkshire Police* [1991] 4 All ER 907
at 917, [1992] 1 AC 310 at 400. Authoritative though that statement is, I   c
question whether it can be held to preclude a claim by the child for psychiatric
disorder in present circumstances if that claim is otherwise soundly based. I
give three reasons. (1) Lord Ackner acknowledged in the passage relied on
that future development of the law was to be expected and in *McLoughlin v
O'Brian* [1982] 2 All ER 298 at 320, [1983] 1 AC 410 at 443 Lord Bridge had
warned against the temptation of seeking to freeze the law in a rigid posture.   d
The recent work by Mullany and Handford *Tort Liability for Psychiatric Damage*
(1993) p 202ff suggests some diversity of approach among the major common
law jurisdictions, and it seems unlikely that the last word has been said in this
difficult and contentious area. (2) The problem with which the courts were
attempting to grapple in the 'nervous shock' cases was one of demarcation: e
how to afford redress to those most directly exposed to a calamity without
opening the door to claims by plaintiffs ever more remote from and ever more
distantly related to the victims of the calamity. That is not a problem which
arises in relation to this claim by the child. (3) The child and the mother are
not claiming damages for grief and distress, but for what is said to be a positive
psychiatric illness (see *McLoughlin v O'Brian* [1982] 2 All ER 298 at 311, [1983] 1   f
AC 410 at 431). (4) It would be little short of absurd if the child were held to
be disentitled to claim damages for injury of the very type which the
psychiatrist should have been exercising her skill to try and prevent.

Since the end of the hearing my attention has been drawn to *Everett (pauper)
v Griffiths* [1920] 3 KB 163, a case which was not cited in argument and is not   g
directly in point but which in my view fortifies the conclusions I have reached.
A plaintiff acting in person sued two defendants. The first had signed an order
under the Lunacy Act 1890 for the plaintiff's reception into an asylum as a
pauper lunatic. The second was a medical practitioner on whose certificate the
first defendant had relied. The plaintiff alleged a want of care against each and   h
claimed damages. At the trial a special jury could not agree whether the
defendants had acted with reasonable care, but Lord Reading CJ entered
judgment for the first defendant on the basis that he was immune from suit, as
acting in a judicial capacity, and for the medical practitioner on the grounds
that the cause of the detention was the first defendant's order and not the
medical certificate.   j

The plaintiff's appeal was unsuccessful, but I think, although much turns in
the judgments on the statute in question, that his appeal against the medical
practitioner would in principle succeed today. Scrutton LJ, it is true, held that
the practitioner incurred no legal liability to the person examined as there was
no legal relation between them (see [1920] 3 KB 163 at 195). But Bankes LJ held

that there was a duty to exercise reasonable care in making the examination because—

> 'in a matter of such importance I cannot think that the Legislature could have contemplated any other examination than one conducted with such care as under the circumstances of each case would come up to the standard of what was reasonable.' (See [1920] 3 KB 163 at 184.)

It was, however, doubtful in his view whether the practitioner owed a duty to exercise reasonable skill as well as reasonable care. Atkin LJ, in an eloquent dissenting judgment, felt no doubt (at 216):

> 'Quite apart from general considerations, it appears to me that there was in this case the special relation of doctor and patient between this defendant and the plaintiff, which establishes a duty owed to the plaintiff to take reasonable care in certifying him. I think, moreover, that the duty is not merely a duty to take reasonable care in making inquiries, that is, in ascertaining the necessary data, but includes a duty to exercise reasonable professional skill in forming a conclusion from such data. For what other purpose is a certificate from a medical practitioner required at all?'

I find this judgment persuasive.

The plaintiff failed in his appeal against the first defendant on the ground that he had been honestly satisfied that the plaintiff was a lunatic and a person properly to be detained and that it was therefore immaterial whether or not he had used reasonable care in arriving at his decision. But Atkin LJ dissented on this aspect also, holding that the first defendant also had been bound to take reasonable care to satisfy himself that the plaintiff was a lunatic before signing the order.

The plaintiff appealed to the House of Lords ([1921] 1 AC 631), which unanimously held that the first defendant was immune from liability on the ground favoured by the majority of the Court of Appeal. The House also held, unanimously, that there was no evidence of negligence by the medical practitioner to leave to the jury. The question whether he owed the plaintiff a duty of care was accordingly not argued. Their Lordships were content to assume the existence of a duty without deciding the question, but Viscount Haldane thought it—

> 'probable that if the matter were argued out [the medical practitioner] would be found to have been under a duty to the [plaintiff] to exercise care ...' (See [1921] 1 AC 631 at 657.)

Although I conclude that the child's claim against the psychiatrist should not be struck out as bad in law, I have the gravest doubt whether it can succeed on the facts. It is not said that the psychiatrist's diagnosis of sexual abuse was at fault, and the interview is said to have been skilfully conducted. I question the extent to which she was involved in verifying the family history. If this claim were to proceed, I would invite those acting for the child to review this claim with particular care once discovery is complete.

The mother and the psychiatrist

The psychiatrist would in my view have recognised the mother as someone foreseeably likely to be injured if, as a result of her advice, the child were to be taken away from the mother. But the mother was not in any meaningful sense the psychiatrist's patient. The psychiatrist's duty was to act in the interests of the child, and that might very well mean acting in a way that would be adverse to the personal interests of the mother; she was concerned with those interests only to the extent that they could have an impact on the interests of the child. In this situation of potential conflict, I do not think the psychiatrist can arguably be said to have owed a duty of care to the mother, whose claim it was accordingly right to strike out. The mother accepted, although reserving the point for argument in the House of Lords, that there is no independent tort of interference with parental rights, as held by this court in *F v Wirral Metropolitan BC* [1991] 2 All ER 648, [1991] Fam 69, but it does not seem to me that the mother is seeking to put her case in that way. I reach the same conclusion as Master Topley and Judge Phelan but would not base my decision on this ground.

The child and the local authority

Those who engage professionally in social work bring to their task skill and expertise, the product partly of training and partly of experience, which ordinary uninstructed members of the public are bound to lack. I have no doubt that they should be regarded as members of a skilled profession. Their task is one of immense difficulty, and frequently they are exposed to unjust criticism; but both those things may, to a greater or lesser extent, be said of other professionals also.

In considering the legal relationship between the child and the local authority, much of what I have said above concerning the child's relationship with the psychiatrist is in my view equally applicable. I will not repeat the conclusions already expressed about foreseeability, proximity, witness immunity, public policy, causation and damage, which mutatis mutandis apply in this context also. But a number of additional points arise for consideration.

It was argued that since, as I have accepted, Parliament has omitted to impose on local authorities a specific statutory duty, breach of which will entitle an injured party to recover damages, the courts should not themselves step in to impose such a duty. If there were any indication that Parliament intended no such duty to be imposed, I would agree. But I find no such indication. Parliament's omission is to my mind more readily explained by the extreme difficulty of adequately defining and circumscribing such a duty in a general provision; I can see no reason to suppose Parliament would have wished to deny the child a claim against the local authority on the detailed (if assumed) facts of this particular case. Had it wished to do so it could have adopted some such formula as is found in s 1(4) of the Banking Act 1987:

> 'Neither the Bank nor any person who is a member of its Court of Directors or who is, or is acting as, an officer or servant of the Bank shall be liable in damages for anything done or omitted in the discharge or purported discharge of the functions of the Bank under this Act unless it is shown that the act or omission was in bad faith.'

A less far-reaching variant of this provision, which has been in force at least since 1890, is now to be found in s 139(1) and (2) of the Mental Health Act 1983 :

> '*Protection for acts done in pursuance of this Act.*—(1) No person shall be liable, whether on the ground of want of jurisdiction or on any other ground, to any civil or criminal proceedings to which he would have been

a   liable apart from this section in respect of any act purporting to be done in pursuance of this Act or any regulations or rules made under this Act, or in, or in pursuance of anything done in, the discharge of functions conferred by any other enactment on the authority having jurisdiction under Pt VII of this Act, unless the act was done in bad faith or without reasonable care.

b   (2) No civil proceedings shall be brought against any person in any court in respect of any such act without the leave of the High Court; and no criminal proceedings shall be brought against any person in any court in respect of any such act except by or with the consent of the Director of Public Prosecutions.'

c
It is hard to suppose that Parliament did not envisage the possibility of claims by plaintiffs complaining that they were wrongly taken, or not taken, into care. Nothing, so far as I can see, was done to curb or preclude such claims. Nor, although much reliance was placed on the authority in argument, do I read *A v Liverpool City Council* [1981] 2 All ER 385, [1982] AC 363 as bearing on this
d   question.

The local authority argued that the child's claim against it was a public law claim which could be pursued only by seeking judicial review. This is not on the facts a very attractive argument. On the material available to the mother, it seems unlikely she could have obtained leave to move. Had she done so, she
e   would have been very unlikely to succeed without access to the transcript or knowledge of what it said, and the judge's order stood in her way. By the time she had the transcript she would have been out of time and had no need of a remedy anyway. But I think the argument is also bad in law. The child is seeking to enforce a private law claim for damages. She is not seeking to impugn the legal validity of any public law act of the local authority. If she can
f   show that the local authority owed her a duty of care, I see no reason why she should not pursue her claim as she has (see *Davy v Spelthorne BC* [1983] 3 All ER 278, [1984] AC 262 and *Roy v Kensington and Chelsea and Westminster Family Practitioner Committee* [1992] 1 All ER 705, [1992] 1 AC 624). I do not on this point share the view of the judge below. Nor was I impressed by the
g   supplementary submission that the child should be confined to a complaint to the local government ombudsman or the Criminal Injuries Compensation Board.

One argument on public policy was addressed to us which seemed to have more relevance to the local authority than to the health authority and the
h   psychiatrist. If a duty of care were imposed on the local authority, and claims such as the child's were permitted to continue, the already overstretched resources of local authorities, human and financial, would be diverted from the valuable purpose of looking after children and wasted on the sterile processes of litigation. One must accept that this must, to a greater or lesser extent, be
j   so, and a somewhat similar argument found favour in *Hill v Chief Constable of West Yorkshire* [1988] 2 All ER 238 at 244, [1989] AC 53 at 63. But this is an argument frequently (and not implausibly) advanced on behalf of doctors; it has not prevailed. Other professions resist liability on the ground that it will in the end increase the cost to the paying customer; that resistance has not on the whole been effective either. Save in clear cases, it is not for the courts to decide how public money is best spent nor to balance the risk that money will be

wasted on litigation against the hope that the possibility of suit may contribute
towards the maintenance of the highest standards.

The mother and the local authority

I do not think the mother's claim against the local authority is legally
distinguishable from her claim against the psychiatrist. It must suffer the same
fate.

The children and the county council

The responsible officers of the county council must, I think, have foreseen
that the children were liable to suffer damage or injury if their cases were
carelessly handled and evaluated. Their relationship with the children was less
proximate than that of the social worker and the psychiatrist with the child in
the Newham case, inasmuch as no direct contact between the county council
and the children is pleaded, but in the language used by Megarry V-C in *Ross v
Caunters (a firm)* [1979] 3 All ER 580 at 587, [1980] Ch 297 at 308 it can fairly be
said that their contemplation of the children was 'actual, nominate and direct'.
It is true of course that the children complain against the county council
because they were wrongly *not* taken into care whereas the child claims against
the psychiatrist and the local authority because she was: this may make the
children's task even harder, but it cannot bear on the existence or
non-existence of a duty of care. It was suggested that the county council could
not be under a duty to protect the children against harm caused by third parties
(their parents), and that the county council could not be held liable for its
omissions. But if the county council owed the children any duty, as I think it
did, such duty must have embraced a duty to take reasonable care to protect
the children against sources of harm of which (on the facts pleaded) the county
council was very well aware by taking such steps (if any) as were justified to
move the children out of harm's way. Any other conclusion would be an
affront to common sense.

The particulars of injury pleaded on behalf of the children were criticised on
the same grounds as in the Newham action. There may well be doubt whether
the claims on behalf of the two younger children are sustainable in law. But I
think the claims pleaded on behalf of the three older children allege psychiatric
disorder and also physical injury. I would not strike out any of these claims.

The public law argument was put a little differently in this case. It was
pointed out that if the county council could be shown to be blatantly ignoring
its statutory duties, it would have been open to the children to seek an order of
mandamus to compel compliance. That is theoretically correct. But the
children's parents would not have been likely to move the court on their
behalf. The NSPCC, a good neighbour or the Official Solicitor (if approached)
might no doubt have done so, but this did not happen and the Official Solicitor
was not approached until later. There must be a probability that the most
vulnerable will be the least able to invoke the protection of the law. I do not
think the theoretical availability of a public law remedy deprives the children
of their right to pursue a private law claim, nor do I think it supports the
inference that Parliament intended there to be no such private law claim.

The provision under the Children Act 1989 of a procedure for entertaining
complaints and representations (described by this court in *R v Brent London BC,
ex p Sawyer* [1993] CA Transcript 1392 as 'relatively speedy and inexpensive')
causes one to consider whether that procedure was intended to preclude any

claim by private action. I cannot think so. It provides a valuable means of trying to ensure that errors are not made and abuses are corrected, but it should not in my view deprive a person of his ordinary right to sue for damages.

I would for my part allow the appeals of the child and the children insofar as they rely on alleged breaches of a common law duty of care.

STAUGHTON LJ. The critical questions in these two appeals are in my opinion only two in number. (1) Did the local authority, in each case, owe a statutory duty to the various plaintiffs which is enforceable by a claim for damages in private law? (2) Did the various defendants owe a duty of care to the plaintiffs at common law, so that damages can be awarded for breach?

Of the other questions argued before us, (3) I do not accept the submission (which appealed to Judge Phelan ([1993] 2 FLR 575) and Master Topley) that the defendants in the Newham case can rely on witness immunity as an answer to the claim against them. My reasons for that conclusion are the same as those given by Sir Thomas Bingham MR.

As to (4), causation, I would have held that this raised issues of fact in the Newham case which must go for trial. It must be a possible view of the facts that the conduct of the psychiatrist and the social worker was the cause of the year's separation between mother and daughter. It cannot be said as a matter of law that the orders of the Newham justices and the judge of the Family Division must necessarily be regarded as the cause of the separation.

Finally there is the issue (5), whether the nature of the harm said to have been suffered by the various plaintiffs is excluded from compensation on the ground that it was not the result of any sudden occurrence. On that question it is unnecessary, in the event, for me to express an opinion and I prefer not to do so.

(1)   A private law claim for breach of statutory duty

There is a great mass of authority on the question whether a statute, when it imposes a duty, also creates a right to damages in private law for breach of that duty. A useful anthology is to be found in the speech of Lord Jauncey of Tullichettle in *Hague v Deputy Governor of Parkhurst Prison, Weldon v Home Office* [1991] 3 All ER 733 at 748–750, [1992] 1 AC 58 at 168–171. The fact that no other remedy is provided is an indication that there may be a right to damages for breach, but is not conclusive.

It must always be a matter for consideration whether the legislature intended that private law rights of action should be conferred upon individuals in respect of breaches of the relevant statutory provision. The fact that a particular provision was intended to protect certain individuals is not of itself sufficient to confer private law rights of action upon them; something more is required to show that the legislature intended such conferment.

When we speak of the intention of Parliament we may often mean, in effect, the intention of the government department which sponsored a Bill, or of the parliamentary draftsman who wrote it, or of members who prepared amendments. But in any case it is an objective assessment, founded on the language of the statute and the terms of its other provisions, and on an assessment of the reasons which would have motivated the legislature to confer, or not to confer, a right to damages for breach.

In *Cutler v Wandsworth Stadium Ltd (in liq)* [1949] 1 All ER 544 at 549, [1949] AC 398 at 410 Lord du Parcq said:

> 'To a person unversed in the science, or art, of legislation it may well seem strange that Parliament has not by now made it a rule to state explicitly what its intention is ... There are, no doubt, reasons which inhibit the legislature from revealing its intention in plain words. I do not know, and must not speculate, what those reasons may be.'

One can, I think, legitimately infer that it might have been politically embarrassing to insert in the Children Act 1989 a section reading 'No local authority shall be liable to a child for negligence in performing its duties under this Act, or in failing to do so'. Some members might have hesitated to vote for so explicit a disclaimer. Would there have been embarrassment and hesitation if instead the section had said that the local authority *was* to be liable? One cannot tell, as Lord du Parcq implied, and must not speculate.

For a number of reasons which I shall consider later, it would appear that in recent times there has been some slight hardening of the courts' approach, against finding a remedy in damages for breach of statutory duty. Thus in *R v Inner London Education Authority, ex p Ali* (1990) 2 Admin LR 822 at 830–831 Woolf LJ in the Divisional Court expressly indorsed the following passage in the judgment of Simon Brown J in *R v Mid-Glamorgan CC, ex p Greig* (1988) Independent, 1 June:

> 'As it seems to me, by no means all breaches of statutory duty by public authorities give rise to any private law claim whatever, irrespective of whether the relevant statute contains default provisions. In my judgment it is only in certain exceptional and well-recognized circumstances that someone, even if particularly damnified by an authority's non-compliance with a statutory duty, can claim damages for such breach.'

That was again indorsed by Otton J in another case, *E (a minor) v Dorset CC* (7 April 1983, unreported).

There may be a number of reasons for the trend against enforcement in private law, if such it be. It is of course no new phenomenon that statutes enact duties on public officials which may impinge on the lives of every citizen. That happens in education, in the health service, and in child care itself since 1889. But it can certainly be said that there has been no decrease in the process. By contrast it has, in recent times, become all too clear that the private enforcement of civil rights is only available on a somewhat capricious basis. Disregarding corporate plaintiffs, only the very rich or the very poor among private individuals can afford to bring a civil action. It is unlikely that Parliament is primarily concerned with enforcement only by those two classes when it enacts legislation.

There are, of course, means of enforcement other than a civil suit when a duty is enacted by statute. Take for example s 17(1) of the 1989 Act: 'It shall be the general duty of every local authority ... (a) to safeguard and promote the welfare of children within their area who are in need ...' In the first place, the members and employees of a local authority will know of that section; it is to be hoped that they will enforce it upon themselves. Secondly, if they do not, the Secretary of State or members of Parliament or the National Society for the Prevention of Cruelty to Children can draw their attention to the duty and any specific need for it to be observed. Newspapers can do the same; and there is the sanction of severe criticism by the press or a public inquiry when an error is made. There is the local government ombudsman. There are also the remedies of public law. These are invoked, for example, in relation to statements under s 7 of the Education Act 1981, which deal with the special educational needs of particular children. Finally the 1989 Act itself contains its own remedies. Section 26(3) provides that every local authority shall establish a procedure for considering representations and complaints. By s 84 the Secretary of State may declare a local authority to be in default if it has failed to comply with any duty under the 1989 Act, and give directions to ensure compliance.

I bear in mind that the cause of action in the Newham case is said to have arisen in 1987 and 1988, before the 1989 Act was passed; and that the Bedfordshire case covers a period before and after it came into force in October 1991. For that very reason counsel for Bedfordshire did not rely on alternative remedies in the statute. Nevertheless it is, as it seems to me, open to serious question whether Parliament ever envisaged that the various statutes with which we are concerned would be enforced by a private civil suit, as opposed to the other remedies which I have mentioned.

The subject matter of a statute may by itself be of a nature such as to render the existence of a private remedy unlikely. Thus in *E (a minor) v Dorset CC* Otton J struck out private claims in respect of the statement process in the Education Act 1981. Both plaintiffs had alleged negligence, and E also relied on breach of statutory duty. Otton J reviewed the authorities on statutory duty at some length. He said:

> 'Generally the courts are reluctant to allow an action in tort against a public authority where the duty in question is a general statutory responsibility for the public welfare. Hence no action lies against the Minister of Education for breach of his duty "to promote the education of the people of England and Wales" ...'

That may have been a reference to an article by Sir Thomas Barnes 'Crown Proceedings Act 1947' (1948) 26 Can BR pp 390–391. Otton J concluded :

> 'The Education Acts do not expressly provide for a civil remedy. I [can] see no basis to imply or infer such a remedy. The nature of the duties where breaches are alleged fall under the general responsibilities of the local education authority.'

At the start of an impressive argument Mr Faulks for Newham London Borough Council referred us to *A v Liverpool City Council* [1981] 2 All ER 385, [1982] AC 363. That case was concerned with wardship when a child was in the care of the council. But I find it of some assistance on the more general consideration whether Parliament can have intended to provide a private law remedy to children for breach of the local authority's duty. Thus Lord Wilberforce said ([1981] 2 All ER 385 at 388–389, [1982] AC 363 at 372–373):

> 'Parliament has by statute entrusted to the local authority the power and duty to make decisions as to the welfare of children without any reservation of reviewing power to the court ... In my opinion Parliament has marked out an area in which, subject to the enacted limitations and safeguards, decisions for the child's welfare are removed from the parents and from supervision by the courts ... The court's general inherent power

is always available to fill gaps or to supplement the powers of the local authority; what it will not do (except by way of judicial review where appropriate) is to supervise the exercise of discretion within the field committed by statute to the local authority.'

Another case in much the same field is *T (a minor) v Surrey CC* [1994] 4 All ER 577. There a child was injured by a child-minder, who had been registered by the local authority pursuant to statute. The child's claim against the local authority failed in so far as it was based on breach of statutory duty, but succeeded on other grounds. Scott Baker J again followed what Simon Brown J had said in *R v Mid-Glamorgan CC, ex p Greig*, and said:

'I can find nothing in the present Act to indicate such an intention. I detect a considerable reluctance on the part of the courts to impose upon local authorities any liability for breach of statutory duty other than that expressly imposed in the statute.'

In my judgment the statutory duties relied on in these two appeals are in the nature of public law functions, the expression used by Lord Bridge of Harwich in *Cocks v Thanet DC* [1982] 3 All ER 1135 at 1138, [1983] 2 AC 286 at 292 and adopted by Otton J in *E (a minor) v Dorset CC*. They involve to a large extent an exercise by the local authority of its own judgment or discretion, with a view to invoking the assistance of the courts (or not doing so).

For all these reasons I conclude that the statutory provisions in question here do not give rise to a private law remedy in damages.

(2) Duty of care at common law

The involvement of Newham London Borough Council and of Bedfordshire County Council comes about entirely by statute. Neither authority has by the common law any right or duty to interfere in the lives of children within its area. At common law a local authority, like a private citizen, may see a child in need but pass by on the other side. One would therefore expect that any duty of care is to be found, if at all, in the statute; if the statute on its true interpretation provides none, then none should be owed by the local authority.

The law does not entirely accord with that view, but tends towards it. In *Yuen Kun-yeu v A-G of Hong Kong* [1987] 2 All ER 705 at 713, [1988] AC 175 at 195 Lord Keith of Kinkel said:

'In these circumstances their Lordships are unable to discern any intention on the part of the legislature that in considering whether to register or deregister a company the commissioner should owe any statutory duty to potential depositors. It would be strange that a common law duty of care should be superimposed on such a statutory framework.'

The same sentiment can, I think, be detected in the judgment of Otton J in *E (a minor) v Dorset CC*.

One can compare what was said by Lord Scarman in *Tai Hing Cotton Mill Ltd v Liu Chong Hing Bank Ltd* [1985] 2 All ER 947 at 957, [1986] AC 80 at 107:

'Their Lordships do not believe that there is anything to the advantage of the law's development in searching for a liability in tort where the parties are in a contractual relationship.'

In the field of private law I would, if I may, heartily agree with that view. For decades it has been the practice that anybody suing upon a contractual duty of care should plead that the defendant is tortiously liable in the alternative. Or more accurately his lawyer does that, for nobody except a lawyer would dream of such unnecessary elaboration. If there is a contractual relationship which includes no obligation to use reasonable skill and care, that seems to me a powerful argument for not holding the defendant liable for negligence at common law.

We were told that what Lord Scarman said has not met with universal acceptance; and in any event the analogy with the present appeals is of more value as an illustration than a compelling argument. But, like Lord Keith, I start from the position that it would be strange if the common law provides a duty when the statute does not.

Mr Munby QC for the plaintiffs in the Newham action based the common law claim on the duty to use reasonable skill and care which every professional person owes to his client, customer or patient (see *Sidaway v Bethlem Royal Hospital Governors* [1985] 1 All ER 643, [1985] AC 871). For this purpose he was at pains to emphasise that both the psychiatrist and the social worker were professional persons; that the exercise upon which they were engaged, including in particular the task of discovering *who* had abused the child, was properly called diagnosis; and that the children (and also the mother in the Newham case) were their clients, customers or patients. I have reservations about that approach.

In particular, I do not consider that the child was, in law and for all purposes, the patient of the psychiatrist in the Newham case. No doubt the medical profession would regard the child as the patient for some purposes, such as the duty of confidentiality. But the child had not sought the psychiatrist's services, nor had her mother as the person with parental responsibility on her behalf; those services had been thrust upon them. The child was no more the patient than an applicant for life insurance who is examined by the company's doctor, or the errant motorist who is deprived of a small quantity of blood by the police surgeon. In all those cases the medical person without doubt owes *some* duty to the person being examined or treated. We have been asking the wrong question, whether *any* duty is owed. The right question is, *what* duty? It is a duty to use reasonable skill and care so as not to cause harm in the course of examination or treatment. But the general duty to perform the task allocated with reasonable skill and care—whether it be 'diagnosing' the name of an abuser, or assessing the expectation of life, or producing a blood sample for analysis—is in my opinion owed to the person who engages the doctor to perform that task. That is the health authority or the local council in the first case, the insurance company in the second, and the police authority in the third.

Much the same can be said of the social worker. He no doubt regards the child as his patient for many purposes. But it was not the child or her mother on her behalf who engaged his services, any more than the criminal engages a probation officer. They were thrust upon her. As with doctors, I can readily accept that the social worker owes *some* duty to the person in his care; for example, he should not advise or encourage a child to engage in some activity which has a hidden danger, such as taking drugs or running across the road. But in the advice which he gives to the local authority as to the child's

problems and needs, his general professional duty is owed to the local
authority which engaged him, rather than to the child.

Sidaway's case and the general duty of professional persons are thus in my
judgment of no assistance to the plaintiffs in these cases. One must look
elsewhere for a duty of care, in accordance with the principles which
determine the boundaries of liability for negligence. In the case of the two
local authorities one starts upon that task, as I have said, against the
background that their involvement is derived from statute and yet the statute
provides no duty of care. I doubt if the same can be said in favour of the
psychiatrist and the health authority; or at any rate the point is less clear in
their case.

Following the recent decisions in the *Yuen Kun-yeu* case, *Caparo Industries plc
v Dickman* [1990] 1 All ER 568, [1990] 2 AC 605 and *Murphy v Brentwood DC*
[1990] 2 All ER 908, [1991] 1 AC 398 we are to ask ourselves whether damage
was foreseeable, whether there was proximity or neighbourhood, and whether
it is just and reasonable that the law should impose a duty (see *Caparo* [1990] 1
All ER 568 at 573–574, [1990] 2 AC 605 at 617–618 per Lord Bridge). For the
purpose of answering those questions, or at any rate the third of them, in a
novel situation we are to ask ourselves whether the imposition of a duty would
be incremental development from established categories (see [1990] 1 All ER
568 at 585, [1990] 2 AC 605 at 633 per Lord Oliver and *Murphy* [1990] 2 All ER
908 at 915, [1991] 1 AC 398 at 461 per Lord Keith).

The question whether it will be just and reasonable to extend an established
category to some new situation can give rise to a number of familiar
arguments, to which there are a number of familiar answers. For example, it
is often said that a new development will open the floodgates to litigation: to
that the answer is either a denial, or the assertion that if there is so much
negligence there ought to be so much litigation, and the courts must cope with
it. It may be said that the legal aid authorities will fund unjustified claims,
resulting in hardship to defendants; in answer, that is a fault of the legal aid
system, and should not be met by denying a cause of action to all. Similarly it
is said that child plaintiffs will be able to delay bringing claims against local
authorities until many years later when they reach the age of 21; the answer is
that the fault lies in the law of limitation of actions, and not in an incremental
duty of care. Again it may be said that professional people with difficult tasks
to perform should only be held liable if they really are negligent, but in practice
will be blamed for mere errors of judgment—or at any rate some payment will
have to be made to settle such cases; that again will be attributed to error in the
operation of the law rather than error in its substance.

To all those points the answer given is sound in logic. But I fear that the time
has come to recognise that it is unsound in practice. If a new duty of local
authorities is established in these appeals, I do not doubt that many claims will
be brought, placing further strain on an already stretched system (which will
be provided with no more resources). I do not doubt that many claims with
little or no prospect of success will be financed by the legal aid fund. Nor that
many will be delayed for years, perhaps until the plaintiff is 21. Nor that many
claims will be settled, or even decided in favour of a plaintiff whose
misfortunes attract sympathy, although there has been no more than an error
of judgment.

When Lord Keith in *Rowling v Takaro Properties Ltd* [1988] 1 All ER 163, [1988] AC 473 spoke of the danger of overkill, he may have had in mind primarily defensive practices, such as requiring foundations for a building which are quite unnecessarily elaborate.   Certainly that danger is very important in medical negligence cases: high standards of duty and vast awards of damages result in unnecessary tests and other procedures at great expense, as experience in the United States has shown.   This is the exercise of a function being carried on in a detrimentally defensive frame of mind (see *Hill v Chief Constable of West Yorkshire* [1988] 2 All ER 238 at 243, [1989] AC 53 at 63 per Lord Keith).   But the other disadvantages which I have described can also in my view be called overkill.   A further problem mentioned in *Hill's* case is that time, trouble and expense will be required for the investigation of claims, to the prejudice of the defendants' budget for their proper functions—policing in that case, caring for children in this.   Again the purist would say they must be given more money. And again I say that very probably they will not be, this time with less fear of being accused of scepticism.   The claims may, I suspect, on occasion be for six-figure sums.

One advantage that is claimed for imposing a duty of care is that it encourages people not to be negligent.   I very much doubt if that is the case. The great expansion of tortious liability over the last hundred and fifty years has had the remarkable feature that the direct financial consequences almost invariably fall on someone whose purse is assumed to be bottomless, such as an insurance company or a large commercial concern or an organ of central or local government.   It is, I imagine, rare for a private individual to find himself paying substantial damages for negligence (but see *Lister v Romford Ice and Cold Storage Co Ltd* [1957] 1 All ER 125, [1957] AC 555).   And even if psychiatrists and social workers were likely to have to pay damages personally, I do not suppose that they would be any less caring for children in need than they are already; they might, as I have said, adopt defensive practices; but I doubt if their general level of care would change.   Indeed I would hope that they are already careful people.

The law of negligence has travelled some way beyond affording a remedy for injury in shops or factories, and on railways or roads.   Medical negligence, for example, is now a substantial and significant category.   But I would not go so far as to impose a private duty on local authorities performing their public law function of caring for children in need.   Nor would I impose a general duty of the same nature on doctors and health authorities participating in the same process.   I recognise that, in the Newham case, the mother is entitled to feel a sense of outrage that her child was wrongly taken from her for a year, the more so if that was done negligently; and the child may indeed be scarred by this trauma.   But I doubt whether money is the appropriate remedy for either of them; what they need, or at any rate the mother needs, is vindication for herself and perhaps the solace of a reproach to the psychiatrist and the social worker.   But whether that is right or not, I would decline to make a monetary award.   That conclusion appears to me to be in line with the decision of this court in *F v Wirral Metropolitan BC* [1991] 2 All ER 648, [1991] Fam 69.

Since preparing this judgment I have considered the decision of the Court of Appeal, and also of the House of Lords, in *Everett (pauper) v Griffiths* [1920] 3 KB 163; affd [1921] 1 AC 631.   My views remain unchanged.

These appeals must in my opinion be dismissed.

PETER GIBSON LJ. Since 1932 Parliament has seen fit to confer on local authorities functions for the protection of children. Those functions have been progressively extended in subsequent years by legislation culminating with the Children Act 1989. They are extremely demanding, primarily because of the number of children involved and the delicate and difficult decisions, usually taken after multidisciplinary consultation, that are entailed in the child care process. We were given some statistics taken from official publications: 39,600 children on the Child Protection Register in 1992; 55,000 children in care on 31 March 1992; 15,407 children who were the subject of applications under the public law provisions of the Children Act 1989 in the year ended 30 June 1993.

Against that background the questions raised by these two appeals in circumstances which appear not to have been the subject of previous litigation can at once be seen to be of general importance. The primary question in both appeals is whether a child has a sustainable cause of action for damages for negligence or breach of statutory duty against a local authority in respect of what it did or failed to do in the performance of its social services functions in relation to children. In the Newham case there are two further questions. (1) Does the child have such a cause of action against a health authority and the psychiatrist it employed who participated in the investigation into whether the child had been sexually abused? (2) Does the child's mother have such a cause of action against all or any of the local authority, the health authority and the psychiatrist?

I adopt with gratitude the exposition by Sir Thomas Bingham MR of the facts, actual or assumed to be true for the purposes of these appeals.

I find it convenient to start with the Bedfordshire case because of the wider range of statutory duties relied on than in the Newham case. In each case I shall consider breach of statutory duty before negligence.

THE BEDFORDSHIRE CASE

Breach of statutory duty

Whether a breach of statutory duty can give rise to a private law cause of action for damages depends on the intention of Parliament, to be ascertained from a consideration of the statute as a whole. I too regret that Lord du Parcq's plea in *Cutler v Wandsworth Stadium Ltd (in liq)* [1949] 1 All ER 544 at 549, [1949] AC 398 at 410 that that intention should be explicitly stated in the legislation creating the statutory duty has been ignored, and we are again faced with what Lord Denning MR in *Ex p Island Records Ltd* [1978] 3 All ER 824 at 829, [1978] Ch 122 at 134–135 called 'a guesswork puzzle'. There are various matters which in any given case may be determinative, such as the nature and language of the statutory duty and the existence or absence of other remedies. But the fact that a particular provision was intended to protect certain individuals is not of itself sufficient to confer private law rights of action upon them: something more is required to show that the legislation intended such conferment (see *Hague v Deputy Governor of Parkhurst Prison, Weldon v Home Office* [1991] 3 All ER 733 at 750, [1992] 1 AC 58 at 170–171).

In the statement of claim a large number of statutory provisions are pleaded as relevant to the claim of breach of statutory duty, but Mr Levy QC, appearing for the plaintiff children, relied in his argument on only the following provisions.

First, he referred us to ss 1(1), 1(2)(a) and 2(2) of the Children and Young Persons Act 1969. Section 1(1) allows a local authority, which 'reasonably a believes' that there are grounds for the court making a protective order, such as a care order, in respect of a child (such grounds including the avoidable prevention or neglect of the child's proper development or the avoidable impairment or neglect of his health or his ill-treatment—s 1(2)(a)), to bring the child before a juvenile court. But the only duty imposed on the local authority to be found in the provisions relied on is that in s 2(2) and it only arises on the fulfilment of the condition precedent:

b

'If it appears to a local authority that there are grounds for bringing care proceedings in respect of a child or young person who resides or is found in their area ...'

It is not pleaded that that subjective condition has been satisfied and I cannot c see that this duty can be said to have been breached.

Second, he relied on s 2(1)(b) and (c) of the Child Care Act 1980. This imposes a duty on a local authority to receive a child into its care 'Where it appears to a local authority' (amongst other things) that the circumstances of paras (b) and (c) of s 2(1) obtain. I make the same comment on that as on the d reliance on the duty under the 1969 Act.

Third, he relied on a number of provisions of the Children Act 1989, which he subdivided into three parts.

The first part consisted of certain provisions of Pt III of the Act, viz ss 17(1), 20, 22, 23, 24 and Pt I of Sch 2. Of these, s 17(1) imposes what is in terms called—

e

'the general duty of every local authority ... (a) to safeguard and promote the welfare of children within their area who are in need; and (b) so far as is consistent with that duty, to promote the upbringing of such children by their families, by providing a range and level of services appropriate to those children's needs.'

f

Section 17(2) introduces the 'specific duties and powers set out in Part I of Schedule 2'. But they are conferred on the local authority '[f]or the purpose principally of facilitating the discharge of their general duty under [s 17]'. The specific duties in Pt I of Sch 2 include duties to 'take reasonable steps to identify the extent to which there are children in need within their area ...' (para 1), to g 'take reasonable steps, through the provision of services under Part III of [the 1989] Act, to prevent children within their area suffering ill-treatment or neglect ...' (para 4) and to—

'take reasonable steps designed—(a) to reduce the need to bring—(i) h proceedings for care or supervision orders with respect to children within their area ... (iii) any family or other proceedings with respect to such children which might lead to them being placed in the authority's care ...' (See para 7.)

In my opinion the unspecific language of what Mr Levy accepted was only a j target duty in s 17(1) and of the ancillary provisions in Sch 2, leaving, as they do, the local authority with wide scope to exercise its subjective judgment, strongly indicates that Parliament did not intend to confer a private law remedy for any breach of its duties.

Similar comments can be made about s 20 (a duty on a local authority to provide accommodation for any child in need within its area who appears to it to require accommodation as a result of certain specified events). As for ss 22,

23 and 24, they are not relevant, relating as they do to children already looked after by the local authority, when the complaint here is that the council failed to act.

The second part consists only of s 31 in Pt IV of the 1989 Act. Although it is pleaded in para 8 of the statement of claim that the local authority has a duty pursuant to ss 31 to 42 to apply to the court for a care order or a supervision order in respect of any child likely to satisfy the criteria of s 31, no such duty is imposed by s 31 or any of the other sections of Pt IV, which specify the power of the court to make, and the scope and effect of, such orders.

The third part consists of ss 43, 44 and 47 in Pt V of the 1989 Act. Sections 43 and 44 do not impose duties: they indicate what the court may do by child assessment orders or orders for the emergency protection of children. Section 47(1) imposes a duty but in subjective terms:

'Where a local authority ... (b) have reasonable cause to suspect that a child who lives, or is found, in their area is suffering, or is likely to suffer, significant harm, the authority shall make, or cause to be made, such enquiries as they consider necessary to enable them to decide whether they should take any action to safeguard or promote the child's welfare.'

Similarly in s 47(8) :

'Where ... a local authority conclude that they should take action to safeguard or promote the child's welfare they shall take that action (so far as it is both within their power and reasonably practicable for them to do so).'

Such subjective language, in my view, points away from the conferment of a right to sue for breach of statutory duty.

In relation to the duties under the 1989 Act, it is also relevant to note the availability of other remedies. In particular, the representations procedure required to be established by every local authority under s 26(3) was clearly intended by Parliament to ensure that any grievance of (amongst others) a child or the parent of a child would be investigated with an independent person participating in the consideration of that grievance. In addition the Secretary of State has power to cause inquiries to be held into any matter connected with the local authority's functions affecting children (s 81) and further a default power is given to the Secretary of State who can give directions enforceable by mandamus (s 84).

The existence of these provisions, as well as the ability of the aggrieved person to proceed by way of judicial review, militates against any inference of the conferment by Parliament of a right to sue for damages for breach of statutory duty under the 1989 Act.

Accordingly I agree with Turner J's conclusion ((1993) Times, 24 November) that a claim for breach of statutory duty cannot be sustained.

Negligence

It is pleaded on behalf of the plaintiff children that the council 'owed a duty of care to the Plaintiffs as children living in their area about whom serious reports of neglect and damage were made to the [council]' and that—

'Pursuant to their duty of care the [council] were required to take all necessary steps to protect the Plaintiffs from neglect and harm by exercising their statutory powers under the [statutory] provisions referred to above or otherwise, or by wardship proceedings or by invoking the inherent jurisdiction of the court.' (See paras 10 and 11 of the statement of claim.)

Mr Levy did not address us on the alleged breach of duty to take wardship proceedings or to invoke the inherent jurisdiction of the court, and in my judgment it is impossible to sustain this part of the claim in negligence.

What, therefore, the claim in negligence comes to is an assertion that the council owed a duty of care to the children, living as they did in the council's area, when serious reports of neglect and damage had been made to the council and that it should have exercised its statutory powers to protect the children. That seems to me to recognise, as is the fact, that the only reason why the council was involved at all was because of the statutory functions imposed on the council and that the complaint of the children is as to the way those functions were exercised. If, as I have held, no action for breach of statutory duty lies in respect of what the council did or failed to do in exercise of those functions, it is not immediately obvious why a common law claim in negligence against the council for failing to exercise its statutory powers or duties should lie.

I would echo the remark made by Lord Keith in *Yuen Kun-yeu v A-G of Hong Kong* [1987] 2 All ER 705 at 713, [1988] AC 175 at 195, albeit in a different context: 'It would be strange that a common law duty of care should be superimposed upon such a statutory framework.' So too Otton J in the context of an action for breach of statutory duty and negligence in relation to a local authority's educational functions, having found no action for breach of statutory duty would lie, said: 'I am satisfied that the allegations of negligence are co-extensive with the breach of statutory duty contended for' and struck out the claim in negligence as not disclosing a reasonable cause of action (see *E (a minor) v Dorset CC* (7 April 1993, unreported)). Similarly, in an action for breach of statutory duty under the Nurseries and Child-Minders Regulation Act 1948 and negligence, Scott Baker J said in *T (a minor) v Surrey CC* [1994] 4 All ER 577 at 600: 'In my judgment, the issues of breach of statutory duty and common law negligence in respect of the exercise by the local authority of its power under this Act run very much hand in glove' and, having held that the claim for breach of statutory duty failed, he refused to recognise a duty of care owed by the local authority (save in respect of negligent misstatement). In the present case Turner J pointed out: 'The allegations of negligence do not add to the allegations of fact that are said to amount to breaches of statutory duty.'

Should the law nevertheless now recognise for the first time a duty of care owed by a local authority to a child within its area, when in the exercise of its statutory functions, it takes a decision as to whether or not to intervene to protect the child? I accept that an action for damages for negligence differs from the assertion of a public law right by judicial review proceedings and so cannot be struck out as an abuse of the process (see e g *Davy v Spelthorne BC* [1983] 3 All ER 278, [1984] AC 262). But that does not help to resolve the question whether in a particular novel situation the law should recognise a duty of care as owed by a public body to an individual. On the incremental approach, now laid down as correct for the development of the law of negligence, if the plaintiffs' action is to go ahead, the court must, I apprehend, answer in the affirmative the question whether the situation as between the

council and the children is one in which it is 'fair, just and reasonable' that the
council should owe a duty of care to the children in the decisions it reaches in
the exercise of the statutory functions relied on by the children (see *Caparo
Industries plc v Dickman* [1990] 1 All ER 568 at 574, [1990] 2 AC 605 at 618 per
Lord Bridge).

No doubt those who exercise the statutory functions on behalf of the council
are specialists professing skills, and, by analogy with other situations where the
law has recognised that a duty of care is owed by the professional to his patient
or client, it can be, and has been, argued with force that a duty of care should
be found here as well. Further I accept that a duty of care is more readily found
to be owed where the negligence results in personal injury rather than mere
economic loss. It is also argued that the recognition of a duty of care will
promote higher standards in the general public interest.

But there are other considerations which point in the other direction. In an
action against the police in *Hill v Chief Constable of West Yorkshire* [1988] 2 All ER
238 at 243, [1989] AC 53 at 63 Lord Keith, in stating why on the particular facts
of that case a liability in negligence should not be entertained, said:

'The general sense of public duty which motivates police forces is
unlikely to be appreciably reinforced by the imposition of such liability so
far as concerns their function in the investigation and suppression of
crime. From time to time they make mistakes in the exercise of that
function, but it is not to be doubted that they apply their best endeavours
to the performance of it. In some instances the imposition of liability may
lead to the exercise of a function being carried on in a detrimentally
defensive frame of mind. The possibility of this happening in relation to
the investigative operations of the police cannot be excluded.'

He then referred to the manner of conduct of police investigations, which he
said—

'must necessarily involve a variety of decisions to be made on matters of
policy and discretion, for example as to which particular line of enquiry is
most advantageously to be pursued and what is the most advantageous
way to deploy the available resources ... Many such decisions would not
be regarded by the courts as appropriate to be called in question, yet
elaborate investigation of the facts might be necessary to ascertain
whether or not this was so. A great deal of police time, trouble and
expense might be expected to have to be put into the preparation of the
defence to the action and the attendance of witnesses at the trial. The
result would be a significant diversion of police manpower and attention
from their most important function, that of the suppression of crime.' (See
[1988] 2 All ER 238 at 244, [1989] AC 53 at 63.)

Similar points can be taken in relation to the performance by local
authorities of their statutory functions when deciding whether or not to
intervene in relation to a child. Society rightly attaches the highest importance
to the welfare of children, and no doubt it was for that reason that local
authorities were given their statutory functions; but the philosophy of the
legislation relating to children and in particular that of the Children Act 1989 is
that the local authority should not intervene save where it is necessary. If the
law were now to recognise a duty of care owed to the children by the local
authority in taking decisions on interventions, there is a significant risk of the

a exercise of such functions being carried on in a detrimentally defensive frame of mind. I repeat that such decisions are delicate and difficult. I do not doubt that reasonable persons may often reach different conclusions on the same matter, and the nature of the matter is such as to arouse strong emotions. Further, if litigation were encouraged by a duty of care being held to exist, a major diversion of resources to defending such actions is likely to ensue. I *b* cannot see that this is fair, just or reasonable, particularly when one bears in mind the existence of other remedies. Throughout the period of the alleged negligence the remedy of judicial review was available. For my part I do not accept Mr Levy's submission that it provided an unrealistic remedy, given the wide concern which, it is pleaded, the children's plight aroused among so many individuals as well as a knowledgeable organisation like the National *c* Society for the Prevention of Cruelty to Children. Of course the court will be slow to interfere in an area in which Parliament has left so much to the discretion and judgment of the local authority, but if the council's failures to act were as clear-cut as is pleaded, I do not see why an application for judicial review could not have been brought at the instance of one of the concerned *d* persons. Further, since the Children Act 1989 came into force the representations procedure under s 26 could easily and without formality have been invoked so as to ensure that the children's complaint was investigated properly.

In *Yuen Kun-yeu* [1987] 2 All ER 705 at 716, [1988] AC 175 at 198 Lord Keith described as having much force an argument that if a duty of care was to be *e* imposed on (amongst others) social workers, it would be much better if the liability was introduced by the legislature, which is better suited than the judiciary to weigh up competing policy considerations. I respectfully agree.

For these reasons, despite the considerable sympathy that I feel for the children, I consider that Turner J was right to hold that the claim in negligence *f* should be struck out.

THE NEWHAM CASE

Breach of statutory duty

The only statutory duties alleged in the amended statement of claim to have *g* been breached are those specified in ss 1 and 18 of the Child Care Act 1980.

In relation to s 1 it is pleaded in para 30(a) of the amended statement of claim that the local authority failed to make available such advice, guidance and assistance as would have promoted the welfare of the child by diminishing the need to receive her or keep her in care. A duty to that effect is imposed by s 1(1) *h* on a local authority, but consistently with the imprecise terms of that duty the headnote to s 1 reads 'General duty of local authorities to promote welfare of children', and s 1(1) goes on to say that any provisions made by a local authority under the subsection may, if the local authority think fit, include provision for giving assistance in kind or, in exceptional circumstances, cash. *i* Such language makes this duty an unlikely one to have been intended by Parliament to give rise, on its breach, to a civil action.

In relation to s 18 it is pleaded in para 30(b) that the local authority failed to give first consideration to the need to promote the welfare of the child. There is a duty, described in the sidenote to s 18 as a general duty, in those terms *j* imposed by s 18(1) on a local authority but only in relation to a child already in its care.

Mr Munby QC in his argument for the child and the mother made clear that
the essential claim that they make is that as a result of the social worker,
employed by the local authority, and the psychiatrist wrongly identifying the
abuser of the child and their erroneous advice to the local authority, the child
was taken into care and separated from the mother. In other words, that
essential breach of duty occurred before the child was taken into care. I do not
see how this provision can be relied on to establish a breach of statutory duty.
In any event, having regard to the general nature of the duty and the imprecise
terms in which it is couched, I find it impossible to believe that a breach of such
a duty was intended sub silentio by Parliament to give rise to a private law
claim in damages.

In my judgment therefore, Judge Phelan ([1993] 2 FLR 575) was right to hold
that no claim for breach of statutory duty can arise.

Negligence

Mr Munby's primary argument was in support of the claim in negligence.
He submitted that the claims of the child and the mother were very simple,
being claims against professional persons for damages for personal injuries, to
which the principles laid down in *Sidaway v Bethlem Royal Hospital Governors*
[1985] 1 All ER 643, [1985] AC 871 applied. He stressed that both the child and
the mother had been the subject of diagnostic interviews carried out by the
social worker and the psychiatrist and that both were 'patients' to whom the
ordinary duty of care was owed by the social worker and the psychiatrist, being
persons professing skills.

I am not able to accept those submissions, persuasively though they were
advanced. I shall consider first the position of the psychiatrist vis-à-vis the
child. The psychiatrist's involvement came about because the local authority
arranged an appointment for the child to be examined by the psychiatrist, and,
as is pleaded in para 9 of the amended statement of claim, 'The purpose of the
interview was to ascertain if [the child] had been sexually abused and, if so, the
identity of any abuser'.

To my mind it is plain that the local authority's purpose in arranging the
examination was to enable it to decide whether or not to intervene in the
performance of its statutory functions. A local authority has no power or duty
at common law to intervene in relation to a child in its area, and can only
exercise a statutory function if it is to make such an intervention. Although the
amended statement of claim contains no reference to any Act other than the
1980 Act, I apprehend that it was in performance of its functions under the
Children and Young Persons Act 1969 that the local authority was considering
intervening. In particular, the local authority would have been concerned to
know whether the circumstances of the child were such that it should apply
under s 28 of the 1969 Act for a place of safety order or under ss 1 and 2 of that
Act for a care order. The psychiatrist's task was to advise the local authority.

In these circumstances it seems to me inapt to regard the psychiatrist as
under the same duty of care when exercising her professional skills in relation
to the child as if the child had been referred to the psychiatrist in order that
advice or treatment be given to the child or, for that matter, her mother. True
it is that the advice related to and foreseeably affected the child and the mother
and that for some limited purposes the child is properly to be regarded as the
psychiatrist's patient. Thus the psychiatrist would owe the child a duty of
confidentiality, though even that would be modified to allow the psychiatrist

a
to report to the local authority. But I cannot see that the psychiatrist owed the child or her mother a duty of care in relation to the advice the psychiatrist gave to the local authority, as it was never intended that the psychiatrist should give that advice to the child or her mother. Similarly, if I propose to effect a policy on my life with insurers who require me to be medically examined by a doctor who will advise them, that doctor owes me no duty of care in the advice which

b
he gives the insurers, even though for purposes of confidentiality he will treat me as his patient.

If the psychiatrist owed no duty of care to the child in relation to the advice given to the local authority, it is hard to see how the psychiatrist owed a duty of care to the mother. I do not accept that the mother was the subject of a diagnostic interview by the psychiatrist. It is simply pleaded in para 18 of the

c
amended statement of claim that after the conclusion of the interview with the child, the mother was brought into the presence of the psychiatrist and the social worker to be told the findings and conclusions reached by them, viz that the child had been sexually abused by the third plaintiff. I do not overlook that it is also pleaded in para 21 that the social worker and the psychiatrist

d
concluded that the mother would be unable to protect the child from further abuse by the third plaintiff, but it is not pleaded that the mother was interviewed for that purpose or at all.

In my judgment therefore, the claims by both the child and the mother against the health authority and the psychiatrist were rightly struck out by the judge.

e
The more significant and difficult question is whether the local authority owed the child or the mother a duty of care at common law such that its breach can give rise to an action in negligence. More specifically, can the negligent mistake which was made by the social worker in identifying the abuser of the child and which (I shall assume) caused personal injury to the child and her

f
mother, whilst not amounting to an actionable breach of statutory duty, give rise to an action for damages?

It is impossible not to feel strong sympathy for both the mother and the child, deprived as they were of each other for a period of a year, particularly after the trauma of the abuse which had correctly been identified as having occurred. But, for reasons similar to those which have persuaded me in the

g
Bedfordshire case, I have reached the conclusion that no duty of care was owed by the local authority to the mother or the child in relation to the error that occurred. In my judgment the situation as between the local authority and the mother and the child was a novel situation not falling within a category previously recognised as giving rise to a duty of care. The social worker who

h
made the error and wrongly advised the local authority on the identity of the abuser was carrying out the statutory function of the local authority to make inquiries. Moreover it is, in my opinion, relevant to note that it was an error that might have been expected to come to light in the consequent court proceedings. It is something of a mystery why the mother's legal advisers did

j
not seek to obtain the videotape evidence of the interview with the child at or before those proceedings or at any rate long before the video was in fact seen and the error recognised. An application to see the video could have been made at any time. Where a decision by the local authority cannot be implemented save by obtaining an order of the court and in those proceedings the approach of the court is not that adopted in adversarial proceedings but has the welfare of the child as the paramount consideration, it seems to me that the

justification for recognising a new duty of care as owed to the child by the local
authority in its decision-taking process is the less.   *a*

For these reasons therefore I would hold that the claim in negligence against
the local authority cannot succeed.

Conclusion

Having reached these conclusions on the grounds which I have endeavoured   *b*
to explain, I find it unnecessary to say anything on the other points argued
before us. I would dismiss both appeals.

Appeals dismissed. Leave to appeal to the House of Lords granted.

c

L I Zysman Esq   Barrister.

E (a minor) v Dorset County Council
and other appeals
d

COURT OF APPEAL, CIVIL DIVISION
SIR THOMAS BINGHAM MR, EVANS AND ROSE LJJ
7, 8, 9, 10 MARCH, 29 APRIL 1994

e

*Education – Local education authority – Statutory duty to provide special education
– Breach – Right of action for damages – Local education authority failing to assess
and provide for special educational needs – Plaintiff suffering consequent damage –
Whether plaintiff entitled to bring private law claim for damages – Whether
plaintiff limited to administrative channels for redress – Education Act 1944, s 8 –* *f*
Education Act 1981, s 7.

*Negligence – Duty to take care – Existence of duty – Education authority – Children
– Child with special education needs – Education authority under statutory duty to
provide special education for such children – Employees of education authority
failing to diagnose or assess child's learning difficulties accurately and failing to* *g*
*provide appropriate education – Whether employees owing duty of care to child –
Whether child having cause of action for negligence.*

In the first action the plaintiff, E, brought proceedings against a local education
authority alleging breach of statutory duty on the grounds that the authority   *h*
had failed to ascertain that he suffered from a learning disorder which required
special educational provision, that it had wrongly advised his parents and that
even when pursuant to s 7[a] of the Education Act 1981 it later acknowledged E's
special needs, it had wrongly decided that the school E was then attending was
appropriate to meet his needs. E further alleged that the authority, in breach   *j*
of its common law duty, had failed to recognise or make adequate inquiries
into his specific learning difficulties or make proper provision for his condition.
He claimed damages for the expense incurred by his parents in placing him at
a special school where his particular educational needs were addressed and his

---

a   Section 7, so far as material, is set out at p 663 *c d*, post

condition diagnosed and treated. On the authority's application E's claim was struck out by the judge as disclosing no reasonable cause of action.

In the second action the plaintiff, M, brought proceedings against a local education authority claiming damages for negligence on the grounds that the headmaster of the local primary school which he had attended had failed to refer him either to the authority for formal assessment of his learning difficulties, which were consistent with dyslexia, or to an educational psychologist for diagnosis, that the teachers' advisory centre to which he was later referred had also failed to identify his difficulty and that such failure to assess his condition (which would have improved with appropriate treatment) had severely limited his educational attainment and prospects of employment. On the authority's application M's claim was struck out by the master as disclosing no reasonable cause of action and on appeal by M that order was affirmed by the judge.

In the third action the plaintiff, R, brought proceedings against a local education authority claiming damages for breach of statutory duty under the Education Act 1944, the 1981 Act and the Education (Special Educational Needs) Regulations 1983 on the grounds that although he did not have any serious disability and was of at least average ability the authority had either placed him in special schools which were not appropriate to his educational needs or had failed to provide any schooling for him at all with the result that his personal and intellectual development had been impaired and he had been placed at a disadvantage in seeking employment. On the authority's application his claim was struck out as disclosing no reasonable cause of action.

The plaintiffs appealed.

Held – (1) The duty imposed by the 1944 and 1981 Acts and the 1983 regulations was, as expressly provided for in s 8[b] of the 1944 Act as amended, to secure that a suitable school was available which a child requiring primary or secondary education could attend. That duty was enforceable by judicial review proceedings brought by or on behalf of the child. In the case of children with special educational needs the 1981 Act and the 1983 regulations prescribed a detailed code for identifying, assessing and providing for such children and made ample provision for involving parents in decisions affecting their children and gave them a right of appeal to an appeal committee and to the Secretary of State if they wished to challenge decisions affecting their children. Those decisions were also subject to judicial review on appropriate grounds. It was therefore clear that Parliament intended any complaint by parents or children of breach of the duties under the 1981 Act and the 1983 regulations should be pursued through administrative channels and not by a private law action for damages or injunction. Although by contrast the relevant provisions of the 1944 Act did not lay down a detailed code and the duties laid on authorities were couched in general terms, there was no indication that Parliament intended any complaint by children or their parents of breach of those duties to be enforceable by a private law action for damages or injunction. It followed that the appeals against the orders striking out the claims for breach of statutory duty would be dismissed (see p 650 *f* to *j*, p 656 *g h*, p 658 *g*, p 665 *d* to *g* and p 671 *c d*, post); *Gateshead Union v Durham CC* [1918] 1 Ch 146 considered.

---

b   Section 8, so far as material, is set out at p 661 *g* to *j*, post

(2) Teaching and making educational provision for children with learning difficulties was not purely a function of the state, since a local education authority, when making an assessment of special educational needs was required to seek educational, medical and psychological advice from professional persons possessing special qualifications or skills who owed a duty of care not only to the local education authority which employed them but also to the children and their parents to take reasonable care to give correct advice to the best of their ability and skill. It was at least arguable that there would be foreseeability of injury and proximity if such professional persons acted carelessly in relation to the children and there were no considerations of fairness and justice which prevented a child which suffered actionable damage or loss as the result of negligent advice from being able to recover damages from the professional person giving the advice and vicariously from the authority which employed that person. It followed that the plaintiffs' claims were not unarguable or incontestably bad and therefore their appeals against the orders striking out their claims in negligence against the authorities would be allowed (see p 657 c to e j to p 658 c g, p 665 h, p 669 c d j and p 671 c d, post); M (a minor) v Newham London BC, X and ors (minors) v Bedfordshire CC [1994] 4 All ER 602 distinguished.

Per curiam. Where the legal viability of a cause of action is unclear (perhaps because the law is in a state of transition), or in any way sensitive to the facts, an order to strike out should not be made (see p 649 f g and p 665 h j, post).

Notes

For construction of a statute to ascertain whether a civil action lies in respect of a breach of a duty imposed by the statute, see 45 *Halsbury's Laws* (4th edn) para 1282.

For nature of negligence and the duty to take care generally, see 34 *Halsbury's Laws* (4th edn) paras 1–5, and for cases on the subject, see 36(1) *Digest* (2nd reissue) 7–64, *1–325*.

For the Education Act 1944, s 8, see 15 *Halsbury's Statutes* (4th edn) (1990 reissue) 117.

For the Education Act 1981, s 7, see ibid 296.

For the Education (Special Educational Needs) Regulations 1983, see 6 *Halsbury's Statutory Instruments* (1993 reissue) 316.

Cases referred to in judgments

Anns v Merton London Borough [1977] 2 All ER 492, [1978] AC 728, [1977] 2 WLR 1024, HL.

Bradbury v Enfield London Borough [1967] 3 All ER 434, [1967] 1 WLR 1311, CA.

Ching v Surrey CC [1910] 1 KB 736, [1908–10] All ER Rep 305.

Cocks v Thanet DC [1982] 3 All ER 1135, [1983] 2 AC 286, [1982] 3 WLR 1121, HL.

Cumings v Birkenhead Corp [1971] 2 All ER 881, [1972] Ch 12, [1971] 2 WLR 1458, CA.

Cutler v Wandsworth Stadium Ltd (in liq) [1949] 1 All ER 544, [1949] AC 398, HL.

Equal Opportunities Commission v Secretary of State for Employment [1994] 1 All ER 910; [1994] 2 WLR 409, HL.

Gateshead Union v Durham CC [1918] 1 Ch 146, CA.

Hague v Deputy Governor of Parkhurst Prison, Weldon v Home Office [1991] 3 All ER 733, [1992] 1 AC 58, [1991] 3 WLR 340, HL.

Home Office v Dorset Yacht Co Ltd [1970] 2 All ER 294, [1970] AC 1004, [1970] 2
WLR 1140, HL.
Jones v Dept of Employment [1988] 1 All ER 725, [1989] QB 1, [1988] 2 WLR 493,
CA.
Lonrho plc v Fayed [1991] 3 All ER 303, [1992] 1 AC 448, [1991] 3 WLR 188, HL.
Lyme Regis Corp v Henley (1834) 2 Cl & Fin 331, [1824–34] All ER Rep 503, 131
ER 1103, HL.
M (a minor) v Newham London BC, X and ors (minors) v Bedfordshire CC [1994] 4 All
ER 602, [1994] 2 WLR 554, CA.
Meade v Haringey London Borough [1979] 2 All ER 1016, [1979] 1 WLR 637, CA.
O'Reilly v Mackman [1982] 3 All ER 1124, [1983] 2 AC 237, [1982] 3 WLR 1096,
HL.
Padfield v Minister of Agriculture, Fisheries and Food [1968] 1 All ER 694, [1968] AC
997, [1968] 2 WLR 924, HL.
R v Inner London Education Authority, ex p Ali (1990) 2 Admin LR 822, DC.
R v Mid-Glamorgan CC, ex p Greig (1988) Independent, 1 June.
R v Secretary of State for Education and Science, ex p Davis [1989] 2 FLR 190, DC.
R v Surrey CC Education Committee, ex p H (1984) 83 LGR 219, CA.
Van Oppen v Bedford Charity Trustees [1989] 3 All ER 389, [1990] 1 WLR 235, CA.
Watt v Kesteven CC [1955] 1 All ER 473, [1955] 1 QB 408, [1955] 2 WLR 499, CA.
Wilford v West Riding of Yorkshire CC [1908] 1 KB 685.
Williams v Eady (1893) 10 TLR 41, CA.
Wood v Ealing London Borough [1966] 3 All ER 514, [1967] Ch 364, [1966] 3 WLR
1209.

Cases also cited or referred to in skeleton arguments
A v Liverpool City Council [1981] 2 All ER 385, [1982] AC 363, HL.
Butler (or Black) v Fife Coal Co Ltd [1912] AC 149, HL.
Bux v Slough Metals Ltd [1974] 1 All ER 262, [1973] 1 WLR 1358, CA.
Calveley v Chief Constable of the Merseyside Police [1989] 1 All ER 1025, [1989] 1 AC
1228, HL.
Caparo Industries plc v Dickman [1990] 1 All ER 568, [1990] 2 AC 605, [1990] 2
WLR 358, HL; *rvsg* [1989] 1 All ER 798, [1989] QB 653, CA.
Davy v Spelthorne BC [1983] 3 All ER 278, [1984] AC 262, HL.
De Falco v Crawley BC [1980] 1 All ER 913, [1980] QB 460, CA.
Drummond-Jackson v British Medical Association [1970] 1 All ER 1094, [1970] 1
WLR 688, CA.
Hedley Byrne & Co Ltd v Heller & Partners Ltd [1963] 2 All ER 575, [1964] AC 465,
HL.
Holtom v London Borough of Barnet (1993) Times, 30 September.
Hubbuck & Sons Ltd v Wilkinson Heywood and Clark Ltd [1899] 1 QB 86, [1895–9]
All ER Rep 244, CA.
Landau v Werner (1961) 105 SJ 1008, CA.
Lonrho Ltd v Shell Petroleum Co Ltd (No 2) [1981] 2 All ER 456, [1982] AC 173, HL.
Moore (a minor) v Hampshire CC (1981) 80 LGR 481, CA.
Murphy v Brentwood DC [1990] 2 All ER 908, [1991] 1 AC 398, HL; *rvsg* [1990] 2
All ER 269, [1991] 1 AC 398, CA.
Palmer v London Borough of Harrow [1992] PIQR 296.
Phillips v Britannia Hygienic Laundry Co Ltd [1923] 2 KB 832, [1923] All ER Rep
127, CA.
R v Hampshire Education Authority, ex p J (1985) 84 LGR 547.

R v Secretary of State for Education and Science, ex p Lashford [1988] 1 FLR 72, CA.
Rawsthorne v Ottley [1937] 3 All ER 902.
Reffell v Surrey CC [1964] 1 All ER 743, [1964] 1 WLR 358.
Rich (Marc) & Co AG v Bishop Rock Marine Co Ltd, The Nicholas H [1994] 3 All ER 686, [1994] 1 WLR 1070, CA.
Rich v London CC [1953] 2 All ER 376, [1953] 1 WLR 895, CA.
Smith v Eric S Bush (a firm), Harris v Wyre Forest DC [1989] 2 All ER 514, [1990] 1 AC 831, HL.
T (a minor) v Surrey CC [1994] 4 All ER 577.
Thornton v Kirklees Metropolitan BC [1979] 2 All ER 349, [1979] QB 626, CA.
West Wiltshire DC v Garland (Cond and ors, third parties) [1993] 4 All ER 246, [1993] Ch 409.
Wyatt v Hillingdon London BC (1978) 76 LGR 727, CA.

Interlocutory appeals

E (a minor) v Dorset CC

The plaintiff, E, a minor proceeding by his father as next friend, appealed with the leave of the judge from the order of Otton J dated 7 April 1993 whereby he ordered under RSC Ord 18, r 19, or alternatively the inherent jurisdiction of the court, that the plaintiff's statement of claim against the defendant, the Dorset County Council, seeking damages for breach of statutory duty under the Education Acts and common law negligence for failure to provide appropriate special education be struck out on the grounds, inter alia, that it disclosed no reasonable cause of action. The facts are set out in the judgment of Sir Thomas Bingham MR.

Christmas v Hampshire CC

The plaintiff, Mark John Christmas, appealed with the leave of the judge, from the order of Otton J dated 7 April 1993, whereby he dismissed the plaintiff's appeal from the order of Master Murray dated 21 September 1992 ordering under RSC Ord 18, r 19, or alternatively the inherent jurisdiction of the court, that the plaintiff's statement of claim against the defendant, the Hampshire County Council, seeking damages for common law negligence for failure to provide appropriate special education be struck out, on the grounds, inter alia, that it disclosed no reasonable cause of action. The facts are set out in the judgment of Sir Thomas Bingham MR.

Keating v Bromley London BC

The plaintiff, Sefton James Keating (known as Richard), appealed with the leave of the deputy judge from the order of Peter Weitzman QC sitting as a deputy judge of the Queen's Bench Division of the High Court dated 30 July 1993 whereby he ordered under RSC Ord 18, r 19, or alternatively the inherent jurisdiction of the court, that the plaintiff's statement of claim against the defendant, the Bromley London Borough Council, seeking damages for breach of statutory duty under the Education Acts and common law negligence for failure to provide appropriate education be struck out on the grounds, inter alia, that it disclosed no reasonable cause of action. The facts are set out in the judgment of Sir Thomas Bingham MR.

a John Friel (instructed by *A E Smith & Son*, Stroud) for E.
Cherie Booth (instructed by *Veitch Penny*, Exeter) for Dorset.
Beverley Lang and Tom Croxford (instructed by *Bindman & Partners*) for Mark.
Cherie Booth (instructed by *Peter Robertson*, Winchester) for Hampshire County
    Council.
b Roger Ter Haar QC and John Greenbourne (instructed by *Teacher Stern Selby*) for
    Richard.
Tim Kerr (instructed by *Walter Million*, Bromley) for Bromley London Borough
    Council.

Cur adv vult

c 29 April 1994. The following judgments were delivered.

SIR THOMAS BINGHAM MR. In each of the three actions which give rise to
these appeals the defendant is an education authority. The ages of the plaintiffs
today range from 16 to 22. Each of them complains of acts done or not done
d by the education authority during his minority. Damages are claimed for
breach of statutory duty and common law negligence or (in one case) common
law negligence alone.

In each case the plaintiff's statement of claim has been struck out as
disclosing no reasonable cause of action and his action has been dismissed.
e There has been no investigation of the facts, some of which are very much in
issue. In accordance with standard practice, the argument has proceeded here
and below on the assumption that the facts pleaded by the plaintiff are true and
capable of proof. I shall refer to the plaintiffs respectively (at their request) as
E, Mark and Richard.

f *E v Dorset County Council*
    E was born on 8 February 1978. He is now aged 16. He proceeds by his
father as next friend. The facts relied on by E (so far as they can be gathered
from the pleading and from earlier judgments) appear to be as follows.
    E was a child with special educational needs. In November 1985 (when he
g was approaching the age of eight) his parents consulted the county council's
psychology service about his problems, which they believed to be caused by
dyslexia. They were advised that he did not suffer from a specific learning
difficulty. Following exchanges between E's parents and the county council,
as a result of E's severe and complex learning difficulties the county council
made a statement of special educational needs in respect of him under the
h Education Act 1981. A final statement was made on 6 July 1987. This identified
the local primary school he was attending as the appropriate school for him.
An educational psychologist employed or engaged by the county council
advised E's school and his parents on his specific problems and the means by
which his condition could be relieved. Until September 1987 E's parents
i accepted this advice and in reliance on it left him at the local school he was then
attending. In September 1987 E's parents, having realised that the
psychologist's advice was negligent and wrong, placed him at a private school
where all his problems and needs were addressed and his condition fully
diagnosed and treated. He thereafter remained at that private school, his
parents meeting the fees.

E's parents appealed under s 8 of the Education Act 1981 against the July 1987 statement. Their main complaint was that the statement of E's special educational needs and the proposed provision to meet those needs addressed only his literacy and not his numeracy difficulties. The appeal was allowed by the appeal committee, which in effect upheld the parents' complaint and remitted the matter to the county council. On 2 September 1988 a second final statement was produced by the county council. This recognised E's special educational needs as arising from difficulties in the fields of literacy and numeracy. It specified the special educational provision to be made for his literacy problems, which it concluded could be met (without outside support) at a named county council school. It did not make provision to meet his numeracy problems and it was later held that this school (nominated by the county council as appropriate for E) could not offer such provision. E's parents appealed to the Secretary of State against that statement and he rejected the appeal, but on 14 January 1991 Nolan J quashed the statement because it made no special educational provision for E's acknowledged numeracy problem and the judge referred the matter back to the Secretary of State. The Secretary of State appealed and on 8 May 1991 the Court of Appeal dismissed his appeal. On 27 June 1991 E's parents sought further directions from Nolan LJ (as he had now become) since the Secretary of State had not yet determined the appeal remitted to him earlier in the year. That application was dismissed. On 22 July 1991 a further statement was produced naming a maintained school as appropriate for E. He has since attended that school and no continuing complaint is made.

E issued proceedings in 1992. His statement of claim has been amended and a proposed reamendment was considered by the judge, although leave to reamend was not given. In the reamended statement of claim E alleges that the county council failed, in breach of its statutory duty, to diagnose or make provision for his special educational needs (particularly in respect of numeracy), or to refer him to an experienced educational psychologist, or to appreciate or act on the advice of its educational psychologist. E also alleges that the county council acted in breach of its common law duty of care in failing to recognise his condition, failing to make proper provision for his special educational needs, advising his parents that the provision for his needs at the local school he was attending was adequate when it was not, wrongly advising his parents to leave him at that local school, failing to inquire adequately into the true extent of his special educational needs and his specific learning difficulties, advising his parents in November 1985 that he did not suffer from a specific learning difficulty, failing to inquire whether adequate facilities existed in Dorset to help him, advising his parents that he had no numeracy problems and no significant emotional reactions, failing to diagnose his specific learning difficulties and advise his parents of their extent, and causing his parents to persevere until September 1987 in an inadequate placement.

The main claim in this case is a financial one. It is for some £30,000, expense to which (it is alleged) E's parents were put because they were obliged to place E at a fee-paying school which could meet his special educational needs. But it is alleged in passing that E failed to make progress and became upset and disturbed.

The county council applied to strike out E's statement of claim. Otton J heard this application jointly with the similar application made in *Christmas v Hampshire County Council*. He acceded to it. E now appeals.

Christmas v Hampshire County Council

Mark Christmas was born on 13 December 1973. He is now aged 20. The facts pleaded in his statement of claim are, in summary, as follows.

From 1978 to 1984 (aged about 5–11) Mark attended a local Church of England primary school. He showed severe behavioural problems and learning difficulties and had particular difficulty learning to read. His symptoms were consistent with the learning difficulty known as dyslexia. His parents expressed their concern to the headmaster and other members of the teaching staff on numerous occasions and asked for advice and further investigation into Mark's condition. The headmaster advised that Mark had no special learning difficulty and that his problems would be resolved if he exercised greater self-discipline and practised his reading.

In June 1984 the headmaster referred Mark to the Mid-Hampshire Teachers' Centre for an assessment of his learning difficulties, stating that Mark's achievements did not match his ability. He asked whether anything could be done before Mark went on to secondary school the following year. In July 1984 the headmaster reported to Mark's father that 'The Advisory Teacher felt that Mark had no serious handicaps, but that it was mainly a question of a good deal of regular practice'. The headmaster passed on the advisory teacher's suggestions for Mark's reading practice and thereafter Mark received assistance in reading practice from a teacher provided by the centre.

In 1985 Mark completed his primary education. Because of his learning difficulties his parents sent him to a private school specialising in remedial problems.

In 1988 Mark was assessed to determine whether he had special educational needs within the meaning of the Education Act 1981. In January 1989 the statement of special educational needs stated that Mark was of average ability but that he was 'significantly underachieving in literacy and especially in terms of his spelling skills and accuracy' and that this could be regarded as 'a severe specific learning difficulty'. Mark's learning difficulty was commonly known as dyslexia. Special educational provision for his learning difficulties was recommended.

Mark remained at the private school he was already attending but the county council paid his fees from the spring term of 1989. He left school in June 1990 aged 16.

On 7 February 1992 Mark, now aged 18, issued proceedings against the county council. In his statement of claim he pleads that the county council, their servants and agents owed him a duty to use reasonable skill and care in their assessment of his educational needs and problems. He alleges breach against the headmaster of the primary school in failing to refer him to the county council for a formal assessment of his educational needs and to an educational psychologist experienced in the diagnosis of specific learning difficulties. He also alleges breach against the centre in 1984–85 in failing to ascertain that Mark had a specific learning difficulty, failing to assess his learning difficulty, failing to diagnose his dyslexia and failing to refer him or recommend his parents to refer him to an educational psychologist. Mark makes no claim based on breach of statutory duty.

Mark pleads that if his condition had been correctly diagnosed, appropriate remedial treatment would have been instituted and his educational handicap and the behavioural problems it generated would have been substantially ameliorated. The failure to diagnose and treat his learning difficulty during his primary education has meant that he has been disadvantaged in realising his potential and as a result his vocational opportunities and prospects are significantly restricted. He has been forced into badly paid employment and his future advancement and earning capacity are likely to be prejudiced. No claim is made to recover any private school fees paid by the parents.

On the county council's application Master Murray ordered that the statement of claim be struck out and the action dismissed. On 7 April 1993 Otton J (who heard this appeal jointly with the defendant's application in *E v Dorset County Council*) dismissed Mark's appeal against that order.

Keating v Bromley London Borough Council

Sefton James Keating (known as Richard) was born on 24 May 1971. He is now aged 22. The facts pleaded in his statement of claim (most dates being approximate and some, according to the borough, wrong) are as follows.

From September 1976 to June 1977 (aged about 5–6) Richard attended a local primary school. From June 1977 to May 1979 (aged about 6–8) he was not registered at and did not attend any school. From May 1979 to July 1982 (aged about 8–11) he attended a special school. In September 1982 he went to another special school which he continued to attend until it closed in 1985. From September 1985 (when he was 14) to November 1986 he was not registered at and did not attend any school. From November 1986 to June 1987 he attended an ordinary secondary school.

Richard issued proceedings against the borough in 1993 when he was aged 21. In his statement of claim he pleads that from June 1977, when the borough removed, or caused, or permitted his removal from the local primary school, until 1986 the borough failed to provide for him a place at any school, or a place at any reasonably appropriate school, but only places at special schools. He also pleads that from June 1977 to May 1979 and from September 1985 to November 1986 the borough failed to provide a place for him at any school. The borough is said to have been in breach of its duty under ss 7, 8, 33 and 34 of the Education Act 1944 and the Handicapped Pupils and Special Schools Regulations 1959, SI 1959/365, and ss 2, 4, 5 and 7 of the Education Act 1981 and the Education (Special Educational Needs) Regulations 1983, SI 1983/29. Breach of a common law duty to take reasonable care in and about the exercise of its functions under these provisions is also alleged against the borough, detailed particulars being pleaded. In the particulars it is alleged that the borough failed to make proper inquiries into or assessments of Richard's educational capacity.

Richard alleges that as a result of these breaches he was deprived of any reasonable education and suffered impairment of his personal and intellectual development and suffered distress. It is said that although Richard is of at least average ability and should have been capable of passing GCSE or A level examinations and thereafter undertaking further education or training, his educational attainments are no more than those of an average 10-year old. He claims damages on these grounds. He also claims to recover the cost of private tuition provided by his parents between 1977 and 1986.

On 30 July 1993 Mr Peter Weitzman QC, sitting as a deputy judge of the Queen's Bench Division, ordered that the statement of claim be struck out. Richard appeals.

Striking out

It is clear that a statement of claim should not be struck out under RSC Ord 18, r 19 as disclosing no reasonable cause of action save in clear and obvious cases, where the legal basis of the claim is unarguable or almost incontestably bad. It was argued by Mr Ter Haar QC, for Richard, that this procedure was inappropriate in a case such as his, raising issues which were novel and difficult. Relying in particular on *Lonrho plc v Fayed* [1991] 3 All ER 303 at 312–313, [1992] 1 AC 448 at 469–470, he urged the undesirability of courts attempting to formulate legal rules against a background of hypothetical facts and pointed to the potential unfairness to plaintiffs if their cases were finally ruled upon before they were able, with the benefit of discovery, to refine their factual allegations. If a summary procedure for determination of legal issues were to be adopted at all, it should (he submitted) follow joinder of issues on the pleadings and discovery, and should be by decision on an issue of law suitable for determination without a full trial under RSC Ord 14A. The defendants answered that their applications do in effect raise an issue of law for decision by the court: if they cannot show the plaintiffs' claims to be plainly bad, then their applications must fail; but if they can show that, then it is preferable in the interests of all concerned that the claims should be dismissed now before the costs of a full trial are incurred.

There is great force in both these arguments. I share the unease many judges have expressed at deciding questions of legal principle without knowing the full facts. But applications of this kind are fought on ground of a plaintiff's choosing, since he may generally be assumed to plead his best case, and there should be no risk of injustice to plaintiffs if orders to strike out are indeed made only in plain and obvious cases. This must mean that where the legal viability of a cause of action is unclear (perhaps because the law is in a state of transition), or in any way sensitive to the facts, an order to strike out should not be made. But if, after argument, the court can be properly persuaded that no matter what (within the reasonable bounds of the pleading) the actual facts the claim is bound to fail for want of a cause of action, I can see no reason why the parties should be required to prolong the proceedings before that decision is reached. The court is of course bound to approach each pleaded cause of action separately, and need not reach the same decision on each.

Two of these plaintiffs rely on alleged breaches of statutory duties owed to them by the education authorities and said to be actionable in a private law action for damages at the suit of a pupil damnified by the authority's breach. The relevant authorities deny that the statutory duties in question can give rise to any private law action for damages. There is here, as it seems to me, a clear-cut issue between the parties. There is clear authority governing the courts' approach to the issue of construction which is raised. The court is able, now as well as later, to review the statutory provisions relied on and any previous case law and decide whether these provisions, if breached, give rise to a private law claim for damages or not. This decision will not be sensitive to the actual facts. I do not think the court would be justified, particularly at this stage, in declining to rule on the issue.

All three plaintiffs rely on alleged breaches of a common law duty of care said to have been owed to them by the authorities or their servants and agents for whom the authorities are legally responsible. Whether such duties were owed is, or may be, more problematical. If it is clear, whether by statute or from previous authority, that the relationship between the parties is not or cannot be such as to give rise to a duty of care, then the court can safely strike out the statement of claim. If, however, that is not clear, or the answer may depend on the exact relationship of the parties and what passed between them and what each knew, did or said at any time, or the court is unable safely to decide whether (on the facts pleaded) it is just and reasonable to impose a duty of care, then the case is not one in which a striking out order can be appropriate.

Breach of statutory duty

I gratefully adopt and need not repeat the summary given by Evans LJ of the relevant provisions of the Education Acts 1944 and 1981 and of the 1983 regulations. I agree with his analysis of them.

In *Hague v Deputy Governor of Parkhurst Prison, Weldon v Home Office* [1991] 3 All ER 733 at 750, [1992] 1 AC 58 at 170 Lord Jauncey of Tullichettle, having reviewed a number of well-known authorities, said:

'My Lords, I take from these authorities that it must always be a matter for consideration whether the legislature intended that private law rights of action should be conferred upon individuals in respect of breaches of the relevant statutory provision. The fact that a particular provision was intended to protect certain individuals is not of itself sufficient to confer private law rights of action upon them, something more is required to show that the legislature intended such conferment.'

If Parliament has conferred other rights, exercisable by individuals, to procure observance of the statutory duty, that will weigh against the inference that Parliament intended to confer a private right to claim damages.

It is evident that the 1981 Act and the 1983 regulations prescribe a detailed code for identifying, assessing and providing for children with special educational needs. This code makes ample provision for involving parents in decisions affecting their children and gives parents a right of appeal to an appeal committee and to the Secretary of State if they wish to challenge decisions made or not made. It seems to me quite plain that Parliament intended any complaint by children or their parents of breach of these duties to be pursued through these administrative channels and not by a private law action for damages or an injunction. After exhausting these remedies, children or parents would of course be entitled, on appropriate grounds, to seek leave to move for judicial review, but that would not of itself carry with it any right to recover damages.

The relevant provisions of the 1944 Act did not lay down a detailed code. The duties laid on local education authorities were, indeed, couched in very general terms. But I find no indication that Parliament intended any complaint by children or their parents of breach of these duties to be enforceable by private law action for damages or an injunction. Since that Act did not provide the specific remedies now available that inference is weaker than on the present legislation, but it still seems to me (looking at the 1944 Act alone) to be an inescapable inference.

If, despite these conclusions, one is to hold that these statutes, and particularly the 1981 Act, did confer an actionable private law right for damages it must be because authority compels or points towards that conclusion. It was argued for E and Richard that authority does have that effect. This makes it necessary to examine those authorities.

In *Wilford v West Riding of Yorkshire CC* [1908] 1 KB 685 the main dispute was between the managers of a public elementary school and a local education authority. The main issues were whether a direction given by the authority was within its powers and whether the court's jurisdiction was ousted by the terms of the Education Act 1902. Channell J held that the direction was ultra vires and that the court's jurisdiction was not ousted. He granted the plaintiffs an injunction. To that extent the case involved what would today be called a pure public law issue. The case is relied on because certain parents of children at the school were also plaintiffs and the judge held that they had rights (albeit qualified) to have their children admitted to public elementary schools (see [1908] 1 KB 685 at 704). But he added that 'the right is one which could hardly be dealt with practically' and 'I do not see my way to giving them any relief against the defendants, and I am not quite sure that I am asked to do so, or, if I am asked, what it is which is asked'. He made no award of damages to the parents. I cannot regard this as persuasive authority on the existence of a private law action for damages for breach of statutory duty.

Ching v Surrey CC [1910] 1 KB 736, [1908–10] All ER Rep 305 arose out of personal injury suffered by a pupil at a public elementary school because the school premises had not been kept in proper repair. The jury found that the injury could have been avoided had proper care been taken, and the Earl of Halsbury regarded the case as one of negligence (see [1910] 1 KB 736 at 741, [1908–10] All ER Rep 305 at 307). The substantial question in the case, according to him, was: who was responsible for the negligence? His answer, with which Fletcher Moulton and Farwell LJJ agreed, was that the defendants were responsible because the 1902 Act laid on them the duty to maintain the school and keep it efficient. It may be correct to regard this as an action for breach of statutory duty, but it does not seem to me to advance the argument very much since the decision is plainly explicable on other grounds.

Gateshead Union v Durham CC [1918] 1 Ch 146 is an authority very heavily relied on by E and Richard. The plaintiffs were poor law guardians responsible for a number of children. The defendants were the local education authority. The defendants, with support from the board of education, threatened to exclude the children from their public elementary school unless the plaintiffs made a special annual payment towards the cost of maintaining the school. The plaintiffs refused and issued proceedings claiming declarations that the children were entitled to attend the school and that the defendants were not entitled to refuse them admission and an injunction. Neville J refused the plaintiffs relief, holding that the defendants' only obligation was to comply with a code of regulations made in 1912, and that it was for the board of education to determine whether the requirements of the code had been observed.

The Court of Appeal reversed that decision. Swinfen Eady LJ said (at 159–160):

> 'I am of opinion that the Acts which require a parent to cause his children to attend school give him the right to comply with their provisions and enable him to insist that the child which he tenders shall be permitted to "attend" school—that is, to be and remain at the school—during school

hours and receive the instruction which similar children receive, and that the defendants have not any right to refuse to receive his child unless they receive some payment or money contribution. He is entitled to free education for his child—that is, education without making any payment whatever. The accommodation in the school cannot be said to have been made "available" for children if they are refused admission unless and until their parents comply with some request to pay money which the statutes do not confer upon the local education authority any right to demand.'

Warrington LJ gave judgment to similar effect (at 164):

'The result, in my opinion, of the statutory provisions so far mentioned is that the defendants are not entitled to exact as a condition of the attendance of a child at one of their schools the payment of money in any form whatever, unless the case is within one of the exceptions to the prohibition contained in s. 2 of the Act of 1891. But the matter does not rest there, for by the joint effect of the statutes and of the by-laws made under them by the defendants the parent of every child of not less than five nor more than fourteen years of age is required under penalties to cause such child to attend school unless there is a reasonable excuse for non-attendance. This seems to me to imply a corresponding obligation on the part of the local education authority to permit the attendance of the child subject only to the conditions expressed or implied in the statutes, which in my opinion, as I have already said, do not include the payment of money.'

The case is, however, chiefly relied on for the observations of Scrutton LJ (at 167):

'Neville J. has, if I understand his judgment, taken the view that he cannot imply a right in the parent and correlative duty in the education authority because the Acts expressly state the duty and there can be no implication. But it seems to me that a statutory obligation to provide education without fee and without religious restriction, if broken, gives a right of action to any person specially injured by the breach of such an obligation though he is not expressly mentioned in the statute. A parent is a person specially injured by any unauthorized exclusion of his child from the free education to which he is entitled, and therefore a person entitled to sue for such a breach of statutory obligation. By similar reasoning in *Ching* v. *Surrey County Council* the county council, who are bound by statute to maintain the school, are held liable in damages to a child injured by defective condition of the school which they have failed to maintain.'

It is clear that the plaintiffs in this case were in the same position as a parent, and the decision recognised the right of a parent to complain if his child is wrongfully excluded from a public elementary school. But there was no claim for damages, as on the facts there could not be, and no damages were awarded. It does not appear that *Ching's* case was relied on in argument, and only Scrutton LJ referred to it. The dispute was of a public law nature. The decision would make it impossible to argue that a parent may not enforce (subject to any defences) the statutory duty laid on a local education authority, but it is tenuous authority for holding that breach of such a duty will found a civil action for damages.

In *Watt v Kesteven CC* [1955] 1 All ER 473, [1955] 1 QB 408 a parent sent his sons to private schools of his own choosing and not to a private school nominated by the defendants at which they were willing to pay the fees. He sought a declaration that the defendants were under a statutory duty to provide education at the schools which the boys had attended, an order of mandamus directing them to carry out their duty and repayment of the tuition fees he had paid. He failed at first instance and on appeal. By this time, of course, the 1944 Act was in force. Denning LJ held that no breach of the Act was shown. He added ([1955] 1 All ER 473 at 476–477, [1955] 1 QB 408 at 424–425):

> 'This being so, the appeal must be dismissed: and there is no need to consider the question which was much debated before us whether a breach of s. 76 gives rise to a cause of action for damages. It could not itself do so, but only in connection with the exercise of some other power or duty in which the general principle was not observed. In view of *Gateshead Union v. Durham County Council*, I should not like to say that there can be no cases under the Act in which an action would lie, but I do not think an action lies in this case. It is plain to me that the duty under s. 8 (to make schools available) can only be enforced by the Minister under s. 99 of the Act and not by action at law. That being so, a breach of s. 76 in the exercise of s. 8 can also only be enforced by the Minister and not by action at law.'

Parker LJ similarly felt it was unnecessary to resolve this question ([1955] 1 All ER 473 at 480, [1955] 1 QB 408 at 429–430):

> 'Finally, the point remains whether the breach of the obligation imposed by s. 76 [of the Education Act, 1944] enables a parent who has suffered injury to bring a civil action. While it is plain that the breach of some provisions of the Act would not give rise to a cause of action, I am certainly not prepared to say that no breach of any obligation imposed by the Act affords a cause of action to a parent who has suffered damage. To do so would be to fly in the face of authority and in particular in the face of the decision in *Gateshead Union v. Durham County Council*, a decision of this court. It is necessary, I think, in every case to consider the duty in question and, where the allegation is that there has been a breach of s. 76, to consider the duty in connection with which it is shown that the provisions of s. 76 have not been observed. Assuming, contrary to the conclusion I have reached above, that there is an obligation to pay full tuition fees at an independent school of the parent's choice, it seems to me that *Gateshead Union v. Durham County Council* is directly in point and that an action would lie. On the other hand, if, as I think, the duty under s. 8 is merely to secure that facilities are available, the only remedy for a breach of that duty would be by action by the Minister on complaint under s. 99. I would dismiss the appeal.'

Birkett LJ agreed with both judgments. This decision gives no support to the suggestion that an action can be founded on breach of s 8 alone, nor that any right under it can be enforced by private action. Nor does it hold that damages are recoverable for any breach of the statutory duties imposed by the Act.

In *Wood v Ealing London Borough* [1966] 3 All ER 514 at 522, [1967] Ch 364 at 384, Goff J held:

> '… any breach of s. 8, whether absolute or because of the impact of s. 76, can only result in a failure to discharge the statutory duty of providing sufficient schools, and the only remedy for that, apart possibly from the case of an individual plaintiff able to show that he or she had suffered damage, which is not the case before me, is by complaint to the Secretary of State under s. 99.'

For that conclusion the judge relied on *Watt v Kesteven CC.* In *Bradbury v Enfield London Borough* [1967] 3 All ER 434, [1967] 1 WLR 1311 the Court of Appeal granted the plaintiffs (who included a number of parents) an interlocutory injunction restraining a local education authority from acting in breach of its statutory duty, but the dispute was of a public law nature and there was no claim for damages. In *Cumings v Birkenhead Corp* [1971] 2 All ER 881, [1972] Ch 12 the plaintiffs' complaint was that the education authority had acted unreasonably and beyond its powers. This claim was rejected. It was held that if a complaint lay it should be made to the minister. Again, the dispute was of a public law nature and there was no claim for damages.

Meade v Haringey London Borough [1979] 2 All ER 1016, [1979] 1 WLR 637 was another decision on which E and Richard strongly relied. Schools in Haringey had been closed for some weeks by strike action. A complaint to the Secretary of State under s 99 of the 1944 Act had proved unavailing. Some parents issued proceedings claiming a mandatory order that the local education authority perform its duty under s 8 of the 1944 Act and associated declarations. Goulding J refused interlocutory relief. By the time the appeal came on for hearing the industrial dispute had been resolved, and the parents' appeal was accordingly dismissed.

Lord Denning MR expressed his opinion in these terms ([1979] 2 All ER 1016 at 1024–1025, [1979] 1 WLR 637 at 647):

> 'But if the public authority flies in the face of the statute, by doing something which the statute expressly prohibits, or by failing to do something which the statute expressly enjoins, or otherwise so conducts itself, by omission or commission, as to frustrate or hinder the policy and objects of the Act, then it is doing what it ought not to do—it is going outside its jurisdiction—it is acting *ultra vires.* Any person who is particularly damnified thereby can bring an action in the courts for damages or an injunction, whichever be the most appropriate. Instances from the House of Lords are when the corporation of Lyme Regis failed to perform its public duty to repair the sea wall, in consequence of which some cottages were flooded (see *Lyme Regis Corpn v Henley* (1834) 2 Cl & Fin 331, [1824–34] All ER Rep 503); and when the Minister of Agriculture failed to refer a complaint to a committee of investigation and thereby so conducted himself as to frustrate the policy and objects of the Act (see *Padfield v Minister of Agriculture, Fisheries and Food* [1968] 1 All ER 694, [1968] AC 997); and when an officer of the Home Office (who was in charge of borstal boys) was guilty of an act of omission contrary to his instructions, by reason of which an individual suffered damage, the Home Office were liable because it was ultra vires both the officer and the Home Office (see *Home Office v Dorset Yacht Co Ltd* [1970] 2 All ER 294 at 332–333,

[1970] AC 1004 at 1068–1069 by Lord Diplock); likewise when the inspector of a local authority acted outside the ambit of the discretion delegated to him (see *Anns v London Borough of Merton* [1977] 2 All ER 492 at 503–504, [1978] AC 728 at 755 by Lord Wilberforce).'

I cannot regard this passage as supported by the authority relied on. The *Lyme Regis* case is far removed from the present cases on its facts; it appears to me that it is possibly to be regarded as a case on public nuisance. In *Padfield* the plaintiffs' claim was for mandamus, not damages. In *Dorset Yacht* and *Anns v Merton London Borough* the liability of the public authority rested on proof of negligence, not breach of statutory duty. Nor can *Gateshead* be regarded as a case in which it was held that 'the parents were held entitled to sue for damages and, if need be, an injunction' (see [1979] 2 All ER 1016 at 1024, [1979] 1 WLR 637 at 646, per Lord Denning MR).

Eveleigh LJ did not express agreement with Lord Denning's judgment. He went no further than to say that a parent whose child was attending a school had a particular interest in the school being open and was entitled to relief if the school were closed without just and reasonable excuse (see [1979] 2 All ER 1016 at 1028, [1979] 1 WLR 637 at 651). Sir Stanley Rees also expressed no agreement with Lord Denning MR. He held that if the parents proved a breach by the authority of their statutory duty under s 8, which they could do by showing that the authority had acted ultra vires or by misfeasance, they would be entitled to an appropriate declaration (see [1979] 2 All ER 1016 at 1035, [1979] 1 WLR 637 at 658). I do not think this decision can be regarded as sound authority for the wider principles sought to be extracted from it.

R v Mid-Glamorgan CC, ex p Greig (1988) Independent, 1 June is closer to the present cases. It was an application for judicial review by an 18-year-old applicant. He claimed damages for a local education authority's breach of statutory duty. His damage comprised a claim for reimbursement of a term's school fees and compensation for loss of the benefit of appropriate education and consequential diminution in the quality of his life. One of the issues Simon Brown J had to address was whether damages were in principle recoverable for the breach of statutory duty alleged. He reviewed a number of the cases and then said:

> 'In the last analysis, however, I believe that the essential objection to a damages claim in this context is not the existence of the default provisions but rather the want of any good cause of action. As it seems to me, by no means all breaches of statutory duty by public authorities give rise to any private law claim whatever irrespective of whether the relevant statute contains default provisions. In my judgment it is only in certain exceptional and well-recognised circumstances that someone, even if particularly damnified by an authority's non-compliance with a statutory duty, can claim damages for such breach. I have in mind circumstances where non-compliance involves also the commission of a recognised tort such as trespass, false imprisonment or negligence, or when the authority is actuated by malice as in a case where it knows that it does not possess the power it purports to exercise. But I am certainly not to be taken in this judgment to be exploring exhaustively the limits of the concept of administrative tort. Turning to the instant case, I conclude that even had I found the respondents to be in breach of their s 8 duty to this applicant, even indeed had this been so exceptional a case as perhaps to enable the

court to declare that Lucton alone would have provided suitable education for William, no damages claim would have been sustainable save only perhaps to the extent of the fees actually paid privately for that education. The case would then have been strictly comparable to that of the homeless person under consideration by Lord Bridge in his speech in *Cocks v Thanet DC* [1982] 3 All ER 1135 at 1138, [1983] 2 AC 286 at 292–293: "Once a decision has been reached by the housing authority which gives rise to the temporary, the limited or full housing duty, rights and obligations are immediately created in the field of private law. Each of the duties referred to, once established, is capable of being enforced by injunction and the breach of it will give rise to a liability in damages. But it is inherent in the scheme of the 1977 Act that an appropriate public law decision of the housing authority is a condition precedent to the establishment of the private law duty."'

The judge did not therefore rule out a claim for damages, but he left little room for one.

In *R v Secretary of State for Education and Science, ex p Davis* [1989] 2 FLR 190 the Queen's Bench Divisional Court (Watkins LJ and Auld J) held that the Secretary of State had no power to make any order which would have the effect of enabling parents to make an enforceable money claim against a local education authority for school fees they had incurred before a statement relating to a child had been made.

The applicant in *R v Inner London Education Authority, ex p Ali* (1990) 2 Admin LR 822 was seeking (by way of judicial review) damages for the interference which he claimed had occurred in his son's education. It was held that the duty imposed by s 8 of the 1944 Act was intended to enure for the public in general and was not intended to give the individual litigant a cause of action. Specific indorsement was given to certain of the observations of Simon Brown J in *Greig*'s case quoted above and the application was dismissed.

In the course of argument considerable reference was made to other authorities dealing with different subject matters, particularly the homelessness legislation. I accept of course that guidance on matters of principle may be derived from cases dealing with different subject matters but where, as here, the question to be answered turns on the effect Parliament intended specific legislative provisions to have it is dangerous to stray very far from the provisions with which one is immediately concerned. None of the cases relied on in my judgment compels a conclusion that any of the statutory provisions in question here was intended to confer a private law right of action for damages for breach of statutory duty. While some statements in some of the cases give E and Richard some assistance, the overwhelming balance of authority is against them. I do not doubt that they can enforce (or could have enforced) the statutory duties they rely on, subject to exhaustion of other remedies and proof of breach, by judicial review, but the Acts confer no right to damages.

Negligence

In Mark's case, allegations of negligence are clearly and explicitly pleaded against his headmaster and a teacher supplied by the Mid-Hampshire Teachers' Centre. Hampshire County Council is sued as being responsible for both.

In the cases of E and Richard, the allegations of negligence are less specific, no doubt because the plaintiffs lack the information necessary to particularise their complaints. It would, however, appear that E complains of negligence by an educational psychologist employed by Dorset County Council, county council officials and teachers. I infer that Richard alleges negligence against officials of the borough and also possibly teachers and educational psychologists. Both E and Richard repeat as particulars of negligence the particulars of statutory duty already pleaded.

Having held that the statutory provisions relied on by E and Richard did not confer a private law right of action for damages, I would not be willing to hold that common law duties of care existed to identical effect. But allegations of carelessness against individuals for whom the education authorities are responsible raise more difficult questions, partly because of the plaintiffs' understandable difficulty in pleading the facts accurately and specifically at this stage.

It would seem to me at least arguable that some of these individuals would be in a position to foresee injury to the plaintiffs if they acted carelessly in relation to them. It would also seem arguable that some of these individuals would have been in a proximate position vis-à-vis the plaintiffs. I have in mind a psychologist examining a plaintiff and advising on his learning capacity; a teacher advising on a plaintiff's learning capacity; or an official receiving reports on one of the plaintiffs and considering or advising what ought to be done. Since there is no precedent for a claim against psychologist, teacher and official in these circumstances, the next stage in the conventional analysis is to ask whether it is just and reasonable to impose a duty on them or any of them in this context.

The plaintiffs say that a psychologist interviewing and advising on a child is in very much the same position as a psychiatrist or any other doctor examining or advising a patient: he is a person exercising a skilled calling and bound by law to show reasonable care and skill in doing so. They say much the same of the teacher. They accept of course that teachers, however dedicated and gifted, cannot rectify inequalities of endowment between one pupil and another; teachers have no duty to ensure that any pupil achieves his full potential; and they are not liable, as no professional person is liable, for mere errors of judgment. But it is said that as trained and skilled professionals they would owe a duty to detect and react appropriately to gross deviations from normality in a pupil's learning performance or behaviour in circumstances where an ordinarily competent teacher would do so. Officials of local education authorities are similarly said to owe the subjects of their decisions and actions a duty to exercise reasonable care and skill.

The education authorities argue strongly against the imposition of such a duty. They say, for reasons similar to those which found favour with the majority in *M (a minor) v Newham London BC, X and ors (minors) v Bedfordshire CC* [1994] 4 All ER 602, [1994] 2 WLR 554, that it would not be just and reasonable to impose such a duty. They rely on the reasoning of the majority in that case to contend further that a common law duty should not be imposed on those whose involvement is as a result of statute, where Parliament itself has not imposed such a duty, and that those acting for a local education authority owed a duty to it and not to the plaintiff (see [1994] 4 All ER 602 at 628–630, 634–636, 638, [1994] 2 WLR 554 at 581–583, 587–588, 591).

To the extent that this reasoning is applicable to the different circumstances of these cases it is of course binding, and even if not binding it may point towards the correct answer. But the circumstances are in my view so different as to make transposition hazardous. The teaching of, and making educational provision for, children with learning difficulties cannot be seen as purely a function of the state. It is hard to say that those who give their advice to parents, or know that their advice will be communicated to parents, owe a duty only to their employer and not to those parents and their children. In the absence of evidence it is hard to weigh the more general considerations to which reference was made.

I do not think it possible to hold as a matter of law that no duty can be owed by any of the individuals for whom it is sought to hold the education authorities liable to these plaintiffs. I am not therefore of opinion that the claims should be struck out at this stage as disclosing no reasonable cause of action. I wish to make it quite clear to the plaintiffs and their parents that I am not holding in their favour that a duty of care was owed to them or any of them. I am only holding that on the pleadings as they stand I do not conclude that these claims are unarguable or almost incontestably bad.

I should refer to a separate ground advanced for striking out Richard's claim. This was that he had suffered no loss which would found a claim to compensation in tort. Whereas in contract a plaintiff may sue for an unrealised gain, in tort he can sue only for loss, and it was said that he had suffered none. I would accept that certain elements pleaded as damage by Richard (for example, the allegation that he suffered distress and that he is a shy, diffident person) cannot be compensated in damages, and similar points may be made about E's claim that he was 'upset'. It is also quite clear that none of the plaintiffs can recover damages for a congenital defect. If, however, a plaintiff can show: (1) that the adverse consequences of his congenital defect could have been mitigated by early diagnosis of the defect and appropriate treatment or educational provision; (2) that the adverse consequences of his congenital defect were not mitigated because early diagnosis was not made, or appropriate treatment not given or provision not made, with resulting detriment to his level of educational attainment and employability; and (3) that this damage is not too remote, I do not regard the claim for damage to be necessarily bad. In any event, I did not understand it to be argued by the education authorities (if, contrary to their submission, any duty was owed) that the claims made by E and Richard for recovery of school fees were bad in principle.

I would allow the appeals by all three plaintiffs against the striking out of their claims for damages for common law negligence. I would dismiss the appeals by E and Richard against the striking out of their claims for damages for breach of statutory duty.

EVANS LJ. It has not been easy to identify and define the damage for which the plaintiffs seek compensation from the defendants, who are local education authorities. I begin therefore with a summary of the claims as I understand them to be.

E is alleged to have been in need of special educational provision between 1985, when he was aged $7\frac{1}{2}$ and his parents first consulted an educational psychologist employed by the defendants, and 1992, when the Secretary of State determined that his learning difficulties could be met within a mainstream school with additional support. No complaint is made about that 1992 assessment. From September 1988 (aged 10) until 1992 he was educated privately at Egington school which provided for his special needs. The fees were paid by his parents. The claim is for damages representing the cost of that period of private schooling together with general damages for personality upset and behavioural disorder which is alleged to have been caused by the failure to provide for his special needs between 1985 and 1988 and by the delay in providing them thereafter. It is asserted on his behalf that Egington was the special school to which he would have been sent at the cost of the defendants if they had performed their statutory duties at least from 6 July 1987 when a statement of special needs was first made pursuant to the Education Act 1981.

The 1981 Act and the regulations made under it came into operation on 1 April 1983 and so they applied throughout the relevant period in this case.

Mark attended a primary school between 1978 (aged 5) and 1984. He is said to have exhibited severe behavioural problems and learning difficulties which were consistent with the condition known as dyslexia. His parents expressed their concern to the teaching staff and to the headmaster but they were assured that no special teaching was necessary. Eventually in 1984 however the headmaster referred him to the defendants' teachers advisory service who reported that he had no serious handicaps. The headmaster passed this onto his parents. They were dissatisfied and arranged for Mark to attend a private school at Frensham. He was assessed under the 1981 Act in 1988 and 'statemented' in January 1989 as requiring special educational provision on account of 'a severe specific learning difficulty', namely dyslexia. The defendants then undertook responsibility for the fees at Frensham school.

The claim is for the cost of private education between 1985 and 1989 and for general damages representing the short and long-term consequences of the delay in diagnosing his dyslexia. It is alleged that because of this delay there was a failure to ameliorate his condition and that the literary deficit cannot now be cured. His earning capacity, it is alleged, both present and future is greatly reduced.

Richard was born on 24 May 1971. He has had a much interrupted history of schooling. An outline account is given in the statement of claim, showing that in June 1977 (aged 7) he was removed from primary school and thereafter until 1986 (aged 15) he either received no schooling or attended two special schools for short periods. Eventually in 1986 an educational psychologist advised that he could and should attend an ordinary school.

The defendants in this action issued their summons to strike out the statement of claim before serving a defence or giving discovery or volunteering any details of the plaintiff's education so far as it is known to them. It is said on their behalf that they challenge the accuracy of the plaintiff's account. This they are entitled to do but it makes the factual issues even more difficult to identify than they might otherwise be. In particular, if the plaintiff was removed from primary school and thereafter required to attend special schools, both before and after 1983 when the 1981 Act came into operation, then the inference must be that some form of assessment was carried out by them, or on their behalf, but we have no knowledge of this.

The claim is for general damages for impairment of the plaintiff's personal and intellectual development and for distress which he has suffered and continues to suffer by reason of the spasmodic and, as is alleged, inappropriate schooling which he received between 1977 and November 1986. He is said to be of average academic ability and to have had an average educational potential, which would have been realised by a reasonably normal education but which is now lost.

DYSLEXIA

We were told by Miss Lang, counsel for Mark, that dyslexia is a neurological dysfunction and is congenital. If untreated, dyslexics suffer from a 'relatively worsening retardation' so that although they make progress in reading and spelling they do so at a rate which is slower than the rate of normal children and they therefore fall more and more behind. Moreover, if treatment is too long delayed, the condition becomes irremediable and the child or young adult can never achieve the standard which otherwise he might have done.

We were not referred to specific expert evidence, but it may also be the case that a physical defect which causes reading difficulties if untreated, for example defective eyesight or a squint, can result in the same process of relatively worsening retardation in the learning process.

Miss Lang's helpful note also states that behavioural problems associated with dyslexia become increasingly severe over time if the dyslexia is not treated because of continued frustration and loss of confidence. In time the child becomes disturbed and can suffer psychological harm of a kind which is sufficiently serious to constitute an identifiable mental illness.

INJURY, LOSS AND DAMAGE

The issue raised by the defendants' applications is whether the claims should be struck out at this stage of the proceedings. The question whether the injury, loss and damage alleged by the plaintiffs is actionable in law depends partly upon the cause of action upon which they rely—the test is different, for example, as between a breach of contract and the tort of negligence—and partly upon expert evidence when medical or psychological injury is alleged, as it is here. No such evidence is deployed at this preliminary stage and the claims could only be struck out on this ground if it was clear that damages for injury of the kind alleged cannot be recovered as a matter of law.

Two specific issues are raised as matters of principle. First, that the allegations of learning difficulties and behavioural problems do not amount to physical or psychological injury for which the defendants can be held responsible in law. Rather, it is submitted that the plaintiffs suffer or may suffer from congenital defects in their learning processes which do not amount to an injury for which damages can be awarded. In my judgment, this submission goes too far. If the plaintiffs suffer or have suffered from a pathological or psychological condition which accounts for the learning difficulties and other problems which they have experienced, then I can see no reason in principle why that should not be recognised as a form of injury for which compensation may be awarded, if the necessary conditions for liability are proved. Whether or not this is proved will depend upon evidence to be given at the trial.

The second objection taken by Mr Tim Kerr for the defendants in Richard's case is that damages for the torts alleged by the plaintiffs cannot be awarded, as he submits, for the loss or non-realisation of an expected gain, or for the defendant's failure to confer a benefit upon the plaintiff, as distinct from causing identifiable damage or loss. There may be much to be said for this as a general proposition but in my judgment it does not amount to an invariable rule. It can be tested in this way. The closest analogy to the duties of care which the plaintiffs allege against a head teacher (Mark) or an educational psychologist (E) is the admitted duty which is owed by a school teacher in respect of the physical well-being, health and safety, of the pupil (see *Van Oppen v Bedford Charity Trustees* [1989] 3 All ER 389, [1990] 1 WLR 235), or by a doctor to his patient. If the pupil or the patient is injured or shows symptoms of a physical illness which the teacher or the doctor negligently fails to notice or to treat, or to arrange medical treatment in the case of the teacher, then clearly the damages recoverable in tort as well as in contract will include compensation for the consequences of that failure, including the consequences of delay in obtaining proper treatment. If the submission was correct, it would mean that no damages could be recovered in tort where the injury or illness became no worse, even though the failure to treat it or the delay in treating it meant that it was slower to heal or be cured than otherwise it would have been.

CAUSE OF ACTION

The causes of action relied upon by E and Richard are breach of statutory duty and negligence; in the case of Mark, negligence alone.

(1) *Breach of statutory duty*

(a) The Education Acts

The Education Act 1944 established what s 7 described as a 'statutory system of public education'. It was the direct successor of the Education Act 1902, which had designated county councils (including county borough councils) as the local education authorities in their areas. The 1902 Act transferred to the local education authorities the powers and duties of school boards which had been established under the Elementary Education Act 1870. Thus the responsibility of local authorities for providing a 'system of public education' can be traced back to the 1870 Act.

The purposes of the statutory system of education introduced by the Education Act 1944 are expressed in s 7 of the Act, as follows:

'... it shall be the duty of the local education authority for every area, so far as their powers extend, to contribute towards the spiritual, moral, mental, and physical development of the community by securing that efficient education ... shall be available to meet the needs of the population of their area.'

The basic statutory duty of the authority is to secure that sufficient schools are available in its area. Section 8 of the Education Act 1944 provides:

'(1) It shall be the duty of every local education authority to secure that there shall be available for their area sufficient schools—(a) for providing primary education ... and (b) for providing secondary education ... and the schools available for an area shall not be deemed to be sufficient unless they are sufficient in number, character and equipment to afford for all pupils opportunities for education offering such variety of instruction and training as may be desirable in view of their different ages, abilities, and aptitudes, and of the different periods for which they may be expected to remain at school, including practical instruction and training appropriate to their respective needs.'

Section 8(2) of the 1944 Act in its original form read as follows:

'In fulfilling their duties under this section, a local education authority shall, in particular, have regard ... (c) to the need for securing that provision is made for pupils who suffer from any disability of mind or body by providing, either in special schools or otherwise, special educational treatment, that is to say, education by special methods appropriate for persons suffering from that disability ...'

Sections 33 and 34 provided for arrangements to be made for the education of pupils requiring special educational treatment and made it the duty of every local education authority to ascertain what children in their area require special educational treatment by the means set out in s 34.

(b) The 1981 Act

The Education Act 1981 introduced a new and much expanded scheme for the provision of special education for children with special educational needs. We were told by Mr Ter Haar QC for Richard that the Act gave expression to a new philosophy. First, even pupils with special educational needs may be better served if they are placed in ordinary or mainstream schools, and secondly, it is important to ensure that special provision is made available for all children who are in need of it, hence the detailed identification and assessment procedures under the Act and the Education (Special Educational Needs) Regulations 1983, SI 1983/29, made under it. The 1981 Act became effective on 1 April 1983.

The scheme of the Act is as follows. Section 8(2)(c) of the 1944 Act was amended to read '[Shall have regard] to the need for securing that special educational provision is made for pupils who have special educational needs' (s 2(1)). Sections 2 and 3 specify the kinds of special provision which may be made: in an ordinary school (s 2(2)) or 'otherwise than in a school' (s 3). The procedure for identifying and assessing children with special educational needs is set out in s 4 and following.

First, identification. It is the duty of every local education authority 'to exercise their powers under this Act with a view to securing that, of the children for whom they are responsible, those with special educational needs which call for [the authority] to determine the special educational provision that should be made for them are identified by the authority' (s 4(1)). This may be called the general statutory duty with regard to children with special needs. It is owed to the children defined in s 4(2), that is to say those who are in the area of the authority and who are *either* (a) registered as a pupil at a school maintained by the authority (or in one additional category not relevant in the present case), *or* (b) 'brought to their attention as having, or as probably having, special education needs', and not registered as above.

Express provision is made in s 9 of the Act for parents to request an assessment of the educational needs of their child.

Section 5 requires the authority, first, to form an opinion as to whether the child does have, or probably has, special educational needs in respect of which some special provision should be made. If it does form such an opinion, then it must make an assessment in accordance with the section. Section 5(1) reads as follows:

'Where, in the case of a child for whom a local education authority are responsible, the authority are of the opinion—(a) that he has special educational needs which call for the authority to determine the special educational provision that should be made for him; or (b) that he probably has such special educational needs; they shall make an assessment of his educational needs under this section.'

The following subsections provide that the parents must be notified and consulted (sub-ss (2) and (5)), and if the authority decides that no special provision need to be made, the parents likewise must be notified and they have a right of appeal to the Secretary of State, who may direct the authority to reconsider its decision (sub-ss (6) to (8)). Section 5, therefore, is concerned with 'assessment'.

The next stage in the process is described in s 7. Having made the assessment, the authority must form a further opinion as to whether it should determine the special provision that should be made for the child. If it does so, then it must make a statement of the special needs and of the special provision to be made for them, and maintain the statement thereafter. Section 7(1) reads:

'Where an assessment has been made in respect of a child under section 5, the local education authority who are responsible for the child shall, if they are of the opinion that they should determine the special educational provision that should be made for him, make a statement of his special educational needs and maintain that statement in accordance with the following provisions of this Act.'

Hence the expression that a child becomes 'statemented' under the Act.

The form of a statement is specified in Sch 1, Pt II, para 3 of the Act. It must give details of the authority's assessment of special educational needs, and it must specify the special educational provision to be made for the purpose of meeting those needs. The prescribed form is in the schedule to the 1983 regulations. It may include what is called 'non-educational provision' for the special needs.

The remaining subsections of s 7 are of some significance in the present appeals. Section 7(2) provides that in any case where the authority maintains a statement in respect of a child, then it is the duty of the authority to arrange that the special educational provision specified in the statement is made for him, but with this proviso 'unless his parent has made suitable arrangements'. This recognises both the continuing involvement of the parent and the fact that he or she may choose to make other arrangements which are suitable for the child's needs.

The parent's role is also emphasised by sub-s (3) and following. He must be notified in writing and may make representations, which the authority is bound to consider at a meeting with the parent and the appropriate persons, including those who gave the relevant advice; and the statement may be made in the form originally proposed, or in a modified form, or the authority may determine not to make a statement.

There follows express provision for appeals, first to an appeal committee (s 8(2)) and then to the Secretary of State (s 8(6)).

(c) The 1983 regulations

Apart from detailed requirements for the form and contents of statements made under s 7(1) of the Act (reg 10), the relevant provisions are those concerned with the process of assessment under s 5. These regulations are made pursuant to the directive in Sch 1, Pt 1 of the Act, which refers expressly to medical, psychological and educational advice.

Regulation 4 requires the authority to seek—

'(a) educational advice as provided in Regulation 5; (b) medical advice as provided in Regulation 6; (c) psychological advice as provided in

Regulation 7, and (d) any other advice which the authority consider desirable in the case in question for the purpose of arriving at a satisfactory assessment ...'

Educational advice has to be sought primarily from the head teacher of a school which the child has attended at some time within the preceding 18 months (reg 5(1)(a)), and medical advice from a 'fully registered medical practitioner' designated or nominated in accordance with reg 6. Psychological advice must be sought—

'(a) from a person regularly employed by the education authority as an educational psychologist, or (b) from a person, in the case in question, engaged by the education authority as an educational psychologist.' (See reg 7(1).)

In addition, reg 8 lists other matters which the authority must take into consideration. These include representations from and any evidence submitted by the child's parents.

There is no provision for the advice which must be sought by the authority to be given to the parent or the child, but the parent's views and any evidence submitted by him must be made available to the person from whom advice is being sought (see reg 4(4)). Moreover, the statement must set out the advice which the authority has received and taken into consideration, as well as the representations, evidence and information upon which it has acted (see reg 10(1)(d)). Before making a statement, the authority must send a copy of the statement which it proposes to make to the parent, and as already noted above it must then take account of any further representations from the parent and, where appropriate, it must arrange meetings which will enable the parent to discuss the relevant advice with the person who gave it (see s 7(3) and following).

Finally, reg 9 provides for a mandatory reassessment at the age of 13.

Comment

The Acts place duties upon local education authorities which are nowhere said to be owed to any individual nor is any individual given the express right to enforce them by action at law. If any of these duties is broken, and a claim is brought by any person who alleges that he has suffered special damage by reason of the breach, then it becomes necessary to consider whether the statute confers such a right upon him as a matter of inference in accordance with the principles set out in *Cutler v Wandsworth Stadium Ltd (in liq)* [1949] 1 All ER 544, [1949] AC 398 and *Hague v Deputy Governor of Parkhurst Prison, Weldon v Home Office* [1991] 3 All ER 733, [1992] 1 AC 58.

Clearly, the Acts envisaged that schools would continue to exist in the private sector and that parents who could make the necessary financial arrangements with such schools would thereby discharge their statutory duty under s 36 of the 1944 Act. In those cases, there would be no actual requirement for the authority to provide free education for that child. Only if the parent appears to be failing to perform his duty is the authority required to intervene by serving a school attendance order under s 37 of the 1944 Act.

Nevertheless, if the child does require primary or secondary education the authority has the express duty under s 8 to secure that a suitable school is available which the child can attend. It is unnecessary in the present appeals to determine the precise implications of this duty; whether there is, for example, a duty to provide a certain minimum standard of education, and if so, how it is to be measured. The express obligation is to secure that a place is available at a suitable school.

If this duty is not performed, then I have no doubt that it may be enforced by means of legal proceedings commenced by or on behalf of the child. The correct form of proceedings in the light of the House of Lords' decision in *O'Reilly v Mackman* [1982] 3 All ER 1124, [1983] 2 AC 237, is an application for judicial review under RSC Ord 53 which is governed by the requirements of the rules. The first question of law which arises in these appeals is whether the child or its parents has any statutory claim for damages or other remedy apart from the application for judicial review. If they had such a claim before the introduction of Ord 53, then nothing in that order or in *O'Reilly v Mackman* has taken it away (see *Equal Opportunities Commission v Secretary of State for Employment* [1994] 1 All ER 910 at 929, [1994] 2 WLR 409 at 427, per Lord Browne-Wilkinson).

Claim for damages for breach of statutory duty

I agree entirely with the judgment of Sir Thomas Bingham MR that the plaintiffs are not entitled to proceed with claims for damages for breach of statutory duty in the circumstances of any of these three cases. I would add only the following by way of general comment. The claim for damages, in my judgment, is not an alternative remedy which may be asserted when a breach of statutory duty is alleged and proved. Damages are an essential part of the cause of action in tort, when it exists. The damages claim is brought in order to recover compensation for failure to perform the statutory duty, rather than to compel performance of the obligation itself.

Before turning to the question whether there is a cause of action in negligence, it is important to note that the statutory duties placed upon the authority are nowhere defined in terms of a duty of care. They are, for example, to secure that schools are available (s 8 of the 1944 Act) and to form opinions (ss 5(1) and 7(1) of the 1981 Act). There is no warrant, in my judgment, for imposing any statutory duty of care upon the authority itself. The second question which arises is whether any of the individuals who play parts in the statutory processes owes a duty of care to the child or the parents which can be enforced by them.

(2) Negligence

Here too I agree entirely with the judgment of Sir Thomas Bingham MR. It is sufficient for the purposes of these appeals to hold, as I do in respectful agreement with him, that the claims in negligence ought not to be struck out as being doomed to failure and inevitably bad. I agree also with his statement of the correct approach which should be adopted to striking-out applications such as these.

We heard full argument on the legal issues arising in relation to the claims in negligence, and what follows represents my provisional views on these issues.

Individual employees of the authority and independent persons who act as the authority's agents, or who are consulted in a professional capacity by the authority, clearly are likely to owe a duty of care to the authority, subject to the terms of their contract of employment or any other contract between them and the authority. There is nothing in the Acts, in my judgment, which entitles the child or the parent to enforce those duties of care, or to claim damages for the consequences of any breach. Nor, as a matter of general principle, can the child or parent enforce any such contractual terms, not being a party to the relevant contract. Therefore, any duty of care owed independently of the contract must also arise independently of the statute, in other words, out of some relationship between the child or parent on the one hand and the alleged tortfeasor on the other hand. If any such duty of care does arise, there is nothing in the Acts, in my judgment, which limits or excludes it, nor is there any reason why the authority, if it was the employer of the tortfeasor at the relevant time and the negligence occurred in the course of the employment, should not be vicariously liable to the child or parent in the usual way.

The tort of negligence is established if the facts show that the defendant owed a duty of care towards the plaintiff, that the defendant was negligent in breach of that duty, and that the breach caused damage to the plaintiff which was not too remote a consequence of the negligence, in law. These appeals provide a timely reminder that the plaintiff's concerns arise in precisely the opposite order to the lawyer's approach. He will allege that he has suffered damage as a result of negligent conduct by the defendant, and only if this can be established will it become necessary to consider whether, in addition to the question of remoteness, the defendant owed the plaintiff at the relevant time a duty of care.

I prefer the latter approach in the present appeals for this reason. Each of the three components of the cause of action in negligence is the subject of dispute: whether the alleged damage is of a kind recognised by the law; the identity of the individual or individuals alleged to have been negligent; and whether that individual or those individuals owed the plaintiff a duty of care. It is necessary to identify the individual before the duty can be established, and the person responsible for the damage cannot be identified until the damage itself has been defined.

The statutory duties of the local education authorities are performed by individuals on their behalf. None of these duties is imposed directly on the individuals, or upon them personally, and the suggestion that they each owe a duty of care to the plaintiffs or other individuals affected by their duties is contrary to the well-established rule that the individual officer of a public authority is not liable unless misfeasance, not merely negligence, is proved against him:

> '... it is a general principle that, if a government department or officer, charged with the making of decisions whether certain payments should be made, is subject to a statutory right of appeal against his decisions, he owes no duty of care in private law. Misfeasance apart, he is only susceptible in public law to judicial review or to the right of appeal provided by the statute under which he makes his decision.' (See *Jones v Dept of Employment* [1988] 1 All ER 725 at 736, [1989] QB 1 at 22 per Glidewell LJ.)

So the plaintiffs must establish that there were individuals employed by the defendants upon whom the common law imposed a duty of care in the performance of their duties independently of the statute and that this duty was owed to the plaintiffs. If there was such a duty and it was broken, then the defendants are vicariously liable to them for its breach.

The next question, therefore, is whether the plaintiffs have identified or can identify any individuals with whom they had dealings and who may have owed to them such a duty of care. The position seems to be as follows. E identifies an educational psychologist employed by the defendants to whom he was first referred in 1985. Whether the subsequent failures to make sufficient provision for his special needs until 1992, as has been held in judicial review proceedings, was the result of advice given by this person, or of some other advice, or an administrative decision is unclear. Mark identifies two persons—the headmaster at his primary school and the consultant employed by the defendants at their advisory teachers' centre. Richard cannot identify any individual, but the facts he alleges in the statement of claim suggest that the defendants in his case received advice from one or other of the categories of experts referred to in the 1983 regulations, at least after the regulations came into operation on 1 April 1983.

When making an assessment, the education authority must seek educational advice from a qualified teacher, and whenever possible from a recent head teacher (see regs 4(1)(a) and 5); medical advice from a duly registered medical practitioner (see regs 4(1)(b) and 6); and psychological advice from a person employed or engaged by the authority as an educational psychologist (see regs 4(1)(c) and 7). In each of these cases, the person by whom advice is given professes a special qualification or skill. The fourth category is 'any other advice which the authority consider desirable in the case in question for the purpose of arriving at a satisfactory assessment' (see reg 4(1)(d)). This may or may not involve a professional person. If it does, then that person is in the same position as the other professionals referred to under the previous heads.

When these persons are asked for their advice, they must owe to the authority a duty to exercise a reasonable degree of professional skill and care, as an implied term of the contract under which they are engaged or employed. The duty may also arise in tort, as for example when the child's former head teacher is not employed by the authority in question. Although owed to the local authority it must be a duty to take reasonable care to give correct advice to the best of the person's ability and professional skills.

If the advice given was negligent and as a result the authority suffered loss, then there would be no reason in principle why the authority should not recover damages for that negligence, whether in contract or in tort (economic loss being prima facie recoverable for negligent advice).

Likewise, if the advice given is negligent and it is the child which suffers actionable damage or loss, there is no reason in principle in my judgment why that loss should not be recovered as damages for tort. The objection taken by the defendants in the present case is that the professional person consulted by the authority or to whom the child has been referred owes no duty of care to the child. The necessary degrees of foreseeability and proximity are admitted to exist. But the law should not impose a duty, it is submitted, which is owed to the child.

General considerations of fairness and justice point clearly, in my opinion, towards such a duty being imposed. It is uncomfortable to think of the doctor, educational psychologist or the head teacher being constrained by an awareness that he could be held liable in damages if he was negligent towards his employer but was immune if he was negligent towards the child. He might even find it difficult to distinguish between a duty owed to the child as well as the authority and one owed to the authority alone. He would either exercise the necessary degree of professional skill and care, or he would not.

The matter can be tested in this way. If the doctor or other professional was consulted privately by the child's parents, he would owe a duty of care towards them as his employer. This duty would be to exercise professional skill and care in the best interests of the child and in my view the same duty would also be owed to the child.

The same applies in my judgment when the employer is not the parents but the education authority. The basis for the duty owed to the child is not the contract under which the professional person is consulted, nor the statutory requirement that the authority should consult him, but the relationship which is brought about between them. Put another way, the consultant owes a duty in tort to the child as his patient, or as the person in whose interests his professional advice is sought and given. Nothing in the statutes prevents this duty from arising or from being enforced in the usual way.

The second objection taken by the defendants is that the majority judgment of this court in *M (a minor) v Newham London BC, X and ors (minors) v Bedfordshire CC* [1994] 4 All ER 602, [1994] 2 WLR 554 prevents us from holding that a duty of care was owed to the plaintiffs in the circumstances of this case. The judgment of course is binding upon us and the question is whether the factual situation is the same. In both cases, the defendants are local authorities who are alleged to have been in breach of statutory duties in respect of the child on whose behalf the proceedings are brought. In the *Newham* case it was the social services legislation, including the Children Act 1989. The defendants included a consultant child psychiatrist employed by the health authority who interviewed the child and examined her in order to ascertain whether she had been sexually abused, as they were concerned to find out.

The majority of the Court of Appeal (Staughton and Peter Gibson LJJ) held that no duty of care was owed to the child either by the psychiatrist or by the social workers who were involved in the case. As regards the psychiatrist, which is the relevant comparison in the present cases, the reason given by Staughton LJ was that the child could not be regarded as the patient of the psychiatrist, except for the purposes of confidentiality and a limited duty not to cause harm in the course of the examination or treatment. 'The child was no more the patient than an applicant for life insurance who is examined by the company's doctor, or the errant motorist who is deprived of a small quantity of blood by the police surgeon' (see [1994] 4 All ER 602 at 629, [1994] 2 WLR 554 at 582). Peter Gibson LJ drew the same analogy with an applicant for life insurance. The child had not been referred to the psychiatrist 'in order that advice or treatment be given to the child, or for that matter, her mother' (see [1994] 4 All ER 602 at 638, [1994] 2 WLR 554 at 591). It was never intended that the psychiatrist should give them the advice which she gave to the local authority.

There are significant differences, in my view, between the situation of a doctor who is asked to examine a child in order to report to the local authority whether or not there is evidence of sexual abuse, so that the local authority can decide whether or not to exercise its statutory powers to remove the child from his home or take other steps to prevent any recurrence of suspected abuse, and of a doctor or other specialist who is asked to advise whether the child suffers from a medical including psychological disorder which requires special treatment and what form the treatment should take. But it is unnecessary to explore these differences further because the former case was held in both the majority judgments to be equivalent to that of a doctor acting for an insurance company who examines an applicant for life insurance. The question which arises is whether the present case is within that same category, or not.

In my judgment it is not, for reasons which reflect the considerations I have referred to above. The insurance company's doctor undertakes by contract to examine and report upon the physical condition of the applicant. He does not undertake by contract or otherwise to treat the applicant, and it may well be the case—I do not know the answer to this—that it would be a breach of professional etiquette towards the applicant's own doctor if he was to offer or undertake any form of treatment, including professional advice. In these circumstances, there clearly is a limited relationship between him and the applicant and this is reflected in the limited scope of the duty of care which he owes to the applicant in tort.

In the present case, on the other hand, the doctor or specialist is engaged not merely to report but to advise on the best interests of the child. The advice is a form of treatment, and in my judgment the child and its parents as well as the authority are entitled to expect that the advice will be carefully and competently given.

For these reasons, I would hold that the *Newham* case is clearly distinguishable from the present and that the educational psychologist identified in the pleadings in E's case, and the unidentified professionals who it must be inferred were involved in Richard's case, owed the plaintiffs in those actions a duty of care.

A different allegation is made by Mark. It is that the head teacher of the primary school which he was attending and the advisory teacher employed by the authority owed him a duty to use reasonable skill and care in their assessment of his educational needs and problems. As for the head teacher, it is established by authority that a school teacher is bound to take such care of his pupils as a careful father would take of his children (see Liell and Coleman *Law of Education* (9th edn, 1993) para 54, citing *Williams v Eady* (1893) 10 TLR 41 and Harris *The Law Relating to Schools* (1990) p 250). The standard of care required may be in some respects higher than that of a parent, because the teacher may have or reasonably be expected to have specialist knowledge by reason of his wider experience and professional qualifications (see *Van Oppen v Bedford Charity Trustees* [1989] 3 All ER 389 at 414, [1990] 1 WLR 235 at 266 per Croom-Johnson LJ). The duty clearly includes exercising reasonable skill and care to safeguard the pupil against physical harm. It does not extend to protecting the child or his parents from economic loss (see *Van Oppen's* case).

At this point, the issues as to damage and duty overlap. In my judgment, for the reasons given at the outset, the failure to treat or the delayed treatment of dyslexia does arguably give rise to a form of injury which can support a claim for damages for negligence in tort. It follows from this that the school teacher's duty to exercise reasonable skill and care to safeguard the pupil from injury includes a duty to be aware of symptoms which a reasonably careful parent or a reasonably skilled and careful teacher would regard as symptoms either of dyslexia or, more generally, of a need for specialist advice. The parent or the teacher can then put the statutory processes for identification, assessment and 'statementing' into operation.

This degree of skill and care seems to me to be no less than the parent could reasonably expect from a private school where the duty would be regulated by an implied (or possibly express) term of the contract between parents and school and in any event, in my judgment, would be owed in tort to the child. If the school failed to notice and report upon specific problems which indicated or might indicate a dyslexic condition, or the child's need for special educational provision, then it seems to me that the parents and the child would have legitimate cause for complaint.

The private school parallel is supported by this extract from O'Connor LJ's judgment in *Van Oppen v Bedford Charity Trustees* [1989] 3 All ER 389 at 416, [1990] 1 WLR 235 at 268:

'When one considers the duty owed by a school to its pupils one finds first of all the duties which the law imposes on all schools because they are schools. These duties are of general application whether the school be provided by the state, or privately, and regardless of whether it be fee-paying or free.'

I respectfully agree.

Miss Booth for the defendants in two of the cases, E and Mark, relied upon the following passage from the judgment of Slade LJ in *R v Surrey CC Education Committee, ex p H* (1984) 83 LGR 219 at 235:

'... there is no question of Parliament having placed the local authority under an obligation to provide a child with the best possible education There is no duty on the authority to provide such a Utopian system, or to educate him or her to his or her maximum potential ...'

It is clear that neither the local authority as the provider of education under the (public) statutory system, nor a school which undertakes by contract to provide private education, is under a duty expressed in these terms. Equally in my judgment, there must be some duty on a private school to provide a minimum standard of education, if only as an implied term of the contract between the school and the parents. This question, however, does not arise in the present case, because the duties of the defendants are imposed by statute and, for the reasons given above, whilst the child and his parents can enforce proper performance of those duties, they cannot claim damages or other compensation for the consequences of past failures of the authority to perform them.

The question which does arise is whether a teacher employed by the authority, for whom the authority is vicariously liable, owes a duty of skill and care in relation to the child's education which goes beyond the duty to safeguard his or her physical and, I would add, mental well-being. Suppose that there was no allegation of dyslexia or some equivalent dysfunction in the present case, but merely an allegation that the child with better teaching could have achieved higher academic standards, or improved examination results, or a more highly paid career. Could it be held that the teacher, if he had failed to teach with reasonable skill and care, and the authority as his employer, was liable in damages in such a case? My provisional view is that the answer must be No, because the plaintiff in such an action could not show any measurable injury other than economic loss, and it is established by the judgment in *Van Oppen*'s case that no claim lies in negligence in respect of such loss. In the present case, however, it is unnecessary to express a concluded view, because it is of the essence of each of the cases that the plaintiff either suffered from what I will call congenital psychological damage which was not properly treated or was caused similar damage as a result of misdiagnosis by unidentified expert advisers to the defendants.

MEASURE OF DAMAGES

I return finally to the question whether the plaintiffs are entitled to recover, not merely general damages in respect of the injury which they allege, but also special damages representing the cost of education in private schools, which was incurred by the parents of E and Mark.   There are two potential difficulties. First, the fees were paid by the parents, not by the plaintiff himself. If this was the only objection, or if the claims for breach of statutory duty could be established, then I would hope that it could be overcome.   The second difficulty is that it may be argued that the fees were incurred because the parents chose to educate the child outside the statutory system, as they were entitled to do.   This could give rise to an issue as to causation; but it has not been raised by the defendants, and I therefore need say no more about it.

ROSE LJ. For the reasons given by Sir Thomas Bingham MR, I agree that the appeals of all three plaintiffs against the striking out of their claims for damages for common law negligence should be allowed and that the appeals of E and Richard against the striking out of their claims for damages for breaches of statutory duty should be dismissed.

Appeal in Christmas v Hampshire County Council allowed.   Appeals in E v Dorset County Council and Keating v Bromley London Borough Council allowed in part. Leave to appeal to the House of Lords granted to all parties.

L I Zysman Esq   Barrister.

Practice Note

QUEEN'S BENCH DIVISION
LORD TAYLOR OF GOSFORTH CJ, SCOTT BAKER AND LONGMORE JJ
25 OCTOBER 1994

Practice – Crown Office list – Time estimates – Skeleton arguments and paginated bundles – Failure to observe time limits for lodging skeleton arguments and paginated bundles – Late Crown Office papers resulting in adjournment of hearing may be penalised in costs.

LORD TAYLOR OF GOSFORTH CJ delivered the following practice note at the sitting of the court.

The following arrangements will take effect immediately.

Applications for leave to apply for judicial review and for leave to appeal under s 289 of the Town and Country Planning Act 1990

Where the documents in support of an application for leave exceed ten pages, they must be paginated and indexed in a convenient bundle.   In addition, a list must be provided of the pages essential for reading by the court. Where only part of a page needs to be read, that part should be indicated, by side lining or in some other way, but not by highlighting.

Substantive hearings

As a case reaches the top of Part B of the Crown Office List the applicant/appellant's solicitors will be informed by letter that the case is likely to be listed, at short notice, with effect from a date specified in the letter (the 'warned date'). It is the responsibility of the applicant/appellant's solicitors to inform the respondent and all interested parties of the likelihood of the case being listed at short notice.

In cases where a fixed date is given, it is the responsibility of the applicant/appellant's solicitors to inform the respondent and all interested parties of the fixed date.

The applicant/appellant's solicitors are also responsible for providing a paginated, indexed, bundle for the use of the court. The bundle must be lodged with the Crown Office at least *five* clear working days before the 'warned date' or, where a fixed date has been given, at least *five* clear working days before the fixed date.

Advocates are required to lodge skeleton arguments in the Crown Office. Advocates for the applicant must lodge, and serve, their skeleton arguments at least *five* clear working days before the 'warned date' or the 'fixed date', as appropriate. Advocates for the respondent or other party wishing to be heard must lodge, and serve, their skeleton arguments at least *three* clear working days before the 'warned date' or the 'fixed date', as appropriate. The skeleton argument must quote the Crown Office reference number and the 'warned date' or the 'fixed date', as appropriate and contain (a) the time estimate for the complete hearing, including delivery of judgment (whether or not an estimate has been given earlier); (b) a list of issues; (c) a list of propositions of law to be advanced (together with the authorities relied upon in support, with page references to passages relied upon); (d) a chronology of events (with reference to the paginated bundle prepared for the court); (e) a list of the essential documents for advance reading by the court, with page references to passages relied upon; (f) a list of dramatis personae where the number of people who feature in the documents warrants it.

The above time limits must be strictly observed. Failure to do so may result in adjournment and may be penalised in costs.

Advocates may however supplement their skeleton arguments up to one working day before the hearing.

Where a case is due to be listed for hearing before a Divisional Court two copies of the skeleton argument and paginated bundle are required. Where the case is due to be listed for hearing before a single judge only one copy of each is required.

Amendment of grounds and further affidavits

Any notice of intention to seek leave to amend the grounds or relief or to rely upon further affidavits must be given to the other party(ies) and the Crown Office, together with the proposed amendments or affidavits, no later than *five* clear working days before the 'warned date' or the 'fixed date', as appropriate.

If notice is not given at that time, the court will be reluctant to exercise its powers to allow amendment or the use of further affidavits, save in exceptional circumstances.

Dilys Tausz   Barrister

Filmlab Systems International Ltd and another v Pennington and others

CHANCERY DIVISION

ALDOUS J

22 JUNE, 2 JULY 1993

Counsel – Payment of costs by counsel personally – Costs incurred unreasonably or improperly – Timing of application for wasted costs order – Legally aided defendants making interlocutory application on advice of counsel – Application dismissed by judge as 'wholly misconceived' – Plaintiffs applying for wasted costs order against defendants' counsel – Whether counsel committing error that no reasonably well-informed and competent member of Bar could have made – Whether interlocutory order for wasted costs appropriate – Supreme Court Act 1981, s 51(6).

The plaintiffs issued proceedings against the defendants alleging inter alia breach of contract and infringement of copyright. The defendants, who had been granted legal aid to defend the action, applied for specific discovery of software and documents (before the time when an order for discovery would normally have been made) in support of their applications for orders striking out the plaintiffs' claims as either disclosing no reasonable cause of action or being an abuse of the process of the court and for an order discharging the Anton Piller order which the plaintiffs had obtained earlier. The judge rejected the principal applications before dismissing the wide-reaching application for discovery as 'wholly misconceived' and ordered the defendants to pay the plaintiffs' costs on an indemnity basis, directing that, because the defendants were legally aided, the order should not be enforced without the leave of the court. The plaintiffs concluded that those costs had been unreasonably incurred and, appearing before a different judge, applied for a wasted costs order pursuant to s 51(6)[a] of the Supreme Court Act 1981 (as substituted by s 4 of the Courts and Legal Services Act 1990) against the defendants' counsel on the ground that he had acted unreasonably or had been negligent in advising the defendants' solicitors to apply for discovery at that stage in the proceedings.

Held – An application for a wasted costs order under s 51(6) of the 1981 Act should not, save in exceptional circumstances, be sought against a party's legal representative until after trial, since it was only at that time that the question whether the legal representative had committed an error of judgment which no reasonably well-informed and competent member of his profession could have made (which applied regardless of whether the representative was acting for a legally aided or for a fee-paying client) could be evaluated properly in the context of the case as a whole and on the basis of evidence, not inference. On the facts, the plaintiffs had not established that advice to apply for discovery of the type that was sought was an error which no reasonably well-informed and competent member of the Bar could have made in the absence of an analysis of the factual background against which it was given. Indeed, it would not be possible until after trial to look at the application in its context of the whole

---

a   Section 51(6) is set out at p 677 *e*, post

proceedings. If, for example, it turned out that the plaintiffs' case was hopeless, the application could be seen as an attempt (albeit with a slim chance of success) to shorten the proceedings at an early stage and so could be viewed as one which competent counsel would try. It followed that the application would therefore be dismissed (see p 677 h to p 678 c g h and p 680 a to d j, post); dictum of Lord Diplock in *Saif Ali v Sydney Mitchell & Co (a firm) (P, third party)* [1978] 3 All ER 1033 at 1043 and of Dillon LJ in *Orchard v South Eastern Electricity Board* [1987] 1 All ER 95 at 105–106 considered.

Per curiam. A further reason why applications for wasted costs orders should not be made at an interlocutory stage is the danger that legal advisers may be prevented from continuing to act objectively for their clients, thus effectively depriving clients of the advisers of their choice, and the consequent danger of wasted costs applications being abused by one party in harassing the other side's legal advisers in such a way as to affect the course of justice (see p 678 j to p 679 c, post).

Notes

For costs generally, including solicitors' personal liability for costs, see 37 *Halsbury's Laws* (4th edn) paras 712–725, and for cases on the subject, see 37(3) *Digest* (1983 reissue) 268–270, 4524–4534.

For counsel's duty of care, see 3(1) *Halsbury's Laws* (4th edn) paras 528–530 and 37 ibid para 511, and for cases on the subject, see 3(2) *Digest* (2nd reissue) 512–547, 4176–4201.

For the Supreme Court Act 1981, s 51 (as substituted by s 4 of the Courts and Legal Services Act 1990), see 11 *Halsbury's Statutes* (4th edn) (1991 reissue) 1217.

Cases referred to in judgment

Orchard v South Eastern Electricity Board [1987] 1 All ER 95, [1987] QB 565, [1987] 2 WLR 102, CA.

RHM Foods Ltd v Bovril Ltd [1982] 1 All ER 673, [1982] 1 WLR 661, CA.

Saif Ali v Sydney Mitchell & Co (a firm) (P, third party) [1978] 3 All ER 1033, [1980] AC 198, [1978] 3 WLR 849, HL.

Application

The plaintiffs, Filmlab Systems International Ltd and Bios Systems Ltd, by a notice of motion dated 5 January 1993 (and amended on 2 February), applied for an order that initially solicitors and then counsel instructed on behalf of the first and third defendants, Brian John Pennington and Derek James Ruddock, should personally pay the costs of a motion for discovery which had been moved on their behalf before Vinelott J on 15 October 1992 in an action for breach of contract and infringement of copyright on the ground that the costs had been unreasonably incurred. The second defendant, Metachrome Images Ltd, which went into receivership in 1991, and the fourth defendant, Bucks Motion Picture Laboratories Ltd, took no part in the proceedings. The facts are set out in the judgment.

Martin Howe (instructed by *Wedlake Bell*) for the plaintiffs.
Michael Burton QC (instructed by *Reynolds Porter Chamberlain*) for the defendant's counsel.

Cur adv vult

2 July 1993. The following judgment was delivered.

ALDOUS J. This is an application by the plaintiffs for what is called a 'wasted costs order' under s 51(6) of the Supreme Court Act 1981 as amended by s 4 of the Courts and Legal Services Act 1990.

The first plaintiff, Filmlab Systems International Ltd, was formed in 1979. It supplies equipment to the film processing industry, mainly to the moving picture film industry. The second plaintiff, Bios Systems Ltd, was formed in August 1986 to provide software to the first plaintiff and if possible to others.

Dr Pennington, the first defendant, started work for the first plaintiff some time in 1984 as a self-employed consultant. Mr Ruddock, the third defendant, was appointed as the first plaintiff's engineering and production manager in August 1989 and left its employ in November of that year. The second defendant, Metachrome Images Ltd, was formed on 14 August 1989 and on 18 August Dr Pennington and Mr Ruddock became its directors.

In about the middle of 1990 the first plaintiff heard a rumour that Mr Ruddock had established a competing company. This was subsequently confirmed to be true, when the plaintiffs found that the second defendant was exhibiting a competing colour film analyser at an exhibition. On 1 May 1990 Mr Varian, the technical director of the first plaintiff, complained to Dr Pennington about what he regarded as undue delay on his part in carrying out work on software for the plaintiffs. Dr Pennington informed him that the delay had been caused by damage to a hard disk drive on his computer which had resulted in him losing the relevant source code. He told Mr Varian the name of the service company that had replaced the disk. Subsequently, the first plaintiff purchased the faulty disk drive from the service company. They had suspicions that Dr Pennington was behaving in breach of his contract and therefore sent it to a company which specialised in recovering data from faulty disk drives.

The analysis of the received data was difficult and time consuming. However, the plaintiffs concluded that Dr Pennington was infringing the plaintiffs' copyright and that the source code used by Dr Pennington would contain substantial sections copied from works of the plaintiffs. They therefore applied for Anton Piller type relief.

At a hearing on 30 July 1991 Harman J ordered that the defendants should allow the plaintiffs to enter their premises and make copies of certain software and also that the defendants should deliver to the plaintiffs copies of certain codes. That order was executed.

The second defendant went into receivership in 1991 and the fourth defendant, Bucks Motion Picture Laboratories Ltd, is taking no part in these proceedings.

On 16 January 1992 the plaintiffs served their statement of claim. In that statement of claim, they allege breach of contract and infringement of copyright and claim injunctions and ancillary relief.

The second and third defendants applied for and were granted legal aid. A defence and counterclaim were served on their behalf on 30 September 1992. They deny the plaintiffs' claim, allege that the plaintiffs have been guilty of offences under the Computer Misuse Act 1990, that the plaintiffs had infringed the defendants' copyright and had misused confidential information. They also allege that the plaintiffs were in breach of their obligations to make full and frank disclosure of all relevant matter at the hearing on 30 July 1991. The defendants also allege that the plaintiffs have conspired to injure the defendants and have thereby caused the second defendant to be put into receivership. They claim injunctions, exemplary damages and other relief.

On 2 October 1992 the defendants issued two notices of motion. The first sought that by 4.30 pm on 12 October the plaintiff should (1) deliver up to the defendants' solicitors a true copy of the diskettes containing recovered data and programs from the defendants' hard disk that was supplied to the plaintiffs pursuant to the disk recovery contract in about May 1991; (2) disclose to the defendants' solicitors the names and addresses of all persons to whom certain programs or data that were recorded on that disk were disclosed; (3) supply to the defendants' solicitors copies of correspondence passing between the plaintiffs and the disk recovery company; and (4) deliver to the defendants, upon terms as to confidence, a copy of the current source code and object code of all programs and data being marketed by the plaintiffs together with associated maintenance and user manuals, promotional material and training documentation.

The second notice of motion sought an order that (1) the statement of claim be struck out under RSC Ord 18, r 19, as disclosing no reasonable cause of action and/or being otherwise an abuse of the process of the court; (2) the order of Harman J be discharged; (3) an interim payment of £95,000 towards the damages suffered by the defendants; (4) an inquiry as to damages under the cross-undertaking as to damages and (5) costs.

Those motions were stood over to come on for hearing on 15 October 1992. On that date Vinelott J heard the first motion relating to discovery and by agreement stood the second motion over generally. That motion has not been brought back before the court.

Vinelott J heard the first motion for about one and a half hours. In his judgment he said:

'In this application the defendant seeks specific discovery of documents before the time when an order for discovery would be made in the ordinary course. The order for discovery is sought on three grounds. First, there is an application, yet to be heard, to strike out the proceedings as disclosing no cause of action. No evidence is capable of being heard on that ground. Secondly, it is sought to strike out the proceedings as an abuse of the process of the court. It seems to me to be quite misconceived to seek wide-reaching discovery in order to show that an action is an abuse of the process of the court. It is for the person seeking the order striking out to make his case. The third ground is the defendants are now seeking to set aside an Anton Piller order and for damages said to result from an Anton Piller order which it is claimed ought never to have been made. It is impossible, I think, at the moment to make an order for discovery in relation to that claim. The evidence on it has not yet been filed. It is by no means clear precisely what the allegations are or what the issues are. It will be for the judge who hears that application, which is both to set aside the order and for damages under the cross-undertaking (they clearly go together), to decide whether it should be heard at the same time as the trial or the trial of the action or immediately after it, or whether if it is heard separately there should not be points of claim. At the moment it is hopelessly ill-defined. If and when points of claim are directed then there will be defined issues on which an order for discovery can be sought. To come here now with a wide-reaching application for discovery in support of ill-defined issues is, in my judgment, wholly misconceived. I will do nothing except dismiss the application.'

He ordered that the motion be dismissed and that the first and third defendants should pay the plaintiffs their costs of the motion, such costs to be taxed if not agreed, but the order for costs should not be enforced without leave of the court. He also ordered that the first and third defendants' costs be taxed pursuant to the Legal Aid Act 1988.

The plaintiffs concluded that the costs of the first motion had been unreasonably incurred and issued a notice of motion on 5 January 1993, seeking an order that the defendants' solicitors should pay the costs of the motion. That motion was stood over to come on as a motion by order. It was amended on 2 February 1993, by order of Mummery J, so as to add the defendants' counsel as a respondent. This resulted from evidence filed, which stated that the defendants' solicitors acted on the advice of counsel. Before me that was accepted to have been the position. Therefore the plaintiffs did not pursue this application against the solicitors and only sought to recover the costs of the motion for discovery from the defendants' counsel.

The ability to recover wasted costs from counsel and solicitors stems from s 51 of the Supreme Court Act 1981, as amended by s 4 of the Courts and Legal Services Act 1990. The relevant parts of that section are as follows:

'... (6) In any proceedings mentioned in subsection (1), the court may disallow, or (as the case may be) order the legal or other representative concerned to meet, the whole of any wasted costs or such part of them as may be determined in accordance with rules of court.

(7) In subsection (6), "wasted costs" means any costs incurred by a party—(a) as a result of any improper, unreasonable or negligent act or omission on the part of any legal or other representative or any employee of such a representative; or (b) which, in the light of any such act or omission occurring after they were incurred, the court considers it is reasonable to expect that party to pay ...'

It is not alleged that the defendants' counsel acted improperly, but it is alleged that he acted unreasonably or was negligent. Thus I must decide: (1) were costs wasted as a result of any unreasonable or negligent act of the defendants' counsel and, if so, (2) should those costs or any part be paid by the defendants' counsel?

The duties of counsel were examined at length in *Saif Ali v Sydney_Mitchell & Co (a firm) (P, third party)* [1978] 3 All ER 1033 at 1043, [1980] AC 198 at 220, where Lord Diplock said:

'No matter what profession it may be, the common law does not impose on those who practise it any liability for damage resulting from what in the result turns out to have been errors of judgment, unless the error was such as no reasonably well informed and competent member of that profession could have made.'

I believe that in that passage Lord Diplock set out the test that I have to apply. Vinelott J held that the application for discovery was misconceived which suggests that there may have been an error of judgment. Even so, the plaintiffs must show that there was an error and that it was one that no reasonably well-informed and competent member of the Bar could have made. Before going on to decide whether the plaintiffs have established that such an error occurred, I must refer to the three matters that were raised by counsel.

Counsel for the plaintiffs drew to my attention the effect that legal aid was having on the plaintiffs in this case. As the only active defendants have legal aid, it follows that, if the plaintiffs are successful, they are unlikely to be able to recover the costs of the action or any misconceived application that the defendants make. That of course is in the mind of the court, but even so the test under the section must be the same whether the legal representative, against whom an order for costs is sought, is representing a legally aided client or not. No lawyer who acts in the public interest by accepting legally aided clients, should stand any greater risk of being ordered to pay costs than if he acted for a paying client. In any case, the fact is irrelevant in this case, as it was not suggested that the defendants' counsel had been influenced in his advice by the fact that the defendants were legally aided.

In *Orchard v South Eastern Electricity Board* [1987] 1 All ER 95 at 105–106, [1987] QB 565 at 580 Dillon LJ pointed out that the charge of acting unreasonably or negligently was a serious one. He said:

'Such a charge ought not to rest solely on inference without evidence. I appreciate that, as already mentioned, defendants who wish to make such a charge against solicitors for the plaintiff have a difficulty in getting evidence because of the rules of legal professional privilege. Those rules of privilege also, however, hamper the solicitor in seeking to justify his own conduct of the case. The justification of privilege lies in the field of public policy; that a defendant may thereby be precluded from making out a claim that his costs should be paid by the plaintiff's solicitor personally is part of the price which has to be accepted from rules designed to ensure that a litigant has freedom to consult with his lawyers before his case comes before the court.'

In that passage, Dillon LJ pointed to the difficulty of providing the necessary evidence to establish the serious charge of acting unreasonably or negligently. That is particularly applicable to a case such as this, where the proceedings have not been concluded and are moving slowly to trial. Not only is it difficult to prove negligence when hampered by the rules of privilege, but it is particularly difficult to rely upon inference before the trial has taken place. What may seem to be a misconceived application could, after trial, be seen as an application which was worth trying as it would have saved considerable time and money if it had succeeded. It is therefore unlikely that applications for wasted costs orders will succeed in civil litigation until after the case has been completed. It is only at that time can the conduct of the legal representatives be assessed in a correct context.

Another reason why wasted costs orders should not be sought until after trial, except in exceptional circumstances, is illustrated by the facts of this case. Due to the claim against him, counsel for the defendants decided that he should not continue to represent the defendants. Thus the defendants have effectively been deprived of counsel of their choice by the plaintiffs application. This problem was alluded to by Donaldson MR in *Orchard*'s case [1987] 1 All ER 95 at 104, [1987] QB 565 at 577:

'There is one final matter which cannot be ignored. Whilst there can be no objection to an application under RSC Ord 62, r 8 at the conclusion of a hearing, given appropriate facts, it is quite another matter where such an application is threatened during or prior to the hearing. Objectivity is a vital requirement of professional advisers. Hence, for example, the rejection of contingency fees and the impropriety of a solicitor acting for co-defendants. Threats to apply on the basis that the proceedings must fail not only make the solicitor something in the nature of a co-defendant, but they may well, and rightly, make him all the more determined not to abandon his client, thereby losing a measure of objectivity.'

Dillon LJ contemplated that claims for wasted costs orders could be attempts to harass the other side's legal advisers which might amount to a contempt of court (see [1987] 1 All ER 95 at 106, [1987] QB 565 at 581).

The line between what amounts to an act which prejudices the course of justice or is an attempt to prejudice the course of justice and what amounts to the exercise of a right to obtain compensation for wasted costs can be difficult to draw. Although the right to seek and obtain wasted costs orders is not limited under the statute, I envisage that it would rarely be wise or right to seek to obtain such an order until after trial. Further, I do not envisage that the right to seek and obtain such an order could or should be affected by waiting until after trial before making a claim; although on rare occasions it might be desirable to inform the legal representative that such an order might be sought.

The plaintiffs' case is based on inference. In particular, it is based upon the terms of the order sought and the plaintiffs' contention that no reasonable counsel could have suggested that such an application be made at that time. In essence, they submitted that discovery of the type sought is only made before the issues have been clarified by pleadings in exceptional circumstances as in *RHM Foods Ltd v Bovril Ltd* [1982] 1 All ER 673, [1982] 1 WLR 661. There was, they submitted, no justification for the application to be made at that time. There were no exceptional circumstances, the discovery sought was vast in range and scope and such documents, which the defendants were entitled to, could have been obtained by agreement or by an order from the master on the summons for directions.

Counsel for the defendants' counsel submitted that the documents under para 1 should have been disclosed pursuant to RSC Ord 24, r 10, and the fact that the notice of motion did not refer to that rule was irrelevant as the letter of 30 September 1992 from the defendants' solicitors made it quite clear that those documents were being sought under that order.

The offer to hand over the faulty disk made in the plaintiffs' solicitors letter of 14 October 1992, was not a satisfactory offer as the faulty disk might no longer show what the plaintiffs had obtained from it. Further, the other documents, if ordered, could have provided evidence leading to the plaintiffs' case being struck out. The application for discovery was considered to be misconceived at the particular time but that does not mean that counsel made an error that no competent counsel could make. In an adversarial system, legal advisers can propose applications some of which may be held to be misconceived. Competent counsel consider the chances of an application succeeding, the cost of such an application and the advantages that can be achieved both to the plaintiffs and the defendants if the application succeeds. They also take into account their duties to the court and if necessary the legal aid fund. That advice can result in a range of advice, from ' this application will succeed' through 'it is worth a try' to/or 'it will fail'.

Although competent counsel would know that discovery before the issues had been defined would only be ordered in exceptional circumstances, the plaintiffs have not established that advice to apply for discovery of the type that was sought was an error that no reasonably well-informed and competent member of the Bar could have made. I suspect that such a member of the Bar would appreciate that it was very unlikely that anything other than the documents in para 1 of the motion would be ordered to be disclosed at that stage, but to go further and conclude that such a person would not have suggested applying at the same time for the other orders, requires analysis of the factual background against which the advice and decision were taken. That is not before the court and could not be before the court. Further, it is not possible to look at the application in the context of the whole proceedings. If it turned out at trial that the plaintiffs' case was hopeless, then the application could be seen as an attempt to shorten the proceedings at an early stage; no doubt an attempt which had a slim chance of success. In those circumstances, the attempt might be seen as one which competent counsel would try.

Finally, I come to the application by counsel who appeared for the defendants' counsel that I should take account of letters passing between the parties' solicitors which were headed 'without prejudice'. In those letters, the plaintiffs' solicitors offered terms upon which the motion for costs could be disposed of. It was suggested that those letters were admissible and relevant to the exercise of the discretion when deciding whether to make a wasted costs order and also as indicating the value that the plaintiffs placed upon their application.

In the result, it is not necessary for me to decide whether those letters are admissible, but I believe that it would have been wrong for me to take them into account. They contain negotiations in the actual dispute and a decision by me to pull away the shield of 'without prejudice' would prevent parties negotiating freely in the future.

The correspondence, however, does illustrate one of the matters to which I have referred. One of the terms of settlement sought by the plaintiffs' solicitors was that the defendants' counsel should undertake to withdraw from any further part in the action. That was accepted by counsel for the plaintiffs to have been an inappropriate term to put forward by way of settlement and it was appropriate for the defendants to reject it. As it happens that request played no part in the defendants' choice of counsel, as the defendants' counsel had already decided to withdraw from the action. However, it illustrates the way that a party may, while the action is in being, seek a course which could affect the course of justice. A person is entitled to counsel of his choice and it is not up to the other side to seek to impose terms or to harass so as to persuade that counsel to be taken off or withdraw from the case. That error of judgment on behalf of the plaintiffs' advisers would not have arisen if the application for the wasted costs order had been left until after trial.

I conclude that the motion should be dismissed and I will hear counsel as to the appropriate order as to costs.

Application dismissed.

Paul Magrath   Barrister.

R v Horsham District Council and another, ex parte Wenman and others

QUEEN'S BENCH DIVISION (CROWN OFFICE LIST)

BROOKE J

2, 13, 14 JULY, 1 OCTOBER 1993

Counsel – Payment of costs by counsel personally – Costs incurred negligently – Jurisdiction to order counsel to pay wasted costs – Unmeritorious application for judicial review – Whether counsel negligent in conduct of judicial review proceedings – Whether wasted costs order appropriate – Supreme Court Act 1981, s 51(6).

In January 1991 a local authority, H, decided to issue enforcement notices and stop notices against a group of gipsies to prevent the unauthorised development of a local site as a permanent gipsy encampment. On instructions from the gipsies, an assistant solicitor with the respondent firm of solicitors lodged appeals against the enforcement notices and requested a public inquiry into the matter. At that point H also decided to institute High Court proceedings for injunctive relief to restrain the gipsies in their use of the land and mandatory relief which would in effect require them to move off the site. On 6 March the gipsies' solicitors instructed A, a junior counsel of over 20 years' experience practising in common law chambers, in connection with the proceedings. A's view was that H's decision to institute proceedings had been taken on pure planning grounds without any proper consideration of the statutory protection afforded to gipsies and was therefore open to judicial review. The solicitors subsequently obtained legal aid to defend the proceedings and A filed a defence and counterclaim, contending inter alia that H's decision to seek relief from the High Court was ultra vires. The planning inquiry into the objections to the enforcement notices commenced in July and when the inquiry was completed the gipsies instituted separate proceedings for judicial review against H and also against a second local authority, WS, alleging that WS was in breach of its duty under s 6 of the Caravan Sites Act 1968 to provide adequate accommodation for gipsies. The gipsies' legal advisers failed to make any written complaint prior to instituting judicial review proceedings against WS, mainly because they considered that WS's inevitable response would be to deny their clients' claims. On 12 September the planning inspector published his decision in which he stated that even if H's provisions for gipsies were inadequate and even if H were to owe all the appellant gipsies a duty under s 6 of the 1968 Act, the serious harm to the rural appearance and character of the area of countryside affected by the encampment together with the highway and amenity objections were sufficiently compelling for the appeals against the enforcement notices to be dismissed. That decision was not forwarded to the Crown Office. On 21 October a single judge granted leave to apply for judicial review on the papers. Thereafter, the judge hearing the applications dismissed them and made an order for costs against those of the gipsies who were legally aided and granted both local authorities liberty to apply unde RSC Ord 62, r 11[a], if so advised, for orders that their costs be paid by th gipsies' legal advisers. The local authorities duly issued summonses fo payment of their costs by A and the firm of solicitors.

Held – (1) The court had jurisdiction under s 51(6)[b] of the Supreme Cour Act 1981 (as substituted by s 4 of the Courts and Legal Services Act 1990) t provide redress for all who had incurred expense in civil and criminal case as a result of the negligence of lawyers and therefore to make wasted cost orders against counsel and solicitors who had been negligent in the conduc of judicial review proceedings. In particular, any solicitor or counsel holdin themselves out as competent to handle judicial review proceedings would b taken as being familiar with the warning on the Crown Office's standar form, which was used to grant leave to apply ex parte, that legal adviser should reconsider the merits of the application once they had received th respondent's evidence. They should also note (i) that lawyers acting for party should not regard it as unnecessary to write a letter before actio merely because they believed it was inevitable that the response would den their clients' claim, (ii) that judicial review proceedings were wholl inappropriate for the resolution of issues of disputed fact and (iii) that a material matters should be placed before the judge who was being invited t grant leave to apply for judicial review ex parte (see p 699 *d* to *f*, p 702 *b* to *d* p 703 *d*, p 710 *f* to *j*, p 711 *e* and p 714 *a*, post).

(2) On the facts, there were grounds on which the validity of H's origin; decision to institute High Court proceedings could have been properl challenged and, in those circumstances, there were no grounds for making wasted costs order in H's favour. H's application would accordingly b dismissed (see p 705 *a c d* and p 714 *a*, post).

(3) The history of the proceedings against WS revealed departures fror proper practice and there were therefore grounds for making a wasted cos' order against A. WS's claim would nevertheless be dismissed, since the ne wasted costs regime only came into effect on 1 October 1991, by which tim all of the most elementary errors had already been made. Moreover, it woul be wrong to make a wasted costs order against the solicitors, who, in th period up to 1 October, had acted on the advice of A, whom they considere to be experienced in the relevant areas of law, and to that extent they had nc been negligent in the conduct of the proceedings. WS's application again; the solicitors would also be dismissed (see p 710 *e*, p 713 *b* and p 713 *g* t p 714 *a*, post).

Notes
For acquiring leave to apply for judicial review, see 37 *Halsbury's Laws* (4t edn) paras 568, 572.

For jurisdiction of the court to order costs against a legal representativ personally, see 37 *Halsbury's Laws* (4th edn) para 719, and 44 ibid paras 259 262, and for cases on the subject, see 44 *Digest* (Reissue) 421–444, *4587–4831*.

---

a　Rule 11, so far as material, provides: '(1)(a) Where the Court decides to make an order und section 51(6) of the Supreme Court Act 1981 disallowing wasted costs or ordering a leg representative to meet such costs or part of them, it shall, subject to paragraph (4), specify in tl order the costs which are to be so disallowed or met …'
b　Section 51(6) is set out at p 699 *a*, post

For the Caravan Sites Act 1968, s 6, see 32 *Halsbury's Statutes* (4th edn) 503.
For the Supreme Court Act 1981, s 51 (as substituted by s 4 of the Courts and Legal Services Act 1990), see 11 *Halsbury's Statutes* (4th edn) (1991 reissue) 1217.

Cases referred to in judgment

Abraham v Jutsun [1963] 2 All ER 402, [1963] 1 WLR 658, CA.

Antonelli v Wade Gery Farr (1992) Times, 29 December; *rvsd sub nom Ridehalgh v Horsefield* [1994] 3 All ER 848, [1994] Ch 205, [1994] 3 WLR 462, CA.

Associated Provincial Picture Houses Ltd v Wednesbury Corp [1947] 2 All ER 680, [1948] 1 KB 223, CA.

Avon CC v Buscott [1988] 1 All ER 841, [1988] QB 656, [1988] 2 WLR 788, CA.

Barrister (wasted costs order), Re a (No 1 of 1991) [1992] 3 All ER 429, [1993] QB 293, [1992] 3 WLR 662, CA.

Davy-Chiesman v Davy-Chiesman [1984] 1 All ER 321, [1984] Fam 48, [1984] 2 WLR 291, CA.

Fozal v Gofur (1993) Times, 9 July, [1993] CA Transcript 680.

Fray v Voules (1859) 1 E & E 839, 120 ER 1125.

Gupta v Comer [1991] 1 All ER 289, [1991] 1 QB 629, [1991] 2 WLR 494, CA.

Holden & Co (a firm) v CPS [1990] 1 All ER 368, [1990] 2 QB 261, [1990] 2 WLR 1137, CA.

Locke v Camberwell Health Authority [1991] 2 Med LR 249, CA.

Midland Bank Trust Co Ltd v Hett, Stubbs & Kemp (a firm) [1978] 3 All ER 571, [1979] Ch 384, [1978] 3 WLR 167.

Orchard v South Eastern Electricity Board [1987] 1 All ER 95, [1987] QB 565, [1987] 2 WLR 102, CA.

R v Chief Constable of the Merseyside Police, ex p Calveley [1986] 1 All ER 257, [1986] QB 424, [1986] 2 WLR 144, CA.

R v Dept of Transport, ex p Presvac Engineering Ltd (1991) Times, 10 July, [1991] CA Transcript 688.

R v Hereford and Worcester CC, ex p Smith (28 April 1988, unreported), Crown Ct.

R v Legal Aid Board, ex p Hughes (1992) 24 HLR 698, CA.

R v Paine (1792) 22 State Tr 357.

R v Secretary of State for the Environment, ex p Lee (1985) 54 P & CR 311.

R v Secretary of State for the Environment, ex p Ward [1984] 2 All ER 556, [1984] 1 WLR 834.

R v Secretary of State for the Home Dept, ex p Brown (1984) Times, 6 February.

R v Wychavon DC, ex p Saunders (27 July 1992, unreported), QBD.

Saif Ali v Sydney Mitchell & Co (a firm) (P, third party) [1978] 3 All ER 1033, [1980] AC 198, [1978] 3 WLR 849, HL.

Saxton (decd), Re [1962] 3 All ER 92, [1962] 1 WLR 968, CA.

Sinclair-Jones v Kay [1988] 2 All ER 611, [1989] 1 WLR 114, CA.

West Glamorgan CC v Rafferty [1987] 1 All ER 1005, [1987] 1 WLR 457, CA.

Summonses

The respondents, Horsham District Council (Horsham) and West Sussex County Council (West Sussex) by summonses dated 28 January 1993 and 27 January 1993 respectively, applied with leave under RSC Ord 62, r 11 for orders that their costs be paid personally by counsel and solicitors who had acted on behalf of the applicants, Frank Wenman and a group of gipsies, in separate judicial review proceedings brought against Horsham and West

Sussex, which Brooke J had dismissed as unmeritorious on 7 May 1992 and 20 May 1992 respectively. The summonses were heard in chambers but judgment was given by Brooke J in open court. The facts are set out in the judgment.

David Elvin (instructed by *Ian Davison*, Horsham) for Horsham.
Roger McCarthy (instructed by *Michael Holdsworth*, Chichester) for West Sussex.
James Munby QC and *Francis Macleod Matthews* (instructed by *Richards Butler*) for counsel.
Roger Hiorns (instructed by *Lance Kent & Co*, Chesham) for the solicitors.

Cur adv vult

1 October 1993. The following judgment was delivered.

BROOKE J. There are before the court two summonses seeking what have now come to be known as wasted costs orders against a barrister (whom I will call 'A') and a firm of solicitors who acted, in one capacity or other, for some gipsies in judicial review proceedings which I heard last year. The successful respondents in those proceedings, the Horsham District Council and the West Sussex County Council, later issued the summonses which are before me now. The hearing of the summonses took place before me in chambers for three days in July, but since they raised issues of considerable complexity and interest arising from comparatively new legislation, the parties agreed that I should give judgment in open court, while not actually naming the barrister and solicitors in my judgment. Since I was moving away from the privacy of chambers, and since I am dismissing these two applications, I considered this was a fair course to take when I balanced the public interest in access to a judgment given in open court against the interests of the barrister and the solicitors in preserving the privacy of a hearing in chambers.

The history is a complicated one. In early May 1992 I heard a number of applications for judicial review or for leave to apply for judicial review. The applicants were Mr Frank Wenman and a number of other people, all of whom claimed to be gipsies entitled to the protection afforded to gipsies by the Caravan Sites and Control of Development Act 1960 and the Caravan Sites Act 1968 (the Caravan Sites Acts). The solicitors acted as their solicitors throughout the proceedings, and A was instructed as counsel on their behalf between early March 1991 and the end of March 1992. He then dropped out due to a conflict of professional engagements, and the applicants were thereafter represented by other counsel against whom no application for any wasted costs order is made.

As I have said, Horsham and West Sussex were the respondents to these applications. In the main proceedings Webster J granted leave ex parte to the applicants to apply for judicial review against both of them on 21 October 1991. Horsham, but not West Sussex, sought unsuccessfully to have that leave discharged at a hearing before Hutchison J in late January 1992, when expedition of the proceedings was ordered. When the matter came before me, it was agreed between counsel that since the issues concerning the two respondents were quite distinct, although they all related to the applicants wish to live as gipsies in West Sussex, I could and should hear them separately. On 7 May 1992 I dismissed the application for judicial review against Horsham in an extempore judgment (the Horsham proceedings). On 20 May 1992 I dismissed the application for judicial review against West Sussex (the West Sussex proceedings).

The Horsham proceedings were concerned, and concerned only, with the legal validity of Horsham's decision to institute proceedings in the High Court against the applicants on 29 January 1991 when it was believed that the applicants were likely to evince themselves totally unwilling to comply with stop notices issued by Horsham as the local planning authority. Horsham was then engaged in trying to stop them establishing a permanent gipsy encampment with access roadways and associated hardstandings without the benefit of planning permission on land some of them owned at Pulborough. Before the application for leave to apply for judicial review was lodged on 11 September 1991 there had been a five-day planning inquiry into an appeal by most of the applicants against those enforcement notices, and the planning inspector issued his decision dismissing that appeal on 12 September.

At the start of the proceedings, on 5 May 1992, I heard a second application by the applicants against Horsham. This was an application for leave to apply for judicial review of Horsham's original decision to embark on enforcement notice procedure against the applicants in January 1991. I refused leave on the grounds, inter alia, that it was now far too late to mount such a challenge.

Finally, on 7 May, I adjourned yet another application by the applicants for leave to apply for judicial review against Horsham. This related to the way in which Horsham had handled the applicants' application for housing under Pt III of the Housing Act 1985. This was adjourned on an undertaking by Horsham that its housing committee would reconsider the matter.

For the sake of completeness I should make it clear that I refused relief to the applicants in the Horsham proceedings on a preliminary issue which related to the fact that their application was first issued seven and a half months after the decision impugned, while I dismissed the application in the West Sussex proceedings on the merits. In both the Horsham and the West Sussex proceedings I made the usual order for costs against those of the applicants who were legally aided and an order for legal aid taxation of the costs of those applicants. I also granted both respondents liberty to apply under RSC Ord 62, r 11, if so advised, for orders that their costs be paid by the applicants' legal advisers.

I must now set out the history in more detail, so far as it is relevant to the matters I have to decide. By the end of January 1991 it had come to Horsham's attention that a number of people had brought their caravans onto land owned by some of them at Gerrards Rough, near Pulborough, and were engaged in constructing hardstandings and access roads and in other acts of unauthorised development on the site. On 29 January Horsham's director of planning law, acting under delegated powers, decided to take steps to stop what was going on. Accordingly he authorised the chief solicitor to issue enforcement notices and stop notices. He also authorised him to take injunctive proceedings to restrain such breaches of planning control and/or to require compliance with planning control and any consequential proceedings as might be appropriate.

The following day nine of the gipsies met a solicitor (whom I will call 'Mrs B') at the solicitors' firm for the first time. Mrs B had originally enrolled as a solicitor in 1958 and she had had ten years' experience in practice before she married. Soon afterwards she stopped practising and it was only in October 1990 that she had been encouraged to return to the law by a partner in the solicitors' firm (whom I will call 'Mrs C'). Mrs B's services were particularly needed to assist in relation to matters concerning gipsies, in which field of practice Mrs C had developed a good deal of experience, and between then and March 1991 Mrs B attended at the firm's offices on a voluntary basis in order to obtain the experience she needed in order to return to practice, particularly in the fields of litigation and legal aid. From April onwards she had a practising certificate again, and she was employed as an assistant solicitor by the firm. Her duties at the firm embraced planning, wills, general litigation and legal aid work, but although her work was general in nature a large part of it concerned dealing with gipsies, mainly in the context of advising small gipsy families or individuals. This was the first time she had dealt with such a large number of gipsies in an individual matter.

At first her new clients were concerned only with two enforcement notices which had been served on them on 29 January, backed by stop notices. On their instructions Mrs B lodged appeals against the enforcement notices requesting a public inquiry. A further enforcement notice was served on 13 February, again backed by a stop notice, and since the gipsies were not deterred by any of these notices, on 21 February Horsham issued a High Court writ, indorsed with a statement of claim, pursuant to s 222 of the Local Government Act 1972, against six named defendants and other persons unknown. These were later increased by amendment to 22 named defendants. On the same day Horsham also issued a summons for interlocutory injunctions returnable on 7 March.

On 6 March the solicitors instructed A for the first time in connection with these proceedings. A is a junior counsel of over 20 years' considerable experience practising in common law chambers. Mrs C chose him for this case since she had worked with him for a number of years in connection with gipsies. The emphasis of A's practice was on contract and commercial work including building contract, judicial review (acting both for and against local authorities), property and housing work and all aspects of negligence including professional negligence. He had also for a number of years been instructed by different solicitors in a steady flow of cases involving the rights and duties of gipsies, six of which have been reported. The issues in such cases typically involved the interrelationship between administrative law, the planning process, and the statutory rights of gipsies. He has told me he believes that through his experience in the field he has gained some insight into the attitude and approach of the Department of the Environment and local and district authorities and into the behaviour of gipsies themselves. He has also become aware of many of the special difficulties which barristers and solicitors face in representing them.

Mrs B, for her part, has told me that she always understood A to have particular expertise, not only in relation to the law relating to gipsy matters which is contained in the Caravan Sites Act 1968 but also in understanding the culture of gipsies as a group within society. She has said she found herself to be greatly indebted to him for his advice and experience.

The terms and date of Horsham's resolution to institute legal proceedings were known to the gipsies and their lawyers when Horsham's affidavit in the interlocutory proceedings was served about the beginning of March, so that everything else being equal it would be unlikely that a court would sympathetically entertain a judicial review challenge to the validity of that resolution if it was not issued in or before the first week of June (see Ord 53, r 4(1): strictly, the three-month period mentioned in that paragraph would expire on 29 April).

A appeared for the gipsies before Cresswell J in chambers the following day to resist not only injunctive relief, which would restrain them in their use of the land, but also mandatory relief, which would direct them to remove off it their caravans, mobile homes and so on. This application was adjourned on appropriate undertakings, which stopped short of undertakings to remove the caravans (orders to the same effect were made against those who did not give undertakings), and directions were given for a timetable for the service of pleadings and the taking of other steps in the action. In practical terms, therefore, unless the gipsies broke their undertakings, Horsham resigned itself to awaiting the outcome of the inquiry into the enforcement notice appeal, while taking appropriate steps to keep the High Court action moving in accordance with the judge's directions.

Mrs B obtained emergency legal aid certificates for some of her clients limited to defending the High Court proceedings, and on 21 March she and Mrs C visited the site to meet their clients and take their detailed instructions. On 3 April A received instructions to draft a defence in the High Court proceedings as a matter of urgency, and he settled a defence and counterclaim the following day. The defence consisted largely of non-admissions and denials, but in para 7 it was pleaded that Horsham's decision to seek relief from the High Court and to start these proceedings was ultra vires and/or *Wednesbury* unreasonable (see *Associated Provincial Picture Houses Ltd v Wednesbury Corp* [1947] 2 All ER 680, [1948] 1 KB 223). The counterclaim referred to the defendants as being homeless gipsies in priority need for housing accommodation, for whom the plaintiffs had failed to provide accommodation or to ensure there was a place where they were entitled or permitted to place their caravans. It also contended that the plaintiffs were in breach of their duties to the defendants under the Housing Act 1985 and the Caravan Sites and Control of Development Act 1960 and counterclaimed appropriate relief.

A explained to me that there appeared to him that there was a continuing deficit in the number of sites in the county. The decision to apply for injunctive relief meant that his clients would be evicted from their occupation of the land, and this decision appeared to have been taken hastily on pure planning grounds without any proper investigation or consideration of the needs of the gipsies and without reference to the 1968 Act or to the advice contained in Department of the Environment circulars 28/77 and 57/78. He felt that Horsham appeared to have failed to investigate the personal position of those on site, and seemed unaware of the hardship which would be caused to them if they had to move from the site without places on official sites. It had not apparently considered that in taking enforcement proceedings it would render the gipsies and their children homeless, nor did it appear to have gone on to consider to what, if any, obligations under the

1985 Act this might give rise, or how it might seek to fulfil such obligation, or to alleviate the position by the exercise of its powers to provide sites itself under the 1960 Act.

A's view was that if the underlying decision to institute proceedings was unlawful—and he had an additional point that, on the information then available, the appropriate delegated authority had not been given to initiate injunctive proceedings—then Horsham would have had no authority to bring them and was unlikely to be granted a discretionary injunction by the court. Because these arguments raised public law issues which could only be ventilated in judicial review proceedings, he was of the opinion that the correct approach would be to apply to adjourn the application for an injunction pending judicial review. He relied on the Court of Appeal decision in *Avon CC v Buscott* [1988] 1 All ER 841, [1988] QB 656 for the proposition that the court could be expected to grant such an adjournment provided that the challenge was tenable.

The *Avon* case was one in which the county council had sought and obtained a final order for possession from a High Court judge in Ord 113 proceedings, and the Court of Appeal explained what should happen if in such proceedings a public law challenge was made to the local authority' conduct. Lord Donaldson MR said ([1988] 1 All ER 841 at 845, [1988] QB 656 at 663):

> 'When a defendant is seeking, in effect, to strike out an action on the basis of a public law right, he should, in my judgment, proceed by way of an application for judicial review, thus ensuring that the matter is dealt with speedily as a preliminary point and in a manner which gives the public authority and the public which it serves the protection enshrined in the judicial review procedure. If an application had been made to Stuart-Smith J for an adjournment to enable judicial review proceedings to be taken, he would have had to have asked himself whether there was any real chance of leave to apply being granted. If he had thought that there was a real possibility, he should, and I am sure that he would, have granted an adjournment.'

A has explained that at this early stage he also considered whether the proceedings should properly be linked with an application for declaratory and/or mandatory relief against West Sussex in respect of its duties under s 6 of the 1968 Act. He believed that of itself a successful application against West Sussex would potentially bring a number of practical benefits to his clients, but before such proceedings could be launched he needed to obtain details of the unauthorised gipsy encampments in West Sussex over a reasonable period, so as to apply the test for identifying a breach of statutory duty which was suggested in the reported cases.

In this context he had in mind a passage in the judgment of Mann J in *R Secretary of State for the Environment, ex p Lee* (1985) 54 P & CR 311, and the comments on that passage by the Court of Appeal in *West Glamorgan CC Rafferty* [1987] 1 All ER 1005, [1987] 1 WLR 457.

In the *West Glamorgan* case Ralph Gibson LJ quoted Mann J ([1987] 1 All ER 1005 at 1017, [1987] 1 WLR 457 at 471):

> 'Mann J had said: "In my judgment, the correct approach is to ask simply whether, at the moment the question is to be answered, there is adequate accommodation for gipsies residing in or resorting to the area

If the answer is No, then whether the breach of duty should be visited by relief is a matter of discretion. So simple an approach seems to me appropriate, having regard to the language of the statute and to the consideration that the court is not dealing with a mere technicality but with the ability of people to have secure accommodation for their homes (as presumably Parliament intended) and with the removal of the often grossly injurious environmental impact on the public and local residents of unauthorised gipsy encampments."'

Ralph Gibson LJ continued:

'I agree with the approach described by Mann J, and the words used by him, provided that the meaning of the phrase "adequate accommodation for gipsies residing in or resorting to their area" and the date by reference to which the adequacy of available accommodation is to be tested are first made clear. In my judgment Parliament clearly, and at least, intended to impose on a county council an obligation to exercise its powers under the 1960 Act so as to provide accommodation for the number of gipsies known to be habitually residing in or resorting to its area in the ordinary course of the year, on the basis that at any time, in considering whether that obligation has been broken, the adequacy of accommodation provided would be tested by reference to the number of gipsies known to the council to be so residing or resorting over a preceding period of time of reasonable length. That period of time would be assessed by reference to the time necessary for a county council to exercise its powers to provide accommodation.'

A has added that he was very conscious that one approach might lie in applying to the Secretary of State, inviting him to exercise his powers under s 9 of the 1968 Act and to revoke the designation which he knew that West Sussex possessed under s 12. However, against the background of the tight timescale then operating, his experience did not lead him to think that this would provide an effective approach. So far as he was aware, the Secretary of State had only ever given two directions in the preceding 22 years. Yet the undisputed evidence which was revealed in the cases in which he had been involved showed that virtually every county had been in constant breach of its duties under s 6 throughout the life of the statute, and he felt that there was not, therefore, much prospect that a direction would be granted: even if it was, it was likely to be long after his clients had been forced to leave the land. He had in mind one case in which a direction was not made until eight years after representations were first made, and another when two and a half years elapsed from first complaint to ultimate direction.

Horsham served a very brief reply and defence to counterclaim a fortnight later, and on 3 May A wrote an advice on the merits for the legal aid authorities, not only in relation to the continued defence of the High Court proceedings but also in relation to proposed judicial review proceedings. In this advice he also referred to the position vis-à-vis West Sussex, to which I have already referred. He did not yet have the information about unauthorised site use in West Sussex which he needed in order to give positive advice.

In May 1991 lists of documents were exchanged in the High Court proceedings and in June some outstanding further and better particulars were served. On 17 June legal aid was refused for judicial review proceedings against Horsham. On 25 June Horsham issued a judge's summons applying for an order for the whole or parts of the defence and counterclaim to be struck out and for interlocutory judgment on its claim, either in default of defence (if it was struck out), or under Ord 14. So far as I am aware, no affidavit was served in support of this summons, but it appears that Horsham was alleging at the time that Mrs B's clients had been breaching the undertakings they had given in March.

Mrs B accordingly visited the site again on 29 June. Part of her time was spent in activities connected with the forthcoming public inquiry on the enforcement notice appeal, including the preparation of evidence for that inquiry. However, she also discussed with her clients the prospect of judicial review proceedings, and on her return she asked for further advice from A on this aspect of the matter.

A still did not have the necessary statistical information in relation to West Sussex. His new advice on the merits of an application against Horsham was forthcoming on 8 July, and four days later emergency legal aid was granted to eight of her clients to apply for leave and, if granted, to seek a judicial review of Horsham's decision in January.

In the course of my judgment in the Horsham proceedings I summarised the history and said at this point:

> 'It should be observed that counsel advised then that there were reasonable grounds for bringing proceedings by way of judicial review and it was then, in my judgment, incumbent on the applicants to proceed to apply for leave for judicial review very promptly rather than wait until, at the forthcoming planning inquiry, which was fixed to start on 30 July, they might find by way of cross-examination further evidence to substantiate their case.'

I referred in this context to some comments made by Purchas LJ in *R v Dept of Transport, ex p Presvac Engineering Ltd* (1991) Times, 10 July.

A received instructions to settle the requisite proceedings on 12 or 13 July, and Mrs B has told me that she had a discussion with A on 15 July, in which it was decided not to start judicial review proceedings straightaway. Horsham was not then told of the existence of the legal aid certificates. It was thought that there would be little point in making an immediate application and, indeed, that their clients might be criticised for making it. It appeared to be a real possibility that a favourable outcome of the planning inquiry might dispose of the problem completely and render the issue relating to the commencement of the injunction proceedings irrelevant since planning permission might be obtained. A also pointed out to her that the evidence at the inquiry might show that consideration had been given to the needs of gipsies in deciding to enforce the enforcement notices by way of injunction proceedings, in which case any application for judicial review on that ground would be pointless. They believed that it was highly unlikely that the planning inquiry would be adjourned since local residents were anxious that it should go ahead and preparations were well under way. Mrs B told me that she believed that both she and A were conscious of the need to avoid wasteful duplication of proceedings.

A has given a similar explanation of his thoughts at that time, which were bolstered by his knowledge that Department of the Environment inspectors had latterly proved quite willing to accord full weight to the special considerations applicable to gipsies and to overrule the objections of local authorities and to override local planning policies. He gave me one very striking instance of this. His judgment went along these lines:

> 'If the planning inquiry resulted in a favourable outcome, then the judicial review proceedings would be redundant, and in that way the cost to the legal aid fund would be reduced. On the other hand the short delay pending the planning inquiry might reduce the chance of success in the judicial review application.'

This assessment was considered reasonable by Hutchison J in January 1992 when he refused to strike out the judicial review application. In his judgment, which I read for the first time in July 1993, Hutchison J was influenced by the fact that there was a paucity of information as to the nature of the matters which Horsham had taken into account on 29 January and that the applicants could reasonably anticipate, as indeed proved to be the case, that that matter might be elucidated to some extent at the hearing. He does not refer to the 1985 judgment of Purchas LJ, which frowned heavily on delays caused by this sort of fishing expedition, and this was not cited to Hutchison J in the written skeleton arguments he received nor, so far as I know, in oral argument.

So far as the High Court proceedings were concerned, there had been another interlocutory skirmish on 11 July before Hidden J, who adjourned what were now cross-summonses to strike out each party's pleadings after some of the defendants gave undertakings that they would abide by the undertakings they had given four months earlier.

By the time the planning inquiry started on 30 July, A had obtained the statistical information he had been seeking concerning the unauthorised encampments in West Sussex. I have seen a copy of his opening submissions at the inquiry. These show that he knew that West Sussex was designated in April 1982 as making satisfactory provision for gipsies in the county, and he knew that in 1980 and 1981 it had doubled the number of available pitches. However, he also knew that at counts made in July 1982, 1987, 1988 and 1990 there were, respectively, 10, 18, 17 and 19 unauthorised pitches in West Sussex, and he drew from these figures the conclusion that there had been a persistent under-provision in the county. This, and West Sussex's settled position that it had no plans to provide any further caravan sites for gipsies, led him to the view, in reliance on the dictum of Mann J in *ex p Lee*, that West Sussex was in breach of its duty under s 6(1) of the 1968 Act.

There are two features of the evidence at the planning inquiry which I must mention. The first is that A cross-examined Horsham's principal planning officer about the considerations which he had in mind when the council decided to take enforcement action on 29 January. A formed the view, which Mrs B shared, that these answers were deeply unsatisfactory, and they strengthened his confidence in the merits of judicial review of Horsham's decision to start High Court proceedings.

The second is that Mr Hunter, who was West Sussex's officer chiefly responsible for gipsy matters, also gave evidence at the inquiry. A has told me that his view of the effect of this evidence was that it strongly supported the contention that West Sussex was and had been for many years in breach of its obligations under s 6 of the 1968 Act.

When the public inquiry ended, the gipsies' legal advisers were pessimistic about the likelihood of a favourable decision by the planning inspector. On the other hand, they believed that their clients' case that Horsham had not taken all relevant considerations into account the previous January, and that West Sussex was in breach of its duties under s 6 of the 1968 Act, had been strengthened by the evidence given at the inquiry. In the light of this, they received their clients' instructions to take judicial review proceedings against West Sussex as well. An extension to the existing legal aid certificates was therefore sought on 15 August and granted on 3 September. Soon after the planning inquiry was over, A left with his family on a three-week summer holiday from which he returned on Monday, 2 September to settle the judicial review proceedings, which he had received instructions to settle (as against Horsham at any rate) in mid-July.

To avoid further delay while the legal aid position as against West Sussex was sorted out, A settled and sent back to the solicitors the following day the draft documents needed for proceedings against Horsham alone. At the end of that week he was told that the legal aid position as against West Sussex had been cleared, and on the following Wednesday, 10 September, he sent back to the solicitors redrafted proceedings as against both respondents. On the same day he spoke to the solicitors, and as a result of that conversation he drafted what have euphemistically been called letters before action to both respondents. This was the applicants' first written contact with West Sussex, and they received their letter after the application for leave to apply for judicial review had been lodged with the Crown Office. At about the same time a letter, also drafted by A, was sent for the first time to the Secretary of State complaining of a breach of statutory duty by West Sussex.

Finally, the last thing which occurred before the Form 86A was lodged at the Crown Office was that Mrs B swore an affidavit in support of the judicial review applications. This was extremely short and consisted essentially of hearsay verification of the facts and matters set out in the 22 paragraphs of grounds for relief in the Form 86A statement. In essence, the applicants repeated as against West Sussex the submissions A had made at the start of the planning inquiry, including the bald statement that between 1981 and 1991 each of the applicants, 18 in number, had resorted to West Sussex but had not been provided with any adequate accommodation by the county council in breach of its duty under s 6 of the 1968 Act. As against Horsham, the earlier history was described, and full grounds were set out for the contention that Horsham had not taken into account all relevant matters (including the hardship likely to be suffered by dispossessed gipsies who had nowhere to go) and had reached a decision to start High Court proceedings which was *Wednesbury* unreasonable. Its decision to start enforcement notice and stop notice procedures was not challenged.

Finally, the delay was said to be excused by the fact that the applicants were not aware until early March of the decision by Horsham on 29 January in relation to proceedings, by the delay in obtaining legal aid against each respondent, and by the fact that it was not until the planning inquiry in early August that the applicants were aware of the nature of the information Horsham relied upon when it decided to start proceedings.

On 12 September 1991 the planning inspector published his decision. For all practical purposes the 18 gipsy appellants were the same as the 18 applicants for judicial review, with some variants for family members and omitting a non-existent lady called 'Mrs Brown', whose name had crept into both sets of court proceedings. Paragraphs 41 to 45 of the decision letter set out in detail that part of the gipsies' arguments which related to Caravan Sites Acts considerations. Paragraphs 53 to 56 set out the local authorities' response. Paragraphs 76 to 78 set out the inspector's findings. He accepted that several relations of the two main families who occupied plots on the site were probably gipsies, and he accepted that these people probably resorted to the area of West Sussex and to some, but inconclusive, extent to Horsham. He found that there were several families on the site among the appellants whose travelling and resorting habits were unknown, and concluded that it was unclear whether West Sussex owed any duty under s 6 of the 1968 Act to, at best, more than half of the appeal site owners.

When he looked at the evidence about unauthorised encampments in West Sussex since 1982 (and he recited the figures of unauthorised caravans at six-monthly counts since January 1987, which averaged 14, with fluctuations between 19 at one end and 6 at the other) he found that the evidence was inconclusive on the question whether West Sussex had continued to meet the needs of gipsies other than those who passed through the area briefly. What was missing from the counts was any detail as to the residing or resorting habits of the gipsies found in the counts. He thought that until the July 1991 count, which included the appeal site, the figures for unauthorised gipsy caravans in West Sussex did not seem to be unduly high. In para 78 of his decision letter he said:

> 'I note the misgivings expressed on behalf of the Appellants about the general state of site provision for gipsies in the country. But I am not persuaded that the situation in West Sussex, and the needs of the Appellants, together with the normal presumption in favour of development, are such that planning permission should be granted for the use of the appeal land as a caravan site in the light of the policy conflict, the serious harm to the rural appearance and character of this area of countryside and the highway and amenity objections discussed above. Even if there was a proven need for additional gipsy accommodation, it would not have to be on this site. There is no cogent reason which justifies this development in the countryside. I conclude that even if the County Council's provisions for gipsies were inadequate and that if they were to owe all the Appellants a duty under Section 6 of the 1968 Act, the above objections are sufficiently compelling to turn away these appeals.'

I have not the slightest doubt that any solicitor who was experienced in Crown Office procedure would have realised that a copy of the inspector's decision should have been sent to the Crown Office immediately. If this was not done, the duty of uberrima fides on an ex parte application would not have been fulfilled, and the single judge would not have the whole picture before him when deciding whether or not to grant leave. This was particularly important in this case because no reference was made to the alternative remedy of complaint to the Secretary of State pursuant to s 9 of the 1968 Act, and I am very doubtful whether Webster J would have granted leave ex parte on paper to the applicants, particularly in relation to the application against West Sussex, if he had had the inspector's findings after a five-day planning inquiry drawn to his attention. The inspector's report disclosed a much fuller picture than the comparatively brief assertions, deposed to by Mrs B on hearsay in her very short affidavit, contained in the Form 86A statement. Nor was Webster J told that no written complaint of any kind had been made to West Sussex or the Secretary of State on behalf of any of the applicants before Form 86A was lodged at the Crown Office on 11 September.

Mrs B's explanation of her failure to write to West Sussex at any time between February 1991 and 12 September 1991, notwithstanding that the possibility of proceedings against them had been in the air for six months, was in these terms:

'I considered that the application for judicial review related to a pre-existing failure of [West Sussex] to comply with their duties under the Act and not some breach that was suddenly arising in September 1991. I would have been very surprised if the response of [West Sussex] had been to say that if only we had given them more notice they would have provided my clients with a site and indeed that was not their response.'

A's reaction on this issue was in similar terms. He said that he recollected some of the gipsies saying at the planning inquiry that numerous informal requests had been made in the past, usually to wardens who operated the sites provided by West Sussex, and the response was always that there were no pitches available. Since few gipsies in his experience could read or write, it would not surprise him if no written applications were made. And since West Sussex was at all times satisfied that it had fulfilled its duties under the 1968 Act, he found it difficult to see what difference prior written requests to West Sussex for caravan site provision would have made.

After the two respondents had been served with notice of motion at the end of October, their reactions were different. Horsham decided to apply to have the grant of leave set aside, and issued a summons for such an order, alternatively for an order for an expedited hearing, on 22 November. This summons was supported by an eight-page affidavit sworn by Horsham's chief solicitor, Mr Davison, to which were exhibited over 300 pages of supporting documents, including the inspector's decision. It is clear from the final paragraph of Mr Davison's affidavit that Horsham still wished to make use of the existing High Court proceedings to obtain orders for the clearance of the site after the extended time allowed by the inspector for compliance with the enforcement notices had expired.

West Sussex for its part wrote to the applicants' solicitors on 2 December seeking detailed information in respect of each of their clients about their habits of life and places of residence over the last five years, with particular reference to any connections with West Sussex. Mrs B responded by saying that the legal aid certificate under which her firm acted hardly covered the extensive investigation which West Sussex was seeking. However, she provided three short paragraphs of general comments and enclosed copies of ten of the proofs of evidence she had prepared in connection with the planning inquiry in August. She said that a high proportion of her clients were illiterate and quite unable to keep diaries of their sojourns. In a response written on 16 December West Sussex asked for information similar to that contained in the proofs in relation to the nine applicants for judicial review for whom proofs had not been provided. It also asked for full details of the repeated applications allegedly made to authorised sites, and asked some questions about the applicants' willingness to accept individual pitches on sites as they became available. These were not forthcoming.

This letter was followed on 24 December by a substantial affidavit sworn by West Sussex's county secretary, Mr Godfrey. I have described the general effect of this evidence in my judgment in the West Sussex proceedings, which is now reported, and there is no need for me to repeat this now. For present purposes, I need only refer to the following points which Mr Godfrey made in his affidavit.

(1) He maintained that West Sussex was not in breach of s 6 of the 1968 Act, that over a 12-month period there was a turnover rate of about 10% on official sites, resulting in about 12 vacancies a year, and that the Department of the Environment had in the past been satisfied with the adequacy of site provision in West Sussex since its designation in 1982. (2) None of the applicants had made any request to West Sussex for accommodation on an official site prior to the judicial review application, and in the absence of such a request West Sussex had no reasons to consider its s 6 duty in relation to them, or even to consider whether they were truly gipsies or whether they resided in or resorted to West Sussex. (3) In the same way, they had made no complaint to the Secretary of State before the judicial review proceedings were launched. (4) There was insufficient detail in their solicitors' original letters in September 1991 to show whether they fell within the language of the 1968 Act and whether they wished to stay in West Sussex if moved from their present site. (5) He said that although West Sussex was not complacent, site provision there compared very favourably with the overall national provision; he referred to the inspector's findings and the monitoring policies which had been in place since 1982. (6) If the court considered that there was a substantial complaint of site inadequacy, then that was a matter which could and should be dealt with by the Secretary of State under his s 9 powers: the Secretary of State would have the opportunity to investigate matters in detail. (7) He maintained that the application against West Sussex was simply a device by which the applicants might pursue their dispute with Horsham, and the fact that they had not even approached West Sussex in the past indicated that they had no real interest in obtaining authorised site places in the county. (8) Alternatively, if they genuinely wanted to obtain authorised site provision or accommodation in the county, it took a long time to find and establish authorised sites and relief by way of judicial review was inappropriate.

Finally, Mr Godfrey commented on detailed aspects of the grounds for relief. He referred to the very recent correspondence and said that judicial review should not be granted in relation to a decision which the council had never been invited to make before recourse was had to the court, and which it could not in any event consider until the applicants had provided all the relevant information.

In the third week of January 1992 there was a two-and-a-half-day hearing before Hutchison J, who dismissed Horsham's application to strike out the judicial review proceedings, but ordered an expedited hearing. Now that I have had an opportunity to read his judgment I can see that Hutchison J considered that the applicants could be excused for waiting till after the planning inquiry before launching their judicial review proceedings in relation to the legal validity of the January decision to start High Court proceedings, and that he also considered that this was not one of those very clear cases in which the courts are willing, and ought, to strike out leave granted at an ex parte hearing. I should add that I have seen the very full written skeleton argument used by A in the hearing before Hutchison J, and

I am not at all surprised that on the material and on the arguments before him he considered that he should not strike out the application against Horsham. Soon after this hearing, the start of the substantive applications against both respondents was fixed for 5 May.

I must now say something about the exchange of affidavits and the other events which occurred before the main hearing started. Horsham served two affidavits in early December as their response to the judicial review application, and there was a flurry of affidavit evidence in January as between the gipsies and Horsham in advance of the hearing before Hutchison J and for the purposes of that hearing.

On 8 and 9 April three more affidavits were forthcoming from Horsham. One related to housing and homelessness matters, one to the way in which the January 1991 decision had been taken, and the third brought the recent history up to date. This showed that the extended periods of time allowed by the planning inspector had now expired, so that the occupation of the land as a gipsy caravan site was now illegal and a criminal offence under planning law. At the end of January, following the hearing before Hutchison J, the council had resolved to use its powers under s 178 of the Town and Country Planning Act 1990 in order to achieve compliance with planning law, and because the gipsies consistently indicated that they intended to obstruct the council when it exercised its enforcement powers, a new writ was issued and served at the end of March. On 10 April, however, Horsham undertook to the court that it would not seek to exercise its new rights until after the hearing of the judicial review application, which was now imminent.

So far as West Sussex was concerned, there was no response at all to Mr Godfrey's affidavit for three and a half months, and it prepared for the expedited hearing on the basis that his evidence was unanswered. West Sussex was not sent copies of the affidavits which were being exchanged between Horsham and the gipsies. On 21 April 1992, just under two weeks before the hearing, Mrs B swore an eight-page affidavit in which she joined issue with much of what Mr Godfrey had said. So far as she made assertions of fact in her affidavit, these were all hearsay. Despite the findings of the planning inspector and the scepticism of West Sussex, assertions of disputed fact were prefaced by the words 'I am informed by the Applicants and verily believe that ...' I do not know how the gipsies' advisers envisaged that the court, which is a court of supervisory jurisdiction only, was going to handle these vague, inadmissible assertions of disputed fact at the substantive hearing. At about the same time, the gipsies' advisers made last-minute written requests for wide-ranging discovery to both Horsham and West Sussex. Mr Godfrey replied to Mrs B's affidavit on 1 May.

Mrs B has explained to me that at each stage in dealing with the evidence which was served in the judicial review proceedings she considered what she enigmatically described as 'these matters' with counsel. She acknowledges that there were some delays in serving affidavit evidence in reply because A was extremely busy. She knew that the fact that A was so busy was leading to delays but she did not consider it appropriate to change counsel since A had been so closely involved in the case and her clients had expressed considerable confidence in him and wished him to deal with the matter.

A problem had arisen from the fact that in early February 1992 A had been delivered the brief in a building contract arbitration which was thought likely to last four to seven days. In the event, the issues widened and it eventually ran for many months. On 24 March he had to explain to the solicitors that he would have to be released from this case, and a junior member of his chambers took over his responsibilities. By then, the Legal Aid Board had granted authority to instruct leading as well as junior counsel at the substantive hearing. A took no further part in the proceedings except to help his successor to draft 'certain further affidavits' on 15 April.

The Easter break then followed, and it must by then have been realised by counsel who now had the carriage of the proceedings that there were some serious weaknesses in their tackle. For one thing, the legal validity of the decision to take enforcement notice proceedings had never been challenged. Their clients were now committing criminal offences under planning law by remaining on the site after their appeals against the enforcement notices had been dismissed and no appeal had been lodged against the inspector's decision, and the time for complying with the enforcement notices had long since expired. For another, they had no admissible evidence at all in the proceedings as against West Sussex in which there were substantial areas of disputed fact.

They sought to remedy the first of these omissions by settling the new application, in which they sought to challenge the validity of the decision to issue enforcement notices, which I heard and dismissed at the start of the substantive hearing. They sought to remedy the second of these deficiencies (while at the same time providing evidence in their new applications against Horsham) by causing Mr Frank Wenman, the gipsies' leader, to swear three affidavits between 22 April and 5 May.

The second of these affidavits displayed vividly the scale of the disputes of fact as between the gipsies and West Sussex. Mr Wenman asserted, on hearsay, that ten other men, some but not all of whom were parties to the present proceedings, had lived in and travelled in West Sussex for most of their lives. Mr Hunter, West Sussex's experienced gipsy liaison officer, maintained for his part that until they occupied the site near Pulborough he had never come across any of them before.

As I have said, I dismissed both the applications in the judicial review proceedings. So far as the Horsham proceedings were concerned, I was strongly influenced by the considerations that no effective challenge had been made to the validity of the decision to invoke enforcement notice procedure, and that the High Court proceedings in March 1991 were issued as an interim measure because the gipsies were flagrantly ignoring the stop notices pending the decision on the planning appeal. This had now been decided against them, and once their extended time for complying with the enforcement notices had run out, Horsham had a new, even stronger right to require them to restore the site to its previous condition and to remove their caravans. In those circumstances, a post-mortem inquiry, initiated seven and a half months afterwards into the thinking of Horsham's director of planning law when he decided to authorise High Court proceedings in January 1991, appeared to me to fulfil no useful purpose: in those circumstances the granting of relief would be detrimental to good administration (see s 31(6) of the 1981 Act). I should add, in fairness to A, that I might not have expressed myself in quite the same terms both in this judgment and in my West Sussex judgment if I had known some of the additional matters he has put before me during the present application.

In my judgment in the West Sussex proceedings I was influenced by the fact that no complaint had been made to West Sussex before the judicial review proceedings were brought. West Sussex was one of the few counties which had been designated as making adequate provision under the 1968 Act, the present gipsies had received no support from any body representative of gipsies, and it was wholly inappropriate to resort to judicial review proceedings in a case in which there were issues of disputed fact and Parliament had given the Secretary of State a supervisory role if there was ground for complaint that any county council was failing to comply with its statutory duty.

In due course both respondents made applications for wasted costs orders against A and against the solicitors, and I must now turn to consider the jurisdiction which the court possesses to make such orders.

Before the enactment of the Courts and Legal Services Act 1990 the courts had no power to make such an order on the application of a party to litigation against counsel instructed on the other side. He was not an officer of the court over whom the court could exercise a disciplinary jurisdiction. Nor did he owe any duty of care to his lay client's opponent (see *Orchard v South Eastern Electricity Board* [1987] 1 All ER 95 at 99, [1987] QB 565 at 571 per Donaldson MR).

So far as solicitors were concerned, Ord 62, which relates to costs, contained rules which gave effect to the court's disciplinary powers over solicitors as officers of the court who owe duties to the court. During the period immediately before 1 October 1991, when the relevant provisions of the 1990 Act came into effect, Ord 62, r 11 gave the court power to order a solicitor to pay 'wasted costs' to the other side where it appeared that 'costs have been incurred unreasonably ... in any proceedings or have been wasted by failure to conduct proceedings with reasonable competence'.

In *Davy-Chiesman v Davy-Chiesman* [1984] 1 All ER 321, [1984] Fam 48 the Court of Appeal held that a solicitor is in very many circumstances protected from personal liability if he has acted on the advice of experienced counsel properly instructed. However, this protection is not total, since a solicitor is highly trained and expected to be experienced in his particular fields of law and he does not abdicate all responsibility whatever by instructing counsel ([1984] 1 All ER 321 at 335, [1984] Fam 48 at 67 per Dillon LJ).

In *Locke v Camberwell Health Authority* [1991] 2 Med LR 249 at 254 Taylor LJ summarised the position of litigation solicitors before the 1990 Act in these terms:

'(1) In general, a solicitor is entitled to rely upon the advice of counsel properly instructed. (2) For a solicitor without specialist experience in a particular field to rely on counsel's advice is to make normal and proper use of the Bar. (3) However, he must not do so blindly but must exercise his own independent judgment. If he reasonably thinks counsel's advice is obviously or glaringly wrong, it is his duty to reject it. (4) Although a solicitor should not assist a litigant where prosecution of a claim amounts to an abuse of process, it is not his duty to attempt to assess the result of a conflict of evidence or to impose a pre-trial screen on a litigant's claim. (5) The jurisdiction to order costs against a solicitor personally is one which falls to be exercised with care and discretion and only in clear cases.'

Section 4 of the 1990 Act substituted a new s 51 of the 1981 Act. This now provides, so far as is relevant:

'... (6) In any proceedings ... the court may disallow, or (as the case may be) order the legal or other representative concerned to meet, the whole of any wasted costs or such part of them as may be determined in accordance with rules of court.

(7) In subsection (6), "wasted costs" means any costs incurred by a party—(a) as a result of any improper, unreasonable or negligent act or omission on the part of any legal or other representative or any employee of such a representative; or (b) which, in the light of any such act or omission occurring after they were incurred, the court considers it is unreasonable to expect that party to pay ...

(13) In this section "legal or other representative", in relation to a party to proceedings, means any person exercising a right of audience or right to conduct litigation on his behalf.'

The relevant rules of court are to be found in Ord 62, r 11. These are designed to ensure that no order may be made unless those against whom it is sought have had a reasonable opportunity to appear and show cause why it should not be made, and they also enable to court to direct an inquiry by a taxing officer if it thinks it appropriate.

The appropriate approach of a court in these cases is to ask itself three questions: (i) was there an improper, unreasonable or negligent act or omission by the legal representative concerned, (ii) if so, has a party as a result incurred costs, (iii) if so, should the court exercise its discretion to make a wasted costs order in respect of all or part of such costs (see *Re a barrister (wasted costs order) (No 1 of 1991)* [1992] 3 All ER 429 at 435, [1993] QB 293 at 301).

It goes without saying that there must be a clear causal connection between the conduct in question and the costs thereby incurred (see *Antonelli v Wade Gery Farr* (1992) Times, 29 December per Turner J).

It was also common ground that in this context, although no common law duty of care was owed to the other side, a 'negligent act' entailed an error that no reasonably well-informed and competent member of the profession in question would have made, and not merely an error of judgment on some matter upon which the opinions of reasonably informed and competent members of the profession might have differed (for this test, see *Saif Ali v Sydney Mitchell & Co (a firm) (P, third party)* [1978] 3 All ER 1033 at 1041, [1980] AC 198 at 218 per Lord Diplock).

Before I describe the complaints which have been made in the present case, there are some preliminary observations which I need to make in relation to the position of counsel and solicitors acting for legally aided clients or clients with limited means in relation to the likely costs of contested High Court proceedings.

In general, a client is entitled to pursue litigation with little prospect of success. In *Fray v Voules* (1859) 1 E & E 839 at 848, 120 ER 1125 at 1129 Erle J said: 'The client, and not the attorney, is the dominus litis.' Counsel must always remember that it is his professional duty not to set his name to a plea which he does not consider to be 'properly arguable' (see the *Code of Conduct of the Bar of England and Wales* para 606). Subject to this, a rich plaintiff may instruct lawyers to bring proceedings on his behalf even though the prospects of success are minimal, the recoverable damages will be slim and the costs will be out of proportion to the likely damages. Counsel is on the cab-rank and provided that he acts with reasonable professional competence there can be no question of a wasted costs order being made against him even if his client fails and has to pay all his opponent's costs (para 209 of the *Code of Conduct*).

It is necessary to be cautious about judicial dicta in cases involving solicitors which were decided before a change in the relevant costs rule took effect in 1986. The former provisions of Ord 62, r 8(1) referred to cases in which 'costs are incurred improperly or without reasonable cause or are wasted by undue delay or by any other misconduct or default', and under that regime the misconduct in question had to be serious, not merely an error of an order which constituted or was equivalent to negligence (see *Orchard v South Eastern Electricity Board* [1987] 1 All ER 95 at 99–100, [1987] QB 565 at 571–572, a case decided under the previous regime where Donaldson MR provides a useful summary of the earlier authorities).

I have not the slightest doubt that the rule change in 1986 and the change in the statutory regime in 1990 were intended to reflect contemporary feeling that it was wrong that solicitors, and now counsel, should cause financial loss to others when they acted below the standards reasonably to be expected of their profession, and that that loss should not be recoverable, even if the people who suffered it were on the opposite side in contested litigation. Accordingly, I now approach with great caution the passage in Donaldson MR's judgment in *Orchard*'s case [1987] 1 All ER 95 at 100, [1987] QB 565 at 572, in which he said:

> 'In the context of a complaint that litigation was initiated or continued in circumstances in which to do so constituted serious misconduct, it must never be forgotten that it is not for solicitors or counsel to impose a pre-trial screen through which a litigant must pass before he can put his complaint or defence before the court. On the other hand, no solicitor or counsel should lend his assistance to a litigant if he is satisfied that the initiation or further prosecution of a claim is mala fide or for an ulterior purpose or, to put it more broadly, if the proceedings would be, or have become, an abuse of the process of the court or unjustifiably oppressive.'

The first part of this passage is unexceptional even when cases under the new costs regime fall to be decided. It echoes *Abraham v Jutsun* [1963] 2 All ER 402 at 404, [1963] 1 WLR 658 at 663, where Lord Denning MR said:

> 'Appearing, as the [solicitor advocate] was, on behalf of an accused person, it was ... his duty to take any point which he believed to be fairly arguable on behalf of his client. An advocate is not to usurp the province of the judge.'

Even though these comments were made under the old costs regime, they are, in my judgment, equally valid today and go to the very heart of the duty of the fearless advocate as expounded by Thomas Erskine just over 200 years ago in *R v Paine* (1792) 22 State Tr 357 at 412.

However, in the second part of the citation from *Orchard*'s case, Donaldson MR was concentrating on what would constitute serious misconduct, which is a more rigorous test than the present test of negligence.

If solicitors or counsel are acting for a client who is seeking legal aid, then it is for the Legal Aid Board to decide whether it is appropriate to allocate public money to help their client to advance his case. With their expert help, the client must satisfy the board that he has reasonable grounds for taking proceedings (s 15(2) of the Legal Aid Act 1988), and even if he does so his application may still be refused if in the particular circumstances of the case it appears to the board unreasonable that he should be granted representation (s 15(3)). The first of these tests has been described as 'the legal merits test' in the notes for guidance in the *Legal Aid Handbook 1992* p 47, which provides this advice:

> 'The area office must be satisfied that, on the facts put forward and the law which relates to them, there is a case ... which should be put before a court for a decision. The availability and strength of evidence to support the facts alleged will be taken into account. However, the area officer sees only one side of the case. It is for the court to adjudicate on the issues although the area office must be satisfied that the applicant has reasonable grounds for taking ... the proceedings. The likelihood of success is a factor which the area office must bear in mind but it is of the essence of litigation that there are two opposing points of view on which the court is required to adjudicate. Litigation is also notoriously uncertain so that any attempt to restrict legal aid to certainties or near certainties would not only be doomed to failure (if the aim was 100 per cent. success rate) but would also be a denial to many applicants of an opportunity to obtain justice. The aim therefore must be not to be over-cautious but not to grant legal aid for cases where there is little or no hope of success. If legal aid is granted in hopeless cases it raises the expectations of assisted persons too high, forces opponents to defend their rights and wastes public money, perhaps doubly if costs are awarded against the fund.'

One of the criteria which the board suggests should be satisfied is that the solicitor would advise the client to take the proceedings privately, i e if he had means which were adequate to meet the likely costs of the case, or would make payment of the likely costs possible, although something of a sacrifice.

In *R v Legal Aid Board, ex p Hughes* (1992) 24 HLR 698 at 702–703 the majority of the Court of Appeal took the view, expressed by Lord Donaldson MR, that the tests to be applied in judicial review cases by the board and by the single judge (when deciding whether to grant leave) are not essentially different. Each has to consider whether the applicant has reasonable grounds, the one for the grant of legal representation at public expense, the other for starting proceedings which will inevitably involve the respondents in cost and, in the case of central government or local authorities, administrative uncertainty.

Part X of the Civil Legal Aid (General) Regulations 1989, SI 1989/339, sets out the mechanisms by which a certificate may be revoked or discharged, and these mechanisms are often invoked by non-legally aided opponents who feel that the grant or continuance of the legal aid certificate in proceedings against them is unreasonable.

It follows, therefore, that the only difference between the case of the lay client who has the means to support the litigation and the case of the lay client who has to seek legal aid is that in the latter case, if he is to receive the services of a lawyer paid for by the taxpayer, he has to satisfy the board, on the legal merits test, that he has reasonable grounds for taking the proceedings and the board must refrain from deciding to withhold representation because it is unreasonable to grant it (see the *Legal Aid Handbook 1992* pp 48–51). If legal aid is granted, the legally aided litigant and his advisers are in the same position as against the other party to the proceedings as the non-legally aided litigant (see s 31(1)(b) of the Legal Aid Act 1988; *Re Saxton (decd)* [1962] 3 All ER 92, [1962] 1 WLR 968). Provided his legal advisers exercise reasonable standards of competence and do not act improperly or unreasonably, there can be no question of a wasted costs order being made against them.

In civil litigation, counsel is usually required to advise again on the merits of the case after pleadings and discovery have been completed and the scope of the initial legal aid certificate usually extends no further than this stage. In judicial review proceedings, after leave is initially granted ex parte, the merits of the proceedings often take on a very different complexion once the respondents have served their evidence. For this reason, the Crown Office's standard form JRJ, which was used by Webster J when he granted leave in the present case, contains the following warning on its face:

'Where leave to apply has been granted, applicants and their legal advisers are reminded of their obligation to reconsider the merits of their application in the light of the respondent's affidavit.'

This warning is derived from a passage in the judgment of Hodgson J in *R v Secretary of State for the Home Dept, ex p Brown* (1984) Times, 6 February, which is in these terms:

'It is highly desirable for counsel and solicitors instructed by an applicant for judicial review to give further careful consideration to the merits of the application once they had received notice of the respondent's evidence, even though leave to move for judicial review had already been obtained. If that were done, much time, expense and disappointment in the hearing of hopeless applications would be saved.'

Although no reference to this case appears in *The Supreme Court Practice 1991*, the warning appears in leading textbooks on judicial review and on the form in standard use by the Crown Office, and in my judgment any solicitor or counsel holding themselves out as competent to handle judicial review proceedings in 1991–92 should be taken as being familiar with it. One of the reasons for the warning, as Hodgson J pointed out, is to avoid the wasting of time and incurring of expense in connection with hopeless applications.

In his powerful submissions for A, Mr Munby QC submitted that too ready a resort to the wasted costs order jurisdiction, and the threat or fear of such applications, might lead to three wholly undesirable results. First, lawyers might allow their judgment in advising their clients, and their willingness to carry a case forward, to be prejudicially affected by considerations of their own financial position, thus inhibiting bona fide claimants from putting their case before the court at all: a wedge might be driven between plaintiffs and their legal advisers, which would inhibit the giving of favourable advice for fear of personal liability. Secondly, lawyers might lose their objectivity and might, in consequence, become more determined than ever not to abandon their clients. And thirdly, there was a real danger that the bringing, or the threat, of such applications might 'frighten' legal representatives acting for legally aided clients and lead to the latter being treated less favourably than privately paying clients, especially at the 'cutting edge'.

These would of course be real grounds for concern if the courts were indeed to resort too readily to this new jurisdiction. But in my judgment, these concerns should not deflect the courts from making a wasted costs order in an appropriate case. If this new statutory regime was to lead those who hold themselves out as competent to practise in as complex a field of litigation as judicial review to decide that they do not in fact have the competence to enable them to avoid the risk of wasted costs orders against them, or to take more active steps to pursue continuing education than is now the norm in order to ensure that they continue to possess the standards of the reasonably competent practitioner in this field, then it must be assumed that these welcome developments were the intention, and hope, of Parliament when it passed the 1990 Act.

It should be remembered that that Act was passed against the background of a disagreement between the civil and criminal divisions of the Court of Appeal on the question whether the new, more severe, 1986 costs regime in civil litigation was ultra vires (contrast *Sinclair-Jones v Kay* [1988] 2 All ER 611, [1989] 1 WLR 114 with *Holden & Co (a firm) v CPS* [1990] 1 All ER 368, [1990] 2 QB 261: a dispute later resolved in *Gupta v Comer* [1991] 1 All ER 289, [1991] 1 QB 629). In substituting negligence for serious misconduct as the threshold test for wasted costs orders in both criminal and civil cases, Parliament must have intended to provide redress for all who incurred expense in civil or criminal cases which was caused by the negligence of lawyers on either side, and been willing to tolerate any adverse consequences of this new policy with equanimity. It is, after all, no more than the risk to which other professional people who do not possess the advocate's immunity in court have customarily exposed themselves. Fears about defensive medicine have not led Parliament to restrict the doctor's duty at common law to compensate those who have suffered loss because he has fallen below the standards of care reasonably to be expected of him.

The wording of the new provisions of s 51(6) of the 1981 Act is, in my judgment, quite clear. It is undeniable that they create a new regime of wasted costs orders which may be novel and unwelcome to barristers. On the other hand, Draco, the Athenian law-maker who fixed the penalty of death for almost all crimes, including petty theft, would have been surprised to find his name attached to this new statutory provision by Macpherson J in *Re a barrister (wasted costs order) (No 1 of 1991)* [1992] 3 All ER 429 at 435, [1993] QB 293 at 301.

It was suggested to me in argument that although this new statutory regime came into force in October 1991 there are still many barristers and solicitors in everyday practice who are unaware of its possible effect on them, despite a rousing attempt by Popplewell J to waken them in July 1992, to which I will refer below (see *R v Wychavon DC, ex p Saunders* (27 July 1992, unreported)). This consideration cannot, in my judgment, deflect a court from giving effect to the Parliamentary intention in connection with any complaints which arise from 1 October 1991 onwards. I should add that the provisions of the 1990 Act had no retrospective effect (see *Fozal v Gofur* (1993) Times, 9 July).

One further matter must always be remembered before a court makes such an order, and this is the effect of the incidence of legal professional privilege. This belongs to the lay client, and it is for him, and him alone, to waive. The privilege attaches to the contents of confidential communications passing between a barrister and his professional or lay client for the purpose of requesting or giving legal advice (see 3(1) *Halsbury's Laws* (4th edn reissue) para 526 and the cases cited at note 1). It does not attach to the fact that on a particular day solicitors sent instructions to counsel to advise, or to the date on which they received that advice, or to what they did or did not do in the conduct of the proceedings in consequence of receiving that advice.

The existence of legal professional privilege may inhibit a barrister or solicitors in defending themselves against a claim for a wasted costs order made by the other side. This is why the Court of Appeal has said that in cases in which privilege has not been waived justice requires that they should be given the benefit of the doubt (see *Orchard v South Eastern Electricity Board* [1987] 1 All ER 95 at 100, 101, 105–106, [1987] QB 565 at 572, 574, 579–580 per Donaldson MR and Dillon LJ).

I turn now to the grounds on which the wasted costs orders are sought. I should say at once that I am indebted to counsel for their very clear skeleton submissions, both at the start of the hearing and in reply, which must have saved at least four hours of time at the hearing. I am also indebted to them for making available to me disks containing the material from their computer databases which contained those skeleton arguments. This help must have saved me at least a full day's work in the preparation of this judgment.

Mr Elvin, for Horsham, relied heavily on some of the views I expressed in my judgment in the Horsham proceedings in support of Horsham's application for wasted costs orders against A and/or the solicitors. I had held that if a judicial review challenge was to be mounted at all, it should have been mounted as soon as legal aid was obtained in July, and the gipsies' advisers should not have allowed more time to go by while they used the planning inquiry in part as a fishing expedition to see if more evidence might turn up to support a case which was already long out of time. I was also heavily influenced by my view that the s 222 High Court proceedings were proceedings for what was essentially interlocutory relief in support of planning law. A quite new situation had emerged when the enforcement notice appeal was dismissed without an appeal to the High Court, and an inquiry into what was in the mind of Horsham's director of planning when he decided to authorise the seeking of interim relief in the High Court against anticipated flagrant breaches of stop notices in January 1991 would be wholly academic 15 months later. In those circumstances the granting of any of the relief sought over four months out of time would be detrimental to good administration.

However, I see that Hutchison J took a different view from me at the interlocutory stage. I also see that Horsham went on seeing its High Court proceedings as an appropriate vehicle for seeking a final order for clearing the site after the planning appeal had failed and did not, until after the hearing before Hutchison J, envisage issuing a new writ to enforce the new rights which it now possessed. Because the validity of the course it had taken in invoking enforcement notice procedure had never been challenged, it would have been open to Horsham to put in a quite short affidavit in response to the judicial review application, pointing out (a) that the application was well out of time; and (b) that as it now had the benefit of winning the planning appeal, it would have statutory powers to clear the land without a court order as soon as the extended period for complying with the enforcement notices had expired, and the present application was wholly academic. It could then have proceeded pursuant to its new rights, no doubt making it quite clear on the face of any new resolution that it had taken into account all the considerations of fact and law it could reasonably have been a expected to take into account when deciding to move gipsies off land which they were not authorised to use for a gipsy encampment, and its position would have been impregnable.

In my judgment, there was certainly material on which the validity of Horsham's original decision could have been properly challenged. This was the view of Webster J, of Hutchison J and of the Legal Aid Board. I have b considerable sympathy with Horsham, because it was a complicated factual and legal situation and they were faced with very determined opponents. The moral of this saga may be that it would be wise for all local authorities to adopt the growing practice of setting out in clear terms the criteria they will use when deciding to move gipsies off land in their local authority area and to make it clear on the face of any resolution to take enforcement or c possession action that they have had those criteria well in mind and the way in which they have applied them on the facts before them. However that may be, I can see no grounds for making a wasted costs order in Horsham's favour in these circumstances. I should add, for completeness, that I heard interesting arguments about the meaning of the description of acts as d 'improper' and 'unreasonable' in s 51(7) of the 1981 Act. I do not consider that there was anything improper, unreasonable or negligent in the conduct of the proceedings against Horsham by any of the applicants' lawyers, and I dismiss Horsham's application.

West Sussex's complaints are more formidable. It must be remembered that it had the benefit of a designation by the Secretary of State that it was e making adequate provision for the gipsies residing in or resorting to its county area and in this respect its position was very different to that of other local authorities who feature in the reported cases concerning gipsies with which A was obviously familiar.

In *R v Secretary of State for the Environment, ex p Lee* (1985) 54 P & CR 311 f Hertfordshire was still more than 100 pitches short of the total number of pitches agreed to be necessary. Complaints had been made both to the council and to the Secretary of State at least a year before judicial review proceedings were started, and both were parties to the proceedings.

In *West Glamorgan CC v Rafferty* [1987] 1 All ER 1005, [1987] 1 WLR 457 West Glamorgan had made no sites at all available, although at least 85 g pitches appeared to be needed. Complaints had been made on behalf of gipsies generally, if not by these particular gipsies, to both the council and the Secretary of State on numerous occasions before issue was joined in court proceedings, and both were parties to the judicial review proceedings.

In *R v Hereford and Worcester CC, ex p Smith* (28 April 1988, unreported) the h court was concerned with both Hereford and Worcester and Surrey County Councils. In the former, the council was not even half way towards its target of 230 local authority pitches. Surrey, for its part, was two-thirds of the way towards its target of 340 pitches, which had recently been increased to 370. The Secretary of State's decisions not to issue directions under s 9 of the 1968 j Act were being challenged in the proceedings, to which he was a party, and both he and the county councils were well aware of the complaints being made about inadequate provision long before the judicial review proceedings were launched.

These two counties also featured in other reported cases which I was shown, and a consideration of all these cases reveal the willingness of this court to intervene by declaratory relief where county councils are incontrovertibly in breach of their statutory duties under the 1968 Act and

attempts to seek redress from the Secretary of State, who is charged with
supervisory jurisdiction over these matters by Parliament, have failed.

West Sussex complain that this was not that type of case at all. They
accept that any redress they may have against A in relation to wasted costs
must relate to matters postdating 1 October 1991. They have divided their
complaints into two periods.

The first period relates to the period between March 1991 and the
commencement of the judicial review proceedings on 12 September 1991. It
is now clear on the evidence that throughout that period A was
contemplating the possibility of proceedings against West Sussex, provided
that he received evidence that the county's actual provision of pitches could
be shown to fall short of the numbers needed to satisfy its statutory duty.
Once he had received evidence of annual counts which suggested an average
annual shortfall of 10%, then he considered it was appropriate to issue
proceedings without more.

West Sussex make six complaints in relation to this period. First, no
proper steps were being taken to produce evidence that the applicants, and
each of them, were gipsies, and that they were persons resorting to or
residing in West Sussex whose needs that county should have taken into
account when considering the performance of its statutory duty. Next, no
steps were taken to obtain information about gipsy counts, or indeed about
anything else relating to the situation in West Sussex, either from the county
itself or from the Secretary of State, to whom these figures were regularly
sent. Thirdly, neither West Sussex nor the Secretary of State were told from
March 1991 onwards that the applicants, and each of them, were persons
who claimed an association with West Sussex, so that suitable inquiries
could be made into their history and needs. As a corollary to this, no
complaint was made to either of these authorities to the effect there was an
actual or apparent breach of s 6 of the 1968 Act going on. Nor were either of
them invited to take steps to remedy the alleged breach, if any. Finally, West
Sussex contend that the applicants' legal advisers had wholly failed to grasp
the fact that any judicial review proceedings were likely to be contested, that
merely to point to a 10% shortfall would not be sufficient to prove a breach
of duty, and that they needed to prepare evidence accordingly. If they were
in any doubt about this before the planning inquiry, those doubts must have
been dispelled by the evidence given by Mr Hunter at the inquiry, after being
confronted with the figures for gipsy counts, that the county was not in
breach of duty.

When A settled the application against West Sussex he included four
claims for relief on Form 86A. Three of these were abandoned by leading
counsel at the outset of the hearing before me in May 1992, because it was
accepted that the county council owed no duty under the 1968 Act to specific
individuals, and that an order of mandamus directing the council to perform
its duties was inappropriate. The only viable claim that was left was an
application for a declaration that West Sussex was in breach of statutory duty
under s 6 of the 1968 Act.

Mr McCarthy, who appeared for West Sussex, makes a number of specific
criticisms of A and of the solicitors in relation to the next period, between
6 August and 10 September 1991. It will be remembered that before going on
holiday A had taken the view that the planning appeal was likely to fail but
that there was now an arguable case against West Sussex in judicial review

proceedings which his clients wished to bring, and he had advised the solicitors to seek and obtain legal aid for that purpose, which they duly did. Mr McCarthy's criticisms reflected the failure to take steps, at any rate after legal aid was available, to obtain direct admissible evidence from each of the applicants for whom they acted establishing their locus standi to make a complaint against West Sussex; the failure to write to West Sussex or to the Secretary of State setting out the gipsies' complaints before legal proceedings were started, and, in A's case, confusion in his mind about the relationship between a county council and individual gipsies which led to his settling three, out of four, claims for relief against West Sussex which stood no possible chance of success.

Mr McCarthy submitted that it was this failure to think out clearly what the gipsies' case, if any, against West Sussex really entailed that led to 11 substantive mistakes being made at the very start of the proceedings, and the effect of these mistakes persisted throughout the proceedings.

It is, of course, trite law that when Parliament has provided an alternative remedy it is only in an exceptional case that judicial review should be granted. The modern practice has been set out by the Court of Appeal in R v Chief Constable of the Merseyside Police, ex p Calveley [1986] 1 All ER 257, [1986] QB 424. I have described in my judgment A's attitude to the way in which, in his experience, the Secretary of State had exercised his powers in the past and why A thought that this dilatory approach by a minister to his duties would not be of any practical use to his clients, but none of this appears in Form 86A or in the very brief supporting affidavit.

The first four errors on which West Sussex rely, therefore, are: (1) the inclusion of a claim for mandamus and for one type of declaration (based on a supposed duty to individual gipsies) which could not possibly succeed; (2) the failure to refer to the statutory remedy (of complaint to the Secretary of State) in Form 86A or in the affidavit in support; (3) the failure to set out any reasons why the statutory remedy was inappropriate and that this was an exceptional case of the type referred to in ex p Calveley; (4) the failure to file any evidence showing why the statutory remedy was thought to be inappropriate.

The fifth criticism, which echoed a criticism made by Horsham, centred round the failure to send the planning inspector's conclusions to the Crown Office at any time between mid-September, when his report was received, and the last week in October, when Webster J granted leave. It will be remembered that the planning inspector expressed considerable scepticism as to whether any duty at all was owed to half the applicants, and that he was by no means satisfied that it could be shown that West Sussex was in breach of duty because there was no evidence about the constitution of the 10% shortfall seen in the half-yearly counts.

The sixth criticism went to the failure to file any admissible evidence at all in support of the judicial review application. Any reasonably competent practitioner, Mr McCarthy submitted, knows that hearsay evidence is only admissible on interlocutory applications (see Ord 41, r 5(2)).

All these criticisms, of course, related to the period before 1 October 1991 when the new wasted costs regime came into effect, and counsel agreed that I should be careful not to rest my decision on these matters except in so far as it could be shown that there was an occasion or occasions after 1 October 1991 when A and/or the solicitors ought to have reconsidered these points and that in some way these earlier failings can properly be added to the later complaints (for the general principle that, if the relevant conduct took place before a certain date, it makes no difference that the lawyers involved continued to act for the client after that date, see *Midland Bank Trust Co Ltd v Hett, Stubbs & Kemp (a firm)* [1978] 3 All ER 571 at 583–584, [1979] Ch 384 at 403 per Oliver J).

The remaining five criticisms related to: (1) the failure to deal in a suitable manner with West Sussex's letters in December 1991 seeking information about the applicants' status, background and plans; (2) the failure to re-evaluate the prospects of success after receiving West Sussex's evidence; (3) the failure up to the hearing (except for an affidavit sworn a week before the hearing which itself contained a lot of hearsay and was not served on West Sussex before the hearing started) to file any admissible evidence in support of the applicants' case; (4) the failure to assess in a realistic manner whether there was any substantial prospect of success against West Sussex; and (5) the failure to bear in mind that some of the applicants were legally aided with negligible means and that the remainder were of unknown means. (For the avoidance of doubt, I should make it clear that no point was taken before me that the solicitors should be made personally liable in relation to the order for costs made against the non-existent Mrs Brown whose name appeared in the list of applicants for whom the solicitors purported to act.)

The real gravamen of Mr McCarthy's complaint was that in all the circumstances a thorough review of the merits of the applicants' case against West Sussex should have been conducted by A and the solicitors after Mr Godfrey's affidavit was served in late December. If this had been done, no reasonably competent solicitors and counsel would have considered it appropriate to continue the proceedings, which I described as 'wholly without merit' in my judgment, and his clients should be entitled to recover their wasted costs from the time when the proceedings ought reasonably to have been abandoned.

Mr McCarthy reasonably points out that Mr Godfrey's affidavit put no less than nine factual issues in dispute. Despite this, nothing at all was done in the next four months to prepare and serve any admissible evidence showing that the applicants (or any of them) were gipsies residing in or resorting to West Sussex within the meaning of the 1968 Act; that they had made any application at all to West Sussex before the proceedings were started; or indeed that they would remain in West Sussex if compelled to leave their present site.

Furthermore, in spite of Mr Godfrey putting in issue all the matters on which West Sussex was to win a runaway victory at the substantive hearing, nothing at all was done at this stage of the proceedings to prepare and serve any evidence in reply which established that there was any justification for the failure to approach West Sussex, or the Secretary of State, before the proceedings started, or that the statutory remedy was unsuitable, or that exceptional circumstances existed which justified judicial review as a suitable alternative to the remedy provided by Parliament. Nor was any evidence filed to rebut the charge that the claim against West Sussex was anything other than a tactical device in the dispute with Horsham.

Even more formidably, it is said that no thought was given as to how the factual disputes between the applicants and West Sussex could be resolved in judicial review proceedings; no admissible evidence was filed in response to

the factual points put in issue by Mr Godfrey; and Mrs B's hearsay affidavit
sworn in mid-April did not address any of the issues relating to the
availability of an alternative remedy.

A has told me in his affidavit that nothing in the evidence of Mr Godfrey
led him to the view that the case could no longer be pursued. Mr McCarthy
submits that this view might have been tenable if A had had in mind and
acted on the need to prove all the matters to which I have just referred.
Whatever might have been in A's mind, the failure to put any evidence
before the court was bound to prove fatal to the application, and no
reasonably competent practitioner in A's position could have failed to take
effective steps to try to remedy the glaring deficiencies in the grounds for
relief and in the evidence filed in support of the application long before trial
bundles were prepared and briefs delivered. It was hardly surprising that Mr
McCarthy also referred me to the passage in my judgment in which I said:

> 'I regard this legally aided application to the court in the absence of any
> prior complaint to the Secretary of State or to the county council, and in
> the apparent absence of any adequate inquiry into the applicants'
> previous history, to be wholly unjustified.'

I will first consider the strength of these complaints against A, as the
barrister charged with the conduct of these proceedings, and I will turn to the
position of the solicitors at the end. Mr Munby cautioned me not to make
findings of negligence against A because problems over legal professional
privilege made it impossible for A to say everything in his defence which he
might want to say. Between October 1991 and March 1992 there was no
guidance from any decision of the court as to the appropriate approach to be
adopted by counsel in cases like these. He submitted that at all times the case
against West Sussex was 'properly arguable' and that it could not be said that
no reasonably competent barrister could have taken the view that the case
did not continue to be properly arguable even after Mr Godfrey's affidavit
was served.

Mr Munby accepted that I should be entitled to find, as I do, that Mr
Godfrey's affidavit had been sent by the solicitors to counsel by mid-January
1992. I have described how no affidavit evidence in response emerged for
three months thereafter, notwithstanding the direction for an expedited
hearing, and in so far as this was due to delays by A, to which Mrs B referred,
caused by pressure of other work, he did not try to excuse them on that
account. Paragraph 601(b) of the *Code of Conduct* provides that a barrister
must not undertake any task which he does not have adequate time and
opportunity to prepare for or perform, or which he cannot discharge within
a reasonable time having regard to pressure of other work. However, he
submitted that I did not know, and could not know, what might have been
passing between A and his solicitors during this period, whether A was
expressing concern about evidential deficiencies, and whether or not it was
A's fault that these deficiencies were not put right.

Mr Munby also submitted that there were barristers who were reasonably
competent in the conduct of judicial review proceedings who might have
taken the view that the reasons why the alternative statutory remedy was
inappropriate could have been explained orally by counsel at the hearing and
did not have to be supported by evidence or explained in Form 86A. If A had
advised his clients that they no longer had a case against West Sussex, he was
at risk of a claim against himself, Mr Munby said, for damages for negligence

or of a complaint to the Bar Council for not observing the cab-rank rule. I do not, incidentally, regard this as one of his best points.

Mr Munby also reminded me of A's evidence that he had difficulty in remembering his mental processes when he came to defend himself in these proceedings 12 months later, and that I should also bear in mind a point made by A that practitioners are now finding that there are wide variations in the approach of different judges assigned to the Crown Office list. Paragraph 203 of the *Code of Conduct* provides that a practising barrister 'must promote and protect fearlessly and by all proper and lawful means his lay client's best interests and do so without regard to his own interests or to any consequences to himself or to any other person'. If a barrister reasonably believes that a case is properly arguable and that there are some judges who would be willing to hold that it should succeed, then it would be intolerable, Mr Munby rightly submitted, that he or she should have a wasted costs order made against them after their clients' claim was, in the event, dismissed.

Mr Munby rightly reminded me that it has been the combination of imaginative counsel and innovative judges which have given the common law its strength to develop over the centuries. He submitted that the courts should be very slow to make wasted costs orders against counsel which might lead to penalise the imaginative and make them less likely to take arguable points which had never been argued before. There would, he submitted, be great dangers if a client is denied access to a court with his lawyer if the criteria for making wasted costs orders are set too high.

I have taken all these matters into account. In my judgment, the history of these proceedings against West Sussex reveals areas of sloppiness of thought or departures from proper practice which are becoming all too commonplace in the conduct of judicial review proceedings before single judges today.

I will give a few examples. Lawyers acting for a party should not regard it as unnecessary to write a letter before action merely because they believe it to be inevitable that the response will deny their clients' claim. Litigation, which is inordinately expensive and time-consuming, should ordinarily be regarded as a weapon of last resort, not of first resort. A fortiori, judicial review proceedings, in which the High Court is invited to supervise the way in which inferior bodies perform duties imposed on them by statute, should not ordinarily be embarked on before the inferior body has received a complaint and been given an opportunity to say whether or not it accepts it, and if it does not, to give its reasons for its stance. How can it be right to embark on such proceedings (other than in quite exceptional emergency circumstances, or when a wealthy client, who has been warned of the costs consequences of proceeding too precipitately, insists on proceeding without a letter before action) without airing one's grievance in writing first and assessing the reasonableness of the answer one receives?

Next, judicial review proceedings are wholly inappropriate as the forum for the resolution of issues of disputed fact. The evidence at the planning inquiry, as recounted in the inspector's report, showed that this case bristled with such issues. What was the history of the applicants (and each of them)? Were they gipsies within the meaning of the 1968 Act? Could they prove that they resided in or resorted to West Sussex to an extent to which, in accordance with the 1968 Act and cases decided under it, West Sussex should take their existence into account when it considered the adequacy of site provision in the county? West Sussex had the rare distinction of being a county council designated as having made adequate provision for its gipsies, and the judgment of Woolf J in *R v Secretary of State for the Environment, ex p Ward* [1984] 2 All ER 556 at 565, [1984] 1 WLR 834 at 844–845 set out the way in which that very experienced judge understood Parliament to have intended the provisions contained in ss 6 to 12 of the Act to work. Mr Hunter's evidence at the planning inquiry showed that there would be a multitude of issues of disputed fact to be resolved, if anyone disputed what he had said. Were the people shown as occupying unauthorised sites at the various counts not only gipsies, but also gipsies who could properly be described as residing in or resorting to West Sussex? If so, how rapidly did West Sussex find places for them on authorised sites, and could it be established that West Sussex had failed to provide authorised sites quickly enough? Had complaints been made to West Sussex, or to the Secretary of State, before these proceedings started, about the adequacy of provision in the county, and what was the fate of those complaints? Was the situation one in which the inability of this court to resolve issues of disputed fact could possibly lead it to make any declaration in judicial review proceedings, still less in the absence of any investigation by a body qualified to carry out such an investigation? Parliament had after all given both West Sussex and the Secretary of State the power, duty and resources to carry out investigations like this.

Thirdly, it is commonplace that in proceedings like these all material matters must be placed before the judge who is being invited to grant leave ex parte. How could it be right not to draw the judge's attention to the alternative statutory remedy or to explain why this was thought to be inadequate? Or to fail to draw his attention to the effect of the evidence given by Mr Hunter at the planning inquiry or to send him a copy of the planning inspector's report when it became available? Or to fail to alert him to the fact that no letter before action of any kind had been sent to West Sussex or the Secretary of State before Form 86A was lodged and to try and give adequate reasons for this omission?

I do not want to prolong this already overlong judgment by referring to other errors of an elementary kind which were committed by those who were responsible for the conduct of these proceedings. It appeared to me that an enthusiasm to do everything which might be done for gipsies occupying land in defiance of the wishes of the local planning authority led to a situation in which A, who held himself out as competent to advise the gipsies and their solicitors (who, at any rate so far as Mrs B was concerned, possessed nothing approaching the same experience), overlooked a lot of fairly basic principles of practice and procedure which he would not ordinarily have overlooked.

But all these considerations do not of themselves persuade me that I should make wasted costs orders when I bear in mind that this new jurisdiction over barristers did not come into effect until 1 October 1991, after all the most elementary of the errors had already been made. I am conscious that I am severely handicapped in my effort to do justice by not being able to penetrate the cloak of legal professional privilege. I was told by counsel that an Official Referee in similar circumstances had recently cut this Gordian knot by reading the instructions to counsel and counsel's advices without showing them to the other side, but I do not know enough about the facts of that case to understand how he was persuaded that he had jurisdiction to do so.

In my judgment, the crucial period, so far as the case against A is concerned, is the period between mid-January and mid-March 1992 when he had received Mr Godfrey's affidavit and had the responsibility of advising on the future conduct of the application. It was at this point, as form JRJ would have reminded him, that he was under an obligation to reconsider the merits of his clients' application in the light of Mr Godfrey's affidavit.

It is easy to say what steps he ought to have taken, and I accept that most of Mr McCarthy's criticisms are well-founded, if indeed A did not advise along these lines. He ought to have taken steps to ensure that Mr Godfrey's evidence was met, point by point, with admissible evidence or, if such evidence was not available, to consider whether he ought to advise that the case against West Sussex was no longer properly arguable. I do not consider that a higher test (such as 'stood a substantial prospect of success') is appropriate in these circumstances.

If all this had been done successfully, no doubt some of the applicants would have fallen out, and there would have been a residuum of a few applicants who could show a prima facie case on affidavit that (a) they were gipsies; (b) that they had resorted to West Sussex with a frequency that entitled their needs to be taken into account when West Sussex considered the adequacy of their site provision; and (c) that they had in the past been turned away by the wardens of authorised sites in West Sussex with no suggestion that there was space on any authorised site elsewhere in the county.

If the evidence had been improved in this way, I do not see how I could hold that an application based on a contention that West Sussex, with its regular 10% shortfall on gipsy counts, was in breach of statutory duty was not arguable, even if I do not consider that the argument had much prospect of success. A has said that he believed that the law was in a state of continuing development, that it had moved forward since *R v Secretary of State for the Environment, ex p Ward*, and that later decisions by Mann J and Henry J revealed a greater willingness to allow a gipsy to apply for declaratory relief notwithstanding the existence of the alternative statutory remedy. He also took the view that even if, as his successors had accepted before me, the dicta of Woolf J in *ex p Ward* accurately represented what A described as the true position, then s 9 of the 1968 Act would not have provided a 'convenient remedy' given the urgency of the present case.

Although I do not share A's view of the law in the circumstances of the present case, it seems to me that it would be wrong for me to hold that the points on which he would have relied if he had continued to handle the case himself were not properly arguable, and, for what it is worth, the legal aid authorities appear to have thought they were.

If, on the other hand, the evidence turned out not to be susceptible of improvement, then I am far from satisfied that any advice by A that the case against West Sussex was no longer properly arguable would have saved West Sussex any money at that late stage. Mr Wenman was a doughty fighter, and he had been granted leave to bring judicial review proceedings which he was then entitled to see through to a hearing in court unless the grant of leave was discharged. I consider it probable that if the case had proceeded under legal aid against Horsham he would have wished to try his luck against West

Sussex as a litigant in person, and in those circumstances I could not be satisfied that any negligence by A between January and March 1992 in itself caused any expenditure by West Sussex which otherwise would not have been incurred.

Accordingly, with some hesitation and no great enthusiasm, I dismiss West Sussex's claim for a wasted costs order against A. I should make it clear that the position might have been very different if the new wasted costs regime had been in place throughout 1991. This case has disclosed so many departures from good practice that the Bar Council would do well, in my judgment, to arrange for the preparation and publication of a statement of the professional standards to be expected of counsel having the conduct of judicial review proceedings in modern times, if barristers are to be helped to avoid the heavy financial penalties A has so narrowly escaped.

I repeat the warning given by Popplewell J in *R v Wychavon DC, ex p Saunders* (27 January 1992, unreported), when he referred to the scandalous two-year delays which are still disfiguring the conduct of judicial business in the Crown Office list:

> 'One of the matters which contributes to this very great delay is the large number of unmeritorious claims which are brought. This has two consequences: first, those who do have meritorious claims are delayed; and secondly, the vast majority of unmeritorious claims are financed at public expense and the cost to the public exchequer is now out of control ... There appears to be a view that almost every perceived wrong should have its remedy by way of judicial review ... It is important that the profession, both members of the Bar and solicitors, should be aware of the provisions of the Courts and Legal Services Act 1990. They may well find themselves having to pay substantial amounts by way of costs to the successful party if they do not give reasonable advice ... The standard to be applied in awarding costs against solicitors has varied. Now the position is abundantly clear. If either a solicitor or a member of the Bar wastes costs by any improper, unreasonable, or negligent act or omission, he or she is liable to pay the wasted costs. It is important that members of the Bar who have hitherto been exempt from this type of order should be fully aware that the court will not hesitate to make such an order in an appropriate case.'

I turn now, briefly, to the claim by West Sussex for a wasted costs order against the solicitors. The case against them ranged over much the same ground as the case against A. I remind myself of the governing principles set out by Taylor LJ in *Locke v Camberwell Health Authority* [1991] 2 Med LR 249 and I am unable to hold that there were negligent acts or omissions by the solicitors on their own account (ie when they were not acting on A's advice) which could be characterised as more than errors of judgment, or which could be shown in themselves to have caused West Sussex to incur expenditure which they would not otherwise have incurred.

They had selected junior counsel who was experienced in this class of litigation, and in so far as they acted on his advice in the period up to 1 October 1991 it would in my judgment be wrong to make an order against them personally under the costs regime in force up to then. I should add that improper conduct has not been alleged, and I have taken the view that where the conduct of either adviser was not negligent, it would be wrong to categorise it as unreasonable in the circumstances of this case.

For these reasons, these applications for wasted costs orders are all dismissed.

Applications dismissed.

Dilys Tausz   Barrister.

CTN Cash and Carry Ltd v Gallaher Ltd

COURT OF APPEAL, CIVIL DIVISION

SIR DONALD NICHOLLS V-C, FARQUHARSON AND STEYN LJJ

15 FEBRUARY 1993

Contract – Duress – Economic duress – Commercial pressure – Supplier lawfully threatening to discontinue purchaser's credit facilities if purchaser failed to pay sum allegedly owed – Purchaser settling account and claiming economic duress – Money not in fact owed by purchaser to supplier – Supplier acting in bona fide belief that money owing – Whether purchaser entitled to recover payment – Whether categories of duress encompassing 'lawful act duress'.

The plaintiff company ran a cash and carry business from warehouses in six towns in the north of England. A feature of the business was the sale of cigarettes, which they purchased in consignments from the defendant distributors. The defendants were not contractually bound to sell cigarettes to the plaintiffs and each sale was under a separate contract on the defendants' standard terms of business. The defendants had also arranged credit facilities for the plaintiffs, which they had absolute discretion to withdraw. In November 1986 the manager of one of the plaintiffs' warehouses placed an order for a consignment of cigarettes at a price of £17,000. By mistake, the defendants delivered the goods to the wrong warehouse. The parties subsequently agreed that the defendants would arrange for the transfer of the goods to the warehouse which had placed the original order, but before that could happen the entire consignment of cigarettes was stolen from the plaintiffs' premises. The defendants, believing that the goods had been at the plaintiffs' risk at the time of the theft, invoiced them for the price of the stolen goods. The plaintiffs initially rejected the invoice, but later paid it after the defendants had made it clear that unless they did so their credit facilities would be withdrawn. The plaintiffs issued a writ claiming repayment of the £17,000 on the ground that they had paid the money under duress, namely the defendants' threat to stop the plaintiffs' credit facilities in future dealings. The deputy judge held that they had no cause of action and had failed to make out a case for economic duress. The plaintiffs appealed.

Held – Although in certain circumstances a threat to perform a lawful act coupled with a demand for payment might amount to economic duress, it would be difficult, though not necessarily impossible, to maintain such a claim in the context of arm's length commercial dealings between two trading companies, especially where the party making the threat bona fide believed that its demand was valid. Any extension of the categories of duress to encompass 'lawful act duress' in a commercial context in pursuit of a bona fide claim would be a radical move with far-reaching implications and would introduce a substantial and undesirable element of uncertainty in the commercial bargaining process, in the sense that it would enable bona fide settled accounts to be reopened when parties to commercial dealings fell out. On the facts, the defendants were entitled in law to vary the terms on which they contracted with the plaintiffs by withdrawing credit facilities and they had made their demand for payment in good faith, genuinely and not unreasonably believing that they were owed the sum in question. It followed that the defendants' conduct did not amount to duress and that the plaintiffs' appeal would accordingly be dismissed (see p 717 *h*, p 718 *a* to *c*, p 719 *a* to *j* and p 720 *d*, post).

Notes

For contracts entered into under duress, see 9 *Halsbury's Laws* (4th edn) paras 296, 297, and for cases on the subject, see 12(1) *Digest* (2nd reissue) 216–221, 1741–1764.

Cases referred to in judgments

Mutual Finance Ltd v John Wetton & Sons Ltd [1937] 2 All ER 657, [1937] 2 KB 389.
National Westminster Bank plc v Morgan [1985] 1 All ER 821, [1985] AC 686, [1985] 2 WLR 588, HL; *rvsg* [1983] 3 All ER 85, CA.
Thorne v Motor Trade Association [1937] 3 All ER 157, [1937] AC 797, HL.
Universe Tankships Inc of Monrovia v International Transport Workers' Federation [1982] 2 All ER 67, [1983] 1 AC 366, [1982] 2 WLR 803, HL.

Cases also cited or referred to in skeleton arguments

Atlas Express Ltd v Kafco (Importers and Distributors) Ltd [1989] 1 All ER 641, [1989] QB 833.
B & S Contracts and Design Ltd v Victor Green Publications Ltd [1984] ICR 419, CA.
Barton v Armstrong [1975] 2 All ER 465, [1976] AC 104, PC.
D & C Builders Ltd v Rees [1965] 3 All ER 837, [1966] 2 QB 617, CA.
North Ocean Shipping Co Ltd v Hyundai Construction Co Ltd, The Atlantic Baron [1978] 3 All ER 1170, [1979] QB 705.
Occidental Wordwide Investment Corp v Skibs A/S Avanti, The Siboen and Sibotre [1976] 1 Lloyd's Rep 293.
Pao On v Lau Yiu [1979] 3 All ER 65, [1980] AC 614, PC.
Smith v William Charlick Ltd (1924) 34 CLR 38, Aust HC.
Vantage Navigation Corp v Suhail and Saud Bahwan Building Materials LLC, The Alev [1989] 1 Lloyd's Rep 138.

Appeal

The plaintiffs, CTN Cash and Carry Ltd, appealed from the decision of Judge Kershaw QC, sitting as a deputy judge of the High Court, made on 8 August 1991, whereby he held that the plaintiffs had no cause of action against the defendants, Gallaher Ltd, and had failed to make out a case for economic duress. The facts are set out in the judgment of Steyn LJ.

Hilary Heilbron QC and *Digby Jess* (instructed by *Simon A Holt & Co*, Preston) for the plaintiffs.

Philip Raynor (instructed by *Addleshaw Sons & Latham*, Manchester) for the defendants.

STEYN LJ (giving the first judgment at the invitation of Nicholls V-C). A buyer paid a sum of money to his supplier. The sum of money was in truth not owed by the buyer to the supplier. The buyer paid the sum as a result of the supplier's threat to stop the buyer's credit facilities in their future dealings if the sum was not paid. The supplier acted in the bona fide belief that the sum was owing. Does the doctrine of economic duress enable the buyer to recover the payment? In a judgment given on 8 August 1991 Judge Michael Kershaw QC gave a negative answer to this question. This appeal challenges the correctness of the deputy judge's conclusion.

The plaintiffs used to carry on a 'cash and carry' business from warehouses in six Lancashire towns, including Preston and Burnley. A feature of the plaintiffs' cash and carry business was the sale of cigarettes. The plaintiffs bought consignments of cigarettes from the defendants. The defendants were apparently the sole distributors in England of popular brands such as Silk Cut and Benson & Hedges. The dealings between the plaintiffs and the defendants took place on the defendants' standard terms of business. It was not a case of what is sometimes called a 'requirements contract', ie a transaction obliging the seller to make periodic deliveries of goods ordered pursuant to its terms. The defendants were not contractually bound to sell any cigarettes to the plaintiffs. The terms of business regulated separate contracts made from time to time. In their absolute and unfettered discretion the defendants sometimes granted credit facilities to customers. Such facilities were effective until withdrawn. The defendants granted such credit facilities to the plaintiffs.

On 20 November 1986 the manager of the plaintiffs' warehouse in Preston placed an order for a large consignment of cigarettes. The invoice value of the order inclusive of VAT was of the order of £17,000. By mistake an employee of the defendants put the address of the plaintiffs' warehouse in Burnley on the delivery note. On 24 November 1986 the defendants' driver delivered the goods to the plaintiffs' warehouse in Burnley. The goods were unloaded. Mr Nuttall, an assistant branch manager of the plaintiffs, signed the delivery note. Shortly afterwards, Mr Nuttall discovered that the delivery was intended for the Preston warehouse and not the Burnley warehouse. He telephoned the defendants' dispatch department about the matter. Eventually it was agreed that the defendants would arrange for the carriage of the goods from Burnley to Preston. The defendants were to undertake the carriage of the goods to Preston on 28 November 1986. Unfortunately, there was a robbery at the Burnley warehouse on the day before. The entire consignment of cigarettes was stolen. In due course the defendants delivered a new consignment of cigarettes to the Preston warehouse and the plaintiffs paid for it.

The question was, who should suffer the loss resulting from the theft of the goods at the Burnley warehouse? On 8 December 1986 the defendants invoiced the plaintiff for the price of the stolen goods. Although property in the goods had not passed to the plaintiffs, the deputy judge found that the defendants thought in good faith that the goods were at that time at the plaintiffs' risk. The deputy judge's finding is not challenged on this appeal. The plaintiffs *a* rejected the invoice. The dispute about the price of the stolen goods lingered on for some time.

In the second half of 1988, or in 1989, Mr Hayes of the defendants discussed the matter with Mr Kitt, the financial director of the plaintiffs. There was an issue of fact as to what was said. The deputy judge found as a matter of fact: (a) that Mr Hayes made it clear to Mr Kitt that unless the plaintiffs paid for the

b stolen goods the defendants would not in future grant credit to the plaintiffs; (b) that the plaintiffs regarded payment for the stolen goods as the lesser of the two evils and paid the disputed invoice for that reason.

By a writ issued in September 1989 the plaintiffs claimed repayment of the £17,000. The parties continued to deal with one another until January 1991. The plaintiffs deducted the sum in question from their last payment to the

c defendants.

The deputy judge said that at the end of the trial the only issue was whether the plaintiffs were entitled to recover the original payment of £17,000 and to set off that sum against their admitted liability for underpayment in respect of the goods ordered and received in the final weeks of trading. That issue was

d unfortunately not pleaded, but the defendants were content for the deputy judge to decide the issue.

On appeal the plaintiffs accept that, if the case for duress does not succeed, the claim for repayment must fail. It seems to me not to matter whether the correct analysis of the facts is that an agreement was made that the plaintiffs would pay the sum in question or whether payment is to be regarded simply as

e a unilateral act of the plaintiffs. In either event the claim must succeed if the case of duress is made out; if that case is not made out, the claim must fail.

Miss Heilbron QC, who appeared for the plaintiffs, submitted that the deputy judge erred in rejecting the plea of duress. She submitted that the payment was made under illegitimate pressure. She emphasised that there was

f objectively no legal basis for demanding the price of the goods, and the threat of withdrawing the credit facilities was made solely in order to obtain the payment. The threat was powerful because the removal of credit would have seriously jeopardised the plaintiffs' business. The clear purpose, she said, was to extort money to which the plaintiffs were in truth not entitled. In the circumstances, the threat was illegitimate and the case of duress was made out.

g Miss Heilbron cited a number of authorities which illustrate developments in this branch of the law. While I found the exercise of interest, I was reminded of the famous aphorism of Oliver Wendell Holmes that general propositions do not solve concrete cases. It may only be a half-truth, but in my view the true part applies to this case. It is necessary to focus on the distinctive features of

h this case, and then to ask whether it amounts to a case of duress.

The present dispute does not concern a protected relationship. It also does not arise in the context of dealings between a supplier and a consumer. The dispute arises out of arm's length commercial dealings between two trading companies. It is true that the defendants were the sole distributors of the

j popular brands of cigarettes. In a sense the defendants were in a monopoly position. The control of monopolies is, however, a matter for Parliament. Moreover, the common law does not recognise the doctrine of inequality of bargaining power in commercial dealings (see *National Westminster Bank plc v Morgan* [1985] 1 All ER 821, [1985] AC 686). The fact that the defendants were in a monopoly position cannot therefore by itself convert what is not otherwise duress into duress.

A second characteristic of the case is that the defendants were in law entitled to refuse to enter into any future contracts with the plaintiffs for any reason whatever or for no reason at all. Such a decision not to deal with the plaintiffs would have been financially damaging to the defendants, but it would have been lawful. A fortiori, it was lawful for the defendants, for any reason or for no reason, to insist that they would no longer grant credit to the plaintiffs. The defendants' demand for payment of the invoice, coupled with the threat to withdraw credit, was neither a breach of contract nor a tort.

A third, and critically important, characteristic of the case is the fact that the defendants bona fide thought that the goods were at the risk of the plaintiffs and that the plaintiffs owed the defendants the sum in question. The defendants exerted commercial pressure on the plaintiffs in order to obtain payment of a sum which they bona fide considered due to them. The defendants' motive in threatening withdrawal of credit facilities was commercial self-interest in obtaining a sum that they considered due to them.

Given the combination of these three features, I take the view that none of the cases cited to us assist the plaintiffs' case. Miss Heilbron accepted that there is no decision which is in material respects on all fours with the present case. It is therefore unnecessary to disinter all those cases and to identify the material distinctions between each of those decisions and the present case. But Miss Heilbron rightly emphasised to us that the law must have a capacity for growth in this field. I entirely agree.

I also readily accept that the fact that the defendants have used lawful means does not by itself remove the case from the scope of the doctrine of economic duress. Professor Birks, in *An Introduction to the Law of Restitution* (1989) p 177, lucidly explains:

'Can lawful pressures also count? This is a difficult question, because, if the answer is that they can, the only viable basis for discriminating between acceptable and unacceptable pressures is not positive law but social morality. In other words, the judges must say what pressures (though lawful outside the restitutionary context) are improper as contrary to prevailing standards. That makes the judges, not the law or the legislature, the arbiters of social evaluation. On the other hand, if the answer is that lawful pressures are always exempt, those who devise outrageous but technically lawful means of compulsion must always escape restitution until the legislature declares the abuse unlawful. It is tolerably clear that, at least where they can be confident of a general consensus in favour of their evaluation, the courts are willing to apply a standard of impropriety rather than technical unlawfulness.'

And there are a number of cases where English courts have accepted that a threat may be illegitimate when coupled with a demand for payment even if the threat is one of lawful action (see *Thorne v Motor Trade Association* [1937] 3 All ER 157 at 160–161, [1937] AC 797 at 806–807, *Mutual Finance Ltd v John Wetton & Sons Ltd* [1937] 2 All ER 657, [1937] 2 KB 389 and *Universe Tankships Inc of Monrovia v International Transport Workers' Federation* [1982] 2 All ER 67 at 76, 89, [1983] 1 AC 366 at 384, 401). On the other hand, Goff and Jones *Law of Restitution* (3rd edn, 1986) p 240 observed that English courts have wisely not accepted any general principle that a threat not to contract with another, except on certain terms, may amount to duress.

We are being asked to extend the categories of duress of which the law will take cognisance. That is not necessarily objectionable, but it seems to me that an extension capable of covering the present case, involving 'lawful act duress' in a commercial context in pursuit of a bona fide claim, would be a radical one with far-reaching implications. It would introduce a substantial and undesirable element of uncertainty in the commercial bargaining process. Moreover, it will often enable bona fide settled accounts to be reopened when parties to commercial dealings fall out. The aim of our commercial law ought to be to encourage fair dealing between parties. But it is a mistake for the law to set its sights too highly when the critical inquiry is not whether the conduct is lawful but whether it is morally or socially unacceptable. That is the inquiry in which we are engaged. In my view there are policy considerations which militate against ruling that the defendants obtained payment of the disputed invoice by duress.

Outside the field of protected relationships, and in a purely commercial context, it might be a relatively rare case in which 'lawful act duress' can be established. And it might be particularly difficult to establish duress if the defendant bona fide considered that his demand was valid. In this complex and changing branch of the law I deliberately refrain from saying 'never'. But as the law stands, I am satisfied that the defendants' conduct in this case did not amount to duress.

It is an unattractive result, inasmuch as the defendants are allowed to retain a sum which at the trial they became aware was not in truth due to them. But in my view the law compels the result.

For these reasons, I would dismiss the appeal.

FARQUHARSON LJ. I agree.

SIR DONALD NICHOLLS V-C. I also agree. It is important to have in mind that the sole issue raised by this appeal and argued before us was duress. The plaintiff claims payment was made by it under duress and is recoverable accordingly. I agree, for the reasons given by Steyn LJ, that that claim must fail. When the defendant company insisted on payment, it did so in good faith. It believed the risk in the goods had passed to the plaintiff company, so it considered it was entitled to be paid for them. The defendant company took a tough line. It used its commercial muscle. But the feature underlying and dictating this attitude was a genuine belief on its part that it was owed the sum in question. It was entitled to be paid the price for the goods. So it took the line: the plaintiff company must pay in law what it owed, otherwise its credit would be suspended.

Further, there is no evidence that the defendant's belief was unreasonable. Indeed, we were told by the defendant's counsel that he had advised his client that on the risk point the defendant stood a good chance of success. I do not see how a payment demanded and made in those circumstances can be said to be vitiated by duress.

So that must be an end to this appeal. I confess to being a little troubled at the overall outcome. At a late stage of the trial the defendant's counsel accepted that the risk in the goods had not in law passed to the plaintiff. Hence, and this must follow, the defendant company was not, and never had been, entitled to be paid for the goods. The risk remained throughout on the

defendant. What also follows is that the basis on which the defendant had
sought and insisted on payment was then shown to be false.

In those circumstances I confess to being a little surprised that a highly
reputable tobacco manufacturer has, so far, not reconsidered the position. A
claim for restitution based on wrongful retention of the money, once the risk
point had been established, was not pursued before us, no doubt for good
reasons. But on the sketchy facts before us, and I emphasise that we have heard
argument only from the plaintiff, it does seem to me that prima facie it would
be unconscionable for the defendant company to insist on retaining the money
now. It demanded the money when under a mistaken belief as to its legal
entitlement to be paid. It only made the demand because of its belief that it
was entitled to be paid. The money was then paid to it by a plaintiff which, in
practical terms, had no other option. In broad terms, in the end result the
defendant may be said to have been unjustly enriched. Whether a new claim
for restitution now, on the facts as they have since emerged, would succeed is
not a matter I need pursue. I observe, as to that, only that the categories of
unjust enrichment are not closed.

I too would dismiss this appeal.

Appeal dismissed.

Celia Fox Barrister.

Afzal and others v Ford Motor Co Ltd and other appeals

COURT OF APPEAL, CIVIL DIVISION

NEILL, BELDAM AND STEYN LJJ

12, 13, 14, 18 APRIL, 18, 27 MAY 1994

*County court – Arbitration – Reference of proceedings to arbitration – Automatic
reference – Suitability of claims for arbitration – Claims against employers seeking
damages for minor injuries sustained in workplace – Number of employees
intentionally overstating amount of claim to avoid automatic reference to
arbitration – Grounds on which reference might be rescinded – Whether intentional
overstatement of claim a misuse of process – Factors to be considered – CCR Ord 19,
rr 3, 4.*

In 22 actions the plaintiff employees brought claims against their various
employers seeking damages in respect of minor personal injuries sustained in
the workplace. In most cases the claims did not exceed £1,000 and under CCR
Ord 19, r 3[a] any proceedings in which the sum claimed or amount involved did
not exceed that sum would be automatically referred for arbitration by the
district judge, unless he was satisfied that he should order trial in court on the
grounds, inter alia, that a difficult question of law or a question of fact of

_____

a   Rule 3 is set out at p 729 *f* to p 730 *b*, post

a exceptional complexity was involved (r 3(2)(a)), or that it would be unreasonable for the claim to proceed to arbitration having regard to its subject matter, the size of any counterclaim, the circumstances of the parties or the interests of any other person likely to be affected by the award (r 3(2)(d)). In 16 of the claims, which were all brought against the same motor company, the employees applied for the reference to arbitration to be rescinded and the cases b tried in court, contending that compulsory arbitration was unsuitable for personal injury claims, particularly in cases involving employers' liability, since the issues of liability involved were too complex for summary resolution and, since Ord 19, r 4[b] strictly limited the costs recoverable in arbitrated claims, trade unions would be deterred from assisting claimants, who would then be at a serious disadvantage in negotiating compensation settlements out of c court. The judge granted the employees' applications on the basis of Ord 19, r 3(2)(d) and ordered that all the claims should be tried in court in view of the subject matter and the circumstances of the parties and, in particular, the fact that the employees, as line workers, could not be expected to frame their own claims in industrial accident cases (where breaches of statutory duty, medical d evidence and discovery might play a large part) without legal representation. The motor company appealed, contending that the judge had applied the wrong test because he had not shown, pursuant to r 3(2)(d), that it was unreasonable for the claims, as a class of case involving employers' liability, to be referred to arbitration and that, while a reference to arbitration could be rescinded under r 3(2)(a) if the case raised difficult questions of law or involved e exceptionally complicated facts, no such considerations arose in the cases under review.

The remaining claims were all heard in court. In three of the cases, the plaintiff employees sought to pre-empt the automatic reference to arbitration by claiming damages limited to £3,000, even though there was no reasonable prospect of recovering more than a few hundred pounds and, in each case, the f trial judge held that the claim should have been dealt with by arbitration and awarded only those costs appropriate to an automatic reference to arbitration. The appellants in all six cases appealed either against the court's reference of the claim to arbitration, its refusal to refer the claim to arbitration, or its award of costs.

g **Held** – (1) The small claims arbitration procedure was intended to improve access to justice and, accordingly, the court should not rescind an automatic reference to arbitration under CCR Ord 19, r 3(1) merely because a question of law was involved or the facts were complex, since r 3(2)(a) made it clear that a h question of law had to be difficult and a question of fact exceptionally complex for a claim to be tried in court. Moreover, it was not a proper interpretation of the rules to reintroduce those matters under r 3(2)(d) as subject matter that made it unreasonable for the claim to proceed to arbitration, since the reference to 'subject matter' in r 3(2)(d) meant something of sufficient importance to one or more of the parties to justify trial in court, such as, for

j

---

b   Rule 4, so far as material, provides: '... (2) No costs [including solicitors' charges] shall be allowed as between party and party in respect of any proceedings referred to arbitration under rule 3, except—(a) the costs which were stated on the summons ... the costs of enforcing the award, and (c) such further costs as the district judge may direct where there has been unreasonable conduct on the part of the opposite party in relation to the proceedings or the claim therein ...'

example, a claim for damages for trespass which might have far-reaching
consequences for the rights of the parties, a claim involving ownership of a
family heirloom, or test cases in which the rights of others were likely to be
affected by the award. The law applicable in employers' liability claims was
often straightforward and although the facts could be complex, in most
instances the question was whether the employer had taken reasonable care or
exposed the employee to an unnecessary risk of injury and the medical issues
were unlikely to be complex where the sum claimed or the amount involved
was less than £1,000. Furthermore, the hardship of an employee representing
himself against his legally represented employer was one faced in all cases
where the financial resources of the parties were unequal and was a matter for
the arbitrator to take into account in the procedure to be adopted for
arbitration, rather than being a decisive factor against proceeding to arbitration
in the first place. It followed that it was wrong to approach employers' liability
claims involving amounts of below £1,000 as a class of case which was, in
general, unsuited to arbitration and that therefore the judge's rescission of the
reference to arbitration in the 16 claims against the motor company could not
be supported. The motor company's appeals would accordingly be allowed
and the cases would be remitted for individual consideration by the district
judge (see p 733 *j* to p 734 *g*, p 735 *c d* and p 747 *g h*, post).

(2) The intentional overstatement of the amount involved in a claim to
avoid a procedure which had been laid down by Parliament and incorporated
in rules of the court was a clear misuse of process. The test for determining
whether a claim had been unjustifiably inflated to avoid automatic reference to
arbitration was whether the plaintiff could reasonably expect to be awarded
more than £1,000 and, if not, it would be an abuse of the process of the court
to claim damages limited to £3,000. Moreover, since the rules relating to
payment into court did not apply where the amount involved was under
£1,000, there was no reason why a defendant faced with an inflated claim
should not state in his defence that the claim could not reasonably exceed
£1,000 and should be automatically referred to arbitration and, in cases where
liability was admitted, the injuries were simple and the medical report agreed,
there was no reason why the defendant should not state his estimate of the
amount involved. The parties should also bear in mind that the overstatement
of the amount of damages claimed or the raising of a speculative and
unsupportable defence might be regarded as unreasonable conduct under CCR
Ord 19, r 4(2)(c). Applying those guiding principles, the court made similar
rulings in the related appeals to those made in the 16 motor company appeals
(see p 735 *g*, p 736 *j* to p 737 *a j* to p 738 *a*, p 740 *c*, p 741 *a*, p 742 *d*, p 743 *g*, p 744 *b*,
p 745 *g* and p 747 *c* to *g*, post); *Hobbs v Marlowe* [1977] 2 All ER 241 considered.

Notes
For automatic reference of small claims to arbitration, see 10 *Halsbury's Laws*
(4th edn) para 273A.

Cases referred to in judgment
Cunningham v BL Components Ltd [1986] CA Transcript 391.
Hobbs v Marlowe [1977] 2 All ER 241, [1978] AC 16, [1977] 2 WLR 777, CA and
    HL.
Hopkins v Rees & Kirby Ltd [1959] 2 All ER 352, [1959] 1 WLR 740.
MacShannon v Rockware Glass Ltd [1978] 1 All ER 625, [1978] AC 795, [1978] 2
    WLR 362, HL; *rvsg* [1977] 2 All ER 449, [1977] 1 WLR 376, CA.

a *Motley v Courtaulds plc* [1990] CA Transcript 77.

Semtex Ltd v Gladstone [1954] 2 All ER 206, [1954] 1 WLR 945.

Appeals

Sokhal v Ford Motor Co Ltd and other appeals

b The defendant employer, Ford Motor Co Ltd, appealed from the decision of Judge Paynter Reece made in the Romford County Court on 28 September 1993 granting the applications of 16 plaintiff employees, Rajiv Kumar Sokhal, John Baxter, Mark David Robinson, Antonio Luongo, Narottamal Shah, Anthony Prince, Naresh Kumar, Charles Elliott Browne, Michael John Humphries, Moses Clint Friday, Keith Russell Pratt, Stephen John Ahern, *c* William Palmer, Diane Jean Bowen, Alfred Thompson and Qaiser Mahmood, that the automatic reference to arbitration pursuant to CCR Ord 19 of their claims for damages for personal injuries sustained in the workplace be rescinded. The facts are set out in the judgment of the court.

Willingham v Kimberley Clark Ltd

d The defendant employer, Kimberley Clark Ltd, appealed from the order of Judge Paynter Reece made in the Romford County Court on 24 February 1993 dismissing their application that the claim brought by the plaintiff employee, James Robert Willingham, for damages for personal injury sustained in the workplace and limited to £3,000 be struck out as a misuse of the process of the *e* court or alternatively that the proceedings be referred to arbitration pursuant to CCR Ord 19. The facts are set out in the judgment of the court.

Caldwell v Wiggins Teape Fine Papers Ltd

The defendant employer, Wiggins Teape Fine Papers Ltd, appealed from the *f* order of Judge Paynter Reece made in the Romford County Court on 30 June 1992 allowing the appeal of the plaintiff employee, Roy Caldwell, from the order of District Judge Hales that no costs should be awarded to the plaintiff in his claim for damages for personal injury sustained in the workplace limited to £3,000 except those allowable on an automatic reference to arbitration pursuant to CCR Ord 19. The facts are set out in the judgment of the court.

g

Green v British Gas plc

The plaintiff employee, George Christopher Green, appealed from the order of Judge Mettyear made in the Kingston upon Hull County Court on 5 July 1993 awarding him in his claim against the defendant employer, British Gas plc, for *h* damages for personal injury sustained in the workplace limited to £3,000, only those costs which would have been recoverable on an automatic reference to arbitration pursuant to CCR Ord 19. The facts are set out in the judgment of the court.

j

Featherstone v Ideal Standard Ltd

The plaintiff employee, Geoffrey Arthur Featherstone, appealed from the decision of Judge Cracknell made in the Kingston upon Hull County Court on 5 May 1993 awarding him in his claim against the defendant employer, Ideal Standard Ltd, for damages for personal injury sustained in the workplace, only the costs appropriate to an automatic reference to arbitration pursuant to CCR Ord 19. The facts are set out in the judgment of the court.

Afzal v Ford Motor Co Ltd

Joyce v Ford Motor Co Ltd

The defendant employer, Ford Motor Co Ltd, appealed from the decision of Judge Paynter Reece made in the Romford County Court on 20 October 1992 dismissing their appeal from the decision of District Judge Finn on 30 March 1992 rescinding the automatic reference to arbitration pursuant to CCR Ord 19 of the claims of the plaintiff employees, Mohammed Afzal and Leonard John Joyce, for damages for personal injury sustained in the workplace. The facts are set out in the judgment of the court.

John Slater QC and *William Vandyck* (instructed by *A E Wyeth & Co*, Dartford) for Ford Motor Co and Ideal Standard.

Jeffrey Burke QC and *Robert Sherman* (instructed by *Robin Thompson & Partners*, Ilford) for the plaintiff employees.

Christopher Purchas QC and *Simon Brown* (instructed by *Kennedys*, Brentwood) for Kimberley Clark and Wiggins Teape.

Simon Jackson (instructed by *Alan Jackson,* Leeds) for British Gas.

Cur adv vult

27 May 1994. The following judgment of the court was delivered.

BELDAM LJ. Before the court are 22 appeals which raise questions of procedure under the provisions for the automatic reference to arbitration of small claims in the county court. Each of the claims is by a plaintiff employee supported by his trade union, and is made against his employer whose interests are handled by its employer's liability insurers. It is contended by the defendant employers that the claims brought against them do not involve more than £1,000 because there is no reasonable prospect of the plaintiff receiving a larger sum in damages. In many cases it is said that the injuries are slight, involve few, if any, continuing symptoms, the claims do not depend on complex questions of law or fact and ought therefore to be dealt with under the regime for automatic arbitration laid down by CCR Ord 19.

Such arbitration is strongly resisted by solicitors instructed at the request of the trade unions to act on the employees' behalf. They boldly assert that there is hardly any claim for damages for personal injuries which is suitable to be dealt with by way of compulsory arbitration, still less any employers' liability claim. The subject matter is too important to the individual plaintiff. In most, if not all, cases of accidents at work, the issues of liability involved are too complex for summary resolution. Many may raise issues of expert medical opinion. The procedure for such arbitration with limited discovery from the defendant would be unfair. The denial of a right to recover the cost of legal advice and representation from the defendant will deter trade unions from supporting their members in such claims, whereas insurers will inevitably continue to bear the cost of such representation. Without legal advice, the employee acting as his own lawyer will be at a grave disadvantage, will be unable adequately to present his claim, will not know whether an offer of compensation is reasonable and some may be forced to abandon a justifiable claim by an unscrupulous insurer raising an untenable defence. At present a very high proportion of such claims (97%) are compromised without recourse to the court. This high settlement ratio reflects the value of the legal assistance a provided to employees by the trade unions. It helps to remove cases from the court's workload but, if on settlement the employers' insurers insist that no costs are recoverable because the claim was one which unless compromised would have been subject to automatic arbitration, the trade unions will be forced to withdraw the support they have traditionally given to their members and many claims which might have been compromised will have to be b arbitrated.

BACKGROUND TO THE APPEALS

Where by negotiation it has proved impossible to reach agreement with the employer's insurers, solicitors for the employee have sought to pre-empt automatic reference to arbitration under the rules by placing a value on the c damages claimed substantially in excess of £1,000 even though there may be no reasonable prospect of the plaintiff recovering more than a few hundred pounds. This tactic has, insurers' solicitors argue, placed them in a dilemma. If they do not serve a defence, the plaintiff, after the appropriate time has elapsed, is entitled to sign judgment for damages to be assessed. Under the d rules the claim is not in that case automatically referred to arbitration and the plaintiff's advisers are entitled to lodge a bill of costs for taxation. These costs can include the ordinary allowable costs of a represented party, including advice and preparation and may do so subject to discretionary powers on taxation even though the amount of the plaintiff's claim is substantially less than £1,000. In some instances the amount of the costs claimed has been very e much greater than the damages recovered.

Employers' solicitors regard such costs as unjustifiable and have sought by several means to avoid having to pay them. The first step has been to serve a defence, whether or not there is any prospect of its success. Next, they have applied to the court for an order that the claim is one automatically referred to f arbitration notwithstanding the amount claimed. Their right to take this course or to seek such an order is disputed by the employees' solicitors. Another counter adopted by employers' solicitors has been to make a payment into court of their estimate of the value of the claim, applying at the same time for the claim to be treated as automatically referred to arbitration.

If the employer's application is successful, the employee's solicitors will be g unable to recover their costs. So they, in turn, have applied to the court to rescind automatic arbitration if it is applicable. But even if such an application is successful, under the rules, legal costs incurred in such a case before an order is made for trial in court are irrecoverable.

It is against that background that in 16 of the cases now before the court h claims were made by employees of Ford Motor Co Ltd at Dagenham in the Romford County Court for damages for personal injury suffered at work. On a provisional assessment they appear to be properly described as small claims within the £1,000 limit. In all the cases a defence had been filed. Solicitors, Messrs Robin Thompson & Partners, acting for the plaintiffs on the instruction j of the trade union, applied to the district judge for an order that the cases be tried in court. The applications were referred by the district judge to Judge Paynter Reece. In the judgment it is said that the district judge referred the applications exercising powers under CCR Ord 50, r 3. As the claims had been referred automatically for arbitration by the district judge, the applications would appear to have been made under Ord 13 and the power of the district judge under Ord 13, r 7 to refer the matter to the judge would seem to have

been more appropriate. On Tuesday, 28 September 1993 Judge Paynter Reece
gave judgment. He granted the employees' applications and ordered that all
the claims should be tried in court—

> 'on the basis that it is unreasonable for the claim to proceed to
> arbitration having regard to the subject matter and the circumstances of
> the parties in particular as I have endeavoured to outline them.'

Later it will be necessary to examine his reasons more closely.

In two of the other appeals he reached a similar conclusion. In *Caldwell v
Wiggins Teape Fine Papers Ltd* on 30 June 1992 in Romford County Court Judge
Paynter Reece set aside an order of the deputy district judge allowing the
plaintiff, who had accepted a payment into court of £410, only the costs
recoverable on an automatic arbitration and awarded the plaintiff his costs on
scale 1.

In *Willingham v Kimberley Clark Ltd*, at the same court on 24 February 1993,
he dismissed an application by the defendant that the plaintiff's action, in
which he claimed damages limited to £3,000, should be struck out or stayed as
a misuse of the process of the court, the defendant contending that there was
no reasonable likelihood of the plaintiff recovering more than £1,000.

In others of the appeals before the court, judges faced with similar questions
have arrived at different conclusions. In *Featherstone v Ideal Standard Ltd* Judge
Cracknell in the Kingston upon Hull County Court, after awarding the plaintiff
£800 damages, limited the costs to those recoverable on an automatic reference
to arbitration. In *Kavanagh v Ideal Standard Ltd* Mr Recorder Dobkin in the
same court on 13 October 1993 allowed an appeal by the defendant from the
order of District Judge Hill rescinding a reference to arbitration and ordered
that the case proceed by way of arbitration. It is unnecessary for the court to
consider this case further, for the parties to the appeal have agreed to terms on
which the appeal should be withdrawn.

In *Green v British Gas plc* Judge M K Mettyear on 5 July 1993 allowed an appeal
from Deputy District Judge Brown who had awarded the plaintiff costs on
scale 1 after he had accepted a sum of £875 paid into court by the defendants.

The appeals thus require the court to consider whether under the County
Court Rules 1981 it would be unreasonable to allow claims for damages for less
than £1,000 to proceed to automatic arbitration when such claims are made by
an employee against his employer.

Questions raised in argument also require us to consider the procedure to be
adopted where the plaintiff's claim, though not limited to £1,000 by him,
appears to the defendant or to the court to involve a sum which does not
exceed £1,000.

DEVELOPMENT OF SMALL CLAIMS ARBITRATION

As early as 1952 in Philadelphia, court-annexed arbitration was proposed as
an alternative to court trial as a way of resolving modest legal disputes. In the
1960s and 1970s many states in the United States of America began to introduce
similar procedures. The main reasons for seeking a less complex system of
resolving claims were the long delays due to congestion of court lists and
burgeoning legal costs out of proportion to the sums involved. Evidence
accrued that access to justice was being deterred and it was considered that a
simpler if less perfect system of justice ought to be available for such cases.

In England and Wales similar pressure led Parliament in 1973 in s 7 of the Administration of Justice Act 1973 to extend the powers of county courts to refer matters to arbitration. Section 7(1)(a) amended s 92 of the County Courts Act 1959 by substituting sub-s (1):

'A county court may, in such cases as may be prescribed, order any proceedings to be referred to arbitration (whether with or without other matters within the jurisdiction of the court in dispute between the parties) to such person or persons (including the judge or registrar) and in such manner and on such terms as the court thinks just and reasonable.'

The first rules made in September 1973 enabled a party to apply for an order referring the proceedings to arbitration. The registrar had power to deal with the application without hearing any party to the proceedings if the sum claimed or amount involved did not exceed £100. However, at any time before the application was heard a party could apply in writing to the registrar to refer the application to the judge. In cases where a party was charged with fraud, the order was not to be made without his consent. A practice direction under Ord 48, r 1, issued by Lord Hailsham LC to secure uniformity, suggested a list of terms on which a reference to arbitration should be made, though the list was not intended to be exhaustive (see [1973] 3 All ER 448, [1973] 1 WLR 1178). Among the terms were:

'(1) The strict rules of evidence shall not apply in relation to the arbitration. (2) With the consent of the parties the arbitrator may decide the case on the basis of the statements and documents submitted by the parties. Otherwise he should fix a date for the hearing. (3) Any hearing shall be informal and may be held in private. (4) At the hearing the arbitrator may adopt any method of procedure which he may consider to be convenient and to afford a fair and equal opportunity to each party to present his case ... (6) With the consent of the parties and at any time before giving his decision and either before or after the hearing, the arbitrator may consult any expert or call for an expert report on any matter in dispute or invite an expert to attend the hearing as assessor. (7) The costs of the action ... shall be in the discretion of the arbitrator ...'

The rules already contained provisions restricting the amount of the costs which the court could order the unsuccessful party to pay. The costs were assessed in accordance with scales depending on the amount claimed or recovered. Under Ord 47, r 5(4), where the sum of money did not exceed £100, no solicitors' charges were to be allowed as between party and party unless (a) the judge granted a certificate under Ord 47, r 13 that a difficult question of law or a question of fact of exceptional complexity was involved, (b) the sum exceeded £5, in which case the court allowed the charges of the plaintiff's solicitor's costs as stated on the summons, the cost of enforcing any judgment or order and any costs which were certified by the court to have been incurred through the unreasonable conduct of the opposite party, and (c) the claim made in the proceedings was for damages for personal injuries exceeding £5.

This was the framework provided by the County Court Rules for arbitration and costs when it was first introduced. The registrar in addition had power to carry out an inspection, to enforce the attendance of witnesses, to conduct the inquiry in the same manner as nearly as the circumstances permitted as if it were the hearing of an action and could exercise the same powers as a judge to order discovery and production of documents and to control the conduct of the inquiry.

It is also relevant to note that Ord 20, r 1 provided:

'Any party to an action or matter may give notice to any other party that he admits the truth of the whole or any part of the case of the other party, and no costs incurred after the receipt of the notice in respect of the proof of any matters admitted therein shall be allowed.'

Over the years a number of changes have been introduced into the procedure but essentially small claims arbitration has remained within the framework originally laid down.

By 1978 the rules provided that a reference should only be made on the application of a party to the proceedings. Such an application could be made by the plaintiff in his particulars of claim or by the defendant in his defence and in any proceedings in which the sum claimed or the amount involved did not exceed £100 and an application for a reference was made by the parties in that manner the proceedings were to be referred for arbitration by the registrar. But by Ord 19, r 1(5), on such an application being made, the other party could within 14 days apply to the registrar to rescind the reference and it was then provided that—

'the registrar shall, if he is satisfied that a charge of fraud against a party is in issue in the proceedings or that for any other reason the proceedings are unsuitable to be referred to arbitration, rescind the reference accordingly.'

Provisions were made for the procedure to be followed after such rescission.

In 1981 the County Court Rules were redrafted. The new rules included significant changes to Ord 19. In addition to the rule that reference should only be made to arbitration on the application of a party to the proceedings, Ord 19, r 2(3) and (4) provided:

'(3) Any proceedings in which the sum claimed or amount involved does not exceed £500 shall stand referred for arbitration by the registrar upon the receipt by the court of a defence to the claim, but the registrar may, on the application of any party, refer the proceedings for arbitration by the judge or by an outside arbitrator.

(4) Where any proceedings are referred for arbitration by the registrar under paragraph (3), he may, on the application of any party, rescind the reference if he is satisfied—(a) that a difficult question of law or a question of fact of exceptional complexity is involved; or (b) that a charge of fraud is in issue; or (c) that the parties are agreed that the dispute should be tried in court; or (d) that it would be unreasonable for the claim to proceed to arbitration having regard to its subject matter, the circumstances of the parties or the interests of any other person likely to be affected by the award.'

Order 19, r 5 contained provisions for the conduct of the reference and incorporated, subject to any directions of the court, the provisions of r 9(a) to (e). The terms of reference were those already noticed, including the fact that the hearing should be informal and the strict rules of evidence should not apply. The arbitrator could adopt any method of procedure which—

'he may consider to be convenient and to afford a fair and equal opportunity to each party to present his case.' (See Ord 19, r 5(2)(4).)

However, the discretion of the arbitrator to award costs was removed in claims involving £500 or less. In such cases Ord 19, r 6 provided:

> 'No solicitors' charges shall be allowed as between party and party in respect of any proceedings referred to arbitration under rule 2(3), except— (a) the costs which were stated on the summons or which would have been stated on the summons if the claim had been for a liquidated sum; (b) the costs of enforcing the award, and (c) such costs as are certified by the arbitrator to have been incurred through the unreasonable conduct of the opposite party in relation to the proceedings or the claim therein.'

By the end of 1991 Ord 19, r 2(4) had been amended to include a power of the district judge to rescind a reference to arbitration of his own motion. If he was minded to do so, however, notice had to be given to the parties of the ground on which he proposed to rescind the arbitration so that they could make representations. If a notice of objection was given by either party, a day was fixed for a hearing of the objections. Only if no notice was given could he rescind of his own motion.

Further, on 1 July 1991 the sum of £1,000 was substituted for £500 for claims automatically referred to arbitration. These changes in the County Court Rules show how the rules of procedure developed an automatic reference to arbitration for small claims. By the County Court (Amendment No 2) Rules 1992, SI 1992/1965, the rules relating to such arbitrations were completely recast. Provision was made for lay representation and automatic reference of small claims was dealt with in Ord 19, r 3:

> '(1) Any proceedings in which the sum claimed or amount involved does not exceed £1000 (leaving out of account the sum claimed or amount involved in any counterclaim) shall stand referred for arbitration by the district judge upon the receipt by the court of a defence to the claim.
>
> (2) Where any proceedings are referred for arbitration by the district judge under paragraph (1), he may, after considering the defence and whether on the application of any party or of his own motion, order trial in court if he is satisfied—(a) that a difficult question of law or a question of fact of exceptional complexity is involved; or (b) that fraud is alleged against a party; or (c) that the parties are agreed that the dispute should be tried in court; or (d) that it would be unreasonable for the claim to proceed to arbitration having regard to its subject matter, the size of any counterclaim, the circumstances of the parties or the interests of any other person likely to be affected by the award.
>
> (3) Where the district judge is minded to order trial in court of his own motion—(a) the proper officer shall notify the parties in writing specifying on which of the grounds mentioned in paragraph (2) the district judge is minded to order trial in court; (b) within 14 days after service of the proper officer's notice on him, a party may give written notice stating his reasons for objecting to the making of the order; (c) if in any notice under sub-paragraph (b) a party so requests, the proper officer shall fix a day for a hearing at which the district judge—(i) shall decide whether to order trial in court, and (ii) may give directions regarding the steps to be taken before or at any subsequent hearing as if he were conducting a preliminary

appointment or, as the case may be, a pre-trial review; and, in the absence
of any request under sub-paragraph (c), the district judge may in the
absence of the parties order trial in court.

(4) For the purposes of paragraph (1), "a defence to the claim" includes
a document admitting liability for the claim but disputing or not admitting
the amount claimed.'

Order 19, r 4 strictly limits the costs recoverable in small claims. No solicitors'
charges, sums allowed to a litigant in person or fee or reward charged by a lay
representative are recoverable in small claims automatically referred to
arbitration but, in addition to the three heads of costs formerly allowed,
expenses incurred by a party or witness travelling to or from the hearing are
recoverable, a sum not exceeding £29 in respect of a party or witness's loss of
earnings when attending a hearing and a sum not exceeding £112·50 in respect
of the fees of an expert. But if a trial in court is ordered, legal costs incurred
after the order may be recovered.

By Ord 19, r 5 the district judge is to be the arbitrator unless the court orders
otherwise. Rule 6 provides for preparation for the hearing. In particular, r 6(3)
provides:

'Where proceedings stand referred to arbitration, the following
directions shall take effect—(a) each party shall not less than 14 days before
the date fixed for the hearing send to every other party copies of all
documents which are in his possession and on which that party intends to
rely at the hearing; (b) each party shall not less than 7 days before the date
fixed for the hearing send to the court and to every other party a copy of
any expert report on which that party intends to rely at the hearing and a
list of the witnesses whom he intends to call at the hearing.'

The circumstances in which a preliminary appointment may be held are
limited, but the district judge has a discretion from time to time to amend or
add to any directions which he has already given. Further, since 26 October
1992, the provisions of Ord 11 relating to payment into court do not apply to
proceedings which stand referred to arbitration under Ord 19, r 3.

Order 19, r 7 contains rules for the conduct of the hearing of an arbitration:

'(1) Any proceedings referred to arbitration shall be dealt with in
accordance with the following paragraphs of this rule unless the arbitrator
otherwise orders.

(2) The hearing may be held at the court house, at the court office or at
any other place convenient to the parties.

(3) The hearing shall be informal and the strict rules of evidence shall
not apply; unless the arbitrator orders otherwise, the hearing shall be held
in private and evidence shall not be taken on oath.

(4) At the hearing the arbitrator may adopt any method of procedure
which he may consider to be fair and which gives to each party an equal
opportunity to have his case presented; having considered the
circumstances of the parties and whether (or to what extent) they are
represented, the arbitrator—(a) may assist a party by putting questions to
the witnesses and the other party; and (b) should explain any legal terms
or expressions which are used.

(5) If any party does not appear at the arbitration, the arbitrator may, after taking into account any pleadings or other documents filed, make an award on hearing any other party to the proceedings who may be present.

(6) With the consent of the parties, and at any time before giving his decision, the district judge may consult any expert or call for an expert report on any matter in dispute or invite an expert to attend the hearing as assessor.

(7) The arbitrator may require the production of any document or thing and may inspect any property or thing concerning which any question may arise.

(8) The arbitrator shall inform the parties of his award and give his reasons for it to any party who may be present at the hearing.'

Rule 8 declares the award of an arbitrator to be final subject to misconduct of the arbitrator or error of law and cases in which the award has been made in the absence of a party.

Over a period of 20 years, therefore, Parliament has provided and the County Court Rules Committee, in the light of experience, has developed a scheme for court-based automatic arbitration for claims in which the amount involved does not exceed £1,000. The present rules contain a code of practice and procedure applicable to such claims. Parliament's object was described by Lord Diplock in *Hobbs v Marlowe* [1977] 2 All ER 241 at 256, [1978] AC 16 at 40–41. He said:

'Parliament and the rule committee in introducing the small claims scheme and amending the rules as to costs recoverable from the other party, gave effect to a public policy that as a general rule a person seeking to enforce a claim for less than £100 should act as his own lawyer with such assistance as is available to him at the office of the county court, the local citizens' advice bureau or consumer advice centre or, if he chooses to instruct a lawyer, should do so at his own expense and not at the expense of the person against whom the claim is made. I say as a general rule, because under CCR Ord 47, r 13, the county court judge retains a discretion to award costs on such scale as he thinks fit if he certifies that a difficult question of law or a question of fact of exceptional complexity is involved.'

We now return to the judgment of Judge Paynter Reece in the 16 cases brought by employees of the Ford Motor Co in the Romford County Court. The claims did not exceed £1,000. Notice in the prescribed form N18A had been sent to the parties stating that the cases were to be dealt with by arbitration but the plaintiffs' solicitors applied to the district judge to rescind the reference. As stated, the district judge had referred the application to Judge Paynter Reece. The judge regretted that the district judge had not come to his own conclusion, but he said:

'I know from previous cases and from speaking to him what the district judge's general views are: that, generally speaking, these industrial accident cases are not best dealt with by arbitration. They are not suitable for a plaintiff to deal with in person. Apart from the inequality of an individual plaintiff against Ford and its insurers as a defendant (always likely to be represented by a high-ranking employee or solicitors), it is absurd to say that plaintiffs can be expected properly to frame their own claims in industrial accident cases where breaches of statutory duty, medical evidence and discovery may all play a large part. To expect a line worker to do that without a solicitor is absurd. I am firmly of the view that these sorts of claims, generally speaking, are not the sort of claims that Ord 19 is designed for.'

Although the judge acknowledged that there was nothing in the rules to this effect, he said:

'Generally in Ford's cases it is unreasonable for the cases to proceed to arbitration or even to have started out as arbitration.'

After repeating that there might be occasional cases which were suitable, he said that, generally speaking, they were not proper matters to be dealt with by arbitration. He considered the submissions of the parties, and said:

'There is a great deal of law involved in and about what goes on in the workplace. There is a great deal of expertise and procedure involved in personal injury accident litigation. Thankfully, experienced solicitors and counsel tend to deal with them, on the whole, on both sides and they make them simple.'

The judge thought they were the sort of cases better dealt with by trial and presented by counsel or solicitors. That was his view after looking at the individual cases.

In none of the cases were the facts so simple or straightforward that they should be dealt with by way of arbitration. Even a case in which there was an admission of liability and agreed medical evidence with only the question of quantum to be decided was not a suitable case. The court could be very much assisted by having counsel there to put comparable cases for quantum. Even though small amounts of damages were claimed and the cases were comparatively simple, it was still going to be necessary to have discovery or experts to give evidence and it was not sensible to consider that a line man could prepare his case as well as doing his job at the same time.

Earlier in his judgment the judge had recorded that in their submissions the plaintiffs relied on Ord 19, r 3(2)(d), arguing that it would be—

'unreasonable for the claim to proceed to arbitration having regard to its subject matter and ... the circumstances of the parties.'

After announcing his decision to order that all the cases be tried in court, the judge was asked by counsel to clarify the basis of his decision and he said:

'No, it is Ord 19, r 3(2)(d) I am basing myself on. The subject matter includes questions of law and questions of fact. I am not so sure that I would say that they were exceptional questions. It is all part of r 3(2)(d) in my opinion and there is no question of fraud or anything like that and the parties are not agreed.'

Counsel for the appellants submitted that the judge erred in deciding the cases on that basis. There are no good reasons to suppose that it would be unreasonable for cases of employers' liability as a class to be referred to arbitration. Indeed, most cases, particularly where the sums involved were small, were entirely suitable for arbitration. It was wrong to say that difficult questions of law or complicated facts were concerned. If difficult questions of law or exceptionally complicated facts were concerned in a particular case, the case could in any event be referred under r 3(2)(a). The judge had to be satisfied that it was *unreasonable* for the claim to proceed for arbitration. He had applied the wrong test. Moreover, in so far as he relied on inequality of representation, the inequality would be no greater than in any case in which one party chose to be represented at his own expense and the other party did not. The rules did not prevent parties from being represented at their own expense.

Further, counsel pointed to the change in the rules relating to costs in personal injury actions. After 1981 such actions were placed on the same footing as regards costs as other actions and no solicitors' charges were recoverable if the sum claimed or the amount involved was less than £500.

In short, counsel submitted that there was no justification for the judge's approach that all, or virtually all, actions for personal injury against Ford or any other employer were too complicated for arbitration. The judge ought to have exercised his discretion in each case and this he had failed to do. Further, in so far as he did exercise a discretion, he had taken into account matters which were irrelevant to its exercise.

Counsel for the plaintiffs sought to uphold the judge's exercise of his discretion. His first submission was that, if no costs were to be recoverable for advice and initiation of proceedings, trade unions would no longer be able to support their members. Many injured plaintiffs would thereby be denied access to justice. Even if employees did bring their own claims, they would be hopelessly outgunned by the lawyers acting for insurers. Employees would have no advice whether to accept an offer of compensation made and no means of knowing whether it was reasonable or not. Full discovery was unobtainable in small claims and was often a vital factor in securing justice for the injured employee. Employees would not know how to obtain a medical or an expert's report and would have no funds with which to do so. The present tactics adopted by insurers' legal representatives, for example by filing a defence denying liability where in truth none was available, would be likely to cause the unadvised employee either to abandon his claim or accept an inadequate compromise. Such tactics caused employees' legal representatives to claim a sum exceeding the limit to avoid the consequences of automatic arbitration. In short, the judge was right to hold that, save in the most exceptionally simple cases, claims by employees, and indeed all claims for personal injury, were unsuitable for arbitration.

We have no doubt that the judge was wrong to approach small employers' liability claims as a class of case which it was unreasonable to allow to proceed to arbitration. When he said that he did not think that in any of the cases 'the facts are now so simple or straightforward that they should be dealt with by way of arbitration', he may have been misled by the elaboration introduced by the traditional pleadings which had been filed on both sides. If he had concentrated on an underlying assertion to be found in virtually every case that the employer had exposed the employee to a risk of injury of which he knew or ought to have known, the cases might well have appeared less complex.

Court-based small claims arbitration is intended to be a greatly simplified procedure for determining claims. The district judge remains an adjudicator and the process adversarial but, as the code makes clear, the aim of the procedure is to get away from the rigid rituals which characterise ordinary litigation and which have dictated the arguments of the parties in the appeals. The following points seem to us significant in interpreting the rules.

(1) The district judge cannot rescind an automatic reference to arbitration under Ord 19, r 3(1) merely because a question of law is involved or the facts are complex. Rule 3(2)(a) makes it clear that the question of law has to be one of difficulty and a question of fact one of exceptional complexity if the claim is to be regarded as one which should be tried in court. It is not a proper interpretation of the rules to reintroduce these matters by themselves under r 3(2)(d) under the guise of subject matter which makes it unreasonable for the claim to proceed to arbitration. 'Subject matter' refers to the nature of a claim generally but in the context of the other provisions of r 3(2) we take it to refer to some quality of the subject matter of the claim of sufficient importance to the parties or to one of them to justify trial in court; for example, a claim for damages for trespass which could have far-reaching consequences for the rights of the parties or a claim involving ownership of a family heirloom. Cases which may be regarded as 'test' cases could be catered for under r 3(2)(d) as cases in which the interests of other persons are likely to be affected by the award.

(2) The law applicable in employers' liability claims is often straightforward. In most instances the question for decision is whether the employer has taken reasonable care or has exposed the employee to an unnecessary risk of injury. The issues can, of course, be complicated if the fault alleged is breach of statutory duty but often liability on the part of the employer is more easily established by such breach. Equally, the facts of such cases may be complex, but they are not in the majority of cases. Nor are the medical issues involved likely to be complex where the amount involved is less than £1,000.

(3) The hardship of an employee representing himself against his legally represented employer is a hardship likely to be faced in all cases where the means of the parties are unequal. Whether the threat to withdraw support from union members would in fact be carried out is, we think, questionable bearing in mind the well-deserved reputation of trade unions for the splendid work they have done for their members in this sphere in the past. We feel sure that on reflection many trade unions will explore the possibility of a simpler process of helping members in putting forward small claims than by the granting of full legal representation in all cases. On the other side, it seems equally questionable whether employers' liability insurers will regard it as commercially justifiable to incur the considerable expense of legal representation at the hearing of such claims which will be irrecoverable.

It is difficult to see how inequality of representation is a proper factor to be taken into account as one of the circumstances of the parties under r 3(2)(d). The rule for the conduct of the hearing, r 7(4), provides:

'At the hearing the arbitrator may adopt any method of procedure which he may consider to be fair and which gives to each party an equal opportunity to have his case presented; having considered the circumstances of the parties and *whether (or to what extent) they are represented*, the arbitrator—(a) may assist a party by putting questions to the witnesses and the other party; and (b) should explain any legal terms or expressions which are used.'

The rule suggests that the circumstances of the parties and whether they are represented are separate considerations for the arbitrator. The circumstances of the parties may, for example, include physical disability, poor sight, pronounced stammer or inability to read. Since the question whether a party is or is not represented is a matter for the arbitrator to take into account in the procedure he adopts for the arbitration, it cannot be a decisive factor against arbitration.

(4) The code also contemplates that cases which need a degree of expert understanding will be subject to compulsory arbitration. For example, Ord 19, r 7(6) permits an arbitrator with the consent of the parties to consult an expert or call for an expert's report and under Ord 19, r 4(3)(c) the fee of an expert may be awarded as costs.

For these reasons, we consider the judgment of Judge Paynter Reece rescinding arbitration in the 16 cases cannot be supported. It was suggested that the court ought in the circumstances to exercise its own discretion in the individual cases and for this purpose the appellants divided them into two groups: those in which liability was admitted, medical evidence was agreed and the injuries were slight and those in which liability was not admitted but the medical evidence was agreed and there was no question of expert inspection nor any issue relating to special damage. We do not consider that this would be a satisfactory way of dealing with the 16 cases. In our judgment they should be remitted for individual consideration by the district judge.

Before passing to the questions raised in the remaining appeals, it is convenient to consider the other general questions raised in the course of argument.

MISUSE OF PROCESS

Mr Burke QC for the employees stoutly resisted the suggestion that it was a misuse of the procedure in the County Court Rules to place a value, for example £3,000, on the sum claimed as damages to avoid the consequence of automatic reference to arbitration. He submitted that in so doing a plaintiff's advisers were seeking to obtain no more than a legitimate juridical advantage. He likened it to forum shopping for the purpose of obtaining a higher award of damages as, for example, was done in *MacShannon v Rockware Glass Ltd* [1978] 1 All ER 625, [1978] AC 795. We would reject such an analogy. The intentional overstatement of the amount involved in a claim to avoid a procedure which has been laid down by Parliament and incorporated in rules of the court is in our judgment a clear misuse of process. In *Hobbs v Marlowe* [1977] 2 All ER 241, [1978] AC 16 to recover costs and solicitors' charges which would have been irrecoverable if the claim had been limited to the amount which the plaintiff actually had at stake, solicitors instructed on behalf of the plaintiff claimed the cost of repairs to his motor car already paid under a knock for knock agreement by the plaintiff's own insurers. The county court judge having found that the claim was raised solely for the purpose of increasing the claim for costs without any financial or other benefit to the plaintiff, deprived the plaintiff of the costs, describing the conduct as an abuse of the process of the court. Lord Diplock said ([1977] 2 All ER 241 at 255–256, [1978] AC 16 at 40):

> 'My Lords, the expressions "abuse of the process of the court" and "misconduct" are terms of art when used in connection with the way in which litigation is carried on by the parties. In upholding the judge's reasons for depriving the plaintiff of his costs the Court of Appeal was at

pains to emphasise that in bringing this action to find out whether, if put to the test of litigation, the tactics that had been adopted on behalf of the AA to get the insurers of the other party to pay the charges of the AA solicitors in connection with an uninsured small claim of an AA member, would prove successful, Amery-Parkes & Co were not guilty of any impropriety. For my part I would endorse that too, and would describe the increase of the claim from £73·53 to £301·12 by the less emotive term "a misuse" of the process of the court but one which fully justified the county court judge depriving the plaintiff of his costs other than those which would had been recoverable had the claim been restricted to the amount which was actually at stake, viz £73·53.'

Further, in *Motley v Courtaulds plc* [1990] CA Transcript 77 the question arose for decision in this court. The plaintiff had succeeded in a claim for damages against her employers for a cut little finger sustained when the finger accidentally came against a sharp protruding screw on a sewing machine. She was treated in the works' sick berth with sterile adhesive strips and a tetanus booster injection. She did not have to go to hospital and had no time off work. She recovered £250. Her particulars of claim had stated that the damages were limited to £3,000. It was, said Ralph Gibson LJ, a claim for a typical small personal injury in a factory. The judge awarded the plaintiff costs on the scale appropriate to the sum recovered (scale 1). The defendants submitted that the judge was wrong to award such costs because of the provisions of Ord 19, rr 2(3) and 6.

The defendant had made an application to the deputy registrar before the hearing for the plaintiff's claim to be limited to £500. The application was made to forestall a suggestion that the defendants had consented to trial. On appeal the defendants contended that there had been deliberate inflation of the amount claimed for the purpose of securing an award of costs.

Counsel for the plaintiff submitted that there had been no inflation so as to constitute misuse of process. Basing himself on the passage from the speech of Lord Diplock in *Hobbs v Marlowe* [1977] 2 All ER 241 at 255–256, [1978] AC 16 at 40, Ralph Gibson LJ (with whom Dillon LJ agreed) held that it was a misuse of the process of the court to inflate a claim for the purpose of avoiding the effect of Ord 19, r 6.

WHAT IS THE APPROPRIATE TEST TO BE APPLIED FOR MISUSE OF PROCESS?

Some time was taken in the hearing of these appeals in discussion of the appropriate test to determine when there had been unjustifiable inflation of the claim to avoid arbitration. Ralph Gibson LJ had referred to the plaintiff claiming a sum 'greater than could be expected to be awarded by the court'.

An alternative formulation in *Cunningham v BL Components Ltd* [1986] CA Transcript 391 was that the claim was unjustifiably inflated if the plaintiff could not reasonably have expected to recover more than the amount stated in the rule (£500). Mr Burke suggested that the proper test to be adopted was whether it was clear to the plaintiff's advisers that no judge would award more than that amount. He referred to *Hopkins v Rees & Kirby Ltd* [1959] 2 All ER 352, [1959] 1 WLR 740.

We do not consider that there is any significant difference in these alternative criteria. But nevertheless we would adopt the following as the most satisfactory formula: 'Could the plaintiff reasonably expect to be awarded more than £1,000?' If the plaintiff could not reasonably expect to be awarded more than £1,000, it is a misuse of process to claim damages limited to £3,000.

WHAT COURSE SHOULD THE DEFENDANT ADOPT?

In the course of the appeal the appellants canvassed the courses open to a defendant faced with a small claim in which the damages claimed were inflated to avoid the no-costs rule. Should a defendant follow the course taken by the defendant in *Hobbs v Marlowe*? If so, could he ask the court to strike out the claim for misuse of process? Could he seek to stay the action? Or could he seek an order from the district judge limiting the amount of the plaintiff's claim? If he were to indorse the overstatement of the amount involved by treating the claim at its face value and make a payment into court, the plaintiff, it was argued, could accept the money and lodge a bill of costs for taxation up to the time of receiving the payment and thus secure the advantage of costs to which he ought not to be entitled. Whether the plaintiff could successfully adopt this course, we consider later in the judgment.

None of the suggested courses provide a satisfactory solution and some of them have been authoritatively said to be inappropriate. Much of the discussion was conditioned by the conventional approach to actions tried in court. The code contained in the rules to Ord 19 is intended to provide a different framework which, if adopted and applied by the parties with common sense, should be adequate to overcome any of these difficulties. The automatic reference of small claims takes place when the 'amount involved' does not exceed £1,000. As Mr Burke pointed out, there is no provision in the rules requiring the plaintiff to limit his claim to £1,000. No doubt the Rules Committee thought that those with small claims would try to comply with, rather than circumvent, the rules and would benefit from the simplified procedure and the saving of costs.

In cases in which the court receives a defence, it is implicit in r 3(1) that the amount 'involved' in an unliquidated claim must depend upon an assessment of the amount by the court. With his particulars of claim, the plaintiff is required by Ord 6, r 5 to file a medical report and a statement of the special damages claimed.

By r 3(4), for the purpose of para 1, a defence to the claim includes a document admitting liability for the claim but disputing or not admitting the amount claimed. It is implicit in Ord 19, r 3(3) that if the district judge is to consider whether to rescind the claim referred to arbitration under r 1 without referring to the parties, he should decide whether the claim involves more than £1,000. If the defence states that it does not, the district judge, according to his view of the case, will either send notice to the parties in prescribed form N18A, or N19, stating that the matter is referred to arbitration, or refer the matter for trial with the appropriate notice under Ord 19, r 3(3)(a). If either party contests his decision, he may apply to the district judge under rr 3(2) or 3(3)(b) respectively.

As the rules relating to payment into court do not apply where the amount involved is under £1,000, we see no reason why a defendant faced with an inflated claim should not state in his defence that the claim cannot reasonably exceed £1,000 and should be automatically referred to arbitration. Further, where liability is admitted, the injuries are simple and the medical report is agreed, there is no reason why the defendant should not state his estimate of the amount involved. In small claims arbitration the parties are expected to

state their cases informally. One way or another we think that parties seeking
to take advantage of the benefits of small claims arbitration could easily *a*
overcome the difficulties which appeared of such concern in argument. The
question for the district judge would be no more difficult than those he would
have to consider if of his own motion or on the application of a party he had to
consider whether to order trial in court. An interpretation of the rules cannot
be justified which would require every case to proceed to trial and to the award *b*
of the judge to decide whether there had been a misuse of the process of the
court.

In *Motley v Courtaulds plc* [1990] CA Transcript 77 Dillon LJ in the course of
his judgment said:

> 'The appeal before us is part of a continuing war over the costs of small *c*
> claims between the employer's insurance company and the trade union.
> The appeal before the other division of this court is part of a continuing
> war, which has already involved all too many appeals to this court,
> between motor accident insurers and legal expenses insurers. In each case
> the nominal parties to the appeals have little, if any, direct interest in the
> outcome. In all cases of this type there is a good deal of manoeuvring *d*
> between the parties: many technical points are taken and many technical
> applications are made, such as the application to the deputy registrar by
> the defendants in this case, seeking to obtain an order limiting the amount
> of the plaintiff's claim so that it would stand automatically referred for
> arbitration pursuant to Ord 19, rr 2, 3 and 6. That was a claim which the *e*
> registrar plainly had no jurisdiction to entertain. All this tends to promote
> delay and increase costs.'

Ralph Gibson LJ also remarked that the registrar had no jurisdiction in 1990
to limit the plaintiff's claim. But the district judge does have power to tell the
parties when the claim is automatically referred to arbitration, and uses the *f*
prescribed forms to do so. In a case where there is misuse of process the court
must be able to ensure that cases which should be automatically referred to
arbitration do not go to trial. It seems to us that it is contrary to the intent and
purpose of Ord 19 that the district judge should be powerless to prevent a
misuse of process.

g

SHOULD THE COURT GIVE GUIDELINES?

It was suggested that it would be helpful to the legal advisers of trade unions
and insurers if the court were to lay down guidelines for the kind of cases in
which it could be said that 'it would be unreasonable for the claim to proceed
to arbitration'. *h*

In our judgment the rules already contain the appropriate criteria to guide
the judgment of those who Finnemore J once described as 'seasoned warriors'
(see *Semtex Ltd v Gladstone* [1954] 2 All ER 206 at 209, [1954] 1 WLR 945 at 950).

To attempt to lay down within the criteria stated in the rules categories of
case which should be tried in court would be to usurp the function expressly *j*
given by Parliament to the Rules Committee under s 75 of the County Courts
Act 1984.

WHAT IS THE EFFECT OF A PAYMENT INTO COURT?

In five of the six additional cases, the defendants sought to use the procedure
for payment into court. For a defendant the object of a payment into court is

to protect himself from the costs of proceedings by placing the plaintiff at risk of having to pay the defendant's costs if he does not accept the money paid into court in satisfaction of his claim. When after 1981 the discretion of the arbitrator to award costs was removed and Ord 19, r 6 provided that no solicitors' charges should be allowed as between party and party unless the registrar certified that there had been unreasonable conduct, the rules for payment in, in a case in which the sum paid in was within the amount at which a claim would be automatically referred to arbitration, could serve little purpose. Order 11, r 3(7) made it clear that the provisions of that order did not affect the restriction on the allowance of costs under Ord 19, r 6, now r 4. If the plaintiff recovered more than the amount automatically referred, a payment into court was of no effect. If he did not, he could not in any event recover more than the costs permitted under Ord 19. The court had no power to award any greater costs. Nor could the plaintiff be ordered to pay the defendant's costs after the date of acceptance of the payment in unless the district judge certified that there had been unreasonable conduct on his part in relation to the proceedings. Unless the district judge was satisfied that the plaintiff had no reasonable prospect of being awarded a sum in excess of the limit for automatic arbitration, he would have no grounds for certifying that the plaintiff had been guilty of unreasonable conduct merely by failing to accept the offer. Thus from a defendant's point of view a payment into court was simply a formal offer to compromise the claim at the figure stated. Mr Burke argued that the provisions of Ord 11 applied where notice of acceptance was given within the 21 days allowed to enable the plaintiff under Ord 11, r 3(5)(a) to lodge for taxation a bill of costs incurred by him up to the time of giving notice of acceptance. This, argued Mr Burke, enabled the plaintiff to recover solicitors' and other legal charges incurred up to the time of acceptance.

In our view this provision of Ord 11 cannot invest the court with a power to award costs where it has none. The words of Ord 19, r 4(2) are mandatory. The mere fact that the plaintiff may lodge a bill of costs and seek to argue that they should be recoverable under one or other of the heads allowed under Ord 19 does not in our view enable the court to award costs other than those permitted by Ord 19, r 4. Nor can we see that any different considerations arise where the plaintiff fails to give notice within the 21 days limited for acceptance.

No doubt these reasons led the Rules Committee in 1992 to disapply the provisions of Ord 11 to claims automatically referred to arbitration altogether.

THE ADDITIONAL CASES

Featherstone v Ideal Standard Ltd

On 29 August 1991 whilst the plaintiff was packing a bath in a cardboard carton, a fellow employee, not paying attention to what he was doing, spilt some hot glue onto the plaintiff's left hand. The plaintiff, a 33-year-old packer, suffered excruciating pain for a while. The top layer of skin was removed, the burn was dressed and bandaged by a first-aider. He continued to have dressings for ten days and after about two weeks the wound had healed. He was put on light work for 48 hours and suffered no loss of earnings. He was left with a reddened scar at the base of the thumb which, two months after the accident, was progressively fading. Apart from this he had no symptoms.

He claimed damages by summons on 2 January 1992. By 28 April 1992 the defendants had paid £600 into court. On 6 July 1992 they admitted liability but disputed damages. The medical report was already agreed. In November 1992 the defendant's solicitors suggested that the claim was one to be dealt with by small claims arbitration. The plaintiff's solicitors disagreed and the trial of the issue of damages was held before Judge Cracknell on 5 May 1993. He awarded £800 damages. The payment into court was therefore inadequate and irrelevant to the judge's decision on costs. In exercising his discretion on costs he considered that the plaintiff had no reasonable expectation of recovering more than £1,000 and that the claim ought to have been dealt with by small claims arbitration. Accordingly he only awarded the plaintiff costs appropriate to an automatic reference under Ord 19, r 4. The plaintiff appeals against Judge Cracknell's order.

We can see no error in the judge's approach to the question of costs which would entitle this court to interfere with the award and would dismiss the appeal.

Willingham v Kimberley Clark Ltd

The plaintiff, a 50-year-old machine operator, was replacing the lid of a glue tank on 12 August 1991 at the defendant's factory at Aylesford in Kent when the underside of his right forearm came into contact with hot glue and he sustained a burn. He claimed it was the employer's fault because the lid of the glue tank was defective. He went to the works' surgery where the nurse dressed the burn. He returned to work. The burn needed dressing for about two weeks and was sufficiently painful for the plaintiff to have to take painkillers for ten days. He did not consult his doctor. His hobbies were interfered with for about four weeks. There were no permanent or residual symptoms or disabilities when the burn had healed.

On 20 November 1992 solicitors instructed on the plaintiff's behalf issued a county court summons in the Romford County Court. They claimed damages limited to £3,000 and asked in the summons that the case be decided by trial. There were no special damages claimed. On 2 December the defendant's solicitors applied for the action to be struck out as a misuse of the process of the court or in the alternative that the proceedings be referred to arbitration and transferred to the Maidstone County Court in whose jurisdiction the cause of action arose.

The defendant's application was referred by the district judge to Judge Paynter Reece. On 24 February 1993 Judge Paynter Reece dismissed the defendant's application and ordered that the defendant pay the costs of the application.

The judge gave no formal judgment but the reasons for his decision appear clearly from affidavits put before the court on the appeal. Firstly, he said that the Romford County Court was not in the habit of referring personal injury cases to arbitration. Secondly, although cases such as the one before him could be suitable for arbitration, if they were referred the defendant could deprive the plaintiff of his pre-reference costs at a stroke. Thirdly, he said that the particular claim was unsuitable for arbitration, adding, 'How can a line worker draft particulars of claim and understand breaches of statutory duty?'

There was a possibility that the plaintiff's claim might turn out to be worth more than £1,000 and there was no requirement for the plaintiff to limit his claim to £1,000. If he had to do so, the plaintiff's solicitor would 'kiss goodbye to all the costs the plaintiff had incurred'.

Accordingly he declined either to strike out the claim, order its amendment or declare that it was automatically referred for arbitration and made no order on the defendant's request that the case be transferred to Maidstone County Court.

For reasons already given, we consider the judge exercised his discretion on wrong principles and that the appeal should be allowed. We do not consider that there was any reasonable prospect of the damages exceeding £1,000 and the matter accordingly should be automatically referred to arbitration. However, should the case proceed, the district judge will have to determine whether the arbitration should be at Romford or at Maidstone County Court.

Afzal v Ford Motor Co Ltd

Mohammed Afzal was a fitter employed at Ford Motor Co's engine plant at Dagenham to carry out tests on engines in the hot testing plant. On 23 October 1990 in the course of his work he disconnected a fuel injector pipe and, as he did so, fuel under pressure shot up into his face and splashed his eye.

It was an unpleasant experience for him but he sustained no special damage. His eye was intermittently painful for four weeks. In March 1991 solicitors instructed on his behalf wrote claiming from the defendants. Negotiations ensued. On 24 July the plaintiff's solicitors sent a medical report and indicated that, unless an acceptable offer was received, they would institute proceedings within 14 days. The defendant's insurers responded with an offer of £450 but stated that they would make no payment for costs. In November particulars of claim were delivered limiting the damages claimed to £3,000. The claim alleged negligence and breach of statutory duty. On 11 December the defendants served a defence denying liability and putting damages in issue and gave notice of payment into court of the sum of £450. In January 1992 the plaintiff's solicitors, with the consent of the defendants, amended their particulars of claim to limit the claim to £1,000. The claim therefore was clearly within Ord 19, r 3(1) and was automatically referred to arbitration but notwithstanding this the parties embarked on extensive discovery and on 6 March 1992 the plaintiff applied to the court to rescind the automatic arbitration. On 27 March the defendants abandoned their defence on liability. On 30 March District Judge Finn made an order rescinding the arbitration on the ground that it would be unreasonable for it to proceed to arbitration. He commented that personal injury actions were not suitable for arbitration. The defendants appealed the district judge's decision to Judge Paynter Reece who heard argument on 22 May 1992. He reserved his decision and gave judgment together with his judgment in *Joyce v Ford Motor Co Ltd* on 22 October 1992.

Whilst the judge considered that the district judge's comment that personal injury actions were not suitable for arbitration was too wide, he thought that in the context the district judge was clearly speaking of industrial injury cases of which Afzal's was typical. He added:

> 'While each case turns on its own facts, that does not mean one cannot form a general view as to what is appropriate in the category of case in which this particular one falls.'

He added to the district judge's reason the fact that:

> 'Awards made by this court in these actions frequently provide guidance to others in the plaintiff's union, as well as to the defendants and their insurers as to the level of awards that can reasonably be expected and even though not reported can be a useful guidance to both parties in settling

similar claims ... as thankfully the vast majority are. It is therefore all the more important that both parties should be able to be legally represented to put their best arguments forward ... a consideration which is an amalgam of the majority of the matters referred to in Ord 19, r 2(4)(d).'

On the grounds stated earlier in this judgment, the judge was in our opinion wrong to uphold rescission of the automatic arbitration in this case. At the time when the order for rescission was made by the district judge, the only issue for decision was the amount of the damages. The district judge could not be satisfied that any of the reasons under r 3(2) justified an order for trial rather than arbitration. In the kind of small claim made by an employee against his employer, of which Afzal's case is a paradigm example, a district judge ought to be able to assess the amount of an award. Of course, so long as it is the policy of a particular court to require such cases to be assessed by the judge, the district judge's experience will be limited but no doubt it will not be long before the district judge accustomed to arbitrate in such cases will become equally experienced. His award will provide equally good guidance to employees and to employers and to those to whom they choose to turn for advice. The amount involved in this case did not exceed £1,000 and accordingly the provision for automatic reference to arbitration applied. We would accordingly allow the appeal.

Green v British Gas plc

In this case the plaintiff appeals against an order for costs made by Judge Mettyear on 5 July 1993. In an accident at work on 4 April 1990 the plaintiff, a 45-year-old fitter employed by the defendant, sustained a strain of the muscles of his lower abdomen when lifting a pipe with others in the course of his work. He was absent from work for a period of three to four weeks. His special damage amounted to £97·91. In a medical report 18 months later, Mr Korab-Karpinski expressed the opinion that the muscular strain had improved considerably whilst he was off work, that he still experienced minor twinges of discomfort during his work but that the injury was unlikely to give rise to any long-term consequences. On examination he had been unable to detect any abnormalities. Solicitors instructed for the plaintiff issued a summons on 13 March 1992. The medical report was served with the summons. Damages were claimed 'limited to £3,000'. Payments into court were made which by 1 April 1993 totalled £875. By that date the provisions of Ord 11 no longer applied to claims automatically referred to arbitration under Ord 19, r 3. The plaintiff indicated that he wished to accept the sum and on 20 May 1993, as if the provisions of Ord 11 applied, he gave notice of his intention to accept the sum offered and on 2 June applied for an order for payment to him of £875 paid into court and that the defendant should pay his costs of the action up to the time of his giving notice of acceptance, which his solicitors indicated amounted to no less than £2,044·92. The defendant resisted the application for costs. The matter came before the district judge on 21 June 1993. He awarded the plaintiff costs on scale 1. The defendant appealed to the judge. Judge Mettyear allowed the appeal and awarded the plaintiff only those costs which would have been recoverable under Ord 19, r 4(2) on an automatic reference to arbitration under r 3. He did so on the basis that the claim to damages limited to £3,000 was a misuse of process; he held that there was no reasonable expectation that general damages would be more than £750, he took into account that wide variations may occur in cases at the lower end of the scale of damages for personal injuries but nevertheless stated:

> 'I am firmly of the view, as I expressed already, that there was no reasonable expectation that a sum of more than £1,000 would be recovered.'

He could see no evidence that the plaintiff's advisers ever thought that more than £1,000 would be awarded. He inferred that the plaintiff's advisers, who had failed to put forward any figure in the course of correspondence, had simply failed to turn their mind to the question of amount. Had they done so, they would have concluded that there was no realistic prospect of obtaining more than £1,000. Based on a note of a decision of the district judge, he found that the district judge had misdirected himself by failing to apply the correct test of reasonable expectation of an award in excess of £1,000.

Before this court the plaintiff argued that the figure of £875 he had accepted was so close to the £1,000 limit that it was not open to the judge to say that there was no reasonable expectation of an award in excess of £1,000. The judge applied the wrong test and should have asked himself, as suggested by Glyn-Jones J in *Hopkins v Rees & Kirby Ltd* [1959] 2 All ER 352, [1959] 1 WLR 740, whether it would have been clear to the plaintiff and his advisers that no judge would award damages of more than £1,000.

As earlier stated, we see no significant difference in the suggested tests and reject this criticism of the judge's decision. The mere fact that the sum finally accepted came within a measurable distance of the £1,000 is not in itself a reason to hold that the plaintiff's advisers could reasonably have expected to recover more than £1,000. The judge was entitled to decide that on the basis of the medical reports before him, there was no such reasonable expectation. He was justified in holding that the statement claiming damages limited to £3,000 was a misuse of process. On the basis of the judge's finding, the claim did not involve more than £1,000 and it was accordingly automatically referred to arbitration under Ord 19, r 3.

The provisions of Ord 19, r 4(2) are clear that the court had no power to allow costs other than those provided for in the rule. Neither the district judge nor the judge could make an order for payment of costs by one party to the other except to the extent contained in r 4(2) and (3). We would uphold the order of Judge Mettyear allowing the defendant's appeal and ordering the defendant to pay the plaintiff's costs of £155.

A question was raised in argument whether an appeal could be brought against the exercise of the discretion of the district judge in awarding costs in a claim referred to arbitration and whether the judge on appeal from the district judge's order had power to award the defendants their costs on scale 1. As the district judge had no power to award any costs other than those allowed by Ord 19, r 4, he made an error of law and his award could be set aside under Ord 19, r 8. Ord 19, r 8(3) sets out the procedure to be adopted. Once the award is entered as a judgment of the court and the application to set it aside has been made, the powers of the judge are those contained in Ord 37, r 6(1):

> 'Any party affected by a judgment or final order of the district judge may, except where he has consented to the terms thereof, appeal from the judgment or order to the judge, who may, upon such terms as he thinks fit,—(a) set aside or vary the judgment or order or any part thereof, or (b)

give any other judgment or make any other order in substitution for the judgment or order appealed from, or (c) remit the action or matter or any question therein to the district judge for rehearing or further consideration, or (d) order a new trial to take place before himself or another judge of the court on a day to be fixed.'

In our view the judge had power to make provision for the costs of the appeal and we can see no ground to disturb his order that the plaintiff should pay the defendants their costs of the appeal.

Caldwell v Wiggins Teape Fine Papers Ltd

On 6 November 1990 while the plaintiff, a machine operator employed by the defendant, was adjusting the locking nuts on part of the machine, another operator caused a knife on the machine to descend, trapping the plaintiff's right thumb. The pulp of the thumb was crushed and the wound bled profusely. It was very painful and he was off work for eight days. The wound was cleaned and dressed at hospital. He suffered a superficial skin loss over the pulp of the right thumb about 7 mm by 3 mm. It took two weeks to heal and when healed the plaintiff was free of pain. There was no visible scar but there was a slight dulling of sensation in the centre of the pulp of the thumb which had improved by August 1991 and was expected to resolve completely. The accident happened at the defendant's factory at Dover. The plaintiff issued a county court summons in the Romford County Court on 26 November 1991. He claimed damages limited to £3,000. On 18 December 1991 the defendant paid £410 into court before defence and on 6 January 1992, after the time for acceptance had expired, it served a defence alleging contributory negligence. On 9 January 1992 the plaintiff gave notice of acceptance of the sum in court and on 31 January the defendant applied to the court for an order that no costs should be awarded except those allowable on an automatic reference. District Judge Hales accepted the defendant's contentions, sensibly refusing to be beguiled by citation of numerous decisions which, it was claimed, required him to apply different tests whether the claim should have been the subject of automatic arbitration. He said:

'I have come to the view that whichever of the tests I have mentioned, or suggested, is applicable, the maximum value of this claim—that is, if the plaintiff had succeeded on all issues—could not have been more than £750. The plaintiff accepted the payment into court with alacrity as soon as his solicitors received the defence ... I have no doubt ... that the full value of this case, taking all relevant matters into account, is not only well within the arbitration limit—in my judgment no more than £750—but also that the plaintiff's advisers were fully alive to this, not only before the defence but at the time of the issue of the summons.'

Accordingly he held that there was a misuse of the process of the court by inflating the claim, which was clearly within the arbitration limit, in an attempt to avoid the arbitration costs rules. So he awarded the plaintiff only the costs which would have been recoverable on such an arbitration. The plaintiff appealed to Judge Paynter Reece, who said:

'I have come to the conclusion that, having seen the medical evidence in this case, although it might be unlikely, and although I am not saying that, in this court in front of me, this plaintiff would have recovered more than £1,000 or indeed as much as £750, it is impossible to say that he could not have on a reasonable assessment of the case received more than £1,000.'

He concluded:

'I have come to the conclusion that the district judge was wrong in his assessment of the possible damages. It is not plain to me what test he was applying. He refers to a number of different tests to which he had made reference and refers to his own test which I have read out. I think he should have applied the test which I have referred to, that is, looked at by a reasonable solicitor, could the plaintiff possibly have recovered at trial more than £1,000? If he had, he would have come to the conclusion: "It may be unlikely but it is certainly possible."'

In our judgment, the test applied by the district judge was one of common sense which he was entitled to apply. The kind of excessive refinements adverted to by the judge should have no place in the district judge's decision whether in all the circumstances the claim was one which, but for misuse of process, would have been automatically referred to small claims arbitration. We have no doubt that the costs involved in arguing the fine distinctions referred to by the judge would greatly exceed the amount at stake and no sensible person would incur them.

As the provisions of Ord 11 for payment into court had not then been disapplied to a claim automatically referred to arbitration under Ord 19, r 3, the plaintiff argued that on giving notice of acceptance he was entitled under Ord 11, r 3(5)(a) to lodge for taxation a bill of the costs incurred by him up to the time of his giving notice of acceptance. He argued that it is implicit in those circumstances that he is entitled to be paid taxed costs, to include legal advice in the preparation of his claim and the settling of the summons and particulars. Aside from the reasons we have already stated for rejecting this argument, one obvious purpose of specifying in the rules the allowances which may be awarded and the amounts which may be claimed for costs is to obviate the expense of taxation. In our judgment, the court has no power to award costs other than those referred to in the rules and we would allow the appeal and restore the order of the district judge. The defendant is entitled to his costs of the appeal to Judge Paynter Reece on scale 1.

Joyce v Ford Motor Co Ltd

The amount involved in this claim was £650, but it was said that the issues were complicated by the fact that the plaintiff incurred legal costs when the limit for claims automatically referred to arbitration was £500.

The plaintiff was employed at the defendant's factory at Dagenham. Whilst showing a new recruit around the premises on 8 June 1990, he tripped over a flat bed trailer, injuring his left shin and bruising and grazing his right leg. His wound was cleaned and dressed in the medical department. He limped for about a fortnight and had some disturbance of sleep for approximately a week. Apart from some slight itching of the scar in warm weather, he had no discomfort or other symptoms as a result of his injury. Solicitors instructed for him by his trade union wrote to the employer claiming damages on 4 September 1990. At the request of the defendant's insurers the plaintiff's solicitors obtained and sent a medical report and gave details of the nature of the claim. On 1 July 1991 the limit for claims to be automatically referred to arbitration was increased from £500 to £1,000. The plaintiff's summons was issued on 25 November 1991 and it included particulars of claim limiting the damages to £3,000. The special damages claimed were only £30·55. On 23 December 1991 the defendant admitted liability to pay damages for the injury and loss proved by the plaintiff and paid £650 into court. The plaintiff did not give notice of acceptance within the 21 days limited by Ord 11, r 3(2) and accordingly, after the parties had failed to agree upon terms on which the plaintiff should be at liberty to accept the £650 paid into court, on 18 February 1992 the plaintiff applied to the court for an order that he be allowed to accept the sum and that it should be paid out to him, and for an order that the defendant pay his costs on scale 1 up to the date when he accepted the money paid into court.

The application was heard on 30 March 1992 by District Judge Finn, who held that the amount involved in the claim did not exceed the £1,000 limit and that had the claim been properly limited it would automatically have been referred to arbitration with a consequent limitation on recovery of costs. Of his own motion he said that he would rescind the automatic reference to arbitration and he ordered that the plaintiff be at liberty to accept the sum in court, that the defendant pay his costs on scale 1 up to the date of acceptance and that thereafter the plaintiff should pay the defendant's costs.

In the light of his finding that had the claim been properly limited it would automatically have been referred to arbitration and of the fact that no issue save that of costs remained for the decision of the arbitrator since the plaintiff had agreed to accept the £650 offered, we cannot see what justification he could have had for ordering trial and rescinding the reference. As we have held, he had no power to award costs except those provided for by Ord 19, r 4.

The defendant appealed to Judge Paynter Reece who heard the appeal with the appeal in *Afzal*'s case and on 22 October dismissed the appeal. For the reasons already stated in this judgment, we would allow the appeal from the order of Judge Paynter Reece and would quash the order for costs made by the district judge. We would substitute for the order of the district judge an order that the defendant pay to the plaintiff the costs recoverable under Ord 19, r 4(2). Finally, we must consider the order made by the district judge that after the date of notice of acceptance of the sum offered, the plaintiff should pay the defendant's costs. The district judge, having rescinded the automatic arbitration, was treating the claim as if the provisions of Ord 11 applied. It was argued by the defendant that it was entitled to its costs of the application before the district registrar because he had held there had been a misuse of the process of the court. Accordingly he ought to have held that under Ord 19, r 4(2)(c) there had been unreasonable conduct on the part of the plaintiff in relation to the proceedings or the claim. When the application was made to the district judge the plaintiff was no longer contending that the amount involved exceeded £1,000. As the district judge did not consider whether the plaintiff had been guilty of unreasonable conduct in connection with the proceedings, this court has to decide whether in all the circumstances the plaintiff should be required to pay the defendant's costs before the district judge. For the plaintiff it was said that when he initially made his claim, the amount involved (£650) exceeded the amount (£500) which would result in automatic reference to arbitration. However, by the time proceedings were commenced the amount involved was below the limit (£1,000). He had already incurred legal costs, the costs of obtaining a medical report and of stating the nature of his claim at the request of the defendant. Whilst it is true that until he accepted the £650 the plaintiff had been guilty of misuse of process, the defendant, after the plaintiff had accepted the sum offered, chose to be represented at the hearing before the district judge to argue the question of costs when there was no power to order the plaintiff to pay the defendant's costs after acceptance of the money paid in. The question is whether, in the exceptional circumstances of the plaintiff accepting a sum which exceeded the limit for arbitration when the claim was originally notified to the defendant, his application to the district judge amounted to unreasonable conduct. In all the circumstances we do not think that the plaintiff should be ordered to pay the defendant's costs of that hearing.

Although this disposes of the appeals before the court, we feel a short summary of the aspects of procedure discussed in this judgment may help the parties to small claims to take advantage of automatic arbitration in the county court.

(a) Where a plaintiff cannot reasonably expect to receive more than £1,000, there is no reason why he should not state in the summons (Form N2) that his claim does not exceed £1,000. If, for any of the reasons stated in the rules the plaintiff considers the case should not proceed to arbitration, he can indicate his objection in the Form N2.

(b) If the damages claimed in a summons are not so limited or are stated to be limited to a figure exceeding £1,000 and the defendant considers that the amount involved does not exceed £1,000, he should include a statement to that effect in his defence and ask for the claim to be automatically referred to arbitration.

(c) There is no reason why the defendant should not state in his defence the amount he considers to be involved.

(d) The district judge will then form his own opinion of the amount involved and inform the parties of his decision by sending the appropriate form; alternatively he may regard the case as one in which an application for trial has been made and decide to hear the parties.

(e) The parties should bear in mind that the overstatement of the amount of damages claimed or the raising of a speculative and unsupportable defence may be regarded as unreasonable conduct under Ord 19, r 4(2)(c).

Finally, we desire to emphasise that the small claims arbitration procedure is intended to improve access to justice. For many people a small claim for damages for an injury sustained at work will be their only experience of the working of the system of justice. If those who advise employees and employers in such claims disregard the objects of the small claims arbitration procedure, the law as a whole is likely to be brought into disrepute. If it is seen that in a significant class of claims procedural battledore and shuttlecock is costing far more than the amount of the damages recovered, the reputation of justice must suffer. In the handling of small claims it is just as much a misuse of the process of the court for a defendant to file a defence denying liability when he knows there is none as it is for a plaintiff to overstate the amount involved in the claim for the purpose of avoiding arbitration. Each tactic disguises the real questions at issue for an improper reason. The discretion given to the district judge under r 4 (2)(c) to allow costs where there has been unreasonable behaviour by either party is intended to reinforce the need for restraint. The problems perceived by the parties and exhaustively discussed in these appeals could, we feel, be easily overcome by a spirit of co-operation to make the small claims arbitration work fairly and effectively.

Appeals allowed in the 16 Ford cases. Appeals dismissed in Green v British Gas and Featherstone v Ideal Standard. Appeals allowed in Willingham v Kimberley Clark, Caldwell v Wiggins Teape and Joyce v Ford Motor Co.

Wendy Shockett   Barrister.

IBM United Kingdom Ltd v Prima Data International Ltd

CHANCERY DIVISION

SIR MERVYN DAVIES QC SITTING AS A JUDGE OF THE HIGH COURT

18, 19, 20, 25 JANUARY 1994

Practice – Pre-trial or post-judgment relief – Anton Piller order – Privilege against self-incrimination – Action for damages for conspiracy – Risk of criminal prosecution – Order for disclosure of information and documents relating to alleged conspiracy – Order including proviso to safeguard defendant's right to claim privilege against self-incrimination – Defendant electing not to claim privilege – Whether proviso an effective safeguard of defendant's rights.

In 1992 the director of the defendant company entered into agreements with the plaintiff company, IBM, for the purchase of computer equipment worth £653,087·10. The sale was negotiated on terms which precluded the company from selling on the IBM equipment without first having incorporated it into its own product. The company subsequently failed to pay for the equipment supplied under the contracts and in March 1993 IBM obtained judgment under RSC Ord 14 for the amount outstanding. IBM's attempt thereafter to enforce the judgment failed when it was revealed that the company had no assets, and resulting investigations disclosed that (contrary to representations made by the director and company secretary) the company was not in the business of making its own products and that the company had sold the IBM equipment directly to third parties in its unaltered state and at a price lower than the invoice price. IBM later issued proceedings against inter alia the company and its director, claiming damages for conspiracy to extract goods without payment, and obtained an order ex parte including Anton Piller and Mareva relief. The proviso to the Anton Piller sections of the ex parte order requiring the director to disclose and deliver up specified items relating to dealings arising from the sale transaction stated that, prior to execution of the order, the supervising solicitor should (i) explain the meaning and effect of the order to the director in everyday language, (ii) advise him of his right to obtain legal advice on the consequence of allowing search and seizure and (iii) explain that he might be entitled to claim privilege against self-incrimination so that the order would have effect only in so far as such privilege was not claimed. The director elected not to invoke the privilege against self-incrimination, which had been explained to him in accordance with the proviso requirements, and the Anton Piller order was duly executed. The director then applied for an order setting aside the Anton Piller sections of the ex parte order, contending that the order ought not to have been made because the proviso safeguards against self-incrimination were inadequate in view of the risk of criminal prosecution for conspiracy and that, at the time of execution, he had not fully understood the privilege against self-incrimination.

Held – An Anton Piller order which would expose a defendant to a real risk of criminal prosecution for conspiracy could only properly be made and served on the defendant if it contained a proviso which adequately protected the defendant's right to claim privilege against self-incrimination. The order would not however be executed until (a) the defendant had been informed of his right to claim privilege in everyday language and properly understood his rights as preserved by the order, namely that there would be no entry if he claimed privilege and (b) the defendant then expressly declined to claim that right. On the facts, although it was plain that the director was in danger of criminal proceedings for conspiracy, the form of the Anton Piller order had preserved his privilege against self-incrimination and its scheme had been faithfully observed. The director's application to set aside those sections of the ex parte order requiring him to disclose and deliver up specified items in his possession, custody or power would accordingly be dismissed (see p 760 *d* to *fh* to p 761 *b*, post).

Rank Film Distributors Ltd v Video Information Centre [1981] 2 All ER 76 applied.

A T & T Istel Ltd v Tully [1992] 3 All ER 523 considered.

Notes

For compliance with Anton Piller orders and the privilege against self-incrimination, see 24 *Halsbury's Laws* (4th edn) (reissue) para 875.

Cases referred to in judgment

A T & T Istel Ltd v Tully [1992] 3 All ER 523, [1993] AC 45, [1992] 3 WLR 344, HL.
R v Boyes (1861) 1 B & S 311, [1861–73] All ER Rep 172, 121 ER 730.
Rank Film Distributors Ltd v Video Information Centre [1981] 2 All ER 76, [1982] AC 380, [1981] 2 WLR 668, HL.
Sociedade Nacional de Combustiveis de Angola UEE v Lundqvist [1990] 3 All ER 283, [1991] 2 QB 310, [1991] 2 WLR 280, CA.
Spokes v Grosvenor and West End Railway Terminus Hotel Co Ltd [1897] 2 QB 124.
Tate Access Floors Inc v Boswell [1990] 3 All ER 303, [1991] Ch 512, [1991] 2 WLR 304.

Cases also cited

Bishopsgate Investment Managment Ltd (in prov liq) v Maxwell, Cooper v Maxwell, Mirror Group Newpapers plc v Maxwell [1992] 2 All ER 856, [1993] Ch 1, CA.
Hytrac Conveyors Ltd v Conveyors International Ltd [1982] 3 All ER 415, [1983] 1 WLR 44, CA.

Motion

Iain McKenzie Holloway, the second defendant to a writ dated 22 December 1993 in which the plaintiff, IBM United Kingdom Ltd (IBM), claimed damages for conspiracy, by a notice of motion dated 11 January 1994, sought an order to set aside those parts of an ex parte order granted to IBM by Warner J on 21 December 1993 which related to Anton Piller relief on the ground that compliance with the order would expose him to the risk of prosecution for conspiracy. The first and third defendants, Prima Data International Ltd (the company of which Mr Holloway was director) and Peter James Culshaw (who was the company secretary) took no part in the application. The facts are set out in the judgment.

Paul Ashwell (instructed by *Howlett Clarke Cushman,* Brighton) for Mr Holloway.
Philip Heslop QC and *Robert Miles* (instructed by *Herbert Smith*) for IBM.

Cur adv vult

25 January 1994. The following judgment was delivered.

SIR MERVYN DAVIES QC. This is a motion by the second defendant to set aside part of an ex parte order made by Warner J on 21 December 1993. The plaintiff is IBM United Kingdom Ltd (IBM). The defendants are (1) Prima Data International Ltd (PDI), (2) Mr Iain McKenzie Holloway, (3) Mr Peter James Culshaw and (4) Bluepatch Ltd. The writ in the action was issued on 22 December 1993. IBM claims: (1) against the first, second and third defendants, damages for a conspiracy pursuant to which they induced the plaintiff to supply components to PDI between August and November 1992 by making false representations about the intended use of such components and about the nature of PDI's business; (2) against the second and third defendants, damages for misrepresentations in connection with the matters set out in (1); and (3) against the second, third and fourth defendants, a declaration that all money, assets and property received by them, derived from the sale proceeds of components supplied to PDI by IBM, are held by them upon a constructive trust by IBM together with an order to account. I need not refer to the other relief claimed.

On the day before the issue of the writ an application was made to Warner J for an ex parte order including Anton Piller and Mareva relief. The application was supported by an affidavit intended to be sworn by Mr A J T Willoughby, a solicitor in the firm of Messrs Herbert Smith, acting for IBM. The affidavit was sworn on 23 December. There are 18 exhibits to the affidavit. The affidavit shows that IBM, as is well known, makes and sells computer equipment. Contracts are made which on occasion bind the purchaser not to sell the IBM equipment purchased otherwise than by incorporating the equipment into its own product.

In 1992 IBM was approached by Mr Culshaw and Mr Holloway on behalf of PDI. Three contracts followed and, pursuant to the contracts, IBM equipment worth £653,087·10 was supplied to PDI. The contracts were made following certain misrepresentations said to have been made by Mr Culshaw and Mr Holloway. I need not now mention the misrepresentations. In any event, they are now conveniently set out in the statement of claim. It does not appear that the misrepresentations were framed in consequence of any information acquired by enforcing the ex parte order.

I have referred to the fact that PDI did not pay for the equipment supplied. On 10 March 1993 a writ was issued against PDI in the Queen's Bench Division claiming the sum I have mentioned with interest. Judgment was obtained under RSC Ord 14 eventually for the whole sum.

On 15 July 1993 a writ of fieri facias was issued. The sheriff's office made a nil return. It appears that PDI has no assets. In these circumstances IBM instructed inquiry agents to seek to ascertain how PDI apparently dissipated £650,000 or so worth of assets. Inquiries made disclosed, says Mr Willoughby, that: (1) contrary to representations made, PDI did not have a business of making its own products; (2) PDI sold the IBM products directly to third parties and at prices lower than the prices at which IBM invoiced the products to PDI; (3) between March 1992 and January 1993 Mr Holloway and members of his family received about £230,000, Mr Holloway being the managing director of PDI; (4) the only substantial receipts by PDI during that period were from sales of components supplied to PDI by IBM; (5) Mr Holloway caused Bluepatch, the fourth defendant, to be incorporated in 1993. Its directors are Mr Holloway's son and daughter and a third person. Such stock and assets as PDI had were transferred to Bluepatch for, it is said, no consideration. Bluepatch trades from the address previously used by PDI; and (6) Mr Holloway is interested in a large number of companies, many incorporating the words 'Prima Data' and some being offshore companies. In these circumstances, says Mr Willoughby, the plaintiff company believes that it has been the victim of a scheme to extract products from it when there was never any intention to pay for them.

After giving that general picture Mr Willoughby, in his affidavits, turns to some detail of the situation. The documents filed at Companies House concerning PDI say that it is a £100 company incorporated on 12 February 1992. Mr Holloway owns 50 shares and 50 shares are held by Miss K L Culshaw. Mr Holloway is the only director. Mr Culshaw was the company secretary. Mr Holloway is or was a director of 17 companies including PDI, 12 of which include the words 'Prima Data' in their name, e g Prima Data Group Ltd, Prima Data Direct Ltd, Prima Data GmbH in Germany etc. Registered details of the English companies are exhibited. The affidavit goes on to detail the negotiations of IBM supplying components to PDI.

Mr Patrick Noakes was the principal person negotiating on behalf of IBM and his contracts were with Mr Holloway and Mr Culshaw. Mr Noakes at one stage, on 14 September 1992, visited the premises at 85 South Coast Road, Peacehaven. The premises were in disrepair but Mr Noakes was told that PDI had just bought the premises and there was to be a completion of building works.

In para 48 of his affidavit Mr Willoughby states that a representative of IBM, Mr Littlecote, met a Mr Simon Wells in Strasbourg. It appears that Mr Wells had been invited by Mr Culshaw and Mr Holloway to join PDI as a consultant. Mr Wells provided IBM with some documents. I should say that Mr Holloway regarded Mr Wells as being completely untrustworthy. However that may be, Mr Wells supplied to IBM two diskettes containing computer ledgers for PDI together with hard copy print-outs under ten headings such as, 'purchase ledger', 'day books', 'purchase invoices', 'day book sales invoices' etc.

The print-outs are exhibited and cover 162 pages. It is said, and it appears to me to be the case, that substantially the whole of the PDI's revenue was derived from the onward sale of IBM products. There are annotations on the print-out. These were made by Mr Wells and are said to be payments out to Mr Holloway or to members of his family.

I was taken through Mr Willoughby's affidavit in all its completeness and I was referred to a number of the exhibits. It came as no surprise to me that

Warner J made the ex parte order, which I will now mention. The order was made, as I have said, on 21 December 1993. As I understand, no relief was sought against Mr Culshaw. The order takes up 13 pages.

After recitals usually seen in Anton Piller or Mareva orders one comes to para 1 under 'IT IS ORDERED'. Paragraph 1 orders Mr Holloway to permit entry to 14 Fairlight Avenue (that is where Mr Holloway resides with his wife). Entry is to be for the purpose of looking for, inspecting, etc all documents as specified in Sch 2 to the order, ie 'the specified items'.

The schedule indicates that the specified items are bank statements, ledgers, correspondence and other documents of whatever description relating to dealings arising from the sale of components by the plaintiff to PDI.

Proviso (i) says that the order is to be served by Mr Paul Rawlinson of the firm of Messrs Baker & McKenzie acting as the supervising solicitor in accordance with the current Anton Piller practice.

Proviso (ii) must be set out in full. It states:

'before any persons enter [14 Fairlight Avenue] pursuant to this Order the Supervising Solicitor shall offer to explain to the Second Defendant the meaning and effect of this Order in everyday language and shall also advise the Second Defendant of his right to obtain legal advice before permitting entry provided such advice is obtained at once (such advice to include an explanation that the Second Defendant may be entitled to avail himself of the privilege against self-incrimination); and so that the provisions of paragraphs 1, 2, 3 and 4 of this Order shall have effect only in so far as such privilege is not claimed by the Second Defendant.'

The words that follow the semi-colon were, so I am told, added by Warner J to the draft that was put before him by counsel for IBM. There follow paras 2, 3, 4 and 5 of the order. They read:

'2. That the Second Defendant do disclose forthwith to the plaintiff's Solicitors the whereabouts of all Specified Items that are in his possession, custody or power.

3. That the Second Defendant do forthwith deliver to the plaintiff's Solicitors all Specified Items in his possession, custody or power.

4. That if any of the Specified Items exist in computer readable form only, the Second Defendant shall cause them forthwith to be printed out and shall deliver the print-out to the plaintiff's Solicitors or, failing a printer, shall cause it forthwith to be displayed to the plaintiff's Solicitors in any readable form.

5. That until 12th January 1994 or further Order herein the Second Defendant be restrained from doing any of the following acts, namely altering, destroying, moving or tampering with any of the Specified Items or causing, or permitting the same to occur, save in compliance with paragraphs 1 and 3 above.'

I am told that Mr Holloway offers an undertaking in the terms of para 5, but paras 2, 3 and 4 are objected to. Other material parts of the order as affecting Mr Holloway are paras 13 and 16, which read:

'13. That the First Defendant do by a director or other officer within fourteen days of service upon it of this order swear and serve on the plaintiff's Solicitors a further Affidavit setting forth details of what has become of all and any sums derived by it (whether directly or indirectly) from the sale of components supplied to it by the Plaintiff between 1st August 1992 and 30th November 1992, such Affidavit to exhibit all relevant documents within the categories set forth in Schedule 2 to this Order within the possession, custody or power of the First Defendant.

16. That the Second Defendant do within fourteen days of service upon him of this Order swear and serve on the plaintiff's Solicitors a further Affidavit setting forth details of what has become of all and any sums derived from the sale by the First Defendant of components supplied to it by the Plaintiff between 1st August 1992 and 30th November 1992 and any property which represents any such sums, such Affidavit to exhibit all relevant documents within the categories set forth in Schedule 2 to this Order within the possession, custody or power of the Second Defendant.'

The order was also directed against Bluepatch. The action has been discontinued as against Bluepatch but in view of what has taken place it is necessary to take account of the order as it affected Bluepatch.

In para 6 Bluepatch was required by a director or other responsible officer or by a person in control of 85 South Coast Road to permit the second supervising solicitor, in this case Mr Willoughby, to enter 85 South Coast Road for the purpose of inspecting the same specified items as are referred to in para 1 of the order.

There follow some provisos as to the mode of execution of the order but I do not set out such provisos. The order was also directed against PDI. I need not refer to that aspect of the order, save to say that I have continued, until judgment, the order made against PDI.

The Anton Piller order was executed as to 14 Fairlight Avenue (Fairlight) and 85 South Coast Road (No 85) on 22 December 1993. I understand that documents were taken, photographed and retained. The return date for the ex parte order was 12 January 1994. Following execution of the order both supervising solicitors made reports for submission to the court. The reports detail the events that took place and I seek to summarise the principal events as set out in a useful document put before me by Mr Heslop QC for IBM.

The mode of execution adopted was that Mr Rawlinson and three others attended at Fairlight at about 11.30 am on 22 December while Mr Willoughby, with three others, went to No 85 at about the same time. It will be appreciated that Mr Rawlinson was concerned with the order against Mr Holloway in respect of Fairlight and Mr Willoughby was concerned with the order against Bluepatch in respect of No 85.

Mr Rawlinson, in approaching Fairlight, was informed that Mr Holloway was at No 85. At this time Mr Willoughby approached No 85 and found that Mr Holloway was there. Mr Willoughby identified himself and told Mr Holloway of the proceedings, including the making of the ex parte order.

Mr Willoughby told Mr Holloway that the order required Mr Holloway to allow entry into Fairlight for the search of the specified items I have mentioned and, further, that the order required Bluepatch to allow entry into No 85.

There was then the arrival at No 85 of Mrs Gail McCallum. Mrs McCallum is a daughter of Mr Holloway and a director of Bluepatch. Mrs McCallum reported the presence of Mr Rawlinson's team at Fairlight. Mr Holloway said he would be seeking legal advice and that Mrs McCallum was to contact Miss Hilary Nelson of Messrs Howlett Clarke, Cushman, the solicitor who would act for Bluepatch.

Mr Holloway said he wished Mr Willoughby to speak to his daughter's solicitor. Accordingly, Mr Willoughby spoke to Miss Nelson. Miss Nelson said that she was not sure she could accept instructions because no one appeared to have sufficient funds to pay her and she doubted whether she would get an emergency legal aid certificate.

However that may be, Mr Willoughby explained the basis of IBM's claim as being one of conspiracy and of course referred to the ex parte order. The paragraphs concerning entry into Fairlight and No 85 were read out. Mr Willoughby suggested that it would be helpful if she or her representative could come to No 85. Mr Willoughby drew attention to the fact that Mr Holloway and Bluepatch had the right to seek legal advice and that Mr Rawlinson had to tell Mr Holloway of his right to take legal advice about a possible claim to privilege against self-incrimination.

Following that conversation Mr Willoughby served Mrs McCallum with the order. By this time it was 12.15 pm. At that stage Mr Willoughby served the order on Mr Holloway explaining that Mr Rawlinson would deal with the formalities. He explained that the order could not be executed at Fairlight otherwise than under the supervision of Mr Rawlinson. Proviso (i) to para 1 of the order lays down that Mr Holloway was to be served by Mr Rawlinson. Mr Ashwell for Holloway said he did not wish to take any point on that.

There was then, at 12.20 pm, another telephone conversation between Mr Willoughby and Miss Nelson. He said that Mr Holloway was indicating that he would not allow a search of Fairlight but that he, Mr Willoughby, would arrange for Rawlinson to come to No 85. The premises are, as I understand, not a great distance from each other.

Mr Rawlinson arrived at No 85 at about 1.07 pm. Until then he had been waiting near Fairlight. Mr Rawlinson began explaining the order to Mr Holloway. The explanation is said to have lasted for almost an hour. Mr Rawlinson's general impression was that Mr Holloway understood the meaning of the order. Mr Holloway was advised to call a solicitor. He was told he was entitled to invoke the privilege against self-incrimination in relation to any entry into Fairlight. Mr Rawlinson's affidavit, sworn on 13 January, states that he explained to Mr Holloway that he was entitled to refuse to comply with paras 1, 2, 3 and 4 of the order if he believed that to do so would be likely to expose him to a risk of criminal prosecution (see para 5).

Thereupon, Mr Holloway told Mrs McCallum to go to Fairlight and tell his wife that Fairlight was to be searched. Mr Rawlinson said he interrupted Mr Holloway because he wanted to explain again the point about self-incrimination. Again, at 1.44 pm Mr Rawlinson went over Mr Holloway's right to obtain legal advice and his right to avail himself of the privilege against self-incrimination, ie that Mr Holloway was entitled to choose not to comply with paras 1, 2, 3 and 4 of the order if he believed that there was a risk that to do so would expose him to a risk of criminal prosecution.

Mr Holloway asked to speak to Mr Rawlinson alone. He did so. He asked what Mr Rawlinson's advice would be if he, Mr Holloway, did have incriminating documents. Mr Rawlinson said he regarded that to be an hypothetical question. Anyway Mr Rawlinson replied that Mr Holloway could rely on privilege and not allow a search of Fairlight and that even so he, Mr Holloway, could not rule out the possibility of a criminal investigation. Mr Holloway then said he had no choice but to allow a search to proceed. He was again advised to take professional advice.

While Mr Rawlinson was engaged with Mr Holloway, as I have set out, Mr Willoughby was explaining the order to Mrs McCallum and to Mr David Brierly, a co-director of Bluepatch. Mr Willoughby spoke of self-incrimination as respects Bluepatch (although the provision about incrimination had been deleted from the order as respects Bluepatch). Since Bluepatch is not before me and in fact the action has been discontinued against Bluepatch I need take this aspect of the affair no further.

After all the extensive preliminaries Mr Willoughby and his team at 2.50 pm began a search at No 85 with the consent of Mrs McCallum and some members of the Rawlinson team helped Mr Willoughby in that task. At 4.28 pm Mr Rawlinson and his team went from No 85 to Fairlight accompanied by Mr Holloway. There there took place a search which lasted only about 15 minutes. Very few material documents were found there.

Mr Rawlinson returned to No 85. The search there, under Mr Willoughby's supervision, went on till about 6.20 pm, so the search team was engaged at No 85 for over three hours. I understand that many documents were taken, photocopied, and returned.

The supervising solicitors' reports are before the court. That of Mr Rawlinson is dated 5 January 1994 and is 'PR.1' to his affidavit sworn on 13 January. That of Mr Willoughby is filed in court. I understand that copies of both reports were sent to Mr Holloway before 10 January.

The next step to mention is the notice of motion issued by Mr Holloway. It is dated 11 January. Therein Mr Holloway seeks an order that paras 2, 3, 4, 5, 13 and 16 of the order of Warner J dated 21 December 1993 be dissolved. There is an affidavit in support sworn on 11 January 1994. It will be recalled that the return date of the order of 21 December was 12 January.

In para 3 of the affidavit Mr Holloway says that one of the grounds of his motion is that he is advised 'that there is a real risk of prosecution for conspiracy which is the primary claim in the generally endorsed writ'. I quote paras 4, 5 and 6 of the affidavit:

'4. I have read two reports on the execution on 22nd December of the order. One is by the independent supervising solicitor Paul Rawlinson of Baker & McKenzie. It is dated 5th January 1994. The other is by the second supervising solicitor, Anthony J.T. Willoughby of Herbert Smith. It is undated. I received them on 10th January 1994. They both report accurately what took place in my presence. In particular they are correct in stating that both Mr. Willoughby and Mr. Rawlinson informed me that I had the right to obtain legal advice and that Mr. Rawlinson explained to me that I was entitled to claim privilege against self-incrimination. They correctly relate that I said that I would be seeking legal advice and would be applying for emergency legal aid. I did speak to Hilary Nelson, a solicitor and partner in the firm of Howlett Clarke Cushman, by telephone on 22nd December but I was mainly concerned about the involvement of Bluepatch Ltd (the Fourth Defendant) and did not talk to her about self-incrimination.

5. Mr. Rawlinson's explanation of the privilege against self-incrimination was just one of the many complexities of the order that was explained and one of the many legalities that was discussed. I did not fully understand what the privilege against self-incrimination meant and what the consequence of allowing the search and seizure might be, though I did think that if I refused to allow the search I might go to prison and Mr.

Rawlinson told me that that was one potential consequence of not complying with the order. I was in a state of shock and confusion. My principal concerns were for the distress that a search of our home would cause my wife, the unjustified involvement of Bluepatch, of which my daughter Gail McCallum is a director and my concern to explain that IBM had been misled by Simon Wells as to the way in which the business of PDI had been carried on.

6. I made no conscious decision to waive privilege against self-incrimination and did not intend to do. I was granted Legal Aid by a certificate dated 31st December received by me on 6th January. I have now received legal advice and I wish to invoke that privilege and ask that all the Specified Items seized by reason of my not invoking that privilege on the day of the search be returned.'

I should mention that Mr Holloway swore another affidavit on 12 January 1994. He did so as a director of PDI and it is an affidavit of means. He states that on 10 January 1993 PDI issued a statutory demand against Prima Data Group seeking payment of £465,999·30. I see no significance in that in the context of the motion before me. Mr Holloway has also sworn an affidavit of his own means which appear to be meagre.

On IBM's side there is a response to Mr Holloway's affidavit from which I have just quoted. It is an affidavit by Mr Rawlinson sworn on 13 January 1994. Mr Rawlinson says that he has served over one dozen Anton Piller orders in the United Kingdom and in Hong Kong and that he has acted as a supervising solicitor in the High Court on three occasions. I think I should, as I did in the case of the Holloway affidavit, quote from Mr Rawlinson's affidavit at length:

'4. As indicated on page 3 of my report at 'PR 1', I commenced my explanation of the Order to Mr Holloway at approximately 1.10 pm and completed my explanation at approximately 2.07 pm. It took me, therefore, almost an hour to explain the provisions of the Order to Mr Holloway in detail and my general impression, throughout my explanation, was that Mr Holloway understood its provisions and effect. Except where otherwise indicated below, a trainee solicitor from Baker & McKenzie, James McGregor, was present throughout my explanation to Mr Holloway of the Order and took a summary note of the conversation. I have discussed this account of my explanation of the Order to Mr Holloway with Mr McGregor and he confirms that, to the best of his recollection, it is accurate.

5. I refer to page 4 of my report. At 1.25 pm it is noted that I was continuing to explain to Mr Holloway the undertakings contained in pages 2 and 3 of the Order. On page 5 of my report, it is noted that I first mentioned the privilege against self-incrimination to Mr Holloway in the course of completing my explanation of the undertaking before explaining the body of the Order. I recall that I was conscious of my obligation to explain the point before entering any premises (although I had been invited into the premises at 85 South Coast Road by Mr Holloway). I explained to Mr Holloway that he was entitled to refuse to comply with paragraphs 1, 2, 3 and 4 of the Order (contained on pages 4 to 5 of the Order) if he believed that to do so would be likely to expose him to a risk of criminal prosecution. I explained that paragraphs 1 to 4 concerned the proposed search at the premises at 14 Fairlight Avenue for items listed in

Schedule 2 (which I then described to Mr Holloway); the disclosure of the whereabouts of the items listed in Schedule 2; the delivery up of the items listed in Schedule 2; the delivery up of computer programs containing information about the items listed in Schedule 2. Mr Holloway told me that he had no documents at his home and that all documents were kept at the premises at 85 South Coast Road.

6. I then reverted back to page 3 of the Order and I then proceeded to read through paragraph 1 of the Order, on page 4, concerning the provision permitting the search of the premises at 14 Fairlight Avenue. I recall (and it is noted in my report at 1.36 pm) that Mr Holloway told his daughter to go home and tell Mrs Holloway what was happening and that we were going to search his home. I interrupted because I wanted to explain, again, the privilege against self-incrimination and the remaining parts of the Order.

7. It is noted in my report that, at 1.44 pm, I explained to Mr Holloway his right to obtain legal advice and the privilege against self-incrimination. I recall reading aloud to Mr Holloway paragraph 1(ii) of the Order which contained the obligation to explain to Mr Holloway the meaning and effect of the Order in everyday language, to advise Mr Holloway of his right to obtain legal advice before permitting entry and that such advice was to include an explanation that Mr Holloway may be entitled to avail himself of the privilege against self-incrimination. I explained that this meant that he was entitled to choose not to comply with paragraphs 1 to 4 of the Order (the parts which required immediate action by Mr Holloway) if he believed that there was a risk that to do so would expose him to a risk of criminal prosecution. I recall that, at this point, Mr Holloway asked Mr McGregor to allow me to speak to Mr Holloway in private. Mr Holloway then asked me what my advice would be if he were to have any incriminating documents at his home premises. I verily believe that Mr Holloway asked me this question hypothetically and was not suggesting that he had any documents. I answered that he would be able to rely on the privilege against self-incrimination and not permit the search to take place at his home but he could not rule out the possibility of a criminal investigation being pursued. Mr Holloway then said that he felt he had no choice but to allow the search to proceed. I advised him that he should take independent legal advice on what to do and that my duty was to explain the Order to him as fairly and objectively as possible. Mr Holloway then asked me to continue my explanation of the Order and invited Mr McGregor to rejoin us.

8. As is apparent from my report and the report of Mr Willoughby, Mr Holloway stated on several occasions throughout the day that he had nothing to hide and that, in view of the fact that he had known for some time that he was being investigated, stated that he would have got rid of documents before the search if he had had any incriminating documents.'

Mr Ashwell, for Mr Holloway, did not complain of the way in which the order was executed. Mr Ashwell's principal submission in support of the motion was that, there being plainly a risk of self-incrimination by Mr Holloway, the order dated 21 December 1993 ought not to have been made because the safeguards therein against self-incrimination are inadequate and do not reflect authority. He said it would not have been possible to make an order embracing adequate safeguards against prosecution. That submission was well developed by Mr Ashwell.

Mr Heslop for IBM submitted that the order was consistent with the concern expressed by the courts as to the effect of pleading privilege in civil cases: see eg Lord Templeman in *A T & T Istel Ltd v Tully* [1992] 3 All ER 523 at 530, [1993] AC 45 at 53, where he says—

> 'I regard the privilege against self-incrimination exercisable in civil proceedings as an archaic and unjustifiable survival from the past when the court directs the production of relevant documents and requires the defendant to specify his dealings with the plaintiff's property or money.'

(See also [1992] 3 All ER 523 at 534, [1993] AC 45 at 58 per Lord Griffiths and *Sociedade Nacional de Combustiveis de Angola UEE v Lundqvist* [1990] 3 All ER 283 at 302–303, [1991] 2 QB 310 at 338 per Browne-Wilkinson V-C.) With proviso (ii) to para 1 of the order in mind, Mr Heslop went on to say that Mr Holloway having been told by the supervising solicitor of his right to invoke privilege decided not to do so. In that way, it was said, the order in para 1, having been conditional on Mr Holloway's consent, then became unconditional.

There was then the point, said Mr Heslop, that privilege having been discarded (so as to make the order unconditional) Mr Holloway could not, days later, change his mind and ask the court to allow him to invoke privilege.

The impact of the plea of privilege in civil actions and in particular at the stage of any Anton Piller or Mareva application has been much remarked. As well as the two instances I have mentioned above there are, as is well known, many other instances, all the remarks being unfavourable. However that may be, the privilege may be exercised and usually has its effect despite any distaste expressed (see eg Lord Griffiths' dissenting judgment in *A T & T Istel Ltd v Tully* [1992] 3 All ER 523 at 533, [1993] AC 45 at 58). Parliament has to some extent accepted a need to amend the law. There is s 31 of the Theft Act 1968 and s 72 of the Supreme Court Act 1981 (see *Istel* [1992] 3 All ER 523 at 530, [1993] AC 45 at 54). But the plea of privilege can still be invoked when there is a risk of prosecution for conspiracy. That is the position here.

Therefore, one arrives at the conclusion that, if an Anton Piller order drafted in the usual form is made against a defendant, the defendant can decline to comply if he can show that to comply may expose him to a risk of prosecution or conspiracy. (I do not now pause to consider the conflict between asserting the privilege and failing to comply with an order of the court.)

The situation has been so far recognised that the courts do not now make Anton Piller orders when the complaint against the defendant includes a conspiracy allegation. In *Tate Access Floors Inc v Boswell* [1990] 3 All ER 303 at 316, [1991] Ch 512 at 532 Browne-Wilkinson V-C said:

> 'But if, as is likely too often to be the case, there is a real risk of a conspiracy charge, the judge will not be able to make an Anton Piller order at all and in consequence vital evidence will be destroyed.'

Earlier in that case Browne-Wilkinson V-C said ([1990] 3 All ER 303 at 314, [1991] Ch 512 at 530):

> 'In the ordinary case, it is up to the defendant to put forward the claim to privilege. However, [*Rank Film Distributors Ltd v Video Information Centre* [1981] 2 All ER 76, [1982] AC 380] establishes that, where an ex parte order is sought which might in practice preclude the defendant from

raising the claim to privilege before the order is executed, the judge should not have made the ex parte order at all (see [1980] 2 All ER 273 at 286, 289, [1982] AC 380, 416, 419 per Bridge and Templeman LJJ). The Court of Appeal set aside the ex parte order and the House of Lords upheld their decision. Therefore, in any case in which the *Rank Film* decision applies, an Anton Piller order should not be made at all.'

IBM's advisers in this case well appreciated the difficulty of obtaining an Anton Piller order in this case in light of the authorities I have mentioned. No doubt they noted the particular circumstances in which orders were upheld in the *Istel* case. The situation in that case differs markedly from the situation here. Nevertheless an order was upheld in the *Istel* case despite an invoking of privilege because the defendant was regarded as being adequately protected against prosecution (see e g [1992] 3 All ER 523 at 541–542, [1993] AC 45 at 67 per Lord Lowry). One sees in the *Istel* case the involvement by letter of the Crown Prosecution Service.

There are then some observations of Lord Wilberforce in *Rank Film Distributors Ltd v Video Information Centre* [1981] 2 All ER 76 at 82, [1982] AC 380 at 443. He said:

'The appellants argued that, even if, in principle, the privilege against self-incrimination is capable of attaching in cases such as the present, that should not prevent the order for information and production being made; the defendant should be left to raise the question of privilege, if he wishes, and if necessary the court should rule on it. The difficulty is, however, that the orders are intended to take effect immediately on the arrival of the plaintiff's representatives (including, under existing practice, a solicitor) at the defendant's premises, and if the defendant were to refuse to comply, even in reliance on the privilege, he might, at least technically, be liable in contempt. I do not think that this problem is for this House to resolve. Attention can merely be drawn to it, and in due course, no doubt forms of order will be worked out which will enable the orders to be as effective as practicable while preserving the defendant's essential rights. All that this House can do is to decide that the privilege against self-incrimination is capable of being invoked. I would so decide.'

One sees there that Lord Wilberforce supposed that '... no doubt, forms of order will be worked out which will enable the orders to be as effective as practicable while preserving the defendant's essential rights'. In this situation the question is, as I see it, as follows. (A) Have the plaintiffs devised a form of order that (a) enables the plaintiffs to enter and search but (b) preserves the privilege of the second defendant? If the answer to that question is Yes then of course there will arise another question, (B) which is whether or not in operating the order the scheme of the order was truly and faithfully observed? Addressing question (A), one sees in particular proviso (ii) to para 1 of the order.

Mr Heslop appeared for IBM before Warner J. I am told that the risk of incrimination for conspiracy was well in mind. Warner J would have been perfectly well aware of the usual course of refusing an Anton Piller order when conspiracy is alleged. The learned judge was, I am told, content to accept proviso (ii) as shown in the copy before me with its handwritten amendments and additions. I understand that the judge was particularly concerned to add the handwritten words at the end of proviso (ii). So it was that the learned judge made the order.

The matter comes before me with the advantage of hearing argument for Mr Holloway. Mr Ashwell submitted persuasively that the order is not such an order as has ever been made and ought not to have been made. He relied, in particular, on the words of Browne-Wilkinson V-C in *Tate Access Floors Inc v Boswell* [1990] 3 All ER 303 at 314, [1991] Ch 512 at 530 that I have already quoted stressing the words, which I quote again: 'Therefore, in any case in which the *Rank Film* decision applies, an Anton Piller order should not be made at all.' However, it seems to me that that sentence (and the later sentence) must be taken in context (see [1990] 3 All ER 303 at 316, [1991] Ch 512 at 532). One notes that Browne-Wilkinson V-C is saying, as I understand, that an ex parte order should not be made if the order is an order 'which might in practice preclude the defendant from raising the claim to privilege before the order is executed' (see [1990] 3 All ER 303 at 314, [1991] Ch 512 at 530).

In my view, the order against Mr Holloway was not an order which in practice might have precluded him from raising privilege before the execution of the order. On the contrary, the clear meaning of proviso (ii) is that Mr Holloway was to be told of his right to claim privilege and that there was to be no execution of paras 1 to 4 of the order if privilege was claimed. Paragraphs 1 to 4 of the order are the only parts of the order relevant to a privilege claim by Mr Holloway.

My conclusion from the foregoing is that an Anton Piller order may properly be made in the terms of para 1 with its provisos. The order may be served but may not be executed until (a) the defendant is told of his privilege right and (b) the defendant then expressly declines to claim that right. In short, the order means that the supervising solicitor must say to the defendant, 'I have a search order but I cannot execute it if you tell me that the search may result in disclosing matters showing that you have been involved in a conspiracy'. It seems to me that the form of order adequately protects the defendant's privilege while at the same time allowing search if privilege is not claimed.

Of course that is not the end of the story. Defendants are bemused by the appearance of solicitors bearing 13-page orders in legal language. A supervising solicitor must ensure that the defendant properly understands his rights as preserved by the order, ie that there will be no entry if the defendant claims privilege and the meaning of privilege must be explained. Everyday language must be used—see proviso (i).

So the question is whether or not Mr Holloway adequately understood that he could refuse to permit an entry into Fairlight by invoking a claim of privilege. I note that there was no entry into Fairlight until 4.38 pm. Mr Holloway had been in conversation with either Mr Willoughby or Mr Rawlinson since 11.42 am. The reports by Messrs Willoughby and Rawlinson and in particular the affidavit of Mr Rawlinson sworn on 13 January 1994, together with the affidavit of Mr Holloway, must all be taken into consideration. I have quoted or summarised extensively from those documents above.

It would have been helpful to see the witnesses in person but neither side sought cross-examination. However, I feel able to assume that Mr Holloway is a businessman of some experience. In the circumstances, I am satisfied that Mr Rawlinson did adequately explain the position to Mr Holloway and Mr Holloway understood what was said to him. At the end of his affidavit Mr

Rawlinson says: 'I also believe that Mr Holloway understood my explanation of his right to rely on the privilege against self-incrimination.' I quote again these words from para 5 of Mr Rawlinson's affidavit:

'I explained to Mr Holloway that he was entitled to refuse to comply with paragraphs 1, 2 and 3 of the Order (contained on pages 4 to 5 of the Order) if he believed that to do so would be likely to expose him to a risk of a criminal prosecution.'

Thus I find that both my questions (A) and (B) are answered in the affirmative and so I decline to set aside paras 2, 3 and 4 of the order.

The notice of motion also seeks a setting aside of paras 13 and 16 of the order. I have already set them out above. Mr Ashwell submits that Mr Holloway is not obliged to comply with either of those paragraphs because compliance may expose him to the risk of prosecution.

In considering this submission it of course not necessary to consider the special wording of para 1 of the order. It is not too late now to consider a privilege claim as to paras 13 and 16. The information sought in para 13 is the same as that sought in para 16, save that para 16 includes the words 'and any property which represents any such sums'. The particular difference between the paragraphs is (a) that para 13 is directed to PDI and orders that PDI, by a director or other officer, give details of what has become of sums derived from the sale of IBM components, (b) that para 16 is directed to Mr Holloway himself as respects virtually the same information. In this situation it is convenient to take para 16 first. Mr Heslop said, as I understand, that to raise a plea of privilege as to para 16 there must be before the court an affidavit in which the privilege is claimed and in which the grounds for claiming privilege are set out. He referred to *Spokes v Grosvenor and West End Railway Terminus Hotel Co Ltd* [1897] 2 QB 124. If that is so, I think that Mr Holloway passes that test. First, there is Mr Holloway's affidavit sworn on 11 January 1994 in which he claims privilege.

There is then the fact that there are ample grounds for seeing that Mr Holloway is at risk to prosecution for conspiracy—so much appears from the evidence put in by IBM. The fact that the likely risk is shown by the plaintiff's rather than the defendant's evidence seems to me to be of no consequence if the defendant chooses to invoke privilege. Staughton LJ in *Sociedade Nacional de Combustiveis de Angola UEE v Lundqvist* [1990] 3 All ER 283 at 291–292, [1991] 2 QB 310 at 324, quoting from *R v Boyes* (1861) 1 B & S 311 at 330, [1861–73] All ER Rep 172 at 174, considers the standard of proof for a claim to privilege against self-incrimination. The theme for that standard is said to be:

'"... the Court must see, from the circumstances of the case and the nature of the evidence which the witness is called to give, that there is reasonable ground to apprehend danger to the witness from his being compelled to answer."'

Item (iii) of Staughton LJ's judgment reads:

'... if the fact of the witness being in danger be once made to appear, great latitude should be allowed to him in judging for himself of the effect of any particular question.'

In my opinion, the danger of a criminal prosecution has appeared from the evidence before me very plainly so latitude must be allowed to Mr Holloway. Looking at para 16 and, with the knowledge derived from the IBM's evidence, it seems to me that if Mr Holloway is properly to comply with para 16 he may be obliged to make known some important facts that bear on establishing whether or not he has acted criminally. Since that is so, I do not think that para 16 should be allowed.

The same applies to para 13 as respects Mr Holloway; but since para 13 is directed to PDI it may remain in the order with the qualification that PDI is not to require Holloway to be its representative for the purposes of complying with para 13.

I add that Mr Heslop said that the plea of privilege should not be allowed either as respects paras 13 or 16 because such information as would be forthcoming from a compliance with those paragraphs would not increase the risk of Mr Holloway being prosecuted having regard to what IBM already know. I am not satisfied that that is so.

Application dismissed.

Celia Fox   Barrister.

Re H (a minor) (guardian ad litem: requirement)

FAMILY DIVISION

BOOTH J

15, 16 MARCH 1993

Ward of court – Practice – Official Solicitor – Official solicitor appointed as guardian ad litem – Application by ward of court to continue proceedings without guardian ad litem – Whether ward having 'sufficient understanding' to participate in proceedings as a party without guardian ad litem – Whether appropriate for Official Solicitor to act as amicus curiae – Family Proceedings Rules 1991, r 9.2A.

In 1992 the parents of H, a 15-year-old boy, moved to France, having first made arrangements for H to stay with the family of R. About three months later R, who ran a dance academy which H attended, was arrested and charged with serious sexual offences against another boy. H however refused to live with his parents. As a result, H's parents commenced wardship proceedings and obtained orders granting them care and control of H, with leave to them to remove him to France, and an injunction restraining R from having any contact with H. The Official Solicitor was also appointed on his own application as guardian ad litem to H. The parents' attempt to keep H in France failed and he ran away and returned to England. Thereafter H totally rejected his parents, who believed that he was wholly under the influence of R. H, who was subsequently joined as a defendant in the wardship proceedings, later applied under r 9.2A[a] of the Family

---

a   Rule 9.2A, so far as material, provides: '(4) Where a minor … wishes to … defend the remaining stages of the proceedings without a … guardian ad litem, the minor may apply to the court for leave for that purpose and for the removal of the … guardian ad litem …

(6) … the court shall grant the leave sought [under para 4 above] and, remove the … guardian ad litem if it considers that the minor concerned has sufficient understanding to participate as a party in the proceedings concerned … without a … guardian ad litem.'

Proceedings Rules 1991 to continue the proceedings without the Official Solicitor acting as his guardian ad litem on the ground that he had 'sufficient understanding' to participate as a party to the proceedings without his assistance. In support of his application, H relied on the fact that, prior to their departure, his parents had considered that he had sufficient intellect to decide to remain in England, that recent school reports spoke highly of his academic ability and that when the case came to be determined he would be $15\frac{1}{2}$ years old. H's parents and the Official Solicitor opposed the application, contending that H was under the influence of R and his family and was unable to express his own independent views.

Held – When deciding whether a ward of court had sufficient understanding to participate as a party in proceedings, in the sense of being able to give instructions and make decisions as the need arose, the court would consider all the circumstances of the case in the light of what had already happened as well as what was likely to happen in the future course of the proceedings, without taking into account what it might or might not consider to be in the best interests of the child. In such circumstances, there was clearly a role for the Official Solicitor to play when removed from the post of guardian ad litem, and the role of amicus curiae should be extended to allow him to give the court independent and objective advice on the interests of the child. It would however be inappropriate for the Official Solicitor, when invited to take that role, to be joined as a party to the proceedings. On the facts, the court was satisfied that H's capacity to hold and express his own views had not been destroyed by R's influence and that fact, together with H's already high degree of involvement in the proceedings, meant that he had the necessary understanding to be allowed to participate in the proceedings without a guardian ad litem. The Official Solicitor would therefore be removed as guardian ad litem to H (who would then be allowed to instruct his own solicitors in the proceedings) and invited, subject to his consent, to act as amicus curiae (see p 765 d to f, p 766 h to p 767 d j to p 768 e g, post).

Re H (a minor) (care proceedings: child's wishes) [1992] 2 FCR 330 and dictum of Sir Thomas Bingham MR in *Re S (a minor) (independent representation)* [1993] 3 All ER 36 applied.

Notes

For role of Official Solicitor in family proceedings, see 5(2) *Halsbury's Laws* (4th edn) (reissue) paras 830–831.

Cases referred to in judgment

H (a minor) (care proceedings: child's wishes), Re [1992] 2 FCR 330.
S (a minor)(independent representation), Re [1993] 3 All ER 36, [1993] Fam 263, [1993] 2 WLR 801, CA.

Application

A 15-year-old ward of court, H, applied under r 9.2A of the Family Proceedings Rules, SI 1991/1247, to continue wardship proceedings, which had been brought on 16 June 1992 on the ex parte application of his parents whereupon they had been granted care and control of H, without the assistance of the Official Solicitor (who on 19 October 1992 had been appointed as H's guardian ad litem upon his own application) on the ground that he had 'sufficient understanding' to participate as a party in the proceedings. The application was heard and judgment was given in chambers. The case is reported by permission of Booth J. The facts are set out in the judgment.

Michael Lane (instructed by *Bates Wells & Braithwaite*, Sudbury) for the parents.
Richard Bond (instructed by the *Official Solicitor*) for the guardian ad litem.
Anthony J Kirk (instructed by *Gross & Co*) for H.

BOOTH J. This is an application by H, who was born on 6 January 1978, so he is now 15 years and 2 months of age. He is a ward of court. The originating summons was issued on 16 June 1992 by the plaintiffs, his parents. On 21 July 1992 the Official Solicitor was appointed on his own application to act as guardian ad litem for H. H was not then made a party to the proceedings. That, I think, must have been an oversight or misunderstanding of the procedures. He ultimately became a party on 19 October 1992, acting then through his guardian ad litem, the Official Solicitor. The application before me is that H be allowed to continue to defend the proceedings without the Official Solicitor acting as his guardian ad litem; in other words that the Official Solicitor be removed from that position according to r 9.2A(4) of the Family Proceedings Rules 1991, SI 1991/1247, as amended by SI 1992/456. That raises an issue as to whether H has sufficient understanding to participate in the proceedings without a guardian ad litem in accordance with r 9.2A(6).

This is an exceptional case. It is exceptional because of the facts which give rise to the proceedings. It is exceptional because the procedure so far followed has already allowed H to play a part far greater in the proceedings than is usual or desirable. He has, for example, sworn two affidavits, one of 25 September 1992 and one of 14 October 1992. He has written letters to a circuit judge and to the Official Solicitor's representative, and he has made an application to discharge or vary an injunction.

The basic facts are these. In 1984 the parents, H and his sister, a girl aged 13, moved to Bury St Edmunds. H had for long been interested in dancing and started to attend an academy of dancing run by R, a married man with two children and three foster children. In September 1991 H started to attend King Edward Grammar School and at the same time continued to attend the academy. Some time during 1990 or 1991 H's mother and father decided to move permanently to France. It became apparent that H did not want to leave Bury St Edmunds and arrangements were made for him to stay with the family of R and social services were informed of this arrangement.

In February 1992 the parents and sister went to France, H remaining in the home of R.

Early in May 1992 the parents were informed that social services had removed H from the home of R, who had been arrested and charged with serious sexual offences against another 14-year-old boy. R is now awaiting trial, which is to commence on 10 May 1993 in London on seven counts, including buggery and indecent assault. In May 1992 the mother and father removed H from England to France and wanted him to stay in that country with them. On 3 June he ran away and returned to England. That led to wardship proceedings being started on 16 June and orders were made on the ex parte application of the parents by which care and control of H was granted to the mother and father with leave to them to remove him to France. An injunction was made restraining R from having any contact with H. As a result of that order the parents took H to France. On 28 July H again ran away and returned to England. He has ever since remained here and eventually went to live with a Mr and Mrs P. On 5 August H took a large number of paracetamol tablets and immediately telephoned a friend. It is said that the reason he took the tablets was that he was worried that his parents would locate his whereabouts. He then became a patient of Dr Astel, a child and adolescent psychiatrist.

The present situation is that H continues to stay with Mr and Mrs P and to attend King Edward School. He has limited access to the academy but apparently there is no question of his going elsewhere for lessons or practice. Applications by R and by H himself for the discharge or variation of the injunction against R having contact with H have been refused. H now totally rejects his parents and his parents believe that H is wholly under the influence of R, his family and associates. The parents' view is shared by Dr Ian Weir, a consultant in child, adolescent and family psychiatry, instructed by the Official Solicitor. It is the view of Dr Weir that any relationship between H and R is highly detrimental to H. It is agreed however that H's future should be decided after the trial of R, which is due to start in May 1993, and the wardship originating summons will be set down for hearing on 5 July. The application to remove the Official Solicitor as guardian ad litem is opposed by the parents, who have been represented in it, and it is also opposed by the Official Solicitor who, too, is represented.

H has been present in court throughout the hearing and his case is presented by counsel, instructed by his solicitor. It is accepted on behalf of H that if the Official Solicitor is removed as guardian ad litem he should remain in the case as amicus and undertake the role requested of him by the court.

The approach to be taken by a court to an application such as this was fully canvassed by the Court of Appeal in *Re S (a minor) (independent representation)* [1993] 3 All ER 36, [1993] Fam 263. The test is clear. The court must be satisfied that H, in this instance, has sufficient understanding to participate as a party in the proceedings without a guardian ad litem. Participating as a party, in my judgment, means much more than instructing a solicitor as to his own views. The child enters the arena among other adult parties. He may give evidence and he may be cross-examined. He will hear other parties, including in this case his parents, give evidence and be cross-examined. He must be able to give instructions on many different matters as the case goes through its stages and to make decisions as the need arises. Thus a child is exposed and not protected in these procedures. It has yet to be determined how far the court has power, if it has any power, in such circumstances to deny a child access to the hearing. The child also will be bound to abide by the rules which govern other parties, including rules as to confidentiality.

Expert evidence was given in support of and in opposition to the application before me. Dr Astel supported it on behalf of H with a report dated 10 March and made with specific reference to this application. The doctor stated in that report that he was of the view that H had sufficient understanding to instruct his own solicitor and that it was important that H had (and in addition, the doctor said, feels he has) a conduit for expressing his views. The doctor said:

> 'I have gained the consistent impression from H in now many individual sessions that he has not felt that the Official Solicitor has expressed his own views. Having such a conduit will, in my opinion, help him feel that justice is being done, to accept and comply with provisions made for him and reduce the risk of rash and unwise actions.'

The doctor went on in that report, as he did during the course of his oral evidence, strongly to recommend the retention of the Official Solicitor in the proceedings, albeit not as guardian ad litem for H, but as an independent advisor to the court. Dr Astel said in the course of his evidence that he had seen H on some 17 sessions and repeated that he considered that H had sufficient understanding and that it was important that he should have his own say by his own counsel. I have to say that the doctor appeared to have little concept of what it meant for a child to be a party participating in proceedings. But he was clear in his view that H knew his own mind and was expressing his own views and not the views which have been planted in his mind by R. Dr Astel very fairly took the view that if, contrary to his opinion, H's mind had been substantially or wholly brainwashed by R, then his view of the situation as to H's independent representation would be different. Dr Weir took a very different view from Dr Astel. He first made a report to the Official Solicitor, a full report, on 7 January 1993, and in para 4 of that report said that despite H's physical maturity and intelligence:

> 'I would say that R has abused H's juvenile dependency over a period of
> years in order to achieve a situation in which he is largely in control of H's
> thoughts, feelings and actions.'

That evidence was the tenor of the oral evidence which Dr Weir gave to me. He took the view that H was not of sufficient understanding to participate as a party in these proceedings because, as the doctor put it, 'he is so powerfully under the influence of R and of his associates'.

The doctor took the view that he was not able to make a wise choice as to his future and did not see the dangers posed by R and the influence of R's family. Dr Weir also expressed the view that H had been given far too much freedom for his own good and had no ability to see the pros and cons of the situation.

There was no other oral evidence before me but Mr Kirk, on behalf of H, relied in support of the application upon affidavit evidence filed by the parents from which it is clear that, prior to their departure for France, they had taken the view that H was of sufficient intellect to decide to remain in England and they had accordingly left him here. Reliance is also placed upon up-to-date reports from the King Edward School which speak highly of H's academic ability there or indeed at any school he might attend. Reliance is placed upon the fact that H is now over the age of 15 and by the time that this case comes to be determined will be $15\frac{1}{2}$ years. Relied on in opposition to this application is not only the evidence of Dr Weir but also the report of the social services department of Suffolk County Council that was made on a direction given under s 37 of the Children Act 1989 to the effect that R and his family have greatly influenced H in the view of the social worker making that report.

The test as to whether a particular child has sufficient understanding to participate as a party in proceedings must, in my judgment, be considered in the light of all the circumstances of the case and in the light of what has already happened as well as what is likely to happen in the course of the proceedings in the future. In this case, while the evidence points to a strong influence by R and his family and associates upon H's views, it is impossible, as I judge it, on the evidence before me to find that the views that H presently holds are not his own to such an extent that he is not able to present them as his case. Adopting the words of Thorpe J in *Re H (a minor) (care proceedings: child's wishes)* [1992] 2 FCR 330 at 340: has that influence, I ask, been 'so intense as to destroy the capacity to give coherent and consistent instructions ?'

In my judgment, the evidence does not at this stage go that far, despite the opinion of Dr Weir. H has maintained a consistent view of what is in his best interests over many months, during which there is no evidence that he has had contact with R. To make a finding that H's ability to think for himself has been so far overborne by R in my judgment would be to run the risk of pre-judging on insufficient evidence an issue which may be crucial to the outcome of the case. I bear in mind, too, that H has already been involved in the proceedings to a much greater degree than is desirable for any child and considerable confusion has led to dubious procedures. It would now be artificial if H were not able to put his own case to the court and to test the evidence against it. The Official Solicitor has, quite properly, come to a view contrary to that of H as to what is in H's best interests but, in the circumstances of this case, it would be difficult, as I see it, for the Official Solicitor through his counsel to undertake the task of presenting H's case and testing the case against it to any great degree. Unless H is able to put his case, it is, I think, unlikely that he would accept any decision which was contrary to his wishes.

In those circumstances, I am satisfied that H has sufficient understanding to participate as a party in the proceedings and should be permitted to do so. It is not for this court, in applying that test, to take into account what the court may or may not consider to be in the best interests of the child.

The result of this decision will be that the Official Solicitor will cease to act as guardian ad litem and the question then arises what role, if any, should he continue to have in these proceedings. In *Re S (a minor)* Sir Thomas Bingham MR clearly envisaged that it would be open to the court in such circumstances to ask the solicitor for his continuing assistance as amicus. I refer to the particular passage of his judgment in which he said:

'The case does indeed cry out for the application of an objective, experienced judgment such as the Official Solicitor and those whom he consults are peculiarly well fitted to supply. Had the judge, surprisingly, decided to grant S's request, he would undoubtedly have sought the continuing assistance of the Official Solicitor as an amicus [for S], so the gain to S [that is of the Official Solicitor ceasing to act as S's guardian ad litem] might in any event have been small.' (See [1993] 3 All ER 36 at 47, [1993] Fam 263 at 280.)

I am told by Mr Bond representing the Official Solicitor, that the appointment of the Official Solicitor as amicus, in circumstances such as have arisen in this case, has already been made by a High Court judge in an as yet unreported case. It is however a new role for the Official Solicitor. Traditionally the role of amicus was fulfilled by counsel who advised the court at its request on questions of law and procedure and who was generally instructed by the Attorney General. The role did not extend to making independent investigations or calling evidence and indeed there is some doubt as to whether counsel acting as amicus could properly call evidence. An amicus does not have the right to appeal any decision of the court if the advice he tenders to the court is rejected. That is a very different role from that of the guardian ad litem, whose duty it is to represent the interests of the child, to make inquiries, to instruct expert witnesses and to present the child's case to the court. Clearly, there is a role for the Official Solicitor to play in those cases where a child is allowed to instruct his own solicitors and present his own case as there is such a role for a panel guardian ad litem, appointed in public law proceedings, who finds himself or herself in a situation when he or she is removed from that post. It may be of vital importance to the court to have independent and experienced assistance.

In this case I deem it to be so vital that such assistance is given to the court at the hearing of the originating summons in July. The Official Solicitor can assist with independent and objective advice and participation in what will be a sensitive and difficult confrontation between the child and his parents. He can instruct his own adviser and, as he has already instructed Dr Weir, it is important that that doctor's evidence should be placed before the court. The Official Solicitor can advise the court on points of law which may arise and he may more easily obtain the disclosure of documents, as for example, the documents relating to the criminal proceedings against R. The Official Solicitor can also advise in relation to the part to be taken by persons other than parties to the proceedings, again by way of example, R against whom there is an injunction in relation to the ward but who is not a party to the originating summons.

The role of amicus must, in my judgment, be extended now to cover the wide range of assistance which it may be appropriate for the Official Solicitor to give to the court in the light of the new procedures. In that role the Official Solicitor will be subject to the directions of the court and by its direction must be furnished with all necessary authority to carry out such investigations and inquiries as the court requires. He must receive all papers, reports and other documents in the case and must be able to apply for such directions and make such applications as he thinks fit. In that capacity however he acts not as guardian ad litem of the child. Although he may carry out similar inquiries with a view to advising on the child's best interests he does not represent the child. He is strictly in the position of an independent advisor to the court. That being so, I do not consider that it is appropriate for the Official Solicitor, when invited to act as amicus to be joined as a party to the proceedings.

It will only be in those difficult cases where the court needs such independent assistance that the Official Solicitor would be requested to act as amicus. In my judgment, it should be for him to decide whether or not to consent to do so. There may be cases when, contrary to the initial view of the court, he feels unable for one reason or another to assist, or he may feel that he can add little to the information already before the court. That is not a situation which is likely to occur with any frequency. Nevertheless, the Official Solicitor should not be deprived of the ability which he has always had of exercising his own judgment in relation to his appointment.

For those reasons, I will remove the Official Solicitor as guardian ad litem for H to enable H to instruct his own solicitors and through his solicitor and counsel present his case to the court, but I will invite the Official Solicitor, subject to his consent to do so, to act as amicus to the court.

Application allowed.

Carolyn Toulmin   Barrister

R v Deakin

COURT OF APPEAL, CRIMINAL DIVISION

FARQUHARSON LJ, McKINNON AND LAWS JJ

12, 15 APRIL 1994

Criminal evidence – Competence as witness – Mentally handicapped witness – Expert evidence as to mentally handicapped witness's competence – Expert evidence heard in presence of jury –Whether expert evidence of witness's capacity to tell the truth a question of admissibility – Whether expert evidence of witness's capacity to tell the truth should be heard by judge alone in absence of jury.

The appellant was charged with indecent assault upon the complainant, a 34-year-old woman with Downs Syndrome, who was living in a home for the mentally handicapped where the appellant was employed as a care assistant. Before the jury was empanelled the judge was invited to rule as to whether the complainant was competent to give evidence and adjourned the case in order to obtain psychologists' reports. Two psychologists found that the complainant was capable of telling the truth and the judge decided that the jury should hear their evidence. The judge directed the jury that in his opinion the complainant was a competent witness but that it was for them to decide whether or not her account was truthful. The appellant was convicted. He appealed, contending that the decision on the competence of the complainant to give evidence was a question of admissibility and so fell to be resolved by the judge in the absence of the jury and that the psychologists' testimony as to the complainant's competence should not have been given in the presence of the jury, since their acceptance of the complainant's account of events would have influenced the jury to accept it.

Held – The rule that the jury should hear all the evidence given in a case and that questions relating to the competence of a witness ought to be answered by the witness himself in the presence of the jury did not apply to expert evidence as to a witness's capacity to tell the truth, since such evidence turned on the question of admissibility and was a matter for the judge alone and would not assist the jury in deciding whether to accept his evidence by observing the manner of his answers to questions. In the circumstances, the calling of the psychologists in the presence of the jury was an irregularity but since the appellant had suffered no prejudice thereby no miscarriage of justice had occurred. The appeal would therefore be dismissed (see p 774 *j* to p 775 *d* and p 776 *a b e j*, post).

R v Reynolds [1950] 1 All ER 335 distinguished.

Notes

For competence of a witness under general incapacity, see 17 *Halsbury's Laws* (4th edn) paras 231–232.

For function of judge and jury in questions of admissibility, see ibid paras 22, 29, and for a case on the subject, see 15(2) *Digest* (2nd reissue) 523, 23530.

Cases referred to in judgment

Demirok v R (1977) 137 CLR 20, Aust HC.

R v Dunne (1930) 21 Cr App R 176, CCA.
R v Norbury (1992) Times, 7 May, CCA .
R v Reynolds [1950] 1 All ER 335, [1950] 1 KB 606, CCA.
R v Robinson (Raymond) (1993) Times, 25 November, CCA.

Cases also cited or referred to in skeleton arguments
R v Galbraith [1981] 2 All ER 1060, [1981] 1 WLR 1039, CA.
R v Hayes [1977] 2 All ER 288, [1977] 1 WLR 234, CA.
R v Yacoob (1981) 72 Cr App R 313, CA.

Appeal against conviction
Richard Albin Deakin appealed with the leave of the full court (Nolan LJ, Tuckey and Latham JJ) granted on 12 October 1993 against his conviction in the Crown Court at Birmingham on 4 June 1992 before Simon Brown J and a jury by a majority of ten to two of indecent assault, contrary to s 14(1) of the Sexual Offences Act 1956, for which he was sentenced to three years' imprisonment. The facts are set out in the judgment of the court.

Timothy Barnes QC and *Richard Martin* (assigned by the *Registrar of Criminal Appeals*) for the appellant.
Mark Eades (instructed by the *Crown Prosecution Service*, Stafford) for the Crown.

Cur adv vult

15 April 1994. The following judgment of the court was delivered.

FARQUHARSON LJ. On 2 June 1992 the defendant appeared before Simon Brown J in the Crown Court at Birmingham. He was then facing an indictment containing three charges: the first, alleged rape, the second, indecent assault and the third, unlawful sexual intercourse with a mental defective.

During the course of the trial the judge directed acquittals on counts 1 and 3 because he was not satisfied that penetration of the complainant had been proved. On 4 June 1992 the jury convicted him on count 2. All the charges have been founded on the same incident which took place on 25 May 1991. At that time the complainant was 34 years of age. She suffered from Downs Syndrome and was living in a home for the mentally handicapped in Stafford. She occupied, with three others, accommodation which was separate from the main building and intended for the use of patients who, to a limited degree, were able to look after themselves. The appellant was employed at the home as a care assistant. The case for the prosecution depended on the complainant's evidence, supported to some degree by the medical and scientific evidence. The complainant's account was in general terms as follows: namely that at some time between 7 pm and 8.30 pm on the evening of 25 May, the appellant had gone to 1 North Avenue and made his way to the complainant's bedroom. He there committed a series of indecent assaults upon the complainant. The latter described how the appellant had handled her breasts, placed his penis in her mouth and in her genital area. The complainant did not tell any of the other staff of these events that evening. It was on 26 May that another member of staff thought that her behaviour was strange and observed blood on her face. In answer to questions, the complainant gave the account set out above. She was examined on 28 May by Dr Haig-Ferguson who found that she had bruises above her right eye, cheek and forehead. There was no damage to her genitalia.

Stains were found on the duvet cover from her bedroom which were found, in turn, to come from semen. A blood sample was taken from the appellant and a DNA analysis was carried out. The scientist's evidence was that there was more than a 500,000:1 chance that the semen on the duvet cover had come from the appellant. As the defence pointed out, however, it could not be established that the semen stain was caused on 25 May without relying on the evidence of the complainant.

It was the defence case that the appellant had not been guilty of any indecency. He agreed during the interview by the police that he had gone to the complainant's room on the evening of 25 May and indulged in what can be described as a certain amount of horseplay. The complainant is an affectionate woman and certain incidents of tickling and the like had occurred between them. In his interview the appellant had told the police that he might have gone just a bit over the top. It was a rule of the home that male staff should not enter unaccompanied the bedrooms of female patients.

The case was first listed for trial before Blofeld J on 26 March 1992. Before a jury was empanelled the judge was invited to give a ruling as to whether the complainant was competent to give evidence, bearing in mind her mental handicap. It was submitted that the judge should have followed the usual practice of satisfying himself of the complainant's competence by putting the necessary questions to her when she came to be sworn before the jury. The judge declined to take that course saying that in the case of a witness suffering from Downs Syndrome it was necessary that he should have a report before him from one or more psychologists. The case was accordingly adjourned. When it was relisted before Simon Brown J there were two reports available to the judge from consultant psychologists, namely Mr Paul Britton and Mrs Dawes-Gamble.

In general terms, the psychologists were in agreement that the complainant was competent to give evidence, but might become upset if questions were put to her suggesting she was lying or was in some other respect at fault. The defence disputed the complainant's competence and submitted that any question on that issue should be put to her in the presence of the jury. It was conceded that the decision whether she should give evidence was for the judge to make, but Mr Barnes QC argued that any questions to the consultant psychologists on this issue should be put in the absence of the jury.

This argument was buttressed by the fact that there were a number of serious inconsistencies in the complainant's account of events which it is necessary to set out.

First, she complained at one point that the appellant had indecently assaulted her 'lots of times', and on other occasions that he had done so only once before and that her complaints had been ignored. Members of the staff said that there had been no previous complaints, otherwise they would, of course, have been investigated.

Secondly, that on the night in question the appellant had struck her with a broomstick, and that a member of the staff had entered the room and taken the stick away. The complainant asserted that she had reported the assault to a senior officer at the home on the same evening. Both these allegations were denied by those concerned.

Thirdly, that the appellant had made further indecent assaults upon her on the following day, 26 May, which was inconsistent with other evidence adduced by the prosecution.

The judge heard submissions on the issue of whether the psychologists should give evidence in the absence or in the presence of the jury. In the result he decided that the jury should hear the evidence of the psychologists as well as the complainant. After the evidence had been given, the judge decided that the complainant was a competent witness. He was careful to explain to the jury the limitations of that decision. He said:

> 'It is not, it seems to me, appropriate or desirable to give a reasoned decision, but I have come to a clear conclusion on the matter. I hold that this complainant is a competent witness. That merely means, and I have in effect said as much to the jury already, that in my opinion I have been required to form a present judgment on the point. I believe she has the capability of giving a rational and truthful account, but that, let me make superabundantly plain, does not begin to prejudge the ultimate question which is, will she be giving a truthful account, and that is absolutely and exclusively for you to decide and I shall direct you about that later. I merely decide that the case goes ahead on the footing that her evidence is properly fit to be heard and assessed by you the jury. Do you follow that? I am sure you do.'

It is this issue which is the subject of the first ground of appeal. The thrust of the argument on behalf of the appellant is that the judge's decision on the competency of the complainant to give evidence was, in reality, a question of admissibility. Like all questions of admissibility of evidence, it fell to be resolved by the judge in the absence of the jury. Mr Barnes accepts that the posing of the necessary questions to the witness as to her understanding of the need to tell the truth must take place in the presence of the jury. The law on that point is well established. But counsel argues that the same considerations do not apply to evidence of third parties testifying as to a witness's competence. While the jury will be assisted by hearing a witness's answers to questions about her understanding of the truth when it comes to assess the witness's credibility, the same considerations do not apply to third parties. Mr Barnes asks forensically what the purpose would be of calling the evidence of the psychologists before the jury, as their evidence is not relevant to any issue that the jury have to resolve. As a general rule, the evidence of one witness, however expert, as to the credibility of another will not be admitted. In effect the psychologists' evidence was directed not to the complainant's credibility but to her competence to give truthful evidence. Both witnesses when giving their evidence were careful not to go beyond their remit. A few illustrations from the transcript of their evidence makes this clear.

Mr Paul Britton (the first psychologist) was asked by the judge:

> 'Q. In your opinion is she capable of distinguishing between fact and fiction, between truth and lies? A. She is if she is asked with sufficient patience, if language is used that is appropriate for her level of

understanding ... I do believe that she understands that it is important that she tells the truth here today.'

In cross-examination, he was asked:

'Q. Is she capable of giving a truthful account? A. She is capable of giving a truthful account, Yes. She is, however—it is possible to confuse her if one if one wanted to.
Q. Is she capable of making things up? A. Oh Yes.'

Later there is this exchange:

'Q. She is, Mr Britton, can we agree this, severely handicapped? A. 'I find her to be severely handicapped, Yes.'

Then appears the passage:

'I think that she would be distressed because she would feel that you were saying that you believed that she was telling lies. I don't think, as I indicated previously, she fully understands the role of the court, so there would be some personal distress for her, but if the matter was pursued, as I say, with patience and sensitivity, I know of no reason why you would not be able to explore those matters.'

And this answer:

'... I am still confident she is able to tell the truth. I am not saying she will. I am saying that she is able to tell the truth.'

Later, the witness says:

'On occasions she would give answers to questions that were contradictory to answers that she had given previously, but overall I am quite content that she is capable of knowing the difference between right and wrong and telling the truth and telling lies.'

While recognising that these citations are taken out of context, it is clear that the experts are not giving any opinion as to the complainant's credibility. Mr Barnes recognises that the two psychologists did not step over this line when giving their evidence and accepts that the judge's warning to the jury cited above was both fair and clear. However, counsel asserts that the impression must have been given to the jury that the psychologists were of the opinion that the complainant's account was truthful. He supports this submission by pointing out that their evidence was given on the basis of interviews with the complainant, each of some four hours in length, when the complainant's account of the alleged assault must have been the sole topic. The jury would then readily infer from the psychologists' opinion that they accepted the complainant's account and would themselves accept it however unconvincing her evidence was in the witness box. While recognising that it was a matter for the judge's discretion whether he heard the evidence of the psychologists in the absence of the jury, on the facts of this case the discretion could only be exercised in one way, that is to say consistently with his submissions that on a question of admissibility the jury should not hear the evidence.

The difficulty that lies in the way of the appellant's argument is the decision of this court in R v Reynolds [1950] 1 All ER 335, [1950] 1 KB 606.

There, the accused was charged with an indecent assault on a girl aged 11. The question arose whether she was fit to be sworn. In the absence of the jury a school attendance officer gave evidence of the background of the child. The court held that this amounted to a material irregularity and quashed the conviction. Lord Goddard CJ, giving the judgment of the court, said ([1950] 1 All ER 335 at 337, [1950] 1 KB 606 at 610):

'No member of this court has ever known of a case in which a witness has been called to inform the court whether or not a child is fit to give evidence. I am not saying that there may not be cases—perhaps this was one—in which the judge or chairman may want some such assistance, especially if he hears that the child is at a particular sort of school. It is not on that ground that the court thinks that there has been a fatal mistake here. The reason why the court decided in *R. v. Dunne* ((1930) 21 Cr App R 176) that the evidence of the child must be given in the presence of the jury was because, although the duty of deciding whether the child may be sworn or not lies on the judge and is not a matter for the jury, it is most important that the jury should hear the answers which the child gives and see her demeanour when she is questioned by the court, for that enables them to come to a conclusion as to what weight they should attach to her evidence. If that be the reason why the court in *R. v. Dunne* held that it was essential that the evidence should be given in the presence of the jury, it is *a fortiori* so, it seems to me, when some witness is called to assist the court by relating his experience of the child and the impression he may have formed of her. The jury then would have all the facts before them with regard to the child's truthfulness or reputation for truthfulness ... It should be regarded as most exceptional that any evidence should be given in a criminal trial not in the presence of the jury.'

That decision has been followed many times in the 40 years since it was given, but was criticised in an Australian case, *Demirok v R* (1977) 137 CLR 20 at 31, where Gibbs J said:

'If evidence which the judge has to consider on the voir[e] dire in deciding a question of competence or admissibility is likely to be prejudicial to the accused, it should be received in the absence of the jury.'

It is evident from the transcript of the submissions made on this issue that the judge considered the point to be a difficult one. As already stated, he decided that the evidence of the psychologists should be given before the jury. He gave no reasons for his decision, but he may well have been influenced by the decision in *R v Reynolds* [1950] 1 All ER 335, [1950] 1 KB 606.

With diffidence we have come to the conclusion that in the circumstances of this case the evidence should have been heard in the absence of the jury for the following reasons.

(1) Questions of admissibility of evidence are for the judge to decide.

(2) If, after hearing the evidence and the submissions on the issue in the presence of the jury, the judge decides against admitting the evidence in question, the jury would have difficulty in excluding from their mind the evidence which the judge had ruled out. In the present case, this consideration was not significant as the prosecution would not have

proceeded if the judge had decided not to admit the evidence of the complainant.

(3) The rule, if it be a rule, that the jury should hear all the evidence given in a case does not here apply because at the time the evidence of the psychologists was given, the complainant was not a witness. It was of course only after hearing the evidence that the judge was able to rule on the complainant's competence to give evidence.

(4) While acknowledging that it is right in law that questions relating to the competence of the witness in question should be answered by the witness himself in the presence of the jury, different considerations arise in relation to the evidence given by 'third party' experts. In the former case, the jury may be assisted in deciding whether to accept the evidence of the complainant by observing the manner of his or her answers to the judge's questions. The evidence of the experts is in an altogether different category.

(5) The jury would not be assisted in deciding the issue before them by hearing the expert evidence, which was concerned with the capacity of the complainant to tell the truth. As Mr Barnes put it in argument, 'What good would it do?'

In *Demirok v R* the court was able to dispose of the decision in *R v Reynolds* by saying that it had not settled the practice in Australia even if it had done so in England. That course is not open to us, but we think that the decision can be readily distinguished from the present case. The issue before the court in *Reynolds* was whether the child complainant was fit to be sworn. The judge heard the evidence of the school attendance officer concerning the background of the child, particularly of her home and her school. The judge then ruled that the child should be sworn. It was not a 'competence' case save to the extent that the issue was whether the child understood the meaning of taking the oath. The present case is different, the evidence being directed to the capacity of the complainant to tell the truth. Furthermore there is no parallel between a lay witness giving evidence of a child's background, which would have no relevance to the question which the jury had to decide, and the expert psychologists concerned with the witness's competence.

We have had drawn to our attention two comparatively recent decisions of this court where it appears that the judge heard evidence of a child's competence in the absence of the jury. In *R v Norbury* (1992) Times, 7 May the evidence was given by a social worker and by police officers who had been present when the complainant (a child of six) was interviewed. The judge also looked at videotapes of those interviews. He made his own inquiries of the child in court in accordance with the usual practice. The judge ruled that the child's evidence should not be given on oath but admitted under s 38(1) of the Children and Young Persons Act 1933. No point appears to have been taken about the propriety of the relevant evidence being heard by the judge in the absence of the jury.

In *R v Robinson* (1993) Times, 25 November an educational psychologist was called to give evidence on the voire dire to determine whether the complainant (aged 15) was a competent witness in view of her mental retardation. The case concerned a different point, but once again there was no challenge to the witness giving such evidence at that stage.

While it hardly amounts to a practice, these examples show that expert evidence of the kind with which we are concerned is heard on the voire dire.

We feel justified therefore in drawing a distinction between expert evidence and that tendered in R v Reynolds.

Accordingly, we conclude that the calling of the two educational psychologists to give their evidence in the presence of the jury amounted to an irregularity. The further question is whether it is a material irregularity within the meaning of s 2(1) of the Criminal Appeal Act 1968.

It is quite clear from the passages already cited that in giving their evidence the two psychologists were careful not to usurp the role of the judge and to confine themselves to the area of their own expertise. Moreover, the judge in his ruling carefully explained to the jury their role in the case. On this basis it is difficult to see what prejudice the appellant suffered as a result of the jury hearing this evidence. Mr Barnes felt it incumbent upon him to cross-examine the experts before the jury about the shortcomings of the complainant's account of the alleged assault and the inconsistencies already referred to, to see if the experts had given sufficient weight to those matters in their assessment of the complainant's capacity to tell the truth. That was a professional decision which we do not criticise but, as Mr Eades points out these matters were opened up at the instance of the defence.

However that may be, Mr Barnes argues, as already pointed out, that the jury may well have drawn the conclusion that the experts believed that the complainant was telling the truth. After giving careful consideration to these arguments and to the factors which have already been cited, we feel that there was no prejudice to the appellant in the jury hearing the evidence of the experts, and we hold that there was here no material irregularity. Even if we are wrong about this, we would have no hesitation in applying the proviso of s 2 of the 1968 Act.

Two further points were raised by Mr Barnes. He complains that the judge gave him no opportunity to make submissions on the effect of the expert evidence after it had been given. He argues that it was incumbent upon the prosecution to prove that the complainant was a competent witness and he should have been permitted to address the arguments at that stage. We do not feel that there is much substance in this complaint. The matter had been argued before the judge at great length at an earlier stage on the basis of the experts' reports, and it is difficult to see that further arguments would have added anything.

Mr Barnes also contended that the judge should have withdrawn the indecent assault count from the jury, as he had the other two counts, at the end of the prosecution case. Without entering into a further review of the evidence, in our judgment the combination of the complainant's evidence with all its imperfections and the DNA analysis, together with the statements of the appellant during his interviews with the police, entitled the judge to take the course he did of leaving that count to the jury. The appeal is therefore dismissed.

Appeal dismissed.

Carolyn Toulmin   Barrister

Pounds v Pounds

COURT OF APPEAL, CIVIL DIVISION

NEILL, HOFFMANN AND WAITE LJJ

31 JANUARY, 1, 2, 24 FEBRUARY 1994

Divorce – Financial provision – Consent order – Consent order approved by registrar before decree nisi – Order sealed subsequent to decree nisi but dated prior to decree nisi – Whether consent order valid – Whether consent order to be amended under the slip rule – RSC Ord 42, r 3(2).

Following the breakdown of the marriage and in anticipation of a decree nisi being granted the husband and wife negotiated a 'clean break' settlement by which all future maintenance claims on either side were to be extinguished in return for the husband's surrender of his interest in the former matrimonial home. The agreement was placed before the registrar, who accepted that it was suitable for incorporation into a clean break consent order dismissing all financial claims on both sides. The registrar accordingly initialled the order, but it was not at that point drawn up. The decree nisi was duly pronounced and a month later the court issued a perfected and sealed order. As a result of a clerical error the order had been dated the day the registrar approved and initialled the draft consent order and not the day when the order was sealed. Shortly thereafter the wife changed her mind about the agreement and consulted new solicitors, who applied to set aside the order on the ground that it was a nullity since it carried a date antecedent to that of the decree nisi. The judge held (i) that the registrar had no power on a date before decree nisi to direct that the order should be made on a date subsequent to decree nisi, (ii) that a consent order was only valid if some 'judicial act' (such as a fresh consideration by the registrar) had intervened on or after the date of decree nisi and (iii) that the order was a nullity which could not be amended under RSC Ord 20, r 11[a] (the slip rule) and would therefore be set aside. The husband appealed.

Held – A district judge in a special procedure undefended divorce where the pronouncement of the decree nisi was still pending had power under RSC Ord 42, r 3(2)[b] to approve a draft financial consent order in advance of the decree nisi and to direct that the order should take effect at a date on or after the day on which the decree nisi was to be pronounced. Moreover, the judge's approval of the draft order was the only judicial act required to validate the consent. In particular, there was neither the scope nor the necessity for any judicial act' or fresh appraisal of the merits of the order after decree nisi, since the approval it had received was a continuing one and the only further step required was that the order should be drawn up and sealed and given its true date, the sealing date. If through inadvertence the date of the order was stated to be the date of the judge's approval of the draft order rather than the date of sealing, that error could be corrected under the slip rule. It followed that the consent order had been validly made and that the order would be amended

_____

a   Rule 11 is set out at p 784 *d*, post

b   Rule 3(2), so far as material, is set out at p 784 *b c*, post

under the slip rule by inserting the date of sealing in place of the date of the registrar's approval of the draft order. The appeal would accordingly be allowed (see p 782 *j* to p 783 *e*, p 784 *e f*, p 790 *g* to *j*, p 791 *e* to *g*, p 792 *a* to *e* and p 793 *c*, post).

Board (Board intervening) v Checkland [1987] 2 FLR 257 and *Munks v Munks* [1985] FLR 576 considered.

Notes

For consent orders embodying spouses' agreement on financial provisions, see 13 *Halsbury's Laws* (4th edn) para 1158.

For amendment of accidental mistakes in orders, see 37 *Halsbury's Laws* (4th edn) para 279.

Cases referred to in judgments

Board (Board intervening) v Checkland [1987] 2 FLR 257, CA.

Camm v Camm (1982) 4 FLR 577, CA.

Day v Day [1979] 2 All ER 187, [1980] Fam 29, [1979] 2 WLR 681, CA.

Edgar v Edgar [1980] 3 All ER 887, [1980] 1 WLR 1410, CA.

Hyman v Hyman [1929] AC 601, [1929] All ER Rep 245, HL.

Keystone Knitting Mills' Trade Mark, Re [1929] 1 Ch 92, [1928] All ER Rep 276 CA.

Livesey (formerly Jenkins) v Jenkins [1985] 1 All ER 106, [1985] AC 424, [1985] 2 WLR 47, HL.

Munks v Munks [1985] FLR 576, CA.

Appeal

By notice of appeal dated 2 August 1993, Malcolm Pounds (the husband appealed from the decision of Singer J made on 20 April 1993 whereby he allowed an application by the respondent, Valerie Pounds (the wife), to set aside a clean break consent order bearing the purported date of 11 December 1990 and made in divorce proceedings by Mr Registrar Elliott sitting at the Northampton County Court on the ground that, as it bore a date antecedent to that of the decree nisi, it was made without jurisdiction. The facts are set out in the judgment of Waite LJ.

Peter Duckworth (instructed by *Max Engel & Co*, Northampton) for the husband.
Ellen Solomons (instructed by *Toller Hales & Collcutt*, Wellingborough) for the wife.

Cur adv vul

24 February 1994. The following judgments were delivered.

WAITE LJ (giving the first judgment at the invitation of Neill LJ). This appeal arises from the efforts of a husband and wife after marriage breakdown to achieve a 'clean break' settlement of their financial claims. Like most couples their principal asset was the home they had once both lived in and still jointly owned. Their solicitors, with the help (on the wife's side) of counsel, were able to negotiate an agreement under which all future maintenance claims on either side were to be extinguished in return for the husband's surrender of his interest in the matrimonial home, so that the whole of it would become the wife's sole property.

So long as that bargain remained an out-of-court agreement, it would be impossible to claim for it the finality which both sides hoped to achieve. The common law will not enforce, and statute law renders void, any provision in an agreement purporting to restrict rights to apply to a court for an order giving financial relief. Far from being clean, the break would become liable to a painful rejoining if either side, whether because of second thoughts or because of changed circumstances, became dissatisfied with the bargain. The only safe way of making their agreement watertight would be to incorporate it in an order of the court. It would then become immutable save in the event of a radical change of circumstance, or of one party's consent to it being later found to have been obtained through the other's fraud or material non-disclosure. The couple's solicitors therefore negotiated a draft order giving the court's approval of the agreement. Two matters had to be resolved, however, before the necessary consent order could be obtained.

One related to timing. Ever since divorce was introduced into our legal system in 1857, it has been an absolute requirement that no order for permanent (as opposed to interim) financial support can be made until the decree nisi has been pronounced. The purpose, no doubt, was to avoid any step that might hinder a reconciliation, for which the door would need to be kept open until the moment of decree. The value of such a requirement is still recognised, as can be seen from Lord Mackay LC's consultation paper *Looking to the Future: Mediation and the ground for divorce* (Cm 2424), which proposes to retain it in principle, while for the first time introducing a power to dispense with it in 'special circumstances' (see Pt 6, para D20).

The other related to proof of the fairness of the agreement. In most areas of our law, parties to litigation who are sui juris and independently advised can settle their differences on terms which are included by agreement in an order or rule of court (so as to be enforceable thereafter through the court process without the necessity to start fresh proceedings) with the authority of a judge who may not be aware of the terms of the deal at all (for example, when they are indorsed on counsel's brief), still less be concerned with any question as to their suitability or fairness. That is not so in financial proceedings between husband and wife, where the court does not act, it has been said, as rubber stamp. The judge will be concerned, whether the order be made by consent or imposed after argument, to be satisfied that the criteria of ss 25 and 25A of the Matrimonial Causes Act 1973 have been duly applied.

When in this case the spouses' solicitors came to court to have their agreement approved, it was appreciated by everyone that effect could not be given to such approval there and then. This was because the decree nisi had not yet been pronounced, and was not due to be pronounced until a few days later. Nevertheless the registrar (or district judge as he would now be called), who already had in his possession the court file containing the affidavits of means of the parties and who had been supplied that day with the statutory particulars designed to enable the compromise to be judged in the light of the s 25 and 25A criteria, felt able to say that the agreement was a suitable one for incorporation into a clean break consent order dismissing all financial claims on both sides. The registrar accordingly initialled the order, but it was not at that point drawn up. The decree nisi was duly pronounced a few days later, and then a month passed before the order was produced by the court in its final form as a perfected and sealed order. The date appearing on the perfected order was not the date of its sealing. The court official had assigned to it the date of the occasion when the proceedings had last been before the registrar that is to say the day on which he had approved and initialled the draft consent order. No one at that stage noticed that there was anything amiss.

Not long afterwards the wife changed her mind about the agreement. She changed her solicitors too. They were quick to spot that the consent order carried a date antecedent to that of the decree nisi. Before Singer J they contended successfully that the order was consequently a nullity. The judge ruled that there was no possibility of amending it under the slip rule, and set it aside on the ground that it had been made without jurisdiction. That opened the way for the wife to assert that the original agreement was not binding on her, and that it should now be set aside because its terms were unjust. Consequent evidence and argument about the fairness of the original agreement, the quality of the advice given to the wife by her former solicitor and the terms of any new order which should be made by the judge if he thought the original agreement was unjust, extended the length of the hearing substantially. In the upshot, the judge ruled that the original agreement had been unjust, on the ground that there was such a disparity between the income and pension rights of the husband and the modest earning powers and expectations of the wife as to make it an unsuitable case for any clean break order at all. The wife should not therefore be held to it, and a fresh order should be made to include provision for periodic maintenance for the wife which would keep her future maintenance claims alive.

The appellant husband now contends, in this court, that the judge was wrong on both counts.

Before describing in more detail the circumstances in which the impugned order was made, it will be useful to look at the procedural background, which was helpfully explained by counsel in the course of their clear and well-researched submissions.

The nature and function of the special procedure for undefended divorce

In outward form English divorce law still does its best to emphasise the institutional solemnity of marriage by insisting that it can be ended only by a judicial pronouncement, and that the terms of any financial compromise accompanying or following divorce are judicially approved. In practice procedural corners have had to be cut in the interests of saving time, expense and heartache within a system that has to accommodate more than 150,000 unopposed divorce petitions annually.

One such development has been the enlargement of what began as a 'special' procedure until it became the norm for most unopposed divorces. It still bears the superficial hallmarks of a full-scale judicial process, in that the proceedings are spoken of as a 'cause' and there is reference in the rules to their outcome as a 'trial'. Closer inspection reveals that such descriptions have more pageantry than substance. Although the special procedure as now laid down by the Family Proceedings Rules 1991, SI 1991/1247, does not greatly differ, I will refer, in summarising it, to the rules which were in operation at the dates in 1990 and 1991 relevant to the present case, namely the former

Matrimonial Causes Rules 1977, SI 1977/344 (as amended), and I will refer to he district judge by his then title of registrar.

Following presentation of the petition, the petitioner's solicitor lodges an application for 'directions for trial' together with a standard affidavit in the form required to verify the particular ground alleged in the petition. In routine cases (ie where no problem of costs or of approving arrangements for the children arises) the registrar gives 'directions for trial' by entering the cause in he special procedure list and thereafter considers the evidence filed by the petitioner. If he is satisfied that the petitioner has sufficiently proved the contents of the petition and is entitled to the decree sought and any costs prayed for, he will make and file a certificate to that effect. The court then sends notification to the parties of the date, time and place fixed for the pronouncement of the decree nisi. The parties are also told that their attendance at the pronouncement of decree is not necessary. The actual process of pronouncement of the decree has become reduced to a very brief ceremony of a purely formal character in which decrees are listed together in batches for a collective mention in open court before a judge who speaks (or nods) his assent. The right to a decree absolute six weeks thereafter is automatic, on the application of either party. (A more detailed summary of the procedure will be found in *Rayden and Jackson on Divorce* (16th edn, 1991) p 334.)

The procedures for dissolution of marriage on unopposed petitions in England have thus become truncated over the years to the point that the sole truly judicial function in the entire process is that of the registrar when granting his certificate. Everything that follows is automatic and administrative, and the open court pronouncement of the decree is a pure formality, to which the pronouncing judge (who under current procedures may himself be a district judge) has no option but to consent. If any party attends the ceremony of pronouncement and objects, the judge's powers are accordingly limited to directing that the petition shall be stood out of the pronouncement list, to enable some substantive application to be made to vary or discharge the registrar's certificate (see *Day v Day* [1979] 2 All ER 187, [1980] Fam 29).

Financial consent orders

When the House of Lords ruled in *Livesey (formerly Jenkins) v Jenkins* [1985] 1 All ER 106, [1985] AC 424 that the duty of disclosure of assets was owed by spouses not only to each other but to the court, it did so upon the basis that it was the function of the court in every case, whether it was proceeding by consent of the parties or after a contested hearing, to be satisfied that the provision made by the order fulfilled the criteria laid down by s 25 of the 1973 Act. It is clear, however, that this was intended to be an assertion of general principle only, and not to impose on the court the need to scrutinise in detail the financial affairs of parties who came to it for approval of an independently negotiated bargain. It could not be otherwise, for earlier that year Parliament had specifically enacted a more cursory regime for the scrutiny of consent orders. Section 7 of the Matrimonial and Family Proceedings Act 1984 inserted into the 1973 Act a new section, s 33A, of which sub-s (1) reads as follows:

> 'Notwithstanding anything in the preceding provisions of this Part of this Act, on an application for a consent order for financial relief the court

may, unless it has reason to think that there are other circumstances into which it ought to inquire, make an order in the terms agreed on the basis only of the prescribed information furnished with the application.'

The 'prescribed information' is that required by r 76A of the 1977 rules (now re-enacted and amended by r 2.61 of the 1991 rules), which provides:

'(1) ... there shall be lodged with every application for a consent order ... two copies of a draft of the order in the terms sought, one of which shall be endorsed with a statement signed by the respondent to the application signifying his agreement, and a statement of information (which may be made in more than one document) which shall include—(a) the duration of the marriage, the age of each party and of any minor or dependent child of the family; (b) an estimate in summary form of the approximate amount or value of the capital resources and net income of each party and of any minor child of the family; (c) what arrangements are intended for the accommodation of each of the parties and any minor child of the family (d) whether either party has remarried or has any present intention to marry or to cohabit with another person ... (f) any other especially significant matters ...'

Forms for use in supplying those particulars were prescribed by practice direction: the form in force for present purposes being that annexed to the *Practice Direction (divorce: consent orders: statement of information)* [1990] 1 All EF 382, [1990] 1 WLR 150. They run to no more than two pages, and the space allowed in the boxes for financial information is very restricted indeed.

The effect of s 33A and the rules and directions made under it is thus to confine the paternal function of the court when approving financial consent orders to a broad appraisal of the parties' financial circumstances as disclosed to it in summary form, without descent into the valley of detail. It is only if that survey puts the court on inquiry as to whether there are other circumstances into which it ought to probe more deeply that any further investigation is required of the judge before approving the bargain that the spouses have made for themselves. It is interesting to note that although this statutory limitation might be thought to provide an exception to the principle asserted in *Livesey (formerly Jenkins) v Jenkins* [1985] 1 All ER 106, [1985] AC 424 it was not apparently so regarded by the House of Lords, where Lord Brandon preferred to describe it as a 'step in the right direction' (see [1985] 1 All ER 106 at 118, [1985] AC 424 at 444).

The timing of consent orders

It is common ground that the effect of a financial consent order is to exercise one or more of the powers under ss 23 or 24 of the 1973 Act. Those powers are only capable of being exercised 'On granting a decree ... or at any time thereafter'. The effect of these words is to deny jurisdiction to the court to make a consent order at any date before the pronouncement of decree nisi (we have already indicated in the course of argument our rejection of M Duckworth's submission that this temporal limit was in any way abated by s 33A so as to authorise consent orders taking effect before the date of decree).

The obtaining of a financial consent order, like that of a decree nisi, involves a judicial exercise at one stage only. That occurs at the point where the registrar signifies his approval of the draft order. If a decree has already been pronounced, he can make the order there and then. The approval date and the order date will in that instance be the same.

If, on the other hand, the pronouncement of decree is still pending, the registrar's judicial function will include, in addition to the approval of the draft order, the necessity to choose between two possible courses of action in regard to the subsequent machinery required to bring into being an order giving effect to the draft which he has approved.

One course (and this we were told by counsel is the course followed in the great majority of cases) is to include a statement of his approval of the draft order on the face of the certificate which he is giving for the purposes of the decree. If that path is followed, the draft order will automatically become a consent order of the court at one and the same moment as the decree is pronounced.

The other course is to direct that the draft order shall come into being as a substantive order at a date on or after the day on which a decree nisi is to be pronounced.

Whichever of those two courses is selected, no further judicial function is required. The administrative wheels simply turn. If the first course is chosen, no difficulty is likely to arise (although I shall mention in a moment one unfortunate case where it did). The draft order will enter the file that goes into court on pronouncement day, and the court staff will arrange for the decree nisi and consent order to be printed out together, both bearing the same date, ie the date of pronouncement of the decree. If, however, the second course is chosen, there is a risk that the administrative wheels may turn too soon, with the result that the order is made (disastrously) before the day on which the decree is eventually pronounced.

Board (Board intervening) v Checkland [1987] 2 FLR 257 is a case in which it had been intended to follow the first course (ie have the order pronounced at decree nisi) and shows how even under that (safer) procedure administrative slips are liable to occur. It also provides an instructive illustration of the general perils that can beset any draft consent order while it remains in the limbo that lies between approval and perfection. The parties submitted to the court an agreed application for a lump sum order on 17 May. Their decree nisi had not yet been pronounced, but was due for pronouncement in the following month. The registrar indorsed the application 'by consent order as prayed on decree nisi' and gave informal instructions that the order should not be made until decree nisi. In due course a decree was pronounced on 17 June. In the meantime, however, someone on the court staff had come across the agreed application with the registrar's indorsement on it. He or she was unaware of (or had overlooked) the informal instructions that had been given for the order not to be drawn up until decree nisi. So it came about that on a day in May or early June (which is not mentioned in the law report but which I shall call 'the actual order date'), while a decree nisi was still awaited, the consent order was perfected and sealed. The date attributed to it was 23 May (the date of the registrar's indorsement of approval). The order was held by the Court of Appeal to have been made without jurisdiction. It is to be noted that it would have been pointless in that case to amend the date on the face of the order under the slip rule by substituting the actual order date, for the actual order date was itself fatally antecedent to the date of pronouncement of decree nisi.

The dating of orders

Consent orders made in the matrimonial jurisdiction are not subject to any special rules as to their dates of operation or as to their amendment on the ground of error in their drawing up, but are subject to the general rules which are as follows.

RSC Ord 42, r 3 provides:

'(1) ... a judgment or order of the Court ... takes effect from the day of its date.

(2) Such a judgment or order shall be dated as of the day on which it is pronounced, given or made, unless the Court ... orders it to be dated as of some other earlier or later day, in which case it shall be dated as of that other day.'

It was not disputed that this rule applies equally in the county court.

Order 20, r 11 (reproduced for the county court as CCR Ord 15, r 5) generally called the 'slip rule', reads:

'Clerical mistakes in judgments or orders, or errors arising therein from any accidental slip or omission, may at any time be corrected by the Court on motion or summons without an appeal.'

The two features of those rules relevant to this case are: (i) the court has power under Ord 42, r 3(2) when initially making an order to direct in advance (or retrospectively) that its order shall bear some date other than that of the day on which it is actually pronounced and (ii) it is settled law that an order which is a nullity, because it was made (or directed to be dated) on a day when the court had no jurisdiction to make it, cannot have validity conferred on it retrospectively by use of the slip rule to change its date to a day on which the court, had it chosen that day on which to make (or date) its order, would have had jurisdiction to make it (see *Re Keystone Knitting Mills' Trade Mark* [1929] 1 Ch 92, [1928] All ER Rep 276, *Munks v Munks* [1985] FLR 576 and *Board (Board intervening) v Checkland* [1987] 2 FLR 257).

Such is the procedural background against which I can now turn to describe the circumstances of the consent order that was obtained in the present case.

The parties were married in October 1960. They had three sons, all of whom are now adult and in their twenties. By December 1988 their marriage had broken down after 28 years. The husband was then aged 51 and the wife 46. He was the regional manager of a building society with a salary in the region of £30,000 pa, and she had been working part-time as an auxiliary nurse earning £3,200 pa. She had however suffered a recent whiplash injury in a motor accident, which might affect her ability to continue nursing work for the future.

The wife remained in occupation of the matrimonial home in Northampton, which was in their joint names. It had a value of about £140,000 and was subject to a low-rate mortgage from the husband's employers of £20,000, secured on an endowment policy. In the summer of 1989 the circumstances of each of them changed. The wife was advised that she would have to give up nursing because of the continuing effects of her accident, and she was able to find work as a mobile warden for sheltered accommodation. The husband accepted voluntary retirement terms from his employers under which he received a lump sum net of tax of £53,600, the bulk of which he invested (with the help of a low-interest mortgage of £15,000 from his former

employers) in the purchase of a home of his own for £59,000. He also received
a pension starting at £17,773 but subject to periodic increase. He was able to
get new work as an administrator (first for the police and later for a firm of
solicitors) at a gross salary in the region of £12,000 pa. The parties' invested
savings were worth around £17,500.

In the summer of 1990 the wife issued her formal claim for financial relief in
the divorce proceedings which she had by then instituted. Affidavits of means
were filed. Their accuracy has not been criticised (this being a case where no
criticism is made of the husband for non-disclosure of assets or putting the
wife under unfair pressure to settle on his proposed terms). In the negotiations
which were then already on foot the husband expressed his wish for a clean
break settlement. The stance taken by the wife was that she wanted to remain
in the matrimonial home, although her solicitor advised her that if the case
went to court at a contested hearing the judge would regard that property as
being too large for her needs and would probably insist on a sale. In the end,
after the wife had consulted counsel, terms were agreed in early December
1990 for a clean break on the basis that the wife would take the entire interest
in the matrimonial home. The two solicitors drew up a very simple form of
draft order which recited the husband's undertaking to redeem the mortgage
on the former matrimonial home and continued:

> 'BY CONSENT IT IS ORDERED THAT: 1. The Respondent do within ...
> days from today transfer to the Petitioner all his estate and interest in [the
> former matrimonial home]',

and then set out orders in standard form dismissing the claims of each party for
financial relief against the other and making no order as to costs.

An appointment was duly taken out with the registrar for approval of that
document on 11 December 1990. The state of the divorce proceedings at that
point was that the registrar had given his certificate on 31 July 1990 but
(unusually) had not at the same time given directions for trial. The result was
that when the solicitors attended the appointment on 11 December, no date
for pronouncement of decree had yet been fixed.

Each of them had prepared, before they went into the registrar's room,
forms giving the r 76A particulars. The information, though succinct, was
accurate. The value of the former matrimonial home, the mortgage on it, the
like particulars of the husband's new home, the surrender value of his
insurance policies, his annual income from pension (£13,530) and earnings
(£6,348) and the wife's annual earnings (£2,892) were all mentioned. The
forms were handed in at the outset of the appointment.

The solicitors were not engaged with the registrar for long. In the evidence
which they gave to the judge about the appointment, one of them thought it
had lasted 10, the other for 15, minutes. At the end of the appointment the
registrar completed and slightly altered para 1 of the draft so that it read:

> 'The Respondent do within 28 days from ~~today~~ *Decree Absolute* transfer
> to the Petitioner all his estate and interest in [the former matrimonial
> home].'

He also added the following handwritten indorsement: '11.12.90. Both
solicitors appearing and consenting. Terms of Order approved' and initialled
it.

In regard to the discussions leading up to that indorsement, it was common
ground on the solicitors' evidence that there had been some talk at first about

procedure, because all three of them (the registrar and both solicitors) were aware that no decree nisi had yet been pronounced. As to exactly what else was discussed the wife's former solicitor was unable to be specific; when asked how the matter was presented to the registrar generally—what he was told, what discussion there was about the order—he said he had no recollection. The husband's solicitor was able to give a slightly fuller account. After he had been referred in evidence to the registrar's indorsement on the draft order, the relevant questions and answers-in-chief were as follows:

'Q. What was the registrar's solution to the problem about the decree nisi? A. The registrar said that he would approve the order in principle but would let it lie on the file until the decree nisi was granted.

Q. Do you recall whether, before giving such approval, there was any talk about the merits? A. Yes, there was some talk.

Q. Did the registrar appear to read the r 76A statement beforehand? A. To the best of my knowledge, he did.

Q. Can you say whether ... he read the affidavit? A. I am not in a position to say.

Q. Do you go, and have you in the past gone, frequently before [the registrar] on pre-trial reviews? A. Yes, I have.

Q. Can you say what his practice is normally in relation to reading affidavits? A. I find that generally he has acquainted himself with the background of the case prior to the review.

Q. Did he express on this occasion any comment on the provision made by the draft order? A. Yes. I recollect that he thought the terms were reasonably generous.

Q. Presumably, therefore, he found no difficulty in approving it? A. I was not aware of any difficulty.'

When it was put to him in cross-examination that the 'problem of the decree nisi and the lack of it caused some consternation', the witness answered:

'I was not aware of any particular consternation. It was raised before I went in and, as I recollect, [the registrar] took it fairly calmly, approved the order and said it would lie on the file.'

The next day (12 December) the registrar gave directions for trial in the divorce suit by appointing 18 December as the day for pronouncement of decree nisi. He did not make any change to his certificate to refer to the proposed consent order or give any direction that the approved draft should be before the court on the day of pronouncement.

The result was that when, on 18 December, the decree nisi was duly pronounced in open court, no reference at all was made to the approved draft order. Nor was any reference to it to be found in the decree nisi as drawn up. The draft order simply lay where the registrar had directed it should lie, on the court file.

About a month later, the wife's solicitor wrote to the court on 21 January saying 'we do not seem to have received the ancillary relief order which should have been issued after decree nisi' and asked for a copy of it. That inquiry led the court staff to remove the draft order from the file and use it as the basis of a sealed and perfected order which was sent to the parties on 25 January. The judge made a finding that the perfection of the order took place on a day (to which I shall refer as 'the sealing date') falling between 21 and 25 January. The perfected order read (so far as relevant) as follows:

> 'BEFORE MR REGISTRAR [naming him] SITTING AT [the court address] ON 11 DECEMBER 1990
>
> UPON HEARING Solicitors for both parties
>
> UPON the Respondent's undertaking to redeem the mortgage of [the former matrimonial home] before the transfer hereinafter ordered to be made by him
>
> BY CONSENT IT IS ORDERED that:
>
> 1. The Respondent do within 28 days from Decree Absolute transfer to the Petitioner all his estate and interest in [the former matrimonial home].'

The remaining paragraphs of the order as perfected followed the terms of the draft order, including the paragraph dismissing the claims of the parties to financial relief.

It will be remembered that the mortgage on the former matrimonial home (which the husband had undertaken to discharge) was partly secured by an endowment insurance policy. It had a surrender value (£6,866) which it was proposed to apply in part satisfaction of the amount required to redeem the mortgage (which then stood at £8,000). The policy having been effected in the parties' joint names, the wife's signature was required on the formal surrender of the policy. She refused to give it, objecting that this went beyond anything that had been agreed in the consent order. The husband's solicitors insisted that she was bound to do so, as part of the mechanics of giving effect to the consent order. The wife maintained her objections. That impasse was eventually resolved in May 1991 when the mortgagee of its own motion applied the proceeds of the policy towards redemption of the mortgage, the balance of which was paid off by the husband.

When the husband then sought to have the decree made absolute, the wife objected. She instructed new solicitors, who on reading the file noted that the consent order purported to bear a date (11 December 1990) antecedent to the date of decree nisi. On 18 September 1991 they wrote to the husband's solicitors pointing this out, referring to *Board (Board intervening) v Checkland* [1987] 2 FLR 257, and saying that the consent order must be regarded as a nullity. The husband's solicitor was very surprised by this news. In his reply he stated that his recollection was that at the appointment of 11 December 'the Order was approved in principle but would not be made until such time as Decree Nisi was pronounced'. Something must, he agreed, have gone wrong. He did not at that time know what the exact history of the drawing up of the order had been. That (as I shall later describe) only came to light as a result of detective work by Singer J in the county court file. So it is not surprising that the husband's solicitor felt bound at that stage to agree that the order had been made without jurisdiction. As for the registrar himself, his response when the matter of the date of the consent order was taken up with him was to write to the parties' solicitors on 2 October 1990 saying 'I agree that my order of 11.12.90 is a nullity (despite both solicitors being present and consenting)' and stating that he would consider the matter on 30 October.

On that day the registrar had the husband's solicitors and the wife's new solicitors before him. The husband's solicitors felt bound (for the reasons I have described) to accept that the consent order had been a nullity and to allow the wife's application for financial relief to be reopened. The order made by the registrar accordingly recited 'the order purporting to have been made on 11 December 1990 being a nullity' and proceeded to give directions for the filing of further evidence and directed an exchange of valuations. On 3 March 1992 the husband gave notice in the proceedings to the wife to show cause why the agreement contained in the consent order should not be carried into effect, and on 14 July 1992 the registrar directed that all proceedings should be transferred to the Family Division.

They came in due course before Singer J. At that point the husband's advisers were still disposed to accept that the consent order must have been a nullity, on account of its purported date. The judge, at an early stage of the hearing, called for the county court file. His eye lit upon the correspondence which disclosed the history in the drawing up of the order which I have related, and which was to lead to the finding to which I have already referred, namely that the consent order was not in fact perfected until the sealing date.

That discovery prompted Mr Duckworth, the husband's counsel, to submit that the consent order was a fully effective order since it had been made on the sealing date, a date which was subsequent to the date of decree nisi. The purported attribution to it of the wrong date (being the date of the registrar's original approval of the draft) was an obvious clerical error which could, and should, be readily corrected under the slip rule by substituting the order's true date, which was the sealing date. The judge rejected that submission. He made an order formally setting aside the consent order, and proceeded to deal on its merits with the husband's application to enforce the agreement to which that order had purported to give effect.

That led to a detailed investigation by the judge of the justice of the agreement on lines approved by the Court of Appeal in *Edgar v Edgar* [1980] 3 All ER 887, [1980] 1 WLR 1410 and *Camm v Camm* (1982) 4 FLR 577. The wife's former solicitor was closely questioned on his own advice and the instructions he had given to counsel—a form of inquiry which appeared to be justified by the references (on the part of Ormrod LJ in the authorities just mentioned) to the quality of the legal advice tendered to the wife as being a relevant consideration. The judge concluded that this was not a case in which a clean break could have been reached consistently with fairness to the wife, in view of the disparity between the parties' respective incomes and income potential. He declined to uphold the agreement embodied in the purported consent order, and substituted an order that the wife should be entitled, in addition to a property transfer order in respect of the husband's share in the former matrimonial home, to periodic maintenance at the rate of £6,300 until further order (reducible to £5,700 in the event that the husband should nominate in her favour the death in service benefit to which he was entitled under his pension arrangements).

In stating his grounds for setting aside the consent order as a nullity, the judge first acknowledged that this case was different from *Munks v Munks* [1985] FLR 576 and *Board (Board intervening) v Checkland* [1987] 2 FLR 257 in that—

'here this order was in fact drawn up and sealed, as I have found, at a date when there was jurisdiction to make the order, although the document was then backdated to a time when there would have been no jurisdiction to make it. The question is therefore not so much, when was

an order made, but rather, was an order made? For if it can properly be
held that this order was made at the time in January 1991 when it was in
fact produced, then there was jurisdiction to make it ...'

He then proceeded to answer the question thus posed as follows:

'Submissions, which I shall summarise, were made to me by Mr
Duckworth to the effect that the drawing up of the order in late January
1991, as I have found was when that was done, was purely an
administrative action carried out by one of the court's staff, validly to
reflect what transpired at the hearing on 11 December 1990, and that the
antedating of the order did not affect its validity and could be corrected
under the slip rule. He advanced detailed arguments in support of this
basic proposition and put it in its historical context so far as the applicable
rules are concerned. But the essence of his case on this point can, I hope,
fairly be stated as succinctly as I just have. This is a submission which I
find to be ill-founded. It ignores what seems to me to be the fundamental
factor that the making of an order, as opposed to the preparation of a
document which reflects its terms, is a judicial act. A document to recite
the terms of the order reflecting the agreement can only properly have
been prepared after the decree nisi, if a judicial act on or after the
pronouncement of decree nisi had resulted in an order in those terms. I
am unable to construe from the events as we know them that there was
any occasion when this took place. First, we know that on 11 December
1990 the district judge and both solicitors were aware that there was no
jurisdiction to make an order there and then. The only record of what
transpired are the words written by the registrar on the draft, "terms of
order approved". Given that those words could not have been intended
to indicate that an order was made there and then, they can no more easily
be construed to reflect an intention without more ado to make an order in
futuro. Next, we know, and I have already referred to the fact, that the
registrar did not adopt the course which was open to him of amending his
certificate so that on decree the judge would make an order in the agreed
terms. Next, it might be argued, and was by Mr Duckworth, that the
registrar intended that after the decree nisi an order in terms of the draft
should be drawn without any further judicial act. I am not satisfied that it
would have been open to the registrar to take that course. He would
effectively have been making an order then on 11 December 1990, not to
be drawn up until a subsequent date. To my mind that is precisely
equivalent to making the order then, but delaying the production of the
document recording it. That is precisely what the 1973 Act provides is an
ineffectually premature attempt to exercise jurisdiction which has not yet
come into existence. It is of course true that circumstances sometimes
arise where the terms of a consent order are indicated to a judge who then
directs that the order shall not be drawn up until some future event has
occurred. This is a useful device where, for instance, a condition
precedent to the effectiveness of the agreement has not yet occurred so
that the agreement may fail. But if and when the document to reflect such
an order is drawn up, it will bear upon it the date of the hearing before the
judge and not the date when the document is prepared. Finally, as one
way in which it would have been possible effectively to produce a valid
order in this case, the registrar might have taken steps to secure that the

file should be returned to him once the decree nisi had been pronounced when, without requiring the attendance of parties or solicitors, he might have decided to make an order in the terms of which he had already signified approval. The order he would then have made, when drawn as a document, would then have borne the date when he exercised that judicial function. But there is nothing to indicate that this was the course which the registrar either suggested he would take, intended to take, or did take. I therefore conclude that there was no judicial occasion after the moment of pronouncement of the decree which could have justified the court staff in drawing an order which no judge or registrar had ever effectively directed should be made. Thus I answer No to the question earlier posed: "Was an order made?".'

My interpretation of that reasoning is that the judge found the consent order invalid on one or other or both of the following grounds. (1) The registrar had no power on a date before decree nisi to direct that the order should be made on a date subsequent to decree nisi. (2) A consent order is only valid if some 'judicial act' is brought to bear upon it on or after the date of decree nisi.

It is necessary, in considering the first ground, to bear in mind that there are several ways in which an order may be made operative at a date subsequent to that on which it receives judicial approval. One is for the court to direct that the order shall not be drawn up and perfected until the future date or eventuality has occurred. Another is to state on the face of the order that it shall not become operative until the future date or eventuality. Yet another is to direct in advance under Ord 42, r 3(2) that the order is to be dated as of some later day than that on which it is pronounced. In the first two cases the order bears the date on which it is pronounced. In the last case the order bears the date which it has been directed to bear.

The evidence of the husband's solicitor was that the registrar at the hearing on 11 December 1990 'said that he would approve the order in principle but would let it lie on the file until the decree was granted'. That evidence was not contradicted by the wife's solicitor, and I do not understand it to have been rejected by the judge. The language used by the registrar may have been informal, but the sense of it, to my mind, is plain enough. He gave advance approval to the order on that day (11 December) upon the footing that such approval would remain inchoate, and would not become the subject of any order of the court, until a date falling after the pronouncement of decree nisi. That seems to me to be a perfectly valid method of enabling consent orders to be made after decree nisi with the benefit of an approval obtained before decree nisi. Indeed that would appear to be precisely the process which comes into play whenever the parties adopt the more common practice to which I have already referred, namely taking a consent order on the same occasion as the pronouncement of the decree. The registrar (now district judge) in such cases first approves the draft consent order in advance of the decree nisi, and then, as part of his 'directions for trial', dispatches it to the 'trial hearing', at which it will receive automatic approval from the judge or district judge who is given formal responsibility for pronouncing the decree. The judge's first ground for finding the order invalid was therefore in my judgment erroneous.

When the judge used the expression 'judicial act' he intended, I am sure, to use it in the sense in which it would normally be understood, that is to say as describing an action which is not merely formal but requires an independent judgment by its maker as to whether the act should be done or not. It has been noted already that in the streamlined procedures which now obtain for unopposed divorce, the scope for any 'judicial act' in that sense is very restricted indeed. In the suit itself, the only steps which can properly be called judicial acts are the giving by the registrar of his directions for trial and his certificate: all that follows is either administrative or formal. That applies even to the culminating event in the whole process—the pronouncement of the decree itself; because although that is in a limited sense a judicial action (in that the rules require it to be performed by a judicially qualified person), the pronouncer has no discretionary power (save adjournment) and acts as a virtual cipher (see *Day v Day* [1979] 2 All ER 187, [1980] Fam 29). Similarly, in regard to the obtaining of a consent order, the only relevant 'judicial act' is that of the registrar when he certifies his approval and gives any necessary directions as to when and how such approval is to be incorporated into an order of the court. The procedures that follow are vital, for without them the desired approval can never be given legal effect, and they will need to be carried out carefully and conscientiously by people with suitable skill and training; but none of them will involve a fresh or independent judgment being brought to bear on the merits of granting the approval itself. The judge appears to have accepted in this case that the registrar's approval was duly given on 11 December 1990, but to have taken the view that such approval was incapable of forming the basis of a consent order after decree nisi unless some further 'judicial act' had intervened thereafter (such as a fresh consideration by the registrar). In my judgment there was neither the scope nor the necessity for any fresh appraisal, after decree nisi, of the merits of the proposed consent order. The approval it had already received was a continuing one, and the only further step required after decree nisi was that it should be drawn up and sealed and given its true date—the sealing date. The judge's second ground for finding the order invalid was therefore also erroneous.

It follows that, for the reasons indicated and with regret at having to take a different view from a judge with acknowledged expertise in this field, I consider that the consent order was validly made; that the attribution to it of the date of the appointment before the registrar instead of the date of sealing was a pure clerical error; and that the judge ought to have ordered the consent order to be amended under the slip rule by inserting the sealing date as its true date.

It is unnecessary, in view of that conclusion, to deal with the second limb of the appeal and go into the question whether the judge was right to have set aside the agreement which (with professional advice) had been reached between the parties. I am grateful, none the less, for the interesting arguments that were addressed to us under this head. They demonstrated that the question of the setting aside of out-of-court financial agreements is an extremely problematic area of the law. It is better to stay out of it, and enjoy the relative security and peace of mind which an order approved by the court can supply. All the more reason, therefore, that such orders should be drawn up and dated with the utmost care, to avoid a recurrence of the problems which arose in the present case and which must have involved much additional anxiety and expense for the parties. A putting together of heads by chief clerks and district judges ought to make it possible, for those who have not done so already, to devise for their court files and computers a suitable warning system to prevent any financial consent order being inadvertently allocated a date antecedent to the decree nisi. The present case provides an object lesson in pointing to the serious consequences which are liable to follow if such precautions are overlooked.

I would allow the appeal and substitute for the order made by the judge a direction that the consent order purportedly dated 11 December 1990 be amended under the slip rule by changing the date to 25 January 1991.

HOFFMANN LJ. I agree that this appeal should be allowed for the reasons given by Waite LJ. The judge said of the words 'terms of order approved' written by the district judge on the draft consent order:

> 'Given that those words could not have been intended to indicate that an order was made there and then, they can no more easily be construed to reflect an intention without more ado to make an order in futuro.'

Why not? One should, I think, attribute meaning and, if possible, validity, to what the district judge was doing. The fact that he had written the words on the draft seems to me clearly to show that he did not contemplate any more judicial ado on his part; not, at any rate, unless some change of circumstances was drawn to his attention. He knew, as the judge found, that he could not make an order with immediate effect. Therefore, to give any meaning to what he was doing, he must have intended that the order would take effect as from a future date. This he had power to do under RSC Ord 42, r 3. In my judgment it is what he did.

There is more than one lesson to be learned from this case. The first, as Waite LJ has pointed out, is the need for care in drawing up orders. The second concerns the grounds upon which the court may refuse, as the judge did in this case, to give effect to an agreement between the parties which has not yet been incorporated in a valid consent order. In view of our conclusion that there was a valid consent order, we have not had to express a view on this aspect of the matter and I shall not do so. But it does seem to me that the law is in an unsatisfactory state. There are in theory various possible answers to the problem. One might be that an agreement between the parties, at least where each has independent legal advice, is binding upon them subject only to the normal contractual remedies based on fraud, misrepresentation, undue influence etc. At present, the policy of the law as expressed in *Hyman v Hyman* [1929] AC 601, [1929] All ER Rep 245 is against such a solution. The court retains its supervisory role and only its order gives finality. Another answer might be that when parties are negotiating with a view to an agreement which will be embodied in a consent order, everything should be treated as without prejudice negotiation until the order is actually made. In the latter case, the parties would know that until the court had given its imprimatur, nothing which they had negotiated was legally binding or even admissible. If one of them changed his or her mind, they would have either to go back to the negotiating table or litigate the matter de novo. This may be tiresome, as in the case of a house purchase where one party changes his or her mind before contracts are exchanged. But the parties would at least know where they stood. The result of the decision of this court in *Edgar v Edgar* [1980] 3 All ER 887, [1980] 1 WLR 1410 and the cases which have followed it is that we have as it seems to me, the worst of both worlds. The agreement may be held to be binding, but whether it will be can be determined only after litigation and may involve, as in this case, examining the quality of the advice which was given to the party who wishes to resile. It is then understandably a matter for surprise and resentment on the part of the other party that one should be able to repudiate an agreement on account of the inadequacy of one's own legal advisers, over whom the other party had no control and of whose advice he had no knowledge. The appellant's counsel, who has considerable experience in these matters, told us that he reckoned that in Northampton an agreement has an 80% chance of being upheld but that attitudes varied from district judge to district judge. In our attempt to achieve finely ground justice by attributing weight but not too much weight to the agreement of the parties, we have created uncertainty and, in this case and no doubt others, added to the cost and pain of litigation.

NEILL LJ. I agree that this appeal should be allowed for the reasons given by Waite LJ.

Appeal allowed.

L I Zysman Esq   Barrister.

Mathew v T M Sutton Ltd

CHANCERY DIVISION

CHADWICK J

15, 17 JUNE 1994

Interest – Sale of pawned articles – Surplus proceeds – Unredeemed articles sold by pawnbroker – Surplus proceeds withheld by pawnbroker pending third party claim to ownership of articles – Surplus proceeds paid to pawnor without interest – Pawnor claiming interest in equity on surplus proceeds for period between sale and payment – Whether pawnbroker liable for interest – Whether fiduciary relationship between parties.

On five separate occasions the plaintiff, M, entered into agreements with the defendant pawnbroker under which he pawned silver articles and jewellery as security for loans made to him under the agreements. Each agreement was regulated by the Consumer Credit Act 1974 and specified a six-month term for the loan and a credit charge of 3 to 3·5% per month. The agreements also provided that if the articles were not redeemed by the redemption dates specified, the pawnbroker could sell them and, if the proceeds exceeded the amount owed, M would receive the surplus balance. When M failed to redeem the articles as agreed, the pawnbroker sold them at auction in May and June 1989 and gave M notice of the surplus balance payable to him. The pawnbroker did not however pay the surplus balance of £2,044·43 to M until the end of May 1993, because a claim to the ownership of the pawned articles which had been made in 1989 was not abandoned or released until that date. M subsequently claimed interest on the sum paid at the rate of 3% per month for the period between June 1989 and May 1993. M later brought proceedings against the pawnbroker, claiming that, in the absence of any contractual term regulating the position, the pawnbroker was liable in equity to pay interest on the money withheld.

Held – There was a fiduciary relationship between a pawnbroker and a pawnor in view of the nature of a pawn or pledge of personal property, which involved a transfer of the possession of personal property from the pawnor to the pawnbroker by way of security under which the ownership of the property remained in the pawnor, subject only to the special interest to which the pawnbroker was entitled for the purpose of protecting and realising his security. Moreover, there was no reason why the beneficial interest of the pawnor in the pawned articles should be extinguished to any greater extent than was necessary to give effect to the pawnbroker's right to realise his security, and no reason why that interest should not be transferred from the articles which had been sold to the proceeds of sale and so remain attached to the surplus in the pawnbroker's hands. It followed that the fiduciary relationship necessary to found jurisdiction to award interest in equity existed between the pawnbroker and pawnor in relation to any surplus arising on the sale of pawned articles so that, in the absence of any contractual term regulating the position, the pawnee was liable to pay interest on the surplus. On the facts, the pawnor was entitled to receive interest on the £2,044·43. However, since the pawnbroker had not placed the surplus proceeds in an interest-bearing account pending the outcome of the third party claim, but had probably used the funds in his business, the interest rate payable would be ascertained on inquiry as to what use he had actually made of the money and the interest rate obtained (see p 800 *g* to *j*, p 801 *d e j* and p 802 *g* to p 803 *a*, post).

Dictum of Lord Denning MR in *Wallersteiner v Moir (No 2)* [1975] 1 All ER 849 at 855 applied.

Notes

For the right to interest, see 32 *Halsbury's Laws* (4th edn) paras 106–110, and for the rate usually allowed by the courts, see ibid para 112.

For the Consumer Credit Act 1974, see 11 *Halsbury's Statutes* (4th edn) (1991 reissue) 15.

Cases referred to in judgment

Attenborough & Son v Solomon [1913] AC 76, [1911–13] All ER Rep·155, HL.
Banner v Berridge (1881) 18 Ch D 254.
Bartlett v Barclays Bank Trust Co Ltd (No 2) [1980] 2 All ER 92, [1980] Ch 515, [1980] 2 WLR 430.
Burdick v Garrick (1870) LR 5 Ch App 233, LC and LJ.
Coggs v Bernard (1703) 2 Ld Raym 909, [1558–1774] All ER Rep 1, 92 ER 107.
Jay's the Jewellers Ltd v IRC [1947] 2 All ER 762.
Morley (Inspector of Taxes) v Tattersall [1938] 3 All ER 296, CA.
Wallersteiner v Moir (No 2) [1975] 1 All ER 849, [1975] QB 373, [1975] 2 WLR 389, CA.

Summons

The plaintiff, Thomas Mathew, obtained leave from Warner J on 14 March 1994 to bring an action by writ claiming, in respect of articles pawned by him to the defendant pawnbroker, T M Sutton Ltd, and subsequently sold by the defendant: (i) a declaration that the defendant was liable to pay interest on the surplus proceeds arising on those sales in respect of the period from sale to payment of the surplus to the plaintiff, (ii) an inquiry as to the rate or rates at which such interest was properly payable and (iii) payment of any sum found due to him as a result of such an inquiry. On 20 April 1994 the plaintiff issued a summons (treated as a summons made pursuant to RSC Ord 14A) seeking the same relief as sought in the writ. The facts are set out in the judgment.

The plaintiff appeared in person.
The defendant did not appear.

Cur adv vult

17 June 1994. The following judgment was delivered.

CHADWICK J. The defendant in this action, T M Sutton Ltd, carries on the business of pawnbroker at 156 Victoria Street, London SW1. In late 1987, and again in the early months of 1988, the plaintiff, Mr Thomas Mathew, made use of the loan facilities which the defendant provided. On five separate occasions the plaintiff delivered articles of silver and jewellery to the defendant in pawn and as security for loans made to him. On each occasion the plaintiff and the defendant entered into a credit agreement, or agreements, which were regulated by the Consumer Credit Act 1974.

The agreements (of which there were six in all) each contained a description of the property in pawn and particulars of the amount of the loan, the total charge for credit for the full contractual term of that loan (which was six months), the annual percentage rate and the total amount payable. A summary of the six agreements is set out below:

Date	Agreement No	Loan	Credit charge	Annual percentage rate	Total amount payable
		£	£		£
10 Dec 1987	Z07056	1,500	270·00	39·2	1,770·00
5 Jan 1988	Y22311	225	47·28	46·4	272·28
15 Jan 1988	Z07122	2,000	360·00	39·2	2,360·00
18 Jan 1988	Z07125	3,000	540·00	39·2	3,540·00
18 Jan 1988	Z07128	5,500	990·00	39·2	6,490·00
5 Apr 1988	Y22783	400	72·00	39·2	472·00
		12,625	2,279·28		14,904·28

In each case (save in the case of agreement Y22311, where the relevant rate was 3·5% per month) the credit charge for the six-month period of the loan was computed on the basis of simple interest at the monthly rate of 3%. The annual percentage rate is based on the same monthly rate, but compounded at the end of the first six months.

On the face of each agreement there was a 'Notice to Customer'. The notice specified a date on or before which the articles could be redeemed.

That date was, of course, a date six months after the date of the agreement. The notice also contained the following paragraphs:

'Unredeemed Articles.

An article not redeemed within the redemption period becomes our property, if the credit (or credit limit) is not more than £25 and the redemption period is 6 months.

In any other circumstances it may be sold by us, but it goes on being redeemable until it is sold. Interest is payable until the actual date of redemption. Where the credit (or credit limit) is more than £50 we must give you 14 days' notice of our intention to sell.

When an article has been sold you will receive information about the sale. If the proceeds (less expenses) are more than the amount that would have been payable to redeem the article on the date of sale you will be entitled to receive the surplus. If they are less than that amount you will owe us the shortfall.'

Those paragraphs reflect the provisions in ss 120 and 121 of the 1974 Act. In particular, s 121(3) and (4) of that Act provides:

'(3) Where the net proceeds of sale are not less than the sum which, if the pawn had been redeemed on the date of the sale, would have been payable for its redemption, the debt secured by the pawn is discharged and any surplus shall be paid by the pawnee to the pawnor.

(4) Where subsection (3) does not apply, the debt shall be treated as from the date of sale as equal to the amount by which the net proceeds of sale fall short of the sum which would have been payable for the redemption of the pawn on that date.'

Each agreement also contained, on the reverse side, the standard terms upon which the loan was made. So far as material, these included the following:

'1. Loan and deposit of articles.

We agree to lend you the sum referred to overleaf for six months on the terms set out in this agreement ... You agree to deposit with us the articles referred to overleaf until you have repaid the loan and all other sums which may be due to us under this agreement.

2. Reclaiming your pawned articles.

When you wish to reclaim your pawned articles you must pay to us the "Total Amount Payable" referred to overleaf. If we allow you to reclaim your articles after the specified redemption date, you must also pay us interest, calculated on a monthly basis, at a rate equivalent to the annual percentage rate referred to overleaf on the amount of the loan unpaid from the Redemption Date to the date of payment.'

Mr Mathew did not redeem the articles pawned by the redemption date specified in any of the six agreements. In due course the defendant caused the articles to be sold at auction. Those sales took place on 16 May 1989 and on 9 June 1989.

The defendant computed the amounts which would have been payable under each of the agreements if the articles pawned had been redeemed on the date of the relevant sale and gave notice to the plaintiff of the amounts of the surplus payable to him or (in the case of agreements Y22783 and Z07128) of the reduced amounts of the debt. The amounts notified were:

Agreement No	Net proceeds of sale	Amount payable for redemption on date of sale	Surplus/(debt)
	£	£	£
Z07056	3,690·65	2,273·88	1,416·77
Z07125	5,556·66	4,432·85	1,123·81
			2,540·58
Y22783	529·60	586·87	(57·27)
		Surplus at 16 May 1989	2,483·31
Y22311	761·30	360·00	401·30
Z07122	3,972·00	3,007·34	964·66
			1,365·96
Z07128	6,454·50	8,259·34	(1,804·84)
			(438·88)
		Surplus carried over	2,483·31
		Surplus at 9 June 1989	2,044·43

The amounts that would have been payable for redemption on the date of sale appear to have been calculated on the basis set out in standard condition 2 of the agreements, using a daily rate of interest equivalent to 3% per month (or 3·5% per month in the case of agreement Y22311). The amounts have not been challenged by the plaintiff.

The defendant did not, immediately following the sale of the articles, make payment to the plaintiff of the balance which was acknowledged to be due. The reason for the defendant's failure or refusal to do so appears to be that a claim to ownership of the articles pawned had been made on 10 April 1989 by the permanent trustee of Princess Olga Romanoff (Mrs Thomas Mathew). The permanent trustee had been appointed by the issue in Scotland of an act and warrant dated 22 December 1988. That claim was not abandoned or released until the end of May 1993. Payment of the balance acknowledged to be due was made by the defendant to the plaintiff in cash on 26 May 1993 (£1,044·43) and 28 May 1993 (£1,000).

The plaintiff, understandably perhaps in the light of the substantial sums in respect of interest for which he had been debited by the defendant, took the view that the defendant ought to pay interest on the surplus moneys which it had been holding since 16 May and 9 June 1989. On 2 June 1993 the plaintiff sent to the defendant a demand, described as a 'Bill of Interest', claiming interest at the rate of 3% per month on the sum of £2,044·43 held by the defendant from 9 June 1989 until 27 May 1993. Shortly thereafter, and in the absence of any response from the defendant, the plaintiff served on the defendant a statutory demand for that sum. On 25 June 1993 the defendant's solicitors rejected the plaintiff's claim. They wrote:

'The principal sums upon which your claim for interest is based were returned to you in May of this year. Those sums were payable in accordance with the conditions set out in the various agreements into which you entered on pawning the articles in question. There is no provision in those contractual documents for the payment of interest by our client. Furthermore, and on account of the principal sums having been paid, you have no entitlement to statutory interest by way of alternative. Accordingly, your claim has no basis in law and our client has no obligation to you whatsoever.'

In a 'without prejudice' letter of the same date, while maintaining that the claim had no basis in law, the defendant's solicitor wrote—

'our client nonetheless recognises that morally it would not be unfair for you to be compensated by an *ex gratia* payment so as to reflect the interest that you would have been able to earn had the moneys been earlier returned to you. Our client is prepared, therefore, on that basis, to pay the sum of £639·68.'

That sum, which was offered in full and final settlement of any claim to interest which the plaintiff might have, was not accepted by the plaintiff. The offer was renewed on 22 October 1993 in the amount of £695·80, being an amount recalculated to the end of October 1993. That offer has not been accepted.

The plaintiff is subject to an 'all proceedings order' made against him on 15 February 1991 under s 42(1) of the Supreme Court Act 1981. That order was not made as a result of any proceedings between the plaintiff and the defendant; nevertheless, its effect has been that the plaintiff has been unable to commence any proceedings against the defendant without the leave of the High Court. After a couple of false starts—occasioned, I think, by the plaintiff's misconceived notion that he could take steps to enforce his claim by the issue of a winding-up petition—the plaintiff obtained leave from Warner J on 14 March 1994 to bring an action by writ in this division claiming against the defendant (i) a declaration that the defendant is liable to pay him interest in respect of the period from the sales of the articles pawned to the payment of the surplus on those sales, (ii) an inquiry as to the rate or rates at which such interest is properly payable and (iii) payment of any sum found due to him on the taking of such an inquiry. The plaintiff served his writ and statement of claim on 21 March 1994.

On 20 April 1994 the plaintiff issued the summons which is now before me. The summons seeks the same relief as the writ. It is, I think, properly to be treated as a summons for judgment. The defendant has served no defence and has not chosen to be represented at the hearing. Nevertheless, affidavits have been filed on its behalf in which the defendant, through its solicitors, has asked the court to treat the plaintiff's application as if made pursuant to RSC Ord 14A, to determine the question whether or not interest was payable on the surplus proceeds of sale in favour of the defendant and to dismiss the action.

Order 14A, r 1(1) gives the court power to—

'determine any question of law ... arising in any cause or matter at any stage of the proceedings where it appears to the Court that—(a) such question is suitable for determination without a full trial of the action, and (b) such determination will finally determine (subject only to any possible appeal) the entire cause or matter or any claim or issue therein.'

I am satisfied that those conditions are met. Rule 1(3) requires that the court shall not determine any question under Ord 14A unless the parties have had an opportunity of being heard on the question or have consented to an order or judgment on such determination. I am satisfied that the defendant has had an opportunity to be heard, has decided not to take advantage of that opportunity and is content that I should determine the question whether or not interest is payable on the surplus proceeds of sale without a full trial. The plaintiff has appeared before me in person and has given me such assistance as he can. Nevertheless the question is a question of law on which I would have been assisted by submissions from counsel. It is a matter of some regret that I have to decide the question—which must be of some general importance to the defendant and to others who carry on business as pawnbrokers—without the benefit of opposing submissions on the law.

The first question for decision is whether, in the absence of any contractual term regulating the position, interest is payable by a pawnbroker on surplus moneys remaining in his hands after the discharge of the debt out of the proceeds of sale of the pawned articles.

It is, I think, convenient to take the general principles governing the right to interest from the statement in 32 *Halsbury's Laws* (4th edn) paras 106–110, under the title 'Interest on money':

> '**106.** *Interest in general.* Interest is the return or compensation for the use or retention by one person of a sum of money belonging to or owed to another ...
>
> **108.** *When interest is payable at common law.* At common law interest is payable (1) where there is an express agreement to pay interest; (2) where an agreement to pay interest can be implied from the course of dealing between the parties or from the nature of the transaction or a custom or usage of the trade or profession concerned; (3) in certain cases by way of damages for breach of a contract (other than a contract merely to pay money) where the contract, if performed, would to the knowledge of the parties have entitled the plaintiff to receive interest. Except in the cases mentioned, debts do not carry interest at common law.
>
> **109.** *Equitable right to interest.* In equity interest may be recovered in certain cases where a particular relationship exists between the creditor and the debtor, such as mortgagor and mortgagee, obligor and obligee on a bond, personal representative and beneficiary, principal and surety, vendor and purchaser, principal and agent, solicitor and client, trustee and beneficiary, or where the debtor is in a fiduciary position to the creditor ...
>
> **110.** *Interest under statute.* A right to interest is conferred by statute in many cases ...'

The existence of an obligation on the pawnee to pay to the pawnor the surplus moneys remaining in his hands after the discharge of the debt out of the sale of the pawned articles is not in doubt. Whatever may have been the position under the Pawnbrokers Act 1872—see, in particular, s 22 of that Act—the position in relation to agreements regulated by the 1974 Act is spelt out in s 121(3): any surplus shall be paid by the pawnee to the pawnor. There is no need under the 1974 Act for the pawnor to make demand for payment. Nevertheless, there is no basis upon which it could be held that interest is payable at common law. There is no express agreement; there is no course of dealing (of which I am aware) from which an agreement could be implied; it has not been suggested that interest is payable by pawnbrokers by custom or usage of the trade. In my view the plaintiff's claim to interest at common law must fail.

I am satisfied, also, that there is no basis for a claim to interest under statute. The 1974 Act contains no provision for the payment of interest on a surplus, either in s 121(3) or at all. There is no statutory provision, of which I am aware, upon which the plaintiff could rely other than s 35A of the 1981 Act. That section provides:

'(1) Subject to rules of court, in proceedings (whenever instituted) before the High Court for the recovery of a debt or damages there may be included in any sum for which judgment is given simple interest, at such rate as the court thinks fit or as rules of court may provide, on all or any part of the debt or damages in respect of which judgment is given, or payment is made before judgment ...'

In my view the defendant's solicitors were correct when they asserted, on 25 June 1993, that there could be no entitlement to statutory interest—by which I take them to mean interest under s 35A of the 1981 Act—because the principal amount of the surplus had been paid before the plaintiff issued his writ in these proceedings. This must, I think, be the effect of the words 'in proceedings ... for the recovery of a debt ... there may be included ... simple interest ... on the debt'. Section 35A does not enable the court to entertain a claim for interest alone in circumstances where there was no debt (or claim for damages) which could itself be the subject of the proceedings in which the claim for interest is made.

The principles upon which interest may be awarded in equity were considered in *Wallersteiner v Moir (No 2)* [1975] 1 All ER 849 esp at 855, [1975] QB 373 esp at 388 per Lord Denning MR:

'Equity awards [interest] whenever money is misused by an executor or a trustee or anyone else in a fiduciary position—who has misapplied the money and made use of it himself for his own benefit.'

It is necessary, therefore, to consider whether a pawnbroker is in a fiduciary position in relation to the pawnor in respect of the surplus moneys remaining in his hands after the discharge of the debt out of the proceeds of sale of the pawned articles. In my view there is a fiduciary relationship: the pawnbroker holds the surplus upon trust for the pawnor. This follows, I think, from the nature of a pawn or pledge of personal property.

A pawn or pledge involves a transfer of the possession of personal property from the pawnor to the pawnee by way of security; the ownership in the property remains in the pawnor subject only to the 'special interest' to which the pawnee is entitled for the purpose of protecting and realising his security. As Viscount Haldane LC said in *Attenborough & Son v Solomon* [1913] AC 76 at 84, [1911–13] All ER Rep 155 at 158:

'When the person who owns the chattel makes a pledge of it to a pawnbroker he is not purporting to part with the full property or giving any thing which is in the nature of a title to that property to the pawnee, excepting to a limited extent. The expression has been used that the pawnee in such a case has got a special property in the chattel. My Lords, that is true in this sense, that the pawnbroker is entitled to hold the chattel upon the terms that when the possession has been lawfully given to him it is not to be taken away from him, and that if default is made in the redemption of the pledge, or it may be in the payment of interest, he may go further and by virtue of his contract, assuming it to be valid, sell the chattel. But the contract of pawn is simply an illustration of that contract of bailment of which Holt C.J. gave the famous exposition in the great case of *Coggs* v. *Bernard* ((1703) 2 Ld Raym 909, [1558–1774] All ER Rep 1); and it rests upon this foundation, that the property remains in the bailor, and that the bailee, whether it be a bailment by way of pawn or in any other form, simply takes at the outside a right to the possession dependent on the validity of the title of the bailor with the other rights possibly superadded to which I have referred.'

When the pawned articles are sold by the pawnee, under the power now conferred by s 121(1) of the 1974 Act, the property in those articles passes to the purchaser. The proceeds of sale are paid to the pawnee; indeed, in the usual case, they will be received by the pawnee in the form of money credited to his bank account. But there is no reason why the beneficial interest of the pawnor in the pawned articles should be extinguished to any greater extent than is necessary to give effect to the pawnee's right to realise his security. In particular, there is no reason why the beneficial interest of the pawnee should not be transferred from the articles which have been sold to the proceeds of sale and so remain attached to the surplus in the hands of the pawnee after he has discharged the debt out of the proceeds of sale.

This analysis is, I think, consistent with the decision of Atkinson J in *Jay's the Jewellers Ltd v IRC* [1947] 2 All ER 762. The question in that case was whether a surplus remaining after the realisation of the pawned property should be treated for the purposes of excess profits tax as trade receipts of the pawnbroker in the year in which the surplus arose or in the year in which the pawnor lost his right to demand payment under s 22 of the 1872 Act. Atkinson J, after referring to the judgment of Lord Greene MR in *Morley v Tattersall* [1938] 3 All ER 296, said:

> 'As a matter of law, these monies when received were not the [pawnbroker's] monies at all; they belonged to their clients, and if a client came in the next day and demanded his money they would have to pay it away.' (See [1947] 2 All ER 762 at 765.)

Further, there is, as it seems to me, no reason in principle why the position of a pawnee in relation to a surplus after realisation of the article pawned should be more favourable than that of a mortgagee who has realised the mortgaged property. The position of a mortgagee is now governed by s 105 of the Law of Property Act 1925; but the statutory trust imposed by that section reflects the position which had been recognised in equity (see *Banner v Berridge* (1881) 18 Ch D 254 at 269).

It follows, therefore, that I hold that the fiduciary relationship necessary to found jurisdiction to award interest in equity does exist between pawnee and pawnor in relation to the surplus, if any, arising on the sale of the pawned articles. Accordingly, I will make the declaration sought in para (1) of the writ in this action.

The question then arises: at what rate or rates should interest be payable. The principle is set out in the judgment of Lord Hatherley LC in *Burdick v Garrick* (1870) LR 5 Ch App 233 at 241–242:

'... the Court does not proceed against an accounting party by way of punishing him for making use of the Plaintiff's money by directing rests, or payment of compound interest, but proceeds upon this principle, either that he has made, or has put himself into such a position as that he is to be presumed to have made, 5 per cent., or compound interest, as the case may be. If the Court finds ... that the money received has been invested in an ordinary trade, the whole course of decision has tended to this, that the Court presumes that the party against whom relief is sought has made that amount of profit which persons ordinarily do make in trade, and in those cases the Court directs rests to be made.'

That principle was applied by the Court of Appeal in *Wallersteiner v Moir (No 2)* [1975] 1 All ER 849 at 855–856, 863, 870, [1975] QB 373 at 388, 397, 406. It is clear, however, that courts of equity are no longer confined to a conventional or historic rate of 5%, with or without rests. In *Wallersteiner v Moir (No 2)* interest was awarded at 1% above the official bank rate or minimum lending rate in operation from time to time, compounded with yearly rests (see [1975] 1 All ER 849 at 856, 864–865, [1975] QB 373 at 388, 398–399). In *Bartlett v Barclays Bank Trust Co Ltd (No 2)* [1980] 2 All ER 92, [1980] Ch 515 Brightman LJ held that a proper rate of interest to be awarded, in the absence of special circumstances, to compensate beneficiaries and trust funds for non-receipt from a trustee of money that ought to have been received, is that allowed from time to time on the court's short-term investment account, established under s 6(1) of the Administration of Justice Act 1965. He did not direct compound interest.

The question in the present case is whether interest should be awarded at a rate which is linked to some independent commercial rate, say, bank rate or the rate allowed on the short term investment account; or whether I should order an inquiry for the purpose of ascertaining what use was made by the defendant of the money which it held as a fiduciary and what return was earned by the defendant upon it.

In my view this is an appropriate case for an inquiry. It would have been open to the defendant to place the surplus proceeds of sale upon an interest bearing account—distinct from any account in which it held its own moneys—to await the outcome of the claim made by the permanent trustee. If that had been done—and, as it seems to me, that is what should have been done—the defendant would be accountable for the interest earned on that account. No more and no less. If that was not done, then it must, at the least, be likely that the defendant used the surplus in its business. That business includes the lending of money at rates which have been equal to, or in excess of, 3% per month. If the defendant was, in fact, able to and did obtain a return equivalent to 3% per month on what (on this hypothesis) was the plaintiff's money, I can see no reason why the plaintiff should be required to accept a lesser return.

Accordingly, I propose to make a declaration that the defendant is liable to pay to the plaintiff interest (i) on the sum of £2,483·31 from 16 May 1989 until 9 June 1989, (ii) on the sum of £2,044·43 from 9 June 1989 until 26 May 1993 and (iii) on the sum of £1,000 from 26 May 1993 until 28 May 1993. Further, I will direct an inquiry (1) as to what use was made by the defendant between 16 May 1989 and 28 May 1993 of the moneys representing the proceeds of sale of the pawned articles, (2) what return, if any, was obtained by the defendant by its use of those moneys and (3) at what rate or rates interest ought to be paid to the plaintiff.

Order accordingly.

Celia Fox   Barrister.

Crédit Suisse v Beegas Nominees Ltd

CHANCERY DIVISION

LINDSAY J

28–30 JUNE, 1, 2, 5–9, 12–15, 19–21 JULY, 2 SEPTEMBER 1993

Landlord and tenant – Covenant – Covenant to repair – Breach – Landlord's covenant to 'maintain repair amend renew' and 'otherwise keep in good and tenantable condition' – Inherent defect in building – Water leaking through anodised aluminium and glass cladding – Whether landlord in breach of covenant – Whether landlord liable for cost of putting building into tenantable condition – Whether landlord's liability extending to replacement of cladding.

The plaintiff bank was the tenant of newly constructed commercial premises, the outside walls of which were clad in anodised aluminium and glass panels. The principal covenant of the lease, cl 5(c), provided for the landlord 'To maintain repair amend renew ... and otherwise keep in good and tenantable condition' the structure of the building, including its walls. The covenant was subject to the proviso that the landlord would not be liable to the tenant for 'any defects or want of repair hereinbefore mentioned' unless the landlord had had notice thereof. The plaintiff complained that water frequently leaked into the building through the cladding, that the cladding was defectively constructed and that the principal covenant was wide enough to require the landlord to undertake the necessary works to make the building finally watertight, even though it had not been so when the plaintiff first took possession under the lease, and indeed never had been. The plaintiff ceased paying rent and brought proceedings against the landlord, claiming damages for inconvenience and losses resulting from the breach of covenant. The landlord counterclaimed for the arrears of rent and service charge.

Held – (1) A covenant which required the landlord to keep the building in 'good and tenantable condition' was wide enough to require him to put it into that condition even if it had never been so tenantable, since those words (in keeping with the parallel obligation to 'amend' and 'renew' and the phrase 'defects or want of repair' in the proviso) went beyond merely to 'repair' and the obligation was not just to keep the building in good and tenantable condition, but to put the building into that condition which, given the property's age, character and locality, would make it reasonably fit for the occupation of a reasonably minded tenant of the class likely to take it. Moreover, the required condition in which the premises were to be put and kept was to be judged not by reference to the actual state of the building at the date of the demise, but rather to the requirements of a hypothetical reasonably minded tenant of the class likely to take that building (see p 821 *a* to *g*, p 822 *e* and p 823 *a* to *e*, post); *Proudfoot v Hart* [1886–90] All ER Rep 782 and *Lurcott v Wakeley* [1911–13] All ER Rep 41 considered.

(2) On the facts, it was beyond doubt that the building's cladding (which was conceded to be within the subject matter of the principal covenant) had not, during the tenant's occupancy, been put into, nor kept in, the putative necessary 'good and tenantable condition'. Even if the only solution to the long-standing problem was to dismantle the existing cladding and replace it entirely with a newly designed system, the plaintiff would merely be getting what the hypothetical reasonably minded tenant would always have expected. Moreover, the total recladding of the premises (which could not then be regarded as being of a wholly different kind from the premises which had originally been demised) fell within the obligation to 'amend' and 'renew', which clearly extended to incorporate a total replacement of the subject matter to which it related. The landlord was accordingly in breach of its covenant either as to 'good and tenantable condition' or at least to 'amend' and 'renew' the structure of the building. The damages to be awarded to the plaintiff for inconvenience and loss, when assessed, would however reflect the landlord's counterclaim for arrears of rent and service charge (see p 823 *e* to *h*, p 824 *b* to *f*, p 826 *b* to *d f* to *j*, p 831 *d e*, p 833 *b* and p 834 *b c*, post).

Notes

For landlord's obligations towards the tenant, see 27(1) *Halsbury's Laws* (4th edn reissue) paras 328–341.

For covenants generally, see ibid paras 371–426, and for cases on the subject, see 31(2) *Digest* (2nd reissue), 170–177, 5872–5915.

Cases referred to in judgment

Amalgamated Investment and Property Co Ltd (in liq) v Texas Commerce International Bank Ltd [1981] 3 All ER 577, [1982] QB 84, [1981] 3 WLR 565, CA.
Anstruther-Gough-Calthorpe v McOscar [1924] 1 KB 716, [1923] All ER Rep 198, CA.
A/S Awilco of Oslo v Fulvia SpA di Navigazione, The Chikuma [1981] 1 All ER 652, [1981] 1 WLR 314, HL.
Bailey (C H) Ltd v Memorial Enterprises Ltd [1974] 1 All ER 1003, [1974] 1 WLR 728, CA.
Barrett v Lounova (1982) Ltd [1989] 1 All ER 351, [1990] 1 QB 348, [1989] 2 WLR 137, CA.
Battishill v Reed (1856) 18 CB 696, 139 ER 1544.
Calabar Properties Ltd v Stitcher [1983] 3 All ER 759, [1984] 1 WLR 287, CA.
Collins v Flynn [1963] 2 All ER 1068.
Dodd Properties (Kent) Ltd v Canterbury City Council [1980] 1 All ER 928, [1980] 1 WLR 433, CA.
Keen v Holland [1984] 1 All ER 75, [1984] 1 WLR 251, CA.
Lurcott v Wakeley [1911] 1 KB 905, [1911–13] All ER Rep 41, CA.
McDougall v Easington DC [1989] 1 EGLR 93, CA.
Mira v Aylmer Square Investments Ltd [1990] 1 EGLR 45, CA.
Norwegian American Cruises A/S v Paul Mundy Ltd, The Vistafjord [1988] 2 Lloyd's Rep 343, CA.

Norwich Union Life Insurance Society v British Railways Board [1987] 2 EGLR 137.

Plough Investments Ltd v Manchester City Council, Plough Investments Ltd v Eclipse Radio and Television Services Ltd [1989] 1 EGLR 244.

Post Office v Aquarius Properties Ltd [1985] 2 EGLR 105; *affd* [1987] 1 All ER 1055, CA.

Proudfoot v Hart (1890) 25 QBD 42, [1886–90] All ER Rep 782, CA.

Ravenseft Properties Ltd v Davstone (Holdings) Ltd [1979] 1 All ER 929, [1980] QB 12, [1979] 2 WLR 897.

Smedley v Chumley & Hawke Ltd (Warrell, third party) (1981) 44 P & CR 50, CA.

Stent v Monmouth DC [1987] 1 EGLR 59, CA.

Torrens v Walker [1906] 2 Ch 166, [1904–7] All ER Rep 800.

Action

The plaintiff tenant, Crédit Suisse, by a writ issued on 4 April 1990, claimed damages against the defendant landlord, Beegas Nominees Ltd, for alleged breaches of a repairing and maintenance covenant in the underlease of commercial premises at No 66 St James's, London SW1. The facts are set out in the judgment.

Jonathan Gaunt QC and *Richard Gray QC* (instructed by *Fladgate Fielder*) for the tenant.

Brian Knight QC and *Martin Rodger* (instructed by *Braby & Waller*) for the landlord.

Cur adv vult

2 September 1993. The following judgment was delivered.

LINDSAY J. This case is between tenant and landlord and concerns water leaking from the exterior into a very striking modern office and residential building known as No 66 St James's, London SW1. The building is sometimes referred to as 'Map House' but, to some, a little unfairly, it is also known (by reason of its almost circular towers or turrets and metallic appearance) as the 'Rocket Ship'. The freehold of the building is owned by the defendant landlord and it is still let, as to parts up to and including the fourth floor, to, and was earlier occupied by, the plaintiff tenant. Above the fourth floor (which is residential) there is a residential penthouse which is not let to the plaintiff and which plays little part in the events. I shall be principally concerned with the ground to fourth floors. The ground floor and the first to third floors are offices and the ground floor was used by the plaintiff as its West End banking hall. The total approximate area let to and previously occupied by the plaintiff is some 8,120 sq ft. Number 66, as my reference to the 'Rocket Ship' may have suggested, presents an unusual appearance. It is on a corner site at the corner of St James's Place and St James's; it is roughly 'L' shaped with the left and lower faces of the 'L' facing those respective streets. At the corner of the 'L' there is a tower describing a good portion of a circle and capped at the top by a sloping and very tall elliptical window some two storeys or so high. Less emphatic turrets with similar sloping windows mark the other ends of the 'L'. On the outside of the building there are a number of circular or rectangular vertical ducts, which are made of or are clad in metal to match in appearance the dark bronze anodised aluminium which clads the rest of the building. Each

of the three turrets has set in it on each floor with which I am concerned curved
double glazing units. In between those curved units, on each of the flat lengths
of the 'L', are flat double glazing units on each floor. The penthouse's outer
walls slope sharply away from the street rather as would a mansard roof and
almost all the ducts bend in conjunction with those outer walls of the
penthouse. Number 66 was completed in the very early 1980s and, like much
of modern architecture, it has both adherents and opponents, but all, I
apprehend, would agree that it is in a prominent position on a major
thoroughfare in the capital city, an area (and here I quote from a brochure
produced by the plaintiff's agents) 'now recognised as a premier office location
by many well established and international organisations'.

The questions which arise for decision relate principally to a covenant in the
plaintiff's underlease which is of a kind usually (but without necessarily
thereby completely indicating its true nature) called a repairing covenant.
Water leaks from the exterior to the interior, says the plaintiff tenant, because
there are now and have been breaches of the repairing covenant in relation to
the aluminium cladding of the building.

As it may become material to consider the class of tenant which at and
around the time of the relevant demise would be likely to take the underlease
of No 66, I should mention that the first underlessee was J Rothschild & Co Ltd
and the surety, Charterhouse J Rothschild plc. Rothschild's assignee was the
plaintiff, Crédit Suisse, a bank with a rating of AAA at Moody's for its
long-term deposits, one of the world's strongest banks and the third largest and
most profitable of Swiss banks. The landlord defendant is custodian trustee of
the British Gas Corp Pension Scheme. The scheme's property manager has the
supervision, through agents, of literally hundreds of tenancies and the scheme
has immense resources. I am entitled to regard the defendant as a respectable
landlord, well able out of its own resources to finance any of the works to
which I will later need to turn in more detail.

The convenient course will be for me to divide this judgment into a number
of broad headings as follows. (i) A description of the cladding and the
technical terms which are used in relation to it. (ii) The conveyancing title
with which I shall be concerned, giving, in particular, the relevant terms of the
plaintiff's underlease. (iii) A chronology of the relevant events. (iv) Breach
or nay: whether on the true construction of the underlease and in the events
which have happened the defendant has breached the terms of the repairing
covenant in the underlease? (v) If the answer to breach or nay is breach, then
the next subject will be damages: were any suffered and if they were, how
should they be computed?   (vi) Estoppel.   (vii) The counterclaim.
(viii) Finally, I shall mention a point on the pleadings and then attempt to
summarise my conclusions.

The cladding

Number 66's two faces to the streets are clad in bronze-coloured anodised
aluminium panels each of which interlocks both vertically and horizontally
with its neighbours. On the turrets or towers at the three extremities of the 'L'
shape of No 66 there are curved panels but the rest of the panels are flat. Each
separate flat panel is 3·3 m high and 1·2 m wide. It is convenient to have the
outline of a ladder in mind; the 3·3 m lengths are, so to speak, the vertical sides
of the ladder and the 1·2 m pieces are as if the rungs, but, unlike a ladder, the
rungs are infrequent and not at regular intervals. The sides of the ladder are

called 'mullions', which are basically hollow vertical rectangular tubes, an inner and an outer, with additions and plates designed to link into the neighbouring mullions in such a way as also to accommodate horizontal expansion and contraction between one panel and the next. The mullions also have horizontal divisions to accommodate expansion and contraction in the vertical plane as between one panel and the next. As for the 'rungs', the two most important are called 'transoms'. The gap between the head transom and the sill transom (one above and the other below a window) is a space designed to be fitted with one of the double glazing units (DGUs) used at No 66. Each transom is, in effect, a rectangular hollow tube with additions designed to link to the adjoining mullions and to accommodate the DGU intended for that cladding unit. These additions create the double glazing rebate. Each transom in a flat panel is fixed to its neighbouring mullions by, as it transpires, screws from the mullions passing into receptacles called 'screw ports' in the transom. A typical DGU is 1·9 m tall in the flat cladding panels; the rest of the 3·3 m height of each flat cladding unit consists not only of the head and sill transoms (one immediately above and one immediately below the window, as I have described) but also of horizontal flat plates of aluminium filling in the rest of the ladder and covered in part by other plates in a rather angular 'C' shape with the open end of the letter C pointing in towards the building. The C section plates are largely or perhaps entirely cosmetic. These horizontal plates running above the head transom and beneath the sill transom are sometimes referred to as 'spandrels', a term used in particular to distinguish between these horizontal pieces and the horizontal transoms. The cladding panels I have described are commonly fixed to stanchions set in the concrete floors of No 66, stanchions which are themselves embedded in and covered by the concrete of the flooring. Apart from the DGUs, the cladding units, which are something of the order of 9 inches in depth inside to out, represent generally the totality of what lies between the fresh air outside and a person standing in No 66. In large part, the anodised bronze finish of the cladding units framing the windows is what one would see looking out from No 66 to the outside but parts even of the internal faces of the cladding units are invisible from within No 66 by reason of the concrete floors of the building and also by reason of suspended ceilings added beneath the upper floors.

[His Lordship then made further reference to the structural design of the cladding units before turning to consider the conveyancing title to the property. He continued:]

The conveyancing title

On 14 December 1977 an agreement was made between Samuel Properties (Developments) Ltd (the developer) and Williams & Glynn's Trust Co Ltd (the fund) in its capacity as custodian trustee of the central fund of the Gasworkers' Pension Scheme. The fund was to buy the corner site known as 66–67 St James's St and 1 St James's Place. I shall call the site and the premises eventually built there 'No 66'. If the fund was able to buy No 66 then the developer was to proceed to erect a building there for shopping, office and residential use. The fund was to finance the development. On completion of the building the fund was to grant the developer a 99-year lease with an option for further renewal. This development agreement made provision for a 'certificate of practical completion' and 'certificate of final completion'. The developer was required to submit plans for the building to be erected. The fund was not unreasonably or unnecessarily to withhold its consent to the developer's plans but withholding of approval on the ground (inter alia) that the building would, in the opinion of the fund, be unlikely to be readily lettable was not to be deemed unreasonable. The fund's surveyors were to have liberty to inspect the site to view the state and progress of the building works. The developer bound itself to endeavour to negotiate the first underlettings of No 66 to a tenant approved by the fund. The 99-year term was to begin on the date of the certificate of practical completion. There were later supplemental agreements which I need not mention. The fund did acquire the freehold of No 66 and the development thus proceeded.

The approved plans provided for a building readily separable into a residential penthouse on its fifth and sixth floors and the rest, which I shall call 'the offices'. I shall need to say something later about the class of building which emerged or was intended to emerge as No 66 but, to continue with the conveyancing side of the matter, the developer found an underlessee for the offices, J Rothschild & Co Ltd, who, on 7 July 1981, agreed to take an underlease. I shall refer to this agreement more fully below. The building was, at that date, still far from completion. On 16 July 1982 a certificate of partial practical completion was signed (as to the offices) and on 10 November 1982 a further one was signed as to common parts servicing the offices. Rothschilds cannot have been in occupation long. It is unclear precisely when they moved in or out; they began paying rent from July or August 1982, presumably under the agreement for an underlease, but by August 1983 they were minded to move out. As yet no headlease from the fund to the developer had been granted but that emerged on 25 June 1984. Then, on 28 January 1985, the developer granted Rothschilds a 25-year term from 25 July 1983 (which had been the date of practical completion of the penthouse). This is the underlease under which the plaintiff holds and to which I shall need to return later in greater detail. On the same day, 28 January 1985, the developer sold its interest in the headlease of 25 June 1984 to the fund, subject to and with the benefit of the Rothschilds' agreement for an underlease. The intention and the result was that the developer's headlease would be surrendered by operation of law leaving Rothschilds holding under the terms of their underlease but directly from the fund. On 26 June 1985 Rothschilds assigned their underlease of the offices at No 66 to the plaintiff for the unexpired residue of their term. The fund had consented to the assignment. The fund and the plaintiff agreed some minor amendments to the underlease to reflect that the plaintiff would wish to use the ground floor of No 66 for retail banking purposes, a change of use for which planning permission was thought to be necessary. The changes included that when the rent review came round if, by then, planning permission had been granted for this intended use then the review would look toward whichever would yield the highest rack rental of office, showroom and, as was now to added, banking use. At the time of the assignment to the plaintiff the rent payable under the underlease was £200,000 pa, subject to review.

By virtue of the Royal Bank of Scotland Act 1985 the undertaking of the fund was vested in the Royal Bank of Scotland plc. Presumably there was included the property held by the fund as custodian trustee; certainly the case has proceeded on that footing. In that way (as it would seem to be) the Royal Bank of Scotland became custodian trustee of the British Gas Corp Pension Scheme, which I take it was a new name for or included the central fund of the erstwhile Gasworkers' Pension Scheme. On 15 May 1980 the Royal Bank of Scotland transferred the freehold of No 66 to Beegas Nominees Ltd, the defendant, to hold the same as trustee of the British Gas Corp Pension Scheme. Thus it is that the plaintiff holds No 66 for the residue of the term of the underlease of 28 January 1985 until 2008 of the defendant upon the terms, with slight modification, of the underlease. That suffices to deal with title. I must now look at the underlease in more detail.

In the underlease the terms 'tenant' and 'landlord' were expanded in conventional ways to include the respective successors in title of J Rothschild & Co Ltd and the developer and hence the plaintiff and the defendant fall within those respective definitions. Rent is payable quarterly in advance on the usual quarter days. In addition to 'ordinary' rent a service charge described as 'further and additional rent' is payable, as well as a contribution to insurance. The tenant's annual service charge was to equal 75% of certain specified outgoings incurred by the landlord performing his, the landlord's, repairing covenant in the year in question, as to the ascertainment of which outgoings there are detailed provisions. It is plain from those quantification provisions that the landlord was to be able to recoup outgoings other than only those that were of a periodically recurring nature. The remaining 25% of the specified outgoings were, in effect, attributed to the penthouse and to be recoverable from its tenant. If all went well the landlord would thus recover all its outgoings of a repairing kind.

The tenant covenants to repair and keep the interior and all landlord's fixtures and fittings in good and substantial repair, to decorate and to yield up the premises in such state and condition as should in all respects be consistent with a full and due performance by the tenant of the tenant's covenants.

The landlord is entitled to enter No 66 to inspect the state of repair and condition and may by notice require the tenant to make good his shortcomings in that respect. The landlord is expressly entitled to enter No 66 to do work which is its responsibility within its covenants. There is a user clause which (in the event which, I apprehend, happened, of planning permission being granted for retail banking on the ground floor) reads as follows:

> '16(a). NOT to occupy and use the demised premises or any part thereof or permit the same to be used except as to the ground floor and basement thereof for a shop for retail sales (or upon planning permission being granted as offices or showrooms) [or for banking purposes] as to the first second and third floors as offices and as to the fourth floor for residential purposes ...'

I understand the fourth floor was used for residential purposes during the plaintiff's occupancy and that all other user was within the prescribed terms. The user clause and other clauses expressly forbad a number of uses and practices in a manner consistent with an intention on the landlord's part to preserve the value and tone of the premises and there is a covenant against alienation in a full form, including a provision that the landlord should be able to withhold consent to sub-underletting where the rent to be paid by the sub-underlessee 'is less than the full rack rent and is not reviewable upwards only'.

Turning to the landlord's covenant, the crucial one for the purposes of the case is found at cl 5(c), which, with the omission of parts which need not now be read (but with my emphasis added) is as follows:

'(c) (Subject to the payment by the Tenant of the rents and service charge) To maintain repair amend renew cleanse repaint and redecorate and *otherwise* keep in good and tenantable condition:
  (1) the structure of the Building and in particular the roof's foundations and walls thereof but excluding nevertheless therefrom ... (ii) the internal faces of boundary walls that enclose the demised premises ...
  (2) the boundary walls ... of and in the curtilage of the Building ...
  PROVIDED THAT the Landlord shall not be liable to the Tenant for any *defect or* want of repair hereinbefore mentioned unless the Landlord has had notice thereof nor in respect of any obligation hereunder that is to be construed as falling within the ambit of any of the Tenant's covenants hereinbefore contained.'

I shall call the passage I have read 'the principal covenant'. In cl 5(d) the landlord goes on (using the same phrases as in the principal covenant) to covenant to maintain repair amend renew cleanse repaint and redecorate and otherwise keep in good and tenantable repair the common parts and service facilities. Different verbs of obligation are used in different parts; for example cl 5(e)(1) has 'to supply maintain repair and renew', cl 5(e)(2) has 'supply provide purchase maintain renew replace repair and keep in good and serviceable order and condition', cl 5(g)(1) reverts, in relation to the heating and air conditioning and lighting, to the phrase 'maintain repair amend renew cleanse and otherwise keep in good and tenantable condition' as used in the principal covenant, as does cl 5(h) in relation to the lifts.

Clause 6 represents several pages of provisions which include, at cl 6(12)(b), that the landlord should not be liable for any breach of the express or implied covenants for renewals, repair and maintenance until it shall have written notice of such repairs being necessary and then only after a lapse of a reasonable time for the carrying out of the same. There is also an express provision that the landlord should not be liable to make any refund to the tenant in the event of any breach of the landlord's express or implied covenants. No particular written notice is pleaded as complying with cl 6(12)(b) but it has been acknowledged by the defendant that it takes no point as to that absence. There are a number of communications which could amount to notice within cl 6(12)(b) but in any event the case has proceeded as if, so long as notice shall have been clear, it matters not whether it shall have been oral or written.

Clause 7 of the underlease dealt with review of the rent at the expiration of the fifth year and thereafter at five-yearly intervals. The rent can never move downwards; it will always be either as it shall have been in the preceding five years or higher. There is no express assumption of a basis that the landlord shall have performed his covenants.

The third schedule, in addition to passing on to the tenant, as I have mentioned, 75% of the costs incurred by the landlord in discharging the obligations under, inter alia, the principal covenant, provides also for the landlord similarly to pass on:

'2. The cost of periodically inspecting examining maintaining overhauling and where necessary replacing any and every part of the Building and the appurtenances thereof ...'

referred to in, inter alia, the principal covenant.

Whilst I shall need at some point to refer back to the clauses in the underlease which I have already cited and indeed, to some other clauses, that, for the moment, suffices to describe the conveyancing background of the case before me.

The relevant events: a chronology

[His Lordship then set out a detailed chronological account of the relevant events, of which what follows is a shortened version:]

In 1979 Messrs Josef Gartner were invited to supply and fit the curtain wall cladding to the building. Terms were agreed and the building was erected with Gartners' cladding forming a high proportion of its external surfaces, particularly those fronting to St James's and St James's Place.

Annexed to the agreement for the underlease, made as a draft on 7 July 1981, between the developer and Rothschilds, was a form of underlease in the form which was later granted. The developer was there described as landlord, which was expressed to include the estate owner for the time being of the reversion. The term tenant extended to persons deriving title under Rothschilds. There was a covenant with Rothschilds that the site works described in the plans and specifications approved by Rothschilds' surveyors would be done in good and substantial and workmanlike manner and in accordance with those plans. Prior to the certificate of practical completion a 'snagging list' was to be drawn up in consultation with the tenant's surveyors, who could hold up the issue of the certificate of practical completion. Under cl 19 of the agreement for an underlease the developer as landlord should, to the reasonable satisfaction of the tenant, make good as soon as practicable all defects and wants of repair appearing within two years after practical completion, all those in the 'snagging list' or otherwise which were such that the contractor was liable to remedy them within the defects liability period there referred to.

On 16 July 1982 the certificate of partial practical completion relating to basement, ground floor and the first to fourth floors was signed by the architects. Rothschilds began to pay rent as from July or August 1982, though a formal underlease was not for the moment granted.

In late October 1982 the architects were receiving complaints that in heavy rainfalls the building leaked. The architects instructed Gartners to keep their men on site until the facade was made completely watertight. Schedules of leaks were prepared. Gartners blamed blocked drainage holes within the cladding and glazing and suggested cleaning the drainage holes.

On 10 November 1982 the architects signed a further certificate of partial practical completion. The leaks continued, but by March 1983 the contractors understood from Gartners that the remedial work had been attended to, and on 10 March 1983 Rothschilds confirmed to the architect that no further ingress of water had occurred.

By early August 1983 Rothschilds had decided that the premises were unsuitable for their requirements and they told the developer of their intention to vacate. They did not tell the developer that leaks were still occurring or that they were moving out because of them. On 9 November 1983 the architects drew up a schedule of defects at the end of the defects liability period. No leaks were mentioned as such, although some discolouration was mentioned in relation to a sill.

The architects did not issue a certificate as to the making good of defects because, although between March 1983 and March 1984 there were no complaints of leaks, from April 1984 there were further complaints of leaks and Gartners were again called in. Until the defects in the cladding were made good, the architects felt it right to withhold a final certificate from the contractors.

Meanwhile the plaintiff, Crédit Suisse, was studying the building and its suitability for its wish to have a private banking presence in the West End. The plaintiff was acting through agents, Messrs Dron & Wright, whose Mr Gordon advised them on 18 December 1984 that the costs of maintenance and repair of such a building would be likely to be higher than for a more conventianal building. The landlord's agents, then called Harold Williams Bennett & Partners, advised the landlords that it would be to their advantage in valuation terms to have a tenant of the plaintiff's stature in occupation.

With the plaintiff's approval Dron & Wright brought in consulting engineers, the ZMG Partnership, to advise as to the building's structural suitability. They were asked to include the cladding within the subject matter of their report. ZMG brought in Bickerdike Allan Partners, specialist engineers with particular experience in relation to cladding. On 4 March 1985 Dron & Wright, in a preliminary report to the plaintiff, warned it of problems with the cladding and of the likelihood of high maintenance costs. On 8 March 1985, Dron & Wright sent the plaintiff the final report of ZMG into which Bickerdike Allan's report was incorporated. ZMG reported that No 66 was generally well-designed and should not require more than the normal routine maintenance and expense to be expected for a structure of its kind, but Bickerdike Allan had real doubts, saying leakage through windows was a serious problem affecting about a third of the windows. This threatened not only the cosmetic appearance of things but also the failure of DGUs. They warned that No 66 could involve a lessee in substantial maintenance and remedial costs and disruption. The defendant's agents passed the report to Gartners, describing the problem as one which required urgent rectification.

On 26 June 1985 Rothschilds assigned the underlease to the plaintiff, although the plaintiff did not for the time being move in. Gartners continued principally to blame blocked weepholes and said they had taken steps to unblock them. But the building continued to leak. The plaintiff complained to the landlord's agents, who on 11 September told the plaintiff that they had in mind beginning investigation and remedial works as a matter of urgency. They would be looking for an indemnity from the developer. The developer did not accept liability to the landlord and, other arguments apart, cited Gartners' belief that the blocked weepholes caused the leakage and that their blockage was caused by the landlord's poor maintenance and cleaning. The landlord then instructed its own engineers, Messrs Mott Hay & Anderson, who were handed a copy of the earlier ZMG report.

By late January 1986 Mott Hay had received Gartners' drawings which, it was found, did not show drainage holes of the kind which Gartners had been asserting existed and had compiled a list of leaks and inspected the building in rainy conditions. They recommended the external application of black silicon mastic to the windowsills, without prejudice to further investigation and remedial action elsewhere.

The landlord's agents studied this report and their building surveyor, Mr Richard Bennett, concluded that the problem of water leaks was becoming widespread and that the application of mastic could be regarded only as a temporary repair. None the less, on 4 March 1986, the landlord's solicitors indicated to the developers that unless they heard that the developers were themselves arranging the mastic application as recommended by Mott Hay then the landlord would itself go ahead with the application of mastic and with further investigations.

On 10 March 1986 Mott Hay sent their final report to their clients' agents. They understood that the cladding included drainage holes not shown on Gartners' drawings. As a priority they still advised the application of silicon mastic and they still needed to make further investigations as to the causes of leaks other than those at windowsills. They had not found any cause of leaks other than such as would, in their view, be held to be the responsibility of the installer of the cladding. They followed up their report on 19 March 1986 with a specification of the immediate remedial works considered necessary to overcome the majority of the leaks. They thought these works would cost some £9,000 to £11,000.

The developer's reaction to the landlord's indication that the landlords themselves would do the remedial works if the developer did not was to warn that so doing might release other parties from claims that might otherwise be made against them, presumably thus referring to Gartners, who, in correspondence between themselves and the developer, were declining to accept any responsibility, especially referring to the failure, as they said it was, of the owners or occupiers to keep the drainage holes properly cleaned. The outcome was that the landlord did not proceed with the works which its own engineers had suggested, the mastic sealant; this work, as was said, was put 'on hold'. Gartners were still insisting that blocked drainage holes were the root cause. Although they had put the matter 'on hold', in correspondence the landlord's solicitors continued to threaten that the remedial steps recommended by Mott Hay would be taken in order to meet what they indicated was their duty to mitigate, presumably referring to mitigation of such damage as might be claimed by the plaintiff. Something like an impasse now existed. Without a full inspection involving an opening up of the cladding it was unlikely that the root cause of the leaks would be traced, but Gartners, insisting that poor maintenance and blocked drainage holes were the causes and were not their responsibility, would not open up the cladding until they had been paid in full; the developer's architects and contractors would not have been keen to see Gartners paid in full unless and until their cladding system was verified to be sound. The landlord wished to press ahead with an investigation into causes but the developer was fearful that opening up might involving losing Gartners' guarantee and in the meantime the tenant's premises leaked, although the tenant had understood that the landlord would see the problem cured.

The evidence of Mr Murray [the tenant's premises maintenance manager] was that every time it rained, water leaked into No 66. Promotional material on the ground floor was destroyed or rendered useless. Water ran down a cable into an electricity distribution box. The staff laid towels and cloths on window sills in an attempt to absorb water and had from time to time to stop work to mop up. Carpets became wet and were stained. Baskets and bins were set to catch drips. Machinery was moved in, away from windows. The facade of the building was cleaned by specialist industrial cleaners, who had been directed to pay special attention to weepholes. Yet still the tenant was experiencing serious water penetration.

By 9 June 1987 the developers saw fit to serve writs against the architects, Gartners and others; the writs had been issued almost a year earlier. This development led to Gartners declining to attend further site meetings which had been arranged in the hope of a more thorough investigation of the causes of the problems. However, on 4 August 1987 Gartners made proposals for remedial works, which involved sealing all expansion joints to mullions, considering the use of silicon in place of mastic seals, sealing expansion joints and so on. The developers introduced yet further experts into the equation and in the meantime the tenant was suffering water ingress of a kind which damaged carpets and left water on windowsills.

Even Gartners were by now beginning to be less certain that the blockage of drainage holes was a material factor. Indeed, the very existence of the drainage holes of the kind to the blocking of which Gartners had attributed the problem began to be questioned by some. Gartners' drawings showed only a few drainage holes but they had been representing to others that there were drainage holes not shown on the drawings and to those who had questioned this Gartners had replied that the drawings did not show the holes because they were incorporated into their work as a matter of standard practice.

On 7 January 1988 the tenant's executive board met. The board decided in principle to move the West End office elsewhere. The decision was not dictated solely or, I would think, even principally by the state of the building; but the fact, as the board recorded it, that during the frequent rainy periods parts of the building became uninhabitable, was plainly a contributory factor feeding into the decision.

In February 1988 Mott Hay, under the heading 'Suggested remedial works', advised their clients, the landlords, of alternative remedial measures. The first was removal of the entire cladding system and its replacement by a redesigned system. The alternative included removal of the existing system, replacement of mullions and transoms by redesigned ones, the drilling of drainage holes and the reassembly of the units with fresh seals.

On 1 March 1988 two cladding panels were removed from the building, in Gartners presence, but no clear cause of the leakage was found. By now the tenant was in touch with surveyors and estate agents, Messrs Conway Relf, with a view to considering a disposal of the underlease at No 66. It was recognised that the then current rent payable of £200,000 pa would shortly come up for review. The first rent review date would be 25 July 1988. The market was buoyant; the likelihood was the landlord would wait until as late as possible to begin the review negotiations so as best to take advantage of the rising market. Conway Relf, by their Mr Berrill, advised the tenant to settle the review before disposing of the underlease. Any incomer, he said, would want to know for certain the rent he would need to pay. On 25 May 1988 the landlord's agents gave notice to the tenant of an intention to increase the rent with effect from 25 July 1998. By July the landlord's agents were proposing an increase to £385,000.

The tenant decided to sell the lease and to return its private banking operations to Bishopsgate. By 31 August 1988 the decision had been taken to vacate No 66 as from 1 November 1988. Amongst the reasons for the move was dissatisfaction with No 66 as being technically deficient.

In January 1989 the landlord's and tenant's agents agreed a new rent for £365,000, roughly £45 per sq ft. The tenant confirmed the acceptability of this new rent and began marketing the underlease.

Letting boards were put up at the premises and a brochure prepared and circulated to, inter alios, major banks and building societies. Advertisements were placed in the Financial Times and the Estates Gazette. Interest was widely shown and offers began to come in. Knight Frank & Rutley, as agents acting for Coast Securities, offered a premium of £50,000. They indicated that their client was in a position to move very quickly. Other serious offers were received but the offerors were told that the tenant was proceeding with another party but that they would be informed, should negotiations with that other party prove abortive.

On 6 March 1989 Knight Frank & Rutley for Coast indicated that they had been instructed to carry out a building survey. The tenant's solicitors when answering the inquiries before contract of Coast's solicitors, quite properly, felt that the problem of water penetration ought to be mentioned, but added that the purchaser must rely on its own survey. The inquiries also raised the question of whether there was any breach of covenant by either landlord or tenant; the answer was given that the tenant was aware of none but it was added that the purchaser was to take subject to any breach there might be. On 7 March 1989 Coast's solicitors specifically asked for information as to the dispute between the landlord and the suppliers of the cladding. On 3 March 1989 the landlord had issued a writ in the Queen's Bench Division, headed 'Official Referees' Business', against the developer for breach of the development agreement of 14 December 1977. There were other proceedings in Queen's Bench between the developer and six defendants, including Gartners, and arrangements were made for those two sets of proceedings to proceed together.

On 9 March 1989, the deadline date for exchange, the tenant's solicitors faxed the landlord's solicitors indicating that the proposed assignees had asked for a letter to be produced from the landlord acknowledging that the cost of remedying any defect in the building in respect of water penetration would be borne by the landlord and would not be passed on as part of the service charge. The landlord's solicitors were warned that the prospective assignee was threatening to withdraw if such a letter was not produced. The tenant's solicitors warned that failure to supply such a 'comfort letter' could cause the tenant yet further damage. On 15 March 1989 the landlord's solicitors indicated they were unable to give the tenant the acknowledgment it sought. Conway Relf, attempting as best they could to keep the deal with Coast alive, suggested a reduction of the asked-for premium and also the giving of an indemnity to Coast.

At the end of March 1989 the tenant again instructed Bickerdike Allan, whose Mr Josey reported on 5 April 1989 that the disruption to an occupier, inevitably to be associated with the making good of such defects as he found, was likely to be substantial.

On 7 April 1989 the landlord's agents informed Knight Frank & Rutley that they were unable to give any assurance as to whether the tenant would be liable for any of the costs of rectification of the water penetration and that they could not give any indication as to how the remedial works would be undertaken. Bickerdike Allan's report was sent to Knight Frank & Rutley, who on 11 April 1989 wrote to confirm that Coast had instructed them to withdraw from negotiations.

Conway Relf, having revived contact with the other offerors, admitted when asked why the first offeror had withdrawn that it was because of the problem of water penetration. Conway Relf advised the plaintiff that they could not seriously expect to secure a tenant in the circumstances and recommended that the building be withdrawn from the market and that they carefully review their position. On 21 April 1989 the tenant instructed Conway Relf to withdraw No 66 from the market.

On 14 June 1989 the tenant's solicitors wrote a letter before action to the landlord's solicitors, asserting that had the premises been in repair the tenant could have assigned them and for a premium. The tenant had been advised, they said, that they would set off against future liability for rent any claim for damages that they might have. They indicated that rent would not be paid from and including 24 June 1989, although they indicated also that they were still willing to assist with the landlord's proceedings against the contractors and others. Attempts to ascertain the causes of the leaks were proceeding in the context of the landlord's action against the developers (by now called 'Clayform' rather than by their earlier name, Samuel Developments).

On 17 August 1989 twelve individuals met, representing eight parties or firms. Glazing was removed and metal was cut away and the majority agreed that the cladding was not a fully drained system and differed from Gartners' drawings. The landlord was represented at this meeting by Crocker Tooth Associates, cladding experts, who had come on the scene in connection with preparation of the landlord's statement of claim against the developers and contractors. It was agreed that further tests were necessary. An opening up of further cladding in the presence of Miss Tooth of Crocker Tooth Associates and Mr Josey of Bickerdike Allan (for the tenant) was arranged for late November 1989.

On 1 December 1989 the landlord's solicitors understood that the landlord (without admitting that the tenant was entitled to withhold the same) was not going to proceed for the unpaid rent and service charges and was going to include such losses in its claim against the developers, which by then had been fixed to come on before the Official Referee in February 1991. However, by March 1990 the landlord had been advised not to delay seeking rent and service charges from the tenant and the landlord then demanded some £333,000 or so in March, a claim which had grown to £447,000-odd by April. On 4 April 1990 the tenant issued the writ in the present action.

On 8 March 1991 heads of agreement were signed to settle the actions between the landlord and its developer and the architect and between the developer and the architect and others including Gartners. The tenant had assisted the landlord in pressing those claims. The landlord was to appoint an architect to devise a new cladding scheme for No 66 which Gartners, after removing the existing cladding, were to design, manufacture and erect to the reasonable satisfaction of the landlord's architects and at Gartners' cost. The new system was to include a thermal break. Gartners were, to an agreed extent, to indemnify the landlord against the tenant's claims against it in the present action. If a building contract for the new cladding was not to be entered into within a specified period then, unless an extension to the specified period were to be agreed, Gartners would be obliged to pay the landlord £2·3m

by a date in March of 1993. By a consent order in Tomlin form before Judge
a John Newey QC hearing official referees' business on 8 March 1991, all
proceedings as to cladding in that court were stayed. Gartners paid the
landlord's costs. These arrangements were incorporated in the schedule to the
Tomlin order in the usual way.

The architects chosen by the landlord for devising the new cladding were
b Broadway Malyan. One of their objects was to produce a design that dispelled
the stigma which by now attached to No 66 and to make it readily marketable
and capable of reoccupation. If the recladding was in something other than
matching materials, such as masonry, planning permission would be
necessary; but in July 1991 the Royal Fine Arts Commission commended the
masonry solution and indicated that other proposals would be wholly
c unacceptable. Broadway Malyan's proposals for cladding bore scarcely any
resemblance to the Rocket Ship. The landlord instructed quantity surveyors
who costed various alternatives. The cost of replicating the existing cladding
but to an improved specification and with thermal breaks was in August 1992
estimated to be £940,000 although a simplified proposal could be achieved for
d about £685,000. Gartners foresaw difficulties and devised an alternative
overcladding scheme. The landlord had instructed new engineers by now and
they, Messrs Emmer Pfennigger Partners, went round the building in January
1993 with Miss Tooth, the landlord's cladding expert. Emmer Pfennigger
reported that Gartners' overcladding proposal was unworkable. By now it was
February 1993. The deadline, if £2·3m was not to become payable by Gartners,
e approached. In March 1993 Emmer Pfennigger costed a satisfactory proposal
for recladding at £1,154,516.

[It seemed unlikely that Gartners would be used in any new scheme. So far
as it was relevant to any question before the court, his Lordship proposed to
proceed on the basis that the landlord would recover the £2·3m together with
f any interest due from Gartners under the heads of agreement and Tomlin
order. To this day no final certificate as to the completion of the whole of
No 66 has been granted. His Lordship having concluded his chronology of
relevant events, of which the above is a shortened version, continued:]

Breach or nay?
g   I shall deal first with a number of minor arguments on the construction of
the underlease.

I am invited by Mr Knight QC for the landlord to proceed on the basis of
giving commercial effect to the principal covenant. He cites *C H Bailey Ltd v
Memorial Enterprises Ltd* [1974] 1 All ER 1003 at 1009, [1974] 1 WLR 728 at 735
h per Sir Eric Sachs. I thus approach the underlease having in mind that the
arrangements likely to have been intended to have been made by business
people will be businesslike arrangements. But I do not see the notion as going
further than that; it does not enable me to give other than a natural meaning
to the words used, although, doubtless, where two natural meanings equally
beckon I should, in this context, prefer the more businesslike.
j   Mr Knight invites me, in connection with terms commonly referred to in the
authorities, to give a construction consistent with that derivable from those
authorities because inconsistency is undesirable, he says, in standard forms of
commercial contracts. Plainly, I should accept guidance from authorities but I
do not regard this lease as a standard form of contract. Although certain words
recur in the authorities dealing with different repairing covenants and
although some guidance can thus be derived from other cases, there is a world

of difference between the case before me and cases where the courts properly
strive for consistency as to the construction of, say, the printed standard form
terms of the New York Produce Exchange: see eg *A/S Awilco of Oslo v Fulvia
SpA di Navigazione, The Chikuma* [1981] 1 All ER 652, [1981] 1 WLR 314 to which
Mr Knight referred.

It is argued that the fact that this is a landlord's covenant (but with recovery
under the service charge) should not be a factor pressing me towards some
construction other than that which would obtain had it been an identical
covenant on the tenant's part. My attention was drawn to *Torrens v Walker*
[1906] 2 Ch 166 at 174, [1904–7] All ER Rep 800 at 804. There Warrington J held
that the principle (applicable to a tenant's repairing covenant) that a lessee was
not bound to give back to the lessor at the end of the term a different thing
from that which had been demised to him, was matched, in a landlord's
covenant, by one under which the lessor would not be bound by a similar
covenant to give to the lessee during the term a different thing from that which
the lessee had taken at the beginning of the tenancy. There was, he held, no
difference in principle. The case does not, so far as material, go beyond that,
but it does seem correct to me that unless other circumstances compel
otherwise, similar words must have similar effect whether they be found in a
landlord's or in a tenant's covenant.

It is an irony in this case that the landlord has been saying that it would be
wrong to give a wide effect to the landlord's covenant for repair because, as the
expense of compliance is passed on to the tenant, so to do would, says the
landlord, unreasonably burden the tenant. The tenant, by contrast, hopeful
that, even if given works are within the principal covenant and hence
ordinarily within the service charge, it none the less has a prospect of escaping
the need to pay for extraneous reasons, presses for a wide construction of the
landlord's covenant. I am also invited to recognise, as did Scott J in *Plough
Investments Ltd v Manchester City Council, Plough Investments Ltd v Eclipse Radio
and Television Services Ltd* [1989] 1 EGLR 244 that, when the covenant is cast in
the way it is in the underlease here, the landlord's obligation to repair,
although nominally an obligation, is in a sense a right. It enables the landlord
to keep its building in repair at the tenant's expense and, as to works within the
covenant, it is the landlord rather than the tenant who determines how the
work is to be done. A tenant who might, had the choice been his, have got
away, so to speak, with a cheap solution to a given problem as to repair, might
find, under this form of a landlord's covenant, that a more expensive solution
is foist upon him by way of the landlord's choosing to employ it. I bear this in
mind but I do not see it as having a force sufficient to drive me away from the
ordinary meaning of words.

The tenant argues that it is not to be expected that the parties left a gap in
their obligations such that work needing to be done should transpire to be an
obligation neither of the tenant nor of the landlord. That is far from obvious
to me; parties can overlook some needs or even deliberately shy away from
some problems. Mr Gaunt QC for the tenant argued that if the necessary
works were not within the landlord's obligations then, as neither were they
within the tenant's, the situation would be that no one was responsible for
them which, he said, would be uncommercial. I was taken to *Barrett v Lounova
(1982) Ltd* [1989] 1 All ER 351 at 356–357, [1990] 1 QB 348 at 358. In that case
the Court of Appeal upheld the implication, in a demise of a house which
contained an express covenant that the tenant should keep the interior in good

order, of an obligation on the landlord to repair the outside. However, what
persuaded Kerr LJ to uphold the implication was not so much that if there were
no such implication no one would be responsible for the upkeep of the outside,
as the fact that if the outside were not kept up then in time the express
covenant by the tenant as to the interior could no longer be complied with, and
yet it was plain that the tenant did have to comply with it throughout the
whole term. It was that, rather than a gap such that otherwise no one would
have had to keep up the exterior, which enabled the court to imply an
obligation to keep the outside in repair. *Barrett v Lounova (1982) Ltd* might assist
a court in coming to a businesslike conclusion and in filling a gap where the
language of a lease can fairly be construed either to leave a gap or to fill it but
it cannot be authority for a proposition that whenever one encounters what
seems to be an unbusinesslike gap then the court is able or obliged to fill it.

The landlord refers to the ability of the landlord to enter during the term and
argues that such entry is limited to entry for works of repair strictly so called,
which thus points to the principal covenant also being limited only to works of
repair. However, cl 4(11)(d) permits entry 'for the purpose of carrying out the
Landlord's obligations hereunder' and Pt III of the second schedule reserves to
the landlord the right to enter not merely for the purposes of 'repairing' but
also—

> 'for the purpose of carrying out any work or doing anything whatsoever
> comprised within the Landlord's obligations herein contained ... for which
> the Tenant is liable hereunder to make a contribution ...'

The argument thus rebounds on the landlord; if the draughtsman has seen fit
to give entry for works under the landlord's obligation but which are other
than of repair strictly so called, then surely the principal covenant must
correspondingly go beyond works only of repair? The lease is over 45 pages of
single spaced typescript and I am far from confident that its draughtsmanship
is of a quality such that one can derive very much from this sort of exercise,
which requires a contrast to be made between references, for example, on p 12,
with those some 30 pages or so later. However, what little weight this point
does have ends up, as I see it, as being in the tenant's favour.

The landlord argues that it is wrong to look at the eight verbs in the principal
covenant and to see each one as intended to add to the meaning ascribable to
each of the others. In *Post Office v Aquarius Properties Ltd* [1987] 1 All ER 1055 at
1059 the covenant included 'well and substantially to repair ... amend ... renew
and keep in good and substantial repair and condition' yet the Court of Appeal
and Hoffmann J below ([1985] 2 EGLR 105) ruled on the case on the basis that
the words 'keep in good and substantial repair' were the critical words.
However, it is trite law, as the *Aquarius* case [1987] 1 All ER 1055 at 1064
acknowledges, that the parties to a lease may agree such provisions as they
choose and the *Aquarius* case cannot be authority for a proposition that
separate words are not to be given separate meanings where that is possible, if
only because the Court of Appeal was careful to indicate that no reliance had
been placed in the argument before them on any contention that the words
'amend', 'renew', or 'condition' added anything to the words which Hoffmann
J had taken to be the critical words: see *Post Office v Aquarius Properties Ltd*
[1987] 1 All ER 1055 at 1059, 1065, 1066 per Ralph Gibson, Slade LJJ and Sir
Roger Ormrod respectively agreeing.

The landlord sought to advance the same argument by reference to *Norwich
Union Insurance Society v British Railways Board* [1987] 2 EGLR 137, a rent review

case in which the arbitrator had adjusted the new rent downwards to reflect
that the covenant to repair was especially onerous upon the tenant. The
covenant for repair included not only 'To keep the demised premises in good
and substantial repair and condition' but also 'when necessary to rebuild
reconstruct or replace the same' (see [1987] 2 EGLR 137 at 138). The 1968 lease
was for a term of 150 years from 1964. With an irony corresponding to that
which I have mentioned as present in this case, the landlord was there arguing
that the covenant was to be construed so as to lighten the apparent burden on
the tenant; the added words 'rebuild', 'reconstruct' and 'replace' should not, he
urged, be taken as imposing obligations substantially beyond those in a
conventional covenant for repair and hence should be limited to the rebuilding
etc of subsidiary parts only of the building. In rejecting that, Hoffmann J
concluded that the covenant had two distinct parts; one involved the concept
of repair, the other, distinctly and separately, of rebuilding, reconstructing and
replacing, and that both were imposed on the tenant. However, and this is the
point most relied upon by Mr Knight, Hoffmann J said (at 138):

> 'Now I accept that in the construction of covenants such as this one
> cannot, for the reasons I have already given, insist upon giving each word
> in a series a distinct meaning. Draftsmen frequently use many words
> either because it is traditional to do so or out of a sense of caution so that
> nothing which could conceivably fall within the general concept which
> they have in mind should be left out. I also accept that if the language is
> not entirely clear the covenant should not readily be assumed to impose
> unusual obligations. In the ordinary way a covenant in a lease to rebuild
> the entire premises would be unusual.'

The 'reasons already given' included that the lease in that case employed
what Hoffmann J described as 'a torrential style of drafting'. As Hoffmann J
held that the obligation upon the tenant did, on the language of that covenant,
extend to a rebuilding of the whole building he was plainly not of the view that
added words can never add to the meaning. The argument that added words
should lead to added meaning had not needed to be pressed: *Lurcott v Wakeley*
[1911] 1 KB 905, [1911–13] All ER Rep 41, for example, was not, it seems, cited
to the learned judge, who in any event accepted, of course, that according to
normal rules of construction, additional words should be given some
additional meaning. *Norwich Union Life Insurance Society v British Railways Board*
is not and could not be authority for a proposition that that normal rule does
not apply to repairing covenants. Even where there is a torrent, each stream
of which it is comprised can be expected to have added to the flow.

Mr Knight, for the landlord, refers to Slade LJ's remarks in *Post Office v
Aquarius Properties Ltd* [1987] 1 All ER 1055 at 1066 that clear words are needed
to impose a contractual obligation on a tenant to remedy defects in the original
construction of the building 'at least at a time before these have caused any
damage. This is not an obligation which tenants under a commercial lease
might reasonably be expected readily to undertake'. Slade LJ does not say, of
course, that if clear words to that effect are found they can be overridden.
Moreover, as will later appear, I shall hold there to have been damage to the
subject matter of the principal covenant.

I now turn to more central issues of construction. As Fletcher Moulton LJ
emphasises in *Lurcott v Wakeley* [1911] 1 KB 905 at 915, [1911–13] All ER Rep
41 at 44, the duty of the court is to give a proper and full effect to

each word used in repairing covenants.   Atkin LJ indorsed this approach in
Anstruther-Gough-Calthorpe v McOscar [1924] 1 KB 716 at 731, [1923] All ER Rep
198 at 204.   I see the verbs 'amend' and 'renew' as capable of going outside the
verb 'repair', especially where, as here, the use of the phrase 'defects *or* wants
of repair' in the proviso to the principal covenant shows that some meaning
beyond repair is contemplated.   Moreover, and again having regard to that
phrase in the proviso, I see the words '*otherwise* keep in good and tenantable
condition' as having a potential going beyond repairs strictly so called (by
which I mean works of a kind which would fall within a covenant merely 'to
repair').   Just as did Fletcher Moulton LJ in *Lurcott v Wakely* [1911] 1 KB 905 at
916, [1911–13] All ER Rep 41 at 45 ('keep in good condition'), I shall first take
the phrase as to tenantable condition in the principal covenant and look at it as
if it were a separate covenant.

A number of points emerge.   Firstly, although *Proudfoot v Hart* (1890) 25 QBD
42, [1886–90] All ER Rep 782 has lost ground as to some parts of its reasoning
and has been said often to have been misunderstood, the notion illustrated by
it that a covenant to keep in a specified state includes an obligation to put into
that state has been acted upon, by now, in probably hundreds of cases and still
survives.   The obligation here is thus not merely to keep in good and
tenantable condition but that the landlord should put the building into that
condition.

Next, to transpose dicta directed to 'tenantable repair' to the expression
'good and tenantable condition' then the expression refers to such condition
as, having regard to the age, character and locality of the property, would make
it reasonably fit for the occupation of a reasonably minded tenant of the class
who would be likely to take it: see *Proudfoot v Hart* (1890) 25 QBD 42 at 55,
[1886–90] All ER Rep 782 at 786-787 and *Lurcott v Wakeley* [1911] 1 KB 905 at
921, [1911–13] All ER Rep 41 at 47, though one cannot lower the nature of that
condition by reference to deterioration in the expectations of the hypothetical
tenant consequential upon a deterioration in the class of tenants after date of
the lease: see *Anstruther-Gough-Calthorpe v McOscar* [1924] 1 KB 716 at 731,
[1923] All ER Rep 198 at 204.

Next, whilst I accept the inevitability of the conclusion of the Court of
Appeal in *Post Office v Aquarius Properties Ltd* [1987] 1 All ER 1055 that one
cannot have an existing obligation to repair unless and until there is a disrepair,
that reasoning does not apply to a covenant to keep (and put) into good and
tenantable condition.   One cannot sensibly proceed from 'no disrepair, ergo no
need to repair' to 'no disrepair, ergo no need to put or keep in the required
condition'.   Leaving aside cases, such as this, where there is special provision
for there to have been prior knowledge or notice in the covenantor, all that is
needed, in general terms, to trigger a need for activity under an obligation to
keep in (and put into) a given condition is that the subject matter is out of that
condition.

Next, where, as here, one has not only the verbs other than 'repair' but a
context showing that 'defects' in express contradistinction to 'repairs' are
within the covenant, the great body of law debating whether a given
shortcoming is or is not a repair or is or is not an inherent defect such that
remedying it goes beyond repair does not, in my judgment, apply.   Of course,
as with covenants to repair, questions as to the age, nature and class of the
subject matter to be put and kept in the specified condition have to be borne in
mind: see Fletcher Moulton LJ's examples in *Lurcott v Wakeley* [1911] 1 KB 905
at 916, [1911-13] All ER Rep 41 at 45 of the difference between keeping in

condition (in 1911) the Mauretania and a 'tramp that has been at sea for fifteen years'. So cases on 'repair' cannot be wholly discarded but, as I see it, it is no *a* necessary escape from liability under a covenant to put and keep in a specified condition that the work needed in order that that condition should be achieved is not a repair strictly so called. Nor do I see as important on this part of the landlord's covenant that the work required to achieve the given condition is of a particular great cost. I can see that that may well affect and has been *b* frequently taken to affect whether the work is one of 'repair' but I do not see it as material to an obligation to put and keep in a given condition. I have not understood any authority cited to me as disabling me from giving to the words of the covenant '*otherwise* keep in good and tenantable condition' the meaning which *Proudfoot v Hart* and *Lurcott v Wakeley* ascribe to similar phrases, nor as obliging me to attach to these words all the qualifications, which have been *c* held to circumscribe or affect an obligation to 'repair'.

It may perhaps be (but it is, as I mention below, unnecessary for me to decide) that a proper limitation on the obligation to put and keep in tenantable condition is that the landlord cannot be required to provide the tenant with something 'of a wholly different character from that which had been let': see *d* *McDougall v Easington DC* [1989] 1 EGLR 93 at 96. I thus say nothing as to that.

Next, if the meaning I have attributed to 'good and tenantable condition' is right, then the required condition in which the premises are to be kept and into which they are to be put falls to be judged not (if they differ) by reference to the actual state of the building as at the date of the demise but rather to what at that time were the requirements as to condition of the hypothetical reasonably *e* minded tenant of the class likely to take that building. There is warrant in *Smedley v Chumley & Hawke Ltd* (*Warrell, third party*) (1981) 44 P & CR 50 at 56–57 for the court to have regard, in relation to a new building, as the starting point in judging whether the effect of the words in question would be to yield something different to that which had been demised, not to what was the state *f* at the demise but what was contemplated as then being the state. The extensive foundation work done in that case providing a concrete raft, bracing it with concrete piles driven in, placing joists on the raft and then lowering the building onto that new foundation was held to be such—

'that after the works were done the difference to the premises was that *g* the walls and roof were in the condition that both parties contemplated as their necessary condition at the date of the lease'. (See 44 P & C R 50 at 57 per Cumming-Bruce LJ.)

If that is appropriate in a case where reference to a hypothetical reasonably *h* minded tenant was not in play, a fortiori it is relevant when the requirements as to condition of such a tenant are introduced. *Anstruther-Gough-Calthorpe v McOscar*, by its emphasis that the later lowered expectations of the subsequent hypothetical tenants are not to lower the standard beneath that applicable at the time of the demise, itself thus makes the point that it is expectation or contemplation which is important. Of course, in most circumstances the *j* hypothetical required condition and the actual condition as at the date of the lease will coincide. If there is no reason to regard the actual tenant as other than a reasonably minded member of the class likely to take the building of the kind in question and if he has inspected before he takes the lease it can reasonably be inferred, if the parties are silent on the point and if the surrounding circumstances add nothing, that the building reached the standard that the hypothetical tenant would have thought fit for his occupation. But so far as concerns good and tenantable condition, I cannot see it as relevant minutely to examine into whether, on the very day of the lease, No 66 was or was not watertight and if it was not, why it was not. If, as I think it is, the relevant standard of condition is what I shall call the putative condition, namely the condition that the tenant of the class I have described would require, then what is important is not so much the state of fact as at the date of the demise but what the tenant in particular then thought was the fact or, in the absence of direct evidence as to that, what it can be inferred the tenant is likely then to have thought in relation to the condition of the building. I cannot see it ought to be effective to lower the standard of condition in which the landlord has to keep the building beneath the putative condition were it to be proved, for example, that the building leaked on 28 January 1985 or 25 July 1983 (the date from which the term ran) if it could be claimed that the tenant reasonably believed that the new building was then good or would have had no reason to think that it was poor or if he understood or expected that the building was in the course of being, or was to be, made good by the landlord. The yardstick by which the necessary condition is, on this basis, to be ascertained is derived from the putative requirements of the reasonably minded tenant and so it is not to be lowered either by proof that the actual tenant was deceived or delayed in his receipt of that which he could be inferred to have expected.

Turning to what that hypothetical tenant might have expected, I cannot think that any tenant of the class of 'undoubted covenant' that the landlord would have then been looking for, taking in 1985 a wholly new and expensive architect-designed office and residential building in such a prime site as that occupied by No 66 would have required of the cladding of No 66 anything less than that it should be very substantially watertight. Short of the cladding being put into and kept in that state, it seems to me the building would not be reasonably fit for the occupation of such a tenant.

If I am right so far, then the chief question becomes a relatively simple one. Beyond any doubt the cladding at No 66 (which is conceded to be within the subject matter of the principal covenant) has during the plaintiff's occupancy not been put into, nor has it been kept in, the good and tenantable condition which I have supposed to be the putative necessary condition. The failed DGUs, the water stains on carpets, the buckets and bins needing to be placed to collect drips, the wet and stained windowsills, the stained and salt encrusted mullions, the spoiled display material and the bursting tungsten lamp all thus testify. Moreover, the chronology shows the landlord was sufficiently put on notice from 1984 on.

Nor, moving on to another point, can I regard No 66, even with a wholly new and redesigned cladding system, as being of a wholly different kind from that which had been let. Although, as will have been seen from the chronology, the landlord's engineers, Mott Hay, advised the application of black mastic, that seems since to have been regarded as only a temporary solution at best and probably not comprehensive even so long as it lasted. The landlord has not pressed that it would suffice to apply and reapply mastic from time to time. It may be a further factor that the building has acquired a 'stigma', as it has been described, the consequence of which is that short of comprehensive works being *seen* to have been done it will be poorly regarded by the agents letting in the area. Rather, the experts agree that the dismantling of the whole existing cladding and its entire replacement by a newly designed system is the only practical solution. Where what a sensible man would do would be thus comprehensively to eliminate the shortcomings in a way which would avoid repetition of temporary works, that factor, so long as the making-good of the defect does not involve a substantial rebuilding of the whole subject matter of the covenant, tends to put the works into the category of 'repair': see *Stent v Monmouth DC* [1987] 1 EGLR 59 at 65. I would not regard the replacement of the cladding as amounting to a substantial rebuilding of the whole subject matter of the covenant, which extended to the whole structure of the building, including its foundations. The cladding is but the exterior of two faces of the 'L' shape of the building. If it were wholly to be replaced with watertight cladding, the tenant would merely be getting what the hypothetical reasonably minded tenant would always have expected and what, I have no doubt, Rothschilds also thought they were contractually entitled to and would be getting and what the landlord hoped to be demising, namely a modern building completed to a good specification with anodised aluminium cladding faces which were watertight. It is for this reason I do not need to decide whether the 'wholly different character' argument applies to 'good and tenantable condition' *McDougall v Easington DC* [1989] 1 EGLR 93 at 96; even if I assumed it did apply, the point would fail on the facts. Nor, if I am wrong in disregarding cost, would I think that the cost of dismantling the present cladding and replacing it with wholly new and redesigned cladding, a cost of some £1·2m, would be such to put the works (if this be relevant) beyond the description of 'repair', given the value of No 66 as demonstrated by a rent which has varied between £200,000 to £365,000 and in the light of No 66 having had a capital value (on an assumed basis of being in repair) of as much as £7m.

Accordingly, in my judgment, and looking for the moment just to the obligation comprised within the words 'and otherwise keep in good and tenantable condition' the landlord is in breach, and has long been in breach, of the principal covenant. I should add that if, contrary to my views as to the proper yardstick being what I have called the putative condition at or about the time of the lease, the true measure were instead to be the actual condition then or thereabouts, then even so I should hold the landlord to be in breach. I shall need to go further into this subject below but I shall be holding that an earlier and better condition of the building has not been maintained. Leaks have got worse, DGU failures have increased, encrustations have grown worse and, of course, (though this relates to a period before the demise) the leak-free year between March 1983 and March 1984 presents a state that had not yet been regained.

If I am right to have regarded the words 'keep in good and tenantable condition' in the way that I have, then there is no need to ask in more detail why the building leaks. It is enough on that basis that it has leaked to the extent that it has. But if the verbs 'repair and renew' in the principal covenant are to be fastened upon, then, as to the verb 'repair,' as *Post Office v Aquarius Properties Ltd* [1987] 1 All ER 1055 shows, if the landlord is to be liable to 'repair' there must first be a disrepair. It is thus relevant, lest I am wrong on 'tenantable condition' and if 'renew' adds nothing material to 'repair', to find out why it is that the building leaks in order to ascertain whether there is some disrepair. Equally, it would be appropriate to see if what needs to be done to make the building appropriately watertight can fairly be described as work of 'repair' or of 'amendment' or of 'renewal' and whether the work falls outside *a* all or some of such descriptions as being, for example, the remedying of some inherent design or other defect which has afflicted the building from its outset.

To assist on such questions as these I received evidence by way of both written reports and oral evidence from two experts as well as such indications as one can glean from the correspondence and earlier reports which I have described in the chronology.

b [His Lordship, having set out the evidence of the landlord's expert, Miss Elizabeth Tooth RIBA, a chartered architect and principal of Crocker Tooth Associates, and the plaintiff's expert, Mr Josey, an associate of Bickerdike Allan Partners, as to the causes and possible solutions of the problem, continued:] What, then, are the conclusions which I should draw from all this evidence? I accept the situation as to leaks has got progressively worse in recent years but

c I am not convinced that proving that the leaks have got worse necessarily shows that the problem is one of repair strictly so called or that it is not one of inherent bad design or of initial bad construction. It does not seem to me to follow, for example, that an initial shortcoming in design or construction should reveal itself by symptoms which are observably of a steady frequency

d and of unincreasing severity, especially where variable factors such as wind and weather are material. Nor does it seem to me to follow from the starting point that one cannot be obliged to repair that which is not in disrepair that where there is disrepair the work that is needed to make it good must necessarily be described as work of repair. Still less does it necessarily prove that what is needed is work of repair for it to be shown that 'deterioration' has

e taken place. The cladding is not designed for ease of dismantling, for reduction to its component parts or for the replacement of the thin seals, which I accept have existed between many of its material parts. Failed seals cannot be made good by a smear of sealant on their faces nor can sealant, to any useful degree, be forced in between the assembled components.

f On the technical and other evidence I have heard I conclude as follows.

(i) There has been actual damage caused to the subject matter of the principal covenant in the sense that DGUs have failed and there have been encrustations and stains on the faces of the internal mullions and sills. The landlord itself alleged this and other damage to No 66 in its proceedings against others in the Official Referees' court.

g (ii) The damage has been caused by water penetration into the cladding and its passage from the cladding into the interior and, in the cases of DGUs, by penetration into the glazing rebates and from there into the DGUs themselves.

(iii) There were, from the outset, grave shortcomings in design and to a lesser extent, of construction in the cladding and glazing systems, which had a

h propensity to leak.

(iv) Seals have failed and amongst the causes of the penetration of water an important one is the failure of seals. In large part their failure has occurred after and has grown worse over the time since the building was demised.

(v) In the sense that the failure of seals is the failure of subsidiary parts, it

j can be described as a disrepair and some at least of the damage to the subject matter of the covenant which has occurred can be attributed to the failure of the seals.

(vi) However, even if I should thus describe the cladding as being in a state of disrepair I would none the less not think it right to speak of the total removal of the existing system and its entire replacement with a new and redesigned system as work of mere 'repair'. The question is established to be one of degree and, in my judgment, the whole cladding system, whilst well-short of being the whole subject matter of the covenant, is too substantial and important a portion of the whole subject matter of the principal covenant for its complete removal, redesign and replacement to be regarded as an operation in respect only of a subordinate or subsidiary part: see Buckley LJ in *Lurcott v Wakeley* [1911] 1 KB 905 at 924, [1911–13] All ER Rep 41 at 49.

(vii) However, I would think it right to describe such remedial work as a 'renewal' and within the obligation to 'repair amend renew' in the principal covenant, again bearing in mind that the proviso, by its reference to 'defects or want of repair', indicates a possibility of liability outside mere repair. In a covenant which appears to go beyond mere repair and which, in so doing, refers to renewal, 'renewal' can be taken to embrace reconstruction even of the entirety of the subject matter of the covenant: see Buckley LJ in *Lurcott v Wakeley*. I do not see it as a necessary part of a renewal (in contrast with a restoration) that the new should be exactly as was the old, particularly where the old had proved defective. The fact that the new cladding will be to a different design does not, in my view, deny it the description of being a renewal. On this basis, whether I am right or wrong as to the total recladding being outside 'repair', I find it within the obligation to 'amend, renew'. I am conscious of the argument that if 'renew' is to be given a separate meaning beyond 'repair' then there is probably no stopping point short of its ability to require the rebuilding of the whole subject matter of the covenant: see *Collins v Flynn* [1963] 2 All ER 1068. However, the landlord in a case such as the present would be likely to have wished that and the tenant, whilst recognising the size of the potential burden on him, could well have thought, in relation to a new architect-designed building thought to have been completed to a high specification, that the likelihood of that burden actually turning into a present liability during the 25 years of the underlease was so remote as to be discounted. Thus if the word 'renew', in a context plainly going beyond repair, can properly extend, as I believe it can, as far as a total replacement of the subject matter to which it relates, then I see no good reason why it should not here do so. If it is asserted that clear words would be needed for such a conclusion I would say that in a context, as here, where 'defects' are within the covenant as alternatives to 'repairs', the words 'amend' and 'renew' are clear enough.

It is not as if the work proposed will extend the practical life of the building. The new cladding, said Miss Tooth, would last 60 years, the normal life of the building. I note that in *Ravenseft Properties Ltd v Davstone (Holding) Ltd* [1979] 1 All ER 929, [1980] QB 12 the covenant included an obligation to 'renew' but Forbes J found it unnecessary to give the word any separate consideration (see [1979] 1 All ER 929 at 938, [1980] QB 12 at 22).

Accordingly, even if I am wrong in seeing the landlord as being in breach of its covenant as to good and tenantable condition, I would find it to have been being in breach of its obligations to 'renew' and to 'amend'. It would only be if I were constrained by authority to regard the clear apparent extension of the principal covenant beyond a liability merely to 'repair' that I would conclude the landlord not to be in breach, but I find no such constraint. Indeed, so far from finding such constraint, I have already cited high authority for the propriety of giving a proper and full effect to each word used.

On the basis that the landlord is in breach, I turn next to the subject of damages.

Damages

The plaintiff argues that if No 66 had been begun to be put into tenantable condition (or amended, or renewed, or as the plaintiff would have it also, repaired) within a reasonable time after the landlord had received notice of such 'renewal, repair and maintenance' (cl 6(12) of the underlease) then that work would have been completed long before the tenant came to market its underlease of No 66 in early 1989 and, in the buoyant conditions of the time, the likelihood is, says the plaintiff, that the underlease would have been promptly assigned for a premium of £85,000 or thereabouts. It is not said that, in a lease of this kind, it need not have been foreseen that the tenant might wish to assign: see *Mira v Aylmer Square Investments Ltd* [1990] 1 EGLR 45.

I hold, as Mr Berrill of Conway Relf and Mr Castle of Dron & Wright deposed, that the problems encountered on the attempt at disposition were entirely due to shortcomings in the state of No 66 which I hold would not have existed had the principal covenant been duly performed. It cannot be doubted but that the landlord had notice of severe leaks from 1985 at the latest. Its own engineers, Mott Hay, reported to it in 1985 and 1986. Mott Hay's recommendations for further investigations were not fully pursued. Had they been and had the cladding been investigated in detail its lack of drainage would have come to light literally years before that was discovered and the need wholly to renew the cladding would similarly have been revealed as the only real solution years before that eventually emerged. I hold that, had the landlord taken reasonable steps to cure the breaches of its obligations under the principal covenant within the time allowed by the underlease, then No 66 would have been assigned by the tenant in or about the first week of March 1989 and for a premium of £85,000 or so, the figure which Conway Relf, on the tenant's behalf, were pressing to obtain from Knight Frank & Rutley's client, Coast Securities.

Mr Gaunt for the plaintiff cited in this context *Calabar Properties Ltd v Stitcher* [1983] 3 All ER 759 at 766–767, [1984] 1 WLR 287 at 295–296, where Stephenson LJ says :

> 'In measuring and assessing any tenant's damages for breach of a landlord's repairing covenant the court must, I think, always start with the fundamental principle that they are "so far as is possible by means of a monetary award, to place the plaintiff in the position which he would have occupied if he had not suffered the wrong complained of, be that wrong a tort or a breach of contract". I take that statement from the judgment of Donaldson LJ in *Dodd Properties (Kent) Ltd v Canterbury City Council* [1980] 1 All ER 928 at 938, [1980] 1 WLR 433 at 456 ... So the true measure of damages for persons owning or occupying land, whether in tort or contract, depends on the position of the plaintiffs and all the circumstances in which they have suffered loss and damage, in the light of the fundamental principle to which I have referred.'

I willingly accept, as that citation suggests, that there is no one inflexible form of computation to be applied to all breaches but that the court is to look as best it can to the particular position which the plaintiff in the case before the court would have occupied if he had not suffered the wrong in question.

Building on that citation from the *Calabar* case, the plaintiff seeks damages under three heads. First, there is general damages for inconvenience. As to this, the plaintiff points to the inconvenience suffered by customers and, more particularly, by staff of the bank. The plaintiff argues that the breach was complete by 1986 and that compensation under this head is payable in respect of the period from then until the plaintiff moved out of the premises in late 1988. I would not put the breach quite so early but I would see it as occurring by or at the beginning of 1987. I am thus asked to make an award in respect of nearly two years' inconvenience. Mr Gaunt, for the plaintiff, seeks to use the landlord's own expert's view as a guide, that expert, Mr Hayward, having suggested that the premises were halved in rental value by reason of their state or, upon some assumptions little related to reality, that the premises were reduced by some 20% in rental value. Mr Gaunt modestly claimed only the lesser basis of 20%. However his modesty, I apprehend, was not true modesty but was arrived at from an awareness that the drop of 50% in value would produce a figure that would likely be seen to be hopelessly high for general damages of the kind in question. In my judgment, the 20% basis is also unacceptable; I am unconvinced one can evaluate inconvenience to a tenant in occupation by reference simply to the diminution in prospective letting value to some hypothetical other tenant. General damages are notoriously at large but, doing the best I can to have regard to the inconvenience suffered by staff and customers in these expensive and prestigous premises over the period I have described, I fix general damages at £40,000.

The plaintiff's second head of damage includes the lost premium and costs incurred in the abortive attempts to dispose of the underlease in 1989. I have already indicated I would expect a premium of £85,000 to have been achieved and I find this to be within the plaintiff's special damage suffered. As for the costs incurred in the abortive attempt to dispose of the underlease, the landlord says that such costs would have been incurred even had the premises been in the best order and condition and even had the assignment gone ahead. However, it is to be borne in mind that those costs were incurred but that they profited the tenant not one iota and that the tenant will incur a further set of costs when it does come, albeit belatedly, to underlet the premises once they are put into good order. (It is accepted that, because of the fall in rents, an assignment, at all events without a 'negative premium', cannot realistically be supposed to be possible.) I accept these wasted costs are to be recovered by the tenant. The landlord must pay therefore a series of sums (the precise sums, I understand, are or will be agreed) in respect of fees of Messrs Dron & Wright, Bickerdike Allan, Conway Relf and Fladgate Fielder. Also within this second head is a whole range of outgoings cleaning, storage, security, rates, fire protection, electricity, water and heating services which the tenant has borne since early March 1989 which would not have been borne, at any rate by him, had the underlease been assigned. I am by no means confident of the individual figures agreed as they have changed from time to time in the course of argument and I have not received the final schedule from the defendants, which I had understood I was to receive. If there are difficulties on these figures then they can be mentioned to me but I apprehend the current figure down to September 1993 and, including the abortive costs I have mentioned, is £260,173·37 plus £6,305·12 VAT.

To such, and subject to the effect of the counterclaim, which I deal with below, must be added rent, insurance and service charges payable by the tenant after the date at which, had the principal covenant been honoured, the tenant would have disposed of the property. The relevant figure is of the order of £1,551,250. Again, if a precise figure is not agreed then I will hear counsel on the point. Insurance required by the underlease in the period which is to be added to the special damage to be payable by the landlord is of or about £17,130·02 and service charges add a further £170,529·07.

Still within the tenant's second head are two forms of claims as to interest. They are, I think, affected by my finding the first week of March 1989 as the date of the putative disposal of the underlease but rather than my attempting to put a value on these claims or fully describing them, the simpler course is for me merely to indicate that if interest is not agreed then I will hear counsel further on the subject.

The third head of loss claimed by the plaintiff is occasioned by its remaining liable under the underlease for the rest of the term to 2008. This liability is to be computed on the basis referred to during the hearing as option 2B, under which (the landlord having given evidence on this subject which I accept) it is assumed that, irrespective of recovery from Gartners or others, the landlord will now very shortly set about a total recladding of No 66.

Option 2B is an elaborate table (happily largely agreed as to the figures) which assumes the tenant remains tenant until 2008 but assumes also that as soon as is practicable after No 66 is put into good order the tenant will sub-underlet at the best rent obtainable to a description of tenant of a kind to whom the landlord would be likely to permit a sub-underletting. The present tenant is to bear rates, service charges and insurance until the putative new tenant comes in. In the fullness of time the putative incoming tenant will suffer upwards-only rent reviews. The plaintiff, under option 2B, never pays a greater rent to the landlord than the £365,000 pa which it now pays, as both experts agree that 1983 rent levels are unlikely to be reached again throughout the whole term until 2008. The plaintiff tenant bears service charges until the putative new tenant takes them over. These putative incomings and outgoings of the tenant are, in option 2B, converted to a net cash flow in or out, quarter by quarter, down to 2008 and that net cash flow is discounted back to today's date at an agreed rate of 8% pa. Today's pound is thus worth a hundred pence whereas that to be paid in 2008, for example, is now worth 32p.

Option 2B assumes that the specifying of the necessary recladding works and their execution will be followed first by a period for the marketing of the underlease and then (in the conditions foreseen as likely) by the incoming tenant needing to be given an initial 'rent holiday'. The experts differed as to the precise length of 'rent holiday' likely and of the marketing period needed. The plaintiff's computation assumes No 66 does not come on stream as a yielder of rent till the quarter day, 25 March 1997. I accept on the evidence that that is the probability, as seen from today. Although, looking to the rest of the period from 25 March 1997 to mid-2008, the experts differed in only one part of their respective computations, because one is looking to expenses likely over a relatively long period even a small difference can yield a large difference in the resulting cash figure. The one difference is this: both experts expect the first rental, when, after the necessary works and the 'rental holiday', No 66 will first yield rent, to be £170,000 pa, which is also what they both see as the rent which would be the value of the premises today were they in good condition. Both experts are content to accept that as a matter of general experience over a long period rents can be expected to increase by 7% pa in respect of premises such as No 66 in a location such as No 66's. There will be two reviews (upwards only) of the rent that the putative incoming subtenant will need to pay in 1998 and in 2003. The difference between the experts in relation to the rent increases likely on those rent reviews is as to from what date the expected 7%

p a increase should be taken to operate. The landlord says that that 7% should be computed to run as from today whereas the tenant urges that it should run from the date of the supposed letting to the putative tenant in 1995. I prefer the landlord's view; if the 7% figure is a figure generally observable over a long term I see no good reason to delay the start of that long term. The fact that this approach leads to a conflict between the view that the premises, if in good order, would be worth £170,000 p a today but only that same figure in 1995 when they are relet is simply a conflict between a generally observable pattern and what is specifically expected in the relatively short term in this particular case. If, as seems accepted and indeed inevitable, the rent in the longer term is to be computed by reference to what is generally observed, then the adoption of that general position seems to me to lead to a computation increasing from today at 7% p a from today's figure of £170,000 p a.

Option 2B is computed on the basis (which I accept to be correct) that the tenant's tenancy of No 66 since it left the premises in November 1988 has been of no value whatsoever to it and, moreover, is incapable of being turned to value. Any sub-underlessee of the kind who might have been willing to pay something to be in possession in the short term of premises in such disorder would, on the evidence, have been a tenant an underletting to whom the landlord would not for a moment have countenanced.

Mr Knight, for the landlord, whilst agreeing many of the figures in option 2B, resisted it in principle and submitted that any award of damages in respect of the liability of the tenant to pay rent, insurance and service charges in respect of No 66 after the date of my judgment would be wrong. The principal covenant, he urges, is a continuing covenant under which damages may be awarded from time to time as they accrue. The tenant cannot, he says, sue for future unascertained damages. He relies on *McGregor on Damages* (15th edn, 1988) para 979 on this point. The tenant can come back and sue as often as it likes, he says, so long as any breach of the landlord's covenant (which is denied) continues. Mr Gaunt's answer is that what the tenant here invites to be assessed is not further losses flowing from future breaches but future losses from a past breach, the breach from 1987 or so to March 1989 which had the consequence that the tenant, instead of being able to dispose of the premises, was unable to rid itself of them, with the consequences, on the evidence, that it will be unable to shift liability for rent and so on during the rest of the term to 2008. Mr Gaunt argues that if the tenant were to fail now fully to claim for these losses it would be in difficulties were it to attempt to recover them later; the landlord could in such a case reply 'res judicata'. I accept Mr Gaunt's argument and I do not see *Battishill v Reed* (1856) 18 CB 696, 139 ER 1544 as barring that conclusion. In that case the plaintiff, who held the reversion in some premises, complained that some tiles in the eaves of his property had been removed by the defendant and that a taller building had been erected so close by on the immediately adjoining land by the defendant that water no longer fell as it had onto and from his eaves. Although the cost of replacing the tiles was only 30s the plaintiff claimed that the 40s paid into court was not enough. The jury found it was sufficient. On appeal it was argued that the plaintiff ought to have been allowed to give evidence to show that the saleable value of his premises had been materially depreciated by the defendant's wrongful acts. The plaintiff had suffered a permanent injury, it was argued, in being prevented from raising the level of his property, if so minded, and had suffered a diminution in its market value, evidence of which should have been admitted. The crucial difference between that case and this (although it is a difference only one of the four judges expressly brought out) is that the plaintiff there did not aver that he had wished to sell his reversion. Cresswell J, in finding that the evidence of diminution in value was properly excluded said (18 CB 696 at 715, 139 ER 1544 at 1552):

> 'So, here, the consideration of the subject might have been very different if the plaintiff had alleged and proved an attempt to sell the premises, which had failed in consequence of the nuisance.'

Williams J, next following, began by saying that he was entirely of the same opinion, as did Willes J (see 18 CB 696 at 716, 717, 139 ER 1544 at 1552). By contrast, the evidence before me did show an attempt to dispose which failed in consequence of the landlord's breach of covenant. In the light of that crucial difference I do not see the tenant as properly to be confined, as was the plaintiff in *Battishill v Reed*, to initial nominal damages coupled with the ability to bring second and subsequent actions, perhaps for increasing damages, so long as the defendant's default should continue.

I am thus in a position to award general and special damages to the tenant broadly as I have mentioned them, although I recognise that I may need to be addressed further as to the final detail if figures are not agreed in the light of my findings. More importantly, as I shall mention below, there is a counterclaim by the landlord to be borne in mind and this will have an effect on the total damages to be awarded because of the indemnity or set off I shall there discuss.

Estoppel

The tenant submits that the landlord is estopped, by way of an estoppel by convention, from denying that he has been and still is liable to remedy such defects as have caused the ingress of water. Mr Gaunt relies on *Amalgamated Investment and Property Co Ltd (in liq)v Texas Commerce International Bank Ltd* [1981] 3 All ER 577 at 584, [1982] QB 84 at 121 per Lord Denning MR and on *Norwegian American Cruises A/S v Paul Mundy Ltd, The Vistafjord* [1988] 2 Lloyd's Rep 343 at 351–352, where Bingham LJ said:

> 'I do not propose to essay a definition of estoppel by convention. It is sufficient for the purposes of this case to adopt the description given by the Court of Appeal in *Keen v. Holland* ([1984] 1 All ER 75 at 81–82, [1984] 1 WLR 251 at 261), of the essential nature of the *Amalgamated* case, and to say that it applies where (1) parties have established by their construction of their agreement or their apprehension of its legal effect a conventional basis, (2) on that basis they have regulated their subsequent dealings, to which I would add (3) it would be unjust or unconscionable if one of the parties resiled from that convention.'

In the light of my earlier conclusions I may take this further argument in the tenant's favour fairly shortly. I am willing to treat the underlease as if it was an agreement between the landlord and the tenant, which it was not, but even so I do not find the facts necessary to establish a convention as to its construction or effect. In the context that a landlord may indicate a willingness to do works outside his strict obligation and in a context, as here, in which the landlord believes he may have a good case to get others to do works or to recover the expense of works from others, merely to point to a landlord's apparent willingness to do works or have them done is not, of itself, material sufficient to show a convention as to the effect of the underlease. The landlord by its agents used expressions such as that it was taking most seriously the question of repairs, that it would draw up a scheme for investigation and remedy and that it seemed important to try to identify the problems with the cladding and get them put right without waiting for a lengthy battle or litigation as to responsibility (which the landlord's agents, be it noted, indicated *they would have to pursue in due course*) . The landlord's agents said they were in contact with their client and its solicitors with a view to initiating the necessary further investigation and remedial works as a matter of urgency, but, as the landlord also made clear, it was pursuing the developer to have the defects remedied and was maintaining a pressure on the developer to that end. Nowhere do I find that the landlord was indicating it would see the defects made good by reason of its liabilities under the principal covenant or under the underlease generally. Nowhere is the meaning and effect of the principal covenant discussed or assumed. Nowhere at any time relevant to estoppel is the ordinary consequence of the landlord's liability under the principal covenant, namely the tenant's liability under the service charge, discussed or assumed. Mr Murray, the tenant's premises maintenance manager, undoubtedly and rightly believed that the landlord was a substantial pension fund which had accepted that it would get the necessary work done but he did not assert that allied to that was that it had accepted that the work had to be done by reason of the principal covenant. The tenant asserts that not once in the correspondence did the landlord ever deny its responsibility to do the necessary works or have them done, but not once, either, was it ever accepted in the correspondence that the landlord was so responsible by way of the principal covenant or otherwise under the underlease. Had it been material for me to deal with estoppel as a matter of decision I would have held the estoppel to fail because the first of Bingham LJ's three ingredients is missing. I would not have been satisfied, either, that the second was present, and in the absence of those first two, the third would not have arisen.

The counterclaim

The current rent is £365,000 p a. Option 2B is computed on the basis that the tenant will be liable for and will pay that rent punctually quarter by quarter till the expiry of the underlease in 2008. There is and can be no counterclaim as to future rent. As to past rent after the date, early March 1989 (which I have accepted as the date at which the tenant would have assigned if the premises had been in the proper order), down to the September quarter day in 1993, this has not been paid, after June 1989, by the tenant. I have mentioned, as a head of loss by the tenant, that it was liable for rent over this period, a liability which amounts to some £1,642,500 when added together with the further sums for service charges and insurance. If that total were to be allowed as a head of recoverable damage by the tenant then the landlord would need to be put in a position in which he was to be paid that money.

However, the tenant's claim was expressed not only as damages in respect of that global liability but, alternatively, for indemnity against that liability. Although any potential difference in the net effects between, on the one hand, my giving judgment on damages and ordering payment to the landlord on his counterclaim and, on the other, my simply setting one against the other, has not been the subject of any argument, I take it to be tacitly accepted that either way the overall effect is zero and that the more convenient course is not to award a sum and then a counter-sum but to proceed on the basis that no damages are to be awarded to the tenant in respect of rents, insurance and service charges payable prior to the September 1993 quarter day and that no rent etc is to be ordered payable to the landlord for that period either. On that basis I need grant no separate relief on the landlord's counterclaim but rather adjust the tenant's damages downwards by deleting the part otherwise attributable to rents, insurance and service charges payable prior to September 1993 and not paid.

Pleadings and conclusion

At the end of Mr Castle's oral expert evidence on behalf of the plaintiff I asked whether his schedule of the computation of future losses suffered by the tenant reflected that if the landlord had been liable under the principal covenant to do the various works and if they had been done then their cost would have been passed on to the tenant under the service charge. I was told that neither Mr Castle's figures nor those of Mr Hayward, the landlord's expert, reflected that possibility. This troubled me because, if the measure of damages was to include reference to what the tenant's position would have been if only the landlord had not breached the covenant, it seemed to me that that position would include that the tenant would become liable by way of service charge. I later raised the point with Mr Gaunt who was, I think, entitled to answer, as he did, that it was not clear the landlord would even attempt so to recover and that it was for the landlord to plead factors which reduced the damages (if any) payable by him and that nothing of the kind was pleaded. Mr Gaunt also then outlined some other reactions he would need to enlarge upon were the landlord to seek to have his prospective recovery by way of service charge brought into account. Some while later, after Mr Knight had completed his speech and when Mr Gaunt had nearly finished his reply at the very end of the case, Mr Knight applied further to amend the defence and counterclaim on the basis that the landlord would indeed seek to recover under the service charge and that it wished to deduct from the tenant's computation (known as option 2B) that part (said to be 75%, under the service charge) of the cost of the recladding works (£1·2m) which the landlord had sworn would now be put in hand. The prospective future deduction would need to be discounted back to give its present value. No expert or other evidence had been directed to these ideas and I was not confident that there could have been no relevant evidence directed to them. Moreover, the tenant, were the point to be raised, would have wished to argue that for the landlord to recover from the tenant for such works would have led to an unjust entitlement, a double recovery, because it had already recovered therefor from Gartners, or was about to do so.

Questions of subrogation were said to arise and the landlord was set to argue that recovery from Gartners was res inter alios acta. None of these questions had been explored earlier. Had I felt that any true hardship or material injustice would have been visited on the landlord if I refused it leave to amend I would have given leave even though an adjournment for amendment of pleadings for further argument and, not improbably, for further evidence would have ensued. However, if I make no deduction from the damages to reflect prospective recovery under the service charge then the landlord will be entirely free to seek to recover from the tenant the 75% (if that is appropriate) of whatever the true cost of the works within the covenant proves to be, when it is eventually done. Even if there were to be an injustice to the landlord here (and that is far from clear, given the tenant's arguments against double recovery and other arguments, perhaps including subrogation and estoppel, against its liability under the service charge) it would be shortlived. In all the circumstances I refused the landlord leave further to amend. There was, at the same time, another subject as to which the landlord sought to amend but in the event, which happened, that Mr Gaunt opposed it, it was not pressed and I need say no more about it.

So, by way of conclusion, I hold the landlord to be, and long to have been, in breach of the principal covenant, that substantial damages are to be awarded to the tenant and that, because of the landlord's counterclaim, the sum finally to be awarded is to take into account that the tenant, whilst liable under the underlease for rent, service charges and insurance, has in fact paid no rent since June 1989 and other sums, if at all, only sporadically. As I hand this judgment down whilst sitting as vacation judge the convenient course will be for further discussion as to the precise awards in the light of this judgment and as to other questions, such as to costs, to be the subject of a restored short hearing in the new term.

Judgment for the tenant.

Paul Magrath Esq   Barrister.

Connaught Restaurants Ltd v Indoor Leisure Ltd

COURT OF APPEAL, CIVIL DIVISION

NEILL, SIMON BROWN AND WAITE LJJ

25 JUNE , 19 JULY 1993

Landlord and tenant – Covenant – Payment of rent – Payment of rent 'without any deduction' – Meaning of 'deduction' – Landlord's breach of covenant causing tenant damage – Tenant withholding payment of rent – Landlord claiming possession of premises and arrears of rent – Tenant counterclaiming for damages in respect of disruption to business – Whether tenant entitled to claim equitable right of set-off – Whether right of set-off excluded by words 'without any deduction'.

In 1983 the landlord demised part of its leasehold premises to the tenant for a term of twelve and a half years. The underlease contained a covenant requiring the tenant to pay the agreed rent 'without any deduction' and the landlord's covenants in common form (including the covenant for quiet enjoyment). From November 1987 the tenant suffered severe damage caused by flooding from the landlord's retained section of the building, which, in turn, caused major disruption to its business. In June 1989 the tenant withheld rent of £12,500, which was due for the quarter, and paid no further instalments thereafter. The landlord subsequently brought proceedings for possession of the demised premises and arrears of rent. In defence, the tenant contended that it had an equitable right of set-off arising from the landlord's breach of covenant and counterclaimed for damages. The judge held that the tenant's right of set-off had been excluded by the covenant for the payment of rent 'without any deduction'. He therefore gave judgment for the landlord for £202,690 in unpaid rent, plus interest and costs, and judgment for the tenant on its counterclaim for damages of £435,760, plus interest and costs, for serious breaches of covenant by the landlord. The tenant appealed, contending that it was the real victor and deserved a more favourable result in terms of costs and interest.

Held – Clear words were needed to exclude a tenant's remedy of an equitable right of set-off. The word 'deduction' however could not be accurately described as a clear word. It was a useful and flexible word, which could be employed either in the strict sense to describe the process of subtraction with which it was grammatically associated, or in a broader sense to describe the result where one claim was set off against another and a balance struck, but it was heavily dependent on its context and if the context afforded no guidance, it necessarily suffered from ambiguity. It followed that the simple expression 'without any deduction' was insufficient by itself, in the absence of any context suggesting the contrary, to operate by implication as an exclusion of the tenant's equitable right of set-off. On the facts, the provision in the lease that rent should be paid 'without any deduction' was insufficiently clear to exclude the tenant's equitable right to set off a claim for damages for the landlord's breach of covenant against the rent due. The tenant's appeal would accordingly be allowed (see p 843 *a* to *g j* and p 844 *a e* to *j*, post).

Grant v NZMC Ltd [1989] 1 NZLR 8 at 13 considered.
Famous Army Stores v Meehan [1993] 1 EGLR 73 disapproved.

Cases referred in judgment

Akehurst v Stena Sealink Ltd (17 February 1993, unreported) QBD.
British Anzani (Felixstowe) Ltd v International Marine Management (UK) Ltd [1979] 2 All ER 1063, [1980] QB 137, [1979] 3 WLR 451.
Famous Army Stores v Meehan [1993] 1 EGLR 73.
Federal Commerce & Navigation Co Ltd v Molena Alpha Inc, The Nanfri, The Benfri, The Lorfri [1978] 3 All ER 1066, [1978] QB 927, [1978] 3 WLR 309, CA.
Gilbert-Ash (Northern) Ltd v Modern Engineering (Bristol) Ltd [1973] 3 All ER 195, [1974] AC 689, [1973] 3 WLR 421, HL.
Grant v NZMC Ltd [1989] 1 NZLR 8, NZ CA.
Hanak v Green [1958] 2 All ER 141, [1958] 2 QB 9, [1958[2 WLR 755, CA.
S L Sethia Liners Ltd v Navigiagro Maritime Corp, The Kostas Melas [1981] 1 Lloyd's Rep 18.
Lee-Parker v Izzet [1971] 3 All ER 1099, [1971] 1 WLR 1688.
Sapsford v Fletcher (1792) 4 Term Rep 511, [1775–1802] All ER Rep 126, 100 ER 1147.
Young v Kitchin (1878) 3 Ex D 127.

Notes

For deductions allowed from rent, see 27(1) *Halsbury's Laws* (4th edn reissue) para 234.
For set-off against rent, see 13 *Halsbury's Laws* (4th edn) paras 284–286.

Appeal

Indoor Leisure Ltd (the lessees) appealed from the decision of Judge Bowsher QC hearing official referees' business made on 10 June 1992 whereby he gave judgment (i) for Connaught Restaurants Ltd (the lessors) in their action for unpaid rent of £202,690 plus interest in respect of the demised premises, being part of the basement of the Connaught Room, Great Queen Street, London

WC2 and (ii) for the lessees on their counterclaim for damages of £435,760 plus interest for breach of covenants which had resulted in loss and damage to their business on the grounds that the judge had erred in holding that the covenant in the underlease to pay rent 'without any deduction' excluded the lessees' right of set-off and that he ought to have given judgment with costs for the lessees in the lessors' action for rent and judgment with costs for the lessees on their counterclaim in a sum representing the excess of the damages over the rent, with interest on that balance. The facts are set out in the judgment.

Colin Rimer QC and *Robert Powell-Jones* (instructed by *McBride Wilson & Co*) for the lessees.
Kim Lewison QC and *Mark Warwick* (instructed by *Howard Kennedy*) for the lessors.

WAITE LJ. This appeal raises the question whether a provision in a lease that the rent should be paid 'without any deduction' had the effect of excluding the lessees' equitable right of set-off. There were serious breaches of covenant by the lessors, causing the lessees to cease payment of rent. The damages for breach of the lessors' covenants have now become quantified by unchallenged findings of the court below, and it is accepted that they substantially exceed any arrears of rent that became owing to the lessors as a result of the lessees' decision to stop payment. It is also accepted that at the time when the lessees ceased paying rent, the damages to which they were then entitled for breach of covenant already exceeded the amount of the rent due on that, and on every subsequent, occasion when rent was withheld.

On 10 June 1992 Judge Bowsher QC, hearing official referees' business, gave judgment for the lessors in their action for rent unpaid in the sum of £202,690, and judgment for the lessees on their counterclaim for damages for breach of covenant in the sum of £435,760. Interest was awarded in the claim in the sum of £44,832, and in the counterclaim in the sum of £52,323, bringing the judgments on the claim and counterclaim to a total (in round figures) of £247,500 and £488,000 respectively. Each party was awarded the costs of the claim and counterclaim respectively (on an indemnity basis in the case of the lessees' costs of the counterclaim) and the two sets of costs were ordered to be set off against each other.

In their appeal to this court the lessees contend that the judge was wrong to have expressed the result in the form of judgments favourable to each party on the claim and counterclaim respectively. The real victors were the lessees, who established a substantial surplus of damages over rent. The judge ought therefore, they say, to have given judgment with costs for the defendant lessees in the plaintiff lessors' action for rent, and judgment with costs for the defendant lessees on their counterclaim in a sum representing the excess of the damages over the rent, with interest on that balance.

An order in that form would produce a substantially more favourable result for the lessees, in terms not only of costs but also of interest. It is accepted by the lessors that if the lessees' right of equitable set-off has not been excluded by the lease, the appellant lessees are entitled to have the order expressed in that way. The sole issue in the appeal is therefore whether the lessees' right of set-off has or has not been excluded. The judge held, albeit with expressed reluctance, that it had been so excluded. The appellant lessees claim that he was wrong.

The relevant lease is an underlease dated 7 December 1983 and made between the respondent landlords, Connaught Rooms Ltd of the first part, the appellant tenants, Indoor Leisure Ltd of the second part, and certain sureties for the lessees of the third part. The demised premises were part of the basement of the Connaught Rooms at Great Queen Street, London WC2. The term was for $12\frac{1}{2}$ years from October 1983 to February 1996. The lessors hold the leasehold reversion to the entirety of the Connaught Rooms under a lease expiring at a date well into the next century. The lessees carry on the business of a snooker and health club at the demised premises.

Clause 2 of the underlease demised the premises to the lessees for the term already mentioned and continued:

'... PAYING FIRST (a) for the period from the 18th day of October 1983 to the 18th day of October 1984 the yearly rent of £32,500·00 (b) for the period from the 18th day of October 1984 to the 25th day of December 1986 the yearly rent of £40,000·00 and (c) thereafter the yearly rent payable under the Third Schedule such rent to be paid without any deduction (except as required by any Act) by four equal quarterly payments in advance the first payment to be made on the execution of this Underlease and to be in respect of the period from the 18th day of October 1983 to the next succeeding usual quarter day ...'

The same clause then set out five further categories of payment to be treated as rent—namely contributions to the cost of insuring, heating and maintaining the main building and so on. Neither side has sought to attach any significance to these additional rents. Each of them was expressed to be payable 'on demand', but there was no equivalent reference to payment 'without any deduction'.

The lessees' covenants were set out in cl 3 of the underlease, and read, so far as relevant, as follows:

'THE TENANT covenants with the Landlord:

Rent (1) To pay the Rents at the times and in manner aforesaid without any deduction (except as aforesaid) and if so required by banker's standing order

Outgoings (2)(A) To defray (or in the absence of direct assessment on the Premises to pay to the Landlord a fair proportion of) all existing and future rates taxes assessments charges and outgoings payable in respect of the Premises or any part thereof by any estate owner landlord tenant or occupier thereof ...

Requirements of any Act or competent authority (17) To comply in every respect with the provisions of any Act or the requirements of any competent authority in respect of the Premises or any part thereof or in respect of the occupation or user thereof and to indemnify the Landlord against all claims demands expenses and liability in respect thereof and to pay all costs charges and expenses incurred by the Landlord in connection with any such provision or requirement.'

The third schedule contained provision for review of the principal rent at specified review dates during the term of the demise.

Clause 4 of the underlease contained the lessors' covenants in common form including the covenant for quiet enjoyment and there is no dispute that these covenants, as well as those implied into the underlease by law, provided the basis for the lessors' liability in damages.

The events leading up to these proceedings are not in dispute and can be summarised as follows. Following a change of ownership of the share capital of the lessors in the summer of 1987, the premises demised to the lessees by the underlease began from November 1987 to suffer severe damage caused by flooding from the lessors' retained portion of the building. The damage continued down to the date of the hearing before the judge and caused major disruption to the lessees' business. There is no appeal from the judge's findings that the bulk of this damage was suffered as a result of breaches by the lessors of the lessors' covenant in the underlease. In June 1989 the lessees withheld the rent of £12,500 due for that quarter in respect of the principal rent and paid no further instalments thereafter. Throughout the period from June 1989 to the date of judgment on 2 June 1992 the amount of damage for which the lessors were liable for breach of the lessors' covenants substantially exceeded the amount of any rent accruing due from the lessees. The primary meaning of the verb 'to deduct' is given in the *Shorter Oxford Dictionary* as 'To take away or subtract from a sum or amount' and of the noun 'deduction' as 'The action of deducting or taking away; subtraction; that which is deducted'. The relevant issue before the judge, and before this court on appeal, has been the effect of the use, in the words of demise and in the covenant for payment of the principal rent, of the formula 'without any deduction [except as required by any Act]'. The lessors contend that the effect of that formula was to operate as a contractual exclusion of the lessees' equitable right of set-off for all purposes. The lessees contend that it operated only to exclude such deductions from rent as they would have been entitled—but not statutorily bound—to make under the general law and by statute, and had no application to rights of equitable set-off arising from breaches of covenant by the lessors.

These opposing contentions have been ably urged by Mr Rimer QC for the appellant lessees and Mr Lewison QC for the respondent lessors. There are two propositions of law as to which they are in agreement, namely: (1) the lessees were entitled in equity to set off unliquidated claims for damages for breach of covenant against the rent accruing due under the underlease on the basis approved in *British Anzani (Felixstowe) Ltd v International Marine Management (UK) Ltd* [1974] 2 All ER 1063, [1980] QB 137; and (2) it was open to the parties to exclude this equitable right of set-off by express words or by implication from the language of the contract as embodied in the underlease. There is however a starting presumption that neither party intends to abandon any remedies for breach arising by operation of law and clear language must be used if this presumption is to be rebutted (see *Gilbert-Ash (Northern) Ltd v Modern Engineering (Bristol) Ltd* [1973] 3 All ER 195 at 215, 220, [1974] AC 689 at 717, 723 per Lord Diplock and Lord Salmon).

There, however, the agreement between counsel ends. Their submissions were first addressed to the general instances which are to be found in the authorities of the use by judges indiscriminately of the expressions 'deduction' and 'set-off' to describe the state of affairs which arises when a claim is matched, or partly matched, with a cross-claim to which rights of set-off are accorded in equity. It will be sufficient to refer to three of those instances only.

Hanak v Green [1958] 2 All ER 141, [1958] 2 QB 9 is the chief authority establishing the principle—conceded in this case—that where the result of applying rights of equitable set-off is to produce an excess of the amount of the cross-claim over the amount of the claim, the counterclaiming defendant is entitled to judgment in the action as well as judgment for the balance in the counterclaim. The basis for that, as Morris LJ said, was that the 'defendant had an equitable set-off which defeated the plaintiff's claim' (see [1958] 2 All ER 141 at 152, [1958] 2 QB 9 at 26). He described that conclusion, however, as resulting from the authorities he had cited earlier in his judgment, including *Young v Kitchin* (1878) 3 Ex D 127 and specifically the observation in that case of Cleasby B that the defendant could not recover anything from the plaintiff but was entitled 'by way of set-off or deduction from the plaintiff's claim, to the damages which he had sustained ...' (see (1878) 3 Ex D 127 at 130).

Lord Denning MR, in a passage of his judgment tracing the historical genesis of the right of equitable set-off, said in *Federal Commerce & Navigation Co Ltd v Molena Alpha Inc, The Nanfri, The Benfri, The Lorfri* [1978] 3 All ER 1066 at 1077–1078, [1978] QB 927 at 974:

> 'But the courts of equity, as was their wont, came in to mitigate the technicalities of the common law. They allowed deductions, by way of equitable set-off, whenever there were good equitable grounds for directly impeaching the demand which the creditor was seeking to enforce ...'

Goff J, in holding that by the principle of equitable set-off a charterer may set off certain claims against hire even where the contract did not expressly give him the right to do so, said in *S L Sethia Liners Ltd v Naviagro Maritime Corp, The Kostas Melas* [1981] 1 Lloyd's Rep 18 at 26:

> 'Furthermore the exercise of a right of deduction or set-off is essentially an act of self-help ...'

We were invited by Mr Rimer to view those instances of use by judges of the word 'deduction' in the context of equitable set-off as reflecting no more than the fact that it happens to be the most convenient and succinct term available in the English language to describe what occurs in most cases as a result of set-off being applied. It is a useful shorthand term which may permissibly be employed, notwithstanding that it may involve a technical misuse of language, to describe the operation of the set-off process whenever the court is dealing with a case in which there is no necessity to draw any distinction between the separate processes of set-off on the one hand and deduction—properly so called in its strict grammatical sense—on the other. Mr Lewison urged us to take the contrary view of those instances as indicating a deliberate development by the judges of the expression 'deduction' into a term of art embracing, when used in the context of a lease, rights of set-off in addition to rights of strict subtraction.

The argument next turned to cases where issues arose that were more closely comparable to that in the present case. In none of the authorities so far mentioned was the court required to decide whether, in the particular document under consideration, there was any material distinction to be drawn between the terms 'deduction' on the one hand and 'set-off' on the other. Nor is there any reported instance where that question has arisen in this court. There are, however, two decisions at first instance and one Commonwealth authority in which it did become necessary to grapple with the issue, and they must now be mentioned.

The appellants in *Grant v NZMC Ltd* [1989] 1 NZLR 8 were lessees under a lease providing for the payment of rent 'free and clear of exchange or any deduction whatsoever'. They had an unliquidated claim against the lessors in damages for alleged misrepresentation by the lessors inducing their acceptance of the lease, on the strength of which they had withheld rent and on which they had sought unsuccessfully to rely at first instance when resisting a claim to summary judgment based on the non-payment of rent. The New Zealand Court of Appeal allowed the appeal, holding firstly that the cross-claim was sufficiently linked to the claim to found a case for equitable set-off and, secondly, that the relevant words in the lease did not amount to a contractual exclusion of such rights of set-off. The second holding was stated in these terms by Somers J giving the judgment of the court (at 13):

> 'The more difficult question is whether the words of the lease as to payment of rent "free and clear of exchange or any deduction whatsoever" amount to … a contract [to exclude a right of equitable set-off]. No case was cited to us as to the effect of those or similar words and those we have found (some are referred to in *Hill and Redman's Law of Landlord and Tenant* (15th ed, 1970) p 341 are not helpful). Statute apart, the recognised deductions which a tenant may make against his rent are those authorised by the lease itself and those in respect of moneys paid by the tenant which it was the landlord's obligation to pay. The latter include moneys outlaid on repairs covenanted to be, but not in fact done by the landlord (as in *Lee-Parker v Izzet* ([1971] 3 All ER 1099, [1971] 1 WLR 1688) in which the right to deduct was described as one of "ancient common law") and moneys payable by the landlord, the failure to pay which imperils the tenant's possession (as in *Sapsford v Fletcher* ((1792) 4 Term Rep 511, [1775–1805] All ER Rep 126) and the other cases mentioned in 27 *Halsbury's Laws of England* (4th ed) para 232, note 7). The covenant to pay rent without deduction may embrace such matters. It is not easy to envisage any other subject-matter to which they relate. We do not think the word "deduction" is clear enough to hold that it was agreed that a set-off of the kind claimed by [the appellants] could not be made. The word "deduction" does not in its natural sense embrace a set-off.'

It is common ground between counsel in the present case that the New Zealand court was wrong to cite non-payments, or reduced payments, of rent made in a *Lee-Parker v Izzet* situation as an instance of the kind of 'recognised deduction' to which the term 'deductions' when construed in its narrowest grammatical sense might be expected to apply. The principle which operates in that situation is that the tenant, by carrying out himself the repairs which ought to have been done by the landlord, becomes entitled to have his expenditure treated as though it had itself been a direct payment of rent; so that strictly speaking no question of equitable set-off arises at all, and the process of giving credit for the cost of repairs carried out by the tenant in arriving at the figure for rent outstanding is one of recoupment rather than deduction—see Goff J in *Lee-Parker v Izzet* [1971] 3 All ER 1099 at 1107, [1971] 1 WLR 1688 at 1693, although I note that the term 'deduction' appears to have found its way, doubtless for the sake of brevity, into the judge's formal order (see [1971] 3 All ER 1099 at 1110, [1971] 1 WLR 1688 at 1695). It is common ground also that the New Zealand Court of Appeal's references to the cases of *Sapsford v Fletcher* and the other authorities cited in 27 *Halsbury's Laws* (4th edn) para 232, note 8 to which they referred were of no direct assistance to their conclusion.

Mr Rimer urges us, nevertheless, to take the view that the New Zealand Court was right in its basic approach to the case, starting as they did from what he asserts to be the correct premise, namely that the word 'deduction' does not in its natural sense embrace a set-off. Mr Lewison submits that this decision was, quite simply, wrong and should not be followed.

We have been shown the transcript of a judgment of Clarke J in interlocutory proceedings between landlord and tenant heard in chambers in *Akehurst v Stena*

Sealink Ltd (17 February 1993, unreported), the opening paragraph of which reads:

> 'The clause in this agreement ... reads—"The tenant for itself and its successors hereby covenants with the landlord in the manner following, that is to say—1(a) to pay to the landlord the yearly rent hereby reserved and any revised and additional rents, without any deduction" etc. In my judgment that means without any deduction of any kind, and that would include any deduction by way of equitable set-off. That appears to me to be plain on the true construction of that provision.'

It is common ground that nothing further of relevance was said in the remainder of that judgment. The transcript affords very little indication of the precise circumstances with which the judge was dealing, and there is no way of knowing whether there were any other provisions in the tenancy agreement, in addition to the very brief excerpt quoted by the judge, which might have been of potential relevance when construing the provision he was required to consider. The judge gave leave for the case to be reported, but with understandable hesitation in view of the brevity of his judgment.

There had in fact been an earlier decision at first instance on a similar provision, although it was not reported until March 1993. It was that of Steyn J in *Famous Army Stores v Meehan* [1993] 1 EGLR 73 when he was sitting in Liverpool on appeal from an order of the district registrar who had granted summary judgment under RSC Ord 14 on a landlord's claim for arrears of rent. The defendant tenant had sought to plead equitable set-off in respect of damages allegedly suffered as a result of failure by the landlord to carry out the works necessary to achieve eligibility for, and thereafter to obtain, a fire certificate. The district registrar decided that set-off had been excluded by the lease, and the judge upheld his decision. The relevant passage in the judgment reads as follows (at 74):

> 'It is axiomatic that the right of set off may be excluded by agreement. It is also clear that clear express words are required to rebut the presumption that neither party intends to abandon any remedies or breach of contract which may arise by operation of law: see *Gilbert-Ashe (Northern) Ltd v Modern Engineering (Bristol) Ltd* ([1973] 3 All ER 195 at 215, [1974] AC 689 at 717). The tenants were granted a rent-free period of three months, thereafter rent instalments were payable. The lease provided in clause (1), and repeated in clause (2)(i), that the payment of rent was to be made "without any deductions". It was agreed that the words "except as aforesaid" which were inserted in clause (2)(i) were inserted by mistake and can safely be ignored. It has not been pleaded or suggested in argument that in the context the words "without any deductions" have been impressed with any special meaning by custom or usage. No implication of any term has been put forward. The question for decision is simply a point of construction ...'

The judge then referred to the fact that neither side relied on surrounding circumstances creating a special context and continued:

> 'The question is simply what the words "without any deductions" in the context of the rent payable under this lease would convey to the ordinary speaker of English. It seems to me that the ordinary meaning of "without any deductions" is that the rent must be paid in full and that there must be

no deductions of any kind which otherwise might be permissible by law. The ordinary meaning of the words is therefore wide enough to exclude any right of set off under this lease ...'

He then dealt with certain arguments raised by the defendant and concluded the judgment by saying:

'On behalf of the defendants one further matter was urged on me. It was said that if I resolved this issue in favour of the plaintiff it would come as a surprise to conveyancers. It is not possible for the court to poll conveyancers on this issue. In truth their answers may not be harmonious: some may say "Yes," others "No" and a yet larger body possibly "I do not know." There is no decision on the point and there are no *obiter dicta* to provide guidance. The point was apparently argued [counsel at this hearing are agreed that the judge must have intended to say "not argued"] In *British Anzani (Felixstowe) Ltd v International Marine Management (UK) Ltd* ([1979] 2 All ER 1063, [1980] 1 QB 137). In that case there is no reasoned decision on the point. In the absence of a reasoned decision *Anzani* can be of no assistance. One is driven back to the starting point of the process of construction, namely the ordinary meaning of the relevant words in the lease. In my judgment, the words in question exclude a right of set off: there was, therefore, no defence to the claim for judgment under Ord 14 in respect of the rent ...'

The judge then concluded with these words:

'Finally, I simply add that, when announcing my decision, I made it clear that I grant leave to appeal in this case since it is a point of some importance to conveyancers and it would be of benefit to conveyancers to have the judgment of the Court of Appeal on the matter.'

Those last two cases—which Mr Lewison asked us to uphold and Mr Rimer urged us not to follow—conclude the relevant authorities. One further topic was raised in argument to which it is necessary, finally, to refer. It is the question of whether any light is shed upon the meaning of the phrase 'any deduction' in the relevant provisions in this underlease by the words of exception which immediately follow them in brackets 'except as required by any Act'.

There are instances where a tenant is empowered by statute to make deductions from rent. They include s 23 of the Income and Corporation Taxes Act 1988 (deduction of tax collected from a derivative lessee), the Law of Distress Amendment Act 1908 (deduction of sums paid by an underlessee to preserve his goods from distress levied on his superior lessee), ss 212 and 305 and Sch 13 to the Highways Act 1980 (deduction of street works charges levied on the lessee as 'occupier') and s 291(2) of the Public Health Act 1936 (deduction of the cost of works recovered from an 'occupier' by a public health authority).

This statutory context is relied on by Mr Rimer as showing the *species* of deduction that was in the mind of the draftsman of the underlease when framing the prohibition against deductions from rent—that is to say the process of deduction properly and grammatically so called which takes place whenever Parliament authorises (as it has done in the instances just mentioned) a subtraction or recoupment from rent. The validity of that argument is not, he submits, affected by the fact that (as Mr Lewison was quick to point out) all but one of the four possible heads of statutory deduction—the exception being payments in avoidance of distress—were excluded already by the lessees' covenant to defray all outgoings in cl 3(2)(A) and (17) of the underlease, which I have already quoted.

I can now turn, after that account of the authorities and the arguments, to the considerations to be applied in construing the provision in this underlease prohibiting 'any deduction' from rent. They should in my judgment be the following. (1) Clear words are needed to exclude a tenant's remedy of an equitable right of set-off. (2) The word 'deduction' has never achieved the status of a term of art, but is an expression employed (both in everyday speech and in the language of the courts) at one moment in its strict sense to describe the ordinary process of subtraction with which it is grammatically associated, and at other moments in a broader sense to describe the result which follows when one claim is set against another and a balance is struck. It is thus a useful and a flexible word, but heavily dependent upon the context in which it is used for an accurate understanding of the sense in which it is being employed. If the context happens to be one that affords no guidance as to its intended meaning, it becomes an expression that necessarily suffers from ambiguity. It cannot, in short, be accurately described as a 'clear' word. (3) It follows that the simple expression 'without any deduction' is insufficient by itself, in the absence of any context suggesting the contrary, to operate by implication as an exclusion of the lessee's equitable right of set-off. (4) Added words of exception or qualification are relevant to the construction of such a phrase, but they too are subject to the general requirement of clarity and will only be effective to displace the lessee's right of equitable set-off if their effect is to create a clear context for exclusion.

Issues of construction are seldom easy, and are bound to depend in the last analysis upon the impression left in the mind of the judge when the language used by the parties is examined in the light of authority. When the considerations I have just mentioned are applied to the wording used in the present case, the impression left on my mind is that the parties to this lease used language that was insufficiently clear to carry the implication of an intention to exclude the lessees' equitable right of set-off. The words of exception in brackets do nothing to cure the want of clarity; they tend if anything (for the reasons urged by Mr Rimer) to provide a slight indication that the parties did not have set-off in mind when they were framing the prohibition against deduction.

A conclusion once reached in a construction case is not improved by elaboration. I do not think it is necessary for me to add more to it than this general comment which may be of assistance to those who are involved in the drafting of leases. The term 'deduction' is one of those words for which the convenience of flexibility has been achieved at the price of some inherent ambiguity. Draftsmen who are concerned to exclude the lessee's equitable right of set-off would therefore be well advised to do so explicitly. They will find useful guidance in that regard in Mr Lewison's publication on the drafting of leases, *Drafting Business Leases* (3rd edn, 1989).

It will be implicit in what I have said that the decisions in *Famous Army Stores v Meehan* [1993] 1 EGLR 73 and *Akehurst v Stena Sealink Ltd* (17 February 1993, unreported) should not in my judgment be followed and that the approach, though not the entire reasoning of the New Zealand court in *Grant v NZMC Ltd* [1989] 1 NZLR 8 was correct.

I would for my part allow the appeal and substitute for the order made by the judge the form of order prayed by the amended notice of appeal with any necessary amendments that may be agreed by counsel.

NEILL LJ. I agree that this appeal should be allowed for the reasons given by Waite LJ. I only add a short judgment of my own because we are differing from the decision of Judge Bowsher QC.

It seems that the obligation to pay a periodic rent reserved under the reddendum in a lease is capable of being reduced in a number of different circumstances. These circumstances include the following. (1) A contractual provision for a deduction in the lease. (2) A statutory provision for a deduction: see eg s 3 of the Law of Distress Amendment Act 1908 and s 23(5) of the Income and Corporation Taxes Act 1988. It may be noted that any agreement not to allow a deduction of tax under s 23(5) of the 1988 Act is void: see s 106(2) of the Taxes Management Act 1970. (3) A payment made by the tenant by way of proper expenditure on repairs which the landlord has neglected to carry out; in that event the payment will be regarded pro tanto as payment of the rent, and will certainly be an answer to an action for the rent and possibly an answer to a claim to distrain: see *Lee-Parker v Izzet* [1971] 3 All ER 1099 at 1107, [1971] 1 WLR 1688 at 1693. (4) The exercise of an equitable right of set-off: see *British Anzani (Felixstowe) Ltd v International Marine Management (UK) Ltd* [1979] 2 All ER 1063, [1980] 1 QB 137. (5) The exercise of a statutory right of set-off: see eg s 17 of the Agricultural Holdings Act 1986 .

The question which arises in this case is whether the word 'deduction' in the phrase in the reddendum 'To be paid without any deduction (except as required by any Act) ...' is to be construed so as to enable the lessors to claim the rent in full despite the existence of an equitable right of set-off in respect of breaches of the lessors' covenants.

As Waite LJ has demonstrated, it is a simple matter to find authorities where judges have used indiscriminately the expressions 'deduction' and 'set-off' to describe the state of affairs which arises when a claim is matched, or partly matched, by a cross-claim to which rights of set-off are accorded in equity. It seems to me, however, that where, as here, it is necessary to examine the use of the word 'deduction' more closely the distinction between a contractual or statutory 'deduction' and an equitable right of set-off becomes apparent. As I understand it though the matter was not fully examined, it is still the general rule of the law of distress that apart from deductions authorised by contract or statute a set-off cannot be used to reduce the amount for which a landlord is entitled to distrain: see 13 *Halsbury's Laws* (4th edn) para 286; 27 ibid para 232. Furthermore, I share the view of the Court of Appeal in New Zealand in *Grant v NZMC Ltd* [1989] 1 NZLR 8 at 13 that 'the word "deduction" does not in its natural sense embrace a set-off '. Accordingly I too am satisfied that the lessees are entitled to rely on their equitable set off.

I would only note in conclusion that it may be that, though the point is not relevant to this underlease, ss 119, 120 and 349 of the 1988 Act provide examples of deductions from the rent which are required to be made by statute.

SIMON BROWN LJ. I agree with both judgments.

Appeal allowed.

Wendy Shockett   Barrister.

Eller v Grovecrest Investments Ltd

COURT OF APPEAL, CIVIL DIVISION
NEILL, HOFFMANN AND WAITE LJJ
15 FEBRUARY 1994

Landlord and tenant – Claim for rent – Distress for rent – Set-off – Cross-claim for damages – Whether tenant entitled to invoke set-off against claim by landlord to levy distress.

The plaintiff was the tenant of premises on an industrial estate. For some time he had complained, to no effect, of alleged acts of nuisance and breach of covenant by the landlord and in July 1992 he decided to put pressure on the landlord by withholding his rent. The landlord sent in bailiffs to distrain on his goods and chattels and the plaintiff was obliged to sign a walking possession agreement to prevent their physical removal. He then applied ex parte for an injunction to restrain the landlord from proceeding with the distraint, contending that in equity he owed no rent because he was entitled to set off his claims for damages for nuisance and breach of covenant. The injunction was granted ex parte, but on the landlord's application it was discharged on the grounds that although the tenant had an arguable cross-claim and, since it arose out of the same lease as the claim for rent, they were sufficiently closely connected to give rise to an equitable set-off, he was bound by authority to hold that set-off did not affect a landlord's right to distrain. The plaintiff appealed.

Held – As a matter of fair dealing between the parties a tenant was entitled to invoke a right of set-off, for example by way of an arguable claim for damages for breach of covenant, against a claim by the landlord to levy distress. It followed that the appeal would be allowed and that the plaintiff was entitled to an injunction to restrain the landlord from proceeding with the distraint (see p 850 *a* to *g* and p 852 *f* to p 853 *c*, post).

Dictum of Lord Denning MR in *Federal Commerce and Navigation Co Ltd v Molena Alpha Inc* [1978] 3 All ER 1066 at 1078 applied.

Notes
For set-off against rent, see 13 *Halsbury's Laws* (4th edn) paras 284–286.

Cases refered to in judgments

Absolon v Knight (1743) Barnes 450, 94 ER 998.
American Cyanamid Co v Ethicon Ltd [1975] 1 All ER 504, [1975] AC 396, [1975] 2 WLR 316, HL.
British Anzani (Felixstowe) Ltd v International Marine Management (UK) Ltd [1979] 2 All ER 1063, [1980] QB 137, [1979] 3 WLR 451.
Brown v Holyoak (1733) Barnes 290, 94 ER 920.
Cia Sud Americana de Vapores v Shipmair BV, The Teno [1977] 2 Lloyd's Rep 289.
Federal Commerce and Navigation Co Ltd v Molena Alpha Inc [1978] 3 All ER 1066, [1978] QB 927, [1978] 3 WLR 309, CA; *affd* [1979] 1 All ER 307, [1979] AC 757, [1978] 3 WLR 991, HL.
Gibbs v Cruikshank (1873) LR 8 CP 454.
Hanak v Green [1958] 2 All ER 141, [1958] 2 QB 9, [1958] 2 WLR 755, CA.

Laycock v Tufnell (1787) 2 Chit 531.
Sanxter v Foster (1841) Cr & Ph 302, 41 ER 506, LC.
Stumore v Campbell & Co [1892] 1 QB 314, [1891–94] All ER Rep 785, CA.
Townrow v Benson (1818) 3 Madd 203, 56 ER 484.
Waters v Weigall (1795) 2 Anst 575, 145 ER 971, Exch.

Appeal

The plaintiff, Adrian Eller, appealed from the order of Sir Peter Pain, sitting as a deputy High Court judge, made on 30 July 1992, discharging the injunction granted ex parte by Morland J on 10 July 1992 restraining the defendant, Grovecrest Investments Ltd, the landlord of premises situated at West Hendon of which the plaintiff was the tenant, from proceeding with distraint against the plaintiff's goods and chattels for unpaid rent. The facts are set out in the judgments of Hoffmann LJ.

Richard Davison (instructed by Titus Miranda) for the plaintiff.
The defendant did not appear.

HOFFMANN LJ (delivering the first judgment at the invitation of Neill LJ). The question in this appeal is whether set-off against a claim for rent can be invoked against a landlord exercising the ancient common law remedy of distress.

The plaintiff was the tenant of premises on a small industrial estate in West Hendon. He complained for some time of what he said were acts of nuisance and breach of covenant by his landlord. In July 1992 he lost patience and decided to put pressure on the landlord by withholding his rent. The landlord sent bailiffs to distrain upon his goods and chattels. The tenant was obliged to sign a walking possession agreement to prevent their physical removal. He then applied ex parte to Morland J for an injunction to restrain the landlord from proceeding with the distraint. He said that in equity he owed no rent because he was entitled to set off his claims for nuisance and breach of covenant. Morland J granted the injunction, but, on the landlord's application, Sir Peter Pain discharged it. He held that the tenant had an arguable cross-claim for the purposes of the American Cyanamid guidelines (see American Cyanamid Co v Ethicon Ltd [1975] 1 All ER 504, [1975] AC 396). He also accepted that, as it arose out of the same lease as the claim for rent, they were sufficiently closely connected to give rise to an equitable set-off in accordance with the principle in Hanak v Green [1958] 2 All ER 141, [1958] 2 QB 9. It followed that if the landlord had been suing for rent, the tenant, if he had made good his cross-claim, would have had a complete defence (see British Anzani (Felixstowe) Ltd v International Marine Management (UK) Ltd [1979] 2 All ER 1063, [1980] QB 137). But, said the deputy judge, he was bound by authority to hold that set-off did not affect a landlord's right to distrain. Against that decision the tenant appeals. The judge agreed to continue the injunction pending appeal on condition that the tenant paid the money into court. This was done. Meanwhile, the action has not been pursued.

Mr Davison for the tenant told us that the landlord company was in financial difficulties. It has not appeared to oppose the tenant's appeal. So Mr Davison has ably put before us the arguments which he thinks could be made on the landlord's behalf as well as those for the tenant. We are greatly indebted to him.

In 13 *Halsbury's Laws* (4th edn) paras 284–286 it is said that the amount for which a landlord can distrain may be reduced by payments made on the landlord's behalf with his express or implied authority. But otherwise 'the general rule of law is that there is no right to set off against or deduct from the rent distrained for sums due from the landlord to the tenant or payments made on behalf of the landlord' (para 286). Five old cases, to which I shall return, are cited in support.

These authorities can be understood only against the background of the principles which governed set-off at common law and equity before the Judicature Acts. At common law, a defendant could resist a money claim on the ground that he had already paid money to the plaintiff's use. That was the basis of the rule in *Halsbury's Laws* which allows sums paid on the landlord's behalf to be deducted from the rent for which he can distrain. But no cross-claim could be set off in any proceedings until the Insolvent Debtors Relief Act 1729 (2 Geo II c 22), which provided in s 13:

'… where there are mutual Debts between the Plaintiff and the Defendant … one Debt may be set off against the other, and such Matter may be given in Evidence upon the General Issue, or pleading in Bar, as the Nature of the Case shall require …'

In *Brown v Holyoak* (1733) Barnes 290, 94 ER 920 the Court of Common Pleas decided this statute did not enable a tenant to rely on a debt under a simple contract against his landlord's action for rent on a parol lease. The reason was that because rent issued out of land, it was treated as a special debt and 'a debt of inferior nature cannot be set off against a superior demand'.

This technical distinction was abolished two years later by s 5 of the Debtors Relief (Amendment) Act 1735 (8 Geo II c 24), which provided—

'by virtue of [the 1729 Act] mutual Debts may be set against each other, either by being pleaded in Bar, or given in Evidence on the General Issue, in the Manner therein mentioned, notwithstanding that such Debts are deemed in Law to be of a different Nature …'

Nevertheless, set-off under the statute was restricted to mutual debts and did not, for example, allow the set-off of a claim for unliquidated damages such as the tenant makes in this case.

In *Absolon v Knight* (1743) Barnes 450, 94 ER 998 the Court of Common Pleas considered whether the statute applied to distraint. The common law procedure for challenging a distraint was for a tenant whose goods and chattels had been distrained to give security for the rent and bring an action for replevin. The landlord's defence, by which he pleaded the rent due, was called the avowry. This could be challenged by various pleas on the part of the tenant, such as riens in arrere, that no rent was owing. The difficulty for the tenant was that the 1729 Act was procedural rather than substantive. Set-off was a defence which could be pleaded in an action of contract or debt for a liquidated sum. But replevin was an action in tort and the statute could not be made to fit into its system of pleading. Accordingly, the tenant's attempt to plead a mutual debt against the landlord's avowry failed. A similar attempt in the King's Bench was equally unsuccessful in *Laycock v Tufnell* (1787) 2 Chit 531.

So much for the position at common law. The Court of Chancery approached set-off on a wider basis and would relieve a debtor against a common law liability when he had a cross-claim 'so directly connected with [the claim] that it would be manifestly unjust to the claimant to recover without taking into account the cross-claim' (see *Cia Sud Americana de Vapores v Shipmair BV, The Teno* [1977] 2 Lloyd's Rep 289 at 297 per Parker J). The procedural remedy given by the Court of Chancery was to injunct the plaintiff from bringing or proceeding with his common law action until the cross-claim had been taken into account. But as Morris LJ pointed out in *Hanak v Green* [1958] 2 All ER 141 at 147, [1958] 2 QB 9 at 18–19:

> 'The court of equity would not act merely because there were cross-demands. The assistance of the court of equity would only be given to someone who could show some equitable ground for being protected against his adversary's demand.'

So, for example, if the alleged set-off would have been valid under the 1729 Act a court of equity would not usurp the jurisdiction of a common law court by trying the action.

In *Waters v Weigall* (1795) 2 Anst 575, 145 ER 971 the tenant claimed to have spent money on repairs which he said should have been done by the landlord. He claimed that the Court of Exchequer, in the exercise of its equity jurisdiction, should therefore restrain the landlord from proceeding with his claim for rent. MacDonald CB said:

> 'I do not see how you entitle yourself to the interposition of this Court. If the landlord is bound in law or equity to repair ... and you were right in expending this sum in repairs for him, it is money paid to his use; and may be set off against the demand for rent. If you fail in making out these points, your ground of relief is destroyed in equity, as well as at law.'

These principles, with their heavily procedural and jurisdictional content, were the background to *Townrow v Benson* (1818) 3 Madd 203, 56 ER 484. The plaintiff was tenant of a five hundred acre farm in Lincolnshire at a rent of £500 a year. When he entered into the tenancy he, at the landlord's request, paid the previous tenant £1,200 in respect of his claim to tenant-right for standing crops amd manure. He said that it was a condition of this payment that he should be paid a similar sum when he quit the holding. But when he did so, the landlord refused to pay him anything. His own claim to tenant-right was valued at £692 and he wanted to set off at least this amount against his liability for rent. The landlord distrained for rent and the tenant gave security for the rent by bond and brought an action for replevin. Instead of proceeding to plead to the avowry at common law, the tenant applied to the Court of Chancery for an injunction to restrain the landlord from enforcing the replevin bond. The landlord demurred to the bill for want of equity. Mr Horne for the landlord said:

> 'Here the set-off, if any, might have been made available at law. It is a legal set-off, and therefore cannot be enforced in this Court.' (See 3 Madd 203 at 209, 56 ER 484 at 486.)

In view of *Absolon v Knight* (1743) Barnes 450, 94 ER 998 and *Laycock v Tufnell* (1787) 2 Chit 531, I rather doubt whether Mr Horne meant that a statutory set-off could have been pleaded at law in the replevin action. He was probably saying that the true basis of the tenant's claim was that his payment to the previous tenant had been money paid to the landlord's use, which (like the money spent on repairs in *Waters v Weigall*) could have been relied upon at law even before the statute to reduce or extinguish the landlord's claim to rent.

Mr Agar for the tenant, conceded that 'There is not, perhaps, any case where a legal set-off has been enforced in a Court of Equity' but he claimed that the tenant had an equitable claim to stand in the shoes of the previous tenant. Leach V-C does not seem to have thought much of this argument. He said in *Townrow v Benson* (1818) 3 Madd 207 at 209–210, 56 ER 484 at 486–487:

> 'The tenant here claims to set off a legal demand against the distress of his landlord for rent. The policy of the law does not permit a set-off against a distress for rent; and a Court of Equity must follow the law, and cannot relieve against the rule of law, where the claim to set off is founded on a legal demand. It is not necessary to consider how the case might be if the tenant had a counter demand, not at law, but in equity.'

This is a very compressed report, but it seems to me that when the Leach V-C says that 'the policy of the law does not permit set-off against a distress for rent', he is referring to the way in which the statute had been construed in *Absolon v Knight* and *Laycock v Tufnell* to exclude its application to replevin. His remark that equity must follow the law meant, I think, that in the case of a legal cross-claim which could be pleaded as a defence to an action, but not to an avowry, equity should not subvert the statutory distinction by injuncting a landlord from enforcing the replevin bond. But he expressly left open the case of a purely equitable set-off.

There is some slight indication of willingness of the Court of Chancery to injunct a distraint on purely equitable grounds in *Sanxter v Foster* (1841) Cr & Ph 302, 41 ER 506. The tenant there sought relief against liability to pay an additional rent on the grounds that it was penal. Shadwell V-C granted an interlocutory injunction to restrain the landlord from levying a distress. Lord Cottenham LC, on appeal, discharged the injunction on the facts and because the tenant could not support the cross-undertaking in damages, but there is no suggestion that it was wrong in principle to interfere with the remedy of distraint. And if a court of equity could do so in order to enforce relief against penalties and forfeitures, why not to enforce an equitable set-off?

I have now discussed three of the five cases cited by *Halsbury's Laws* in support of the proposition that there is no set-off against rent for the purposes of distraint. The other two, in my judgment, take the matter no further. All the cases are before the Judicature Acts. These, it was said by the Court of Appeal in *Stumore v Campbell & Co* [1892] 1 QB 314, [1891–4] All ER Rep 785, were not intended to alter the rights of the parties in set-off, but only to affect procedure. In the case of set-off, however, procedure was usually what had determined whether or not a set-off was available in a particular court. Collapsing the procedural distinctions between common law and equity, debt and replevin, undermines the basis upon which most of the older cases were decided. Thus, the fact that set-off under the 1729 Act could not apply to replevin was purely on account of the fact that its procedure could not be fitted into the replevin cause of action. The statute itself was repealed over a century ago and only its principle was preserved. The refusal to allow a set-off in *Townrow v Benson* turned entirely upon the jurisdictional division between the courts of common law and the Court of Chancery.

Accordingly, I see no reason why the present case should not be decided in accordance with principle rather than by following cases based upon procedural distinctions of long ago.

There is encouragement to take this course in *Federal Commerce and Navigation Co Ltd v Molena Alpha Inc* [1978] 3 All ER 1066 at 1078, [1978] QB 927 at 974, where Lord Denning MR said:

'It is now far too late to search through the old books and dig them out. Over 100 years have passed since the Supreme Court of Judicature Act 1873. During that time the streams of common law and equity have flown together and combined so as to be indistinguishable the one from the other. We have no longer to ask ourselves: what would the courts of common law or the courts of equity have done before the Supreme Court of Judicature Act 1873? We have to ask ourselves: what should we do now so as to ensure fair dealing between the parties?'

What fair dealing requires seems clear enough. It is contrary to principle that a landlord should be able to recover more by distress than he can by action. As Mr Davison pointed out, it would mean that a landlord whose application for judgment under RSC Ord 14 in a claim for rent was defeated by an arguable cross-claim could leave court and immediately enforce his claim by levying a distress. The injustice will be even greater if the landlord, as there is reason to believe may be the case in these proceedings, is in financial difficulties. The money recovered from the tenant by distress will, on insolvency, be distributed among the creditors while the tenant will have to be satisfied with a dividend in respect of his cross-claim.

In my judgment, therefore, this court is free to hold that set-off is available against a claim to levy distress. Mr Philip Wood, in his comprehensive book on *English and International Set-Off* (1989) para 4.86 says that this is the better view. I agree. I would, therefore, allow the appeal and restore the injunction granted by Morland J

WAITE LJ. I agree.

NEILL LJ. There are numerous statements in the textbooks and elsewhere to the effect that no cross-claim by a tenant can be used by way of set-off so as to restrict the landlord's right to distrain on the tenant's property to enforce a claim for arrears of rent. This appeal raises the question whether these statements accutately represent the law.

In these proceedings Mr Adrian Eller seeks an injunction to restrain Grovecrest Investments Ltd (the landlords) from exercising the remedy of distress in respect of unpaid rent and rates. Mr Eller complains of breaches of covenant and asserts that his cross-claims for damages exceed the sum claimed by the landlord by way of rent and rates. It is argued that these cross-claims can be used as an equitable set-off so as to support the defence that at the date of the distress no sum was due to the landlord at all.

Sir Peter Pain rejected Mr Eller's contention. He held that he was bound by authority to find that an equitable set-off provided no defence to a distraint. In his judgment the deputy judge continued:

'[An equitable set-off] may provide a defence to an action for rent but that a distraint exists is an ancient right independently of the right to sue for one's rent and a right which the landlord has retained throughout the ages. It seems to me, somewhat to my regret, that I must treat that as still being good law on the basis of *Townrow v Benson* (1818) 3 Madd 203, 56 ER 484.'

In this court the landlords have not appeared. In these circumstances a heavy burden was placed on Mr Davison for the tenant to ensure that the court was referred to the relevant authorities and that any arguments available to support the judge's decision were put forward. The court is grateful to Mr Davison for the help which he gave us.

It is not in dispute in the present proceedings that if the landlords had brought an action to recover rent and rates, or had claimed possession on the basis that the rent and rates were in arrears, Mr Eller could have set up his claims for damages by way of equitable set-off within the principles formulated by Morris LJ in *Hanak v Green* [1958] 2 All ER 141, [1958] 2 QB 9 and applied by Forbes J in *British Anzani (Felixstowe) Ltd v International Marine Management (UK) Ltd* [1979] 2 All ER 1063, [1980] QB 137. Sir Peter Pain felt constrained by authority, however, to hold that a similar equitable set-off could not be relied on where the landlord exercised the remedy of distress as a means of self-help.

Mr Davison submitted that there was no satisfactory reason why, if an equitable set-off could be relied upon in an action for rent, such a set-off should be disregarded where the landlord distrained.

It is necessary to remember that before the passing of the statutes of set-off in the time of George II there was no right of set-off in an action at law. The two statutes which were passed at that time—the Insolvent Debtors Relief Act 1729 (2 Geo II c 22) and the Debtors Relief (Amendment) Act 1735 (8 Geo II c 24)—were do prevent the imprisonment, as a debtor, of a person who was not truly indebted because there was a mutual debt owing to him by his creditor.

The introduction of the statutory right of set-off represented an important development, but the set-off was only available in the circumstances prescribed in the statute, that is, in respect of debts or liquidated demands due between the same parties in the same right. It followed, therefore, that a claim for damages for tort or in pursuit of a remedy in respect of some tortious liability could not be used by way of a set-off under the statutes. Thus, in *Laycock v Tufnell* (1787) 2 Chit 531 it was held that a plaintiff in an action in replevin could not plead a set-off in response to a claim for rent because an action for replevin is for the tortious taking of goods (cf *Gibbs v Cruikshank* (1873) LR 8 CP 454 at 459 per Bovill CJ).

It would appear that another effect of the strict rules governing a statutory set-off at law was that in the eighteenth and nineteenth centuries, before the Judicature Acts 1873 and 1875, courts of equity were very reluctant to intervene where the position of the parties inter se was regulated by their rights at law. A useful illustration of this reluctance is provided by the decision in *Townrow v Benson* (1818) 3 Madd 203, 56 ER 484 to which the deputy judge referred. In that case the plaintiffs sought an injunction to restrain proceedings at law for rent on the ground that the landlord was indebted to them in a sum which was more than the amount of the rent. Leach V-C refused the application for an injunction holding that it was against the policy of the law to allow a set-off against a distress for rent and that in these circumstances a court of equity would not intervene. It is unnecessary for the purpose of this judgment to consider whether Leach V-C was correct in concluding that at law a set-off could not be asserted against a distress for rent in any circumstances, because the plaintiffs had the additional difficulty that the agreement under which their claim to a 'tenant-right' was made was not in writing.

The position was different, however, where the set-off relied on was a true equitable set-off and one which was not even arguably within the statutes. In the course of his judgment in *British Anzani (Felixstowe) Ltd v International Marine Management (UK) Ltd* [1979] 2 All ER 1063 at 1071–1073, [1980] QB 137 at 149–151 Forbes J referred to cases where the courts of equity had intervened in cases of ejectment where the tenant had an equitable set-off for unliquidated damages. He concluded ([1979] 2 All ER 1063 at 1073, [1980] QB 137 at 151):

> 'A consideration of all these cases leads me to the conclusion that except in cases of distress or replevin equity has never refused to interfere to protect a tenant whose landlord was bringing proceedings based on non-payment of rent, if the tenant had a bona fide cross-claim for unliquidated damages against the landlord, provided that he was not covered by an existing common law remedy and that the ordinary rules pertaining to equitable set-off were obeyed.'

It will be seen that in this paragraph Forbes J made a specific exception of cases of distress and replevin. For my part, however, I can find no satisfactory basis for excepting these cases from the general proposition which he set out. It is, of course, true that the remedy of distress took the form of self-help and that, therefore, any court proceedings would be those instituted by the tenant, either by an action for replevin or by a claim for an injunction. One can see, therefore, that in a system where rules of procedure were very strict it would be difficult to found a claim on the basis of an equitable right which could only be invoked, if at all, by way of defence. In principle, however, I can see no reason to distinguish between the position of a landlord who is asserting his rights in respect of arrears of rent by a claim for possession or by an action in debt, on the one hand, and that of a landlord who is asserting identical rights, but who is availing himself of the remedy of distress. In both cases the proper question to be determined is, looking at the state of account between the parties in the light of their rights under the lease, is any sum due to the landlord. In the present case the cross-claim by Mr Eller arises out of the same contract as the claim for rent and is directly connected with it. In my judgment it would be manifestly unjust to allow the landlords to recover without taking into account the cross-claim which, it is clear, is capable of existing as an equitable set-off. I can, therefore, see no reason why at the present day this equitable set-off should not be used to establish the true state of account between Mr Eller and his landlords and thus to found a claim for an injunction.

It is noteworthy that in *Townrow v Benson* itself Leach V-C left open what the position would have been if the cross-claim by the plaintiffs had been equitable. He said ((1818) 3 Madd 203 at 210, 56 ER 484 at 487):

> 'It is not necessary to consider how the case might be if the tenant had a counter demand, not at law, but at equity.'

Accordingly, for these reasons and for the reasons more fully explained by Hoffmann LJ, I, too, would allow this appeal. It seems to me that to do so would be fully in accord with the approach suggested by Lord Denning MR in

Federal Commerce and Navigation Co Ltd v Molena Alpha Inc [1978] 3 All ER 1066 at 1078, [1978] QB 927 at 974, where he said:

'It is now far too late to search through the old books and dig them out. Over 100 years have passed since the Supreme Court of Judicature Act 1873. During that time the streams of common law and equity have flown together and combined so as to be indistinguishable the one from the other. We have no longer to ask ourselves: what would the courts of common law or the courts of equity have done before the Supreme Court of Judicature Act 1873? We have to ask ourselves: what should we do now so as to ensure fair dealing between the parties?'

Appeal allowed.

Wendy Shockett   Barrister.

Thomas and another v Countryside Council for Wales

QUEEN'S BENCH DIVISION
ROUGIER J
6, 7, 8, 9, 23 JULY 1993

Compensation – Measure of compensation – Arbitration – Appeal against award – Site of special scientific interest – Statutory restriction on use of land – Correct test for compensation of loss – Whether standard rules governing measure of tortious or contractual liability applicable – Factors to be considered – Wildlife and Countryside Act 1981, ss 28, 50.

The appellants were experienced sheep farmers. Their farm comprised 371 inland acres, but they also had grazing rights over 117 acres of cliff land, which provided shelter for the sheep and was of particular value in the management of their sheep farming activity. The respondent local authority, exercising powers under s 28 of the Wildlife and Countryside Act 1981, declared the cliff land to be an area of special scientific interest and issued a notice requiring the appellants to limit drastically the pasturing of sheep there. As a result, the appellants radically altered their farming policy, reducing their flock and converting much of the inland acreage to arable use. Under s 50(2)[a] of the 1981 Act the compensation payable was to be determined in accordance with guidelines issued jointly by the Department of the Environment and the Welsh Office. Paragraph 16[b] of the guidelines provided that annual compensation payments should reflect 'net profits foregone'. The appellants were dissatisfied with the terms of compensation offered by the local authority for net profits foregone and referred the issue to arbitration. The

---

a   Section 50(2), so far as material, provides: '... payments shall be of such amounts as may be determined by the [Countryside Council] in accordance with guidance given by the Ministers.'
b   Paragraph 16, so far as material, is set out at p 857 *b*, post

arbitrator calculated the 'net profits foregone' by reference to the difference between the profit which the appellants would have earned had they been allowed to continue as before and the maximum income the farm could produce under the restrictions, the sole criterion being that of finance. The appellant appealed under s 1 of the Arbitration Act 1979, contending that the arbitrator had applied the wrong formula under para 16 of the guidelines and that he had erred in rejecting their claim for capital losses.

Held – The wording of the ministerial guidelines was intended to equate the manner of assessing compensation payable to a landowner/occupier under s 50 of the 1981 Act in respect of statutory restrictions imposed on his use of land which had been declared an area of special scientific interest with the normal law applicable to cases of contractual or tortious liability. The basis for the measure of damages was therefore compensation for pecuniary loss which directly and naturally flowed from the breach, although a plaintiff could not call on a defendant to pay the full direct consequence unless he himself had acted reasonably to mitigate his loss. The amount of compensation payable should accordingly be assessed by asking (i) what could the landowner/occupier have achieved, (ii) what had he achieved and (iii) whether any act or omission on his part had been unreasonable and of such a nature that the difference between (i) and (ii) could no longer be said to be caused by the restriction. However, the question whether the landowner/occupier had acted reasonably was not to be answered solely in terms of the commercial optimum, and should take some account of other circumstances, including individual personal factors of amenity and even aesthetic preference. It followed that the arbitrator's assessment of 'net profits foregone' by the appellants was wrong in law, since he had failed to consider whether the appellants' decision to adopt the farming policy they did was reasonable. The arbitrator's rejection of the additional claim for capital losses was similarly flawed in so far as he had applied the wrong test in assessing the loss of profits. The appeal would therefore be allowed and the award would be remitted to the arbitrator for reconsideration in the light of the correct test (see p 860 *c e* to *g*, p 861 *a* to *c j* and p 864 *h j*, post).

British Westinghouse Electric and Manufacturing Co Ltd v Underground Electric Railways Co of London Ltd [1911–13] All ER Rep 63 applied.

Notes

For measure of compensation, see 12 *Halsbury's Laws* (4th edn) para 1126, and for cases on the general principle of compensation, see 17 *Digest* (Reissue) 87–90, *32–46*.

For the Arbitration Act 1979, s 1, see 2 *Halsbury's Statutes* (4th edn) (1992 reissue) 651.

For the Wildlife and Countryside Act 1981, ss 28, 50, see 32 *Halsbury's Statutes* (4th edn) 218, 240.

Cases referred to in judgment

British Westinghouse Electric and Manufacturing Co Ltd v Underground Electric Railways Co of London Ltd [1912] AC 673, [1911–13] All ER Rep 63, HL.

Lloyds and Scottish Finance Ltd v Modern Cars and Caravans (Kingston) Ltd [1964] 2 All ER 732, [1966] 1 QB 764, [1964] 3 WLR 859.

Sotiros Shipping Inc v Sameiet Solholt, The Solholt [1983] 1 Lloyd's Rep 605, CA.

Universal Petroleum Co Ltd (in liq) v Handels- und Transportgesellschaft mbH [1987] 2 All ER 737, [1987] 1 WLR 1178, CA.

Appeal

David Joseph Harry Thomas and Elizabeth Marilyn Harry Thomas appealed with leave against an arbitration award made on 6 August 1992 on a reference to arbitration under s 50(3) of the Wildlife and Countryside Act 1981 of an offer of compensation made by the Welsh Countryside Council in respect of statutory restrictions which had been placed on the appellants' use of land under s 28 of the 1981 Act on the grounds that the arbitrator's method of assessing the compensation payable was wrong in law and that his rejection of their additional claim for capital losses was similarly flawed. The appellants further applied under s 1(5) of the Arbitration Act 1979 for the matter to be remitted to the arbitrator requiring him to make further findings of fact and to give full reasons for his decisions. The facts are set out in the judgment.

C A Brodie QC and *Keith Lindblom* (instructed by *John Owen*, Llandeilo) for the appellants.
Keith Bush (instructed by the *Treasury Solicitor*) for the respondent.

Cur adv vult

23 July 1993. The following judgment was delivered.

ROUGIER J. This appeal is brought by the appellants with leave of the court against an arbitration award made pursuant to s 50(3) of the Wildlife and Countryside Act 1981. Principally, the appeal concerns the question of the proper measure of compensation to be paid to a landowner whose use of land is affected by powers exercised by what was originally the Nature Conservancy Council and which has now been subdivided into various regional councils, the respondent, as its name suggests, being that responsible for the Principality.

The appellants are farmers, whose main enterprise is sheep farming. They are experienced and have a good reputation—a factor remarked upon by the arbitrator in making his award. Their farm is called Paviland Manor Farm, comprising 371 inland acres, and they have grazing rights over a further 117 acres of cliff land, all at Rhossili, which is at the south-west corner of the Gower peninsula. Whether one calls the adjoining sea the Bristol Channel or the Atlantic matters little; the wind and the rain sweep in from the west and shelter is at a premium. This fact is of importance since strangely enough it was the cliff land which provided shelter for the appellants' flock of sheep and thereby had particular value in the management of their sheep farming activity. At the relevant time, which was in 1986 or 1987, the appellants had expanded their flock to some 1,100 ewes and were planning to increase the numbers to something like 2,000. To cater for the increase they had recently built a bothy on the inland part of the farm at a cost of some £29,000.

The respondent may broadly be described as the authority responsible for conservation and the protection of wildlife in the area. Its powers are derived from the Wildlife and Countryside Act 1981, a measure passed with the objective, amongst others, of preventing undue exploitation and consequent damage to the flora and fauna of this country. In order to be able to carry out this objective, the relevant authority is given powers under s 28 to declare certain areas to be those of special scientific interest and, by appropriate notification, to ban or limit any operations which appear to them to be likely to damage the countryside unacceptably. The cliff land at Rhossili had been declared an area of special scientific interest and it comes as something of a surprise to learn that the activity which incurred the displeasure of the respondent was that of pasturing sheep. But so it was: on 23 October 1986 it gave formal notification to the appellants pursuant to s 28(1) of the 1981 Act that this time-honoured form of husbandry had to be drastically limited. Owing to the crucial importance of the cliff land, clearly compliance with the notification would entail drastic alteration to the appellants' sheep farming and their plans for the future.

It is necessary briefly to describe the various steps which led to the arbitration, all of which are provided for by the 1981 Act. First, any owner or occupier of land who has been served with notification is prevented from carrying out any of the operations specified for four months, and then only if he has served a counter-notice that he proposes to carry out the operations proscribed (see s 28(5)). The method whereby the council can enforce any ban or limitation is described as a management agreement and the 1981 Act provides for the parties to enter into such an agreement by negotiation. Before a long-term management agreement can be finalised, the parties wil enter into short-term management agreements and, if no long-term agreement is negotiated, the council or other relevant authority next makes a formal offer to enter into a management agreement by virtue of s 50(1). This offer has to specify the terms including the terms as to payment which the council is prepared to make in order to compensate the owner or occupier for the restrictions being imposed on his land. By s 50(2) the payments are stated to be determined in accordance with guidelines issued by the ministers (the Department of the Environment circular 4/83, Welsh Office circular 6/83). If the owner/occupier is dissatisfied with the terms of payment offered he can require the matter to be referred to arbitration by virtue of s 50(3), and that is what happened in this case. During the course of the unsuccessful negotiations the respondent commissioned a report from a Mr Hollington, which it disclosed to the appellants. This report is in the nature of a feasibility study and addresses the problem of how the land might be farmed subject to the restrictions. Therein it will be seen that Mr Hollington considered two possibilities: the first to reduce the existing flock to some 640 ewes and convert a part of the land to arable; the second was to reduce the flock to a mere 220 ewes with a consequently greater conversion to arable. In terms of cost, Mr Hollington gave it as his opinion that the first alternative would limit the loss to be sustained by approximately £2,000 more than would the second alternative. It is necessarily implicit in his report that he considered both options to be viable.

The relevant terms of the guidelines are as follows. Paragraph 13 provides:

'For the purposes of the long-term agreement, owners and owner-occupiers may choose *either* lump sum payment *or* annual payments … Only annual payments are available to *tenants* …'

Paragraph 14 provides:

'Payment, at the commencement of the agreement, of a single *lump sum* for the management agreement over a 20-year period … *The amount should be equal to the difference between the restricted and unrestricted value of the owner or owner-occupier's interest,* calculated having regard to the rules for assessment in respect of the compulsory acquisition of an interest in land, as set out in Section 5 of the Land Compensation Act 1961 ...'

Paragraph 16, headed 'Annual payments: (owners or owner-occupiers)' provides: 'Payment of *annual sums* for an agreement over a 20-year period ... *The payments should reflect net profits forgone because of the agreements* ...' By para 18 it is stated that individual assessment will be appropriate in most cases to calculate the sums payable.

Later in the document, under a heading entitled 'Other Factors Determining Payment', para 29 provides:

'*Fees:* On completion of a management agreement the offeror should pay the reasonable costs of the offeree incurred in retaining professional advisers to assist him in connexion with the agreement.'

Paragraph 30, 'Other costs', provides:

'A management agreement may also provide for payment:—(a) for expenditure reasonably incurred within the previous 12 months of the date of notification which has been rendered abortive or in undertaking work rendered abortive by the agreement (subject to minimising loss—see paragraph 11 above); (b) for any loss or damage directly attributable to the agreement; in so far as ... no relevant payment is available under other provisions of these guidelines.'

Under the heading 'Minimising loss', para 11 states:

'From the date of initial notification of his proposed operation, an owner or occupier should not take any action which may increase the sum eventually payable to him under these guidelines, e g entering into any contract or commitment with third parties relating to the proposed work ...'

This paragraph earns few prizes for drafting.

The appellants' appeal is brought pursuant to s 1 of the Arbitration Act 1979 and is advanced on two basic grounds. (1) That in determining the measure of net profits foregone because of the agreements within the terms of para 16 of the guidelines, the arbitrator, as a matter of law, applied the wrong formula when he calculated the loss by reference to the difference between what the appellants could have earned had they continued with the proposed expansion of their sheep farming activity compared with what they could earn by switching to a farming policy which would maximise profits, without taking into account any considerations other than those which were purely financial.   It is contended that this is an incorrect interpretation of the combined effect of paras 11 and 16 of the guidelines. (2) That the arbitrator erred in rejecting various heads of claim for lost capital expenditure on the basis that, the appellants having opted for annual payments, they were not entitled to payments under paras 29 and 30 of the guidelines.

Contained in the appeal is also an application pursuant to s 1(5) of the 1979 Act that the matter be remitted to the arbitrator for him to make further primary findings of fact which are necessary and to give reasons which both parties had asked him to do. To apply to remit in this fashion at the same time as appealing the findings seems to me to be putting the cart, if not in front of, at least beside the horse, but the appellants were given leave, so I am told, under both subsections, and Mr Bush for the respondent, after some initial hesitation, does not seek to argue that I should not deal with both aspects at the same time.

I now turn to consider the relevant terms of the arbitrator's award. At the outset it should be mentioned that, although this is an award made in relation to a proposed long-term agreement, it is only referable to the three years from 1 September 1987 to 31 August 1990. As a further background fact it should be recorded that the appellants, faced with the restrictions which were being imposed upon their use of the cliff land, made a considered judgment that any substantial sheep farming operation would not be viable, and therefore altered their farming policy radically and in essence adopted the second possibility which had been described by Mr Hollington in his report. Nobody has suggested that the appellants took their decision other than in good faith and backed by their own not inconsiderable experience of farming in the area. More importantly, the respondent accepted that this decision was not to be regarded as an action which might 'increase the sum eventually payable to them' within the terms of para 11 of the guidelines. The parties appeared to have agreed that the wording of para 11 was intended solely to deal with actions taken in bad faith with the deliberate intention of increasing the eventual compensation. Whether or not that is the correct interpretation must abide some later dispute. Fortunately, for present purposes, it is not necessary for me to construe the proper meaning of para 11. I content myself with the prophecy that it is likely to give trouble in the future.

The formula adopted by the arbitrator for assessing the net profits foregone can be deduced from the following passages in the award. First para 12, where he states:

'In reaching my decision I first considered whether the farming policy adopted by the claimants was the optimum in the circumstances and secondly what might the claimants have achieved from the sheep unit had the restrictions not been imposed.'

Later, in para 15, we find the following:

'It must be assumed that any farmer managing his holding properly will be looking to a farming policy that will maximise profits. The farmer can, and is free to, farm the holding as he wishes provided he can afford the losses that may result but the respondents are not obliged to work out the profits foregone on other than their view properly established as to the optimum farming system resulting from the imposition of the restrictions. The accounts for the years 1989 and 1990 show very large losses which I consider show that the policy adopted was not the optimum.'

And finally, in para 17(2):

'The claimants are free to adopt any farming policy they wish to choose but the respondents are required only to consider under the heading "Profit Foregone" the effect on those profits arising from the restrictions imposed ... I consider that a viable, although reduced, flock could have been maintained using the inland areas after the imposition of the restrictions.'

From these passages it is clear that in order to assess the net profits foregone, the arbitrator first estimated the profit which the appellants would have earned had they been allowed to continue as before, and as the second half of the equation he assessed what was the maximum income the farm could produce, the sole criterion being that of finance; no other considerations entered the picture.

In my judgment that approach is wrong in law. It would have appealed to Mr Gradgrind but it does not appeal to me. There are several reasons which can be advanced for this, but the following will suffice. (1) Paragraph 16 of the guidelines makes it clear that the question of loss is to be looked at as a matter of causation; this is in accordance with the general principles of law applicable to damages for tortious acts or breaches of contract and the equation adopted by the arbitrator goes far beyond any principle of damages applicable to such cases. (2) Farming activities can vary in profitability from year to year; one of the principal variables being the level of subsidies on particular activities. Bearing in mind that this was a calculation designed to fix the level of annual payments, it might well be that one particular strategy would be the commercial optimum one year but not the next. (3) In determining the proper meaning to be ascribed to the words of para 16, I consider it permissible to look at the entire compensation structure provided for. That which is found in the short-term agreement is: 'to pay the owner for any reasonable financial loss arising as a consequence of this agreement.' It would, in my judgment, be strange indeed if compensation under the long-term agreement was computed on a formula which was likely to be more disadvantageous to the owner/occupier. (4) Paragraph 18 of the guidelines makes it clear that individual assessment will be appropriate in most cases. This seems to me to be incompatible with any proposition that the only yardstick is purely commercial. Even the respondent, albeit in an alternative proposition, was prepared to concede that it must take their farmer as it found him with his preferences and perhaps in some cases his lack of competence. A basis of computation of loss which involves the notional transmutation of perhaps a somewhat inefficient farmer to one of maximum competence would obviously work great injustice. I must not lose sight of the fact that this is a situation where a statutory body is given arbitrary power to interfere with the manner in which the ordinary citizen is going about a perfectly lawful occupation on his own land. Such interference, while doubtless well intentioned, is always susceptible to somewhat overzealous application, even at times to abuse. Take the case of a farmer who farms sheep and nothing else because that is what he wishes to do. Restrictions are placed upon him which will entail a very considerable diminution of the number of sheep he is able to farm; bowing to the inevitable he takes advice and is told that rather than continue with a limited herd he will make more money if he converts his entire farm to turnips and mangoldwurzels. Is he not to be allowed to say: 'I don't like turnips and mangoldwurzels; I don't like their smell, I don't like the mud that they produce, and I fail to see why this intrusive body, "drest in a little brief authority", should come and radically alter the amenities and tenor of the life that I have led for many years.' Are not such arguments to be heard? If the answer is No then the world will have grown grey indeed. For these reasons the matter must be remitted to the arbitrator for him to apply the correct test.

This naturally leads to the question what is the correct test? The appellants' first contention was that any obligation on the part of an owner/occupier was limited to and exhaustively defined by the terms of para 11 of the guidelines. Freed from the necessity of determining just what para 11 meant, Mr Brodie QC for the appellants boldly submitted that his clients were entitled to be compensated in full, whatever altered farming policy they chose to adopt, provided they did not fall foul of the restriction imposed by para 11. As an alternative, he submitted that the whole question was to be equated pari passu with the standard law governing damages for breach of contract or for tort, and mitigation.

I have to reject his first submission. I think that the wording of the guidelines, although far short of ideal, was intended to equate the manner of assessing compensation with the normal law applicable to cases of contractual or tortious liability. To that extent, para 11 is in fact surplusage. A further consideration that has influenced me is that, whereas the parties during the course of the arbitration adopted an interpretation of para 11 which was extremely sensible, I am far from persuaded that in the face of the actual wording, it was correct. It seems to me that on a somewhat less sympathetic construction of the words any course of action by a farmer which subsequently turned out to be uneconomic might well fall foul of the paragraph, in which case the farmer would be worse off than he would be under the ordinary law.

Under the normal law of contract and tort the fundamental basis for the measure of damages is compensation for pecuniary loss which directly and naturally flows from the breach. The authority so far as breach of contract is concerned is to be found in *British Westinghouse Electric and Manufacturing Co Ltd v Underground Electric Railways Co of London Ltd* [1912] AC 673 at 689, [1911–13] All ER Rep 63 at 69. There is, however, a qualification that a plaintiff suing for breach of contract or, for that matter, for tort cannot call upon a defendant to pay the full direct consequences unless he himself has acted reasonably to mitigate the loss. It is sometimes loosely described as a plaintiff's duty to mitigate. In *MacGregor on Damages* (15th edn, 1988) para 275 it is stated:

'The first and most important rule is that the plaintiff must take all reasonable steps to mitigate the loss to him consequent upon the defendant's wrong and cannot recover damages for any such loss which he could thus have avoided but has failed, through unreasonable action or inaction, to avoid. Put shortly, the plaintiff cannot recover for avoidable loss.'

With respect to the learned author, the word 'must', implying some sort of duty, may not be strictly accurate. If he wishes to claim the full measure of his loss, a plaintiff must act reasonably, but, as was recently pointed out in *Sotiros Shipping Inc v Sameiet Solholt, The Solholt* [1983] 1 Lloyd's Rep 605 at 608, a plaintiff is under no duty to mitigate his loss. He is completely free to act as he judges to be in his best interests. The significance of his failure to act in a reasonable manner is merely that he cannot then call upon the defendant to pay for losses which he might have avoided had he taken reasonable steps to do so. For the purposes of the present remission to the arbitrator I would stress that fundamentally the matter is one of causation—that is to say the assessment of the loss which has naturally flowed as a result of the restrictions.

Questions to be asked are as follows. (1) What could the appellants have achieved? This is one which the arbitrator has already determined. (2) What have the appellants achieved? (3) In between those two poles, has any act or omission of the appellants been unreasonable and of such a nature as to lead one to say that the difference between (1) and (2) can no longer be said to be caused by the restrictions? Put another way, was the appellants' decision to adopt the farming system which they did a reasonable one? That question is not to be answered solely in terms of the commercial optimum. Obviously profitability is a factor, and an important one, but in an occupation such as farming any test of reasonableness should take some account of other circumstances including individual personal factors of amenity, even of aesthetic preference. The question of what is reasonable is entirely one of fact for the arbitrator. However, in view of the contents of the report by Mr Hollington, some assistance as a matter of law may be derived from the concluding remarks of the judgment in *Lloyds and Scottish Finance Ltd v Modern Cars and Caravans (Kingston) Ltd* [1964] 2 All ER 732 at 741, [1966] 1 QB 764 at 782, where, without stating a definite proposition of law, the court expressed grave doubt whether, if a plaintiff acted upon the suggestion of the defendant, he could ever be said to have acted unreasonably. Whether or not the two possibilities described by Mr Hollington amounted to a suggestion made by the respondent will again be a matter of fact for the arbitrator.

I next turn to deal with the appellants' second ground of appeal concerning the capital costs disallowed by the arbitrator. These are to be found, together with such reasons as the arbitrator gave, at para 18 of the award. Herein the appellants' primary submission was that the award demonstrated on its face that, in disallowing the various items listed under para 18, the arbitrator had done so on the basis that lump sums could not be claimed if the claimants had exercised the option open to them to select annual payments rather than a lump sum payment.

Had this been the basis of the arbitrator's reasoning, I should have had no hesitation in holding that he was in error: paras 29 and 30 of the guidelines seem to me to be a clear indication that, over and above the annual payments, or for that matter the limited basis of the lump sum recoverable under para 4, certain further items of capital expenditure are recoverable. But I think that Mr Bush is correct when he submits that para 18 of the award, taken as a whole, does not indicate that the arbitrator was at fault in that regard; it was only item (c), described as 'Loss in Capital Value of the Holding', which he disallowed on that basis. It is nevertheless necessary to consider the various items listed under para 18 of the award to see if, as the plaintiffs contend, there are errors of law on their face. I will deal with them in turn, leaving item (c) until last.

Sub-paragraph (a) is in a separate category. Sub-paragraph (b): the capital costs resulting from the need to purchase machinery and improvements have been disallowed on the basis that these costs would not have arisen if the appellants had retained sheep on the inland areas, that is to say had adopted the first of the two possibilities mentioned by Mr Hollington in his report. Since I have held that the arbitrator applied the wrong test in deciding that the appellants could not claim any losses over and above those which would have been sustained had they adopted that suggestion, it necessarily follows that

his approach to this item was erroneous also. If, on the remission, the
arbitrator comes to the conclusion that the appellants acted reasonably, it will
be necessary for him to examine this item of claim afresh. Further, contrary
to what is set out in the last sentence under sub-para (b), it is not necessary to
incorporate any award under this head in the annual calculation of profit
foregone since, as I have already tried to indicate, paras 29 and 30 of the
guidelines allow for capital costs of this nature as separate items.

Sub-paragraph (d): here again the arbitrator seems to give two reasons: the
first, namely that reflected by the words; 'this building would be essential if a
flock of sheep was retained', reflects the same error of approach as that
described under sub para (b). The arbitrator continues, however, by saying
'even without the flock the building is of such a construction that it adds value
to the holding as it could be adopted for other uses of value to the farm.
Again, the wrong test has been applied; the arbitrator should ask himself
whether the appellants would be unreasonable if they did not use the building
for other uses of value; this distinction, however, may well turn out to be
more academic than real.

Sub-paragraph (e): the forced sheep sale. The arbitrator states:

> '... in a letter dated 22 July 1987 from Mr D.J. Harry Thomas to Mr
> Thompson, land agent to the N.C.C., it is made quite clear that the advice
> of their auctioneer was that because of the number of ewes involved a sale
> on the farm was likely to produce better prices.'

The arbitrator continues that he considers the advice was understandable
because of the quality of the stock and the reputation of the appellants. But
that again is a wholly incorrect reason for disallowing the claim. This matter
too must be considered in the light of whether or not the appellants acted
reasonably in changing to the farming policy which they did. It is implicit in
the arbitrator's remarks under this sub-paragraph that he considers that the
appellants acted reasonably in selling on their farm rather than at auction, so
that if, on remission, he comes to the conclusion that the appellants did act
reasonably in their selection of an alternative farming strategy, this too is a
claim which must be entertained.

Sub-paragraph (f) has not been pursued in this appeal. Sub-paragraph (g):
here the arbitrator does not deal with this on the basis that it is a claim which
does not fall within his remit. In view of the terms of para 29 of the guidelines
this again must be classed as an error. Sub-paragraph (h): this has not been
contended for.

I return therefore to sub-para (c), which, in the way in which it has been
dealt with, gives rise to some difficulty. It is necessary to set out the
arbitrator's findings verbatim as follows:

> 'Loss in capital value of the holding: no evidence to substantiate the
> valuations put forward on behalf of the claimants was put forward. The
> valuation was therefore not tested before me and in any case the
> guidelines are quite explicit about the claim to be either profit foregone
> or lump sum payment.'

Two criticisms are made of this, both, as it seems to me, valid. To start
with, I am told, and there is no dispute about this, that in fact evidence was
put before the arbitrator in the form of a report from a Mr Jeremy, whom the
appellants did not call. Granted that the respondents objected to the report

being put in evidence, nevertheless the arbitrator allowed it. A reading of it reveals that the arbitrator appears to have been under a misapprehension. What was being claimed was not the loss in capital value of the land by reason of the restrictions from the very moment the restrictions were imposed—that indeed would be attempting to claim both annual payments and lump sum payments, and would be impermissible. On the contrary, what was being claimed was the diminution of the capital value of the land after the management agreement had run its course. For the sake of convenience this has been referred to as residual capital loss. The report of Mr Jeremy places this at £55,000, which was the figure claimed in the appellants' original notice of claim.

This gives rise to the following problem: as expressed, there is no discernible error of law or, for that matter, of approach in the way in which the arbitrator has dealt with the loss in capital value under para 18(c). Am I entitled to go behind the curtain, as it were, in order to satisfy myself that the arbitrator's finding was based on a misapprehension as to the nature of the claim being made? Mr Bush has drawn my attention to the judgment of the Court of Appeal in *Universal Petroleum Co Ltd (in liq) v Handels- und Transportgesellschaft mbH* [1987] 2 All ER 737, [1987] 1 WLR 1178. This report contains a definitive statement of the limitations of the right to challenge an arbitrator's award imposed by s 1 of the 1979 Act. In particular the court stressed that primary findings in an award could not be challenged unless there was misconduct by the arbitrator, or a lack of jurisdiction, or he had failed to accede to the request of the parties on a specific matter. It was stressed that the arbitrator's primary findings of fact were immune from review apart from those circumstances and in particular that evidence could not be introduced in order to challenge those findings. Any error open to challenge had to be visible in the award itself rather than arise from the arbitration. Having considered the entirety of the judgment, however, I have reached the conclusion that the case is not strictly in point where the present issue is concerned. The Court of Appeal were dealing with the strict limitations on the power to challenge findings of primary fact by an arbitrator. Paragraph 18(c) of the award makes no primary findings of fact other than the incorrect one that no evidence was put forward in support of the claim. For my part I do not consider that looking at the way in which the original claim was framed comes under the heading of taking account of matters which are extrinsic to the award. The claim is, in essence, the progenitor of the award itself. In my judgment it surely must be permissible to consider precisely what was being claimed in order to go one further and consider whether the arbitrator in fact dealt with that particular claim. To put it another way, though one cannot query whether the arbitrator got his facts right, it must surely be open to a party to contend that he failed to perform his task. In this instance, although the claim was rather baldly stated in its pleaded form as a claim for the capital value of the land, nevertheless the sum of £55,000 was specifically mentioned and reference was made to Mr Jeremy's report. This, I consider, was sufficient to bring that report within the ambit of the claim, and once that position is arrived at, it is quite clear that the appellants were only claiming for the residual capital loss. This is a matter which the arbitrator failed to appreciate and accordingly this again must be submitted to him for reconsideration.

Finally, I come to the third issue raised in the appeal, namely the contention that the matter should be remitted to the arbitrator for him to make further findings of fact and to give his reasons for arriving at the award which he did. I can deal with this fairly shortly. It should be said at once that, since the arbitrator was specifically asked to state his reasons, sadly, it is apparent that he has not done so. Apart from the bare statement that he has considered this, that or the other factor, he has merely given figures for the three years in question. It has been quite impossible for either party to determine just how the arbitrator has arrived at those figures. Whilst accepting Mr Bush's submission that an arbitrator cannot be expected to make every single minute finding of fact involved in a fairly complex award, yet where the whole purpose of the arbitration is to calculate and arrive at a specific sum or sums of money payable by way of compensation, then the steps and calculations by which those sums are arrived at in my judgment must amount either to primary findings of fact or at least to reasons. In the present award virtually no reasons have been given; Mr Bush himself, when asked point blank how one could determine the method whereby the arbitrator had arrived at the three figures referred to, was unable to supply an answer, nor could anyone else.

But that is by no means conclusive. Section 1(5) of the 1979 Act has also drastically limited the circumstances in which an award can be remitted for further findings. Section 1(5) states, in its relevant terms:

'... if an award is made and, on an application made by any of the parties to the reference ... it appears to the High Court that the award does not or does not sufficiently set out the reasons for the award, the court may order the arbitrator or umpire concerned to state the reasons for his award in sufficient detail to enable the court, should an appeal be brought under this section, to consider any question of law arising out of the award.'

The foregoing words envisage a two-stage process: first the court has to determine whether the reasons given for the award are sufficient. That I have already done and held them insufficient. But secondly the court cannot order the matter to be remitted for further findings or reasons unless satisfied that these would enable it to determine whether or not an error of law had been committed. Despite Mr Brodie's submissions on the point, I remain quite unconvinced that even if the arbitrator gave the precise reasons for the award at which he arrived, which principally would be a matter of mathematics, any question of law would be likely to arise.

For these reasons I do not think that the application under s 1(5) can succeed. But for the reasons which I have endeavoured to express, I take the view that this appeal must succeed, and the matter must be remitted to the arbitrator for his further consideration after applying what I have stated to be the correct test when interpreting the meaning of the words 'profits foregone because of the restrictions' in para 16 of the guidelines.

Appeal allowed.

K Mydeen Esq   Barrister

Barclays Bank plc v Glasgow City Council
Kleinwort Benson Ltd v Glasgow City Council

QUEEN'S BENCH DIVISION (COMMERCIAL COURT)

HIRST J

19, 20, 27 FEBRUARY 1992

COURT OF APPEAL, CIVIL DIVISION

LLOYD, MANN AND STEYN LJJ

17, 18 MAY 1993

Conflict of laws – Jurisdiction – Challenge to jurisdiction – Restitution – Banks entering into interest rate swap agreements with local authorities – Agreements declared void ab initio – Banks bringing restitutionary claims in England against local authority domiciled in Scotland – Scottish authority challenging jurisdiction of English court – Whether English court having special jurisdiction over banks' claims – Whether transactions matters 'relating to a contract' or 'relating to tort' – Whether Scottish authority 'one of a number of defendants' – Whether reference to European Court for clarification of special jurisdiction provisions appropriate – Civil Jurisdiction and Judgments Act 1982, Sch 2, art 3, Sch 4, arts 2, 5(1)(3), 6(1).

Contract – Restitution – Interest rate swap agreement – Bank entering into interest rate swap agreements with local authority – Agreements ultra vires the local authority and void – Whether bank entitled to recover payments made.

The defendant, a Scottish local authority, entered into a number of interest rate swap agreements with the plaintiff banks. Following the House of Lords ruling that such agreements were ultra vires the local authorities and void ab initio, the plaintiff banks brought a number of actions in England, seeking to recover from the defendant and other English local authorities various sums of money which had been paid out under the interest rate swap transactions by way of claims for restitution. The defendant however challenged the jurisdiction of the English court and applied for an order dismissing the actions on the ground that it was domiciled in Scotland for the purposes of the Convention on Jurisdiction and the Enforcement of Judgments in Civil and Commercial Matters 1968 (set out in Sch 1 to the Civil Jurisdiction and Judgments Act 1982) and should be sued in the courts of Scotland pursuant to s 16(1)[a] of and art 2[b] of Sch 4 to the 1982 Act, which made provision for the allocation of jurisdiction within the United Kingdom. The banks contended that they were entitled to sue the defendant in England on the basis of the special jurisdiction provisions of arts 5[c] and 6[d] of Sch 4 to the Act, which provided (i) that a person could be sued in 'matters relating to a contract' in the courts for the 'place of performance of the obligation in question' (art 5(1)) and in 'matters relating to tort', where the harmful event occurred (art 5(3)) and (ii) that 'one of a number of defendants' could be sued in the courts of another part

---

Section 16(1) is set out at p 869 *a* to *c*, post
Article 2, so far as material, is set out at p 869 *d*, post
Article 5, so far as material, is set out at p 869 *f* to *h*, post
Article 6, so far as material, is set out at p 869 *h j*, post

of the United Kingdom where any one of them was domiciled (art 6(1)). The judge granted the defendant's application and struck out the banks' actions holding that agreements which had been declared void ab initio as contracts were not open to classification as 'matters relating to a contract' under art 5(1) so as to allow jurisdiction in the courts of the country of performance of the obligations arising from the transactions. He further held that a claim for unjust enrichment did not fall within the terms of art 5(3) and that art 6 did not apply, since the words 'one of a number of defendants' envisaged a claim by the same plaintiff and therefore did not apply to different defendants in a large number of different unconsolidated actions initiated by different plaintiffs. One of the banks appealed.

Held – (1) On its true construction, the rule laid down in art 6(1) of Sch 4 to the 1982 Act applied in circumstances where it would be expedient to hear and determine a number of related actions together in order to avoid the risk of irreconcilable judgments resulting from separate proceedings. The banks were unable to rely on the special jurisdiction provisions of art 6(1), since the large number of separate actions comprising the interest rate swap litigation would not be heard and determined together and, even if there were a prospect of irreconcilable decisions at first instance or on intermediate appeal, the House of Lords would be able to give a single final decision which would be binding in both England and Scotland, with no possibility of irreconcilability. I followed that the judge's ruling on the art 6(1) point was correct. The bank's appeal on that ground would accordingly be dismissed (see p 885 e to j, post) *Kalfelis v Bankhaus Schröder Münchmeyer Hengst & Co* Case 189/87 [1988] ECR 5565 applied.

(2) However, the question of the scope of art 5(1) and (3) of Sch 4 to the 1982 Act and their relationship to each other would be referred to the Court of Justice of the European Communities for a preliminary ruling under art 3 of the 1971 Protocol on the Interpretation of the 1968 Convention, albeit that no question of Community law as such was involved, since, in the absence of clear guidance from the European Court, the court would be unable to resolve the difficult questions of construction raised by the special jurisdiction provision and thereby determine the bank's appeal on that ground (see p 889 b to h, post) *Gmurzynska-Bscher v Oberfinanzdirektion Köln* Case C-231/89 [1990] ECR I-4003 applied.

Notes

For jurisdiction of the courts with respect to the 1968 convention on recognition and enforcement of EC judgments, see 8 *Halsbury's Laws* (4th edn) para 768B.

For the Civil Jurisdiction and Judgments Act 1982, s 16, Sch 2, art 3, Sch 4 arts 2, 5, 6, see 11 *Halsbury's Statutes* (4th edn) (1991 reissue) 1113, 1158, 1190, 1191.

Cases referred to in judgments

Arcado SPRL v Haviland SA Case 9/87 [1988] ECR 1539.
Davenport v Corinthian Motor Policies at Lloyds 1991 SLT 774, Ct of Sess.
Effer SpA v Kantner Case 38/81 [1982] ECR 825.
Engdiv Ltd v G Percy Trentham Ltd 1990 SLT 617, Ct of Sess.

Ets A de Bloos SPRL v Société en Commandite par actions Bouyer Case 14/76 [1976] ECR 1497.

Gmurzynska-Bscher v Oberfinanzdirektion Köln Case C-231/89 [1990] ECR I-4003, ECJ.

Gubisch Maschinenfabrik KG v Palumbo Case 144/86 [1987] ECR 4861.

Hazell v Hammersmith and Fulham London BC [1991] 1 All ER 545, [1992] 2 AC 1, [1991] 2 WLR 372, HL; *rvsg* [1990] 3 All ER 33, [1990] 2 QB 697, [1990] 2 WLR 1038, DC and CA.

Ivenel v Schwab Case 133/81 [1982] ECR 1891.

Kalfelis v Bankhaus Schröder Münchmeyer Hengst & Co Case 189/87 [1988] ECR 5565.

Martin Peters Bauunternehmung GmbH v Zuid Nederlandse Aannemers Vereniging Case 34/82 [1983] ECR 987.

Reichert v Dresdner Bank (No 2) Case C-261/90 [1992] I L Pr 404, ECJ.

Shearson Lehman Hutton Inc v TVB Treuhandgesellschaft für Vermögensverwaltung und Beteiligungen mbH Case C-89/91 [1993] I L Pr 199, ECJ.

Somafer SA v Saar-Ferngas AG Case 33/78 [1978] ECR 2183.

Tesam Distribution Ltd v Schuh Mode Team GmbH [1990] I L Pr 149, CA.

Union Transport plc v Continental Lines SA [1992] 1 All ER 161, [1992] 1 WLR 15, HL.

Westdeutsche Landesbank Girozentrale v Islington London BC, Kleinwort Benson Ltd v Sandwell BC [1994] 4 All ER 890; *affd in part* [1994] 4 All ER 890, [1994] 1 WLR 938, CA.

Cases also cited or referred to in skeleton arguments

Arab Bank Ltd v Barclays Bank (Dominion Colonial and Overseas) [1954] 2 All ER 226, [1954] AC 495, HL.

Bank of Scotland v Seitz 1990 SLT 584, Ct of Sess.

Dumez France and Tracoba v Hessische Landesbank (Helaba) Case C-220/88 [1990] ECR 49, ECJ.

Duval (Charles) & Co Ltd v Gans [1904] 2 KB 685, CA.

Eider, The [1893] P 119, CA.

Gascoine v Pyrah (1991) Times, 26 November.

Handelskwekerij G J Bier BV v Mines de Potasse d'Alsace SA Case 21/76 [1976] ECR 1735.

Industrie Tessili Italiana Como v Dunlop AG Case 12/76 [1976] ECR 1473.

Jakob Handte GmbH v Traitements mécano-chimiques des Surfaces Case C-26/91) [1992] ECR 3967, ECJ.

Lipkin Gorman (a firm) v Karpnale Ltd [1992] 4 All ER 512, [1991] 2 AC 540, HL; *rvsg in part* [1992] 4 All ER 409, [1989] 1 WLR 1340, CA; *rvsg in part* [1992] 4 All ER 331, [1987] 1 WLR 987.

Marc Rich & Co AG v Societa Italiana Impianti PA, The Atlantic Emperor [1989] 1 Lloyd's Rep 548, CA.

Mercury Publicity Ltd v Wolfgang Loerke GmbH (1991) Times, 21 October, [1991] CA Transcript 1036.

R v International Stock Exchange of the UK and the Republic of Ireland Ltd, ex p Else (1982) Ltd, R v International Stock Exchange of the UK and the Republic of Ireland Ltd, ex p Roberts [1993] 1 All ER 420, [1993] QB 534, CA.

Shenavai v Kreischer Case 266/85 [1987] ECR 239.

Shevill v Presse Alliance SA [1992] 1 All ER 409, [1992] 2 WLR 1, CA.

Applications

The plaintiffs, Barclays Bank plc and Kleinwort Benson Ltd (the banks), by writs issued on 6 August 1991 and 6 September 1991, brought proceedings against the defendant local authority, Glasgow City Council (Glasgow), seeking restitution of sums totalling £389,431 and £807,230·31 respectively, being moneys had and received by Glasgow under interest rate swap agreements which were ultra vires the local authority and void ab initio. By summonses dated 16 October 1991 Glasgow sought, against each bank, (i) a declaration that the English court had no jurisdiction over it in respect of the subject matter of the claims and (ii) an order that the actions be dismissed since it was domiciled in Scotland for the purposes of the Convention on Jurisdiction and the Enforcement of Judgments in Civil and Commercial Matters 1968 and should be sued in the courts of Scotland pursuant to s 16 of and art 2 of Sch 4 to the Civil Jurisdiction and Judgments Act 1982. The applications were heard together in chambers, but judgment was delivered by Hirst J in open court. The facts are set out in the judgment.

Tom Beazley (instructed by *Clifford Chance*) for the banks.
Jonathan Tecks (instructed by *William Sturges & Co*) for Glasgow.

Cur adv vult

27 February 1992. The following judgment was delivered.

HIRST J.

Introduction

The applicants in these two summonses, the City of Glasgow District Council (Glasgow), have been sued in two separate actions by Barclays Bank plc and Kleinwort Benson Ltd respectively (the banks), in the case of Barclays for £389,431 in relation to sums paid under one single interest rate swap agreement, and in the case of Kleinwort Benson for £807,230·31 in relation to sums paid under seven interest rate swap agreements.

Following from the decision of the House of Lords in *Hazell v Hammersmith and Fulham London BC* [1991] 1 All ER 545, [1992] AC 1 that all such transactions were ultra vires the local authority concerned and void ab initio, the banks claim the return of the above-mentioned sums on a restitutionary basis on the footing that the consideration for which the respective agreements were concluded has wholly failed; that the payments were made under a mistake of fact so that it is unjust and unconscionable that Glasgow should be entitled to retain them; that the sums are money had and received for the use of the banks; that the sums are held by the council on implied or resulting or constructive trusts of the bank; and that the banks are entitled to trace them.

In the present summonses Glasgow seeks declarations that the court has no jurisdiction over it in respect of these claims, and asks the court to order that the actions be dismissed.

These are two of a very large number of similar actions brought by various banks against various local authorities, in respect of which a lead action order has been made to which I refer below. I am giving this judgment in open court at the request of all parties.

Rules governing the court's jurisdiction

Section 16(1) of the Civil Jurisdiction and Judgments Act 1982 stipulates as follows:

> 'The provisions set out in Schedule 4 (which contains a modified version of Title II of the 1968 Convention) shall have effect for determining, for each part of the United Kingdom, whether the courts of law of that part, or any particular court of law in that part, have or has jurisdiction in proceedings where—(a) the subject-matter of the proceedings is within the scope of the 1968 Convention as determined by Article 1 (whether or not the Convention has effect in relation to the proceedings); and (b) the defendant or defender is domiciled in the United Kingdom or the proceedings are of a kind mentioned in Article 16 (exclusive jurisdiction regardless of domicile).'

It is common ground between the parties that these two actions were both within the ambit of art 1, which of course comprises 'civil and commercial matters', and that Sch 4 therefore applies to determine the court's jurisdiction. Article 2 of Sch 4 provides as follows:

> 'Subject to the provisions of this Title, persons domiciled in a part of the United Kingdom shall ... be sued in the courts of that part.'

It is therefore also common ground that prima facie Glasgow must be sued in Scotland because of course it is domiciled in Scotland, and that the banks are only entitled to sue in England if they can bring themselves within the special jurisdiction laid down in arts 5 and 6 of Sch 4.

These articles, so far as relevant, provide:

> *'Special jurisdiction*
>
> ARTICLE 5
>
> A person domiciled in a part of the United Kingdom may, in another part of the United Kingdom, be sued:
>
> (1) in matters relating to a contract, in the courts for the place of performance of the obligation in question ...
>
> (3) in matters relating to tort, delict or quasi-delict, in the courts for the place where the harmful event occurred or in the case of a threatened wrong is likely to occur ...
>
> (8) in proceedings—(a) concerning a debt secured on immovable property; or (b) which are brought to assert, declare or determine proprietary or possessory rights, or rights of security, in or over movable property, or to obtain authority to dispose of movable property, in the courts of the part of the United Kingdom in which the property is situated.
>
> ARTICLE 6
>
> A person domiciled in a part of the United Kingdom may, in another part of the United Kingdom, also be sued:
>
> (1) where he is one of a number of defendants, in the courts for the place where any one of them is domiciled ...'

Section 16(3)(a) of the 1982 Act provides as follows:

> 'In determining any question as to the meaning or effect of any provision contained in Schedule 4—(a) regard shall be had to any relevant principles laid down by the European Court in connection with Title II of the 1968

Convention and to any relevant decision of that court as to the meaning or effect of any provision of that Title ...'

Article 5(1): the rival submissions

The decision on this paragraph turns on the proper construction of the crucial words, 'in matters relating to a contract', it not being disputed that the place of performance of the obligation in question (if it exists) was England.

Mr Tecks submitted that the authorities of the Court of Justice of the European Communities cited below show that the crucial words refer to obligations which have their basis in contract or in a closely similar nexus such as that existing between an association and its members, so that the matters in question must be contractual or closely akin to contractual. In the present case, he submitted, the House of Lords has now conclusively ruled that there is not and never was a contract, and it is thus apparent on the plain words of art 5(1) itself that these restitutionary claims cannot possibly be properly classified as matters relating to a contract. This principle, he submitted, is further exemplified by the line of the Court of Justice authority which shows that the jurisdiction of the court may be invoked under this article where there is a dispute between the parties as to whether a contract in fact exists, but only if that dispute is real and genuine.

Mr Beazley for the banks submitted: (i) the Court of Justice authorities have laid down that the wording of the Schedule is to be given an independent interpretation and is not to be construed in accordance with national law. (ii) There is a general overriding principle that the Schedule must be interpreted by reference principally to the system and objectives of the Brussels Convention in order to ensure that it is fully effective; in order to strengthen in the Community the legal protection of persons therein established; and in order to contribute to the proper administration of justice within the Community by preventing parallel proceedings before the courts of different contracting states, and avoiding conflict between decisions which might result from permitting such parallel proceedings to continue. (iii) So far as art 5(1) itself is concerned, he submitted that it is clearly established by Court of Justice decisions that it reflects the close links created by the contract between the parties thereto, and the need to resolve all difficulties which may arise in connection with the contract in the same court in a country which has a close connection with the case, ie the court in the country where the obligation in question has to be performed. (iv) Although the claims in these actions are not made for the performance of the obligations under the contracts or as a result of their breach, they do concern matters relating to a contract, since the court is determining the consequences of the nullity of the contracts, particularly with regard to the contractual matters of total failure of consideration and payments under a mistake.

In support of his interpretation of art 5(1) Mr Beazley relied on the following additional points. (a) The provision of art 10(1)(e) in the Convention on the Law applicable to Contractual Obligations 1980 (the Rome Convention) enacted into English law by the Contracts (Applicable Law) Act 1990, that the law applicable to a contract shall govern inter alia 'the consequences of nullity of the contract', supports the view that on the proper independent interpretation of art 5(1) the consequences of nullity must be treated as within the scope of the phrase 'matters relating to a contract'. (b) In English law the choice of law rules governing claims for restitution are influenced by the claim

eing connected with a contract, having regard to the English conflict of laws
ule that the proper law of the obligation to restore a benefit, if the obligation
rises in connection with a contract, is the proper law of the contract: see *Dicey
nd Morris on the Conflict of Laws* (11th edn, 1987) p 1350, r 203.
:) Quasi-contractual claims, at least where there is a contract involved,
hould probably fall per se under art 5(1) (see the opinion of the editors of *Dicey
nd Morris*, p 1341 to this effect, and the decision of the Scottish courts that a
tatutory claim to contribution falls within that article in *Engdiv Ltd v G Percy
'rentham Ltd* 1990 SLT 617 at 621). (d) In the case of a claim for the return of
ioneys paid under an ineffective contract, there is no artificiality in deducing
n implied promise to pay, even though the old theory that restitution was
ased on the concept of such an implied promise is now largely discredited.

'he European Court cases and the Rome Convention
    In *Martin Peters Bauunternehmung GmbH v Zuid Nederlandse Aannemers
'ereniging* Case 34/82 [1983] ECR 987 at 991 the Supreme Court of The
Jetherlands referred to the Court of Justice the following question:

> 'Does Article 5(1) of the [Brussels] Convention apply to claims which are
> made by an association constituted under private law possessing legal
> personality against one of its members in a matter relating to obligations
> in regard to the payment of a sum of money and which have their basis in
> the relationship between the parties by virtue of membership, such
> relationship arising from the defendant party's joining the association as a
> member by virtue of a legal transaction entered into for that purpose?'

The court's decision, so far as relevant, was as follows:

> '9. Thus the concept of matters relating to a contract serves as a
> criterion to define the scope of one of the rules of special jurisdiction
> available to the plaintiff. Having regard to the objectives and the general
> scheme of the Convention, that it is important that, in order to ensure as
> far as possible the equality and uniformity of the rights and obligations
> arising out of the Convention for the Contracting States and the persons
> concerned, that concept should not be interpreted simply as referring to
> the national law of one or other of the States concerned.
> 10. Therefore, and as the Court ruled on similar grounds in relation to
> the words "the operation of a branch, agency or other establishment"
> referred to in Article 5(5) of the Convention (judgment of 22. 11. 1978 in
> Case 33/78 *Somafer v Saar-Ferngas AG* [1978] ECR 2183), the concept of
> matters relating to a contract should be regarded as an independent
> concept which, for the purpose of the application of the Convention, must
> be interpreted by reference chiefly to the system and objectives of the
> Convention, in order to ensure it is fully effective.
> 11. In this regard it should be pointed out that although Article 5 makes
> provision in a number of cases for a special jurisdiction which the plaintiff
> may choose, this is because of the existence, in certain clearly-defined
> situations, of a particularly close connecting factor between a dispute and
> the court which may be called upon to hear it, with a view to the
> efficacious conduct of the proceedings.
> 12. In that context, the designation by Article 5(1) of the Convention of
> the courts for the place of performance of the obligation in question
> expresses the concern that, because of the close links created by a contract

between the parties thereto, it should be possible for all the difficulties which may arise on the occasion of the performance of a contractual obligation to be brought before the same court: that for the place of performance of the obligation.

13. In that regard it appears that membership of an association creates between the members close links of the same kind as those which are created between the parties to a contract and that consequently the obligations to which the national court refers may be regarded as contractual for the purpose of the application of Article 5(1) of the Convention.

14. Since under national legal systems it is usually stipulated that the place in which the association is established is to be the place of performance of obligations arising out of the act of becoming a member the application of Article 5(1) of the Convention also has practical advantages: the court for the place in which the association has its seat is in fact usually the best fitted to understand the documents of constitution rules and decisions of the association, and also the circumstances out of which the dispute arose.' (See [1983] ECR 987 at 1002–1003.)

In *Arcado SPRL v Haviland SA* Case 9/87 [1988] ECR 1539 at 1541 the Cour d'Appel in Brussels referred the following question to the Court of Justice:

'Are proceedings relating to the wrongful repudiation of an (independent) commercial agency agreement and the payment of commission due under such an agreement proceedings in matters relating to a contract within the meaning of Article 5(1) of the Brussels Convention of 27 September 1968?'

The court's decision, so far as relevant, was as follows:

'10. As the Court held in its judgment of 22 March 1983 in Case 34/82 (*Martin Peters Bauunternehmung GmbH v Zuid Nederlandse Aannemers Vereniging* [1983] ECR 987) the concept of "matters relating to a contract" serves as a criterion to define the scope of one of the rules of special jurisdiction available to the plaintiff. Having regard to the objective and the general scheme of the Convention, it is important that, in order to ensure as far as possible the equality and uniformity of the rights and obligations arising out of the Convention for the Contracting States and the persons concerned, that concept should not be interpreted simply as referring to the national law of one or other of the States concerned.

11. Consequently, the concept of "matters relating to a contract" is to be regarded as an independent concept which, for the purpose of the application of the Convention, must be interpreted by reference principally to the system and objectives of the Convention in order to ensure that it is fully effective.

12. There is no doubt that a claim for the payment of commission due under an independent commercial agency agreement finds its very basis in that agreement and consequently constitutes a matter relating to a contract within the meaning of Article 5(1) of the Convention.

13. The same view must be taken of a claim for compensation for the wrongful repudiation of such an agreement as the basis for such compensation is the failure to comply with a contractual obligation.

14. As regards, more particularly, the right of a self-employed commercial agent to notice, its contractual nature and therefore the contractual nature of the compensation in lieu of notice were recognized in Articles 15 and 17 of Council Directive 86/653 of 18 December 1986 on the coordination of the laws of the Member States relating to self-employed commercial agents (Official Journal 1986, L 382, p. 17).

15. In addition, Article 10 of the [Rome] Convention on the Law applicable to Contractual Obligations of 19 June 1980 (Official Journal 1980, L 266, p. 1) confirms the contractual nature of judicial proceedings such as those in point inasmuch as it provides that the law applicable to a contract governs the consequences of a total or partial failure to comply with obligations arising under it and consequently the contractual liability of the party responsible for such breach.' (See [1988] ECR 1539 at 1554–1555.)

In *Union Transport Group plc v Continental Lines SA* [1992] 1 All ER 161, [1992] WLR 15 the House of Lords held that under art 5(1) of the Brussels onvention the court's jurisdiction was to be determined by the place of erformance of the principal obligation in the contract, applying the Court of stice's decision in *Ets A de Bloos SPRL v Société en commandite par actions Bouyer* ase 14/76 [1976] ECR 1497, described in the speech of Lord Goff as follows:

'That case was concerned with an exclusive distribution agreement, under which Bouyer, a French company, conferred on de Bloos, a Belgian company, exclusive distribution rights for Bouyer's products in Belgium, Luxembourg and Zaire. De Bloos commenced proceedings against Bouyer in Tournai in Belgium claiming, on the ground that Bouyer had committed a unilateral breach of the contract, an order for the dissolution of the agreement and damages. Bouyer invoked the convention. The court held that the place where the goods were to be delivered and where bills were payable was Bouyer's registered office in France, and on that basis the court declined jurisdiction. On appeal, the Court of Appeal at Mons referred the matter to the European Court. The European Court held that the word "obligation" in art 5(1) refers to the contractual obligation forming the basis of the legal proceedings, and that, in a case such as *de Bloos*, where the plaintiff asserts the right to be paid damages and seeks dissolution of the contract on the ground of the wrongful conduct of the other party, the obligation referred to in art 5(1) is still that which arises under the contract, the non-performance of which is relied upon to support such claims. It followed that regard must be had to the contractual obligation under consideration, and not to the contract as a whole.' (See [1992] 1 All ER 161 at 165, [1992] 1 WLR 15 at 19.)

In *Gubisch Maschinenfabrik KG v Palumbo* Case 144/86 [1987] ECR 4861, which r Beazley relied on as laying down the broad general principles which should e applicable, and which concerned the interpretation of art 21 of the Brussels onvention, the Court of Justice stated as follows (at 4874 (para 8)):

'According to its preamble, which incorporates in part the terms of Article 220, the Convention seeks in particular to facilitate the recognition and enforcement of judgments of courts or tribunals and to strengthen in the Community the legal protection of persons therein established. Article 21, together with Article 22 on related actions, is contained in Section 8 of Title II of the Convention; that section is intended, in the

interests of the proper administration of justice within the Community, t
prevent parallel proceedings before the courts of different Contractin
States and to avoid conflicts between decisions which might resu
therefrom. Those rules are therefore designed to preclude, in so far as
possible and from the outset, the possibility of a situation arising such a
that referred to in Article 27(3), that is to say the non-recognition of
judgment on account of its irreconcilability with a judgment given in
dispute between the same parties in the State in which recognition
sought.'

In *Effer SpA v Kantner* Case 38/81 [1982] ECR 825 the Court of Justice he
that a plaintiff may invoke the jurisdiction of the courts of the place o
performance of a contract in accordance with art 5(1) even where the existenc
of the contract on which the claim is based is in dispute between the parties.

In *Tesam Distribution Ltd v Schuh Mode Team GmbH* [1990] I L Pr 149 the Cou
of Appeal had to apply *Effer SpA v Kantner* in a case where the plaintiff produce
evidence, controverted by the defendant, that a contract existed. Stocker I
interpreted the *Effer SpA* case as follows (at 165):

> '[44] If in order to decide the question of jurisdiction it is necessary t
> determine finally whether a contract exists or not it would seem to follo
> that if the conclusion arrived at was that no contract existed then e
> *hypothesi* the conditions of *Article 5(1)* would not be met and the Cou
> would have no jurisdiction. It would seem to follow from that that th
> unsuccessful plaintiff can sue again in the court of the defendant
> domicile. I do not read the decision in EFFER v. KANTNER as having tha
> effect which would be contrary to the form in which the question pose
> was answered in that decision. Moreover, *vide* the comments cited i
> *Schlosser* [OJ 1979 No C 59 p. 71], and perhaps inferentially from the EFFE
> decision on an interlocutory application the U.K. court would be bound t
> decide the jurisdiction issue as a preliminary one on the informatio
> placed before it.
>
> [45] In my view the effect of the EFFER v. KANTNER decision is that a cou
> other than a court of the defendant's country of domicile cannot accep
> jurisdiction on the mere assertion or pleading of the plaintiff. There mu
> be evidence adduced from which a conclusion could properly an
> genuinely be drawn that a contract existed and that the place o
> performance was the country in which the action was brought. Onc
> jurisdiction can properly be established on this basis then the effect o
> *Article 5(1)* in the light of the EFFER v. KANTNER decision is that the court ha
> jurisdiction finally to determine the issues between the parties. If after fu
> trial the conclusion is that no contract existed then since the court ha
> jurisdiction to try the issue that determination is final and binding upo
> the parties.'

Nicholls LJ expressed a similar view and O'Connor LJ agreed (see [1990] I L F
149 at 158).

In the Rome Convention, art 10(1), provides as follows:

> 'Scope of the applicable law
> 1. The law applicable to a contract by virtue of Articles 3 to 6 and 12 o
> this Convention shall govern in particular: (a) interpretation; (t
> performance; (c) within the limits of the powers conferred on the court b

its procedural law, the consequences of breach, including the assessment of damages in so far as it is governed by rules of law; (d) the various ways of extinguishing obligations, and prescription and limitation of actions; (e) the consequences of nullity of the contract.'

The report of Professor Giuliano and Professor Lagarde (OJ 1980 C282, p 1 p 33) and which by virtue of s 3(3) of the 1990 Act may be considered in certaining the meaning or effect of any provision of the Rome Convention, plains the genesis of sub-para (e):

'Subparagraph (e) also makes the consequences of nullity subject to the applicable law. The working party's principal objective in introducing this provision was to make the refunds which the parties have to pay each other subsequent to a finding of nullity of the contract subject to the applicable law. Some delegations have indicated their opposition to this approach on the grounds that, under their legal systems, the consequences of nullity of the contract are non-contractual in nature. The majority of delegations have nevertheless said they are in favour of including such consequences within the scope of the law of contracts, but in order to take account of the opposition expressed provision had been made for any Contracting State to enter a reservation on this matter: (Article 22(1)(b)).'

reservation to this effect is continued in s 2(2) of the 1990 Act, which provides at inter alia para 10(1)(e) of the Rome Convention shall not have the force of w in the United Kingdom.

alysis and conclusions
The House of Lords having held that the swap transactions were void ab tio, the suggestion that the restitutionary claims in these actions are in atters relating to a contract seems to me to be placing a very severe strain deed on the language of art 5(1).
I can find nothing either in *Martin Peters Bauunternehmung GmbH v Zuid derlandse Aannemers Vereniging* Case 34/82 [1983] ECR 987 or in *Arcado SPRL Haviland SA* Case 9/87 [1988] ECR 1539 to support such a conclusion. Mr azley relied particularly on the *Peters* case, which he submitted shows that ere does not have to be an actual contract in order to bring the case within : 5(1); but the relationship in that case between the association and its embers was a consensual relationship which was manifestly very closely akin an actual contract and in no way comparable, in my judgment, to the sition here where there is no contract.
Mr Beazley also relied on the general statements of principle in the *Peters* se [1983] ECR 987 at 1002 (paras 9 and 10) quoted above, which he submitted hoed the general principles laid down in *Gubisch Maschinenfabrik KG v lumbo* Case 144/86 [1987] ECR 4861; these are important principles, to which ll weight must be given, but they cannot in my judgment warrant the court acing a construction on the words of art 5(1) which they cannot reasonably ar, and moreover they must be balanced against another general principle, d down for example in *Kalfelis v Bankhaus Schröder Münchmeyer Hengst & Co* se 189/87 [1988] ECR 5565 at 5585, that the special jurisdictions enumerated arts 5 and 6 of the Brussels Convention constitute derogations from the inciple that jurisdiction is vested in the courts of the state where the fendant is domiciled, and as such must be interpreted restrictively (see also ra 8 of the same judgment).

In the *Arcado* case a commercial agency agreement was in existence, and th ratio of the Court of Justice was that a claim for compensation for wrongf repudiation found its very basis in that contract and hence was within th scope of art 5(1). This does not assist Mr Beazley.

In my judgment, the *Peters* and the *Arcado* cases are both consistent with M Tecks's proposition that there must be either a contractual relationship givin rise to actual contractual obligations, or a consensual obligation similar to contract (as in the *Peters* case) giving rise to a comparable obligation, for th case to fall within the crucial test in art 5(1).

This conclusion is, I think, reinforced by the *Ets A de Bloos* and *Uni Transport plc* cases, showing that the word 'obligation' in art 5(1) refers to th contractual obligation forming the basis of the legal proceedings; and also I the interpretation by the Court of Appeal of the *Effer SpA* case in *Tesa Distribution Ltd v Schuh Mode Team GmbH* [1990] I L Pr 149, showing that whe there is no evidence of the existence of a contract, and therefore no real dispu as to its existence, the court has no jurisdiction under art 5(1).

So far as the Rome Convention is concerned, I of course accept that it legitimate and appropriate to take its provisions into account in construing a 5(1) (the *Arcado* case [1988] ECR 1539 at 1555 and see, also, *Ivenel v Schwab* Ca 133/81 [1982] ECR 1891 at 1900). However, the Rome Convention cann properly be treated as determinative of the construction of art 5(1).

Moreover, in the present case, as Mr Tecks submitted, the court is in n judgment entitled in construing Sch 4 to the 1982 Act, which is dealing wi jurisdictions within the United Kingdom, to take into account the fact that th United Kingdom has derogated from the Rome Convention by excludin art 10(1)(e) from the law of the United Kingdom. Mr Beazley suggested that do this would be adopting an isolationist attitude, but I am unable to acce this submission, particularly since Sch 4 itself is a modified version of counterpart in the Brussels Convention, which has been adapted in substanti respects to fit United Kingdom requirements, for example by the addition the last 12 words to art 5(3), and by the insertion of the entirely new art 5(8) (which Mr Beazley relies in the present case.

In my judgment, when dealing with the Rome Convention in relation persons of United Kingdom domicile under Sch 4, as in the present case, th court can and should likewise take into account substantive derogations fro the Rome Convention in the law of the United Kingdom, especially one directly apposite as that presently in question.

Furthermore, looking at the question of the wider European context, I a not satisfied that art 10(1)(e) of the Rome Convention is a good guide to th interpretation of the crucial words in art 5(1) of Sch 4. It was no doubt prop and necessary for the Rome Convention to stipulate a proper law applicable the consequences of nullity of the contract in order to embody comprehensive conflicts of law code; but it by no means follows that th consequences of nullity are matters relating to a contract, since ex hypothe no contract existed; nor is art 10(1)(e) comparable with art 10(1)(c) (which is th sub-paragraph cited in the *Arcado* case) or indeed with sub-paras (a), (b) and (of art 10(1), since in all these instances there is a contract in existence.

So far as Mr Beazley's other points are concerned: (a) I do not accept that th English choice of law rule is relevant, since we are not here dealing with choice of law problem. (b) I do not accept quasi-contractual claims, ev where a contract is involved, are properly to be treated as falling per se with

t 5(1), having regard both to the general considerations I have already
lvanced in my analysis of the cases such as the *Peters* case and also because it
difficult to locate a place of performance for a quasi-contractual obligation.
is noteworthy that the textbook writers are not unanimous on this point (see
aye *Civil Jurisdiction and Enforcement of Foreign Judgments* (1987) p 490, where
.e author doubts whether actions in quasi contract on the ground of unjust
arichment fall within art 5(1) and cites in the footnote German and French
uthorities expressing conflicting views). (c) I do not think *Engdiv Ltd v G Percy
'entham Ltd* 1990 SLT 617 assists Mr Beazley, since both the pursuers seeking
ontribution and the defenders resisting it were parties to the building contract
issue in the case, so that it was difficult to resist the submission that the claim
r contribution in that case was in a matter relating to a contract. (d) I do not
ink Mr Beazley can draw any comfort from the old implied contract theory
 restitution cases, since as he himself recognises that theory is now
scredited.

For all these reasons, I have come to the conclusion, and I hold, that the
anks have failed to bring themselves within art 5(1).

ticle 5(3)

At first sight it would seem difficult to bring a restitutionary claim within
is article, and Mr Beazley's case depends entirely on the construction which
: seeks to put on the Court of Justice decision in *Kalfelis v Bankhaus Schröder
ünchmeyer Hengst & Co* Case 189/87 [1988] ECR 5565. In that case the
andesgerichtshof referred two questions to the Court of Justice, the first of
hich is relevant to art 6(1) below, and the second of which is presently
levant and was in the following terms (at 5569):

> '(2)(a) Must the term "tort" in Article 5(3) of the EEC Convention be
> construed independently of the Convention or must it be construed
> according to the law applicable in the individual case (*lex causae*), which is
> determined by the private international law of the court applied to?
> (b) Does Article 5(3) of the EEC Convention confer, in respect of an action
> based on claims in tort and contract and for unjust enrichment, accessory
> jurisdiction on account of factual connection even in respect of the claims
> not based on tort?'

The reference arose out of an action brought by the plaintiff against a
amber of banks and other defendants, based on contractual liability, tort, and
ajust enrichment. The decision of the Court of Justice, so far as relevant, was
 follows:

> '15. With respect to the first part of the question, it must be observed
> that the concept of "matters relating to tort, delict or quasi-delict" serves
> as a criterion for defining the scope of one of the rules concerning the
> special jurisdictions available to the plaintiff. As the Court held with
> respect to the expression "matters relating to a contract" used in Article
> 5(1) (see the judgments of 22 March 1983 in Case 34/82 *Peters v ZNAV*
> [1983] ECR 987, and of 8 March 1988 in Case 9/87 *SPRL Arcado and SA
> Haviland* [1988] ECR 1539), having regard to the objectives and general
> scheme of the Convention, it is important that, in order to ensure as far as
> possible the equality and uniformity of the rights and obligations arising
> out of the Convention of the Contracting States and the persons

concerned, that concept should not be interpreted simply as referring the national law of one or other of the States concerned.

16. Accordingly, the concept of matters relating to tort, delict quasi-delict must be regarded as an autonomous concept which is to interpreted, for the application of the Convention, principally by referen to the scheme and objectives of the Convention in order to ensure that t latter is given full effect.

17. In order to ensure uniformity in all the Member States, it must recognized that the concept of "matters relating to tort, delict a quasi-delict" covers all actions which seek to establish the liability of defendant and which are not related to a "contract" within the meaning Article 5(1).

18. It must therefore be stated in reply to the first part of the seco question that the term "matters relating to tort delict or quasi-delic within the meaning of Article 5(3) of the Convention must be regarded an independent concept covering all actions which seek to establish t liability of a defendant and which are not related to a "contract" within t meaning of Article 5(1).

19. With respect to the second part of the question, it must be observe as already indicated above, that the "special jurisdictions" enumerated Articles 5 and 6 of the Convention constitute derogations from t principle that jurisdiction is vested in the courts of the State where t defendant is domiciled and as such must be interpreted restrictively. must therefore be recognized that a court which has jurisdiction und Article 5(3) over an action in so far as it is based on tort or delict does n have jurisdiction over that action in so far as it is not so based.

20. Whilst it is true that disadvantages arise from different aspects of t same dispute being adjudicated upon by different courts, it must pointed out, on the one hand, that a plaintiff is always entitled to bring l action in its entirety before the courts for the domicile of the defenda and, on the other, that Article 22 of the Convention allows the first cou seised, in certain circumstances, to hear the case in its entirety provid that there is a connection between the actions brought before the differe courts.' (See [1988] ECR 5565 at 5584–5587.)

Mr Beazley submitted that the court's decision in paras 17 and 18 of t judgment (which is also reflected in the answer given to the question in t court's ruling) is conclusive in his favour and determinative of the constructi of art 5(3); and that in consequence art 5(1) and (3) is to be construed mutually exclusive, but as all-embracing so far as actions to establish any ki of liability of the defendants are concerned. I am unable to accept tl interpretation of the judgment. It seems to me that the judgment must be re as a whole, and that paras 19 to 20, dealing with question 2(b) and complete inconsistent with Mr Beazley's construction, seeing that if he were right a 5(3) would become a 'catch-all' provision, and liability not based on tort del or quasi-delict would fall within it, notwithstanding the explicit statement the contrary in the last two lines of para 19.

In my judgment, the word 'liability' in paras 17 and 18 must be interpret as connoting liability within the scope of the art 5(3) categories, ie liability tort, delict or quasi-delict. On this construction, which I do not think do violence to paras 17 and 18, the judgment as a whole is completely consiste I should add that the court's answer in para 19 to question 2(b), which referr

ɔ claims in 'tort and contract *and for unjust enrichment*' would seem to have the
ffect of ruling out the third heading since it is a restitutionary claim not based
n tort (my emphasis). This construction of art 5(3) is, I think, reinforced, as
1r Tecks submitted, by the consideration that the words, 'harmful event',
vhile completely appropriate for claims in tort or delict or quasi-delict, seem
10st inappropriate for restitutionary claims.

For these reasons I have come to the conclusion and I hold that the banks
liled to bring their case within art 5(3).

rticle 6(1)

The issues under this sub-paragraph turn on the Court of Justice's answer to
1e first question in the *Kalfelis* case [1989] ECR 5565 at 5569, which was:

> '(1)(a) Must Article 6(1) of the EEC Convention be interpreted as
> meaning that there must be a connection between the actions against the
> various defendants?   (b) If Question (a) must be answered in the
> affirmative, does the necessary connection between the actions against the
> various defendants exist if the actions are essentially the same in fact and
> law (einfache Streitgenossenschaft), or must a connection be assumed to
> exist only if it is expedient to hear and determine them together to avoid
> the risk of irreconcilable judgments resulting from separate proceedings
> (for example, in cases of "notwendige Streitgenossenschaft" (compulsory
> joinder))?'

The court's judgment so far as relevant on this question was:

> '8. The principle laid down in the Convention is that jurisdiction is
> vested in the courts of the State of the defendant's domicile and that the
> jurisdiction provided for in Article 6(1) is an exception to that principle. It
> follows that an exception of that kind must be treated in such a manner
> that there is no possibility of the very existence of that principle being
> called in question.
>
> 9. That possibility might arise if a plaintiff were at liberty to make a
> claim against a number of defendants with the sole object of ousting the
> jurisdiction of the courts of the State where one of the defendants is
> domiciled. As is stated in the report prepared by the committee of experts
> which drafted the Convention (Official Journal C 59, 5.3.1979, p.1), such a
> possibility must be excluded. For that purpose, there must be a
> connection between the claims made against each of the defendants.
>
> 10. In order to ensure, as far as possible, the equality and uniformity of
> the rights and obligations under the Convention of the Contracting States
> and of the persons concerned, the nature of that connection must be
> determined independently.
>
> 11. In that regard, it must be noted that the abovementioned report
> prepared by the committee of experts referred expressly, in its explanation
> of Article 6(1), to the concern to avoid the risk in the Contracting States of
> judgments which are incompatible with each other.   Furthermore,
> account was taken of that preoccupation in the Convention itself, Article
> 22 of which governs cases of related actions brought before courts in
> different Contracting States.
>
> 12. The rule laid down in Article 6(1) therefore applies where the actions
> brought against the various defendants are related when the proceedings
> are instituted, that is to say where it is expedient to hear and determine

them together in order to avoid the risk of irreconcilable judgment resulting from separate proceedings. It is for the national court to verif in each individual case whether that condition is satisfied.' (See [1989 ECR 5565 at 5583–5584.)

In the present swap litigation there are a very large number of separat actions, in all of which banks are plaintiffs, and in nearly all of which Englis local authorities are defendants. They are not combined together in a singl trial but are regulated by an order of Steyn J on 31 July 1991 as follows:

'1. The parties listed in schedule 2 here to shall be the lead actions in th rate swaps litigation. 2. (1) All other rate swap actions (whether or nc presently constituted), including any third party proceedings in suc actions (whether against local authorities, brokers or otherwise) shall b stayed generally after the close of pleadings in each action of thirty part proceeding (as the case may be) save for third party proceedings in lea actions against third parties. (2) For the purposes of this order "rate swap action" shall mean an action arising out or in connection with any of th kinds of transaction described in App A to the judgment of the Division; Court in *Hazell v Hammersmith and Fulham London BC* [1990] 3 All ER 33 ; 63–64, [1990] 2 QB 697 at 739–740, involving a local authority and one c more other parties (whether or not including a local authority). 3. Partie in actions other than the lead actions shall be at liberty to incorporate i their pleadings such part or parts of the pleadings in the lead actions ; they may wish to adopt.'

Schedule 2, listing the lead cases, is in the following terms:

'INTEREST RATE SWAPS LITIGATION.
Lead cases:
1. Barclays v. Hammersmith & Fulham (1991/318) Hammersmith an Fulham v. BZW (1991/654); 2. Chemical v. Hammersmith and Fulhar (1991/205); 3. Citicorp v. Sandwell (1991/454); 4. Midland v. Birminghar (1991/440) Samuel Montagu v. Birmingham (1991/422); 5. Samue Montagu v. Welwyn Hatfield (1991/423); 6. NCNB National Bank c North Carolina v. Hammersmith and Fulham (1991/434).'

Cases 1 and 4 have recently been settled, but the other four cases are sti continuing. As a result there will be two separate lead action trials, the firs combining cases 3 and 5, followed by the other comprising cases 2 and 6.

The selection of the lead cases was aimed to ensure that the great majorit of the very important points of law which are at issue in all cases ar authoritatively decided, and it is hoped that, as a result, clear guidance will b given to the large number of remaining cases which are stayed, leading t settlements (or at least the elimination of some issues common to the lea cases) and the avoidance of multiplicity of litigation. However, the lea actions are not strictly test cases, and while there is a reasonable prospect tha the above aspiration will be fulfilled, there may well be individual issues arisin in some of the other cases which will in any event need to be litigated (eg a individual local authority defendant's particular case on change of positio giving rise to an estoppel).

In the first group of lead actions the position is as follows. (1) There are very large number of major points of law which have to be decided on th manifold issues which arise under the various heads of restitutionary clain

(2) there appear to be no or no significant disputes on the common issues of fact affecting the swaps cases generally, and indeed those matters covered by an agreed general statement of fact which has been placed before the court; (3) there are discrete factual issues arising in individual cases (eg on change of position, since individual local authorities dealt with the money received under swap transactions in several different ways, which are variously relied upon as furnishing a change of position defence). The same is likely to apply to the second group.

Mr Beazley invites me to give a very broad interpretation to para 12 of the *Kalfelis* judgment [1988] ECR 5565 at 5584, and to say that all these swap actions fall broadly within the test that it is expedient to hear and determine them together; he argues that the use of the plural in that paragraph shows that the principle there laid down covers several defendants in groups of actions as well as several defendants in an individual action; and he submits that there is a risk here of irreconcilable judgments, seeing that both at first instance and thereafter, if the cases proceed up to the appellate process, different decisions may be reached in England and Scotland respectively, on the questions of English law which arise (there is no suggestion that Scottish law applies to these actions).

I very much doubt, though it is unnecessary for me to decide the point, that the use of the plural in para 12 was intended to connote different defendants in several different unconsolidated actions, since there was only one single action in being in the *Kalfelis* case, and para 13 (not quoted above) would seem to envisage a claim by the same plaintiff, unlike the present litigation where there are a very large number of different plaintiff banks in different actions. But leaving that aside, as I have already explained, the court will not be 'hearing and determining the swap cases together' and I do not think those words can be stretched so as to include the present procedural arrangements.

Furthermore, I am not satisfied that there is a risk of irreconcilable decisions. As already noted, there is no question of there being conflicting decisions on the common issues of facts which arise. So far as the issues of English law are concerned, it is, as Mr Beazley fairly recognised, almost inevitable that these cases, in view of the very difficult legal problems and of the very large sums of money at stake, will, unless settled, proceed in the end (as did *Hazell's* case) to the highest court; thus even if there was a prospect of irreconcilable decisions at first instance or on intermediate appeal (which I do not think is likely) the final arbiters in the House of Lords will be able to give one single decision which will be binding in both England and Scotland, and with no possibility of irreconcilability.

For these reasons I have come to the conclusion, and I hold, that the banks have failed to bring themselves within art 6(1).

Article 5(8)

I can deal with this very shortly. In order to come within this paragraph, Mr Beazley must satisfy the court at least that he has an arguable case that the property which the banks seek to trace is situated in England. He submits that he can do this, seeing that, as is common ground, the money was originally paid into one of Glasgow's bank accounts in London, but otherwise he is unable to produce any evidence in support of this contention.

The evidence from Glasgow on the other hand, contained in an affidavit of Julieanne Wight, who is a solicitor of the Supreme Court and who has the conduct of these cases on behalf of Glasgow is as follows:

'The bank account in question has existed for at least forty years. It was set up for the administrative convenience of the London banks and the Defendant and has been used principally in connection with the buying and selling of stocks and shares on the London market. The account is and has been no more than a conduit, the Defendant holding its funds with a Scottish bank in Glasgow. As a matter of practice, monies paid into the account would be transferred from it to the account in Scotland if not immediately, then certainly within a matter of days, for amalgamation with the general fund. Accordingly, there is no possibility that any monies paid into the account by Barclays Bank PLC or Kleinwort Benson Limited would still be there now, the last payments made by those parties pursuant to the interest rate swaps transactions having been made in September 1989 and September 1987 respectively.'

I accept this evidence, and it follows that there is no arguable case that the moneys sought to be traced are now situated in England.

It follows, and I hold, that the banks are unable to bring themselves within art 5(8).

Conclusion

The banks having failed to bring themselves within any of the special jurisdictions laid down in arts 5 or 6, art 2 prevails, and Glasgow must be sued in their court of domicile in Scotland. I am therefore prepared to grant the relief sought by Glasgow and will hear counsel as to the exact terms of the declarations.

I cannot part from this case without expressing my profound gratitude to both counsel for their very clear, able and concise arguments.

Applications granted.

Appeal

One of the plaintiff banks, Kleinwort Benson Ltd, appealed from Hirst J's decision.

Tom Beazley (instructed by *Clifford Chance*) for the bank.
Michael Burton QC and *Jonathan Tecks* (instructed by *Lewis Silkin*) for Glasgow.

LLOYD LJ delivered the following judgment of the court. In 1981 there came into existence a new type of financial transaction known as an interest rate swap contract. Such contracts are of many kinds. But in its simplest form it consists of an agreement between two parties whereby one pays to the other, over a period of months or years, sums calculated by reference to the difference between a fixed rate of interest and the current market rate of interest from time to time. The party paying the fixed rate of interest is called the fixed rate payer. The party paying a floating rate of interest is called the floating rate payer. The typical transaction was well described by Hobhouse J in *Westdeutsche Landesbank Girozentrale v Islington London BC, Kleinwort Benson Ltd v Sandwell BC* [1994] 4 All ER 890. The contract does not involve a loan. The principal sum is purely notional and exists solely for the purpose of calculating the obligations of the parties to pay differences. The essential feature of the transaction is that it is a futures contract, the financial outcome of which depends on future movements in interest rates. The transaction could be used as a genuine hedge transaction, or it could be used for speculation.

As the market developed and became more complex the British Bankers Association and the Foreign Exchange Currency Deposit Brokers Association saw the need for a set of standard terms and conditions for use by bankers and others. These were published in 1985.

From about 1982 interest rate swap contracts came to be used by a number of local authorities. The City of Glasgow District Council entered the market in about 1982. There was a single transaction with Barclays Bank and seven transactions with Kleinwort Benson Ltd. In *Hazell v Hammersmith and Fulham London BC* [1991] 1 All ER 545, [1992] 2 AC 1 the House of Lords held that all such transactions were ultra vires and unlawful, since the councils did not have any express power to enter into such transactions, nor could they be said to be conducive or incidental to the discharge of the councils' borrowing powers. So a power could not be implied by virtue of s 111 of the Local Government Act 1972.

In the course of the hearing before the House of Lords it was pointed out by counsel who appeared for the banks that if swap transactions were held to be unlawful, the banks would be involved in great difficulty. They expressly reserved the right to argue in subsequent proceedings that since they were not themselves tainted by legality, they could retain or recover payments made in pursuance of all ultra vires contracts. Lord Templeman, who gave the leading speech in the House of Lords, did not rule out recovery by the banks. But he said that the consequences of any ultra vires transaction might depend on the facts of each case.

Not surprisingly, therefore, the decision of the House of Lords in *Hazell's* case was followed by a flood of claims. Well over 200 actions were started in the commercial court. In most of them the plaintiff was a bank and the defendant a local authority. Judges of the commercial court took charge of the litigation. Lead actions were selected for trial so that important issues, common to many of the cases, could be decided. A list of all the parties involved was set out in the schedule to an order made by Steyn J on 31 July 1991.

The first of the lead actions to reach trial was *Westdeutsche Landesbank Girozentrale v Islington London BC*, to which I have already referred. Hobhouse J held in that case that the plaintiffs were entitled at common law to recover £1,145,525 from the defendants, the Islington London Borough Council, as money had and received by the defendant to the plaintiff's use, or alternatively as money which belonged to the plaintiffs in equity, and which the plaintiffs were, therefore, entitled to trace in the defendant's hands.

The writ in the present action was issued on 6 September 1991. We are no longer concerned with the parallel action brought against the defendants by Barclays Bank. The sum claimed by Kleinwort Benson, resulting from seven interest swap transactions, between 7 and 22 September 1982, amounted to £807,230. The basis of the claim was the same as that which succeeded in the *Westdeutsche Landesbank* case. The nature of the claim can be characterised as a claim in restitution founded on the principles of unjust enrichment.

The special feature of the present case is that the defendants are domiciled in Scotland. On 16 October 1991 the defendants issued a summons by which they claimed a declaration that the English courts, and in particular the

Commercial Court in London, where almost all the other actions are being tried, including other actions in which Kleinwort Benson are plaintiffs, has no jurisdiction to hear this particular claim. If the plaintiffs wish to pursue their claim against these defendants, they must do so in Scotland.

One may be forgiven for wondering why it matters, since it is common ground that the transactions are all governed by English law and that the proceedings are very likely to end up in the House of Lords, wherever they are tried at first instance. But no doubt the defendants considered that they had certain advantages in being sued in the courts of their own domicile, just as the plaintiffs see advantages of convenience to them, if all the actions in which they are plaintiffs are tried in the same jurisdiction in London. In addition, the defendants say that there is a point of principle involved. Whatever may be the motives of the parties, an objection to the English jurisdiction has been taken and the point must be decided.

Hirst J decided the point in favour of the defendants. The plaintiffs now appeal to this court.

Section 2 of the Civil Jurisdiction and Judgments Act 1982 provides that the Convention on Jurisdiction and the Enforcement of Judgments in Civil and Commercial Matters 1968 shall have the force of law in the United Kingdom. But since the 1968 convention set out in Sch 1 to the Act applies to states, and since there is more than one jurisdiction within the United Kingdom, provision had to be made for the allocation of jurisdiction within the United Kingdom. This is done by s 16 of the Act. Section 16 provides:

'(1) The provisions set out in Schedule 4 (which contains a modified version of Title II of the 1968 Convention) shall have effect for determining, for each part of the United Kingdom, whether the courts of law of that part, or any particular court of law in that part, have or has jurisdiction in proceedings where—(a) the subject-matter of the proceedings is within the scope of the 1968 Convention as determined by Article 1 (whether or not the Convention has effect in relation to the proceedings); and (b) the defendant or defender is domiciled in the United Kingdom or the proceedings are of a kind mentioned in Article 16 (exclusive jurisdicion regardless of domicile).'

Article 2 of Sch 4 provides:

'Subject to the provisions of this Title, persons domiciled in a part of the United Kingdom shall ... be sued in the court of that part.'

Prima facie, therefore, the defendants must be sued in Scotland. But arts 5 and 6 of Sch 4, which correspond to arts 5 and 6 of the 1968 convention, provide for special jurisdiction in certain cases. Article 5 provides:

'A person domiciled in a part of the United Kingdom may, in another part of the United Kingdom, be sued: (1) in matters relating to a contract, in the courts for the place of performance of the obligation in question ... (3) in matters relating to tort, delict or quasi-delict, in the courts for the place where the harmful event occurred or in the case of a threatened wrong is likely to occur.'

It was argued in the court below that since the House of Lords has decided that the contracts in question are all ultra vires and therefore void ab initio, or a nullity, the claim for restitution is not a claim relating to a contract within the meaning of art 5(1). A claim cannot be said to relate to a contract where no contract has in law come into existence. The learned judge accepted that argument.

Turning to art 5(3), the judge held that a claim for unjust enrichment does not relate to tort, delict or quasi-delict. Accordingly, he decided both points under art 5 in favour of the defendants.

There was a further point under art 6. Article 6(1) provides:

> 'A person domiciled in a part of United Kingdom may, in another part of the United Kingdom, also be sued: (1) where he is one of a number of defendants, in the courts for the place where any one of them is domiciled.'

In *Kalfelis v Bankhaus Schröder Münchmeyer Hengst & Co* Case 189/87 [1988] ECR 5565 at 5584 (para 12) the Court of Justice of the European Communities stated the following principle:

> 'The rule laid down in Article 6(1) therefore applies where the actions brought against the various defendants are related when the proceedings are instituted, that is to say where it is expedient to hear and determine them together in order to avoid the risk of irreconcilable judgments resulting from separate proceedings. It is for the national court to verify in each individual case whether that condition is satisfied.'

The judge, in the course of his judgment, observed that the swap litigation has involved a very large number of separate actions. He traced the procedural arrangements which have been made for the trial of these actions. He then continued (p 881, ante):

> 'I very much doubt, though it is unnecessary for me to decide the point, that the use of the plural in para 12 was intended to connote different defendants in several different unconsolidated actions, since there was only one single action in being in the *Kalfelis* case, and para 13 ... would seem to envisage a claim by the same plaintiff, unlike the present litigation where there are a very large number of different plaintiff banks in different actions. But leaving that aside, as I have already explained, the court will not be "hearing and determining the swap cases together" and I do not think those words can be stretched so as to include the present procedural arrangements. Furthermore, I am not satisfied that there is a risk of irreconcilable decisions. As already noted, there is no question of there being conflicting decisions on the common issues of facts which arise. So far as the issues of English law are concerned, it is, as Mr Beazley fairly recognised, almost inevitable that these cases, in view of the very difficult legal problems and of the very large sums of money at stake, will, unless settled, proceed in the end (as did *Hazell's* case) to the highest court; thus even if there was a prospect of irreconcilable decisions at first instance or on intermediate appeal (which I do not think is likely) the final arbiters in the House of Lords will be able to give one single decision which will be binding in both England and Scotland, and with no possibility of irreconcilability. For these reasons I have come to the conclusion, and I hold, that the banks have failed to bring themselves within art 6(1).'

I say at once that I can see no reason to doubt that, as far as art 6(1) is concerned, the judge correctly applied the principles stated in the *Kalfelis* decision to the unusual circumstances of the present case.

But arts 5(1) and 5(3) raise more perplexing problems. They arise out of the perennial difficulties of classification and, in particular, the difficulty of classifying the restitutionary remedies afforded by English law in a European context.

As to art 5(1), Mr Beazley's submissions were broadly as follows. (1) The Court of Justice has decided that the wording of the article must be given an independent interpretation in accordance with the objectives of the convention, and is not to be construed narrowly in accordance with national law (see *Martin Peters Bauunternehmung GmbH v Zuid Nederlandse Aannemers Vereniging* Case 34/82 [1983] ECR 987 and *Arcado SPRL v Haviland SA* Case 9/87 [1988] ECR 1539).

(2) Article 5(1) does not require the existence of a binding contract. It is enough that there are close links of the same kind as those which are created between parties to a contract: see the *Peters* case. Mr Beazley points out that whereas the English text of art 5(1) refers to 'a contract', the French text refers to 'en matière contractuelle'. He submits that the relationship which, in English law, gives rise to a claim in quasi contract is sufficiently close to come within art 5(1). He refers us in that connection to Collins *The Civil Jurisdiction and Judgments Act 1982* (1983) p 53:

> 'Whether a matter relates to a contract will not usually gives rise to a difficulty. There is a sufficiently common core on the meaning of contract to result in the term being given a Community interpretation. Thus the fact that in English law a contract must be supported by consideration has not been an obstacle to the enforcement in England of contracts or agreements not so supported. There will be borderline cases, such as quasi-contractual claims, which have also given rise to difficulty under R.S.C., Ord. 11. Such claims are probably included under Art. 5(1), at least where they are very close in nature to contractual claims or where they arise out of a contract. Thus there can be little doubt that claims arising out of an ineffective contract or claims for necessary goods supplied to a person under incapacity are covered by Art. 5(1); other claims may be closer to tort claims, and included, if at all, under Art. 5(3).'

(3) Article 10 of the Convention on the Law applicable to Contractual Obligations 1980 (the Rome Convention), which has the force of law by virtue of s 2 of the Contracts (Applicable Law) Act 1990, provides:

> 'The law applicable to a contract by virtue of Articles 3 to 6 and 12 of this Convention shall govern in particular: (a) interpretation; (b) performance; (c) within the limits of the powers conferred on the court by its procedural law, the consequences of breach, including the assessment of damages in so far as it is governed by rules of law; (d) the various ways of extinguishing obligations, and prescription and limitation of actions; (e) the consequences of nullity of the contract.'

In the *Arcado* case [1988] ECR 1539 at 1555 (para 15) the Court of Justice referred to art 10 of the Rome Convention as confirmation of the contractual nature of the proceedings in that case. By the same token, art 5(1) should, says Mr Beazley, be construed so as to include the consequences of nullity of a contract, thereby harmonising the two conventions.

(4) Matters relating to a contract in art 5(1) must bear the same meaning as 'proceedings concerning a contract' in art 13. If proceedings concerning a

contract do not cover the consequences of nullity of a contract there will be a serious gap in the protection afforded to consumers by s 4 of the convention.

As to art 5(3), both parties relied on the *Kalfelis* decision. One of the questions in the *Kalfelis* decision was as follows ([1988] ECR 5565 at 5582):

> '2(a) Must the term "tort" in Article 5(3) of the EEC Convention be construed independently of the the Convention, or must it be construed according to the law applicable in the individual case (*lex causae*), which is determined by the private international law of the court applied to? (b) Does Article 5(3) of the EEC Convention confer, in respect of an action based on claims in torts and contract and for unjust enrichment, accessory jurisdiction on account of factual connection even in respect of the claims not based on tort?'

Paragraphs 17 and 18 of the judgment are as follows (at 5585):

> '17. In order to ensure uniformity in all the Member States, it must be recognized that the concept of "matters relating to tort, delict and quasi-delict" covers all actions which seek to establish the liability of a defendant and which are not related to a "contract" within the meaning of Article 5(1).
>
> 18. It must therefore be stated in reply to the first part of the second question that the term "matters relating to tort, delict or quasi-delict" within the meaning of Article 5(3) of the Convention must be regarded as an independent concept covering all actions which seek to establish the liability of a defendant and which are not related to a "contract" within the meaning of Article 5(1).'

Mr Beazley submits that the *Kalfelis* decision is thus a clear decision that all actions in which the plaintiff is seeking to establish the liability of a defendant, which are not related to a contract, come within art 5(3).

In support of that argument he refers us to the opinion of Mr Advocate General Darmon in *Shearson Lehman Hutton Inc v TVB Treuhandgesellschaft für Vermögensverwaltung und Beteiligungen mbH* Case C-89/91 [1993] I L Pr 199. After referring to the facts of the *Kalfelis* case, Mr Advocate General Darmon continued (at 215):

> 'The action [in the *Kalfelis* case] was based on both contractual liability (for breach of duties of information) and liability in tort (for conduct contrary to proper commercial practice). The claim was also based on unjust enrichment on the ground that futures contracts such as those for silver do not bind the parties. In reply to a question concerning the interpretation of "matters relating to tort, delict or quasi-delict," the term used in Article 5(3) of the Convention, the Court held that: [this] term ... must be regarded as an independent concept covering *all* actions, which seek to establish the liability of a defendant and which not do not concern "matters relating to a contract" within the meaning of Article 5(1), thereby including in "matters relating to tort, delict or quasi-delict" actions based on unjust enrichment.' (Advocate General Darmon's emphasis.)

In the earlier case of *Reichert v Dresdner Bank (No 2)* Case C-261/90 [1992] I L Pr 404 Mr Advocate General Gullman drew attention to the different versions of art 5(3) in other languages which he set out in the course of his opinion. He then said (at 414):

'It is clear from the Court's settled case law that a provision should not
be interpreted in isolation, taking account only of its wording in the
language of the proceedings, but that it should be interpreted in the light
of the wording of all the language versions in order to ensure uniform
interpretation.'

Mr Beazley pointed out that the Portuguese version of art 5(3) reads 'em
matéria excontratual', which presumably means in non-contractual matters, or
in matters not relating to contract. The same appears to be the meaning of the
Danish version of art 5(3). *Reichert's* case concerned an action paulienne in
French law. After the referring to *Kalfelis v Bankhaus Schröder Münchmeyer
Hengst & Co*, the court said (at 423):

'[16] In paragraph 17 of the same judgment the Court also held that, in
order to ensure a uniform approach in all the member-States, it should be
accepted that the concept of "tort, delict or quasi-delict" covers any action
which seeks to establish the liability of a defendant and which is not
connected with a "matter relating to a contract" within the meaning of
Article 5(1) ...
[20] Under these circumstances, an action like the *action paulienne* of
French law cannot be regarded as an action which seeks to establish the
liability of a defendant in the sense understood in *Article 5(3)* of the
Convention and is not therefore within the scope of that article.'

Mr Beazley argued that if the claim for restitution in this case does not come
within art 5(1), then it is clearly an action 'which seeks to establish the liability
of the defendant' within art 5(3), as explained by the court in the *Kalfelis* case.

Mr Burton, on the other hand, relies on paras 18 and 19 of the *Kalfelis*
judgment. They read as follows ([1988] ECR 5565 at 5585–5586):

'18. It must therefore be stated in reply to the first part of the second
question that the term "matters relating to tort, delict or quasi-delict"
within the meaning of Article 5(3) of the Convention must be regarded as
an independent concept covering all actions which seek to establish the
liability of a defendant and which are not related to a "contract" within the
meaning of Article 5(1)
19. With respect to the second part of the question, it must be observed,
as already indicated above, that the "special jurisdictions" enumerated in
Articles 5 and 6 of the Convention constitute derogations from the
principle that jurisdiction is vested in the courts of the State where the
defendant is domiciled and as such must be interpreted restrictively. It
must therefore be recognized that a court which has jurisdiction under
Article 5(3) over an action in so far as it is based on tort or delict does not
have jurisdiction over that action in so far as it is not so based ...
21. In those circumstances, the reply to the second part of the second
question must be that a court which has jurisdiction under Article 5(3)
over an action in so far as it is based on tort or delict does not have
jurisdiction over that action in so far as it is not so based.'

Question 2(b), says Mr Burton, assumes that a claim for unjust enrichment
is not within art 5(3). By answering the question in the way it did in paras 19
and 21 the court confirmed that assumption to be correct. The word 'liability'
in paras 17 and 18 of the judgment must, therefore, be read as meaning 'liability
in respect of tort, delict or quasi-delict,' which is what the judge held. Indeed,

Mr Burton goes further than the judge. He submits that the court in the *Kalfelis* case not only decided that unjust enrichment does not come within art 5(3); it also decided, in effect, that a claim for unjust enrichment is not within art 5(1) either.

It is common ground that if art 5(1) applies, then London is the place of the performance of the obligation in question. If, on the other hand, art 5(3) applies, it is common ground that London is the place where the harmful event has occurred. Accordingly, a decision on the scope of art 5(1) and (3), and their relationship to each other, is clearly necessary to enable us to dispose of this appeal.

Then comes the question whether in those circumstances we ought to refer this case to the Court of Justice for a preliminary ruling under art 3 of the 1971 Protocol, as set out in Sch 2 to the 1982 Act. Mr Burton points out a difference in language between s 3 of the Act, whereby we are bound to apply the principles laid down in the Court of Justice, and s 16(3) of the Act, whereby we are enjoined to have regard to those principles. But in the end, Mr Burton accepted that there is no real distinction, and that we do have jurisdiction to ask for a preliminary ruling. The question is whether that is desirable on the facts of the present case. In my view it is. The questions which arise under art 5(1) and (3) are difficult and important. The answers are far from plain. There is, as yet, no clear guidance provided by the European Court on the points which have been argued before us. The textbooks to which we have been referred, including Kaye *Civil Jurisdiction and Enforcement of Foreign Judgments* (1987) p 490 (footnote at p 745), Cheshire and North *Private International Law* (12th edn, 1992) p 301, *Dicey and Morris on the Conflict of Laws* (11th edn, 1987) vol 2, p 341 and Collins *The Civil Jurisdiction and Judgments Act 1982* do not speak with one voice.

We were told that this is the first case to be referred by an English court where the contest is whether the English courts or the Scottish courts have jurisdiction. But there is precedent for the course we propose to take, provided by the German courts, in *Gmurzynska-Bscher v Oberfinanzdirektion Köln* Case C-231/89 [1990] ECR I-4003. A question arose as to the meaning of a term taken from the Common Customs Tariff and used as part of German tax law. Although no question of Community law as such was involved, it was held that the court had jurisdiction to give a ruling under art 177 of the EEC Treaty in order to ensure uniformity of interpretation. The same reasoning applies to the present case. The only questions which need to be referred are those arising under art 5(1) and (3). I have already held that the judge's decision on art 6(1) was plainly correct.

We will now hear counsel on the form which those questions should take. I should perhaps add that I have overlooked the decision of the Inner House in Scotland in *Davenport v Corinthian Motor Policies at Lloyds* 1991 SLT 774 upon which Mr Burton relied.

Appeal dismissed in part. Questions referred to the Court of Justice of the European Communities for preliminary ruling accordingly

K Mydeen Esq   Barrister.

Westdeutsche Landesbank Girozentrale v Islington London Borough Council
Kleinwort Benson Ltd v Sandwell Borough Council

QUEEN'S BENCH DIVISION (COMMERCIAL COURT)
HOBHOUSE J
12–14, 18–21, 25–28 JANUARY, 12 FEBRUARY 1993

COURT OF APPEAL, CIVIL DIVISION
DILLON, LEGGATT AND KENNEDY LJJ
7, 8, 13, 14, 17 DECEMBER 1993

Contract – Failure of consideration – Recovery of money paid – Lump sum payment made by bank to local authority under interest rate swap agreement – Payments also made by local authority pursuant to agreement – Agreement being ultra vires the local authority and void – Whether local authority liable to pay bank balance of lump sum paid – Whether local authority liable to pay compound interest on balance – Whether local authority liable to pay compound interest from date of payment of lump sum.

Contract – Restitution – Interest rate swap agreement – Bank entering into interest rate swap agreement with local authority – Agreement ultra vires the local authority – Whether bank entitled to recover balance of lump sum payment.

The plaintiff bank entered into a ten-year interest rate swap agreement with the defendant local authority commencing on 18 June 1987. The interest payments, which were payable half-yearly, were calculated on a notional principal sum of £25m by reference to the difference between the fixed rate of interest (payable by the bank) and the floating London Inter-Bank Offered Rate (payable by the local authority). Additionally, the bank agreed to pay the local authority a lump sum of £2·5m on the commencement date as the first of the fixed rate payments. At the same time, the bank entered into a parallel swap transaction with a second bank in order to hedge its potential liabilities under the arrangement with the local authority. By June 1989 the local authority had made four payments to the bank under the swap agreement, totalling £1,354,474·07. However, on 1 November 1989 the Divisional Court of the Queen's Bench Division held, in an unrelated case subsequently upheld by the House of Lords in January 1991, that interest rate swap transactions were outside the powers of local authorities and void ab initio. Thereafter the local authority made no further payments. The bank subsequently brought an action against the local authority, claiming inter alia repayment of £1,145,525·93, being the amount of the initial lump sum payment of £2·5m less the payments made by the local authority, and interest as from 18 June 1987. The judge held that the bank was entitled to recover the balance of the £2·5m payment on the ground that there had been no consideration for the lump sum payment since the underlying agreement was ultra vires and void and since the bank had not intended to make a gift of the money. The judge also took account of the fact that the bank had received £2·5m under the parallel swap transaction and that it was not until the local authority stopped payment under its own agreement that the bank began to be out of pocket and awarded the bank compound interest on the lump sum from the later date of 1 April 1990. The local authority appealed, contending that the money was not recoverable either as money had and received or on the ground of unjust enrichment, since, by making four payments to the bank, the consideration for the £2·5m had not wholly failed and that if the money was indeed recoverable the award of interest should be limited to simple interest only. The bank cross-appealed, contending that the judge should have awarded interest from 18 June 1987 rather than 1 April 1990.

Held – (1) A bank which had made a lump sum payment to a local authority under an interest rate swap agreement which was ultra vires the local authority and void ab initio was entitled to recover the balance of the money in quasi contract as money had and received or on the ground of unjust enrichment at the expense of the bank as owner of the money, since there had been no consideration for the payment by the bank. Since, contrary to the expectations of the parties, the swap transactions and contract were from the outset ultra vires and void, the purpose for the payment of the lump sum had wholly failed and consequently that sum had, from the time the local authority received it, been held on a resulting trust for the bank, which was therefore entitled in equity to the return of the balance of the lump sum. The bank was also entitled to interest on the money awarded under a restitutionary remedy, and since the local authority had from the beginning held the money in a fiduciary position on resulting trust for the bank it was appropriate that the award should be compound interest, having regard to the fact that the local authority had spent the money on its ordinary purposes and that, if it had not received the lump sum payment, it would have borrowed an equivalent sum at compound interest in order to meet its expenditures. It followed that the local authority's appeal would accordingly be dismissed (see p 962 *e* to *h*, p 963 *c*, p 967 *b c*, p 969 *c* to *f*, p 970 *f* to *h* and p 971 *f g*, post); *Sinclair v Brougham* [1914–15] All ER Rep 522 and *Lipkin Gorman (a firm)* v *Karpnale Ltd* [1992] 4 All ER 512 applied; *Woolwich Building Society v IRC (No 2)* [1992] 3 All ER 737 considered.

(2) Furthermore, the date from which interest should run was the date of receipt of the money by the local authority, since it was from that date that the local authority had had the use of the whole of the bank's money. Accordingly, the fact that the bank had received an equivalent lump sum payment under a parallel swap agreement which staggered the point at which it began to suffer loss was irrelevant to the question of when interest should begin to run, as was any suggestion that the local authority should be absolved from paying interest to the bank over the period while the decision on local authority swap transactions was being tested in the courts. In those circumstances, the local authority would be charged compound interest on the balance from time to time outstanding of the money it had received from the bank as from 18 June 1987. The bank's cross-appeal would therefore be allowed (see p 963 *c* to *g*, p 964 *e* to *g j*, p 967 *b c* and p 971 *d* to *g*, post).

Notes

For a local authority's power to incur expenditure, see 28 *Halsbury's Laws* (4th edn) paras 1245, 1247, and for cases on the subject, see 33 *Digest* (Reissue) 31–34, 96–104.

Cases referred to in judgments

Aries Tanker Corp v Total Transport Ltd [1977] 1 All ER 398, [1977] 1 WLR 185 HL.

Barclays Bank Ltd v W J Simms Son & Cooke (Southern) Ltd [1979] 3 All ER 522, [1980] QB 677, [1980] 2 WLR 218.

Barlow Clowes International Ltd (in liq) v Vaughan [1992] 4 All ER 22, CA.

Beauchamp (Earl) v Winn (1873) LR 6 HL 223.

Beauforte (Jon) (London) Ltd, Re [1953] 1 All ER 634, [1953] Ch 131, [1953] 2 WLR 465.

Bell v Lever Bros Ltd [1932] AC 161, [1931] All ER Rep 1, HL.

Bilbie v Lumley (1802) 2 East 469, [1775–1802] All ER Rep 425, 102 ER 448.

Blackburn and District Benefit Building Society v Cunliffe Brooks & Co (1882) 22 Ch D 61, CA; *affd* (1884) 9 App Cas 857, HL.

BP Exploration Co (Libya) Ltd v Hunt (No 2) [1982] 1 All ER 925, [1979] 1 WLR 783; *affd* [1982] 1 All ER 925, [1981] 1 WLR 232, CA; *affd* [1982] 1 All ER 925, [1983] 2 AC 352, [1982] 2 WLR 253, HL.

Bradford Advance Co Ltd v Ayers [1924] WN 152, DC.

Bromley v Holland (1802) Coop G 9, 35 ER 458.

Bromley London BC v Greater London Council [1982] 1 All ER 129, [1983] 1 AC 768, [1982] 2 WLR 62, CA and HL.

Brougham v Dwyer (1913) 108 LT 504, DC.

Burdick v Garrick (1870) LR 5 Ch App 233.

Byne v Vivian (1800) 5 Ves 604, 31 ER 762.

Campbell v Hall (1774) 1 Cowp 204, [1558–1774] All ER Rep 252, 98 ER 1045.

Chandler v Webster [1904] 1 KB 493, CA.

Chase Manhattan Bank NA v Israel-British Bank (London) Ltd [1979] 3 All ER 1025, [1981] Ch 105, [1980] 2 WLR 202.

Churchill v Bertrand (1842) 3 QB 568, 114 ER 625.

Coltman, Re, Coltman v Coltman (1881) 19 Ch D 64, CA.

Cook v Addison (1869) LR 7 Eq 466.

Cooper v Phibbs (1867) LR 2 HL 149.

Cotman v Brougham [1918] AC 514, [1918–19] All ER Rep 265, HL.

Cowper v Godmond (1833) 9 Bing 748, 131 ER 795, cf 3 Moo & S 219, CP.

Davies v Rees (1886) 17 QBD 408.

Davis v Bryan (1827) 6 B & C 651, 108 ER 591, cf 9 Dow & Ry 726.

Dew v Parsons (1819) 2 B & Ald 562, 106 ER 471.

Diplock's Estate, Re, Diplock v Wintle [1948] 2 All ER 318, [1948] Ch 465, CA; *affd* sub nom *Ministry of Health v Simpson* [1950] 2 All ER 1137, [1951] AC 251, HL.

Fibrosa Spolka Akcyjna v Fairbairn Lawson Combe Barbour Ltd [1942] 2 All ER 122, [1943] AC 32, HL.

Flood v Irish Provident Assurance Co Ltd [1912] 2 Ch 597n, Ir CA.

General Tire and Rubber Co v Firestone Tyre and Rubber Co Ltd [1975] 2 All ER 173, [1975] 1 WLR 819, HL.

Green v Farmer (1768) 4 Burr 2214, 98 ER 154.

Guardian Ocean Cargoes Ltd v Banco do Brasil SA (No 3) [1992] 2 Lloyd's Rep 193.

Guardian Permanent Benefit Building Society, Re (1882) 23 Ch D 440, CA.

Hanak v Green [1958] 2 All ER 141, [1958] 2 QB 9, [1958] 2 WLR 755, CA.

Hazell v Hammersmith and Fulham London BC [1991] 1 All ER 545, [1992] 2 AC 1, [1991] 2 WLR 372, HL; rvsg [1990] 3 All ER 33, [1990] 2 QB 697, [1990] 2 WLR 17, 1038, DC and CA.

Henriksens Rederi A/S v PHZ Rolimpex [1973] 3 All ER 589, [1974] QB 233, [1973] 3 WLR 556, CA.

Hicks v Hicks (1802) 3 East 16, 102 ER 502.

Hoffman v Cooke (1801) 5 Ves Jun 623, 31 ER 772.

Holbrook v Sharpey (1812) 19 Ves 131, 34 ER 467.

Hudson v Robinson (1816) 4 M & S 475, 105 ER 910.

Huggins v Coates (1843) 5 QB 433, 114 ER 1313.

Kiriri Cotton Co Ltd v Dewani [1960] 1 All ER 177, [1960] AC 192, [1960] 2 WLR 127, PC.

Leslie (R) Ltd v Sheill [1914] 3 KB 607, [1914–15] All ER Rep 511, CA.

Liggett (B) (Liverpool) Ltd v Barclays Bank Ltd [1928] 1 KB 48, [1927] All ER Rep 451.

Linz v Electric Wire Co of Palestine Ltd [1948] 1 All ER 604, [1948] AC 371, PC.

Lipkin Gorman (a firm) v Karpnale Ltd [1992] 4 All ER 512, [1991] 2 AC 548, [1991] 3 WLR 10, HL.

London Celluloid Co, Re (1888) 39 Ch D 190, CA.

Lonrho Ltd v Shell Petroleum Co Ltd [1981] 2 All ER 456, [1982] AC 173, [1981] 3 WLR 33, HL.

Madras Official Assignee v Krishnaji Bhat (1933) 49 TLR 432, PC.

Molton v Camroux (1849) 4 Exch 17, 154 ER 1107, Ex Ch.

National Bank of Greece SA v Pinios Shipping Co No 1, The Maira [1990] 1 All ER 78, [1990] 1 AC 637, [1989] 3 WLR 1330, HL.

National Pari-Mutuel Association Ltd v R (1930) 47 TLR 110, CA.

National Permanent Benefit Building Society, Re, ex p Williamson (1869) LR 5 Ch App 309.

Newbigging v Adam (1886) 34 Ch D 582, [1886–90] All ER 975, CA; affd (1888) 13 App Cas 308, HL.

North Central Wagon Finance Co Ltd v Brailsford [1962] 1 All ER 502, [1962] 1 WLR 1288, Assizes.

Oatway, Re, Hertslet v Oatway [1903] 2 Ch 356.

Orakpo v Manson Investments Ltd [1977] 3 All ER 1, [1978] AC 95, [1977] 3 WLR 229, HL.

Pepper (Inspector of Taxes) v Hart [1993] 1 All ER 42, [1993] AC 593, [1992] 3 WLR 1032, HL.

Phoenix Life Assurance Co, Re, Hoare's Case (1862) 2 John & H 229, 70 ER 1041.

President of India v La Pintada Cia Navegacion SA [1984] 2 All ER 773, [1985] AC 104, [1984] 3 WLR 10, HL.

Queens of the River Steamship Co Ltd v River Thames Conservators (1899) 15 TLR 474.

Rolled Steel Products (Holdings) Ltd v British Steel Corp [1985] 3 All ER 52, [1986] Ch 246, [1985] 2 WLR 908, CA.

Roscoe (James) (Bolton) Ltd v Winder [1915] 1 Ch 62.

Rover International Ltd v Cannon Film Sales Ltd (No 3) [1989] 3 All ER 423, [1989] 1 WLR 912, CA.

Rowland v Divall [1923] 2 KB 500, [1923] All ER Rep 270, CA.

Rugg v Minett (1809) 11 East 210, 103 ER 985.

Seddon v North Eastern Salt Co Ltd [1905] 1 Ch 326, [1904–7] All ER Rep 817.

Sharp Bros v Chant [1917] 1 KB 771.
Shove v Webb (1787) 1 Term Rep 732, 99 ER 1348.
Sinclair v Brougham [1914] AC 398, [1914–15] All ER Rep 622, HL.
Solle v Butcher [1949] 2 All ER 1107, [1950] 1 KB 671, CA.
Steele v Williams (1853) 8 Exch 625, 155 ER 1502.
Stocks v Wilson [1913] 2 KB 235.
Tilley's Will Trusts, Re, Burgin v Croad [1967] 2 All ER 303, [1967] Ch 1179, [1967] 2 WLR 1533.
Tower Hamlets London BC v Chetnik Developments Ltd [1988] 1 All ER 961, [1988] AC 858, [1988] 2 WLR 654, HL
Twyford v Manchester Corp [1946] 1 All ER 621, [1946] Ch 236.
Walker v Clements (1850) 15 QB 1046, 117 ER 755.
Wallersteiner v Moir (No 2) [1975] 1 All ER 849, [1975] QB 373, [1975] 2 WLR 389, CA.
Wenlock (Baroness) v River Dee Co (1887) 19 QBD 155, CA.
Westminster City Council, Re [1986] 2 All ER 278, [1986] AC 668, [1986] 2 WLR 807, HL.
Woolwich Building Society v IRC (No 2) [1992] 3 All ER 737, [1993] AC 70, [1992] 3 WLR 366, HL; *affg* [1991] 4 All ER 577, [1993] AC 70, [1991] 3 WLR 790, CA.
Wrexham Mold and Connah's Quay Rly Co, Re [1899] 1 Ch 440, CA.

Cases also cited or referred to in skeleton arguments

A-G v Alford (1855) 4 De GM & G 843, 43 ER 737, LC.
Ashbury Railway Carriage and Iron Co Ltd v Riche (1875) LR 7 HL 653.
Birkbeck Permanent Benefit Building Society, Re [1912] 2 Ch 183, CA.
Butterworth v Kingsway Motors Ltd (Hayton, third party, Kennedy, fourth party, Rudolph, fifth party) [1954] 2 All ER 694, [1954] 1 WLR 1286, Assizes.
Central Transportation Co v Pullman's Palace Car Co (1891) 139 US 24, US SC.
Craven-Ellis v Canons Ltd [1936] 2 All ER 1066, [1936] 2 KB 403, CA.
David Securities Pty Ltd v Commonwealth Bank of Australia (1992) 175 CLR 353, Aust HC.
Hooper Grain Co v Colonial Assurance Co [1917] 1 WWR 1226, Man KB.
Miller v Race (1758) 1 Burr 452, 97 ER 398.
Morgan Guaranty Trust Co v Lothian Regional Council (1993) Times, 30 November, Ct of Sess.
Moses v Macferlan (1760) 2 Burr 1005, [1558–1774] All ER Rep 581, 97 ER 676.
Nissan v A-G [1969] 1 All ER 629, [1970] AC 179, HL.
Pavey & Matthews Pty Ltd v Paul (1987) 69 ALR 577, Aust HC.
Pearce v Brain [1929] 2 KB 310, [1929] All ER Rep 627, DC.
Space Investments Ltd v Canadian Imperial Bank of Commerce Trust Co (Bahamas) Ltd [1986] 3 All ER 75, [1986] 1 WLR 1072, PC.
United Australia Ltd v Barclays Bank Ltd [1940] 4 All ER 20, [1941] AC 1, HL
Valentini v Canali (1889) 24 QBD 166, [1886–90] All ER Rep 883, DC.
Warman v Southern Counties Car Finance Corp Ltd (W J Ameris Car Sales, third party) [1949] 1 All ER 711, [1949] 2 KB 576.

Actions

Westdeutsche Landesbank Girozentrale v Islington London BC
The plaintiff bank, Westdeutsche Landesbank Girozentrale (Westdeutsche), by a writ issued on 15 April 1991, claimed restitution of money which it had paid to the defendant, Islington London Borough Council (Islington), under an

interest rate swap agreement dated 16 July 1987 which Islington had purported
to enter into with Westdeutsche, but which was in fact ultra vires Islington and
void ab initio. The facts are set out in the judgment.

Kleinwort Benson Ltd v Sandwell BC

The plaintiff merchant bank, Kleinwort Benson Ltd, by an amended writ
reissued on 13 January 1993, claimed restitution of sums of money which it had
paid to the defendant, Sandwell Borough Council (Sandwell), under four
interest rate swap agreements which Sandwell had purported to enter into
with Kleinwort Benson between 1983 and 1987, but which were in fact ultra
vires Sandwell and void ab initio.   On 21 December 1992 Hobhouse J had
ordered that the court should determine as a preliminary issue whether the
matters pleaded in the amended points of defence and counterclaim, which
related principally to the questions whether consideration for the money paid
to Sandwell had wholly failed and whether Kleinwort Benson was entitled to
an equitable proprietary remedy, were capable in law of amounting to a
defence and that that issue should be argued at or immediately after the
Westdeutsche action. The facts are set out in the judgment.

Jonathan Sumption QC and *George Leggatt* (instructed by *Travers Smith
Braithwaite*) for Westdeutsche.
Elizabeth Appleby QC and *Hodge Malek* (instructed by *Nabarro Nathanson*) for
Islington.
Richard Southwell QC, Rhodri Davies and *Nicholas Lavender* (instructed by *Clifford
Chance*) for Kleinwort Benson
John Dyson QC and *Mark West* (instructed by *Sharpe Pritchard*, agents for *F N
Summers*, Warley) for Sandwell.

Cur adv vult

12 February 1993. The following judgment was delivered.

HOBHOUSE J.   On 1 November 1989 the Divisional Court delivered its
judgment in *Hazell v Hammersmith and Fulham London BC* [1990] 3 All ER 33,
[1990] 2 QB 697. Mr Hazell was the district auditor and he was challenging the
legality of the accounts of the Hammersmith Council for the years ending 31
March 1988 and 1989.   The transactions which were called into question were
what have been called interest rate swaps.   The council had entered into a large
number of such transactions, almost entirely on a speculative basis, with other
councils and with various banks.   An interest rate swap can take a large number
of forms, as are set out in the appendix to the Divisional Court judgment (see
[1990] 3 All ER 33 at 63–66, [1990] 2 QB 697 at 739–743). In its simplest form,
an interest rate swap contract involves an agreement by two parties to make to
each other on specified dates over a period of time, usually a number of years,
a series of payments calculated by reference to the differences between a fixed
rate of interest and whatever may be from time to time the current market rate
of interest upon a notional sum of principal.   The party whose liability is
calculated by reference to the fixed rate is called the 'fixed rate payer' and the
party whose liability is calculated by reference to the varying market rate is
called the 'floating rate payer'. It does not involve any contract of loan and the
'principal' sum is purely notional and exists solely for the purpose of

calculating the obligations of the parties to pay differences. The essential feature of the transaction is that it is a futures contract, the financial outcome of which depends upon future movements in interest rates. Accordingly it can be used as a hedging transaction by a party who has entered into an actual loan transaction under which he will pay or receive certain interest when that party wishes to protect himself against the consequences of market movements which might either cause him loss or deprive him of profit; this is called a 'parallel' swap. Similarly the notional sum referred to in the contract might be expressed in two different currencies and therefore involve movements in the parity of currencies as well as in rates of interest. There are many other uses to which the mechanism of interest rate swap contracts can be put. They can enable parties with access to different money markets with different merits and demerits to come together so that they can, by entering into a swap contract, take advantage of the interest rate features which are of advantage to each of them. An interest rate swap contract may also be structured so as to provide a form of off-balance sheet borrowing by providing for the payment by one party of an initial sum (the 'up-front payment', or, as it was sometimes called, a 'front-end premium') which will be balanced by an adjustment of the parties' liabilities during the remainder of the life of the contract. Thus the contract might provide for the fixed rate payer to pay an immediate sum of £1m and during the next ten years of the contract to pay one per cent less than would otherwise have been the appropriate rate (or the floating rate payer might be required to pay a higher rate than otherwise would have been the case).

Interest rate swap contracts first came into use in about 1981 and began to be used by some local authorities from about 1982. A sophisticated market gradually developed involving institutions in the position of market makers and a corps of money brokers. The normal principles of prudence applied so that a party dealing in the swaps market would keep a balanced book and not take up open positions save within well-controlled limits. A party who was genuinely using the contract as a hedge would appear to have an open position but it would, in truth, be covered by an actual loan transaction already entered into. As the market developed and became more complex it was recognised that it needed to become more organised and the British Bankers Association, in association with the Foreign Exchange Currency Deposit Brokers Association, formulated in 1985 a set of standard terms and conditions which those associations recommended should be used. They were called the 'BBAIRS terms'. These terms provided for standard contracts forms with standard clauses for the basic interest rate swap contracts. It was part of the standard terms that the contract should be governed by English law and that each party should represent and warrant to the other that:

'(i) It has full power and authority (corporate and otherwise) to enter into this agreement and to exercise its rights and performance obligations hereunder and has obtained all authorisations and consents necessary for it so to enter, exercise rights and perform obligations and such authorisations and consents are in full force and effect; (ii) the obligations expressed to be assumed by it under this agreement are legal and valid obligations binding on it in accordance with their terms ...'

In respect of single currency swaps there was a standard clause, which provided:

'If the fixed rate payer is obliged to pay any sum to the floating rate payer
... on the same day as the floating rate payer is obliged to pay any sum to
the fixed rate payer ... such sum shall not be paid and instead the party
liable to pay the greater of such sums shall on such day pay to the other
party in the same manner a sum in the same currency equal to the excess
of such greater sum over the other sum.'

The parties to interest rate swap contracts were normally regular
participants in the money markets and, accordingly, of recognised solvency.
Local authorities in the United Kingdom are also regarded in the market as
being institutions of unquestioned solvency.   Nor was there seen to be any
legal risk.   For ordinary financial institutions this was obviously correct.   For
local authorities it was assumed that interest rate swaps could legitimately be
entered into as an ancillary to the exercise by a local authority of its borrowing
and lending powers.   This was the effect of advice received by the Chartered
Institute of Public Finance and Accountancy in the latter part of 1983.   Where
money was being lent to a local authority, legal risk was negatived by the
provision in para 20 of Sch 13 to the Local Government Act 1972:

'A person lending money to a local authority shall not be bound to
inquire whether the borrowing of the money is legal or regular or whether
the money raised was properly applied and shall not be prejudiced by an
illegality or irregularity, or by the misapplication or non-application of any
of that money.'

The assumption that swaps contracts were ancillary to the exercise of the
borrowing power of local authorities continued to be acted on uncritically
until 1987.   In August 1987 the Audit Commission and its officers made
statements strongly critical of the accounting devices being adopted by local
authorities, including the use of front-end premium swaps; they also
questioned whether local authorities could say that they were engaging in debt
management when they were acting as intermediaries in a chain of swaps
contracts.   Local authorities 'have no general power to act as a financial
institution seeking a profit for the benefit of ratepayers ... The participation of
a local authority as an intermediary in a swap transaction solely with a view to
realising a profit is not within the powers of that authority.   To be lawful, the
authority's participation would have to be genuinely ancillary to the
management of that authority's existing debt'.   In September 1987 the
Municipal Journal carried an article quoting these and similar opinions.

In 1988 the Audit Commission obtained the advice of counsel on the
question of the legality of local authorities entering into interest rate swap
contracts.   Counsel's opinion was, in summary, that it was only contracts that
were actual hedging transactions in relation to actual loans that fell within the
powers of a local authority; any other type of interest rate swap contract was
not within the powers of a local authority under the 1972 Act.   On 14 July 1988
the Audit Commission issued a press release publicising the advice that it had
received and warning that auditors might challenge items arising from
transactions that were not permitted by the statute.

On 22 February 1989 Mr Hazell directed that Hammersmith Council should
cease further activity in interest rate swaps, including payments under existing
swaps, unless supported by a legal opinion and he issued a public interest
report in respect of the activity of that council on the swaps market under

s 15(3) of the Local Government Finance Act 1982. On 29 May 1989 Mr Hazell started the proceedings against Hammersmith Council for a declaration that the swaps contracts were illegal and for an order for the rectification of the accounts of that council for the years 1986/7 and 1987/8. The Divisional Court unanimously held that all interest rate swap contracts were ultra vires, that is to say outside the powers of a council under the 1972 Act. It made the declaration asked for by the district auditor and directed that the council's accounts be rectified accordingly. Various banks which had an interest in upholding the validity of the contracts to which they were counter-parties had been allowed to intervene and argue that the contracts were within a local authority's powers. The banks appealed to the Court of Appeal. On 22 February 1990 the Court of Appeal ([1990] 3 All ER 33, [1990] 2 QB 697) delivered its judgment, holding that contracts which were 'parallel' contracts, that is to say contracts genuinely hedging actual loans, were capable of being within the powers of local authorities but that all other forms of swap contract were ultra vires. The Court of Appeal accordingly varied the order of the Divisional Court. The district auditor and the council both appealed to the House of Lords. On 24 January 1991 the House of Lords ([1991] 1 All ER 545, [1992] 2 AC 1) unanimously allowed the appeal and restored the judgment of the Divisional Court.

The leading speech was delivered by Lord Templeman. He emphatically rejected the argument that an interest rate swap contract could ever be regarded as ancillary or incidental to the exercise of the power to borrow and lend money or that it could properly be described as 'debt management'. He said ([1991] 1 All ER 545 at 558–559, [1992] 2 AC 1 at 34–35):

'Debt management is not a function. Debt management is a phrase which has been coined in this case to describe the activities of a person who enters the swap market for the purpose of making profits which can be employed in the payment of interest on borrowings. The expression "debt management" could be employed to describe the duty of a local authority to consider from time to time whether it should change a variable PWLB [Public Works Loan Board] loan to a fixed interest loan, whether it should redeem one loan and take out another, whether when a new borrowing is contemplated the borrowing should be at a variable or fixed rate taking into account all the other borrowings of the local authority. Debt management is a phrase which describes prudent and lawful activities on the part of the local authority. If swap transactions were lawful a local authority would be under a duty to consider entering into swap transactions as part of its duty of debt management. But if a swap transaction is not lawful then it cannot be lawful for a local authority to carry out a swap transaction under the guise of debt management … For the banks it was argued that swap transactions are akin to insurance which enables provision to be made for possible risks. By insurance, an assured sacrifices a premium which, when aggregated with premiums from other assured, will form a pool from which the insurer will indemnify the unfortunate victim (if any) who suffers from the risk insured against. A swap contract based on a notional principal sum of £1m under which the local authority promises to pay the bank £10,000 if [the London Inter-Bank Offered Rate] rises by 1% and the bank promises to pay the local authority £10,000 if LIBOR falls by 1% is more akin to gambling than insurance. The Court of Appeal was impressed by the argument that if swap transactions were unlawful a local authority could not take advantage of reductions in interest rates. But the success of swaps depends on a successful forecast of future interest rates ... The greater the volatility of interest rates, the greater the risk of loss to a local authority as a result of swap transactions.'

He further supported his opinion by a detailed examination of the provisions of Sch 13 to the 1972 Act.

At one point in his speech Lord Templeman referred to an argument which had been advanced by the banks that the decision of the Divisional Court, if upheld, would produce unjust and impractical consequences. He said ([1991] 1 All ER 545 at 560, [1992] 2 AC 1 at 36):

'The major problem concerns the activities of the council, which indulged in speculation on a vast and admittedly unlawful scale. It may not follow that, as between the council and the banks, payments made by the council ... can be recovered by the council. Nor does it follow that payments received by the council ... cannot be recovered by the banks. The consequences of any ultra vires transaction may depend on the facts of each case. The banks have expressly reserved the right to argue in any proceedings arising out of a swap transaction that the banks are not tainted by illegality and that, for a variety of reasons which cannot now be canvassed, payments made pursuant to swap transactions can be retained by the banks or recovered from the council.'

The judgment of the Divisional Court upheld by the House of Lords being that all interest rate swap contracts were ultra vires the local authorities, it followed that no such contract could be enforced by or against any local authority. Following the decision of the House of Lords, well over 200 actions have been commenced with a view to establishing that sums previously paid by or to a local authority under any such contract could be recovered from the recipient. In most of those actions the plaintiff was a bank or similar institution and the defendant was a local authority; in some the roles were reversed; in others both parties were local authorities. There were also third party proceedings. Judges of this court have made various orders to marshal those actions. Certain lead actions were selected for trial; it was directed that the remainder should be stayed on certain terms pending the determination of the lead actions. Hirst J made a costs sharing order. A proportion of the actions have since settled and all those listed for trial in 1992 also settled. Accordingly other actions were selected as lead actions and I directed that these should so far as necessary be successively tried during the current year. They have been selected so as to involve as far as possible the decision also of the points of law and principle which are involved in the other cases and so as to provide a basis upon which they can be settled or, if they cannot be settled, expeditiously tried and disposed of.

I am now concerned with two of the lead actions. In the first, the plaintiff is Westdeutsche Landesbank Girozentrale (Westdeutsche) and the defendant is Islington London Borough Council (Islington). It concerns the payments that were made under a single contract entered into on 16 June 1987. There is a claim and a counterclaim. The trial has been a full trial of the action on agreed statements of facts supplemented by oral evidence called by both sides.

The other action is that between Kleinwort Benson Ltd as plaintiff and Sandwell Borough Council (Sandwell) as defendant. Here, the trial has been of certain of the issues of law arising on the pleadings. The pleadings have been supplemented by agreed statements of fact but there has been no oral evidence. The action concerns the payments made under four contracts dated respectively 6 July 1983, 10 September 1986, 11 November 1986 and 10 November 1986. There are claims and counterclaims. The purpose of hearing the arguments upon these issues of law in the Sandwell action at the same time as the trial of the Islington action is to broaden the factual base upon which the basic restitution issues have to be considered and so that the decision should not turn upon any peculiarity of the Westdeutsche-Islington contract. The Sandwell case also gives rise to an issue of limitations of actions.

THE ISLINGTON ACTION

The writ was issued on 15 April 1991. The plaintiff, Westdeutsche, is a bank incorporated in Germany with its head office in Dusseldorf and a branch in London. Westdeutsche is, after the German government, the largest permanent issuer of Deutschmark fixed rate bonds and is one of the largest inter-bank market participants. It has a strong funding ability and a high credit standing; accordingly it is an attractive counter-party for other banks in the swap market. It had engaged in the swaps market since the summer of 1983 and had been active since then, particularly in swap contracts involving a variety of major currencies and with contracts of up to 15 years' duration. However, prior to its contract with Islington, it had not entered into any swap contract with a local authority in Great Britain.

On 16 June 1987 Mr Peter Goodwin, an investment banker employed in its London branch, was telephoned by a firm of swap brokers asking whether Westdeutsche would be interested in becoming a party to a '£100 million' swaps transaction with an unnamed local authority. After the proposal was outlined to him Mr Goodwin responded that he would not be prepared to enter into the contract unless the broker could match it with a balancing transaction with another counter-party and the 'principal' was limited to £25m. Mr Goodwin's reasons for giving this response were purely reasons of financial prudence. He did not want to take any open position and he wished to limit the size of any individual contract. It never occurred to him that there might be any legal risk involved in the transaction. Although Westdeutsche had not been entering into contracts with English local authorities, local authorities were, and had been for a number of years, well-established participants in the swap market in London and Mr Goodwin had never heard of any question being raised as to their capacity to enter into such contracts. The equivalent local authorities in Germany were regular participants in the swap market there. He throughout assumed that any reputable local authority would certainly not enter into any transaction which it was not within its powers to undertake. Had he thought for a moment that there was any legal risk involved in the contract he would never have entered into it. Mr Goodwin was cross-examined by Miss Appleby QC on behalf of Islington so as to suggest that he had knowingly at the time of entering into this contract accepted a risk that it might be unenforceable. He firmly rejected that suggestion. I accept his evidence. He was concerned only with the commercial and solvency risk. He took appropriate steps to protect his bank against the commercial risk and he rightly regarded local authorities in the United Kingdom as presenting no insolvency risk.

Later, on 16 June 1987 the broker came back to Mr Goodwin with a satisfactory balancing transaction which would give to Westdeutsche the security it required and a satisfactory turn. The broker disclosed that the local authority was Islington and that the other counter-party was Morgan Grenfell & Co Ltd of London. Telexes were exchanged between Mr Goodwin and the broker confirming the two contracts. They were essentially back-to-back contracts. Both were on the BBAIRS terms with a notional principal amount of £25m. Each was to run for ten years starting 18 June 1987 with semi-annual payments. Upon the Islington contract Westdeutsche was the fixed rate payer at a rate of 7·5% pa and Islington was the floating rate payer at the domestic sterling LIBOR rate. On the Morgan Grenfell contract Westdeutsche was the floating rate payer at the domestic sterling LIBOR rate and Morgan Grenfell was the fixed rate payer at a rate of 7·74% pa. Accordingly the 'turn' of Westdeutsche was 0·24% pa on a notional figure of £25m. There was a further feature of both agreements: each provided for the fixed rate payer to pay to the floating rate payer on the commencement date, 18 June 1987, an additional sum of £2·5m. Under the scheme of the contracts this was expressed to be the first of the fixed rate payments and it was calculated against a discount in the later fixed rate payments. If there had been no discount, the appropriate fixed rate of interest for the ten-year period would have been 9·43% pa. £2·5m represented the advancement of periodic semi-annual payments of 1·93% pa on £25m over ten years.

From the point of view of Westdeutsche, the pair of transactions were without risk and provided an assured return. From the point of view of Morgan Grenfell and Islington, they respectively represented a ten-year interest rate swap with Morgan Grenfell as the fixed rate payer and Islington as the floating rate payer, combined with an advance by Morgan Grenfell and an advance to Islington of £2·5m. The contracts did not purport to be and were not expressed as contracts of loan but simply as interest rate swap contracts. This feature was vital to the reason of Islington for entering into the swap contract.

Islington is and was at all material times a local authority governed by the 1972 Act. It was 'rate-capped' for the three financial years 1985/6, 1986/7 and 1987/8. Islington had not previously entered into many swap contracts. In 1982 and 1983 it had entered into seven, but none between that time and the summer of 1987, when only one of the earlier contracts was still running.

It was the duty of a local authority under s 2 of the General Rate Act 1967 and its successors to prepare a balanced budget in advance of each financial year, starting 1 April, that is to say a budget where the budgeted expenditure was fully covered by revenue. Owing to the fact that Islington as a matter of council policy was unwilling to reduce expenditure and had had its powers of raising revenue from its ratepayers limited as a result of being rate-capped, Islington had had to resort to a number of financial and accounting devices to supplement its income. This gave rise to a situation which was the subject of repeated comment by the district auditor including a Public Interest Report dated 26 January 1987. He referred to the fact that his previous advice had not been heeded and that the short term expediencies which had been adopted would exacerbate problems for the future. Various measures taken could not be repeated; some were not in accord with best accounting practice; others would merely serve to increase the council's indebtedness and commit progressively more future resources in respect of past services. The reliance of the council on deferred purchase arrangements had particular significance for its future financial situation. It had entered into such arrangements totalling £197m with finance companies. This had enabled the council to incur increased capital expenditure at the expense of later accounting years, with particular burdens having to be borne by the revenue account in those years. He drew attention to the very serious financial consequences that would ensue for the council unless it altered its budgeting policy and stated that it was essential that the council face these serious problems when considering the rate that it would be setting for the year 1987/8.

It was against this background that the relevant committee of the council considered the matter on 19 March 1987 with a report from its director of finance, Mr Stenning. Mr Stenning's report referred to what the district auditor had said and acknowledged that accounting devices had been used. However, in making his recommendation how a budget shortfall of over £29m should be dealt with, he proposed that various council properties should be disposed of on a long lease for 75 years and that the council should then lease those properties back on a shorter lease of about 20 years with an initial rent-free period of three years. This he estimated would yield a capital payment of £150m which could be used to generate income of £15m in a full year. That increase in income would only last three years, after which it would become an increase in expenditure of over £12m pa. Accordingly, it was a short-term device to increase income available to the council over a three-year period at the cost of significantly increasing the burden to be borne by the expenditure account, and therefore the ratepayers (or charge payers), in later years. It thus was a device which had the effect of borrowing from later revenue accounts for the benefit of earlier revenue accounts. Mr Stenning also provided the council with figures which projected the overall shortfall on the council's revenue account resulting from the policies adopted in previous years. The projected shortfall of 1991/2 was £136·4m. The only alternative which Mr Stenning offered to the adoption of the lease/leaseback scheme was various cuts in expenditure together with rent increases to council tenants. The council approved a budget prepared on the basis that the lease/leaseback transaction would be entered into. Within a short time after the start of the new financial year Mr Stenning ascertained that he would not after all be able to implement the lease/leaseback scheme during the financial year 1987/8. (It was in fact implemented during the following financial year, 1988/9.)

Accordingly Mr Stenning was faced with the problem of finding a figure of the order of £15m as a revenue item from some other source. The solution he chose was to enter into seven interest rate swap contracts with a total notional 'principal' of £175m on terms which included up-front payments totalling £19·36m. The contract with Westdeutsche was one of the seven and they were each on similar terms with Islington as the fixed rate payer and the other party as the floating rate payer. The other six contracts were each with another local authority; the contract with which the present action is concerned was the only one with a bank. As previously explained, the effect for Islington of these swap contracts was similar to the net revenue effect of the lease/leaseback proposal: there would be an increase in revenue for the current year at the expense of the revenue accounts for later years.

It appears that Mr Stenning entered into the seven swap contracts without referring to the council for approval and that approval was not in fact given until 8 October 1987. Nothing however turns in the present case on any question whether or not Mr Stenning originally had the authority to enter into those contracts. However, there were two material points which arose in relation to the treatment of the £19m up-front payments which had been paid into the council's bank accounts. It was essential to the scheme which Mr Stenning had adopted that he should treat them as revenue payments so that they could be taken into account as such during the current year. He chose to treat them as if they were payments of interest by third parties on money which the council had lent to third parties during the current year. This was not the true state of affairs and it had two consequences.

The first and less serious consequence was that the accounts made no provision for the implicit deferred expenditure represented by the discount on the 'fixed interest' payments the council was to receive in later years. Prudent accounting practice would adopt a system of accruals and spread the benefit of the up-front payment over the years so as to balance the burden and the benefit in each year. Further, if that was not to be done, the accounts should, in order to give a fair view of the financial state of the council, at least have contained a note that the £19m credited to the accounts in 1987/8 represented an advance on sums that would have to be debited to the accounts through the succeeding nine years. The Deputy Controller of the Audit Commission had publicly deplored the taking of an up-front payment into the revenue account of a single year. The same view was expressed by the district auditor in a letter to the council dated 31 July 1967. However, the council having been informed that counsel instructed by the borough solicitor had advised that it was ultimately a question for the discretion of the council, decided in October to take the credit for the whole of the £19m into the 1987/8 accounts.

Besides choosing to credit the whole of the up-front payments to 1987/8, Mr Stenning also chose to treat the sums as if they were payments of interest on money which had been lent out by the council. This of course they were not. No loan of any capital sum was involved in any of the swap contracts and the 'principal' was wholly notional. This error gave rise to a breach of the statutory accounting requirements and to a wrong assessment by the council of its entitlement to housing subsidy for the year 1987/8 and the following years.

Under s 148(3) of the 1972 Act the council was required to carry all receipts to the general rate fund of the council. Under para 15 of Sch 13 to the Act the council was empowered to introduce a scheme to establish and operate a loans fund for the purpose of defraying any expenditure which it was authorised by or under statute to meet out of moneys borrowed by the council and for the repayment or redemption of debt. The council had such a scheme, 'The Consolidated Loans Fund Scheme 1967'. Under that scheme a consolidated loans fund was constituted including within that fund an interest account. Paragraph 24(2) provided, so far as material, that the interest account of the consolidated loans fund should be credited with 'interest earned by the investments of the loans fund'. There was no provision which empowered or entitled the council to credit the up-front payments to the consolidated loans fund. It is clear that Mr Stenning never gave his mind to the statutory requirements or to the scheme which the council had adopted. The defendant's witnesses at the trial accepted that the payments could not properly have been credited to the consolidated loans fund.

Under the relevant legislation the housing subsidy to which the council is entitled in any given year is calculated by reference to a complicated formula dependent on a number of factors. One factor is the average net cost of the council's borrowings in the relevant year. Thus there should be taken into account the interest which the council has to pay upon money which it has borrowed and the interest which it receives on money which it has lent. If the net interest burden is higher, the subsidy entitlement is increased; conversely if it is lower, the subsidy entitlement is reduced. Mr Stenning chose, mistakenly, to treat the sums received under the swap contracts as if they were interest payments received on moneys lent out by the council and he intended in later years to treat the sums paid by the council under those contracts as if they were payments of interest on sums lent to the council. Accordingly he assumed, wrongly, and so advised the council, that the subsidy entitlement of the council for the year 1987/8 would be reduced by about £11·62m but would be increased in later years by about £2m pa (assuming that the council would be having to pay under the swap contracts about £3·35m pa). Thus, on Mr Stenning's advice, the council failed to claim the full housing subsidy to which it was entitled for the year 1987/8 and was planning to claim greater subsidies than it would be entitled to for the following years. Under the relevant regulations a council's application for housing subsidy is treated as provisional, as are any payments made, until the claim has been certified by the district auditor. The relevant claims on the basis adopted by Mr Stenning were never certified by the district auditor and I will have to revert to this aspect when considering the change of position defence which has been raised by Islington.

Mr Stenning gave evidence at the trial. He was not an impressive witness and certain aspects of his evidence were clearly unsatisfactory. He demonstrably misunderstood the correct accounting approach in relation to the treatment of the sums payable under the swap contracts and their irrelevance to the council's housing subsidy claims. The explanation may be that Mr Stenning as an officer of the council was subject to political control which limited his freedom of action. It may be that he had never given his mind to considering what was the correct nature of the swap contracts which he had entered into during the summer of 1987. He was however perfectly frank that the purpose of those contracts was not any aspect of debt management or the hedging of any loan contracts; it was simply another device which was designed to increase the revenue available during the current year albeit at the cost of reducing the net revenue available in later years. It was also expressly recognised (mistakenly) that an effect of the contracts was that housing subsidy entitlement would be postponed from the current year to later years. It appears that in July and August Mr Stenning was in part justifying his accounting treatment of the up-front payments by saying that they might be reversed out. He was unable to give any explanation of those statements and there was no basis for supposing that they could be reversed out nor on what terms.

The documentation for the swap contract between Westdeutsche and Islington was prepared, as is normal, after the contract had been made and was not actually signed until September or October. It followed the BBAIRS scheme with amendments. It recited that 'the floating rate payer [that is to say Islington] has certain liabilities in respect of which it is obliged to pay interest at a fixed rate and wishes to exchange such obligations for obligations to make payments at a floating rate of interest'. This recital purports to state that so far as Islington was concerned the contract was a hedging transaction. This was not in accordance with the facts. The contract also included the standard warranty of capacity (which I have quoted earlier); it is recognised by the plaintiffs in this action that it was ultra vires the council to give this warranty just as it was ultra vires the council to enter into the contract as a whole. Clauses 1, 2 and 3 of the contract make it clear that the status of and the consideration for the making of the up-front payments is no different from the status and consideration for any of the other payments to be made by Westdeutsche to Islington under the contract. The up-front payments were, as a matter of contract, merely the first of a number of payments to be made by the fixed rate payer to the floating rate payer under the contract. It is also clear from cl 3 of the contract that when the semi-annual payments fell to be made there was only a single net liability by one party to the other, although in determining which party was liable to make the payment and the amount of the payment there should first be a calculation of the notional amount of the variable interest amount and then it would be the difference between that sum and the fixed interest amount that would be payable the one way or the other. The contract as signed departed from the normal BBAIRS scheme in that it did not acknowledge any contemplation by the floating rate payer that the fixed rate payer might have any back-to-back agreement with another party.

Under the contract the following payments were made:

Date	Payment by Westdeutsche £	Payment by Islington £	Calculation £
18.06.87	2,500,000		
18.12.87		172,345·89	1,112,414·38
			− 940,068·49
20.06.88		229,666·09	1,180,008·56
			− 950,342·47
19.12.88		259,054·56	1,193,986·07
			− 934,931·51
19.06.89		693,407·53	1,628,339·64
			− 934,931·51
Totals	2,500,000	1,354,474·07	

Net payment £1,145,525·93 by Westdeutsche to Islington.

The last payment made was thus a payment made by Islington to Westdeutsche on 19 June 1989. No payment was made in December 1989 in view of the Divisional Court decision which by then had been given. How matters were dealt with thereafter by Islington and Westdeutsche will be discussed under the heading 'Change of position'.

The claims and counterclaims in the action have been formulated in a number of ways. Each side has at one time put its case on the basis of treating its claim as being for the full amount of the 'fixed interest' or 'floating interest' sums notwithstanding that the contract only imposes a liability to pay net sums and that was all that was actually paid. Thus Westdeutsche has claimed a total of £6,260,273·98 and Islington has counterclaimed a total of £5,114,748·05. This approach cannot be supported. It is contrary to the facts and the express contract; it has no basis in any principle of unjust enrichment. The figures which can properly form the subject matter of the claim and counterclaim are respectively £2,500,000 and £1,354,474·07, being the aggregate of the actual payments made. By the conclusion of the trial this was the case of both parties and I will have to deal with it on that basis although it cannot seriously be disputed that on any principle of unjust enrichment these figures must be netted off against each other and that the reality of the case is an alleged enrichment of Islington at the expense of Westdeutsche in the sum of £1,145,525·93.

The legal basis upon which Westdeutsche makes its claim in the action and, so far as necessary, Islington makes its counterclaim is put under the following heads. (1) The claim for money had and received: (a) money paid for a consideration that has wholly failed, (b) money paid by the plaintiff to the defendant which has been applied by the defendant in the discharge of its legal liabilities and (c) money paid under a mistake. (2) In equity, the 'proprietary' right to trace the money into the assets of the defendant and for an order that the relevant sum should be repaid out of those assets.

The claim to money had and received on the ground of total failure of consideration was developed in argument in a way that in my judgment altered its character to a claim based upon the payment of money under a void contract or alternatively money paid without consideration and without any intention to make a gift. The defences raised by Islington are: (i) the money was paid by Westdeutsche voluntarily assuming the risk that the contract would be unenforceable or void; (ii) the money was paid under a mistake of law and therefore is irrecoverable (regardless of whether the plaintiff can establish one of its other bases of claim); and (iii) change of position.

As against Islington's counterclaim Westdeutsche has also pleaded the defence of change of position. Each side has also advanced arguments in favour of or against the award of simple interest or compound interest on any sums that may be held to be repayable.

The issues of fact which have arisen are very limited. The allegation that Westdeutsche, through Mr Goodwin, voluntarily assumed the risk that the contracts would be unenforceable or void was not made out on the evidence and I find that there was no contemplation of the existence of any such risk and that no such risk was, as a matter of fact, voluntarily assumed. The other limited issues of fact related to the defence of change of position and the ability to trace and I will revert to the evidence on those aspects later in the judgment.

The issues of law were those which were raised by each of the bases of claim which were put forward but they were fundamentally what was the nature and extent of the rights of one party against the other in respect of payments made under a contract which was wholly void on the ground of ultra vires. They also raised the question whether such a situation gives rise to a right to trace in equity and what are the limits of that equitable tracing remedy.

THE SANDWELL ACTION

The writ in the action was issued on 3 April 1991. The plaintiff, Kleinwort Benson, is and was at all material times a participant in the money markets in lending to private and public sectors and in the interest rate swaps markets. Between 1982 and 1988 it entered into some 70 swap transactions with 36 local authorities. The defendant council, Sandwell, is the district council for a district in the West Midlands created as part of the 1974 local government reorganisation. It is governed by provisions of the 1972 Act. Between 1982 and 1987 Sandwell entered into some 50 swap transactions with a variety of parties. The action between Kleinwort Benson and Sandwell is concerned with four swap transactions entered into between 1983 and 1987.

The first swap

This was entered into on 6 July 1983 through brokers. Substantive terms of the swap were: (i) a notional principal of £5m; (ii) Kleinwort Benson to pay Sandwell a fixed rate of $11\frac{3}{8}$% half-yearly; (iii) Sandwell to pay Kleinwort Benson a floating rate of LIBOR quarterly; and (iv) the swap to have a life of five years, with the last payment to be made on 15 July 1988. When the end of a quarter did not coincide with the end of a half year, Sandwell made payments to Kleinwort Benson; when the end of a quarter and the end of a half year coincided, net payments were made by Kleinwort Benson.

The payments that were made were as follows:

Date	Kleinwort Benson £	Sandwell £	Cumulative payments by Kleinwort Benson £
17.10.83		127,962·33	(127,962·33)
16.01.84	170,625·00		42,662·67
16.04.84		118,424·66	(75,761·99)
16.07.84	172,183·22		96,421·23
15.10.84		150,368·15	(53,946·92)
15.01.85	152,037·68		98,090·76
15.04.85		153,339·04	(55,248·28)
15.07.85	123,099·32		67,851·04
15.10.85		151,232·88	(83,381·84)
15.01.86	140,993·15		57,611·31
15.04.86		161,044·52	(103,433·21)
15.07.86	153,095·03		49,661·82
15.10.86		127,405·82	(77,744·00)
15.01.87	142,765·35		65,021·35
15.04.87		137,157·53	(72,136·18)
15.07.87	158,938·35		86,802·17
15.10.87		115,787·67	(28,985·50)
15.01.88	156,746·58		127,761·08
15.04.88		112,191·78	15,569·40
15.07.88	180,753·42		196,322·72
	1,551,237·10	1,354,914·38	196,322·72

The contract ran its full course with all the intended payments being made. The total of the payments made by Kleinwort Benson was £1,551,237·10 and the total of the payments made by Sandwell was £1,354,914·38. Thus the overall result was that Kleinwort Benson has paid to Sandwell £196,322·72 more than Sandwell has paid to Kleinwort Benson. The payments made subsequent to 3 April 1985 were made within the six-year period before the issue of the writ and accordingly no question of limitation of action arises in respect of them. But in respect of the first three payments by each side under the contract a question of the limitation of actions has arisen. The first three payments by Kleinwort Benson total £494,845·90 and the first three by

Sandwell total £396,755·14. Therefore the net amount referable to those payments is £98,090·76 paid by Kleinwort Benson to Sandwell.

Accordingly, the additional points which arise from the first swap are whether it makes any difference that the contract has run its full course and is entirely executed and secondly what is the relevance, if any, of the Limitation Acts to any cause of action which either party may have in respect of the payments made under the first swap.

The second swap

The second swap was entered into on 10 September 1986 and provided for: (i) a notional principal of £5m; (ii) a floating rate of BBAIRS sterling settlement rate payable by Sandwell half-yearly; (iii) a fixed rate of 10·3125% payable by Kleinwort Benson half-yearly; and (iv) a life of ten years from 11 September 1986 until 11 September 1996. The BBAIRS terms were incorporated. Payments were made on this contract until the autumn of 1989. They were:

Date	Kleinwort Benson £	Sandwell £
11.03.87	7,748·29	
11.09.87	12,602·74	
11.03.88		4,674·66
11.09.88	27,718·32	
13.03.89		51,421·24
11.09.90		68,561·65
Totals	£48,069·35	£124,657·55

Hence Sandwell has made net payments to Kleinwort Benson of £76,588·20. Sandwell counterclaims this sum against Kleinwort Benson on the basis that if it is unable to rebut the bases of claim put forward by Kleinwort Benson in respect of the other swaps, it must follow that it is entitled to recover in respect of the second swap. Kleinwort Benson does not dispute that conclusion, subject to any special defences that may be open to it.

The only additional point which arises therefore from the second swap is whether it makes any difference, where there have been payments both ways, that the party making the net claim is the local authority rather than the bank.

The third and fourth swaps

The third and the fourth swaps raise exactly the same points and there is no need to make any distinction between them. Accordingly they can be taken together.

The third swap was entered into on 11 November 1986 and provided for: (i) a notional principal of £5m; (ii) Kleinwort Benson to pay Sandwell a fixed rate of 11·42% half-yearly; (iii) Sandwell to pay Kleinwort Benson a floating rate of LIBOR half-yearly; and (iv) the swap was to have a life of ten years with the payments being made semi-annually starting with 11 May 1987 and ending with 11 November 1996. The BBAIRS terms were incorporated.

Before the time arrived for making the first payment under this swap contract the parties entered into a further agreement which had the effect of reversing it out. The 'reverse' swap was entered into on 10 February 1987 and provided for: (i) a notional principal of £5m; (ii) Sandwell to pay Kleinwort Benson a fixed rate of 10·38% half-yearly; (iii) Kleinwort Benson to pay Sandwell a floating rate of LIBOR half-yearly; and (iv) the swap was to have a

life of approximately nine years nine months with the first payment to be made
on 11 May 1987 and the last to be made on 11 November 1996.

It was thus an exact reversal of the 11 November 1986 contract save that
Kleinwort Benson was left with a net obligation to make semi-annual
payments equivalent to interest on a notional amount of £5m at a rate of 1·04%
p a.   It was further a term of the February agreement that the respective
liabilities of the parties under the two agreements should be set off against each
other and that the sole surviving obligation should be that of Kleinwort Benson
to pay the specified net sums on specified dates.   (The payment to be made on
11 May 1987 had also to take into account that the reversing agreement had not
been entered into until 10 February 1987 and therefore there was a difference
between the fixed and floating rates to be taken into account for the period 11
November to 10 February.)

The payments that were made under the reversed third swap by Kleinwort
Benson were:

Date	Kleinwort Benson
	£
11.05.87	16,507·88
11.11.87	26,213·70
11.05.88	25,928·77
11.11.88	26,213·70
11.05.89	25,786·30
	120,650·35

Accordingly under the third swap Sandwell has made no payments to
Kleinwort Benson, and Kleinwort Benson has made payments to Sandwell
totalling £120,650·35.

The fourth swap was entered into on 10 November 1986 and was in all
respects the same as the third swap, except that the fixed rate was 11·35% p a.
The reverse swap was dated 19 February 1987 and was in all respects the same
as for the third swap except that the fixed rate was 10·25% p a.   Accordingly the
resulting liability of Kleinwort Benson had to be calculated by reference to a
fixed rate difference of 1·1% p a.   The payments made by Kleinwort Benson to
Sandwell under the reversed fourth swap were:

Date	Kleinwort Benson
	£
11.05.87	9,902·40
11.11.87	27,726·03
11.05.88	27,424·66
11.11.88	27,726·03
11.05.89	27,273·97
	120,053·09

Accordingly Kleinwort Benson has made payments under the fourth swap as
reversed which total £120,053·09, and Sandwell has made no payments to
Kleinwort Benson.

The defendant, Sandwell, accepts that both the third and fourth swaps and
the contracts by which those swaps were reversed were ultra vires the council.
Further, it does not allege or submit that the contracts of reversal amounted in
any way to an accord and satisfaction or anything akin to a settlement
agreement, nor does it say that any of the payments should be treated as

payments to 'close a transaction'. Accordingly, the additional question raised by the third and fourth swaps is whether it makes any difference to the bank's right to recover that payments have only been made one way, that is by the bank to the local authority, and no payments have been made by the local authority to the bank.

The Sandwell issues

The reamended points of claim of Kleinwort Benson plead the contracts and the fact that in accordance with the decision of the House of Lords in the *Hammersmith* case all the relevant contracts were beyond the capacity of Sandwell. It pleads that in the premises:

'(a) the property in the payments made by the plaintiff to the defendant has remained in the plaintiff; and/or (b) such payments have been made by the plaintiff for a consideration which has totally failed; (c) such payments were made by the plaintiff on the basis of a mistaken belief that they were being made pursuant to a binding contract between the plaintiff and the defendant. Accordingly the defendant has had and received the sums paid by the plaintiff to the use of the plaintiff, the plaintiff is entitled to restitution of all such payments and the defendant has at all times since receipt and now holds them on trust for the plaintiff.'

It also claims on the basis that the payments received by Sandwell were spent by Sandwell on defraying its lawful liabilities or expenditure, and/or on the basis that the sums can be traced in the hands of Sandwell and Kleinwort Benson is entitled in equity to a charge upon and/or repayment from the assets of Sandwell. Kleinwort Benson says it will give credit against its claim for restitution (save for its proprietary claim) for the payments made by Sandwell to it. Kleinwort Benson also claims interest and/or compound interest.

The reamended points of defence and counterclaim admit that all the relevant contracts were ultra vires and the defendant pleads the following defences so far as are presently material.

The limitation upon the capacity of Sandwell existed for the benefit and/or the protection of Sandwell and the rate and community charge payers within its district.

It denies that the property in the payments has remained in Kleinwort Benson and that the consideration for the moneys has wholly failed.

It says that the moneys paid are in any event irrecoverable as having been paid under a mistake of law (namely as to the capacity of the defendants to contract and/or the lawfulness of the agreements and each of them).

The payments, being made purportedly pursuant to void contracts, amounted in law to gifts to the defendant and are therefore irrecoverable from the defendant.

The property in all the money paid passed to the defendant upon payment and were mixed with other of the defendant's moneys and have since been paid out or spent (in whole or in part).

'In the premises, in so far as the same is alleged, it is denied that the plaintiff is entitled to trace any money paid by it into any money and/or property held by the defendant.'

It is denied that the plaintiff has any proprietary interest in the said funds, such that it is entitled in equity to a charge upon them or to a rateable share therein.

In respect of the first swap the plaintiff's claim in respect of the first three payments is time-barred under ss 5 and/or 36 of the Limitation Act 1980.

Other defences are raised with which I am not presently concerned (including an allegation of illegal gaming) and which involve mixed questions of fact and law. I am not concerned with what was the actual mistaken state of mind of the relevant employees of Kleinwort Benson at the time the various payments were made. Nor am I concerned with the defences of change of position which are pleaded by Sandwell (and Kleinwort Benson). It is not in dispute following the speeches of the House of Lords in *Lipkin Gorman (a firm) v Karpnale Ltd* [1992] 4 All ER 512, [1991] 2 AC 548 that a defence of change of position is potentially available to a defendant in a case such as the present. Whether or not it succeeds will depend upon the facts of each case. I am not concerned with the counterclaim, but it raises similar bases of claim as those which the plaintiff has raised against the defendant.

In its points of reply and defence to counterclaim the plaintiff has pleaded in response to the limitation defence that, in so far as the claim is based upon relief from the consequences of a mistake, the plaintiff is entitled to rely upon s 32 of the 1980 Act. I am not concerned with that issue. It also pleads that the principles of set-off will either render inapplicable or irrelevant the defence of limitation under s 5 of the Act. This point has been argued before me and raises a further question of the construction of s 35 of that Act.

The issues which have been ordered to be tried are preliminary issues of law and the Sandwell action raises the same fundamental issues as are raised in the Islington action but in relation to contracts and payments that are factually different from the contract involved in the Islington action. The legal argument in the two cases has been conducted on the basis that all counsel have had full access to the skeleton arguments submitted by all the other counsel and to the daily transcripts. Accordingly I heard argument from leading counsel for Westdeutsche and for Islington and then from leading counsel for Kleinwort Benson and for Sandwell. Each counsel has, where appropriate, adopted the arguments of another or responded to an adverse argument. The relevant points have therefore been fully argued by the counsel for all parties and I am grateful to them and the members of their respective teams for the very considerable thought and research that has gone into the presentation of those arguments and the preparation of the very large number of authorities which it has been necessary to refer to. As will be appreciated, the issues of mixed fact and law raised by the Islington case went beyond those which it was necessary for counsel in the Sandwell action to deal with. Similarly, the limitation and associated issues only arose in the Sandwell action and were not the subject of any argument by counsel in the Islington action. The present trials were not concerned with any alleged defences under the Gaming Acts. Islington conceded that no such defence was available to it and that the relevant contract was not unlawful.

THE SCHEME OF THE JUDGMENT

This judgment will be sub-divided into a number of sections. The first, under the heading 'Preliminaries', will deal with various matters, a number of them of fundamental importance, which underlie the examination of the plaintiffs' various bases of claim. The second section will, under the heading 'Money had and received', deal with the common law causes of action and remedies. The third section, under the heading 'Equitable tracing', will deal with the equitable proprietary rights and remedies. The fourth section will deal with the defence of 'Limitation of actions', relevant only to the first Sandwell swap. Fifthly, the defences of 'Change of position', as raised by the parties to the Islington action, will be dealt with. Finally, there will be the question of 'Interest'. Questions of fact will to some extent have to be dealt with both under the heading of equitable tracing and under the heading of change of position. As regards Islington, both these headings require findings of fact regarding the accounting practices and finances of Islington from the time it received the sum of £2·5m from Westdeutsche on 18 June 1987 down to the date of this judgment.

(1) Preliminaries

(a) The historical perspective

The cases cited during the course of the argument extended over a period of more than 200 years. Inevitably they included lines of authority which are hard to reconcile and individual decisions and dicta which are, or appear to be, inconsistent. Further the law has developed in a radical fashion over the period and that development has become even more marked in recent years with the decisions of the House of Lords in the *Lipkin Gorman* case and *Woolwich Building Society v IRC (No 2)* [1992] 3 All ER 737, [1993] AC 70. Up until even the second decade of this century and the decision in *Sinclair v Brougham* [1914] AC 398, [1914–15] All ER Rep 622, it was normal to categorise the remedy of restitution under the common law as an aspect of quasi contract depending upon implied contract. This approach had a historical derivation from the cause of action in indebitatus assumpsit and meant that if there was some objection to the implication of a promise by the recipient of a benefit to reimburse the party at whose expense that benefit had been enjoyed then, because no contract could be implied, no remedy was given by the common law.

There has not been, and still is not, any general cause of action in English law for restitution for unjust enrichment. In *Orakpo v Manson Investments Ltd* [1977] 3 All ER 1 at 7, [1978] AC 95 at 104 Lord Diplock said:

'My Lords, there is no general doctrine of unjust enrichment recognised in English law. What it does is to provide specific remedies in particular cases of what might be classified as unjust enrichment in a legal system that is based on the civil law.'

In *Lipkin Gorman (a firm) v Karpnale Ltd* [1992] 4 All ER 512 at 532, [1991] 2 AC 548 at 578 Lord Goff said:

'The recovery of money in restitution is not, as a general rule, a matter of discretion for the court. A claim to recover money at common law is made as a matter of right; and, even though the underlying principle of recovery is the principle of unjust enrichment, nevertheless, where recovery is denied, it is denied on the basis of legal principle.'

In *Woolwich Building Society v IRC (No 2)* [1992] 3 All ER 737 at 754, [1993] AC 70 at 165 he said:

'Where a sum has been paid which is not due, but it has not been paid under a mistake of fact or under compulsion ... it is generally not recoverable.'

Similarly, in equity the existence of any unqualified remedy has been rejected. In *Re Diplock's Estate, Diplock v Wintle* [1948] 2 All ER 318 at 346–347, [1948] Ch 465 at 520–521 the Court of Appeal said:

'Regarded as a pure piece of machinery for the purpose of tracing money into a mixed fund or into property acquired by means of a mixed fund, a declaration of charge might be thought to be a suitable means of dealing with any case where one person has, without legal title, acquired some benefit by the use of the money of another—in other words, any case of what is often called "unjust enrichment." The opinion of LORD DUNEDIN in *Sinclair* v. *Brougham* ([1914] AC 398 at 437, [1914–15] All ER Rep 622 at 640) appears to us to come very nearly to this, for he appears to treat the equitable remedy as applicable in any case where a superfluity, expressed or capable of being expressed in terms of money, is found to exist. Such a view would dispense with the necessity of establishing as a starting point the existence of a fiduciary or quasi-fiduciary relationship or of a continuing right of property recognised in equity. We may say at once that, apart from the possible case of LORD DUNEDIN'S speech, we cannot find that any principle so wide in its operation is to be found enunciated in English law.'

However, there are also judicial dicta which can be taken as recognising a general principle of unjust enrichment. The best known of these is the oft-quoted statement of Lord Wright in *Fibrosa Spolka Akcyjna v Fairbairn Lawson Combe Barbour Ltd* [1942] 2 All ER 122 at 135, [1943] AC 32 at 61. It was quoted by Lord Browne-Wilkinson in *Woolwich* [1992] 3 All ER 737 at 780–781, [1993] AC 70 at 196–197, where he also placed it in its context in English law at the present day.

'Although as yet there is in English law no general rule giving the plaintiff a right of recovery from a defendant who has been unjustly enriched at the plaintiff's expense, the concept of unjust enrichment lies at the heart of all the individual instances in which the law does give a right of recovery. As Lord Wright said in [the *Fibrosa* case]: "The claim was for money paid for a consideration which had failed. It is clear that any civilised system of law is bound to provide remedies for cases of what has been called unjust enrichment or unjust benefit, that is, to prevent a man from retaining the money of, or some benefit derived from, another which it is against conscience that he should keep. Such remedies in English law are generically different from remedies in contract or in tort, and are now recognised to fall within a third category of the common law which has been called quasi-contract or restitution." In the present case the concept of unjust enrichment suggests that the plaintiffs should have a remedy. The Crown demanded and received payment of the sum by way of tax alleged to be due under regulations subsequently held by your Lordships' House to be ultra vires (see [1991] 4 All ER 92, [1990] 1 WLR 1400). The payment was made under protest. Yet the Crown maintains that it was under no legal obligation to repay the wrongly extracted tax and in consequence is not liable to pay interest on the sum held by it between the date it received the money and the date of the order of Nolan J. If the Crown is right, it will be enriched by the interest on money to which it had no right during that period. In my judgment, this is the paradigm of a case of unjust enrichment. As in so many other fields of English law, the occasions on which recovery is permitted have been built up on a case by case basis.'

In the *Woolwich* case the House of Lords (by a majority) applying the general principle to the facts of that case held that the law should give a remedy even though in doing so they were going beyond any previously decided case.

Since the Judicature Acts in the last century the systems of law and equity have been fused and must now be regarded as a single system although, in any individual case, the nature of the remedy which is asked for and the right or interest which it is claimed should be recognised and given effect to must be considered. Thus it may still be necessary to establish some kind of fiduciary relationship between a defendant and a plaintiff but there is no need, in the context of restitution for unjust enrichment, to treat the action for money had and received and an action for an equitable remedy as any longer depending upon different concepts of justice. Indeed, such an approach was recognised in the late 18th and early 19th centuries and was vividly expressed by Bayley J in *Davis v Bryan* (1827) 6 B & C 651 at 655, 108 ER 591 at 592:

'This appears to be a clear case on principles both of law and honesty. This is an action for money had and received, and I learned many years ago that such an action could not be maintained, if it were against equity and good conscience that the money should be recovered.'

A similar statement is to be found in the speech of Lord Goff in *Lipkin Gorman* [1992] 4 All ER 512 at 534, [1991] 2 AC 548 at 581, where he comments that a more broadly based approach to the law of restitution enables the courts to take into account the true merits of the cases of both parties to the relevant transaction. In considering whether or not a defence of change of position should now be recognised by the law, and deciding that it should, he said:

'... the recognition of change of position as a defence should be doubly beneficial. It will enable a more generous approach to be taken to the recognition of the right to restitution, in the knowledge that the defence is, in appropriate cases, available; and, while recognising the different functions of property at law and in equity, there may also in due course develop a more consistent approach to tracing claims, in which common defences are recognised as available to such claims, whether advanced at law or in equity.'

A court should not now find itself in the same position as the House of Lords in the *Fibrosa* case where they were unable to give effect to the merits of both the plaintiffs' and the defendants' case, to the disadvantage of the defendants, a situation which was remedied by Parliament in the Law Reform (Frustrated Contracts) Act 1943.

I have been extensively referred by counsel to the decisions of courts, often of the highest authority, in other common law jurisdictions. They show that on occasions those courts have either taken or declined to take some step in the development or application of the law of restitution. I have been referred to some judgments displaying outstanding scholarship which contain particularly valuable discussions. However, I hope that I will not be thought disrespectful to either the arguments of counsel or those authorities if I do not refer to them in this judgment. I have to decide the present cases upon the present state of the law of England.

(b) Ultra vires

It was not in dispute before me that the present case is concerned with acts which were ultra vires the local authority in the proper use of that term. The authority lacked the necessary capacity and therefore its acts were without legal effect. It is not to be confused with a case of excess of authority (see *Rolled Steel Products (Holdings) Ltd v British Steel Corp* [1985] 3 All ER 52, [1986] Ch 246). The purported contracts never came into existence and were from the start wholly void.

It was also common ground at these trials that no illegality was involved. The purported contracts were not illegal and there is no overriding principle of illegality or public policy which prevents the recognition of whatever restitutionary rights and remedies may be available to the parties. Further, I am not concerned with contracts which are binding in honour only and which the courts will not recognise as, for example, gaming contracts. In such situations the courts will not intervene and money paid pursuant to an obligation binding in honour only is to be treated as a gift (see *Lipkin Gorman* [1992] 4 All ER 512 at 531, [1991] 2 AC 548 at 577 per Lord Goff).

The object of the doctrine of ultra vires is, as was pointed out by Lord Templeman in *Hammersmith and Fulham* [1991] 1 All ER 545 at 560, [1992] 2 AC 1 at 36, citing *Cotman v Brougham* [1918] AC 514, [1918–19] All ER Rep 265, the protection of the public. In relation to a company, it protected subscribers to the company and those who were relying upon the credit of a company. In the case of local authorities, it exists for the better regulation of local authorities in the public interest and, in relation to their revenue-raising powers, for the protection of their ratepayers (or charge payers). It does not exist for the benefit of those in the position of the banks in these cases and the banks are not entitled to rely upon any such principle (cf *Kiriri Cotton Co Ltd v Dewani* [1960] 1 All ER 177, [1960] AC 192). Although it must be the primary duty of the members of a council and its officers to see that the council does not act ultra vires, the third party, however innocent, cannot escape the consequences of such lack of capacity. Lord Sumner in *Sinclair v Brougham* [1914] AC 398 at 451–452, [1914–15] All ER Rep 622 at 648, in a passage upon which Miss Appleby, counsel for Islington, relied, said that everybody concerned 'must all be taken to have known of the legal invalidity [of the relevant transactions] ... All must equally abide by the legal consequences of this invalidity'. This statement is simply a statement of the legal consequences of the doctrine of ultra vires. It does not involve any actual knowledge on the part of the third party nor does it involve any imputation to the third party of a willingness to enter into a void transaction. Once the transaction is held to have been void from the outset and the third party has been held to have no rights under the purported contract, the effect of the doctrine of ultra vires is exhausted and it is from that starting point that the question of restitution has to be considered.

(c) The passing of property in money

It was not in dispute that the legal property in the various sums of money which were paid to each other by the parties to these actions passed to the recipient. They were paid into mixed funds and thereafter became in law the property of the recipient. The case of the banks is that the sums of money nevertheless remained in equity the property of the banks. The proprietary claims made by the banks rest entirely upon the contention that equity would say that it was unconscionable that the councils should retain the moneys. Thus the banks submit that the present cases illustrate the principle of unjust enrichment and that both law and equity should recognise this and, further, that they disclose a sufficient fiduciary relationship between the recipient and the payer to give rise to equitable remedies. It is not alleged that the councils received the money as trustees or as constructive trustees, nor do the banks rely upon any allegation of actual or constructive knowledge on the part of the councils that they were not entitled to receive the moneys. The banks' case is put upon the same basis as, they submit, was accepted in *Sinclair v Brougham* and was held to give rise to the equitable charge upon the assets of the society in that case.

This gave rise in its turn to an argument whether different principles applied if the recipient was solvent or insolvent. Miss Appleby submitted that the payer of a sum of money might have more extensive rights to recover that sum if he were seeking to share in an insolvent fund as opposed to seeking to get an order for repayment from a solvent defendant. She gained some support for this submission from the fact that Lord Parker appears to have left the point open in *Sinclair v Brougham* [1914] AC 398 at 449, [1914–15] All ER Rep 622 at 647, when discussing the order made in *Re Guardian Permanent Benefit Building Society* (1882) 23 Ch D 440, and from the order made in *Re Jon Beauforte (London) Ltd* [1953] 1 All ER 634, [1953] Ch 131. However, I reject this argument: the basis of a claim on a fund must be the availability of a remedy against the legal owner of that fund. Where the recipient of the money is solvent there is no reason, provided that the continuing existence of the equity can be recognised, why the remedy should not be granted. The problem is whether or not the equitable right to repayment ever existed and whether it continues to have efficacy at the time that the remedy is sought. In a case of insolvency the added factor is that there are other claimants upon an inadequate fund: the competing equities of those claimants have to be considered. That was the exercise which was undertaken, for example, in *Sinclair v Brougham*. But it is absurd to suggest that had the society in *Sinclair v Brougham* been solvent the House of Lords would not have recognised the right of the plaintiffs to recover the payments that they had made and would not have ordered restitution. Accordingly, contrary to the argument of Miss Appleby, the cases where a payer of money has been held entitled to share in the distribution of an insolvent fund are authorities upon which a claimant can rely when seeking restitution from a solvent defendant. The distinction between purely personal remedies and equitable remedies which are categorised as proprietary (although equity acts in personam), will cease to be material save for the fact that as the law at present stands the equitable remedy depends upon an ability to trace (see *Re Diplock's Estate* [1948] 2 All ER 318 at 346, [1948] Ch 465 at 521 and *Barlow Clowes International Ltd (in liq) v Vaughan* [1992] 4 All ER 22 at 42 per Woolf LJ). With this qualification regarding the availability of the remedy, there is no reason why the existence of the right in law and in equity should not be assimilated. Thus if a certain category of mistake suffices to give rise to an equitable right to restitution there is now no adequate reason why that right should not now be generally recognised.

In *Chase Manhattan Bank NA v Israel-British Bank (London) Ltd* [1979] 3 All ER 1025, [1981] Ch 105, in the reverse position of equity following the law, Goulding J held that the equitable remedy of tracing was available in an insolvent winding up to a plaintiff who had paid money under a mistake of fact on the ground that he retained an equitable property in the money and the conscience of the recipient was subjected to a fiduciary duty to respect his proprietary right. Miss Appleby submitted that that case was wrongly decided but it is clearly correct.

(d) Sinclair v Brougham

The plaintiffs before me relied upon *Sinclair v Brougham* [1914] AC 398, [1914–15] All ER Rep 622 as being an authority which showed that they were entitled to recover both by way of money had and received and in equity. The defendants on the other hand submitted that *Sinclair v Brougham* showed that the plaintiffs' claims could not succeed. It is therefore necessary for me to consider what was decided in *Sinclair v Brougham* and what propositions of law were involved in the decision. The speeches in the House of Lords have been the subject of analysis in *Re Diplock's Estate* and were again considered in the *Chase Manhattan* case.

The case arose out of the winding up of the insolvent Birkbeck Permanent Building Society. The society had been formed under the Building Societies Acts. Those Acts laid down what were to be the objects of the society and the purposes for which it could borrow and lend money. The powers of the society did not include the capacity to carry on a banking business or to borrow money for the purposes of or as part of such a business. However, from an early stage the society did undertake a banking business, becoming commonly known as the 'Birkbeck Bank'. After the banking business had been carried on successfully for a considerable number of years the society got into difficulties and in 1911 an order was made for it to be wound up. Questions of priority arose in the winding up between the outside creditors of the society, the contributors to the society (the shareholders), and the bank customers (the depositors) who had accounts in credit with the society. The assets of the society were sufficient to enable the outside creditors to be paid in full and this was done. The point arising for decision was how the remainder of the fund should be distributed as between the contributors and the depositors. The fund was insufficient to enable both classes to be paid in full. The decision of the House of Lords was that, subject to one qualification, the two classes of claimants should share rateably in the remainder of the fund on an equal basis. The qualification was that the order made gave the liberty to any individual contributor or depositor to trace, if he could, his own money specifically into any particular asset.

The case therefore concerned ultra vires transactions and the claim of the depositors was a claim for the repayment of sums paid under a void contract. The depositors were mistaken in their assumption that there was a relationship of banker and customer between the society and themselves. No argument seems to have been founded on the categorisation or relevance of this mistake. Only Lord Sumner referred to it, after having decided on another ground that the claim in money had and received could not succeed. He said ([1914] AC 398 at 452, [1914–15] All ER Rep 622 at 648):

'To the other dificulties of such claims I will allude shortly. There was no mistake of fact. The facts were fully known so far as was material. The rules and objects of the society were accessible to all. The only mistake made was a mistake as to the law, or that mistake of conduct to which all of us are prone, of doing as others do and chancing the law.'

His approach undoubtedly reflected the common law rule that unless some mistake as to some specific fact could be identified then the mistake must be categorised as a mistake of law.

The ground upon which the claim in money had and received failed in the House of Lords was that to permit it to succeed would be contrary to the statute which restricted the capacity of the society. To succeed the depositors must persuade the court to imply a contract to repay since the implication of such a contract was considered at that time to be an essential basis of a cause of action in money had and received. The society had no capacity to promise to repay the moneys lent to it by the depositors, whether such a promise was actual or was to be implied. Viscount Haldane LC founded his decision upon the fact that the taking of deposits from banking customers was the equivalent to taking a loan from them and that to order the repayment of the deposit would be the equivalent of enforcing an ultra vires contract of loan. He said ([1914] AC 398 at 414–415, 417, [1914–15] All ER Rep 622 at 628–629, 630):

'To hold that a remedy will lie in personam against a statutory society, which by hypothesis cannot in the case in question have become a debtor or entered into any contract for repayment, is to strike at the root of the doctrine of ultra vires as established in the jurisprudence of this country … When it speaks of actions arising quasi ex contractu it refers merely to a class of action in theory based on a contract which is imputed to the defendant by a fiction of law. The fiction can only be set up with effect if such a contract would be valid if it really existed … it appears to me that as a matter of principle the law of England cannot now, consistently with the interpretation which the Courts have placed on the statutes which determine the capacity of statutory societies, impute the fiction of such a promise where it would have been ultra vires to give it.'

Lord Parker said ([1914] AC 398 at 440, [1914–15] All ER Rep 622 at 642):

'It has been settled in the cases of *National Permanent Benefit Building Society, Blackburn and District Benefit Building Society* v. *Cunliffe Brooks & Co.* and *Wenlock* v. *River Dee Co.* that an ultra vires borrowing by persons affecting to act on behalf of a company or other statutory association does not give rise to any indebtedness either at law or in equity on the part of such company or association. It is not, therefore, open to the House to hold that in such a case the lender has an action against the company or association for money had and received. To do so would in effect validate the transaction so far as it embodied a contract to repay the money lent. The implied promise on which the action for money had and received is based would be precisely that promise which the company or association could not lawfully make.'

Lord Sumner said ([1914] AC 398 at 452, [1914–15] All ER Rep 622 at 648):

'The depositors' case has been put, first of all, as consisting in a right enforceable in a common law action. It is said that they paid their money under a mistake of fact, or for a consideration that has wholly failed, or that it has been had and received by the society to their use. My Lords, in my opinion no such actions could succeed. To hold otherwise would be indirectly to sanction an ultra vires borrowing. All these causes of action are common species of the genus assumpsit. All now rest, and long have rested, upon a notional or imputed promise to repay. The law cannot de jure impute promises to repay, whether for money had and received or otherwise, which, if made de facto, it would inexorably avoid.'

The decision in *Sinclair v Brougham* that the personal claim in money had and received could not succeed therefore depended upon the fact that the relevant transactions were characterised as borrowing transactions and the recognition that, because of the statute, a promise to repay could not be implied. That situation is clearly distinguishable from the present cases. The banks do not seek directly or indirectly to enforce the ultra vires contracts. Their claims are the reverse of that. They do not allege or need to allege any promise to repay. They simply say that the councils have received their money under void contracts and that they should have it back.

Cases which involved similar arguments were cited to the House of Lords in *Sinclair v Brougham*. They were *Re Phoenix Life Assurance Co, Hoare's Case* (1862) 2 John & H 229, 70 ER 1041 and *Flood v Irish Provident Assurance Co Ltd* [1912] 2 Ch 597n. In those cases repayments of sums paid under void contracts had been ordered. The House of Lords, without either approving or disapproving those decisions, distinguished them on the ground that they were concerned with contracts of insurance and not contracts which involved the lending and repayment of money.

Lord Parker, having referred to the decisions on ultra vires borrowing, said ([1914] AC 398 at 440, [1914–15] All ER Rep 622 at 642):

'At the same time there seems to be nothing in those decisions which would bind the House, if they were considering whether an action would lie in law or in equity to recover money paid under any ultra vires contract which was not a contract of borrowing; for example, money paid to a company or association for the purchase of land which the company had no power to sell and the sale of which was therefore void, or money paid to the company or association by way of subscription for shares which it had no power to issue. In such cases the implied promise on which the action for money had and received depends would form no part of, but would be merely collateral to, the ultra vires contract.'

Therefore *Sinclair v Brougham* on the money had and received claim is an authority which is more in favour of than adverse to the banks' claims in money had and received (although the speech of Lord Sumner does include a dictum about mistake of fact which is unhelpful to the banks).

The other part of the decision in *Sinclair v Brougham* was the decision on the claim to trace in equity. The speech which has subsequently been adopted as containing the authoritative statement of the reasoning which led to the success of this claim is that contained in the speech of Lord Parker. He recognised that the starting point must be some fiduciary relationship which sufficed to give rise to an equity but the relationship could arise simply from the circumstances in which the money was received. Further, it is implicit in his speech that once the money has been taken into a mixed fund and treated as part of the general assets of the recipient the nature of the equity becomes an equitable charge upon those assets for the repayment of the sum received.

Prima facie, the equity will continue to subsist so long as those assets continue to exist. Despite the fact that the depositors had paid the relevant sums of money to the society over varying periods and the society had meanwhile been using those sums of money in the course of its ultra vires business and had ultimately become insolvent, no problem appears to have been felt in tracing such sums through to the remaining assets. A distinction was drawn in this connection betweeen such general tracing based upon a general equitable charge and the more specific tracing which would be involved in tracing a particular payment through to a particular asset so as to give that claimant a proprietary right in respect of that specific asset which would therefore not any longer be treated as one of the general assets of the society.

Lord Parker said ([1914] AC 398 at 441–442, [1914–15] All ER Rep 622 at 642–643):

> '... it appears to be also well settled that the lender in an ultra vires loan transaction has a right to what is known as a tracing order. A company or other statutory association cannot by itself or through an agent be party to an ultra vires act. If its directors or agents affecting to act on its behalf borrow money which it has no power to borrow, the money borowed is in their hands the property of the lender. At law, therefore, the lender can recover the money, so long as he can identify it, and even if it has been employed in purchasing property, there may be cases in which, by ratifying the action of those who have so employed it, he may recover the property purchased. Equity, however, treated the matter from a different standpoint. It considered that the relationship between the directors or agents and the lender was a fiduciary relationship, and that the money in their hands was for all practical purposes trust money. Starting from a personal equity, based on the consideration that it would be unconscionable for any one who could not plead purchase for value without notice to retain an advantage derived from the misapplication of trust money, it ended, as was so often the case, in creating what were in effect rights of property, though not recognized as such by the common law.'

He identifies the nature of the right of property as being an equitable charge. In discussing *Re Guardian Permanent Benefit Building Society* (1882) 23 Ch D 440 he identified the relevant equity:

> 'The equity lay in this, that it would be unconscionable for the society to retain the amount by which its assets had been increased by, and in fact still represented, the borrowed money. It would be inequitable for the society to take advantage of the misapplication by its agents of money belonging to others and held by them in a fiduciary capacity.' (See [1914] AC 398 at 444, [1914–15] All ER Rep 622 at 644.)

In *Re Diplock's Estate* [1948] 2 All ER 318 at 357, [1948] Ch 465 at 540 the Court of Appeal summarised the equity recognised in *Sinclair v Brougham*:

> 'There, a sufficient fiduciary relationship was found to exist between the depositors and the directors by reason of the fact that the purposes for which the depositors had handed their money to the directors were by law incapable of fulfilment.'

As regards tracing, Lord Parker said ([1914] AC 398 at 448, [1914–15] All ER Rep 622 at 646):

'Here is a mass of assets arising in the course of an ultra vires business carried on by the directors and agents of the society. There are, on the one hand, liabilities, how or for what purpose incurred is not in evidence. No one claims any interest in the assets except the ultra vires lenders, the members of the society and the creditors, in respect of the liabilities to which I have referred. The ultra vires lenders and the members are willing that these liabilities and the costs of the liquidation, which are in effect costs of administering the fund, shall be first paid. If this is done, what is left may be taken to represent in part the moneys of the ultra vires lenders and in part the moneys of the society wrongfully employed in the business. The equities of the ultra vires lenders and of the society are equal, and it follows that the remainder of the assets ought to be divided between the ultra vires lenders and the society rateably, according to the capital amount contributed by such lenders and the society respectively.'

I consider that this line of reasoning bears a close analogy to the present case. The councils have to act through their officers. The officers purport to enter into contracts on behalf of the council which are in fact not contracts at all. Pursuant to those supposed contracts the officers of the council who have the day-to-day control of the council's banking accounts cause to be credited to those accounts sums paid by the banks. Those sums were paid to discharge supposed liabilities of the banks to the councils but they could not be applied for that purpose. The fiduciary relationship arose at the time of payment and affects the funds in the possession of the council. The funds having been absorbed into the general assets of the council, the equity is represented by an equitable charge upon those assets. *Sinclair v Brougham* is accordingly a direct authority in favour of the payer having an equitable right against the recipient and having a right to trace into the general assets of the recipient which is of the nature of an equitable charge upon those assets.

(e) The annuity cases

The arguments in this case have drawn attention to a line of authorities relating to the right of restitution in respect of payments made under annuity contracts which were void or voidable. They are clearly relevant to the legal issues which I have to decide in the present case in relation to the claim for money had and received. Surprisingly they seem to have escaped the notice of those who have written on the law of restitution and are only briefly noted in 9 *Halsbury's Laws* (4th edn) para 669 as an example of total failure of consideration.

In 1777 the Grants of Life Annuities Act was passed 'for registering the grants of life annuities and for the better protection of infants against such grants'. The preamble recited: 'whereas the pernicious practice of raising money by the sale of life annuities hath of late years greatly increased, and is much promoted by the secrecy with which such transactions are conducted', and the relevant substantive provision was that a memorial of any instruments creating an annuity or rentcharge should be enrolled in the High Court of Chancery within 20 days of its execution, that the memorial should contain certain particulars and that failing such enrolment 'every such deed bond instrument or other assurance shall be null and void to all intents and purposes'. There then followed eight other sections which are not presently material. The 1777 Act was repealed and the material provision re-enacted in identical terms by the Annuity Act 1813. There was an 'explanatory' Act in 1822 and the relevant provisions were repealed in 1854 by the Usury Laws Repeal Act.

Counsel have cited to me some 20 reported cases which were decided between 1787 and 1849 concerning the right to recover money which had been paid by either or both the parties under instruments which had not been registered. The consideration of these authorities is complicated by the fact that until *Davis v Bryan* (1827) 6 B & C 651, 108 ER 591 the courts appear to have treated the unregistered instruments as wholly void ab initio regardless of who was at fault in failing to procure the statutory registration complying with the requisite statutory form. *Davis v Bryan* and later cases developed an approach which, no doubt realisticallly, treated the obligation to register as being an obligation of the grantee. From this it was reasoned that the grantee could not take advantage of his own default and treat the transaction as void unless the grantor had himself disclaimed or set aside the transaction. The analysis was therefore adopted that the effect of the Act was to make the transaction voidable ab initio by the grantor and that the causes of action arising from such avoidance only accrued at the date of such avoidance; this was relevant to the question of limitation of actions (see *Cowper v Godmond* (1833) 9 Bing 748, 131 ER 795, *Churchill v Bertrand* (1842) 3 QB 568, 114 ER 625, *Huggins v Coates* (1843) 5 QB 433, 114 ER 1313 and *Molton v Camroux* (1849) 4 Exch 17, 154 ER 1107; see also *Re London Celluloid Co* (1888) 39 Ch D 190). However, it was common to all these cases that the effect of the statute and/or the avoidance of the transaction was that the whole transaction was void ab initio.

The primary importance of this line of cases is that the transactions gave rise to payments both ways, that is to say both by the grantor and the grantee. When the transaction had been determined to be void, the moneys paid either way were treated as being recoverable in an action for money had and received. This was first recognised in *Shove v Webb* (1787) 1 Term Rep 732, 99 ER 1348, where the action was for money had and received and a defence of illegality was rejected. In delivering the opinion of the court Ashurst J said (1 Term Rep 732 at 735, 99 ER 1348 at 1349):

> 'In regard to the money paid as part of the consideration; as the security is not set aside for any fraud in the transaction, but merely for a mistake or omission in form, it becomes unconscientious in the party to retain it, and is therefore recoverable on the count for money had and received to the plaintiff's use.'

After some intervening decisions which were not wholly consistent with each other but on the whole adopted the same view, the relevant principle was again clearly stated in *Hicks v Hicks* (1802) 3 East 16, 102 ER 502. It was an action for money had and received to recover back £711, the consideration money paid many years ago for an annuity granted by the defendant to the plaintiff. The annuity had been paid for more than six years but had recently been set aside by the court on the application of the defendant for a defect in the memorial of registry.

> 'The defendant pleaded a set-off of more money paid to the plaintiff's use than was due to him: and this appeared at the trial to be true, provided

the defendant was at liberty to set off all the payments which had been made to the plaintiff in respect of the annuity for more than six years past; which Lord Ellenborough held that he might, the plaintiff not having replied the Statute of Limitations.' (See 3 East 16, 102 ER 502.)

Accordingly, the defendant obtained the verdict. Erskine on behalf of the plaintiff moved to set aside the verdict, contesting the right of the defendant to set off the sums which he had paid to the plaintiff against the plaintiff's demand for the original consideration, 'which had failed'. Lord Ellenborough CJ giving judgment said (3 East 16 at 17, 102 ER 502 at 502):

> 'This was either an annuity or not an annuity. If not an annuity, the sums paid on either side were money had and received by the one party to the other's use. If the consideration of the annuity be money had and received, it must be money had and received with all its consequences; and therefore the defendant must be at liberty to set off his payments as such, on the same score.'

The courts of Chancery applied the same principles and gave equivalent remedies of account which led to a complete restitution (see *Byne v Vivian* (1800) 5 Ves 604, 31 ER 762, *Hoffman v Cooke* (1801) 5 Ves Jun 623, 31 ER 772 and *Bromley v Holland* (1802) Coop G 9, 35 ER 458).

These authorities therefore establish that the right of restitution existed in respect of payments made under void contracts even though there were payments both ways and therefore on a contractual analysis there was no 'total failure of consideration'. Also, they are not cases which depended upon any submission or finding of mistake of fact. The cause of action at common law was an action for money had and received. (This was expressly confirmed in *Cowper v Godmond* (1833) 9 Bing 748, 131 ER 795; cf 3 Moo & S 219.) The reasoning of the common law judges expressly had regard to what was conscionable and by inference reflected the analogy between the common law 'use' and the fiduciary concept recognised by equity. There was also a complete convergence of the principles applied by the common law and Chancery courts. *Hicks v Hicks* also establishes the general principle that restitution must be mutual and that the nature of the remedy is a form of mutual restitutio in integrum, that is to say, putting the parties back into their original positions. This is an earlier example of the same principle as that applied in *Newbigging v Adam* (1886) 34 Ch D 582 at 595, [1886–90] All ER Rep 975 at 984 in relation to the law of rescission, where Bowen LJ stressed that there ought to be 'a giving back and taking back on both sides'.

Sandwell relied upon *Davis v Bryan* (1827) 6 B & C 651, 108 ER 591 as showing that there should not be a right of recovery in respect of the first Sandwell swap. The first Sandwell swap differs from the other transactions with which the present actions are concerned in that it ran its full course and all the payments contemplated by it were in fact made. In *Davis v Bryan* the plaintiff was the executrix of a person who had purchased an annuity for his life from the defendant who had regularly paid the annuity up to the time of the death of the grantee. However, no memorial of the grant of the annuity had ever been enrolled. The executrix of the grantee then sued for the repayment of the sum paid by the grantee to the grantor as money had and received by the defendant to the use of the grantee. The action failed.

The judgments appear to be based on three grounds. (See also the report at 9 Dow & Ry 726.) Firstly, they applied a general principle of conformity to equity and good conscience which was implicit in the action for money had and received. It was unconscionable that a party should wait to see how the contract turned out before deciding whether or not to adopt it. 'The testator received the whole of that which he bargained for, and now his representative says that the contract was void from the beginning. Is there any thing like good conscience in the claim?' Secondly, faced with a need to distinguish *Hicks v Hicks*, they formulated the proposition that the grantee who had failed to register the transaction could not himself unilaterally avoid it; in *Hicks v Hicks* the transaction had already been avoided in earlier proceedings upon the insistence of the grantor and 'the grantee was therefore at liberty to contend for the same thing'. Thirdly, it was said that a fully executed contract could not be rescinded. (See 6 B & C 651 at 655–656, 108 ER 591 at 592.)

Of these reasons, it is for the second that *Davis v Bryan* has been treated as authority in the later cases. There is no other authority that the mere fact that the relevant contract is no longer executory is of itself a bar to the remedy of restitution unless it be the now discredited doctrine in *Seddon v North Eastern Salt Co Ltd* [1905] 1 Ch 326, [1904–7] All ER Rep 817, which turned upon a proposition that the remedy of rescission was confined to the rescission of contracts, not conveyances. In my judgment, *Davis v Bryan* does not establish any proposition of assistance to Sandwell in relation to the first Sandwell swap save that in any action for money had and received it is always necessary to have regard to considerations of equity and good conscience.

(2) *Money had and received*

(a) Total failure of consideration

The phrase 'failure of consideration' is one which in its terminology presupposes that there has been at some stage a valid contract which has been partially performed by one party. It is essentially a concept for use in the law of contract and provides a common law remedy governed by rigid rules granted as of right where the contract becomes ineffective through breach or otherwise. The rules that govern the application of the principle include the technical concept of an 'entire' consideration, what amounts in law to a total failure of consideration, and the absence of defences to the action for the recovery of money paid for a consideration which has wholly failed. In the case of ultra vires transactions such as those with which I am concerned where there is not and never has been any contract, I prefer to use the phrase 'absence of consideration'. I note that this was the phrase used by the House of Lords in the *Woolwich* case [1992] 3 All ER 737, [1993] AC 70 and has been used by other judges in the past, although it is right to say that the phrase 'failure of consideration' has very frequently been used in connection with void contracts (see e g the argument in *Fibrosa Spolka Akcyjna v Fairbairn Lawson Combe Barbour Ltd* [1943] AC 32 at 36).

Adopting for the moment the contractual approach, what amounts to a total failure of consideration was authoritatively considered by the House of Lords in the *Fibrosa* case. That case concerned a frustrated contract under which the buyer had made an advance payment of the price but had not received any goods or actual benefit in return and under which, prior to its frustration, the seller had incurred expense in starting to manufacture the goods which would, after the completion of their manufacture, have become the subject of the sale.

It was argued that the consideration for the advance payment was the promises of the seller and that they had been valid promises; it was said that the principle was confined to cases where the contract was avoided (so that the promises were avoided as well). Viscount Simon, having referred to the opinion expressed in *Chandler v Webster* [1904] 1 KB 493 that the doctrine of failure of consideration only applied to contracts which had been avoided as oppposed to frustrated, and having distinguished contracts under seal, continued ([1942] 2 All ER 122 at 129, [1943] AC 32 at 48):

> '... when one is considering the law of failure of consideration and of the quasi-contractual right to recover money on that ground, it is, generally speaking, not the promise which is referred to as the consideration, but the performance of the promise. The money was paid to secure performance and, if performance fails, the inducement which brought about the payment is not fulfilled.'

Accordingly the relevant failure of consideration for the application of this principle is the failure of performance on the part of the opposite party. If the opposite party has at least partially performed his obligations under the contract so as to confer some benefit upon the claimant, then the claimant cannot rely upon the principle. Further, it is clear from the speeches in the House of Lords and the overruling of *Chandler v Webster* that, whilst the principle was properly applied in cases where contracts had been avoided ab initio, it was not confined to such cases.

Applying the principle stated in the *Fibrosa* case, the banks cannot say that the contractual principle enables them to recover on any of the contracts save for the third and fourth Sandwell swaps. On the the third and fourth Sandwell swaps there were only payments one way and there was never any performance by Sandwell. Accordingly, in respect of those two transactions, Kleinwort Benson is entitled to say, on the basis of the contractual principle, that there has been a total failure of consideration and that they should be entitled to recover all sums paid under those two swaps at common law as money had and received. As regards the Islington swap and the second Sandwell swap, there has been partial performance by both sides and both sides have received benefits under the 'contract'. As regards the first Sandwell swap, the contemplated contract was in fact fully performed and neither party can, on the contractual approach, say that there was any failure of consideration, let alone any total failure. Therefore the contractual principle of total failure of consideration does not suffice to give any right to recover the sums paid under those contracts.

(b) Void contracts and absence of consideration

To get round the difficulty that they could not satisfy the test stated in the *Fibrosa* case, the plaintiffs advanced various arguments which all in the end amounted to the proposition that, where there has never been any contract in law, as is the case where the purported contract is ultra vires one party, any sums paid under that contract can in principle be recovered. They recognised that if ordering the repayment of sums paid amounted to indirectly enforcing the ultra vires contract, as was the case in *Sinclair v Brougham*, the prima facie right to repayment could not be recognised, but they relied in particular upon what was said by Lord Parker, which expressly recognised that where no question of indirectly enforcing an ultra vires contract was involved there might well be a right of recovery (see [1914] AC 398 at 440, [1914–15] All ER Rep 622 at 642).

They were also able to rely upon the decision of the Divisional Court in *Brougham v Dwyer* (1913) 108 LT 504. This case also involved the ultra vires banking business of the Birkbeck Building Society. The plaintiff was the liquidator of the society and the defendant was a customer of the supposed bank. It appears that the defendant had had an active current account with the society for some time and that at the date of the liquidation the account was £32 2s 2d overdrawn. The county court judge had declined to distinguish between ultra vires and illegality and had given judgment for the defendant. The Divisional Court allowed the appeal and held that the plaintiff was entitled to recover the amount of the overdraft as money had and received by the defendant to the use of the society. The distinction between ultra vires and illegality was underlined, and the basis of recovery was spelt out by Lush J (at 505):

> 'It turned out that in point of law the building society were incompetent to make such a contract, and it followed that the contract which the directors thought they were making was not a contract at all, but was simply a transaction which in point of law did not exist. The consequence was that the defendant had received moneys belonging to the building society under a transaction which had no validity of any sort or kind. If the matter stood there, I should have thought it plain that there being no contract an action for money had and received would lie. The case appears to me to be on all fours with one in which money has been advanced on something which was thought to be a contract, but as to which it turns out there has been a total failure of consideration ... the action was main-tainable, and the defendant had no answer to it. It was an action brought for money lent under a transaction which was thought to be valid but which was in fact not valid. On principle I can see no possible reason why such an action should not be maintainable, and the Court of Appeal in *Re Coltman* ((1881) 19 Ch D 64) clearly decided that in a case such as the present assuming the contract not to be illegal, there would be no answer to the action.'

What Lush J says must of course be read subject to what was said by the House of Lords in *Sinclair v Brougham*, but it confirms the basic proposition that in the absence of some special factor money paid under an ultra vires contract can be recovered as money had and received in the same manner as can money paid for a consideration that has totally failed. This is so even though no question of mistake of fact arises and there were mutual dealings under the supposed contract which would preclude the application of what I have chosen to characterise as the ordinary contractual principle.

The same conclusions are also powerfully supported by the annuity cases and, in particular, *Hicks v Hicks*.

The two cases referred to in the speeches in *Sinclair v Brougham*, that is to say *Re Phoenix Life Assurance Co, Hoare's Case* (1862) 2 John & H 229, 70 ER 1041 and *Flood v Irish Provident Assurance Co Ltd* [1912] 2 Ch 597n, were concerned with purported insurance contracts which were entered into ultra vires the powers of the relevant insurance company. In the *Phoenix Life Assurance* case the claimants were allowed to prove in the liquidation for the premiums that they had paid on the basis that they would have been recoverable at law as money had and received. *Flood's* case was similar save that the insurance company was not in liquidation. The premiums paid on the void policies were held to be recoverable as being money paid without consideration. The *Phoenix Life Assurance* case was cited and treated as having been decided upon the same basis. These cases are accordingly consistent with both sides' submissions. The language used assists the banks; the facts show that the application of the *Fibrosa* test would have led to the same conclusion.

The banks also relied upon the decision of Cairns J in *North Central Wagon Finance Co Ltd v Brailsford* [1962] 1 All ER 502, [1962] 1 WLR 1288. The facts were somewhat complicated. In summary they were that in 1955 the defendant, Brailsford, entered into what purported to be a hire-purchase contract with the plaintiffs in respect of an Albion lorry which was in fact already owned by the defendant. Under that agreement the plaintiffs advanced £1,000, which was used by the defendant to purchase a second lorry. Matters then proceeded for some two and a half years on the basis of the supposed hire-purchase agreement and variations of it. Substantial payments were made by or on behalf of the defendant to the plaintiffs. However, by the beginning of 1958 there was still money apparently owing by the defendant to the plaintiffs. The plaintiffs sued for the money outstanding under the supposed hire-purchase agreement. The defendant objected that it was in truth an unregistered bill of sale and therefore void. The court upheld that contention and it followed that the claim on the supposed contract could not succeed. However, an alternative claim for the repayment of the £1,000 as money had and received by the defendant to the use of the plaintiffs was allowed. Cairns J dealt with the point very shortly. He said ([1962] 1 All ER 502 at 507, [1962] 1 WLR 1288 at 1293–1294):

> 'I now turn to the plaintiffs' alternative claim for money had and received. In *Davies* v. *Rees* ((1886) 17 QBD 408), it was held that a bill of sale which is void for want of form is void for all purposes, but nevertheless it was held at first instance, and not contested on appeal, that the money could be recovered by the lender with reasonable interest. In *Bradford Advance Co., Ltd.* v. *Ayers* ([1924] WN 152), BAILHACHE, J., held that the money could be recovered, not on the basis of any oral agreement leading up to the bill of sale, but as money had and received. In my view, the same considerations apply where money is advanced on a bill of sale which is void for non-registration.'

Cairns J held that the plaintiffs were entitled to recover from the defendant the sum advanced, 'less repayments and other proper credits, with interest' (see [1962] 1 All ER 502 at 509, [1962] 1 WLR 1288 at 1295). This case will not stand up to any analysis on the basis of satisfying the *Fibrosa* test. Benefits had been given and received and the approach of the court was not to deny the remedy but to take them into account in evaluating the computation of the amount of the remedy. Similarly, it is not a case which was based in any way upon any mistake of fact.

The argument of the banks was formulated in a number of ways. The simplest was that contained in the skeleton argument of Mr Southwell QC for Kleinwort Benson: 'Payments made under a void contract do not amount to consideration for the purposes of the law of restitution.' In support of that proposition he cites two Gaming Act cases, which in my judgment do not assist since payments for honour are in law gifts (see the *Lipkin Gorman* case), and

Brailsford's case and *Hicks v Hicks,* which are clear authorities in favour of the proposition. The argument developed by Mr Sumption QC was that it is necessary to ask whether the payer got the benefit for which he bargained. 'What the bank bargained for was payments which would discharge a legal obligation and which the bank was entitled lawfully to receive. What it obtained were payments made under a void agreement which Islington was prima facie entitled to recover back.'

In support of that submission Mr Sumption relied primarily upon two cases. The first, *Rowland v Divall* [1923] 2 KB 500, [1923] All ER Rep 270, in which the purchaser of a motor car was suing the seller for the return of the price on the basis that, although the motor car had been delivered to the buyer and in fact on-sold by him, the seller had never passed a good title in the car to him. The price was held to be recoverable as money paid for a consideration that had wholly failed and the benefit which he had had through having the possession of the motor car for a period of time was disregarded. I do not find that case of assistance. It has to be contrasted with the decision of the Privy Council in *Linz v Electric Wire Co of Palestine Ltd* [1948] 1 All ER 604, [1948] AC 371, where a similar claim failed on the ground that there was not a total failure of consideration. In *Linz's* case what the plaintiff had paid for was a number of preference shares which had been invalidly issued. Such decisions depend upon an analysis of whether the defendant's breach was fundamental to the particular contractual transaction and, by necessary implication, whether the plaintiff was in the circumstances precluded from treating the contract as rescinded. In *Linz's* case it was held that 'she got exactly that which she bargained to get' (see [1948] 1 All ER 604 at 606, [1948] AC 371 at 377). In *Rowland v Divall* it was considered that the buyer did not get what he bargained for. This is very different from the present case where there was in truth no bargain at all and problems of deciding what was the essential part of the bargain do not arise and there can be no question whether the plaintiff's conduct has affected his right to treat the contract as rescinded.

The second case relied upon by Mr Sumption was more helpful and, indeed, was illustrative of a principle recognised in a number of other cases. The case was *Rover International Ltd v Cannon Film Sales Ltd (No 3)* [1989] 3 All ER 423, [1989] 1 WLR 912, which concerned a supposed contract which was void because at the time it was entered into one of the purported parties had not yet been incorporated. Surprisingly, it appears that neither of the parties was aware of this fatal flaw in their relationship and over a period of time mutually conducted themselves on the basis that the contract existed. Rover had paid five instalments totalling over $US300,000. Cannon provided films to Rover which Rover proceeded to dub with a view to taking advantage of the contractual provision which entitled them to share in the profits of the marketing of those films. All members of the Court of Appeal held that Rover were entitled to recover the sums that they had paid on the ground that they had been paid under a mistake of fact. They also held that Rover was entitled to recover a quantum meruit in respect of the work which it had done on the films. Kerr LJ, with whom Nicholls LJ agreed, also held that Rover had a right to recover the money paid on the ground of total failure of consideration. Kerr LJ referred to the *Fibrosa* case and *Rowland v Divall* and to a similar case where a party letting a car under a hire-purchase agreement had had no title to the car (see [1989] 3 All ER 423 at 433, [1989] 1 WLR 912 at 924). Kerr LJ said that the case before him was a fortiori to those cases: '... delivery and possession [of the films] were not what Rover had bargained for ... Due to the invalidity of the agreement Rover got nothing of what they had bargained for, and there was clearly a total failure of consideration' (see [1989] 3 All ER 423 at 434, [1989] 1 WLR 912 at 925). He continued:

> 'This equally disposes of counsel for the respondents' ingenious attempt to convert his concession of a quantum meruit, in particular the element of reasonable remuneration, into consideration in any relevant sense. Rover did not bargain for a quantum meruit, but for the benefits which might flow from cl 6 of the schedule. That is the short answer to this point.'

This case illustrates that for the purposes of the law of failure of consideration it is contractual performance that must be looked at and that collateral benefits received do not deprive the payer of his remedy. Similarly, compensation by way of quantum meruit or under some form of quasi contract is not a relevant benefit at all. It does not arise under the relevant contract. It is awarded by the court independently, on the basis that there is no effective contract and has been no contractual compensation. However, again, the analysis of Kerr LJ is essentially contractual.

In my judgment, the correct analysis is that any payments made under a contract which is void ab initio, in the way that an ultra vires contract is void, are not contractual payments at all. They are payments in which the legal property in the money passes to the recipient, but in equity the property in the money remains with the payer. The recipient holds the money as a fiduciary for the payer and is bound to recognise his equity and repay the money to him. This relationship and the consequent obligation have been recognised both by courts applying the common law and by Chancery courts. The principle is the same in both cases: it is unconscionable that the recipient should retain the money. Neither mistake nor the contractual principle of total failure of consideration are the basis for the right of recovery.

Where payments both ways have been made the correct view is to treat the later payment as, pro tanto, a repayment of the earlier sum paid by the other party. The character of the remedy, both in law and equity, is restitution, that is to say putting the parties back into the position in which they were before. Accordingly, the remedy is only available to a party on the basis that he gives credit for any benefit which he has received. He must give credit for any payments which have been made by the opposite party to him and, where the court thinks appropriate, pay a quantum meruit or quantum valebat. The same conclusion follows from the application of the principle of unjust enrichment: in so far as the recipient has made cross-payments to the payer, the recipient has ceased to be enriched.

This formulation is explicitly the basis of the decisions in the annuity cases and the decision of the Divisional Court in *Brougham v Dwyer* (1913) 108 LT 504. It is implicit in the decision in *Brailsford's* case [1962] 1 All ER 502, [1962] 1 WLR 1288. It is also fully consistent with the many judicial statements of the general principle which underlies the law of restitution and unjust enrichment which are typified by the statement, already quoted, of Lord Wright in the *Fibrosa* case [1942] 2 All ER 122 at 135, [1943] AC 32 at 61.

The application of the principle is subject to the requirement that the courts should not grant a remedy which amounts to the direct or indirect enforcement of a contract which the law requires to be treated as ineffective.

Since the obligation which law and equity require the conscience of the
receiver to recognise is in effect an obligation to repay money, it is hard to
think of any situation where this qualification will be relevant save where the
void contract was one which purported to create a debtor and creditor
relationship, as was the case in *Sinclair v Brougham*. Since *Sinclair v Brougham*
was decided on the basis of applying this qualification, it is a decision which
tends to confirm the formulation. The existence of the qualification and its
relevance in *Sinclair v Brougham* was repeated by Lord Sumner in *R Leslie Ltd v
Sheill* [1914] 3 KB 607 at 613, [1914–15] All ER Rep 511 at 515.

The right to recover payments is also subject to any available defences.
Generally speaking, those are any defences which affect the equity. This is
again either explicit or implicit in the annuity cases and, since the *Lipkin
Gorman* case, includes, as an application of that approach, the defence of
change of position.

Since the right of recovery, although based on equitable principles, has been
recognised by the common law courts and has been held to be capable of
founding an action for money had and received, it can form a proper basis for
a legally recognised right of recovery in personam in the present cases. If,
contrary to my view, there were some distinction to be drawn between the
right to restitution as recognised in law and in equity, any such distinction
should not now affect the outcome of a case where no question of insolvency
arises; the principles of both law and equity should be applied in a unified
fashion so as to provide the appropriate remedy.

This decision is sufficient to establish the prima facie right of the plaintiffs to
recover in both of the actions which are before me. It also follows from the fact
that I consider that the correct analysis is absence of consideration and not
failure of consideration that it is not open to Kleinwort Benson to assert an
absolute right of recovery on the third and fourth Sandwell swaps on the basis
of a right to recover money paid for a contractual consideration that has wholly
failed to which there are no defences; it will be open to Sandwell to seek to
raise a defence of change of position. Likewise, it follows that it is irrelevant
to the existence of a cause of action in connection with the payments made
under the first Sandwell swap that the supposed contract was in fact fully
performed and there was no failure of consideration at all in the contractual
sense.

(c) Mistake

The issue is what relevance, if any, mistake has in these cases. The plaintiffs
submit that mistake gives them an additional ground on which they may base
their claim. The defendants submit that the character of the mistake is such
that it gives them a defence to the claims, however based. The element of
mistake affecting the payment made by Westdeutsche to Islington has been the
subject of evidence. The element of mistake in the Sandwell action is at the
moment solely a matter of pleaded allegations and may hereafter have to be the
subject of evidence and findings of fact.

In the Islington case the evidence of Mr Goodwin, which I accept, is that he
made the assumption that any reputable local authority would not enter into
transactions which it was not empowered to do. He accordingly believed that
the swap contract was a proper contract for Islington to undertake and he was
confirmed in this belief by the fact that so far as he knew local authorities had
been engaging in the swaps market for a number of years as ordinary

participants in that market. Thus he reasonably assumed that in making his agreement with Islington he was, on behalf of Westdeutsche, entering into a legal contract with Islington. Mr Goodwin is a commercial man, not a lawyer. It is unrealistic to investigate or analyse his thought processes as if he were a lawyer. In reality, to say that his mistake was a mistake of fact or a mistake of law is not to make a finding of fact about what he actually thought but is to place a potentially arbitrary legal categorisation upon what he did. In a case where a representation is made it is possible objectively to construe and categorise the representation and the respects in which it was false. In some cases of mistake it may be possible to undertake the same exercise. In many cases where there has simply been an underlying assumption it is not possible. It can, however, be said that Westdeutsche has not proved that Mr Goodwin made any mistake as to any actual fact.

In the Sandwell case the allegation in the points of claim is that the 'payments were made by the plaintiff on the basis of a mistaken belief that they were being made pursuant to binding contracts between the plaintiff and the defendant'. In the points of defence, the defendant pleads:

'It is not admitted that the plaintiff was mistaken as to any material matter of fact; if, which is not admitted, the plaintiff was mistaken, then it is averred that it was mistaken as to a matter or matters of law (namely the capacity of the defendant to contract and/or the lawfulness of the agreements and each of them).'

There is no evidence or allegation in either case that the relevant bank was mistaken as to any actual fact. It is clear that the critical matter of which they were unaware was the provisions of the 1972 Act and their effect as was subsequently to be declared by the Divisional Court and the House of Lords. Lack of knowledge of a statutory provision and its legal effect is an error of law (see *Bilbie v Lumley* (1802) 2 East 469, [1775–1802] All ER Rep 425, *Sharp Bros v Chant* [1917] 1 KB 771 and *National Pari-Mutuel Association Ltd v R* (1930) 47 TLR 110). The plaintiffs accept that in this court I am bound by authority to hold that a mistake of law does not give a right to recover money at common law as money had and received. They reserve the right to challenge this position if necessary in an appellate court.

They did, however, advance two arguments by means of which they sought to submit that these cases did not apply. The first argument relied on such cases as the *Kiriri Cotton* case [1960] 1 All ER 177, [1960] AC 192, in which the character of the legislation is examined to see whether the relevant provision has been passed for the protection of a party and therefore it is to be inferred that such a party should be entitled to recover a sum which the statute provided that he should not have to pay. His ignorance of the statutory protection to which he was entitled can be relied upon as justifying his recovery of the payment from the party under a duty to comply with the statute notwithstanding that the payer's mistake would have to be characterised as a mistake of law. This line of authority, particularly as developed by certain Commonwealth decisions, adopts a similar approach to that stated by Lord Diplock in *Lonrho Ltd v Shell Petroleum Co Ltd* [1981] 2 All ER 456 at 461, [1982] AC 173 at 185 for determining whether a criminal provision in a statute should be construed so as to give an implied civil remedy. The 1972 Act is not such an Act. It was not passed for the benefit of the banks and the relevant provisions are not designed to protect persons dealing with the local

authorities. In so far as Lord Denning in the *Kiriri Cotton* case treated the
landlord as primarily responsible for the mistake and as having, as between
himself and the tenant, the duty of observing the law so as to give the tenant
the right to recover payments that he had made to the landlord, again the
principle applied in the *Kiriri Cotton* case does not apply to the position of a
local authority under the 1972 Act. The Act defines the powers of the council
and it must be part of the reponsibilities of the members and officers of the
council to observe the provisions of the Act. But it cannot be said, where a
question of capacity is involved and no question of the statutory provisions
existing for the protection of the payer of the relevant money, that any
distinction is to be drawn between the way that the statute affects the payer
and the payee.

The second argument relied upon the well-known statement of Lord
Westbury in *Cooper v Phibbs* (1867) LR 2 HL 149 at 170:

> 'The result, therefore, is, that at the time of the agreement for the lease
> which it is the object of this Petition to set aside, the parties dealt with one
> another under a mutual mistake as to their respective rights. The
> Petitioner did not suppose that he was, what in truth he was, tenant for life
> of the fishery. The other parties acted upon the impression given to them
> by their father, that he (their father) was the owner of the fishery, and that
> the fishery had descended to them. In such a state of things there can be
> no doubt of the rule of a Court of equity with regard to the dealing with
> that agreement. It is said, "*Ignorantia juris haud excusat;*" but in that maxim
> the word "*jus*" is used in the sense of denoting general law, the ordinary
> law of the country. But when the word "*jus*" is used in the sense of
> denoting a private right, that maxim has no application. Private right of
> ownership is a matter of fact; it may be the result also of matter of law; but
> if parties contract under a mutual mistake and misapprehension as to their
> relative and respective rights, the result is, that that agreement is liable to
> be set aside as having proceeded upon a common mistake.'

Similarly, in *Earl Beauchamp v Winn* (1873) LR 6 HL 223 at 233 Lord Chelms-
ford said:

> 'The cases in which Equity interferes to set aside contracts are those in
> which either there has been mutual mistake or ignorance in both parties
> affecting the essence of the contracts, or a fact is known to one party and
> unknown to the other, and there is some fraud or surprise upon the
> ignorant party.'

The same type of point can be illustrated from the language used by Dillon LJ,
but not by the facts of the case, in *Rover International Ltd v Cannon Film Sales Ltd*
(*No 3*) [1989] 3 All ER 423 at 440, [1989] 1 WLR 912 at 933:

> 'On the facts this is, in my judgment, a classic case of money paid under
> a mistake of fact. The instalments were paid because Rover mistakenly
> believed, as did Cannon, that there was a contract between them, and in
> order to satisfy Rover's obligations under that contract.'

There can be no doubt that it would be hard to think of a more fundamental
mistake than that evidenced by the present case. The parties believed there
was a contract when in truth there was no contractual relationship between
them at all. It is the type of mistake that negatives intention. It satisfies the

formulation of Sir John Simon (in argument) in *Bell v Lever Bros Ltd* [1932] AC 161 at 166:

> '[When] the parties contract upon a contractual assumption which is false and which on the facts is found to lie at the very root of the contract. Then, if the assumption is not true, the contract is avoided.   The assumption must be contractual and fundamental.'

However, this line of argument is not open to me in the present case. Despite the obvious desirability of reformulating the law so that it recognises that the relevance of mistake is to the validity of the relevant transaction and the voluntariness of any payment purportedly made under it and the presence or absence of a need to prove some element of duress (see the *Woolwich* case and its treatment of *Twyford v Manchester Corp* [1946] 1 All ER 621, [1946] Ch 236), the present state of the law is that the broader view of mistake can only be used for the purpose of invoking equitable remedies. Accordingly, for the purposes of the common law claim to money had and received, a mistake which is not a mistake as to some actual fact does not suffice of itself to give a cause of action.

The defendants submitted that if money has been mistakenly paid by one party to another and the mistake is not a mistake of fact in the strict sense then, because the mistake must be categorised as a mistake of law, it must follow that the money cannot be recovered and that the recipient has a defence to the payer's claim for money had and received.

This argument depends upon the simple slogan: 'money paid under a mistake of law cannot be recovered.'   This is a misunderstanding of the relevant principles. A plaintiff has first of all to establish a basis of recovery. As the law at present stands, a mistake of law does not provide a ground for recovery on the basis of money had and received.   But if a plaintiff does establish a prima facie right of recovery on some ground other than mistake, then the relevant question becomes whether or not the payment was 'voluntary' or made to 'close the transaction'. It may be that the payer, in making a voluntary payment or a payment to close a transaction, has taken a mistaken view of the law, but that is not the reason why he cannot recover the payment. The essence of mistake of law is that it does not provide a basis of recovery: it is not that, without more, it provides a defence to a claim for money had and received.

That this is the law has recently been reconfirmed by the House of Lords in the *Woolwich* case [1992] 3 All ER 737, [1993] AC 70. That case did not involve any question of mistake but in the Court of Appeal differing views as to the relevance of mistake of law had been expressed. Ralph Gibson LJ had said that although mistake of law does not give any right of recovery it likewise does not of itself bar recovery if a right of recovery exists independently of the mistake, whereas Glidewell and Butler-Sloss LJJ appeared to have preferred the view that a mistake of law precludes any recovery (see [1991] 4 All ER 577 at 626, 602, 636, [1993] AC 70 at 129, 101, 140). In the House of Lords Lord Goff said ([1992] 3 All ER 737 at 764, [1993] AC 70 at 177): '... I do not consider that the principle of recovery should be inapplicable simply because the citizen has paid the money under a mistake of law.'

Lord Slynn said, commenting upon the judgments of Glidewell and Butler Sloss LJJ ([1992] 3 All ER 737 at 787, [1993] AC 70 at 205):

'I do not, however, agree that this principle cannot apply where there is a mistake of law. That is the situation where the relief is most likely to be needed and if it is excluded not much is left.'

Accordingly, the submission of the defendants before me that the mistake which was made in the present cases, being a mistake which has to be characterised as a mistake of law, bars the plaintiffs' right to recover in money had and received must be rejected.

(d) Voluntary assumption of risk

If the facts were that these payments had been made with a conscious appreciation that the contracts were or might be void, that would normally suffice to negative any right of recovery. They would be voluntary payments. But, unless there was such an actual conscious appreciation, the principle cannot be applied. It does not suffice that a fully informed investigation of the legal position leading to the correct conclusions in law would have disclosed that the councils did not have the capacity to enter into the contracts. A situation has to be disclosed which is tantamount to a willingness to make a gift of the money to the recipient.

On the evidence in the Islington case there clearly was no voluntary assumption of risk in any relevant respect and in the Sandwell case it does not appear that the points of defence show any basis for a different conclusion. However, in the Sandwell case the court has not yet been concerned with any question of fact.

(e) Money used to discharge liabilities

The submission of the plaintiffs is that where a recipient of money uses the money to discharge or reduce liabilities of the recipient to others, then the payer is entitled to be reimbursed by the recipient. This argument has obvious attractions and satisfies a general concept of unjust enrichment. The recipient has had the benefit of the money. If he had not had the plaintiff's money he would have had to pay his creditor. Let him now therefore pay the plaintiff instead.

Any plaintiff who is going to advance this argument must establish the necessary factual basis by evidence (see Re National Permanent Benefit Building Society, ex p Williamson (1869) LR 5 Ch App 309 and Blackburn and District Benefit Building Society v Cunliffe Brooks & Co (1882) 22 Ch D 61). This, Westdeutsche has not succeeded in doing. It accepts that the burden of proof is upon it. On the evidence in the Islington case, Islington has a wide range of classes of expenditure. Some do represent pre-existing debts; others represent discretionary expenditure. It was not possible on the evidence to say what the actual money which Islington received from Westdeutsche was actually spent on. As a matter of accounting, because it was credited to the interest account of the consolidated loans fund, it could therefore have been said to have been applied to the payment of interest charges, or the repayment of principal, on some part of the borrowings of the council. But this is merely an accounting exercise and does not correspond to what may actually have happened to the relevant money. No specific indebtedness can be identified. It is not possible to make a finding of fact that any identified indebtedness of the council was in fact discharged or reduced by the application of the money which Islington received from Westdeutsche. Therefore the basis of claim fails upon the facts.

In the Sandwell case the plaintiff's pleadings are similarly unspecific and there is at present no indication that Kleinwort Benson will be able to discharge any burden of proof that lies upon it. However, in any event, it appears to me that this line of argument is mistaken. It reflects a principle which has been adopted in cases concerning borrowings where it may provide a basis for recovery in respect of ultra vires loans, usually cases where the defendant's borrowing powers are said to have been exceeded. In cases where the claim depends upon tracing, it forms a part of the tracing remedy. In other cases where the defendant might otherwise have a defence to the claim, the principle may negative that defence. For example, it may show that what would otherwise appear to be an excess of the defendant's borrowing powers did not in fact increase the indebtedness of the defendant; or it might negative a defence of change of position.

The most striking example of the application of the principle as a defence lies in a wholly different field where the cause of action relied upon was nevertheless still debt. In *B Liggett (Liverpool) Ltd v Barclays Bank Ltd* [1928] 1 KB 48, [1927] All ER Rep 451 the plaintiff was a customer of the bank and was suing for the credit balance in his current account. The bank had debited to that account a cheque which had not been properly drawn in accordance with the mandate. However, the cheques had been drawn in favour of creditors of the plaintiff and their payment discharged liabilities of the plaintiff to those creditors. Normally the bank, not having complied with the mandate, would have had no defence to the customer's claim. However, Wright J allowed the bank to raise an equitable defence and be given the benefit of the claims of the creditors against the plaintiff. An inquiry was ordered.

The cases in which the principle gives an independent right of recovery are the cases involving ultra vires or unauthorised borrowing. The effect of these cases was summarised by Lord Parker in *Sinclair v Brougham* [1914] AC 398 at 440–441, [1914–15] All ER Rep 622 at 642. He referred to *Re National Permanent Benefit Building Society, ex p Williamson*, *Blackburn and District Benefit Building Society v Cunliffe Brooks & Co*, *Baroness Wenlock v River Dee Co* (1887) 19 QBD 155 and *Re Wrexham Mold and Connah's Quay Rly Co* [1899] 1 Ch 440 and said:

'Accepting the principle that no action or suit lies at law or in equity to recover money lent to a company or association which has no power to borrow, the question remains whether the lender has any other remedies. On this point the result of the authorities may be stated as follows: First, it appears to be well settled that if the borrowed money be applied in paying off legitimate indebtedness of the company or association (whether the indebtedness be incurred before or after the money was borrowed), the lenders are entitled to rank as creditors of the company or association to the extent to which the money has been so applied. There appears to be some doubt as to whether this result is arrived at by treating the contract of loan as validated to the extent to which the borrowed money is so applied, on the ground that to this extent there is no increase in the indebtedness of the company or association, in which case, if the contract of loan involves a security for the money borrowed, the security would be validated to a like extent; or whether the better view is that the lenders are subrogated to the rights of the legitimate creditors who have been paid off … It is still open to your Lordships' House to adopt either view, should the question actually come up for determination.'

The principle so stated does not assist in the present cases. Its relevance, if any, is as an aid to the plaintiffs' argument on equitable tracing.

(f) Conclusion upon the claims for money had and received

Subject to the defences of change of position and, in respect of the first Sandwell swap, the defence of limitation of actions and to any other defences which may exist in the Sandwell action with which I am not presently concerned, the plaintiffs are entitled to recover from the defendants the net sums claimed in money had and received. The essential basis upon which they are entitled to recover is that the sums were paid without consideration under contracts which were ultra vires the defendants and were void ab initio. The fact that the first Sandwell swap 'contract' was fully performed does not make any difference. The payments made had exactly the same status as the other payments the subject matter of these actions. The lapse of time between the making of the payments under the first Sandwell swap and the issue of the writ and the trial are of course relevant to any question of limitation of actions and may be relevant to any question of change of position or other equitable defence. It does not, however, show that there was not a cause of action in money had and received. On the second Sandwell swap the council can assert a claim for money had and received in the same way as the bank can on the other swaps. On the third and fourth Sandwell swaps the bank would be able to formulate a claim for money had and received based upon total failure of consideration but I do not consider that that is the correct basis of that claim: the correct basis, as for the other swaps, is absence of consideration and it is potentially open to the same defences as the claims on the other swaps.

(3) *Equitable tracing*

(a) Constituents

The constituents of the right to trace in equity and the equitable remedy are firstly the identification of some fiduciary relationship between the plaintiff and the recipient of the money and secondly the ability to trace the payment into the assets of the recipient (or his representative) as they exist at the time of trial.

(b) The fiduciary relationship

There is no objection to the existence of a fiduciary relationship that the common law should recognise a right to recover the relevant payments as money had and received (see *Chase Manhattan Bank NA v Israel-British Bank (London) Ltd* [1979] 3 All ER 1025, [1981] Ch 105). Equity will follow the law: indeed, equity will provide remedies where the common law remedies are inadequate. The existence of concurrent remedies at common law and in equity has been recognised in the annuity cases. The ability of equity to provide a remedy where the common law cannot is illustrated by *Sinclair v Brougham* itself.

Miss Appleby relied upon *Stocks v Wilson* [1913] 2 KB 235 for the submission that in a case such as the present, notwithstanding *Sinclair v Brougham*, the equitable remedy ought not to be allowed. It was a case of a sale of goods which were not necessaries to an infant who had fraudulently misrepresented his age. The judgment of Lush J supports the case of the plaintiffs. He said (at 242–243):

'What the Court of Equity has done in cases of this kind is to prevent the infant from retaining the benefit of what he has obtained by reason of his fraud. It has done no more than this, and this is a very different thing from making him liable to pay damages or compensation for the loss of the other party's bargain. If the infant has obtained property by fraud he can be compelled to restore it; if he has obtained money he can be compelled to refund it.'

The equity and the equitable remedy can subsist with a void transaction and there is a distinction between the grant of the remedy and the enforcement of a contract.

Under the heading 'Mistake', on the basis of the authorities that are presently binding upon me, I have felt unable to treat the mistake that was made in the present cases as being of a character which of itself gives a right to recover the money as money had and received. However, it is clear that the character of the mistake is one which will be regarded as fundamental in equity and thus capable of giving rise to equitable remedies. This is implicit in *Sinclair v Brougham*. It is also covered by formulations such as that to be found in *Cooper v Phibbs*. The parties thought that they were in contractual relations, whereas no contract ever existed between them or was capable of existing. There is no reason in principle why the consequences of such a mistake should not be the subject of equitable relief (see also *Solle v Butcher* [1949] 2 All ER 1107, [1950] 1 KB 671). It is not necessary for the banks to put forward a case of mistake as the basis for their right to trace in equity; but, if it were, the mistake made would be capable of founding a claim for equitable relief as was the mistake made in the *Chase Manhattan* case. In equity it is not necessary that the mistake should be a mistake as to any actual fact.

However, the present case is indistinguishable from *Sinclair v Brougham*. The fiduciary relationship comes into existence and the equity is created at the time that the payee receives the money. Thereafter the question becomes one of ability to trace and of the continued existence of the equity. The equity may be lost or become qualified by change of circumstances or the intervention of third parties or third party interests or by the lapse of time. Further payments between the same parties in respect of the same transaction clearly affect the equity, just as, in my judgment, they affect the claim for money had and received. In the present cases, where there have been cross-payments in respect of the same swap, reverse payments pro tanto reduce or reverse the pre-existing equity. Since the payments were made pursuant to the same void transaction, they fall to be looked at together and there is no equity in respect of one payment independent of the equity in respect of the others.

The equities relied upon in the present cases do not depend upon knowledge or notice. However, once the holder of the relevant money becomes aware of the equity in favour of the payer of that money, he may become affected by more specific equities of the character of a constructive trust. Nothing in the present cases turns upon such a point but it may not be irrelevant to the consideration of a defence of change of position. The knowledge of the voidness of the relevant transactions existed from at the latest the decision of the Divisional Court.

In the present cases therefore, the plaintiffs and, where relevant, the defendants can establish the fiduciary relationship and the equity which as at the time of the making of the payments gave rise to the right to the equitable remedy of tracing.

(c) Tracing

The question here is the ability to trace. As a matter of principle this question arises in both the Islington and the Sandwell actions. But I have only received evidence in the Islington action. Therefore all that I say in relation to the Sandwell action will be subject to any evidence that may be adduced, and any admissions that may be made, in that action.

Once the equity has been held to exist the burden of proof is upon the holder of the fund to prove what has happened to it. Miss Appleby originally accepted the proposition that: 'the primary rule is that a beneficiary can claim the whole of the mixed fund, save that which the fiduciary can identify as his own; the effect of this is that the onus of distinguishing the assets is on the fiduciary.' She accepted that this was the effect of *Madras Official Assignee v Krishnaji Bhat* (1933) 49 TLR 432 and *Re Tilley's Will Trusts, Burgin v Croad* [1967] 2 All ER 303, [1967] Ch 432. However, she later refined that submission to tracing money in mixed accounts, as opposed to following money into and out of assets that might have been purchased by a defendant who had received the plaintiff's money. In my judgment the qualification is inappropriate. The principle derives from the intermixture of moneys which are considered to be held in a fiduciary capacity with those that are not subject to any equity. If the relevant fiduciary wishes to say that he does not still hold the relevant moneys or that he does not hold any asset which could represent the relevant moneys (*Re Oatway, Hertslet v Oatway* [1903] 2 Ch 356) or that he does not hold further moneys which represent the proceeds of the sale of that asset, he must discharge that burden of proof. Where no question of insolvency arises and where the claimant is simply asking that the fiduciary account for the money that he has received, the fiduciary cannot, by failing to account, escape liability. *Sinclair v Brougham*, *Re Tilley* and the *Chase Manhattan Bank* case each illustrate the grant to a plaintiff of a general tracing remedy of the nature of an equitable charge upon the defendant's assets (and in contrast to the right to trace into a specific asset), notwithstanding the inability to trace individual specific sums through the accounts of the defendant (or the recipient) down to the date of trial. The position may be different where the claimant is seeking to share in the increased value of assets which the fiduciary has acquired (as was the actual case in *Re Tilley's Will Trusts*) or, where there are competing claims on an inadequate fund, the claimant is having to assert his right to a prior claim on that fund, or is asserting his right to have some equitable proprietary right over some individual asset. In such cases the claimant may have to discharge some burden of proof. But in the simpler class of case, such as that with which I am concerned, the position is as summarised by Stuart V-C in *Cook v Addison* (1869) LR 7 Eq 466 at 470, as quoted by Ungoed-Thomas J in *Re Tilley's Will Trusts* [1967] 2 All ER 303 at 306, [1967] Ch 1179 at 1183:

'It is a well-established doctrine in this court, that if a trustee or agent mixes and confuses the property which he holds in a fiduciary character with his own property, so that they cannot be separated with perfect accuracy, he is liable for the whole.'

Ungoed-Thomas J adds:

'If a trustee mixes trust assets with his own, the onus is on the trustee to distinguish the separate assets and, to the extent that he fails to do so, they belong to the trust.'

It was also the effect of the judgment of Ungoed-Thomas J that the order in which sums were drawn out of or paid into an account was irrelevant to tracing in equity.

Miss Appleby submitted that on the facts of the Islington case the right to trace had been lost. She relied upon *James Roscoe (Bolton) Ltd v Winder* [1915] 1 Ch 62 and *Barlow Clowes International Ltd (in liq) v Vaughan* [1992] 4 All ER 22. If a fund can be shown to have been exhausted, then the right to continue to trace within that fund stops. Thus if a bank account goes into overdraft, later payments into that bank account do not recreate a right to trace within that account. (Mr Sumption did not seek to support the statement to the contrary in *Snell on Equity* (29th edn, 1991) p 301, which is perhaps to be treated as an example confined to express trusts or as illustrating a right of a beneficiary to be subrogated to the rights of the discharged creditor—I do not have to consider this.)

Islington ran a number of bank accounts at a branch of the Co-operative Bank plc. These various accounts were a matter of convenience and the Co-operative Bank had a right to combine them and to set off debits in one account against credits in another. The evidence was that the £2·5m paid by Westdeutsche to Islington on 18 June 1987 was credited to a general account for income, No 61090101, and that on a number of subsequent occasions that account has been overdrawn. It was also the evidence that at times the aggregate of the accounts of Islington with the Co-operative Bank have been overdrawn. Indeed it was the evidence that this was the position overnight on several dates in June and July 1987 after the £2·5m sum had been received and there was specific evidence of an overall debit balance on 16 November 1987. Accordingly, if one was merely to look at the bank accounts, Islington would be able to say that the bank accounts had been exhausted at various times and that accordingly the right to trace within those accounts was lost.

However, that is not the end of the matter because the beneficiary is entitled to ask what has been done with the sums taken out of those accounts. If they have been used to acquire an asset he is entitled to a charge upon that asset. If that asset should subsequently be sold and the proceeds of sale repaid into one of the fiduciary's bank accounts, the beneficiary is entitled to follow those proceeds of sale. Such a situation is illustrated by the facts of the present case. On occasions when the accounts only contained small credits or were in overdraft, Islington had in fact lent money out on the market on a short-term basis (presumably at an advantageous rate of interest). On this scenario, what was happening was that the credits in the account (which were debts owing by the bank to Islington) were converted into debts owing to Islington by persons dealing on the money market and on the repayment of those debts they were converted back again into debts owing by the Co-operative Bank to Islington, and the rights of Westdeutsche will certainly not have been lost. The mere fact that a given bank account or group of bank accounts may not be in credit does not mean that the right of a beneficiary to trace through the assets of a fiduciary has been lost. If the fiduciary wants to say that the relevant moneys must have been dissipated, he must prove that that is the only possible conclusion on the evidence.

Islington has not attempted to undertake the exercise of proving the impossibility of tracing the sum it received from Westdeutsche through its overall assets. There is good reason for this. It would almost certainly be an impossible and fruitless exercise. There would always be assets, the property of Islington, which could be said to be capable of representing the original £2·5m. Miss Appleby has objected that this conclusion produces a result in the present case which is little different from the recognition of a personal remedy against Islington. In a case where there are no competing equities and no question of insolvency I find nothing surprising in this result. Indeed it is the appropriate result. The character of the equity upon which Westdeutsche relies is that in conscience Islington should repay the £2·5m to Westdeutsche out of the assets which Islington has. At no time since 1987 has Islington had insufficient assets to enable it give effect to the equity. Therefore the equity has survived. Similarly, in terms of an equitable charge, there have throughout been assets which could be the subject of the charge.

As I have previously said, during the period since 1987, Islington has undoubtedly spent substantial sums on items of discretionary expenditure. But it has not shown, nor attempted to show, that such expenditure has at any time led to a situation where Islington was without assets. It is no doubt also the case that during the relevant period Islington has expended substantial sums on discharging its lawful indebtedness to others. Before a court could come to the conclusion that the equity of Westdeutsche had been extinguished, it would in my judgment be necessary to consider whether or not the principles recognised by Lord Parker analogous to subrogation could not be relied upon by Westdeutsche. This would be a further difficulty in the way of Islington if it were seeking to prove that the equitable rights of Westdeutsche had been wholly lost, albeit that the right might become solely personal and cease to be proprietary.

Accordingly, Westdeutsche is entitled, subject to the defence of change of position, to the equitable remedy of tracing against Islington and, since Islington's assets are more than sufficient to satisfy any equitable charge upon them of £2·5m, to have an order that Islington pay that sum to Westdeutsche. In so far as it depends upon questions of law the conclusion in the Sandwell action must be the same.

(4) *Limitation of actions*

(a) Set-off and the Sandwell first swap

The argument under the Limitation Acts depends upon the premise that each cause of action in money had and received, or analogous equitable claim, must be treated as having accrued at the date when the relevant sum was paid. As appears from the table on p 907 of this judgment, three payments were made by Kleinwort Benson and three by Sandwell outside the six-year period preceding the issue of the writ. The three payments paid by Kleinwort Benson totalled £494,845·90 and the three by Sandwell totalled £396,755·14. Therefore as at six years before the issue of the writ Kleinwort Benson had paid £98,090·76 more to Sandwell than Sandwell had paid to Kleinwort Benson. By the time the first swap had run its full course in July 1988 Kleinwort Benson had paid to Sandwell £196,322·72 more than Sandwell had paid to it. For the reasons that I have given earlier in this judgment I consider that the claim of Kleinwort Benson, whether put in money had and received or in equity, is in truth only for the net sum of £196,322·72. Its claim has to give credit for the payments that it has received. As is implicit in the action for money had and received on the ground of unjust enrichment and as was expressly held in *Hicks v Hicks* (1802) 3 East 16, 102 ER 502, the claim cannot be asserted without at the same time giving credit for any payments received. As a matter of the principle of unjust enrichment, the defendant has only been enriched in the net sum and the enrichment has only been at the expense of the plaintiff in the net sum.

Following this analysis through, and looking again at the table on p 907, it can be seen that the enrichment of the parties fluctuated. After the first payment made on 17 October 1983 it was Kleinwort Benson which was enriched to the tune of £127,962·33. After the second payment on 16 January 1984, it was Sandwell that was enriched in the sum of £42,662·67. On 15 January 1985 Kleinwort Benson was the party which was enriched but by 15 April of that year it had become Sandwell. The position oscillated back and forth and it was not until 1988 that Kleinwort Benson ceased to be at any time enriched at the expense of Sandwell and the position emerged as being one where Sandwell was enriched at the expense of Kleinwort Benson. The last payment made by Sandwell, £112,191·78, paid on 15 April 1988, merely served to reduce the amount by which Sandwell had been enriched; it did not result in any enrichment of Kleinwort Benson. Accordingly, the position was analogous to that of a running account between the two parties. Only one underlying transaction was involved—the first Sandwell swap contract. The successive payments merely altered the location and extent of the enrichment which existed from time to time. The earlier payments had long since ceased to give any cause of action to either party. They were merely part of the previous dealings between the parties which were relevant to ascertaining what, if any, cause of action either party had at a later date.

Although Mr Southwell for Kleinwort Benson refused to put his case in this way, it is legitimate to test the defence of limitation of actions by asking what would have been the position if Kleinwort Benson had in its points of claim solely asserted causes of action arising from the payments made on 15 January and 15 July 1988. These two payments totalled well over £300,000 and were more than sufficient to support a claim for £196,000. No defence of limitation of actions could be or has been raised in respect of the payments made by Kleinwort Benson to Sandwell in 1988. The only basis for a defence of limitation of actions would be if the last payment made by the plaintiff had been made over six years before the issue of the writ.

An argument was developed which submitted that a way in which Sandwell could rely upon the limitation period would be to say that in calculating the equitable defences, or set-off, to be taken into account one should go back to 3 April 1985 and no further. What would be the equity in such an approach escapes me. Where there have been a whole succession of payments one way and the other in respect of a single underlying transaction, both equity and justice require that one should have regard to the totality of those payments and the resultant overall benefit and detriment and not have regard to some arbitrary cut-off point unless there is some statutory provision which requires one to do so.

The argument actually advanced on behalf of Kleinwort Benson reached a similar destination but by a more complicated route. It said its claim was for the £1·5m, being the total of all the payments that it had made to Sandwell; Sandwell pleaded limitation in respect of the first three payments and counterclaimed for all the payments that it, Sandwell, had made totalling about £1·3m; in defence to the counterclaim Kleinwort Benson is entitled to set off all its own payments including the first three: the net result is an entitlement of Kleinwort Benson to recover the net sum of about £196,000. As will be appreciated, I consider that this analysis is over-complicated and wrong in principle. At no time during the history of this transaction has there been a cause of action for more than the net balance existing at any given time.

Two points of construction of the Limitation Act 1980 have been argued. That under s 5 becomes academic in view of the analysis which I have adopted; that under s 35 is still material but is effectively concluded by what I have already said. No point arose under s 32. Both sides accept that that section can only be relevant where the cause of action relied upon is based upon mistake.

(b) Limitation Act 1980, s 5

I will take this point shortly. Section 5 provides:

> 'An action founded on simple contract shall not be brought after the expiration of six years from the date on which the cause of action accrued.'

The question is whether the words 'action founded on simple contract' are sufficiently broad to cover an action for money had and received.

The 1980 Act was a consolidating act and re-enacted a similarly worded provision in the 1939 Act. The 1939 Act had replaced earlier Acts including the Limitation Act 1623. Under s 3 of that Act one of the categories of action for which limitation periods were provided was 'all actions ... upon the case'. Actions for money had and received were actions upon the case. The 1939 Act was drafted so as to avoid references wherever possible to the old causes of action. It was partly a consolidating and partly an amending statute.

In *Re Diplock's Estate, Diplock v Wintle* [1948] 2 All ER 318 at 343, [1948] Ch 465 at 514 the 1939 Act was referred to because a defence of limitation of actions was raised. The Court of Appeal said:

> 'We assume ... that the words "actions founded on simple contract" must be taken to cover actions for money had and received, formerly actions on the case, and, as such, covered in express terms by the Limitation Act, 1623. The assumption must, we think, be made, though the words used cannot be regarded as felicitous.'

Weak though this statement is, I consider that it can only be read as the expression of an opinion that the words must be construed as including actions for money had and received. The word 'simple' is used to exclude an action upon a specialty, for which a period of 12 years was prescribed.

The alternative to the view of the Court of Appeal would have to be that the intention of the legislature in 1939 was that there should be no limitation period for any common law action based upon quasi contract. Such an omission would be clearly contrary to the general purpose of the Act; yet that is the submission of Kleinwort Benson before me. In view of what the Court of Appeal have said, the 1939 Act must be regarded as ambiguous and that in turn, under the more liberal approach to the construction of statutes adopted by the House of Lords in *Pepper (Inspector of Taxes) v Hart* [1993] 1 All ER 42, [1993] AC 593, allows the court to look at the genesis of the Act, including any clear statements in Hansard. This is a case where the relevant statutory provision can be said to be ambiguous or obscure or, potentially, to lead to absurdity. I have accordingly been referred to the reports in Hansard of the two occasions when the Bill was introduced into the House of Commons in 1938 and 1939 by the then Solicitor General, Sir Terence O'Connor. On both occasions he made it clear that the purpose of the Bill was to give effect to the recommendations in 1936 of the Law Revision Committee as set out in their Fifth Interim Report (Cmd 5334). That committee, chaired by Lord Wright, had recommended, among other things: '(1) that the period for all actions founded in tort or simple contract (including quasi-contract) ... should be six years ...' (para 37). From this it appears that the intention of the committee, of the Solicitor General (who had also been a member of the committee), and of the House of Commons was that actions in quasi contract should be subject to a six-year time limit and that the expression 'simple contract' should be understood as including quasi contracts.

Accordingly, I consider that I should follow the opinion expressed by the Court of Appeal in *Re Diplock's Estate* and that s 5 of the 1980 Act should be construed as having the same effect as the equivalent provision in the 1939 Act. It follows that if, which is not the case, Kleinwort Benson were having to rely upon causes of action in money had and received which had accrued more than six years before 3 April 1991 such causes of action would be time-barred.

It is common ground betweeen the parties that in so far as s 5 applies, then under s 36 the same limitation period should apply to any claim for equitable relief by analogy and that there remains a jurisdiction to refuse relief 'on the ground of acquiescence or otherwise'. This does not however alter the position since what Kleinwort Benson is seeking to trace in support of its equitable remedy includes sums of money which were received by Sandwell within the six-year period.

(c) The Limitation Act 1980, s 35

Section 35 provides:

> '(1) For the purposes of this Act, any new claim made in the course of any action shall be deemed to be a separate action and to have been commenced .... on the same date as the original action.
>
> (2) In this section a new claim means any claim by way of set-off or counterclaim ...'

The question is what is the meaning of the word 'set-off' in this section. Does it include equitable set-offs? Here again the relevant provision is in the material respects a re-enactment of a provision of the 1939 Act, which read:

> '**28.** For the purposes of this Act, any claim by way of set-off or counterclaim shall be deeeemed to be a separate action and to have been commenced on the same date as the action in which the set-off or counterclaim is pleaded.'

Among the previous statutory provisions repealed by the 1939 Act was s 4 of the Statute of Frauds Amendment Act 1828, which had applied the provisions of the 1623 Act to 'the Case of any Debt on Simple Contract alleged by way of Set-off on the Part of any Defendant, either by Plea or Notice or otherwise'.

Historically, therefore, the contemplation of such provisions was the legal set-off of debts under the statutory provisions which permitted such set-offs. In the language of the 1939 and 1980 Acts, the relevant provision is still expressed in the terms 'any claim' by way of set-off or counterclaim. Accordingly, as a matter of language what is contemplated is something which is, or can be expressed as, a 'claim', not something which has a mere status as a defence. As will be appreciated from what I said earlier, the principle of taking into account the net effect of payments both ways for the purpose of ascertaining what is the right of a plaintiff to a remedy of money had and received, or in equity, does not involve any claim by the opposite party: it is truly a qualification of the plaintiff's right to recover and, if it depends upon facts pleaded and proved by the defendant, the defendant has done no more than raise a defence.

It does not appear that s 28 of the 1939 Act resulted from any recommendation of the Law Reform Committee. The only reference to this topic appears to be in para 24(a) of the report:

'It should be pointed out, however, that a person cannot appropriate to the payment of a statute barred debt any money of the debtor's which he happens to find in his hands, e.g., money had and received in respect of a different transaction altogether. That would be an attempt to "set-off" the debt and so would be defeated by section 4 of the Statute of Frauds Amendment Act 1828 which provides that the Limitation Act shall apply to any debt under a simple contract alleged by way of set-off.'

Apart from again treating an action for money had and received as an action to recover a debt under a simple contract, this passage is no more than a quotation from the 1828 Act and, because it refers to money received 'under a different transaction altogether', it is clearly not intended to refer to equitable set-off. This passage is fully consistent with construing s 28 of the 1939 Act as referring to legal set-off, not equitable set-off, but it is not sufficiently clear to provide a basis for the resolution of an ambiguity.

Section 28 of the 1939 Act gave effect to the law as it had been held to be in *Walker v Clements* (1850) 15 QB 1046, 117 ER 755, a case which involved an alleged legal set-off of various cross-claims. The construction of the 1939 Act was discussed, obiter, in *Henriksens Rederi A/S v PHZ Rolimpex* [1973] 3 All ER 589, [1974] QB 233, where the Court of Appeal was concerned with an attempt to set off a claim for damages for breach of a contract of carriage of goods by sea against a claim for freight. It held that no right of set-off could exist to a claim for freight. However, they also considered what they took to be the effect of a procedural time bar (see now *Aries Tanker Corp v Total Transport Ltd* [1977] 1 All ER 398, [1977] 1 WLR 185) in relation to a defence of equitable set-off such as that typified by *Hanak v Green* [1958] 2 All ER 141, [1958] 2 QB 9. In this context Lord Denning MR expressed the view, without argument, that s 28 did not apply to a defence of equitable set-off. The two other members of the court expressly disassociated themselves from what he had said. Lord Denning MR said ([1973] 3 All ER 589 at 593, [1974] QB 233 at 245):

'In point of principle, when applying the law of limitation, a distinction must be drawn between a matter which is in the nature of a *defence* and one which is in the nature of a *cross-claim*. When a defendant is sued, he can raise any matter which is properly in the nature of a *defence*, without fear of being met by a period of limitation. No defence, properly so-called, is subject to a time-bar. But the defendant cannot raise a matter which is properly the subject of a *cross-claim*, except within the period of limitation allowed for such a claim. A cross-claim may be made in a separate action, a   or it may be made by way of set-off or counterclaim. But on principle it is always subject to a time-bar.' (Lord Denning MR's emphasis.)

He stressed the use of the word 'claim' in s 28 and continued:

b   'The word "set-off" is not defined in s 28; but I think it is used to denote a legal set-off and not an equitable set-off. That is, a legal set-off as permitted by the statutes of set-off. These apply only "where the claims on both sides are liquidated debts or money demands which can be ascertained with certainty at the time of pleading": see Bullen and Leake (*Precedents of Pleadings* (3rd edn, 1868) p 679). These cross-claims must arise out of separate transactions ... If there is no separate transaction, but only opposing demands arising out *of the same transaction*, then no

c   question of set-off, properly so called, arises.' (Lord Denning MR's emphasis.)

He referred to *Halsbury's Laws of England*, *Green v Farmer* (1768) 4 Burr 2214, 98 ER 154 and *Walker v Clements*.

d   At the conclusion of his judgment Cairns LJ referred to what Lord Denning MR had said and observed ([1973] 3 All ER 589 at 601, [1974] QB 233 at 254):

'No argument to this effect was presented at the Bar and I am not to be taken to accede to this interpretation of the statute. But it does not affect the result of this appeal.'

e   Roskill LJ associated himself with what Cairns LJ had said (see [1973] 3 All ER 589 at 609, [1974] QB 233 at 264).

In the textbooks the view expressed by Lord Denning MR is generally accepted. Having heard the argument in the present case, I also consider it to be correct. I reach this conclusion both as a matter of the construction of the

f   actual wording of the statute and as a matter of principle where the set-off raised is truly a matter of defence, as explained in the *Aries Tanker* case. If a plaintiff, in equity, is not entitled to assert his cause of action without at the same time giving credit to the defendant for the relevant matters, no question of any claim being made by a defendant against the plaintiff arises and the sole question is what is the proper claim that the plaintiff should make against the

g   defendant. In the present case, as I have held, Sandwell has no claim in respect of the first swap against Kleinwort Benson so on any view s 35 of the 1980 Act cannot have any application.

But even if there were something capable of founding a cross-claim, it would still be necessary to consider whether it could be raised as an equitable defence

h   and whether the plaintiff was bound in conscience and in equity to take that matter into account before enforcing his own claim. The relevant provision of the 1980 Act then becomes s 36 and in particular s 36(2). If the lapse of time between the matter which constitutes the basis of the equitable set-off and either the accrual of the plaintiff's cause of action or the commencement of the

j   action is such that the grant of an equitable set-off no longer conforms to equity, then the relief can and should be refused. Given a true case of equitable set-off in the first place, it is very unlikely that any narrow margin between a period of six years under the 1980 Act as applied to a defendant's defence and as applied to the plaintiff's cause of action will give rise to any qualification of the defendant's right to equitable relief. But if there should be any such case it falls to be dealt with under s 36, not s 35.

Accordingly, the 1980 Act does not provide Sandwell with any defence to the *a* plaintiff's claim in respect of the payments made under the first swap. The lapse of time may of course be relevant to the defence of change of position, but that is a quite separate defence from any which is raised under the 1980 Act.

(5) *Change of position*

(a) The principle *b*

Lipkin Gorman (a firm) v Karpnale Ltd [1992] 4 All ER 512, [1991] 2 AC 548 was the first case in which the courts of this country expressly recognised that the defence of change of position was available to a claim which was based upon restitution, or unjust enrichment. In that case a partner, called Cass, with a firm of solicitors (the plaintiffs) had stolen money and gambled it away at the *c* defendants' gaming club. The solicitors sued the defendants to recover the money. The House of Lords allowed the solicitors to recover the money subject to giving credit for the net winnings which had been paid to and retained by Cass. It was in this context—whether credit should be given for the winnings repaid to Cass—that the defence of change of position was considered and upheld, pro tanto. All members of the House of Lords indorsed *d* the existence of the defence in principle. They declined to define it in terms which would prevent its free development on a case by case basis by courts which subsequently had to make decisions with regard to the defence.

Lord Goff posed the question:

e

> 'In these circumstances, it is right that we should ask ourselves: why do we feel that it would be unjust to allow restitution in cases such as these? The answer must be that, where an innocent defendant's position is so changed that he will suffer an injustice if called upon to repay or to repay in full, the injustice of requiring him so to repay outweighs the injustice of denying the plaintiff restitution. If the plaintiff pays money to the *f* defendant under a mistake of fact, and the defendant then, acting in good faith, pays the money or part of it to charity, it is unjust to require the defendant to make restitution to the extent that he has so changed his position. Likewise, on facts such as those in the present case, if a thief steals my money and pays it to a third party who gives it away to charity, *g* that third party should have a good defence to an action for money had and received. In other words, bona fide change of position should of itself be a good defence in such cases as these.' (See [1992] 4 All ER 512 at 533, [1991] 2 AC 548 at 579.)

He observed: *h*

> 'I am most anxious that, in recognising this defence to actions of restitution, nothing should be said at this stage to inhibit the development of the defence on a case by case basis, in the usual way. It is, of course, plain that the defence is not open to one who has changed his position in *j* bad faith, as where the defendant has paid away the money with knowledge of the facts entitling the plaintiff to restitution ...' (See [1992] 4 All ER 512 at 534, [1991] 2 AC 548 at 580.)

In such a situation, considerations of constructive trust would no doubt also be relevant. Lord Goff then proceeded to state a general principle:

a
'At present I do not wish to state the principle any less broadly than this: that the defence is available to a person whose position has so changed that it would be inequitable in all the circumstances to require him to make restitution, or alternatively to make restitution in full. I wish to stress, however, that the mere fact that the defendant has spent the money, in whole or in part, does not of itself render it inequitable that he

b
should be called upon to repay, because the expenditure might in any event have been incurred by him in the ordinary course of things. I fear that the mistaken assumption that mere expenditure of money may be regarded as amounting to a change of position for present purposes has led in the past to opposition by some to recognition of a defence which in fact is likely to be available only on comparatively rare occasions.' (See [1992]

c
4 All ER 512 at 534, [1991] 2 AC 548 at 580.)

He also pointed out that the recognition of the existence of the defence should also permit the courts to 'develop a more consistent approach to tracing claims, in which common defences are recognised as available to such claims, whether advanced at law or in equity'. (See [1992] 4 All ER 512 at 534, [1991] 2

d
AC 548 at 581.)

    The defence of change of position is thus in essence a recognition that the cause of action in restitution or unjust enrichment, whether expressed in common law or equitable terms, is based upon equitable principles and that it is essential that, in evaluating the equity of the position, the court should take

e
into account the position of the defendant as well as that of the plaintiff. That the defence involves similar considerations to those involved in the tracing remedy and to the concept of unjust enrichment is even more clearly illustrated by the reasoning of Lord Templeman in the same case, in a speech which was also agreed to by the other members of the House. He said ([1992]

f
4 All ER 512 at 517, [1991] 2 AC 548 at 559–560):

g
    'In the course of argument there was a good deal of discussion concerning tracing in law and in equity. In my opinion, in a claim for money had and received by a thief, the plaintiff victim must show that money belonging to him was paid by the thief to the defendant and that the defendant was unjustly enriched and remained unjustly enriched. An innocent recipient of stolen money may not be enriched at all: if Cass had paid £20,000 derived from the solicitors to a car dealer for a motor car priced at £20,000, the car dealer would not have been enriched. The car dealer would have received £20,000 for a car worth £20,000. But an innocent recipient of stolen money will be enriched if the recipient has not

h
given full consideration. If Cass had given £20,000 of the solicitors' money to a friend as a gift, the friend would have been enriched and unjustly enriched because a donee of stolen money cannot in good conscience rely on the bounty of the thief to deny restitution to the victim of the theft. Complications arise if the donee innocently expends the stolen money in

j
reliance on the validity of the gift before the donee receives notice of the victim's claim for restitution. Thus, if the donee spent £20,000 in the purchase of a motor car which he would not have purchased but for the gift, it seems to me that the donee has altered his position on the faith of the gift and has only been unjustly enriched to the extent of the secondhand value of the motor car at the date when the victim of the theft seeks restitution. If the donee spends the £20,000 in a trip round the world,

which he would not have undertaken without the gift, it seems to me that
the donee has altered his position on the faith of the gift and that he is not   *a*
unjustly enriched when the victim of the theft seeks restitution.'

He then pointed out that the gaming club was in the same position as a donee
of the money staked but had repaid winnings to Cass and only retained a lesser
net sum. His conclusion was that although the solicitors had lost a greater sum   *b*
through the conduct of Cass, the defendants had only been enriched to the
extent of their net receipts.

The question therefore becomes one of asking to what extent the defendant
remains unjustly enriched at the expense of the plaintiff at the date that action
is brought; and the question has to be answered having regard to the extent to
which the position of the defendant has changed since he received the relevant   *c*
money and whether such change would make it inequitable in all the
circumstances to require him to make restitution or, alternatively, restitution
in full.

It is not in dispute that the principles stated in the *Lipkin Gorman* case are to
be applied so far as material in both of the actions before me. But that   *d*
application depends upon the facts proved or admitted in any case and
therefore I have only to consider the actual application of the principle in the
Islington case. Its further consideration in the Sandwell case will have to await
the further trial (should that prove necessary). In the Islington case the defence
has been relied upon both by the plaintiff, Westdeutsche, and the defendant,
Islington.   *e*

(b) The defence: Westdeutsche

Westdeutsche relied upon the defence in relation to the counterclaim of
Islington for the repayment of the various sums which Islington had paid to
Westdeutsche. The factual basis was that on the same day as Westdeutsche   *f*
had made the contract with Islington, Westdeutsche had made a back-to-back
contract with Morgan Grenfell. Under that contract Westdeutsche had
received an initial payment on 18 June 1987 of £2·5m but thereafter had been
required to make semi-annual payments to Morgan Grenfell so that as at the
end of the year 1992 Westdeutsche had paid to Morgan Grenfell £3,180,091·76
more than it had received from Morgan Grenfell. The contract between   *g*
Westdeutsche and Morgan Grenfell was wholly unaffected by any question of
want of capacity or illegality and is to continue, unless terminated by
agreement of the parties, until 18 June 1997. The reliance of Westdeutsche
upon the defence is misconceived for a number of reasons.

First, Islington has no counterclaim against Westdeutsche. Westdeutsche   *h*
has not been enriched at the expense of Islington. Therefore the allegation of
such a defence has no relevance. Secondly, there has been no alteration of the
position of Westdeutsche since it received the sums paid to it by Islington. The
change of position of Westdeutsche occurred on 16 June 1987, when it entered
into the contract with Morgan Grenfell. That contract was, as a legal   *j*
transaction, wholly independent of Westdeutsche's transaction with Islington.
The supposed existence of the contract between Westdeutsche and Islington
had provided the motive for Westdeutsche to enter into a contract with
Morgan Grenfell, but that was all. Therefore there has been no change of
position of Westdeutsche relevant to any claim which Islington might have
had against it. Thirdly, whilst it is presently correct that Westdeutsche as the

a floating rate payer under its contract with Morgan Grenfell is presently out of pocket, it does not follow that this will be the final outcome of that contract. While high interest rates have prevailed on the sterling market in London, the contract has been disadvantageous to the floating rate payer. If the situation becomes one where low interest rates prevail then the contract will become advantageous to the floating rate payer; Westdeutsche will start to be in a

b position where it receives payments rather than has to make them and it is perfectly possible that this may fairly quickly extinguish and reverse the loss of £3m. To assert that Westdeutsche will have made a loss through entering into the Morgan Grenfell contract is simply a speculation.

c (c) The defence: Islington

Islington adduced evidence to support its case on change of position, in particular the evidence of Mr Graney, who succeeded Mr Stenning as director of finance in April 1992. Mr Graney was a satisfactory witness of whom no criticism is to be made. The case of Islington in relation to change of position was argued effectively under three heads.

d The first was that it was wrong in principle to allow any action in money had and received or any remedy of equitable tracing as against a local authority because a local authority's affairs were essentially conducted on an annual basis and to carry over any liability from one year to another, or to require one year to compensate for a benefit received in an earlier year was contrary to

e principle and should not be permitted. This argument, as presented by Miss Appleby, was put forward primarily as providing an analogy with *Sinclair v Brougham* [1914] AC 398, [1914–15] All ER Rep 622 and the recognition in that case that considerations of statutory, or public, policy might override the grant of the restitutionary remedy. In *Sinclair v Brougham* the remedy could not be

f used so as to get round the statutory provision and permit the indirect enforcement of the ultra vires borrowing contracts. So, Miss Appleby argued, in the present type of case to order restitution would be inconsistent with a statutory policy that the finances of local authorities should be regulated on an annual basis. In my judgment, this argument is better considered as an aspect of change of position. At the time that the payment of £2·5m was made, this

g argument would have not provided any defence to a claim for its repayment. It is only because subsequent accounting years have come and gone that the factual basis of the defence arises. That is why I discuss this argument under the heading of the change of position defence.

The second argument is that it would be unjust to expect the charge payers

h for the current year, 1992/3, or the council tax payers for the year 1993/4 to pay for a benefit which was received by the council in the year 1987 and indirectly by the residents in the borough for that year or the following year. Obviously the individual residents of any borough or local authority district will be constantly changing, including those who receive the benefit of council

j expenditure and those who are affected by the council's revenue-raising powers. I have no evidence as to the extent of the turnover in the residents of Islington but it is obvious that, as between the year 1987 and the present day, there must have been changes. There was also uncontradicted evidence that if the sum of £1,145,525·93 had been added to the community charge levied for 1992/3 there would have had to have been an increase of 2·7% in the charge levied, which would have amounted to £10·37 for each ordinary charge payer.

This argument raises similar considerations to that involved in the first argument and they are most conveniently considered together.

The third argument depended upon the treatment of housing subsidy. Owing to the error of Mr Stenning and others in 1987, the sum of £2·5m was treated as if it was interest received by the council upon a capital loan made by the council to a third party and was therefore included in the calculation of the council's entitlement to housing subsidy for that year so as to reduce it by the sum of £1·41m. It was also an effect of what Mr Stenning did that in subsequent years, by reason of the payments that would then be expected to be made by Islington to Westdeutsche under the swap contract and their treatment by Islington in the same mistaken way, that the entitlement of Islington to housing subsidy in those later years would be increased. The case of Islington was that the underpayment of housing subsidy for the year 1987/8 had been lost and, therefore, that that loss constituted a material change in the position of Islington. On the true state of the law as it has now been ascertained, and upon the evidence which has been placed before me I do not find that that subsidy underpayment has been lost. It is clear that the original returns put in by Islington were wrong. They were never certified by the district auditor in their erroneous form and questions were in any event raised upon by them by the department. The same applies to the claims as they were originally put in for the succeeding years and in which the subsidy claim was wrongly inflated. The appropriate claims have now been put in on a correct basis and have been certified by the district auditor. No basis has been made out before me for a finding that the payments of subsidy will not be appropriately adjusted and indeed it is implicit in the evidence of the Islington witnesses that they believe that that is what will occur. The balance of probabilities is that the adjustment will be made.

On this state of the facts, the highest that Islington can put its case in respect of change of position in relation to the housing subsidy aspect is that they have lost the use of the money during the intervening period. It therefore enters into the analysis not as a defence to the principal claim made by Westdeutsche but to the additional claim by Westdeutsche that it should be awarded interest upon whatever amount of restitution Islington is ordered to pay.

However, I consider that the question of loss of interest on housing subsidy is not sufficient to affect the equity as between the plaintiffs and the defendants in the Islington action. Firstly, the failure to calculate the subsidy entitlement properly in the year 1987/8 arose purely from the failure of the officers of the council to fulfil their duty to make a proper claim for housing subsidy for that year. The consequences of that failure should, in justice, be solely for Islington to bear. There is no basis for saying that they ought in justice to be borne by Westdeutsche. Further, the treatment of housing subsidy by the council was one which overtly adopted a policy of reducing the entitlement for the current year for the benefit of later years. The postponement of subsidy arose from a decision of the council which was designed to have that effect. It does not alter the equities as between the plaintiff and the defendant. The defendant has produced a calculation which purports to set off the interest losses arising from an underpayment of subsidy of about £1·41m in 1987/8 and overpayments of subsidy of £494,000 in 1988/9 and £191,000 in 1989/90, in each case calculated down to the end of December 1992, so as to show a net loss of interest in the sum of £501,000. This was a notional figure calculated by reference to the average seven-day market rate during each year. When the council receives

the adjustment of its subsidy payments from central government, it will not
receive any payment of interest to compensate it for this loss of the use of its
money. The figures therefore are not de minimis, but they do not in principle
affect the right to restitution but are only to be taken into account in so far as
they affect the question of an award of interest in favour of the plaintiff against
the defendant.

I now turn to the first and second arguments and the question of the
principle of annual accounting. The defendant's submission was that it is a
fundamental principle of local authority accounting that each year should be
looked at separately and that the revenue raised for each year should only be
for the purposes of that year's expenditure and correspondingly expenditure
should only be included in the accounts of a given year that is attributable to
that year. In support of this proposition Miss Appleby cited *Tower Hamlets
London BC v Chetnik Developments Ltd* [1988] 1 All ER 961, [1988] AC 858, *Re
Westminster City Council* [1986] 2 All ER 278, [1986] AC 668 and *Bromley London
BC v Greater London Council* [1982] 1 All ER 129, [1983] 1 AC 768, which contain
a general affirmation of the principle of annual accounting and the specific
decision that the power to tax, the right of the Greater London Council to raise
precepts, could only be properly exercised in any given year in relation to
expenditure which was properly referable to that year.

However, this submission of the defendant begs the question what are the
expenditure items which have properly to be covered in any given year. These
are conveniently set out in s 2 of the General Rate Act 1967 which, although
now repealed, is in similar terms to the subsequent Acts. It provided that the
rating authority should set rates which—

> 'will be sufficient to provide for such part of the total estimated
> expenditure to be incurred by the authority during the period in respect of
> which the rate is made as is not to be met by other means or by means of
> excepted rates, including in that expenditure any sums payable to any
> other authority under precepts issued by that other authority, together
> with such additional amount as is in the opinion of the rating authority
> required to cover expenditure previously incurred, or to meet contin-
> gencies, or to defray any expenditure which may fall to be defrayed before
> the date on which the moneys to be received in respect of the next
> subsequent rate made under this subsection will become available.'

This provision confirms the evidence of the witnesses that if at the end of
any given year the council has a deficit on its income and expenditure account
then it must carry forward that deficit to the following year and take that
deficit into account in setting its budget for the following year. Thus, far from
it being the case that the law precludes the inclusion of previous expenditure
in the calculation of the revenue to be collected in any given year, the law
requires that it shall be taken into account and expressly contemplates that the
residents will in the subsequent year either have to pay an increased rate (or
other charge) to the council or suffer a diminution in the expenditure of the
council during that year. Therefore the legal proposition relied upon by the
defendant is not made out.

Further, it was accepted that councils are under an obligation to conduct
their financial affairs and prepare their accounts prudently and in accordance
with good accounting practice. The formal accounting requirements have been
made more specific during the period in question and it is not material to
investigate (as the plaintiffs were inclined to do) the degree to which full

disclosure of the council's financial affairs had been made in its published
abstract of accounts. What was established on the evidence and on the *a*
statutory provisions was that a council should conduct its affairs prudently and
therefore include appropriate provisions, take into account accruals, and not
allocate income to years to which it was not referable. Thus, in preparing a
given year's accounts, reserves should be established to cover future
expenditure to which the council is committed and cover contingencies and *b*
where income is only partly referable to a current year it should not be credited
in full to that year. It was not correct to treat the benefit of the receipt of the
£2·5m in 1987 as solely referable to that year although in fact the council chose
to credit it in full to that year. The benefit of that payment in truth belonged
also to the succeeding nine years. If an accounting approach had been adopted
which had reflected the true position, a substantial proportion of the £2·5m *c*
would have remained in the accounts of the council as the contract had run for
less than three years before payments were stopped.

Further, the statutory provision which I have quoted requires a council to
take into account any expenditure which it may have to defray before the time
when it will next levy and receive revenue. It must therefore make provision *d*
for anticipated expenditure. That in fact is what the defendants, and other
councils, were advised to do by the Audit Commission in respect of any
restitution claims that they might be liable to face. They were advised to make
provision for the payment of those claims in the year or years when they
anticipated that they would have to pay them. Islington did make provision.
Initially it did this by crediting the payments which it would otherwise have *e*
made to a 'suspense code' in its accounts. The payment which would have
been due (had the contract been valid) to Westdeutsche on 18 December 1989
was £872,602·74. A similar approach was apparently adopted in relation to the
other 1987 swap contracts. The next payment which would have fallen due to
be made by Islington to Westdeutsche was similarly treated so that by the time *f*
of the decision of the House of Lords, Islington had approximately £1·8m set
aside under a suspense code to make payments which it had originally
expected to make under its contract with Westdeutsche.

Accordingly, as at the time that the House of Lords delivered its decision, the
defendant had set aside out of budgeted sums for the years 1989/90 and 1990/1 *g*
sums which in the aggregate were more than sufficient to meet the restitution
liability which I have held was the consequence of the decision of the House of
Lords. This is the end of the defendant's change of position argument on the
facts. It had been planning to make payments to the plaintiff and it had
budgeted for them. It had expected the liability to make those payments to be *h*
a contractual liability. In fact, its liability was a liability to make restitution,
that is to say to repay to the plaintiff the balance of a sum which it had
previously received from the plaintiff. The only change in the position of the
defendant was that the legal basis for the liability to make the payment was
different from that which it had assumed and the sum which it was actually
going to have to pay (subject to the question of interest) was less than that *j*
which it was prepared to pay.

The defendant apparently had not adopted the same approach in respect of
the other 1987 swap contracts which it had entered into with other local
authorities as intermediaries. Following the Divisional Court judgment it had
realised that those contracts were inevitably doomed and it had accordingly,
after taking account of a housing subsidy adjustment, made a provision of

a £2·049m in the council's accounts for the year ending 31 March 1990 against a liability to make restitution in respect of those swaps. The note to the balance sheet included in the abstract of accounts included the sentences:

> 'The Court of Appeal ruling would appear to make the swaps with other local authorities illegal as they acted as intermediaries. This represents six of the large swaps; the remaining one with the banks is thought to be
b > legal.'

The 'remaining one' is the Westdeutsche contract. What happened thereafter was summarised by Mr Graney in his evidence. The defendant estimated that its total restitution liability in respect of all the 1987 swaps could be of the order of £9·9m and against that it thought it prudent to make a provision in its budget
c for 1992/3 of £4·8m, with another £4·8m in its budget for 1993/4. Mr Graney frankly accepted that the making of provisions was affected by the likely date that it was expected that cases would be tried and that certain provisions had been released when it had been found that they would not be needed in a given year. Further, it would be necessary for Islington to know by March of this
d year what the decision in this case would be so that it could take into account whatever liability was or was not held to exist in setting its budget for 1993/4.

The submission therefore that the defendant council, Islington, has changed its position since it received the sum of £2·5m in such a way that it would become unjust and inequitable for it now to be ordered to repay to the plaintiff the sum of £1,145,525·93 does not bear examination on the facts. It
e has at all material times been in a position to make such repayment out of budgeted sums and in so far as it may find, if such be the case, that it has in the year 1993/4 to increase the revenue which it raises from local government tax payers in its borough, that situation will have come about solely because it has chosen to release funds which it previously held which were more than
f sufficient to meet the liability.

The remaining points on change of position overlap in a similar way with the matters discussed in relation to the remedy of tracing. The evidence of the defendant has not disclosed any significant alteration of the position of the defendant as a result of its having assumed that it was entitled to receive the sum of £2·5m from Westdeutsche in the summer of 1987. Large though the
g sum may appear to be, its immediate financial impact was reduced to about £1·1m as a result of Mr Stenning's choice to treat it as resulting in a reduction of about £1·4m in the housing subsidy entitlement of the council for the first year. It was not proved that Islington would in fact have made any significant differences in its expenditure for the year 1987/8 if that £1·1m had not been
h available. In fact as matters turned out at the end of that year the council was left with a significant excess of income over expenditure owing to certain special factors. Further, the sums involved are in any event very small in relation to the overall turnover of the council in any given year and in relation to the overall value of the council's net current assets. The arguments of the defendant were theoretical rather than based upon actuality. The accounting
j practices adopted by the council and Mr Stenning signally failed to give weight to the prudence, or the principle, of distinguishing between one accounting year and another. The devices adopted were openly devised so as to transfer revenue from one year to another in order to meet current expenditure at the revenue cost of later years. The scale on which such devices were being adopted makes insignificant any distortion which might have resulted from the need to give restitution in respect of this contract. The effect of the decision of

the Divisional Court was to require that councils' accounts should be rectified
so as to accord with the law. The accounts of the council for the relevant years
had not been certified by the district auditor by the time of the Divisional Court
judgment. They have had to be rectified in any event.

The defence of change of position raised by Islington accordingly fails.

(6) Interest

The result of my judgment is that Westdeutsche is entitled to an order that
Islington pay to it the sum of £1,145,525·93. The court has the power to award
simple interest on that sum under s 35A of the Supreme Court Act 1981 (see *BP
Exploration Co (Libya) Ltd v Hunt (No 2)* [1982] 1 All ER 925, [1979] 1 WLR 783;
affd [1982] 1 All ER 925, [1983] 2 AC 352 and *Woolwich Building Society v IRC (No
2)* [1992] 3 All ER 737, [1993] AC 70). It is also apparent from the *Woolwich* case
that the restitutionary remedy should normally include an award of interest.
The defendant has been enriched by having the use of the plaintiff's money
during the relevant period. An assessment of that enrichment is the interest
which that money has earned in the hands of the defendant or, to put the same
point in another way, the reduction in the defendant's interest bill which the
defendant has enjoyed by reason of having had the plaintiff's money. But I
have also held that the plaintiff is entitled to the equitable remedy of tracing
and I have the jurisdiction as part of that remedy to order that the defendant
shall repay the relevant sum together with compound interest.

The plaintiff's cause of action originates from the making of the payment on
18 June 1987. However, I regard it as inappropriate that, in a case such as this
which depends upon equitable principles, the award of interest should date
back to that time. Both parties were conducting themselves at that time on the
basis that the contract was valid and the plaintiff was not in fact out of pocket
for the £2·5m. The plaintiff had received an equivalent sum from Morgan
Grenfell under its contract with that bank. It was not until after the decision
of the Divisional Court and the defendant stopped payment that the plaintiff
began to be actually out of pocket. The defendant should have made payment
to the plaintiff on 18 December 1989 and 18 June 1990. It did not do so and
thereby it failed to repay to the plaintiff the balance of the original sum of
£2·5m and it instead retained that sum in every sense at the expense of the
plaintiff.

There is a logical argument that can be advanced by the plaintiff that I should
be concerned solely with the question whether or not during this early period
the defendant was enriched and not with any collateral transaction into which
the plaintiff had entered and with which the defendant was in no way
concerned. I accept the logic of this argument but I do not consider that it has
sufficient regard to the discretionary nature of the remedy which I am being
asked to provide, the award of interest, and the question whether it is just that
the defendant should be ordered to pay interest to the plaintiff at a time when
both the plaintiff and the defendant were labouring under a bona fide mistake
and at a time when the plaintiff was not actually out of pocket. I do not
consider that it is just that such an award of interest should be made. This also
makes largely academic the defendant's point on the postponement of the
housing subsidy.

From the time of the Divisional Court judgment the parties were no longer
in the same position. The decision of the Divisional Court was that all swap
contracts were void. The defendant should have known that on the basis of
that decision its contract with the plaintiffs was void and indeed it should have

a realised that that remained the position after the decision of the Court of Appeal. The case for some award of interest from 18 December 1989 is unanswerable. By 18 June 1990 the council had actually set aside a fund which was more than sufficient to meet its liability to make restitution to the plaintiff. It has kept that sum and has not made any restitution. In this situation I see no reason why I should not exercise my equitable jurisdiction to award compound

b interest. Simple interest does not reflect the actual value of money. Anyone who lends or borrows money on a commercial basis receives or pays interest periodically and if that interest is not paid it is compounded (eg *Wallersteiner v Moir (No 2)* [1975] 1 All ER 849, [1975] QB 373 and *National Bank of Greece SA v Pinios Shipping Co No 1, The Maira* [1990] 1 All ER 78, [1990] 1 AC 637). I see no reason why I should deny the plaintiff a complete remedy or allow the

c defendant arbitrarily to retain part of the enrichment which it has unjustly enjoyed. There are no special factors which have to be taken into account. No question of insolvency is involved nor is there any basis for any persuasive argument to the contrary.

I consider that the appropriate order that I should make is that the entire

d sum which I have ordered should be paid by the defendant to the plaintiff should be paid with compound interest calculated from 1 April 1990 (an intermediate date between December and June) with six-monthly rests. Any residual argument which the defendant has in relation to its housing subsidy point is more than sufficiently taken account of by my postponement of the starting date for interest to April 1990.

e The parties have not addressed me upon the rate of interest. Since I am exercising my equitable jurisdiction to award compound interest, it is the position of the defendant which must be primarily looked at. It has to account for the benefit which it has received, or must be taken to have received, from having the plaintiff's money during the relevant period. In connection with

f the loss of use of the housing subsidy, the defendant, through its chief accountant, Mr Beaton, put forward an interest calculation on the basis of average seven-day rates. For the year 1990/91 the rate he gives is 14·42% pa, for 1991/92 it is 10·98%, for the period April 1992 to January 1993 it is 9·72%. Subject to further evidence or some other agreement between the parties, these are the rates which should be used for the purpose of the calculation of

g the compound interest.

CONCLUSIONS

The Islington action

In the Islington action I hold that the plaintiff is entitled to an order that the

h defendant do pay to it the sum of £1,145,525·93, being the net balance which has not to date been repaid of the £2·5m paid by the plaintiff to the defendant on 18 June 1987. The plaintiff is entitled to recover that sum either as money had and received by the defendant to the use of the plaintiff or as money which in equity belongs to the plaintiff and which it is entitled to trace in the hands of the defendant and have repaid to it out of the present assets of the defendant.

j The basis of the plaintiff's claim, whether at common law or in equity, is that the defendant has been unjustly enriched at the expense of the plaintiff and that in conscience the defendant must repay to the plaintiff, save in so far as it has already done so, the sum which it received from the plaintiff. The right to restitution arises from the fact that the payment made by the plaintiff to the defendant was made under a purported contract which, unknown to the plaintiff and the defendant, was ultra vires the defendant and wholly void.

There was no consideration for the making of the payment. The fact that the plaintiff's mistake was not a mistake as to any actual matter of fact does not preclude the plaintiff from recovery. The plaintiff's payment does not fall to be categorised as a voluntary payment. Although a defendant to an action in which restitution is being sought on the ground of unjust enrichment may seek to rely upon any material change of circumstance as a defence to the claim, Islington was unable to show any facts which entitled it to rely upon that defence. Since the plaintiff was entitled to invoke equitable remedies against the defendant, it was entitled to ask the court to award it compound interest, not merely simple interest. In the exercise of my discretion I have ordered that the principal sum be repaid by the defendant to the plaintiff with compound interest calculated at six-monthly rests from 1 April 1990 down to the date of this judgment.

The Sandwell action

On the preliminary issues ordered to be tried in the action between Kleinwort Benson and Sandwell, I hold: (1) that the plaintiff's points of claim disclose a good cause of action both in money had and received and at equity against the defendant in respect of the balance in their favour of the payments made under the first Sandwell swap and the payments made under the third and fourth Sandwell swaps, and that prima facie the defendant has equivalent rights against the plaintiff in respect of the balance outstanding in favour of the defendant on the second Sandwell swap; (2) that it is not necessary to the establishment of the cause of action that the plaintiff should be able to show that there has been a total failure of consideration in the contractual use of that term as typified by the *Fibrosa* case; but, if it were necessary, it has shown such a failure in respect of the third and fourth swaps; however, this will not increase its rights against the defendant; (3) the basis upon which the plaintiff is entitled to recover is that the relevant payments were made under purported contracts which, unknown to the plaintiff and the defendant, it was outside the capacity of the defendant to make and were wholly void; (4) the payments were made without any consideration; (5) it is not necessary for the plaintiff to show that it was mistaken about any actual fact and it does not provide the defendant with a defence that the plaintiff's mistake was not one as to any actual fact; (6) the mere fact that all the payments contemplated by the first Sandwell swap were in fact made does not, without more, provide the defendant with an answer to the plaintiff's claim in connection with that swap; and (7) the limitation of actions defence raised by the defendant in respect of the first Sandwell swap does not give the defendant any defence either in whole or in part to the plaintiff's claim in respect of the payments made under that swap.

Judgment for Westdeutsche in the first action. Preliminary issues answered accordingly in the second action.

Appeal and cross-appeal

Islington appealed and Westdeutsche cross-appealed on the ground that interest ought to run from 18 June 1987 and not 1 April 1990. Kleinwort Benson and Sandwell took no part in the proceedings. The facts are set out in the judgment of Dillon LJ.

Trevor Philipson QC, Brian Doctor and *Andrew Burrows* (instructed by *Nabarro Nathanson*) for Islington.
Jonathan Sumption QC and *George Leggatt* (instructed by *Travers Smith Braithwaite*) for Westdeutsche.

Cur adv vult

17 December 1993. The following judgments were delivered.

DILLON LJ. This is an appeal by the defendant in the action, the Islington London Borough Council (Islington), against a judgment of Hobhouse J, sitting in the Commercial Court on 12 February 1993, whereby it was adjudged that Islington pay the plaintiff in the action, the respondent to this appeal, Westdeutsche Landesbank Girozentrale (Westdeutsche), the sum of £1,591,894·74, being as to £1,145,525·93 principal and as to £446,368·81 interest thereon.

The main issue on the appeal is whether Islington is liable to pay Westdeutsche the principal, the amount of which is not in dispute. But there is a subsidiary issue on the appeal as to interest, namely whether the judge was entitled to order Islington to pay Westdeutsche compound, and not merely simple, interest on the principal. There is also an issue raised by Westdeutsche by a respondent's notice that interest ought to run from an earlier date, 18 June 1987, rather than the date, 1 April 1990, selected by the judge.

The judge's judgment from which this appeal is brought was delivered after the trial of this action which was heard at the same time as another action between a different bank, Kleinwort Benson Ltd, and a different local authority, the Sandwell Borough Council. We are not concerned at all on this appeal with that other action.

The present action arises out of an interest rate swap 'agreement' made on 16 June 1987 between Islington and Westdeutsche. How interest rate swap arrangements such as that between Islington and Westdeutsche were supposed to work is concisely set out by Lord Templeman in *Hazell v Hammersmith and Fulham London BC* [1991] 1 All ER 545 at 550, [1992] 2 AC 1 at 24. The contract was described as—

> 'an agreement between two parties by which each agrees to pay the other on a specified date or dates an amount calculated by reference to the interest which would have accrued over a given period on the same notional principal sum assuming different rates of interest are payable in each case. For example, one rate may be fixed at 10% and the other rate may be equivalent to the six-month London Inter-Bank Offered Rate (LIBOR). If the LIBOR rate over the period of the swap is higher than 10% then the party agreeing to receive "interest" in accordance with LIBOR will receive more than the party entitled to receive the 10%. Normally neither party will in fact pay the sums which it has agreed to pay over the period of the swap but instead will make a settlement on a "net payment basis" under which the party owing the greater amount on any day simply pays the difference between the two amounts due to the other.'

The arrangement between Islington and Westdeutsche was to run for ten years starting on 18 June 1987 and the interest sums were to be calculated on a notional principal sum of £25m and to be payable half-yearly. Westdeutsche was to be the fixed rate payer at a rate of 7·5% pa and Islington was to be the floating rate payer at the domestic sterling LIBOR rate. Additionally, Westdeutsche as the fixed rate payer was to pay Islington as the floating rate payer on 18 June 1987 a sum of £2·5m.

So far as Westdeutsche was concerned, this arrangement with Islington was backed by an arrangement with Morgan Grenfell & Co Ltd, involving a like notional principal sum and a like payment of £2·5m by the fixed rate payer, under which Westdeutsche was the floating rate payer and Morgan Grenfell was the fixed rate payer, but nothing in my judgment turns, on this appeal, on that counter-arrangement, which was unquestionably valid as between its parties.

The actual payments made between Westdeutsche and Islington were the following:

Date	Payment by Westdeutsche to Islington £	Payment by Islington to Westdeutsche £
18.06.87	2,500,000	172,345·89
18.12.87		229,666·09
20.06.88		259,054·56
19.12.88		693,407·53
Totals	2,500,000	1,354,474·07

If the total of the payments by Islington is deducted from the £2·5m paid to Islington by Westdeutsche, the balance left is the £1,145,525·93, which is the principal for which the judge awarded Westdeutsche judgment against Islington.

The trouble that has arisen for the parties is that in *Hazell's* case, as is well known, the district auditor challenged the power of the Hammersmith and Fulham London Borough Council, or any other local authority, to enter into interest rate swap transactions. The proceedings in *Hazell's* case were started on 29 May 1989. The Divisional Court ([1990] 3 All ER 33, [1990] 2 QB 697) held that interest rate swap transactions by local authorities were ultra vires, and that view was unanimously upheld by the House of Lords on 24 January 1991. The transactions are not illegal, but they, and the contracts purporting to embody them, are ultra vires the local authority and void.

Since *Hazell's* case was brought against the local authority by the district auditor, the courts did not have to decide the effect of the transaction having been ultra vires and void. In the present case the court does have to decide the effect since Westdeutsche claims against Islington repayment of the balance of its £2·5m paid to Islington, viz the £1,145,525·93, with interest on the balance from time to time outstanding from 18 June 1987, the day on which the £2·5m was paid to Islington.

Islington accepts that Westdeutsche never had any intention of making a gift to Islington of the £2·5m or of any part of that sum. Consequently, Islington accepts that if the legal consequences of *Hazell's* case had become known and clear to the parties before 18 December 1987, when Islington made its first payment of 'interest' to Westdeutsche, Islington would have been bound to repay the whole of the £2·5m to Westdeutsche (with interest) as money paid for a consideration which had wholly failed.

A fortiori, if interest rates at the time had been such that the first four six-monthly 'interest' payments had been paid by Westdeutsche as the fixed rate payer to Islington (instead of having actually been paid the other way round), Islington would have been bound to repay to Westdeutsche the total of the £2·5m and the 'interest' payments (assumedly) paid by Westdeutsche to Islington.

But it is Islington's case that as Islington has made the four 'interest' payments to Westdeutsche—for the purposes of the argument one payment would have been enough—Westdeutsche can recover nothing and Islington can keep the £1,145,525·93. I find such a conclusion repugnant to common sense.

Islington's case is, in effect, that common sense or fairness do not come into it because the categories of case in which money can be recovered in quasi contract as money had and received or on grounds of unjust enrichment have been laid down long ago and the only recognised category which Westdeutsche can hope to invoke is that of 'money paid for a consideration which has wholly failed'.

That is of course a well-known category for cases in which the full amount of money paid by one party to a contract or intended contract can be recovered. It applies not merely where the supposed contract has for some reason been void or was voidable and has been rescinded, but also where there was a valid contract, but there has been a fundamental breach by the other party and so the payer can get his money back instead of merely having to claim damages. It is clear from *Fibrosa Spolka Akcyjna v Fairbairn Lawson Combe Barbour Ltd* [1942] 2 All ER 122, [1943] AC 32 (a case of frustration) that by 'the consideration has wholly failed' is meant that the performance promised has not been provided.

Thus it is said for Islington that the performance promised by Islington to Westdeutsche has in part been satisfied or provided because Islington has made the four 'interest' payments to Westdeutsche (and one would have been enough) and so the consideration has not wholly failed and so Westdeutsche cannot recover the balance of the £2·5m.

The judge held that the balance fell to be repaid on the different ground that, as the swap transaction and the agreement for it were ultra vires and void, there was no consideration for the payment of the £2·5m by Westdeutsche to Islington and so, as Westdeutsche never intended to make a gift of the money to Islington, the money was recoverable as money paid for no consideration.

That is an approach recently developed by the House of Lords in *Woolwich Building Society v IRC (No 2)* [1992] 3 All ER 737, [1993] AC 70. That case concerned a claim by the building society to recover from the Revenue money paid to the Revenue under protest by the building society, which had asserted throughout that the regulation under which the money was claimed by the Revenue was ultra vires. Lord Goff of Chieveley referred to reinterpretation to reveal a different line of thought pointing to the conclusion that money paid to a public authority pursuant to an ultra vires demand should be repayable, without the necessity of establishing compulsion, on the simple ground that there was no consideration for the payment (see [1992] 3 All ER 737 at 754, [1993] AC 70 at 166). In relation to a decision of Lord Mansfield CJ in *Campbell v Hall* (1774) 1 Cowp 204, [1558–1774] All ER Rep 252 he said that 'the simple fact remains that recovery was stated to be founded upon absence of consideration for the payment'. Lord Browne-Wilkinson dealt with the same argument in the *Woolwich* case [1992] 3 All ER 737 at 781, [1993] AC 70 at 197:

'As in so many other fields of English law, the occasions on which recovery is permitted have been built up on a case by case basis. For present purposes there are in my judgment two streams of authority relating to moneys wrongly extracted by way of impost. One stream is founded on the concept that money paid under an ultra vires demand for a tax or other impost has been paid without consideration. The other stream is based on the notion that such payments have been made under compulsion, the relative positions and powers of the two parties being unequal. The stream based on the concept of payment without consideration stems from what Lord Mansfield CJ said in *Campbell v Hall* (1774) 1 Cowp 204, [1558-1774] All ER Rep 252 and is reflected in the decision in *Dew v Parsons* (1819) 2 B & Ald 562, 106 ER 471. In *Steele v Williams* (1853) 8 Exch 625 at 632, 155 ER 1502 at 1505 Martin B said that the payment in that case was not a voluntary payment but was "more like the case of money paid without consideration". In *Queens of the River Steamship Co Ltd v River Thames Conservators* (1899) 15 TLR 474 Phillimore J founded his decision on the fact that there was no consideration for the payment. Although this stream seems subsequently to have run into the sand, I find the approach attractive: money paid on the footing that there is a legal demand is paid for a reason that does not exist if that demand is a nullity. There is in my view a close analogy to the right to recover money paid under a contract the consideration for which has wholly failed.'

The same concept, that a payment can be recovered if there was no consideration for the payment, seems to have been relied on by Robert Goff J (as he then was) in *Barclays Bank Ltd v W J Simms Son & Cooke (Southern) Ltd* [1979] 3 All ER 522, [1980] QB 677. In that case the bank had honoured its customer's cheque in favour of the defendant, but had done so under a mistake of fact, forgetting that the customer had cancelled its mandate to honour the cheque. It was held that the bank could recover the amount of the cheque from the defendant, because the payment without mandate was not effective to discharge the drawer's obligation on the cheque and (as I understand the case) the payee therefore gave no consideration for the payment.

The *Woolwich* case and *Barclays Bank v Simms* were both cases in which it would be more accurate to say that there had been no consideration for the payment than to say that the consideration had wholly failed; the transactions in issue did not obviously involve any consideration or performance, moving from the payee to the plaintiff, in the sense of the phrase 'the consideration has wholly failed'.

In the *Fibrosa* case [1942] 2 All ER 122 at 137, [1943] AC 32 at 64–65 Lord Wright, in referring to the concept that the consideration has wholly failed, spoke of where 'the consideration, if entire, has entirely failed, or where, if it is severable, it has entirely failed as to the severable residue, as in *Rugg* v. *Minett* ((1809) 11 East 210, 103 ER 985)'. *Rugg v Minett* is also referred to by Viscount Simon LC as an instructive decision (see [1942] 2 All ER 122 at 129, [1943] AC 32 at 48). Lord Atkin described it as being a case where the buyer had paid part of the purchase price on a sale of turpentine in casks, where the property in some casks had passed while in the seller's warehouse but some had not (because the casks had not yet been filled) and the purchaser was entitled to recover as money had and received the proportion properly attributable to the *a* casks in which the property had not passed when they were destroyed by fire (see [1942] 2 All ER 122 at 131, [1943] AC 32 at 52–53). Viscount Simon LC's account indicates that the plaintiff's payment in advance had been a sum of money on account of his purchases generally. Plainly there had been no total failure of consideration in respect of the whole of the payment in advance on account of the purchases generally, since the title to the casks which had been

b filled had passed to the plaintiff. But the court severed the consideration and held that the part attributable to the casks which had not been filled had wholly failed.

Mr Philipson QC contends that the true interpretation of *Rugg v Minett* is that the plaintiff had bought separately a number of lots of casks, sold separately at an auction sale, and that he recovered his payments in respect of

c those lots separately purchased which were destroyed by the fire before they were filled because they had been bought by separate bids and thus separate contracts at the auction. That was not how the case was interpreted by the House of Lords, nor, as I read the report, is it the basis on which the judges who heard the case decided it.

d I do not see why a similar process of severance should not be applied where what has happened, in a purely financial matter, is that there has been a payment of money one way and a payment of smaller sums of money the other way. The effect of severance is that there has been a total failure of consideration in respect of the balance of the money which has not come back.

e Severance apart, however, to hold that as the interest swap transaction and contract were ultra vires and void there was no consideration for the payment by Westdeutsche of the £2·5m and therefore the balance which has not so far been repaid by Islington can be recovered by Westdeutsche in quasi contract as money had and received or on the grounds of unjust enrichment is

f warranted by early cases decided under the Grants of Life Annuities Act 1777.

It appears that before that Act was enacted a practice had developed whereby a person desiring to raise money would grant, ie sell, an annuity to a grantee in consideration of a capital sum paid to the grantor by the grantee. The Act imposed various restrictions on such transactions, including a requirement that a memorial of the document which granted the annuity,

g containing prescribed details, must be enrolled in the Court of Chancery within 20 days of the execution of the document. In default of compliance the document was to be 'null and void to all intents and purposes'. As a result of the 1777 Act there were a number of cases and the law was established that if there had been non-compliance the grantor was entitled to have the annuity

h set aside, but the grantee was entitled to have his capital premium repaid to him with interest, subject to giving credit for the instalments of the annuity which he had received.

In *Hicks v Hicks* (1802) 3 East 16, 102 ER 502 the action was brought by the plaintiff for money had and received to recover the consideration money paid

j many years ago for an annuity granted by the defendant to the plaintiff which had been paid for several years but had been recently set aside by the court on the application of the defendant for a defect in the memorial of registry. The defendant claimed to set off the payments of the annuity which the plaintiff had received. Lord Ellenborough CJ upheld that claim. He said (3 East 16 at 17, 102 ER 502):

'This was either an annuity or not an annuity. If not an annuity, the
sums paid on either side were money had and received by the one party to
the other's use. If the consideration of the annuity be money had and
received, it must be money had and received with all its consequences; and
therefore the defendant must be at liberty to set off his payments as such,
on the same score.'

What Lord Ellenborough CJ there said was applied by Grant MR in *Holbrook
v Sharpey* (1812) 19 Ves 131 at 132, 34 ER 467. He also said:

'Either all the payments, made under a void annuity deed, must be
considered as purely voluntary, in which case none of them could be
recovered back; or they are all money had and received to the use of the
grantor, and therefore to be all returned or accounted for.' (See 19 Ves 131
at 133, 34 ER 467 at 468.)

The payments were not to be considered as purely voluntary because they
had been intended to be made for the consideration expressed in the annuity
deed. That is equally the case with the payments each way in the present case.
Neither party intended to make a gift to the other.

In *Lipkin Gorman (a firm) v Karpnale Ltd* [1992] 4 All ER 512 at 521, [1991] 2 AC
548 at 564 Lord Templeman approved another statement by Lord Ellenborough CJ in *Hudson v Robinson* (1816) 4 M & S 475 at 478, 105 ER 910 at 911
that 'an action for money had and received is maintainable whenever the
money of one man has, without consideration, got into the pocket of another'.

It must follow, in my judgment, on the authorities referred to, that
Westdeutsche is entitled to recover the balance of the £2·5m from Islington as
money had and received, or, as it is now called, as Lord Goff pointed out in
Lipkin Gorman [1992] 4 All ER 512 at 527, [1991] 2 AC 548 at 572 'unjust
enrichment at the expense of the owner of the money'.

It is unnecessary to explore in this case what intricacies there may be in
applying the concept of 'money paid for a consideration which has wholly
failed' in other cases where the consideration for a payment of money is
something other than the payment of other money and is not severable.

The same result can be achieved on equitable, as opposed to common law,
grounds. Since, contrary to the expectation of the parties, the swap transaction
and contract are, and were from the outset, ultra vires and void, the purpose
for which the £2·5m was paid by Westdeutsche to Islington has wholly failed,
and the £2·5m has, from the time Islington received it, been held on a resulting
trust for Westdeutsche: see the speech of Viscount Haldane LC in *Sinclair v
Brougham* [1914] AC 398 at 418, [1914–15] All ER Rep 622 at 630, where he
referred to the claim of the depositors in the ultra vires banking business of the
Birbeck Permanent Benefit Building Society as 'a claim to ... recover property
with which, in equity at all events, they had never really parted'. He further
stated ([1914] AC 398 at 420–421, [1914–15] All ER Rep 622 at 632):

'The Court of Chancery could and would declare, even as against the
general creditors of the wrong-doer, that there was what it called a charge
on the banker's debt to the person whose money had been paid into the
latter's bank account in favour of the person whose money it really was ...
It was, as I think, merely an additional right, which could be enforced by

a the Court of Chancery in the exercise of its auxiliary jurisdiction, wherever money was held to belong in equity to the plaintiff.'

Sinclair v Brougham was, so far as is relevant for present purposes, summed up by Lord Greene MR in *Re Diplock's Estate, Diplock v Wintle* [1948] 2 All ER 318 at 357, [1948] Ch 465 at 540–541 as follows:

b   'There, a sufficient fiduciary relationship was found to exist between the depositors and the directors by reason of the fact that the purposes for which the depositors had handed their money to the directors were by law incapable of fulfilment.'

So interpreted, *Sinclair v Brougham* is a direct parallel to the present case.
c Thus in equity also Westdeutsche is entitled to the return of the balance of the £2·5m.

Under the *Woolwich* case Westdeutsche is also entitled to interest on the money awarded it by a restitutionary remedy. Prima facie the date from which interest should run is the date of the receipt of the £2·5m by Islington, viz 18
d June 1987: see the judgment of Robert Goff J in *BP Exploration Co (Libya) Ltd v Hunt (No 2)* [1982] 1 All ER 925 esp at 975, [1979] 1 WLR 783 esp at 846. Robert Goff J pointed out, however, that the power to award interest was discretionary, and there was certainly no rule that interest would invariably run from what he called the date of loss. He then referred to three main groups of case in which the court in the exercise of its discretion might depart from the
e fundamental principle.

In the present case, the judge gave two reasons for awarding Westdeutsche interest from a date later than 18 June 1987. The first is that Westdeutsche had received an equivalent sum of £2·5m from Morgan Grenfell under the swap arrangement with Morgan Grenfell, and it was not until Islington stopped
f payment under its own swap arrangement with Westdeutsche after the decision of the Divisional Court in *Hazell's* case that Westdeutsche began to be out of pocket. But, though Westdeutsche had arranged the interest swap with Morgan Grenfell to limit its exposure under the supposed interest swap with Islington, that is irrelevant to the present question, because the consequence of the fact that the swap transaction between Westdeutsche and Islington was
g ultra vires and void makes the actual transaction between Westdeutsche and Islington in respect of which interest is claimed by Westdeutsche completely different from the intended swap under the void swap contract. The swap with Morgan Grenfell is res inter alios acta.

The second reason given by the judge for his choice of date from which
h interest is to run is that 'By 18 June 1990 the council had actually set aside a fund which was more than sufficient to meet its liability to make restitution to the plaintiff. It has kept that sum and has not made any restitution' (see p 955, ante). That is factually wrong, however, in so far as it suggests that Islington had set money apart to make restitution to Westdeutsche. Islington never did
j any such thing, even in respect of the instalment which Islington would have had to pay to Westdeutsche under the swap arrangement, if it had been valid, on 18 December 1989 (which was the next after the last instalment actually paid). The most that Islington did was to credit such interest payments to a suspense account code; but that was a mere accounting entry, not supported by any actual fund, indicating a liability which Islington might have to meet. In fact the instalment of 18 December 1989 would have had to be paid on any

view, unless Islington succeeded in its unmeritorious contention in these
proceedings that because it was discovered that the swap arrangements were *a*
void it was absolved from making any further payment to Westdeutsche.
Accordingly, I cannot regard the fact that the accounting entry was made,
without payment, as an indication of merit on Islington's part which should
warrant mitigating Islington's liability to pay interest on money had and
received.   *b*

Mr Philipson relies, for Islington, on a passage in the speech of Lord
Wilberforce in *General Tire and Rubber Co v Firestone Tyre and Rubber Co Ltd*
[1975] 2 All ER 173 at 188, [1975] 1 WLR 819 at 836, where he said:

> 'Where a wrong-doer has failed to pay money which he should have
> paid, justice, in principle, requires that he should pay interest over the *c*
> period for which he has withheld the money. But other considerations
> may enter into it. In a commercial setting, it would be proper to take
> account of the manner in which and the time at which persons acting
> honestly and reasonably would pay.'

Mr Philipson urges that Islington could not be expected to repay anything *d*
more than it had actually paid, before Islington knew that the interest swap
contract was ultra vires and void, and he urges further that Islington did not
really know that until the decision of the House of Lords in *Hazell*'s case [1991]
1 All ER 545, [1992] 2 AC 1 (which was not given until 24 January 1991), though
Mr Philipson is content to accept the judge's date of 1 April 1990 in the absence
of any challenge to that date in Islington's notice of appeal.   *e*

As I see it, the judge's exercise of his discretion as to the date is flawed,
because he took into account the two factors I have mentioned in arriving at
his date of 1 April 1990. This court has therefore to exercise its own discretion.

I see no merit in the suggestion that Islington should be absolved from
paying interest to Westdeutsche over the period while the correctness of the *f*
decision of the Divisional Court in *Hazell*'s case [1990] 3 All ER 33, [1990] 2 QB
797 (which was given on 1 November 1989) was being tested in the higher
courts. As to the earlier period from 18 June 1987, the overriding factor is, in
my judgment, that from 18 June 1987 Islington had the use of the whole of
Westdeutsche's £2·5m, the whole of which it spent. Accordingly, I would fix
the date from which interest is to run as 18 June 1987.   *g*

Then should the interest award be simple or compound interest? It is
common ground that only simple interest can be awarded under s 35A of the
Supreme Court Act 1981. By contrast, the Chancery courts have awarded
compound interest when they thought that justice so demanded, including
where money had been withheld or misapplied by a trustee or anyone else in a *h*
fiduciary position: see *President of India v La Pintada Cia Navegacion SA* [1984] 2
All ER 773 at 779, [1985] AC 104 at 116 per Lord Brandon of Oakbrook.

In the present case, Islington was, on the true view that the swap agreement
with Westdeutsche was ultra vires and void, a person in a fiduciary position
from the outset, 18 June 1987: see the alternative analysis above founded on the *j*
statements of Viscount Haldane LC in *Sinclair v Brougham* [1914] AC 398 at 420,
[1914–15] All ER Rep 622 at 631–632 and Lord Greene MR's analysis of that case
in *Re Diplock's Estate* [1948] 2 All ER 318 at 357, [1948] Ch 465 at 540.

The leading case in the last century on the Chancery practice of charging an
accounting party with compound interest is *Burdick v Garrick* (1870) LR 5 Ch
App 233 (where in fact compound interest was not charged). In that case,

Giffard LJ said (at 243): 'The question of interest clearly depends upon the amount which the person who has improperly applied the money may be fairly presumed to have made.'

Lord Hatherley LC put it at slightly greater length, when he said (at 241–242):

> '… the Court does not proceed against an accounting party by way of punishing him for making use of the Plaintiff's money by directing rests, or payment of compound interest, but proceeds upon this principle, either that he has made, or has put himself into such a position as that he is to be presumed to have made, 5 per cent., or compound interest, as the case may be. If the Court finds … that the money received has been invested in an ordinary trade, the whole course of decision has tended to this, that the Court presumes that the party against whom relief is sought has made that amount of profit which persons ordinarily do make in trade, and in those cases the Court directs rests to be made.'

It has to be noted that in considering what profit a person is to be taken to have made, the court takes into account the economic and financial conditions of the time. In *Burdick v Garrick* and other nineteenth century cases 5% interest was regarded as a very high rate but in more recent years prevailing interest rates have been much higher, and this has been recognised by the Chancery court in its awards. In *Wallersteiner v Moir (No 2)* [1975] 1 All ER 849 at 856, [1975] QB 373 at 388 Lord Denning MR, after citing from Lord Hatherley LC, said:

> 'The reason is because a person in a fiduciary position is not allowed to make a profit out of his trust; and, if he does, he is liable to account for that profit or interest in lieu thereof.'

Buckley LJ set out substantially the same position and agreed that Dr Wallersteiner ought to be charged compound interest (see [1975] 1 All ER 849 at 863–864, [1975] QB 373 at 397–398). Scarman LJ stated that the question whether the interest to be awarded should be simple or compound depends upon evidence as to what the accounting party has or is to be presumed to have done with the money and he cited the passage I have just read from the judgment of Lord Hatherley LC in *Burdick v Garrick*. He continued ([1975] 1 All ER 849 at 871, [1975] QB 373 at 406):

> 'Dr Wallersteiner was at all material times engaged in the business of finance. Through a complex structure of companies he conducted financial operations with a view to profit. The quarter million pounds assistance which he obtained from the two companies in order to finance the acquisition of the shares meant that he was in a position to employ the money or its capital equivalent in those operations. Though the truth is unlikely ever to be fully known, shrouded as it is by the elaborate corporate structure within which Dr Wallersteiner chose to operate, one may safely presume that the use of the money (or the capital it enabled him to acquire) was worth to him the equivalent of compound interest at commercial rates with yearly rests, if not more. I, therefore, agree that he should be ordered to pay compound interest at the rates, and with the rests, proposed by Lord Denning MR and Buckley LJ.'

Finally, in *Guardian Ocean Cargoes Ltd v Banco do Brasil SA (No 3)* [1992] 2 Lloyd's Rep 193 at 199 a bank defendant which had been ordered to refund certain sums to the plaintiff was ordered by Hirst J to pay compound interest because it must 'be presumed to have used the money for normal banking purposes as part of its working capital, and thus to have been in a position to earn compound interest'.

I come then to the facts in so far as they are relevant to the claim for compound interest. We have had a good deal of argument about equitable tracing and how far it is possible to trace the £2·5m from Islington's bank account into which it was initially paid into other assets of Islington acquired out of moneys in that bank account or into a general charge on Islington's assets, and about whether the onus is on Westdeutsche as the claimant to prove tracing or on Islington as the fiduciary to disprove it. I find none of these matters relevant to the issue with which we are concerned. The starting point is, as indicated above, that Islington became accountable in equity for the £2·5m which it received for purposes which were by law incapable of fulfilment: see *Re Diplock's Estate* [1948] 2 All ER 318 at 357, [1948] Ch 465 at 540 per Lord Greene MR. Since it is beyond doubt that Islington is solvent, that personal liability in equity subsists whether or not tracing to establish some particular or general charge is possible.

The Westdeutsche account into which the money was initially paid became, as Mr Philipson said, exhausted on at least one occasion and went into overdraft although it was later replenished. Ignoring sophisticated possibilities of tracing, the money initially received by Islington from Westdeutsche was spent by Islington on its ordinary purposes. That is not surprising and Islington's statutory activities are not the sort of activities which are calculated to be carried on at enormous financial profit to Islington.

The other side to that coin is, however, that if Islington had not received the £2·5m from Westdeutsche under the intended swap transaction, Islington would have had to borrow an equivalent sum. In modern conditions that borrowing would have had to have been from a bank or similar institution and would in the ordinary way of business have been at compound and not merely simple interest.

Islington had been three times rate-capped, and it is said, no doubt correctly, that it was more difficult for a rate-capped council to borrow. It is said that one of the attractions to Islington of the interest rate swap scheme was that it was an alternative to borrowing as a way of obtaining finance. But the only alternative to borrowing which would have been open to Islington in the absence of the rate swap scheme would have been to cut its expenditure by the equivalent amount. It is, however, plain that the members of Islington did not want to cut their expenditure further, if they could avoid it; no doubt they had already cut expenditure over the years when Islington had been rate-capped.

We also have the evidence of Mr Stenning, Islington's director of finance at the time, in his witness statement that 'we did not repay any debt with the money but did not have to borrow as much. By the end of the financial year, the money had effectively been spent'. Under cross-examination Mr Stenning agreed that Islington would have borrowed more, if it had not received the payment from Westdeutsche, in order, in effect, not to have to reduce its expenditure by the same amount.

This equates to the position envisaged by Scarman LJ in the passage which I have cited from his judgment in *Wallersteiner v Moir (No 2)* [1975] 1 All ER 849 at 870, [1975] QB 373 at 406, where he said that one may safely presume that the use of the money which Dr Wallersteiner obtained from the two companies in that case was worth to him the equivalent of compound interest at commercial rates.

In these circumstances it is appropriate, in my judgment, and consistent with authority, that Islington should be charged compound interest on the balance from time to time outstanding of the money it received from Westdeutsche. No issue has been raised as to the rates of interest.

Accordingly I would dismiss Islington's appeal and allow Westdeutsche's cross-appeal by respondent's notice as to the date from which interest is to run. The necessary alteration should be made to the judge's order when the calculations have been made.

LEGGATT LJ.

Unjust enrichment

The parties believed that they were making an interest swaps contract. They were not, because such a contract was ultra vires the local authority. So they made no contract at all. Islington say that they should receive a windfall because the purpose of the doctrine of ultra vires is to protect council taxpayers whereas restitution would disrupt Islington's finances. They also contend that it would countenance 'unconsidered dealings with local authorities'. If that is the best that can be said for refusing restitution, the sooner it is enforced the better. Protection of council taxpayers from loss is to be distinguished from securing a windfall for them. The disruption of Islington's finances is the result of ill-considered financial dispositions by Islington and its officers. It is not the policy of the law to require others to deal at their peril with local authorities, nor to require others to undertake their own inquiries about whether a local authority has power to make particular contracts or types of contract. Any system of law, and indeed any system of fair dealing, must be expected to ensure that Islington do not profit by the fortuity that when it became known that the contract was ineffective the balance stood in their favour. In other words, in circumstances such as these they should not be unjustly enriched.

It is common ground that the interest swaps and Islington's payments were ultra vires the local authority, and that the contract was therefore void ab initio; that there was no illegality involved; and that the legal property in the money which was paid by the parties to each other under the swap contract passed to the recipient.

Where A has in his possession the money of B under a void transaction, B should be entitled to reimbursement unless some principle of law precludes it. If the transaction was a contract, initially valid, the question will arise whether it has been partially performed. If so, the failure of consideration will not be total. But if the transaction was entered into by both parties in the belief, which proves unfounded, that it was an enforceable contract, in principle the parties ought to be restored to the respective positions from which they started. To achieve that, where there have been mutual payments the recipient of the larger payment has only to repay the net excess over the payment he has himself made.

Hobhouse J said (p 929, ante):

'In my judgment the correct analysis is that any payments made under a contract which is void ab initio, in the way that an ultra vires contract is void, are not contractual payments at all. They are payments in which the legal property in the money passes to the recipient but in equity the property in the money remains with the payer. The recipient holds the money as a fiduciary for the payer and is bound to recognise his equity and repay the money to him. This relationship and the consequent obligation have been recognised both by courts applying the common law and by Chancery courts. The principle is the same in both cases: it is unconscionable that the recipient should retain the money. Neither mistake nor the contractual principle of total failure of consideration are the basis for the right of recovery.'

In my judgment that formulation is wholly accurate, provided that the contract in question is not a borrowing contract. If it were a borrowing contract, it would fall foul (as the judge recognised) of the principle in *Sinclair v Brougham* [1914] AC 398, [1914–15] All ER Rep 622 that restitution will not be ordered where to do so would have the effect of enforcing a void contract. That is not the case here. In relation to a contract other than a borrowing contract the effect of restitution is to put the payer into the position in which he would have been if the transaction had never been entered into.

The judge's conclusion was supported, as he found and as Dillon LJ has demonstrated, by the annuity cases. There have been other manifestations of the principle, culminating in *Woolwich Building Society v IRC (No 2)* [1992] 3 All ER 737, [1993] AC 70, although the decision in that case could be treated as confined to cases of money paid pursuant to an unlawful demand by a public authority which is thereby unjustly enriched. But the principle for which Westdeutsche contend has been exemplified in *North Central Wagon Finance Co Ltd v Brailsford* [1962] 1 All ER 502, [1962] 1 WLR 1288 in which Cairns J held money paid on a bill of sale which was void for non-registration to be recoverable as money had and received after giving proper credits. In *Rowland v Divall* [1923] 2 KB 500, [1923] All ER Rep 270 the buyer of a car, who had used it for several months, was held entitled when the seller proved to have had no title to it to sue for the price paid as money had and received because the buyer had received no part of what he contracted to receive, namely the property and right to possession. In *Rover International Ltd v Cannon Film Sales Ltd (No 3)* [1989] 3 All ER 423 at 433, [1989] 1 WLR 912 at 923 Kerr LJ expressed the test as being 'whether or not the party claiming total failure of consideration has in fact received any part of the benefit bargained for under the contract or purported contract'. That seems to me to be the test to apply here.

As Westdeutsche submitted, the fact that the payer had received a benefit did not mean that there had been no total failure of consideration, if the payer did not get the benefit for which he bargained. What in this case Westdeutsche bargained for were payments which would discharge a contractual obligation and which Westdeutsche were entitled lawfully to receive. What they obtained were payments made under a void agreement, which in equity remained the property of Islington and which even at law they were always entitled to recover back.

Islington criticised this formulation as artificial, contending that if the formulation of counsel for Westdeutsche in the court below, which appears to have been indorsed by Hobhouse J, is that Islington must also show absence of consideration, then the argument is circular. The payments by Westdeutsche were tainted by 'absence of consideration' because they received payments from Islington which were recoverable because Islington received payments from Westdeutsche, which are recoverable by Westdeutsche, and so on. Islington argued that Westdeutsche here did not bargain for the right to receive repayment of their payment to Islington. No doubt it hoped to do so. It bargained for participation in a series of risks on specified days in the future on each of which the prevailing London Inter-Bank Offered Rate would be compared with 7·5% and, if the risk favoured Westdeutsche, a payment would be made by Islington, and vice versa. It bargained for the risk-taking twice a year for ten years. It got two years. There was no total failure of consideration, only partial. It was so held by Hobhouse J.

There can have been no consideration under a contract void ab initio. So it is fallacious to speak of the failure of consideration having been partial. What is meant is that the parties did, in the belief that the contract was enforceable, part of what they would have been required to do if it had been. As it was, they were not performing the contract even in part: they were making payments that had no legal justification, instead of affording each other mutual consideration for an enforceable contract. In my judgment, the payments made are in those circumstances recoverable by Westdeutsche, in so far as they exceed the payments made by Islington, as money had and received to the use of Westdeutsche by which Islington have been unjustly enriched.

The proprietary claim in equity

All of the components of Westdeutsche's claim in equity were viewed in a sense favourable to Westdeutsche by the House of Lords in *Sinclair v Brougham* with the result that: (1) in equity the money remained the property of Westdeutsche; (2) mere receipt by Islington of money which was not theirs constituted them fiduciaries; (3) Westdeutsche's equitable right in relation to the money in Islington's hands which remained Westdeutsche's was in the nature of an equitable charge; and (4) since Islington are solvent, Westdeutsche can recover in full.

Interest

Where money has been withheld by a person in a fiduciary position the court has power to award compound interest: see *Burdick v Garrick* (1870) LR 5 Ch App 233, as explained by Scarman LJ in *Wallersteiner v Moir* (*No 2*) [1975] 1 All ER 849 at 870, [1975] QB 373 at 406. The court is concerned to ensure that the fiduciary does not make a profit from the use of money that was not his. The fiduciary may be proved or presumed to have used the money profitably. Here there was no proof that Islington used the money to lend or invest advantageously. Hobhouse J said (p 939, ante):

> 'On occasions when the accounts only contained small credits or were in overdraft, Islington had in fact lent money out on the market on a short-term basis ...'

I do not take the phrase 'On occasions when' to mean 'Whenever'. There simply was no proof of what the money was used for. If a fiduciary is engaged in trade or investment business it may readily be presumed that compound interest was earned. But a local authority uses its money for a multitude of purposes, and indeed one of the reasons why Islington entered into the interest swap was to obtain the benefit of the money paid 'up front' in advance of the dates when they might have received parts of it by way of interest payments.

There was no evidence of any intention to lend or invest this payment, although it may well have been Islington's policy to lend out on short-term deposits money that would otherwise have been lying idle on current account. About his decision to award compound interest the judge said only (p 955, ante):

'Anyone who lends money or borrows money on a commercial basis receives or pays interest periodically and if that interest is not paid it is compounded ...'

Islington had the advantage of £2·5m in their hands that turned out not to have been theirs. They must yield up the financial benefit which they derived from doing so. To accord Westdeutsche no more than simple interest would not represent commercial reality. If Islington had lent the money out, they would have earned compound interest. But there is no evidence that they did so, except sporadically. I do not regard the judge's description of Islington as having 'actually set aside a fund' as helpful. That implies that there was an actual fund in the sense of cash in a bank account or otherwise earmarked. But there only ever was a book entry. That will have had accounting consequences, but they are not shown in themselves to have resulted in a liability to pay compound interest.

The evidence about the position in which Islington found themselves was given by Mr Stenning (Islington's director of finance at the time). He acknowledged in cross-examination that if Islington had not received swap premiums they would have borrowed more. He also accepted that the possibility of making economies was not a realistic option for 1987/8, and that Islington for political reasons desired not to make the savings necessary to avoid the need to raise money. It is said that, rate-capped as they were, they would have had difficulty in borrowing the sum of £2·5m, and that that was why they adopted the 'financial device' of interest swaps. But, whatever difficulty they might have encountered, the fact is that Islington had the benefit of £2·5m which was not theirs. The value of it to them cannot be less than it would have cost them to borrow it, if they had been permitted to do so. Indeed, the advance of the sum of £2·5m was in consideration of a reduction in the amount of fixed interest which Westdeutsche were obliged to pay annually to Islington under the interest-swap contract. The use of £2·5m was needed by Islington, was acquired by them as what they believed was a legitimate alternative to a loan, and was worth to them what they would have had to pay in interest to borrow that sum. Since they have paid no interest on it the value to them of the use of the money has been the amount of such interest at the rates current from time to time and compounded. It is undeniable that during the relevant period Westdeutsche would have lent the money out on that basis if they had not parted with it to Islington.

It is common ground that interest will generally be awarded from the date of accrual of the cause of action: see BP Exploration Co (Libya) Ltd v Hunt (No 2) [1982] 1 All ER 925 at 975, [1979] 1 WLR 783 at 846. The three exceptions envisaged by Robert Goff J were (1) when the position of the defendant demands it, (2) when the conduct of the plaintiff does so, and (3) when it would be unjust in all the circumstances to award interest from the date of loss. Mr Philipson QC does not suggest that it would be unjust to apply the normal rule, nor does he contend that Westdeutsche were blameworthy, although he does point to the fact that so long as Westdeutsche believed the contract to be enforceable they pressed Islington to comply with it. But Islington neither paid the net balances of interest as they fell due nor tendered repayment of the sum of £2·5m. Mr Philipson relies on Lord Wilberforce's comment in *General Tire and Rubber Co v Firestone Tyre and Rubber Co Ltd* [1975] 2 All ER 173 at 188, [1975] 1 WLR 819 at 836:

> 'In a commercial setting, it would be proper to take account of the manner in which and the time at which persons acting honestly and reasonably would pay.'

But this was said in the context of a commercial practice under which royalties in respect of use before grant of a patent are not expected to be paid before grant, from which it followed that it was appropriate to award interest only from the date of grant. No such practice inhibits the award of interest in this case from the date when Islington would first have had to pay it if the money had been borrowed.

The judge would have awarded compound interest for the whole period if he had not felt constrained by two arguments to make it run only from 1 April 1990. But Mr Philipson did not feel able to support either of them. The fact that neither party initially realised that the contract under which the money had been paid was ultra vires is immaterial. Nor can it affect Islington's liability to pay interest on the money that they should not have had that Westdeutsche had laid off their liability by means of a protective contract with Morgan Grenfell. That was nothing to do with Islington: it was res inter alios acta.

No objection has been taken in this court to the rates at which the judge awarded interest: he did so on the basis of average seven-day rates, calculated separately for each fiscal year. In my judgment it is just that, having had the use of the money, Islington should pay compound interest at average seven-day rates (calculated by the fiscal year) on such part of Westdeutsche's advance of £2·5m as from time to time remained outstanding during the successive periods beginning one day after the receipt by Westdeutsche from Islington of credit for each net payment of interest. I would dismiss the appeal, allow Westdeutsche's cross-appeal, set aside the award of interest, and substitute the order which Dillon LJ has indicated.

KENNEDY LJ. I have read the judgments of Dillon and Leggatt LJJ and agree with them.

Appeal dismissed. Cross-appeal allowed. Leave to appeal to House of Lords refused.

23 May 1994. The Appeal Committee of the House of Lords gave Islington leave to appeal.

Mary Rose Plummer   Barrister.

Kleinwort Benson Ltd v South Tyneside Metropolitan Borough Council

QUEEN'S BENCH DIVISION (COMMERCIAL COURT)

HOBHOUSE J

22, 23 FEBRUARY, 1, 2, 3, 12 MARCH 1993

Contract – Failure of consideration – Recovery of money paid – Interest rate swap agreements entered into between bankers and local authority – Agreements ultra vires local authority and void ab initio – Whether bankers entitled to recover money paid under agreements to local authority – Whether claim time-barred – Whether fact that bankers hedged liabilities under parallel contracts and recouped part or whole of losses invalidating claim for restitution – Whether bankers able to show that local authority had been unjustly enriched at their expense – Whether compound interest recoverable – Limitation Act 1980, ss 5, 29(5).

Contract – Restitution – Interest rate swap agreement – Bankers entering into interest rate swap agreements with local authority – Agreements ultra vires the local authority and void – Whether bankers entitled to recover payments made.

Between 1983 and 1986 the plaintiff bankers entered into five interest rate swap contracts (KB1 to KB5) with the defendant local authority which involved payments by both parties. The plaintiffs also entered into parallel hedging transactions to offset its potential liabilities under swap contracts KB1 and KB2. Only KB2 ran its full course because on 1 November 1989 the Divisional Court held, in an unconnected case subsequently upheld by the House of Lords in January 1991, that such transactions were ultra vires the local authorities and void ab initio. Thereafter, the local authority made no further payments under the swap contracts, but paid the sums due into an interest bearing account held with its bankers. In March 1991 the plaintiffs issued a writ against the local authority, claiming restitution of over £1·6m as money paid under the contracts and compound interest thereon. The local authority accepted that prima facie it was under a personal liability to make restitution in law and in equity to the plaintiffs, but contended (i) that the six-year time limit provided for in s 5[a] of the Limitation Act 1980 applied in respect of one of the payments made under KB1, with the result that the plaintiffs' claim had to be limited to the £582,257·19 paid within that period and that a claim for £8,784·25 made outside the six-year period was time-barred, (ii) that the fact that the plaintiffs had hedged their supposed liabilities under KB1 and KB2 and recouped their losses (either in whole or in part) invalidated their claim, since they could not show that the local authority had been unjustly enriched at their expense, (iii) that the criteria necessary for the grant of a restitutionary remedy were not satisfied in the case of KB5, since the complex structure of the underlying transactions in effect precluded any restoration of the parties to their original position and (iv) that it was not open to the court to award compound interest to the plaintiffs where only remedies in personam were involved. The plaintiffs contended that, in evaluating their net claim, the court should have

---

a   Section 5 provides: 'An action founded on simple contract shall not be brought after the expiration of six years from the date on which the cause of action accrued.'

regard to the payments made in connection with all five swap contracts so as to arrive at some aggregated position which would obviate the need to refer to any individual time-barred payment, that the four payments made by the local authority under KB1 were payments 'in respect of' the plaintiffs' right to recover in full money had and received from the local authority within s 29(5)^b of the 1980 Act, which provided that where any right of action accrued to recover any debt in circumstances where the person liable for the claim made any payment 'in respect of' it, that right would be treated as having accrued on and not before the date of payment, and that they were entitled to an award of compound interest on the basis of their equitable right in personam to recover the payments made under the swap contracts.

Held – (1) Having regard to the fact that each interest rate swap contract was an independent transaction it was clear that no right of set-off or aggregation existed as between one contract and another. Accordingly, in evaluating the plaintiffs' net claim, each swap contract both in law and in equity had to be looked at separately, with the result that the plaintiffs were not entitled to aggregate or set off payments made under the contracts so as to arrive at an overall aggregate position which would have enabled them not to have to refer to any time-barred payments. It followed that to succeed in full in respect of the payments they had made in connection with the first swap contract the plaintiffs could only rely on payments which had been made within the six-year period (see p 979 h j, post).

(2) In deciding whether a payment amounted to an acknowledgement of a debt for the purposes of s 29(5) of the 1980 Act, the court would look at the act and intention of the debtor to see whether the payment was made 'in respect of' a particular debt and therefore at the actual position as understood by the parties at the time of the payment, without reference to the analysis which the law might place on that payment. Since the four payments made by the local authority to the plaintiffs in relation to the first interest rate swap contract were made in supposed discharge of a legal liability under that contract and not 'in respect of' any liability for money had and received, they did not constitute an acknowledgement by the local authority of a liability to make restitution to the plaintiffs of sums earlier received by the local authority and therefore could not be treated as having been made in respect of that liability. The plaintiffs' claim in respect of the payments made under the first swap contract would accordingly be limited to £582,257·19 (see p 981 b d e, post); dictum of Buckley J in *Re Footman Bower & Co Ltd* [1961] 2 All ER 161 at 164 applied; *Westdeutsche Landesbank Girozentrale v Islington London BC, Kleinwort Benson Ltd v Sandwell BC* [1994] 4 All ER 890 considered.

(3) In considering whether a plaintiff was entitled to restitution as against a defendant on the ground of unjust enrichment at the expense of the plaintiff, the question whether the plaintiff had entered into related contracts or parallel transactions (although relevant to the right to compensation) had nothing to do with the principle of restitution. Accordingly, the fact that the plaintiffs had followed a hedging strategy in parallel to the interest rate swap transactions entered into with the local authority was irrelevant to the recognition of a restitutionary remedy in personam, which simply required the plaintiffs to show that they were the payers of the money at issue, that the local authority

b   Section 29(5), so far as material, is set out at p 980 a b, post

had been unjustly enriched and that there was no obstacle to restitution. The plaintiffs were therefore entitled to claim restitution in respect of the payments made under the first two swap contracts and the fact that they had recouped their losses in hedging transactions did not provide a defence to their claim. However, the plaintiffs' claim in respect of the fifth swap contract failed, since it would not be appropriate to order a partial restitution because the parties could not be restored to their previous position and both had enjoyed benefits arising out of the transaction (see p 985 *a* to *d*, p 987 *f g* and p 990 *c* to *f*, post); dictum of Lord Wright in *Fibrosa Spolka Akcyjna v Fairbairn Lawson Combe Barbour Ltd* [1942] 2 All ER 122 at 135 and of Lord Goff in *Lipkin Gorman (a firm) v Karpnale Ltd* [1992] 4 All ER 512 at 532 applied; *Air Canada v British Columbia* (1989) 59 DLR (4th) 161 considered.

(4) The court would only award simple interest in cases where the plaintiff was confined to personal rights and remedies analogous to those recognised at common law in an action for money had and received and had no proprietary equitable remedy against the defendant, who no longer had his property, albeit that the plaintiff was relying on a restitutionary remedy. It followed that the plaintiffs' claim to be awarded compound interest independently of any proprietary claim would be rejected. The plaintiffs were accordingly entitled to judgment for the sum of £1,470,945·30 (being the amount of the original claim less the time-barred payment under KB1 and the KB5 payments) with simple interest thereon at 1% above base rate. Simple interest would be awarded as from 1 January 1990, since by that time the local authority should have honestly and reasonably appreciated that repayment ought to be made because the plaintiffs' causes of action had all fully accrued and a judgment on the correct view of the law had been given (see p 994 *g* to *j*, p 995 *a b g*, p 996 *f* to p 997 *b d e*, post); dictum of Lord Wilberforce in *General Tire and Rubber Co v Firestone Tyre and Rubber Co Ltd* [1975] 2 All ER 173 at 188 applied; *Westdeutsche Landesbank Girozentrale v Islington London BC* [1994] 4 All ER 890 considered.

Notes

For a local authority's power to incur expenditure, see 28 *Halsbury's Laws* (4th edn) paras 1245, 1247, and for cases on the subject, see 33 *Digest* (Reissue) 31–34, 96–104.

For the Limitation Act 1980, ss 5, 29, see 24 *Halsbury's Statutes* (4th edn) (1989 reissue) 653, 679.

Cases referred to in judgment

A-G v Alford (1855) 4 De GM & G 843, 43 ER 737, LC.

Air Canada v British Columbia (1989) 59 DLR (4th) 161, Can SC.

Amministrazione delle Finanze dello Stato v SpA San Giorgio Case 199/82 [1983] ECR 3595.

BP Exploration Co (Libya) Ltd v Hunt (No 2) [1982] 1 All ER 925, [1979] 1 WLR 783; *affd* [1982] 1 All ER 925, [1981] 1 WLR 232, CA; *affd* [1982] 1 All ER 925, [1983] 2 AC 352, [1982] 2 WLR 253, HL.

Bray v Ford [1896] AC 44, [1895–9] All ER Rep 1009, HL.

Bromley v Holland (1802) Coop G 9, 35 ER 458.

Burdick v Garrick (1870) LR 5 Ch App 233.

Diplock's Estate, Re, Diplock v Wintle [1948] 2 All ER 318, [1948] Ch 465, CA; *affd* sub nom *Ministry of Health v Simpson* [1950] 2 All ER 1137, [1951] AC 251, HL.

Fibrosa Spolka Akcyjna v Fairbairn Lawson Combe Barbour Ltd [1942] 2 All ER 122, [1943] AC 32, HL.

Footman Bower & Co Ltd, Re [1961] 2 All ER 161, [1961] Ch 443, [1961] 2 WLR 667, Ch D.

General Tire and Rubber Co v Firestone Tyre and Rubber Co Ltd [1975] 2 All ER 173, [1975] 1 WLR 819, HL.

Hazell v Hammersmith and Fulham London BC [1991] 1 All ER 545, [1992] 2 AC 1, [1991] 2 WLR 372, HL; *rvsg* [1990] 3 All ER 33, [1990] 2 QB 697, [1990] 2 WLR 17, 1038, DC and CA.

Hoffman v Cooke (1801) 5 Ves Jun 623, 31 ER 772.

Lipkin Gorman (a firm) v Karpnale Ltd [1992] 4 All ER 512, [1991] 2 AC 548, [1991] 3 WLR 10, HL.

London Chatham and Dover Rly Co v South Eastern Rly Co [1892] 1 Ch 120, CA; *affd* [1893] AC 429, HL.

Lonrho plc v Fayed (No 2) [1991] 4 All ER 961, [1992] 1 WLR 1.

Mason v New South Wales (1959) 102 CLR 108, Aust HC.

O'Sullivan v Management Agency and Music Ltd [1985] 3 All ER 351, [1985] QB 428, [1984] 3 WLR 448, CA.

President of India v La Pintada Cia Navegacion SA [1984] 2 All ER 773, [1985] AC 104, [1984] 3 WLR 10, HL.

Shearson Lehman Hutton Inc v Maclaine Watson & Co Ltd (No 2) [1990] 3 All ER 723.

Surrendra Overseas Ltd v Government of Sri Lanka [1977] 2 All ER 481, [1977] 1 WLR 565.

Wallersteiner v Moir (No 2) [1975] 1 All ER 849, [1975] QB 373, [1975] 2 WLR 389, CA.

Westdeutsche Landesbank Girozentrale v Islington London BC, Kleinwort Benson Ltd v Sandwell BC [1994] 4 All ER 890; *affd in part* [1994] 4 All ER 890, [1994] 1 WLR 938, CA.

Woolwich Building Society v IRC (No 2) [1992] 3 All ER 737, [1993] AC 70, [1992] 3 WLR 366, HL.

Action

The plaintiffs, Kleinwort Benson Ltd, by a writ issued on 27 March 1991 brought an action against the defendants, South Tyneside Metropolitan Borough Council, partly in their own right and partly as the successors of the Tyne and Wear Metropolitan County Council, claiming restitution of payments which they had made to the defendants in connection with interest rate swap contracts which were in fact ultra vires the defendants and void ab initio. The facts are set out in the judgment.

Richard Southwell QC, Rhodri Davies and *Nicholas Lavender* (instructed by *Clifford Chance*) for the plaintiffs.
Anthony Mann QC and *David Bean* (instructed by *Sharpe Pritchard,* agents for *D J Freeman*) for the defendants.

Cur adv vult

12 March 1993. The following judgment was delivered.

HOBHOUSE J. This action, like those which were the subject of the judgment which I handed down on 12 February 1993 in *Westdeutsche Landesbank Girozentrale v Islington London BC, Kleinwort Benson Ltd v Sandwell BC* [1994] 4 All ER 890 (which I will call 'Swaps 1') concerns the rights of restitution in connection with void transactions which had been entered into between a bank and a local authority. In the Swaps 1 judgment I have set out the background to the decisions of the Divisional Court, Court of Appeal and House of Lords in *Hazell v Hammersmith and Fulham London BC* [1990] 3 All ER 33, [1990] 2 QB 697 (DC and CA); [1991] 1 All ER 545, [1992] 2 AC 1 (HL), in which it was held that interest rate swap contracts were ultra vires local authorities under the Local Government Act 1972 and were accordingly wholly void. In Swaps 1, which concerned certain transactions of the council of the London borough of Islington and the borough council of Sandwell, I held that where money had been paid under a supposed contract which was in truth wholly void, the payer was prima facie entitled to recover that sum either as money had and received by the payee to the use of the payer or as money which in equity continued to belong to the payer and which the payee was in equity bound to repay and which the payer was entitled to trace into the assets of the payee. The basis of the payer's claim, whether at common law or in equity, was that the payee had been unjustly enriched at the expense of the payer and that in conscience the payee must repay to the payer the sum which he had received from the payer. The right to restitution arose from the fact that the payment was made without consideration under a contract which was, unknown to both parties, wholly void and not that the payer had been operating under any mistake as to any specific fact. In respect of one of the transactions involving the Sandwell council (the first Sandwell swap) a defence of limitation of actions was raised by the council; although I held that the claim for money had and received fell within s 5 of the Limitation Act 1980, I held that that provision did not, on the facts of that case, provide the council with a defence to the claim of the plaintiff bank. In the action against the Islington council, I held that the relevant payments of the plaintiff bank were to be traced into the assets of the council as at the date of trial and that accordingly the bank was entitled in equity to an order against the defendant council that it pay the appropriate sum to the bank out of its assets as part of the equitable remedy of tracing. In this connection the plaintiff bank had also asked for an order that such sum be paid together with compound interest and I ordered that compound interest should be paid.

In the present action the plaintiffs are Kleinwort Benson Ltd, who were also the plaintiffs in the Sandwell action, and the defendants are the South Tyneside Metropolitan Borough Council, who are sued partly in their own right and partly as the statutory successors of the Tyne and Wear Metropolitan County Council, which ceased to exist on 1 April 1986. For present purposes it is not necessary for me to distinguish between the two councils and I will refer simply to them as 'the defendants'. The claims which are made by Kleinwort Benson in this action against the defendants relate to payments made by Kleinwort Benson to the defendants in connection with five interest rate swap contracts. It is convenient to number these KB1 to KB5:

Swap	Date	Start	Finish	Last payment	Net claim
KB1	17/6/83	27/6/83	27/6/90	27/6/89	£591,241·04
KB2	11/11/83	15/11/83	16/5/88	16/5/88	£46,647·26
KB3	10/5/84	5/3/84	5/3/94	5/9/89	£384,563·34
KB4	22/3/84	30/3/84	30/3/94	29/9/89	£457,227·38
KB5	12/12/86	12/12/86	[21/11/96]	N/A	£123,675·62

Total Claim: £1,603,405·04

The only swap contract that ran its full course was KB2; KB1, KB3 and KB4 were still uncompleted at the time of the decision of the Divisional Court in *Hazell's* case. All these swaps involved payments both ways. KB5 comes into a special category, to which I will revert. Kleinwort Benson also claim compound and/or simple interest.

With one qualification, both parties to this trial have presented their arguments on the basis that, subject to appeal, the law is as stated in the judgment in Swaps 1 and I have not sought to re-argue the matters there considered and decided. On this basis the defendants accept that prima facie they are under a personal liability to make restitution in law and in equity to the plaintiffs. The defendants have expressly abandoned certain of their pleaded defences. Thus, they have abandoned alleged defences of estoppel, voluntary assumption of risk, illegal gaming, and change of position. The defendants do not admit that the plaintiffs are able to trace the relevant payments and accordingly dispute the availability of any tracing remedy. The question of tracing in the present matter is undoubtedly more complicated and difficult than it was in the Islington case on account of the fact that certain of the payments were made to, or for the account of, the now defunct county council; the plaintiffs have also alleged that at a later stage a fund was set up by the defendants which amounted to a trust fund in which the plaintiffs are entitled to share. It has therefore been sensibly agreed between the present parties that the trial of any question of the availability of the tracing remedy and its extent shall be stood over to be tried on another occasion should the need arise. Accordingly, the present trial has proceeded on the basis that the defendants are, in principle, under a personal liability to the plaintiffs either because South Tyneside was itself the party initially liable or that it is the statutory successor to the personal liabilities of the county council. It has also been agreed between the parties that any claim of the plaintiffs based upon 'discharge of liabilities' (that is to say the basis of claim considered in Swaps 1) should likewise be deferred to a later trial, should the need arise.

The issues which have to be determined at the present trial are accordingly: (1) whether the defendants have a defence of limitation of actions under s 5 of the Limitation Act 1980 to part of the plaintiffs' claim in respect of the payments made under KB1. This defence involved an application of my decision in Swaps 1 in relation to the first Sandwell swap and a contention by the present plaintiffs that they are entitled to rely upon s 29(5) of the 1980 Act. The defendants have abandoned any further limitation defence in relation to KB1 or KB2 and KB3; (2) whether the fact that the plaintiffs hedged their supposed liabilities under KB1 and KB2 and recouped, either in whole or in part, their losses invalidates the plaintiffs' claim to restitution on the basis that the plaintiffs cannot show that the defendants have been unjustly enriched at the expense of the plaintiffs. This argument of the defendants raises a fundamental question whether, and to what extent and under what circumstances, it is an answer to a claim based upon the principle of unjust enrichment that the plaintiff has not at the end of the day suffered the loss. It is analogous to the question raised in compulsion cases of 'passing on' where the payer of the wrongful impost or tax has passed on the burden to his customers. The defendants have abandoned a similar defence to the claims in respect of KB3 and KB4; (3) whether, upon the special facts of KB5, the plaintiffs can make out a claim for restitution on the ground of unjust enrichment at the expense of the payer. This argument turns upon the particular circumstances of that transaction but it also involves a consideration of what is the fundamental principle; (4) what award of interest should be made in favour of the plaintiffs. It is not in dispute that simple interest can properly be awarded, subject to a suitable starting date and rate, but the defendants do dispute that it can be proper to make any award of compound interest. They submitted that this was clear where only personal remedies were involved, as must be assumed to be the case for present purposes, and they further questioned whether, even where tracing remedies were available, as was the case in the Islington action, it is open to a court to award compound interest. This argument in turn gave rise to a consideration of what was the nature of the personal remedy that was recognised in equity as opposed to the common law cause of action in money had and received.

The trial of this action took place upon agreed facts supplemented by affidavit evidence and documents. No oral evidence was called and there was no material issue of fact. It is therefore convenient to take the issues that arise in the order in which I have just stated them and to refer to the facts that are relevant to each issue at that time.

(1) LIMITATION OF ACTIONS

In the *Sandwell* case the defendant council raised a defence of limitation of actions in respect of the claim of the plaintiff bank in relation to the payments that had been made under an interest rate swap contract dated 6 July 1983 ('the first Sandwell swap'). The writ in the action had been issued on 3 April 1991 and accordingly any cause of action which had accrued prior to 3 April 1985 was liable to be time-barred. The payments which had been made under that contract dated from 17 October 1983 through to 15 July 1988. Because of the way that that contract was structured payments were made quarterly first one way and then the other. These are set out in the table in Swaps 1 [1994] 4 All ER 890 at 907. At the end of the period, having regard to all the payments that had been made both ways, the bank had paid to the local authority £196,322·72 more than the local authority had paid to the bank. I held that the bank's claim must be viewed as a claim for that net balance although the cause of action in money had and received had to be related to payments actually made. I gave my reasons why the defence could not succeed in that case (see [1994] 4 All ER 890 at 955).

The six-year time limit provided for in s 5 of the Limitation Act 1980 applies to an action for money had and received and by analogy to an equivalent equitable action. The cause of action in money had and received arises when the relevant money is paid by the plaintiff to the defendant. If a plaintiff has to rely upon a payment which he has made more than six years before the issue of the writ, then any cause of action based upon that payment is, pro tanto, time-barred. In the *Sandwell* action, the plaintiff (like the plaintiffs in the present action in connection with KB2 and KB3) did not need to rely upon any

time-barred payment; its cause of action could be based upon payments made
within the six-year period. On the facts of that case the plaintiff did not need
to rely upon any payment it had made earlier than 1988. As at 31 December
1987 the plaintiff had received in aggregate a greater sum from the local
authority than it had paid to the local authority. It was only the last payments
which gave rise to the unjust enrichment in respect of which the plaintiff was
suing in that action. No defence of time-bar was available.

Turning to the facts of the present case, the writ in the action was issued on
27 March 1991 so that causes of action which accrued before 27 March 1985 are
prima facie time-barred. The payments made under swap KB1 were as follows:

Date	The plaintiffs £	The defendants £
28.12.1983	94,520·55	
27.06.1984	107,517·12	
27.12.1984	89,306·51	
27.06.1985	79,469·18	
27.12.1985		84,606·16
27.06.1986		56,095·89
29.12.198	114,041·10	
29.06.1987		11,686·64
29.12.1987	141,010·27	
27.06.1988	153,416·09	
28.12.1988	94,520·55	
27.06.1989		130,171·24
	873,801·37	282,559·93

The net payment made by the plaintiffs to the defendants is £591,241·44 and
this is the sum which the plaintiffs claim in the present action from the
defendants in respect of this swap. However, within the six-year period, the
plaintiffs had only paid to the defendants £582,257·19. To justify the full claim
the plaintiffs have to have recourse also to the payment made on 27 December
1984, outside the six-year period. Accordingly, the defendants submit that the
plaintiffs' claim in respect of the payments made under KB1 must be limited to
£582,257·19 and the claim for £8,784·25 is time-barred. (The defendants accept
that no defence can be based on the fact that the first two payments were also
made outside the six-year period.)

The plaintiffs accept that this is the effect of the judgment in Swaps 1 but
they submit, firstly, that in evaluating what their net claim in the present
action is, one should have regard to the payments made in connection with all
five of the interest rate swaps concerned in this action so as to arrive at some
overall aggregated position which enables them not to have to refer to any
time-barred payment. This argument must be rejected. Each interest rate
swap contract was an independent transaction and no right of set-off or
aggregation exists or existed as between one contract and another. Each
contract, both in law and in equity, must be looked at separately and to succeed
in full in respect of the payments they have made in connection with KB1, the
plaintiffs may only rely upon payments which they have made within the
six-year period.

The second answer which the plaintiffs sought to make was to rely upon s 29(5) of the Limitation Act 1980, which provides:

'... where any right of action has accrued to recover—(a) any debt or other liquidated pecuniary claim ... and the person liable or accountable for the claim acknowledges the claim or makes any payment in respect of it the right shall be treated as having accrued on and not before the date of the acknowledgement or payment.'

The plaintiffs submit that the four payments made by the defendants to them in relation to KB1 between December 1985 and June 1989 are payments 'in respect of' the right of the plaintiffs to recover in full money had and received from the defendants. It is not in dispute that when the defendants were making these payments they thought that they were discharging a legal liability under the KB1 contract. They did not realise at that time that it was void and they were wholly unaware of any restitutionary right that the plaintiffs might have against them. Therefore the plaintiffs' argument has to be put on the basis of what is now known to be the legal position and the effect which the law would now attach to those payments. 'Where payments both ways have been made the correct view is to treat the later payment as, pro tanto, a repayment of the earlier sum paid by the other party' (see Swaps 1 [1994] 4 All ER 890 at 929). The question therefore becomes whether for the purposes of answering the question posed by s 29(5) one has to have regard to the actual position as understood by the parties at the time of the part payment or whether it suffices to have regard to an analysis which the law places on that payment although the parties were at the material time unaware of it.

This was effectively the point which had to be considered in *Re Footman Bower & Co Ltd* [1961] 2 All ER 161, [1961] Ch 443 and *Surrendra Overseas Ltd v Government of Sri Lanka* [1977] 2 All ER 481, [1977] 1 WLR 565. In the winding up in *Re Footman Bower & Co Ltd* the relevant claimant had supplied goods to the company over a period of more than six years and the company had from time to time made payments on account generally. Buckley J held that such payments were sufficient to start the limitation period running afresh. He referred to the law as it had existed prior to the passing of the Limitation Act 1939:

'Before that Act there was no statutory provision that in the case of a simple contract debt part payment should stop time running under the Limitation Act, 1623. For a payment to have this effect it was necessary that it should amount to an acknowledgment of the debt and import a new promise to pay the outstanding balance. The mere act of the creditor appropriating a payment to a statute-barred debt could not have this effect, for such an acknowledgment and promise could only come from the debtor. Since the enactment of the Limitation Act, 1939, the position has been different, for s. 23(4) now contains a statutory provision applicable to simple contract debts whereby any payment in respect of a debt will make time start to run afresh in respect of that debt. There is no longer need to establish a new promise to pay. In my judgment, however, one must still look at the act and intention of the debtor to see whether the payment is made in respect of the particular debt. Payment in s. 23(4) is dealt with in close conjunction with acknowledgment. Just as an acknowledgment can only acquire that character by the act of the debtor or his agent, so also, I think, a payment, for the purposes of s. 23(4), can only acquire the characteristic of being made "in respect of" the debt by the act of the debtor or his agent.   Consequently, in my judgment, appropriation by a creditor of a sum received from the debtor towards satisfaction of a particular debt, be it statute-barred or not, cannot make such appropriation a "payment in respect thereof" within the meaning of s. 23(4).' (See [1961] 2 All ER 161 at 164, [1961] Ch 443 at 449.)

Therefore Buckley J was deciding that it was still necessary to look at the act and intention of the debtor to see whether the payment was made in respect of the particular debt. Kerr J in the *Surrendra Overseas* case followed and applied *Re Footman Bower & Co Ltd*. He said ([1977] 2 All ER 481 at 491, [1977] 1 WLR 565 at 577):

'A part payment, like an acknowledgment, must be evidence of an admission of liability for the debt claimed.'

It is accordingly clear that unless one can conclude that the payments made by the defendants to the plaintiffs evidence an acknowledgment by the defendants of a liability to make restitution to the plaintiffs of sums earlier received by the defendants, the payments cannot be viewed as having been in respect of that liability.   As previously stated, it is not in dispute that the relevant payments were made by the defendants to the plaintiffs in supposed discharge of a liability under an interest rate swap contract and not in respect of any liability for money had and received. Accordingly, the plaintiffs' answer to the limitation defence fails and the plaintiffs' claim in respect of the payments made in connection with KB1 must be limited to £582,257·19.

(2) UNJUST ENRICHMENT AT THE EXPENSE OF THE PLAINTIFFS (SWAPS KB1 and KB2)

The defendants' contention under this head is that in considering whether or not a plaintiff should be entitled to restitution as against a defendant on the ground of unjust enrichment at the expense of the plaintiff, one should examine the position of the plaintiff and see whether in truth the enrichment has occurred at his expense.   This is the opposite side of the coin to the argument which the courts have recognised by reference to a defendant's position: whether by reason of some change of position it is still correct to say that the defendant has been unjustly enriched (see Swaps 1 [1994] 4 All ER 890 at 946–948) and the citations there from the speeches in *Lipkin Gorman (a firm) v Karpnale* [1992] 4 All ER 512 at 517, 533, 534, [1991] 2 AC 548 at 559–560, 579, 580, 581). The defendants submit that where a payer has hedged his liabilities under the relevant swap contract and has thereby succeeded in recouping the losses that he otherwise would have suffered by reason of having entered into that swap contract, he should not be allowed to say that the enrichment of the payee was at his expense. They accept that where there have been hedging transactions, but these have not been successful in recouping the payer's loss, then the payer should still be entitled to claim restitution from the payee; where there has been partial recoupment, they say that that fact should be taken into account in assessing the degree to which the payee should make restitution to the payer. (This argument is illustrated by KB1 where the net payment made by the plaintiffs to the defendants amounted to £591,241·44 and the sums received by the plaintiffs under the hedging transaction which the defendants say is relevant were £306,942·99; the defendants have also abandoned their defence in relation to KB3 and KB4, where the related transactions resulted in additional losses to the plaintiffs.)

In the early stages of the London interest rates swap market, banks often operated as intermediaries between counter-parties who might themselves be intermediaries or might be a party who had entered into an actual transaction of borrowing or lending. The intermediary would deal simultaneously as principal with both counter-parties, the contracts precisely off-setting one another except for a profit margin, or turn, for the intermediary. The parties on either side of the intermediary would be aware of the way that the market usually operated but would not necessarily know at any stage whether there was any other party with whom the intermediary was dealing or its identity. Intermediaries would however usually try to avoid taking interest rate risks and therefore would try to ensure that both legs of the transaction into which they were entering were concluded simultaneously.

From about 1983 some banks began to take open positions and accept interest rate risks. Consequently, a bank would not necessarily enter into a matching transaction with another. However, the general considerations of market prudence would still apply and hedging mechanisms would be used to protect the overall position of the bank. There are a number of ways in which this might be done. It might hedge its position into a related exchange traded instrument or a marketable security such as a gilt or a bond. The hedge might be merely an interim measure or might be intended to be kept in place for a longer period. Accordingly, a bank or similar institution when entering into an interest rate swap transaction might be doing so simply as an intermediary with a pair of matching transactions or it might be doing so as part of a business in which it was prepared to hold positions and to hedge its overall position in a more general fashion.

From about 1985 market-makers began to appear with institutions offering to enter into interest rate swap contracts as the fixed rate payer or fixed rate receiver. Such banks, which were always relatively few in number, would have a spread between the terms on which they offered to pay or receive fixed interest sums. As referred to in the Divisional Court's judgment in *Hazell v Hammersmith and Fulham London BC* [1990] 3 All ER 33, [1990] 2 QB 697 more sophisticated types of swap transaction were also developed. Banks, whether acting as market-makers or on some more limited scale, would still have to have regard to their overall book of contracts and the extent to which it involved an interest rate risk and then would have to consider whether to leave this risk unprotected to any extent and what hedging or other protective measures to take either in the shorter or longer term.

The present plaintiffs, Kleinwort Benson, are and were at the times material to these proceedings a participant in the money markets in lending to private and public sector institutions and in the interest rate swaps market. They have not been a market-maker. Between 1982 and 1988 Kleinwort Benson entered into 79 swap transactions with 36 local authorities. Their initial involvement in the market followed the pattern which I have referred to of generally avoiding having any open position with an interest rate risk. Accordingly, they would generally only enter into an interest rate swap transaction if they could find a directly matching transaction. This was not however invariably the case. When they were left with an open position it would usually be hedged. The hedge might be another interest rate swap contract or it might be by purchasing or selling gilt securities which were the most liquid fixed rate asset available though other fixed rate transactions might be used. The bank's position would be watched from day to day so as to assess what the overall effect of its portfolio of contracts was in relation to its portfolio of hedging securities held at any given time. Sophisticated criteria were used to assess the overall position of the bank so as to run its book in such a manner as to take advantage of fluctuations in interest rates as between swaps and gilts and achieve a profit. Hedging was undertaken not by reference to any individual transaction but by relation to the whole portfolio.

Turning to the particular transactions to which the defendants seek to refer, in KB1 the contract was to run for seven years with the bank as the fixed rate payer and the council as the floating rate payer. The notional principal was £15m. The transaction did not run its full term as the judgment of the Divisional Court in *Hazell's* case intervened and no payments were made after 27 June 1989. The contract had been made on 17 June 1983. It was not immediately covered. About a week later, Kleinwort Benson took the opportunity to enter into a swap with Hill Samuel Ltd, with Hill Samuel as the fixed rate payer and Kleinwort Benson as the floating rate payer. The period was the same but the notional principal was £10m. The turn for Kleinwort Benson was 0·375%. The contract with Hill Samuel ran its full course. The two final payments under it were made by Kleinwort Benson to Hill Samuel and amounted to £315,547·95. Overall, Hill Samuel paid to Kleinwort Benson £306,942·99 more than Kleinwort Benson paid to Hill Samuel under this contract. It was profitable to Kleinwort Benson. It is this profit which the defendants before me say should be taken into account.

However the position is not quite as simple as that. On 24 June 1983 Kleinwort Benson also entered into a contract with the Ford Motor Credit Co and lent them £5m at a fixed rate of 12·25% for seven years. Further, during the life of this swap, Kleinwort Benson were continuing to run their book and to take into account their overall position in deciding what hedging transactions they should enter into from time to time.

KB2 illustrates a straightforward pair of matched transactions effectively entered into by Kleinwort Benson on the same day. For both, the notional principal was £2m and the period four and a half years with the last payment to be made on 16 May 1988. In its contract with the defendants, Kleinwort Benson was the fixed rate payer and the defendants the floating rate payer. In its contract with the other party (PK Christiania), Kleinwort Benson was the floating rate payer and the counter-party the fixed rate payer. The turn of Kleinwort Benson was only 0·125%. Both contracts ran their full course. Under its contract with the defendants, Kleinwort Benson made net payments of £46,647·26 and in the matching contract Kleinwort Benson received net payments from the counter-party of £57,907·54. Thus, taking the two transactions together, Kleinwort Benson was not out of pocket.

It is also relevant to evaluate the defendants' arguments against a wider background. The plaintiffs before me have drawn attention to what happened in relation to KB3 and KB4. Here the hedging transactions were complex. Some were favourable to Kleinwort Benson and others were not: the overall effect was that on those hedging transactions Kleinwort Benson paid out about £614,974·48 more than they received. This illustrates the complexity of a bank's position and the fact that hedging transactions can not be looked at in isolation from one another and without having regard to the overall position of the bank. Hedging transactions involve a complex of decisions on an ongoing basis and ultimately the inquiry becomes one of whether the bank has been running its interest rate business, including the relevant parts of its gilt-edged and bond businesses, at a profit or a loss. The argument of the defendants essentially involves looking behind the curtain to the way in which the relevant plaintiff runs its business overall.

A further feature of the market which has existed since an early stage and corresponds to a similar situation in the commodity and other markets is that it is possible to assess the positive or negative value of any given contract at any given time by reference to the current market levels ('mark to market'). This facility can be used merely to value the contract for internal or accounting purposes or it can be used in relation to a sale or close out of the contract. Thus although a contract may have a life of, say, ten years it does not follow that it will run that full term and will not be closed out by some further agreement which takes into account the current market position. This again underlines the dynamic character of any party's portfolio of contracts.

The position therefore is that a participant in the interest rate swap market may, in relation to any individual contract, have entered into another contract which it is easy to link with the first or may have adopted a more complex approach either by reference to the gilts market or to some overall hedging strategy. Further, a bank may revise or adjust its strategy from time to time.

The principles to be applied

The underlying principle is that of unjust enrichment:

> 'It is clear that any civilised system of law is bound to provide remedies for cases of what has been called unjust enrichment or unjust benefit, that is, to prevent a man from retaining the money of, or some benefit derived from, another which it is against conscience that he should keep.' (See *Fibrosa Spolka Akcyjna v Fairbairn Lawson Combe Barbour Ltd* [1942] 2 All ER 122 at 135, [1943] AC 32 at 61 per Lord Wright.)

Applying this principle, the Swaps 1 judgment held that, where money has been paid under a void transaction, the payee was in principle bound in law and in equity to repay the sum to the payer (see [1994] 4 All ER 890 at 955–956). The enrichment of the payee arises from his receipt of the payment. The money which the payee received was the money of the payer. The payment transferred the legal title in the money from the payer to the payee but because the transaction was void the money remained in equity the money of the payer. It is in recognition of this that law and equity say that the money should be repaid to the payer. Where, as in all these cases, the relevant plaintiff is the party who has paid the relevant sum or sums, he thereby establishes his title to sue. It was his money and he is asking that it should be restored to him.

In *Lipkin Gorman* [1992] 4 All ER 512 at 532, [1991] 2 AC 548 at 578 Lord Goff said:

> 'The recovery of money in restitution is not, as a general rule, a matter of discretion for the court. A claim to recover money at common law is made as a matter of right; and, even though the underlying principle of recovery is the principle of unjust enrichment, nevertheless, where recovery is denied, it is denied on the basis of legal principle.'

What is the legal principle which the defendants invoke? It can only be some unspecific principle which derives not from the law of restitution but from some concept of compensation. The essential feature in what the defendants here are asking the court to do (and other defendants in similar actions) is to make an assessment of the loss suffered by the relevant plaintiff as if one were investigating a right to compensation. The argument involves problems of remoteness. Even in the simplest cases where parties are dealing on a market, other individual contracts are in principle too remote to be taken into account. Compensation is assessed by reference to the market, not by reference to individual contracts. Where the position is more complex and it is not a question of looking at individual contracts but at the overall position of the plaintiff which may change from time to time, the problems of remoteness become self-evident and the risk of entering into an infinite regress likewise become apparent.

But the primary answer is that such considerations may be relevant to compensation but are not relevant to restitution. Here there is no problem about recognising a restitutionary remedy in personam against the defendants in favour of the plaintiffs. What contracts or other transactions or engagements the plaintiffs may have entered into with third parties have nothing to do with the principle of restitution. Therefore it suffices in the present case for the plaintiffs to show that they were the payers of the relevant money, that the defendants were unjustly enriched by the payments and that there is no obstacle to restitution. The problems which arise in different classes of case and are referred to in the textbooks, where the defendant has enjoyed some less tangible benefit and it does not derive from a payment made by the plaintiff to the defendant, do not arise for consideration in this case.

In support of their argument the defendants relied upon the decision of the majority of the Supreme Court of Canada in *Air Canada v British Columbia* (1989) 59 DLR (4th) 161. The airlines had paid a tax upon the purchase of gasoline which it had at the time been ultra vires the government of the Province of British Columbia to exact. The majority refused the right to recover the tax on a number of grounds including that the airlines may have passed on to their customers the burden of the tax and that the measure of the restitutionary recovery was the gain made by the province at the airlines' expense. There was no argument but that the province had been enriched through the imposition of the unconstitutional tax. Counsel for the airlines argued that the 'passing on' defence should only be available where the tax has been specifically charged to other identified parties so as to make those parties the true taxpayers. It was submitted that otherwise the fact that a tax may have been passed on is no ground on which to deny recovery; though the airlines may have increased their prices to raise the revenue to pay the tax, resulting higher prices may have had an impact on sales volume which may in turn have had an out-of-pocket impact on the airlines' profit.

La Forest J, who gave the judgment with which the majority agreed, quoted Professor George C Palmer *The Law of Restitution* (1986 Supplement) p 255:

'There is no doubt that if the tax authority retains a payment to which it was not entitled it has been unjustly enriched. It has not been enriched at the taxpayer's expense, however, if he has shifted the economic burden of the tax to others. Unless restitution for their benefit can be worked out, it seems preferable to leave the enrichment with the tax authority instead of putting the judicial machinery in motion for the purpose of shifting the same enrichment to the taxpayer.' (See 59 DLR (4th) 161 at 193.)

La Forest J commented (at 193–194):

> 'The law of restitution is not intended to provide windfalls to plaintiffs who have suffered no loss. Its function is to ensure that where a plaintiff has been deprived of wealth that is either in his possession or would have accrued for his benefit, it is restored to him. The measure of restitutionary recovery is the gain the province made at the airlines' expense. If the airlines have not shown that they bore the burden of the tax, then they have not made out their claim. What the province received is relevant only in so far as it was received at the airlines' expense. This alone is sufficient to deny the airlines' claim.'

The reasoning of La Forest J is thus essentially compensatory and seems to reflect a public policy approach that the plaintiff in such a situation must prove a loss in its business not merely that it was the payer of the tax.

The dissenter, Wilson J, adopted a different approach. She said (at 169–170):

> 'My colleague ... says, in effect, that the appellants would be receiving a "windfall" if they received their money back because in all likelihood they have already recouped the payments made on account of the *ultra vires* tax from their customers. In terms of my colleague's analysis, the appellants are unable to show that the unjust enrichment of the province was at their expense. In my view there is no requirement that they be able to do so. Where the payments were made pursuant to an unconstitutional statute there is no legitimate basis on which they can be retained.'

The difference between these two opinions appears essentially to be one of a policy approach to unconstitutional taxation. However it is clear that Wilson J did not accept the compensatory approach adopted by La Forest J.

In Australia, in *Mason v New South Wales* (1959) 102 CLR 108, the High Court of Australia allowed the recovery of sums unlawfully exacted by the government of the state from carriers by road under a statute which was ultra vires. The plaintiffs' claim in money had and received succeeded. Windeyer J said (at 146):

> 'It was argued that, even if they were otherwise entitled, the plaintiffs were in some way estopped from recovering because they had "passed on" to their customers the amounts paid for permits and are thus, it was said, not themselves at a loss. I can see no basis for this contention ... If the defendant be improperly enriched on what legal principle can it claim to retain its ill-gotten gains merely because the plaintiffs have not, it is said, been correspondingly impoverished? The concept of impoverishment as a correlative of enrichment may have some place in some fields of continental law. It is foreign to our law. Even if there were any equity in favour of third parties attaching to the fruits of any judgment the plaintiffs might recover—and there is nothing proved at all remotely suggesting that there is—this circumstance would be quite irrelevant to the present proceedings. Certainly it would not enable the defendant to refuse to return moneys which it was not in law entitled to collect and which *ex hypothesi* it got by extortion.'

Kitto J said (at p 129):

'What happened between them and their customers is irrelevant: it was still their money that they parted with, and there is nothing to account for their parting with it except the pressure they were under. In my opinion they are entitled by law to have it back.'

These decisions were cited to the House of Lords in *Woolwich Building Society v IRC (No 2)* [1992] 3 All ER 737, [1993] AC 70. The question of the 'passing on' defence did not arise in that case but Lord Goff, who was attracted by the judgment of Wilson J, said:

'It will be a matter for consideration whether the fact that the plaintiff has passed on the tax or levy so that the burden has fallen on another should provide a defence to his claim. Although this is contemplated by the Court of Justice of the European Communities in [*Amministrazione delle Finanze dello Stato v SpA San Giorgio* Case 199/82 [1983] ECR 3595], it is evident from *Air Canada v British Columbia* that the point is not without its difficulties; and the availability of such a defence may depend on the nature of the tax or other levy. No doubt matters of this kind will in any event be the subject of consideration during the current consultations with the Law Commission.' (See [1992] 3 All ER 737 at 764, [1993] AC 70 at 177–178.)

This shows that in the law of taxation special considerations may apply and that there may be taxes, as for example VAT, where it may be possible to say that the plaintiff was in the position of a collector of the tax and was not a payer. I am not concerned with such complications which are peculiar to the law of taxation and to the payment of sums under compulsion.

In the present case I am concerned with payments made under void transactions where there is no question but that the relevant plaintiff made the payment on his own account and out of his own money. If the plaintiff is to be denied his remedy in respect of the sum which he has paid to the defendant and which it is unjust that the defendant should retain, it must be upon a basis that is relevant to the law of restitution and not some principle borrowed from the law of compensation. Further, the application of the principle, if it is to be adopted, must respect the principles of remoteness recognised in the law of compensation. The defendants' 'passing on' defence in respect of the payments made in connection with swaps KB1 and KB2, and any similar defence in any other action, fails on both these counts and does not provide an answer to the plaintiffs' claim.

(3) SWAP KB5

This point depends upon the special facts of this transaction which are to be derived primarily from the contemporaneous documentation since none of the persons actually involved has much independent recollection of what occurred. It concerns a consideration of the position of both parties and the circumstances under which the relevant payments were made. It includes an examination of the payer's position but it does so not in terms of considering what if any loss he has suffered but rather whether or not the criteria for the grant of restitution are satisfied.

The story starts on 21 November 1986 when the defendants entered into two interest rate swap contracts with Barclays Bank plc. They each had a notional principal of £5m, making £10m in all, and were on the same terms. Their commencement date was 21 November 1986 and they were to have a life of ten years with the final payment to be made on 21 November 1996. The first payment was not to be made until 21 November 1987. Barclays Bank was the fixed rate payer at a rate of 11·90% and the defendants were the floating rate payer at the London Inter-Bank Offered Rate with the rate for the first year being agreed at 10·9%. After the first year the floating rate payer would make payments semi-annually whereas the fixed rate payments would be made annually throughout.

This contract was of course ultra vires the defendants and created no legal rights; it was void and unenforceable. However, owing to movements in interest rates shortly after 21 November, the contract achieved a marketable value because the inter-bank market rate had moved from 11·9% to 11·44% so that there was a differential between the fixed rate which Barclays Bank was to pay to the defendants and the current market rate. Capitalised, this gave the contract a value of about £120,000. The defendants decided to take this profit.

On 12 December 1986 the defendants entered into a contract (KB5) with the plaintiffs. The terms were exactly the same as those of the contract which they had with Barclays Bank save that the commencement date was to be 12 December 1986. As a consideration for the defendants entering into that contract with them the plaintiffs undertook to pay to the defendants the sum of £120,000. Unlike the up-front payment that was included in the interest rate swap contract between the plaintiffs and the defendants in the Islington action, the promise by the plaintiffs to pay the sum of £120,000 was truly a collateral promise.

It is also clear that from the outset it was intended that the plaintiffs should take over the defendants' contract with Barclays Bank. The agreed facts state (para 77):

> 'When the swap was entered into it was agreed that in due course, subject to the consent of all parties, [the defendants] would drop out of the transaction and a swap would be established directly between [the plaintiffs] and Barclays Bank (with which [the defendants] had already entered into two swaps …).'

In the brokers' letters of confirmation they said:

> 'In parallel with this transaction [the plaintiffs] will pay to [the defendants] the sum of £120,000. It is agreed that in due course, subject to mutual consent of all parties concerned, assignment of the swap by [the defendants] will take place … Documentation already in place. Assignment to take place subject to Barclays Bank Plc agreeing at some future date to [defendants] assigning the underlying swap.'

In their own internal documentation, the dealing slip of the plaintiffs originally described the counter-party as Barclays Bank and included the statement '£120,000 to L.A. South Tyneside on assignment'. This again confirms the contemplation that the counter-party would be Barclays Bank and the link between the £120,000 payment and the transfer of the Barclays Bank contracts. It appears that the plaintiffs quite specifically preferred to have a bank as their counter-party rather than a local authority and this was part of their motivation at the time of entering into swap KB5. In a document written in June or July 1987, one of the defendants' officers referred to the November contract with Barclays Bank and said: 'The swap was subsequently sold to Kleinwort Benson for an up front fee of £120,000 on 12/12/86.' Thus although the form of the swap contract entered into between the plaintiffs and the defendants was on the face of it a conventional free-standing contract, it in reality formed part of a wider agreement under which it was agreed that: (a) the defendants would procure a direct contract between Barclays Bank and the plaintiffs, and (b) the plaintiffs would pay to the defendants £120,000.

The swap contract itself and the collateral agreement were ultra vires the defendant council and wholly void. It was a financial transaction undertaken with a view to profit which was not within the powers of the defendants. Further, it had as its subject matter the supposed contract between Barclays Bank and the defendants which existed in fact but likewise had no legal existence as a contract between those parties. Had they known it Barclays Bank could have disclaimed any legal liability under that supposed contract.

However, none of the three parties was aware of the relevant limitation upon the powers of local authorities and, in accordance with their intention, the three parties in June 1987 entered into a further group of agreements whereby the defendants were released from their respective contracts with Barclays Bank and the plaintiffs, and the plaintiffs entered into a substitute, or novated, contract direct with Barclays Bank. The documentation, as was usual, was completed subsequent to the making of those revised agreements; the agreements were all backdated to 12 December 1986. Barclays Bank were able to obtain from the plaintiffs a reduction of 0·05% in the fixed rate which Barclays Bank were to pay to the plaintiffs. No express explanation of this adjustment was given but, on the evidence, it seems most likely that it was accounted for by the fact that the plaintiffs were gaining a bank as a counter-party in place of a local authority. But whatever it was, and it may have been part of some other adjustment between Barclays Bank and the plaintiffs, having regard to other transactions between them, it does not alter the fact that the essential character of the June 1987 contract was an assignment and novation of the contracts entered into during the previous year and that the plaintiffs had obtained that for which they had bargained in December 1986, namely an interest rate swap contract on the stated terms with Barclays Bank.

The defendants were involved in some financial adjustments with Barclays Bank to take account of the fact that the starting date of the 1986 contracts was different. These are not material. As between the plaintiffs and the defendants, the plaintiffs did not pay the £120,00 in December 1986, perhaps because they contemplated that it would only be paid when they had taken over the contract with Barclays Bank. However the defendants demanded its payment and the plaintiffs paid the sum on 26 March 1987. It was and is accepted that the sum ought to have been paid earlier and subsequently on 24 October 1987 the plaintiffs paid the defendants the sum of £3,675·62 by way of interest to compensate the defendants for the late payment. Accordingly, the total payments which the plaintiffs made to the defendants in connection with swap KB5 was £123,675·62. The question is whether the defendants should repay that sum to the plaintiffs.front-end payment

Other things being equal the sum should be repaid. The relevant transactions were ultra vires the defendant council and they have been enriched when they should not have been. However the plaintiffs got the substance of what they were paying for, a valid and enforceable contract with Barclays Bank. In the *Fibrosa* sense there was no failure of consideration at all; the substance of the consideration was performed. No suggestion has been made that Barclays Bank are claiming back, or that the plaintiffs may be required to repay to Barclays Bank, the various sums which it has received from Barclays Bank. On the contrary, the contract was performed by Barclays Bank and on 7 November 1990 Barclays Bank paid to the plaintiffs £180,000 in order to close out that and another contract.

The tripartite nature of the relevant transactions and the inability of the plaintiffs to put all the parties back into their original position raises the question whether the restitutionary remedy should be granted. This is not a case like the second Sandwell swap or KB2 where, although the transaction has run its full term, the parties can be restored to their previous position. Here they cannot and the only proposal of the plaintiffs is simply that, without more, the defendants should repay to them the sum of £123,675·62. I consider that this claim by the plaintiffs does not satisfy the criteria necessary for the grant of a restitutionary remedy. There has been a change of circumstance which has the practical effect of precluding restitutio in integrum. It has the effect of disqualifying the plaintiffs from their entitlement to the restitutionary remedy. It is true that this conclusion leaves in the hands of the defendants a sum of money which they ought not to have received. But likewise, to order that the defendants repay that sum to the plaintiffs would mean that the plaintiffs would be enabled both to keep the benefit which they have gained from the supposed contract and to recover the price which they paid to obtain that benefit. In my judgment, the principle of restitutio in integrum is fundamental to this part of the law of restitution (see Swaps 1 [1994] 4 All ER 890 at 955–956). In the present connection both the plaintiffs and the defendants have enjoyed benefits directly arising out of the relevant transactions. The party which it might be said has been unjustly impoverished, Barclays Bank, is not before the court. The benefits enjoyed by the plaintiffs and the defendants should remain where they are. It is not appropriate that the court should intervene and order a partial restitution. Therefore the plaintiffs' claim against the defendants in respect of the payments they made in connection with swap KB5 fails.

(4) INTEREST

Compound interest

It is not in dispute that, in respect of a cause of action in money had and received, simple interest can be awarded under s 35A of the Supreme Court Act 1981. That section gives no power to award compound interest. It is also common ground that the only power to award compound interest can be in relation to some right or remedy recognised by equity and then only in accordance with the principles established in the courts of equity.

In Swaps 1, compound interest was awarded in favour of the plaintiffs in the Islington case. It is necessary to see on what basis that was done. Compound interest was there awarded as part of the equitable remedy of tracing. This was a proprietary remedy proceeding on the premise that the property of the defendants was subject to an equitable charge to repay out of that property the sums which had been received from the plaintiffs. Compound interest was only awarded from a date after which it had been established, as a result of the decision of the Divisional Court in *Hazell v Hammersmith and Fulham London BC* [1990] 3 All ER 33, [1990] 2 QB 697, that the relationship of the parties was not contractual and at a time when the defendants had in their hands a reserve of funds created by reference to the relevant transaction in the expectation that it would or might be necessary to make further payments to the plaintiffs on one basis or another and when those sums were more than sufficient to enable the defendants to make the appropriate repayment to the plaintiffs. Further the rate of interest was fixed on the basis of a conservative view of the interest rate that, on the defendants' own evidence, was being earned by them at the relevant times on their own money. Therefore the compound interest was awarded as part of the proprietary equitable remedy of tracing money in the hands of the defendants and of requiring them to account to the plaintiffs for the profit which they had thereby made. It was awarded from a time at which it could be fairly said that the defendants were withholding the plaintiffs' money and at a rate which represented the value of the retained money to the defendants. Such an award fell four square within the recognised equitable principles permitting the award of compound interest.

Where simple interest is being awarded different principles apply as are fully set out in the judgment of Robert Goff J (as he then was) in *BP Exploration Co (Libya) Ltd v Hunt (No 2)* [1982] 1 All ER 925 at 974 [1979] 1 WLR 783 at 845:

> 'The fundamental principle is that interest is not awarded as a punishment, but simply because the plaintiff has been deprived of the use of the money which was due to him.'

He quoted Lord Wilberforce in *General Tire and Rubber Co v Firestone Tyre and Rubber Co* [1975] 2 All ER 173 at 188, [1975] 1 WLR 819 at 836:

> 'Where a wrong-doer has failed to pay money which he should have paid, justice, in principle, requires that he should pay interest over the period for which he has withheld the money.'

Robert Goff J continued ([1982] 1 All ER 925 at 975, [1979] 1 WLR 783 at 846):

> 'It is for this reason that interest will generally run from the date of accrual of the cause of action in respect of money then due or loss which then accrues; and in respect of loss which accrues at a date between accrual of the cause of action and judgment, from such date ... But the power to award interest is discretionary, and there is certainly no rule that interest will invariably run from the date of loss.'

He quoted Lord Wilberforce in *General Tire* [1975] 2 All ER 173 at 188, [1975] 1 WLR 819 at 836:

> 'In a commercial setting, it would be proper to take account of the manner in which and the time at which persons acting honestly and reasonably would pay.'

But he added ([1982] 1 All ER 925 at 976, [1979] 1 WLR 783 at 847):

> 'There must have been many cases in the Commercial Court in which, although the quantum of damages was in doubt until the date of judgment, interest was awarded from the date of loss. Similarly, the mere fact that it is doubtful whether the plaintiff's claim will succeed, and it is reasonable to contest his claim, will not generally require any departure from the general principle; nor generally will any doubt, however justified, as to the principles of law which will be applied.'

The rate of simple interest is assessed on a compensatory basis being that at which a plaintiff would need to borrow in order to replace the funds pending judgment. Thus the difference between an award of compound and simple interest may be less dramatic than is at first assumed. Under an award of simple interest, the rate may well be higher and the period may be longer. Although in the present case the question of compound interest has been fully argued it is probable that the choice of starting date and rate for the award of interest has a greater impact upon the amount of the judgment than whether or not the interest is compounded.

In the present case, upon the hypothesis that no tracing remedy is available, the plaintiffs have to say that the equitable right in personam is one which carries with it a power to award compound interest. In the present case, as in Swaps 1, the plaintiffs make no allegation of fault against the defendants nor is any express, implied or constructive trust relied on. The plaintiffs base their case upon the formulation in the judgment in Swaps 1 [1994] 4 All ER 890 at 929:

> 'In my judgment the correct analysis is that any payments made under a contract which is void ab initio, in the way that an ultra vires contract is void, are not contractual payments at all. They are payments in which the legal property in the money passes to the recipient but in equity the property in the money remains with the payer. The recipient holds the money as a fiduciary for the payer and is bound to recognise his equity and repay the money to him. This relationship and the consequent obligation have been recognised by courts applying the common law and by Chancery courts. The principle is the same in both cases: it is unconscionable that the recipient should retain the money.'

The relationship is therefore a fiduciary one which comes into existence at the time the money is received by the payee and gives rise to a personal liability of the payee recognised by equity and, potentially, also to proprietary remedies. The defendants submit that this is not enough to give rise to a jurisdiction to award compound interest.

The starting point must be the concise summary contained in the speech of Lord Brandon in *President of India v La Pintada Cia Navegacion SA* [1984] 2 All ER 773 at 779, [1985] AC 104 at 116:

> 'Third, the area of equity. The Chancery courts, again differing from the common law courts, had regularly awarded simple interest as ancillary relief in respect of equitable remedies, such as specific performance, rescission and the taking of an account. Chancery courts had further regularly awarded interest, including not only simple interest but also compound interest, when they thought that justice so demanded, that is to say in cases where money had been obtained and retained by fraud, or where it had been withheld or misapplied by a trustee or anyone else in a fiduciary position ... Chancery courts only in two special classes of case, awarded compound, as distinct from simple, interest.'

Lord Brandon was not in that case concerned with precisely defining the limits of the jurisdiction in equity to award compound interest; he was simply concerned to point out that it was not a general jurisdiction but was confined to certain classes of case. The use by Lord Brandon of the word 'withheld' is important. He clearly is contemplating an actual withholding by the defendant of money which in equity belongs to the plaintiff: pace Lord Wilberforce above, this is to be contrasted with the phrase used by Robert Goff J in *BP*

Exploration Co (Libya) Ltd v Hunt (No 2) [1982] 1 All ER 925 at 974, [1979] 1 WLR 783 at 845: 'because the plaintiff has been deprived of the use of the money which was due to him.'

Where fraud or breach of trust or some similar equitable obligation is involved, compound interest may be awarded on the basis that the defendant must not be allowed to make any profit from his trust. As it was put by Buckley LJ in *Wallersteiner v Moir (No 2)* [1975] 1 All ER 849 at 863–864, [1975] QB 373 at 397–398:

'It is well established in equity that a trustee who in breach of trust misapplies trust funds will be liable not only to replace the misapplied principal fund but to do so with interest from the date of the misapplication. This is on the notional ground that the money so applied was in fact the trustee's own money and that he has retained the misapplied trust money in his own hands and used it for his own purposes. Where a trustee has retained trust money in his own hands, he will be accountable for the profit which he has made or which he is assumed to have made from the use of the money. In *Attorney-General v Alford* (1855) 4 De GM & G 843 at 851, 43 ER 737 at 741 Lord Cranworth LC said: "What the Court ought to do, I think, is to charge him only with the interest which he has received, or which it is justly entitled to say he ought to have received, or which it is so fairly to be presumed that he did receive that he is estopped from saying that he did not receive it." This is an application of the doctrine that the court will not allow a trustee to make any profit from his trust. The defaulting trustee is normally charged with simple interest only, but if it is established that he has used the money in trade he may be charged compound interest. See *Burdick v Garrick* (1870) LR 5 Ch App 233 at 241 per Lord Hatherley LC, and Lewin on Trusts (16th edn 1964) p 226, and the cases there noted. The justification for charging compound interest normally lies in the fact that profits earned in trade would be likely to be used as working capital for earning further profits. Precisely similar equitable principles apply to an agent who has retained monies of his principal in his hands and used them for his own purposes (*Burdick v Garrick*). The application of this rule is not confined to cases in which a trustee or agent has misapplied trust funds or a principal's property, nor is it confined to trustees and agents. It was enunciated by Lord Herschell in *Bray v Ford* [1896] AC 44 at 51, [1895–9] All ER Rep 1009 at 1011 in these terms: "It is an inflexible rule of a Court of Equity that a person in a fiduciary position ... is not, unless otherwise expressly provided, entitled to make a profit; he is not allowed to put himself in a position where his interest and duty conflict." ... In cases of this kind interest is not, as I understand the law, given to compensate for loss of profit but in order to ensure as far as possible that the defendant retains no profit for which he ought to account.'

Scarman LJ made a similar statement of the law and followed and applied *Burdick v Garrick* (see [1975] 1 All ER 849 at 870–871, [1975] QB 373 at 406). Neither Lord Justice agreed with a wider formulation by Lord Denning MR (see [1975] 1 All ER 849 at 856, [1975] QB 373 at 388).

Burdick v Garrick itself fully supports what Buckley LJ says. It demonstrates that there is a power to award compound interest in cases of fiduciary agency, not simply where there is an express trust, and it also confirms that the basis is that there is a fund to which the fiduciary obligation relates. Compound interest was not in fact awarded in that case because the defendant was a solicitor and the court did not consider that he should be treated as having used the money in business to make a profit.

The relationship between personal and proprietary remedies has been stated in a number of cases including *Re Diplock's Estate, Diplock v Wintle* [1948] 2 All ER 318, [1948] Ch 465 and *Lonrho plc v Fayed (No 2)* [1991] 4 All ER 961, [1992] 1 WLR 1. In *Re Diplock's Estate* [1948] 2 All ER 318 at 347, [1948] Ch 465 at 521 the Court of Appeal said:

> 'The equitable form of relief, whether it takes the form of an order to restore an unmixed sum of money (or property acquired by means of such a sum) or a declaration of charge on a mixed fund (or on property acquired by means of such a fund) is, of course, personal in the sense that its efficacy is founded on the jurisdiction of equity to enforce its rules by acting on the individual. It is, however, not personal in the sense that the person against whom an order of this nature is sought can be made personally liable to repay the amount claimed to have belonged to the claimant. The equitable remedies presuppose the continued existence of the money either as a separate fund or as part of a mixed fund or as latent in property acquired by means of such a fund. If, on the facts of any individual case, such continued existence is not established, equity is as helpless as the common law itself. If the fund, mixed or unmixed, was spent on a dinner, equity, which only dealt in specific relief and not in damages, could do nothing. If the case was one which at common law involved breach of contract, the common law could, of course, award damages, but specific relief would be out of the question. It is, therefore, a necessary matter for consideration, in each case where it is sought to trace money in equity, whether it has such a continued existence, actual or notional, as will enable equity to grant specific relief.'

The Court of Appeal also expressly drew attention to the different consequences as regards interest which might arise from the entitlement to a proprietary remedy (see [1948] 2 All ER 318 at 345, [1948] Ch 465 at 517).

The position is therefore that if a plaintiff is entitled to a proprietary remedy against a defendant who has been unjustly enriched, the court may but is not bound to order the repayment of the sum with compound interest. If on the other hand the plaintiff is only entitled to a personal remedy which will be the case where, although there was initially a fiduciary relationship and the payer was entitled in equity to treat the sum received by the payee as his, the payer's, money and to trace it, but because of subsequent developments he is no longer able to trace the sum in the hands of the payee, then there is no subject matter to which the rationale on which compound interest is awarded can be applied. The payee cannot be shown to have a fund belonging to the payer or to have used it to make profits for himself. The legal analysis which is the basis of the award of compound interest is not applicable. (It is possible that in some cases there might be an intermediate position where it could be demonstrated that the fiduciary had, over part of the period, profited from holding a fund as a fiduciary even though he no longer held the fund at the date of trial and that in such a case the court might make some order equivalent to requiring him to account for those profits; but that is not the situation which I am asked to consider in the present case.)

Although the original equitable right in both situations is the same at the outset, that is to say at the time when the payment was made and received, the two situations do not continue to be the same and are not the same at the time of trial when the remedy comes to be given. The payee no longer has property of the payer. The payer is confined to personal rights and remedies analogous to those recognised by the common law in the action for money had and received. In such a situation only simple interest can be awarded even though the plaintiff is relying upon a restitutionary remedy. Simple interest was awarded in *Woolwich Building Society v IRC (No 2)* [1992] 3 All ER 737, [1993] AC 70 and in *BP Exploration (Libya) Ltd v Hunt (No 2)* [1982] 1 All ER 925, [1979] 1 WLR 783 and both those cases involved an application of restitutionary principles which carried with them remedies in personam (see also *O'Sullivan v Management Agency and Music Ltd* [1985] 3 All ER 351, [1985] QB 428.)

The plaintiffs, in support of their argument in favour of compound interest, relied also upon the annuity cases in the Chancery courts where an account was ordered and the sum found due on the account was ordered to be paid over to the plaintiff. They relied in particular upon *Hoffman v Cooke* (1801) 5 Ves Jun 623, 31 ER 772 and *Bromley v Holland* (1802) Coop G 9, 35 ER 458. These cases indicate that the allowing of interest on the sums in the account was part of the equitable remedy and that rests might be taken in the preparation of the accounts so that interest and other items of receipt and expenditure would from time to time be capitalised in the account. This is not, however, an exercise which depends upon an award of compound interest such as that which the plaintiffs are asking for in the present case and does not assist them. Further, in the present case the plaintiffs have not yet established that they are entitled to have any sum paid to them on the taking on an account. They have claimed an account in the action but this is ancillary to their tracing remedy. On the taking of that account it may be that the plaintiffs can say that an account should be taken of the profits which the defendants have made out of having the plaintiffs' money. An account is not necessary or appropriate where a plaintiff is simply seeking to enforce a personal liability of the defendant (see for example *Snell on Equity* (29th edn, 1991) p 637 and *London Chatham and Dover Rly Co v South Eastern Rly Co* [1892] 1 Ch 120 at 140 per Lindley LJ).

Accordingly, the plaintiffs' claim to be awarded compound interest independently of any proprietary claim must be rejected.

Simple interest: the starting date

The causes of action accrued at the time when the relevant payments were made by the plaintiffs to the defendants which give rise to the final net balance in favour of the plaintiffs. Since the defendants were the floating rate payer, the payments falling to be made in 1989 and 1990 were and would have been payments made by the defendants to the plaintiffs. Payments continued to be made by the defendants to the plaintiffs up to the time of the judgment of the Divisional Court in *Hazell*'s case which was delivered on 1 November 1989. The next payment that would have fallen to be made under the relevant swaps was a payment of £244,417·81 to be made by defendants to the plaintiffs on 27 December 1989 under swap KB1. On 21 December 1989 the defendants had written to the plaintiffs saying that in view of the Divisional Court judgment they would not be making further payments under the relevant swap contracts but would for the time being pay the sums into a 'call' account with their own bankers until the situation was further clarified. The call account was an interest bearing account into which the defendants continued to make payments until May 1991 in connection with swap transactions involving a number of other parties besides the plaintiffs. The attitude of the plaintiffs during this period up and until the decision of the House of Lords in *Hazell's* case in January 1991 was to call upon the defendants to continue to perform the swap contracts or at least to pay the relevant sums into some form of escrow account. The defendants did not accede to these requests. On 21 March 1991 the plaintiffs' solicitors wrote a letter before action demanding repayment of the sums which had been paid by the plaintiffs to the defendants and on 27 March 1991 the writ in this action was issued.

The submissions which have been made by the parties concerning the appropriate starting date of the award of simple interest range from, at one extreme, the original payment dates of the relevant sums through to, at the other extreme, the date of the issue of the writ. I consider that the appropriate approach is to select a date which is appropriate to the totality of the claims for which judgment is to be given for the plaintiffs, that is to say in respect of the payments made under all the transactions except swap KB5. I do not consider that it is appropriate to award interest from an earlier date than 1 November 1989, the date of the decision of the Divisional Court. Down to that date both parties were proceeding upon the basis that the swap contracts were valid, notwithstanding the doubts which had been cast upon them, and the supposed contracts were being performed. The question is whether the starting date for an award of interest should be put back to a later date. In answering this question I have had regard to the principles conveniently summarised by Robert Goff J in *BP Exploration Co (Libya) Ltd v Hunt (No 2)* [1982] 1 All ER 925 at 935–945, [1979] 1 WLR 783 at 796–808.

I consider that the appropriate date to take is 1 January 1990. It is by this time that it could be said, in the words of Lord Wilberforce in *General Tire and Rubber Co v Firestone Tyre and Rubber Co* [1975] 2 All ER 173 at 188, [1975] 1 WLR 819 at 836, that a properly informed defendant would honestly and reasonably have repaid to the plaintiff what he had received from him. Any postponement of repayment was going progressively to cause loss to the plaintiffs who had neither the money which they had paid to the defendants nor the continued performance of the supposed contracts. The defendants, if it be material to consider their position, were correspondingly enjoying a benefit by failing to restore the relevant sums to the plaintiffs. There is certainly no consideration arising from the position of the defendants in the present case which makes it inappropriate to award simple interest against them from 1 January 1990.

The overall relationship between the plaintiffs and the defendants was a commercial one whereby each was seeking to enter into financial transactions which would yield them profit. There is no justification for departing from the normal approach to the award of interest in relation to amounts awarded or adjudged to be due in commercial disputes. By 1 January 1990 the plaintiffs' causes of action had all fully accrued and a judgment had been given from which, on a correct view of the law, it followed that repayment should be made. The defendants were right to stop making payments under the supposed contracts and to refuse the plaintiffs' requests that they do something equivalent to a continued performance of them. But, by the same logic, this does not give a sound basis for refusing the plaintiffs an award of simple interest from the date upon which it ought honestly and reasonably to have been appreciated that the sums ought to be repaid.

Accordingly, I award simple interest from 1 January 1990 on the sums for which judgment is being given in favour of the plaintiffs in this action.

Simple interest: rate

In view of the fact that the relationship between the parties was an essentially commercial one and that the plaintiffs, who have been out of their money, are bankers, there is no reason for departing from the normal Commercial Court approach which is to award interest at 1% above base rate (see *Shearson Lehman Hutton Inc v Maclaine Watson & Co Ltd (No 2)* [1990] 3 All ER 723). I award that the rate of interest should be 1% above base rate.

CONCLUSIONS

On the issues which have been argued before me in this action: (1) the defendants' defence under the Limitation Act 1980 in respect of swap KB1 succeeds so as to reduce the sum for which the plaintiffs are entitled to judgment in respect of the payments made under that swap to £582,257·19; (2) the defendants' 'passing on' defence raised in connection with swaps KB1 and KB2 fails; (3) the defendants' defence to the claim in connection with swap KB5 succeeds on the basis that in the circumstances full restitution is not possible; (4) in respect of their claims in personam the plaintiffs are not entitled to any award of compound interest. Simple interest only should be awarded with a starting date 1 January 1990 and a rate of 1% above base rate.

Accordingly, there will be judgment for the plaintiffs in this action in the sum of £1,470,945·30 together with interest thereon from 1 January 1990 to the date of judgment at base rate plus 1%.

Judgment for the plaintiffs.

Mary Rose Plummer   Barrister.

Torvald Klaveness A/S v Arni Maritime Corp

HOUSE OF LORDS

LORD TEMPLEMAN, LORD ACKNER, LORD MUSTILL, LORD SLYNN OF HADLEY AND LORD WOOLF

27, 28, 29 JUNE, 27 OCTOBER 1994

Shipping – Time charterparty – Last voyage – Late redelivery – Repudiation – Repudiation by late delivery – Charterers' order preventing redelivery on time – Time at which validity of charterers' order for final voyage prior to redelivery to be judged – Whether owners entitled to treat order as repudiatory breach of contract – Whether validity of charterers' order for final voyage to be determined when order given or when order to be performed.

The charterers chartered a vessel under a time charterparty commencing on 8 January 1988. The last day for redelivery was 18 March. The charterers ordered the vessel to deliver a cargo of bauxite at the port of Matanzas on the Orinoco River in Venezuela and on 9 February ordered the vessel to the neighbouring port of Palua to load a cargo of iron ore for delivery to an Italian port prior to redelivery at an authorised port in Europe on or before 18 March. On 25 February the vessel arrived at Palua ready to load but by then another vessel had grounded in the Orinoco causing delays to traffic on the river. If the vessel had left Palua immediately without loading the cargo of iron ore it could have escaped the congestion on the river and could have been redelivered on or soon after the date for redelivery. In those circumstances the owners refused to load and requested fresh orders to enable the vessel to be redelivered on time. On 29 February the charterers refused to give fresh orders and insisted that the order of 9 February for a laden voyage from Palua was valid. The owners treated the conduct of the charterers in ordering and insisting upon loading at Palua as a repudiatory breach of contract and accepted the repudiation. In the event the parties agreed that the vessel would reload at Palua and sail to Italy subject to the charterers paying an agreed higher rate of hire if, at arbitration, it was held that the owners would have been justified in refusing to perform the voyage. The vessel was in fact redelivered eight days late. In the ensuing arbitration the charterers contended that the order of 9 February for a laden voyage from Palua was a valid order. The arbitrator held that the validity of the order for the final voyage was to be judged as at the time when it fell to be complied with on 25 February and not at the time when it was given on 9 February, and that the charterers by giving the order and then refusing to replace it had given an order for a voyage which could not be legitimately given and had thereby repudiated the contract. The arbitrator awarded the owners $US 299,791 and on appeal his award was upheld by the judge. The owners' appeal was upheld by the Court of Appeal on the grounds, inter alia, that an order which if complied with would involve some degree of lateness could not in itself be an actual breach of condition or a repudiatory breach. The charterers appealed to the House of Lords.

Held – The appeal would be allowed for the following reasons—

(1) (Per Lord Templeman) Applying elementary principles of contract, a charterer agreed under the charterparty to redeliver on time and was required

to give orders which ensured that the vessel would be redelivered on time. If the charterer gave an order which would not enable the vessel to be redelivered on time, the owner was entitled to treat that order as a repudiatory breach of contract and if he complied with the order he lost his right to repudiate but was entitled to damages for any late delivery. Accordingly, since the order to load at Palua, if complied with, would have prevented redelivery on time, that order was one which the charterers were not entitled to give and was a repudiatory breach of contract. The owners were therefore entitled to the increased freight rate (see p 1000 *f g* and p 1001 *g* to *j*, post).

(2) (Per Lord Ackner, Lord Mustill, Lord Slynn and Lord Woolf) The time at which the validity of a charterer's order for a final voyage prior to redelivery under a time charterparty was to be judged was primarily the time when the order was to be performed. Under the terms of the charterparty the owner promised to provide the services of the vessel and a service which fell outside the range encompassed by the owner's original promise was not one which he could be compelled to perform. Thus, if and for so long as the services required by the charterer conformed with those which the shipowner promised in advance to render, the specific order created a specific obligation to perform those services when the time arrived, but if circumstances changed, so that compliance with the order called for a service which in the original contract the shipowner never undertook, the obligation to comply fell away. Although the issuing of an invalid order was not an automatic ground of discharge, the persistence of the charterers in an order which because of the changed circumstances of the blockage of the Orinoco had become illegitimate was conduct evincing an intention no longer to be bound by the contract, and hence a repudiation of it. The original order having become ineffectual, the charterers' refusal to replace it with a permissible order showed that they did not intend to perform their obligations under the charter and was an anticipatory breach which entitled the owners to treat the contract as being at an end. The owners were therefore entitled to increased rate of hire (see p 1002 *a*, p 1006 *e* to p 1007 *b*, p1008 *c*, p 1010 *c* to *e* and p 1011 *f* to *h*, post).

Per Lord Mustill (Lord Ackner, Lord Slynn and Lord Woolf concurring). Timely redelivery is probably not a condition of a time charterparty contract and therefore is not necessarily a repudiatory breach, since a short delay in redelivery will not justify the termination of the contract (see p 1002 *a*, p 1009 *h*, p 1010 *a* and p 1011 *g h*, post).

Notes
For redelivery of a vessel on the expiration of a time charterparty, see 43 *Halsbury's Laws* (4th edn) para 436.

Cases referred to in opinions
Alma Shipping Corp of Monrovia v Mantovani, The Dione [1975] 1 Lloyd's Rep 115, CA.

Batis Maritime Corp v Petroleos del Mediterraneo SA, The Batis [1990] 1 Lloyd's Rep 345.

Bunge Corp v Tradax SA [1981] 2 All ER 513, [1981] 1 WLR 711, HL.

Cie Commerciale Sucres et Denrées v C Czarnikow Ltd [1990] 3 All ER 641, [1990] 1 WLR 1337, HL.

Federal Commerce and Navigation Co Ltd v Molena Alpha Inc [1979] 1 All ER 307, [1979] AC 757, [1978] 3 WLR 991, HL.

Hyundai Merchant Marine Co Ltd v Gesuri Chartering Co Ltd, The Peonia [1991] 1
Lloyd's Rep 100, QBD and CA.
Marbienes Cia Naviera SA v Ferrostaal AG, The Democritos [1976] 2 Lloyd's Rep
149, CA.
Motor Oil Hellas (Corinth) Refineries SA v Shipping Corp of India, The Kanchenjunga
[1989] 1 Lloyd's Rep 354, CA.

Appeal

Arni Maritime Corp, the owners of the vessel Gregos, appealed with leave
granted by the Appeal Committee on 23 November 1993 from the decision of
the Court of Appeal (Russell, Hirst and Simon Brown LJJ) ([1993] 2 Lloyd's Rep
335) delivered on 27 May 1993 allowing the appeal of the respondents, Torvald
Klaveness A/S, the charterers of the Gregos under a charterparty dated 30
December 1987, from the judgment of Evans J ([1992] 2 Lloyd's Rep 40)
delivered on 31 January 1992 upholding the award of the arbitrator, Mr Mark
Hamsher, dated 15 February 1991, that the charterers were liable to pay the
owners the sum of $US 299,791·25 for repudiatory breach of the charterparty.
The facts are set out in the opinion of Lord Mustill.

Peter Gross QC and *David Goldstone* (instructed by *Ince & Co*) for the owners.
Kenneth Rokison QC and *Timothy Young* (instructed by *Sinclair Roche &
Temperley*) for the charterers.

Their Lordships took time for consideration.

27 October 1994. The following opinions were delivered.

LORD TEMPLEMAN. My Lords, in a time charter the time for redelivery of
the vessel by the charterer to the owner at the end of the charter is of the
essence of the contract, absent any provision in the contract to the contrary. If
the charterer in the course of the charterparty evinces an intention not to
redeliver the vessel by the date or last date fixed for redelivery, the charterer
will evince an intention no longer to be bound by the contract and will thus
repudiate the contract. The owner may ignore the repudiation and claim
damages resulting from breach of contract by any late delivery or accept the
repudiation, withdraw the vessel from the control of the charterer and claim
damages resulting from repudiation.

In the present case, the charterparty of the vessel Gregos began on 8 January
1988 and the last day for redelivery was 18 March 1988. During the currency of
the charterparty the charterers were entitled to give orders to the master of the
vessel with regard to the loading and sailing of the vessel but they were bound
to give orders which would result in the vessel being redelivered to the owners
not later than 18 March. Orders were lawfully given by the charterers for the
vessel to deliver a cargo of bauxite at Matanzas, a port in Venezuela on the
Orinoco River, and thereafter to load a cargo of iron ore at the neighbouring
port of Palua, also on the Orinoco, for delivery to Fos in Italy prior to
redelivery at an authorised port in Europe on or before 18 March. The Gregos
was ready to load at Palua on 25 February. Following the grounding of the
vessel, Philippine Roxas, in the Orinoco, it was then possible for the Gregos to
escape from the Orinoco unladen in time for redelivery on 18 March. If,
however, the Gregos took on a cargo of iron ore at Palua, as had been ordered,

it was no longer possible for the Gregos to clear the Orinoco until the obstruction of the channel caused by the grounding of the Philippine Roxas had been overcome. In that event, according to the owners, it was not possible for the Gregos to be redelivered by 18 March. The charterers ordered the master to load at Palua. This order, if complied with, would have prevented redelivery by 18 March and was therefore a repudiatory breach of contract. If the master had accepted the order to load at Palua, the owners would have lost their right to accept repudiation and would only have been entitled to damages for late delivery. The master refused to load at Palua and requested fresh orders to enable the Gregos to be redelivered on time. On 29 February the charterers refused to give fresh orders and the owners treated the conduct of the charterers in ordering and attempting to insist upon loading at Palua as a repudiatory breach of contract and accepted that repudiation.

In the arbitration which inevitably followed, the charterers contended that they would have been able to redeliver by 18 March 1988 even if the Gregos had loaded at Palua and unloaded at Fos but this contention was disproved by events and was rejected by the arbitrator. It follows that the charterers were not entitled to order the vessel to be loaded at Palua, that their refusal to give an alternative order evinced an intention no longer to be bound by the contract to redeliver not later than 18 March and that the owners were entitled to accept the conduct of the charterers as a repudiation of the contract. In the event the owners did not suffer any damages from the repudiation but immediately after 26 February, while the charterers were still contending that they were not guilty of breach of contract or repudiatory conduct and that the owners were bound to allow the vessel to be loaded at Palua, the charterers and the owners entered into an agreement whereby the Gregos lifted the iron ore from Palua and the charterers agreed that if the owners were held to be entitled to accept the conduct of the charterers at Palua on 25 February as repudiatory, the charterers would pay the current increase in freight rate over the charterparty rate plus a notional ballast bonus. The arbitrator and Evans J ([1992] 2 Lloyd's Rep 40) found in favour of the owners. The Court of Appeal ([1993] 2 Lloyd's Rep 335) found in favour of the charterers.

There was a good deal of discussion about legitimate and illegitimate last voyages, but to my mind this appeal falls to be determined by the application of elementary principles of contract. The charterer agrees to redeliver on time and must therefore give orders which ensure that the vessel will be redelivered on time. If the charterer gives an order which will not enable the vessel to be redelivered on time, the owner may treat that order as a repudiatory breach of contract. If the owner complies with the order he loses his right to repudiate but is entitled to damages for any late delivery. In the present case, the crucial date was 25 February when the charterers could have given an order which would have enabled redelivery on time but insisted on an order which did not allow the vessel to be redelivered on time. The order to load at Palua on 25 February was a repudiatory breach of contract. If the Gregos had been loaded, pursuant to that order, the owners would have lost their right to repudiate but would have remained entitled to damages for late delivery. The owners accepted the repudiation and withdrew the vessel. The repudiation and the acceptance of repudiation were followed by an agreement between the owners and the charterers whereunder the owners became entitled to the sums awarded by the arbitrator. I would allow the appeal.

LORD ACKNER. My Lords for the reasons given by noble and learned friend Lord Mustill, I, too, would allow this appeal and restore the order of the arbitrator.

LORD MUSTILL. My Lords, in merchant shipping time is money. A cargo ship is expensive to finance and expensive to run. The shipowner must keep it earning with the minimum of gaps between employments. Time is also important for the charterer, because arrangements must be made for the shipment and receipt of the cargo, or for the performance of obligations under sub-contracts. These demands encourage the planning and performance of voyages to the tightest of margins. Yet even today ships do not run precisely to time. The most prudent schedule may be disrupted by regular hazards such as adverse weather or delays in port happening in an unexpected manner or degree, or by the intervention of wholly adventitious events.

Where the charterparty is for a period of time rather than a voyage, and the remuneration is calculated according to the time used rather than the service performed, the risk of delay is primarily on the charterer. For the shipowner, so long as he commits no breach and nothing puts the ship off-hire, his right to remuneration is unaffected by a disturbance of the charterer's plans. It is for the latter to choose between cautious planning, which may leave gaps between employments, and bolder scheduling with the risk of setting aims which cannot be realised in practice.

This distribution of risk holds good during most of the chartered service. As the time for redelivery approaches things become more complicated. (The word 'redelivery' is inaccurate, but it is convenient, and I will use it.) If the market is rising, the charterer wants to have the use of the vessel at the chartered rate for as long as possible. Conversely, the shipowner must think ahead to the next employment, and if, as is common, he has made a forward fixture he will be in difficulties if the vessel is retained by the charterer longer than had been foreseen. This conflict of interest becomes particularly acute when there is time left for only one more voyage before the expiry of the charter, and disputes may arise if the charterer orders the ship to perform a service which the shipowner believes will extend beyond the date fixed for redelivery.

Disputes of this kind have given rise to a considerable body of authority, not entirely easy to reconcile. In the first place there are judgments which lay down rules for deciding what, in the light of the words used in the individual charterparty, is the last permissible date for redelivery. In its early stages, the present case raised an issue of this kind. Next, the courts have discussed the 'legitimacy', as it is often called, of the final voyage (that is, the question whether the charterer's order to perform the voyage is one which the shipowner must obey) in terms of the likelihood that the voyage will end in time to permit redelivery by the last permissible date. Finally, some of the legal consequences of late redelivery have been worked out.

There remain a number of unanswered questions, with which some of which your Lordships are now concerned. The context is a dispute between the owners and the charterers of the vessel Gregos. This was referred to arbitration. In the reasons for his award the arbitrator succinctly described the issues as follows:

'This arbitration concerned a claim by the registered owners for damages flowing from the time charterers' orders for a final allegedly "illegitimate" voyage, in other words, one that could not reasonably be expected to allow redelivery by the end of the charter period. The owners had refused to accept the orders. The parties had then entered into a without prejudice agreement under which the last voyage was performed. I had to determine whether or not the orders for the last voyage were ones that the charterers were entitled to give and, if not, what consequences flowed from the giving of those orders.'

The arbitrator decided that the voyage was not legitimate; that the owners were entitled to refuse the order; that the charterers were thereby in wrongful repudiation of the charter; and that the owners were entitled to a substantial sum by way of damages. From this award the owners obtained leave by consent to appeal to the High Court. Evans J ([1992] 2 Lloyd's Rep 40), sitting as commercial judge, upheld the award but certified that questions of general public importance were involved. By leave, an appeal was brought to the Court of Appeal ([1993] 2 Lloyd's Rep 335), which reversed the orders of Evans J and remitted the matter to the arbitrator for reconsideration in the light of its judgments. An appeal is now brought to this House by leave of your Lordships.

The facts of the dispute were as follows. The Gregos was chartered by Arni Maritime Corporation (the owners) to Torvald Klaveness A/S (the charterers) on terms which, so far as material, were as follows:

'Witnesseth, That the said Owners agree to let and the said Charterers agree to hire the said vessel, from the time of delivery, for about 50 to maximum 70 days ... Vessel ... to be employed in carrying lawful merchandise ... in such lawful trades ... between safe port and ... as the Charterers or their Agents shall direct, on the following conditions ... 8. That the Captain shall prosecute his voyages with the utmost despatch ... The Captain (although appointed by the Owners), shall be under the orders and directions of the Charterers as regards employment and agency ... 11. That the Charterers shall furnish the Captain from time to time with all requisite instructions and sailing directions ...'

In the early stages of these proceedings there was an issue about the meaning of 'maximum 70 days'. Did this allow a margin for later redelivery in unforeseen circumstances? The arbitrator held that there was no room for such a margin. This is now accepted as correct. Thus, the charterers were obliged to redeliver the vessel on or before 18 March 1988, 70 days after her initial delivery into their service on 8 January 1988, or pay damages for breach of contract. (On damages, see *Hyundai Merchant Marine Co Ltd v Gesuri Chartering Co Ltd, The Peonia* [1991] 1 Lloyd's Rep 100.)

The charterers' original contemplation was to employ the vessel first by ballasting her from Antwerp to Trombetas in Brazil to carry a cargo of bauxite to Matanzas, a port in Venezuela on the Orinoco River. Thence the vessel was to proceed up river in ballast to Puerto Ordaz where she would load a cargo of iron ore for Italy, prior to redelivery. Later, this plan was revised in two respects. First, the charterers interposed a second voyage from Matanzas to Trombetas in ballast with a return leg to Matanzas with bauxite, between the first bauxite voyage and the final voyage to Europe. Secondly, this final voyage was now to be from Palua, also on the Orinoco, with iron ore for Fos. The first element of this changed schedule was notified to the owners and complied with. The vessel did lift a second bauxite cargo. The other element, namely the substitution of a laden voyage from Palua to Fos, was notified by the charterers to the master of the vessel on 9 February 1988. If judged when the order was given, compliance with the order could reasonably have been anticipated to allow redelivery by 18 March, the last permissible date.

Three days later things began to go wrong. Another vessel grounded with unusual severity in the Orinoco, causing delays to river traffic which led the owners to warn the charterers that if the plan was adhered to the Gregos could not be redelivered in time. As the arbitrator was later to find, this warning was justified. Even if all had gone well thereafter there would have been a late redelivery of between two and four days. The vessel nevertheless proceeded on the very short ballast leg to Palua from Matanzas. On 25 February 1988 the owners advised the charterers that they declined to perform the laden voyage from the Orinoco to Fos, and called upon the charterers to give revised orders for the final voyage. No such orders were given, and a dispute arose, the charterers insisting and the owners denying that the order of 9 February for a voyage from Palua to Fos remained valid. Whilst the impasse continued the owners began to negotiate a replacement fixture with a concern named Navios involving a rate of freight higher than that provided for under the instant charter, coupled with a bonus to reflect the fact that the vessel was in place at the intended loading port under the substitute employment and did not have to perform a ballast voyage. In the event, the deadlock was broken by a without prejudice agreement between the owners and the charterers. The terms were not before the House, but it was explained in argument that the agreement provided for the performance of the laden voyage to Fos on terms that if, in subsequent proceedings, it was held that the owners were justified in refusing to perform the voyage they would be entitled to a sum reflecting the difference between the chartered rate of hire and the more advantageous terms of the proposed substitute fixture with Navios. Pursuant to the without prejudice agreement the vessel loaded the cargo of iron ore and prepared to sail from Palua, but her departure was further delayed because another vessel grounded in the river ahead of her. In the event, the last laden voyage was not completed until 23 March, and the actual redelivery took place on 26 March— eight days late.

On these facts the matter went to arbitration. The clear and thorough reasons given by the arbitrator for his award reflected a distinction drawn in the arguments before him, and still drawn in the submissions before the House, between two issues. (1) Should the validity of the order for the final voyage be judged as at the time when it was given or as at the time when it fell to be complied with; or on some other date? (2) If the validity of the order was to be judged in the light of matters as they stood on 25 February, so that the voyage was not one for which a legitimate order could be given, what was the effect of (a) the charterers having given the order and (b) their refusal to replace it by another? Two decisions by the arbitrator are no longer challenged. First, that the wording of the charter left no room for a margin beyond the end of the stipulated 70 days. Second, as regards the order for the voyage from Palua to Fos, his conclusion was that if judged as at 9 February the order was reasonable but that due to the intervening delays by 25 February this was no longer the case. On the issues which are still in dispute the arbitrator reasoned as follows.

Essentially, on the ground of common sense, he rejected an argument for the owners that proper voyage instructions could not be given until the vessel was free of her previous cargo, for that would have left only (in the present case) the $1\frac{1}{2}$ hours of the ballast leg to Palua during which the next voyage could be nominated. On the other hand, if it were the law that the order could be given weeks or even months in advance (and the charterers did not suggest a limitation on how in advance it could be given) it would not be sensible to allow the charterers to shelter behind the apparent reasonableness of an order given at a time when it must be anticipated that practical problems were likely to render the theoretical scheduling of the vessel wholly unrealistic. The arbitrator thus concluded that the time for evaluating the propriety of an order previously given was when the voyage was to be commenced. Quite apart from his own reasoning, the arbitrator considered himself bound to arrive at this conclusion by *Marbienes Cia Naviera SA v Ferrostaal AG, The Democritos* [1976] 2 Lloyd's Rep 149. On this basis, the arbitrator held that the order originally given on 9 February, and on which the charterers were continuing to insist, had by 25 February become invalid. The arbitrator then turned to the question whether the giving of the illegitimate order constituted a repudiation of the contract. Given that the anticipated overrun was only a few days he would, in the absence of authority, have considered that there was no repudiation, but regarded himself as compelled by authority to the opposite view. The arbitrator then proceeded to damages, and arrived at an award of $US 299,791·25, comprising the difference between the charter hire and the hire obtainable on the alternative fixture with Navios, plus the bonus which Navios would have paid to recognise the immediate availability of the ship.

This award was upheld on appeal by Evans J. On the first question the learned judge concluded that the time for deciding whether the owner was bound to perform the order was when the time for performance arrived. His Lordship relied principally on practical considerations but stated that the weight of authority supported his conclusion. As to repudiation he had two reasons for upholding the award. First, that timely redelivery was a condition of the contract, and that ordering the vessel on a voyage which would involve a breach of condition must of necessity have been a wrongful repudiation. Secondly, the charterers' persistence with an order for an illegitimate voyage, and the resulting failure to give a lawful order with which the vessel could comply, was in itself a wrongful repudiation.

In the Court of Appeal two reasoned judgments were delivered. After a careful discussion of the reported cases in this field which, in the event, he concluded were indecisive Hirst LJ analysed the first issue principally in terms of convenience and concluded that—

> 'the legitimacy of the last voyage order has to be established at the date
> when it is given, having regard not only to the reasonableness at that date
> of the estimate of the expected duration of the voyage, but also to the
> reasonableness at that date of making an estimate at all ...' (See [1993] 2
> Lloyd's Rep 335 at 346.)

Regarding the second issue, Hirst LJ dealt only with the question whether timely redelivery was a condition of the contract, since he considered that the certified question of law did not extend to the alternative possibility that the giving of an order for an illegitimate voyage was in any event repudiatory. Holding that timely redelivery was not a condition of the contract, Hirst LJ concluded that an order which, if complied with, would involve some degree of lateness could not in itself be an actual breach of condition or a repudiatory breach.

The other reasoned judgment was delivered by Simon Brown LJ, who began with the second issue. On this, Simon Brown LJ considered that the giving of an order for a voyage which will overrun the redelivery date is not a breach of contract at all, although it is ineffectual as a means of compelling the vessel to perform the ordered service. Even if, contrary to this view, such order is a breach, Simon Brown LJ considered that it is not repudiatory because: (1) the shipowners' remedy is to ignore the order; and (2) the charterers' obligation not to insist on an illegitimate last voyage cannot be of more fundamental importance than the obligation to redeliver the vessel by the final date—'an obligation clearly established *not* to be a condition properly so called' (see [1993] 2 Lloyd's Rep 335 at 350; Simon Brown LJ's emphasis).

As regards the first issue, Simon Brown LJ considered that the shipowner is obliged to accept and obey the charterers' last voyage order whenever it is given, save in so far as he is entitled (i) to refuse to obey it if it is illegitimate and (ii) to refuse to commit himself whether or not to obey it if it is given unreasonably early. Russell LJ agreed with both of these judgments. The owners now appeal to your Lordships' House.

I begin with the first issue, concerning the date for judging the validity of the charterers' order. Here, it seems to me that the inquiry has been led astray by concentrating too much on the order and too little on the shipowner's promise to furnish the services of the vessel, which is what the contract is about. Initially, the practical implications of the promise are undefined, since they depend on how in the future the charterer decides to employ the vessel; but they are not unlimited, being constrained from the start as to duration, nature and extent by express terms in the charter (concerning for example the types of cargo to be carried and the geographical limits of trade) and also by important implied terms. Later, when the time for performance has arrived, this broad promise is converted to a series of specific obligations by the charterer's orders for employment, but the constraints expressly or impliedly accepted by the charterer in the original contract continue to apply. Whatever the charterer may order, a service which falls outside the range encompassed by the owner's original promise is not one which he can be compelled to perform; and this is so as regards not only the duration of the chartered service, but also all the other limitations imposed by the charterparty on the charterer's freedom of choice. There is thus to be a measuring of the service called for against the service promised. As a matter of common sense, it seems to me that the time for such measurement is, primarily at least, the time when performance falls due.

My Lords, I have qualified this statement with the words 'primarily at least' because in practice the interests of both parties demand that the charterer is entitled to give orders in advance of the time for performance; and this must entail at least a provisional judgment on the validity of the order. If it can be seen at this early stage that compliance will involve a service which lies outside the shipowner's undertaking the latter can say so at once, and reject the order. But if the order is apparently valid its validity is no more than contingent, since the time for matching the service against the promise to serve does not arrive until the nature of the service is definitively known; and this will not usually be until the service is due to begin, or in some instances until it is already in progress. Thus, if and for so long as the service required conforms with those which the shipowner promised in advance to render the specific order creates a specific obligation to perform them when the time arrives. But only for so long as that state of affairs persists. If circumstances change, so that compliance with the order will call for a service which in the original contract the shipowner never undertook, the obligation to comply must fall away. As I see it, the charterers' order in advance amounts to a continuing requirement, the validity of which may change with the passage of time.

My Lords, this much I conclude simply by considering the general nature of a time charterparty. The conclusion must however be tested by recourse to the authorities and (with appropriate caution) to its practical implications. On the former I need not dwell. Great care has properly been taken in the courts below to see whether there can be found in the decided cases any judicial pronouncement which points unequivocally to a conclusion. For my part I can find none. Certainly, there are several turns of phrase which suggest one or another assumption about when the question of validity should be judged, but I am quite satisfied that in no case was the choice of date in issue, or even in most instances present to the mind of the judges, and I will therefore not stay to quote from them.

Turning to the practicalities, I entirely share the opinion of Saville J in *The Peonia* [1991] 1 Lloyd's Rep 100 that questions of this kind are better decided by looking at what the contract says than by speculating on the practical outcome of preferring one solution to another. Naturally, no judge will favour an interpretation which produces an obviously absurd result unless the words used drive him to it, since it is unlikely that this is what the parties intended. But where there is no obvious absurdity, and simply assertions by either side that its own interpretation yields the more sensible result, there is room for error. The difference of opinion in the present case is an illustration. It is an essential part of the charterers' argument that an order given at a time when it is reasonably anticipated that compliance will not infringe the restrictions imposed by the contract has an immutable contractual effect. Even if circumstances change both parties are committed to the ordered employment unless released by mutual consent. The present charterers must be arguing for this, for if a charterer is free to recall his original order and substitute another the inference is irresistible that he ought to make such a substitution if changed circumstances cause the performance to break the bounds of the shipowner's original promise. What is the commercial convenience of such an inter-pretation? Undeniably, there is this to be said for it, that the parties will have a firm projection of future employment on the basis of which they can both make plans. But powerful considerations point the other way. First, if the charterers are right an order given long in advance will lock both parties into a set of contractual obligations, which may well be compromised by the passage of time, as regards both commercial desirability and physical practicability. This can be in nobody's interest. The only escape would be to hold, as the Court of Appeal has held, that the order cannot be given before it is reasonable to do so, thus diminishing the likelihood of unexpected events. My Lords, with respect I cannot accept this solution for I cannot see how, even after the event, a court or arbitrator could set the criteria for deciding whether an order was premature or apply them to the facts. Still less, in my opinion, should a shipowner be expected in the press of the moment to decide in the light of such criteria, whether to reject the order—a rejection which, if subsequently held by an arbitrator to have been ill-founded, would in all probability be a wrongful repudiation by the shipowner. Secondly, if the order is irrevocable the shipowner may find himself, if circumstances change, obliged to perform a service which he never agreed to undertake. This consequence, unacceptable enough in the context of an order prolonging the service beyond the time stipulated in the contract, could be even more serious when related to some other restriction imposed by the charterparty to which, if the argument is sound, it must equally apply. Furthermore, if the order is irrevocably binding on both sides (which is the logic of the argument) it must follow that a charterer who has reasonably given an order which is later falsified by events is compelled to proceed with a voyage which will inevitably be a breach of contract on his part. This can hardly be in the interests of commerce.

Thus, if the matter is to be decided according to balance of convenience the owners' argument appears to have much the better of it. But I prefer to concentrate on the charterparty itself; and here, for the reasons stated, the analysis leads directly to the conclusion that, as the arbitrator and Evans J decided, the correct date for assessment was 25 February. By then, an order originally permissible had become illegitimate.

I turn to the issue of repudiation. Although the appeal is concerned with an invalid order for a final voyage this is only a special case of an order issued for the performance of a service which lies outside the scope of the shipowner's promise. Since orders for employment and compliance with them lie at the heart of a time charter the question is of general importance, and the solution arrived at should hold good for all types of order. The analysis is not straightforward. There are three different grounds upon which it might be said that where a charterer calls on a shipowner to perform an extra-contractual service the shipowner is entitled to treat himself as discharged. First, the giving of an invalid order is by its nature a repudiatory breach. Second, redelivery after the final date is a breach of contract, and has the character of a breach of condition, entitling the shipowner to treat himself as discharged. It follows, so the argument runs, that an order for a voyage which according to a reasonable prediction will lead to late redelivery must necessarily be a repudiatory breach. Third, the persistence of the charterers in an illegitimate order was conduct 'evincing an intention no longer to be bound' by the contract, and hence a repudiation of it.

When considering the first of these arguments it is necessary to distinguish between two propositions: that the charterer is obliged at the appropriate time to give a valid order for the employment of the ship, and that he is obliged never to give an invalid order. At first sight this distinction may seem mere wordplay, but for present purposes it is essential, as may be seen from the example of a charterer who gives a series of orders, all of them invalid and hence ineffectual. The former proposition entails that since an ineffectual order is the same as no order at all, the charterer becomes in breach only when the time for giving an order for the employment of the vessel has come and gone with no valid order having been given. The consequence of the latter is different, namely that every invalid order is in itself a breach of contract, giving the shipowner an immediate and distinct cause of action on each occasion. In company with Simon Brown LJ I have difficulty in accepting the latter proposition. Certainly, if the shipowner acts on the order and suffers damage he should have an implied right of indemnity at common law. But if he rejects the order and does nothing, to say that he has suffered an actionable breach of contract by the mere receipt of the message seems to introduce an unnecessary complication, and if the matter were free from authority I would hesitate to take this step. There are however a number of judgments, concerned with unsafe ports as well as final voyages, which assert or assume that an illegitimate order is in itself a breach (see eg *The Peonia* [1991] 1 Lloyd's Rep 100, *Motor Oil Hellas (Corinth) Refineries SA v Shipping Corp of India, The Kanchenjunga* [1989] 1 Lloyd's Rep 354 and *Batis Maritime Corp v Petroleos del Mediterraneo SA, The Batis* [1990] 1 Lloyd's Rep 345) and since the proposition appears to have been conceded in the Court of Appeal I will assume it to be correct. It is however quite another matter to say that the duty never to give an invalid order is so fundamental to the working of the contract that the giving of such an order must in every case entitle the shipowner to treat the contract as at an end, even if by rejecting the order he can ensure that it causes him no damage at all. My Lords, although it is well established that certain obligations under charterparties do have the character of conditions I would not for my part wish to enlarge the category unduly, given the opportunity which this provides for a party to rely on an innocuous breach as a means of escaping from an unwelcome bargain. In the present instance I can see no commercial necessity to hold that the issuing of an invalid order is an automatic ground of discharge, and every reason for holding that it does not. I would therefore reject the first of the shipowners' arguments.

I turn to the second argument which concentrates, not on the rejected order itself, but on the hypothetical consequences which would have been likely to ensue if it had been obeyed. It runs as follows. The timely redelivery of the vessel is a condition of the contract; an actual late redelivery, whether long or short, would therefore enable the shipowner to treat the contract as terminated; the invalid order actually given, if obeyed, would probably have caused the vessel to be redelivered late; the breach of condition which this would have entailed must be referred back to the invalid order, even though in fact it was not obeyed. At first sight this argument appears to lead straight to the law on anticipatory breach, and in particular to the discussion in *Federal Commerce and Navigation Co Ltd v Molena Alpha Inc* [1979] 1 All ER 307, [1979] AC 757 of the situation where the threatened breach is not of a fundamental character. On reflection, however, I question whether this analysis is sound, for I am not convinced that the shipowner can at the same time treat the charterer as evincing an intention to commit a breach in the future and yet ensure, by rejecting the order, that no such breach ever takes place.

Quite apart from this however I find it hard to accept that timely redelivery is a condition of the contract. The classification of an obligation as a condition or an 'innominate' term is largely determined by its practical importance in the scheme of the contract, and this is not easily judged in relation to the obligation to redeliver, since the occasions for the cancellation of a charter on the ground of a few days' delay at the end of the chartered service are likely to be few. If the ship is laden when the final date arrives the shipowner will often have obligations to third party consignees which make it impossible for him to cut short the voyage, quite apart from the improbability that he will go to the trouble and expense of arranging for the discharge and receipt of the cargo at an alternative destination, just to save a few days' delay. These problems will not arise if the vessel is ballasting to the redelivery port, but even if the shipowner really wants the vessel back on time, rather than a few days late, he will not usually need to have recourse to a cancellation, since the charterer will have no motive to keep the charter in being, with its obligation to pay hire for an empty ship. Even acknowledging the importance given in recent years to time clauses in mercantile contracts (see e g *Bunge Corp v Tradax SA* [1981] 2 All ER 513, [1981] 1 WLR 711 and *Cie Commerciale Sucres et Denrées v C Czarnikow Ltd* [1990] 3 All ER 641, [1990] 1 WLR 1337). I would incline to the view that this particular obligation is 'innominate' and that a short delay in redelivery would not justify the termination of the contract. For this additional reason therefore I would reject the owners' second argument. It is however unnecessary to express a firm conclusion upon it, given my opinion on the owners' third argument, to which I now turn.

This argument depends, not on the invalid order which was given, but on the valid order which was not. The original order having become ineffectual the charterers were obliged by cl 11 to replace it with one which they were entitled to give. Whether at the time of the cancellation they had committed an actual breach of this obligation is debatable, but at all events the breach was not final, since (if I correctly understand the arbitrator's reasons) there would have been time if all else failed for the charterers to ballast the vessel back to the redelivery area before the final date, or conceivably to issue an order for a revised laden voyage. But it is plain from the facts stated by the arbitrator that the charterers had no intention of doing this, and that the critical time would pass without any valid orders being given. This is the significance of the changed circumstances which rendered the original order invalid. Not that the order constituted a repudiation in itself, but that the charterers' persistence in it after it had become invalid showed that they did not intend to perform their obligations under the charter. That is to say, they 'evinced an intention no longer to be bound' by the charter. This was an anticipatory breach, which entitled the owners to treat the contract as ended.

My Lords, although differently expressed this reasoning accords with that of Evans J. Rather than call up a secondary obligation to give a new order once the old one has failed, I prefer to envisage a continuing primary obligation to give a valid order; but this distinction is largely a matter of terminology and has no practical significance. In expressing this opinion I have not analysed the reported cases, since in none of them was the present question in issue, and your Lordships are free to approach the matter from first principles. I should however place on record that I have taken into account *The Kanchenjunga* [1989] 1 Lloyd's Rep 354, *The Batis* [1990] 1 Lloyd's Rep 345 and *Alma Shipping Corp of Monrovia v Mantovani, The Dione* [1975] 1 Lloyd's Rep 115. In relation to *The Dione* I have particularly noted the statement of Lord Denning MR which corresponds with the view above expressed, but since it was plainly obiter and was not founded on an analysis of the authorities I have thought it preferable not to call it up in support (see [1975] 1 Lloyd's Rep 115 at 188).

In conclusion I must notice a feature of the award which troubled the arbitrator himself, which Hirst LJ relied upon in support of his conclusion that there had been no repudiation, and which was the subject of comment in a valuable article by Brian Davenport QC and Michele White 'Last voyage orders—again: The Gregos' [1994] Lloyd's MCLQ 154. This was what Hirst LJ called the 'windfall damages' attached to the repudiation, a large multiple of those which would have been awarded simply in respect of a few days late redelivery. At first sight, this apparently anomalous result is a good reason for questioning whether the claim for repudiation was soundly based. On closer examination, however, the anomaly consists, not so much in the size of the damages, but in the fact that damages were awarded at all. Imagine that the without prejudice agreement had not been made, and that the owners, having treated the charter as wrongfully repudiated, had accepted a substitute fixture with Navios. If one then asked what loss had the repudiation caused the owners to suffer, the answer would be—none. On the contrary, the charterers' wrongful act would have enabled the owners to make a profit. Even if they had not accepted the substitute employment they might very well have suffered no loss, since they would have been in the favourable position of having their ship free in the right place at the right time to take a spot fixture on a rising market. In neither event would the owners ordinarily recover any damages for the wrongful repudiation. Yet the arbitrator awarded a large sum. The reason was, I believe, that what the arbitrator did was not to award damages but to enforce the terms of the without prejudice agreement, and to remunerate the owners for performing a voyage from which, in consequence of the charterers' wrongful act, they would otherwise have been free. This purely technical distinction would have been of no interest but for the stress laid on the size of an award of some $US 300,000 for the anticipatory repudiation of a contract which, if performance had gone ahead, would have led to a breach yielding a mere $US 35,000 in damages. For the reasons just stated, this comparison is inaccurate. The point really to be made is that if the conduct of the charterers was repudiatory the consequence that they were left without a ship to lift their sub-charterers' cargo may seem out of proportion to the comparatively minor breach which their order, if performed, would have entailed. There is force in this, but not enough to overcome the contractual logic. The fact is that in a volatile market, of which merchant shipping is by no means the only example, a contract breaker may find that the consequences of a breach are multiplied to a surprising degree by adventitious factors. Here, the charterers chose to stand their ground in circumstances where, if they were mistaken, the owners would have the upper hand. I believe that they were mistaken and must suffer the consequences, harsh as they may seem.

For these reasons I would allow the appeal and restore the award of the arbitrator.

LORD SLYNN OF HADLEY. My Lords, for the reasons given by noble and learned friend Lord Mustill, I too would allow this appeal and restore the order of the arbitrator.

LORD WOOLF. My Lords, I have had the advantage of reading in draft the speech of my noble and learned friend Lord Mustill. For the reasons which he gives I would allow the appeal and concur in the order he proposes.

Appeal allowed.

Celia Fox   Barrister.

R v South Hams District Council and another, ex parte Gibb
and other appeals

COURT OF APPEAL, CIVIL DIVISION

NEILL, LEGGATT AND MILLETT LJJ

10, 11, 12, 27 MAY 1994

Local authority – Caravan sites – Provision of caravan sites – Duty of local authority – Duty to provide accommodation for gipsies – Definition of 'gipsies' – Question of whether particular persons 'gipsies' being a matter for the relevant local authority – Whether local authority's decision open to challenge – Caravan Sites Act 1968, s 16.

On its true construction, the definition of 'gipsies' in s 16[a] of the Caravan Sites Act 1968 as 'persons of nomadic habit of life' imports the requirement that there must be some recognisable connection between the wandering or travelling from place to place and the means whereby the persons concerned make or seek their livelihood. The s 16 definition does not therefore apply to persons or individuals who move from place to place merely as the fancy takes them and without any connection between the movement and their means of livelihood. Moreover, the question whether particular persons are gipsies within the meaning of s 16 is pre-eminently a matter for the relevant local authority to determine when considering its duty under s 6[b] of the 1968 Act to provide sites for those who visit the area in cohesive groups and who have some purpose and pattern for their wanderings, and accordingly the local authority's decision on that matter is only open to challenge on an application for judicial review on the ground of irrationality (see p 1020 *h* to p 1021 *e h*, p 1022 *d* and p 1024 *b* to *j*, post).

Garlick v Oldham Metropolitan BC [1993] 2 All ER 65 applied.

Mills v Cooper [1967] 2 All ER 100 considered.

Notes

For the duty of local authorities to provide caravan sites for gipsies, see 46 *Halsbury's Laws* (4th edn reissue) para 621, and for cases on the subject, see 47(1) *Digest* (Reissue) 159–161, 575–580.

For the Caravan Sites Act 1968, ss 6, 16, see 32 *Halsbury's Statutes* (4th edn) 503, 512.

Cases referred to in judgments

Associated Provincial Picture Houses Ltd v Wednesbury Corp [1947] 2 All ER 680, [1948] 1 KB 223, CA.

Berkshire CC v Bird (26 September 1986, unreported), QBD.

Commission for Racial Equality v Dutton [1989] 1 All ER 306, [1989] QB 783, [1989] 2 WLR 17, CA.

---

a Section 16, so far as material, is set out at p 1016 *f* to *h*, post
b Section 6, so far as material, is set out at p 1015 *h j*, post

Garlick v Oldham Metropolitan BC [1993] 2 All ER 65, [1993] AC 509, [1993] 2 WLR 609, HL.

Greenwich London BC v Powell [1989] 1 All ER 65, [1989] AC 995, [1989] 2 WLR 7, HL.

Khawaja v Secretary of State for the Home Dept [1983] 1 All ER 765, [1984] AC 74, [1983] 2 WLR 321, HL.

Mills v Cooper [1967] 2 All ER 100, [1967] 2 QB 459, [1967] 2 WLR 1343, DC.

Mole Valley DC v Smith (1992) 24 HLR 442, CA.

R v Fulham, Hammersmith and Kensington Rent Tribunal, ex p Zerek [1951] 1 All ER 482, [1951] 2 KB 1, DC.

R v Gloucester CC, ex p Dutton (1991) 24 HLR 246.

South Hams DC v Shough (1992) 25 HLR 189, CA.

Appeals

R v South Hams DC and anor, ex p Gibb

John Michael Gibb, by a notice of appeal dated 6 December 1993, appealed with leave from the decision of Harrison J made on 3 November 1993 whereby he ordered that the appellant's motion for judicial review of decisions of the South Hams District Council to institute and pursue proceedings for the recovery of land at Steamer Quay, Totnes, and of the continuing failure of Devon County Council to provide adequate accommodation for gipsies in accordance with s 6(1) of the Caravan Sites Act 1968, be dismissed on the grounds that the judge had erred in holding (i) that the definition of 'gipsies' in s 16 of the Caravan Sites Act 1968 presupposed persons who move from place to place with a purpose in mind, (ii) that the respective local authority had properly considered whether the appellant was a gipsy and (iii) that a decision as to any person being a gipsy could only be made by a local authority and could only be challenged on the basis of unreasonableness. The facts are set out in the judgment of Neill LJ.

R v Gloucestershire CC, ex p Davies

Steven Davies, by a notice of appeal dated 15 November 1993, appealed with leave from the decision of Harrison J made on 3 November 1993 whereby he ordered that the appellant's motion for judicial review of a decision of Gloucestershire County Council to apply for a possession order in relation to land at Hollow Fosse, Gloucestershire, be dismissed on the same grounds as those asserted in the above case. The facts are set out in the judgment of Neill LJ.

R v Dorset CC, ex p Rolls and anor

Ian Rolls and Christian Nicole, by a notice of appeal dated 31 January 1994, appealed with leave from the decision of Laws J made on 27 January 1994 whereby he ordered that the appellants' motion for judicial review of a decision of Dorset County Council to institute proceedings for possession in respect of land at Blackdown, Hardy's Monument, near Dorchester, Dorset, be dismissed on the grounds that the judge had erred in holding (i) that the definition of 'gipsies' in s 16 of the Caravan Sites Act 1968 presupposed persons who move from place to place with a purpose in mind and (ii) that the local authority had properly considered whether the appellants were gipsies. The facts are set out in the judgment of Neill LJ.

David Watkinson (instructed by *Cartridges,* Exeter) for Mr Gibb, and (instructed by *Bobbetts Mackan,* Bristol) for Messrs Davies, Rolls and Nicole.

Timothy Straker (instructed by *Sharpe Pritchard,* agents for *David Incoll,* Totnes, *Philip Jenkinson,* Exeter and *David Jenkins,* Dorchester and instructed by *Ian Wotherspoon,* Gloucester) for the councils.

Cur adv vult

27 May 1994. The following judgments were delivered.

NEILL LJ. In these three appeals the appellants seek judicial review to quash the decisions of the respondent local authorities to issue proceedings against them claiming possession of the pieces of land occupied respectively by the appellants.

In the first appeal the appellant is Mr John Michael Gibb, who has been an occupant of a site at Steamer Quay, Totnes in Devon. The proceedings for possession were brought by South Hams District Council on 31 October 1991. The district council are the owners of the land at Steamer Quay. Devon County Council are also parties to the proceedings.

In the second appeal the appellant is Mr Steven Davies. The proceedings for possession were brought against Mr Davies on 14 July 1992 in relation to his occupation of land at Old Gore Wood, Hollow Fosse, in Gloucestershire. The land is owned by the Gloucestershire County Council as a highway authority, the land being a redundant part of the old A429 road.

In these two appeals the appeals are brought against the order of Harrison J dated 3 November 1993 dismissing the applications for judicial review.

In the third appeal the appellants are Mr Ian Rolls and Mr Christian Nicole. The proceedings for possession were brought by the Dorset County Council in respect of the occupation by the appellants of land at Blackdown, Hardy's Monument, near Dorchester in Dorset. This appeal is brought against the order of Laws J dated 27 January 1994 dismissing the appellants' application for judicial review.

In each of these appeals the following issues arise for consideration. (1) The meaning of the word 'gipsy' in s 16 of the Caravan Sites Act 1968. (2) Whether the court has to decide on the available evidence as a precedent fact whether the individual appellants are gipsies within the meaning of s 16 of the 1968 Act, or whether the court is confined to reviewing on the ordinary *Wednesbury* principles the decisions reached by the three local authorities on the facts (see *Associated Provincial Picture Houses Ltd v Wednesbury Corp* [1947] 2 All ER 680, [1948] 1 KB 223). (3) Whether a district council, when deciding whether or not to bring proceedings for possession, is under a duty to take into account the fact that the relevant county council is in breach of its statutory duty to provide adequate accommodation for gipsies in accordance with s 6 of the 1968 Act. I can turn at once to the first issue.

(1) The meaning of the word 'gipsy' in s 16 of the 1968 Act

In order to consider this issue it is necessary to set out the relevant statutory provisions.

I should refer first to the Caravan Sites and Control of Development Act 1960. Section 24 of the 1960 Act provides:

'(1) A local authority shall have power within their area to provide sites where caravans may be brought, whether for holidays or other temporary purposes or for use as permanent residences, and to manage the sites or lease them to some other person.

(2) Subject to the provisions of this section, a local authority shall have power to do anything appearing to them desirable in connection with the provision of such sites, and in particular—(a) to acquire land which is in use as a caravan site, or which has been laid out as a caravan site, or (b) to provide for the use of those occupying caravan sites any services or facilities for their health or convenience; and in exercising their powers under this section the local authority shall have regard to any standards which may have been specified by the Minister under subsection (6) of section five of this Act.'

Section 24 of the 1960 Act has to be read in conjunction with s 23(2). Section 23(2) has been slightly amended by later primary and secondary legislation, but as originally enacted was in these terms:

'The council of a rural district may make with respect to any land in their area to which this section applies an order prohibiting, either absolutely or except in such circumstances as may be specified in the order, the stationing of caravans on the land for the purposes of human habitation.'

It seems clear that a number of local authorities made use of their powers under s 23(2) of the 1960 Act. One of the consequences of the use of these powers was that gipsies found it increasingly difficult to make use of common land as stopping places on their journeys. In order to deal with this and other problems the 1968 Act was enacted. I should set out the relevant provisions of the 1968 Act.

Counsel for the appellants drew our attention to the long title of the 1968 Act and in particular to the following words:

'An Act ... to secure the establishment of [caravan] sites by local authorities for the use of gipsies and other persons of nomadic habit, and control in certain areas the unauthorised occupation of land by such persons ...'

Part II of the 1968 Act is headed 'Gipsy Encampments'. Section 6 of the 1968 Act (as amended by the Local Government Act 1985) is, so far as is material, in these terms:

'(1) Subject to the provisions of this and the next following section, it shall be the duty of every local authority being the council of a county, metropolitan district or London borough to exercise their powers under section 24 of the [1960 Act] (provision of caravan sites) so far as may be necessary to provide adequate accommodation for gipsies residing in or resorting to their area ...

(4) The powers of a local authority under the said section 24 shall include power to provide, in or in connection with sites for the accommodation of gipsies, working space and facilities for the carrying on of such activities as are normally carried on by them; but subsection (1) of this section shall not apply to the powers conferred by this subsection.'

Section 7 of the 1968 Act contains provisions relating to the functions of district councils. It is sufficient to refer to s 7(1), which provides:

'The duty imposed by section 6(1) of this Act on the council of a county shall extend only to determining what sites are to be provided and acquiring or appropriating the necessary land; and it shall be the duty of the council of the district in which any such site is located to exercise all other powers under section 24 of the [1960 Act] in relation to the site.'

I should refer next to s 9 of the 1968 Act, as substituted by the Local Government, Planning and Land Act 1980. As substituted, s 9 provides:

'The Secretary of State may, if at any time it appears to him to be necessary so to do, give directions to any local authority to which subsection (1) of section 6 of this Act applies requiring them to provide, pursuant to that section, such sites or additional sites, for the accommodation of such numbers of caravans, as may be specified in the directions; and any such directions shall be enforceable, on the application of the Secretary of State, by mandamus.'

Sections 10 to 12 of the 1968 Act contain provisions for the control of unauthorised encampments. It is not necessary to refer to these provisions in detail, but it is to be noted that powers are given under s 12 for areas to be designated in which it is an offence for any person, being a gipsy, to station a caravan, for the purpose of residing for any period, on any land as specified in s 10(1). Section 11 of the 1968 Act empowers magistrates to make orders for the removal of unlawfully parked caravans and their occupants.

Finally I should refer to s 16, which is the interpretation section in the 1968 Act. By virtue of this section 'caravan' has the same meaning as in Pt I of the 1960 Act and means—

'any structure designed or adapted for human habitation which is capable of being moved from one place to another (whether by being towed, or by being transported on a motor vehicle or trailer) and any motor vehicle so designed or adapted, but does not include—(a) any railway rolling stock which is for the time being on rails forming part of a railway system, or (b) any tent ...

"gipsies" means persons of nomadic habit of life, whatever their race or origin, but does not include members of an organised group of travelling showmen, or of persons engaged in travelling circuses, travelling together as such ...'

It seems probable that the statutory definition of 'gipsies' can be traced to the decision of the Divisional Court in *Mills v Cooper* [1967] 2 All ER 100, [1967] 2 QB 459. In that case an information had been preferred against the defendant of an offence contrary to s 127 of the Highways Act 1959. So far as is material, that section provided:

'If, without lawful authority or excuse ... (c) a hawker or other itinerant trader or a gipsy pitches a booth, stall or stand, or encamps, on a highway, he shall be guilty of an offence ...'

In the course of his judgment Lord Parker CJ considered the meaning of the word 'gipsy' in the 1959 Act. He said ([1967] 2 All ER 100 at 103, [1967] 2 QB 459 at 466):

'It was urged that the word "gipsy" should be given its dictionary meaning, as being a member of the Romany race ... I am, however, quite satisfied that "gipsy" in this context cannot bear that meaning ... That a man is of the Romany race is, as it seems to me, something which is really too vague of ascertainment, and impossible to prove; moreover, it is, I think, difficult to think that Parliament intended to subject a man to a penalty in the context of causing litter and obstruction on the highway merely by reason of his race. I think that, in this context, "gipsy" means no more than a person leading a nomadic life with no, or no fixed, employment and with no fixed abode. In saying that, I am hoping that those words will not be considered as the words of a statute, but merely as conveying the general colloquial idea of a gipsy. Looked at in that way, a man might well not be a gipsy on one date and yet be one on a later date.'

Diplock LJ agreed. He said ([1967] 2 All ER 100 at 104, [1967] 2 QB 459 at 467):

'I agree that the word "gipsy" as used in s. 127(c) of the Highways Act, 1959, cannot bear its dictionary meaning of a member of a wandering race (by themselves called Romany) of Hindu origin. If it did, it would mean that Parliament in 1959 had amended the corresponding section of the Highway Act, 1835, s 72, which referred to "gipsy or other person" so as to discriminate against persons by reason of their racial origin alone. It would raise other difficulties too. How pure blooded a Romany must one be to fall into the definition? The section is a penal section and should, I suppose, be strictly construed as requiring pure Romany descent. As members of this race first appeared in England not later than the beginning of the sixteenth century, and have not in the intervening centuries been notorious for the abundance of their written records, it would be impossible to prove Romany origin even as far back as the sixteenth century, let alone through the earlier centuries of their peripatetic history from India to the shores of this island. The section, so far as it referred to "gipsy", would be incapable in practice of having any application at all. Confronted by those difficulties, counsel for the respondent only faintly argued that the word "gipsy" in the context of the section does not bear its popular meaning, which I would define as a person without fixed abode who leads a nomadic life, dwelling in tents or other shelters, or in caravans or other vehicles. If this meaning is adopted, it follows that being a gipsy is not an unalterable status. It cannot be said "once a gipsy always a gipsy". By changing his way of life a modern Borrow may be a gipsy at one time and not a gipsy at another.'

It may be noted that the provisions in s 127(c) of the Highways Act 1959 replaced part of s 72 of the Highway Act 1835, which was in these terms:

'... If any Hawker, Higgler, Gipsy, or other Person travelling shall pitch any Tent, Booth, Stall, or Stand, or encamp upon any Part of any Highway ... every Person so offending in any of the Cases aforesaid shall for each and every such Offence forfeit and pay any Sum not exceeding Forty Shillings, over and above the Damages occasioned thereby.'

It was argued on behalf of the appellants that the word 'gipsies', as defined in s 16 of the 1968 Act, meant no more than persons 'with a tendency or settled practice of leading a wandering life with their homes'. It was important, it was said, to concentrate on the word 'nomadic' rather than the word 'gipsies'. 'Nomadic' in modern usage was apt to describe those who led a wandering life; though it was accepted that originally and etymologically nomads were people who wandered in search of pasture for their animals, this meaning had long since disappeared; it was therefore no longer permissible to restrict the statutory definition of gipsies to those who led a wandering life with an economic purpose in mind.

In order to consider this argument it will be convenient to refer shortly to some of the authorities in which the word 'gipsies' has been considered by the courts in the last ten years or so.

From the authorities to which we were referred one can collect the following formulations. First:

> '[Gipsies] are persons whom the Act contemplates will live in caravans, as no doubt befits a person whose habit of life is nomadic, that is wandering. The term "nomadic" originally applied to members of races or tribes who moved from place to place to find pasture. It still seems to me, even in the statutory definition, to presuppose a type of person who, when he moves from place to place, does so with some purpose in view. A "habit of life" is, in my judgment, a phrase meaning a manner of living so settled as to have become customary. It has, as I have already remarked, been found expedient to distinguish between permanent and transit sites for gipsies. That difference is perhaps reflected in the reference in s 6 of the 1968 Act to "gipsies residing in or resorting to their area", since a gipsy no doubt resides on a permanent site, though he may wander from it from time to time, whereas he resorts to a transit site temporarily … It seems to me that [the word "resorting"] may have the connotation of having recourse to a place for a purpose, whether it be to do work or on the way to a more remote destination. That is at least consonant with the behaviour of a nomad.'

This passage is an extract from the judgment of Leggatt J in *Berkshire CC v Bird* (26 September 1986, unreported). A little later, in rejecting Miss Bird's claim to be a gipsy, the judge added: '… visits to Berkshire have, upon her own account, apparently been casual, if not adventitious and without any avowed purpose.'

Second:

> 'It would be very unwise for a judge, and particularly a judge at first instance, to attempt a tighter definition of the words "gypsies residing in or resorting to their area" than that provided by Parliament. But if on ordinary principles of statutory construction I place myself in the draftsman's chair in 1968 and consider through 1968 eyes the mischief against which Parliament was legislating, it was in my judgment the mischief of the persistent hounding from place to place of people who had a recognisable identity in the social history of this country: people of a nomadic habit of life who either resided in a county as their more or less permanent residence of choice or such people who regularly resorted to a county during the year for a particular purpose, like those who went hop-picking in Kent or strawberry-picking in Somerset at the appropriate

season.' (See *R v Gloucester CC, ex p Dutton* (1991) 24 HLR 246 at 260 per Brooke J.)

Third:

'It is clear from the cases ... that a person may be a traditional gipsy, as that term is commonly understood, but yet not be a gipsy within the definition of the 1968 Act because he or she has lost the nomadic habit of life ... In my view, the definition of gipsy in the 1968 Act is capable of embracing persons other than traditional gipsies so long as they can be said to have a nomadic habit of life. If a "nomadic habit of life" simply means a settled practice of leading a wandering life ... the applicants in these cases may well be able to persuade a local authority that he or she comes within the definition in the 1968 Act. In my opinion, however, those words, and in particular the word "nomadic", import something more than that, something more than just the habit of wandering or travelling ... As the dictionary definition shows, the terms "nomadic" originally applied to members of races or tribes who moved from place to place to find pasture ... the term "nomadic" in the definition in the 1968 Act still presupposes a type of person who moves from place to place with a purpose in mind. In my view, that purpose is a necessary and characteristic part of the life of a nomad in the sense of the original derivation of that word.' (See the judgment of Harrison J in the South Hams and Gloucestershire cases which are now before us.)

Fourth:

'In my judgment, it has to be remembered that the purpose of Pt II of the 1968 Act is to accord rights to gipsies. I cannot think that Parliament intended to confer the benefits of s 6(1) on any person simply because he has no permanent home of his own and makes a habit, seasonal or continuous, of moving from place to place to live. So to conclude would be to hold that Parliament intended to advantage persons who frankly chose to move round the country or county so as to live rent-free on other people's land where possible, and had no other purpose in their travels than doing so ... The term "nomad" has a Greek derivation, from the word meaning "to pasture". Plainly, gipsies nowadays do not have to be itinerant farmers, whether within the s 16 definition or not; but I apprehend that the notion of a nomadic way of life has always meant something more than the mere fact of moving from place to place. In my judgment, the definition contemplates that class of persons whose means of getting an independent living necessarily involves wandering from place to place. I think that the notion of economic independence, or at least of an aspiration to economic independence, is inherent in the idea of nomadic life, as is the notion that the nomad's living is to be got in an activity which requires him to go from place to place.' (See the judgment of Laws J in the Dorset case.)

I should refer also to the speech of Lord Bridge in *Greenwich London BC v owell* [1989] 1 All ER 65, [1989] AC 995. In that case the defendants had their ermanent residence at a caravan site provided by Greenwich London orough Council pursuant to its duty under s 6 of the 1968 Act. However, the efendants did seasonal work fruit-picking away from the site, usually for

four to five months a year. Greenwich London Borough Council gave th
defendants notice to quit on the ground that their licence to occupy the lan
had expired. The defendants resisted the claim for possession on the basis tha
the site was a protected site within the meaning of s 5(1) of the Mobile Home
Act 1983, notwithstanding that the definition of a protected site in s 5(1
excluded land occupied by a local authority as a caravan site for gipsies. Lor
Bridge referred to the Department of Environment circular 28/77 containin
'Notes for the Guidance of Local Authorities in the Implementation of Pt II c
the Caravan Sites Act 1968'. He observed ([1989] 1 All ER 65 at 70, [1989] A
995 at 1011):

> '... passages in the notes ... encourage local authorities to provide site
> to accommodate gipsies in four categories as follows: (1) emergenc
> stopping places ... (2) transit or short-stay sites ... (3) residential sites ... (4
> permanent sites for long-term residential use ... The last of thes
> categories can only have had in contemplation sites such as that a
> Thistlebrook to which gipsies return year after year as their permanen
> residence but from which they set forth at certain seasons to pursue thei
> traditional nomadic way of life.'

It is clear that the statutory definition of 'gipsies' is wider and looser than th
meaning of 'gipsies' in its traditional sense. Moreover, the statutory definitio
applies to 'persons of nomadic habit of life', whatever their race or origin.
therefore see the force of the argument that the term 'gipsies' in s 16 means n
more than persons with a settled practice of leading a wandering life with thei
homes. Furthermore, it may be said that this argument receives some suppor
from the judgment of Nicholls LJ in *Commission for Racial Equality v Dutto*
[1989] 1 All ER 306 at 309, [1989] QB 783 at 796, where he said:

> 'As the judge observed, there are many people who travel around th
> country in caravans, vans, converted buses, trailers, lorries and moto
> vehicles, leading a peripatetic or nomadic way of life. They includ
> didicois, mumpers, peace people, new age travellers, hippies, tinkers
> hawkers, self-styled "anarchists", and others, as well as Romany gipsies
> They may all be loosely referred to as "gipsies", but as a group they do no
> have the characteristics requisite of a racial group within the Act.'

I have come to the conclusion, however, that the interpretation of s 1
advanced on behalf of the appellants cannot be accepted.

In seeking to apply the statutory definition of gipsies it is important to keep
the actual words used in s 16 in the forefront of one's mind. At the same time
it is necessary to take account of the purpose behind Pt II of the 1968 Act and
the extent of the duty imposed by s 6(1). In the light of these considerations I
have come to the conclusion that one can identify the following matters as
being relevant to a decision whether or not any particular group is composed
of gipsies.

(1) The links between members of the group and between the group and
other groups who are either at the site or visit the site. Living and travelling
together in cohesive groups is a feature of nomadic peoples.

(2) The pattern of the journeys made by the group. Though a group of
gipsies may have a permanent residence (*Greenwich London BC v Powell* [1989] 1
All ER 65, [1989] AC 995), a nomadic habit of life necessarily involves travelling
from place to place. Furthermore, as the duty imposed by s 6(1) relates to the

rovisions of adequate accommodation 'for gipsies residing in or resorting to'
1e area of the county council, it is relevant to inquire whether the group visits
tes in the county on a regular basis.

(3) The purpose of the travel. I accept that the word 'nomadic' no longer
as any connection with the concept of 'seeking pasture', but it seems to me
1at in the context of the 1968 Act the word 'nomadic' adds to the words 'habit
f life' a sense of purpose for the travelling. The powers conferred by s 6(4) of
1e 1968 Act are conferred on local authorities as defined in the 1960 Act rather
1an on county councils, but it is to be noted that the power is to provide
vorking space', and 'facilities for the carrying on of such activities as are
ormally carried on' by gipsies. These words seem to me to mean that 'habit
f life' involves purposive activities including work and that travel forms part
f that habit of life.

As Lord Donaldson MR remarked in *Mole Valley DC v Smith* (1992) 24 HLR
42 at 444, the definition in s 16 of the 1968 Act is not 'a particularly happy
efinition'. In my judgment however, in the context of Pt II of the 1968 Act,
1e definition of 'gipsies' in s 16 imports the requirement that there should be
ome recognisable connection between the wandering or travelling and the
1eans whereby the persons concerned make or seek their livelihood. Persons,
r individuals, who move from place to place merely as the fancy may take
1em and without any connection between the movement and their means of
velihood fall outside these statutory definitions. As I read s 6(1) of the 1968
ct, the duty of the county council is to provide sites for those who come in
ohesive groups and who have some purpose and pattern for their wanderings.

I have not been able to construct one simple test by reference to which the
tatutory definition can be applied to particular persons or groups. One can
nly suggest guidelines and point to the purpose behind Pt II of the 1968 Act as
ppears from the relevant sections read as a whole.

I return to the judgments of Harrison and Laws JJ in the cases under appeal.
consider that these judgments are consonant with the approach which I have
1ggested and I consider that they were correct to reject the arguments that the
ocal authorities concerned had misconstrued the meaning of the word gipsies
1 s 16.

I turn therefore to the second and third issues with which I can deal very
hortly.

2) *The issue of precedent fact*

It was accepted on behalf of the appellants that if the local authorities
pplied the right test and if their decisions could only be reviewed on
Vednesbury grounds, the appeals (save for the appeal in the South Hams case
n the third issue) were bound to fail. It was argued on behalf of the appellants,
owever, that the question whether they were gipsies within the meaning of
he 1968 Act was a matter to be determined by the court as a precedent fact. If
he appellants were indeed gipsies within the meaning of s 16, the relevant
ocal authorities had reached their decisions on a wrong basis.

In support of the argument that the court could consider anew whether the
ppellants were gipsies within the meaning of the 1968 Act, counsel referred us
o the decision of the House of Lords in *Khawaja v Secretary of State for the Home
Dept* [1983] 1 All ER 765, [1984] AC 74. In particular counsel drew our attention
o the principle enunciated in the speech of Lord Scarman:

'... the well-established principle that, where the exercise of an executive power depends on the precedent establishment of an objective fact, it is for the court, if there be a challenge by way of judicial review, to decide whether the precedent requirement has been satisfied.' (See [1983] 1 All ER 765 at 780, [1984] AC 74 at 108.)

In addition counsel referred us to Wade *Administrative Law* (6th edn, 198? and to *R v Fulham, Hammersmith and Kensington Rent Tribunal, ex p Zerek* [1951 1 All ER 482, [1951] 2 KB 1.

I do not find it necessary for the purpose of the present case to explore the precise circumstances in which the *Khawaja* principle has to be applied. In my judgment, however, the possibility of applying the principle in a case such a the present is rendered impossible, certainly in this court, by the decision of the House of Lords in *Garlick v Oldham Metropolitan BC* [1993] 2 All ER 65, [199? AC 509. In that case a question arose as to whether an applicant to a housing authority had sufficient mental capacity to make the application. It was held that Parliament must have intended that the detailed investigations which were necessary to establish the applicant's capacity could only be properly carried out by the authorities concerned. The present case seems to me to be a stronger case than the case of Miss Begum (one of the related appeals hear by the House of Lords). I am satisfied that Parliament must have intended that if as a matter of law the local authorities applied the right test, the question whether particular persons or groups were as a matter of fact gipsies within that test was pre-eminently a matter for the authorities concerned.

I turn to the third issue.

(3) *The obligations of South Hams District Council*

South Hams District Council were the owners of the land at Steamer Quay and the proceedings for possession against Mr Gibb and others were brough by the district council. The proceedings for possession were adjourne pending the outcome of the present proceedings for judicial review.

The grant of an adjournment by Judge Willcock QC in the county court wa contested by the district council, and an appeal in a related claim agains another occupier of the land at Steamer Quay, Mr Shough, came before the Court of Appeal.

It was argued on behalf of the appellant in the South Hams case that it wa a relevant circumstance that there was no authorised site in the area of the district council or indeed in the area of the county council to which the appellant could move. It was said that the Devon County Council were in breach of their duty under s 6(1) of the 1968 Act.

In the course of the argument our attention was drawn to a passage in the judgment of Nourse LJ in *South Hams DC v Shough* (1992) 25 HLR 189 at 194:

'A district council, like any other local authority, must administer their land in accordance with the general or particular requirements of statute and, where there is no requirement to the contrary, in the best interests of the inhabitants of their area. Speaking generally, a district council will best serve the interests of the inhabitants as a whole by seeking to recover possession against a trespasser on their land. But there may be a case where statute imposes on them a duty to the trespasser not to evict him, a duty higher than that which is owed to the other inhabitants. In my opinion it is arguable both that such a duty can arise under the 1968 Ac and that one did arise in the circumstances of this case as briefly described by Judge Willcock.'

It cannot be argued in the present case that the district council were in breach of any duty to provide a site under s 6(1) of the 1968 Act. The duty under that section is imposed on county councils. Having considered the relevant sections in Pt II of the 1968 Act I can see no basis for saying that the district council were in breach of any statutory or other duty owed by them to the appellant. Nor can I see that the district council acted unreasonably in a *Wednesbury* sense in seeking to recover possession of the land at Steamer Quay. The appellant had no right to be there. The district council had concluded, reasonably as I see it, that he was not a gipsy.

I would therefore uphold the decision of Harrison J on this aspect of this case also.

In these circumstances I would dismiss the appeals. It will be for consideration whether any consequential orders or directions need to be given.

LEGGATT LJ. The first of the three issues identified by Neill LJ relates to the definition of 'gipsies' in s 16 of the Caravan Sites Act 1968. That definition is said to owe its origin to *Mills v Cooper* [1967] 2 All ER 100, [1967] 2 QB 459. An information was laid against a person alleging that he, being a gipsy, had unlawfully encamped on the highway, contrary to s 127 of the Highways Act 1959. The magistrates dismissed the summons because they were not satisfied that the defendant was a gipsy.

The Divisional Court, allowing the appeal, held that 'gipsy' was to be construed as meaning 'a person leading a nomadic life with no, or no fixed, employment and with no fixed abode' or 'a person without fixed abode who leads a nomadic life, dwelling in tents or other shelters, or in caravans or other vehicles' (see [1967] 2 All ER 100 at 103, 104, [1967] 2 QB 459 at 467, 468 per Lord Parker CJ and Diplock LJ). Common to these definitions are the elements of (a) leading a nomadic life and (b) having no fixed abode. Whereas Lord Parker CJ included also 'no, or no fixed, employment', Diplock LJ referred to what a gipsy lives in.

The present definition adopts the element of leading a nomadic life, makes no reference to employment, and treats the lack of fixed abode as implicit in the need for a caravan site. It also asserts that the Act applies irrespective of race or origin. Yet the term 'gipsy' is used as the word to be defined. The term might have been 'nomads' or 'travellers', but 'gipsies' was preferred. From this it may be inferred that Parliament intended the Act to apply to persons who behave like gipsies without necessarily being Romanies by race or origin.

It is to be noted that the definition is of 'gipsies' in the plural. No doubt that is because the duty conferred on local authorities is to provide sites for gipsies generally and not for individual gipsies. Despite this, and despite the exclusion from the definition of particular groups, the term is not expressly confined to those who travel in groups, and the Act does not stipulate that persons cannot be gipsies unless they do so. Conversely, although the fact that persons travel in groups does not of itself make them gipsies, it may nevertheless be an indication that they are, provided that they are neither showmen nor participants in a circus. One of the principal purposes of the exclusion probably is to avoid the need for provision of sites for shows or circuses.

The definitions relied on in some of the decided cases have now been replaced by those in the *New Shorter Oxford English Dictionary*. 'Gipsy' is there defined (after reference to traditional gipsies) as: 'A person regarded resembling one of this people in looks or way of life.' 'Nomadic', on the oth hand, is now defined as: 'Of, pertaining to, or characteristic of nomads; movir from place to place to find pastures; leading a roaming or wandering life.'

Fitting these definitions together, 'gipsies' at least means persons custor arily leading a wandering life. It will obviously take time before a person wh has not been nomadic can be said to have adopted that lifestyle as a habit. Th question is whether the use of the words 'gipsies' and 'nomadic' imports son further requirement. Little help is afforded by the 1968 Act. But like Harrisc and Laws JJ in the cases under appeal, and as I did myself in *Berkshire CC v Bi* (26 September 1986, unreported), I have come to the conclusion th Parliament must have recognised and assumed the characteristic of noma and also of gipsies that it is in order to make or seek a living that they mov from place to place. It is because they have no fixed abode and no fixe employment that gipsies live in caravans, so that they can both have a hon and go where work is. It may be seasonal or sporadic, regular or occasional; t reach it they must use the caravans in which they live. Living in them as the do for that purpose, they are entitled under the Act to have a site provided fc them in any area in which they reside or to which they resort. In my judgmen however, this privilege is not available to occupants of caravans who do n live in them for that purpose, and whose moves are actuated not by need, bu by caprice. The nomads for whom sites have to be provided live in caravans s that they can travel in them from time to time, as their means of livelihoo requires. That accords with the conclusion to which Harrison and Laws respectively came.

Imprecise though this approach may appear to be, it is due to the fact tha the statutory definition does not provide a rule of thumb for determining wh are gipsies: it provides a description of persons who are to be regarded a gipsies.

As well as agreeing with Neill LJ on the first issue, I agree with him also o the other two issues. The appeals should therefore be dismissed.

MILLETT LJ. I have reservations on the ability of the solitary individual wh lives and travels alone and who has done so all his life to qualify as a gips within the meaning of the Caravan Sites Act 1968. Living and travelling i groups is a distinctive feature not only of Romanies but also of nomadi peoples, and in my view the term nomadic cannot properly be applied to a individual except metaphorically. While, therefore, I agree that the fact tha persons travel in groups does not make them gipsies, and that the lone surviv of a group of gipsies does not cease to be one, I do not think that it would b easy for someone who has never lived and travelled as part of a group to brin himself within the statutory definition.

The question does not, however, arise in the present case, and with th reservations I have expressed, I agree with both judgments.

Appeals dismissed.

Wendy Shockett　Barrister

Fuji Finance Inc v Aetna Life Insurance Co Ltd and another

CHANCERY DIVISION

SIR DONALD NICHOLLS V-C

27, 28, 29 JUNE, 7 JULY 1994

Insurance – Contract of insurance – Nature of contract – Capital investment bond – Policy benefits on surrender or on death of life insured – Whether policy an 'insurance on the life of any person' – Whether contract a policy of life insurance – Life Assurance Act 1774, s 1.

Insurance – Illegality – Restrictions on carrying on insurance business – Insurance company restricted to business of insurance – Benefits under capital investment bond payable on surrender or on death of life assured – Whether insurance company prohibited from issuing policy – Whether policy unenforceable – Insurance Companies Act 1982, s 16.

In October 1986 the plaintiff, a Panamanian investment company, took out a policy known as a capital investment bond with the defendant insurance company and paid out a single premium of £50,000. Under the policy, sums were payable on the death of the life assured, T (the prime mover behind the plaintiff's operations), or the earlier surrender of the policy and, either way, the sums payable were calculated by reference to the value of the units then allocated to the policy. If however the policyholder chose to surrender the policy within the first five years, the amount payable would be subject to a small discontinuation charge. A central feature of the policy was the 'switch' option, which entitled the policyholder to direct the insurers to convert units of an internal fund allocated to the policy to units of another fund. Within six years the policy had soared in value to over £1m due to T's astute use of the switch option. The insurers then altered the procedures of the switch option and thereafter circumstances were no longer such that T could succeed in making only profits and avoiding losses. The plaintiff claimed that that alteration of the policy terms constituted a repudiatory breach of contract and surrendered the policy. The insurers paid out surrender proceeds of £1,110,758, but the plaintiff was not satisfied and commenced an action for damages against them. The insurers denied that they had committed any breach of contract. They contended (i) that the policy was an 'insurance on the life' of T within the meaning of s 1[a] of the Life Assurance Act 1774 and, as such, it was void on the ground that the insured policyholder did not have an insurable interest in the life assured and (ii) that if the policy was not a contract of life insurance, it was unenforceable by virtue of s 16[b] of the Insurance Companies Act 1982, which restricted insurance companies to the business of insurance. Those points were directed to be heard as preliminary issues.

Held – (1) A policy issued by a life insurance company which provided that the same benefits would be payable on the death of the life assured as would be

---

a   Section 1, so far as material, is set out at p 1029 *f*, post
b   Section 16, so far as material, is set out at p 1035 *b*, post

payable on surrender was not a contract of insurance within s 1 of the 1774 Act. To fall within the scope of the s 1 prohibition, the policy had to be an insurance on the life of a person and the policy benefits had to be payable on an event uncertain, either as to its timing or as to its happening at all, and that event had to be dependent on the contingencies of human life. It was only where the principal object of the policy was to insure that the contract as a whole could be called a contract of insurance, and the presence of a minor element of insurance could not turn a contract otherwise of a different nature into a contract of insurance. On the facts, there was no difference between the sum payable on surrender of the policy and the sum payable on death, since in both cases the amount payable was the value of units on the next valuation day after the company received notification of the death or the request for payment. It followed that the policy was not an insurance on the life of T within s 1 of the Act and the presence of a discontinuation charge, as a minor element of insurance, was not sufficient to alter the basic character of the policy. Accordingly, the policy was not rendered void by s 1 because of the absence of a sufficient insurable interest in T's life (see p 1031 b c f, p 1032 c to h, p 1033 j and p 1034 g h, post); *Prudential Insurance Co v IRC* [1904] 2 KB 658 considered.

(2) Although the insurance company was prohibited from issuing the policy by s 16 of the 1982 Act, Parliament was not to be taken to have intended to strike down all contracts entered into in good faith by the insurer in breach of s 16 and render them unlawful and unenforceable. The intended remedy for a default by an insurance company under s 16 lay in the powers of intervention conferred on the Secretary of State by the 1982 Act. It followed that although the policy was not a policy of insurance within s 1 of the 1774 Act, it was not unenforceable by virtue of s 16 of the 1982 Act (see p 1035 c d, p 1036 e and p 1037 b to d, post); *Phoenix General Insurance Co of Greece SA v Halvanon Insurance Co Ltd* [1987] 2 All ER 152 considered.

Notes

For principles common to all insurances, see 25 *Halsbury's Laws* (4th edn reissue) para 2.

For enforcement of illegal contracts, see 9 *Halsbury's Laws* (4th edn) paras 422–428, and for cases on contracts made void or illegal by statute, see 12(1) *Digest* 519–525, 4034–4063.

For the Life Assurance Act 1774, s 1, see 22 *Halsbury's Statutes* (4th edn) (1991 reissue) 7.

For the Insurance Companies Act 1982, s 16, see ibid 181.

Cases referred to in judgment

Flood v Irish Provident Assurance Co Ltd [1912] 2 Ch 597n, Ir CA.
Gould v Curtis [1913] 3 KB 84, CA.
Joseph v Law Integrity Insurance Co Ltd [1912] 2 Ch 581, (1912) 107 LT 538, CA.
National Standard Life Assurance Corp, Re [1918] 1 Ch 427.
Phoenix General Insurance Co of Greece SA v Halvanon Insurance Co Ltd [1987] 2 All ER 152, [1988] QB 216, [1987] 2 WLR 512, CA.
Prudential Insurance Co v IRC [1904] 2 KB 658.

Cases also cited

Griffiths v Fleming [1909] 1 KB 805, [1908–10] All ER Rep 760, CA.
Medical Defence Union Ltd v Dept of Trade [1979] 2 All ER 421, [1980] Ch 82.
Paterson v Powell (1832) 9 Bing 320, 131 ER 635.

Smith v Anderson (1880) 15 Ch D 247, [1874–80] All ER Rep 1121, CA.

Preliminary issue
On 25 March 1994 Master Barratt ordered a hearing of preliminary issues in the action brought by the plaintiff investment company, Fuji Finance Inc, against the defendants, Aetna Life Insurance Co Ltd and Windsor Life Assurance Co Ltd (to which Aetna had transferred its long-term business), seeking damages for repudiatory breach of contract on the ground that Aetna had adversely altered the terms of a capital investment bond providing for the payment of benefits on the death of the life assured or earlier surrender of the policy, which had originally been taken out by Fuji with Tyndall Assurance Ltd (which had subsequently transferred its undertakings and liabilities to Aetna). The preliminary issues to be determined were (i) whether the policy was or was not a policy of insurance, (ii) if it was, whether it was a policy of life insurance within the meaning of s 1 of the Life Assurance Act 1774 and (iii) if the policy did not fall within (i) or (ii), whether it was enforceable under s 16 of the Insurance Companies Act 1982. The facts are set out in the judgment.

Nicholas Underhill QC and *Robert Powell-Jones* (instructed by *Peter Sewell & Co*) for Fuji.
Nigel Davis QC and *Lindsey Stewart* (instructed by *Hartwig*, Croydon) for the defendants.

Cur adv vult

7 July 1994. The following judgment was delivered.

SIR DONALD NICHOLLS V-C.   In recent years many life insurance companies have devised increasingly sophisticated forms of policies designed to make them attractive as investments. Potential investors are wooed with the advantages of these policies: they are tax efficient, they offer protection against inflation and, unlike the traditional forms of life policies, money can be withdrawn instantly and regularly so as to give the policyholder a source of income.

This case concerns one such policy. The case has a most unusual background. In short, the policy in question enabled the policyholder to switch the units allocated to his policy between several funds. For a reason I will explain, the policyholder was able to make switches in circumstances where he always gained and never lost; indeed, every investor's dream. So the policy increased phenomenally in value. The policy appreciated in value at an annual average rate of 90% compound, which equals a tenfold increase every four years. The policy was taken out in October 1986, and a single premium of £50,000 was paid. In less than six years, by June 1992, the policy had soared in value to over £1m.

The insurance company then changed its switching procedures. The policyholder claimed this was a repudiatory breach of contract and surrendered the policy. The surrender proceeds amounted to £1,110,758, and these were paid. The policyholder was not satisfied. He launched this action for damages. The amount of damages being claimed is at large. The insurance company says that if the policy had continued to appreciate at the same rate for the expected lifetime of the life assured the damages could amount to 252 thousand trillion pounds. This is equivalent to the gross national product of the United Kingdom for 460,000 years. In fact, the damages could not exceed the value of the relevant funds of the company. Even so, the sums involved must be very substantial.

The insurance company denies it has committed any breach of contract. One of its defences is that the policy is null and void under s 1 of the Life Assurance Act 1774. A preliminary issue has been directed on this point, and on a further point concerning the effect of contravention of s 16 of the Insurance Companies Act 1982.

The policy

Before I turn to the 1774 Act I must put a little more flesh on the bones. Mr Gary Robert Tait is a sophisticated investor. In 1986 he looked closely at some policies, called investment accounts, being marketed by Tyndall Assurance Ltd. Under these policies sums were payable on the death of the life assured or the earlier surrender of the policy. Either way, the sums payable were calculated by reference to the value of the units then allocated to the policy. The value of the units was the measure, although the amount payable was not necessarily equal to that value. Depending on the circumstances and requirements of a particular policyholder, the amount payable on death might be more than the current value of the policy units. The sum payable on death might, for instance, be 1·5 times the value of the policy units.

In short, the way these policies worked was this. The value of the policy was linked to the price of units of internal funds of Tyndall, these internal funds being identified subdivisions of Tyndall's long-term business fund. The names of the funds indicate their content. I mention some of them: UK equity fund, property fund, fixed interest fund and index-linked fund. The prices of units in the funds were based upon the value of the assets constituting the funds. In some cases, such as the North American equity and Far Eastern funds, the assets were themselves units in a corresponding unit trust, or more than one unit trust, managed by an associated company of Tyndall. The assets in the internal funds were not the property of the policyholder. Units in the funds were notionally allocated to the policy as a means of calculating the value of the policy.

A feature of the policies was a 'switch' option. This option entitled the policyholder to direct Tyndall to convert units of an internal fund allocated to the policy to units of another fund. Suffice to say, switching instructions given by 2.30 pm on (say) Tuesday were carried out at prices published in Wednesday's *Financial Times*. Tyndall fixed those prices at 10 am on Tuesday. They were based on the prevailing stock market prices, in the case of UK equities and fixed interest stocks. So an investor who was well-informed about the movement of prices on the stock exchange could do his own calculations. By this means he could know, after 10 am and before 2.30 pm on Tuesday, the approximate price Tyndall would have fixed at 10 am on Tuesday as the value of the units in some of the funds. He could calculate this for himself, even though the prices struck by Tyndall would not be published until the following day. So when he gave a switching instruction at 2 pm on Tuesday, he was in effect switching at known prices. By this means he could make profits and avoid losses.

Mr Tait is the prime mover behind a Panamanian company, Fuji Finance Ltd. In October 1986 Fuji took out a policy with Tyndall, called a capital investment bond. Before doing so, Mr Tait checked with Tyndall that he had correctly understood the switch option procedure. Fuji paid a single premium of £50,000. The life assured was Mr Tait. He then operated the switch option procedure to great effect, as already mentioned. In March 1987 Tyndall's long-term business was transferred to Aetna Life Insurance Co Ltd.

Fuji's policy was not a particularly large one at the outset. But as the value of the policy grew and the number of switches increased, adverse effects were felt by other policyholders. Some complained about the poor investment performance of the funds. In 1990 Aetna undertook a review of its procedures. In April 1991 the procedures were revised. Mr Tait was told that in future, in order to improve the equitable treatment of all policyholders, Aetna was changing the time at which prices for units in the internal funds would be struck from 10 am to 4 pm. So, in future, an instruction given by Mr Tait at 2 pm on Tuesday would not be carried out by reference to values already determined. This led to Fuji's claim that Aetna had committed a repudiatory breach of contract. In turn, this was followed by Fuji surrendering the policy and commencing this action. On 31 December 1993 Aetna's long-term business was transferred to Windsor Life Assurance Co Ltd.

The Life Assurance Act 1774

The Life Assurance Act 1774 renders null and void life insurances, and certain other insurances, in which the insured does not have an insurable interest. This Act, perhaps surprisingly, is the statute which still governs this aspect of life insurance. The mischief at which the Act was aimed, as recited in the Act, was that by experience it had been found that making insurances on lives or other events in which the assured had no interest 'hath introduced a mischievous kind of gaming'. Section 1 provides:

> ' ... no insurance shall be made by any person ... on the life or lives of any person or persons, or on any other event or events whatsoever, wherein the person ... on whose account such policy ... shall be made, shall have no interest, or by way of gaming or wagering; and ... every assurance made contrary to the true intent and meaning hereof shall be null and void to all intents and purposes whatsoever.'

In the present case Fuji, the policyholder, accepts that it had no insurable interest in Mr Tait's life, at any rate to a greater amount than the £1·1m paid to Fuji when the policy was surrendered. The area of dispute is whether, having regard to its terms and conditions, Fuji's policy is an 'insurance on the life' of Mr Tait for the purposes of s 1. The insurance company, now Windsor, claims that the policy is within the section and is void accordingly. Fuji asserts the contrary.

Insurance on the life of any person

Surprisingly, there seems to be no authority in which the meaning of the key phrase in s 1 'insurance ... on the life ... of any person' has been directly considered. However, there are several cases in which similar or more widely drawn expressions under other statutes have been addressed. Foremost among these is *Prudential Insurance Co v IRC* [1904] 2 KB 658. The question concerned the stamp duty payable on a policy under which a specified sum was payable on the life assured attaining 65 years of age, or a lesser sum on his earlier death. Channell J held this was stampable as a policy of life insurance within the meaning of s 98 of the Stamp Act 1891. Under that Act a policy of life insurance is defined as 'a policy of insurance upon any life or lives or upon any event or contingency relating to or depending upon any life or lives'. That case is well known for Channell J's exposition of what is meant by 'insurance'. In short, and subject to one point I need not mention, he described insurance as a contract whereby a sum of money or some other benefit is payable upon the happening of an event which involves a degree of uncertainty, either as to the happening of the event or as to the date on which the event will occur. In that case the policy, considered as a whole, satisfied those criteria (see [1904] 2 KB 658 at 663). Further, the endowment aspect, even if considered separately, fell within the statutory definition of a policy of life insurance, because money was thereby made payable on a contingency relating to life, the contingency being the insured living to age 65.

Next, chronologically, was the decision of the Irish Court of Appeal in 1910 in *Flood v Irish Provident Assurance Co Ltd* [1912] 2 Ch 597n. The importance of this case, for present purposes, is that it brought out that a contract may be a contract of insurance even though the insurer trades without any risk. The sums payable under the policy, and the amounts payable on the uncertain event, may be so arranged that in purely financial terms the insurer cannot lose. In that case the question was whether a number of policies were outside the objects of the company as 'policies of assurance upon or in any way relating to human life'. The company issued policies for fixed sums payable at the end of a certain number of years if the life assured were still living, in return for the periodical payment of premiums, with a provision that in the event of earlier death a percentage of the premiums would be repaid. Holmes LJ observed that the insured would have done better to lodge the amount paid as premiums in the Post Office Savings Bank from which he or his personal representatives could withdraw the full amount at any time with interest (see [1912] 2 Ch 597n at 601). Despite this, the court held that these were policies of assurance. Further, and plainly, the policies fell within the description of policies of assurance 'upon or in any way relating to human life'. Accordingly the policies were ultra vires the company.

Two years later a similar point came before the English Court of Appeal in *Joseph v Law Integrity Insurance Co Ltd* [1912] 2 Ch 581. The question was whether certain policies fell outside the company's objects, which excluded life insurance within the meaning of the Life Assurance Companies Act 1870. In return for periodic payments, sums were payable at stated intervals if the insured were still alive. If he died before a payment date, the premiums paid since the last payment date were returned. In the court below the policies were held not to be policies of life insurance; they did not insure against risk, the premiums were fixed irrespective of the average duration of life and irrespective of the age or health of the insured, and the contract was properly described as a means of enabling thrifty persons to accumulate a sum of money by small savings (see [1912] 2 Ch 581 at 589). The Court of Appeal reversed this decision. Although the 1870 Act did not expressly define life insurance, that expression was to be understood as including insurance whereby a sum of money is payable on the happening of a contingency depending on the duration of human life. The policies in that case satisfied that test. Accordingly they were ultra vires.

The same approach was adopted by the Court of Appeal in *Gould v Curtis* [1913] 3 KB 84. An insurance policy provided for payment of £100 on the death of the life assured within a stated period of years, and £200 if he were alive at the end of the period. The question was whether this was an insurance by the taxpayer 'on his life' within the meaning of s 54 of the Income Tax Act 1853.

The court held that it was. All three members of the court observed that 'on his life' imports the notion of payment being dependent on the contingency of human life. The phrase includes the case where payment is contingent on survival as well as the case where payment is contingent on death (see [1913] 3 KB 84 at 92, 94–95, 97 per Cozens-Hardy MR, Buckley LJ and Kennedy LJ).

I return to s 1 of the 1774 Act: '... no insurance shall be made ... on the life of any person ...' To be within the scope of this prohibitory section, the contract must be, first, an insurance which, secondly, is on the life of a person. In the *Prudential* case, Channell J enunciated the essence of an insurance for this purpose: a contract under which a sum of money becomes payable on an event which is uncertain as to its timing or as to its happening at all. The second element ('on the life') requires that the uncertain event is one geared to the uncertainties of life. This reading of s 1 accords with the now well-established understanding of what is meant by life insurance.

I appreciate that, as I have already observed, the decided cases were concerned with the application of particular statutory or other definitions concerned with life insurance. However, none of those cases turned on subtle nuances of language. Shining through the cases is a judicial appraisal of the essence of life insurance. Moreover, if one were to seek to compare language, *Joseph's* case would be indistinguishable. There, the company's objects incorporated a reference to the business of life assurance within the meaning of the Life Assurance Companies Act 1870. That Act applied to companies which issued 'polices of assurance upon human life'. I can see no reason for interpreting the similar expression in the 1774 Act differently from the way the Court of Appeal interpreted that expression in the 1870 Act.

Accordingly, in my view, to be within s 1, a sum of money (or other benefit) must be payable on an event uncertain, either as to its timing or as to its happening at all, and that event must be dependent on the contingencies of human life.

The application of s 1 to this policy: the death benefit

I now turn to apply s 1, as so understood, to Fuji's policy. The two key provisions are conditions 5 and 7. Condition 5 reads:

> 'BENEFIT ON DEATH On the death of the Life Assured the Company shall pay the Value of the Units on the Next Valuation Day following receipt by the Company of written notification of death multiplied by the Death Benefit Factor ...'

Condition 7 reads:

> 'BENEFIT ON SURRENDER At any time ... the Policyholder may by notice to the Company in writing surrender the Policy in exchange for a cash sum equal to the Value of Units on the Next Valuation Day following receipt of the notice reduced by the Discontinuance Charge calculated in accordance with the table endorsed on this Policy ...'

In the present case the death benefit factor was one. (That is the figure stated in the policy, and the parties agreed I should decide the preliminary issue on this basis. There may be some question that this figure was a mistake.) Accordingly, and leaving aside for the moment the discontinuance charge, there was no difference at all between the amount payable on request and the amount payable on death. In both cases the benefit payable was the same. In both cases the sum payable was the value of units on the next valuation day after the company received notification of the death or the request for payment.

How, then, is this policy to be characterised? The insurance company submitted that under condition 5 a sum was payable on the death of Mr Tait and that is decisive. The fact that the policy might be surrendered earlier or terms yielding an equivalent payment is neither here nor there. The manner in which the sums payable on death or on earlier surrender were quantified is irrelevant for present purposes.

I am unable to accept this approach. To be within s 1 the contract must not only be 'on life', the contract must also be a contract of 'insurance'. Accordingly it is necessary to identify the uncertain event which triggers a payment by the insurer. I do not see how an event can be regarded as triggering a payment if there is already in existence, irrespective of the happening of that event, an obligation on the insurer to make that very same payment on request. When the event occurs, the insured acquires nothing he did not already have. Nor, I add, does the insured lose anything.

Here, Fuji could at any time have called for payment of a cash sum equal to the value of the units allocated to its policy. On Mr Tait's death all that happened was that the policy came to an end, and the same cash sum became payable whether or not Fuji wished to be paid out. I do not see how the fact that the policy was ended by Mr Tait's death can turn this contract into a contract of insurance if otherwise it would not be such. The death of Mr Tait, like the death of anyone else, is uncertain as to its timing although certain as to its happening. But, under this policy, the happening of that uncertain event did not impose, for better or for worse, an obligation on the insurer to pay an amount otherwise not payable. Nor did the death relieve the insurer from its subsisting obligation to pay the current value of the policy units on request.

Expressed in slightly different language, the position is that under this policy Fuji paid £50,000 to Tyndall as an investment. That, of itself, is neutral. That, of itself, gives no assistance in deciding whether the contract was a policy of insurance. The policyholder could determine the contract at any time by calling for payment of an amount fixed by a formula unrelated to anything save the current value of the units attributed to the policy. The contract was also determined automatically on Mr Tait's death or, more strictly perhaps, when Tyndall was told of his death. In that event, the sum payable was calculated according to the identical formula applicable throughout the whole period of the contract. That is not a contract of insurance. The death of Mr Tait had no effect on the amounts payable or receivable by the parties.

I recognise that Fuji's policy was clothed in the vesture of life insurance. This does not advance matters. This clothing would have been altogether appropriate if the death benefit factor had exceeded one. (In saying this, I am not to be taken as expressing a view on what would be the position if the death benefit factor had been 1·01, a figure canvassed in the course of the submissions.) Had the death benefit factor exceeded one, references to the life assured, his age, the health questionnaire, mortality cost, and so forth, would have been appropriate. But those references in these standard form documents do not assist if, on a proper analysis of the parties' rights and obligations under this particular policy, the policy is not a contract of insurance at all.

In the present case there was no mortality deduction built into the calculation of benefits payable. That is because, as I have indicated, Mr Tait's life was not being insured. The sums payable did not vary according to whether Mr Tait was then alive or dead.   However, speaking in more general terms, it would be wrong to conclude that a mortality deduction from the benefits payable is an essential feature of a contract of life insurance.   The presence of such a deduction is one indicia of life insurance, but the absence of such a deduction does not prove the opposite.   Depending on the way the benefits are calculated, the insurer may not need to build a mortality deduction into the calculation.   As already discussed, a policy may be a policy of life insurance even though the insurer cannot lose.   It is not an essential feature of a life insurance policy that the terms place the insurer at risk of loss in certain events.   However, the absence of a mortality cost calculation in Fuji's policy is relevant in so far as it confirms that the formula for calculating the policy benefits was unaffected by any consideration of the life expectancy of Mr Tait. The mode of calculating the benefits is consistent with the policy not being an insurance on Mr Tait's life.

The application of s 1 to this policy: the discontinuance charge

So far I have left altogether on one side the provision in condition 7 that, on surrender, the amount payable was to be reduced by a discontinuance charge. No such reduction was made on payment on death under condition 5.

The discontinuance charge arises in this way.   Tyndall was, naturally enough, concerned to attract larger rather than smaller single premiums.   So it offered an incentive to those who paid larger sums by initially allocating policy units on a sliding scale according to the size of the premium.   For premiums up to £10,000, the initial allocation of units was 100% or less.   Above £10,000 the initial allocation exceeded 100%.   At the top end were premiums exceeding £25,000.   The percentage of initial premium allocated to units in such cases was 102·5%.   Tyndall was also concerned to recoup allocations made in excess of 100% in the event of the policyholder ending the policy within five years.   In the event of discontinuance within the first year after payment of the premium paid, Tyndall clawed back the whole of the bonus, that is the whole of the percentage allocated in excess of 100%.   The claw back diminished by 0·5% for each completed year.   So, in a case such as Fuji, where there was an initial allocation of 102·5%, the claw back diminished year by year until the policy had been in existence for five complete years.   From then on there was no discontinuance charge.

The effect of these provisions in Fuji's case was that, for the first five years of the policy, there was a difference between the amount payable on surrender and the amount payable on death.   In the latter event, save in the case of suicide within the first year, no discontinuance charge was deductible if payment had fallen due on Mr Tait's death.   But if Fuji had surrendered the policy within five years, a percentage of the units allocated to the policy, varying from 2·5% in the first year to 0·5% in the fifth year, would have been deducted and retained by Tyndall.

Clearly, there is an element of insurance on the life of Mr Tait built into this provision.   In the event of his death within five years, Tyndall became obliged to pay a larger sum than it was obliged to pay if Fuji had chosen to surrender the policy at that time.   Even so, I do not think this can sensibly lead to the conclusion that Fuji's policy is a contract of insurance on Mr Tait's life.   What happened is that, to reflect the advantages larger premiums had for Tyndall, Tyndall allocated a bonus in such cases.   Those who paid large premiums received a marginally greater (up to 2·5%) allocation of units.   Tyndall was concerned that those who received these bonuses should not be able to cash them in straight away: hence the discontinuance charge. I do not think the presence of such a charge, for the period and the amounts involved in Fuji's policy, is sufficient to alter the character of this policy which, in all other respects, is not a contract of insurance. It cannot be that the presence of a minor and insignificant element of insurance suffices to turn a contract otherwise of a different nature into a contract of insurance. If a contract has to be labelled either as a contract of insurance or as not a contract of insurance, then it must be necessary to look at the overall position in the case of a contract with elements of more than one nature. I agree with the suggestion in *MacGillivray and Parkington on Insurance Law* (8th edn, 1988) para 7 that only where the principal object is to insure can a contract as a whole be called a contract of insurance.

I do not overlook Neville J's decision in *Re National Standard Life Assurance Corp* [1918] 1 Ch 427. There the court had to decide whether several classes of policies constituted policies on human life within the definition in s 30 of the Assurance Companies Act 1909 '... any instrument by which the payment of money is assured on death ... or the happening of any contingency dependent on human life'. Under the third class of policies, in return for payment of annual premiums, fixed sums were payable at the end of a stated period of years. Those amounts were payable irrespective of whether the life assured was still alive. The only contingency in the policy relating to the life of the life assured was that his personal representatives had the option to surrender the policy within six months of the policyholder's death, in which case all the premiums were returned. Neville J held that this right of termination, exercisable only by the personal representatives, was a 'contingency dependent on human life', and accordingly the policy fell within the statutory definition of life assurance (see [1918] 1 Ch 427 at 432). I need not embark on a consideration of whether that case was correctly decided. Suffice to say, the option featured in that case was much more central to the parties' bargain than the discontinuance charge on voluntary termination within five years in the present case.

For these reasons, in my view Fuji's policy is not within s 1 of the 1774 Act as an insurance on the life of Mr Tait. Accordingly it is not rendered void by that section because of the absence of a sufficient insurable interest in Mr Tait's life.

I add a footnote on this aspect of the case. I have characterised Fuji's policy as not a contract of insurance despite the presence of an element of insurance. The case was argued before me on the footing that the policy as a whole has to bear one label or the other. I am not to be taken as disagreeing with this approach, but I add this regarding a contract containing both insurance and non-insurance elements. If, in such a case, and contrary to this approach, it is only the insurance element which is void in the absence of an insurable interest, that would still not assist the insurance company here. In the instant case the insurance element was confined to the first five years of the policy. The matters in issue in this action have nothing to do with that aspect of the policy.

The Insurance Companies Act 1982

The defendants have another string to their bow. Tyndall was an insurance company. As such it was required by statute to restrict its business to insurance. Section 16(1) of the Insurance Companies Act 1982 provides:

'An insurance company ... shall not carry on any activities ... otherwise than in connection with or for the purposes of its insurance business.'

The defendants submitted that if, as I have held, Fuji's policy is not a contract of insurance, Tyndall should not have issued the policy. Having been sued in contravention of the statute, the policy is not enforceable. No question about repayment of premiums arises, because Fuji received £1·1m when it surrendered the policy. The effect of the statutory prohibition, it was submitted, is to preclude Fuji from claiming damages for breach of the terms and conditions of the policy.

In my view, Tyndall was prohibited from issuing Fuji's policy by s 16. This section restricts insurance companies to the business of insurance. An insurance company will need to enter into many transactions which are not themselves contracts of insurance. The company will need to obtain premises, employ staff, acquire equipment and so on. These activities are carried on for the purposes of its insurance business or in connection with that business. However, matters stand differently when the company enters into a contract whose raison d'être is that it is a contract of life insurance. In such a case, whether the statute is breached depends simply on whether, indeed, the contract is an insurance contract or not. If not, the insurance company has trespassed beyond its permitted bounds and into forbidden territory, however attractive the other territory may be and however well the two territories can be combined together.

The 1982 Act does not spell out the consequences of a failure to comply with s 16, beyond stating that such a default is not a criminal offence on the part of the insurance company (see s 71(7)). Accordingly, this case raises the not unfamiliar question of whether, by necessary implication, the statute intended to strike down as illegal and unenforceable a contract entered into by one party, here the insurer, in breach of a prohibition aimed at him alone. On this I have the benefit of the guidance provided by the Court of Appeal in *Phoenix General Insurance Co of Greece SA v Halvanon Insurance Co Ltd* [1987] 2 All ER 152, [1988] QB 216. In that case the court was concerned with a prohibition in s 2 of the Insurance Companies Act 1974 (now replaced by s 2 of the 1982 Act) against carrying on an insurance business unless duly authorised. The material words are 'no person shall carry on ... insurance business ...' Insurance business is defined as the business of 'effecting and carrying out contracts of insurance' of the relevant classes. Kerr LJ observed that in such a case of a unilateral prohibition it does not necessarily follow that the contract itself is impliedly prohibited so as to render it illegal and void. He said ([1987] 2 All ER 152 at 176, [1988] QB 216 at 273–274):

'Whether or not the statute has this effect depends on considerations of public policy in the light of the mischief which the statute is designed to prevent, its language, scope and purpose, the consequences for the innocent party, and any other relevant considerations ... The Insurance Companies Act 1974 only imposes a unilateral prohibition on unauthorised insurers. If this were merely to prohibit them from carrying on "the business of effecting contracts of insurance" of a class for which they have no authority, then it would clearly be open to the court to hold that considerations of public policy preclude the implication that such contracts are prohibited and void. But unfortunately the unilateral prohibition is not limited to the business of "effecting contracts of insurance" but extends to the business of "carrying out contracts of

insurance" ... I can see no convincing escape from the conclusion that th
extension of the prohibition has the unfortunate effect that contracts mac
without authorisation are prohibited by necessary implication an
therefore void. Since the statute prohibits the insurer from carrying ou
the contract (of which the most obvious example is paying claims), ho
can the insured require the insurer to do an act which is express
forbidden by statute? And how can a court enforce a contract against a
unauthorised insurer when Parliament has expressly prohibited him fro
carrying it out? In that situation there is simply no room for th
introduction of considerations of public policy.'

In the present case the prohibition is against carrying on any 'activitie
other than those permitted. 'Activities' is every bit as wide and comprehensiv
as the prohibition in the *Phoenix* case. 'Activities', albeit loose and general, is
comprehensive expression in this context. It must be apt to embrace carryin
out a non-insurance contract as well as effecting such a contract. For th
reason I am unable to draw any sensible distinction between the language c
the prohibition in the two sections.

Despite this I am not persuaded that, in the case of s 16, Parliament is to b
taken to have intended to strike down all contracts entered into, perhap
unwittingly by the insurer and in good faith by the insurer, in breach of s 1
In reaching this conclusion I have taken into account several matters. Firs
s 16 appears to have been enacted in order to give effect to directives of th
Council of the European Communities of 24 July 1973 and 5 March 197
These two directives, Directive (EEC) 73/239 and Directive (EEC) 79/26
were concerned to harmonise the legislation of member states in order t
facilitate insurance business and, at the same time, provide adequat
protection for insured parties. To these ends the 1973 directive oblige
member states to require that any relevant undertaking should 'Limit i
business activities to the business of insurance and operations directly arisin
therefrom to the exclusion of all other commercial business' (see art 8, par
1(b)). The 1979 directive contained an equivalent provision. That appears t
be the genesis of s 16.

Secondly, and following on from this, it is to be noted that if a company wer
to incorporate such restrictions into its own constitution, persons dealing wit
the company would still acquire a substantial measure of protection in respec
of their transactions with the company (see s 35, 35A and 35B of the Companie
Act 1985 as amended by s 108 of the Companies Act 1989). Such persons woul
not be left high and dry without adequate recourse against the company whic
entered into the contract.

Thirdly, as already mentioned, the 1982 Act expressly provides that a defaul
under s 16 is not a criminal offence. This is in marked contrast to a breach o
s 2 (see s 14). Section 2 is in Pt 1 of the Act. Section 16 is in Pt 2, heade
'Regulation of insurance companies'. Under Pt 2 the Secretary of State is give
wide powers of intervention in the affairs of an insurance company. He is als
given power to modify Pt 2, including s 16, in relation to particular companies.

Finally, I note that Parliament has revisited these provisions in the light c
the *Phoenix* case. Section 132 of the Financial Services Act 1986 now gives th
court a discretion in certain circumstances to allow a contract made i
contravention of s 2 to be enforced. Parliament has made no such provisio
regarding s 16, although if contracts made by an insurance company in breac

·f s 16 are unenforceable, the case for equivalent treatment for such contracts ·ust be even stronger than the case for contracts made in breach of s 2.

In my view, these features taken together point to the conclusion that ·arliament did not intend that a contract made by an insurance company in ·reach of the restriction in s 16 should be unlawful and unenforceable. Rather, 16 is part of a regulatory framework, in respect of which the Secretary of State ·as wide-ranging powers and responsibilities. The intended remedy for a ·efault by an insurance company under s 16 lies in the powers of intervention ·onferred on the Secretary of State by the same part of the Act in which s 16 ·ppears. Default under s 16 can trigger an exercise of those powers (see 37(2)(b)(i)).

For these reasons, my conclusion is that, although the Fuji policy is not a ·olicy of insurance within the meaning of s 1 of the Life Assurance Act 1774, it · not unenforceable by virtue of the provisions of s 16 of the Insurance ·ompanies Act 1982.

reliminary issues answered accordingly.

Celia Fox   Barrister.

RMC Roadstone Products Ltd v Jester

QUEEN'S BENCH DIVISION
RALPH GIBSON LJ AND SMITH J
2, 13, 28 JANUARY 1994

Iealth and safety at work – Employer's duties – Duty to other person's employees –)uty to conduct undertaking in such a way as to ensure other person's employees not ·xposed to risks to health and safety – Statutory offence – Employer's liability – Imployer engaging independent contractors to carry out repairs to premises – Imployer leaving contractors to work in way they saw fit – Whether contractors' ·ctivity within employer's conduct of its undertaking – Degree of control over ·ontractors' activity necessary to establish liability – Health and Safety at Work etc ·Act 1974, s 3.

·n 1991 the appellant company, which manufactured road-making materials, ·ngaged independent contractors to carry out repair work at its premises. One ·tem of work was to replace some broken asbestos sheets in the side of a ·ransfer tower using, at the contractors' suggestion, old sheets of asbestos, ·which formed part of the roof of an adjacent disused factory. The company's ·rojects manager obtained the owner's permission to remove eight sheets ·rom the roof of a loading bay some 16 feet above the ground. At a meeting ·n the factory site, the projects manager warned the contractors of the dangers ·f working on an asbestos roof, but gave no specific directions on how the ·emoval of the sheets was to be effected. The projects manager also offered to ·upply the contractors with any equipment necessary for the job, but all they ·asked for was a front-loading shovel to lower the sheets from the roof and to ·transport them. One of the contractors, who had been working on the roof

loosening the securing bolts which held the sheets in place, subsequently fe
through a skylight to the ground below and suffered fatal injuries. Th
company was charged with and convicted of an offence under s 33(1)[a] of th
Health and Safety At Work etc Act 1974 of failing to discharge its duty unde
s 3[b] to conduct its business in such a way as to ensure, so far as reasonab!
practicable, that persons not in its employment who might be affected thereb
were not exposed to risks to their health and safety. The company appeale
by way of case stated, contending that the removal of asbestos sheets by th
contractors from the factory premises did not fall within the ambit of th
company's conduct of its undertaking within the meaning of s 3(1), since
was not in a position to exercise complete control over the contractor
activities in carrying out the scheduled work, which were exclusively withi
the conduct of their own undertaking.

Held – An employer's mere capacity or opportunity to exercise control ove
the activity of an independent contractor was not enough to bring that activit
within the ambit of the employer's conduct of his undertaking for th
purposes of s 3 of the 1974 Act. There had to be some exercise of actual contro
(rather than complete control) over the contractor's activity or a common lav
duty to exercise such control before that activity could be said to be part of th
employer's undertaking. Accordingly, if the employer chose to leave th
independent contractor to do the work in the way he saw fit, the work woul
be wholly the contractor's undertaking. If the employer did involve himsel
albeit voluntarily, by for example instructing the contractor to adopt a certai
method of work, or by lending a particular piece of equipment, then it migh
be that his involvement would be within the ambit of his undertaking, and
the system of work proved to be unsafe, or the equipment proved to b
defective and gave rise to a risk to the safety of the contractor, then it migh
also be that the principal would be guilty of failing to discharge his duty unde
s 3 of the Act. On the facts, it was not open to the justices to find that th
activity of removing the asbestos sheets fell within the ambit of the company'
conduct of its undertaking, since the company had made no stipulation as t
how the work was to be done or what equipment was to be used and it wa
under no duty to lay down a safe system of work for the contractors and it ha
not done so. It followed that the appeal would be allowed and the convictio
quashed (see p 1045 *f g*, p 1046 *g h*, p 1047 *e* to *h*, p 1048 *j* to p 1049 *b* an
p 1050 *f g*, post).

R v Swan Hunter Shipbuilders Ltd [1982] 1 All ER 264, *Carmichael v Rosehal
Engineering Works Ltd* 1984 SLT 40 and *Mailer v Austin Rover Group plc* [1989]
All ER 1087 considered.

Notes

For duties of employers to persons other than their employees, see 2(
Halsbury's Laws (4th edn reissue) para 555.

For the Health and Safety at Work etc Act 1974, ss 3, 33, see 19 *Halsbury'.
Statutes* (4th edn) (1994 reissue) 801, 833.

a   Section 33(1), so far as material, provides: 'It is an offence for a person—(a) to fail to discharge
      duty to which he is subject by virtue of sections 2 to 7 ...'
b   Section 3, so far as material, is set out at p 1042 *h j*, post.

Cases referred to in judgments

Mailer v Austin Rover Group plc [1989] 2 All ER 1087, sub nom *Austin Rover Group Ltd v HM Inspector of Factories* [1990] 1 AC 619, [1989] 3 WLR 520, HL.
Carmichael v Rosehall Engineering Works Ltd 1984 SLT 40, HC of Just.
McArdle v Andmac Roofing Co [1967] 1 All ER 583, [1967] 1 WLR 356, CA.
R v Swan Hunter Shipbuilders Ltd [1982] 1 All ER 264, [1981] ICR 831, CA.

Cases also cited

Aitchison v Howard Doris Ltd 1979 SLT 22, HC of Just.
Atterton v Browne [1945] KB 122, DC.
Clare v L Whittaker & Son (London) Ltd [1976] ICR 1.
Clayton v Woodman & Son (Builders) Ltd [1962] 2 All ER 33, [1962] 2 QB 533, CA.
Griffith v Jenkins [1992] 1 All ER 65, [1992] 2 AC 76, HL.
R v Board of Trustees of the Science Museum [1993] 3 All ER 853, [1993] ICR 876, CA.
R v Mara [1987] 1 All ER 478, [1987] 1 WLR 87, CA.
Smith v George Wimpey & Co Ltd [1972] 2 All ER 723, [1972] 2 QB 329, CA.
Stephenson v Johnson [1954] 1 All ER 369, [1954] 1 WLR 375, DC.

Case stated

RMC Roadstone Products Ltd appealed by way of case stated by the justices for the South East London Commission area for the Petty Sessional Division of Bexley, sitting at Bexleyheath, Kent, from the justices' decision on 12 November 1992 whereby, following the laying of an information by the respondent, Desirée Rita Jester, HM Inspector of Factories, they convicted the appellant of an offence under s 33(1) of the Health and Safety at Work etc Act 1974 by reason of its failure to discharge its duty under s 3(1) of the Act to conduct its undertaking to ensure the safety of persons not in its employment, including Hans Derhun, who fell to his death while removing roof sheets from an asbestos cement roof. The questions for the consideration of the Divisional Court were: (1) whether the justices were correct in finding that the prosecutor was not required to provide particulars of the alleged failure to discharge the duty imposed by s 3 of the 1974 Act and that the information was not therefore defective; (2) whether the justices were correct in their opinion that the work being carried out by Mr Derhun formed part of the company's undertaking; and (3) whether the justices were correct in their opinion that the company had failed to conduct its undertaking to ensure the safety of persons not in its employment. The facts are set out in the judgment of Smith J.

David Richardson (instructed by *The Heap Partnership*, Croydon) for the appellant.
William Hoskins and *Dominic Grieve* (instructed by *John Oteino*) for the respondent.

Cur adv vult

28 January 1994. The following judgments were delivered.

SMITH J (giving the first judgment at the invitation of Ralph Gibson LJ). This is an appeal by case stated against the appellant's conviction by the Bexley Magistrates' Court on 12 November 1992 of an offence under s 3(1) of the

Health and Safety at Work etc Act 1974. The case arose out of a tragic acciden in which a Mr Hans Derhun fell to his death while working on a fragile roof ir March 1992.

The information laid by one of HM Inspectors of Factories alleged that or 18 March 1992, at the premises of British Gypsum Ltd, Church Manorway Erith, Kent, the appellant, being an employer within the meaning of the 197⸱ Act, did fail to discharge a duty to which it was subject by virtue of s 3(1) of the 1974 Act, in that it failed to conduct its undertaking so as to ensure the safet‌ of persons not in its employment, including Mr Hans Derhun (now deceased)‌ who were removing roof sheets from an asbestos cement roof, whereby the‌ appellant was guilty of an offence as provided by s 33(1) of the Act and liable to a penalty as provided by s 33(3).

At the hearing the magistrates convicted the appellant, but have stated ⸱ case for the consideration of this court. The magistrates made the following findings of fact.

In 1991 Messrs Derhun and Poulter started a business called 'Iron Age' ir which they did welding, metal work and general repair work. Mr Poulter had never before been in such employment, although he had done his owr household repairs. Mr Derhun was a skilled man and had some experience o‌ working at heights, although always under supervision. He had always worr a safety harness. He had no previous experience of roof work.

In 1991 Iron Age were sub-contracted to a company called 'Abbey Civi‌ Engineering' to carry out welding work on roof support beams on the underside of a roof of the appellant's premises. The appellant supplied the materials.

During this work the appellant's projects manager, Mr Sibley, saw Messrs Derhun and Poulter working at heights of eight to ten metres. He saw and‌ believed that their competence and the provision they made for safety were that of ordinary, prudent general maintenance workers.

On the completion of that work Mr Sibley, on behalf of the appellant, invited Iron Age to tender for various contracts, which they successfully did. One item of work was to replace some broken asbestos sheets in the side of a‌ transfer tower. Originally it was intended that the appellant should obtain‌ some new sheets, but Mr Derhun suggested that use might be made of some old sheets which formed part of the roof of the disused factory of British‌ Gypsum adjacent to the appellant's premises. Mr Sibley obtained permission‌ from British Gypsum for eight sheets to be removed from the roof of a loading bay. They were about 16 feet above ground.

On 17 March 1992 Messrs Derhun, Poulter and Sibley and Mr Durrant, the British Gypsum caretaker, all met on the British Gypsum site. The caretaker pointed out which eight sheets were to be taken. Each measured about 8 ft by 3 ft. Mr Sibley observed that asbestos roofs gave no warning of breaking, but just 'crack and go'. He said they had no load-bearing capacity and one had to be very careful when removing them. He spoke of an occasion in the past when he had refused an instruction to climb onto an asbestos roof and walk on the purlins. He had regarded it as too dangerous.

There was then a discussion about the provision of equipment. Mr Derhun asked Mr Sibley if he and Mr Poulter could borrow the appellant's front-loading shovel to lower the sheets from the roof and to transport them. Permission was granted. Mr Sibley asked if Mr Derhun needed ladders or other equipment, and offered to supply that which was required. Mr Derhun said they had their own ladder, and he did not ask for any other equipment. No specific time limits were laid down by the appellant, nor was the order of work specified. It was implied that Messrs Derhun and Poulter would do the work on such days as they thought fit.

On 18 March 1992 Messrs Derhun and Poulter returned to the site, bringing a single scaffold board from the appellant's premises. They also brought the front-loading shovel, which they climbed upon and used as a means of access to the roof. The work began of cropping the securing bolts and releasing the sheets. Initially both men were working on the roof itself. Mr Poulter walked on the part of the roof where the purlin bolts protruded. Mr Derhun did likewise but he also used the scaffold board. Mr Poulter then climbed into the bucket of the shovel to receive the sheets and lower them to the ground. Mr Derhun stayed on the roof. As they were putting the last sheet into the bucket Mr Derhun fell through the skylight to the ground below and suffered fatal injuries. Precisely what had happened to lead to the accident was not known.

The magistrates found that asbestos sheets are a cheap form of weather protection and are not designed to bear any weight. Walking along the purlin bolts is not a safe method of moving about on such a roof. The minimum safety precaution should have entailed the provision of two crawling boards at least 17 inches wide.

They also found that the asbestos sheets could have been removed without Messrs Derhun and Poulter climbing onto or walking on the roof. A scaffold tower could have been erected below the roof and the bolts cropped from below. Such a scaffold tower could have been hired locally, quite easily and cheaply. This method, said the magistrates '... should have been obvious both to Mr Sibley and to Mr Derhun and Mr Poulter'. It would have greatly reduced the risk to safety.

The magistrates did not make any express finding of fact as to the nature of the appellant's business. However, it has been agreed that the nature of the business, which is that of manufacturer of road-making materials, may be readily and adequately inferred from the company name.

Having set out their findings of fact the magistrates turned to consider the parties' contentions. The first issue was a preliminary point relating to the adequacy of the particulars contained in the information. I shall deal with that issue later in this judgment.

Second, the appellant contended that the removal of asbestos sheets by Messrs Derhun and Poulter from the British Gypsum premises did not fall within the ambit of the appellant's conduct of its undertaking. The respondent contended that it did and that there was therefore a duty on the appellant to take reasonable precautions for the safety of the contractors.

The appellant's third contention was that, if the removal of the sheets did indeed fall within the ambit of its conduct of its undertaking, then the duty which arose was limited to the giving of a warning as to any specific hazards of which it was aware, and to ensuring the safety of any equipment lent by it to the contractors. These duties it had complied with. Mr Sibley had warned the contractors of the danger of walking on fragile asbestos sheets. The respondent replied to this contention that a warning was not enough. The appellant ought to have made inquiries to ascertain whether the contractors were competent and experienced in working on asbestos roofs. The appellant was not entitled to rely on the contractors' own skill and expertise to ensure their own safety. Further, the appellant, being aware through Mr Sibley of the risk of working on an asbestos roof, should have ensured that reasonable safety precautions were taken.

The justices then gave their opinion on each issue. First, they found that the information was not defective. Second, they found that the removal of the asbestos sheets from the roof on the British Gypsum site by contractors at the request of the appellant was part of the appellant's undertaking. They went on to say:

'It was not necessary for the appellant to work and control the site on which the work was carried out for the appellant to exercise complete control of the way in which the contractors carried out the work. The appellant was in a position to give specific directions to the contractors on how the work should be done. The appellant therefore owed the duty to take reasonable precautions to ensure the safety of Mr Derhun.'

They went on to hold that Mr Sibley was aware of the risk to safety in walking on asbestos sheets without proper equipment, that the contractors were not roofing specialists and the appellant could not rely on their skill and expertise to ensure their own safety. The discussion about the danger of walking on an asbestos roof had only served to identify the risk, and this was not a sufficient precaution to ensure Mr Derhun's safety. The appellant could have taken the precaution of providing a scaffold tower and laying down a system whereby the bolts would be undone from below. This would have avoided the risk to the contractors. By implication the justices found that the appellant ought to have taken this precaution as they found that the appellant had failed to discharge its burden of showing that it had 'taken reasonable precautions'. Accordingly, they convicted the appellant.

The case stated posed three questions for the court. These were: (1) were we correct in finding that the respondent was not required to provide particulars of the alleged failure to discharge the duty imposed by s 3(1) of the Act, and that the information was not therefore defective; (2) were we correct in our opinion that the work being carried out by Mr Hans Derhun at the British Gypsum works formed part of the appellant's undertaking; and (3) were we correct in our opinion that the appellant failed to conduct its under-taking to ensure the safety of persons not in the appellant's employment.

I shall leave the question of whether the undertaking was defective due to a lack of particularity and proceed to consider the second and third questions, which require an analysis of s 3 of the Act.

Section 3 provides as follows:

'General duties of employers and self-employed to persons other than their employees

(1) It shall be the duty of every employer to conduct his undertaking in such a way as to ensure, so far as is reasonably practicable, that persons not in his employment who may be affected thereby are not thereby exposed to risks to their health or safety.

(2) It shall be the duty of every self-employed person to conduct his undertaking in such a way as to ensure, so far as is reasonably practicable,

that he and other persons (not being his employees) who may be affected thereby are not thereby exposed to risks to their health or safety ...'

In order to establish prima facie liability under s 3(1) the Crown must, in my judgment, prove three elements. First, they must show that the defendant was an employer. Second, they must prove that the activity or the state of affairs which gave rise to the complaint fell within the ambit of the defendant's conduct of his undertaking. Third, they must show that there was a risk to the health or safety of persons, other than his employees, who were affected by that aspect of his conduct of his undertaking. If these three are proved the conviction will follow unless the defendant is able to satisfy the court on the balance of probabilities that it has done all that was reasonably practicable to comply with the duty imposed (see s 40 of the 1974 Act).

The word 'employer' is not itself defined in the 1974 Act. In s 53(1) (the definition section) 'employee' is defined as an individual who works under a contract of employment. It is said that related expressions are to be construed accordingly. Thus 'employer' must mean one who employs one or more individuals to work for him under a contract of employment. Here the magistrates found that the appellant was an employer. It plainly did employ employees in its business of manufacturing road-making products.

Next, the Crown had to show that the removal of asbestos sheets from the premises of British Gypsum was within the ambit of the appellant's conduct of its undertaking. If it was, then the third element was plainly made out, as the justices found that the system of work for the removal of the sheets was dangerous. Messrs Derhun and Poulter, who were not the appellant's employees, but who were affected by the removal of the asbestos sheets, were indeed exposed to risks to their safety.

The question which falls to be decided is whether the magistrates were right, as a matter of law, when they expressed the opinion that the removal of the asbestos sheets from the British Gypsum roof fell within the ambit of the appellant's conduct of its undertaking. They so found on the basis that the appellant was able to exercise complete control of the way in which the contractors carried out their work, in that it was in a position to give specific directions as to how the work was to be done.

The term 'undertaking' is not defined in the Act, but the dictionary definitions include the expression 'enterprise'. A defendant's undertaking is its business or enterprise.

Counsel accepted that the appellant's business of manufacturing road-making materials carried out at its premises at Erith, Kent, included, as part of the undertaking, the maintenance and repair of the premises. The activity of obtaining asbestos sheets for the repair of its premises, whether they were to be obtained by purchase from suppliers or by arranging for the removal and collection of secondhand sheets from other premises, was for the benefit of the appellant's undertaking. If the appellant had sent its own employees to remove and collect the asbestos sheets, there could be no doubt that the activity of the removal of the sheets would have been an activity of the appellant in the conduct of its undertaking.

However, the appellant did not remove the sheets by its own employees. Mr Sibley arranged for them to be removed by independent contractors. There was no suggestion that Messrs Derhun and Poulter were not genuinely independent. This was not a pretence of self-employment to enable the parties to avoid the incidents of employment. The question which falls to be determined is whether by acting through contractors, instead of using their own employees, the appellant can still be said to have been conducting its undertaking. If it was conducting its undertaking through contractors it owed a duty to ensure the safety of Mr Derhun, and it was properly convicted. There is no criticism made of the justices' approach to the issue of whether or not the appellant did all that was reasonably practicable.

On behalf of the appellant, Mr Richardson submitted that where a person (whom I shall call a 'principal' in order to distinguish him from an employer of employees) engages an independent contractor to carry out work for him, the work or activity carried out is not the principal's conduct of his undertaking, but is wholly the contractor's conduct of his undertaking. He submitted that there could be no overlap between undertakings: an activity is either the principal's or the contractor's conduct of its undertaking. This is because, he submitted, one has to examine who has complete control over what is being done. It is well established that a principal is not entitled to lay down to an independent contractor the manner in which the contract work is to be done. Therefore, he submits, the principal cannot exercise complete control and it must follow that the activities of the contractor are exclusively the conduct of his undertaking.

Mr Richardson derives support for this proposition from an obiter dictum in the speech of Lord Jauncey (with whom three other members of the Appellate Committee of the House of Lords agreed) in *Mailer v Austin Rover Group plc* [1989] 2 All ER 1087, [1990] 1 AC 619. That was a case involving a prosecution under s 4 of the 1974 Act. Before beginning his analysis of s 4 Lord Jauncey reviewed the scheme of the Act. He said ([1989] 2 All ER 1087 at 1096–1097, [1990] 1 AC 619 at 633):

> 'My Lords, before turning to consider in detail the provisions of s 4, reference must be made to the preceding sections of the 1974 Act. Section 1 provides, inter alia: "(1) The provisions of this Part shall have effect with a view to—(a) securing the health, safety and welfare of persons at work; (b) protecting persons other than persons at work against risks to health or safety arising out of or in connection with the activities of persons at work" ... Section 2 imposes duties on an employer in relation to his employees and ... provides: "It shall be the duty of every employer to ensure, so far as is reasonably practicable, the health, safety and welfare at work of all his employees."'

Lord Jauncey then summarised the effect of sub-s (2). He then read s 3(1), which imposes duties on employers in relation to persons who are not their employees, and summarised s 3(2), which imposes duties on the self-employed. He went on:

> 'Failure to discharge a duty imposed by ss 2, 3 or 4 constitutes an offence (s 33) but does not give rise to civil liability (s 47). The onus of proving that it was not reasonably practicable to perform any duty imposed by ss 2, 3 or 4 is placed upon the accused (s 40).'

He then went on as follows—and it is this passage upon which Mr Richardson relies ([1989] 2 All ER 1087 at 1097, [1990] 1 AC 619 at 634):

'Sections 2 and 3 impose duties in relation to safety on a single person, whether an individual or a corporation, who is in a position to exercise complete control over the matters to which the duties extend. An employer can control the conditions of work of his employees and the manner in which he conducts his undertaking.'

He went on to contrast that with the situation which prevailed under s 4, with which we are not concerned.

This passage was cited to the magistrates in the course of submissions, which followed closely those advanced before this court. It appears that the magistrates accepted the proposition that only the activities over which the employer had complete control would fall within the ambit of the conduct of his undertaking.

Mr Hoskins, for the respondent, submitted with some diffidence, bearing in mind the august source of the dictum, that Lord Jauncey was wrong when he spoke of the concept of complete control in respect of the duties under ss 2 and 3. He submitted primarily that the exercise of control was not a necessary feature of the conduct of an undertaking. He drew attention to the fact that no mention is made of 'control' in s 3 of the 1974 Act, whereas in ss 2(2)(d), 4(2), 5(4), 6(7) and 6(8)(a) the statute limits the duty imposed to places or activities under the defendant's control. Mr Hoskins invites us to infer that as there is no mention of control in s 3, the concept of control is an irrelevant consideration. He contends that any activity which is for the benefit of the defendant must be regarded as part of the conduct of his undertaking. Mr Hoskins accepted that if that were so, the manufacture of a special item by an independent contractor at his own premises at the principal's request would be an activity within the ambit of the principal's conduct of his undertaking, even in circumstances where the principal had neither the right, nor the opportunity, to exercise any control whatsoever over the way in which the work was to be done.

I find myself unable to accept that 'conduct of an undertaking' should be so widely construed. Nor am I able to accept that control is irrelevant to the conduct of an undertaking. I find it inconceivable that Parliament should have intended that there should be criminal liability under an offence which is subject to the defence of 'reasonable practicability' for matters over which the defendant has no control.

In the alternative, if the court should not accept his contention that control is irrelevant, Mr Hoskins submitted that complete control is not necessary, only partial control. He submitted that there may be circumstances in which control of an operation is shared by two parties, and where the activity would be within the ambit of both parties' undertaking. For example, where a main contractor instructs sub-contractors to do part of the contract work, both contractors may have some control over the sub-contract work, and each may properly be said to be conducting his undertaking. Similarly, he says where a principal instructs an independent contractor to do something required for the purpose of his undertaking, both the principal and the contractor may have some control over the activities, and each may properly be said to be conducting his undertaking. One must look, submits Mr Hoskins, not at the bare legal position of control. One must examine the realities of commercial life. If the terms of the contract reserve to the principal the right to give instructions as to how the work is to be done, as many building contracts do, then if instructions are given it should be inferred that the principal has some control. Even where the contractual terms do not specifically provide for such control, the principal may in practice exercise control over how the work is done. If he does, he may be said to be conducting his undertaking.

In support of this alternative contention Mr Hoskins relied upon the Scottish authority of *Carmichael v Rosehall Engineering Works Ltd* 1984 SLT 40, which was concerned with a prosecution under s 3(1) of the 1974 Act arising out of the accidental death of a man employed in the defendant's factory under a youth employment scheme operated by the Manpower Services Commission. The court said (at 40):

'We start with the recognition that the duties imposed on employers under ss. 2 and 3 relate to different classes of people. Section 2 concerns employees, who are under the direction and control of the employers in all aspects of the employers' undertaking including the general policy, the organisation and arrangements for the time being in force for carrying out the policy, as well as the actual operation of the work being undertaken. It is not surprising then that the general duties in relation to such employees should be spelt out in practical detail. Section 3 deals with people who are not employees of the employers. They may be engaged in the employers' undertaking in a variety of ways and capacities. For instance, they may be youths operating under the said scheme. They may be employees of contractors or sub-contractors. Their involvement may be varied. The employers do not necessarily have the same direction and control over them as they have over their own employees. When consideration is given to the large variety of situations which could exist it is perhaps not surprising that s. 3(1) is enacted in wider and less specific terms than s. 2. The duty imposed thereunder on the employer is not an absolute one, in that it only arises when it is reasonably practicable in all the circumstances. Each case, therefore, will require to be looked at and decided on its own circumstances. We do not consider that the comparison between the provisions of the two sections avails the respondents in their argument.'

This passage lends some support for the proposition that the defendant's conduct of his undertaking is not limited to those activities over which he has complete control. I find myself attracted to Mr Hoskins's alternative submission and, with great hesitation, I have come to the conclusion that it is well founded and that Lord Jauncey, who did not hear argument on the point, may not have considered all the variety of situations in which a person may share control of an activity which may still be described as the conduct of his undertaking. That would be so in the example which I gave above, in which a main contractor and his sub-contractor may both be said to be conducting their undertakings in respect of the sub-contract work. Difficult decisions might well arise on particular facts. For example, in the present case, if it had been arranged that Messrs Derhun and Poulter were to work on the roof, cropping the bolts, removing the asbestos sheets and handing them down to the shovel driver, an employee of the appellant, whose job it was to receive the sheets and take them to the appellant's premises, I would be of the view that the activity of removing the sheets was Iron Age's undertaking, and the receipt and transport of the sheets was the appellant's undertaking. However, one can see that it might well be arguable that both parties had some control over what was being done and that the whole operation was the undertaking of each of them.

However, it is not sufficient for Mr Hoskins's purposes for him to persuade the court that some activities may be within the ambit of the conduct of an undertaking of more than one employer, and that it is not necessary to show that an employer has complete control over an activity before it can be said that it is part of his undertaking. He must go further and show that in this case there was shared control so that it could be said that the removal of the sheets was part of the appellant's undertaking.

Mr Hoskins further submits, as he must in order to show that the justices' approach was right, that the appellant's capacity to exercise some control over the activity is enough to show that the activity is within the ambit of the conduct of its undertaking. He submits that if it be the case that Messrs Derhun and Poulter were in such a small way of business that they would have complied with any instructions which the appellant gave as to the method of work to be adopted for the removal of the sheets, then one should infer that the appellant was able to exercise some control over the activity. The activity was therefore within the ambit of the appellant's conduct of his undertaking. That, he says, is so, even though the appellant did not in fact give any such instructions, could not, as a matter of law, have insisted upon doing so, and was under no duty to do so under the civil law.

No authority has been cited to us which supports those additional contentions.

I am unable to accept that the mere capacity or opportunity to exercise control over an activity is enough to bring that activity within the ambit of the employer's conduct of his undertaking. Before he can say that an activity is within his conduct of his undertaking, the employer must, in my judgment, either exercise some actual control over it or be under a duty to do so. If the principal chooses to leave the independent contractor to do the work in the way he thinks fit, I consider that the work is not within the ambit of the principal's conduct of his undertaking. It is wholly the contractor's undertaking. If the principal does involve himself, albeit voluntarily—as, for example, by instructing the contractor to adopt a certain method of work, or by lending a piece of equipment—then it may be that his involvement would be within the ambit of his undertaking. If the system of work proved to be unsafe, or the equipment proved to be defective and gave rise to a risk to the safety of the contractor, then it may be that the principal would be guilty of an offence under s 3.

Here the appellant appointed a sub-contractor to do the work of removing the asbestos sheets. The justices found that the only equipment asked for by the contractors and lent by the appellant was the front-loading shovel. No stipulations were made about when the work was to be done. It is implicit in the justices' finding that no stipulations were made as to how the work was to be done, or what equipment was to be used. The appellant left the contractors to do the work in any way they chose. It was under no duty to lay down a safe system of work for the contractors and it did not do so. In those circumstances it seems to me that it was not open to the justices to find that the activity of removing the sheets fell within the ambit of the appellant's conduct of its undertaking.

It seems to me that it could properly have been said that the appellant's act of appointing contractors to do the work for it would fall within the ambit of its conduct of its undertaking. However, once the contractors are appointed and have accepted responsibility for what is to be done, the actual work is not within the ambit of the appellant's undertaking. Here the case was put on the basis that it was the actual work of removing the sheets which was within the ambit of the appellant's undertaking, and not the appointment of the contractors. I have already concluded that the actual work of the contractors could not fall within the ambit of the appellant's undertaking.

Mr Richardson submitted that if the appellant were to be held to be under a duty under the 1974 Act to devise a safe system of work for these independent contractors, it would extend its duty under the criminal law far beyond the limit of his duty under the civil law.

Mr Hoskins submitted that as this is a penal statute, whose objects include the promotion of the health, safety and welfare of persons at work, there is no reason why, as a matter of policy, the duties imposed should not extend beyond the bounds of the duty at common law.

However, Mr Hoskins's submission does not accord with the proposition accepted by the Court of Appeal in *R v Swan Hunter Shipbuilders Ltd* [1982] 1 All ER 264, [1981] ICR 831 that the duties under the Act were not intended to extend beyond the defendant's duties at common law.

In that case Swan Hunter were charged with offences under ss 2 and 3(1) of the 1974 Act. Section 2, as was seen earlier, imposes duties on employers in respect of the health and safety of their own employees. It was alleged that Swan Hunter had failed to advise and instruct sub-contractors working in the yard about the safety procedures which had been laid down for Swan Hunter employees for the handling of oxygen equipment in confined spaces. A sub-contractor's employee left a hose in a confined space overnight, with the result that an explosion occurred when a welder lit his torch the next morning. Several men were killed, some of whom were employed by Swan Hunter and some by other contractors.

The Crown submitted that the 1974 Act was not intended to, and did not, create any new duty which was not already imposed by the civil law. As Swan Hunter were main contractors, they were under a duty at common law to co-ordinate the activities of the sub-contractors so as to ensure the safety not only of their own employees, but also of the employees of sub-contractors (see *McArdle v Andmac Roofing Co* [1967] 1 All ER 583, [1967] 1 WLR 356).

Dunn LJ, giving the judgment of the court, accepted the Crown's submission. At least so far as s 2 is concerned, the proposition that the 1974 Act was not intended to impose a duty which went beyond the common law appears to have been part of the ratio decidendi of the case. However, it is not clear from the two reports, which differ in some small but important respects, whether or not the court held that s 3 was also intended to reflect existing common law duties. If it did, that would be binding on this court. I draw comfort from the fact that the conclusion I have reached on other grounds is consistent with the proposition which the Court of Appeal accepted, at least in relation to s 2.

I turn then to answer the justices' second and third questions. The second question—were we correct in our opinion that the work being carried out by

Mr Hans Derhun at the British Gypsum works formed part of the appellant's undertaking—must be answered in the negative.

The relevance of the third question depends on the correctness of the answer to the second question. It would be inappropriate to examine in detail the reasoning which led the justices to form the conclusion that the appellant failed to conduct its undertaking so as to ensure the safety of persons now being in their employment when I have formed the view that they could not, as a matter of law, have reached the conclusion that what was being done was within the ambit of the appellant's undertaking.

In view of the conclusion I have reached, I shall deal very briefly with the preliminary issue reflected in the justices' first question.

The appellant had alleged that the information was defective in that it did not give such particulars as were necessary for the giving of reasonable information of the nature of the charge, as required by r 100 of the Magistrates' Courts Rules 1981, SI 1981/552.

I have already set out the terms of the information. Before the hearing, at which the appellant had intended to plead not guilty, its solicitors sought particulars of the information. They asked:

'1. What facts and matters are relied on by the prosecution in support of the allegations that at the time of the accident Roadstone (the appellant) was conducting its undertaking in a way which affected Messrs Poulter and Derhun. 2. Please identify the particular undertaking referred to in the summons. 3. Please state precisely what steps it is alleged the appellant should have taken but failed to take so as to ensure the safety of Mr Derhun. 4. In respect of each step identified by the prosecution in answer to 3, please state all facts and matters relied upon.'

The factories inspector, for the respondent, replied as follows.

'In answer to your request for further particulars we make the following points. 1. Facts and matters relied on by the prosecution should be obtained from the statements, which we supplied in full. 2. The undertaking was the manufacture of roadstone products. Such manufacturing will include the maintenance and refurbishment of the jetty. 3. The prosecution do not have to detail all the steps the appellant should have taken, but have to establish that the appellant failed to ensure the safety of persons, including Mr Derhun. If there is a case to answer it is for your client to show that he did all that was reasonably practicable to ensure their safety.'

The respondent had already disclosed a full set of written statements.

The appellant's contention was that the information ought to have specified what steps the respondent would say the appellant should have taken in order to ensure the safety of the persons in question.

The respondent contended that the information was adequate. In particular, there was no burden on the prosecution to show exactly what the employer had done or failed to do to breach his duty. It was enough to show that the employer had failed to ensure the safety of non-employees. It was then for the employer to show that he had done all that was reasonably practicable.

The magistrates ruled that the information gave adequate particulars and was not defective. In my judgment they were right to do so. I have already set out what the prosecutor must prove in order to pass the burden of proof to the defendant. He must prove: (1) the defendant was an employer within the meaning of the 1974 Act; (2) the activity which gave rise to the complaint fell within the ambit of the defendant's undertaking; and (3) that the defendant failed to ensure that persons affected by that aspect of its conduct were exposed to a risk of health or safety. That does not include proving a failure to take any particular steps. It is sufficient to prove the failure to achieve the desired result.

I would therefore conclude that the specific complaint of lack of particularity was not made out.

However, it does seem to me that the appellant could legitimately complain that it came to court not knowing exactly what aspect of its conduct of its undertaking was under scrutiny and criticism.

By a letter dated 30 July it had asked that the prosecutor should identify the undertaking referred to in the summons. The prosecutor replied that the undertaking was the manufacture of roadstone products, and that such manufacture would include the maintenance and refurbishment of the jetty, which was another name for the transfer tower. In fact the case was run on the basis that the actual removal of the asbestos sheets from the British Gypsum site was within the ambit of the appellant's conduct of the undertaking. It was not clear from the information how the case was to be put. It seems to me that, on the rather unusual facts of this case, the summons ought to have included this information. However, that was not the way in which the point was argued before the justices.

I would answer the first question posed by the justices in the affirmative. They were correct in finding that the respondent was not required to provide particulars of the alleged failure to discharge their duty under s 3(1).

This final decision does not affect my overall conclusion resulting from the answers given to the second and third questions as a result of which I would allow this appeal and quash the conviction.

RALPH GIBSON LJ. I agree.

Appeal allowed. The court refused leave to appeal to the House of Lords but certified in accordance with s 1(2) of the Administration of Justice Act 1960 that the following point of law of general public importance was involved in the decision: is the capacity of an employer to exercise some control over work carried out on his behalf by an independent contractor sufficient to bring that work within the ambit of the employer's conduct of undertaking for the purposes of s 3(1) of the Health and Safety at Work etc Act 1974?

16 June 1994.   The Appeal Committee of the House of Lords (Lord Jauncey of Tullichettle, Lord Slynn of Hadley and Lord Nolan) refused leave to appeal.

Dilys Tausz   Barrister.

R v Associated Octel Co Ltd

COURT OF APPEAL, CRIMINAL DIVISION

STUART-SMITH LJ, KAY AND DYSON JJ

13, 24 JUNE, 19 JULY 1994

Health and safety at work – Employer's duties – Duty to other person's employees – Duty to conduct undertaking in such a way as to ensure other person's employees not exposed to risks to health and safety – Statutory offence – Employer's liability – Independent contractors carrying out repair and maintenance work to employer's chemical plant – Contractors' employee injured while carrying out repairs – Whether contractors' activity within employer's conduct of its undertaking – Test of liability – Health and Safety at Work etc Act 1974, s 3.

In 1990 the appellant company, which operated a chemical plant, engaged a firm of specialist contractors to carry out annual maintenance and repair work. As part of the scheduled work, the contractors had to repair the lining of a tank within the chlorine plant, which involved grinding down the damaged areas of the tank, cleaning the dust from the surfaces with acetone and applying fibreglass matting to rebuild those areas. While the contractors' employee was inside the tank, the bulb of the light he was using broke, and the electric current caused the acetone vapour to ignite. There was a flash fire and explosion which badly burned the employee. The company was subsequently charged with and convicted of an offence under s 33(1)[a] of the Health and Safety at Work etc Act 1974 of failing to discharge the duty imposed on it by s 3[b] to conduct its business in such a way as to ensure, so far as reasonably practicable, that persons not in its employment who might be affected thereby were not exposed to risks to their health or safety. The company appealed, contending (i) that the duty imposed by s 3 was coterminous with the duty imposed by the law of tort in respect of the liability of a person to those who were not in his employment and that that did not, save in exceptional cases, involve liability for the acts of independent contractors and (ii) that the effect of s 3 was merely to impose a criminal sanction in those cases where, under the law of tort, the defendant would be liable to the injured man, with the sole modification that the onus of proving negligence was not on the prosecution but on the defendant to show, so far as reasonably practicable, that he had taken all proper care. The Crown contended that that narrow approach was wrong in law and that the words 'conduct his undertaking' in s 3 were not confined to criminalising breaches of the common law duty in tort, but were wide enough to embrace the activities of independent contractors carrying out works of cleaning, repair and maintenance which were necessary for the conduct of the employer's business or enterprise. It further contended that all that was necessary was to show that the repair and maintenance of the chlorine plant was part of the conduct of the company's undertaking and that, on the facts, injury had resulted.

---

a   Section 33(1), so far as material, provides: 'It is an offence for a person—(a) to fail to discharge a
     duty to which he is subject by virtue of sections 2 to 7 ...'
b   Section 3, so far as material, is set out at p 1056 *f g*, post

Held – The word 'undertaking' in s 3(1) of the 1974 Act meant 'enterprise' o 'business' and the cleaning, repair and maintenance of plant, machinery an(buildings necessary for carrying on the employer's business were part of th(conduct of his undertaking for the purposes of s 3(1), whether it was done b' the employer's own employees or by independent contractors. Accordingly if there was a risk of injury to the health and safety of persons not employe(by the employer, whether to the contractor's men or members of the public and a fortiori if there was actual injury as a result of the conduct o that operation, there was a prima facie liability, subject to the defence o reasonable practicability. The question of control might well be relevant t(the issue of whether it was reasonably practicable for the employer to giv(instructions on how the work was to be done and what safety measures wer(to be taken and, in each case, that question was one of fact and degree. Th(ingredients of the s 3 offence were therefore that the accused was (i) a(employer (ii) who so conducted his undertaking (iii) as to expose to risk t(health or safety (iv) a person not employed by him (v) who might be affecte(by such conduct of the accused's undertaking. It followed that the company': appeal against its conviction of the s 3 offence would be dismissed on the basi: of that broad approach (see p 1062 *j* to p 1063 *a f* to *j* and p 1064 *g h*, post).

R v Mara [1987] 1 All ER 478 applied.

RMC Roadstone Products Ltd v Jester [1994] 4 All ER 1037 considered.

Notes

For duties of employers to persons other than their employees, see 2(*Halsbury's Laws* (4th edn reissue) para 555.

For the Health and Safety at Work etc Act 1974, ss 3, 33, see 19 *Halsbury': Statutes* (4th edn) (1994 reissue) 801, 833.

Cases referred to in judgment

Honeywill & Stein Ltd v Larkin Bros (London's Commercial Photographers) Ltd [1934] 1 KB 191, [1933] All ER Rep 77, CA.

McArdle v Andmac Roofing Co [1967] 1 All ER 583, [1967] 1 WLR 356, CA.

R v Board of Trustees of the Science Museum [1993] 3 All ER 853, [1993] 1 WLR 1171, CA.

R v Mara [1987] 1 All ER 478, [1987] 1 WLR 87, CA.

R v Swan Hunter Shipbuilders Ltd [1982] 1 All ER 264, [1981] ICR 831, CA.

RMC Roadstone Products Ltd v Jester [1994] 4 All ER 1037, [1994] ICR 456, DC.

Rylands v Fletcher (1868) LR 3 HL 330, [1861–73] All ER Rep 1, HL.

Appeal

Associated Octel Co Ltd appealed with leave from the decision of Judge Prosser on 19 March 1993 in the Crown Court at Chester whereby it was convicted of an offence under s 33(1) of the Health and Safety at Work etc Act 1974 for failure to discharge its duty under s 3 of the Act to conduct its undertaking in such a way as to ensure that persons other than its employees were not exposed to risks to health and safety, which failure led to the serious injury of Eric Cuthbert, one of the employees of Resin Glass Products, a firm of specialist contractors which had been engaged to carry out annual repairs and maintenance work to the appellant's chemical plant on the ground that the judge had been wrong to reject the appellant's submission of no case to answer. The facts are set out in the judgment of the court.

Raymond Walker QC and *Julian Waters* (instructed by *Hill Dickinson Davis Campbell*, Liverpool) for the appellant.
Hugh Carlisle QC and *Simon Earlam* (instructed by *Kevin O'Reilly*) for the Crown.

Cur adv vult

19 July 1994. The following judgment of the court was delivered.

STUART-SMITH LJ. On 19 March 1993 in the Crown Court at Chester before Judge Prosser and a jury, the appellant company was convicted of an offence of failing to discharge a duty to which it was subject by virtue of s 3 of the Health and Safety at Work etc Act 1974 and was fined £25,000 and ordered to pay £60,000 towards the costs of the prosecution. The appellant now appeals against that conviction with the leave of the single judge.

The prosecution arose from an accident that occurred on 25 June 1990 at the appellant's chemical plant at Ellesmere Port which resulted in serious injury to an employee of a firm of contractors carrying out work at the premises. The firm of contractors, Resin Glass Products Ltd (RGP), was also prosecuted and admitted an offence of failing to discharge the duty imposed by s 2 of the same Act.

It was the appellant's practice to shut down the chemical plant annually for preplanned maintenance and repair. Amongst the work planned for the 1990 shut-down was the repair of the lining of a tank within the chlorine plant, which was situated in a separate building on the site. This work was entrusted to RGP, who were specialist contractors. RGP had for many years carried out work for the appellant and indeed its employees worked at the appellant's sites virtually all the time.

The particular task was assigned by RGP to one of its employees, Eric Cuthbert. It required the grinding down of damaged areas within the tank, cleaning dust from the surfaces after grinding and the application of fibreglass matting with resin to provide a patch. To effect the work, Mr Cuthbert had to enter the tank and it was necessary for him to take in lighting so that he could see to work. Once the grinding was complete, the cleaning was done by removing the surface debris with a brush and then washing any residue off with a solvent, acetone, applied with a paint brush. Acetone is a highly inflammable substance.

Whilst Mr Cuthbert was inside the tank, the bulb of the light that he was using suddenly broke, probably as a result of acetone dripping on it, and the electric current caused the acetone vapour to ignite. There was a flash fire and explosion which badly burned Mr Cuthbert.

Three aspects of the carrying out of the work were highlighted by the factory inspectors as unsafe. The acetone was contained in an open bucket which permitted vapour to be given off. It was suggested that use should have been made of a closed container. Secondly, the lamp was not a safety lamp and the prosecution contended that an air lamp should have been employed. Thirdly, it was said that forced ventilation should have been provided.

Before turning to consider the grounds of appeal and the law relating to aɪ offence of the kind alleged, it is necessary to examine the safety arrangement for the carrying out of this work that were revealed by the evidence. Thiṣ information was provided by documents seized from the appellant on behaḷ of the Health and Safety Executive after notification of the accident anḍ produced by a factory inspector and the evidence of Mr Cuthbert and anotheɪ employee of RGP, who was working with him.

The appellant's chemical plant was designated as a 'major hazard site' anḍ as such was subject to the Control of Industrial Major Accident Hazard Regulations 1984, SI 1984/1902, reg 7 of which required the appellant tọ submit to the Health and Safety Executive a safety report. That report entitled 'Safety Case, Associated Octel Company Limited, Ellesmere Porṭ Site', was produced in evidence. Two parts of the report were highlighted bɣ the prosecution in opening the case to the jury.

As a part of the appellant's health, safety and environmental policɣ contained within the safety case, it was stated that works/departmental/ establishment policy documents must recognise a number of establisheḍ principles, which included:

'Employees, contractors and visitors will be informed, through traininɡ and instruction, of roles, systems of work, practices and procedures sọ that they can carry out work without risk to themselves or others.'

Paragraph 3.2 of App 6 of the safety case contained the statement:

'Construction work is planned and co-ordinated by engineers usinɡ approved contractors. All Contractors employing over two workers oṇ site must include a supervisor. All Contractors working on site must conform to the permit to work system.'

The permit to work system operated by the appellant was proved by itṣ booklet 'Safety Certificates and Permits', which was produced in the same way. Section 5 of that booklet dealt with contractors' permits to work. It stated the purpose of the system as:

'To provide for the effective control of the Contractor's employees anḍ staff within operational areas. To ensure that all Contractor's staff anḍ operating personnel are informed of the adequate precautions to be taken to safeguard the persons detailed to work in operational areas.'

The contractor's permit to work was a three-part document. Section A waṣ to be completed by the project engineer, the chief clerk of works, or some other appointed issuing authority, section B by the maintenance engineer of the area in which the work was to be done, and section C by the safety officer or process foreman.

The procedure for use was defined and the relevant parts read:

'Section A of the Contractor's Permit to Work is completed in order to notify Works staff that certain operations are to take place. Adequate information must be given to enable the authorising Engineer to assess the risks and prescribe the safe working conditions which he does in Section B ... The issuing authority will hand the top copy to the Contractor (or his appointed representative) who will sign as having understood the provisions of the permit and will retain the top copy throughout the course of the work, returning it to the Maintenance Foreman's office each evening and collecting it the next working day after it has been authorised for the current day's work ...'

As well as producing this documentation relating to the appellant's system, the prosecution also produced from the appellant's records a series of documents that related to the specific work resulting in the accident. These included RGP's specification for carrying out the work, which included:

'The vessel would be ground to a rough surface to give good adhesion. This will need extraction and men to wear full suit protection. We would supply the extraction.'

The relevant contractor's permit to work was produced. It related to four separate items of work including the one which resulted in the accident. Section A stated that the work was to be carried out by approximately two men under the control of 'J. Buckley, [the] contractor's supervisor'. The only relevant details of the work given were 'refurbish ejector water tank' in dechlorination plant, No 1 Cell Hall. Details required as to tools or equipment to be used were given as 'Hand tools, grinder' and the question 'Will any spark producing tools or equipment be used?' was answered 'Yes'.

Section B, which was completed and signed by the maintenance engineer, made the requirement 'Each job must have its own Safety Certificate and where appropriate Vessel Entry and Flame Notes'. There was a part which was available for stipulating any additional precautions that were required but nothing additional was added in this section.

The resulting general safety and vessel entry certificates were produced. The latter recorded the carrying out of a test for toxicity within the tank and the result. It provided that entry was permitted provided that safety equipment, as detailed in the general safety certificate, was worn.

The general safety certificate was on the appellant's standard form for such a certificate. It carried the printed requirement 'All precautions detailed below must be taken before job is commenced'. There were a number of preprinted requirements that were completed either by deletion of one of the alternatives 'is/is not required' or by the ticking of a box. In the former category requirements were made in relation to this work by the appellant for use of a scaffold or ladder and for a safety attendant. The wearing of safety equipment was provided for by ticking boxes for a full-face air mask, a protective suit and protective gloves.

There was then a section headed 'Obtain the following equipment before starting work'. One item listed on the form so that it could be specified was an air lamp. None of the items was ticked and the prosecution drew attention to that fact.

A section headed 'Further precautions' was completed by adding: 'Plant shut down. Tank to be drained and washed out. Contact operator before starting work'. The evidence as to how these safety provisions were actually utilised was provided by Mr Cuthbert and the fellow employee who had been working with him. Mr Cuthbert explained that the dust extractor had been connected up the previous week. On the day of his accident, he was instructed by RGP's supervisor, Mr Buckley, to carry out the particular piece of work. They then waited whilst one of the appellant's laboratory technicians carried out the test for toxicity referred to in the vessel entry certificate and ensured that there was no danger arising from any residual chlorine. They then collected the general safety and vessel entry certificates from the appellant's process office, which they read and to which they gave effect.

They were supplied with a face mask and protective overalls drawn from the appellant's safety stores. The electric light used was obtained by Mr Buckley from the appellant's electrician's workshop and handed to them.

The acetone, which Mr Cuthbert gave evidence was always used for washing down the surface before application of the fibreglass throughout the eight-year period that he had worked at the appellant's site, was poured from ten-gallon containers into open-topped buckets for use. The buckets utilised were discarded painters' emulsion buckets which they were in the habit of recovering from bins on site.

Equipped in this manner, RGP undertook the work with the disastrous consequences to which reference has already been made.

Other evidence was called by the prosecution relating to the operation of permit to work systems at other similar sites and to guidance on the operation of such systems given by the Health and Safety Executive. Such evidence could only be relevant to rebut any possible defence that the appellant had done all that was reasonably practicable, the onus of proof of which was, by virtue of s 40 of the 1974 Act, on the appellant.

At the conclusion of the prosecution case, the defence submitted that there was no case to answer. This submission was rejected and the defence elected to call no evidence. There was thus no evidence given to suggest that the documentation produced did not bear the ordinary meaning to be gleaned from the documents themselves, no evidence to contradict the evidence of Mr Cuthbert as to the events that led to his accident, and no evidence in support of a defence of reasonable practicability.

The first question in this appeal is, what are the ingredients of the offence under s 3 of the 1974 Act? That section provides:

'(1) It shall be the duty of every employer to conduct his undertaking in such a way as to ensure, so far as is reasonably practicable, that persons not in his employment who may be affected thereby are not thereby exposed to risks to their health or safety ...'

Mr Walker QC submits that the duty imposed by the section is coterminous with the duty imposed by the law of tort in respect of the activity of a person to those who are not in his employment and that this does not, save in exceptional cases, involve liability for the acts of independent contractors. The effect of the section is merely to impose a criminal sanction in those cases where, under the law of tort, the defendant would be liable to the injured man, with the sole modification that the onus of proving negligence is not on the prosecution since the onus is on the defendant to show, so far as is reasonably practicable, that he had taken all proper care. Section 3, in contrast to s 2, which is concerned with an employer's duty to his own employees, is concerned with the duty owed by an employer to persons not in his employment. Under the law of tort such a person is not in general liable for the acts of an independent contractor whom he has employed to do the work. RGP was, says Mr Walker, such an independent contractor. There are exceptions to this general principle: examples which are not relevant are the rule in *Rylands v Fletcher* (1868) LR 3 HL 330, [1861–73] All ER Rep 1, some cases of nuisance, work on the highway, withdrawal of support for land or buildings and non-delegable duties of care owed by the employer to his own employees. More relevant are cases of the conduct of extra-hazardous operations: see *Honeywill & Stein Ltd v Larkin Bros (London's Commercial Photographers) Ltd* [1934] 1 KB 191, [1933] All ER Rep 77, where a head contractor fails to co-ordinate the activities of sub-contractors; *McArdle v Andmac Roofing Co* [1967] 1 All ER 583, [1967] 1 WLR 356, where the employee of an independent contractor is injured by some defect in the premises under the control of the occupier or by defective plant or equipment provided by him for the purpose of carrying out the contractor's work, a situation governed so far as the 1974 Act is concerned by s 4; or where the employer-principal exercises control over the contractor's operations in the sense that he can tell the contractor's men how they are to do the work and what safety precautions they are to take, or exercises joint or partial control over them in this respect. Since RGP were independent contractors, competent to decide how the work was to be done and what precautions were to be used, Mr Walker submitted that Octel were not at the material time 'conducting their undertaking'. The operation that was being carried out was the conduct of RGP's undertaking. This was the foundation of the submission of no case to answer. Mr Walker submitted that because of an error of law on the part of the prosecution they had never attempted to prove that Octel had exercised the necessary degree of control to bring the case within the section and show that it was the conduct of Octel's undertaking. It is also the foundation of the first ground of appeal that the judge was wrong to reject the submissions of no case to answer.

Mr Carlisle QC for the Crown answers this in two ways. First, he submits that Mr Walker's construction (the narrow approach) is wrong in law; the words 'conduct his undertaking' are not confined to criminalising breaches of the common law duty in tort, but are wide enough to embrace the activities of independent contractors carrying out works of cleaning, repair and maintenance which are necessary for the conduct of the employer's business or enterprise (the wide approach). All that was necessary here was to show that the repair and maintenance of the chlorine plant was part of the conduct of Octel's undertaking, which he says it plainly was, and that, on the facts of this case, injury resulted. It was then for Octel to show that it was not reasonably practicable to prevent it, which they did not attempt. This is the way Mr Carlisle opened the case to the jury. This difference in construction is therefore a matter of great importance. Alternatively, Mr Carlisle submitted that, if the narrow approach is correct in law, there was sufficient evidence here of control by Octel.

In support of this narrow construction Mr Walker relied on *R v Swan Hunter Shipbuilders Ltd* [1982] 1 All ER 264, [1981] ICR 831. The appellants were shipbuilders; their employees were working alongside those of their contractors and sub-contractors. They were aware of the danger of fire if the air became oxygen-enriched. They gave their own employees appropriate instructions to guard against the risk, but they did not give them to contractors' or sub-contractors' employees. One of these had not disconnected the oxygen hose overnight and had left it in a confined area where it should not have been and oxygen leaked out. Next morning a disastrous fire occurred when a welder, not appreciating the danger, used his torch. Swan Hunter were prosecuted and convicted, both under s 2 in respect of their own employees who were working in the ship and under s 3 in respect of the employees of contractors and sub-contractors. Their appeal was dismissed; it was held that, so far as their own employees were concerned, their safety depended upon proper instructions being given to contractors' and sub-contractors' workmen. So far as s 3(1) was concerned, it was held that the obligation was wide enough to include an obligation to provide instruction to the employees of others and was not limited by the words of s 3(3), which dealt with specific cases which might be prescribed by regulations (though none had yet been). There can be no doubt that Swan Hunter were conducting their undertaking of shipbuilding at the time, so the issue with which we are concerned did not arise; the real question, so far as s 3(1) was concerned, was whether the wide words were cut down by s 3(3).

Dunn LJ said ([1982] 1 All ER 264 at 270, [1981] ICR 831 at 839):

> 'Counsel for the Crown submitted that there was nothing revolutionary or novel in the duties imposed by ss 2 and 3 of the 1974 Act. He pointed out that before 1974 there was a duty on the main contractor to co-ordinate the operations at a place of work so as to ensure the safety not only of his own employees but also the employees of sub-contractors.'

There then follows a citation from *McArdle's* case [1967] 1 All ER 583 at 591–592, [1967] 1 WLR 356 at 367–368. The judgment continues ([1981] ICR 831 at 840–841; cf [1982] 1 All ER 264 at 270–271):

> 'So, said Mr. Potts [counsel for the Crown], as Munkman puts it in the latest edition of his *Employer's Liability*, 9th ed. (1979), the duties imposed by the Act of 1974 are modelled on the common law duties of care and do not constitute any significant departure from those duties as was suggested by [counsel for Swan Hunter].
>
> So far as section 3 was concerned, Mr. Potts submitted that subsection (1) simply lays down in statutory form the situation which existed prior to the passing of the Act in a general way. Subsection (3), he submitted, was limited to dealing with certain situations, and in those situations only prescribed information was to be given to persons outside the employment of the contractor conducting the undertaking. Subsection (3) envisages regulations, and in Mr. Potts's submission, there was no inconsistency between the judge's interpretation of subsection (1) and subsection (3), which, in his submission, was quite separate from it. He points out that the words in subsection (1), "It shall be the duty of every employer to conduct his undertaking in such a way as to ensure ..." were very wide in terms and quite apt to cover the provision of information and instruction.
>
> We accept the submissions of Mr. Potts so far as the construction of the section is concerned. In our view the duties are all covered by the general duty in subsection (1) of section 2 ...'

It is not altogether clear whether Dunn LJ is referring in this passage to s 2, s 3 or both. There is a difference between the two reports, the All England Law Reports referring to section*s* in the second line of the last paragraph. After dealing with s 2, Dunn LJ deals with s 3 later on the page and holds that s 3(3) does not cut down the words of s 3(1). But even if, as we think, he was referring to both sections, it is clear, in our judgment, that the statement that s 3(1) did no more than criminalise breaches of the existing duty in tort was obiter and not necessary for the decision of the court. We entirely accept that, so far as s 2 is concerned, both the general duty in s 2(1) and the specific duties set out in s 2(2), relating to such questions as the provision of plant, safe system of work, instructions, safe place of work and method of access, simply echo the common law obligation of an employer to his workman. But s 3(1) is quite different and introduces the concept of 'conducting his undertaking', which is not an expression used in the law of tort to define the scope of liability.

Mr Walker next relied upon a decision of the Divisional Court in *RMC Roadstone Products Ltd v Jester* [1994] 4 All ER 1037, [1994] ICR 456. Smith J gave a judgment with which Ralph Gibson LJ agreed. In that case the appellants required some repairs to be carried out to one of their buildings. The work involved the replacement of corrugated asbestos sheets; they sub-contracted the work to a two-man firm who were regarded as independent contractors. Instead of buying new sheets, this firm suggested that secondhand sheets could be obtained from the roof of a building, not owned or occupied by the appellants. The appellants agreed and the contractors went off to remove these sheets, the appellants supplying a mechanical shovel to assist in lowering the sheets. In the course of the work one of the men fell through the fragile asbestos roof. The system of work was unsafe and inadequate materials provided. Counsel for the respondent, HM Inspector of Factories, submitted that the question of control over how the work was done was irrelevant to the consideration of whether the appellants were conducting their undertaking, the same submission that Mr Carlisle makes in this case. This submission was rejected. Smith J said ([1994] 4 All ER 1037 at 1045, [1994] ICR 456 at 468):

'I find myself unable to accept that "conduct of an undertaking" should be so widely construed. Nor am I able to accept that control is irrelevant to the conduct of an undertaking. I find it inconceivable that Parliament should have intended that there should be criminal liability under an offence which is subject to the defence of "reasonable practicability" for matters over which the defendant has no control.'

Mr Walker relies heavily on this line of reasoning. But with respect to the Divisional Court, we cannot see why it should be inconceivable. The notion of control is something of which the draftsman of the 1974 Act was fully aware (see eg ss 2(2)(d), 4(2), 5(4) and esp s 6(7), s 6 dealing with liability of manufacturers as regards articles and substances for use at work). The question of control over how work is done may be very relevant to the issue whether the employer has taken precautions as far as is reasonably practicable. Nor are we particularly daunted by the spectre, which Mr Walker conjured up, of many employers being prosecuted for the shortcomings of an independent contractor; where an apparently competent independent contractor is engaged, it will often be simpler for an employer to discharge the onus on him to prove that it was not reasonably practicable to do more than was in fact done (s 40). A prosecutor can be liable in costs if he brings a prosecution which never should have been brought because there is a clear defence on these lines.

Furthermore, it is not inconceivable that Parliament intended to create an offence involving criminal liability, subject only to the defence of 'so far as is reasonably practicable'. This is exactly what was done in ss 28 and 29 of the Factories Act 1961, which are concerned with floors being kept free of obstructions and substances likely to cause persons to slip (s 28) and safe means of access and safe places of work (s 29). If the factory occupier entrusts the performance of the duty to an independent contractor, he does not thereby avoid criminal or civil liability for breach. He may, however, obtain indemnity or contribution against civil liability either by contract or under the Civil Liability (Contribution) Act 1978.

The Divisional Court went on to hold that there must be some actual control over how the work is done, though it might be joint or shared control, before the work is within 'the ambit of the employer's undertaking'. Smith J said ([1994] 4 All ER 1037 at 1047, [1994] ICR 456 at 470):

'I am unable to accept that the mere capacity or opportunity to exercise control over an activity is enough to bring that activity within the ambit of the employer's conduct of his undertaking. Before he can say that an activity is within his conduct of his undertaking, the employer must, in my judgment, either exercise some actual control over it or be under a duty to do so. If the principal chooses to leave the independent contractor to do the work in the way he thinks fit, I consider that the work is not within the ambit of the principal's conduct of his undertaking. It is wholly the contractor's undertaking. If the principal does involve himself, albeit voluntarily—as, for example, by instructing the contractor to adopt a certain method of work, or by lending a piece of equipment—then it may be that his involvement would be within the ambit of his undertaking. If the system of work proved to be unsafe, or the equipment proved to be defective and gave rise to a risk to the safety of the contractor, then it may be that the principal would be guilty of an offence under s 3.'

If the *RMC Roadstone* case is correctly decided, then, in our judgment, it is not distinguishable on the basis that the actual work was being carried on outside the appellant's premises, as Mr Carlisle suggested. But he also contended that it was wrongly decided.

We have therefore to consider Mr Carlisle's submissions in favour of the wide approach to the meaning of the words 'conducts his undertaking'. The only authority of this court directly in point is *R v Mara* [1987] 1 All ER 478, [1987] 1 WLR 87. In that case the appellant was the director of a cleaning company, CMS, which provided cleaning services under contract with IS to clean its industrial premises on weekday mornings. The cleaning machines used for this purpose were provided by CMS and left at IS premises over the weekend. The arrangement was that IS employees could use them for cleaning over the weekend. One of these machines had a dangerous electrical defect as a result of which an employee of IS was injured when using it. The appellant was charged with failing to discharge an employer's duty contrary to ss 33(1) and 37(1) of the 1974 Act by consenting to the breach by CMS of its duty under s 3(1). He was convicted; his appeal to this court was dismissed. Parker LJ gave the judgment of the court. He said ([1987] 1 All ER 478 at 481, [1987] 1 WLR 87 at 90–91):

'Next it was submitted that CMS was not, on Saturday morning, conducting its undertaking at all and that the only undertaking then being conducted was the undertaking of IS. Accordingly it was submitted that CMS was not in breach of the duty imposed by s 3(1) and the appellant could not therefore have consented to or connived at any such breach or caused any such breach by his neglect. This submission has more force but, in our judgment, it is not permissible to treat the section as being applicable only when an undertaking is in the process of being actively carried on. A factory, for example, may shut down on Saturdays and Sundays for manufacturing purposes, but the employer may have the premises cleaned by a contractor over the weekend. If the contractor's employees are exposed to risks to health or safety because machinery is left insecure, or vats containing noxious substances are left unfenced, it is, in our judgment, clear that the factory owner is in breach of his duty under s 3(1). The way in which he conducts his undertaking is to close his factory for manufacturing purposes over the weekend and to have it cleaned during the shut down period. It would clearly be reasonably practicable to secure machinery and noxious vats, and on the plain wording of the section he would be in breach of his duty if he failed to do so. The undertaking of CMS was the provision of cleaning services. So far as IS is concerned, the way in which CMS conducted its undertaking was to do the cleaning on weekday mornings and leave its machines and other equipment on the premises in the intervals with permission for IS employees to use the same and knowledge that they would use the same.'

It is clear from this that the court considered that an employer who closes down the factory for manufacturing purposes so that cleaning, repairs and maintenance can be carried out by contractors, is still conducting his undertaking while such operations are being carried out. It is true that the examples that Parker LJ gives of insecure machinery or vats containing noxious substances are matters for which at common law he would be liable as occupier of the premises; but the ratio of the passage is that the employer is conducting his undertaking, even through the agency of contractors and it would be reasonably practicable to ensure the safety of the machines or vats, not that the operation of cleaning the factory is not part of his undertaking or within the 'ambit of his undertaking', to use the phrase adopted in the *RMC Roadstone* case [1994] 4 All ER 1037 at 1041, [1994] ICR 456 at 464.

In *R v Board of Trustees of the Science Museum* [1993] 3 All ER 853, [1993] 1 WLR 1171 the appellants' air-conditioning cooling tower was inspected by officers of the Health and Safety Executive and found to contain the bacteria which caused legionnaires' disease. The appellants were charged under s 3 of the 1974 Act and convicted. The appellants contended at trial that there was no case to answer as no actual risk to the health of the public had been proved. The same point was taken on the appeal which was dismissed. It was held that it was sufficient for the prosecution to prove that members of the public were exposed to a possibility of danger for there to be a risk to the health and safety of members of the public in the vicinity. The decision is not directly in point, but it does show very graphically that the section goes much further than common law liability in tort, since it is concerned with risk of injury and not the actuality of injury. Mr Carlisle relies on two passages in the judgment of

Steyn LJ. The first passage is where he said ([1993] 3 All ER 853 at 859, [1993] 1 WLR 1171 at 1178):

'Subject only to the defence of reasonable practicability s 3(1) is intended to be an absolute prohibition. Bearing in mind the imperative of protecting public health and safety so far as it is reasonably practicable to do so, the result can be faced with equanimity.'

Although Steyn LJ was not dealing with a case involving the activities of independent contractors, classically, liability for the acts of independent contractors is one of the hallmarks of absolute liability. The section is so framed as to achieve a result, namely that persons not employed are not exposed to risks to their health and safety by the conduct of the undertaking. That result could be defeated if, ipso facto, the duty could be delegated to an independent contractor.

In the second passage Steyn LJ, after referring to the Robens Report, *Safety and Health at Work* (Cmnd 5034), which led to the enactment of the 1974 Act, said ([1993] 3 All ER 853 at 858, [1993] 1 WLR 1171 at 1177):

'It was a central thesis of the report that the development control powers of local authorities were insufficient to protect members of the public. The report recommended specific statutory controls exercised directly in the interests of public safety. This approach explains the battery of powers in the 1974 Act. Section 18 and following sections provide for the enforcement of "the relevant statutory provisions" which include s 3(1) (see s 53). Section 20 vested inspectors with a wide ranging power to investigate. Sections 21 and 22 created a power to serve improvement and prohibition notices, a failure to comply with such a notice constitutes an offence. These far reaching statutory powers are linked with s 3(1). It is, therefore, clear that the broad purpose of this part of the legislation was preventive. Section 3 must, therefore, not be read in isolation. The powers set out in ss 20, 21 and 22 are an important contextual aid to the construction of s 3(1).'

Mr Carlisle also sought to pray in aid ss 20, 21 and 22 in support of his construction in this case. He contended that the powers of the inspector would be substantially emasculated if, before he served an improvement notice or prohibition notice, the inspector had to consider nice questions of sole, joint or shared control of the operation in question. There is some force in this submission so far as improvement notices under s 21 are concerned. But s 22, which relates to prohibition notices, is confined by sub-s (1) to:

'... any activities which are being or are [likely] to be carried on by or under the control of any person, being activities to or in relation to which any of the relevant statutory provisions apply'.

But what can be said is that this language is quite different from that used in s 3(1) and shows that the latter is concerned with a wider spectrum than activities under the control of the employer.

In our judgment, Mr Carlisle is right. The word 'undertaking' means 'enterprise' or 'business'. The cleaning, repair and maintenance of plant, machinery and buildings necessary for carrying on business is part of the conduct of the undertaking, whether it is done by the employer's own employees or by independent contractors. If there is a risk of injury to the health and safety of the persons not employed by the employer, whether to the contractor's men or members of the public, and, a fortiori, if there is actual injury as a result of the conduct of that operation there is prima facie liability, subject to the defence of reasonable practicability.

It is to be noted that there is no similar provision in the 1974 Act to the old s 161 of the 1961 Act. Although under s 36 of the 1974 Act, where the commission of the offence under the Act is due to the act or default of some other person than the original person charged, that other person shall be guilty of the offence; but it seems that such a person is guilty in addition to and not in substitution for the first person charged.

But the question of control may be very relevant to what is reasonably practicable. In most cases the employer/principal has no control over how a competent or expert contractor does the work. It is one of the reasons why he employs such a person—that he has the skill and expertise, including knowledge of appropriate safety precautions which he himself may not have. He may be entitled to rely on the contractor to see that the work is carried out safely, both so far as the contractor's workmen are concerned and others, including his own employees or members of the public; and he cannot be expected to supervise them to see that they are applying the necessary safety precautions. It may not be reasonably practicable for him to do other than rely on the independent contractor.

But there are cases where it is reasonably practicable for the employer to give instructions how the work is to be done and what safety measures are to be taken. Examples of such cases are the *Swan Hunter* case [1982] 1 All ER 264, [1981] ICR 831, where the shipbuilders were aware of the special hazards, *McArdle's* case [1967] 1 All ER 583, [1967] 1 WLR 356, where co-ordination of the activities of sub-contractors was necessary for the safety of their men and cases involving defects in plant provided for use of the contractor's men or hazards in the premises of which they may not be aware, though these cases may fall under the specific provisions of s 4 of the 1974 Act.

The question of what is reasonably practicable is a matter of fact and degree in each case. It will depend on a number of factors so far as concerns operations carried out by independent contractors; what is reasonably practicable for a large organisation employing safety officers or engineers contracting for the services of a small contractor on routine operations may differ markedly from what is reasonably practicable for a small shopkeeper employing a local builder on activities on which he has no expertise. The nature and gravity of the risk, the competence and experience of the workmen, the nature of the precautions to be taken are all relevant considerations.

In our judgment, the ingredients of the offence are that the accused is (1) an employer (2) who so conducts his undertaking (3) as to expose to risk to health or safety (4) a person not employed by him (5) who may be affected by such conduct of the accused's undertaking. Where injury in fact results, as in this case, the position can be more shortly stated. (1) and (2) are the same (3) as to injure (4) a person not employed by him.

That is sufficient to dispose of the first ground of appeal since Mr Walker concedes that, if the wide approach is correct, there was clearly a case to answer. But we are also of the opinion that, even on the narrow approach, there was a case to answer. It is immaterial that prosecuting counsel advanced the case on the wider basis—which on this hypothesis can be said to be wrong—if in fact the evidence showed that Octel had assumed a sufficient measure of control over the safety precautions that should be adopted by RGP's men. The documents to which we have referred, which were Octel's documents, on the face of them, showed that Octel was laying down what safety equipment should be used for the work and these did not include an air lamp. If Octel had wished to show that these documents were not what they appeared but were completed by Octel's employee acting, as Mr Walker put it, simply as an amanuensis for RGP, who specified clearly not only how the work was to be done but what safety precautions were to be adopted, then it was incumbent on them to call evidence to this effect.

In the second ground of appeal it is alleged that the judge misdirected the jury in a number of respects. We do not think it is necessary to deal with these criticisms in detail, because most of them proceed on the basis that the narrow approach, and not the wide approach, is correct in law. But even on the narrow approach, we are not persuaded that the judge misdirected the jury. For the reasons which we have given, he was entitled to take the view that the documents showed that Octel had assumed a measure of control; his comment to this effect was no more than comment and left the issue to the jury. In our judgment, the judge did adequately set out the ingredients of the offence, even though this may have involved doing little more than reading the section and the voluntary particulars.

The final ground of appeal is that the judge failed to sum up the case to the jury in a comprehensive manner; it is said that it was confused and confusing so that no reasonable jury could have correctly understood the issues. In some passages extraneous words have crept in; in others it appears that a word or words have been omitted. Even assuming the text is not corrupt, this is not unusual in a summing up which is often largely extempore. We think the sense of these passages is clear. Most of the criticisms that Mr Walker makes under this head were based on the proposition that the narrow approach was correct and that reliance should not be placed on the documents for the purpose of showing that Octel exercised control. We have carefully considered the structure and content of the summing up. In our judgment, a jury who had been carefully taken through the documents in the course of the trial would have had no difficulty in understanding the summing up or the issues they were required to decide.

The appeal is dismissed.

Appeal dismissed.

N P Metcalfe Esq   Barrister.

Brooks v Brooks

COURT OF APPEAL, CIVIL DIVISION

NEILL, HOFFMANN AND WAITE LJJ

16, 17 FEBRUARY, 26 MAY 1994

Variation of settlement (matrimonial causes) – Post-nuptial settlement – Pension scheme – Variation of husband's pension scheme on divorce – Pension scheme containing option allowing husband to surrender part of pension entitlement for benefit of spouse – Pension fund varied to make limited pension provision for wife – Whether pension scheme a post-nuptial settlement – Whether court having jurisdiction to vary husband's pension fund arrangements – Whether court should exercise its jurisdiction to vary scheme – Matrimonial Causes Act 1973, s 24(1)(c).

The husband and wife married in 1977, whereupon the wife gave up her job at her husband's request. The husband was the sole shareholder of a building company through which he had made pension fund arrangements secured by various policies. Legal title to the assets of the pension scheme set up in 1980 under one of the policies was vested with trustees, who were charged with the duty of applying those assets in accordance with its rules. Rule 1(e) of the scheme stipulated that the husband had a right at the date of retirement to surrender a portion of his pension entitlement for the benefit of any spouse of his and/or any other person whom the trustees might consider to be financially dependent on him. In 1989 the marriage broke down when the husband left his wife to live with another woman. At about the same time his company stopped trading and was later struck off the register. The wife petitioned for divorce and a few days later the husband charged his half share of the jointly owned matrimonial home to a bank for the company's debts to the extent of £100,000. The wife, who had no earning/income prospects beyond the state pension for which she would qualify at 60, applied to the court for the husband's pension scheme to be declared a post-nuptial settlement and varied in her favour pursuant to s 24(1)(c)[a] of the Matrimonial Causes Act 1973 on the ground that the pension scheme fund had been built up entirely during the marriage for the benefit of both parties. The husband's assets were limited to the pension funds, which had a total value of £440,000 (with a surplus of £166,000), and his share of the matrimonial home, which had a net value of £247,342. In addition, the husband was receiving income support and had liabilities of a £90,000 mortgage on his new home (which had a negative equity) and debts of £113,000, comprised mainly of the company's overdraft. The district judge treated the pension scheme as a post-nuptial settlement and varied it to provide the wife with a modest annuity and a pension to be paid from the time of the husband's death of one-fifth of the maximum pension available to him. The district judge further ordered that the matrimonial home be sold and that the husband pay the wife a lump sum of £150,000 from the net proceeds of sale and periodic payments of £4,000 pa. The husband appealed, contending (i) that the court had no jurisdiction to vary the pension scheme under s 24(1)(c) of the Act on the ground that the spouse's interest under the r 1(e) option was as a potential appointee under the power of the husband to surrender part of his pension

a   Section 24(1), so far as material, is set out at p 1076 h j, post

rights in her favour and, as such, that interest was not sufficient to render the scheme a post-nuptial settlement and (ii) that the relief granted was unduly favourable to the wife. The judge rejected the argument as to jurisdiction, but allowed the appeal to the extent that he reduced the lump sum payable to the wife to £110,000. The wife appealed from the downward variation order and the husband cross-appealed.

Held – (1) (Hoffmann LJ dissenting) A pension fund scheme which made provision for a husband, on retirement, to surrender a portion of his pension entitlement for the benefit of a spouse was a post-nuptial settlement for the purposes of s 24(1)(c) of the 1973 Act, since it was that power of surrender exercisable by the husband alone which gave the scheme the character of a settlement and it was the inclusion of a spouse within its objects which gave the settlement its nuptial element. The court accordingly had jurisdiction to vary the scheme in matrimonial proceedings to provide a limited pension for the wife on divorce. In practice, however, the court would be most unlikely, save in exceptional circumstances, to allow the variation power to be used to reduce or disturb the rights or potential rights of people outside the marriage. The touchstone test therefore would be to inquire whether any proposed variation of the pension arrangements would be liable to affect the rights of third parties and, if there was any such risk, the court would abandon consideration of any direct interference with the scheme under s 24 and would confine itself to making whatever use it could of its general powers to achieve a compensatory effect in the way envisaged under s 25(2)(h)[b] of the 1973 Act (see p 1076 *a* to *c*, p 1079 *b* to *f* and p 1087 *f* to *j*, post); dictum of Hill J in *Prinsep v Prinsep* [1929] P 225 at 232–233 and of Somervell LJ and of Denning LJ in *Lort-Williams v Lort-Williams* [1951] 2 All ER 241 at 245 considered; *Hargreaves v Hargreaves* [1926] All ER Rep 195 distinguished.

(2) On the facts, although the main purpose of the pension scheme was to provide a pension for the husband as an employee of the company, the husband's power under r 1(e) of the policy to surrender part of the benefits in favour of the wife if he so chose was sufficient to give the scheme the character of a post-nuptial settlement. The fact that the wife had a contingent interest only under the policy was immaterial. Moreover, since no third party rights arose (the bank having indicated that it did not intend to pursue the company for repayment of the loan), there was no objection in principle or policy to the husband's pension scheme being varied under s 24(1)(c) of the 1973 Act to make limited pension provision for the wife. The husband's cross-appeal would accordingly be dismissed. The wife's appeal from the judge's downward variation of the lump sum payment awarded to her on the sale of the former matrimonial home would also be dismissed as the criticisms advanced did not vitiate the judge's conclusions (see p 1079 *h* to p 1080 *a*, p 1081 *a* to *c e f* and p 1088 *f* to *h* post).

Decision of Ewbank J [1993] 4 All ER 917 affirmed.

Notes

For variation of a settlement on divorce, see 13 *Halsbury's Laws* (4th edn) paras 1136, 1138, and for cases on the subject, see 27(3) *Digest* (2nd reissue) 274–295, *10803–10939*.

---

b   Section 25(2)(h) is set out at p 1078 *b*, post

For the Matrimonial Causes Act 1973, ss 24, 25, see 27 *Halsbury's Statutes* (4th edn) (1992 reissue) 760, 763.

Cases referred to in judgments

Dormer (orse Ward) v Ward [1901] P 20, [1900–3] All ER Rep 363, CA.
Hargreaves v Hargreaves [1926] P 42, [1926] All ER Rep 195.
Le Marchant v Le Marchant [1977] 3 All ER 610, [1977] Fam 241, [1977] 1 WLR 559, CA.
Lort-Williams v Lort-Williams [1951] 2 All ER 241, [1951] P 395, CA.
Marsh v Marsh (1878) 47 LJP 34.
Milne v Milne [1981] 2 FLR 286, CA.
Parker v Parker [1972] 1 All ER 410, [1972] Fam 116, [1972] 2 WLR 21.
Prinsep v Prinsep [1929] P 225.
Richardson v Richardson (1978) 9 Fam Law 86, CA.
Ulrich v Ulrich and Felton [1968] 1 All ER 67, [1968] 1 WLR 180, CA.
Vallance v Vallance (1907) 77 LJP 33.

Cases cited or referred to in skeleton arguments

Ainsbury v Millington [1987] 1 All ER 929, [1987] 1 WLR 379n, HL.
Airedale NHS Trust v Bland [1993] 1 All ER 821, [1993] AC 789, HL.
Bosworthwick v Bosworthwick [1927] P 64, [1926] All ER Rep 198, CA.
Bown v Bown and Weston [1948] 2 All ER 778, [1949] P 91.
Browne's Policy, Re [1903] 1 Ch 188.
Callwell v Callwell (1860) 2 Sw & Tr 259, 164 ER 1274.
Cousins v Sun Life Assurance Society [1933] Ch 126, [1932] All ER Rep 404, CA.
E v E (financial provision) [1990] 2 FLR 233.
Edmonds v Edmonds [1965] 1 All ER 379, [1965] 1 WLR 58.
Egerton v Egerton [1949] 2 All ER 238, CA.
Gojkovic v Gojkovic (No 2) [1992] 1 All ER 267, [1992] Fam 40, CA.
Gulbenkian v Gulbenkian [1927] P 237.
Gunner v Gunner and Stirling [1948] 2 All ER 771, [1949] P 77.
Janion v Janion [1929] P 237n.
Jump v Jump (1883) 8 PD 159.
Leadbeater v Leadbeater [1985] FLR 789.
Marsh v Marsh [1993] 2 All ER 794, [1993] 1 WLR 744, CA.
Melvill v Melvill and Woodward [1930] P 159, [1930] All ER Rep 79, CA.
Morgan v Morgan and Kirby [1923] P 1.
Parrington v Parrington [1951] 2 All ER 916.
Pepper (Inspector of Taxes) v Hart [1993] 1 All ER 42, [1993] AC 593, HL.
Smith v Smith [1945] 1 All ER 584.
Sun Life Assurance Co of Canada v Jervis [1944] 1 All ER 469, [1944] AC 111, HL.
Thrells Ltd (in liq) v Lomas [1993] 2 All ER 546, [1993] 1 WLR 456.
Worsley v Worsley (1869) LR 1 P & D 648.

Appeal and cross-appeal

Anne Brooks (the wife) appealed with leave from the decision of Ewbank J ([1993] 4 All ER 917, [1993] Fam 322) made on 2 April 1993 whereby he ordered that the decision of District Judge Plumstead dated 10 December 1992 in ancillary proceedings whereby she ordered, inter alia, (i) that the former matrimonial home be sold and out of the net proceeds of sale the sum of £150,000 be paid to the wife with the balance to the respondent husband, Douglas Ernest Brooks, (ii) that the husband pay the wife periodical payments of £4,000 pa from 1 November 1992 during the parties' joint lives or until the wife's remarriage and (iii) that the trust dated 14 January 1980 under which the husband's company, D E Brooks Ltd, was appointed trustee of his pension scheme be varied under s 24(1)(c) of the Matrimonial Causes Act 1973 to provide the wife with an annuity of £2,618 pa and, after the husband's death, with a pension being one-fifth of the maximum pension available to him, be itself varied so as to provide, inter alia, that the wife receive the sum of £110,000 from the proceeds of sale of the former matrimonial home. The husband cross-appealed contending principally that the court had no jurisdiction to vary the pension fund under s 24(1)(c) of the 1973 Act and that for policy reasons such variation should not be made by a court in the absence of legislation to that effect. The facts are set out in the judgment of Waite LJ.

Martin Pointer (instructed by *Paisner & Co*) for the wife.
John Elvidge (instructed by *Girlings,* Canterbury) for the husband.

Cur adv vult

26 May 1994. The following judgments were delivered.

WAITE LJ (giving the first judgment at the invitation of Neill LJ). This appeal arises from the breakdown of a marriage when the parties were in middle age. The husband is in his sixties and is eligible for substantial benefits from a pension fund. Those include an option to have part of his entitlement applied in providing a pension for a wife. One consequence of the divorce is that the wife has lost all possibility of having that discretion exercised in her favour. She claimed successfully however in financial proceedings against the husband that his pension scheme had the character of a post-nuptial settlement, and on that basis obtained an order varying the pension terms so as to give her vested and indefeasible pension rights of her own. The major questions arising on the appeal are whether the court had jurisdiction to vary the husband's pension fund arrangements; and, if it did, whether it was a misuse of jurisdiction to do so.

The circumstances (to state them first in summary) are that the husband and wife are now aged 64 and 56. He owned a building business of which the wife was for a time an employee. The business had been run through a company effectively owned by the husband, but the company had ceased to trade. During its years of trading the company had established a pension fund for the benefit of the husband which was substantially in surplus. The terms of the fund allowed provision to be made on the husband's nomination for a spouse. The former matrimonial home had an appreciable equity. The husband's new home, by contrast, was subject to a mortgage in excess of its value. The district judge found that the husband had run down his assets deliberately to defeat the wife's claims, and he failed to satisfy the district judge that he had fully disclosed to the wife and to the court such assets as remained to him. The wife had no earning or income prospects beyond the state widow's pension for which she would qualify at 60.

District Judge Plumstead held that she was entitled to treat the pension fund arrangements as a post-nuptial settlement entered into by the husband. She varied the trusts of the scheme and policy which governed it by inserting firstly an immediate annuity for the wife and secondly a dependant's pension payable in the event of his predeceasing her. The former matrimonial home was

ordered to be sold, and the proceeds divided in the proportions of £150,000 to
the wife and the balance to the husband. All the wife's costs were to be paid by
the husband.

The husband appealed against those orders, both generally on the ground
that the provision made for the wife was excessive, and specifically on the
ground that there was no jurisdiction to vary the pension fund provision.
Ewbank J on appeal varied the district judge's order by reducing the wife's
share of the proceeds of sale of the home and also reducing the amount of costs
for which the husband would be liable (see [1993] 4 All ER 917, [1993] Fam 322).
He refused, however, to disturb the order varying the trusts of the pension fund
scheme.

There is now before this court, in consequence, firstly an appeal by the wife
against the judge's reduction of the wife's share of the sale proceeds of the
former matrimonial home and secondly (by respondent's notice) a cross-appeal
by the husband against the variation of the pension fund policy.

The governing legislation can be summarised in this way. The powers of
capital disposition conferred on the court by the Matrimonial Causes Act 1973
are wide-ranging. There is a general duty, when looking to achieve fairness
between the parties (and where there are children giving effect to their best
interests), to apply the principles laid down by ss 25 and 25A. Subject to that
constraint, however, a high degree of flexibility is allowed to the court. Lump
sums of capital may be ordered to be paid by one spouse to the other, and
property vested in one may be ordered to be transferred into the name of the
other. There is power, in certain circumstances, to rewrite the trusts of
settlements under which a spouse is a beneficiary. The extent of that power is
defined by s 24(1) of the 1973 Act, which includes amongst the adjustment
orders which the court is authorised to make at divorce:

> '... (c) an order varying for the benefit of the parties to the marriage and
> of the children of the family or either or any of them any ante-nuptial or
> post-nuptial settlement ... made on the parties to the marriage.'

The husband and wife were 47 and 38 respectively when they married in
January 1977. It was a second marriage for them both. Their matrimonial
home, 8 Sunning Avenue, Sunningdale, was purchased initially by the husband
in his sole name and transferred into the joint names of the spouses in 1989.
The wife did not work (by the husband's wish) but was paid a salary for
nominal services by his builders' business. That business was owned by a
company, D E Brooks Ltd (the company), of which (it is common ground) the
husband is the sole effective shareholder.

Through the company the husband made pension fund arrangements
secured by various policies of which it is necessary only to describe one. On 14
January 1980 the Equitable Life Assurance Society (the society) entered into an
arrangement with the company and with the husband to which I shall refer
hereafter as 'the scheme'. Legal title to the assets of the scheme was shortly
afterwards vested in trustees charged with the duty of applying those assets in
accordance with the rules of the scheme (the rules). The assets in question are
those arising under the policy taken out with the society to fund the scheme
(the policy). The scheme, the policy and the rules were all in a form approved
by the Inland Revenue. The trustees were Mr Moses (the husband's
accountant) and Mrs Evelyn King. I can summarise the gist of the scheme and
of the rules (with acknowledgment to the help given by the affidavit of Mr Mark
McKeown, a solicitor specialising in pension funds) as follows.

Rule 1 deals (by paras (a) to (c)) with the benefits payable to the husband in the event of his retirement on reaching the normal retirement date—specified as the age of 65—and with the contingencies of his retirement before or after that date. In each case he is said to be entitled to 'such pension as the policy will then provide'. Those benefits are expressed to be subject to the limitations imposed by later provisions of the rules (the Inland Revenue maxima).

Rule 1(e) provides:

> '*Optional Form of Pension*
> You will be entitled to elect at the date of your retirement to surrender a portion of the pension to which you would otherwise be entitled in order to provide a non-commutable and non-assignable deferred pension for any one or more of your spouse or any other person whom the Employer may consider to be in any way financially dependent on you, such pension to be payable to such spouse or other dependant for life from the date of your death ...'

Under the rules (as amended in terms set out in the trust deed) the reference in r 1(e) to 'the Employer' is to be taken as meaning the trustees. The effect, accordingly, of r 1(e) is that the husband has the right at the date of retirement to surrender a portion of his pension entitlement for the benefit of any spouse of his and/or any other person whom the trustees may consider to be financially dependent upon him.

Rule 7(c) provides that if and to the extent that the value of the policy may exceed the ceiling of benefit permitted by the Inland Revenue maxima, the excess will be refunded to the employer by the surrender of part or the whole of the policy to the insurer. The expression 'the Employer' for the purposes of para (e) has the primary meaning given to it in the society's letter of 14 January 1980 initiating the scheme and means the company.

The company made significant contributions to the scheme for a number of years. The marriage was happy at first, and the wife conceded in evidence that the husband had been a generous provider. He gave her presents of jewellery and furnished the house very comfortably. She was able to build up a nest egg of invested savings of her own. In the spring of 1989, however, the husband met a very much younger woman with whom he started a relationship, and he left the wife in June of that year.

The district judge made these findings about his attitude in regard to the maintenance of the wife after separation. At first he was cavalier, saying that she could take her half share of the matrimonial home (which had an equity of nearly £250,000) but that was all: she would have to find work to support herself. Later he was deceitful, attempting to charge the Sunningdale home behind her back. Finally, after she had thwarted those attempts and obtained injunctive relief against him in November 1989, he became defiant. In January 1990 he caused the company to cease to trade. By then he had surrendered life policies for a consideration of £41,480, and had purchased a home of his own (called 6 Cross Ashes) at a total cost of £122,000 for which he obtained a mortgage of £90,000. In February 1990 he asserted that he was without means and claimed state benefit in the form of income and mortgage support. In March 1990 he was granted legal aid in these proceedings. He defaulted in the payments of maintenance pending suit and the mortgage instalments and other outgoings on the Sunningdale home for which he had become liable under orders made and undertakings given when the injunction proceedings had been

)efore the court. He nevertheless continued to live on a scale out of all
)roportion to his income, which he financed by running up a large debit
)alance on the company's overdraft account and incurring substantial credit
:ard indebtedness.

At the hearing, the parties made very different impressions on the district
-udge. She found the wife to be fair and reliable. The husband she found to
-ave been an unreliable and at times untruthful witness, saying that she was far
.from satisfied that he had made a full and frank disclosure of his assets.

The asset and potential income position of the spouses with which the court
-was required to deal at that hearing was the following.

EARNING POTENTIAL

The husband was found by the district judge to be still capable of working
and earning. The wife was found to have no future prospect of work, and no
income prospect until she qualifies for a state pension at age 60.

ASSETS

8 Sunning Avenue—market value £280,000 less mortgage (£22,658) and assumed costs of a sale (£10,000)	£247,342
Wife's remaining savings	£3,900
Husband's remaining insurance policies	£15,275
6 Cross Ashes—market value £80,000 subject to outstanding mortgage (including arrears) of £111,531, representing a 'negative equity' or net liability of	£31,531

THE PENSION FUND POSITION

The scheme was not the only pension fund arrangement into which the
husband had entered. The full position was summarised in the affidavit of Mr
Geoffrey Bernstein, a consulting actuary, as follows (the figures being those
which he updated to March 1993):

Valuation of funds

Abbey Life retirement annuities	£18,978
The society scheme	£255,606
Allied Dunbar EPP	£155,586
Allied Dunbar retirement annuity	£9,834
Total (round figures)	£440,000

Maximum benefits

Treating the husband as having retired on 27 January 1990 when the company ceased trading, the maximum benefits now payable to him are	Pension of £23,076 pa
	OR
	lump sum of £40,483
	plus reduced pension of £19,396 pa

Capital cost of providing maximum benefits

Cost of index-linked pension at £19,396 pa	£234,000
Lump sum	£40,000
Total	£274,000

Surplus value of pension funds in excess of
permitted Inland Revenue maxima
  Difference between total value (£440,000)
    and permitted maxima (£274,000)
    produces a total surplus of   £166,000

THE DESTINATION OF THE SURPLUS
  The company has not only ceased to trade. On 29 April 1992 it was struck of
the register. The 'employer' entitled to receive the surplus from the insure:
thus no longer exists as a corporate entity. An application to the Companie:
Court to restore the company to the register would result in the company being
put in funds to the extent of the surplus (£166,000) but would also have the
effect of restoring the claim of the bank (believed to be the company's sole
creditor) to be repaid the amount of the company's overdraft (£100,00(
according to the finding of the district judge). The net surplus would then be
payable to the husband as (effectively) the sole shareholder on a members
voluntary winding up of the revived company. It would, however, be subject
to tax in his hands at 40%.

THE COSTS OF THE PROCEEDINGS
  These were estimated at the hearing before the district judge to amount
already to £100,000. She made a finding that this unusually high figure was
mainly due to the husband's unco-operative attitude to the proceedings,
including obstructiveness in giving discovery.
  I have mentioned already that the wife was for a time an employee of the
company. The district judge was invited by the wife's advisers to consider an
ingenious proposal for taking advantage of that employment history in a way
that would be tax efficient, acceptable to the Inland Revenue and relatively
inexpensive for the husband. Mr Bernstein advised that pension provision for
the wife as an ex-employee could properly take the following form:

  'Assuming that she has no other significant pension entitlements (apart
  from the State scheme), Mrs Brooks could receive a maximum pension in
  respect of her employment with [the company] of £2,618 p.a. payable
  immediately. Alternatively she could have a tax-free lump sum of £5,891
  together with a reduced pension of £2,127 p.a. I have estimated that the
  cost of purchasing an annuity of the latter amount, with pension increases
  in line with the retail prices index, together with the cost of the lump sum
  payment would be £40,000. This can be met from the surplus within the
  pension before it is refunded. Such a pension would be within the Inland
  Revenue's normal limits in respect of Mrs Brooks own employment and I
  would not anticipate any objection from the Inland Revenue to her being
  provided with such a pension.'

  Although, as I shall indicate, the husband strenuously resisted this proposal
both on the ground that the court lacked jurisdiction to impose it and (if there
was jurisdiction) on the merits, no procedural objection was taken. On
representation, some thought was given by the parties' advisers to the question
whether the trustees ought formally to have been joined as respondents, but
that was resolved by Mr Elvidge, counsel for the husband, being given
instructions (even though they were not formally before the court) to oppose
the claim on behalf of the trustees. The husband's solicitors obtained

confirmation for the purpose of this appeal hearing that the bank, as creditor of the company, was content to bide its time and did not wish to be involved in any proceedings at this stage. There did not appear to be any other third party who might have an interest in resisting the claim to award the wife a pension under the scheme.

The district judge was attracted by the proposal that the wife should have pension benefits conferred on her on the lines of Mr Bernstein's advice. She accordingly stated that she would treat the scheme with the society as being a post-nuptial settlement which was capable of being varied to give effect to that proposal.

The district judge's final order, dated 10 December 1992, directed that the former (Sunningdale) matrimonial home should be sold, and the net proceeds of sale divided as to £150,000 to the wife and the balance (approximately £100,000) to the husband. The husband was ordered to pay the wife periodic maintenance at the rate of £4,000 pa. He was also ordered to pay all the wife's costs. In regard to the scheme, the order provided as follows:

'The Trust dated 14th January 1980 under which [the company] was appointed the trustee of the pension scheme which currently is administered by [the society] under [the policy] be varied so as to provide as follows: (a) A proportion of the funds be allocated to provide benefits to the [wife]; the proportion in question being such sum as will with effect from the 1st December 1992 and for her lifetime provide the [wife] with an annuity of £2,618 per annum, but (i) with the [wife] having the right to effect immediate commutation [the order in error reads 'communication'] to a lump sum of such part thereof as may be permitted by the Inland Revenue (such lump sum being then paid from the trust) and (ii) with the pension being indexed in payment during the [wife's] lifetime in accordance with the Retail Prices Index; such pension being secured with a life office of her choice; and (b) A second element of the fund be also allocated to provide benefits for the [wife] and (in coordination with the purchase of a pension for the [husband]) invested with a life office of her choice; the proportion in question being such sum as may be required as at the date hereof to purchase a contingent dependant's pension payable upon the death of the [husband], the pension being one-fifth of the maximum pension available to him from all sources calculated (i) before any commutation by him (ii) before implementation of this order and (iii) upon the basis that he elects to bring all his pensions into payment immediately; and so that that dependant's pension shall be index-linked in accordance with the Retail Prices Index during the lifetime of the [wife].'

The husband, on appeal to Ewbank J, did not seek to overturn any of the district judge's findings of fact. Her order was attacked, however, on the ground that she had no jurisdiction to vary the terms of the scheme, because they did not constitute a 'post-nuptial settlement'; and also on the broader ground that the relief granted (including the costs order) had been unduly favourable to the wife and excessively harsh to the husband. The latter argument succeeded to the extent that the judge on appeal reduced the sum payable to the wife out of the proceeds of sale of the Sunningdale property from £150,000 to £110,000, and made the husband liable only for the costs of the wife incurred before the date when the husband became legally aided. He refused, however, to make any variation in the order against the pension fund and rejected the argument on jurisdiction, holding that the scheme represented a post-nuptial settlement which the court had power to vary.

Although the appeal from Ewbank J has reached this court in the form of an appeal by the wife from the downward variation order and a cross-appeal by the husband from the rejection of his argument on jurisdiction, it will be convenient to deal with the issue raised by the husband's cross-appeal first (because until that has been resolved the issue raised by the appeal as to the rightness of the other orders made by the courts below cannot properly be judged).

Mr Elvidge submits on the cross-appeal that: (1) the scheme established with the society on 14 January 1980 did not amount to a post-nuptial settlement, with the consequence that the court had no power to vary it under s 24(1) of the 1973 Act; alternatively (2) if (contrary to (1)) the court had theoretical power to vary the trusts arising under the scheme, it is a jurisdiction which judges should in practice decline to exercise. Pension funds have traditionally been treated as immune from disturbance by capital provision orders made in the matrimonial jurisdiction. Such immunity is supported by strong considerations of policy and should only be disturbed by Parliament.

I will deal with those submissions in turn.

(1) WAS THE SCHEME A POST-NUPTIAL SETTLEMENT?

The only reference in the scheme to the interests of a spouse are those arising under r 1(e). That is a provision entitling the husband at the date of retirement to surrender a portion of his pension rights in favour of a spouse—alone or in conjunction with any person accepted by the trustees as a financial dependant of the husband. The husband's spouse at the date of retirement has no right to call for such a surrender. She is merely an object of a non-fiduciary power which the husband is free to exercise or not as he thinks fit. The issue can thus be summarised in these very simple terms: so long as the wife remained a wife of the husband she had a potential interest (or spes) in the fund as a potential appointee under the power of the husband to surrender part of his pension rights in favour of herself—alone or in conjunction with any other person acceptable to the trustees as a financial dependant of the husband. Was that interest sufficient to render the scheme a post-nuptial settlement?

The authorities are summarised in *Jackson's Matrimonial Finance and Taxation* (5th edn, 1992) pp 258–259 as follows:

> 'The words "ante-nuptial settlement" and "post-nuptial settlement" are to be given a liberal construction wholly different from the more restricted meaning that would be given to them in a conveyancing instrument or in other contexts. The form of the settlement does not matter: it may be a settlement in the strictest sense of the term, it may be a covenant to pay by one spouse to the other, or by a third person to a spouse. One has to ask the question: Is the settlement upon the husband in the character of husband or upon the wife in the character of wife, or upon both in the character of husband and wife? What matters is that the settlement should provide for the financial benefit of one or other or both of the spouses as spouses and with reference to their married state. Nevertheless, some effect must be given to the word "settlement", and the courts have recognised that it is not to be given the same meaning as if all dispositions made by one spouse in favour of the other or by a third party in favour of a spouse had been expressly included in the scope of the word as used in

the sub-section. The payments made to a spouse in his or her character as a spouse give to those payments the qualification of nuptial, but it does not follow that every payment made and every present given by one spouse to the other constitutes settled property.'

No case has been found by counsel in which the court has been called upon to consider whether rights or potential benefits given to the spouse of an employee under a pension fund scheme had the effect of rendering the scheme a post-nuptial settlement for the purposes of s 24. The question has however been considered in the case of a spouse's interest under a life insurance policy. In *Lort-Williams v Lort-Williams* [1951] 2 All ER 241, [1951] P 395 a husband had taken out a whole-life policy on his life under s 11 of the Married Women's Property Act 1882 for the benefit of 'the widow or children or any of them of the assured in shares and proportions and interest and generally in such manner as the assured shall by will or deed ... appoint'. The policy was held to have been a post-nuptial settlement, so as to entitle a divorcing wife of the husband to apply for its variation. Somervell LJ said ([1951] 2 All ER 241 at 245, [1951] P 395 at 402):

'I agree that the wife's interests under this document are contingent and uncertain for it is dependent on certain factors, but it seems to me that, this document having been taken out during the married life—undoubtedly with the object of creating a fund from which the wife might benefit subject to the exercise of the power of appointment in her favour, it is, *prima facie*, a nuptial settlement in respect of the marriage then existing. It does not cease to be that because it also does something else ... Having regard to the words of the section, however, and applying ordinary common sense, I do not think that a settlement ceases to be a nuptial settlement—in this case a post-nuptial settlement—because in certain contingencies the wife of a subsequent marriage, if there is one, may be the person to take.'

Denning LJ said ([1951] 2 All ER 241 at 245, [1951] P 395 at 403):

'The word "settlement" ... is not used in the conveyancing sense. It includes any provision made by a husband for the future benefit of his wife, if it proceeds on the footing of the then existing marriage. It does not cease to be a settlement on her because the provision is, not absolute, but only contingent, nor does it cease to be a settlement on her because it may in its terms also be applicable for the benefit of a wife by a subsequent marriage.'

There are acknowledged differences between that case and the present. The policy with which the court was there concerned was effected under s 11 of the 1882 Act and was therefore by definition a policy whose whole raison d'être was to benefit a wife and/or children. Here the primary intention of the insurance is to benefit the husband, to which the r 1(e) option of part-surrender in favour of a wife is very much subsidiary. There the transaction was one of conventional life insurance. Here it is complicated by the fact that although the husband is the assured—in the sense that the benefits of the policy are related to his death or retirement—the policy itself is vested in trustees who have powers of their own to define beneficial entitlement (eg in regard to determining who is to be treated as a 'financial dependant' for the purposes of the r 1(e) option). There the whole proceeds of the policy devolved on the beneficiaries. Here the surplus benefits of the policy in excess of the Inland Revenue maxima belong, in the first instance at least, to a separate entity in the form of the company.

None of those, however, are differences which, in my judgment, affect the principle. It is the husband who is entitled to the benefits of the policy up to the ceiling of the Inland Revenue maxima, and it is he alone who within those limits has the power to surrender part of those benefits in favour of a spouse and/or other financial dependant. It is that power which gives the scheme the character of a settlement, and it is the inclusion of a spouse within its objects which gives the settlement its nuptial element. It makes no difference that under the r 1(e) option a spouse has a contingent interest only. I would hold, in agreement with the judge and district judge, that the principle of *Lort-Williams v Lort-Williams* applies to this case by analogy. The scheme amounted to a post-nuptial settlement.

(2) IS THE JURISDICTION TO VARY LIMITED ON POLICY GROUNDS?

Before coming to the arguments that were raised under this head, certain matters of general background should be mentioned.

The history of the jurisdiction

This was helpfully summarised in Mr Pointer's skeleton argument and is undisputed. When secular divorce was introduced into this country by the Matrimonial Causes Act 1857 it included a power to impose a settlement, for the benefit of the innocent spouse and the children of the marriage, upon any property to which a wife guilty of adultery was entitled (see s 45 of the 1857 Act). After that power had been held not to apply to interests under pre-existing settlements, the relevant power was substantially extended by s 5 of the Matrimonial Causes Act 1859, which provided:

'The Court after a final Decree of Nullity of Marriage or Dissolution of Marriage may inquire into the Existence of ante-nuptial or post-nuptial Settlements made on the Parties whose Marriage is the Subject of the Decree, and may make such Orders with reference to the Application of the whole or a Portion of the Property settled, either for the Benefit of the Children of the Marriage or of their respective Parents, as to the Court shall seem fit.'

With only minor changes of wording, that provision has continued through the process of re-enactment in successive Matrimonial Causes Acts down to the 1973 Act, where it now takes its place in s 24(1)(c), which at this point is worth repeating:

'(1) On granting a decree of divorce ... or at any time thereafter ... the court may make any one or more of the following orders, that is to say ... (c) an order varying for the benefit of the parties to the marriage and of the children of the family or either or any of them any ante-nuptial or post-nuptial settlement ... made on the parties to the marriage.'

The range of the jurisdiction

The authorities show that the court treated the jurisdiction from the outset as a wide one. It was not restricted to interests that had vested in possession: contingent, as well as purely discretionary, interests were included (see *Vallance v Vallance* (1907) 77 LJP 33). Nor was the power limited to variation of the rights of the respondent spouse: third party rights could be interfered with. Thus in *Marsh v Marsh* (1878) 47 LJP 34 the court was concerned with a respondent husband who had become bankrupt. That had brought into operation protective trusts under which his life interest under a settlement became subject to a discretion for the trustees to pay income or any part thereof for the maintenance and support of the husband and any wife or children of his. The settlement trustees sought to maintain against the husband's divorced wife that they were entitled in the exercise of that discretion to decline to make any payments of income to her. Hannen P said (at 36):

> 'In this state of things it appears to me that the Court is called upon to exercise its own judgment, whether some other application of the settled funds would not be more just and fitting than one dependent entirely on the will of the trustees if the Court leaves them in possession of their discretionary powers. It cannot control them, however arbitrary or unjust their disposition of the property may be, but it is the duty of the Court to protect the wife, and see that she does not suffer by reason of the misconduct of the husband. This can only be done by securing to her, not only as against her husband but against all other persons, such portions of the settled property as will be sufficient for her and their children's maintenance while they remain under her charge.'

He then proceeded to make an order that the trustees should pay the entire income of the settlement to the wife until remarriage with further provision for the children when they came of age.

Procedural features of the jurisdiction

Rule 2.59 of the Family Proceedings Rules 1991, SI 1991/1247, requires a copy of any application for an order for variation of a settlement to be served, together with the supporting affidavit, on the trustees of the settlement and the settlor if living, and on such other persons, if any, as the district judge may direct. All persons so served may file evidence in answer. The right for any such deponent to be heard in opposition to the claim is not expressly stated but is obviously implied.

Pension funds generally

A large proportion of the national wealth is held, as is well known, by trustees of pension funds. But there is great diversity as between one form of trust and another. Pension schemes come in all shapes and sizes. Some are self-administered. Others are earnings-related. Some are large, involving hundreds or more employees. Others may involve only a single employer and a single employee. All have to comply with complex statutory provisions to satisfy the requirements of the Inland Revenue, requirements which themselves vary according to the type of scheme involved. It was, no doubt, this elaboration and diversity within the structure of the pension fund industry that led the Law Commission, in the report and working papers which preceded the enactment of the 1973 Act, to conclude that although there are undoubted risks of unfairness when a non-working spouse loses through divorce the right to share in pension benefits earned by the working spouse, the problem could not be solved by giving the courts a generalised power to write new terms into pension schemes. It was proposed instead that the courts should be empowered to compensate spouses for loss of pension participation through lump sum and property adjustment orders: see the *Report on Financial Provision in Matrimonial Proceedings* (Law Com No 25) (1969). That proposal is implemented by s 25 of the 1973 Act, which includes in the matters to which the court is specifically required to have regard the following (by sub-s (2)(h)):

'... in the case of proceedings for divorce or nullity of marriage, the value to each of the parties to the marriage of any benefit (for example, a pension) which, by reason of the dissolution or annulment of the marriage, that party will lose the chance of acquiring.'

It is to be noted, however, that capital benefits accruing under a pension scheme are not to be regarded as immune from attack in the matrimonial jurisdiction once they have been acquired. In *Milne v Milne* [1981] 2 FLR 286, for example, an advance order was made, in a case where the husband was due to retire in ten years' time, that the wife should receive one-half of the lump sum entitlement to which he or his estate would become entitled at his retirement or earlier death in service.

Such is the background against which I now turn to consider the opposing arguments as to whether the court, assuming jurisdiction to vary the scheme as a post-nuptial settlement in the present case, was right or wrong in principle to have exercised that jurisdiction.

Mr Elvidge for the husband cites the advance provision ordered in *Milne v Milne* as marking the furthest extent to which any court has up to now been prepared to go in interfering with a spouse's pension entitlement. The usual and proper practice, he submits, is for the court to follow the path indicated by s 25(2)(h) of the 1973 Act and use the wide powers it already possesses of lump sum and transfer to achieve (in conformity with the policy advocated by the Law Commission) a compensatory provision for loss of prospective pension rights. As examples of that he cites *Parker v Parker* [1972] 1 All ER 410, [1972] Fam 116, *Le Marchant v Le Marchant* [1977] 3 All ER 610, [1977] Fam 241 and *Richardson v Richardson* (1978) 9 Fam Law 86. There is nothing, he submits, to distinguish the present case from the countless other cases where a spouse is given contingent rights under the other spouse's pension scheme. To allow the present order to stand would be to invite widespread confusion and uncertainty in the pension fund world.

Mr Pointer, counsel for the wife, submits that the court should look at each case on its merits. The essence of the present case is that the court is here dealing with settled funds subject to a discretion. There is no principle of policy which prevents the court from exercising its wide powers of variation under s 24(1)(c) of the 1973 Act to achieve fairness for the wife in the particular circumstances. Those circumstances include the fact that, subject to any claims of the bank against the surplus funds in excess of the Inland Revenue maxima, the husband is the sole person interested in the entire fund. There is no reason of principle why the court should not vary his interest to the limited extent ordered by the district judge and approved by Ewbank J.

The following principles should in my judgment be applied in determining where the right answer lies as between these opposing submissions.

(1) Private pension schemes are too numerous and too varied to be treated empirically as a class. Questions as to whether: (a) accession by a spouse to membership of a particular scheme will involve the creation of a post-nuptial settlement, or, if it does, (b) the scheme should be varied by the court in the

exercise of its powers under s 24(1)(c) can only be determined on an examination of the terms and circumstances of each particular pension arrangement.

(2) Given the broad interpretation adopted by the courts of a 'post-nuptial settlement' and the wide powers of variation conferred by the statute, it has to be accepted that many pension schemes in which provision is made for an employee's wife or widow would qualify technically as 'post-nuptial settlements' and would theoretically be open to invasion of their funds by the matrimonial jurisdiction. In practice, however, the courts would be most unlikely, save in very unusual and exceptional circumstances, to allow the variation power to be used to reduce or disturb the rights or potential rights of people outside the marriage. Any variation would be limited to the interests of the spouses concerned, and if it could be demonstrated by the fund managers that those rights were incapable of being varied without risk of interference with the interests of others, then it is highly improbable that the court would allow the variation jurisdiction to be used at all.

(3) The touchstone test, therefore, in the vast majority of cases in which the necessary nuptial element is established to bring the provisions of a particular scheme within range of the powers under s 24(1)(c) of the 1973 Act, will be to inquire as to any proposed variation of the pension arrangements whether it would be liable to affect the rights of third parties. If there is any risk that it might, the court will abandon consideration of any direct interference with the scheme terms and will confine itself to making whatever use it can of its general powers with a view to achieving a compensatory effect in the way that is envisaged in s 25(2)(h) of the 1973 Act.

(4) The threshold for determining whether a post-nuptial settlement is involved in, and, if so, whether the court should assume jurisdiction to vary, a particular scheme will normally be the first appointment before the district judge in the hearing of the applicant spouse's financial relief claim. If it is not immediately apparent to the district judge, from the particulars deposed to under r 2.59 of the 1991 rules, whether the rights of persons other than the spouses and their children would be affected by any variation of the relevant pension arrangement, he or she will direct the necessary information to be provided. If it then, or later, appears that third party interests may be affected, directions will be given for the trustees and/or other persons potentially affected to be served with the application and supporting evidence under r 2.59(3). If reasonable objection is then made to the proposed variation by the third parties potentially affected, it is most unlikely that the variation application would be allowed to proceed further.

When the limited variation ordered in the present case is regarded in the light of those principles, it appears to me to pass safely through the narrow mesh in a broad net. If the reasonable assumption is made that the bank as the company's sole creditor will eventually be paid off, the reality of the case is that the husband is entitled (either as pension right holder or as ultimate recipient of the surplus) to the entirety of the pension funds. No third party rights arise. The effect of r 1(e) of the scheme is (for reasons already stated) to subject that portion of the funds which is available to be applied for pension purposes within the Inland Revenue maxima to the status of a post-nuptial settlement. I can see no objection of principle or policy to the scheme being varied under the power under s 24(1)(c) of the 1973 Act in order to make limited pension provision for the wife in the form ordered by the district judge and upheld by the judge on appeal. I would therefore dismiss the cross-appeal.

The appeal itself can be dealt with much more shortly. This was a marriage which had been a second marriage for both parties and had lasted for some 12 years. There are no children. The husband's contribution to the marriage (whatever be said of his conduct after it had broken down) was found to have been satisfactory. The wife gave up a job and her own home to go and live with him and now has no independent earning prospects. The effect of the district judge's order was to give the wife an income of approximately £6,700 pa (made up of £4,000 periodic payments ordered against the husband and £2,700 pension). That falls to be compared to the husband's pension (post variation of the scheme) of £19,400 (rising at age 65 to £26,000) which will leave him with some £15,500 after making the periodic payments to the wife. The wife has no capital assets apart from her interest in 8 Sunning Avenue, beyond a fund of £4,000 obtained from the sale of her porcelain collection. The husband has his pension lump sum (£40,000), life policies worth £15,250, and his present home, 6 Cross Ashes. His liabilities are his overdraft of £13,700 and the notional deficit represented by the negative equity on 6 Cross Ashes, which at current values amounts to some £30,000. It is probably realistic to assume that by the time the surplus pension fund (reduced by the amount required to provide the wife's pension provision) will have passed through the hands of the (revived) company and reached the husband after deduction of the bank's overdraft, there would be little or nothing left for the husband to enjoy from that source. On that basis, the effect of the district judge's order giving the wife £150,000 from the proceeds of sale of 8 Sunning Avenue and the husband the balance of £97,300 was to leave the husband with net capital (so far as disclosed to the court) of £97,300 and the wife with £154,000.

Ewbank J regarded that as unduly favourable to the wife, even making allowance for the finding of the district judge that the husband was still not being wholly truthful about his assets. The effect of his variation of the order (reducing the wife's share of the proceeds of 8 Sunning Avenue to £110,000) was therefore to leave the husband with net capital (so far as disclosed) of £137,000 and the wife with £114,000.

Mr Pointer attacks that variation. There were errors on the figures. The judge had incorrectly, for example, described the husband as having paid £110,000 for his new house, whereas the price he actually paid was £125,000. In describing the husband as having suffered a diminution of the pension fund surplus of £70,000 to provide for the wife's pension, the judge had failed to take account of the fact that the net cost to the husband was 60% of that figure (because that proportion of the surplus would otherwise have been subject to tax in his hands). The judge had moreover placed too high a figure on the husband's prospective liability (calculated down to the date of his legal aid certificate) for the wife's costs.

The judge is also said to have substituted his own views on house values for those of the district judge without any fresh evidence to justify them. The anticipated cost of alternative housing for the wife in the Sunningdale area had been gone into very thoroughly by the district judge. No fresh evidence was produced on that issue to the judge. There was therefore no basis, it is claimed, for Ewbank J to find (as he did) that '£110,000 would be a fair figure for the wife and would meet her needs'.

It is important to bear in mind the nature of the proceeding before Ewbank J. It was an appeal by way of rehearing. The judge was required to give weight to the decision of the district judge, but he was also entitled (and bound) to exercise his own discretion. He plainly took the view that the overall picture left by the district judge's order was unduly favourable in capital terms to the wife. Mr Pointer is certainly entitled to make the points he does about the mathematical detail of some of the judge's reasoning. None of it in my view vitiates the judge's final conclusion. Nor can this experienced judge be criticised for drawing on his own knowledge of the current state of the housing market. Even if the matters complained of did amount to a misdirection (so as to give this court a discretion to substitute an order of its own) I would not myself think it right to award the wife more from the proceeds of sale of the Sunningdale home than the £110,000 ordered by the judge.

So far as costs are concerned, it is common ground that the husband was legally aided from 19 March 1990 (the hearing before the district judge was on 23 October 1992 and before Ewbank J on 2 April 1993). Ewbank J was not, unfortunately, given the correct particulars as to the date when the husband became legally aided. The order that he made, namely that the husband should pay the wife's costs down to the date when he became legally aided, seems to me nevertheless to be entirely the right order in the circumstances. I would not disturb it. The result is that the costs of each party from that date will be the subject of a charge in favour of the Legal Aid Board upon the home they occupy (including any new home bought by the wife). Enforcement of the charge will be deferred under regs 96 and 97 of the Civil Legal Aid (General) Regulations 1989, SI 1989/339, and it does not seem to me to be practicable or desirable to achieve any other result than that.

I would accordingly dismiss both the appeal and the cross-appeal.

HOFFMANN LJ. I had prepared a full judgment explaining why I thought that the pension scheme was not a post-nuptial settlement and why, even if it was, the judge should not have made provision for the wife out of the surplus in the fund. But since Neill and Waite LJJ take a different view, I can state my position quite briefly.

(1) A settlement is 'post-nuptial' if it confers benefits 'upon the husband in the character of husband or on the wife in the character of wife, or upon both in the character of husband and wife' (see *Prinsep v Prinsep* [1929] P 225 at 232).

(2) The pension scheme was a settlement by the company which conferred benefits upon Mr Brooks solely in the character of employee.

(3) The scheme conferred no benefit whatever upon the wife, whether vested or contingent. Instead it conferred upon the husband as employee the benefit of being entitled, if he so elected at retirement date, to surrender part of his pension entitlement in exchange for a pension payable after his death to a spouse or other dependant.

(4) The scheme was therefore not a post-nuptial settlement although it arguably gave Mr Brooks power to create a post-nuptial settlement of part of his own interest by election at retirement date (see *Dormer (orse Ward) v Ward* [1901] P 20, [1900–3] All ER Rep 363 and *Hargreaves v Hargreaves* [1926] P 42, [1926] All ER Rep 195).

(5) The fact that the latter two cases concerned family settlements made before contemplation of the marriage in question was not determinative. They decided that a mere non-fiduciary power to confer a benefit upon a wife only

enabled the principal beneficiary to create an ante-nuptial or post-nuptial settlement if he chose to do so. It did not (even after the exercise of the power) give that character to the original settlement. The decisions would have been the same if the original family settlements had been made after marriage.

(6) *Lort-Williams v Lort-Williams* [1951] 2 All ER 241, [1951] P 395 was a settlement under the Married Women's Property Act 1882 under which the wife was entitled to the whole fund contingently upon her surviving the husband as his widow without issue. The decision of the Court of Appeal i authority for the propositions that (a) 'settlement' has a wide meaning; (b) the question of whether a settlement is 'ante-nuptial' or 'post-nuptial' is decided a at the date of the settlement; and (c) a contingent interest conferred upon a wife as such is sufficient. None of these points is relevant in this case.

(7) *Marsh v Marsh* (1878) 47 LJP 34 and *Vallance v Vallance* (1907) 77 LJP 3. both concerned traditional marriage settlements which plainly conferred benefits upon husband and wife as such.

(8) Even if the pension scheme was a 'post-nuptial settlement', the trusts expressly limited the interest of husband and wife to the maximum allowed under Inland Revenue rules. The rest of the fund belonged to the company.

(9) The fact that the husband was shareholder and director is irrelevant. The company was insolvent and had been struck off for not filing returns. Its assets belonged in theory to the Crown as bona vacantia and in practice (subject to a petition to restore) to its creditors, the bank and the Inland Revenue.

(10) It was not a proper exercise of the judge's discretion to provide for the wife out of someone else's money.

I would therefore allow the cross-appeal.

NEILL LJ. For countless married couples an occupational pension together with the state pension will provide the income on which the couple will live after retirement. Comparatively few couples have other savings which are likely to produce a significant income. Furthermore, for many couples it is the husband's occupational pension which will be the source of this retirement income both during his lifetime and, if the scheme provides for a widow's pension, after his death. In the future the position may change as more and more women obtain employment which is sufficiently well paid to provide them with their own occupational pensions. At present, however, the general imbalance in earnings between men and women means that a very large number of women will depend for their income after their husband's death on widows' pensions resulting from the husband's employment.

It is against this background that one has to examine the position of a wife when there is a divorce. It is a problem which has engaged the attention of those concerned with law reform for many years. For example, in *Matrimonial and Related Proceedings—Financial Relief* (Law Com Working Paper No 9) (1967) the matter was addressed in these terms in para 182:

'There is no doubt that one matter on which there is strong public feeling is the loss of a potential widow's pension that a wife may suffer if she is divorced by or divorces her husband. She may have been married for 20 years or more during which the husband has been a member of a superannuation scheme under which the wife, if she survives him, would be entitled to a pension or lump sum, or, if not entitled, would be the likely recipient of benefits either at the discretion of the trustees or as a result of a nomination by the husband. On the dissolution of the marriage her prospective rights or expectations are normally destroyed, since she can no longer become his widow ... It should be borne in mind, however, that if the wife is divorced while young (and most divorces affect women under 35) the probability is that unless she is handicapped by the care of young children she will be able to find pensionable employment and may well re-marry in due course and thereby acquire a pension expectancy in right of her new husband. When that occurs there is little hardship if she forfeits her expectancy in right of her former husband. The real hardship arises in respect of women left with children to bring up and, more especially, in respect of the older women—those who are 45 or older when divorced. Statistics show that these have a poor expectation of remarriage so that if they lose their hope of an occupational pension in right of the first husband they are likely to lose all hope of an occupational pension; even if they can find pensionable employment, which may not be easy at their age, the pension is likely to be small.'

I turn therefore to the facts of the present case which I can state shortly because of the full account given by Waite LJ in his judgment.

The husband was born in July 1929. He is now 64. The wife was born in February 1938. She is now 56. The parties were married on 6 January 1977. The pension scheme which was established by the Equitable Life Assurance Society's policy No P2007023 was set up in 1980.

The wife issued her petition for divorce on 8 September 1989. At that date the parties had been married for twelve and a half years. The wife was then 51.

On 31 January 1990 D E Brooks Ltd (the company) ceased trading. On 29 April 1992 the company was struck off the register and dissolved pursuant to s 652(5) of the Companies Act 1985.

The rules of the Equitable Life policy set out the benefits payable to the husband on retirement. These were expressed to be subject to the limitations imposed by r 4 of the rules, which contained provisions restricting the total benefits to be provided so that they should not exceed the Inland Revenue limits.

By r 7 it was provided that if at any time a benefit became payable which was in excess of that permitted under the provisions of r 4 the value of the excess might be applied at the discretion of the trustees to augment any other benefit under the policy or to provide benefits in addition to those under the policy, provided that no benefit should be provided which was in excess or in addition to the maximum benefit set out in r 4. It was further provided by r 7(c) that any excess value of the policy should be refunded to the company by the surrender of part or the whole of the policy to the insurer.

I come now to r 1(e), which was in these terms:

'*Optional Form of Pension*
You will be entitled to elect at the date of your retirement to surrender a portion of the pension to which you would otherwise be entitled in order to provide a non-commutable and non-assignable deferred pension for any one or more of your spouse or any other person whom the Employer may consider to be in any way financially dependent on you, such pension to be payable to such spouse or other dependant for life from the date of your death provided that (i) any such deferred pension or the aggregate thereof if more than one is provided shall not exceed the pension you retain

(including the pension equivalent of any lump sum taken under t
provisions of paragraph (f)(i) of this Rule) but may otherwise vary in su
ratio to the pension you retain as you elect, and (ii) if your spouse or oth
dependant shall thereafter predecease you your pension as reduced by a
such surrender and no more shall continue to be paid to you.'

The first question which arises for decision on this part of the case is wheth
the Equitable Life policy constitutes a post-nuptial settlement within t
meaning of s 24(1)(c) of the Matrimonial Causes Act 1973. Section 24(1), so f
as is material, is in these terms:

'On granting a decree of divorce ... or at any time thereafter ... the cou
may make ... (c) an order varying for the benefit of the parties to tl
marriage and of the children of the family or either or any of them a
ante-nuptial or post-nuptial settlement (including such a settlement ma
by will or codicil) made on the parties to the marriage ...'

The court's jurisdiction to alter settlements on divorce was original
introduced by s 45 of the Matrimonial Causes Act 1857 and was extended
pre-existing settlements by s 5 of the Matrimonial Causes Act 1859. Th
jurisdiction to vary such settlements is therefore of long standing and it h
been exercised in a manner which has given a liberal interpretation to the wor
'settlement'. The present position is clearly summarised in a passage
Jackson's Matrimonial Finance and Taxation (5th edn, 1992) pp 258–259:

'The words "ante-nuptial settlement" and "post-nuptial settlement" a
to be given a liberal construction wholly different from the more restricte
meaning that would be given to them in a conveyancing instrument or
other contexts. The form of the settlement does not matter: it may be
settlement in the strictest sense of the term, it may be a covenant to pay b
one spouse to the other, or by a third person to a spouse. One has to as
the question: Is the settlement upon the husband in the character
husband or upon the wife in the character of wife, or upon both in th
character of husband and wife? What matters is that the settlement shoul
provide for the financial benefit of one or other or both of the spouses a
spouses and with reference to their married state. Nevertheless, som
effect must be given to the word "settlement", and the courts hav
recognised that it is not to be given the same meaning as if all dispositior
made by one spouse in favour of the other or by a third party in favour
a spouse had been expressly included in the scope of the word as used i
the sub-section. The payments made to a spouse in his or her character a
a spouse give to those payments the qualification of nuptial, but it does n
follow that every payment made and every present given by one spouse t
the other constitutes settled property.'

In the course of the argument we were referred to the decision of the Cour
of Appeal in *Lort-Williams v Lort-Williams* [1951] 2 All ER 241, [1951] P 395. I
that case the husband had taken out a whole-life policy on his own life unde
s 11 of the Married Women's Property Act 1882 (as amended). It was expresse
to be—

'effected for the benefit of the widow or children or any of them of th
assured in such shares and proportions and interest, and generally in sucl

manner as the assured shall by will or deed ... appoint or may have so appointed.'

ne case is distinguishable from the present case because the policy was in ms issued under s 11 of the 1882 Act and was therefore clearly for the benefit the wife and/or children. There are, however, passages in the judgments nich are of assistance.

It had been argued by counsel for the husband that the life policy did not nstitute a settlement because the interest of the wife was contingent; she had survive the husband and survive him as a widow, and, furthermore, if there ere children, she might take no interest at all if the husband appointed the hole fund to the children. It had also been argued that the life policy was not *nuptial* settlement because the document had no particular marriage in mind it was directed to 'the widow'. Somervell LJ dealt with these arguments as llows ([1951] 2 All ER 241 at 245, [1951] P 395 at 402):

> 'I agree that the wife's interests under this document are contingent and uncertain for it is dependent on certain factors, but it seems to me that, this document having been taken out during the married life—undoubtedly with the object of creating a fund from which the wife might benefit subject to the exercise of the power of appointment in her favour, it is, *prima facie*, a nuptial settlement in respect of the marriage then existing. It does not cease to be that because it also does something else ... I do not think that a settlement ceases to be a nuptial settlement—in this case a post-nuptial settlement—because in certain contingencies the wife of a subsequent marriage, if there is one, may be the person to take.'

enning LJ agreed. It is sufficient to refer to one sentence in his judgment 1951] 2 All ER 241 at 245, [1951] P 395 at 403):

> 'The word "settlement" ... is not used in the conveyancing sense. It includes any provision made by a husband for the future benefit of his wife, if it proceeds on the footing of the then existing marriage.'

In the present case the main purpose of the Equitable Life policy was to rovide a pension for the husband. It cannot be said therefore that, as in ort-Williams v Lort-Williams, the policy was taken out with the object of there eing a fund 'from which the wife might benefit subject to the exercise of the ower of appointment in her favour'. Indeed at the stage when the policy was sued the wife had no more than a prospect that at the date of his retirement ie husband might elect in accordance with r 1(e) of the policy to surrender a ortion of his pension in order to provide a deferred pension for her.

The wife's case is therefore less clear than that of Lady Lort-Williams, who, the marriage subsisted and she survived her husband, was almost certain to btain the benefit of the policy unless she and her husband had children and the usband appointed the whole fund in their favour.

On the other hand, one is entitled to look at the matter at the time when the cheme was established in 1980. At that time the parties had been married only hree years. The pension was designed to provide for the husband and the wife fter his retirement. In addition the scheme provided for a widow's pension if he husband decided to make the necessary election. The funds in the scheme vere therefore funds from which the wife might benefit. Moreover, it was a enefit which she was likely to receive if the marriage continued in being. She

was nearly ten years younger than her husband and had no other pensi
rights. If one had taken an overall view of the family finances in 1980 t
pension rights of the husband and the prospect that the wife might receive
widow's pension would have been important elements in any assessment of t
position. Though the husband's rights were as an employee of the compar
and not as a husband, the wife's prospects were prospects which she enjoyed
a wife.

The cases establish that one is not looking for a 'settlement' in the sense us
by conveyancers, though as Diplock LJ pointed out in *Ulrich v Ulrich and Felt*
[1968] 1 All ER 67 at 72, [1968] 1 WLR 180 at 188 the statutory language 'is mo
appropriate to marriages among the property-owning classes of the nineteen
century than to marriages ... today'. Thus, for example, where a matrimoni
home is said to constitute a settlement one looks to see what intention can I
inferred as to how the property is to be treated. Is it a family asset?

In addition to a number of other authorities I have had the opportunity
consider the decisions of Hill J in *Hargreaves v Hargreaves* [1926] P 42, [1926] *A*
ER Rep 195 and in *Prinsep v Prinsep* [1929] P 225.

In *Hargreaves* the indenture of settlement was executed between th
respondent, his mother and certain trustees on the occasion of his reaching h
majority. The settlement was not expressed to be in contemplation of marriag
nor was any future wife mentioned in the deed, though there were provision
in it which gave the respondent powers of appointment. The responder
subsequently married and shortly before the marriage he exercised his powe
of appointment in favour of the petitioner. The parties were divorced ten yea
later in 1924. The petitioner then sought the variation of the settlement on th
basis that it was an ante-nuptial settlement.

Hill J declined to make an order. He said ([1926] P 42 at 44–45, [1926] All E
Rep 195 at 197):

> '[Counsel for the wife] says that any settlement inter vivos made upo
> either of two people who at any subsequent date marry is a settlemer
> which the Court can deal with under the section, because it is ante-nuptia
> and that any property dealt with by such a settlement is to be regarded *a*
> property settled. In my view that cannot be. This section is dealing wit
> ante-nuptial and post-nuptial settlements, and it refers to marriage.
> refers to it because what it is dealing with is what we commonly know *a*
> a marriage settlement, that is, a settlement made in contemplation of, c
> because of, marriage, and with reference to the interests of married peopl
> or their children.'

In *Prinsep v Prinsep* [1929] P 225 the parties were married in 1912. On the da
before the marriage an ante-nuptial settlement was executed settling fund
brought into settlement by the husband's mother. In 1920 the husband'
mother brought into settlement further substantial trust funds amounting i
value to over £86,000. The trustees were empowered to apply the income fo
the benefit of the husband (who was styled 'principal beneficiary') and his issu
by any marriage and any wife of his. There were a number of other provision
to which it is unnecessary to refer including certain powers of appointmen
reserved to the husband.

The parties were divorced in 1928 and a question arose as to whether the
1920 settlement was a post-nuptial settlement within s 192 of the Supreme

ourt of Judicature (Consolidation) Act 1925. Hill J dealt with the matter (at 32–233):

'Is [the settlement] upon the husband in the character of husband or in the wife in the character of wife, or upon both in the character of husband and wife? If it is, it is a settlement on the parties within the meaning of the section. The particular form of it does not matter. It may be a settlement in the strictest sense of the term, it may be a covenant to pay by one spouse to the other, or by a third person to a spouse. What does matter is that it should provide for the financial benefit of one or other or both of the spouses as spouses and with reference to their married state. Is the settlement of August 25, 1920, of that character? It was made at a time when there was a husband, Mr. Prinsep, and there was a wife, Mrs. Prinsep, and there was also a child of the marriage. In terms, it has in contemplation Mr. Prinsep, whom it designates "principal beneficiary," but it also has in contemplation his then wife, Mrs. Prinsep, and any future wife and his child and any future children. The trustees are, however, given a very wide discretion.'

It seems to me that the decision in *Hargreaves v Hargreaves* [1926] P 42, [1926] ll ER Rep 195 is clearly distinguishable from the present case. The settlement n *Hargreaves v Hargreaves* was not expressed to be in contemplation of marriage or was the petitioner mentioned in it at all. In the present case, on the other and, the parties were married at the time when the scheme was established nd the policy gave the wife the prospect of a widow's pension, if the husband o elected, which she would enjoy by virtue of the fact that she was the wife.

It is my present view that it might be very difficult to show that a pension cheme established before marriage was an ante-nuptial settlement unless clear vords were used to show that it was made in contemplation of the marriage.)nce, however, a marriage has taken place it seems to me that it can be more asily shown that there is a sufficient nexus between the married state and a ension scheme so that the scheme can be regarded as a post-nuptial settlement f the wife has an interest in the scheme or has a prospect of obtaining some enefit from it in her capacity as a wife. It is true that there is no evidence that he policy was issued *because* of the marriage. It is also true, as I have mentioned arlier, that the pension scheme was a scheme for the husband as an employee f the company. I have come to the conclusion, however, that if one looks at he matter at the time when the Equitable Life policy was issued and pays roper regard to the husband's obligations to provide for the wife, the benefit vhich the wife might expect to receive as wife from the funds represented by he policy moneys was sufficient to give the policy the status of a post-nuptial ettlement. Looked at broadly, the policy was part of the family assets from vhich she could expect to obtain some benefit in the future.

I turn to the second question raised on the husband's cross-appeal. Was the udge entitled to vary the trusts of the policy in the way that he did?

It is necessary to set out the relevant facts. (1) At the date of the judgment n April 1993 the funds available from the Equitable Life policy and the other oolicies was £440,000. (2) Because of the Inland Revenue rules the whole sum of £440,000 could not be used for the husband's pension. The cost of the maximum benefit to which the husband would be entitled was £274,000. (3) There was therefore a surplus of £166,000, which, if no further action were taken, would prima facie be returned to the company in accordance with r 7(c

This surplus would be subject to taxation. (4) The husband is the on shareholder in the company and, subject to any claims by creditors of t company, would be entitled to the net surplus after deduction of tax. (5) At t time of the dissolution of the company it owed the sum of £100,000 to Lloy Bank plc. According to the letter from Paisner & Co dated 17 February 199 however, it is not the intention of Lloyds Bank to proceed against the compar because it would involve the bank in the costs of resurrecting the compan (6) The husband, however, provided security for the debt to Lloyds Bank in t form of his half share of the former matrimonial home. But the bank indicate that they are unlikely to take any action against the husband unless he were receive 'a windfall'. (7) The cost of providing the wife with a pension, ordered by the district judge, is £46,000. The cost of providing a continge dependant's pension is £30,000. The total sum of £76,000 would reduce t gross surplus payable to the company, or via the company to the husband, £90,000. As, however, the surplus would be taxable, the net effect on t surplus if a pension were provided for the wife would be £45,600. (8) Th Inland Revenue are, I understand, prepared to approve the provision of pension for the wife. This approval is based on the fact that she was former an employee of the company.

We are not concerned in this case with a pension fund from which t pensions of a number of other individuals may become payable. The fund w established to provide a pension for the husband and, if he elected, for h spouse or dependants. This is an important feature of this case because entirely agree with the view expressed by Waite LJ that, certainly as a gener rule, the court should not attempt to vary the terms of a pension scheme if th rights of third parties are likely to be affected.

Accordingly, as there are no children of the marriage, I would have had n doubt that the court would have been justified in varying the terms of th policy had there been no outstanding creditors of the company. It is th existence of the outstanding debt to Lloyds Bank which has caused me anxiety.

In the end, however, I have come to the conclusion that in the particula circumstances of this case the variation made by the judge was justified. It ha been made clear on behalf of the bank that they do not intend to pursue th company because it will involve the expense of resurrecting it. Meanwhile, th bank's rights against the husband, even if they are not enforced, remain intact.

Accordingly, for these reasons, I would dismiss the husband's cross-appea As to the appeal by the wife and the appeal on costs I am content to express m agreement with the decision and reasons of Waite LJ. In these circumstances would dismiss both the appeal and the cross-appeal.

Appeal and cross-appeal dismissed. Leave to appeal to the House of Lords granted.

Wendy Shockett   Barrister